Frommer's®

South America

5th Edition

by Shawn Blore, Alexandra de Vries, Nicholas Gill, Eliot Greenspan, Charlie O'Malley, Christie Pashby, Jisel Perilla, & Neil Edward Schlecht

Wiley Publishing, Inc.

Published by:

WILEY PUBLISHING, INC.

111River St.
Hoboken, NJ 07030-5774

ISBN 978-0-470-59155-0
Editors: Matt Brown, Melinda Quintero & Jennifer Reilly
Production Editor: Eric T. Schroeder
Cartographer: Andy Dolan
Photo Editor: Richard Fox
Production by Wiley Indianapolis Composition Services

Front cover photo: Iguazú Falls, Iguazú National Park, Argentina ©Etcheverry Collection / Alamy Images
Back cover photo: San Felipe Neri convent in Sucre, Bolivia ©Patrick Escudero / AGE Fotostock, Inc

For information on our other products and services or to obtain technical support, please contact our Customer Care Department within the U.S. at 877/762-2974, outside the U.S. at 317/572-3993 or fax 317/572-4002.

Wiley also publishes its books in a variety of electronic formats. Some content that appears in print may not be available in electronic formats.

Manufactured in the United States of America

5 4 3 2 1

CONTENTS

4 ARGENTINA 70

5 BOLIVIA 175

6 BRAZIL 227

11 PERU 616

12 URUGUAY 724

13 VENEZUELA 748

INDEX 808

LIST OF MAPS

ABOUT THE AUTHORS

A native of California, **Shawn Blore** has lived and worked in a half dozen countries and traveled in at least 50 more (but who's counting?). Long a resident of Vancouver, Shawn has for the past few years made his home in Rio de Janeiro. He is an award-winning magazine writer and the author of *Vancouver: Secrets of the City* and co-author of *Frommer's Brazil* and *Frommer's Portable Rio de Janeiro.*

Alexandra de Vries made her first journey to Brazil at the ripe old age of 1 month. (Alas, few of her food reviews from that trip survive.) In the years since, Alexandra has returned many times to travel, explore, and live in this amazing country. Alexandra co-writes *Frommer's Brazil* and *Frommer's Portable Rio de Janeiro* about her all-time favorite place to visit.

Writer and photographer **Nicholas Gill** is based in Lima, Peru and Brooklyn, New York. His work regularly appears in publications such as the *New York Times, Conde Nast Traveler, Caribbean Travel & Life,* and *World Hum.* He has also contributed to *Frommer's Chile & Easter Island* and *Frommer's Central America* and written *Frommer's Honduras.*

Eliot Greenspan is a poet, journalist, and travel writer who took his backpack and typewriter the length of Mesoamerica before settling in Costa Rica in 1992. Since then, he has traveled almost ceaselessly around Latin America, writing articles and guidebooks to feed his travel habit. He feels particularly at home in the neotropics—in its rain and cloud forests, on its rivers, and under its seas. Eliot is the author of *Frommer's Ecuador, Frommer's Costa Rica, Frommer's Belize*, and *Costa Rica Day by Day.*

Charlie O'Malley is a writer and wine enthusiast who can be found living in Argentina, when he's not traveling the rest of South America. He has also worked on *Frommer's Central America, Nicaragua & El Salvador*, and *Argentina.*

Christie Pashby is the author of *Frommer's Banff and Jasper National Parks* and a contributing writer to *Frommer's Argentina* and *Frommer's Chile & Easter Island.* She divides her time between the Canadian Rockies and Patagonia, where she runs a small guiding business with her husband.

Jisel Perilla worked with a nonprofit microcredit organization in Medellín, Colombia, and has written about, lived in, and traveled throughout much of Latin America. She currently resides in the Washington, D.C., area and is the author of *Frommer's Panama.*

Neil Edward Schlecht first trekked to Machu Picchu in 1983 as a college student, while spending his junior year abroad in Quito, Ecuador. The author of more than a dozen travel guides (including *Frommer's Peru* and *Buenos Aires Day by Day*) and a photographer, he has lived for extensive periods in Brazil and Spain. He now resides in Litchfield County, CT.

HOW TO CONTACT US

In researching this book, we discovered many wonderful places—hotels, restaurants, shops, and more. We're sure you'll find others. Please tell us about them, so we can share the information with your fellow travelers in upcoming editions. If you were disappointed with a recommendation, we'd love to know that, too. Please write to:

Frommer's South America, 5th Edition
Wiley Publishing, Inc. • 111 River St. • Hoboken, NJ 07030-5774

AN ADDITIONAL NOTE

Please be advised that travel information is subject to change at any time—and this is especially true of prices. We therefore suggest that you write or call ahead for confirmation when making your travel plans. The authors, editors, and publisher cannot be held responsible for the experiences of readers while traveling. Your safety is important to us, however, so we encourage you to stay alert and be aware of your surroundings. Keep a close eye on cameras, purses, and wallets, all favorite targets of thieves and pickpockets.

FROMMER'S STAR RATINGS, ICONS & ABBREVIATIONS

Every hotel, restaurant, and attraction listing in this guide has been ranked for quality, value, service, amenities, and special features using a **star-rating system.** In country, state, and regional guides, we also rate towns and regions to help you narrow down your choices and budget your time accordingly. Hotels and restaurants are rated on a scale of zero (recommended) to three stars (exceptional). Attractions, shopping, nightlife, towns, and regions are rated according to the following scale: zero stars (recommended), one star (highly recommended), two stars (very highly recommended), and three stars (must-see).

In addition to the star-rating system, we also use **seven feature icons** that point you to the great deals, in-the-know advice, and unique experiences that separate travelers from tourists. Throughout the book, look for:

Finds Special finds—those places only insiders know about

Fun Facts Fun facts—details that make travelers more informed and their trips more fun

Kids Best bets for kids, and advice for the whole family

Moments Special moments—those experiences that memories are made of

Overrated Places or experiences not worth your time or money

Tips Insider tips—great ways to save time and money

Value Great values—where to get the best deals

The following **abbreviations** are used for credit cards:

AE American Express
DC Diners Club
DISC Discover
MC MasterCard
V Visa

TRAVEL RESOURCES AT FROMMERS.COM

Frommer's travel resources don't end with this guide. **Frommers.com** has travel information on more than 4,000 destinations. We update features regularly, giving you access to the most current trip-planning information and the best airfare, lodging, and car-rental bargains. You can also listen to podcasts, connect with other Frommers.com members through our active-reader forums, share your travel photos, read blogs from guidebook editors and fellow travelers, and much more.

1

The Best of South America

Whether you're an archaeology buff, an outdoor adventurer, or a partier in search of a good time, South America presents so many diverse travel options that it'll make your head spin. We'll help you plan a memorable trip, starting with our highly opinionated lists of the best experiences the continent has to offer.

1 THE MOST UNFORGETTABLE TRAVEL EXPERIENCES

- **Visiting Iguazú (Iguaçu) Falls:** One of the world's most spectacular sights, Iguazú boasts more than 275 waterfalls fed by the Iguazú River, which can (and should) be visited from both the Argentine and the Brazilian (where it is spelled Iguaçu) sides. In addition to the falls, Iguazú encompasses a marvelous subtropical jungle with extensive flora and fauna. See "Puerto Iguazú & Iguazú Falls" in chapter 4 and "Foz do Iguaçu" in chapter 6.
- **Traveling the Wine Roads of Mendoza:** Mendoza offers traditional and modernist wineries, set among vines that run into the snowcapped Andes. The wineries are free to visitors and easily accessible along leafy thoroughfares known as *los Caminos del Vino.* Over 100 wineries offer tours, but most are by appointment only. See "Mendoza" in chapter 4.
- **Traversing the Salar de Uyuni by Land Cruiser:** The world's largest salt desert and its surroundings in southwest Bolivia are one of the most unusual and fascinating places on planet earth: islands of cacti, red flamingo-filled lagoons, steaming geysers, herds of vicuñas, and hotels made of salt. See "Salar de Uyuni" in chapter 5.
- **Celebrating Carnaval in Rio:** The biggest party in the world. Whether you dance it out on the streets, watch the thousands of participants in their elaborate costumes in the samba parade, or attend the fairy-tale Copacabana Palace ball, this is one event not to miss! See "Rio de Janeiro" in chapter 6.
- **Observing Red Macaws at Sunset:** The sunset over the red rock formations in the Chapada dos Guimarães north of Cuiabá in Brazil is a magical experience in itself. Even more special is the view of scarlet macaws working the thermals off the sheer cliffs in the warm glow of the setting sun. See "The Pantanal" in chapter 6.
- **Exploring the Madcap Streets of Valparaíso:** The ramshackle, sinuous streets of Valparaíso offer a walking tour unlike any other. Part of the fascination here is viewing the antique Victorian mansions and colorful tin houses that line terraced walkways winding around precipitous hills; yet also as worthwhile is spending the night here in one of the city's new boutique hotels and savoring the local cuisine at one of Valparaíso's

gourmet restaurants. As well, Valparaíso's bars, which seem to have authored the word "bohemian," are what have brought this city notoriety. See "Around Santiago & the Central Valley" in chapter 7.

- **Sailing Past the Islands and Fjords of Southern Chile:** Quietly sailing through the lush beauty of Chile's southern fjords is an experience that all can afford. There are two breathtaking trajectories: a 3-day ride between Puerto Natales and Puerto Montt, and a 1- to 6-day ride to the spectacular Laguna San Rafael Glacier. Backpackers on a shoestring (as well as those who need spiffier accommodations) all have options. These pristine, remote fjords are often said to be more dramatic than those in Norway. Farther south, a small cruise line takes passengers through Tierra del Fuego and past remote glaciers, peaks, and sea lion colonies, stopping at the end of the world at Cape Horn. See "The Chilean Lake District" in chapter 7.
- **Visiting Colombia's Paradise on Earth:** The Eje Cafetero, with its plantain- and coffee-terraced slopes, verdant mountains, and quaint Spanish-style colonial farm houses, remains one of the most traditional parts of the country. (Remember: Red pillars and shutters for Liberals, blue for Conservatives.) The lush vegetation, wild orchids, and perfect weather will make you think you're in some kind of earthly paradise. Here, you can lie back in a hammock and listen to the birds chirp, visit the hot springs of nearby Santa Rosa, or horseback ride through the endless coffee plantations—a world removed from the hectic Colombian cities. See "El Eje Cafetero" in chapter 8.
- **Watching Blue-Footed Boobies Dance for Love in the Galápagos:** Birds are usually shy, especially during mating season. But in the Galápagos Islands, where wild animals have no fear of humans, you can watch male blue-footed boobies spread their wings, lift their beaks, and dance wildly in a performance known as "sky pointing," all in hope of attracting a mate. If the female likes what she sees, she'll do the same. It's a scene right out of a *National Geographic* documentary. See "The Galápagos Islands" in chapter 9.
- **Floating on Lake Titicaca:** Lake Titicaca, the world's highest navigable body of water, straddles the border between Peru and Bolivia. To locals, it is a mysterious and sacred place. A 1-hour boat ride from Puno takes you to the Uros Islands, where communities dwell upon soft patches of reeds. Visitors have a rare opportunity to experience the ancient cultures of two inhabited natural islands, Amantani and Taquile, by staying with a local family. You won't find any cars or electricity here, but there are remarkable local festivals. The views of the oceanlike lake, at more than 3,600m (11,800 ft.) above sea level, and the star-littered night sky alone are worth the trip. Even better, for those with a bit of adventure and extra time, are kayaking on Titicaca and spending the night on private Isla Suasi. See "Puno & Lake Titicaca" in chapter 11.
- **Gazing upon Machu Picchu:** However you get to it—whether you hike the fabled Inca Trail or hop aboard one of the prettiest train rides in South America—Machu Picchu more than lives up to its reputation as one of the most spectacular sites on earth. The ruins of the legendary "lost city of the Incas" sit majestically among the massive Andes, swathed in clouds. The ceremonial and agricultural center, never discovered or looted by the Spanish, dates from the mid-1400s but seems even more ancient. Exploring the site is a thrilling experience, especially at sunrise, when dramatic rays of light creep over the

mountaintops. If you've already been to Machu Picchu, try trekking to one of the "new" lost Inca cities, such as Choquequirao. See "The Sacred Valley of the Incas" in chapter 11.

- **Visiting Punta del Este in Summer:** As Porteños (residents of Buenos Aires) will tell you, anyone who's anyone from Buenos Aires heads to Punta del Este for summer vacation. The glitzy Atlantic coast resort in Uruguay is packed with South America's jet set from December through February and offers inviting beaches and outstanding nightlife. See "Punta del Este" in chapter 12.
- **Enjoying the Splendor of Angel Falls:** From the boat ride through rapids in a dugout canoe, to the steep hike from the river's edge to the base of the falls, to a swim in the cool waters at the foot of this natural wonder and back again, this is an amazing experience, with spectacular views and scenery throughout. See "Canaima, Angel Falls & the Río Caura" in chapter 13.
- **Riding El Teleférico in Mérida,** Venezuela: The world's highest and longest cable car system will bring you to the summit of Pico Espejo at 4,765m (15,629 ft.). If you've ever wanted to get into thin air without the toil of actually climbing there, this is the way to go. Go early if you want the best views. But be careful: The effects of altitude can be felt, whether or not you actually climb. See "Mérida, the Andes & Los Llanos" in chapter 13.

2 THE BEST SMALL TOWNS & VILLAGES

- **San Martín de los Andes,** Argentina: City planners in San Martín had the smart sense to do what Bariloche never thought of: limit building height to two stories and mandate continuity in the town's Alpine architecture. The result? Bariloche is crass whereas San Martín is class, and the town is a year-round playground to boot. The cornucopia of hotels, restaurants, and shops that line the streets are built of stout, cinnamon-colored tree trunks or are Swiss-style gingerbread confections that all seem right at home in San Martín's blessed, pastoral setting. Relax, swim, bike, ski, raft, hunt, or fish—this small town has it all. See "The Argentine Lake District" in chapter 4.
- **Cafayate Wine Town,** Argentina: This small, sandy village in the Argentine Northwest is surrounded by multicolored mountain ranges and red rock desert. Vineyards punctuated by tall cactus sentinels stretch into the foothills. Home to the delicious white wine Torrontes, Cafayate offers beautiful luxury wine lodges or more down-to-earth family-run hotels. See "Salta & the Northwest" in chapter 4.
- **Isla del Sol,** Bolivia: There are actually several small villages on the Sun Island, but in total, only a few thousand people live here. There are no cars and barely any telephones. At rush hour, things get very chaotic: You may have to wait a few minutes while the locals herd their llamas from one end of the island to the other. Spend a day here, and you'll feel as if you have taken a trip back in time. See "Lake Titicaca" in chapter 5.
- **Porto de Galinhas,** Brazil: This village of three streets in a sea of white sand is the perfect spot to learn to surf. You'll never get cold, while steamed crab and fresh tropical juices between waves do wonders to keep you going. See "Recife & Olinda" in chapter 6.
- **Morro de São Paulo,** Brazil: Situated on a green lush island just a boat ride away from Salvador, this sleepy village

offers some of the best laid-back beach life on the northeast coast of Brazil. Car-free and stress-free, Morro de São Paulo offers the perfect mix of deserted beaches, watersports, and fun nightlife in an idyllic setting. See "A Side Trip from Salvador" in chapter 6.

- **San Pedro de Atacama,** Chile: Quaint, unhurried, and built of adobe brick, San Pedro de Atacama has drawn Santiaguinos and expatriates the world over to experience the mellow charm and New Age spirituality that waft through the dusty roads of this town. San Pedro is home to some of the most inspired eco-lodges in South America. Its location in the driest desert in the world makes for starry skies and breathtaking views of the weird and wonderful land formations that are just a stone's throw away. See "The Desert North" in chapter 7.
- **Pucón,** Chile: Not only was Pucón bestowed with a stunning location at the skirt of a smoking volcano and the shore of a glittering lake, it's also Chile's self-proclaimed adventure capital, offering so many outdoor activities that you could keep busy for a week. But if your idea of a vacation is plopping yourself down on a beach, Pucón also has plenty of low-key activities, and that is the real attraction here. You'll find everything you want and need without forfeiting small-town charm (that is, if you don't come with the Jan–Feb megacrowds). Timber creates the downtown atmosphere, with plenty of wood-hewn restaurants, pubs, and crafts stores blending harmoniously with the forested surroundings. See "The Chilean Lake District" in chapter 7.
- **Villa de Leyva,** Colombia: You'd be hard-pressed to find a place more picturesque than Villa de Leyva, one of the earliest towns founded by the Spanish. At 500 years old, Villa de Leyva is nearly unspoiled by the ravishes of time. Offering green and white colonial-style churches, cobblestone plazas, delightful bed-and-breakfasts, a thriving arts community, and pristine countryside, it's no wonder Villa de Leyva has become the weekend getaway of choice for upscale Bogotános. Villa de Leyva makes a great base for exploring the spectacular Boyacá countryside and participating in all sorts of adventure sports and eco-opportunities, from repelling and kayaking to nature walks through the nearby desert and waterfalls. See "A Side Trip from Bogotá: Villa de Leyva" in chapter 8.
- **Otavalo,** Ecuador: This small indigenous town is famous for its artisans market. However, it also serves as a fabulous base for a wide range of adventures, activities, and side trips. Nearby attractions include Cuicocha Lake, Peguche Waterfall, Mojanda Lakes, and Condor Park. See "Otavalo & Imbabura Province" in chapter 9.
- **Ollantaytambo,** Peru: One of the principal villages of the Sacred Valley of the Incas, Ollanta (as the locals call it) is a spectacularly beautiful place along the Urubamba River; the gorge is lined by agricultural terraces, and snowcapped peaks rise in the distance. The ruins of a formidable temple-fortress overlook the old town, a perfect grid of streets built by the Incas, the only such layout remaining in Peru. See "The Sacred Valley of the Incas" in chapter 11.
- **Colca Valley Villages,** Peru: Chivay, on the edge of Colca Canyon, is the valley's main town, but it isn't much more than a laid-back market town with fantastic hot springs on its outskirts. Dotting the Colca Valley and its extraordinary agricultural terracing are 14 charming colonial villages dating to the 16th century, each marked by its handsomely decorated church. Yanque, Coporaque, Maca, and Lari are among the most attractive towns. Natives in the valley

are descendants of the pre-Inca ethnic communities Collaguas and Cabanas, and they maintain the vibrant style of traditional dress, highlighted by fantastically embroidered and sequined hats. See chapter 11.

- **Colonia del Sacramento,** Uruguay: Just a short ferry trip from Buenos Aires, Colonia is Uruguay's best example of colonial life. The old city contains brilliant examples of colonial wealth and many of Uruguay's oldest structures. Dating from the 17th century, this beautifully preserved Portuguese settlement makes a perfect day trip. See "A Side Trip to Colonia del Sacramento" in chapter 12.
- **Mérida,** Venezuela: Nestled in a narrow valley between two immense spines of the great Andes Mountains, this lively college town is a great base for a wide range of adventure activities. Its narrow streets and colonial architecture also make it a great place to wander around and explore. See "Mérida, the Andes & Los Llanos" in chapter 13.

3 THE BEST OUTDOOR ADVENTURES

- **Discovering Iguazú Falls by Raft:** This is a place where birds like the great dusky swift and the brilliant morpho butterfly spread color through the thick forest canopy. You can easily arrange an outing into the forest once you arrive in Iguazú. See "Puerto Iguazú & Iguazú Falls" in chapter 4.
- **Raging Down the Mendoza River:** Mendoza offers the best white-water rafting in Argentina, and during the summer months, when the snow melts in the Andes and fills the Mendoza River, rafters enjoy up to Class IV and V rapids. Rafting is possible year-round, but the river is colder and calmer in winter months. See "Mendoza" in chapter 4.
- **Biking the Most Dangerous Road in Bolivia:** The 64km (40-mile) road that descends nearly 1,800m (5,900 ft.) from the barren high-plateau area of La Paz to the lush tropical area of Los Yungas is considered one of the most dangerous roads in the world. It's unpaved, narrow, and carved out of the edge of a cliff (without any guardrails). The road recently has become a popular mountain-biking challenge. The views are unbelievable, but don't stare at them too long—you have to keep an eye out for speeding trucks coming at you from the other direction. See "La Paz" in chapter 5.
- **Horseback Riding in the Pantanal:** The world's largest flood plain is best explored cowboy style—on horseback. Spend some time quietly observing the many large bird species, and every now and then take off on a fast gallop through the wetlands, startling alligators and snakes underfoot. See "The Pantanal" in chapter 6.
- **Hang Gliding in Rio:** Running off the edge of a platform with nothing between you and the ground 800m (2,600 ft.) below requires a leap of faith, but once you do, the views of the rainforest and beaches are so enthralling that you almost forget about the ground until your toes touch down on the sand at São Conrado beach. See "Rio de Janeiro" in chapter 6.
- **Kayaking the Brazilian Amazon:** Perhaps the best way to really get in touch with the rainforest is by good old sea kayak. Drifting down an Amazon tributary, you have the time to observe the rainforest; to search the trees for toucans, macaws, and sloths; and to scout the water for anaconda and caiman. On daytime hikes, you explore and swim in

rarely visited Amazon waterfalls. To truly make like a researcher, you can hoist yourself 60m (200 ft.) into the treetops and spend some time exploring the rainforest canopy. See "Manaus & the Amazon" in chapter 6.

- **Trekking in Torres del Paine:** This backpacking mecca just keeps growing in popularity, and it's no wonder. Torres del Paine is one of the most spectacular national parks in the world, with hundreds of kilometers of trails through ever-changing landscapes of jagged peaks and one-of-a-kind granite spires, undulating meadows, milky, turquoise lakes and rivers, and mammoth glaciers. The park has a well-organized system of *refugios* and campgrounds, but there are also several hotels, and visitors can access the park's major highlights on a day hike. See "Southern Patagonia" in chapter 7.
- **Snorkeling in the Galápagos:** The sea lions in the Galápagos are a curious bunch. Once you put on a snorkeling mask and flippers, these guys will think you're one of the gang and swim right up to you. When you aren't playing with sea lions, you'll have the chance to see hammerhead sharks, penguins, sea turtles, and some of the most colorful fish in the world. See "The Galápagos Islands" in chapter 9.
- **Hiking the Inca Trail:** The legendary trail to Machu Picchu, the Camino del Inca, is one of the world's most rewarding eco-adventures. The arduous 43km (27-mile) trek leads across phenomenal Andes Mountain passes and through some of the greatest natural and man-made attractions in Peru, including dozens of Inca ruins, dense cloud forest, and breathtaking mountain scenery. The trek has a superlative payoff: a sunset arrival at the glorious ruins of Machu Picchu, laid out at your feet. Hikers averse to crowds can also embark on one of the newer alternative treks in Cusco's Andes, such as Salcantay or Ausangate. See "The Sacred Valley of the Incas" in chapter 11.
- **Exploring the Peruvian Amazon:** More than half of Peru is Amazon rainforest, and the country has some of the richest biodiversity on the planet. Cusco is the gateway to the southeastern jungle and two principal protected areas, **Tambopata National Reserve** and the **Manu Biosphere Reserve.** Manu is the least accessible and least explored jungle in Peru, with unparalleled opportunity for viewing wildlife and more than 1,000 species of birds, but it's not easy or cheap to get to. Iquitos leads to the accessible northern Amazon basin, with some of the top jungle lodges in the country. Eco-travelers can fish for piranhas and keep an eye out for pink dolphins, caiman, and tapirs. One of the best jungle experiences is viewing the dense forest from the heights of a rickety canopy walkway. See "The Southern Amazon: Manu & Tambopata" and "Iquitos & the Northern Amazon" in chapter 11.
- **Scuba Diving in Los Roques, Venezuela:** Los Roques offers much of the same coral, marine life, and crystal clear waters as the rest of the popular Caribbean dive destinations, but it's still virtually undiscovered. **Ecobuzos** (**✆ 0295/262-9811;** www.ecobuzos.com) is the best dive operator on the archipelago. See "Los Roques National Park" in chapter 13.
- **One-Stop Adventure Travel from Mérida,** Venezuela: With a half-dozen or so peaks 4,500m (14,760 ft.) and above, raging rivers, and a couple of very competent adventure tour outfitters, you can go climbing, trekking, mountain biking, white-water rafting, horseback riding, canyoneering, and even paragliding out of Mérida. You may need a couple of weeks to do it all, but both **Arassari Treks** (www.arassari.com) and **Natoura**

Adventure Tours (www.natoura.com) can help you come up with an adventure package to fit your budget, skill level, and time frame. See "Mérida, the Andes & Los Llanos" in chapter 13.

4 THE MOST INTRIGUING HISTORICAL SITES

- **Manzana de las Luces,** Buenos Aires, Argentina: The Manzana de las Luces (Block of Lights) served as the intellectual center of the city in the 17th and 18th centuries. This land was granted in 1616 to the Jesuits, who built San Ignacio—the city's oldest church—still standing at the corner of Bolívar and Aslina streets. It's worth a visit to see the beautiful altar. See p. 93.
- **Teatro Colón,** Buenos Aires, Argentina: The majestic Teatro Colón, completed in 1908, combines a variety of European styles, from the Ionic and Corinthian capitals and French stained-glass pieces in the main entrance to the Italian marble staircase and exquisite French furniture, chandeliers, and vases in the Golden Hall. The Colón has hosted the world's most important opera singers. See p. 96.
- **Tiwanaku,** Bolivia: The Tiwanaku lived in Bolivia from 1600 B.C. to A.D. 1200. Visit the Tiwanaku archaeological site, which is about 2 hours from La Paz, and you'll see proof of some of the amazing feats of this pre-Columbian culture. The stone-carved Sun Gate could gauge the position of the sun. The technologically advanced irrigation system transformed this barren terrain into viable farmland. The enormous and intricately designed stone-carved monoliths found here give testament to the amazing artistic talents of these people. Much here still remains a mystery, but when you walk around the site, it's exciting to imagine what life must have been like here for the Tiwanaku. See "La Paz" in chapter 5.
- **Potosí,** Bolivia: Once one of the richest cities in the world and now one of the poorest, Potosí is a fascinating but tragic place. A silver mining town that once bankrolled the Spanish empire, Potosí is a high-altitude relic featuring beautiful church architecture and primitive mining, both of which you can experience firsthand. See "A Side Trip to Potosí" in chapter 5.
- **Brasília,** Brazil: Built from scratch in a matter of years on the red soil of the dry *cerrado,* Brasília is an oasis of modernism in Brazil's interior. Marvel at the clean lines and functional forms and admire some of the best modern architecture in the world. See "Brasília" in chapter 6.
- **Pelourinho,** Brazil: The restored historical center of Salvador is a treasure trove of baroque churches, colorful colonial architecture, steep cobblestone streets, and large squares. See "Salvador" in chapter 6.
- **San Pedro de Atacama, Chiu Chiu,** and **Caspana,** Chile: The driest desert in the world has one perk: Everything deteriorates very, very slowly. This is good news for travelers in search of the architectural roots of Chile, where villages such as San Pedro, Chiu Chiu, and Caspana boast equally impressive examples of 17th-century colonial adobe buildings and the sun-baked ruins of the Atacama Indian culture; some sites date from 800 B.C. Highlights undoubtedly are the enchanting, crumbling San Francisco Church of Chiu Chiu and the labyrinthine streets of the indigenous fort Pukará de Lasana. See "The Desert North" in chapter 7.

- **Cartagena,** Colombia: Declared a UNESCO World Heritage Site in 1984, the old walled city of Cartagena is the greatest living outdoor museum dedicated to Spanish colonial history. A walk through one of Cartagena's narrow cobblestone streets, complete with centuries-old Spanish mansions, flower-strewn balconies, and horse-drawn carriages showing tourists around town, might make you feel as if you've stepped onto the set of a colonial-era *telenovela.* Best of all, the finest attractions—the plazas, the fortress, and most of the churches—are free. See "Cartagena & the Atlantic Coast" in chapter 8.
- **Quito's Old Town,** Ecuador: When you walk around old Quito, you will feel as if you have stepped back in time. The oldest church here dates from 1535, and it's still magnificent. La Compañia de Jesús only dates from 1765, but it is one of the most impressive baroque structures in all of South America. It's rare to find a city with so many charming colonial-style buildings. When you wander through the streets, it really seems as if you are walking through an outdoor museum. See "Quito" in chapter 9.
- **The Nazca Lines,** Peru: One of South America's great enigmas are the ancient, baffling lines etched into the desert sands along Peru's southern coast. There are trapezoids and triangles, identifiable shapes of animal and plant figures, and more than 10,000 lines that can only really be seen from the air. Variously thought to be signs from the gods, agricultural and astronomical calendars, or even extraterrestrial airstrips, the Nazca Lines were constructed between 300 B.C. and A.D. 700. See "Lima" in chapter 11.
- **Cusco,** Peru: Cusco, the ancient Inca capital, is a living museum of Peruvian history, with Spanish colonial churches and mansions sitting atop perfectly constructed Inca walls of exquisitely carved granite blocks that fit together without mortar. In the hills above the city lie more terrific examples of Inca masonry: the zigzagged defensive walls of Sacsayhuamán and the smaller ruins of Q'enko, Puca Pucara, and Tambomachay. See "Cusco" in chapter 11.
- **Iglesia de San Francisco,** Caracas, Venezuela: This is the church where Simón Bolívar was proclaimed El Libertador in 1813, and the site of his massive funeral in 1842—the year his remains were brought back from Colombia some 12 years after his death. Begun in 1575, the church shows the architectural influences of various periods and styles, but retains much of its colonial-era charm. See p. 769.

5 THE BEST MUSEUMS

- **Museo Nacional de Bellas Artes,** Buenos Aires: This museum contains the world's largest collection of Argentine sculptures and paintings from the 19th and 20th centuries. It also houses European art dating from the pre-Renaissance period to the present day. The collections include notable pieces by Manet, Goya, El Greco, and Gauguin. See p. 95.
- **MALBA–Colección Costantini,** Buenos Aires: This stunning new private museum houses one of the most impressive collections of Latin American art anywhere. Temporary and permanent exhibitions showcase such names as Antonio Berni, Pedro Figari, Frida Kahlo, Candido Portinari, Diego Rivera, and Antonio Siguí. Many of the works confront social issues and explore

questions of national identity. See p. 94.

- **Museu de Arte Sacra,** Salvador: When you walk into this small but splendid museum, what you hear is not the usual gloomy silence but the soft sweet sound of Handel. It's a small indication of the care curators have taken in assembling and displaying one of Brazil's best collections of Catholic art—reliquaries, processional crosses, and crucifixes of astonishing refinement. The artifacts are shown in a former monastery, a simple, beautiful building that counts itself as a work of art. See p. 308.
- **Pinacoteca do Estado,** São Paulo: A sunlit joy to be in, the Pinacoteca is one of the best curated art collections in Brazil. Renovated in 1997, the roof and many interior walls were removed, replaced with a latticework of glass and open spaces, and connected by a series of catwalks. It's the perfect place for anyone wanting to see and understand Brazilian art. See p. 289.
- **Museo Arqueológico Padre Le Paige,** San Pedro de Atacama: This little museum will come as an unexpected surprise for its wealth of indigenous artifacts, although the museum's famous mummies have been taken off display due to ethical questions. Still, considering that the Atacama Desert is the driest in the world, this climate has produced some of the best preserved artifacts in Latin America, on view here. See p. 416.
- **Museo del Oro,** Bogotá: With over 20,000 pieces of gold, the Museo del Oro offers the largest collection of its kind in the world, providing a visual history of Colombia and Latin America from the pre-Columbian era to the Spanish conquest. Taking a guided tour of the museum is one of the best ways to learn about the indigenous groups that inhabited modern-day Colombia before the arrival of the Spaniards. Whatever you do, don't leave Bogotá without visiting the gold room, a dazzling display of 8,000 pieces of gold. See p. 482.
- **Fundación Guayasamín,** Quito: Oswaldo Guayasamín was Ecuador's greatest and most famous modern artist. His striking large paintings, murals, and sculptures had an impact on artists across Latin America and around the world. This extensive museum displays both his own work and pieces from his collection. Combined with the neighboring **Capilla del Hombre,** this is a must-see for any art lover or Latin American history buff. See p. 540.
- **Museo de la Nación,** Lima: Lima is the museum capital of Peru, and the National Museum traces the art and history of the earliest inhabitants to the Inca empire, the last before colonization by the Spaniards. In well-organized, chronological exhibits, it covers the country's unique architecture (including scale models of most major ruins in Peru) as well as ceramics and textiles. See p. 641.
- **Monasterio de Santa Catalina** and **Museo Santuarios Andinos,** Arequipa: The Convent of Santa Catalina, founded in 1579, is the greatest religious monument in Peru. More than a convent, it's an extraordinary and evocative small village, with Spanish-style cobblestone streets, passageways, plazas, and cloisters, where more than 200 sequestered nuns once lived (only a handful remain). Down the street at the Museo Santuarios Andinos is a singular exhibit: Juanita, the Ice Maiden of Ampato. A 13-year-old girl sacrificed in the 1500s by Inca priests high on a volcano at 6,380m (20,926 ft.), Juanita was discovered in almost perfect condition in 1995. See p. 707.
- **Museo de Arte Contemporáneo,** Caracas: Occupying 13 rooms spread out through the labyrinthine architecture of

The Best of Sensuous South America

Your trip will not be complete until you indulge in at least one of the following uniquely South American experiences:

- **Get High in Bolivia:** With the world's highest capital city, highest commercial airport, and highest navigable lake, Bolivia's air is so thin it will make your head spin. But Bolivia is also home to the infamous coca leaf, a perfectly legal, extremely nutritious source of energy and an antidote to altitude sickness. To learn the complete history of the coca leaf (and for free samples), stop in at the **Museo de la Coca** in La Paz. See p. 191.
- **Be the Girl (or Boy) from Ipanema:** Rio may have other beaches, but Ipanema is still the one with the best people-watching. Grab a spot, and food, drink, and eye candy will come to you. See "Rio de Janeiro" in chapter 6.
- **Feel the Beat in Brazil:** At night the historic heart of Salvador comes alive with music. Most impressive of all are the Afro blocos, the all-percussion bands that create such an intense rhythm with their drums that it sends shivers down your spine. See "Salvador" in chapter 6.
- **Soak in Chilean Hot Springs:** The volatile Andes not only builds volcanoes; it also produces steaming mineralized water that spouts from fissures, many of which have been developed into hot springs, from rock pools to full-scale luxury resorts. Most hot springs seem to have been magically paired by nature with outdoor adventure spots, making for a thankful way to end a day of activity. The Lake District is a noted "hot spot," especially around Pucón. See "The Chilean Lake District" in chapter 7.
- **Enjoy an Orgy of Sights, Sounds, and Smells in Ecuador:** The outdoor **artisans market in Otavalo** is an assault on your senses. The colors and textures of the intricate textiles mix with the sounds of musicians playing reed pipes, as you walk among the scents of herbs and flowers offered up for sale. See p. 558.
- **Feel the Wind Beneath the Condor's Wings in Peru:** Colca Canyon is the best place in South America to see giant Andean condors, majestic birds with wingspans of up to 3.5m (11 ft.). From a stunning lookout point nearly 1,200m (4,000 ft.) above the canyon river, you can watch as the condors appear, slowly circle, and gradually gain altitude with each pass, until they soar silently above your head and head off down the river. A truly spine-tingling spectacle, the flight of the big birds may make you feel quite small. See "Arequipa" in chapter 11.
- **Stroke a roughly 4m (13-ft.) Anaconda in Venezuela:** There's no guarantee you'll wrangle an anaconda—many lodges frown on direct contact—but you can get awfully close. Try a stay at **Hato El Cedral** (p. 804); sightings of the large anaconda here are common, particularly in the dry season. If you're lucky, you'll see a "mating ball," several males and one female entwined in a writhing ball of anaconda lust.

Caracas's Parque Central, the permanent collection here features a small but high-quality collection of singular works by such modern masters as Picasso, Red Grooms, Henry Moore, Joan Miró, and Francis Bacon, as well as a good representation of the conceptual works of Venezuelan star Jesús Soto. See p. 769.

6 THE BEST FESTIVALS & CELEBRATIONS

- **Carnaval,** Argentina, Brazil, Colombia, and Uruguay: The week before the start of Lent, Mardi Gras is celebrated in many towns in Argentina, although to a much lesser extent than in neighboring Brazil. In addition to Rio's incredible party, Salvador puts the emphasis on participation: The action is out on the streets with the blocos, flatbed trucks with bands and sound systems leading people on a 3-day dance through the streets. Barranquilla, Colombia's fourth-largest city, boasts the world's second-largest Carnaval after Rio, and here you can enjoy many events such as the parade of floats, the crowning of Miss Carnaval, and African-inspired dances. Carnaval is celebrated throughout Uruguay with a passion topped only by Brazil. Montevideo spares no neighborhood parades, dance parties, and intense Latin merrymaking. See chapters 4, 6, 8, and 12.
- **Festival of the Virgen de la Candelaria,** Bolivia and Peru: The Virgen de la Candelaria is one of the most beloved religious icons in Bolivia. On February 2, parades and parties erupt in Copacabana in her honor. The festivities, which are some of the liveliest in Bolivia, combine a mixture of Catholic and ancient local influences. Puno, perhaps the epicenter of Peruvian folklore, imbues its festivals with a unique vibrancy; their celebration of the Virgin is one of the greatest folk religious festivals in South America, with a 2-week explosion of music and dance, and some of the most fantastic costumes and masks seen anywhere. See "Lake Titicaca" in chapter 5 and "Puno & Lake Titicaca" in chapter 11.
- **New Year's Eve,** Brazil and Chile: Join up to a million revelers on Copacabana Beach for one of the largest celebrations in Brazil; fireworks, concerts, and the religious ceremonies of the Afro-Brazilian Candomblé make for an unforgettable New Year's Eve. In Chile, Valparaíso rings in the new year with a spectacular bang, setting off a fireworks display high above the city's shimmering bay for the throngs of visitors who blanket the hills. Pablo Neruda used to spend New Year's here, watching the exploding sky from his home high on a cliff. The yearly event is absolutely hectic, so come early and plan on staying late. See "Rio de Janeiro" in chapter 6 and "Around Santiago & the Central Valley" in chapter 7.
- **Inti Raymi,** Ecuador and Peru: June 24 to 29, the fiestas of San Pablo, San Juan, and Inti Raymi (a sun festival celebrating the summer solstice) all merge into one big holiday in the Otavalo area. For the entire week, local people celebrate with big barbecues, parades, traditional dances, and bonfires. In Peru, it takes over Cusco and transforms the Sacsayhuamán ruins overlooking the city into a majestic stage. See "Otavalo & Imbabura Province" in chapter 9 and "Cusco" in chapter 11.
- **Mendoza Wine Harvest Festival:** The first weekend of every March, Argentina's Malbec region celebrates the bumper harvest with wine, women,

and song. Parades, concerts, and a carnival-like atmosphere culminate in a grand open-air spectacle of music, dance, and fireworks. See "Mendoza" in chapter 4.

7 THE BEST HOTELS

- **Alvear Palace Hotel,** Buenos Aires (✆ **011/4808-2100**): Decorated in Empire- and Louis XV–style furnishings, this is the most exclusive hotel in Buenos Aires. Luxurious guest rooms and suites have chandelier lighting, feather beds, silk drapes, and beautiful marble bathrooms; service is sharp and professional. See p. 103.
- **El Hostal de su Merced,** Sucre (✆ **0104/6442-706**): Sucre is one of the most historic cities in Bolivia, so it makes sense to stay in a historic hotel. El Hostal de su Merced is housed in an elegant 300-year-old mansion. All the rooms have charming antiques, crystal chandeliers, and lace curtains. See p. 212.
- **Hotel Sofitel,** Rio de Janeiro (✆ **0800/241-232** or 021/2525-1232): Considered Rio's best hotel, the Sofitel combines old-world elegance and style with one of the city's best locations, across from the Copacabana Fort and steps from Ipanema. See p. 264.
- **Tropical Manaus** (✆ **0800/701-2670** or 092/3659-5000): The Tropical Manaus is without a doubt *the* hotel in town. Set in its own piece of rainforest on the banks of the Rio Negro, the hotel is built in an elegant colonial style. Rooms are spacious and the amenities are top notch; archery lessons, a zoo, wakeboard lessons, a wave pool, a salon, and more await you in the middle of the Amazon. See p. 342.
- **Casa Higueras,** Valparaíso (✆ **32/249-7900**): Housed in an eggshell-white, elegant 1940s mansion that descends four floors on a slope of Cerro Alegre in Valparaíso, this hotel boasts one of the most culturally and architecturally interesting views in Chile. It is one of the country's leading boutique hotels, and the combination of luxury lodging, an infinity pool and spa, umbrella-dotted terrace with a restaurant serving fine food, and a handsome, masculine design really earn kudos among travelers seeking something unique. See p. 403.
- **Awasi,** San Pedro (✆ **888/880-3219** in the U.S., or 55/851460): The intimate and stylish Awasi offers chic accommodations, out-of-the-ordinary excursions around San Pedro de Atacama, a spa, and fabulous cuisine. With just eight suites, the hotel encourages guests to get to know each other, and so it is not ideal for travelers seeking absolute anonymity, but suites—which come with indoor and outdoor showers—are large enough to escape to your own private paradise. The hotel, built of adobe and decorated with local art, is centered around an oasis-style pool and outdoor dining area and bar. See p. 417.
- **Hotel de la Opera,** Bogotá (✆ **1/336-2066**): A rarity among Bogotá's mostly modern, though uninspiring, lodging options, this is a truly charming hotel. In the heart of La Candelaria, Bogotá's historic center, the de la Opera is a stunning restoration of two formerly dilapidated mansions once belonging to influential families. Old-world elegance blends effortlessly with modern-day amenities to make this Italian-style hotel the place to stay in Bogotá. Be sure to book in advance. See p. 486.
- **The Sofitel Santa Clara,** Cartagena (✆ **5/664-6070**): Conveniently located

within the walled-city neighborhood of San Diego, the Sofitel Santa Clara is housed in a 400-year-old building and boasts one of the city's best spas. The interior courtyards and tastefully decorated rooms give the hotel a decidedly romantic, exclusive feel. See p. 510.

- **La Mirage Garden Hotel & Spa,** Otavalo (✆ **800/327-3573** in the U.S. and Canada, or 06/2915-237; www.mirage.com.ec): This luxurious hotel is one of Ecuador's finest. The manicured gardens make this place feel like a mini-Versailles, while the rooms are all palatial-style suites. Ancient Ecuadorian treatments are the specialty at the spa. See p. 562.
- **Royal Palm Hotel,** Santa Cruz, Galápagos (✆ **05/2527-409;** www.royalpalmgalapagos.com): This luxurious resort almost seems out of place in the remote and rustic Galápagos. The villas are truly sumptuous, each with a private Jacuzzi and an enormous bathroom with hardwood floors. Large windows open up to the lush tropical landscape and the awesome stretch of the Pacific in the distance. See p. 595.
- **Hotel Monasterio,** Cusco (✆ **084/241-777**): Carved out of a 16th-century monastery, itself built over the foundations of an Inca palace, this Orient Express hotel is the most dignified and historic place to stay in Peru. With its own gilded chapel and 18th-century Cusco School art collection, it's an attraction in its own right. Rooms are gracefully decorated with colonial touches, particularly the rooms off the serene first courtyard. See p. 666.
- **Machu Picchu Pueblo Hotel,** Aguas Calientes (✆ **800/442-5042** or 084/211-122 for reservations): It's not next to the ruins, but this rustic hotel is a compound of bungalows ensconced in lush tropical gardens and cloud forest, and it's the nicest place in Aguas Calientes. With lots of nature trails and guided activities, it's also great for naturalists. And after a day at Machu Picchu, the spring-fed pool is a great alternative to the thermal baths in town. Junior suites, with fireplaces and small terraces, are the most coveted rooms. See p. 689.
- **Belmont House,** Montevideo (✆ **2/600-0430**): A hotel in Montevideo's peaceful Carrasco neighborhood, Belmont House offers its privileged guests intimacy and luxury close to the city and the beach. Small elegant spaces with carefully chosen antiques and wood furnishings give this the feeling of a private estate. See p. 736.
- **The Conrad Resort and Casino,** Punta del Este (✆ **042/491111**): This resort dominates social life in Punta del Este. Luxurious rooms have terraces overlooking the two main beaches, and there's a wealth of outdoor activities, from tennis and golf to horseback riding and watersports. See p. 745.
- **Jungle Rudy Campamento,** Canaima (✆/fax **0286/962-2359** in Canaima, or 0212/754-0244 in Caracas; www.junglerudy.com): The accommodations here are decidedly simple—no television, air-conditioning, or telephones. However, the setting, on the banks of the Río Carrao above Ucaima Falls, is spectacular. See p. 809.

8 THE BEST LOCAL DINING EXPERIENCES

- **Grilled Meat in Argentina:** Widely considered the best *parrilla* (grill restaurant) in Buenos Aires, **Cabaña las Lilas** (✆ **011/4313-1336**) is always packed. The menu pays homage to Argentine beef cuts, which come exclusively from the restaurant's private *estancia* (ranch). The steaks are outstanding. See p. 107.

- ***Salteñas* in Bolivia:** In almost every town in Bolivia, the locals eat *salteñas* for breakfast. These delicious treats are made with either chicken or beef, spiced with onions and raisins, and all wrapped up in a doughy pastry shell. Most people buy them from vendors on the street. See chapter 5's "Tips on Dining" on p. 184.
- **Street Food in Brazil:** Whether you want prawns, chicken, tapioca pancakes, coconut sweets, or corn on the cob, it can all be purchased on the street for next to nothing. Indulge—don't be afraid to try some of the best snacks that Brazil has to offer. See chapter 6.
- **Prawns on Ilhabela:** Ilhabela has the most succulent, sweet, and juicy prawns in all of Brazil. Enjoy them grilled, sautéed, or stuffed with cheese—they're as good as they come. See "São Paulo" in chapter 6.
- **Fish in the Pantanal:** Anywhere in the Pantanal you can try the phenomenal bounty of the world's largest flood plain. *Paçu, dourado,* and *pintado* are just a few of the region's best catches. See "The Pantanal" in chapter 6.
- **The Mercado Central in Santiago:** The chaotic, colorful central fish-and-produce market of Santiago should not be missed by anyone, even if you are not particularly fond of seafood. But if you are, you'll want to relish one of the flavorful concoctions served at one of the market's simple restaurants. See p. 379.
- ***Bandeja Paisa* in Medellín:** This tasty Antioquian dish of soup, rice, beans, avocado, salad, sausage, plantain, shredded beef, eggs, *arepa,* and *chicharrón* (pork rinds) will leave you stuffed for the rest of the day. See chapter 8.
- **Fresh Fruit Drinks in Ecuador:** The tropical coastal climate in Ecuador is perfect for growing fruit. Almost every restaurant offers a wonderful selection of fresh local fruit, including pineapple, orange, passion fruit, coconut, blackberry, banana, and a variety of typical Ecuadorian fruits such as *guanábana* and *naranjilla.* My favorite is the **tamarillo (tree tomato),** which is often served as a breakfast drink. See chapter 9.
- ***Ceviche* in Peru:** Peruvian cuisine is one of the most distinguished in the world. Though cooking varies greatly from Andean to coastal and Amazonian climes, there are few things more satisfying than a classic Peruvian *ceviche:* raw fish and shellfish marinated in lime or lemon juice and hot chili peppers, served with raw onion, sweet potato, and toasted corn. It's wonderfully refreshing and spicy. (And if that's not adventurous enough for you, you can always try *cuy,* or guinea pig.) The perfect accompaniment is either *chicha morada,* a refreshment made from blue corn, or a pisco sour, a frothy cocktail of white grape brandy, egg whites, lemon juice, sugar, and bitters—akin to a margarita. See chapter 11.
- **Ice Cream at Heladería Coromoto,** Mérida (© **0274/252-3525**): This shop holds the Guinness world record for the most ice-cream flavors. Be adventurous and sample a scoop of smoked trout, garlic, beer, avocado, or squid ice cream. The count currently exceeds 900 flavors, with roughly 100 choices available on any night. See p. 800.

9 THE BEST MARKETS

- **San Telmo Antiques Market,** Buenos Aires: The Sunday market is as much a cultural event as a commercial event, as old-time tango and *milonga* dancers take to the streets with other performers. Here you will glimpse Buenos Aires much as it was at the beginning of the 20th century. See p. 90.

- **The Witches' Market,** La Paz: This is one of the most unusual markets in South America. The stalls are filled with llama fetuses and all sorts of good-luck charms. Locals come here to buy magic potions or small trinkets that will bring them wealth, health, or perhaps a good harvest. You'll be sure to find unique gifts here for all your friends at home. See p. 194.
- **Mercado Adolpho Lisboa,** Manaus: The Mercado Adolpho Lisboa is a vast waterside cornucopia featuring outrageously strange Amazon fish, hundreds of species of Amazon fruits found nowhere else, traditional medicine love potions, and just about anything else produced in the Amazon, all of it cheap, cheap, cheap. See p. 341.
- **Mercado Central,** Santiago: It would be a crime to visit Chile and not sample the rich variety of fish and shellfish available here, and this vibrant market is the best place to experience the country's love affair with its fruits of the sea. Nearly every edible (and seemingly inedible) creature is for sale, from sea urchins to the alien-looking and unfamiliar *piure,* among colorful bushels of fresh vegetables and some of the most aggressive salesmen this side of the Andes. See p. 379.
- **Angelmó Fish and Artisan Market,** Puerto Montt: Stretching along several blocks of the Angelmó port area of Puerto Montt are rows and rows of stalls stocked with arts and crafts, clothing, and novelty items from the entire surrounding region. This market is set up to buy, buy, buy, and it imparts little local color; don't be afraid to bargain. The fish market next door is loud, colorful, and full of treasure, making it more appealing than the street-side stalls. See p. 440.
- **Otavalo,** Ecuador: Otavalo is probably one of the most famous markets in South America for good reason: You won't find run-of-the-mill tourist trinkets here. The local people are well known for their masterful craftsmanship—you can buy alpaca scarves, handwoven bags, and a variety of other exquisite handmade goods. See "Otavalo & Imbabura Province" in chapter 9.
- **Pisac,** Peru: Thousands of tourists descend each Sunday morning on Pisac's liveliest handicrafts market, which takes over the central plaza and spills across adjoining streets. Many sellers, decked out in the dress typical of their villages, come from remote populations high in the mountains. Village officials lead processions around the square after Mass. Pisac is one of the best spots for colorful Andean textiles, including rugs, alpaca sweaters, and ponchos. Some travelers, though, prefer **Chinchero** (also in the Sacred Valley); it's slightly more authentic, the artisans (in village dress) themselves sell their goods, and the setting is dramatic. See "The Sacred Valley of the Incas" in chapter 11.
- **Mercado del Puerto,** Montevideo: The Mercado del Puerto (Port Market) takes place afternoons and weekends, letting you sample the flavors of Uruguay, from empanadas to barbecued meats. Saturday is the best day to visit, when cultural activities accompany the market. See p. 735.
- **Hannsi Centro Artesanal,** El Hatillo: This huge indoor bazaar has everything from indigenous masks to ceramic wares to woven baskets. The selection is broad and covers everything from trinkets to pieces of the finest craftsmanship. Most of the major indigenous groups of Venezuela are represented, including the Yanomami, Guajiro, Warao, Pemón, and Piaroa. See p. 772.

2

South America in Depth

Many outsiders may think of South America as a third-world land of poverty and political instability. And historically, this hasn't been far from the truth. But South America is now beginning to come into its own, both politically and socially. The military dictatorships and guerrilla wars that plagued this region in the 1970s and 1980s are largely things of the past, and a new respect for traditional culture and indigenous people is beginning to ease social tensions—though there's still a long way to go. These social advances are great news for travelers, who are beginning to take notice. The increasing popularity of adventure, archaeological, and ecotourism has brought waves of new visitors to South America, a trend that looks to continue.

1 SOUTH AMERICA TODAY

It's estimated that 385 million people live in South America. The population is extremely diverse, and it would be difficult to generalize about the cultural makeup of the continent. But it is safe to say that of all the different people who live here, a large majority can trace their roots back to Spain, Portugal, Africa, or South America itself. Because of the Spanish and Portuguese influence, mestizos (people of both Amerindian and either Spanish or Portuguese ancestry) are also in the majority. From the late 19th century through 1930, the look of South Americans began to gradually change. Millions of Italians immigrated mainly to Brazil, Argentina, and Uruguay. Significant numbers of Germans, Poles, Syrians, Lebanese, and Japanese began to settle here as well.

THE CULTURAL MAKEUP OF SOUTH AMERICA

Argentina

To understand how Argentina's European heritage impacts its South American identity, you must identify its distinct culture. Tango is the quintessential example: The sensual dance originated in the suspect corners of Buenos Aires's San Telmo neighborhood, was legitimized in the ballrooms of France, and was then reexported to Argentina to become this nation's great art form. Each journey you take, whether into a tango salon, an Argentine cafe, or a meat-only *parrilla,* will bring you closer to the country's true character.

But beyond the borders of Argentina's capital and largest city, you will find a land of vibrant extremes—from the Northwest's desert plateau to the flat grasslands of the pampas. The land's geographic diversity is reflected in its people; witness the contrast between the capital's largely immigrant population and the indigenous people of the northwest. Greater Buenos Aires, in which a third of Argentines live, is separated from the rest of Argentina both culturally and economically. Considerable suspicion exists between Porteños, as the people of Buenos Aires are called, and the rest of the Argentines. Residents of the fast-paced metropolis who consider themselves more European than South American share little in common with the indigenous people of the northwest, for example, who trace their roots to the Incas and take pride in a slower country life.

Bolivia

Bolivia has the highest percentage of indigenous people in all of South America. The country is twice as big as France, but its population is roughly 9 million (about the same as New York City's). And because of the country's rugged vastness, its indigenous groups have remained isolated and have been able to hold onto their traditions. In the rural highlands, lifestyles still revolve around agriculture and traditional weaving. It is also common to see people all over the country chewing coca leaves, a thousands-year-old tradition that is believed to give people energy. The customs of the indigenous people are in full flower not only in rural areas but in cities such as La Paz as well. It is a testament to the tenacity of Bolivian traditions that millions of Bolivians still speak Aymara, a language that predates not only the Spanish conquest of Bolivia but also the Inca conquest. Millions more speak Quechua, the language of the Incas. In fact, only half the population speaks Spanish as their first language. Of course, in the cities there are many mestizos, and most people speak Spanish.

Almost all Bolivians today are Roman Catholic, though traditional indigenous rituals are still practiced, even by devout Catholics. In the 18th and 19th centuries, a distinct "Mestizo Baroque" movement developed, where mestizo artists used indigenous techniques to create religious art. Even today, the mixture of the two influences is evident throughout Bolivian society. In Copacabana, where the Virgin of the Candelaria is one of the most revered Catholic symbols in all of South America, you can climb Calvario, the hill that looms over the cathedral, and receive blessings or have your coca leaves read by traditional Andean priests.

Brazil

Modern Brazil's diverse population is a melting pot of three main ethnic groups: the indigenous inhabitants of Brazil, the European settlers, and the descendants of black slaves from Africa. Within Brazil the blending of various cultures and ethnic groups varies from region to region. Rio de Janeiro's population is composed largely of people of mixed European and African heritage. In Salvador, more than any other area of Brazil, the people are mostly of African descent. Many of the freed slaves settled in this area, and the African influence is reflected in the food, religion, and music. In the Amazon, the cities are populated by migrants from other parts of Brazil, while the forest is predominantly populated by *caboclos* (a mixture of European and Indian ethnicities) and indigenous tribes, many of which maintain their traditional culture, dress, and lifestyle. European immigrants mostly settled the south of Brazil, with a few notable exceptions, such as the large Japanese and Middle Eastern communities of São Paulo.

Brazil remains the largest Roman Catholic country in the world, though Catholicism is perhaps stronger as a cultural influence than a religious force; many Brazilian Catholics see the inside of a church only once a year. Meanwhile, evangelical Protestant churches are growing fast, and African religious practices such as Candomblé remain important, particularly in northern cities such as Salvador.

Brazil is well known for its music; see "South America in Popular Culture: Books, Film & Music" later for details. The cultural center of Brazil is São Paulo, and its rich theater and film scene is begrudgingly envied even by Cariocas (Rio residents). Rio remains the center of Brazil's sizable television industry.

Chile

About 95% of Chile's population is mestizo, a mix of indigenous and European blood that includes Spanish, German (in the Lake District), and Croatian (in southern Patagonia). Other nationalities, such as Italian, Russian, and English, have contributed a smaller influence. Indigenous groups, such as the Aymara in the northern desert and the Mapuche in the Lake District, still exist in large numbers, although fewer than before the Spanish conquest. It is estimated that there are more than a half-million Mapuches, many of whom live on poverty-stricken *reducciones,* literally "reductions," where they continue to use their language and carry on their customs. In southern Chile and Tierra del Fuego, indigenous groups such as Alacalufe and Yagan have been diminished to only a few remaining representatives, and some, such as the Patagonian Ona, have been completely extinguished. One-third of Chile's almost 17 million residents live in the Santiago metropolis alone.

Until the late 1800s, the Roman Catholic Church exerted a heavy influence over all political, educational, and social spheres of society. Today, although more than 85% of the population claims faith in the Catholic religion, only a fraction attends Mass regularly. The church has lost much of its sway over government, but it still is the dominant influence when the government deals with issues such as abortion and divorce. It is estimated that less than 10% of Chileans are Protestants, mostly Anglican and Lutheran descendants of British and German immigrants, and fewer are Pentecostal. The remaining percentage belongs to tiny communities of Jewish, Mormon, and Muslim faiths.

Chile is a country whose rich cultural tapestry reflects its wide-ranging topography. Despite an artistically sterile period during the Pinochet regime, when any form of art deemed "suspicious" or "offensive" (meaning nothing beyond safe, traditional entertainment) was censored, modern art has begun to bloom, and even folkloric art and music are finding a fresh voice. Chile is also known for theater, and visitors to Santiago will find dozens of excellent productions to choose from. The national Chilean dance is the *cueca,* a courtship dance between couples that is said to imitate the mating ritual between chickens! The *cueca* is danced by couples who perform a one-two stomp while flitting and twirling a handkerchief.

Colombia

Colombia's 45 million people live mostly on the high Andean triangle made up of Medellín, Bogotá, and Cali, as well as along the Caribbean Coast. Colombia is a country of incredible diversity: 58% of its citizens are mestizo (a mix of European and indigenous blood), 20% is of mostly European descent, and yet another 20% traces its ancestry to Africa. Moreover, 2% of the population is classified as indigenous, Arab, or "other."

About 90% of Colombians consider themselves Roman Catholic, although there is a growing Protestant and Evangelical movement, and numbers of Mormons, Seventh-day Adventists and Pentecostals are on the rise. There is also a small but significant Jewish population, mostly in Bogotá, Medellín, and Barranquilla.

Colombia has a rich musical, artistic, and literary tradition; see "South America in Popular Culture: Books, Films & Music" later for details. Some of the country's most well-known exports are Fernando Botero, one of the world's highest-paid artists; Nobel-prize-winning writer Gabriel García Márquez; Latin Grammy winners Shakira and Juanes; and actor John Leguizamo.

Ecuador

About 25% of the Ecuadorian population is indigenous. There are 11 indigenous groups, each with its own language and customs. The largest is the Andean Quichua, over two million strong. Still, more than 65% of the population is considered mestizo. Just 3% of Ecuadorians are Afro-Ecuadorian, descendants of African slaves who were forced to work in the coastal areas. Caucasian, Asian, and Middle Eastern immigrants account for the remaining population. The population is about equally divided between the central highlands and the low-lying coastal region. Over the last few decades there has been a steady migration toward the cities, and today 60% of Ecuadorians reside in urban areas. El Oriente (the eastern, Amazon basin region of Ecuador) remains the least populated area in the entire country; only 3% of the population lives here.

In the highland areas, the local people have managed to hold on to their traditional culture. It's very common to see people still celebrating ancient holidays such as Inti Raymi—a festival welcoming the summer solstice. In Otavalo, in the northern highlands, the people still wear traditional clothing, and they have also kept their artisan traditions alive. The finest handicrafts in the country can be found here.

Because of the Amazon basin's isolated location, the locals here were able to escape domination by the Spanish and managed to maintain thousand-year-old rituals and customs. Some groups never had contact with "the outside world" until the 1960s and 1970s. Visitors to the Ecuadorian jungle who are taken to Amazonian villages will find that people here live very much as their ancestors did thousands of years ago.

Much of the art you will see in Ecuador is folk art and crafts. When it comes to modern art, one name reigns supreme—Osvaldo Guayasamín. Renowned throughout Latin America and beyond, many of Guayasamín's most famous pieces are expressions of outrage at the military governments in South America in the 1970s.

Paraguay

Paraguay's population of 6.8 million is 95% mestizo—a mixture of Spanish and Guaraní Indian. Approximately 50% live in urban areas and many exist on subsistence farming. There are approximately 10,000 indigenous Indians living in the north of the country, along with small communities of Mennonites. Some Japanese and Korean immigrants have settled in the south.

Despite the strong Guaraní presence, Paraguayan culture has a distinct European flavor, the legacy of Spanish colonial rule and the Jesuit missions. This is most evident in traditional Paraguayan music; see "South America in Popular Culture: Books, Films & Music" below for details.

Peru

Peru's nearly 30 million people are predominantly mestizo and Andean Indian, but there are also significant minority groups of Afro-Peruvians (descendants of African slaves, confined mainly to a coastal area south of Lima), immigrant Japanese and Chinese populations that are among the largest on the continent, and smaller groups of European immigrants, including Italians and Germans. Their religion is mainly Roman Catholic, though many people still practice pre-Columbian religious rituals inherited from the Incas.

Peru has, after Bolivia and Guatemala, the largest population, by percentage, of Amerindians in Latin America. Perhaps half the country lives in the *sierra,* or highlands, and most of these people, commonly called *campesinos* (peasants), live in either small villages or rural areas. Descendants of Peru's many Andean indigenous groups who live in remote rural areas continue to speak the native languages Quechua (made an official language in 1975) and Aymara or other Amerindian tongues, and for the most part they adhere to traditional regional dress. However, massive peasant migration to cities from rural highland villages has contributed to a dramatic weakening of indigenous traditions and culture across Peru.

Indigenous Amazonian tribes in Peru's jungle are dwindling in number—today, the population is less than two million. Still, many traditions and languages have yet to be extinguished, especially deep in the jungle—though most visitors are unlikely to come into contact with groups of unadulterated, non-Spanish-speaking native peoples.

Peru has one of the richest handicrafts traditions in the Americas. Many ancient traditions, such as the drop spindle (weaving done with a stick and spinning wooden wheel) are still employed in many regions. Terrific alpaca wool sweaters, ponchos, and shawls; tightly woven and brilliantly colored blankets and tapestries; and many other items of great quality are on display throughout Peru.

See "South America in Popular Culture: Books, Films & Music" later for details on the country's literary, film, and music history.

Uruguay

There are 3.4 million Uruguayans, 93% of whom are of European descent. About 5% of the population is of African descent, and 1% is mestizo. The majority of Uruguayans are Roman Catholic. Most live in the capital or one of only 20 other significant towns. Uruguay enjoys high literacy, long life expectancy, and a relatively high standard of living. Despite some economic uncertainty, it remains largely sheltered from the pervasive poverty and extreme socioeconomic differences characterizing much of Latin America.

Uruguay has a rich artistic heritage. Among the country's notable artists are the sculptor José Belloni and the painter Joaquín Torres-García, founder of Uruguay's Constructivist movement.

Venezuela

Venezuela has a population of approximately 27 million people, some 80% of whom live in a narrow urban belt running along the Caribbean coast and slightly inland. Venezuela is a young country, with an estimated half the population under 20 and around 70% under 35. Almost 70% of the population is mestizo. Another 19% are considered white, and 10% are black. While indigenous peoples make up only about 1% of the population, their influence and presence are noticeable. Venezuela has more than 20 different indigenous tribes totaling some 200,000 people. The principal tribes are the Guajiro, found north of Maracaibo; the Pémon, Piaroa, Yekuana, and Yanomami, who live in the Amazon and Gran Sabana regions; and the Warao of the Orinoco Delta.

More than 90% of the population claims to be Roman Catholic, although church attendance is relatively low and Venezuelans are not considered the most devout of followers on the continent. There is a growing influx of U.S.-style Protestant denominational churches, as well as small Jewish and Muslim populations. The country's indigenous peoples were an early target of Catholic missionary fervor, although their traditional beliefs and faith do survive. One of the most interesting religious phenomena in the country is the cult of María Lionza, a unique syncretic sect that combines elements of Roman Catholicism, African voodoo, and indigenous rites.

Although Venezuela has its fair share of European-influenced colonial and religious art, its most important art, literature, and music are almost all modern. Jesús Soto is perhaps the country's most famous artist. A pioneer and leading figure of the kinetic art movement, Soto has major and prominent works in public spaces around Caracas.

2 SOUTH AMERICA PAST & PRESENT

It has been said that 57 million people were living in the Americas when Columbus landed here in 1492. The arrival of the Europeans in this isolated area of the world brought many problems for the local people. With their gunpowder and horses, the Europeans had a distinct military advantage and were able to destroy powerful empires. They also introduced foreign diseases, such as smallpox, measles, and typhus, which wiped out entire communities. But what a boon for the Spanish crown—explorers discovered precious "jewels" here, including corn, potatoes, chocolate, and, of course, gold and silver. Thus began the age of colonialism. Amazingly, 400 years after the Spanish conquest of South America, millions of indigenous people have managed to hold on to their pre-Columbian past. That's what makes South America so unique. Visitors can explore the ruins of old Inca palaces, hike along Inca trails, witness colorful local celebrations that honor the sun or Pachamama (Mother Earth), and visit museums filled with amazing artifacts—gold chest plates, alpaca ponchos, tightly woven textiles, hand-carved silver figurines, wonderfully descriptive ceramic jugs—that give testament to the rich cultural heritage that existed here before the arrival of the Spanish.

ARGENTINA

A Look at the Past

Several distinct indigenous groups populated the area now called Argentina well before the arrival of the Europeans. The Incas made inroads into the highlands of the northwest. Most other groups were nomadic hunters and fishers, such as those in the Chaco, the Tehuelche of Patagonia, and the Querandí and Puelche (Guennakin) of the pampas. Others (the Diaguitas of the northwest) developed stationary agriculture.

In 1535, Spain—having conquered Peru and being aware of Portugal's presence in Brazil—sent an expedition headed by Pedro de Mendoza to settle the country. Mendoza was initially successful in founding Santa María del Buen Aire, or Buenos Aires (1536), but lack of food proved fatal. Mendoza, discouraged by Indian attacks and mortally ill, sailed for Spain in 1537; he died on the way.

Northern Argentina (including Buenos Aires) was settled mainly by people traveling from the neighboring Spanish colonies of Chile and Peru and the settlement of Asunción in Paraguay. Little migration occurred directly from Spain; the area lacked the attractions of colonies such as Mexico and Peru, with their rich mines, a large supply of Indian slave labor, and easy accessibility. Nevertheless, early communities forged a society dependent on cattle and horses imported from Spain, as well as native crops such as corn and potatoes. Pervasive Roman Catholic missions played a strong role in the colonizing process. The Spanish presence grew over the following centuries, as Buenos Aires became a critical South American port.

The years 1806 and 1807 saw the first stirrings of independence. Buenos Aires fought off two British attacks, in battles known as the Reconquista and the Defensa. Around this time, a civil war had distracted Spain from its colonial holdings, and many Argentine-born Europeans began to debate the idea of self-government in the Buenos Aires *cabildo* (a municipal council with minimal powers, established by colonial rulers). On July 9, 1816, Buenos Aires officially declared its independence from Spain, under the name United Provinces of the Río de la Plata. Several years of hard fighting followed before the Spanish were defeated in northern Argentina. But they remained a threat from their base in Peru until it was liberated by General José de San Martín (to this day a national hero) and Simón Bolívar from 1820 to 1824. Despite the drawing up of a national constitution, the territory that now constitutes modern Argentina was frequently disunited until 1860. The root cause of the trouble, the power struggle between Buenos Aires and the rest of the country, was not settled until 1880, and even after that it continued to cause dissatisfaction.

Conservative forces ruled for much of the late 19th and early 20th century, at one point deposing from power an elected opposition party president through military force. Despite the Conservatives' efforts to suppress new social and political groups—including a growing urban working class—their power began to erode. In 1943, the military overthrew Argentina's constitutional government in a coup led by then army colonel Juan Domingo Perón. Perón became president in a 1946 election and was reelected 6 years later. He is famous (although by no means universally applauded) for his populist governing style, which empowered and economically aided the working class. His wife, Eva Duarte de Perón (popularly known as Evita), herself a controversial historical figure, worked alongside her husband to strengthen the voice of Argentina's women. In 1955, the military deposed Perón, and the following years were marked by economic troubles (partly the result of Perón's expansive government spending) and social unrest, with a surge in terrorist activity by both the left and the right. While Perón was exiled in Spain, his power base in Argentina strengthened, allowing his return to the presidency in 1973. When he died in 1974, his third wife (and vice president), Isabel, replaced him.

The second Perónist era abruptly ended with a March 1976 coup that installed a military junta. The regime of Jorge Rafael Videla carried out a campaign to weed out anybody suspected of having Communist sympathies. Congress was closed, censorship imposed, and unions banned. Over the next 7 years, during this "Process of National Reorganization"—a period known as the Guerra Sucia (Dirty War)—the country witnessed a level of political violence that affects the Argentine psyche today: More than 10,000 intellectuals, artists, activists, and others were tortured or executed by the Argentine government. The mothers of these *desaparecidos* (the disappeared ones) began holding Thursday afternoon vigils in front of the Presidential Palace in Buenos Aires's Plaza de Mayo as a way to call international attention to the plight of the missing. Although the junta was overturned in 1983, the weekly protests continue to this day.

Public outrage over the military's human rights abuses, combined with Argentina's crushing defeat by the British in the 1982 Falkland Islands war, undermined the dictatorship's control of the country. An election in 1983 restored constitutional rule and brought Raúl Alfonsín of the Radical Civic Union to power. In 1989, political power shifted from the Radical Party to the Peronist Party (established by Juan Perón), the first democratic transition in 60 years. Carlos Saúl Ménem, a former governor of a province of little political significance, won the presidency by a surprising margin.

A strong leader, Ménem pursued an ambitious but controversial agenda, with the privatization of state-run institutions as its centerpiece. Privatization of inefficient state firms reduced government debt by billions of dollars, and inflation was brought under control. After 10 years as president—and a constitutional amendment that allowed him to seek a second term—Ménem left office. Meanwhile, an alternative to the traditional Perónist and Radical parties, the center-left FREPASO political alliance, had emerged. Radicals and FREPASO formed an alliance for the

October 1999 election, and their candidate defeated his Perónist competitor.

President Fernando de la Rua, not as charismatic as his predecessor, was forced to reckon with the recession the economy had suffered since 1998. In an effort to eliminate Argentina's ballooning deficit, de la Rua followed a strict regimen of government spending cuts and tax increases recommended by the International Monetary Fund. However, the tax increase crippled economic growth, and political infighting prevented de la Rua from implementing other needed reforms designed to stimulate the economy. With a heavy drop in production and steep rise in unemployment, an economic crisis loomed.

The meltdown arrived with a run on the peso in December 2001, when investors moved en masse to withdraw their money from Argentine banks. Government efforts to restrict the run by limiting depositor withdrawals fueled anger throughout society, and Argentines took to the streets in sometimes violent demonstrations. De la Rua resigned on December 20, as Argentina faced the worst economic crisis in its history. A series of interim governments did little to improve the situation, as Buenos Aires began to default on its international debts. On January 1, 2002, Peronist President Eduardo Duhalde unlocked the Argentine peso from the dollar, and the currency's value quickly tumbled.

Poverty and emigration followed. Under popular president Nestor Kirchner (known as "The Penguin" for his Patagonian roots), the situation improved. High commodity prices and a weak peso caused an export boom, not to mention a surge in tourism both national and international.

Argentina Today

In October 2007, Kirchner decided not to run for reelection (he could have easily won a second term) and handed the candidacy to his wife, Senator Cristina Fernández de Kirchner, which she won by a large majority. However, runaway inflation, a paralyzing farmer's dispute, and the overall global downturn has seen the first couple lose some of their sheen and caused the Argentine economy to stumble. Allegations of corruption and rising unemployment mean Nestor Kirchner will have his work cut out for him if he wishes to regain the presidency in 2011.

BOLIVIA

A Look at the Past

Lake Titicaca, the birthplace of the Incas, is one of Bolivia's most sacred and historic sites. But the history of Bolivia begins thousands of years before the arrival of the Incas. The Tiwanaku culture, which eventually spread to the area from northern Argentina and Chile all the way up to southern Peru, was one of the most highly developed pre-Columbian civilizations. From 1600 B.C. to 100 B.C., the Tiwanaku made the important move of domesticating animals, which allowed them to become more productive farmers. From 100 B.C. to A.D. 900, the arts flourished in the Tiwanaku culture. But it wasn't until A.D. 900 to 1200 that the Tiwanaku became warriors and set out to dominate the area that is now Bolivia. A drought destroyed the heart of the Tiwanaku region in the 13th century, and when the Incas swooped down from Peru around 1450, the Tiwanaku had broken up into small Aymara-speaking communities. The Quechua-speaking Incas dominated the area until the arrival of the Spanish in 1525.

Bolivia proved to be the crown jewel of the Spanish empire. As early as 1545, silver was discovered in southern Bolivia. Over the next 200 years, Potosí, home of Cerro Rico (the "rich hill," which was the source of all the silver), became one of the largest and wealthiest cities in the world. Getting rich quickly was the name of the game for most European settlers in Bolivia. Other than the development of Potosí and transportation systems to deliver the silver to the rest of the world, much of Bolivia remained neglected. Indigenous men were forced to work in the mines, often for no pay. This was only the beginning of a system of inequality and sharp class distinctions that to this day exist in Bolivia.

Not surprisingly, the first rumblings for independence arose in the area of Chuquisaca (present-day Sucre, which was then the administrative capital of Potosí). The first revolutionary uprising took place in Chuquisaca in 1809, but Bolivia did not win independence until August 6, 1825.

The age of the republic did not bring much glory to Bolivia. In the next 100-plus years, Bolivia lost its seacoast to Chile in the War of the Pacific (1879–83); in 1903, after a conflict with Brazil, Bolivia was forced to give up its access to the Acre River, which had become a valuable source of rubber; and in the Chaco War (1932–35), Bolivia surrendered the Chaco region, which was believed to be rich in oil, to Paraguay. The high price of silver in the late 19th century and the discovery of tin in the early 20th century kept Bolivia afloat.

After the Chaco War, which drained Bolivia's resources and caused great loss of life, the indigenous people began to distrust the elite ruling classes. In December 1943, the pro-worker National Revolutionary Movement (MNR) organized a revolt in protest of the abysmal working conditions and inflation. This was the beginning of the MNR's reign of power. In 1951, the MNR candidate, Víctor Paz Estenssoro, was elected president, but a military junta denied him power. In 1952, the MNR, with the help of peasants and miners, staged a successful revolution. The MNR managed to implement sweeping land reforms and nationalize the tin holdings of the wealthy. Under the reign of Estenssoro, the government also introduced universal suffrage and improved the educational system.

The MNR managed to hold on to power until a coup in 1964. For the next 20 years, Bolivia became a pawn in the Cold War between the United States and the Soviet Union. A series of military revolts brought power to both leftist and right-wing regimes. In 1971, Hugo Bánzer Suárez became president with the support of the MNR and instituted a pro-U.S. policy. In 1974, because of growing opposition, he set up an all-military government. He was forced to resign in 1978. In the ensuing years, a series of different leaders were unable to deal with the problems of high inflation, growing social unrest, increased drug trafficking, and the collapse of the tin market. Víctor Paz Estenssoro returned to power in 1985. He kept the military at bay and was able to create economic stability. Finally, in 1989, Jaime Paz Zamora, a moderate, left-leaning politician, was elected president; he worked to stamp out domestic terrorism, bringing a semblance of peace to the country. In 1993, a mining engineer, Gonzalo Sánchez de Lozada, was elected president. He worked successfully to reprivatize public business, an effort that actually helped the economy. In 1997, Hugo Bánzer Suárez returned to power. He worked with the United States to eradicate coca growing, with much opposition from local farm workers. The late 1990s marked another period of social unrest for Bolivia, with frequent strikes that paralyzed the nation.

President Gonzalo Sánchez de Lozada was elected president in 2002, but his cooperation with the United States in eradicating coca growing (and thus causing much unemployment) turned most of the country against him. When he signed a deal to export Bolivian gas to the United States and Mexico and transport it via Chile, he sparked a tinderbox of protest among the nation's indigenous people. In late 2003, the anger erupted in violent demonstrations in La Paz and El Alta, the neighboring city. Thousands of peasants flocked to the city from rural areas to participate in the revolt. The situation deteriorated quickly and more than 70 people were killed by the police. On October 17, 2003, more than a quarter of a million protesters rallied in La Paz's Plaza de San Francisco, near the Presidential Palace. Gonzalo Sánchez de Lozada stepped down and fled to Miami; Vice President Carlos Mesa was appointed president. Things returned to normal very quickly but again erupted in early 2005. The gas issue polarized the nation, with the poorer indigenous people accusing the European elite of selling their country's valuable resources.

Bolivia Today

In June 2005, Mesa was forced to resign and Supreme Court judge Eduardo Rodríguez was placed as head of an interim government. In December 2005, former coco farmer Evo Morales was declared Bolivia's first indigenous president. Feared by conservatives for his close relationship with Venezuelan president Hugo Chávez and frequent jabs at the United States, Morales has enjoyed great popularity among the lower classes that make up the bulk of the population. However, a new constitutional assembly has caused uproar in the eastern provinces, and nationalization of the country's gas reserves has scared off foreign investors. A declaration of autonomy by the eastern (richer) provinces has further polarized a society that some say is near a breaking point. It remains to be seen whether Morales can keep both sides happy and his country together.

BRAZIL

A Look at the Past

At the time of the Europeans' arrival in 1500, there were between one million and eight million indigenous people in Brazil, speaking nearly 170 different languages. The Europeans were seeking pau-brasil, a type of wood that could be processed to yield a rich red dye. Coastal Indians were induced to cut and sell timber in return for metal implements such as axes. It was an efficient system, so much so that within a little more than a generation, the trees—which had by then given their name to the country—were all but nonexistent.

But the Portuguese colony soon found a better source of income in sugar, the cash crop of the 16th century. Sugar cane grew excellently in the tropical climate of northeast Brazil. Turning that cane into sugar, however, was backbreaking work, and the Portuguese were critically short of labor. So the Portuguese began to import slaves from West Africa. Brazil was soon one leg on a lucrative maritime triangle: guns and supplies from Portugal to Africa, slaves from Africa to Brazil, sugar from Brazil back to Europe. Within a few decades, colonial cities such as Salvador and Olinda were fabulously rich.

In the early 1700s, gold was uncovered in what would later be Minas Girais. In addition to the miners, the other main beneficiary of the Minas gold rush was Rio de Janeiro, the major transshipment point for gold and supplies. In recognition of this, in 1762, the colonial capital was officially transferred to Rio. It would likely have remained little more than a backwater colonial capital had it not been for Napoleon. In 1807, having overrun most of western Europe, the French emperor set his sights on Portugal. Faced with the imminent conquest of Lisbon, Portuguese Prince Regent João (later King João VI) fled to his ships, opting to relocate himself and his entire court to Brazil. In 1808, the king and 15,000 of his nobles, knights, and courtiers arrived in the rather raw town of Rio. When the king returned to Portugal in 1821, Brazilians—among them the king's 23-year-old son, Pedro—were outraged at the prospect of being returned to the status of mere colony. In January 1822, Pedro announced he was remaining in Brazil. Initially, he planned on ruling as prince regent, but as the year wore on, it became clear that Lisbon was not interested in compromise, so on September 7, 1822, Pedro declared Brazil independent and himself Emperor Pedro I.

Brazil in this period was a deeply conservative country, with a few very wealthy plantation owners, a tiny professional class, and a great mass of slaves to cultivate sugar or Brazil's new cash crop, coffee. Though the antislavery movement was growing worldwide, Brazil's conservative landowning class was determined to hold on to its slaves at all costs. In the 1850s, under heavy pressure from Britain, Brazil finally moved to halt the importation of slaves from Africa, though slavery wasn't officially outlawed until 1888. Seeking a new source of labor, in 1857 Brazil opened itself up to immigration. Thousands poured in, mostly Germans and Italians, settling themselves in the hilly, temperate lands in the south of Brazil.

When reformist army officers and other liberals staged a coup in 1889, the 57-year rule of Pedro II (son of the first emperor) came to an end. The republic that took its place had many of the same ills of the old regime. Corruption was endemic, rebellions a regular occurrence. Finally, in 1930, reformist army officers staged a bloody coup. After several days of fighting, a military-backed regime took charge, putting an end to the Old Republic and ushering in the 15-year reign of the fascinating, maddening figure of Getúlio Vargas.

Vargas began his time in office as a populist, legalizing unions and investing in hundreds of projects designed to foster the industrial development of the country. When the workers nonetheless looked set to reject him in renewed elections, Vargas tore up the constitution and instituted a quasi-fascist dictatorship, complete with a propaganda ministry that celebrated every action of the glorious leader Getúlio. In the early 1940s, when the United States made it clear that Brazil had better cease its flirtation with Germany, Vargas dumped his fascist posturing, declared war on the Axis powers, and sent 20,000 Brazilian troops to take part in the invasion of Italy. When the troops came home at war's end, the contradiction between the fight for freedom abroad and the dictatorship at home proved too much even for Vargas's political skills. In 1945, the army removed Getúlio from power in a very quiet coup. In 1950, he returned, this time as the democratically elected president, but his reign was a disaster, and in 1954, he committed suicide.

In 1956, Juscelino Kubitschek (known as JK) took office, largely on the strength of a single bold promise: Within 4 years, he would transfer the capital from Rio de Janeiro to an entirely new city located somewhere in Brazil's vast interior. The site chosen in Brazil's high interior plateau (the *sertão*) was hundreds of miles from the nearest paved road, thousands from the nearest airport. Undaunted, JK assembled a team of Brazil's top modernist architects—among the best in the world at the time—and 4 years later, the new capital of Brasília was complete.

Democracy, unfortunately, did not fare well in the arid soil of the *sertão.* In 1964, the army took power in a coup, ushering in an ever more repressive military dictatorship that would last for another 20 years. For a time, no one complained much. Thanks to massive government investment, the economy boomed. São Paulo, which had been little more than a market town in the 1940s, exploded in size and population, surpassing Rio to become the heart of Brazil's new manufacturing economy. These were the days of the Brazilian "economic miracle."

In the early '70s, however, it became clear that much of the economic "miracle" had been financed on easy international loans, much of that invested in dubious development projects (roads that disappeared into the forest, nuclear power plants that never functioned) or channeled directly into the pockets of various well-connected generals. The international banks now wanted their money back, with interest. As discontent with the regime spread, the military reacted with ever-stronger repression.

The 1980s were perhaps Brazil's worst decade. Inflation ran rampant, while growth was next to nonexistent. Austerity measures imposed by the International Monetary Fund left governments with little money for basic infrastructure—much less social services—and in big cities such as Rio and São Paulo, *favelas* (shantytowns) spread while crime spiraled out of control.

In the midst of this mess, the army began a transition to democracy. In 1988, in the first direct presidential election in over 2 decades, Brazilians elected a good-looking millionaire named Fernando Collor de Mello. It proved to be a bad move, for Collor was soon found lining his pockets with government cash. The civilian government did prove capable of legally forcing him from office, however, paving the way in 1992 for the election of Fernando Henrique Cardoso.

Though an academic Marxist for much of his career, once in office FHC proved to be a cautious centrist. In his 8 years in office, he managed to reign in inflation, bring some stability to the Brazilian currency, and begin a modest extension of social services to Brazil's many poor.

The main opposition throughout this period was the Workers Party (PT), led by Luiz Inácio Lula da Silva, a charismatic trade unionist with a personal rags-to-riches story. Born into poverty in the Northeast, Lula, as he is usually known, left school to work as a shoeshine boy, got a job in a São Paulo factory, joined the metal workers' union, and began to get involved in politics. During the waning days of Brazil's dictatorship, he and others formed the Workers Party and only just lost Brazil's first democratic election in 1988. Lula persevered, however and, finally, in 2002, in his fourth attempt, was elected Brazilian president, the first democratically elected leftist to hold power in Brazil.

Brazil Today

Hopes for Lula's first term in office were enormous. Confounding expectations of financial markets and right-wing critics, Lula in office proved to be an economic moderate, continuing the tight-money policy of his predecessor. But to the disappointment of his supporters on the left, Lula also proved to be a poor and often absent administrator. Many of the hoped-for reforms—to the distribution of land, to access to education and health care, to environmental policy—were never enacted. His government has been plagued with scandal. Allegations of illegal campaign contributions and diversion of government funds has led to the resignation of a half dozen of Lula's chief ministers.

Lula's one signal accomplishment was a program—called Bolsa Familia—designed to provide basic income support to very low-income families. The popularity of this program, combined with a continued strong economy, was enough to win Lula reelection in 2006. Barred from seeking a third term, Lula is now seeking to position a successor to carry the elections in 2010.

In the cities, things have certainly improved. Governments have paid off the worst of the '80s debts and have funds available to spend on increased policing, better street lighting, and extending services such as sewers, water, and schooling to urban slum dwellers. Though gangs remain stubbornly entrenched in many of the *favelas* of Rio and São Paulo, a new program in Rio de Janeiro is reoccupying *favelas* one by one, removing the gangs and replacing them with community police stations. All in all, the major cities of Brazil are cleaner and safer than they've been in a generation. Though they're a few years yet from matching post-Giuliani Manhattan for safety, Brazil's cities are far and away superior when its comes to sheer *joie de vivre.*

In recent years Brazil's burgeoning growth rate has put the country in the top tier of world economies. Perhaps to showcase its new status, Brazil has won the right to host some of the world's premier sporting events. In 2014, the FIFA Soccer World Cup will be held in nearly a dozen cities across Brazil. Two years later, tens of thousands of athletes and fans will descend on Rio de Janeiro to compete in and watch the 2016 Olympic Summer Games. This will mark the first time the games have ever been held in South America.

CHILE

A Look at the Past

Chile's history as a nation began rather inconspicuously on the banks of the Mapoche River on February 12, 1541, when the Spanish conquistador Pedro de Valdivia founded Santiago de la Nueva Extremadura. At the time, several distinct indigenous groups called Chile home, including the more advanced northern tribes (which had already been conquered by the Incas), the fierce Mapuche warriors of the central region, and the nomadic hunting and gathering tribes of Patagonia. In Spain's eyes, Chile did not hold much interest because of its lack of riches such as gold, and the country remained somewhat of a colonial backwater until the country's independence in 1818, which was led by Bernardo O'Higgins, the son of an Irish immigrant. Spain did, however, see to the development of a feudal landowning system whereby prominent Spaniards were issued a large tract of land and an *encomienda,* or a group of Indian slaves, that the landowner was charged with caring for and converting to Christianity. Thus rose Chile's traditional and nearly self-supporting hacienda, known as a *latifundio,* as well as a rigid class system that defined the population.

Chile experienced an economic boom in the early 20th century in the form of nitrate mining in the northern desert, a region that had been confiscated from Peru and Bolivia after the War of the Pacific in 1883. Mining is still a huge economic force, especially copper mining, and Chile's abundant natural resources have fostered industries in petroleum, timber, fishing, agriculture, tourism, and wine.

Chile enjoyed a politically democratic government until the onset of a vicious military dictatorship, led by General Augusto Pinochet, who took power from 1973 to 1990. In 1970, voters narrowly elected the controversial Dr. Salvador Allende as Chile's first socialist president. Allende vowed to improve the lives of Chile's poorer citizens by instituting a series of radical changes that might redistribute the nation's lopsided wealth. Although the first year showed promising signs, Allende's reforms ultimately sent the country spiraling into economic ruin. On September 11, 1973, military forces led by Pinochet and supported by the U.S. government toppled Allende's government with a dramatic coup d'état, during which Allende took his own life. Upper-class Chileans celebrated the coup as an economic and political salvation, but nobody was prepared for the brutal repression that would haunt Chile for the next 17 years. Most disturbing were the series of tortures and "disappearances" of an estimated 3,000 of Pinochet's political adversaries, including activists, artists, journalists, professors, and any other "subversive" threats. Thousands more fled the country.

Following a "yes" or "no" plebiscite in 1988, Chileans voted to end the dictatorship, and though Pinochet didn't step down as President for another 2 years and he headed the Chilean army for a few more years, since then the country has put great effort into establishing a solid democracy. Today the country is considered the most politically stable in Latin America. Pinochet spent his post presidency years living a cushy life until a banking scandal and judicial inquiries into human rights abuses forced him to spend his last years under house arrest until his death in 2006. Shortly before that, Chile elected its first female president, Michelle Bachelet. The fact that Bachelet was tortured under Pinochet showed just how far the country had come.

Chile Today

At the present, the Chilean economy is stronger and more stable than any other in Latin America. It is rich in natural resources such as copper, forestry, salmon harvesting, and agriculture, and now tourism is becoming an economic heavyweight. In spite of one of the lowest rates of unemployment in Latin America and a relative lack of corruption, Chile still has far to go to solve social problems such as poverty and inadequate education for the majority of its children. Chile also still suffers from an unhealthy dose of classism; however, the country boasts a larger middle class than its neighbors Peru and Bolivia, with about 30% of the population living under the poverty level.

Billionaire centralist businessman Sebastián Piñera became President of Chile in 2010, the first time since the end of the Pinochet regime that power has not been held by the leftist coalition. Experts saw it as an important sign of renewal.

COLOMBIA

A Look at the Past

Colombia has been inhabited for about 12,000 years. Unlike the Inca to the south and the Maya to the north, who developed vast civilizations, the dozens of indigenous groups that inhabited Colombia formed relatively small hunter-gatherer societies. The most notable of these societies were the Muisca, who inhabited the inner Andean region in and around what is today Bogotá, and the Tayronas, who inhabited the Atlantic Coast.

The Spaniards were able to pacify the indigenous peoples of Colombia fairly easily. Alonso de Ojeda was the first European to set foot in Colombia, in 1499, followed in 1525 by Rodrigo de Bastidas. On the northern coast, he founded Santa Marta, Colombia's oldest city. The important port city of Cartagena was begun in 1533 by Pedro de Heredia, a few years before Jiménez de Quesada founded the modern-day capital of Bogotá in 1538. Because Colombia never had a large number of indigenous peoples—and many of them were wiped out by disease after the arrival of the Spaniards—the slave trade began in the late 1500s. Millions of Africans arrived in Colombia via Cartagena, one of Latin America's most important slave-trading posts. For about the next 300 years, Spain ruled Colombia, which was then called the Presidencia del Nuevo Reino de Granada, an area that included modern-day Colombia, Venezuela, and Panama.

Colombia's struggle for independence officially began in 1781 with the Revolución Comunera in the small town of El Socorro. Independence hero Simón Bolívar began his struggle against Spain in 1812, but didn't gain Colombia's independence until the final battle of Boyacá, on August 7, 1819. Thus, Bolívar became Colombia's first president.

Unfortunately, Colombia's independence didn't mean the end of bloodshed. In 1849, the formation of the Liberal and Conservative parties laid the foundation for the conflict that would—and still does—continue to haunt the country. Between 1849 and 1948, nearly half a million Colombians were killed in various insurrections pitting Liberals against Conservatives.

But it wasn't until 1948 that things really got ugly, with La Violencia, a violent time of upheaval that claimed the lives of another 500,000 Colombians in a decade. For several years, there was a period of relative peace, but in 1964, the Revolutionary Armed Forces of Colombia (FARC) was founded, pitting insurgent communists against the ruling elite. Although originally a political organization, the FARC, and later the National Liberation Army (ELN) and the M-19 guerilla groups, soon found their way into the Colombian cocaine trade, resulting in an even greater degree of violence and terrorism. Meanwhile, wealthy landowners, the military, and even government officials encouraged the organization of right-wing paramilitary units, armed groups whose aim was to fight the leftist guerillas. However, like the guerillas, the paramilitaries soon became involved in the drug trade, resulting in frequent, bloody battles between these two factions. Paramilitary power reached its pinnacle during the Pablo Escobar years (1980s and early 1990s), when Escobar and the paramilitaries more or less controlled Colombia through frequent bombings, kidnappings, and assassinations.

In 2002, conservative hard-liner Alvaro Uribe won the presidency, vowing to eliminate the guerillas and, through a peace accord, demobilize the paramilitaries.

Colombia Today

True to his word, President Alvaro Uribe has restored much order in Colombia. In fact, an entire generation of Colombians is experiencing peace for the first time. Once holding the dubious title of being the most dangerous country in the world, President Uribe's government has reduced kidnapping and murder rates by more than 50%. Leftist guerillas have dramatically loosened their grip on Colombian politics and have been pushed out of the cities. (Two of the FARC's seven-member secretariat were killed in a single week in early 2008.) Once afraid to drive long distances because of kidnappings, Colombians are now taking to the road in record numbers as travel becomes safe again.

But it's not all good news: Support is down for President Uribe, and crime rates in major cities have begun to increase slightly. Like many Latin American countries, Colombia also continues to be a country divided by class and stuck in an almost feudal-like society in which the rich rarely interact with the poor and the poor have little chance of upward mobility. Forty percent of Colombians live in absolute poverty, many without life's basic necessities. A small minority of Colombians continue to control most of the country's wealth and resources.

It is unclear if Alvaro Uribe will run for a third term in office, as he already changed the constitution to allow for a second term. Anti-Uribistas say Uribe's government is corrupt and a third term will elevate him to a dictator-like level. Although the Uribe fervor that claimed the country several years ago has subsided substantially, it remains to be seen if any other candidate can maintain Colombia's relative peace.

ECUADOR

A Look at the Past

Before the Spanish arrived in Ecuador in 1533, a group of diverse cultures lived in various areas throughout the country. Many of these cultures, including the Valdivia, Machalilla, and Chorrera, may not have left any written records, but the highly sophisticated pottery, beautifully designed artwork, and gold masks that have been unearthed in Ecuador prove that these cultures were highly developed. By the 16th century, the Incas had conquered the highland areas of the country of Ecuador. At its height, the Inca empire encompassed an estimated 15 million people, belonging to roughly 100 ethnic or linguistic communities, and covered an area of over 6,000 sq. km (2,340 sq. miles), within which were more than 25,000km (15,500 miles) of roads. Cuenca, in southern Ecuador, was the second-most important city in the Inca empire. In 1526, when the Inca leader Huayna Capac died, he divided the empire between his two sons. Huáscar gained control of Cusco and Peru, while Atahualpa inherited control of Cuenca and Ecuador. This split led to a bloody war, which weakened both sides. In part, because of this conflict, when the Spanish arrived in the mid–16th century, they had little trouble defeating the Incas.

Ecuador's indigenous cultures had a hard time under Spanish rule. Newly introduced diseases decimated the local population, and the Spanish system of *encomienda* (forced labor) broke the spirit and the health of the local people. Ecuador wasn't rich in natural resources and therefore wasn't of great value to the Spanish. In the 300 years before independence, Ecuador was alternately governed by the viceroyalty of Peru to the south and the viceroyalty of New Granada in Bogotá to the north.

Ecuador declared independence in 1820, but the independence forces weren't able to defeat the Spanish royalists until the Battle of Pichincha on May 24, 1822. At that time, Ecuador became a part of Gran Colombia, which consisted of Colombia and Venezuela. In 1830, Ecuador seceded from Gran Colombia and became its own republic. The rest of the 19th century was marked by political instability. Conflicts flared between the Conservatives, led by Gabriel García Moreno, and the Liberals, led by Eloy Alfaro. The Conservatives sided with the Catholic Church and Ecuadorians of privilege, while the Liberals fought for a secular government and social reforms.

At the end of the 19th century, Ecuador was getting rich off cocoa exports, and the economy was booming. Later in the early 20th century, when the demand for cocoa decreased, political unrest ensued. In 1925, the military seized power from the former procapitalist leaders. The 1930s were a time of uncertainty for Ecuador: From 1931 to 1940 a total of 14 different presidents spent time at the helm. In 1941, war erupted between Ecuador and Peru over land in the Amazon basin region. In an attempt to settle the dispute, Ecuador signed the Protocol of Rio de Janeiro in 1942 and surrendered much of the disputed land to Peru.

The post–World War II era was a time of prosperity for Ecuador. The country became one of the world's leaders in banana exports. From 1948 to 1960, there were three freely elected presidents who were all able to serve their full terms. In 1952, President José María Velasco implemented social reforms, including improvements in both the schools and the public highways. But in 1960, when Velasco was again elected president, he was faced with a failing economy, and he was unable to hold on to power. During the next 10 years, a series of military juntas controlled the country.

The economy rebounded in the 1970s. Ecuador became the second-largest oil-producing nation in South America, after Venezuela. The oil boom led to an increase in public spending and industrialization. But by the 1980s, when the oil bubble began to burst, the country was again faced with serious economic troubles, including inflation and an insurmountable international debt. In 1986, the price of oil collapsed, and in 1987, an earthquake partially destroyed one of Ecuador's major pipelines.

Rodrigo Borja came to power in 1988. In an attempt to alleviate his country's problems, he increased the price of oil while severely cutting back on public spending. But that wasn't enough—inflation soared, and civil unrest increased. In 1992, in a conciliatory move, the government ceded a large region of the rainforest to the indigenous people. In 1995, Ecuador again disputed its border with Peru in the Amazon area; it wasn't until 1998 that it finally settled with Peru and secured its access to the Amazon. The 3-year war proved to be a drain on the economy. In 1997, a national protest, with overwhelming support of all the Ecuadorian people, succeeded in ousting the corrupt President Abdalá Bucaram. The national congress appointed a new president and reformed the constitution. But again, low oil prices and the devastating effects of El Niño brought the economy to its knees.

In recent years, the instability of Ecuador's executive branch has drawn international attention. Between 1996 and 2006, seven presidents attempted to govern the nation. They all failed to ameliorate the political volatility, either because of a hostile Congress, a military coup d'état, or sheer incompetence.

On July 12, 1998, the mayor of Quito, Jamil Mahuad, was elected president. His biggest success was negotiating a peace treaty with Peru over the country's borders in the Amazon, but he was unable to turn the economy around. His popularity reached a low point on January 9, 2000, when he announced his decision to eliminate the sucre, the national currency, and replace it with the U.S. dollar. On January 21, 2000, the military and police failed to quell chaotic nationwide protests. Mahuad was forced to resign, and his vice president, Gustavo Noboa, became president. Noboa continued on the course of dollarization, and in September 2000, the U.S. dollar became the country's official currency. This move helped to decrease the country's international debt, but it has never really been able to stem inflation.

In April 2005, President Lucio Gutiérrez was fired by Ecuador's congress for interfering with the Supreme Court. He was granted asylum in Colombia and Alfredo Palacio became president. In October 2005, Gutiérrez returned to Quito and was arrested upon his arrival.

Ecuador Today

In 2006, Ecuador went to the polls once more and elected Rafael Correa. The eighth president in 11 years, Correa is a center-left former economist who considers himself a personal friend of Venezuela's Hugo Chávez. He made waves early on in his presidency, winning an April 2007 public referendum allowing him to call a Constituent Assembly to rewrite the national constitution. On September 29, 2008, Ecuadorians voted by a large margin to ratify the new constitution, and President Correa's PAIS Alliance (Alianza PAIS) party controls 74 of the 130 seats in the new Constituent Assembly (national congress), giving it broad powers to enact legislation.

In late 2008, Correa announced that Ecuador would cease interest payments on the country's outstanding international bond debt. So far, the country has been able to buy back over 90% of its bond debt at around 30 cents on the dollar, vastly reducing the country's foreign debt.

Despite the debt reduction and income from higher petroleum prices, the gap between rich and poor remains wide. Estimates vary as to what percentage of the population lives below the poverty line, but most agree the rate is at least 40% and perhaps as high as 70%.

PARAGUAY

A Look at the Past

Pre-Columbian Paraguay was a rich tribal patchwork with mostly Guaraní settled in the south and a band of hunter-gatherers known as Aché inhabiting the subtropical areas that now border Brazil. The Chaco contained a diverse variety of people, known as Abipones, Tobas, Matacas, and Mbayás. Predominately peaceful people, they nevertheless often fought amongst themselves and resisted strongly any Spanish incursions. Indian hostility to foreign settlements continued into the 20th century.

Alejo Garcia was the first European to enter the area in 1524 from the Brazilian side. His discovery of silver in the Andes led to the naming of Río de la Plata (Silver River). Pedro Mendoza, fleeing Indian persecution in Buenos Aires, founded the first settlement at Asunción in 1527. He formed an alliance with the Guaraní and the 350 Spanish men assimilated into Guaraní culture, though eventually the Europeans became the dominant political and economic force.

The arrival of the Jesuits in the late 16th century led to huge social changes, the remains of which can be seen today. The Jesuits had less success in the north where the non-Guaraní tribes resisted strongly and launched raids on the settlements. The Jesuits were eventually expelled by the Spanish in 1767 and the crown lost interest in the Chaco when they realized it held neither gold nor silver or a transit route to Bolivia.

In fact, the Spanish lost interest in the area completely and offered little resistance when independence was declared in 1811. Paraguay's first dictator thus emerged and Dr. José Gaspar Rodríguez de Francia ruled the country with an iron fist and a touch of paranoia from 1814 to 1840. Such was his unpopularity that 30 years after his death, his enemies dug up his remains and threw them into the Río Paraguay.

Carlos Antonio López then led the country for 20 years and ushered in a period of development, prosperity, and military might. This was all squandered by his son Francisco Solano López and his Irish mistress Eliza Lynch when they took power in 1862 and led the country into a disastrous war with Brazil, Argentina, and Uruguay that became known as the War of the Triple Alliance. The result was a catastrophe for Paraguay, with a paranoid and bloodthirsty Solano López meeting his end in the northern jungle and the country decimated; half its population was lost to war, famine, and disease and 150,000 sq. km (58,500 sq. miles) of territory was lost forever.

A period of tumultuous politics followed with the opposing Colorado and Liberal parties engaging in a disordered tug of war for power right up to modern times. The economy slowly recovered with European and Argentine immigration. Agricultural achievements were revived, sovereignty reestablished, and important reforms made.

Then the Chaco War erupted in 1932—a bloody squabble with Bolivia over the piece of northern territory that many thought may hold oil—including Standard Oil and Shell Oil, who were both accused of funding the opposing sides in return for exploration rights. In the end it proved a futile exercise and the area remains populated by isolated Indian tribes and self-sufficient Mennonite communities.

Colorado and Liberal rivalry continued, often taking on the characteristics of a full-scale civil war. Then a military coup in 1954 ushered in the 35-year-long, brutal, corrupt, and repressive dictatorship of General Alfredo Stroessner. It was not until another coup by General Andrés Rodríguez in 1989 and elections in 1991 that Paraguayans could eventually claim to have a "normal," fully fledged democracy.

Juan Carlos Wasmosy became Paraguay's first elected civilian president in 1993. The military menace remained, however, in the shape of General Lino Oviedo. His threat of a coup landed him in jail, but he gained immediate release when his political ally Raúl Cubas won the 1998 election. The pardon caused public disgust followed by outrage at the assassination of critic and Vice President Luis María Argaña in 1999. Cubas and Oviedo eventually joined Stroessner in exile in Brazil and Luis Angel González Macchi assumed power. His initial popularity was soon tarnished with allegations of corruption, not helped by the fact that he drove a stolen BMW.

Paraguay Today

Economic mismanagement, inefficiency, and rampant corruption still dog Paraguayan politics. The Colorado party remains the dominant political force, but it finally relinquished 61 years of the presidency with the election in 2008 of an ex-bishop known as Fernando Lugo. The leader of a loose coalition known as the Patriotic Alliance for Change, Lugo is a political newcomer with very little power base and many challenges facing him. Promising to fight poverty, inequality, and corruption, Lugo's own integrity was called into question in 2009 when it was revealed that he had fathered three children with three different women while still a bishop. Lugo survived the scandal, but it remains to be seen whether he can bring badly needed change to Paraguay, especially in the area of land reform.

PERU

A Look at the Past

Over the course of nearly 15 centuries, pre-Inca cultures settled along the Peruvian coast and highlands. By the 1st century B.C., during what is known as the Formative or Initial Period, Andean society had created sophisticated irrigation canals and produced its first textiles and decorative ceramics. Another important advance was labor specialization, aided in large part by the development of a hierarchical society.

Though Peru is likely to be forever synonymous with the Incas, who built the spectacular city of Machu Picchu high in the Andes, that society, in place when the Spanish conquistadors arrived at the end of the 15th century, was merely the last in a long line of pre-Columbian cultures. The Inca empire (1200–1532) was short lived, but it remains the best documented of all Peruvian civilizations. The Incas' dominance was achieved through a formidable organization and highly developed economic system. They laid a vast network of roadways nearly 30,000km (18,600 miles) total across the difficult territory of the Andes, connecting cities, farming communities, and religious sites. Their agricultural techniques were exceedingly skilled and efficient, and their stonemasonry remains unparalleled.

By the 1520s, the Spanish conquistadors had reached South America. Francisco Pizarro led an expedition along Peru's coast in 1528. Impressed with the riches of the Inca empire, he returned to Spain and succeeded in raising money and recruiting men for a return expedition. In 1532, Pizarro made his return to Peru overland from Ecuador. After founding the first Spanish city in Peru, San Miguel de Piura, near the Ecuadorian border, he advanced upon the northern highland city of Cajamarca, an Inca stronghold. There, a small number of Spanish troops—about 180 men and 30 horses—captured the Inca emperor Atahualpa. The emperor promised to pay a king's ransom of gold and silver for his release, but the Spaniards, having received warning of an advancing Inca army, executed the emperor in 1533. It was a catastrophic blow to the Inca empire.

Two years later, Pizarro founded the coastal city of Lima, which became capital of the new colony, the viceroyalty of Peru. The Spanish crown appointed Spanish-born viceroys the rulers of Peru, but Spaniards battled among themselves for control of Peru's riches, and the remaining Incas continued to battle the conquistadors. Pizarro was assassinated in 1541, and the indigenous insurrection ended with the beheading of Manco Inca, the last of the Inca leaders, in 1544. The Inca Tupac Amaru led a rebellion in 1572, but he met the same fate. Over the next 2 centuries, Lima gained in power and prestige at the expense of the old Inca capital of Cusco and became the foremost colonial city of the Andean nations.

By the 19th century, grumbling over high taxes and burdensome Spanish controls grew in Peru. After liberating Chile and Argentina, José de San Martín set his sights north on Lima in 1821 and declared it an independent nation the same year. Simón Bolívar, the other hero of independence on the continent, came from the other direction. His successful campaigns in Venezuela and Colombia led him south to Ecuador and finally to Peru. Peru won its independence after crucial battles in late 1824.

After several military regimes, Peru finally returned to civilian rule in 1895. Landowning elites dominated this new "Aristocratic Republic." In 1941, the country went to war with Ecuador over a border dispute (just one of several long-running border conflicts). Though the 1942 Treaty of Rio de Janeiro granted the area north of the Marañón River to Peru, Ecuador would continue to claim the territory, part of the Amazon basin, until the end of the 20th century.

Peru's recent political history has been a turbulent mix of military dictatorships, coups d'état, and several disastrous civilian governments, engendering a near-continual cycle of instability. The country's hyperinflation, nationwide strikes, and two guerrilla movements—the Maoist Sendero Luminoso (Shining Path) and the Tupac Amaru Revolutionary Movement (MRTA)—produced violence and terror throughout the late 1980s and early 1990s. Meanwhile, Peru's role on the production end of the international cocaine trade grew exponentially.

With the economy in ruins and the government in chaos, Alberto Fujimori, the son of Japanese immigrants, became president in 1990. Fujimori promised to fix the ailing economy and root out terrorist guerrillas, and in 1992, his government succeeded in arresting key members of both the MRTA and the Shining Path, catapulting the president to unprecedented popularity. Fujimori's strong-arm tactics became suddenly authoritarian, however, shutting down Congress in 1992, suspending the constitution, and decreeing an emergency government (which he effectively ruled as dictator). Still, Fujimori was reelected in 1995.

Most international observers denounced Peru's 2000 presidential election results, which were announced after Fujimori's controversial runoff with Alejandro Toledo, a newcomer from a poor Indian family. Public outcry forced Fujimori to call new elections, but he escaped into exile in Japan and resigned the presidency in late 2000 after a corruption scandal involving his shadowy intelligence chief, Vladimiro Montesinos. Toledo, a former shoeshine boy and son of an Andean sheep herder who went on to teach at Harvard and become a World Bank economist, won the election and became president in July 2001, formally accepting the post at Machu Picchu.

Peru Today

Peru remains a society dominated by elites. Toledo had labeled himself an "Indian rebel with a cause," alluding to his intent to recognize and his support for the nation's Native Andean populations, or *cholos*. Yet Toledo's once-hopeful program Perú Posible did not achieve the results Peruvians had hoped for; his government was mired in corruption and nepotism. Farmers and teachers on strike repeatedly paralyzed Peru, forcing Toledo to declare a national state of emergency. The president limped to the end of his term in 2006.

The Peruvian economy has expanded steadily in the last decade. Former president Alan García—who had also fled Peru after a disastrous term in the 1980s—improbably returned from exile and won the presidency in 2006. A one-time populist, García has positioned himself as a centrist, seeking to put a clamp on inflation and pursuing free-market policies. Most notably, he pushed for a free-trade agreement with the United States, a treaty that was ratified by the U.S. Congress in December 2007 (and which entered into force in February 2009). The Peruvian economy recorded a robust growth rate of 9.2% in 2008, a 15-year high and one of the most impressive in the world, and to date the García presidency (which runs until 2011) has been largely stable and peaceful. The pace of growth dropped by half in 2009, though, and the divide between rich and poor, coastal elites and indigenous highlanders, and modern and traditional continues to loom large.

URUGUAY

A Look at the Past

In 1516, a surprised Spanish sailor discovered the region that would become Uruguay and was followed by Ferdinand Magellan, who in 1520 anchored outside present-day Montevideo. Despite the Spaniards' success in making the journey from home, they were less successful settling in the area, due to resistance from the Charrúa Indians who inhabited the land. Not until the early 17th century, as Spain competed with Portugal for South American territory, did Spanish colonization begin to take hold. Colonia del Sacramento was founded by the Portuguese in 1680. Not to be outdone, the Spanish responded by establishing Montevideo after the turn of the century.

Uruguay's history until the beginning of the 19th century was marked by colonial struggle for the Argentina-Brazil-Uruguay region. In 1811, José Gervasio Artigas initiated a revolt against Spain. The war lasted until 1828, when Uruguay earned its independence from Brazil, to which it had been annexed by the Portuguese. Argentine troops assisted the Uruguayan fighters in defeating the Brazilians, and Uruguay adopted its first constitution by 1830. Political instability dominated the rest of the century, as large numbers of immigrants arrived from Europe. By 1910, the population reached one million.

Uruguay experienced significant political, economic, and social progress under the two presidencies of José Batlle y Ordoñez, who in the early 20th century created what many considered a model social-welfare state. Life seemed to be getting better and better for Uruguayans, who achieved their first World Cup victory in 1930 and again in 1950. By the 1960s, however, Uruguay's charmed reputation as the "Switzerland of South America" was shattered by corruption, high unemployment, and runaway inflation. The instability of Uruguay's economy paved the way for military government, which seized control in 1973 and was responsible for the detention of more than 60,000 citizens during its time in power.

Civilians resumed control of the government in 1984, when Colorado Party leader Julio María Sanguinetti won the presidency. His tenure in office was focused on national reconciliation, the consolidation of democratic governance, and the stabilization of the economy. Violations under the military regime were controversially pardoned in order to promote reconciliation, and a general amnesty was given to military leaders charged with human rights abuses.

The National Party's Luis Alberto Lacalle held the presidency from 1990 to 1995, during which time he reformed the economy in favor of trade liberalization and export promotion. He brought Uruguay into the Southern Cone Common Market (Mercosur) in 1991 and privatized inefficient state industries. Julio María Sanguinetti was reelected in 1995, continuing Uruguay's economic reforms and improving education, public safety, and the electoral system. The economy flagged at the end of the century, exacerbated by the Argentine economic meltdown in 2001. Tourism plummeted a staggering 90%. Currency devaluation followed, and with it a slow recovery.

Uruguay Today

Uruguay's first socialist president, Tabaré Vázquez, took power in March 2005, ushering in a more stable and prosperous period. Ex military leaders were finally taken to court for human rights abuses and the economy brightened, with GDP growing by 30%. In 2006, an environmental dispute broke out with Argentina over two multibillion-dollar paper mills built in Uruguay that the Argentines say will pollute the River Plate. The argument has led to numerous border closures between both countries and looks set to continue for some time.

Despite setbacks like the border closures, Uruguay's economic crisis has certainly passed and the country has become a regional leader in education again, with schemes like every child receiving a free computer. Political maturity is also more evident as another leftist president took over from Vázquez in 2009. Ex-guerrilla José Mujica has promised to continue his predecessor's policies of opening the Uruguayan economy and sharing the country's great wealth with the nation's poor.

VENEZUELA

A Look at the Past

The area we call Venezuela has been inhabited for more than 15,000 years. The earliest indigenous residents were predominantly nomadic; these peoples, descendents of the Carib, Arawak, and Chibcha tribes, left few traces and no major ruins. The most significant archaeological evidence left behind is some well preserved, although largely undeciphered, petroglyphs found in various sites around the country.

In 1498, on his third voyage, Christopher Columbus became the first European to set foot in Venezuela. One year later, Amerigo Vespucci and Alonso de Ojeda, leading another exploration to the New World, dubbed the land Venezuela, or "Little Venice," in honor of (or perhaps making fun of) the traditional indigenous stilt-houses along Lake Maracaibo, which called to mind the namesake city.

Lacking readily apparent gold and silver stores, Venezuela was never a major colonial concern for the Spanish crown. The first city still in existence to be founded was Cumaná, established in 1521. Caracas, the current capital, was founded in 1567. For centuries, the colony was governed from afar by Spanish seats in Peru, Colombia, and the Dominican Republic. The relative isolation and low level of development encouraged a certain amount of autonomy. Perhaps this is why Venezuela figured so prominently in the region's independence struggle.

Venezuela's struggle for independence from Spanish rule began in the early 19th century and took nearly 2 decades to consolidate. The principal figure in the fight was Simón Bolívar, El Libertador—a Venezuelan-born aristocrat considered the "Father of Venezuela" and the person most responsible for ending Spanish colonial rule throughout South America. Taking over in the wake of Francisco de Miranda's death, Bolívar led a series of long and bloody campaigns. In 1819, in the city of Angostura (currently Ciudad Bolívar), the rebel forces declared the independence of Gran Colombia, comprising the current states of Panama, Colombia, Ecuador, and Venezuela. Still, Royalist forces held on, and fighting continued for several more years, culminating in the decisive 1821 Battle of Carabobo. Nevertheless, both Bolívar's good fortune and the fledgling nation were short-lived. By 1830, El Libertador had died as a poor and pitiful figure, and Gran Colombia had dissolved into separate nation-states, including present-day Venezuela.

Over the next century or so, Venezuela was ruled by a series of strongman dictators, or *caudillos,* whose reigns were sometimes interspersed with periods of civil war and anarchy. One of the most infamous dictators was General Juan Vincente Gómez, who ruled from 1908 until his death in 1935. In addition to his cruelty and suppression of dissent, Gómez is best known for having presided over the first period of discovery and exploitation of Venezuela's massive oil reserves. Venezuela quickly became the world's number-one exporter of crude oil. However, there was little trickledown, and most of the wealth generated went to international oil companies and a small local elite.

By 1945, the opposition, led by Rómulo Betancourt, was able to take power and organize elections, granting universal voting rights to both men and women. In 1947, Rómulo Gallegos, the country's greatest novelist, became the first democratically elected president of Venezuela. However, the new democracy was fragile, and Gallegos was overthrown in a military coup within 8 months.

The subsequent military dictator, Colonel Marcos Pérez Jiménez, rivaled Gómez in brutality but will forever be remembered as the architect of modern Venezuela. Pérez Jiménez dedicated vast amounts of oil money to public works projects and modern buildings. In 1958, Pérez Jiménez himself was overthrown and a more stable democracy was instituted. Back in the spotlight, Rómulo Betancourt became the first democratically elected president to finish his term. For decades, Venezuela enjoyed a relatively peaceful period of democratic rule, with two principal parties amicably sharing power.

But Venezuela's almost sole dependence on oil revenues, modern ebbs and flows in international crude prices and production, and internal corruption and mismanagement all took their toll. In 1992, there were two unsuccessful coup attempts, one led by brash paratrooper Lieutenant Colonel Hugo Chávez Frías. Chávez spent several years in prison, but was not out for the count. In 1993, President Carlos Andrés Pérez was found guilty of embezzlement and misuse of public funds, was impeached, and spent more than 2 years under house arrest. More economic woe and political turmoil ensued, and in December 1998, Hugo Chávez, back in the spotlight, was elected president in a landslide.

Venezuela Today

Chávez's folksy populism and leftist rhetoric give him a strong base of support among the poorer classes, although he has faced constant and fierce opposition from much of the political, business, and academic classes, as well as a hostile press. Soon after assuming power, Chávez orchestrated a series of maneuvers, including the dissolution of Congress and the drafting of a new constitution, which have granted him far-reaching powers.

Chávez's early years were marked by frequent public protests both in favor of and against his rule. Several of these protests turned violent, and fatal encounters between opposing sides were not uncommon. This turmoil caused massive capital and intellectual flight. In 2000, Chávez was reelected. However, in 2003, he was briefly ousted in an unsuccessful coup attempt. Soon after, the opposition called for a nationwide referendum on Chávez's rule, which Chávez won in 2004.

Bolstered by these electoral victories, and parallel victories of his party in the legislature, Chávez has been able to further his goals of leading a "Bolívarian revolution," which is an odd amalgam of Marx, Mao, Castro, and Bolívar. However, in December 2007, Chávez suffered a significant setback, with the defeat of constitutional amendments that would have allowed him to be reelected indefinitely.

Nevertheless, Chávez's rhetoric and policies have taken a sharp socialist turn, closely following the Cuban model—even employing many of the same slogans and programs. This shift has included severe curbs on press freedom, a new national school curriculum, and increased antagonism toward the United States. Part of this antagonism towards the United States has been directed at neighboring Colombia, which Chávez claims is being used as a base for an eventual U.S. invasion. Throughout 2009 Chávez has ratcheted up the rhetoric and tensions, going as far as ordering the population to prepare for war.

Thanks to high oil prices, Chávez has plenty of cash. This petro-dollar bonanza has filtered down some, and the country is still experiencing GDP growth, despite the global economic crisis. Nevertheless, critics claim that the benefits to the poor are far too few and often doled out according to political affiliation. Moreover, the country paradoxically faces energy shortages and rationing. Today, Venezuela remains fiercely divided, predominantly along class lines. Chávez's Bolívarian revolution remains a work in progress, and his current term doesn't expire until 2012.

3 THE LAY OF THE LAND

The 10 South American countries that we cover in this book comprise an enormous landmass with an incredibly varied terrain. Details on each country's specific ecosystems and flora and fauna can be found below.

ECOSYSTEMS

ARGENTINA At the heart of Argentina lies the flat, humid pampas, consisting of the central eastern provinces. To the south lies Patagonia, with its alpine Lake District, desolate arid steppes, and spectacular glaciers. The Andes flank the western border and touch every type of geographical zone. The red desert plateaus of Salta province contrast with the temperate lakes of Tafi del Valle and the humid cane fields of Tucuman. Farther south, the provinces of San Juan and Mendoza consist of vast desert scrub with little rain. Mesopotamia consists of the northern border province of Misiones and resembles a jungle frontier. Farther north and east, the land becomes a dry, inhospitable shrub, known as El Chaco, that extends all the way to Bolivia.

BOLIVIA Landlocked in the middle of the South American continent, Bolivia's 1,098,580 sq. km (424,160 sq miles) is nothing less than extreme. Much of the country, including most of the major cities, sits high in the Andes Mountains on the high altitude, cold, windswept Altiplano that begins with Lake Titicaca at the border with Peru and tops out at 6,542m (21,460 ft.) Nevado Sajama. In the southwest the world's largest salt desert, the Salar de Uyuni, and the nearby lagoons and geysers are the country's peak of strange and exotic geography. In complete contrast with the rest of the country, the east and north are hot and humid. Here you'll find the lush green Amazon lowlands and Chaco regions.

BRAZIL Brazil's 190 million citizens inhabit the fifth-largest country in the world, a nation about 10% larger than the continental U.S. The Amazon dominates the northern third of the country—a vast tropical rainforest with the river at its heart. The country's central interior is dominated by the *planalto,* a high dry plateau covered in *cerrado,* a type of dry savanna reminiscent of that of Southern Africa.

West of the *planalto* but south of the Amazon rainforest you find the Pantanal, a wetland the size of France that is one of the best places to see wildlife in the whole of South America. Brazil's Northeast is a land apart. Running roughly from São Luis to Salvador, the coast is dominated by midsize cities and sugar cane and the culture strongly Afro-Brazilian, while on the dry interior plateau those Nordestinos who haven't yet fled to the cities eke out a bare living on the land. Brazil's two chief cities, Rio de Janeiro and São Paulo, stand within a few hundred miles of each other close to the country's south coast. The area has the astonishing natural wonder of Iguaçu Falls, for many visitors a must-see.

CHILE Sandwiched between the Andes and the Pacific Ocean with a width that averages just 180km (112 miles) and some 4,830km (3,000 miles) of land, stretching from the arid northern desert to the wild desolation of Patagonia, Chile encompasses a dazzling array of landscapes and temperate zones. It is hard to believe such variation can exist in just one country; in fact, the only zone not found here is tropical.

The central region of Chile, including Santiago and its environs, features a mild Mediterranean climate, reminiscent of California, while the Atacama region claims the world's driest desert, a beautiful wasteland set below a chain of purple and pink volcanoes and high-altitude salt flats. The Atacama Desert sits at altitudes of 2,000m (6,560 ft.) and up. The extreme climate and the geological forces at work in this region have produced far-out land formations and superlatives such as the highest geyser field in the world.

COLOMBIA The hot and humid eastern third of Colombia starts in Villavicencio and is comprised of dense Amazon forest and unnavigable rivers. The central portion of the country, home to most of the country's largest and most important cities, such as Bogotá and Medellín, and set against the high Andes, incorporates just about every climate and microclimate—from sweltering, low-lying valleys, to snow-peaked mountaintops. Colombia's Atlantic coast is home to the Sierra mountains, the highest seaside mountain chain in the world, as well as the country's most popular beaches. The sweltering Pacific coast is a dense jungle area. Head south toward Ecuador and the mountains become more dramatic, the climate more arid.

ECUADOR Bordered on the north and east by Colombia, on the south and east by Peru, and on the west by the Pacific Ocean, Ecuador covers an area of just under 256,000 sq. km (99,840 sq. miles). The country also includes the Galápagos Islands, 970km (600 miles) due west from mainland coast. There are three primary geographic regions on mainland. The first is La Costa (the Coast), the low-lying area that runs the length of the Pacific coastline, where fertile plains and rolling rivers lead into pleasant Pacific beaches.

The center of the country is called La Sierra (the Mountains), with the Andes Mountains running all the way from north to south. German naturalist Alexander von Humboldt visited Ecuador in the early 19th century and named this central region "Avenue of the Volcanoes," and its star is the 5,897m (19,348 ft.) Volcán Cotopaxi, the world's fourth-highest active volcano. El Oriente (the East) runs from the edge of the Andes to the borders with Colombia and Peru, and contains a chunk of the Amazon rainforest. This area covers over 25% of the country's landmass, but is home to less than 5% of its human population.

The Galápagos archipelago consists of 13 large islands, 17 islets, and several dozen ancient rock formations scattered over 7,500 sq. km (2,925 sq. miles) of ocean. Though famous for its beaches, active volcanoes also rise from several of the islands, reaching altitudes of up to 1,600m (5,250 ft.).

PARAGUAY The Rio Paraguay splits the country into two ecosystems, with the eastern region made up of grassy plains and wooded hills. Here the climate is more temperate, with lots of rainfall. The west can be humid too, especially along the riverbanks and marshes. However, the climate becomes drier as it stretches west into El Chaco, which features vast plains, high temperatures, and low rainfall.

PERU Peruvians are fond of pointing out that their country consists of three distinct geological components: coast, *sierra* (highlands), and *selva* (jungle). Although the largest cities are situated along the coast, the Amazon rainforest, which makes up nearly two-thirds of Peru, and the bold Andes Mountain range dominate the country. The Pacific coastal region is a narrow strip that runs from one end of the country to the other (a distance of some 2,200km/1,360 miles) and is almost entirely desert. The Andes, South

America's longest mountain range, is the most significant feature of the Peruvian landscape. The mountain ranges in the center of Peru, north of Lima, are among the highest in the country. Within Huascarán National Park, the Cordillera Blanca stretches 200km (124 miles) and contains a dozen peaks more than 5,000m (16,400 ft.) tall; the highest is Huascarán, at 6,768m (22,200 ft.). In extreme southern Peru, near Puno and Lake Titicaca, the Andes yield to the Altiplano, the arid high plains, with altitudes of 3,300m (.11,000 ft.). The *selva* ranges from cloud forest in the south to low-lying flatlands in the north. Although 60% of Peru is Amazon rainforest, only about 5% of the country's human inhabitants reside there. Massive Lake Titicaca, shared with Bolivia, is the largest lake in South America and the world's highest navigable body of water (at 3,830m/12,562 ft.).

URUGUAY Uruguay is basically an extension of the Argentine pampas and the rolling hills of southern Brazil. Most of the country is made up of flat, fertile grasslands with little forest but lots of rain. The plains break up into low rolling hills and valleys to the west and north and there are some large lakes near Brazil. The coastal area is notable for extensive dunes and beaches.

VENEZUELA Venezuela sits at the top of the South American continent, and has a total area of 916,445 sq. km (353,841 sq. miles), including a host of offshore islands. The most significant of these islands are Isla Margarita and the Los Roques archipelago. Venezuela's coastal areas are hot and tropical. Its offshore islands are paradisiacal, with soft white sand beaches, rich coral reefs, and clear Caribbean waters.

The Andean mountains run south through the country, beginning along the northwest Caribbean coast. At 5,007m (16,423 ft.), Pico Bolívar is the country's highest mountain, and is just outside the mountain city of Mérida. To the east of the Andes, much of the central part of the country is taken up by Los Llanos (the Plains), a broad expanse of territory amazingly rich in wildlife. Waters from Los Llanos empty into the grand Orinoco River, which reaches the Atlantic Ocean via the vast tropical lowlands of the Orinoco River Delta. Farther south and west, near the world's highest waterfall, Angel Falls, the rain and snowmelt form some of the earliest headwaters of the Amazon River. Much of Venezuela's southern region is taken up by the Gran Sabana, or Great Savannah. This broad and wild area features unique tabletop mountains, or tepuis. Roraima, the largest of these tepuis, was allegedly the inspiration for Arthur Conan Doyle's *The Lost World.*

FLORA & FAUNA

ARGENTINA Unsurprisingly, with such a large variety of ecosystems, Argentina has a huge range of flora and fauna. One of the most spectacular spots for wildlife watching is Esteros de Ibera, a vast wetland south of Iguazú where hundreds of species of birds compete with caiman and swamp deer for your attention. Guanaco and vicuña populate the arid Andes, while big cats like puma and jaguar are not unknown. Patagonia is more famous for its coastal wildlife, including sea lions, elephant seals, and whales. There are many species of trees; even the western deserts host two small squat specimens known as algorroba and quebracha, as well as huge three-fingered cacti. To the humid north you'll find carob and monkey puzzle trees; in the pampas, vast grasslands; and in El Chaco, you'll find a mixture of forest and savanna.

BOLIVIA Owing to Bolivia's drastic changes in altitude, the country has a diverse range of flora—from high altitude shrubbery to green Amazonian rainforest. The desertlike Altiplano is limited to cacti and Ichu, a coarse grass that grows only above 3,500m (11,480 ft.). On the shores of Lake Titicaca plants like tortora reeds, famously used in the construction of the Uros islands, can be found. In the tropical regions in the country's north and east, there's an explosion of diversity in the form of hardwoods, fruits, vegetables, orchids, and Pará rubber trees.

Also owing much to the great divide in altitude, the country's fauna is equally diverse. In the Altiplano, South American camelids such as alpacas, llamas, and vicuñas play prominent roles, as do majestic condors, adorable vicachas, proud pumas, sly Andean foxes, and in the southwest, thousands upon thousands of feeding James, Andean, and Chilean flamingos.

In the north and east, the low-lying tropical forests and Pantanal are home to a wide range of rare species such as caimans, giant river otters, jaguars, spectacled bears, tapirs, and numerous species of monkeys. The bird life is remarkable here, with one of the highest levels of biodiversity on the planet. In protected areas such as Noel Kempff, Amboró, and Madidi national parks you might encounter macaws, herons, toucans, hummingbirds, the Cock of the Rock, and thousands of other species.

BRAZIL The golden lion tamarin—a beautiful squirrel-size primate—is the signature species of Brazil's Atlantic ecosystem, now much endangered. Common tamarins can often be seen in trees and parks in Rio. The coast is also the only place you'll find truly significant mountains. Inland, Brazil rises to a high plateau of from 1,000m to 1,500m (3,280–4,920 ft.) in altitude that rolls all the way to the western foothills of the Andes. In the southern parts of Brazil (Paraná, Santa Catarina, Rio Grande do Sul), this plateau was covered in subtropical rainforest, most of which has long since been converted to cropland. In the center and center west where things are drier (Goiania, Brasília, Mato Grosso do Sul, Mato Grosso, Tocantins), you'll find *cerrado,* dry scrubland forest reminiscent of California chaparral, dotted with beautiful branching Ipe trees—known for bright yellow or purple flowers. Farther west still, on the Paraguay river basin that forms the border with Bolivia, stands the Pantanal. This world's biggest wetland (about the size of Florida) is actually a seasonal flood plain that fills and then slowly drains in response to seasonal rains. It is home to a rich assortment of birdlife—jabiru storks, American woodstorks, red and hyacinth macaws—plus capybara, giant otters, anteaters, and caiman. In the north, the semidesert inland from the coast is known as *sertão.* This is cowboy country, with cattle, bandits (historically), cactus, and not much else.

In the north, covering about a third of the country (Amazonas, Acre, Mato Grosso, Para, Roraima), stands the Amazon rainforest, the richest assortment of plants and animals on earth. Deforestation rates have been reduced in recent years, though a chunk the size of Connecticut still falls to the chainsaw every year.

CHILE Chile's climatic and topographical features correspond to defined botanical regions that boast a rich diversity of flora. Ethereal Atacama, which extends from the far north into Bolivia, is a desolate, lunar landscape where at higher altitudes cacti provide the only vegetation. In the central regions, greater rainfall and a humid environment produce shrubbery and trees with leaves known as sclerohyllous ("hard" leaves that facilitate a greater absorption of water). Predominant tree species include the guayacan, litre, lun, and peumo. The Central Valley is also characterized by hard espinos, a species of cactus, as well as the endangered Chilean palm.

Desert brush lands sweep the Altiplano (a high Andean plateau comprised of basins), which yield to more verdant grasslands on the lower slopes of the Andes. In the region south of the Bío-Bío River, temperate rainforests with high precipitation have yielded over 45 species of endemic trees. Magnolias, laurels, oaks, conifers, and beeches thrive in the dense forests here, but perhaps the most striking is the distinctive monkey puzzle tree (araucaria), Chile's national tree.

COLOMBIA Colombia's bird diversity is second only to Brazil, with over 1,800 species. It is the second-most biodiverse country in the world in terms of species per square mile, and is home to 10% of the world's species. The Amazon region and its rivers feature some of the world's strangest animals and marine life, such as the elusive pink dolphin. Tapirs, pumas, monkeys, wild boars, and caimans are among some of the jungle creatures visitors might spot.

Pine vegetation characterizes the high Andes, while low-lying areas are characterized by tropical vegetation. Colombia is home to over 50,000 plant species, most found in the dense jungle areas in the eastern and Pacific regions of the country.

ECUADOR The biodiversity found within Ecuador's borders is stunning. While it only makes up .02% of the world's landmass, it contains an amazing 10% of the world's plant species. In fact, Conservation International has listed Ecuador as one of just 17 "megadiverse" countries on the planet. Cataloguing of the nation's biological treasures is far from complete, and already scientists have counted 3,800 species of vertebrates, 1,550 species of birds, 320 species of mammals, 350 species of reptiles, 375 species of amphibians, 800 species of freshwater fish, and 450 species of marine fish. Ecuador is a bird-watcher's paradise: A full 18% of the world's bird species can be found in Ecuador, more bird species per square meter than in any other Latin American country. In fact, although Brazil is 30 times Ecuador's size, Ecuador has just as many species of birds. And last but not least, there are over a million species of insects in Ecuador (they're not all ugly—6,000 species are butterflies).

PARAGUAY Rampant deforestation has caused Paraguay to lose much of its wildlife habitat, and native animals like jaguars, deer, giant anteaters, and giant armadillos are now endangered species. In the country's many rivers you'll still find crocodiles, piranhas, and boa constrictors. Plant life includes many types of hardwoods, especially ceiba and quebracho. The Chaco region to the west is made up of scrub and thorn forest.

PERU Nearly two-thirds of Peru is jungle, and many naturalists and biologists believe that Peru's Amazon rainforest holds the greatest diversity in the world. It teems with a staggering roster of wildlife: 400 species of mammals, 2,000 species of fish, 300 reptiles, 1,800 birds, and more than 50,000 plants. The country counts 84 of 103 existing ecosystems and 28 of the 32 climates on the planet among its remarkable statistics. Recent studies have shown that a region just south of Iquitos has the highest concentration of mammals anywhere in the world. Peru's other significant fauna are the great Andean condors, found principally in Colca Canyon, near Arequipa, and the rich marine life of the Paracas National Reserve and Islas Ballestas (Peru's version of the Galápagos Islands), home to communities of endangered Humboldt penguins and sea turtles, sea lions, red boobies, and flamingoes. Coastal Peru south of Lima is also home to one of the greatest population densities of dolphins in the world, with one-third of the world's species identified.

URUGUAY Large wild animals have disappeared from the eastern regions of Uruguay. Foxes, deer, and otters can still be seen in the northern hills, while birdlife such as rheas, swans, and ducks can be found in the pampas and the central and northern lakes. Many indigenous hardwoods such as lapacho and quebracho have given way to introduced plant species such as eucalyptus and acacia.

VENEZUELA Thanks to its large and varied terrain, Venezuela has a stunning wealth of biodiversity. Bird-watchers will enjoy knocking many of the country's 1,200 species off their life lists. Of the most coveted species to spot here are the Andean condor, macaw, several toucan and parrot species, and the hoatzin, a strange and foul-smelling resident of the lowland plains. Meanwhile, over 325 mammals have been recorded, the most spectacular of which include the jaguar, capybara, manatee, and two distinct species of fresh water dolphin. The low, flooded plains of Los Llanos are a prime wildlife viewing spot, where you can see hundreds of bird species, as well as caiman, anaconda, and immense herds of capybara—the world's largest rodent.

With ecosystems that range from tropical lowland rainforest to high Andean paramo, with almost every conceivable permutation in between, Venezuela's flora is abundant and diverse. Thousands of orchid species can be found across the country, and dedicated naturalists will want to visit the Gran Sabana, where a host of endemic species can be found, including many specific to a particular tepui. In the lowland rainforests, large trees like the ceiba can grow as tall as 40m (130ft). Meanwhile, its branches are home to hundreds of species of bromeliads, orchids, and assorted other epiphytes.

4 SOUTH AMERICA IN POPULAR CULTURE: BOOKS, FILMS & MUSIC

For a general primer on South America, Paul Theroux's *Old Patagonian Express: By Train Through the Americas* provides a beautifully written account of his travels throughout the continent. Bruce Chatwin's *In Patagonia* offers an alternate take on the Patagonia region covered in the Theroux work.

If you're interested in a scholarly read, pick up John Charles Chasteen's *Born in Blood and Fire: A Concise History of Latin America.* The book only begins with the arrival of the Europeans in the Americas, but it gives a good overview of the diverse regions of Latin America.

Every traveler to Latin America should read Eduardo Galeano's *Memory of Fire* This astonishing book tells the history of the Americas via poetic prose and a unique style that redefines the form, function, and potential of nonfiction history.

If you'd like a visual overview of South America, *The Motorcycle Diaries,* which chronicles a road trip taken by a young Che Guevara, is a good bet.

ARGENTINA For a review of the country's history, try Nicolas Shumway's *The Invention of Argentina.* Argentine historians Jorge B. Rivera and José Gobello are instrumental in helping demystify modern Argentina. Their books are difficult to find in English; if you read Spanish, try Gobello's *Crónica General del Tango.* Jorgelina Corbatta offers the best account of Argentina's "dirty war" under the military dictatorship from 1976 to 1983 in *Narrativas de la Guerra Sucia en Argentina.*

Jorge Luis Borges sits at the top of Argentine fiction writers; read *Collected Fictions* for an overview of his work. Manuel Puig's *Kiss of the Spider Woman* and Julio Cortázar's *The Winners* are good picks for more contemporary Argentine writing.

Maria Luisa Bemberg is probably the most famous of late-20th-century Argentine filmmakers and specialized in period dramas; she's known for *Camila* and *Miss Mary. The Official Story,* by Luis Puenzo, and *The Night of the Pencils,* by Hector

Olivera, are two powerful dramas about the military dictatorship. *Man Facing Southeast* and *The Dark Side of the Heart* are two compelling movies by Eliseo Subiela. The Italian neorealist style of filmmaking is a strong influence in Argentine cinema, and nowhere is it more evident than in the movies of Pablo Trapero, such as *Crane World* and *El Bonarense. Blessed by Fire,* by Tristan Bauer, is possibly one of the best movies made about the Falklands War, while grifter movie *Nine Queens,* by Fabian Bielinsky, is so good that it was remade in Hollywood.

Unfortunately, Hollywood's take on Argentina is not so illustrious. (The less said about Alan Parker's *Evita,* the better). The best foreign movies about Argentina are those that make the setting speak for itself—two great examples of this are *Happy Together,* by Wong Kar Wai, and *Tango,* by Carlos Saura.

Of course, tango will always be associated with Argentina, but the country has lots more to offer music lovers. *Rock nacional* is the mainstream take on western pop, and *quarteto* and *folklorico* is what gets the locals dancing in the provinces, usually with the aid of a guitar, violin, and occasional synthesizer.

BOLIVIA *The Fat Man from La Paz,* edited by Rosario Santos, is a collection of contemporary short stories by Bolivian writers. The stories provide readers with a vivid picture of life in Bolivia. Che Guevara spent his last days on the run in Bolivia. There are several books detailing his journey. One of the best accounts is the *Complete Bolivian Diaries of Che Guevara and Other Captured Documents* by Ernesto Guevara and Daniel James.

Herbert S. Klein's *Bolivia: The Evolution of a Multi-Ethnic Society* does an excellent job of delving into the government, economics, and history of Bolivia. Klein also touches on art, architecture, and societal relations. For more information about the sophisticated pre-Inca Tiwanaku culture, your best bet is Alan L. Kolata's *The Tiwanku: Portrait of an Andean Civilization.*

For insight into the hard-knock mining life in the mines of Potosí, the documentary *The Devil's Miner* follows a 14-year-old boy as he works long hours to support his family in nothing less than appalling conditions.

The music of Bolivia's Aymara and Quechua Indians defines the country's sound, and dozens of small folk groups have had international success in North America and western Europe, such as Grupo Aymara, Los Jairas, and Bolivia Manta. Quechua singer Luzmila Carpio's records *Kuntur Mallku* and *Arawi* have also earned international praise.

BRAZIL There is no single good general history covering Brazil from 1500 to the present. *Colonial Brazil,* edited by Leslie Bethell, is a scholarly but readable account of Brazil under the Portuguese, while Peter Flynn's *Brazil: A Political Analysis* covers political history from the birth of the first republic to the close of the second dictatorship. For a fascinating introduction to an entire range of topics in Brazil, pick up the excellent anthology *Travelers' Tales: Brazil,* edited by Annette Haddad and Scott Doggett. *Tristes Tropiques* is a classic work of travel writing by the great French anthropologist Claude Lévi-Strauss.

Until he passed away in 2001, Bahian novelist Jorge Amado was considered a serious candidate for the Nobel Prize. His greatest novels include *Dona Flor and Her Two Husbands* and *Gabriela, Clove and Cinnamon.* In a previous generation, Joaquim Maria Machado de Assis wrote fiercely ironic novels and short stories, many set in Rio towards the end of the 19th century. His works available in English include *The Epitaph of a Small Winner.* Brazil's greatest social realist is Graciliano Ramos. His masterpiece *Barren Lives* is considered one of Brazil's finest novels.

Brazil has a long and impressive history of filmmaking, including a number of films by directors who have moved back and forth between Brazil and Hollywood. Hector Babenco is best known in Brazil for *Carandiru,* his excellent film about life in a São Paulo maximum security prison. North American audiences are more likely to have seen his work in *At Play in the Fields of the Lord* or *Kiss of the Spider Woman.* The granddaddy of Brazilian crossover hits has to be *Black Orpheus,* a 1959 retelling of the myth of Orpheus and Euridice, set in a poor neighborhood in Rio during the glorious nights of Carnaval. If you're interested in learning about Rio de Janiero's *favelas,* we recommend watching Fernando Meirelles's *City of God.*

Ever since Vinicius de Moraes and Tom Jobim penned the bossa nova hit "The Girl from Ipanema," Brazil has been a player on the international music scene. Bossa nova and samba were hot in the '50s and '60s, *Tropicalismo*—spearheaded by Brazil's megastars Caetano Veloso and Gilberto Gil—was popular in the '70s. One style that did make it out of Brazil (and maybe shouldn't have) to briefly dominate the dance floors of the late '80s was the Lambada. In the past 10 years, samba has also made a strong comeback, with dozens of clubs opening up in Rio and São Paulo, and *pagode* (a type of samba) bands like Revelação selling double platinum.

Local sounds encompass much more than samba and *pagode*, though, with Brazilian artists playing everything from rap, funk, jazz, and rock to regional rhythms such as the swinging afro-axé pop in Salvador and the fast maracatu in the Northeast. Then there are the regional trends that almost never make it to the rest of the world, among them the uniquely Brazilian country sound known as *sertanejo.* Likely the most unlooked-for trend is the mania for *forró* that has recently swept the country. A happy, upbeat, accordion-infused brand of country, *forró* began in Brazil's poorer northeastern regions, and came to the big cities as poor Nordestino migrants made their way south. And then there's *brega,* a kind of glam version of *forró,* with over-the-top costumes and shamelessly sentimental lyrics.

CHILE A quick, comprehensive guide to all things Chilean, Susan Roraff and Laura Camacho's *Culture Shock! Chile,* explains Chilean etiquette and culture. For history and a look into the Pinochet legacy that came to define modern Chile, try the following books: *A History of Chile, 1808–1994* by Simon Collier and William F. Sater; *A Nation of Enemies: Chile Under Pinochet* by Pamela Constable and Arturo Valenzuela; and *Chile: The Other September 11* by Ariel Dorfman et al.

Chile boasts two literary Nobel Prize winners, Gabriela Mistral and Pablo Neruda; however, most North Americans are probably most familiar with the Chilean export Isabel Allende, whose popular novels such as *Of Love and Shadows* and *House of the Spirits* have been made into major motion pictures. Her more recent books *My Invented Country* and *Inés of My Soul,* are great pretrip primers.

The Pinochet regime placed various limits on artistic liberties, which resulted in a dearth of mainstream cinematic production in the country during much of the late 20th century. At the moment, Chileans are renowned for preferring imported American movies (Hollywood movies that have been filmed or set here include *The Motorcycle Diaries, The Quantum of Solace,* and *Missing*) to home-grown independent productions. However, the success of Sebastian Silva's film *La Nana (The Maid),* which received international recognition at the 2009 Sundance Film Festival, seems to have ushered in a new era of cinematic pride and could be the start of a movie industry renaissance.

Nueva Canción (New Song) is the most significant musical genre in Chile born in the rebellious 1960s. These lyrical songs first became popular in both Chile and

Argentina via the work of troubadours Atahualpa Yupanqui and Violeta Parra. Today, the folk group Illapu, which excels at Andean instrumentals and salsa-tinged ballads, is perhaps the most popular band in Chile. Other popular bands include the heavy rock band Chancho en Piedra, as well as indie rockers Los Bunkers and pop stars La Ley, who enjoy a high profile in both the U.S. and the U.K.

COLOMBIA John Hemmings's *The Search for El Dorado* gives readers insight into the history and conquest of Colombia by the Spanish. For a general overview of Colombia's economy, government, history, geography, destinations, people, and more, try *Colombia, a Country Study Guide,* by USA International Business Publications, which is updated yearly and aimed at businesspeople. To understand the political crisis and never-ending civil war in Colombia, try *Colombia: Fragmented Land, Divided Society* by Frank Safford and Marco Palacios; *The Making of Modern Colombia: A Nation in Spite of Itself* by David Bushnell, Georg Wilhelm, and Friedrich Hegel; or *Bandits, Peasants, and Politics: The Case of "La Violencia"* by Gonzalo Sánchez.

Colombia's—and all of South America's—premiere literary figure is Nobel Prize winner Gabriel García Márquez, known for novels such as *Love in the Time of Cholera* and *One Hundred Years of Solitude,* both of which are widely available. *Vivir para Contarla,* the first volume of his three-part autobiography, is now available in English as *Living to Tell the Tale.*

Maria Full of Grace offers an engaging glimpse into Colombia's drug-running culture. *La Vendedora de Rosas (The Rose Seller),* directed by Victor Gavida and featuring real-life street children as actors, depicts life in the Medellín tough *comunas* (shanty towns). The 2008 movie, *Travel Paraiso,* tells the story of a middle class young man who arrives in New York as an illegal immigrant and touches on aspects of Colombian-American culture in New York. The 2007 movie *Satanas* details the story of Elisio, a Colombian Vietnam veteran who murders dozens of people in an angry rampage.

Due to European, indigenous, and African influences, Colombian music is varied and well known throughout Latin America. Drums dominate the Atlantic and Pacific coasts, and stringed instruments such as the harp and guitar dominate the Andean highlands. Colombia's most well-known artists are the pop stars Shakira, Juanes, and Carlos Vives, all of whom have had international hits. Those wanting a more "authentic" taste of Colombian music will want to check out Carlos Vives' latest album "Clasicos de La Provincia II," featuring vallenatos, Colombia's most popular music style. Salsa lovers will also want to get a hold of one of Joe Arroyo's many CDs.

ECUADOR Ecuador and the Galápagos Islands have captured the imagination of many North American and British writers. Herman Melville's *Las Encantadas* is a collection of various pieces from the 19th century that provide descriptions of the islands themselves, the inhabitants, and the whalers who passed through the area. Kurt Vonnegut's *Galápagos* is a hilarious story about human evolution. It starts off with a story about a small group of people who are shipwrecked and forever stuck on a small isolated island in the Galápagos. It then follows the evolution of these people for a million years into the future.

If you're interested in learning about how Charles Darwin formed his theory of evolution, you should pick up Darwin's *Voyage of the Beagle* or his *Origin of Species.* Michael H. Jackson's *Galápagos: A Natural History* is the best authority on the natural history of plants and animals in the Galápagos.

For contemporary naturalists, the best all-purpose field guide for those visiting Ecuador is David L. Pearson and Les

Beletsky's *Traveller's Wildlife Guide: Ecuador and the Galápagos Islands*. For a quick, simple, and concise history of Ecuador, try reading *In Focus Ecuador: A Guide to the People, Politics, and Culture* by Wilma Roos and Omer Van Renterghem. Linda Newson's *Life and Death in Early Colonial Ecuador* looks at the native people living in Ecuador in the 16th century and discusses how they were affected by both the Inca and Spanish conquests.

Ecuador has a small but budding film industry, but little that has enjoyed any international fame. The 2003 blockbuster *Master and Commander* does feature some excellent location shots of the land and seascapes, and flora and fauna, of the Galápagos Islands. Perhaps the most relevant film for English-speaking visitors is the 2005 docudrama *End of the Spear,* directed by Jim Hanon. Although filmed mostly in Panama, this movie tells the tale of the 1956 Waoroni killing of five missionaries in Ecuador's Amazon basin. The movie even includes cameos by several of the surviving members of the missionary families and members of the Waoroni tribe involved in the events.

Ecuador's music scene is dominated by contemporary imports from around Latin America, the United States, and Europe. However, throughout the country, you'll find discs and performances by a variety of homegrown traditional groups, playing a wide range of folk styles. The traditional music of the Andes features wind instruments such as the guaramo horn, the pifano and pinkullo flutes, and *rondador* (panpipes), supported by percussion. Its distinctive pentatonic scales give it a very haunting feel, and you are likely to hear familiar melodies if you happen upon any Andean bands, either playing in *peñas* (bars) or on public plazas.

PARAGUAY Augusto Roa Bastos is Paraguay´s most famous modern novelist and poet. *Son of Man* and *I the Supreme* are historical works that piece together the country's traumatic past and earned the exiled writer the Cervantes Prize in 1990. Other writers to look out for are Josefina Pla and Gabriel Casaccia.

Paraguayan film was in the doldrums for much of the 20th century, in part because of the repressive censorship of the Stroessner regime. In recent years there have been some signs of a renaissance, most notably in a beautifully shot rural drama called *The Paraguayan Hammock* (2006) by director Paz Encina. The most famous blockbuster to be set in Paraguay (it was also shot in Brazil and Argentina) is the epic, award winning *The Mission* (1996) with Robert De Niro.

Paraguay's most well-known type of music is Guarani folklore. This music has a strong colonial influence and is most notable for the use of giant harps that date back to the 17th century.

PERU Perhaps the classic work on Inca history is *The Conquest of the Incas* by John Hemming, a very readable narrative of the fall of a short-lived but uniquely accomplished empire.

Mario Vargas Llosa, Peru's most famous novelist and a perennial candidate for the Nobel Prize, was nearly elected the country's president back in 1990. *Aunt Julia and the Scriptwriter* is one of his most popular works; *The Real Life of Alejandro Mayta* is a dense meditation on Peruvian and South American revolutionary politics that blurs the lines between truth and fiction; and *Death in the Andes* is a deep penetration into the contemporary psyche and politics of Peru. Another side of the author is evident in the small erotic gem *In Praise of the Stepmother.*

For a glimpse into Peru's recent political history, check out the documentary film *The Fall of Fujimori.*

There is evidence of music in Peru dating back 10,000 years, and musical historians have identified more than 1,000 genres of music in the country. The *música folclórica* that emanates from high in the

Andes Mountains is known for its use of the *quena* (pan flute), played like a recorder; *charango* (from the lute family); and mandolin. The distinctive sounds of this Peruvian music were widely sampled in the Simon and Garfunkel classic "El Cóndor Pasa." That song was based on a melody by a Peruvian composer, Daniel Alomía Robles, who himself had appropriated a traditional Quechua *huayno* folk melody.

Along the coast south of Lima, black Peruvians created a unique mix of African rhythms and Spanish and other European influences, called *música criolla,* in which percussion is fundamental, in addition to strings and vocals. The music is frequently blusier than its jazz-inflected Afro counterparts that developed in Brazil and Cuba. Nicomedes Santa Cruz, Perú Negro, Eva Ayllón, Chabuca Granda, and Susana Baca are a few of the stars of Afro-Peruvian music.

URUGUAY Lawrence Weschler reports on Uruguay's "dirty war" in *A Miracle, A Universe.* Uruguayan journalist Eduardo Galeano examines the consequences of colonialism and imperialism in *Open Veins of Latin America. Blood Pact & Other Stories* is one of the few collections of beloved writer Mario Benedetti available in English. A good place to start tackling the work of essayist José Enrique Rodó is *Ariel.*

The movie *State of Siege* gives a compelling account of Uruguay's "dirty war" and the kidnapping of CIA operative Dan Mitrione.

Tango is an important musical form in Uruguay, and the country lays claim to being the birthplace of Carlos Gardel, the renowned tango artist. The country is also known for *candombe,* a popular form of African percussion music involving groups of drummers who spontaneously gather on street corners every Sunday evening in Montevideo.

VENEZUELA Perhaps no piece of literature is as closely associated with Venezuela as Sir Arthur Conan Doyle's 1912 *The Lost World,* which is set in an area modeled after Venezuela's Amazonas region. *The Lost World* has spawned numerous imitators and literary offspring, and has served as the model for a host of films, including *Jurassic Park.*

Anyone with even the slightest interest in Venezuelan literature should start with Rómulo Gallegos's 1929 classic *Doña Bárbara,* a tale of love and struggle on the Venezuelan plains. Gallegos was a former president and is widely considered the country's principal literary light. Also of interest are Gabriel García Márquez's *The General in His Labyrinth,* a fictional account of Simón Bolívar's dying days, and Isabel Allende's *Eva Luna,* which is set in a town based on the Venezuelan city of Colonia Tovar.

For a glimpse into one of the darker sides of present-day Venezuela—and Latin America, in general—try to see the film *Secuestro Express,* which tells the story of an "express kidnapping" in downtown Caracas, within the context of the country's current political and social situation, or Mariana Rondón's award-winning *Postcards from Leningrad,* which deals with the lives of a couple of children growing up amongst the revolutionary guerrilla movement of 1960's Venezuela.

If you want to take home some Venezuelan music, look for discs by pop crooner Ricardo Montaner, or salsa legend Oscar D'León.

3

Planning Your Trip to South America

The country chapters in this guide provide specific information on traveling to and getting around individual South American countries. In this chapter, we provide you with general information that will help you plan your trip.

1 WHEN TO GO

South America is a huge continent (it crosses both the Equator and the Tropic of Capricorn), and climatic conditions vary widely. In June, when it's freezing cold at the southern tip of Argentina, it's hot and humid in Venezuela. You can take into account, however, that more than 75% of the continent sits south of the Equator, which means that winter usually lasts from June through September and summer from December through March. In high-altitude cities, such as Quito, you can expect cool weather year-round; in the Amazon basin region—in the center of the continent, from Ecuador to Brazil—the weather is hot and humid year-round.

In general, the high season for travel in South America lasts from June through September, from mid-December through mid-January, and during Carnaval, which takes place the week before Ash Wednesday. The ski season in Chile and Argentina reaches its peak in July and August.

HOLIDAYS, CELEBRATIONS & EVENTS

Many of the holidays and festivals in South America correspond to Catholic and indigenous celebrations. (Sometimes they are a mixture of both.) The entire continent seems to turn into one big party zone during Carnaval, usually in February or March. During the solstices and equinoxes, many indigenous groups, which historically have worshipped the sun, organize traditional celebrations throughout South America.

SOUTH AMERICA CALENDAR OF EVENTS

JANUARY

Fiesta de la Santa Tierra, Lake Titicaca (Peru). The main festival on Isla Amantaní sees the population split in two—half at the Temple of Pachamama and the other half at the Temple of Pachatata, symbolizing the islanders' ancient dualistic belief system. Third Thursday in January.

FEBRUARY

Carnaval. The continent's liveliest Carnaval festivities are held in Argentina, Bolivia, Uruguay, and, most famously, Brazil. In Salta, Argentina, citizens throw a large parade, which includes caricatures of public officials and "water bomb" fights. In Oruro, Bolivia, Christian and indigenous myths and legends are woven into the fabric of the elaborate costumes and dances, which helped garner a UNESCO World Heritage rating in 2001. In Uruguay, Montevideo is the center for the main events, including parades, dance parties, and widespread debauchery. In Brazil, it's the party to end all parties—all life comes to a halt for 4 days of nonstop singing, dancing, drinking, and general over-the-top merrymaking. Generally celebrated during the week before the start of Lent.

Festival of the Virgen de la Candelaria. Lively festivities are held in honor of one of the most beloved religious symbols in Bolivia and Peru. In Copacabana, Bolivia, the home of the Virgin, the celebration includes parades and dancing in the street. In Puno, Peru, it's one of the largest and most colorful folk religious festivals in the Americas, with abundant music and dance troupes, many in fantastic costumes and masks. February 2.

Festival de la Canción (Festival of Song), Viña del Mar, Chile. This gala showcases Latin American and international performers during a 5-day festival of concerts held in the city's outdoor amphitheater. The spectacle draws thousands of visitors to an already packed Viña del Mar, so plan your hotel reservations accordingly. Late February.

March

Argentina's Wine Harvest Festival, Mendoza, Argentina. Locally known as Vendimia, the country's celebration of wine, women, and song is centered around its wine capital Mendoza, in the foothills of the Andes. Concerts, parades, street theater, and a hotly contested beauty contest take place throughout the month of February but culminate in a bacchanalian fest with fireworks and gaucho displays during the first week of March.

Iberamerican Film Festival, Bogotá, Colombia. One of the world's largest theater festivals (and South America's biggest) is held every 2 years from mid-March to early April in Bogotá. Over 520 theater companies from around the world are invited to participate.

April

Festival Internacional de Teatro (Caracas International Theater Festival). This festival brings together scores of troupes and companies from around the world and across Venezuela for a 2-week celebration of the theater arts. Performances are held in a variety of theaters (and a plethora of languages) around Caracas, as well as in the streets and plazas. Begun nearly 30 years ago, this is the premiere theater festival in Latin America. For more information, contact the **Ateneo de Caracas** (✆ **0212/573-4400**). Early to mid-April.

Semana Santa, Uruguay. During Holy Week, Uruguay shuts down. In Montevideo and the smaller cities, you'll find gaucho-style barbecues all over the place. During this time, there are also parades, where you'll be able to hear local folk music. Wednesday through Friday before Easter.

May

Fiesta de la Cruz, Peru. The Festival of the Cross features folk music and dance, including "scissors dancers," and processions in which communities decorate crosses and prepare them for the procession to neighboring churches. The *danzantes de tijeras* (scissors dancers) recreate old times, when they performed on top of church bell towers. Today the objective is still to outdo one another with daring feats. Celebrations are especially lively in Lima, Cusco, and Ica. May 2 and 3.

June

Gaucho Parade, Salta, Argentina. The parade features music by folk artists and gauchos dressed in traditional red ponchos with black stripes, leather chaps, black boots, belts, and knives. June 16.

Septenario Festival (Corpus Christi), Cuenca, Ecuador. During this weeklong event, Cuenca is at its most festive. The streets around the main plaza are closed and a carnival atmosphere prevails with games, special food stalls, and nightly fireworks. Thousands of balloons are sent into the sky over the city on closing night. The exact date varies, but is usually mid-June.

Inti Raymi (Festival of the Sun). This Inca Festival of the Sun—the mother of all pre-Hispanic festivals—celebrates the winter solstice and honors the sun god with traditional pageantry, parades, and dances. In Argentina, celebrations take place in towns throughout the northwest on the night before the solstice (around June 20). In Peru, it draws thousands of visitors who fill Cusco's hotels; the principal event takes place on June 24 at the Sacsayhuamán ruins and includes the sacrifice of a pair of llamas. General celebrations continue for several days. In Ecuador, Inti Raymi merges with the fiestas of San Pablo and San Juan to create one big holiday from June 24 to 29 in the Otavalo area.

July

Fiestas Patrias, Peru. A series of patriotic parties mark Peru's independence from Spain in 1821. Official parades and functions are augmented by cockfighting, bullfighting, and Peruvian Paso horse exhibitions in other towns. The best celebrations are in Cusco, Puno, Isla Taquile, and Lima. July 28 and 29.

August

Feria de las Flores, Medellín, Colombia. Likely the largest flower festival in the world, Medellín's biggest annual celebration includes a long list of events such as the Cavalgata de Caballos (Horse Parade), Desfile de Carros Antiguos (Antique Car Parade), and—the most famous and well known—the Desfile de Silleteros, where young and old come out to show-off their hand made *silleteros,* or flower designs, in an hours-long parade. This festival is one of a kind and excitement rivals that of Carnaval in Barranquilla or Cartagena. First week of August.

Independence Day, Bolivia. To celebrate this holiday, Bolivians flock to Sucre, where the leaders of the Bolivian independence movement signed the declaration of independence in 1825. For several days before and several days afterward, there are colorful parades, fireworks, and all sorts of celebrations here. If you can't make it to Sucre, you'll find people partying throughout the country, especially in Copacabana. August 6.

World Tango Championship, Buenos Aires, Argentina. Tango aficionados from all over the world converge on the Tangolopolis of Buenos Aires to strut their stuff and try to walk away with the coveted first-place prize. The less agile can watch or attend the hundreds of events scattered across the city celebrating Argentina's most valued cultural export.

September

Virgen del Valle, Isla de Margarita, Venezuela. The patron saint of sailors, fishermen, and all other seafarers is honored with street fairs and a colorful blessing of the fleet procession. September 8 to 15.

Independence Day and **Armed Forces Day,** Chile. Chile's rich cultural heritage comes to life with plenty of drinking, dancing, rodeos, and military parades. This holiday can stretch into a

3- to 4-day weekend, and the best place to witness celebrations is in the Central Valley south of Santiago. September 18 and 19.

October

El Señor de los Milagros (Lord of the Miracles), Lima, Peru. Lasting nearly 24 hours and involving tens of thousands of participants, many of whom are dressed in purple, this procession celebrates a Christ image painted by an Angolan slave that survived the 1746 earthquake and has since become the most venerated image in the capital. October 18.

November

All Souls' Day and **Independence Day,** Cuenca, Ecuador. The city celebrates both the Day of the Dead and its independence day with parties, art shows, parades, dances in the streets, and food festivals. November 2 and 3.

December

Santuranticuy Festival, Cusco, Peru. Hundreds of artisans sell traditional carved Nativity figures and saints' images at one of the largest handicrafts fairs in Peru in Cusco's Plaza de Armas. December 24.

New Year's Eve, Rio de Janeiro, Brazil. The Copacabana beach is ground zero for an event that attracts more than one million people. The roughly 10km (6 miles) of sand are jam-packed with New Year's revelers, and the entertainment never stops, with concerts and performances all night long leading up to the best fireworks display in the world. The evening is also an important one in the African Candomblé religion; it's the night to make an offering to the sea goddess Yemanjá. Candomblé followers, all dressed in white, offer small boats loaded with flowers, candles, mirrors, jewelry, and other pretty trinkets to the sea in a candlelit ceremony with music and dancing. The sight on the beach is truly spectacular. December 31.

Ferias de Cali, Cali, Colombia: Known as Colombia's hardest partying city, Cali really shows what it's made of during its famous ferias. For 2 long weeks each winter, the streets of Cali become a virtual party ground, full of street vendors, performers and merrymakers. Book your ticket in advance during this time because hotels fill up. Between late December and mid-January.

2 ENTRY REQUIREMENTS

The below passport and visa information in this section is for quick reference; see individual country chapters for complete details about the entry requirements for your destination.

PASSPORTS

A passport is required for entry to all South American countries covered in this book, though passport requirements vary by country. Allow plenty of time before your trip to apply for a passport; processing normally takes 3 weeks but can take longer during busy periods (especially spring). And keep in mind that if you need a passport in a hurry, you'll pay a higher processing fee.

For residents of Australia: You can pick up an application from your local post office or any branch of **Passports Australia,** but you must schedule an interview at the passport office to present your application materials. Call the **Australian Passport Information Service** at ✆ **131-232,** or visit the government website at **www.passports.gov.au**.

For residents of Canada: Passport applications are available at travel agencies throughout Canada or from the central **Passport Office,** Department of Foreign Affairs and International Trade, Ottawa, ON K1A 0G3 (✆ **800/567-6868;** www.ppt.gc.ca).

For residents of Ireland: You can apply for a 10-year passport at the **Passport Office,** Setanta Centre, Molesworth Street, Dublin 2 (✆ **01/671-1633;** www.irlgov.ie/iveagh). Those under age 18 and over 65 must apply for a 3-year passport. You can also apply at 1A South Mall, Cork (✆ **021/272-525**), or at most main post offices.

For residents of New Zealand: You can pick up a passport application at any **New Zealand Passports Office** or download it from their website. Contact the **Passports Office** at ✆ **0800/225-050** in New Zealand or 04/474-8100, or log on to **www.passports.govt.nz**.

For residents of the United Kingdom: To pick up an application for a standard 10-year passport (5-year passport for children 15 and under), visit your nearest passport office, major post office, or travel agency, or contact the **United Kingdom Passport Service** at ✆ **0870/521-0410,** or search its website at **www.ukpa.gov.uk**.

For residents of the United States: Whether you're applying in person or by mail, you can download passport applications from the U.S. Department of State website at **http://travel.state.gov**. To find your regional passport office, either check the U.S. Department of State website or call the **National Passport Information Center** toll-free number (✆ **877/487-2778**) for automated information.

VISAS

A visa is required for travel to Bolivia, Brazil, and Paraguay (see p. 178, 233, and 598 for details); all other countries in this book only require valid passports for short stays.

CUSTOMS

For information about what you can bring with you upon entry, see the "Customs" or "Entry Requirements & Customs" section in individual country chapters.

What You Can Bring Home

For information on what you're allowed to bring home, contact one of the following agencies:

Australian Citizens: A helpful brochure, available from Australian consulates or Customs offices, is *Know Before You Go.* For more information, call the **Australian Customs Service** at ✆ **1300/363-263,** or log on to **www.customs.gov.au**.

New Zealand Citizens: Most questions are answered in a free pamphlet available at New Zealand consulates and Customs offices: *New Zealand Customs Guide for Travellers, Notice no. 4.* For more information, contact **New Zealand Customs,** the Customhouse, 17–21 Whitmore St., Box 2218, Wellington (✆ **04/473-6099** or 0800/428-786; **www.customs.govt.nz**).

Canadian Citizens: For a clear summary of Canadian rules, write for the booklet *I Declare,* issued by the **Canada Border Services Agency** (✆ **800/461-9999** in Canada, or 204/983-3500; **www.cbsa-asfc.gc.ca**).

U.S. Citizens: U.S. Customs & Border Protection (CBP), 1300 Pennsylvania Ave. NW, Washington, DC 20229 (✆ **877/287-8667;** www.cbp.gov).

U.K. Citizens: For information, contact **HM Customs & Excise** at ✆ **0845/010-9000** (from outside the U.K., 020/8929-0152), or consult their website at **www.hmce.gov.uk**.

MEDICAL REQUIREMENTS

See individual country chapters for complete details about the medical requirements for your destination.

Of particular note are acute mountain sickness (AMS), or altitude sickness, in

Andean countries, and the need for yellow-fever vaccinations for travel to Amazon jungle regions in Bolivia, Peru, Ecuador, Colombia, and Brazil.

3 GETTING THERE & GETTING AROUND

GETTING TO SOUTH AMERICA

By Plane

Buenos Aires, Santiago, Lima, and São Paulo receive the greatest number of international flights to South America. If you're planning to explore the entire continent, you might consider starting off at one of these gateways and hooking up there for connecting flights to less-serviced destinations. See the individual country chapters for more detailed information.

GETTING AROUND SOUTH AMERICA

In general, the roads in South America (excepting much of Chile) are often in very poor condition. But there is an enormous network of bus lines, and if you have the time and patience, you can travel easily by bus from one country to another. Because car-rental agencies don't allow cars to be taken across international borders, it's very difficult to drive around the continent. There is also no reliable international train service. All in all, flying makes a lot of sense, especially if you're short on time.

See individual country chapters for complete details on getting around within each country.

By Plane

LAN offers the most comprehensive service in South America. Besides flying to most major cities in Chile and Peru, the airline also offers flights between Argentina, Brazil, Bolivia, Ecuador, Uruguay, and Venezuela. **Taca, Aerolíneas Argentinas,** and **Varig** also have several international routes.

If you plan on traveling between Chile, Argentina, Uruguay, and Brazil, you should consider buying a **Mercosur Air Pass.** The pass allows you to make two stopovers in each country, with a maximum of 10 stopovers. The pass is good for 7 to 30 days. Prices are based on mileage covered. You must buy the air pass outside of South America, and your initial flight must be on Aerolíneas Argentinas, American, Continental, Delta, LAN, TAM, United, or Varig. For more information, contact **Globotur Travel** at ✆ **800/998-5521** or visit **www.globotur.com**.

LAN and American Airlines have joined forces to create the **Visit South America Airpass,** which allows you to travel between Argentina, Bolivia, Brazil, Colombia, Chile, Ecuador, Paraguay, Peru, Venezuela, and Uruguay. You must purchase a minimum of three flight segments, but you can only travel for 60 days or less. Again, fares are based on distance traveled. You must buy the pass in your home country. Contact **LAN** (✆ **800/735-5526;** www.lan.com) or **American Airlines** (✆ **800/433-7300;** www.aa.com) for more information.

By Bus

It's possible to travel from Venezuela all the way to the tip of Argentina by bus. In fact, for most South Americans, buses are the main method of transportation. However, it's hard to find direct international routes. Usually, you take a bus to the border, where you must switch to a bus owned by a company in the country you have just entered. From there, you may have to take a bus to the largest nearby city, where you then can switch to a bus to your final destination. It's not the most efficient way to travel, but it's certainly cheap and a great way to see the countryside.

4 MONEY

At one time or another, inflation has been a thorn in the economies of every South American nation. Because of this, many South American hotels quote their rates in dollars, and in some South American countries, dollars are widely accepted. (Throughout this book, U.S. dollar rates are indicated with the "$.") For specifics on currency and exchange rates, along with information on tipping and taxes, see the individual destination chapters.

ATMS

The easiest and best way to get cash throughout South America is from an ATM (automated teller machine). The **Cirrus** (✆ **800/424-7787;** www.mastercard.com) and **PLUS** (✆ **800/843-7587;** www.visa.com) networks span the continent; look at the back of your bank card to see which network you're on, then call or check online for ATM locations at your destination.

Be sure you know your personal identification number (PIN) and daily withdrawal limit before you depart—you'll need a four-digit PIN throughout much of this region.

Note: Remember that many banks impose a fee every time you use a card at another bank's ATM, and that fee can be higher for international transactions (up to $5 or more). In addition, the bank from which you withdraw cash may charge its own fee. For international withdrawal fees, ask your bank.

Also see the destination chapters throughout this book for specific information on withdrawal limits.

CREDIT CARDS

Credit cards are another safe way to carry money throughout South America. They also provide a convenient record of all your expenses, and they generally offer relatively good exchange rates. You can withdraw cash advances from your credit cards at banks or ATMs but high fees make credit card cash advances a pricey way to get cash. Keep in mind that you'll pay interest from the moment of your withdrawal, even if you pay your monthly bills on time. Also, note that many banks now assess a 1% to 3% "transaction fee" on **all** charges you incur abroad (whether you're using the local currency or your native currency).

Visa, MasterCard, American Express, and, to a lesser extent, Diners Club are all commonly accepted in South America.

South American Currency Conversions

	US$1	Can$1	UK£1	Euro (€)	AUS$1	NZ$1
Argentine peso	0.26	0.27	0.16	0.18	0.28	0.37
Bolivian boliviano	0.145	0.154	0.087	0.10	0.157	0.197
Brazilian real	0.57	0.605	0.344	0.40	0.619	0.779
Chilean peso	.002	.002	.001	.001	.002	.003
Colombian peso	0.52	0.53	0.26	.0003	0.054	0.69
Paraguayan guaraní	0.0002	0.0002	0.00013	0.0002	0.0002	0.00029
Peruvian nuevo sol	0.35	0.36	0.21	0.24	0.37	0.46
Uruguayan peso	0.05	0.054	0.31	0.036	0.56	0.71
Venezuelan bolívar fuerte	0.47	0.50	0.28	0.32	0.51	0.64

Note: Ecuador uses the U.S. dollar.

TRAVELER'S CHECKS

Traveler's checks are hard to cash outside major South American cities, and even in those cities, you may still have problems doing so. Some travelers feel safer carrying a few traveler's checks just in case, though, and they can be bought at most banks in denominations of $20, $50, $100, $500, and sometimes $1,000. Generally, you'll pay a service charge ranging from 1% to 4%.

The most popular traveler's checks are offered by **American Express** (© **800/807-6233,** or 800/221-7282 for card holders—this number accepts collect calls, offers service in several foreign languages, and exempts Amex gold and platinum cardholders from the 1% fee); **Visa** (© **800/732-1322**—AAA members can obtain Visa checks for a $9.95 fee for checks up to $1,500 at most AAA offices, or by calling 866/339-3378; and **MasterCard** (© **800/223-9920**).

5 HEALTH

STAYING HEALTHY

For general information about health issues in South America, log on to the **Centers for Disease Control and Prevention**'s website at **www.cdc.gov/travel**. The CDC advises visitors to South America to protect themselves against hepatitis A and B. See "Health Concerns," in each destination chapter, for country-specific information.

General Availability of Healthcare

Contact the **International Association for Medical Assistance to Travelers** (**IAMAT;** © **716/754-4883** or, in Canada, 416/652-0137; www.iamat.org) for tips on travel and health concerns in the countries you're visiting, and for lists of local, English-speaking doctors. The United States **Centers for Disease Control and Prevention** (© **800/311-3435;** www.cdc.gov) provides up-to-date information on health hazards by region or country and offers tips on food safety. **Travel Health Online** (www.tripprep.com), sponsored by a consortium of travel medicine practitioners, may also offer helpful advice on traveling abroad. You can find listings of reliable medical clinics overseas at the **International Society of Travel Medicine** (www.istm.org).

WHAT TO DO IF YOU GET SICK AWAY FROM HOME

See the "Fast Facts" sections of the destination chapters for information on local hospitals and emergency phone numbers.

Tips **Medical Warning**

The U.S. State Department's Office of Medical Services warns people suffering from the following ailments to exercise caution when traveling to high-altitude destinations such as La Paz, Lake Titicaca, Cusco, and Machu Picchu: **sickle cell anemia, heart disease** (for men 45 or over or women 55 or over who have two of the following risk factors: hypertension, diabetes, cigarette smoking, or elevated cholesterol), **lung disease,** and anyone with **asthma** and on the maximum dosage of medication for daily maintenance, or anyone who has been hospitalized for asthma within a year of their intended trip. It's best to talk with your doctor before planning a trip to a high-altitude destination in South America.

Healthy Travels to You

The following government websites offer up-to-date health-related travel advice.

- **Australia:** www.dfat.gov.au/travel
- **Canada:** www.hc-sc.gc.ca/index_e.html
- **U.K.:** www.dh.gov.uk/en/Policyandguidance/Healthadvicefortravellers
- **U.S.:** www.cdc.gov/travel

For travel abroad, you may have to pay all medical costs upfront and be reimbursed later. (Medicare and Medicaid do not provide coverage for medical costs outside the U.S.) Before leaving home, find out what medical services your health insurance covers. To protect yourself, consider buying medical travel insurance.

Very few health insurance plans pay for medical evacuation. (which can cost $10,000 and up). A number of companies offer medical evacuation services anywhere in the world. If you're ever hospitalized more than 150 miles from home, **MedjetAssist** (✆ **800/527-7478;** www.medjetassistance.com) will pick you up and fly you to the hospital of your choice virtually anywhere in the world in a medically equipped and staffed aircraft 24 hours day, 7 days a week.

If you suffer from a chronic illness, consult your doctor before your departure. Pack **prescription medications** in your carry-on luggage, and carry them in their original containers, with pharmacy labels—otherwise they won't make it through airport security. Carry the generic name of prescription medicines, in case a local pharmacist is unfamiliar with the brand name.

6 SPECIALIZED TRAVEL RESOURCES

In addition to the destination-specific resources listed below, please visit Frommers.com for additional specialized travel resources. Also see the destination chapters for information on country-specific resources.

TRAVELERS WITH DISABILITIES

Except for the most modern and upscale hotels in major cities, most buildings in South America are not well equipped for travelers with disabilities. Where elevators exist, they are often tiny. Many cities in South American streets are crowded and narrow. In the Andes, the high altitude and steep hills slow everyone down. Within individual reviews, you'll find information on ramps, door sizes, room sizes, bathrooms, and wheelchair availability.

A helpful website for accessible travel is **Access-Able Travel Source** (www.access-able.com), which offers detailed destination articles on accessible travel in Peru and a wealth of specific information about Aguas Calientes, Chiclayo, Cusco, Huanchaco, Iquitos, Lima, the Chicama and Moche valleys, Pisac, Trujillo, and Yucay. **Apumayo Expediciones** (✆ **054/246-018;** www.apumayo.com) is way out in front on accessible travel in Peru, offering tours specifically designed for travelers with physical disabilities.

GAY & LESBIAN TRAVELERS

Most countries in South America are Catholic and conservative. However, in most large cities, there is a thriving underground gay community. To avoid offending local sensibilities or inviting possible verbal harassment in other parts of the continent, we recommend being discreet.

The International Gay and Lesbian Travel Association (IGLTA; ✆ 800/448-8550 or 954/776-2626; www.iglta.org) is the trade association for the gay and lesbian travel industry, and offers an online directory of gay- and lesbian-friendly travel businesses and tour operators.

For good, comprehensive information on the current situation in Ecuador, check out **http://quito.queercity.info**, the best English-language online resource for gay travelers to Ecuador, although the site is almost exclusively geared toward men. **Ecuador Gay** (**✆ 02/2529-993;** www.ecuadorgay.com) is a Quito-based travel agency geared specifically towards a gay and lesbian clientele, while **Galápagos Traveller** (**✆ 877/829-9006** in the U.S. and Canada; www.galapagostraveller.com), is a recommended GLB-friendly Ecuadorian travel agency.

SENIOR TRAVELERS

In most South American cultures, there is a deep respect for the elderly. Usually, if you ask for a senior discount, vendors will be happy to help you out. So don't be shy about asking for discounts, but always carry some kind of identification, such as a driver's license, that shows your date of birth. Also, mention the fact that you're a senior when you first make your travel reservations. All major airlines and many hotels offer discounts for seniors. In most cities, people over 60 qualify for reduced admission to theaters, museums, and other attractions, as well as discounted fares on public transportation.

Exploritas (**✆ 800/454-5768;** www.exploritas.org) and **ElderTreks** (**✆ 800/741-7956;** www.eldertreks.com) both offer a variety of options for senior travelers in South America.

FAMILY TRAVELERS

Family values are very important in South America, so if you're traveling with your entire family, you can expect locals to welcome you with open arms. Children are treated with the utmost respect. When you take your kids out to eat, the staff will shower them with attention and make special provisions if your kiddies aren't up to eating exotic food. Rice, potatoes, and chicken are on almost every menu, so you won't have to worry about looking for a McDonald's.

South America is also great for children because the wildlife-watching opportunities are tremendous. Bring your kids to the jungle, and they will be eternally grateful to you for letting them get close to caimans and monkeys. In the Galápagos, swimming with sea lions will be an experience that your children will not soon forget. It's also a good idea to teach your children some South American history before your trip. They will be more willing to visit old cathedrals and museums if they understand the value of what they're seeing.

To locate accommodations, restaurants, and attractions that are particularly kid-friendly, refer to the "Kids" icon throughout this guide.

STUDENT TRAVELERS

Although you won't find any discounts at the national parks, most museums and other attractions around South America do offer discounts for students. It always pays to ask.

The **International Student Travel Confederation (ISTC;** www.istc.org) was formed in 1949 to make travel around the world more affordable for students. Check out its website for comprehensive travel

Staying Safe

Millions of travelers visit South America without any problems. But as in any foreign destination, you should always keep your wits about you. Before you depart, check for travel advisories from the **U.S. Department of State** (www.travel.state.gov), the **Canadian Department of Foreign Affairs** (www.voyage.gc.ca), the **U.K. Foreign & Commonwealth Office** (www.fco.gov.uk/travel), the **New Zealand Ministry of Foreign Affairs** (www.mfat.govt.nz), and the **Australian Department of Foreign Affairs** (www.dfat.gov.au).

Once you're there, keep some common-sense safety advice in mind: Stay alert and be aware of your surroundings; don't walk down dark, deserted streets; and always keep an eye on your personal belongings. Theft at airports and bus stations is not unheard of, so be sure to put a lock on your luggage.

See "Fast Facts: Safety" in each destination chapter for information on country-specific safety concerns and numbers to call in case of an emergency.

services information and details on how to get an **International Student Identity Card (ISIC),** which qualifies students for substantial savings on rail passes, plane tickets, entrance fees, and more. It also provides students with basic health and life insurance and a 24-hour help line. The card is valid for a maximum of 18 months. You can apply for the card online or in person at **STA Travel** (✆ **800/781-4040** in North America; www.statravel.com), the biggest student travel agency in the world; check out the website to locate STA Travel offices worldwide.

If you're no longer a student but are still 25 or younger, you can get an **International Youth Travel Card (IYTC)** from the same people, which entitles you to some discounts. **Travel CUTS** (✆ **800/592-2887;** www.travelcuts.com) offers similar services for both Canadians and U.S. residents. Irish students may prefer to turn to **USIT** (✆ **01/602-1904;** www.usit.ie), an Ireland-based specialist in student, youth, and independent travel.

WOMEN TRAVELERS

Besides the general safety advice offered in each country chapter, women traveling alone in South America should have few problems. Yes, in many cultures here, men have a very macho attitude, and women traveling alone can expect to get intense stares, catcalls, or even be followed for a few blocks by men asking for a date. But for the most part, these men are harmless. A simple *"Déjame en paz"* ("Leave me alone") will send the message that you're not interested.

There have been sporadic, unconfirmed reports of tour guides attacking single women travelers. It's always worth it to pay a few extra dollars to arrange a tour with a reputable travel agency. Talk to your fellow travelers and find out if they have had any problems. If you are attacked, contact the police immediately and notify your embassy. Safety specialists at your embassy will be able to assist you and hopefully work with the police to track down the assailant.

7 SUSTAINABLE TOURISM

South America is one of the planet's prime ecotourism destinations. Many of the isolated nature lodges and tour operators around the country are pioneers and dedicated professionals in the ecotourism and sustainable tourism field. Many other hotels, lodges, and tour operators are simply "green-washing," using the terms "eco" and "sustainable" in their promo materials, but doing little real good in their daily operations. **Responsible Travel** (www.responsibletravel.com) is a great source of sustainable travel ideas with listings on South America; the site is run by a spokesperson for ethical tourism in the travel industry. **Sustainable Travel International** (www.sustainabletravelinternational.org) promotes ethical tourism practices, and manages an extensive directory of sustainable properties and tour operators around the region.

Deforestation is the main threat to South America's fragile ecosystem. Farming has virtually wiped out most of the region's rainforests, and logging is a major threat. Such destruction has been devastating to many species, including man himself, in the form of displaced indigenous tribes, and has led to drinking-water shortages, flash flooding, and mud slides. Though environmental awareness is growing, solving the region's huge environmental problems, including not just deforestation but the effects of overpopulation and industrial pollution, clearly remains an uphill struggle. Your hotel will often be your best bet for finding a place to deposit recyclable waste, especially if you choose a hotel that has instituted sustainable practices.

Volunteer travel has become increasingly popular among those who want to venture beyond the standard group-tour experience to learn languages, interact with locals, and make a positive difference while on vacation in South America. Volunteer options are listed under "Special-Interest Vacations," below.

ARGENTINA

Gold mining in San Juan, soya planting in El Chaco, global warming in South Patagonia, and pulp milling on the River Plate are all hot environmental issues in Argentina at the moment. Despite having one of the best national park systems in the region, the country's protected areas are under threat from encroaching development.

On the bright side is a growing awareness amongst the populace that they are in danger of losing what they have. A forest preservation law was introduced in 2007 prohibiting deforestation, and Mendoza's provincial congress issued a blanket ban on mining, though it was later overturned by the governor. Argentina's main weapon against environmental damage is its utter vastness and underpopulation, yet lax government control, little tradition for conservation, and rampant development are all cause for concern.

BOLIVIA

Bolivia, one of the world's most biodiverse countries on earth, is home to 60 protected areas, including 22 national parks, which covers an impressive 15% of its total territory. Many of the protected areas, however, are in constant threat from oil companies and loggers, who seemingly avoid any crackdowns from the government. The extraction of the significant lithium reserves in southwest Bolivia had led to frequent protests around Uyuni, but thus far they remain untapped. Natural gas reserves, once a significant source of revenue for Bolivia, have lost their value; as buyers in neighboring countries turn elsewhere, new explorations have come to a halt.

Only a few hotels have jumped on the green train in Bolivia thus far, including La Posada del Inca on Isla del Sol (p. 206) and Chalalan Ecolodge (p. 198) in Madidi National Park.

BRAZIL

Brazilian resorts and tour operators do advertise "ecotourism," but in Brazil this means anything that takes place in the outdoors, be it leave-only-footprints nature hikes or churn-up-the-wildlife ATV expeditions. It does not signify lodges or hotels with solar heating or clever ways of dealing with waste water, or even outdoor operators that take particular care of their local ecosystems.

In Brazil's two most vulnerable remaining ecosystems—the Pantanal and the Amazon—there are tourism operators who strive to protect their local ecosystems. In the Pantanal the **Araras Eco Lodge** (p. 350) and the **Jaguar Ecological Reserve** (p. 350) have helped to popularize the private ecological reserve, a Brazilian program through which the government provides tax breaks in return for a landowner committing to preserving a portion of his in perpetuity. The presence of ecotourism operators in the Pantanal has also provided a lobby to counter certain ill-advised development schemes, including the paving of the Transpantaneira highway, and the widening, straightening, and deepening of the Rio Paraguay, the better to transport soybeans to the coast.

In the Amazon, the **Pousada Uakarí** (p. 348) serves as an integral part of the **Mamiraua Sustainable Development Institute** (www.mamiraua.org.br), a project designed to preserve the habitat of the Uakarí monkey while improving the living standards of local human populations living in and around the Uakarí reserve. Other Amazon lodges come nowhere near this standard, though they do provide some local employment for guides and other lodge staff. Unfortunately, the miniscule scale of ecotourism operations in comparison with the employment and revenues generated by the timber and cattle industries has rendered ecotourism a nonplayer in the debate over preserving the Amazon.

However, one could argue that those who experience the Amazon become more likely to lobby to save it. Certainly, awareness of the importance of the Amazon, both globally and in Brazil, has led to the passage in Brazil of a range of reasonably stringent preservation measures, including parks, reserves, Indian reservations, national forest lands, and restrictions on deforestation on private landholdings. The problem in Brazil is that these regulations are often not respected, while enforcement on the ground remains weak. Still, rates of deforestation in the Brazilian Amazon have declined, from a 2004 peak of 27,400 sq. km (16,686 sq. miles, an area somewhat larger than Vermont) to 12,911 sq. km (5,035 sq. miles, an area somewhat smaller than Connecticut) in 2008.

CHILE

The principal environmental problems that confront Chile are deforestation and air, water, and land pollution. Santiago is one of Latin America's most polluted cities, and air pollution there has become an acute problem; children and the elderly and infirm are frequently advised to stay indoors for days on end due to dangerous levels of toxic pollutants that enshroud the capital. Rapid urban expansion, industrial emissions from the copper mining sector, and the increased volume of car traffic are cited as the main causes of Santiago's air pollution. Mining is responsible for releasing the chief air and water pollutants, including sulfur dioxide and arsenic. In 2000, the city faced an unprecedented pollution emergency when over 200,000 vehicles were prohibited from driving on the roads and offending industries were shut down. Fortunately, in the last few years, environmental issues have taken a more prominent role in domestic politics and, while the pace is slow, government initiatives have gone a long way to improving the situation.

The indiscriminate logging of Chile's temperate forests has resulted in the tragic disappearance of thousand-year-old forests. The most publicized case of illegal logging, which has been taken up by environmental agencies, including Greenpeace, is that of the rare alerce tree, which is found in the Andes and can live for up to 3,500 years. Many animals are in serious risk of extinction throughout the country, as well. As of 2001, of the 91 listed mammals in Chile, some 16 species were registered as endangered. Almost 5% of Chile's 298 breeding bird species are threatened with extinction, most notably the tundra peregrine falcon, the Chilean woodstar, and the ruddy-headed goose. Also threatened are four types of freshwater fish and over 250 plant species.

Chile hasn't made great strides in the sustainable accommodations arena, although eco-conscious lodges are popping up in Patagonia and the Lake District.

COLOMBIA

Colombia is facing significant environmental risks. At the current rate of deforestation, experts estimate that Colombia's jungles will completely disappear by the year 2050. The logging, mining, gold, and emerald trade, as well as the illicit coca trade, has caused massive deforestation at a rate of 1.5 to 2 million acres a year. Mountain scraping for farming has caused previously forested and vegetated areas to turn into semi-arid desert zones, and road and home construction in rural areas is threatening the country's biodiversity. In addition, improperly disposed sewage, pesticides, and herbicides have contaminated many of the country's rivers and lakes, making the water undrinkable. Factory and car pollution continues to be a major problem in cities.

ECUADOR

Oil exploration and mining operations continue to be the biggest environmental threats in Ecuador. In addition to impacting the environment, these activities also impact a variety of indigenous groups, whose way of life, culture, and ancestral homelands are severely threatened. This has led to numerous protests, and sometimes violent clashes between indigenous groups and the government. The Galápagos Islands present their own special set of challenges in terms of environmental protection and sustainable development issues. Isolated, unique, and delicate, the Galápagos are threatened by overexposure to tourists, over fishing, and the introduction of non-native species.

PARAGUAY

Deforestation is the main concern in Paraguay, as big agro-businesses come from Brazil and Argentina to clear forests and plant genetically modified plants. On paper the country has an impressive list of parks and reserves, but because of poor public access, underfunded government bodies, and corrupt local officials, it seems the only people that get to enter these biologically diverse areas are ranchers and lumber companies.

PERU

Peru has 72 million hectares (178 million acres) of natural-growth forests—70% in the Amazon jungle region—that comprise nearly 60% of the national territory. Peru has done a slightly better job of setting aside tracts of rainforest as national park reserves and regulating industry than have some other Latin American and Asian countries. The Manu Biosphere Reserve, the Tambopata National Reserve, and the Pacaya-Samiria National Reserve are three of the largest protected rainforest areas in the world, and the government regulates entry of tour groups. Peru augmented the Bahuaja-Sonene National Park, which was created in 1996, by 809,000 hectares (nearly 2 million acres) in 2001. INRENA, Peru's Institute for Natural Resource Management, enforces logging regulations and reseeds Peru's Amazon forests, and in 2008, President Alan García created the country's first Ministry of the Environment. A handful of Peruvian and international environmental and conservation groups, such as ProNaturaleza and Conservation International, are active in Peru, working on sustainable forestry projects.

Yet Peru is losing nearly 300,000 hectares (740,000 acres) of rainforest annually. The primary threats to Peru's tropical forests are deforestation caused by agricultural expansion, cattle ranching, logging, oil extraction and spills, mining, illegal coca farming, and colonization initiatives. Deforestation has shrunk territories belonging to indigenous peoples and wiped out more than 90% of the population. (There were once some six million people, 2,000 tribes and/or ethnic groups, and innumerable languages in the Amazon basin; today the indigenous population is less than two million.) Jungle ecotourism has exploded in Peru, and rainforest regions are now much more accessible than they once were, with more lodges and eco-options than ever. Many are taking leading roles in sustainable tourism even as they introduce protected regions to more travelers.

URUGUAY

Uruguay is often called the most European country in South America, not least because most of its natural forests have been cleared for agriculture and there is little or nothing left of large wildlife indigenous to the region. The few nature reserves that exist offer little out of the ordinary, though there are some seal colonies worth visiting along the coast. The hot environmental issue at the moment is a dispute with Argentina over two massive pulp mills built on the Uruguayan side of the River Plate, which are badly polluting the riverway. The Uruguayans have denied this claim.

VENEZUELA

Since over 90% of Venezuela's population lives in a narrow urban belt along the northern coast, much of the interior is seldom visited and oft forgotten. Still, Venezuela has the third-highest rate of deforestation in South America, and the country's oil industry has caused massive environmental destruction in the Lake Maracaibo area, and to a lesser extent in Los Llanos. Gold, iron, bauxite and coal mining operations have also had a negative impact on the environment. That said, Venezuela has the largest percentage of protected land, with some 55% of its total territory protected in some form or another.

8 SPECIAL-INTEREST TRIPS & ESCORTED GENERAL-INTEREST TOURS

TOUR OPERATORS SPECIALIZING IN SOUTH AMERICA

Organizing a trip to South America can be a royal pain, especially if you don't speak Spanish or Portuguese. These tour companies have connections throughout the entire continent, and their staffs can make all of your travel arrangements for you. Here is a list of some of the best tour operators.

- **Abercrombie & Kent, Inc.** (✆ **800/554-7016;** www.abercrombiekent.com) is one of the most upscale tour companies arranging trips to South America. The company's tours will take you to the best parts of Patagonia, the Galápagos, Peru, Ecuador, Chile, and Argentina.
- **Backroads** (✆ **03/462-2848;** www.backroads.com) is a U.S.-based adventure tour operator specializing in hiking and biking tours, combining active endeavors with varied cultural pursuits and stays at plush inns and bed-and-breakfasts. Their South American itineraries include trips to Ecuador, Argentina, and Peru.

- **Blue Parallel** (✆ **800/256-5307;** www.blueparallel.com) leads private, tailor-made luxury adventure tours across the South American continent, making use of many of the top lodges and resorts in offbeat destinations such as Patagonia and Fernando de Noronha, and offering a "Crossing the Andes" trip from Chile to Argentina.
- **Kon-Tiki Tours & Travel** (✆ **877/566-8454;** www.kontiki.org) is run by an American and Peruvian couple. The company specializes in trips throughout South America, including general highlights, and cultural and spiritual tours. You can choose from more than 30 different itineraries in Peru, Argentina, Bolivia, Brazil, Ecuador, and Chile. Prices include guides and airfare.
- **Ladatco Tours** (✆ **800/327-6162;** www.ladatco.com) specializes in package tours to South and Central America. The company offers Carnaval specials, as well as air-only deals.
- **Overseas Adventure Travel** (✆ **800/493-6824** in the U.S. and Canada; www.oattravel.com) has good-value natural-history and soft adventure itineraries with small groups and naturalist guides. They offer land and cruise packages to a variety of destinations, including Ecuador, Peru, Brazil, Argentina, and Chile.
- **South American Expeditions** (✆ **800/884-7474;** www.adventuresports.com/asap/travel/exped) offers adventure, cultural, off-the-beaten path, and women-only tours to Ecuador and Peru.
- **Tara Tours Inc.** (✆ **800/327-0080;** www.taratours.com) is one of the most experienced agencies offering package tours to South America. Some of the specialties here include archaeology and spiritual journeys. In general, the company's package tours are great deals.
- **Condor Journeys and Adventures** (✆ **01700/841-318;** www.condorjourneys-adventures.com) is a British company that offers tour packages and active vacations throughout South America.
- **Journey Latin America** (✆ **020/8747-8315;** www.journeylatinamerica.co.uk) is one of the premier British travel agencies offering trips to South America. The company can arrange airfare and tour packages throughout the entire continent.
- **Adventure Associates Pty Ltd.** (✆ **02/9389-7466;** www.adventureassociates.com) is the best source in Australia for high-end package tours to South America and Antarctica.

SPECIAL-INTEREST VACATIONS

Here's a list of companies offering educational and volunteer opportunities in South America:

- **AmeriSpan** (✆ **800/879-6640** or 215/751-1100; www.amerispan.com) helps students arrange programs that combine language study, travel, and volunteer opportunities throughout South America.
- **Amigos de las Américas** (✆ **800/231-7796** or 713/782-5290; www.amigoslink.org) is always looking for volunteers to promote public health, education, and community development in rural areas of Latin America.
- **Earthwatch Institute** (✆ **800/776-0188** or 978/461-0081; www.earthwatch.org) supports sustainable conservation efforts of the earth's natural resources. The organization can always use volunteers for its research teams in South America.
- **Habitat for Humanity International** (✆ **229/924-6935,** or check the website for local affiliates; www.habitat.org) needs volunteers to help build affordable housing in more than 79 countries in the world, including most countries in South America.

- **Spanish Abroad, Inc.** (✆ **888/722-7623** or 602/778-6791; www.spanishabroad.com) organizes intensive language-study programs throughout Latin America.

ACTIVE VACATIONS

Many outdoor activities can be arranged easily and cheaply upon arrival in South America. Local operators will have everything you need and can arrange guides and even companions. The nonprofit **South American Explorers** (www.samexplo.org) is a great resource if you're in Lima, Cusco, or Quito.

BIRD-WATCHING Over 3,100 species of birds either live or migrate through South America. Some of the rarest birds in the world live in and near the jungles of the Amazon rainforest. The jungle areas of Brazil, Peru, and Ecuador are among the best bird-watching spots in the world. The Galápagos Islands in Ecuador are also a birder's paradise—albatrosses; penguins; flightless cormorants; red-footed, blue-footed, and masked boobies; and the short-eared owl are just some of the rare birds that you'll see here. Peru's Manu Biosphere Reserve is also impressive: With more than 1,000 bird species recorded here, it has the highest concentration of birdlife on earth.

CLIMBING Many a mountaineer has traveled to South America to scale some of the highest peaks in the world. The snowy peaks of Patagonia offer some of the most challenging climbs on the continent. But you don't have to head all the way down south. In Ecuador, you can climb the glacier-covered Cotopaxi, which, at 5,804m (19,037 ft.), is the highest active volcano in the world.

DIVING The Galápagos Islands, off the coast of Ecuador, offer some of the most exciting diving in the world. You'll have the opportunity to see schools of hammerhead sharks as well as exotic underwater life. Serious divers should consider booking a special diving cruise around the islands. The Caribbean coast off Venezuela is also a popular dive spot.

MOUNTAIN BIKING The 8,050km-long (5,000-mile) Andes mountain range offers some excellent mountain-biking opportunities. From Ecuador down to Patagonia, you'll find mountain-biking outfitters galore. But be careful: The roads are often poorly maintained. Some routes are narrow and open onto steep precipices. It's important to rent a high-quality bike that can deal with the conditions. The South American Explorers Club advises bikers to use Kona, Trek, or Cannondale brand bikes. Cheaper bikes may not be able to survive the rough terrain.

RIVER RAFTING The Amazon is the world's second-longest river, and running it or one of its many tributaries is one of the great thrills in South America. The wildest parts run through Ecuador, Peru, and Brazil. And in central Chile, as the water rages down from the Andes to the Pacific, you'll find some of the wildest white-water rafting anywhere.

SKIING July and August are prime ski season months in South America. The ski areas in Chile and southern Argentina are considered the Alps of South America. In Argentina, the glitterati head to Bariloche, while Chileans consider the ski resorts Valle Nevado (east of Santiago) and Portillo to be sacred ground.

SURFING It's been said that some of the longest breaks in the world exist off the coast of Peru. But small beach towns that cater to the surfing set dot the entire Pacific coast of South America. The Galápagos Islands have also begun to attract serious surfers to their windy shores. Not surprisingly, the Pacific can get quite cold—be sure to bring a wet suit. For warmer waters, surfers should head to the Caribbean coast of Venezuela. Henry Pitter National Park in Venezuela has become a hot spot.

SWIMMING, SNORKELING & OTHER WATERSPORTS The Atlantic coast of South America offers wonderful watersports opportunities. Punta del Este in Uruguay is one of the premier South American beach resorts. From December through March, the Argentine elite come here to sail, swim, water-ski, or just get close to the sea. The warm Caribbean waters off Venezuela are also great for snorkeling, water-skiing, and windsurfing. The Pacific Coast isn't as enticing, but visitors to the Galápagos will find that the snorkeling there is out of this world.

9 STAYING CONNECTED

TELEPHONES

See the individual country chapters for tips on dialing and making calls on land lines.

Your best, cheapest bet for making international calls throughout South America is to head to any Internet cafe with an international calling option. These cafes have connections to Skype, Net-2Phone, or some other **VoIP service.** International calls made this way can range anywhere from 5¢ to $1 per minute—much cheaper than making direct international calls or using a phone card. If you have your own Skype or similar account, you just need to find an Internet cafe that provides a computer with a headset.

CELLPHONES

The three letters that define much of the world's wireless capabilities are **GSM** (Global System for Mobile Communications), a big, seamless network that makes for easy cross-border cellphone use throughout South America. In the U.S., T-Mobile and AT&T Wireless use this quasi-universal system; in Canada, Microcell and some Rogers customers are GSM; and all Europeans and most Australians use GSM. GSM phones function with a removable plastic SIM card, encoded with your phone number and account information. If your cellphone is on a GSM system, and you have a world-capable multiband phone such as many Sony Ericsson, Motorola, or Samsung models, you can make and receive calls across most of South America. Just call your wireless operator and ask for "international roaming" to be activated on your account. Unfortunately, per-minute charges can be high—typically $1–$3 per minute.

For many, **renting** a phone is a good idea. While you can rent a phone from any number of overseas sites, including kiosks at airports and at car-rental agencies, we suggest renting the phone before you leave home. North Americans can rent one before leaving home from **InTouch USA** (✆ **800/872-7626;** www.intouchglobal.com) or **RoadPost** (✆ **888/290-1606** or 905/272-5665; www.roadpost.com). InTouch will also, for free, advise you on whether your existing phone will work overseas; simply call ✆ **703/222-7161** between 9am and 4pm EST, or go to **http://intouchglobal.com/travel.htm**.

Buying a phone can be economically attractive, as many South American nations have cheap prepaid phone systems. Once you arrive at your destination, stop by a local cellphone shop and get the cheapest package; you'll probably pay less than $100 for a phone and a starter calling card. Local calls may be as low as 10¢ per minute, and in many countries incoming calls are free.

INTERNET ACCESS

More and more hotels, resorts, airports, cafes, and retailers are going **Wi-Fi** (wireless fidelity), becoming "hot spots" that offer free high-speed Wi-Fi access or charge a small fee for usage. Most laptops sold today have built-in wireless capability.

Tips Where Are You @?

The @ symbol is hard to find on a Latin American keyboard. You must keep your finger on the "Alt" key and then press "6" and "4" on the number pad to the right. If you're still unsuccessful and at an Internet cafe, ask the assistant to help you type an *arroba*.

To find public Wi-Fi hotspots throughout South America, go to **www.jiwire.com**; its Wi-Fi Finder holds the world's largest directory of public wireless hot spots.

For dial-up access, most business-class hotels in South America offer dataports for laptop modems, and a growing number offer free high-speed Internet access.

Wherever you go, bring a **connection kit** of the right power and phone adapters, a spare phone cord, and a spare Ethernet network cable—or find out whether your hotel supplies them to guests.

10 TIPS ON ACCOMMODATIONS

Upscale travelers are finally starting to get their due in South America. It has taken time, but spurred on by the example and standards of several international chains, and inspired by some award-winning local hotels, service and amenities have been improving across the board, particularly in the upscale market. The region's strong suit is still its moderately priced hotels, though. However, room size and quality vary quite a bit within this price range, so don't expect the kind of uniformity that you may find at home. Almost all the big hotels have free parking lots, while the smaller, budget hotels have street parking.

If you're budget- or bohemian-minded, you can find quite a few good deals for less than $50 a double. ***Note:*** Air-conditioning or central heating is not necessarily a given in many midrange hotels. In general, this is not a problem. A well-placed ceiling fan or heavy blankets are often more than enough to keep things pleasant, unless we mention otherwise in the hotel reviews. And although power outages aren't a regular issue anymore (at least in the region's cities), it is always wise to check out if your hotel has a backup generator in case things get uncomfortable.

Another welcome hotel trend in the area is the renovation and conversion of old homes or historic buildings into small hotels or B&Bs, known as *hosterías* or *posadas.* South America is still riding the ecotourism wave, and you'll find small nature-oriented ecolodges throughout the region, too. These lodges offer opportunities to see wildlife (including sloths, monkeys, and hundreds of species of birds) and learn about tropical forests, high deserts, or other remote wilderness areas. They range from spartan facilities catering primarily to scientific researchers, to luxury accommodations that are among the finest in the country. Keep in mind that although the nightly room rates at these lodges are often quite moderate, prices start to climb when you throw in transportation (often on chartered planes), guided excursions, and meals. Also, just because you can book a reservation at most of these lodges doesn't mean that they're not remote. Be sure to find out how you get to and from the eco-lodge, and what tours and services are included in your stay. Then think long and hard about whether you really want to put up with hot, humid weather; biting insects; rugged transportation; and strenuous hikes to see wildlife.

One uniquely South American lodging type that you might encounter is the *apartotel,* which is just what it sounds like: an apartment hotel where you'll get a full kitchen and one or two bedrooms, along with daily maid service. A *posada* or *hostal* (also called a *hostería*) is a small, usually family-run hotel, not unlike a B&B. If you're visiting an eco-lodge or hotel in any area near the jungle, most accommodations have either screened-in windows or provide mosquito nets. The exceptions are the bare-bones beach shacks along the coast and rustic huts in the jungle.

Hotels listed as expensive throughout this book often offer much cheaper rates for travelers booking through their websites. Your best bet throughout this region is negotiating directly with the hotels themselves, especially the smaller hotels. However, be aware that response times might be slower than you'd like, and many of the smaller hotels might have some trouble communicating back and forth in English. Rates quoted throughout the book reflect double occupancy, and differences between low- and high-season rates are noted wherever possible. (Note that there are some bargains to be had during the low season.)

Also see "Tips on Accommodations" in the country chapters throughout this book for info. For tips on surfing for hotel deals online, visit Frommers.com.

4

Argentina

by Charlie O'Malley

Be prepared to be overwhelmed in Argentina. Its many attractions include the dazzling waterfalls and subtropical jungle of Iguazú; the dry, polychromatic hills of Salta; the frigid scrublands of Patagonia; and the lush, green planes of the pampas. Take a trip down the spine of the Andes and you will pass salt plains, tobacco fields, cactus hills, and bountiful vineyards. The eighth-largest country in the world has 2.6 million sq. km (1 million sq. miles), meaning there's a lot of ground to cover, history to examine, and culture to experience. The diversity of countries that border Argentina—Uruguay, Brazil, Paraguay, Bolivia, and Chile—underscores its rich geography. The people match the landscape and Argentina is a rattlebag of cultures and nationalities, including Andean Incas, jungle-dwelling Indians, European immigrants, and Porteño Jews, to mention just a few.

Argentina contains the most sophisticated city in South America, Buenos Aires. Here you'll find some of the best art and architecture on the planet and a treasure trove of restaurants, bars, and nightspots that would keep the most voracious hedonist occupied for a lifetime.

Argentina had a tumultuous 20th century. It started as one of the richest countries in the world and then underwent a rollercoaster of social upheavals and economic meltdowns, punctuated by Peronist populism and military manhunts. Its boom-and-bust cycle continues, yet that does not deter the millions of visitors it attracts each year, eager to sample a quality of life that few countries can boast.

1 THE REGIONS IN BRIEF

A short visit to Argentina creates the most tantalizing dilemmas: Buenos Aires is a must, but so is Patagonia. Iguazú you have to see, but Mendoza sounds amazing. And what about Salta and the Lake District? One thing is for sure; you cannot see everything unless you have at least a month. Buenos Aires requires at least several days to appreciate. Iguazú from both the Argentine and Brazil sides requires at least 2 full days, though many people are happy to see just the Argentina side on a day trip from the capital. If you choose to head south, you can do it in a week, but you'd spend a good chunk of that time just getting down there. If you only have 2 weeks, split the country in two and save the other half for next time. Look upon it as a good excuse to come back.

BUENOS AIRES & THE PAMPAS Buenos Aires, a rich combination of South American energy and European sophistication, is a city of grand plazas and boulevards. Take time to wander its impressive museums and architectural sites, stroll along its fashionable waterfront, and immerse yourself in its dynamic culture and nightlife. A thick Argentine steak in a local *parrilla* (grill), a visit to a San Telmo antiques shop, a dance in a traditional tango salon—these are the small experiences that will connect you to the city's soul. One-third of Argentines live in greater Buenos Aires.

MENDOZA & THE CENTRAL ANDES **Mendoza** is a gorgeous oasis city of tree-lined avenues and elegant plazas. Open waterways carry melted snow from the ice-tipped Andes in the background, feeding plains of dramatic vineyard country. The province is currently riding a wave of popularity: Argentine wine is experiencing global popularity and visitors are flocking here to visit beautiful wineries and try great regional cuisine. They are also coming to explore **Mount Aconcagua,** the tallest mountain outside the Himalayas, or raft on the famous Rio Mendoza.

MISIONES This small province in the Mesopotamia enjoys a subtropical climate responsible for the region's flowing rivers and lush vegetation. The **Iguazú Falls** are created by the merger of the Iguazú and Paraná rivers at the border of Argentina, Brazil, and Paraguay. In this chapter, I explore Iguazú Falls and review lodging and dining on the Argentine side of the border. You can find similar information on the Brazilian part of the falls in chapter 6.

NORTHWEST The Andes dominate the Northwest, with ranges between 4,800m (15,700 ft.) and 6,900m (22,600 ft.). The two parallel mountain ranges are the Salto-Jujeña, cut by magnificent multicolored canyons called *quebradas.* This region is often compared with the basin and range regions of the southwestern United States, and can be visited from the historic towns of **Salta** and **Jujuy.** A must-see is the wine town of **Cafayate,** a sun-kissed village surrounded by vineyards and palatial wineries.

THE LAKE DISTRICT Argentina's Lake District extends from Junín de los Andes south to Esquel—an Alpine-like region of snowy mountains, waterfalls, forests, and glacier-fed lakes. **San Martín de los Andes, Bariloche,** and **Villa La Angostura** are the chief destinations, but this isn't an area where you stay in one place. Driving tours, boating, skiing—you'll be on the move from the moment you set foot in the region.

PATAGONIA Also known as the Magellanic Region or the Deep South, this dry, arid region at the southern end of the continent has recently soared in popularity. I discuss the Argentine part of Patagonia in this chapter, and the Chilean part is discussed in chapter 7.

Vast, open pampa; the colossal Northern and Southern ice fields; hundreds of glaciers; the jagged peaks of the Andes as they reach their terminus; emerald fiords; and wind, wind, wind—all characterize Patagonia. It's a long way but the journey pays off in the beauty and singularity of the region. **El Calafate** is a tourist-oriented village adjacent to the Perito Moreno Glacier. **El Chaltén** is a village of 200 residents whose numbers swell each summer with those who come to marvel at the towers of mounts Fitzroy, Cerro Torre, and Puntiagudo, for the singular nature of the granite spires that shoot up, torpedo-like, above huge tongues of ice that descend from the Southern Ice Field.

TIERRA DEL FUEGO Even farther south than the Deep South, this archipelago at the southern tip of South America is, like Patagonia, shared by both Chile and Argentina. The main island, separated from the mainland by the Strait of Magellan, is a triangle with its base on the Beagle Channel. Tierra del Fuego's main town is **Ushuaia,** the southernmost city in the world. Many use the city as a jumping-off point for trips to Antarctica or sailing trips around Cape Horn.

2 THE BEST OF ARGENTINA IN 2 WEEKS

This country is so vast, it's wise to sacrifice some locations and not rush. Internal flights are the most convenient but increasingly expensive. Also Buenos Aires is the air transport hub, which means wherever you decide to go, it has to be through the capital, which can be annoying if traveling along the Andes. It is worth considering Argentina's long-distance buses for some of the journeys. Night buses are comfortable—indeed, luxurious—and what you lose in time you save on money plus hotel expenses. Car rentals should only be used for short distances because the regions between major destinations are often flat pampas or desert scrub and don't make for interesting scenery.

Days 1–2: Arrive in Buenos Aires ★★

One of the greatest cities in the world demands your attention for at least 2 days. Put yourself in the lap of luxury at the **Alvear Palace Hotel** (p. 103), and explore the gothic elegance of **Recoleta Cemetery** (p. 91) and the grimy tangolopolis of **San Telmo.** Try to arrive on a weekend, as the city comes alive with antique markets, art fairs, and street performances. In the evening, catch a lavish tango show, or slum it at a neighborhood *milonga.*

Days 3–4: Iguazú Falls ★★★

Fly to **Iguazú** and peer into the abyss. Explore the clever system of walkways that take you so close you can almost touch the white, foaming torrent. Expect to get wet as you take a boat beneath the raging cascade that will drown your screams. Dry off in the nearby **Sheraton** (p. 100), and dine with a spectacular view. The following day, visit the Brazilian side, and do it all over again (don't forget that American and Canadian citizens require a visa to cross over) before returning to Buenos Aires by plane.

Days 5–6: Mendoza Wine Country ★★★

Catch a luxury night bus to the garden city of Mendoza. Spend the day among the tree-lined avenues, leafy plazas, and elegant parks. Enjoy a glass of Malbec on the sunny patio of the **Park Hyatt Mendoza** (p. 129) as you plot your wine tour for the following day.

Day 7: Mount Aconcagua & the Andes

Take a day tour to the Andes. Follow the old Trans-Andean railway as it climbs through the stunning Uspallata valley and learn about its rich cultural and geographical history. At **Aconcagua Provincial Park** (p. 128), take a short hike to view the tallest mountain outside the Himalayas. Visit the picturesque **Puente del Inca** (p. 128) and enjoy a late lunch of kid goat in the mountain town of **Uspallata** (p. 128).

Days 8–9: The Patagonian Glaciers

Go deep south to Patagonia and the town of El Calafate. Enjoy 2 days of all- inclusive pampering at **Los Notros** (p. 165), a luxury lodge with picture windows of the natural wonder that is **Perito Moreno Glacier** (p. 164). Either sit back and enjoy the view, or go for guided ice walks and boat excursions to the wall of jagged blue ice. Watch out for the 10-ton chunks that fall into the water each day.

Days 10–11: Fitzroy ★

Hire a car and go north toward **El Chaltén,** enjoying the granite spires of the Fitzroy mountain range. Stop for a rustic lunch at **Patagonicus** (p. 168) before embarking on an overnight trek with **Fitz Roy Expediciones** (p. 166).

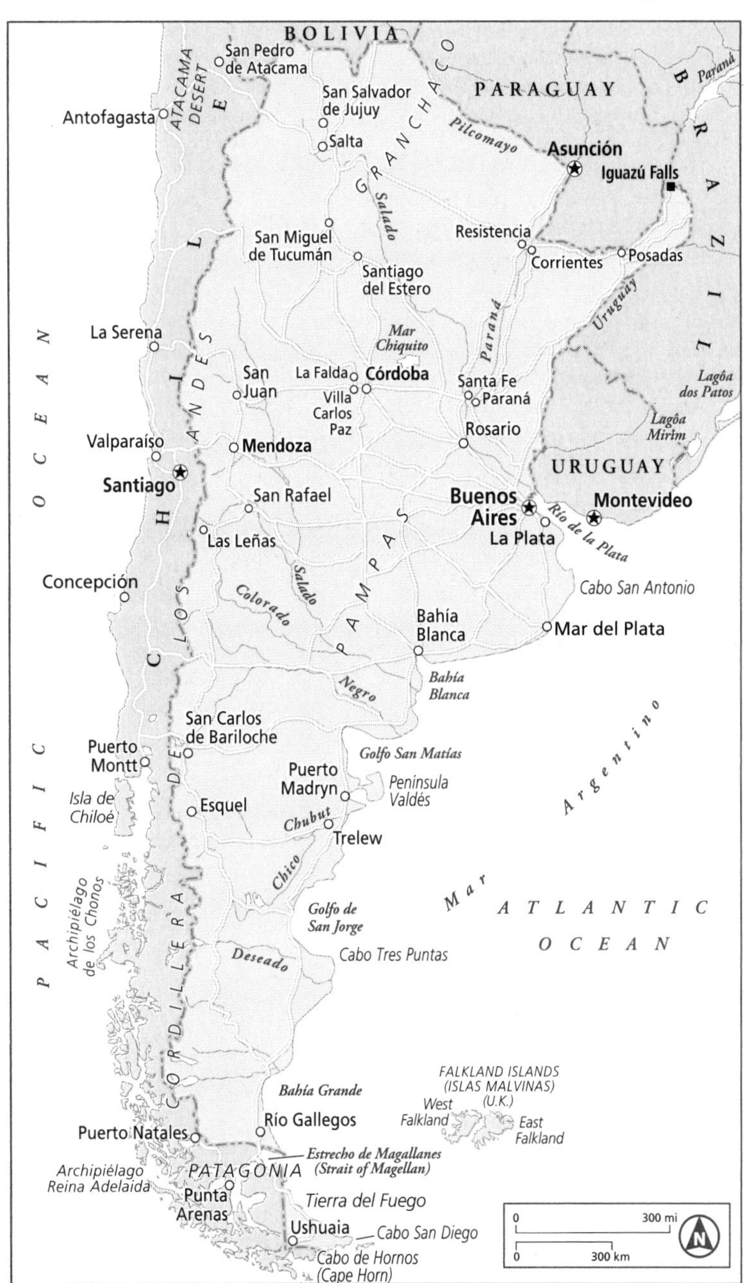
BOLIVIA
San Pedro de Atacama
ATACAMA DESERT
Antofagasta
San Salvador de Jujuy
Salta
PARAGUAY
Pilcomayo
Asunción
Iguazú Falls
GRAN CHACO
Salado
BRAZIL
Paraná
San Miguel de Tucumán
Santiago del Estero
Resistencia
Corrientes
Posadas
Uruguay
La Serena
Mar Chiquito
San Juan
La Falda
Córdoba
Villa Carlos Paz
Santa Fe
Paraná
Lagôa dos Patos
Lagôa Mirim
Valparaíso
Mendoza
Rosario
URUGUAY
Santiago
San Rafael
Buenos Aires
La Plata
Montevideo
Río de la Plata
Las Leñas
Concepción
Colorado
Salado
PAMPAS
Cabo San Antonio
Bahía Blanca
Mar del Plata
Negro
Bahía Blanca
CORDILLERA DE LOS ANDES
PACIFIC OCEAN
San Carlos de Bariloche
Puerto Montt
Golfo San Matías
Isla de Chiloé
Esquel
Puerto Madryn
Península Valdés
Chubut
Trelew
Mar Argentino
Archipiélago de los Chonos
Chico
Golfo de San Jorge
ATLANTIC OCEAN
Deseado
Cabo Tres Puntas
Bahía Grande
FALKLAND ISLANDS (ISLAS MALVINAS) (U.K.)
West Falkland
East Falkland
Río Gallegos
Puerto Natales
Estrecho de Magallanes (Strait of Magellan)
Archipiélago Reina Adelaida
PATAGONIA
Punta Arenas
Tierra del Fuego
Ushuaia
Cabo San Diego
Cabo de Hornos (Cape Horn)
0 300 mi
0 300 km
N

Days ⑫–⑭: The End of the World ★ Fly to **Ushuaia** (there are flights from El Calafate Nov–Mar), the southernmost city in the world. Enjoy your final days in Argentina at **Las Hayas Resort** (p. 172). Cruise the Beagle Channel, where you can view sea lion and penguin colonies. Take a taxi and then a chairlift to the **Glacier Martial** (p. 170). On Day 14, fly back to Buenos Aires for your flight home.

3 PLANNING YOUR TRIP TO ARGENTINA

VISITOR INFORMATION

The central office of the **City Tourism Secretariat,** Calle Balcarce 360, in Monserrat (✆ **11/4313-0187;** www.turismo.gov.ar), is responsible for all visitor information on Buenos Aires but is not open to the general public. Instead, the city uses several kiosks spread throughout various neighborhoods, which have maps and hotel, restaurant, and attraction information. The **Tourist Information Office,** at Av. Santa Fe 883 (✆ **11/4312-2232**), is one of the best located, at the entrance to Retiro Terminal.

The **Buenos Aires City Tourism Office** runs an information hot line (✆ **11/4313-0187**) from 7:30am to 6pm Monday to Saturday, and Sunday 11am to 6pm.

Online Sources

- **www.embassyofargentina.us**: This site includes up-to-date travel information from the Argentine embassy in Washington, D.C.
- **www.turismo.gov.ar**: This Ministry of Tourism site has travel information for all of Argentina, including a virtual tour of the country's tourist regions, shopping tips, links to city tourist sites, and general travel facts.
- **www.mercotour.com**: This Spanish-language travel site focuses on adventure and ecological excursions, and includes information on outdoor activities in both Argentina and Chile.

ENTRY REQUIREMENTS

Since January 2010, citizens of the United States, Canada, the United Kingdom, and Australia are required to pay a $131 entry fee upon entering the country, as well as show a valid passport. At presstime, the fee was required just going through Ezeiza Airport but will be rolled out to all entry points eventually. Travelers from Ireland, New Zealand, and South Africa can enter for free but require a valid passport, with tourist stays of up to 90 days allowed. For more information concerning longer stays, employment, or other types of visas, contact the embassies or consulates in your home country.

Argentine Embassy Locations

In Australia: John McEwen House, Level 2, 7 National Circuit, Barton, ACT 2600 (✆ **02/6273-9111;** fax 02/6273-0500; www.argentina.org.au)

In Canada: Suite 910, Royal Bank Center, 90 Sparks St., Suite 910, Ottawa, ON K1P 5B4 (✆ **613/236-2351;** fax 613/235-2659; www.argentina-canada.net)

In New Zealand: Prime Finance Tower, Level 14, 142 Lambton Quay, Wellington (✆ **04/472-8330;** fax 04/472-8331; www.arg.org.nz)

In the U.S.: 1811 Q St. NW, Washington, DC 20009 (✆ **202/238-6400;** www.embassyofargentina.us)

Telephone Dialing Info at a Glance

- **To place a call from your home country to Argentina,** dial the international access code (011 in the U.S., 0011 in Australia, 0170 in New Zealand, 00 in the U.K.) plus the country code (54), the city or region's area code, and the local number.
- **To make long-distance calls within Argentina,** dial a 0 before the city or region's area code. Note that tariffs are reduced from 10pm to 8am.
- **To place an international call from Argentina,** add 00 before the country code. Holders of **AT&T** credit cards can reach the money-saving USA Direct from Argentina by calling toll-free ✆ **0800/555-4288** from the north, or 0800/222-1288 from the south. Similar services are offered by **MCI** (✆ **0800/555-1002**) and **Sprint** (✆ **0800/555-1003** from the north, or 0800/222-1003 from the south).
- Dial **110** for **directory assistance** (most operators will speak English) and **000** to reach an **international operator.**

In the U.K.: 65 Brooke St., London W1Y 4AH (✆ **020/7318-1300;** fax 020/7318-1301; seruni@mrecic.gov.ar)

CUSTOMS

Travelers coming from countries not bordering Argentina are exempt from all taxes on traveling articles and new articles up to $300, and an additional $300 for goods purchased at Argentine duty-free shops.

MONEY

The official Argentine currency is the **peso** (A$), made up of 100 **centavos.** Money is denominated in notes of 2, 5, 10, 20, 50, and 100 pesos and coins of 1 peso and 1, 5, 10, 25, and 50 centavos. Argentina ended its parity with the dollar in January 2002. At press time, the exchange rate was **3.82 pesos to the dollar.** ***Note:*** U.S. dollars are widely accepted throughout Argentina, especially at hotels. Many hotel rates in this chapter, as well as some tours and airline fares, are quoted in U.S. dollars.

Since devaluation, Argentina has become a bargain for foreign visitors. Though prices have recovered significantly, especially hotel rates, visitors should still be amazed at the quality and value of goods and services. With a few exceptions, prices in this chapter are quoted in dollars, but realize that high inflation and volatile exchange rates will limit their accuracy.

CURRENCY EXCHANGE U.S. dollars are widely accepted in Buenos Aires and can be used to pay taxis, hotels, restaurants, and stores. Do keep some pesos on hand because you might run into spots where you'll need them. U.S. dollars are less useful in rural areas (and places to exchange money less common), so plan ahead. You can convert your currency in hotels, at *casas de cambio* (money-exchange houses), at some banks, and at the Buenos Aires International Airport. Change American Express traveler's checks in Buenos Aires at **American Express,** Arenales 707 (✆ **11/4130-3135**); it is difficult to change traveler's checks outside the capital. I recommend that you carry sufficient pesos (or purchase traveler's checks in pesos) when you venture into small-town Argentina.

Tips Small Change

There are perpetual problems with getting small change throughout Argentina. My best advice is do what the locals do and hoard what coins you can, to use later on buses and for vending machines. And be prepared to be offered candies by corner stores in lieu of change.

If you manage to receive change back, try to hold the left-hand number on the bills under a light. If it doesn't sparkle, you've likely received a fake note.

ATMS ATMs are easy to access in Buenos Aires and other urban areas, but don't bet on finding them off the beaten path. Typically, they are connected to **Cirrus** (✆ **800/424-7787**) or **PLUS** (✆ **800/843-7587**) networks. Many ATMs also accept Visa and MasterCard, less often American Express and Diners Club.

Be aware that most ATMs allow only small withdrawals of as little as $100; although this phenomenon has been going on for a few years, no banks seem to be able to explain the problem and it can cause considerable frustration among travelers. Although many ATMs will actually dispense more than the limit displayed on the screen, the maximum dispensed is 1,000 pesos; you can attempt this twice daily, with varying degrees of success. Always withdraw in multiples of $10 (or 990 pesos) so you can avoid having to make change. Consult your bank before leaving (some have no withdrawal fees), and bear in mind that you'll get charged every time you withdraw money, sometimes up to $5. Finally, I recommend bringing extra dollars and paying by credit card wherever possible.

CREDIT CARDS If you choose to use plastic, Visa, American Express, MasterCard, and Diners Club are the most commonly accepted cards here. However, **bargain-hunters take note:** Some establishments—especially smaller ones—don't like paying the fee to process your credit card and will give you a better price if you pay cash. Credit cards are accepted at most hotels and restaurants, except the very cheapest ones. You cannot use credit cards in many taxis or at most attractions (museums, trams, and so on). To report a lost or stolen **MasterCard,** call ✆ **0800/555-0507;** for **Visa,** call ✆ **0800/666-0171;** for **American Express,** call ✆ **0810/555-2639.**

WHEN TO GO

PEAK SEASON The seasons in Argentina are the reverse of those in the Northern Hemisphere. Buenos Aires and the Lake District are ideal in fall (Mar–May) and spring (Sept–Nov), when temperatures are mild and crowds have yet to descend. The beaches and resort towns are packed with vacationing Argentines in summer (Dec–Mar), while Buenos Aires becomes somewhat deserted. (You decide whether that's a plus or a minus—hotel prices usually drop here in their summer.) Plan a trip to Patagonia and the southern Andes in their summer, when days are longer and warmer. Winter (June–Aug) is the best time to visit Iguazú and the Northwest, when the rains and heat have subsided; but spring (Aug–Oct) is also pleasant, as temperatures are mild and the crowds have cleared out. Mendoza is best visited from November to May, with the wine harvest season beginning in March.

CLIMATE Except for a small tropical area in northern Argentina, the country lies in the temperate zone, characterized by cool, dry weather in the south, and warmer, humid air in the center. Accordingly, January and February are quite hot—often in the high 90s to more than 100°F (35°C–40°C)—while winter (about July–Oct) can be chilly.

PUBLIC HOLIDAYS Public holidays are New Year's Day (Jan 1), Good Friday, Easter, Veterans' Day (Apr 2), Labor Day (May 1), First Argentine Government (May 25), Flag Day (June 20), Independence Day (July 9), Anniversary of the Death of General San Martín (Aug 17), Columbus Day (Oct 12), Feast of the Immaculate Conception (Dec 8), and Christmas (Dec 25). Note that many businesses are also closed on Christmas Eve (Dec 24).

HEALTH CONCERNS

Life in Argentina presents few health concerns. Argentina requires no vaccinations to enter the country, except for passengers coming from countries where cholera and yellow fever are endemic. Some people who have allergies (especially respiratory ones) can be affected by air pollution in the city and the high level of pollen during spring. Because motor vehicle crashes are a leading cause of injury among travelers, walk and drive defensively and always wear a seat belt.

Most visitors find that Argentine food and water is generally easy on the stomach. Water and ice are considered especially safe to drink in Buenos Aires. Be careful with food from street vendors, especially in dodgy neighborhoods of Buenos Aires and in cities outside the capital. The medical facilities and personnel in Buenos Aires and the other urban areas in Argentina are very professional. Argentina has a system of socialized medicine, where basic services are free. Private clinics are inexpensive by Western standards.

ALTITUDE SICKNESS If you visit the Andes, ascend gradually to allow your body to adjust to the high altitude, thus avoiding altitude sickness. Altitude sickness, known as *soroche* or *puna,* is a temporary yet often debilitating affliction that affects about a quarter of travelers to the northern Altiplano, or the Andes, at 2,400m (8,000 ft.) and up. Nausea, fatigue, headaches, shortness of breath, and sleeplessness are the symptoms, which can last from 2 to 5 days. If you feel as though you've been affected, drink plenty of water, take aspirin or ibuprofen, and avoid alcohol and sleeping pills. To prevent altitude sickness, acclimatize your body by breaking the assent to higher regions into segments.

AUSTRAL SUN The shrinking ozone layer in southern South America has caused an onset of health problems among its citizens, including increased incidents of skin cancer and cataracts. If you are planning to travel to Patagonia, keep in mind that on "red alert" days (typically Sept–Nov), it is possible to burn in *10 minutes.* If you plan to be outdoors, protect yourself with strong sunblock, a long-sleeved shirt, a wide-brimmed hat, and sunglasses.

MALARIA & OTHER TROPICAL AILMENTS The Centers for Disease Control and Prevention (www.cdc.gov) recommends that travelers to northwestern Argentina take malaria medication. Yet risk is very low and basic mosquito repellent should be sufficient. Cholera and dengue fever appear from time to time in the Northwest, but such tropical diseases do not seem to be a problem in the sultry climate of Iguazú.

GETTING THERE

Argentina's main international airport is **Ezeiza Ministro Pistarini** (airport code EZE; ✆ **11/4480-0889**), located 34km (26 miles) outside Buenos Aires (allow 1 hr. to get to the city). A departure tax of approximately $20 is included in your ticket price. Passengers in transit and children 1 and under are exempt from this tax. However, visitors are advised to verify the departure tax with their airline or travel agent, as the exact amount changes frequently. Be aware that any immediate domestic connection requires a 1-hour taxi ride to Buenos Aires internal airport **Aeroparque Jorge Newbery Airport** (✆ **11/4514-1515**). This is hard to avoid except when traveling first to Mendoza via Santiago de Chile; this is much more convenient as it does not require an airport change and the connecting flight is 30 minutes over the Andes.

FROM THE U.S. & CANADA Argentina's national airline, **Aerolíneas Argentinas** (✆ 800/333-0276 in the U.S., 0810/222-86527 in Buenos Aires, or 1800/22-22-15 in Australia; www.aerolineas.com.ar), flies nonstop from Miami and New York's JFK. **American Airlines** (✆ 800/433-7300 in the U.S., or 011/4318-1111 in Buenos Aires; www.aa.com) flies nonstop from Miami and Dallas–Fort Worth. **Copa Airlines** (✆ 800/333-0425; www.copa.com) flies nonstop from Houston and New York (Newark). **Delta Airlines** (✆ 800/241-4141 in the U.S., or 0800-666-0133; www.delta.com) flies nonstop from Atlanta and Los Angeles. **LAN** (✆ 866/435-9526 in the U.S. and Canada, or 11/4378-2222 in Buenos Aires; www.lan.com) flies nonstop from Los Angeles, Miami, and New York. **United Airlines** (✆ 800/241-6522 in the U.S., or 0810/777-8648 in Buenos Aires; www.united.com) flies nonstop from Miami; Washington, D.C. (Dulles Airport); Chicago; New York (La Guardia); and Los Angeles. Approximate flight time from Miami to Buenos Aires is 9 hours. **Air Canada** (✆ 888/247-2262 in Canada, or 11/4327-3640 in Buenos Aires; www.aircanada.ca) flies directly from Toronto to Buenos Aires.

FROM THE U.K. & EUROPE **British Airways** (✆ 0845/773-3377 in the U.K., or 11/4320-6600 in Buenos Aires; www.britishairways.co.uk) flies nonstop from London Gatwick to Buenos Aires; approximate flight time is 13 hours. **Air France** (✆ 800/423-7422 in Europe, or 11/4317-4700 in Buenos Aires; www.airfrance.com) flies nonstop from Paris (Charles de Gaulle). **Iberia** (✆ 0845/601-2854 in the U.K., or 11/4131-1000 in Buenos Aires; www.iberia.com) connects through Madrid and Barcelona. **Lufthansa** (✆ 0870/1288-737 in the U.K., or 11/4319-0600 in Buenos Aires; www.lufthansa.com) flies nonstop from Frankfurt. **Aerolíneas Argentinas** (✆ 0800/096-9747; www.aerolinas.com.ar) flies from Madrid, Barcelona, and Rome. **Alitalia** (✆ 0810/777-2548; www.alitalia.com) operates flights from Rome.

FROM AUSTRALIA & NEW ZEALAND **Aerolíneas Argentinas** (✆ **800/22-22-15** in Australia; www.aerolineas.com.ar) flies from Sydney, with a stop in Auckland; approximate flight time from Sydney is 16 hours. **LAN** (✆ **300/36-14-00** in Australia, or ✆ 649/977-2233 in New Zealand; www.lan.com) and **Qantas** (✆ **13-13-13** in Australia or 11/4514-4730 in Buenos Aires; www.qantas.com.au) have service from Sydney to Santiago, with shared service continuing to Buenos Aires on LAN.

GETTING AROUND

By Plane

The easiest way to travel Argentina's vast distances is by air. **Aerolíneas Argentinas** (✆ **0810/222-86527;** www.aerolineas.com.ar) connects most cities and tourist destinations in Argentina, including Córdoba, Jujuy, Iguazú, Mendoza, and Salta. Its only competitor, **LAN** (✆ **11/43782200;** www.lan.com), serves Iguazú, Mendoza, and Bariloche, among others. By American standards, domestic flights within Argentina are very expensive. Expect long delays with Aerolíneas Argentinas, which has an 80% monopoly of the domestic market; the company is inefficient and guilty of outrageous dual pricing, charging foreign travelers as much as 300% more than locals.

In Buenos Aires, domestic flights and flights to Uruguay travel out of **Aeroparque Jorge Newbery Airport** (airport code AEP; ✆ **11/4514-1515**), 15 minutes from downtown. Inexpensive taxis and *remises* (private, unmetered taxis) cost about A$60 to get you to and from the city center. At both airports, only take officially sanctioned transportation and do not accept transportation services from any private individuals. **Manuel Tienda León** (✆ **11/4314-3636**) is the most reliable transportation company, offering buses and *remises* to and from the airports (www.tiendaleon.com.ar).

By Bus

Argentine buses are comfortable, safe, efficient, and surprisingly luxurious. They connect nearly every part of Argentina as well as bordering countries. In cases where two classes of bus service are offered—*semicama* and *cama*—the latter offers wider seats, is very comfortable, and is only 10% more expensive. Some companies offer *cama ejecutivo,* which is basically a full horizontal bed and, again, only 10% more expensive than a *cama.* Most long-distance buses offer clean toilets, air-conditioning, TV entertainment, and dinner/bar service. Bus travel is much cheaper than air travel for similar routes, and for this reason, many people opt for a luxury night bus. My advice is to consider a night bus if you are on a budget and the journey is no more than 16 hours. Even committed air travelers are surprised at just how pleasant the night bus can be, and it is a singular, South American cultural experience. ***One piece of advice:*** Take an extra sweater as some companies can be overly generous with the air-conditioning.

Among the major bus companies that operate out of Buenos Aires are **La Veloz del Norte** (✆ **11/4315-2482**), serving destinations in the Northwest including Salta and Jujuy; **Singer** (✆ **11/4315-2653**), serving Puerto Iguazú and Brazilian destinations; and **T. A. Chevallier** (✆ **11/4313-3297**), serving Bariloche. **Andesmar** (✆ **11/4328-8240;** www.andesmar.com) is a first-class company that goes everywhere, including Santiago de Chile. They serve free wine and conduct on-the-road bingo sessions in case you get bored. Another recommended company is **CATA** (✆ **11/4311-5581;** www.catainternacional.com), which operates between Argentina and Chile and thoughtfully serves a nightcap of whiskey before you drop off.

By Car

Argentine roads and highways are generally in good condition, with the exception of some rural areas. Most highways have been privatized and charge nominal tolls. In cities, Argentines drive exceedingly fast, and do not always obey traffic lights or lanes. When driving outside the city, remember that *autopista* means motorway or highway, and *paso* means mountain pass. Don't drive in rural areas at night, as cattle sometimes overtake the road to keep warm and are nearly impossible to see. Wear your seat belt; it's required by Argentine law, although few Argentines actually wear them. You need an international license to drive in most parts of the country. A car that uses GNC (a hybrid fuel of gas and oil) is 50% cheaper than unleaded gas (known as NAFTA) but requires more frequent filling. ***Beware:*** In remoter areas many filling stations do not serve GNC so you must revert to NAFTA.

The **Automóvil Club Argentino (ACA),** Av. del Libertador 1850 (✆ **11/4802-6061**), has working arrangements with international automobile clubs. The ACA offers numerous services, including roadside assistance, road maps, hotel and camping information, and discounts for various tourist activities.

CAR RENTALS Many international car-rental companies operate in Argentina with offices at airports and in city centers. The major companies are **Hertz** (✆ **800/654-3131**

in the U.S.; www.hertz.com), **Avis** (© **800/230-4898** in the U.S.; www.avis.com), **Dollar** (© **800/800-3665** in the U.S.; www.dollar.com), and **Thrifty** (© **800/847-4389** in the U.S.; www.thrifty.com); see "Buenos Aires," below, for locations in the capital. Car rental will cost about $70 per day for an intermediate-size vehicle, including unlimited miles and 21% tax (ask for any special promotions, especially on weekly rates). Check to see if your existing automobile insurance policy (or a credit card) covers insurance for car rentals; otherwise you should purchase full insurance that costs approximately $10 a day. Be aware that you cannot cross into neighboring countries in rental cars unless you acquire a special permit at the rental agency. **Avis** is the best company to do this with.

TIPS ON ACCOMMODATIONS

Business, boutique, or backpacker? Accommodations in Argentina cover every taste and literally every budget. Even the tiniest towns have excellent camping sites with showers and pools for those on an ultralow budget. Despite the explosion in hotel options in recent years, there are still chronic bottlenecks when it is near impossible to get a decent room. Watch out for spring in Buenos Aires (Oct–Nov) and summer in Mendoza and Patagonia (Dec–Feb). Easter is also always busy, as is the winter break in July, when everybody goes west to ski in Bariloche. Small boutique hotels, winery lodges, and *estancias* are often the first to fill up, so book those well in advance. Prices are also on the rise, but you can get some good off-season bargains in Patagonia and Salta. Quality is generally excellent at properties across the board, with good facilities, including restaurants, though service can be lacking and slow. Hotel rooms in this chapter fall under the price categories of **Very Expensive**, $200 and up; **Expensive**, $120 to $199; **Moderate**, $80 to $119; and **Inexpensive**, $79 and below.

TIPS ON DINING

Argentines can't get enough beef. Indeed, the average citizen eats more than his or her own weight in meat each year. While exporting some of the finest beef in the world, they still manage to keep enough of this national treasure at home to please natives and visitors alike. Argentine meat is regarded as healthier and more free range than its foreign counterparts. A huge sizzling steak is often item number one on many travelers' itineraries when they arrive here.

The Argentine social venue of choice is the *asado* (barbecue). Families and friends gather at someone's home and barbecue prime ribs, pork, chicken, sausages, sweetbreads, kidneys—the list goes on. You can enjoy this tradition while eating out; many restaurants are referred to interchangeably in Spanish as *parrillas* or *parrilladas,* with open-air grills and, occasionally, large spits twirling animal carcasses over a roaring fire. For the full experience, ask for the *parrillada mixta* (mixed grill), which includes many of the items mentioned above. And don't forget the *chimichurri* sauce—an exotic blend of chili and garlic—to season your meat. ***A note on steaks:*** You can order them *bien cocida* (well done), *punto* (medium rare), or *jugoso* (rare, literally "juicy").

But vegetarians exhale: Argentina offers some great alternatives to the red-meat diet. One of the imprints Italians have left on Argentine culture is a plethora of pasta dishes, pizzas, and even *helados* (ice cream), reminiscent of Italian gelato. In addition, ethnic restaurants are springing up throughout Buenos Aires, stretching beyond traditional Spanish, Italian, and French venues to Japanese, Indian, Armenian, and Thai. Ethnic dishes come to life with fresh meats, seafood, and vegetables—the products of Argentina's diverse terrain. If you're just looking for a snack, try an empanada, a turnover pastry filled with minced meat, chicken, vegetables, or corn and varying a bit by region.

Tips **Late-Night Dining**

In Argentina, meal times are, on average, later than English-speaking travelers may be used to. Dinner frequently does not begin until after 9pm, and restaurants stay open until well past midnight.

Meals in this chapter are listed according to **Very Expensive,** A$60 and up; **Expensive,** A$45 to A$60; **Moderate,** A$30 to A$45; and **Inexpensive,** under A$30. Prices shown don't include beverages or tax.

Beverages

An immensely popular afternoon custom is the sharing of *mate,* a tea made from the *yerba mate* herb. In the late afternoon, Argentines pass a gourd filled with the tea around the table, each person sipping through a metal straw with a filter on the end. The drink is bitter, so you might opt to add some sugar. *Mate* is such an important part of daily life in Argentina that if people plan to be out of the house at teatime, they tote a thermos with them. A popular alcoholic drink is the Italian digestif Fernet, served with lashings of ice and cola.

Argentina boasts some spectacular wine-growing regions; the best known is Mendoza, but Salta, San Juan, and La Rioja also produce impressive vintages. Malbec is the best known Argentine red wine and is an engaging companion to any *parrillada mixta.* Torrontes, a dry white wine, has won various international competitions as well. Other grapes to look out for: Tempranillo and Bonarda.

Typical Argentine Dishes

Look for some of these favorites on your menu:

- ***Bife de chorizo:*** Similar to a New York strip steak, but twice as big. Thick and tender, usually served medium rare.
- ***Bife de lomo:*** Filet mignon, 7.5cm (3-in.) thick. Tender and lean.
- ***Buseca:*** Stew with sausages.
- ***Locro criollo:*** Beef stew with potatoes.
- ***Milanesa:*** Breaded meat filet, sometimes in a sandwich.
- ***Panqueques:*** Either dessert crepes filled with *dulce de leche* (caramel) and whipped cream, or salted crepes with vegetables.
- ***Provoletta:*** Charbroiled slices of provolone cheese served at a *parrilla.*

TIPS ON SHOPPING

Porteños (residents of Buenos Aires) consider their city a fashion capital. Buenos Aires boasts the same upscale stores you would find in New York or Paris. The big designer labels are in Recoleta and Belgrano and small, boutique designers in Palermo Viejo. Furs, wool, and leather goods are excellent quality across the country, while Buenos Aires is superb for antiques and vintage clothes. Keep your receipts for invoices over approximately $20 from stores participating in tax-free shopping; you should be able to get a refund of the 21% value-added tax (abbreviated IVA in Spanish) when you leave the country. Forms are available at the airport—desk 25 in Ezeiza. Get forms stamped and go through customs before collecting your refund upstairs. Opt for the cash refund, as credit card processing takes weeks. Technically they can ask to see goods, but this rarely happens since it is impractical—*except* at Aeroparque on flights to Uruguay. Be aware that credits over $170 require an authorization code from the store. Art items will often be flagged by Customs unless accompanied by a special export permit provided by the vender and a certificate of authenticity by the artist. One possible way around the export permit is a letter from the artist saying the item is a gift.

Fast Facts Argentina

American Express Offices are located in Buenos Aires, Bariloche, Salta, San Martín, and Ushuaia. In Buenos Aires, the Amex office is at Arenales 707 (✆ **11/4312-1661**). It's open Monday to Friday 9am to 5pm.

Business Hours Banks are open weekdays from 10am to 3pm. Shopping hours are weekdays 9am to 8pm and Saturday 9am to 1pm. Shopping centers are open daily from 10am to 8pm. Some stores close for lunch.

Doctors & Hospitals The best hospitals in Buenos Aires are **British Hospital,** Perdriel 74 (✆ **11/4309-6400**); **Sanatorio San Lucas,** Belgrano 369, San Isidro (✆ **11/4732-8888**); and **Mater Dei,** San Martín de Tours 2952 (✆ **11/4809-5555**). All have English-speaking doctors on staff.

Electricity If you plan to bring a hair dryer, radio, travel iron, or any other small appliance, pack a transformer and a European-style adapter, since electricity in Argentina runs on 220 volts. Note that most laptops operate on both 110 and 220 volts. Luxury hotels usually provide transformers and adapters.

Embassies & Consulates In Buenos Aires: **Australia,** Villanueva 1400 (✆ **11/4777-6580**); **Canada,** Tagle 2828 (✆ **11/4805-3032**); **New Zealand,** Carlos Pellegrini 1427, 5th Floor (✆ **11/4328-0747**); the **United Kingdom,** Luis Agote 2412 (✆ **11/4803-6021**); and the **United States,** Av. Colombia 4300 (✆ **11/4774-5333**).

Emergencies The following emergency numbers are valid throughout Argentina. For an ambulance, call ✆ **107;** in case of fire, call ✆ **100;** for police assistance, call ✆ **101.**

Internet Access Cybercafes are on every corner in Buenos Aires and are found in other cities as well, so it won't be hard to stay connected while in Argentina. Access is reasonably priced (usually averaging A$7.20 per hr.) and connections are reliably good. The bigger cybercafes usually offer Skype, connected with hand phones attached to monitors. Wi-Fi is ubiquitous, especially in top hotels, cafes, and some city pedestrian streets.

Language Argentina's official language is Spanish, but it's easy to find English speakers in major hotels, restaurants, and shops—particularly in the big cities. Many working-class Argentines speak little or no English, and it's even less common in rural areas.

Liquor Laws The official drinking age in Argentina is 18. Licensing laws are very liberal, though in some city districts stores cannot sell after 11pm.

Maps Reliable maps can be purchased through the **Automóvil Club Argentino,** Av. del Libertador 1850, Buenos Aires (✆ **11/4802-6061** or 11/4802-7071).

Newspapers & Magazines Major local papers are ***Clarín*** (independent), ***Página*** (center-left), and ***La Nación*** (conservative). The ***Buenos Aires Herald*** is the (quite good) local English newspaper. The ***International Herald Tribune*** is widely available at news kiosks around the country. Some hotels in Buenos Aires will deliver a ***New York Times*** headline news fax to your room. ***Time Out Buenos Aires*** is a city-listings magazine, and ***Wine Republic*** (www.wine-republic.com) is Mendoza's English-language publication.

Post Offices & Mail Post offices are generally open Monday through Friday from 8am to 6pm and Saturday from 8am to 1pm. Airmail postage for a letter weighing 7 ounces or less from Argentina to North America and Europe is A$29. Mail takes on average between 10 and 14 days to get to the U.S. and Europe.

Restrooms Public facilities are generally very good; you can duck into hotel lobbies, restaurants, cafes, and shopping centers.

Safety Argentina is the safest country in South America after Uruguay. Nevertheless, petty crime is widespread in Buenos Aires and growing elsewhere. Travelers should be especially alert to pickpockets and purse snatching on the streets and on buses and trains. Street crime is common in the suburbs of the capital and in Buenos Aires province. Avoid demonstrations, strikes, and other political gatherings. Always keep your belongings in sight while dining or drinking. Do not take taxis off the street in Buenos Aires; you should call for a radio-taxi or *remise* (private, unmetered taxi) instead—your hotel, restaurant, or bar will happily call one for you.

Smoking Smoking used to be a pervasive aspect of Argentine society but is now prohibited in bars and restaurants—though this may change from province to province. Where there are no restrictions, you can request a nonsmoking table in a restaurant, and you will usually be accommodated. There is never any smoking on buses or trains, and most hotels prohibit smoking in rooms and public areas.

Taxes Argentina's value-added tax (IVA) is 21%. For tax-free shopping, see "Tips on Shopping," above.

Telephone & Fax Domestic and international calls are expensive in Argentina, especially from hotels (rates fall 10pm–8am). Direct dialing to North America and Europe is available from most phones.

Public phones take either phone cards (sold at kiosks on the street) or coins (less common). Local calls cost 20 centavos to start, and charge more the longer you talk. Telecentro offices—found everywhere in city centers—offer private phone booths where calls are paid when completed. Most hotels offer fax services, as do all Telecentro offices. For international calls, I recommend using phone cards such as Hablemas or Teletel. If you can follow the Spanish instructions, it means a call lasting an hour and 40 minutes to the U.S. can cost as little as A$11. Another good option is the many cybercafes with Skype. See the "Telephone Dialing Info at a Glance" box on p. 75.

Time Zone The country is 1 hour ahead of Eastern Standard Time in the United States in summer and 2 hours ahead in winter. However, daylight saving time is sometimes employed by the eastern provinces.

Tipping A 10% tip is expected at cafes and restaurants. Give at least A$4 to bellhops and porters, 5% to hairdressers, and leftover change to taxi drivers.

Water In Buenos Aires and along the Andes, the water is perfectly safe to drink; if you are traveling to more humid regions in the northeast, it's best to stick with bottled water for drinking.

4 BUENOS AIRES ★★

Shop till you drop amidst South America's swankiest boutique stores and liveliest open air markets. Pose in gilded tango theatres with Belle Epoque interiors. Stroll through museums with cutting-edge art. Party till dawn on a star-studded waterfront. Gamble at an elegant race track or roar with the crowds at a crucible-like soccer stadium. Buenos Aires has often been called the Paris of South America, but it has in fact upstaged its European mentor when it comes to sheer energy, color, and edginess. It is the Mona Lisa with graffiti scrawled across it. It is both raw and beautiful, sophisticated and wild.

Argentina's capital is a city of bold contrasts—be it the glass-and-steel coolness of the Puerto Madero docklands or the smoke-tinged cobblestones and antiques of historic San Telmo. The neo-classical facades and well-groomed avenues of Recoleta stretch into the trendy streets and plazas of Palermo. Avenida De Mayo is a fabled thoroughfare that has seen revolutions and bombings, and fittingly ends at the famous Plaza de Mayo and Casa Rosada (Pink House), the boisterous center of Argentina's tumultuous political scene.

The city's famous cafe life has bloomed into a full-blown gourmet revolution, with countless restaurants serving everything from sushi to Indian and, of course, the famous home-grown beef. Visitors continue to flock to and indeed set up shop in what is the most desirable city to live in within the region. Its allure is only enhanced by its history; Porteños mark the capital's 200-year-old independence from Spain in 2010.

ESSENTIALS

Getting There

BY PLANE See "Getting Around: By Plane," on p. 78.

BY BUS The **Estación Terminal de Omnibus** (also known as Terminal Retiro), Av. Ramos Mejía 1680 (✆ **11/4310-0700**), in the city center near Retiro train station, serves all long-distance buses. The terminal's official website, **www.tebasa.com.ar**, provides useful information on the buses serving the terminal and their destinations.

BY CAR In Buenos Aires, travel by *subte* (subway), *remise,* or radio-taxi is easier and safer than driving yourself. Rush-hour traffic is chaotic, and parking is difficult. If you do rent a car, park it at your hotel or at a nearby garage and leave it there. You really don't need to have one in the city.

Orientation

Although Buenos Aires is a huge city, the main tourist neighborhoods are concentrated in a small section near the Río de la Plata. The Microcentro, which extends from Plaza de Mayo to the south and Plaza San Martín to the north, and from Plaza del Congreso to the west and Puerto Madero to the east, forms the city center. San Telmo, La Boca, Puerto Madero, Recoleta, and Palermo surround the Microcentro. The city layout is fairly straightforward, where *avenidas* signify the broad avenues and *calles* smaller, one-way streets, while *diagonales* cut streets and avenues at 45-degree angles. Each city block extends about 100m (328 ft.), and building addresses indicate the distance on that street.

The **Microcentro** includes Plaza de Mayo (the political and historic center of Buenos Aires), Plaza San Martín, and Avenida 9 de Julio (the widest street in the world). Most commercial activity is focused here, as are the majority of hotels and restaurants. Next to the Microcentro, the riverfront area called **Puerto Madero** boasts excellent restaurants and nightlife as well as new commercial areas. Farther south, **La Boca, Monserrat,** and **San Telmo** are the historic neighborhoods where the first immigrants arrived and tango originated.

The city's most strikingly European neighborhood, **Recoleta,** offers fashionable restaurants, cafes, and evening entertainment amid rich French architecture. It's home to the Recoleta Cemetery, where key personalities such as Evita are buried. To the northwest is **Palermo,** actually made of several different and distinct neighborhoods. Palermo contains lots of parks, mansions, and gardens—making it perfect for a weekend picnic or evening outing. **Palermo Viejo,** further divided into **Palermo SoHo** and **Palermo Hollywood,** is full of funky bohemian boutiques and music bars, as well as the city's chicest restaurants.

STREET MAPS Ask the front desk of your hotel for a copy of "The Golden Map" and "QuickGuide Buenos Aires" to help you navigate the city and locate its major attractions. Before leaving home, you can also get great maps ahead of time from the Buenos Aires–based company **De Dios** (www.dediosonline.com), which has laminated street maps and various themed maps, ranging from tango to shopping. All magazine kiosks sell a tiny invaluable booklet called *Guia T,* primarily for negotiating the city's myriad bus routes but also handy as a walking map guide.

Getting Around

The Buenos Aires metro—called the *subte*—is the fastest, cheapest way to get around. Buses are also convenient, though less commonly used by tourists. Get maps of metro and bus lines from tourist offices and most hotels. (Ask for the "QuickGuide Buenos Aires.") All metro stations and most bus stops have maps.

BY METRO Six *subte* lines connect commercial and tourist areas in the city Monday through Saturday from 5am to 11pm and Sunday and holidays from 8am to 11pm. This is an estimate, and the actual times will vary. The flat fare is A$1.10, with tickets purchased at machines or windows at every station. You can also buy a *subte* pass for A$11, valid for 10 trips. It's always wise to buy spare cards, as they often demagnetize in the intense humidity so common throughout the summer. Line A connects Plaza de Mayo to Primera Junta. This was the city's first line; it still retains the old turn-of-the-20th-century wooden cars, and it is like a moving museum. Line B runs from near Puerto Madero (Av. Leandro N. Alem) to Federico Lacroze. Line C travels between the city's train stations, Retiro and Constitución. Line D runs from Congreso de Tucumán to Catedral. Line E links Bolívar with Plaza de los Virreyes. Neither the Recoleta nor Puerto Madero neighborhoods have *subte* access. Most of Puerto Madero, however, can be reached via the L. N. Alem *subte.* (It's a 5- to 20-min. walk, depending on which dock you're going to.) The H line runs from Avenida Caseros to Avenida Rivadavia. Visit the website **www.subte.com.ar** for more information on the system, as well as downloadable maps and a point-to-point page estimating travel time.

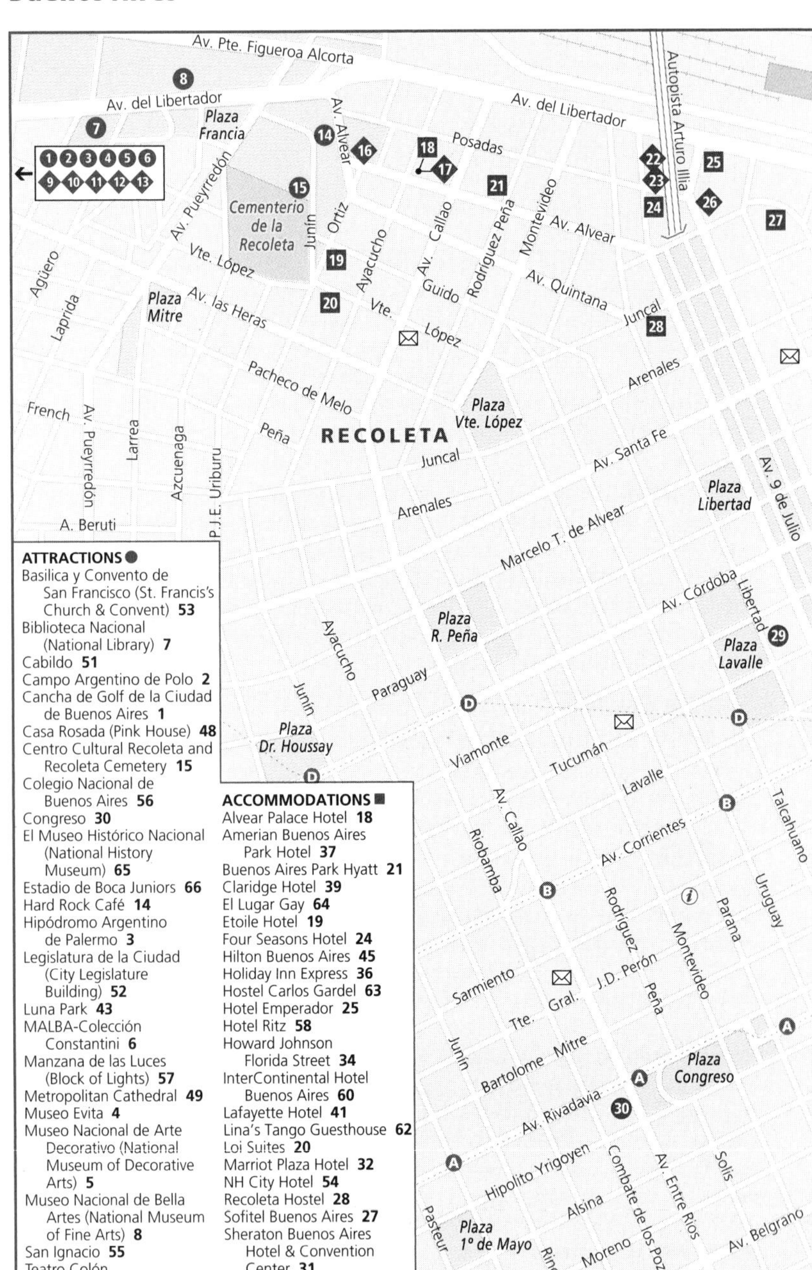
Av. Pte. Figueroa Alcorta
Av. del Libertador
Plaza Francia
Av. Alvear
Posadas
Av. del Libertador
Autopista Arturo Illia
Av. Pueyrredón
Cementerio de la Recoleta
Junín
Ortiz
Ayacucho
Av. Callao
Rodriguez Peña
Montevideo
Av. Alvear
Vte. López
Av. Guido
Av. Quintana
Agüero
Laprida
Plaza Mitre
Av. las Heras
Vte. López
Juncal
Pacheco de Melo
Arenales
French
Av. Pueyrredón
Larrea
Azcuenaga
P.J.E. Uriburu
Peña
RECOLETA
Plaza Vte. López
Juncal
Av. Santa Fe
Arenales
Plaza Libertad
Av. 9 de Julio
A. Beruti
Marcelo T. de Alvear
Av. Córdoba
Libertad
Plaza R. Peña
Plaza Lavalle
Ayacucho
Junín
Paraguay
Plaza Dr. Houssay
Viamonte
Tucumán
Lavalle
Av. Callao
Riobamba
Av. Corrientes
Talcahuano
Uruguay
Rodriguez
Montevideo
Parana
Sarmiento
J.D. Perón
Peña
Tte. Gral.
Junín
Bartolome Mitre
Plaza Congreso
Av. Rivadavia
Hipolito Yrigoyen
Combate de los Pozos
Av. Entre Rios
Solis
Pasteur
Plaza 1º de Mayo
Alsina
Rincon
Moreno
Av. Belgrano
ATTRACTIONS
Basilica y Convento de San Francisco (St. Francis's Church & Convent) 53
Biblioteca Nacional (National Library) 7
Cabildo 51
Campo Argentino de Polo 2
Cancha de Golf de la Ciudad de Buenos Aires 1
Casa Rosada (Pink House) 48
Centro Cultural Recoleta and Recoleta Cemetery 15
Colegio Nacional de Buenos Aires 56
Congreso 30
El Museo Histórico Nacional (National History Museum) 65
Estadio de Boca Juniors 66
Hard Rock Café 14
Hipódromo Argentino de Palermo 3
Legislatura de la Ciudad (City Legislature Building) 52
Luna Park 43
MALBA-Colección Constantini 6
Manzana de las Luces (Block of Lights) 57
Metropolitan Cathedral 49
Museo Evita 4
Museo Nacional de Arte Decorativo (National Museum of Decorative Arts) 5
Museo Nacional de Bella Artes (National Museum of Fine Arts) 8
San Ignacio 55
Teatro Colón (Colón Theater) 29
ACCOMMODATIONS
Alvear Palace Hotel 18
Amerian Buenos Aires Park Hotel 37
Buenos Aires Park Hyatt 21
Claridge Hotel 39
El Lugar Gay 64
Etoile Hotel 19
Four Seasons Hotel 24
Hilton Buenos Aires 45
Holiday Inn Express 36
Hostel Carlos Gardel 63
Hotel Emperador 25
Hotel Ritz 58
Howard Johnson Florida Street 34
InterContinental Hotel Buenos Aires 60
Lafayette Hotel 41
Lina's Tango Guesthouse 62
Loi Suites 20
Marriot Plaza Hotel 32
NH City Hotel 54
Recoleta Hostel 28
Sofitel Buenos Aires 27
Sheraton Buenos Aires Hotel & Convention Center 31
V&S Hostel 40

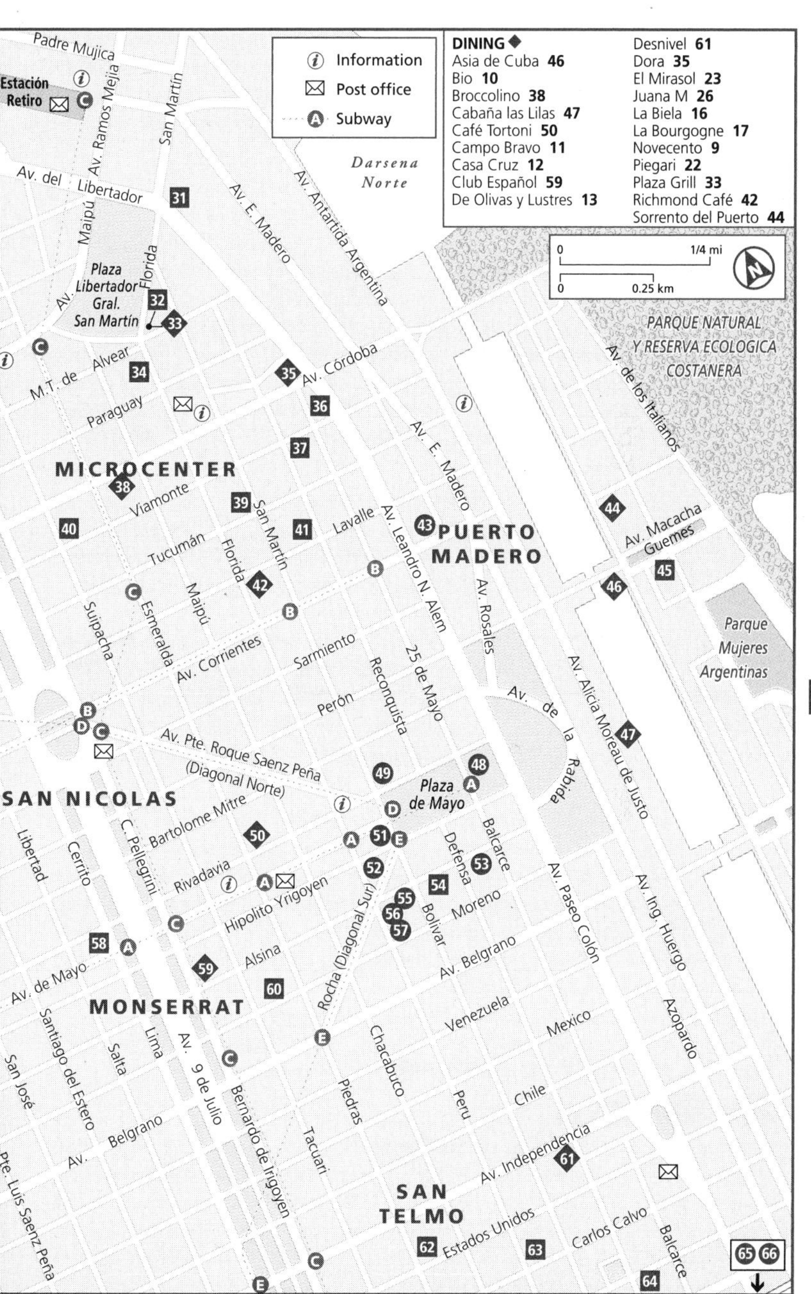
Information
Post office
Subway
DINING
Asia de Cuba 46
Bio 10
Broccolino 38
Cabaña las Lilas 47
Café Tortoni 50
Campo Bravo 11
Casa Cruz 12
Club Español 59
De Olivas y Lustres 13
Desnivel 61
Dora 35
El Mirasol 23
Juana M 26
La Biela 16
La Bourgogne 17
Novecento 9
Piegari 22
Plaza Grill 33
Richmond Café 42
Sorrento del Puerto 44
0
1/4 mi
0
0.25 km
N
Estación Retiro
Padre Mujica
Av. Ramos Mejía
San Martín
Av. del Libertador
Maipú
Florida
Plaza Libertador Gral. San Martín
Darsena Norte
Av. E. Madero
Av. Antártida Argentina
PARQUE NATURAL Y RESERVA ECOLOGICA COSTANERA
Av. de los Italianos
M.T. de Alvear
Paraguay
Av. Córdoba
MICROCENTER
Viamonte
San Martín
Lavalle
Av. Leandro N. Alem
PUERTO MADERO
Av. Macacha Guemes
Tucumán
Florida
Maipú
Suipacha
Esmeralda
Av. Corrientes
Sarmiento
Reconquista
25 de Mayo
Av. Rosales
Parque Mujeres Argentinas
Perón
Av. de la Rabida
Av. Alicia Moreau de Justo
Av. Pte. Roque Saenz Peña (Diagonal Norte)
Plaza de Mayo
SAN NICOLAS
Bartolome Mitre
C. Pellegrini
Libertad
Cerrito
Balcarce
Defensa
Rivadavia
Hipolito Yrigoyen
Rocha (Diagonal Sur)
Bolivar
Moreno
Av. Paseo Colón
Av. Ing. Huergo
Av. de Mayo
Alsina
Av. Belgrano
MONSERRAT
Santiago del Estero
Salta
Lima
Av. 9 de Julio
Venezuela
Mexico
Azopardo
Chacabuco
San José
Bernardo de Irigoyen
Piedras
Peru
Chile
Av. Belgrano
Tacuari
Av. Independencia
Pte. Luis Saenz Peña
SAN TELMO
Estados Unidos
Carlos Calvo
Balcarce

BY BUS Around 140 bus lines operate in Buenos Aires 24 hours a day and are an excellent way to get around the city. It is essential you buy a *Guia T* map booklet at any newspaper kiosk to truly take advantage of all the routes. The minimum fare is A$1.10 and goes up depending on the distance traveled. Pay your fare inside the bus at an electronic ticket machine, which accepts coins only. Many bus drivers, provided you can communicate with them, will tell you the fare for your destination and help you with where to get off.

BY TAXI Fares are relatively inexpensive, with an initial meter reading of A$3.80 increasing 38 centavos every 200m (656 ft.) or each minute. Most of what the average tourist needs to see in the city is accessible for a $6-to-$10 cab ride. *Remises* and radio-taxis are much safer than regular street taxis. Radio-taxis, when hailed on the street, can be recognized by the plastic light boxes that are usually on their rooftops. When heading to an off-the-beaten-path destination, or one along the miles-long *avenidas,* take note of the cross street. ***Be warned:*** Buenos Aires *taxistas* are sharks. Watch out for unwanted city tours as they take you the long way home and provide counterfeit notes when returning change. To request a taxi by phone, consider **Taxi Premium** (✆ **11/4374-6666**), which is used by the Four Seasons Hotel, or **Radio Taxi Blue** (✆ **11/4777-8888**), contracted by the Alvear Palace Hotel.

BY CAR Driving in Buenos Aires is like warfare: Never mind the lane, disregard the light, and honk your way through traffic. It's far safer, and cheaper, to hire a *remise* or radio-taxi with the help of your hotel or travel agent. If you must drive, international car-rental companies rent vehicles at both airports. Most hotels offer parking for a small fee.

The main car rental offices in Buenos Aires are **Hertz,** Paraguay 1122 (✆ **800/654-3131** in the U.S., or 11/4816-8001 in Buenos Aires); **Avis,** Cerrito 1527 (✆ **11/4300-8201**); **Dollar,** Marcelo T. de Alvear 449 (✆ **11/4315-8800**); and **Thrifty,** Av. Leandro N. Alem 699 (✆ **11/4315-0777**). Expect to pay about $65 to $80 per day for an intermediate-size car, including unlimited miles and 21% tax. Add another $10 per day if you require insurance.

ON FOOT Buenos Aires is a walker's city. The Microcentro is small enough to navigate by foot, and you can connect to adjacent neighborhoods by catching a taxi or using the *subte.* If you have several days in Buenos Aires, it makes sense to slice your time into segments for walking tours—so spend a day in the Microcentro, for example; an evening in Puerto Madero; another day in La Boca and San Telmo; and another day in Recoleta and Palermo. Plazas, parks, and pedestrian walkways are omnipresent in the city center. If you'd like a knowledgeable guide to fill you in on this city's fascinating history, you can join a popular walking tour at Rivadavia Avenida and Rodriguez Peña at 11am every day. The 2½-hour tour is free, though tips are welcome. Contact **Buenos Aires Free Tours,** J. Maria Gutierrez 2668 (✆ **11/156-395-3000;** www.buenosairesfreetours.com).

Visitor Information

The central office of the **City Tourism Secretariat,** responsible for all visitor information on Buenos Aires, is at Calle Balcarce 360 in Monserrat (✆ **11/4313-0187;** www.bue.gov.ar), but this office is not open to the general public. Instead, you'll find several kiosks (with maps and hotel, restaurant, and attraction information) spread throughout various neighborhoods. These are found at J. M. Ortiz and Quintana in Recoleta, Puerto Madero, the central bus terminal, Calle Florida 100 (where it hits Diagonal Norte), and other locations in the city center. Most are open Monday through Friday from 10am to

5pm and on weekends, though some open and close later. In addition, individual associations have their own tourist centers providing a wealth of information, such as that for the Calle Florida Business Association in the shopping center Galerías Pacífico and where the pedestrianized shopping street Calle Florida ends at Plaza San Martín. There are branches at Ezeiza International Airport and Jorge Newbery Airport as well, which are open daily from 8am to 8pm.

The **Buenos Aires City Tourism office** also runs an information hot line (✆ **11/4313-0187**), which is staffed from 7:30am to 6pm Monday to Saturday, and Sunday from 11am to 6pm. The city also provides free tours. Though the majority of these tours are in Spanish, a few are conducted in English. To find out more about the tours, call ✆ **11/4114-5791** Monday to Friday from 10am to 4pm.

FAST FACTS It's easier to exchange money at the airport, your hotel, or an independent money-exchange house rather than at an Argentine bank. **American Express,** in a building next to Plaza San Martín at Arenales 707 (✆ **11/4312-1661**), offers the best rates on its traveler's checks. It offers currency exchange for dollars only and is open Monday through Friday from 9am to 6pm. ATMs are plentiful in Buenos Aires. You can also have money wired to **Western Union,** Av. Córdoba 975 (✆ **0800/800-3030;** www.westernunion.com).

For **police** assistance, call ✆ **101;** in case of **fire,** ✆ **100;** for an **ambulance,** ✆ **107;** for an English-speaking hospital, call **Clínica Suisso Argentino** (✆ **11/4304-1081**).

You never have to venture more than a few blocks to find a **post office,** open Monday through Friday from 10am to 8pm and Saturday until 1pm. The main post office (Correo Central) is at Av. Sarmiento 151 (✆ **11/4311-5040**). Another postal alternative is **OCA,** a private company with branches throughout the city.

Unless you are calling from your hotel (which will be expensive), the easiest way to place calls is by going to a **locutorio** (Telecentro office), a version of a public phone system, found on nearly every city block. See "Telephone & Fax" under "Fast Facts: Argentina" for more information.

WHAT TO SEE & DO

Buenos Aires is a wonderful city to explore and is fairly easy to navigate. The most impressive historical sites are located around Plaza de Mayo, although you will certainly experience Argentine history in neighborhoods such as La Boca and San Telmo, too. Don't miss a walk along the riverfront in Puerto Madero, or an afternoon among the plazas and cafes of Recoleta or Palermo. Numerous sidewalk cafes offer respite for weary feet, and there's good public transportation to carry you from neighborhood to neighborhood.

Your first stop should be one of the city tourism centers (see "Visitor Information," above) to pick up a guidebook, city map, and advice. You can also ask at your hotel for a copy of *The Golden Map* and *QuickGuide Buenos Aires* to help you navigate the city and locate its major attractions.

Neighborhoods to Explore

La Boca

La Boca, on the banks of the Río Riachuelo, developed originally as a trading center and shipyard. Drawn to the river's commercial potential, Italian immigrants moved in, giving the neighborhood the distinct flavor it maintains today.

At the center of La Boca lies the **Caminito,** a pedestrian walkway (and a famous tango song) that is both an outdoor museum and a marketplace. Surrounding the cobblestone street are shabby metal houses painted in dynamic shades of red, yellow, blue, and green, thanks to designer Benito Quinquela Martín. Today, many artists live or set up their studios in these multicolored sheet-metal houses. Along the Caminito, art and souvenir vendors work side by side with tango performers—this is one place you won't have to pay to see Argentina's great dance, but you will have to pay exorbitant prices for a beer or snack. Sculptures, murals, and engravings—some with political and social themes—line the street. This Caminito "Fine Arts Fair" is open daily from 10am to 6pm. I think the place has become too much of a tourist trap and has lost much of its authenticity, replaced by tacky vendors and bars that only want to fleece tourists. However, the area was recently revamped for the 2010 national bicentennial celebrations.

To catch an additional glimpse of La Boca's working-class spirit, walk 4 blocks to the corner of calles Del Valle Iberlucea and Brandsen. **Estadio de Boca Juniors**—the stadium for Buenos Aires's most popular *club de fútbol* (soccer club), the Boca Juniors—is here. Go on game day, when street parties and general debauchery take over the garbage-strewn area. Try not to dress like a tourist, as this may attract unwanted attention. For information on *fútbol* games, see the *Buenos Aires Herald* sports section. Use caution in straying too far from the Caminito, however, as the less patrolled surrounding areas can be unsafe. Avoid La Boca altogether at night.

San Telmo

Buenos Aires's oldest neighborhood, San Telmo originally housed the city's elite. When yellow fever struck in the 1870s—aggravated by substandard conditions in the area—the aristocrats moved north. Poor immigrants soon filled the neighborhood, and the houses were converted to tenements, called *conventillos.* In 1970, the city passed regulations to restore some of San Telmo's architectural landmarks. With new life injected into it, the neighborhood has taken on a bohemian flair, attracting artists, dancers, and numerous antiques dealers 7 days a week. While the area maintains a generally rundown air about it, it is rapidly gentrifying.

After Plaza de Mayo, **Plaza Dorrego** is the oldest square in the city. Originally the site of a Bethlehemite monastery, the plaza is also where Argentines met to reconfirm their Declaration of Independence from Spain. On Sundays from 10am to 5pm, the city's best **antiques market ★★★** takes over the square. You can buy leather, silver, handicrafts, and other products here along with antiques, and tango dancers perform on the square. If you are in Buenos Aires on a Sunday, do not miss coming here, as it is alive with people, music, and atmosphere.

San Telmo is full of tango salons, known as *milongas,* as well as show palaces; one of the most notable of the latter is **El Viejo Almacén ★** (at Independencia and Balcarce). During the day, you can appreciate the club as a landmark: An example of colonial architecture, it was built in 1798 and was a general store and hospital before its reincarnation as the quintessential Argentine tango club. Make sure to go back for a show at night (see "Buenos Aires After Dark," later in this chapter). If you get the urge for a beginner or refresher tango course while you're in San Telmo, look for signs advertising lessons in the windows of restaurants and clubs in this area.

Palermo

Palermo is a term used to define a considerable chunk of northern Buenos Aires, but it is composed of several distinct neighborhoods—**Palermo, Palermo Chico, Palermo Viejo** (which is further divided into **Palermo SoHo** and **Palermo Hollywood**), and **Las Cañitas.**

Palermo is a neighborhood of parks filled with magnolias, pines, palms, and willows, where families picnic on weekends and couples stroll at sunset. You might want to think of this part as Palermo Nuevo when compared to Palermo Viejo, described below. Designed by French architect Charles Thays, the parks of Palermo take their inspiration from London's Hyde Park and Paris's Bois de Boulogne. The **Botanical Gardens ★** (✆ **11/4831-2951**) and the **Zoological Gardens ★** (✆ **11/4806-7412**) are both off **Plaza Italia.** Stone paths wind their way through the botanical gardens, and flora from throughout South America fills the garden, with over 8,000 plant species from around the world represented. Next door, the city zoo features an impressive diversity of animals. The eclectic and kitschy architecture housing the animals, some designed as exotic temples, is as delightful as the animals themselves. Peacocks and some of the other small animals are allowed to roam free, and feeding is allowed with special food for sale, making it a great place for entertaining kids.

Palermo Chico is an exclusive neighborhood of elegant mansions off Avenida Alcorta, tucked behind the **MALBA** museum. Other than the museum and the beauty of the homes and a few embassy buildings, this small set of streets has little to interest the average tourist. Plus, there is no subway access to this neighborhood.

Palermo Viejo, once a run-down neighborhood full of warehouses, factories, and tiny decaying stucco homes few cared to live in as recently as 1990, has been transformed into the city's chicest destination. Once you walk through the area and begin to absorb its charms—cobblestone streets, enormous oak-tree canopies, and low-rise buildings giving a clear view to the open skies on a sunny day—you'll wonder why it had been forsaken for so many years. Palermo Viejo is further divided into **Palermo SoHo** to the south and **Palermo Hollywood** to the north, with railroad tracks and Avenida Juan B. Justo serving as the dividing line. The center of Palermo Hollywood is **Plaza Julio Cortázar,** better known by its informal name, **Plaza Serrano,** a small oval park at the intersection of calles Serrano and Honduras. Young people gather here late at night for impromptu singing and guitar sessions, sometimes fueled by drinks from the myriad funky bars and restaurants that surround the plaza. The neighborhood was named Palermo Hollywood because many Argentine film studios were initially attracted by its once-cheap rents and easy parking. Palermo SoHo is better known for boutiques owned by local designers, with some restaurants mixed in. Both areas were historically where Middle Eastern immigrants originally settled, and this presence is still apparent in the businesses, restaurants, and community centers that remain. **Las Cañitas** is a neighborhood adjacent to Palermo Viejo, famous for the polo grounds, and the restaurant-filled street Calle Baez.

Recoleta

The city's most exclusive neighborhood, La Recoleta wears a distinctly European face. Tree-lined avenues lead past fashionable restaurants, cafes, boutiques, and galleries, many housed in French-style buildings. Much of the activity takes place along the pedestrian walkway Roberto M. Ortiz, and in front of the Cultural Center and Recoleta Cemetery. This is a neighborhood of plazas and parks, a place where tourists and wealthy Argentines spend their leisure time outside. Weekends bring street performances, art exhibits, fairs, and sports.

The **Recoleta Cemetery ★★★** (✆ **11/4804-7040**), open daily from 8am to 6pm, pays tribute to some of Argentina's historical figures and is a lasting place where the elite can show off their wealth. Once the garden of the adjoining church, the cemetery was created in 1822 and is the oldest in the city. You can spend hours wandering the grounds that cover 4 city blocks, adorned with works by local and international sculptors. More than 6,400 mausoleums form an architectural free-for-all, including Greek temples and pyramids. Some seem big enough to be small churches. The most popular site is the tomb of Eva "Evita" Perón, which is always heaped with flowers and letters from adoring fans. Many other rich or famous Argentines are buried here as well, including a number of Argentine presidents, various literary figures, and war heroes. As any Argentine will tell you, it's important to live in Recoleta while you're alive, but even more important to remain here in death. Guided English-language tours of the cemetery take place Tuesday and Thursday at 11am, weather permitting.

Adjacent to the cemetery, the **Centro Cultural Recoleta★** (✆ **11/4803-1041**) holds permanent and touring art exhibits along with theatrical and musical performances. Designed in the mid–18th century as a Franciscan convent, it was reincarnated as a poorhouse in 1858, and it served that function until becoming a cultural center in 1979. The first floor houses an interactive children's science museum called **Museo Participativo de Ciencias** (✆ **11/4807-3260**; Mon–Fri 10am–5pm, Sat–Sun 3:30–7:30pm; admission A$3) where it is "forbidden not to touch." The center is open from Monday to Friday from 2 to 8pm, and Saturday and Sunday from 10am to 9pm. Admission is a suggested A$1 donation, and exhibition prices vary from A$3 to A$5.

Buenos Aires Design Center is next door on Pueyrredon and Libertador (✆ **11/5777-6000**; www.designrecoleta.com.ar; daily 9am–5pm; free admission) and features shops specializing in home decor; among the best is Puro Diseño Argentina**.** Buenos Aires's **Hard Rock Cafe,** Ave. Pueyrreddón 2501 (✆ **011/4807-4444;** www.hardrock.com) is nearby.

Plaza de Mayo ★

Juan de Garay founded the historic core of Buenos Aires, the Plaza de Mayo, in 1580. The plaza's prominent buildings create an architectural timeline: the Cabildo and the Metropolitan Cathedral are vestiges of the colonial period (18th and early 19th c.), while the seats of national and local government reflect the styles of the late 19th and early 20th century. In the center of the plaza, you'll find palm trees, fountains, and benches. Plaza de Mayo remains the political heart of the city, serving as a forum for protests. The mothers of the *desaparecidos,* victims of the military dictatorship's war against leftists, have demonstrated here since 1976. You can see them march every Thursday afternoon at 3:30pm.

The Argentine president goes to work every day at the **Casa Rosada (Pink House)** ★★★. It is from a balcony of this mansion that Eva Perón addressed adoring crowds of Argentine workers. You can watch the changing of the guard in front of the palace every hour on the hour, and around back is a small museum (✆ **11/4344-3802**) with information on the history of the building and the presidents of the nation who worked in it. It's open Monday through Friday from 10am to 6pm; admission is free.

The original structure of the **Metropolitan Cathedral** ★★ (✆ **11/4331-2845**) was built in 1745; it was given a new facade, with carvings telling the story of Jacob and his son Joseph, and was designated a cathedral in 1836. Inside lies a mausoleum containing the remains of General José de San Martín, the South American liberator regarded as the "Father of the Nation." (San Martín fought successfully for freedom in Argentina, Peru, and Chile.) The tomb of the unknown soldier of Argentine independence is also here.

The **Cabildo★**, Bolívar 65 (✆ **11/4334-1782**), was the original seat of city government established by the Spaniards. Completed in 1751, the colonial building proved significant in the events leading up to Argentina's declaration of independence from Spain in May 1810. Parts of the Cabildo were demolished to create space for Avenida de

Mayo and Diagonal Sur. The remainder of the building was restored in 1939. The museum is open Tuesday from Friday 12:30 to 7pm, and Saturday to Sunday 2 to 6pm; admission is A$3.80.

A striking neoclassical facade covers the **Legislatura de la Ciudad (City Legislature Building),** at Calle Perú and Hipólito Irigoyen, which houses exhibitions in several of its recently restored halls. The building's watchtower has more than 30 bells. In front of the Legislatura, you'll see a bronze statue of Julio A. Roca, considered one of Argentina's greatest presidents. His legacy, however, also includes the murder of thousands of native Indians in the area surrounding Buenos Aires. For this reason, Argentina is a largely white society in comparison to other South American countries.

Farther down Calle Perú stands the enormous **Manzana de las Luces (Block of Lights)** ★★, Calle Perú 272, which served as the intellectual center of the city in the 17th and 18th centuries. This land was granted to the Jesuits in 1616, who then built **San Ignacio**—the city's oldest church—still standing at the corner of calles Bolívar and Alsina. San Ignacio has a beautiful altar carved in wood with baroque details. Also here is the **Colegio Nacional de Buenos Aires;** Argentina's best-known intellectuals have gathered and studied at the National School, and the name "block of lights" recognizes the contributions of its graduates. Tours are usually led on Saturday and Sunday at 3 and 4:30pm and include a visit to the Jesuits' system of underground tunnels, which connected their churches to strategic spots in the city (admission is A$7.60). The tunnels were also favorite hiding spots for the students when they wanted to get out of class. Over the years, paranoid dictators added to the tunnels, in the event they ever needed to escape a takeover of the nearby Casa Rosada. In addition to weekend tours, the Comisión Nacional de la Manzana de las Luces organizes a variety of cultural activities during the week, including folkloric dance lessons, open-air theater performances, art expositions, and music concerts. Call ✆ **11/4331-9534** for information.

Puerto Madero

Puerto Madero became Buenos Aires's major gateway to trade with Europe when it was built in 1880. But by 1910, the city had already outgrown the port. The Puerto Nuevo (New Port) was established to the north to accommodate growing commercial activity, and Madero was abandoned for almost a century. Urban renewal saved the original port in the 1990s with the construction of a riverfront promenade, apartments, and offices. Bustling and businesslike during the day, the area attracts a fashionable, wealthy crowd. It's lined with restaurants serving Argentine steaks and fresh seafood specialties, and there is a popular cinema showing Argentine and Hollywood films, as well as dance clubs such as **Asia de Cuba.** Several luxury hotels have made their way into the district, but the lack of subway access means cabs are the most convenient way of getting to and from the area. Popular with joggers and strollers is the **Ecological Preserve** ★★, a patch of humid greenery that emerged on a silt bank west of the port.

Plaza San Martín & Environs

Plaza San Martín ★★ is a beautiful park at the end of Calle Florida in the Retiro neighborhood. In summer months, Argentine businesspeople flock to the park on their lunch hour, loosening their ties, taking off some layers, and sunning for a while amid the plaza's flowering jacaranda. A monument to General José de San Martín towers over the scene. The San Martín Palace, one of the seats of the Argentine Ministry of Foreign Affairs, and the Marriott Plaza Hotel, one of the city's grande dames, face the square.

Calle Florida ★★★ is the main pedestrian thoroughfare of Buenos Aires and a shopper's paradise. The busiest section, extending south from Plaza San Martín to Avenida

Corrientes, is lined with boutiques, restaurants, and record stores. You'll find the upscale Galerías Pacífico fashion center here.

Avenida Corrientes★ is a living diary of Buenos Aires's cultural development. Until the 1930s, Avenida Corrientes was the favored hangout of tango legends. When the avenue was widened in the mid-1930s, it made its debut as the Argentine Broadway. Today, Corrientes, lined with cinemas and theaters, pulses with cultural and commercial activity day and night. Here you'll find, at the intersection with 9 de Julio, Buenos Aires's signature monument, the **Obelisco,** built in 1936 to celebrate the 400th anniversary of the city's founding and now a focal point for spontaneous celebrations.

Museums

El Museo Histórico Nacional (National History Museum) ★★ Argentine history from the 16th through the 19th centuries comes to life in the former Lezama family home. The expansive Italian-style mansion houses 30 rooms with items saved from Jesuit missions, paintings illustrating clashes between the Spaniards and Indians, and relics from the War of Independence against Spain. The focal point of the museum's collection is artist Cándido López's series of captivating scenes of the war against Paraguay in the 1870s.

Calle Defensa 1600, in Parque Lezama. ✆ **11/4307-1182.** Free admission. Feb–Dec Tues–Sun noon–6pm. Metro: Constitución.

MALBA–Colección Costantini ★★★ The airy and luminescent Museo de Arte Latinoamericano de Buenos Aires (MALBA) houses the private art collection of Eduardo Costantini. One of the most impressive collections of Latin American art anywhere, its temporary and permanent exhibitions showcase such names as Antonio Berni, Pedro Figari, Frida Kahlo, Cândido Portinari, Diego Rivera, and Antonio Siguí. Many of the works confront social issues and explore questions of national identity. Even the benches are modern pieces of art. Latin films are shown Tuesday through Sunday at 2 and 10pm.

Av. Figueroa Alcorta 3415, at San Martín. ✆ **11/4808-6500.** www.malba.org.ar. Admission A$15 (reduced Wed to A$5). Wed noon–9pm; Thurs–Mon noon–8pm. No Metro access.

Museo Evita ★★ It is almost impossible for non-Argentines to fathom that it took 50 years from the time of her death for Evita, the world's most famous Argentine, to finally get a museum. The Museo Evita opened on July 26, 2002, in a mansion where her charity, the Eva Perón Foundation, once housed single mothers and their children.

The Museo Evita's displays divide Evita's life into several parts, looking at her childhood; her arrival in Buenos Aires to become an actress; her ascension as Evita, first lady and unofficial saint to millions; and finally her death and legacy. You will be able to view her clothes, remarkably preserved by the military government, which took power after Perón's 1955 fall. Other artifacts of her life include her voting card, since it was Evita who gave Argentine women the right to vote. There are also toys and schoolbooks adorned with her image, given to children to indoctrinate them into the Peronist movement. Whether you hate, love, or are indifferent to Evita, this is a museum that no visitor to Argentina should miss.

Calle Lafinur 2988, at Gutiérrez. ✆ **11/4809-3168** or 11/4807-0306. www.evitaperon.org. Admission A$14. Tues–Sun 11am–7pm. Metro: Linea D Plaza Italia.

Museo Nacional de Arte Decorativo (National Museum of Decorative Arts) ★ French architect René Sergent, who designed some of the grandest mansions in Buenos Aires, also designed the mansion housing this museum. The building is itself a work of art, and it will give you an idea of the incredible mansions that once lined this avenue, overlooking the extensive Palermo park system. The building's 18th-century French design provides a classical setting for the diverse decorative styles represented within. Sculptures, paintings, and furnishings make up the collection, and themed shows rotate seasonally.

Av. del Libertador 1902, at Lucena. ✆ **11/4801-8248.** Admission A$5. Tues–Sun 2–7pm. No Metro access.

Museo Nacional de Bellas Artes (National Museum of Fine Arts) ★★ This building, which formerly pumped the city's water supply, metamorphosed into Buenos Aires's most important art museum in 1930. The museum contains the world's largest collection of Argentine sculptures and paintings from the 19th and 20th centuries. It also houses European art dating from the pre-Renaissance period to the present day. The collections include notable pieces by Renoir, Monet, Rodin, Toulouse-Lautrec, and van Gogh, as well as a surprisingly extensive collection of Picasso drawings.

Av. del Libertador 1473, at Agote. ✆ **11/4803-0802.** Free admission. Tues–Sun 12:30–7:30pm. No Metro access.

Other Attractions

Among the city's other attractions is the **Café Tortoni** (p. 111), long a meeting place for Porteño artists and intellectuals. Also see information on the cafe's tango shows on p. 112.

Basílica y Convento de San Francisco (San Francis's Church and Convent) ★ The San Roque parish to which this church belongs is one of the oldest in the city. A Jesuit architect designed the building in 1730, but a final reconstruction in the early 20th century added a German baroque facade, along with statues of St. Francis of Assisi, Dante, and Christopher Columbus. Inside, you'll find a tapestry by Argentine artist Horacio Butler along with an extensive library.

Calle Defensa and Alsina. ✆ **11/4331-0625.** Free admission. Hours vary. Metro: Plaza de Mayo.

Biblioteca Nacional (National Library) ★ Opened in 1992, this modern architectural oddity stands on the land of the former Presidential Residence in which Eva Perón died. (The building was demolished by the new government so that it would not become a holy site to Evita's millions of supporters after her death.) With its underground levels, the library's 13 floors can store up to five million volumes. Among its collection, the library stores 21 books printed by one of the earliest printing presses, dating from 1440 to 1500. Visit the reading room—occupying two stories at the top of the building—to enjoy an awe-inspiring view of Buenos Aires. The library also hosts special events in its exhibition hall and auditorium.

Calle Aguero 2502. ✆ **11/4807-0885.** Free admission. Mon–Fri 9am–9pm; Sat–Sun noon–8pm. No Metro access.

Congreso ★★ Opened on May 12, 1906, after nearly 9 years of work, and built in a Greco-Roman style with strong Parisian Beaux Arts influences, Congreso is the most imposing building in all of Buenos Aires. One of the main architects was Victor Meano, who was also involved in designing the Teatro Colón (below), but he was murdered—the result of a love triangle gone wrong—before completion of either building.

Tours take visitors through the fantastic chambers, which are adorned with bronzes, statues, German tile floors, Spanish woods, and French marbles, and lined with Corinthian columns. The horseshoe-shaped congressional chamber is the largest, with the senatorial chamber an almost identical copy but at one-fifth the size.

Entrance is usually through the Rivadavia side of the building, but it can switch to the Yrigoyen doors, so arrive early and announce to the guards that you are there for a visit. The tour guide will not be called down unless they know people are waiting. This is an incredible building and worth the confusion.

Entre Ríos and Callao, at Rivadavia. ✆ **11/4370-7100** or 11/6310-7100, ext. 3725. Free guided tours in English Mon–Tues and Thurs–Fri 11am and 4pm; simultaneous Spanish and English tours Mon–Tues and Thurs–Fri 5pm. Metro: Congreso.

Teatro Colón ★★★ Known across the world for its impeccable acoustics, the Colón has attracted the world's finest opera performers. Opera season in Buenos Aires runs from April to November. A masterpiece of European style architecture, the Colón has its own philharmonic orchestra, ballet, and choir companies. Sadly, the theater has been closed for multimillion-dollar renovations since 2004 and its reopening has been constantly delayed, thus missing its 100-year anniversary in 2008. City mayor Mauricio Macri has vowed this once cultural giant will reopen in time for Buenos Aires's bicentennial celebrations in 2010, and, at presstime, a tentative date was set for a grand opening in May 2010. The ticket office remains open, as the theater's performers can be seen in venues scattered across the city in different locations. Call (✆ **11/4378-7130**) to see if tours have resumed.

Calle Libertad 621, at Tucumán. ✆ **11/4378-7142.** Prior tour admission fee A$7.50. Prior ticket prices A$12–A$90. Metro: Tribunales.

Spectator Sports & Outdoor Activities

GOLF Argentina has more than 200 golf courses. Closest to downtown Buenos Aires is **Cancha de Golf de la Ciudad de Buenos Aires,** Av. Torquist 1426, at Olleros (✆ **11/4772-7261**), which is 10 minutes from downtown and boasts great scenery and a 71-par course. The **Jockey Club Argentino,** Av. Márquez 1700, San Isidro (✆ **11/4743-1001**), offers two courses (71 and 72 par).

HORSE RACING Over much of the 20th century, Argentina was famous for its thoroughbreds. It continues to send prize horses to competitions around the world, although you can watch some of the best right here in Buenos Aires. In the center of the city, you can see races at **Hipódromo Argentino de Palermo,** Av. del Libertador 4205, at Dorrego in Palermo (✆ **11/4778-2839**), a track made in a classical design with several modern additions. The other big track is **Hipódromo San Isidro,** Av. Márquez 504 (✆ **11/4743-4010**), in the upscale northern suburb of the same name. Check the *Buenos Aires Herald* for schedule information.

POLO Argentina has won more international polo tournaments than any other country, and the **Argentine Open Championship,** held late November through early December, is the world's most important polo event. There are two seasons for polo: March through May and September through December, held at the **Campo Argentino de Polo,** avenidas del Libertador and Dorrego (✆ **11/4576-5600**). Tickets can be purchased at the gate for about A$110 per person. This is one of the most important polo stadiums in the world, and visits by European royalty are not uncommon. Contact the **Asociación Argentina de Polo,** Hipólito Yrigoyen 636 (✆ **11/4331-4646** or 11/4342-8321), for information on polo schools and events.

SOCCER Any sense of national unity dissolves when Argentines watch their favorite clubs—River Plate, Boca Juniors, Racing Club, Independiente, and San Lorenzo—battle on Sunday in season, which runs from February until November. Catch a game at the **Estadio Boca Juniors,** Brandsen 805, in La Boca (✆ **11/4362-2260**), followed by raucous street parties. Ticket prices start at A$10 and can be purchased in advance or at the gate. The match to see is the Superclasico, when arch rivals Boca Juniors and River Plate meet in a gladiator-style spectacle.

SHOPPING

By Neighborhood

MICROCENTRO Calle Florida, the pedestrian walking street in the Microcentro, is home to wall-to-wall shops from Plaza San Martín past Avenida Corrientes. The **Galerías Pacífico** mall is at Calle Florida 750 and Avenida Córdoba (✆ **11/4319-5100**), with a magnificent dome and stunning frescoes. Over 180 shops are open Monday through Saturday from 10am to 9pm and Sunday from noon to 9pm, with tango shows held on Thursdays at 8pm. Food-court restaurants are open later. As you approach Plaza San Martín, you'll find a number of well-regarded shoe stores, jewelers, and shops selling leather goods.

RECOLETA Avenida Alvear is Argentina's response to the Champs-Elysées, and—without taking the comparison too far—it is indeed an elegant, Parisian-like strip of European boutiques and cafes. Start your walk from Plaza Francia and continue from Junín to Cerrito. Along Calle Quintana, French-style mansions share company with upscale shops. Nearby, **Patio Bullrich,** Av. del Libertador 750 (✆ **11/4814-7400**), is one of the city's best malls. Its 69 elegant shops are open daily from 10am to 9pm.

AVENIDA SANTA FE Popular with local shoppers, Avenida Santa Fe offers a wide selection of clothing stores and more down-to-earth prices. You will also find bookstores, ice-cream shops, and cinemas. The **Alto Palermo Shopping Center,** Av. Santa Fe 3253 (✆ **11/5777-8000**), is another excellent shopping spot, with 155 stores open daily from 10am to 10pm. Food-court restaurants are open later.

SAN TELMO & LA BOCA These neighborhoods offer antiques as well as arts and crafts celebrating tango. Street performers and artists are omnipresent. My opinion is that La Boca's souvenirs are overpriced. La Boca is considered dangerous at night, but rapidly gentrifying San Telmo is generally safer.

PALERMO VIEJO The stalking ground of Borges is now awash with trendy bars and restaurants and a plethora of homegrown designer stores, offering everything from funky fashion to chic interior furnishings.

Shopping A to Z

Most stores are open weekdays from 9am to 8pm and Saturday from 9am to midnight, with some stores closing for a few hours in the afternoon. Shopping centers are open daily from 10am to 10pm. You might find some shops open on Sunday along Avenida Santa Fe, but few will be open on Calle Florida.

Almost all shops in Buenos Aires accept credit cards. However, you will sometimes get a better price if you offer to pay with cash, and you won't be able to use credit cards at outdoor markets.

Antiques

Throughout the streets of San Telmo, you will find the city's best antiques shops; don't miss the antiques market that takes place all day Sunday at Plaza Dorrego (see "Markets," below). There are also a number of fine antiques stores along Avenida Alvear in Recoleta, including a collection of boutiques at **Galería Alvear,** Av. Alvear 1777. **Calle Antigua,** calles Defensa 914 and Defensa 974, at Estados Unidos (✆ 11/4300-8782), sells religious art, chandeliers, furniture, and other decorative objects. Credit cards are not accepted. **Galería El Solar de French,** Calle Defensa 1066, is a gallery with antiques shops and photography stores depicting the San Telmo of yesteryear. **Pallarols,** Calle Defensa 1039, San Telmo (✆ 11/4361-7360; www.pallarols.com.ar), belongs to a family of the same name that makes and sells an exquisite collection of Argentine silver and other antiques.

Art

Galería Ruth Benzacar, Calle Florida 1000 (✆ **11/4313-8480;** www.ruthbenzacar.com), is an avant-garde gallery, in a hidden underground space at the start of Calle Florida next to Plaza San Martín. **Cándido Silva,** Defensa 1066 at Humberto1, in Galeria El Solar de French (✆ 11/4361-5053; www.candidosilva.com.ar), offers objects made from wood, marble, and silver and an interesting art collection including local Argentine and some European artists, as well as small antiques and decorative objects.

Cameras

Cosentino, Av. Roque Sáenz Peña 738 (✆ **11/4328-9120**), offers cameras, repairs, and high-quality developing services.

Fashion

Avenida Alvear and Calle Quintana in Recoleta is where you'll find all the big designer names, whilst Palermo Soho is the place for boutiques showcasing Argentine designers. **Florentina Muraña,** Calle Borges 1760, at Pasaje Russel (✆ **11/4833-4137;** www.florentinamurania.com.ar), has in-house feminine designs such as popcorn shag sweaters and crystal jewelry. **Ermenegildo Zegna,** Av. Alvear 1920 (✆ **11/4804-1908**), is a famous Italian chain that sells outstanding suits and jackets made of light, cool fabrics. **Escada,** Av. Alvear 1444 (✆ **11/4814-0292**), sells casual and elegant selections of women's clothing. **Maria Cher,** El Salvador 4724, at Armenia (✆ **11/4833-4736;** www.maria-cher.com.ar) has a sophisticated and fashionable selection of dresses and leather coats.

Jewelry

Cousiño Jewels, Av. San Martín 1225 (✆ **11/4312-2336** or 11/4313-8881), is located in the Sheraton hotel and features a brilliant collection of rhodochrosite, or Inca Rose, a beautiful form of milky-pink quartz. **H.Stern,** Marriott Plaza, Calle Florida 1005 (✆ **11/4318-3083**), or at the Sheraton, Av. San Martín 1225 (✆ 11/4312-6762), is an upscale Brazilian jeweler that sells an entire selection of South American stones, including emeralds and the unique imperial topaz.

Leather

Argentina is one of the world's best leather centers. If you're looking for high-quality, interestingly designed leather goods, especially women's shoes, accessories, and handbags, few places beat Buenos Aires. Many leather stores will also custom make jackets and other items for interested customers. **Ashanti Leather Factory,** Calle Florida 585 (✆ **11/4394-1310**), offers a wide selection of leather goods. Ask for a tour of the basement factory.

Casa López, Marcelo T. de Alvear 640 (✆ 11/4312-8911), is widely considered one of the best *marroquinería* (leather-goods shop) in Buenos Aires. **El Nochero,** Posadas 1245, in the Patio Bullrich Mall (✆ 11/4815-3629), is full of products made with first-rate Argentine leather and manufactured by local workers.

Outdoor Markets

Feria de San Telmo ★★ (www.feriadesantelmo.com), which takes place every Sunday from 10am to 5pm at Plaza Dorrego, is a vibrant, colorful experience that should not be missed. As street vendors sell their heirlooms, singers and dancers move amid the crowd to the music of tangos and *milongas.* Among the 270-plus vendor stands, you will find antique silversmith objects, porcelain, crystal, and other antiques. **Plaza Francia's Fair,** also known as the Recoleta Fair, is in front of the Recoleta Cemetery. You'll find ceramics, leather goods, and arts and crafts amid street musicians and performers. It's held Saturday and Sunday from 9am to 7pm.

Wine Shops

Stores selling Argentine wines abound, and three of the best are **Grand Cru,** Av. Alvear 1718; **Tonel Privado,** in the Patio Bullrich Shopping Mall; and **Winery,** which has branches at L. N. Alem 880 and Av. Del Libertador 500, both downtown.

WHERE TO STAY

Despite the economic downturn, hotels still fill up in the high season, so you should book ahead, even if it is only for your first night or two. Bargains can be had, especially in four-star properties located off the beaten path and in locally owned (rather than international) hotel chains in all categories. Another trend is an explosion in upscale B&Bs and hostels in Palermo Viejo and San Telmo. Always try your luck and ask for a better rate. One trick is to use the Spanish version of a hotel's website when booking online.

Increasingly popular are temporary apartment rentals that can vary from a few nights to several months. Recommended agencies that will help you set this up are **Apartments BA** (✆ 11/5254-0100; www.apartmentsba.com), **ByT Argentina** (✆ 11/4876-5000; www.bytargentina.com), Home in Argentina (✆ 11/4772-4303; www.homeinargentina.com.ar), and Oasis BA (✆ 11/4831-0340; www.oasisba.com).

As for choosing a location, it's a matter of deciding what is best for you and what you want out of your Buenos Aires vacation. For a more thorough discussion of neighborhoods, see the "Neighborhoods to Explore" section, earlier in the chapter.

Microcentro

Very Expensive

Marriott Plaza Hotel ★★ The historic Plaza was the grande dame of Buenos Aires for most of the 20th century, and the Marriott management has maintained much of its original splendor. The intimate lobby, decorated in Italian marble, crystal, and Persian carpets, is a virtual revolving door of Argentine politicians, foreign diplomats, and business executives. The veteran staff offers outstanding service, and the concierge will address needs ranging from executive business services to sightseeing tours. Twenty-six rooms overlook Plaza San Martín, providing dreamlike views of the green canopy of trees in the spring and summer. The hotel's health club is one of the best in the city. Uniquely, guests whose rooms are not ready when they check in are provided access to a special lounge area in the health club where they can rest and shower. Four rooms are available for those with disabilities, but only two offer full access.

Calle Florida 1005 (overlooking Plaza San Martín), 1005 Buenos Aires. ✆ **888/236-2427** in the U.S., or 11/4318-3000. Fax 11/4318-3008. www.marriott.com. 325 units. $258 double; from $318 suite. Buffet breakfast $21. AE, DC, MC, V. Metro: San Martín. **Amenities:** 2 restaurants; cigar bar; concierge; exercise room; health club w/outdoor pool; room service; sauna. *In room:* A/C, TV, hair dryer, minibar.

Sofitel Buenos Aires ★★ This classy French hotel near Plaza San Martín joins two seven-story buildings to a 20-story neoclassical tower dating from 1929, with a glass atrium lobby bringing them together. The lobby resembles an enormous gazebo, with six ficus trees, a giant iron-and-bronze chandelier, an Art Nouveau clock, and Botticcino and black San Gabriel marble filling the space. Adjacent to the lobby you will find an elegant French restaurant, **Le Sud,** and an early-20th-century-style Buenos Aires cafe. The cozy library, with its grand fireplace and dark woods, offers guests an enchanting place to read outside their rooms. These rooms vary in size, mixing modern French decor with traditional Art Deco styles. The beautiful marble bathrooms have separate showers and bathtubs.

Arroyo 841/849, 1007 Buenos Aires. ✆ **11/4909-1454.** Fax 11/4909-1452. www.sofitel.com. 144 units. From $290 double; from $390 suite. AE, DC, MC, V. **Amenities:** Restaurant and cafe; bar; concierge; fitness center; indoor pool; room service. *In room:* A/C, TV, hair dryer, minibar, Wi-Fi.

Expensive

Claridge Hotel ★ The Claridge is living testimony to the once-close ties between England and Argentina. The grand entrance, with its imposing Ionic columns, mimics a London terrace apartment, and the lobby was renovated in a classical style with colored marbles. Guest rooms are spacious, spotless, tastefully decorated, and equipped with all the amenities expected of a five-star hotel. The restaurant's hunting-themed wood-paneled interior is a registered city landmark. Because it occasionally hosts conventions, the Claridge can become very busy. The rates at this hotel can go down significantly when rooms are booked via website promotions, pushing it into the moderate category.

Tucumán 535 (at San Martín), 1049 Buenos Aires. ✆ **11/4314-7700.** Fax 11/4314-8022. www.claridge.com.ar. 165 units. $192 double; from $292 suite. Rates include buffet breakfast. AE, DC, MC, V. Free valet parking. Metro: Florida. **Amenities:** Restaurant; bar; concierge; exercise room; health club w/heated outdoor pool; room service; sauna. *In room:* A/C, TV, minibar.

Sheraton Buenos Aires Hotel and Convention Center ★ The enormous Sheraton is situated in the heart of the business, shopping, and theater district and is an ideal location for business travelers and tour groups. Guest rooms are typical for a large American chain—they're well equipped, but lacking in charm. What the hotel lacks in intimacy, however, it makes up for in the wide range of services offered to guests, regardless of whether they're in town for business or tourism. It shares three restaurants with the neighboring Park Tower Buenos Aires, and its "Neptune" pool and fitness center are among the best in the city. During conference time, the elevators can get overly busy and cause delays.

Av. San Martín 1225 (at Libertador), 1104 Buenos Aires. ✆ **11/4318-9000.** Fax 11/4318-9353. www.sheraton.com. 741 units. $279 double; from $508 suite. Rates include breakfast and access to the spa. AE, DC, MC, V. Valet parking $15. Metro: Retiro. **Amenities:** 3 restaurants; snack bar; piano bar; babysitting; concierge; fitness center w/gym; putting green; 2 pools; room service; wet and dry saunas; 2 lighted tennis courts. *In room:* A/C, TV, hair dryer, high-speed Internet access, minibar.

Moderate

Amerian Buenos Aires Park Hotel ★★ Finds One of the best hotels in the city, this modern hotel (also known as the American Reconquista) is a good bet for tourists as well as for business travelers. The warm atrium lobby looks more like California than

Argentina, and the highly qualified staff offers personalized service. Soundproof rooms are elegantly appointed with wood, marble, and granite, and all boast comfortable beds, chairs, and work areas. The suites, located on their own floor, come with whirlpool bathtubs. Many services are not directly provided by the hotel, such as massage and babysitting, but can be handled on request. The hotel is just blocks away from Calle Florida, Plaza San Martín, and the Teatro Colón.

Reconquista 699 (at Viamonte), 1003 Buenos Aires. ✆ **11/5171-6565.** Fax 11/4317-5101. www.amerian.com. 152 units, including 14 suites. $149 double; from $199 suite. Rates include buffet breakfast. AE, DC, MC, V. Parking $5. Metro: Florida. **Amenities:** Restaurant; pub; concierge; exercise room; room service; sauna. *In room:* A/C, TV, minibar.

Holiday Inn Express ★ This hotel enjoys a convenient Microcentro location close to Puerto Madero and its restaurants and nightlife. Although it doesn't have room service, concierge, or bellhops, the hotel is friendly, modern, and inexpensive. Guest rooms have large, firm beds, ample desk space, and 27-inch cable TVs; half of the rooms boast river views. Coffee and tea are served 24 hours a day, and the buffet breakfast is excellent.

Av. Leandro N. Alem 770 (at Viamonte), 1057 Buenos Aires. ✆ **11/4311-5200.** Fax 11/4311-5757. www.holiday-inn.com. 116 units. From $145 double. Children 17 and under stay free in parent's room. Rates include buffet breakfast. AE, DC, MC, V. Free parking. Metro: L. N. Alem. **Amenities:** Deli; exercise room; sauna; whirlpool. *In room:* A/C, TV.

Howard Johnson Florida Street ★★ (Value) This has a great location off Calle Florida near Plaza San Martín, with access through a shopping-and-restaurant gallery in the hotel's ground level. Guest rooms come equipped with king- or queen-size beds, sleeper chairs, large desks and dressers, and well-appointed bathrooms. Rooms are of an above-average size in this category. Each room has two phones, and local calls and Internet use are free—a rarity in Buenos Aires. There's a small, airy cafe and bar in the lobby, with additional food served in the gallery below. There is no pool or health club on premises, but access is offered free of charge to a nearby facility.

Calle Florida 944 (at Alvear), 1005 Buenos Aires. ✆ **11/4891-9200.** Fax 11/4891-9208. www.hojoar.com. 77 units. $135 double. Rates include buffet breakfast. AE, DC, MC, V. Metro: San Martín. **Amenities:** Restaurant; bar; room service. *In room:* A/C, TV, hair dryer, high-speed Internet access, minibar.

Lafayette Hotel ★ (Kids) The Lafayette Hotel is good value for a mid-price-range hotel, with spacious rooms (some can accommodate an entire family) that are exceedingly clean and well maintained. Each has a desk and all rooms have Wi-Fi access. Street-side rooms are great for people-watching in the Microcentro, though you should expect some noise. Back rooms are quieter but offer no views. The location is ideal for Microcentro's Lavalle and Florida street shopping. The hotel is separated into two different elevator bays, so if staying with friends or family, request rooms in the same division of the hotel.

Reconquista 546 (at Viamonte), 1003 Buenos Aires. ✆ **11/4393-9081.** Fax 11/4322-1611. www.lafayettehotel.com.ar. 82 units, including 6 suites. From $86 double; from $96 suite. Rates include generous buffet breakfast. AE, DC, MC, V. Metro: Florida. **Amenities:** Restaurant; bar; concierge; limited room service. *In room:* A/C, TV, hair dryer, minibar, Wi-Fi.

Inexpensive

V&S Hostel ★★ (Finds) This lovely turn-of-the-20th-century building has lavish touches such as curved doorway entries, stained glass ornamentation, and balconies. Dorms come with a communal kitchen or, if you reserve in time, you can avail yourself of one of six private bedrooms with bathrooms. A patio, library, and TV sitting room are free to mingle in. The property's excellent location makes it one of the best-value hostels in the downtown area.

Viamonte 887 (at Suipacha), 1053 Buenos Aires. ✆ **11/4322-0994.** www.hostelclub.com. 60 units. From $12 per bed; $60 per private room. Rates include continental breakfast. No credit cards. Metro: Lavalle. **Amenities:** Concierge; high-speed Internet; shared kitchen; lockers; Wi-Fi. *In room*: A/C (for a small fee), hair dryer, Wi-Fi (select rooms).

Monserrat

Expensive

Inter-Continental Hotel Buenos Aires ★★★ This luxurious tower hotel is decorated in the Argentine style of the 1930s. The marble lobby is colored in beige and apricot tones, with heavy black and brass-metal accents, and decorated with handsome carved-wood furniture and antiques inlaid with agates and other stones. The lobby's small **Café de las Luces** sometimes offers evening tango performances. The **Restaurante y Bar Mediterráneo** serves healthy, gourmet Mediterranean cuisine on an outdoor patio under a glassed-in trellis. Guest rooms continue the 1930s theme, with elegant black woodwork, comfortable king-size beds, marble-top nightstands, large desks, and black-and-white photographs of Buenos Aires. Some rooms need updating but all have nice touches such as fresh fruit and daily English-language newspapers. The staff is very helpful, if a little inconsistent in quality of service.

Moreno 809 (at Piedras), 1091 Buenos Aires. ✆ **11/4340-7100.** Fax 11/4340-7119. www.buenos-aires.interconti.com. 312 units. $303 double; from $424 suite. AE, DC, MC, V. Parking $10. Metro: Moreno. **Amenities:** Restaurant; wine bar; lobby bar; concierge; exercise room; health club w/indoor pool; room service. *In room:* A/C, TV, hair dryer, minibar, Wi-Fi.

Moderate

NH City Hotel ★★ This hotel's jagged ziggurat exterior calls to mind buildings more associated with Jazz Age New York than with Argentina. Its lobby is a combination of Art Deco and Collegiate Gothic popular in that time period. Many of the rooms vary greatly in size and are on the dark side, with a masculine combination of simple materials in red and black. Others are brighter, with white walls and burnt-sienna offsets. All the bathrooms are spacious and luminous. Its location is very central (close to Plaza de Mayo), but the immediate environment (surrounded by government buildings) is somewhat dead at night. You might also try the **NH Florida,** at San Martín 839 (✆ **11/4321-9850**).

Bolívar 160 (at Alsina), 1066 Buenos Aires. ✆ **11/4121-6464.** Fax 11/4121-6450. www.nh-hotels.com. 303 units, including 50 suites. From $140 double; from $200 suite. Generous buffet breakfast included in rates. AE, DC, MC, V. Parking $16. Metro: Bolívar or Plaza de Mayo. **Amenities:** 2 restaurants; bar; babysitting; concierge; executive floor; small gym facility w/open-air pool deck; room service; sauna; spa. *In room:* TV, hair dryer, minibar, Wi-Fi.

Inexpensive

Hotel Ritz ★ A good location and excellent staff make this hotel one of the best budget options in the city center. Old-world features such as high ceilings, French doors, and brass fixtures, as well as balconies overlooking Avenida de Mayo and 9 de Julio, mean you could do a lot worse for the price. Rooms are large and comfortable, though the bathrooms could do with updating and many come with low water pressure.

Av. de Mayo 1111 (at 9 de Julio), 1085 Buenos Aires. ✆ **11/4383-9001.** 38 units. From $42 double. Rates include continental breakfast. AE, DC, MC, V. Off-site parking $12. Metro: Lima. **Amenities:** Concierge; room service; Wi-Fi. *In room*: A/C, TV.

Puerto Madero

Hilton Buenos Aires ★★ The Hilton is in Puerto Madero and lies within easy walking distance of some of the best restaurants in Buenos Aires, yet feels somewhat isolated from the rest of the city. The strikingly contemporary hotel—a sleek silver block hoisted on stilts—features a seven-story atrium with more than 400 well-equipped guest rooms and an additional number of private residences. Spacious guest rooms offer multiple phone lines, walk-in closets, and bathrooms with separate showers and tubs. Next to the lobby, the **El Faro** restaurant serves California cuisine with a focus on seafood. The hotel has an impressive on-site pool and fitness center. Watch out for hefty late check-out penalty charges and the $20 Internet connection fee, which seems to me an unnecessary expense in these Web-surfing times.

Av. Macacha Güemes 351 (at Malecón Pierina Dealessi), 1106 Buenos Aires. ✆ **800/445-8667** in the U.S., or 11/4891-0000. Fax 11/4891-0001. www.buenos.hilton.com. 418 units. From $230 double; from $401 suite (breakfast included). AE, DC, MC, V. 24-hr. parking $14. No nearby Metro stations. **Amenities:** Restaurant; bar; babysitting; concierge; modern gym facility w/open-air pool deck and light snacks and beverages; room service. *In room:* TV, hair dryer, high-speed Internet access, minibar.

Recoleta

Very Expensive

Alvear Palace Hotel ★★★ In the center of the upscale Recoleta district, the Alvear Palace is the most exclusive hotel in Buenos Aires and one of the top hotels in the world. A gilded classical confection full of marble and bronze, the Alvear combines Empire and Louis XV–style furniture with exquisite French decorative arts. Rooms combine luxurious comforts, such as chandeliers, Egyptian cotton linens, and silk drapes, with modern conveniences such as touch-screen telephones that control all in-room functions. All rooms come with personal butler service, cellphones that can be activated on demand, fresh flowers, fruit baskets, and daily newspaper delivery. Large marble bathrooms contain Hermès toiletries, and most have Jacuzzi tubs. It is expensive, but the website offers discounts. The Alvear Palace is home to one of the best restaurants in South America (**La Bourgogne;** p. 108). Nonguests can indulge in the afternoon lunch buffet in their palm-court-style lobby restaurant, **L'Orangerie.**

Av. Alvear 1891 (at Ayacucho), 1129 Buenos Aires. ✆ **011/4808-2100.** Fax 11/4804-0034. www.alvear palace.com. 210 units, including 85 "palace" rooms and 125 suites. From $575 double; from $684 suite. Rates include buffet breakfast. AE, DC, MC, V. No Metro access. **Amenities:** 2 restaurants; bar; private butler service; concierge; small health club; room service; spa. *In room:* A/C, TV, hair dryer, minibar, free Wi-Fi.

Buenos Aires Park Hyatt ★★★ A main tower facing Posadas Street connects to the mansion Palacio Duhau via a garden, and below ground by an art-filled tunnel. This Hyatt has two lobbies, one in the new tower and another one in the Palace, accessed by a gorgeous double staircase that fronts the building. The side rooms and waiting areas that spill from it are magnificent. Rooms in the Palace exhibit the mix of modern and classical elements found throughout the hotel. Within the tower you'll find leather browns, charcoals, and silver-grays. Rooms are spacious, and suites come with extra bathrooms. Bathrooms in both buildings are enormous, containing a walk-in shower and a bathtub. A wine-and-cheese bar stocks about 45 artisanal cheeses, and the spa and health facilities are enormous.

Av. Alvear 1661 (at Montevideo), 1014 Buenos Aires. ✆ **11/5171-1234.** Fax 11/5171-1235. http://buenos aires.park.hyatt.com/hyatt/hotels/index.jsp. 165 units, including 23 mansion units; 23 suites in both towers. $648 double; from $829 suite; from $2,965 select suites. AE, DC, MC, V. No Metro access. **Amenities:**

3 restaurants; lobby bar; babysitting; concierge; exercise room; health club; heated indoor pool; room service. *In room:* A/C, TV/VCR, hair dryer, minibar, Wi-Fi.

Four Seasons Hotel ★★★ (Kids A French-style garden and a pool separate two buildings—the 12-story Park tower and the Louis XIII–style La Mansión. This is the only outdoor garden pool in all of Recoleta, creating a resortlike feeling in the middle of the city, though much of the pool is in shade until early afternoon. The ample space and safe facilities make it a perfect place for kids. There's also a well-equipped health club on the premises offering spa treatments. The hotel's restaurant, **Galani,** serves excellent Mediterranean cuisine in a casual environment. Spacious guest rooms offer atypical amenities such as walk-in closets, wet and dry bars, stereo systems, and cellphones. Large marble bathrooms contain separate showers and water-jet bathtubs.

Posadas 1086–88 (at Av. 9 de Julio), 1011 Buenos Aires. ✆ **800/819-5053** in the U.S. and Canada, or 11/4321-1200. Fax 11/4321-1201. www.fourseasons.com. 165 units, including 49 suites (7 suites in La Mansión). $636 double; from $926 suite; $1,180 mansion suites. Prices include 21% tax. AE, DC, MC, V. Valet parking $10. No Metro access. **Amenities:** Restaurant; lobby bar; babysitting; concierge; exercise room; health club; heated outdoor pool; room service; large spa. *In room:* A/C, TV/VCR, hair dryer, minibar, Wi-Fi.

Expensive

Hotel Emperador ★★ The theme here is Empire with a modern update; a bust of Julius Caesar overlooks the concierge desk. The lobby evokes a sense of the Old World. Behind the main restaurant, the lobby opens onto a large overgrown patio that has a gazebo and outdoor seating. The decor is attractive but could do with a revamp. All bathrooms are oversized, with cream and green marble. Suite bathrooms are even larger, with separated tub and shower stalls. Each room comes equipped with a large desk and high-speed Internet and Wi-Fi access, which will cost you about $10 a day. Check-in can be slow and check out even slower, so give yourself time. Also, in the high season the breakfast room can be uncomfortably crowded.

Av. del Libertador 420 (at Suipacha), 1001 Buenos Aires. ✆ **11/4131-4000.** Fax 11/4131-3900. www.hotel-emperador.com.ar. 265 units, including 36 suites. $170 double; from $315 suite (includes a Jacuzzi). Rates include buffet breakfast. AE, DC, MC, V. Valet parking $4. Metro: Retiro. **Amenities:** Restaurant; bar; babysitting; concierge; small fitness center w/medium-size indoor heated pool and sauna; room service. *In room:* A/C, TV, hair dryer, minibar, Wi-Fi.

Loi Suites ★★ Part of a small local hotel chain, the Loi Suites Recoleta is a contemporary hotel with spacious, functional rooms and excellent, personalized service. A palm-filled garden atrium and covered pool adjoin the lobby, which is bathed in various shades of white. Breakfast and afternoon tea are served in the "winter garden." Although the management uses the term "suites" rather loosely to describe rooms with microwaves, sinks, and small fridges, the hotel does in fact offer some traditional suites in addition to its more regular studio-style rooms. In-room Internet is free and there are also CD players. A less upscale **Loi Suites** is at Marcelo T. de Alvear 842 (✆ **11/4131-6800**), which is particularly good for kids.

Vicente López 1955 (at Ayacucho), 1128 Buenos Aires. ✆ **11/5777-8950.** Fax 11/5777-8999. www.loisuites.com.ar. 112 units. From $200 double; from $240 suite. Rates include buffet breakfast. AE, DC, MC, V. Parking $12. No Metro access. **Amenities:** Restaurant; exercise room; indoor pool; room service; sauna. *In room:* A/C, TV, CD player, fridge, hair dryer, high-speed Internet access, minibar.

Moderate

Etoile Hotel ★ (Value Located in the heart of Recoleta, the 14-story Etoile is an older hotel with a Turkish flair. It's not as luxurious as the city's other five-star hotels, but it's not as expensive either—making it a good value for Recoleta. The hotel labels itself a five-star but is really a high-quality four-star whose convention facilities allow it to retain a higher rating. Guest rooms are fairly large and are decorated with blue and neutral accents. Executive rooms have separate sitting areas and large, marble-lined bathrooms with whirlpool bathtubs. Rooms facing south offer balconies overlooking Plaza Francia, with a spectacular view of Recoleta Cemetery.

Roberto M. Ortiz 1835 (at Guido, overlooking Recoleta Cemetery), 1113 Buenos Aires. ✆ **11/4805-2626.** Fax 11/4805-3613. www.etoile.com.ar. 96 units. $160 double; from $200 suite. Rates include buffet breakfast. AE, DC, MC, V. Free parking. No Metro access. **Amenities:** Restaurant; concierge; exercise room; rooftop health club w/indoor pool; room service. *In room:* A/C, TV, hair dryer, high-speed Internet access, minibar.

Inexpensive

The Recoleta Hostel ★ Finds This is an inexpensive choice for people who want to be in a beautiful neighborhood but can't ordinarily afford the prices. The rooms (bunk beds only) are simple, with bare floors and walls, beds, and a small wooden desk in the private rooms. Overall, the decor is rather reminiscent of a convent and facilities could be cleaner. Public areas have high ceilings, and there is an outdoor patio for guests' use. Bring your laptop for free Wi-Fi. One gripe: The $6 charge to leave luggage is something most other hostels and hotels would do for free.

Libertad 1216 (at Juncal), 1012 Buenos Aires. ✆ **11/4812-4419.** Fax 11/4815-6622. www.trhostel.com.ar. 70 bed spaces, including 4 in 2 bedrooms with attached bathroom. From $11 per bed; $45 private room with bathroom. Rates include continental breakfast. No credit cards. No Metro access. **Amenities:** Concierge; shared kitchen; lockers; TV room; Wi-Fi. *In room:* Hair dryer.

San Telmo

Inexpensive

El Lugar Gay ★ As the name implies, this small, laid-back hotel accommodates gay clientele (male only). If you qualify, you'll find a charming, old-world building with some modern industrial chic flourishes. Rooms are small and bare and the lobby is on the upper floors via a flight of stairs, but you cannot beat the location in the heart of San Telmo, less than a block from Plaza Dorrego. Some rooms at the back have lovely views of the local church.

Defensa 1120 (at Humberto 1), 1102 Buenos Aires. ✆ **11/4300-4747.** www.lugargay.com.ar. 7 units, some with shared bathrooms. $60–$80 double. Rates include continental breakfast. No credit cards. Metro: Independencia. **Amenities:** Restaurant; bar. *In room:* A/C, TV.

Hostel Carlos Gardel ★ Another old townhouse has been renovated to accommodate budget travelers who don't mind sharing bathrooms, a kitchen, and a rooftop terrace. The famous tango singer adorns walls with stained-glass windows, and a marble staircase leads to dorms where sheets and towels are provided. There are only two rooms with private bathrooms (though there are 45 beds total), so book well in advance if you wish to secure them.

Carlos Calvo 579 (at Peru), 1102 Buenos Aires. ✆ **11/4307-2606.** www.hostelcarlosgardel.com.ar. 9 units. From $12 per bed; $40 per room. Rates include continental breakfast. No credit cards. Metro: Independencia. **Amenities:** Concierge; self-service drink station; free high-speed Internet; shared kitchen; TV room. *In room:* Lockers.

Lina's Tango Guesthouse ★★★ Finds For tango fanatics, this makes a perfect stop, with a helpful live-in owner providing a great introduction to the Tangolopolis. Owner Lina Acuña offers dance classes in this colorful 100-year old building with a garden patio. She'll even take you out on nighttime excursions to the city's many *milongas.* Rooms vary

The Boutique Boom

B&B accommodation in Argentina should not be associated with the fusty, cluttered images we link with such guesthouses back home. In recent years Buenos Aires has seen a surge in small hotels that merge the B&B concept with boutique style, with the result that you end up staying in hip and cosmopolitan homes with a focus on design and luxury and a price often half of what you'd pay at a conventional hotel.

At the vanguard of this movement is **1555 Malabia House ★★**, Malabia 1555 (at Gorriti), Palermo Viejo (✆ **11/4833-2410;** www.malabiahouse.com.ar). Fourteen rooms surround three minigardens to create a designer oasis with Zen-like charm. Rates start at $110. **1890 Hotel Boutique ★**, Salta 1074 (at Carlos Calvo), San Telmo (✆ **11/4304-8798;** www.1890hotel.com.ar), has only six rooms, all decked out in the original features of this 19th-century townhouse. Tall ceilings and windows overlook a garden patio, while the comfortable rooms have stylish bathrooms. Rates start at $100. **Mansión Vitraux,** Carlos Calvo (at Defensa), San Telmo (✆ **11/4300-6886;** www.mansionvitraux.com), has 12 luxurious rooms with decor that varies from minimalist sophistication to oriental opulence. Dinner and wine tastings are served in an atmospheric wine cellar. Rates start at $226.

For high-end film buffs, check out **Jardin Escondido,** Gorrito 4746 (at Armenia), Palermo (✆ **0800/746-3743** in the U.S.; www.coppolajardinescondido.com), a low-key but luxurious property owned by the movie director Francis Ford Coppolla. The six rooms are named after family members and the hotel consists of two freestanding buildings around a communal courtyard. Set up to be rented in suites or in its entirety, individual rooms are possible to rent depending on availability. Rates start at $665 for a downstairs suite.

The award-winning **Bo Bo Hotel,** Guatemala 4882 (at Thames), Palermo (✆ **11/4774-0505;** www.bobohotel.com), is both hip and comfortable, with an excellent restaurant. Rates start at $200. The **Garden B&B,** Piedras 1677 (at Caseros), San Telmo (✆ **11/4300-3455;** www.gardenbuenosaires.com), has an unassuming street entrance that leads to a lush lawn surrounded by four unique rooms. Small, peaceful, and immaculate, the hotel is very much a home away from home—the American owner, Pamela, lives upstairs. Rates start at $85 for a double with shared bathroom.

in size, are painted in bright primary colors, and have original doors and fittings. Three of the eight rooms share bathrooms and there is a communal kitchen and TV room.

Estados Unidos 780 (at Piedras), 1011 Buenos Aires. ✆ **11/4361-6817.** www.tangoguesthouse.com.ar. 8 units, 5 with private bathroom. From $70 double. Rates include continental breakfast. No credit cards. Metro: Independencia. **Amenities:** Breakfast room; self-service kitchen; tango tours. *In room:* Wi-Fi.

WHERE TO DINE

Buenos Aires offers world-class dining, with a variety of Argentine, Italian, and international restaurants. You've heard that Argentine beef is the best in the world; *parrillas* serving the choicest cuts are ubiquitous. Many kitchens have an Italian influence, and you'll find pasta on most menus. The city's most fashionable neighborhood for eating out is Palermo Viejo, where new restaurants are constantly opening—and closing. Additional top restaurants line the docks of Puerto Madero, with the majority focused on seafood. The Microcentro and Recoleta offer many outstanding restaurants and cafes as well. Cafe life is as sacred to Porteños as it is to Parisians.

Porteños eat breakfast until 10am, lunch between noon and 3:30pm, and dinner late—usually after 9pm. Many restaurants require reservations, particularly on weekends. Executive lunch menus are offered most places at noon, but dinner menus are usually a la carte. There is sometimes a small charge for bread and other items placed at the table. In restaurants that serve pasta, the pasta and its sauce are priced separately. Standard tipping is 10%, or more for exceptional service. When paying by credit card, you will often be expected to leave the *propina* (tip) in cash, since many credit card receipts don't provide a place to include it. Many restaurants close between lunch and dinner, and are closed on Monday nights. Call ahead to make sure, as this can also change seasonally.

Puerto Madero

Expensive

Cabaña las Lilas ★★ ARGENTINE Widely considered the best *parrilla* in Buenos Aires, Cabaña las Lilas is always packed. The menu pays homage to Argentine beef, which comes from the restaurant's private *estancia* (ranch). The best cuts are the rib-eye, baby beef, and thin skirt steak. Order sautéed vegetables, grilled onions, or Provençal-style fries separately. Chicken and fish are also part of the offerings, and vegetarians don't have to stay at home, since there is a large selection of very fresh and crisp salads. Service is hurried but professional. This enormous spot offers indoor and outdoor seating, and in spite of its high price, it has a casual and informal vibe.

Alicia Moreau de Justo 516, at Villaflor in Dique 3. ✆ **11/4313-1336.** www.laslilas.com. Reservations recommended. Main courses A$70–A$90. AE, DC, V. Daily noon–midnight. Metro: L. N. Alem.

Moderate

Asia de Cuba ASIAN Though it is certainly not the supertrendy spot it used to be, Asia de Cuba is not a bad choice if you want to dine late and dance even later in a slick waterside location. On Wednesday evenings it is flooded with suited office workers taking advantage of happy hour prices (known as "after office" locally). The sushi-dominated menu is excellent and the drink list is top notch. Asian-style interiors and lounge chairs on the terrace make it a cool place to while away a lazy afternoon after lunch.

Pierina Dialessi 750 and Macacha Guemes, Puerto Madero Este. ✆ **011/4894-1328.** www.asiadecuba.com.ar. Main courses A$35–A$55. AE, MC, V. Daily 1–4.30pm and 9pm–late.

Sorrento del Puerto ★★ ITALIAN The only two-story restaurant in Puerto Madero enjoys impressive views of the water from both floors. The sleek modern dining room boasts large windows, modern blue lighting, and tables and booths decorated with white linens and individual roses. People come here for two reasons: great pasta and even better seafood. The best seafood dishes include trout stuffed with crabmeat or sole with a Belle Marnier sauce. Sorrento has a second location in Recoleta at Posadas 1053 (✆ **11/4326-0532**).

Av. Alicia Moreau de Justo 410, at Guevara on Dique 4. ✆ **11/4319-8731.** Reservations recommended. Main courses A$45–A$70. AE, DC, MC, V. Mon–Fri noon–4pm and 8pm–1am; Sat 8pm–2am. Metro: L. N. Alem.

Recoleta

Expensive

La Bourgogne ★★★ FRENCH The only Relais Gourmand in Argentina, chef Jean Paul Bondoux serves the finest French and international food in the city. Decorated in a modern style, the formal dining room serves the city's top gourmands. To begin your meal, consider a warm foie gras scallop with honey-wine sauce, or perhaps the succulent *ravioli d'escargots.* Examples of the carefully prepared main courses include *chateaubriand béarnaise,* roasted salmon, veal steak, and lamb with parsley-and-garlic sauce.

Av. Alvear 1981, at Ayacucho (Alvear Palace Hotel). ✆ **11/4808-2100.** www.alvearpalace.com. Reservations required. Jacket and tie required for men. Main courses A$45–A$80. AE, DC, MC, V. Free valet parking. Mon–Fri noon–3pm; Mon–Sat 8pm–midnight. No Metro access.

Piegari ★★ ITALIAN Piegari has two restaurants located across the street from each other (under a highway overpass, of all places); the more formal focuses on Italian dishes, while the other (Piegari Vitello e Dolce) is mainly a *parrilla.* Both are excellent, but visit the formal Piegari for outstanding Italian cuisine. Homemade spaghetti, six kinds of risotto, pan pizza, veal scallops, and black salmon ravioli are just a few of the mouthwatering choices.

Posadas 1042, at Av. 9 de Julio in La Recova, near the Four Seasons Hotel. ✆ **11/4326-9654.** Reservations recommended. Main courses A$45–A$80. MC, V. Daily noon–3:30pm and 7:30pm–1am. No Metro access.

Moderate

El Mirasol ★ PARRILLA One of the city's best *parrillas,* this restaurant serves thick cuts of fine Argentine beef. Its glassed dining area full of plants and trellises gives the impression of outdoor dining. A mammoth 2½-pound serving of tenderloin is a specialty. The best dessert is an enticing combination of meringue, ice cream, whipped cream, *dulce de leche,* walnuts, and hot chocolate sauce.

Posadas 1032, at Av. 9 de Julio in La Recova near the Four Seasons Hotel. ✆ **11/4326-7322.** www.el-mirasol.com.ar. Reservations recommended. Main courses A$30–A$60. AE, DC, MC, V. Daily noon–2am. No Metro access.

Juana M (Value) PARRILLA This amazing little *parrilla* is easily overlooked, but you shouldn't miss it. Located in the basement of an orphanage, this neoclassical building is one of the few saved from the highway demolition that created the nearby La Recova. This cavernous industrial-chic space is white and luminous by day. At night, when the space is lit only by candlelight, trendy young patrons flood in, chattering the night away. The menu is simple, high quality, and amazingly inexpensive.

Carlos Pellegrini 1535 (basement), at Libertador, across from the La Recova area. ✆ **11/4326-0462.** Main courses A$30–A$50. AE, MC, V. Daily noon–4pm and 8pm–12:30am. No Metro access.

Inexpensive

La Biela ★★ CAFE Black-and-white photos of Argentine car racers decorate the huge dining room. Artists, politicians, and neighborhood executives (as well as a fair number of tourists) all frequent La Biela, which serves breakfast, informal lunch plates, ice cream, and crepes. The outdoor terrace sits beneath an enormous 19th-century gum tree, opposite the church of Nuestra Señora del Pinar and the adjoining Recoleta Cemetery. La Biela is a protected *bar notable.*

Av. Quintana 596, at Alvear. ✆ **11/4804-0449.** www.labiela.com. Main courses A$25–A$50. V. Daily 7am–3am. No Metro access.

Palermo

Expensive

Casa Cruz ★★ Finds ITALIAN/INTERNATIONAL With its enormous polished-brass doors and lack of a sign on the door, you almost feel like you are entering a nightclub, and inside, the dark modern interior maintains the theme. The impressive round bar leads into a spacious dining area full of polished woods and red upholstery. The menu here is eclectic and interesting. Rabbit, sea bass, Parma ham rolls, and other interesting and exotic ingredients go into the many flavorful dishes.

Uriarte 1658, at Honduras. ✆ **11/4833-1112.** Reservations highly recommended. Main courses A$40–A$60. AE, MC, V. Tues–Sat 8:30pm–3am, later Sat. No Metro access.

Moderate

De Olivas i Lustres ★ MEDITERRANEAN Located in Palermo Viejo, this magical restaurant is a Buenos Aires favorite. The small, rustic dining room displays antiques, olive jars, and wine bottles, and each candlelit table is individually decorated. The reasonably priced menu celebrates Mediterranean cuisine, with light soups, fresh fish, and sautéed vegetables as its focus. For about A$80 each, you and your partner can share 15 tapas-style dishes, brought out individually. The items are meant to contrast and surprise you as the night progresses.

Gorriti 3972, at Medrano. ✆ **11/4867-3388.** Reservations recommended. Main courses A$20–A$45. AE, V. Mon–Sat 8:30pm–1:30am. Metro: Scalabrini Ortiz.

Novecento ★★★ INTERNATIONAL Fashionable Porteños pack the New York–style bistro by 11pm, and waiters rush around with dishes such as salmon carpaccio and steak salad. The pastas and risotto are mouthwatering, but you may prefer a steak au poivre or a chicken brochette. Other wonderful choices include filet mignon, grilled Pacific salmon, and penne with wild mushrooms. Novecento has a sister restaurant in Soho.

Báez 199, at Arguibel. ✆ **11/4778-1900.** Reservations recommended. Main courses A$30–A$53. AE, DC, MC, V. Daily noon–4pm and 8pm–2am; Sun brunch 8am–noon. Metro: Ministro Carranza.

Inexpensive

Bio ★★ Finds VEGETARIAN/MEDITERRANEAN In a nation where meat reigns supreme, finding an organic vegetarian restaurant is a near impossibility. Bio is the exception. Their "meat" is made on the premises from wheat and then marinated to add more flavor. All the ingredients used at Bio are organic, and all are grown or produced strictly in Argentina. Piles of organic cheese line the counters. Quinoa, the ancient Incan grain, is also used in many of the dishes.

Humboldt 2199, at Guatemala. ✆ **11/4774-3880.** Main courses A$25–A$36. AE, MC, V. Tues–Sun noon–3:30pm; daily 8pm–1am (often later Sat–Sun). Metro: Palermo is 4 blocks away.

Campo Bravo ★ Value PARRILLA/ARGENTINE This place serves as the virtual center of the Las Cañitas dining scene. It's relaxed during the day but insane at night. Dining on the sidewalk here, you'll get a great view of the glamorous crowds who get dropped off by taxis to begin their night in this exciting neighborhood. The *parrilla* serves up basic Argentine cuisine, and its enormous slabs of meat are served on wooden boards. Expect long delays for an outside table on weekends. One good thing—they don't close between lunch and dinner, so early diners can enjoy a great meal here with no wait at all for a table.

Báez 292, at Arévalo. ✆ **11/4514-5820.** Main courses A$22–A$45. MC. Mon 6pm–4am; Tues–Sun 11:30am–2:30am (often later Sat–Sun, depending on crowds). Metro: Carranza.

Monserrat

Moderate

Club Español SPANISH The Art Nouveau Spanish Club boasts the most magnificent dining room in Buenos Aires. Despite the restaurant's architectural grandeur, the atmosphere is surprisingly relaxed and often celebratory; don't be surprised to find a table of champagne-clinking Argentines next to you. Tables have beautiful silver place settings, and tuxedo-clad waiters offer formal service. Although the menu is a tempting sample of Spanish cuisine, including the paella and Spanish omelets, the fish dishes are the chef's best.

Bernardo de Yrigoyen 180, at Alsina. ✆ **11/4334-4876.** Reservations recommended. Main courses A$30–A$60. AE, DC, MC, V. Daily noon–4pm and 8pm–midnight. Metro: Carlos Pelegrini.

Microcentro

Expensive

Dora ★★ ARGENTINE/SEAFOOD Nobody comes here for the decor. Dora has been open since the 1940s and is run by the same family that opened it. The specialty at this expensive restaurant is fish, though a few beef, chicken, and pasta dishes are thrown in, too—almost as a second thought. The Cazuela Dora is the specialty—a casserole of fish, shellfish, shrimp, and just about everything else the sea offers thrown into one pot. Appetizers alone are expensive, from A$38 to A$92, but some of the options are made with fresh seafood.

Reconquista 1076. ✆ **11/4311-2891.** Main courses A$30–A$170. V. Mon–Thurs 12:30pm–1am; Fri–Sat noon–2am. Metro: San Martín.

Plaza Grill ★★ INTERNATIONAL For nearly a century, the Plaza Grill has dominated the city's power-lunch scene. The dining room is decorated with dark oak furniture, Indian fans from the British empire, and Villeroy & Boch china place settings. Tables are well spaced, allowing for intimate conversations. Order a la carte from the international menu or off the *parrilla*—the steaks are perfect Argentine cuts. The restaurant's wine list spans seven countries, with the world's best Malbec coming from Mendoza.

Marriott Plaza Hotel, Calle Florida 1005, overlooking Plaza San Martín. ✆ **11/4318-3070.** Reservations recommended. Main courses A$45–A$70. AE, DC, MC, V. Daily noon–3pm and 7pm–midnight; tea service 5–7pm. Metro: San Martín.

Moderate

Broccolino ★ ITALIAN Taking its name from New York's Italian immigrant neighborhood—notice the Brooklyn memorabilia filling the walls—the restaurant has a distinctly New York feel. Three small dining rooms are decorated in quintessential red-and-white-checkered tablecloths, and the smell of tomatoes, onions, and garlic fills the air. The restaurant is known for its spicy pizzas, fresh pastas, and, above all, its sauces (*salsas* in Spanish).

Esmeralda 776, at Córdoba. ✆ **11/4322-7652.** Reservations recommended. Main courses A$22–A$70. Daily noon–4pm and 7–11pm. Metro: Carlos Pelegrini.

Richmond Cafe ★★ CAFE/ARGENTINE The Richmond Cafe, a *bar notable,* is all that is left of the Richmond Hotel, an Argentine-British hybrid that opened in 1917 and once catered to the elite. The menu here is traditionally Argentine with a *confiteria* (cafe) section in the front. You'll find a mix of locals of all kinds here, from workers grabbing a quick bite to well-dressed seniors. The decor is that of a gentlemen's club, full of wood, brass, and red-leather upholstery. Downstairs is a bar area full of billiard tables, and the restaurant offers hearty basics such as chicken, fish, and beef.

Calle Florida 468 at Corrientes. ✆ **11/4322-1341** or 4322-1653. Main courses A$35–A$45. AE, MC, V. Mon–Sat 7am–10pm. Metro: Florida.

Inexpensive

Café Tortoni ★★★ Moments CAFE/ARGENTINE This historic cafe has served as the artistic and intellectual capital of Buenos Aires since 1858. Wonderfully appointed in woods, stained glass, yellowing marble, and bronzes, the place tells more about its history by simply existing than any of the photos hanging on its walls could. This is the perfect spot for a coffee or a snack when walking along Avenida de Mayo. Stop by for one of the nightly tango shows (7:30 and 9:30pm), set in a cramped side gallery where the performers often walk through the crowd.

Av. de Mayo 825, at Esmeralda. ✆ **11/4342-4328.** Snacks A$6–A$30. AE, DC, MC, V. Mon–Thurs 7:30am–2am; Fri–Sat 8am–3am; Sun 9am–1am. Metro: Estación Piedras.

San Telmo

Moderate

Desnivel PARRILLA This place brings new meaning to the phrase greasy spoon, because everything in here seems to be greasy—from the slippery floor to the railings, glasses, and dishes. Even the walls, and the artwork on them, seem to bleed grease. This is one of San Telmo's best *parrillas,* and a flood of locals and tourists keep the place going.

Defensa 855, at Independencia. ✆ **11/4300-9081.** Main courses A$30–A$42. No credit cards. Daily noon–4:30pm and 7:30pm–1am. Metro: Independencia.

BUENOS AIRES AFTER DARK

From the theater shows to dimly lit tango salons, Buenos Aires offers an exceptional variety of nightlife. Porteños eat late and play later, with theater performances starting around 9pm, bars and nightclubs opening around midnight, and no one showing up until after 1am. Thursday, Friday, and Saturday are the big going-out nights, with the bulk of activity in Recoleta, Palermo Viejo, and Costanera. Summer is quieter because most of the town flees to the coast.

Performing arts in Buenos Aires are centered on the highly regarded Teatro Colón, home to the National Opera, National Symphony, and National Ballet. In addition, there are nearly 40 professional theaters around town showing Broadway- and off-Broadway-style hits, Argentine plays, and music reviews. Buy tickets for most productions at the box office or through **Ticketron** (✆ **11/4321-9700**) or **Ticketmaster** (✆ **11/4326-9903**).

The Performing Arts

Theaters, Exhibitions & Other Venues

Asociación Argentina de Cultura Inglesa (British Arts Centre) ★★ Everything from Shakespeare to *Absolutely Fabulous* screenings get shown here, and it is a perfect stop for any homesick English-speaking visitor. Suipacha 1333 (at Arroyo). ✆ **11/4393-2004.** www.aaci.org.ar and www.britishartscentre.org.ar. Tickets $2–$10. Metro San Martin.

Centro Cultural de Borges ★★ Located in the downtown mall Galería Pacifico, this arts center celebrates Argentina's most important man of letters. Art exhibitions, tango classes, a book store, and a ballet school are just some of the attractions you can enjoy between shopping. Viamonte and San Martin. ✆ **11/5555-5359.** www.ccborges.org.ar. Ticket prices vary. Metro San Martin.

Centro Cultural Recoleta (Recoleta Cultural Center) ★ This cultural center is just one door over from the famous Recoleta Cemetery. It hosts Argentine and international art exhibits, experimental theater works, occasional music concerts, and an interactive science museum for children where they are encouraged to touch and play with the displays. Junín 1930, next door to the Recoleta Cemetery. ✆ **11/4803-1041.** No Metro access.

Luna Park Once the home of international boxing matches, the Luna is the largest indoor stadium in Argentina, and as such, it hosts the biggest shows and concerts in Buenos Aires. Buchard 465, at Corriendes. ✆ **11/4311-1990** or 4311-5100. Tickets $6–$30. Metro: L. N. Alem.

Teatro Colón Known across the world for its impeccable acoustics, the Colón has attracted the world's finest opera performers. Opera season in Buenos Aires runs from April to November. The Colón has its own philharmonic orchestra, ballet, and choir companies. Unfortunately, this beautiful theater has been closed for some years now due to never-ending renovations—two deadlines for completion were missed in 2008 and 2010. The ticket office is still open, as the theater's different companies temporarily perform in other venues across the city. Consult the website for more information. Calle Libertad 621, at Tucumán. ✆ **11/4378-7100.** www.teatrocolon.org.ar. Tickets $4–$30. Metro: Tribunales.

Teatro Gran Rex A popular music venue for national and international artists. Av. Corrientes 857 (at Suipacha). ✆ **11/4322-8000.** Metro: Carlos Pellegrini.

Teatro Municipal General San Martín This entertainment complex has three theaters offering drama, comedy, ballet, music, and children's plays. Its lobby often has special exhibitions of photography and art related to the theater and, on its own, is worth a special visit during the daytime. The lobby exhibitions are usually free. Corrientes 1530, at Paraná. ✆ **0800/333-5254.** Tickets $6–$18. Metro: Uruguay.

Teatro Nacional Cervantes This is an ornate Spanish Imperial–style theater house that shows some of the best plays in town. Calle Libertad 815 (at Cordoba). ✆ **11/4816-4224.** Metro: Tribunales.

Teatro Opera A unique and rare example of Art Deco in Buenos Aires, this futuristic theater is located on the city's version of New York City's Broadway (Corrientes St.) and accordingly houses mainstream musicals and plays. Av. Corrientes 860 (at Suipacha). ✆ **11/4326-1335.** Metro Carlos Pellegrini.

The Club & Music Scene

Tango Dance Clubs & Show Palaces

In Buenos Aires, you can *watch* the tango or *dance* the tango. (Perhaps the former will lend inspiration to the latter.) You'll have many opportunities to see the dance during your visit: Tango dancers frequent the streets of La Boca and San Telmo, many high-end hotels offer tango shows in their lobbies and bars, and tango salons blanket the city. The most famous (besides Café Tortoni, p. 111) are in San Telmo and combine dinner and a show. Have a hotel driver or *remise* take you to San Telmo, La Boca, or Barracas at night, rather than taking the Metro or trying to walk.

Tango Palaces

Cafe Tortoni, Av. De Mayo 829 (✆ **11/4342-4328**), has excellent shows at 9pm everyday except Tuesday, in a back room with dinner available. **El Viejo Almacén,** Independencia and Balcarce (✆ **11/4307-6689**), shows traditional Argentine-style tango. Sunday to Thursday shows are at 10pm; Friday and Saturday shows are at 9:30 and 11:45pm. **Esquina Carlos Gardel ★★**, Carlos Gardel 3200 (✆ **11/4876-6363**), is perhaps the most elegant of the city's tango show palaces, held in a restaurant where Carlos Gardel used to dine with his friends. **Señor Tango,** Vieytes 1653 (✆ **11/4303-0212**), is more akin to a Broadway production theater than to a traditional tango salon, but the dancers are fantastic and the owner, who clearly loves to perform, is a good singer.

Tango Clubs & Milongas

El Arranque, Bartolomé Mitre 1759, at Callao (✆ **11/4371-6767**), is so old-fashioned you may have to sit apart from your partner when you're not dancing, and forget about dressing casually. Located in an authentic old hall, it hosts afternoon dancing at 3pm and is therefore perfect for those who like their beauty sleep. **El Beso Nightclub**, Riobamba 416, at Corrientes (✆ **11/4953-2794**), has the feeling of a 1940s nightclub with its hidden street location and upstairs entrance. Be sure to call and reserve a table. **La Glorietta,** Once de Septiembre and Echeverría (✆ **11/4674-1026**), offers tango in the open-air, although it can be slightly touristy. There is a show at 1am on Friday and Saturday. **La Cathedral,** Sarmiento 4006, at Medrano (✆ **11/155325-1630**), has all the atmosphere of an underground rave—except the music is tango instead of techno. **La Viruta**, Armenia 1366, at Cabrera (✆ **11/4774-6357**), may have all the charm of a 1970s high school prom, yet is authentic and cheap and attracts a healthy mix of young locals and foreigners eager to show off their steps. **Salón Canning,** Scalabrini Ortiz 1331 (✆ **11/4832-6753**), is among the most authentic of the city's *milongas.*

Other Dance Clubs

Dancing in Buenos Aires is not just about tango, with the majority of the younger population preferring salsa, *cumbia,* and European beats. The biggest nights out are Thursday, Friday, and Saturday, but the Argentine habit of not hitting the clubs until 2am means many foreigners peak too soon and arrive to empty clubs at midnight. **Asia de Cuba ★**, P. Dealessi 750 (✆ **11/4894-1328** or 4894-1329; www.asiadecuba.com.ar), offers sophisticated drinking and dancing. Some of the entertainment, though, can be wild—of the women-dancing-in-cages variety. **Crobar,** Paseo de la Infanta, Av. del Libertador 3883, at Infanta Isabel, Palermo (✆ **11/4778-1500;** www.crobar.com), is a super club, with overhead walkways and balconies over the main dance floor. It is best on Fridays night, and on Saturdays attracts a younger clientele. **Jet Lounge**, Av. Rafael Obligado 4801, Costanera Norte (✆ **11/4872-5599;** www.jet-lounge.com.ar), has a lounge bar and disco on the waterfront. Thursday nights are best; sushi is served with cocktails to a fashionable clientele all nights. **Maluco Beleza,** Sarmiento 1728, at Rodriguez Peña, Tribunales (✆ **11/4372-1737;** www.malucobeleza.com.ar), offers a colorful slice of Brazilian samba in downtown Buenos Aires. Sunday is reggaeton night. **Niceto Club,** Niceto Vega 5510, at Humboltd, Palermo Viejo (✆ **11/4779-9396;** www.niceto club.com), is one of B.A.'s better established clubs, pumping out everything from *cumbia* to reggaeton. Thursdays and Fridays are best in this two room party spot. **Pachá,** Avenida Rafael Obligado and La Pampa, Costanera Norte (✆ **11/4788-4280;** www.pachabuenos aires.com), needs little introduction to hardcore clubbers and was one of the first clubs to establish the capital as a regular stop for international DJs keen to get people grooving on a waterside terrace under the stars. Go on Saturday for the best experience.

Mar del Plata: Buenos Aires–on-the-Sea

Forty-seven kilometers (29 miles) of Atlantic beach is what attracts eight million holidaymakers to the coastal city of Mar del Plata every summer. Situated 400km (248 miles) south of Buenos Aires, it makes for the perfect escape from the sweltering heat of the capital (Dec–Mar) and offers everything from surfing to golfing, fishing, and horseback riding. Its vibrant nightlife and theater scene also means Porteños have found a home away from home, with sand and sea included. Many people choose to tan on the packed beach of **Playa Grande** or break out their wallets in the city's main **Mar del Plata Casino.** Others walk along the city's waterfont, known as **La Rambla,** or surf at **Waikiki beach.** Additional highlights include the **Fishing Harbour,** where trawlers land their catch, watched by a colony of 800 hungry sea lions; **De los Padres Lakes and Hills,** a picturesque forest with a lake; and **Museo del Mar**, Av. Colón 114 (✆ **223/451-9779**; www.museodelmar.com; daily 9.30am–midnight; admission A$20), which holds live sharks in massive water tanks, plus a small theater and arthouse cinema.

The best place to stay in the area is the open and spacious **Sheraton Mar de Plata,** Alem 4221, 7600 Mar del Plata (✆ **0800/777-7002;** www.sheratonmardelplata.com.ar), or the old and luxurious **Hermitage,** Bd. Ramos 2657, 7600 Mar del Plata (✆ **223/451-9081;** www.hermitagehotel.com.ar). To get to Mar del Plata, you can take a plane, train, bus, or car from Buenos Aires. The journey by bus takes 4 to 5 hours, departing from Retiro station in Buenos Aires. Trains depart from Constitución station in the capital and also take 4 to 5 hours. In the high season there are three flights a day from Jorge Newbery airport, operated by Aerolineas Argentinas.

Gay & Lesbian Dance Clubs

Amerika, Gascón 1040, Palermo (✆ **11/4865-4416;** www.ameri-k.com.ar), is the city's most popular gay club, and even straight people are beginning to come here in droves for the great music. It's open Friday and Saturday only. **Contramano,** Rodríguez Peña 1082, Recoleta (**11/4811-0494;** www.contramano.com), is popular with a mature crowd and was the first gay bar opened in Buenos Aires. **Glam ★**, Cabrera 3046, Palermo (✆ **11/4963-2521;** www.glambsas.com.ar), is young, lively, and popular.

The Bar Scene

Where to start? Where to go? B.A. is hopping with bar life, and below is just a small sample. Be warned that many bars don't get going until very late, so take advantage of bars that run "after office" promotions (postwork happy hours, basically), as they fill up with revelers at a more respectable hour (7–10pm).

The Alamo-Shoeless Joe's, Uruguay 1175, Tribunales (✆ **11/4813-7324;** www.elalamobar.com), is one of the few places you can enjoy a daytime beer with like-minded strangers. It is popular with American expats keeping up with sports back home. **The Kilkenny,** Marcelo T. de Alvear 399, Microcentro (✆ **11/4312-7291**), is more like a rock house than an Irish pub and is packed with both locals and foreigners. **Plaza Dorrego Bar,**

Calle Defensa 1098, San Telmo (✆ **11/4361-0141**), has antique liquor bottles in cases along the walls, and anonymous writings engraved in the wood. **Breoghan Brew Bar,** Pasaje San Lorenzo 389, San Telmo (✆ **11/4362-4750**), is a rare find in B.A.—a microbrewery with 50 varieties of local and imported beers, as well as excellent food.

Bar Guebara, Humberto 463, San Telmo (✆ **11/155751-5550**), is a hole in the wall popular with both local and foreign barflies. **The Shamrock,** Rodríguez Peña 1220, Recoleta (✆ **11/4812-3584**), is packed every night of the week, including Mondays. On weekends, the basement space opens up into a small disco, adding to the fun. **Gibraltar,** Peru 895 (✆ **11/4362-5310**), is a real pub, with draft beer that comes in pint glasses and food such as Thai curry. **Millión,** Parana 1048, Recoleta (✆ **11/4815-9925**), is a lavish, renovated mansion attracting a beautiful crowd. **Post Street Bar,** Thames 1885, at Nicaragua, Palermo (✆ **11/156543-9648**), is a no-nonsense beer haven amongst Palermo's trendier restaurants and designer stores. Graffiti walls and a pizza menu all add to its down-to-earth vibe.

5 PUERTO IGUAZU & IGUAZU FALLS ★★★

1,330km (825 miles) NE of Buenos Aires

"Niagara on Viagra" is how one visitor put it when he saw Iguazú for the first time. Twenty-three kilometers (14 miles) of deafening waterfalls plummet up to 70m (229 ft.) into a giant gorge in a spectacular subtropical setting. The sheer power is overwhelming. You come face to face with raging sheets of water, with sprays so intense it seems as though geysers have erupted from below. Iguazú is a must-see on any trip to Argentina.

It's shocking that this ecological blockbuster is a 90-minute flight from the civilized, cosmopolitan buzz of Buenos Aires. Many people drop into this humid corner of Misiones province on a day trip, or for 2 days max. Yet this fascinating jungle zone of red soil, giant butterflies, and comical toucans has more to offer than jaw-dropping waterfalls. Misiones Province is a heady mix of strong indigenous tribal culture, blond eastern European settlers, and tropical frontierland. Its abundant wildlife and the mystery of its long-fallen Jesuit ruins are worth exploring. With its multitude of isolated national parks and huge swaths of untouched rainforest, it is an ecotourist's paradise, with several genuine jungle lodges. Civilization has encroached in the form of tea plantations and pine forests, yet it is possible to get off the beaten track and visit isolated wonders such as Esteros del Ibera, a vast marshland teeming with wildlife that is fast becoming one of Argentina's hottest destinations.

You can visit the waterfalls on your own, but you will most certainly need a tour operator to explore the jungle. Allow at least 1 full day to explore the waterfalls on the Argentine side, another to visit the Brazilian side, and perhaps half a day for a jungle tour. Most people stay in the sedate, laidback town of **Puerto Iguazú,** 18km (11 miles) from the park.

ESSENTIALS

Getting There

BY PLANE **Aerolíneas Argentinas** (✆ **0810/222-86527** or 3757/420-194; www.aerolineas.com.ar), and **LAN** (✆ **3757/424-296;** www.lan.com) offer up to five daily flights from Buenos Aires to **Aeropuerto Internacional Cataratas** (airport code IGR; ✆ **3757/422-013**); the trip takes 1½ hours. Round-trip fares cost approximately $420, depending on whether any specials are on offer. Aerolíneas Argentinas occasionally offers flights to Iguazú from Ezeiza international airport, usually on Saturday or Sunday. Catch a taxi (for about A$70) or one of the shuttles from the airport to town (A$8), a 20-minute drive.

BY BUS The fastest bus service from Buenos Aires is with **Vía Bariloche** (✆ **11/4315-4456** in Buenos Aires), which takes 18 hours and costs A$226 to A$325 one-way, depending on the seat you choose. (The more expensive fare gets you a fully reclining *cama* [bed] seat.) Less pricey but longer (21 hr.) are **Expreso Singer** (✆ **11/4313-3927** in Buenos Aires) and **Expreso Tigre Iguazú** (✆ **11/4313-3915** in Buenos Aires), which both run for about A$255 one-way. **Puerto Iguazú Bus Terminal,** Calle Córdoba and Avenida Misiones (✆ **3757/423-006**), is in the town center.

Visitor Information

In Puerto Iguazú, obtain maps and park information from the **Parque Nacional** office at Victoria Aguirre 66 (✆ **3757/420-722**), open Monday through Friday from 8am to 9pm. For information on the town, contact the municipal tourist office, at Victoria Aguirre and Brañas (✆ **3757/420-800**). It's open Monday to Friday from 8am to 9pm, Saturday and Sunday from 8am to noon and 3 to 9pm. Visitor information is also available near the national park entrance (see below).

Getting Around

BY BUS **El Práctico** local buses run every 45 minutes daily from 7am to 8pm between the Puerto Iguazú bus terminal and the national park; the cost is A$5.

BY TAXI Taxis are unmetered and relatively expensive, with most drivers charging a flat fee of A$80 wherever you go, whether it's to the airport or park. **Parada 10** (✆ **3757/421-527**) and **Remisses Falls VIP,** Bompland 185 (✆ **3757/420-805**), provide 24-hour taxi service. Within both Puerto Iguazú and the national park, you can easily walk or, in the former, take the narrow-gauge train.

BY CAR The main roads are excellent but be prepared for wretched mud baths if you stray. **Budget Rent a Car,** Paulino Amarante 76, Puerto Iguazú (✆ **3757/421-675;** www.budgetargentina.com), offers small cars for $70 a day.

BY BICYCLE **Internet Yguazu,** Av. Victoria Aguirre 552 (✆ **3757/424-034**), offers bicycles for A$40 a day.

VISITING THE NATIONAL PARK ★★★

Your first stop will likely be the **visitor center** (✆ **3757/491-444**), where you'll find maps and information about the area's flora and fauna. Known as the Centro de Interpretacion, it is .8km (½ mile) from the park entrance, close to the parking lot and footbridges for the waterfall circuits. Adjacent to the visitor center you will find a restaurant, snack shops, and souvenir stores. A natural-gas train takes visitors to the path entrance for the Upper and Lower circuits and to the footbridge leading to Devil's Throat. (If you'd rather walk, footpaths are available, but note that the walk to Devil's Throat is about 3km/1.75 miles.) The visitor center is staffed with a number of English-speaking guides, available for individual and private tours. You may opt to see the falls on your own or with an experienced local guide. A guide is not really necessary, however, unless your time is limited or you want to ask detailed questions about the region's geography and fauna. The entrance fee is A$60, which also covers the train ride, for non-Argentines

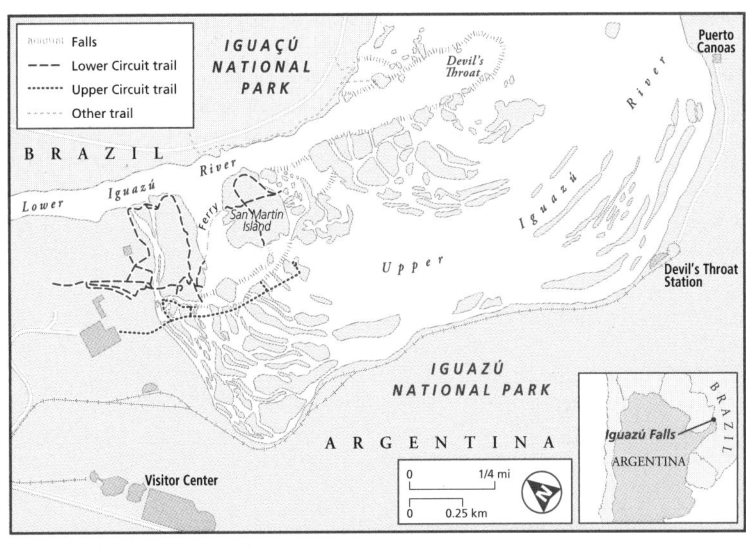

to enter the national park. The national park is open daily 8am to 7pm in summer, and from 8am until 6pm in winter.

The two main paths from which to view the waterfalls are the **Circuito Superior (Upper Circuit)** ★ and the **Circuito Inferior (Lower Circuit)** ★, both of which begin within walking distance (less than .8km/½ mile) from the visitor center. You may want to save your energy, however, and catch the train to the path entrance. There's a small snack shop near the beginning of the trails. The Upper Circuit winds its way along the top of the canyon, allowing you to look down the falls and see the area's rich flora, including cacti, ferns, and orchids. The Lower Circuit offers the best views, as magnificent waterfalls come hurtling down before you in walls of silvery spray. The waterfalls are clearly marked by signs along the way.

The best time to walk the **Upper Circuit** is early in the morning or late in the afternoon, and rainbows often appear near sunset. This .9km (.5-mile) path takes 1 to 2 hours, starting at the viewing tower and leading past **Dos Hermanas (Two Sisters), Bossetti, Chico (Small), Ramírez,** and **San Martín** (the park's widest) falls. You can come right to the edges of these falls and look over them as they fall as far as 60m (197 ft.) below. Along your walk, you can also look across to San Martín Island and the Brazilian side, and you'll pass a number of small streams and creeks.

The 1.8km (1.25-mile) **Lower Circuit** takes 2 hours to walk, leading you first past **Lanusse** and **Alvar Núñez** falls, then along the Lower Iguazú River past the raging **Dos Mosqueteros (Two Musketeers)** and **Tres Mosqueteros (Three Musketeers)** falls. The trail winds its way toward **Ramírez, Chico,** and **Dos Hermanas** falls. Here, you'll find an inspiring view of the **Garganta del Diablo (Devil's Throat)** and **Bossetti** falls. From the Salto Bossetti waterfall, a small pathway leads down to a small pier, where you can catch a free boat to **San Martín Island.**

Once on the island, climb the stairs and walk along clearly marked trails for remarkable views of the surrounding *cataratas* (falls). To the left, you see the enormous **Garganta del Diablo, Saltos Brasileros (Brazilian Falls),** and **Ventana;** to the right, you overlook the mighty **Salto San Martín,** which sprays 30m (98 ft.) high after hitting the river below. This panoramic view looks out at dozens of falls forming an arch before you. San Martín Island also has a small, idyllic beach perfect for sunbathing and swimming.

Garganta del Diablo is the mother of all waterfalls in Iguazú, visible from observation points in both the Brazilian and Argentine parks. You'll notice that the water is calm as it makes its way down the Iguazú River, then begins to speed up as it approaches the gorge ahead. In front of you, Mother Nature has created a furious avalanche of water and spray that is the highest waterfall in Iguazú and one of the world's greatest natural spectacles. You might want to bring a raincoat, because you will get wet.

Outdoor Activities

INSIDE THE PARK The park's official tour operator is **Iguazú Jungle Explorer** (**© 3757/421-696;** www.iguazujunglexplorer.com), located both inside the national park and in the Sheraton Internacional Iguazú (p. 120). This company offers the Nautical Adventure tour (A$100), which visits the falls by inflatable raft; the Ecological Tour (A$50), which takes you to Devil's Throat and lets you paddle rubber boats along the Upper Iguazú Delta; and the Gran Aventura (Great Adventure) tour (A$200). This last tour begins with an 8km (5-mile) safari ride along the Yacoratia Path, the original dirt road that led through the forest and on to Buenos Aires. During the ride, you'll view the jungle's extensive flora and might catch a glimpse of some of the region's indigenous wildlife. You will then disembark at Puerto Macuco, where you'll hop into an inflatable boat with your tour group and navigate 6.5km (4 miles) along the lower Iguazú River, braving 1.6km (1 mile) of rapids as you approach the falls in Devil's Throat Canyon. After a thrilling and wet ride, the raft lets you off across from San Martín Island. From there, catch a free boat to this island with excellent hiking trails and a small beach for swimming and sunbathing. You can combine the Ecological Tour and Great Adventure by buying a full-day Pasaporte Verde for A$230. An increasingly popular tour is a guided walk around the falls under a full moon, where nighttime rainbows appear.

If you want to arrange a private adventure tour for your specific interests, the best outfit is **Explorador Expediciones,** with offices in the Sheraton Internacional Iguazú and in Puerto Iguazú at Perito Moreno 217 (**© 3757/421-632**). The guides are experts on life in the Iguazú jungle. A jungle safari costs A$150 (including mineral water and wildlife literature) and an excursion to the waterfall is A$120, plus the park admission fee. English guides are available, and tours last 2 hours.

OUTSIDE THE PARK **Jungle Fly,** Selva Iriapú s/n (**© 3757/423-330;** reservas@laaldeadelaselva.com), is based in the jungle lodge La Aldea de la Selva, 7km (4 miles) outside town. They specialize in zip-lining and rappelling. **Yguazu Extreme,** Santuario Sta. Maria (**© 3757/423-660;** sanmartin_locations@hotmail.com), also organizes rock climbing and boat excursions on the Parana River. **Iguazú Forest,** Mariano Moreno 58, Puerto Iguazú (**© 3757/421-140;** www.iguazuforest.com), will show you how to climb a waterfall in a nature reserve 7km (4 miles) south of the town while learning more about the birds and butterflies in the area. **Iguazú Adventure** (**© 3757/15-679-475**) is in front of the Hotel Cataratas and combines a *doble aventura* of horseback riding and hiking, and a visit to the indigenous reserve Yriapu. **Cabalgatas Ecológicas** (**© 3757/421-543;** www.cabalgatasecologicas.com) conducts 2-hour horseback jungle excursions that

Border Crossing

Citizens from the United States, Canada, and Australia all must obtain a visa (p. 233) to enter the Brazilian side of the falls, whether for 1 day or 90 days. On the ground, however, some local officials, hotel concierges, tourist agencies, and taxi companies ignore this rule and take you across without formalities. But rules are rules, and it is illegal to enter a country without the proper papers. If you truly want to see the Brazilian side of Iguazú Falls, my advice is to get a visa.

This can be done at short notice in Puerto Iguazú. Visit the Brazilian Consulate, Av. Córdoba 264 (© **3757/421-348**), Monday to Friday 8am to 1pm. The process takes 2 hours and requires a passport.

cost A$80. **Iguazú Water Sports,** Town Port, Puerto Iguazú (© **3757/556-932**), organizes all-day fishing excursions, including riverside *asados* (barbecues), as well as other watersports.

WHERE TO STAY

Puerto Iguazú has witnessed a hotel boom in recent years, with some excellent budget options in the town and more upscale operations appearing on the road to the park. Peak season for hotels in Iguazú extends through January and February (summer holiday) and also includes July (winter break), Semana Santa (Holy Week, the week before Easter), and long weekends.

Expensive

Hotel Cataratas ★ Kids None of the stuffiness you sometimes feel at luxury hotels is evident here. Despite the hotel's unimpressive exterior, rooms are among the most modern and spacious in the area—especially the 30 "master rooms" that feature two double beds, handsome wood furniture, colorful artwork, large bathrooms with separate toilet rooms, and views of the pool or gardens. The hotel's many facilities make this a great choice for families. The hotel lies 4km (2½ miles) from the center of Puerto Iguazú and 17km (11 miles) from the national park entrance. Bus service is available.

RN 12, Km 4, 3370 Misiones. © **3757/421-100.** Fax 3757/421-090. www.hotelcataratas.com. 130 units. $109 double standard; from $189 suite. Rates include buffet breakfast. AE, DC, MC, V. Free parking. **Amenities:** Restaurant; concierge; putting green; gymnasium; Jacuzzi; outdoor pool; room service; spa; tennis court; Wi-Fi. *In room:* A/C, TV, hair dryer, minibar.

Iguazú Grand Hotel Resort & Casino ★ Kids This large, red-brick, mansion-style hotel sits on a low slope with lawns running down to an attractive pool area. The lobby is stunning and elegant, with white pillars and sparkling marble floors. All rooms are huge, almost suite sized. Even the junior suites have 40 sq. m (431 sq. ft.) worth of impeccable decor, stylish period furniture, and ample light. All the bathtubs have a hydromassage. The hotel grounds are delightful and the breakfast buffet is superb.

RN 12, Km 1640, 3370 Puerto Iguazú. © **3757/498-050**. www.casinoiguazu.com. 120 units. $253 junior suite; $342 garden suite. Rates include buffet breakfast. AE, DC, MC, V. **Amenities:** Restaurant; babysitting; casino; concierge; putting green; health club; 3 outdoor pools; room service; spa; tennis court. *In room:* A/C, TV, hair dryer, minibar.

Sheraton Internacional Iguazú Overrated How on earth this typewriter-shaped bunker got to be built in a nature reserve is anybody's guess. The Sheraton enjoys a magnificent and exclusive location inside the national park (read: It's the *only* hotel inside the park). Guests have little need to leave the resort, and you have the added advantage of being able to explore the park when the daily crowds have left. Half of the guest rooms have direct views of the water (the others have splendid views of the jungle). The decor is fairly standard Sheraton-issue and service can be patchy.

Parque Nacional Iguazú, 3370 Misiones. ✆ **0800/888-9180** local toll-free, or 3757/491-800. Fax 3757/491-848. www.sheraton.com. 180 units. $351 double with jungle view; $424 double with view of waterfalls; from $563 suite. Rates include buffet breakfast. AE, DC, MC, V. Free parking. **Amenities:** 3 restaurants; babysitting; basketball court; concierge; fitness center; outdoor and indoor pools; room service; spa; 2 tennis courts; Wi-Fi. *In room:* A/C, TV, hair dryer, minibar.

Moderate

Boutique Hotel de la Fonte This is a small garden hotel with ample grounds and excellent food. From the street it looks like any well-to-do residential home, and, indeed, staying here feels like a weekend sojourn with your Argentine cousins. The rooms are a little old-fashioned, with low beds and heavy curtains, but it's the rambling garden that makes the place. The Italian owners are talented chefs, which comes through in the incredible menu that can be enjoyed in intimate corners of the garden. Boutique Hotel de la Fonte is located on a quiet, residential street just a 5-minute walk from the downtown area.

1 de Mayo and Corrientes s/n, Puerto Iguazú, Misiones. ✆ **3757/420-625.** www.bhfboutiquehotel.com. 8 units. $100 double; $140 double superior with Jacuzzi. Rates include buffet breakfast. AE, DC, MC, V. Free parking. **Amenities:** Restaurant; hot tub; outdoor pool; Wi-Fi. *In room:* A/C, TV, minibar.

Esturión Hotel & Lodge Hotel Esturión is spacious, well equipped, and just a 10-minute walk from the town center. The main building has the look of a modern, tropical schoolhouse and the huge pool and surrounding grounds have a Caribbean feel. Rooms are decent, if a little dated, and some have pleasant balconies. Service can be patchy, however, and do not expect much English.

Av. Tres Fronteras 650, 3370 Puerto Iguazú. ✆ **3757/420-100.** Fax 3757/421-468. www.hotelesturion.com. 128 units. $130 double; $160 suite. Rates include buffet breakfast. AE, DC, MC, V. Free parking. **Amenities:** Restaurant; bar; outdoor pool; Wi-Fi. *In room:* A/C, TV, minibar.

Hotel Saint George ★★ Finds The Saint George is a modern cream-colored property located on one of the town's principal streets. The newer master rooms are much larger than the old standard rooms and worth the extra $10. Sleek flatscreen TVs go nicely with the stylish black minibars, while outside you'll find a lush, ample courtyard with a large kidney-shaped pool. The bathrooms are big, with glass-enclosed showers and separate tubs. The family-owned hotel has one of the best restaurants in town, known as La Esquina.

Av. Córdoba 148, 3370 Puerto Iguazú. ✆ **3757/420-633.** Fax 3757/420-651. www.hotelsaintgeorge.com. 100 units. $154 double; $168 suite. Rates include both dinner and breakfast. AE, DC, MC, V. Free parking. **Amenities:** Restaurant; Jacuzzi; outdoor pool; sauna; Wi-Fi. *In room:* A/C, TV, minibar.

La Aldea de la Selva ★ A sleek wooden walkway leads you through the jungle to this stylish and comfortable boutique hotel that is conveniently located 7km (4 miles) from downtown Puerto Iguazú on the way to the falls. A brilliant blue terraced pool with three levels is surrounded by a wooden deck and greenery. The rooms have pine walls and teak flooring that lead to wide wraparound balconies with thick wooden rails you can lean on—where you can literally reach out and touch the jungle. The bathrooms are immaculate and luxurious, with tiled walls and gleaming-white wash bowls and tubs.

Selva Iriapú s/n, Puerto Iguazú, Misiones. ✆ **3757/425-777.** www.laaldeadelaselva.com. 8 units. $105 double. Rates include buffet breakfast. AE, DC, MC, V. Free parking. **Amenities:** Restaurant; outdoor pool; Wi-Fi. *In room:* A/C, TV, minibar.

Inexpensive

Hosteria Los Helechos *Value* This is the best budget choice located in the heart of town. The pale-yellow building has a simple design but a cozy feel, with wooden window frames looking in on a large lobby complete with a tropical fish tank. The rooms are pretty basic, but some have windows framed in greenery overlooking a plant-filled courtyard.

Paulino Amarante 76, 3370 Puerto Iguazú. ✆/fax **3757/420-338.** www.hosterialoshelechos.com.ar. 60 units. $68 double. AE, DC, MC, V. Free parking. **Amenities:** Restaurant; bar; computer w/Internet in lobby; pool. *In room:* A/C, TV.

Hotel Lilian *Value* Somewhat stark and plain and eerily quiet during the day, the Hotel Lilian is a budget hotel perfectly suitable for budget travelers just passing through for a night or two. Situated on a quiet residential street that is 5 minutes from downtown, it has a big light-filled lobby and rooms that are somewhat small and dark, yet clean and comfortable. The staff is a little shy, which all adds to the hotel's low-key vibe.

Fray Luis Beltran 183, 3370 Puerto Iguazú. ✆/fax **3757/420-968**. hotelliliana@yahoo.com.ar. 24 units. $47 double. Rates include breakfast. No credit cards. Free parking. **Amenities:** Computer w/Internet in lobby. *In room:* A/C, TV.

Residencial Uno Hostel This big, rambling building has basic rooms that come in doubles and dorms. The lobby is dark, cool, and spacious, and outside there is a large garden with a good-size pool. The helpful owners Valeria and Dayan speak good English and the hostel is located on a quiet residential street 5 minutes from the town center.

Beltran 116, Puerto Iguazú. ✆ **3757/420-529.** 23 units. $26 double; $32 double with A/C and TV. Rates include breakfast. AE, DC, MC, V. Free parking. **Amenities:** Bar; pool; Wi-Fi.

Timbó Posada *Finds* This miniature hostel is for those who like a touch of jungle charm. A tiny lobby leads to a beautiful garden, a small pool, and hammocks hanging amid greenery in front of a lovely wooden veranda. Everything is small, compact, and shady, including the rooms and their tiny, basic bathrooms. It is located close to the bars of Calle Brazil.

Av. Misiones 157, Puerto Iguazú. ✆/fax **3757/422-698.** www.timboiguazu.com.ar. 5 units. $50 double. AE, DC, MC, V. Free parking. **Amenities:** Restaurant; bar; pool; Wi-Fi.

WHERE TO DINE

Dining in Puerto Iguazú is casual and inexpensive, provided you look for a meal outside your hotel. Meat, pasta, and pizza are the standard fare, and that does not change much between venues. Take advantage of the good river fish you find in the area, mainly *surubí,* pacu, and dorada, although availability depends on the season.

El Quincho del Tío Querido ★★ Bonpland 110, at Perito Moreno (✆ **3757/420-151**) is in the heart of town and serves excellent *parrilla* and fresh river fish such as dorado or *surubí,* along with live music. Main courses start at A$45. **El Charo,** Av. Córdoba 106 (✆ **3757/421-529**), is large and somewhat soulless, yet produces delicious food such as breaded veal, sirloin steaks, pork chops, catfish, and items from the *parrilla.* It is tremendously popular with tourists and locals alike. Main courses range from A$30

Esteros del Ibera

Esteros del Ibera is a 13,000-sq.-km (5,019-sq.-mile) trough of remarkable wildlife running up the middle of Corrientes, the next province south of Misiones. Dominated by two lakes, Laguna de Luna and Laguna Ibera, it is a morass of waterways and vegetation, with wide-open spaces perfect for spotting abundant wildlife like storks, cormorants, kingfishers, capybaras, caimans, howler monkeys, and anacondas. Spectacular sunsets are just the opening act to incredible night skies, and the utter peace and tranquillity demand that you stay for at least 2 or 3 days.

Most people choose to stay in the sleepy settlement of **Colonia Carlos Pellegrini. Posada de la Laguna** (✆ **3773/499-413;** www.posadadelalaguna.com) is a simple, hacienda-style house with beautifully decorated rooms. Doubles start at $150 per night. **Hosteria Ñandé Retá** (✆ **3773/499-411;** www.nandereta.com) is a little more old-fashioned but has lots of space. **Posada Aguape** (✆ **11/4742-3015** in Buenos Aires, or 3773/499-412 in Corrientes; www.iberaesteros.com.ar) is an upscale facility comprised of four houses with a lakeside location. Here you can stay for 3 days and 2 nights, food and excursions included, for $384 per person. **Lodge Irupé** (✆ **3752/438-312;** www.irupelodge.com.ar) has palm-fronded wood cabins with large decks to enjoy the sunset. Here a double room costs $90.

Like many of Argentina's most fascinating places, getting here can be a problem. There are direct flights from Buenos Aires to Corrientes city and Posadas, but a 5-hour transfer to the park is still required. Colonia Carlos Pellegrini itself is 740km (460 miles) from B.A. You can catch an overnight 8-hour bus from Buenos Aires to Mercedes, which is the nearest large town. Recommended bus companies are **Aguila Dorada Bis** (✆ **11/4311-3700**) and **El Cometa** (✆ **11/4313-7872**). Tickets cost A$150 from Buenos Aires to Mercedes, and the journey takes 8 hours. From Mercedes, you can organize a private transport through your hotel to Colonia Carlos Pellegrini, which is 120km (75 miles) away and takes 3 hours. **El Rayo** (✆ **3773/420-184**) operates a daily minibus service between Colonia Pellegrini and Mercedes costing A$15. It is possible to drive there from Puerto Iguazú or Posadas, but the journey is best done in a 4WD vehicle.

to A$80. **La Rueda** ★, Av. Córdoba 28 (✆ **3757/422-531**), is a small A-frame house with an outdoor patio and casual atmosphere. The diverse menu features pasta, steaks, and fish dishes. Try the *surubí brochette,* a local whitefish prepared with bacon, tomatoes, onions, and peppers, and served with green rice and potatoes. Main courses range from A$30 to A$60.

Color, Av. Córdoba 135 (✆ **3757/420-206**), is one of Iguazú's most popular restaurants and is jammed at night, mostly with tourists. The large and airy indoor part is modern and attractive and there is a street-side courtyard. Try the Argentine favorite *milanesa*—a thick slab of grilled beef or chicken dipped in bread crumbs. Main courses range from A$40 to A$90. **Gustos del Litoral** ★, Av. Misiones 209 (no phone), is a tiny sidewalk restaurant with lots of character offering local river dishes such as *paçu* fish with lemon sauce and saffron-flavored rice. Main courses cost between A$35 and A$60.

PUERTO IGUAZU AFTER DARK

Although it has improved somewhat in recent years, Puerto Iguazú's nightlife is nothing to get your disco flares in a twist about. Most of the bigger restaurants stage live traditional music on weekends, while a series of new bars has popped up along Avenida Brasil, offering late-night alfresco drinking. The slickest of these disco bars is **Jackie Brown,** Av. Brasil 180 (✆ **3757/421-208**). The designer white seating inside goes well with the designer chrome seating outside. This place rocks to techno all weekend until 5am, with a more eclectic mix of pop during the week. Across the street is the more laid-back **La Tribu** ★, Av. Brasil 155 (✆ **3757/421-794**), with tropical Latin beats reverberating around a stylish deck and inside bar with black leather seating. It is open every day from 6pm to 2am. Even more chilled out is **Puerto Bambu,** Av. Brasil 96 (✆ **3757/421-900**). This is a large corner bar with a giant bamboo veranda and a reggae music list that goes well with frequent happy hours. It is open every day from 5pm to 3am. **Cuba Libre,** at Paraguay and Brazil (no phone; cubalibre_iguazu@yahoo.com.ar), has been around the longest and plays tropical beats until late.

6 MENDOZA

710km (440 miles) NW of Buenos Aires; 721km (447 miles) SW of Córdoba

Give yourself time to linger in Mendoza's cafes, plazas, and many fantastic restaurants. This is a city that lives life outdoors, with many public places, cafes, and street-side restaurants that bustle from noon to night. Argentina's loveliest city is in fact an artificial oasis surrounded by desert. A scarce commodity, water is celebrated in the trickling fountains of the city's many lovely plazas, in the shade of the dike-supported trees that line the boulevards, and in the tranquil nature of the residents who reap the benefits of the centuries-old roadside canal system.

Several days trying wine in this garden city will make you curious to see where it comes from. Mendoza has some of the most dramatic wine country in the world, all within 30 minutes of the city. Snow-capped mountains tower over lush vineyards. Leafy lanes hide quaint rustic wineries and olive houses. Modern, high-tech temples to wine offer gourmet cuisine and luxury lodgings. There is plenty for the adventure seeker, too. World-class ski resorts compete with rafting camps for adrenaline junkies, while Mount Aconcagua sits loftily in the background, the highest mountain outside the Himalayas and a place of pilgrimage every year for thousands of ambitious mountain climbers.

ESSENTIALS

Getting There

BY PLANE Mendoza's international airport, **Francisco Gabrielli** (also known as El Plumerillo; airport code MDZ; ✆ **261/520-6000**), lies 8km (5 miles) north of town on Ruta 40. **Aerolíneas Argentinas** (✆ **0810/222-86527;** www.aerolineas.com.ar) offers seven daily arrivals from Buenos Aires. On Monday mornings, a flight departs from Ezeiza International Airport. **LAN** (✆ **0810/999-9526;** www.lan.com) flies to Mendoza from both Buenos Aires (two times a day) and from Santiago, Chile, once in the morning and once in the evening. If Mendoza is your first destination in Argentina, it is much more convenient to fly in via Santiago as it requires no airport change in Santiago, whereas in Buenos Aires you must take a one hour taxi ride from the international airport to the domestic airport.

BY BUS The **Terminal del Sol** (✆ **261/431-3001**), or central bus station, lies just east of central Mendoza. Buses travel to Buenos Aires (12–14 hr.; A$215); Córdoba (12 hr.; A$166); Santiago, Chile (7 hr.; A$90); Las Leñas (7 hr.; A$40); and other cities throughout the region. **Chevallier** (✆ **261/431-0235**), **Expreso Uspallata** (✆ **261/421-3309**), and **Andesmar** (✆ **261/431-0585**) are the main bus companies.

BY CAR The route from Buenos Aires is a long (10 hr.), easy, but boring drive on either the RN 7 or the RN 8. Mendoza is more easily reached by car from Santiago, Chile, along the RN 7, although the dramatic 250km (155-mile) trek through the Andes can be treacherous in winter, when chains are required and the border tunnel is often closed for several days. Give yourself 6 to 7 hours to make the journey from Santiago.

Getting Around

You can easily explore central Mendoza on foot, although you will want to hire a driver or rent a car to visit the wine roads and tour the mountains. Taxis and *remises* (private, unmetered taxis) are inexpensive: Drivers cost no more than A$38 per hour. Traditionally Mendoza is one of Argentina's safest cities, but it has experienced an increase in crime, especially bag snatching. For a *remise,* try **La Veloz Del Este** (✆ **261/423-9090**) or **Mendocar** (✆ **261/423-6666**). For a taxi, call **Radiotaxi** (✆ **261/430-3300**).

If you do rent a car, parking is easy and inexpensive inside the city, with paid parking meters and private lots (called *playas*) clearly marked. The easy-to-navigate city spreads out in a clear grid pattern around Plaza Independencia. Outside the city, road signs are sometimes missing or misleading. The main highways are Highway 40, which runs north-south and will take you to Maipú and Luján de Cuyo, and Highway 7, which runs east-west and will take you to the Alta Montaña Route.

Both **Budget** (✆ **261/425-3114;** www.budget.com) and **Hertz Annie Millet** (✆ **261/448-2327;** www.hertz.com) rent cars at Mendoza's airport. Expect to pay about $55 per day for a compact car with insurance and 200km (124 miles) included. **AutoMendoza** (✆ **261/420-0022;** www.automendoza.com), a locally run company, has flexible rates and will drop a car off wherever you need it. Rates start at $45 per day. You'll get a better deal if you pay in cash. Regular buses depart from various stops in town to the outlying wine areas, but the routes are unfathomable. El Trole, an old-fashioned tram, is fun and cheap, at A$1.20 per ride. It's an easy way to get up to Parque San Martín and back, but exact change is required.

Visitor Information

Mendoza's **Subsecretaría Provincial de Turismo,** Av. San Martín 1143 (✆ **261/420-2800**), is open daily from 9am to 9pm. **Municipal tourist offices,** called Centros de Información, are at Garibaldi near San Martín (✆ **261/423-8745;** daily 8am–1pm), 9 de Julio 500 (✆ **261/420-1333;** Mon–Fri 9am–9pm), and Las Heras 340 (✆ **261/429-6298;** Mon–Fri 9am–1:30pm and 3–7:30pm). They provide city maps, hotel information, and brochures of tourist activities. You will find small visitor information booths at the airport and bus station as well. Information and permits for Aconcagua Provincial Park are available at the **Centro de Informes del Parques,** in Mendoza's Parque San Martín (✆ **261/420-5052**). The office is only open during the climbing season, from

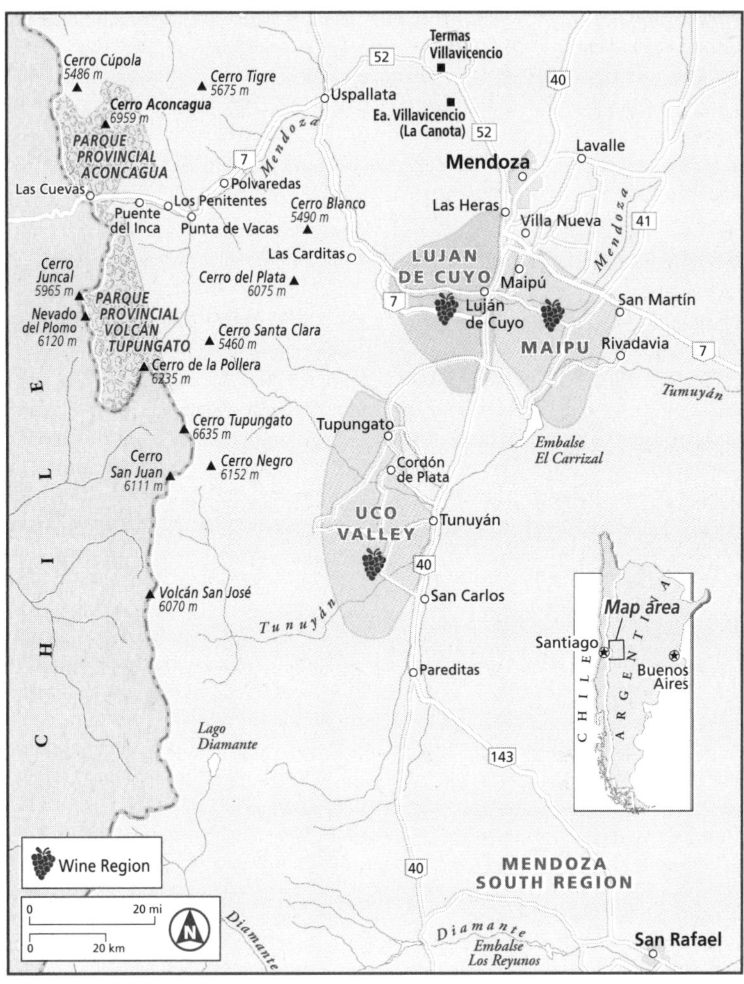

December through March. During the rest of the year, you must contact the **Subsecretaría Provincial de Recursos Naturales** (✆ **261/425-2090/425-8751**). Permits to climb the summit cost A$600 in the months of November and February and A$1,200 to A$1,800 in the high-season months of December, January, and the beginning of February. You must go in person with your passport to obtain one. In addition, several websites offer useful tourist information: **www.turismo.mendoza.gov.ar**, **www.aconcagua.mendoza.gov.ar**, and **www.wine-republic.com** (the latter is also a free bimonthly publication, in English, available all around the city).

FAST FACTS Two reliable exchange houses, both at the corner of San Martín and Catamarca, are **Maguitur** (✆ **261/425-1575**) and **Cambio Santiago** (✆ **261/420-0277**).

 They are open Monday through Friday from 8:30am to 1pm and from 5 to 8:30pm, and Saturday from 9:30am to 1pm. Major banks, with ATMs that have Cirrus and PLUS access, are located around the Plaza San Martín and along Avenida Sarmiento, including **Citibank,** Av. Sarmiento 20 (✆ **261/449-6519**).

For an **ambulance,** dial ✆ **107** or 261/424-8000; for **police,** dial ✆ **101** or 261/429-4444; in case of **fire,** dial ✆ **100. Hospital Central** (✆ **261/420-0600**) is near the bus station at Salta and Alem.

Internet access in most places costs A$2 per hour. The main post office, **Correo Argentino** (✆ **261/429-0848**), is at the corner of Avenida San Martín and Colón. It's open Monday to Friday from 8am to 8pm.

WHAT TO SEE & DO

In Town

Plaza Independencia ★★ marks the city center, a beautiful square with pergolas, fountains, frequent artesian fairs, and cultural events. Following the 1861 earthquake, the new city was rebuilt around this area. Four additional plazas—San Martín, Chile, Italia, and España—are located 2 blocks off each corner of Independence Square. At the center of the square you will find the Julio Quintanilla Theater and the small **Modern Art Museum** (✆ **261/425-7279;** admission A$3.80). On opposite corners of the plaza is the Independencia Theater and the Provincial Legislature. Adjacent to the Alameda, a beautiful promenade under white poplars, **Museo Histórico General San Martín** ★, Remedios Escalada de San Martín 1843 (✆ **261/428-7947**), pays homage to Argentina's beloved hero, who prepared his liberation campaigns from Mendoza. It's open Monday to Friday from 9:30am to 5pm and Saturday 10:30am to 1pm; admission costs A$3. Another museum worth visiting is **Museo Fundacional** ★★, Videla Castillo between Beltrán and Alberdi (✆ **261/425-6927**), 3km (2 miles) from downtown. Chronicling the early history of Mendoza, it's a little short of real artifacts. It's open Tuesday through Saturday from 8am to 8pm, Sunday from 3 to 8pm; admission is A$5. Something quirky to consider is **Museo de Motos Antiguas,** San Juan 646 (✆ **261/429-1469**), a private collection of old motorbikes, including a Che Guevara replica. It's open Monday through Friday 8:30am to 12:30pm and 5 to 8:30pm; admission is A$5.

Almost as big as the city itself, the wonderful **Parque General San Martín** ★★★ has 17km (11 miles) of idyllic pathways and 300 species of plants and trees. A tourist office, near the park's main entrance at avenidas Emilio Civit and Bologne Sur Mer, provides information on all park activities, which include boating, camping, horseback riding (outside the park's perimeters), hang gliding, and hiking. The best hike leads to the top of **Cerro de la Gloria,** which offers a panoramic view of the city and surrounding valley. You can also catch regular minibus tours to the hill if you don't feel like walking. Check out the natural history museum, **Museo Moyano** (✆ **261/428-7666;** admission A$4), the boat-shaped building at the end of the lake. Here you'll find fascinating exhibits, on topics such as giant condors, in a superb building that sorely needs renovating. The museum is open Tuesday to Friday 8am to 1pm and 2 to 7pm, Saturday and Sunday 3 to 7pm. A **zoo** (daily 9am–6pm; admission A$10) is also located inside the park.

Touring the Wineries

Mendoza offers some of the most stunning wine country in the world, with vineyards dominated by a breathtaking backdrop of the snowcapped Andes. The wineries are very spread out but accessible along wine roads known locally as Los Caminos del Vino. These roads are as enticing as the wine itself, weaving and winding through tunnels of trees to vast dry valleys, punctuated by fruit orchards and olive groves. Some roads climb as high as 1,524m (5,000 ft.) in Valle de Uco, while others lead to lower-level vineyards in Maipú. There are over 900 wineries surrounding Mendoza, and numerous wine-growing regions. The most important for visitors are Lujan de Cuyo, Valle de Uco, and Maipú. Different wine roads branch out through these and it is very easy to get lost. Three hundred wineries formally offer tours, but in reality less than 60 have an efficient setup to accept visitors, such as available guides and tasting rooms. The most and the best require prebooking at set times. Most now charge admission of at least A$15, with extra charges if you want to try the better wines.

Lujan de Cuyo is known as La Primera Zone. It is the home of Malbec and where Argentina's most prestigious wineries—both old and knew—are located. It is situated 17km (11 miles) south of the city to the west of the Route 40, hugging the wide, dry Río Mendoza. Here you'll find Chacras de Coria, a beautiful leafy neighborhood where many of Mendoza's most luxurious wine lodges are located. There are a multitude of wineries to visit in Lujan and it is impossible to list them all; the following are my favorites. **Alta Vista,** Alzaga 3972 (✆ **261/496-4684;** admission A$10), is a masterful mix of old and new and produces excellent Malbec and Torrontes. **Achaval Ferrer,** Calle Cobos 2601 (✆ **261/488-1131**), is Argentina's star boutique winery, winning accolades around the world for some very fine blends. **Lagarde,** Ave. San Martín 1745 (✆ **261/498-0011**), has 120-year-old vines and a tiny champagne operation. **Tapiz,** RP15, Agrelo (✆ **261/490-0202**), gives a marvelous tank and barrel tasting and vineyard tour. **Ruca Malen,** RN7, Agrelo (✆ **261/425-7279**), does the best winery lunch in the Southern Hemisphere. **Pulenta Estate,** Ruta 86 (✆ **261/420-0800**), is slick and modern and makes incredible wines. **Clos de Chacras,** Monte Libano, Chacras (✆ **261/496-1285**), is charming and quaint and within walking distance of Chacras plaza.

Valle de Uco is the new frontier in Argentine wine, a high-altitude wine region pushing against the Andes. It is 90 minutes south of Mendoza and definitely worth a visit for its seductive rural atmosphere and dramatic scenery. **O. Fournier,** Los Indios, La Consulta (✆ **261/451-088**), is a modernist masterpiece producing rich Tempranillos and exquisite lunches. **Salentein,** Tupungato (✆ **2622/423-550**), must be visited for its templelike cellar and ultramodern visitor center with art gallery. **Andeluna,** RP89, Gualtallary, Tupungato (✆ **261/429-9299**), has a marvelous old-world-style tasting room and premium wines. **Finca La Celia,** Avenida De Circunvalación, San Carlos (✆ **261/413-4400**), is one of Mendoza's oldest wineries.

Maipú is the closest wine region to the city, 15 minutes away by taxi or bus. Popular for bike tours and large coach tours, it is a big region, with many wineries. The northern part is urban and ugly, but the southern area is beautiful. **Rutini,** Montecaseros 2625, Coquimbito (✆ **261/497-2013**), can be very touristy but has a fascinating wine museum. **Tempus Alba,** Perito Moreno 572 (✆ **261/481-3501**), is more intimate and modern, with a beautiful roof terrace. **Carinae,** Videla Arande 2899, Cruz de Piedra (✆ **261/499-0470**), is small and charming, and its tour is often conducted by the engaging French owners. **Zuccardi,** RP33 Km 7.5 (✆ **261/441-0000**), has excellent tours and delicious barbecue-style lunches amid the vines.

Organized wine tours vary greatly in quality, from run-of-the-mill urban tours with large groups and bad wines to more expensive, personalized excursions with gourmet lunches. **Ampora Wine Tours,** Sarmiento 647 (✆ **261/429-2931;** www.mendozawinetours.com), does quality day tours of all the regions. **Uncorking Argentina,** P. de la Reta

 992 (✆ **261/155-103230;** www.uncorkingargentina.com), offers custom-made tours with small groups.

On the first weekend of every March, Mendoza celebrates the **Fiesta Nacional de la Vendimia (National Wine Harvest Festival).** This includes parades, concerts, folk dancing, and a final, spectacular night during which the festival's queen is crowned. For information on the festival events, the wineries, and Mendoza in general, check out **www.wine-republic.com**, the Web's version of a free bimonthly magazine available around the city.

Outdoor Activities

Turismo Uspallata, Las Heras 699 (✆ **261/438-1092;** www.turismouspallata.com), runs trips to rural *estancias* and sells bus transfers to all the surrounding areas, including San Rafael and Valle de Uco. **Cordon de Plata,** Patricias Mendocinas 1429, Mendoza (✆ **261/423-7423;** www.cordondelplata.com), arranges single- or multiday hiking trips and a day of horseback riding in the Andes with an Argentine barbecue.

Argentina Rafting Expediciones, Amigorena 86 (✆ **261/429-6325;** www.argentina rafting.com), and **Ríos Andinos,** Sarmiento 784, Mendoza (✆ **261/429-5030;** www.riosandinos.com.ar), offer rafting trips ★ from their bases close to Potrerillos lake, 90 minutes west of the city. Grade IV and V rafting on the Mendoza River is possible in the summer months of January and February. Once a month, full moon rafting trips occur, with nightly forays down the river finishing with a lively party. These rafting companies also offer kayaking, trekking, and horseriding trips in the area.

A DAY TRIP TO ACONCAGUA PROVINCIAL PARK

A long sojourn in Mendoza is not complete without taking a trip up through the Andes as far as the Chilean border. This popular excursion is known locally as *Alta Montaña* and involves a 3-hour drive through spectacular mountain scenery to **Aconcagua Provincial Park**, where you can spy the highest mountain outside the Himalayas—Mt. Aconcagua, just shy of 7,000m (22,960 ft.) and an increasingly popular climb. The park is officially open from November to April but it is possible to reach the entrance, where you can see the snow-capped peak, all year round. Other attractions along the way include **Puente del Inca**, a naturally formed bridge over a ravine, **Penitentes Ski Resort**, and **Uspallata**, a mountain town set in a lush green valley. Tour operators **Turismo Uspallata,** Las Heras 699 (✆ **261/438-1092;** www.turismouspallata.com) and **Cordon de Plata,** Patricias Mendocinas 1429, Mendoza (✆ **261/423-7423;** www.cordondelplata.com), arrange day trips to the park with guides, but be warned, it is a long day, starting at 7am and returning to Mendoza at 8pm.

SHOPPING

On Friday, Saturday, and Sunday, an outdoor **handicrafts market** takes place during the day on Plaza Independencia, as do smaller fairs in Plaza España, Las Heras, Belgrano, and along Calle Mitre. Regional shops selling handicrafts, leather goods, gaucho paraphernalia, and *mate* tea gourds line Avenida Las Heras. For high-quality leather, visit **Alain de France,** Andrade 101 (✆ **261/428-5065**). More mainstream stores line Avenida San Martín, and Calle Arístides Villanueva is home to upscale fashion boutiques. The city's best shopping mall is **Palmares Open Mall,** on Ruta Panamericana 2650 in Godoy Cruz (✆ **261/413-9100**). Also outside the city but worth the visit is a huge emporium of

South American handicrafts, **Ayllu,** Ruta Panamericana 8343 (© **261/496-1213;** www.aylluartepopular.com/ar). The city's main food hall is in the **Mercado Central**, on Las Heras and 9 de Julio. This leads to a warren of streets with stalls selling everything from pirated CDs to cowboy hats.

Most shops (except in the malls) close from 1 to 5pm each day for siesta. Some of the best wine boutiques in town include **Marcelinos,** Zapata and Benegas (© **261/429-3648**), and **Sol y Vino,** Sarmiento 664 (© **261/425-6005**). The larger, more conventional chain **Winery**, Chile 890 (© **261/420-2840**), has a good selection of the better-known brands.

WHERE TO STAY

A general boom in hotel building and a downturn in domestic tourism means there are now plenty of rooms here in all brackets, which should see prices come down. Apart-hotels are increasingly popular, and more than 40 hostels also dot downtown Mendoza.

Expensive

The **Park Hyatt Mendoza★★★**, Chile 1124 (© **261/441-1234;** www.mendoza.park.hyatt.com), peers majestically over Plaza Independencia and serves as the cultural heart of Mendoza. Doubles start at $248, but check their website for a 10% discount. **El Portal Suites,** Necochea 661 (©/fax **261/438-2038;** www.elportalsuites.com.ar), has comfortable suites with a clean and modern style and is an especially good option for families. Rates start at $93. **Hotel NH Cordillera,** Av. España 1324 (© **261/441-6464;** www.nh-hotels.com), caters to business travelers and has four floors of crisp, compact rooms, half of which face Plaza San Martín. Doubles start at $150. **Park Suites Apart Hotel,** Mitre 753 (© **261/413-1000;** www.parksuites.com.ar), is a stylish hotel 2 blocks from Plaza Independencia. Single rooms are called "suites," and each room has hardwood floors, a kitchenette, firm mattresses, and a stereo system. Rates start at $85. **Hotel Argentino ★★**, Espejo 455 (© **261/405-6300;** www.argentino-hotel.com), overlooks the Plaza Independencia and is a good value, with elegant and comfortable rooms starting at $94. **Posada de Rosas,** Martínez de Rosas 1641 (© **261/423-3629;** www.posadaderosas.com), is another attractive house with a gorgeous pool situated on a quiet residential street close to the park. Rooms start at $120. For a short-term luxury stay, try **Apartments Mendoza**, Leonidas Aguirre 175 (© **261/569-0079;** www.apartmentsmendoza.com). Rates start at $120.

Moderate

Deptos Mendoza, Leandro N. Alem 41 (© **261/1541-94844;** www.deptosmendoza.com.ar), is a sleek building of steel and brick that offers great value. The apartments are decorated with local art, with a focus on function and lighting. Rates start at $65. **Hotel Cervantes,** Amigorena 65 (© **261/520-0400;** www.hotelcervantesmza.com.ar), has been run by the Lopez family since 1945, and staff members are old-school hotel professionals. From the outside, the place is baroque and traditional with a lovely new garden out back and ample parking. Ask for a "special" room on the fourth floor for more space and style. Rates start at $65 for a double. **La Escondida Bed and Breakfast,** Julio A. Roca 344 (© **261/425-5202;** www.laescondidabb.com), is a family-run, friendly bed-and-breakfast in a pleasant and convenient neighborhood. All rooms have private bathrooms and a light and airy style, but some could do with updating. Insist on a room upstairs. Rooms start at $64.

Winery Lodges

Wine and dine yourself by staying at a luxury winery lodging in the nearby vineyards. The best is **Club Tapiz,** Ruta 60, Maipú (© **261/496-0131;** www.tapiz.com), a converted winery set amid 10 hectares (24 acres) of vineyards. **Finca Adalgisa,** Pueyrredon 2222, Chacras de Coria (© **261/496-0713;** www.fincaadalgisa.com.ar), is another excellent choice, with vineyards and an old family *bodega.* **Lares de Chacras,** Larrea 1266, Chacras de Coria (© **261/496-1061**), is a lovely stone lodge offering deluxe accommodation and an atmospheric wine cellar.

Inexpensive

Damajuana Hostel, Aristides Villanueva 282 (© **261/425-5858;** www.damajuanahostel.com.ar), is like a five-star resort at a rock-bottom price. This hostel is located in the heart of the happening Arístides district and has a huge pool, garden, and barbecue in the backyard. Bunk-bed rates start at $15. **Confluencia Hostel,** España 1512 (© **261/429-0430;** www.hostalconfluencia.com.ar), is one of those rare finds in Argentina, a hostel that doesn't pile them high like sardines. Confluencia has large, bright rooms for three, without a bunk bed in sight. Rooms start at $25.

WHERE TO DINE

Expensive

Francesco Ristorante ITALIAN Francesco is the most elegant and classy Italian restaurant in town. The meat and homemade pasta dishes are equally excellent. The option of combining three stuffed pastas lets you try some of the highlights. Don't miss the tiramisu for dessert. Service is seriously professional here, down to the doting sommelier. The outdoor garden is romantic and lovely, especially on a summer evening.

Chile 1268 (Espejo and Gutiérrez), Mendoza. © **261/429-7182.** www.francescoristorante.com.ar. Reservations recommended. Main courses A$40–A$60. AE, MC, V. Daily 7:30pm–1am.

Moderate

Ana Bistro *Moments* ARGENTINE An attractive, roomy restaurant, Ana Bistro exudes modernity and style. Here you'll find armchairs and sofas spread across wooden platforms and a fragrant garden with a bamboo-covered patio. Dishes include delicious stir-fried chicken and trout *empanadas.* It's a great place for afternoon cocktails.

Av. Juan B. Justo 161. © **261/425-1818.** Dinner reservations recommended. Main courses A$30–A$45. AE, MC, V. Tues–Sun 11am–1am.

Azafrán ★ *Finds* INTERNATIONAL The food here is imaginative, fresh, and eclectic. You may start with the house specialty—a platter of smoked meats and cheeses. For entrees, the rabbit ravioli in champagne sauce is delicate and unusual, and the vegetables and tofu baked in a puff pastry will please any vegetarian. The wood tables and vintage checkered floors give you a sense of dining in an old farmhouse.

Sarmiento 765 (Belgrano and Perú). © **261/429-4200.** Reservations recommended. Main courses A$35–A$45. AE, MC, V. Mon–Sat 11am–1am.

Mi Tierra ARGENTINE This "thematic restaurant" is tucked inside an old townhouse, each room presenting the wines of a different local vineyard. The menu offers local specialties such as goat, young pork, wild boar, and rabbit. The pastas are excellent. For dessert, try the Chardonnay parfait.

Mitre 794 (Pueyrredón and General Lamadrid). ✆ **261/425-0035.** Reservations recommended. Main courses A$35–A$45. AE, MC, V. Daily noon–3:30pm and 8:30pm–12:30am.

MENDOZA AFTER DARK

On any given night and especially in the summer, hundreds of the young and beautiful gather at one of the bars lining Aristides Villanueva in the center of town, before heading to the clubs in Chacras de Coria.

Start the night early at a local wine bar such as **The Vines of Mendoza,** Espejo 567 (✆ **261/438-1031**). The Park Hyatt Mendoza's **Bar Uvas,** Chile 1124 (✆ **261/441-1234**), offers a complete selection of Mendocino wines, a long list of cocktails, and live jazz and bossa nova groups playing most nights.

On Aristides Villanueva, try **Por Acá,** A. Villanueva 557 (no phone), for pizza and microbrewed beers; or **El Abasto,** A. Villanueva 308 (✆ **261/483-4232**), for good old rock 'n' roll. Nightclubs can be found on the principal avenue south to Godoy Cruz, 5 minutes by taxi. **Iskra,** San Martín 905 (✆ **261/15453-1038**), is popular and regularly jammed. **Geo,** San Martín Sur 576 (no phone), is another top disco in this area. Locals flock to **La Reserva,** Rivadavia 32 (✆ **261/420-3531**), on weekend nights for the drag show at midnight. The **Blah Blah Bar,** Paseo Peatonal Alameda, Escalada 2301 Maipú (✆ **261/429-7253**), is great for a late-night drink. ***Note:*** In an effort to keep their wild offspring from staying out so late, the Mendoza powers-that-be have demanded clubs close their doors at 2:30am, though those inside can dance until dawn.

7 SALTA & THE NORTHWEST ★

90km (56 miles) S of San Salvador de Jujuy; 1,497km (928 miles) N of Buenos Aires; 1,268km (786 miles) N of Mendoza

Red deserts, dusty adobe villages, and sparkling white churches are what you'll find in the northwestern part of Argentina. You might indeed think you were in Bolivia or Peru as you savor the indigenous flair of this historical place. Here you'll find the ruins of ancient civilizations—be it the terraced settlements of the Quilmes Indians or the mysterious standing stones of the Tafi tribe. You can gaze upon the wonderful baroque art and colonial splendor of Salta city. Time trips at a more rhythmic pace, like the hoof-clopping music *chacareras,* which pipes from every cafe and car. Salta city itself (pop. 500,000) is a sunny mix of colonial architecture; friendly, gracious people; colorful history; and indigenous pride. Conservative by nature, Salteños let their hair down during Carnaval (Mardi Gras), when thousands come out for a parade of floats celebrating the region's history. And here begins RN 40, that epic Andean roadway that forms the backbone of Argentina. In the Northwest alone it passes by vineyards, cactus hills, rainforests, tobacco fields, sugar-cane country, dinosaur parks, and vast empty salt plains. All this and more make the Northwest of Argentina the very heart of South America.

ESSENTIALS

Getting There

I don't recommend making the long-distance drive to Argentina's Northwest; it's safer and much easier to fly or take the bus, and hire a car when you get there.

BY PLANE Flights land at **Martín Miguel De Güemes International Airport,** RN 51 (airport code SLA; ✆ **387/424-2904**), 8km (5¼ miles) from the city center. **Aerolíneas Argentinas** (✆ **0810/222-86527** or 387/431-0862; www.aerolineas.com.ar) flies three times a day, at 7am, 2:40pm, and 6:30pm. **Andes Líneas Aéreas** (✆ **0810/122-26337** or 387/424-9214; www.andesonline.com) flies from Buenos Aires at 8am every day (some flights make a stop in Córdoba) and **LAN** (✆ **387/424-8881**; www.lan.com) flies twice a day, at midday and in the afternoon. Nonstop flights from Buenos Aires take 2 hours and cost between $190 and $210 each way, depending on the season and availability. A shuttle bus travels between the airport and town for about A$10 one-way; a taxi into town will run about A$22.

BY BUS The **Terminal de Omnibus,** or central bus station, is at Avenida H. Yrigoyen and Abraham Cornejo (✆ **387/401-1143**). Buses arrive from Buenos Aires (18 hr.; A$325) and travel to San Salvador de Jujuy (2hr.; A$28) and other cities in the region. **Chevalier** (✆ **387/431-2819**) and **La Veloz del Norte** (✆ **387/401-2164**) are the main bus companies.

Visitor Information

The tourism office, **Secretaría de Turismo de Salta,** Buenos Aires 93 (✆ **387/431-0950** or 431-0640; www.turismosalta.gov.ar), will provide you with maps and information on dining, lodging, and sightseeing in the region. It can also help you arrange individual or group tours. It's open every day from 9am to 9pm. In Buenos Aires, obtain information about Salta from the **Casa de Salta** in Buenos Aires, Sáenz Pena 933 (✆ **11/4326-1314**). It's open weekdays from 10am to 6pm.

FAST FACTS Exchange money at the airport, at **Dinar Exchange,** Mitre and España (✆ **387/432-2600;** Mon–Fri 9am–1:30pm and 5–8pm; Sat 10am–3pm), or at **Banco de La Nación,** Mitre and Belgrano (✆ **387/431-1909;** Mon–Fri 9am–2pm). Traveler's checks can be changed at **Masventas,** España 666 (✆ **387/431-0298;** www.masventas net.com.ar; Mon–Fri 9am–1:30pm and 5–8pm).

Dial ✆ **911** for police, ✆ **100** for fire, and ✆ **107** for an ambulance. The tourism police are located on Calle Mitre 23 (✆ **387/437-3199;** poltursalta@gobiernosalta.gov.ar).

Saint Bernard Hospital is at Dr. M. Boedo 69 (✆ **387/431-8320**).

Getting Around

Salta city is small and easy to explore on foot, but be careful; drivers here are pedestrian-blind, and the summer sun in the afternoon can be stifling. The **Peatonal Florida** is Salta's pedestrian walking street. The main sites are centered on **Plaza 9 de Julio,** with a monument to General Arenales in the center and a beautiful baroque cathedral at its edge.

BY BUS A great innovation is **Bus Turistico Salta,** 20 de Febrero 796 (✆ **387/422-7798;** www.busturisticosalta.com), a shuttle service that takes visitors around the city in high-tech open-top buses. You can get on and off from any of the 14 stops and get the next bus that comes along, on average, every 25 minutes. The service starts at 9:30am and carries on until 8pm (with a pause from 1–4pm for siesta). Tickets cost A$35 and can be bought on the bus when you board at any of the brightly painted stop signs.

RENTING A CAR **Noa Rent a Car,** Buenos Aires 1 Local 6 (✆ **387/431-0740**), has subcompacts and four-wheel-drives. **Rentacar Noroeste,** Buenos Aires 88, Local 10 (✆ **387/421-8999;** www.rentacarnoroeste.com.ar), is close by and offers reasonable rates. There are several car-rental offices on Caseros street and at the airport, most notably:

The Train to the Clouds

The **Tren a las Nubes (Train to the Clouds)** ★★★ is one of the world's great railroad experiences—a breathtaking ride that climbs to 4,220m (13,842 ft.) without the help of cable tracks. The journey takes you 434km (269 miles), through 21 tunnels and over 13 viaducts and 29 bridges, culminating in the stunning La Polvorilla viaduct. You will cross magnificent landscapes, making your way from the multicolored Lerma valley through the deep canyons and rugged peaks of the Quebrada del Toro and on to the desolate desert plateau of La Puña. The 15-hour ride includes a small breakfast, lunch, and a folkloric show with regional music and dance. The ride makes for a fascinating experience, but be prepared for a very long day, as departure is at 7am and the train returns at 11pm. Always check ahead, as cancellations are common.

For more information, contact **General Belgrano Train Station,** Ameghino and Balcarce (✆ **387/421-5658**), or **Tren a las Nubes Buenos Aires Office,** Av. Córdoba 650 (✆ **11/5246-6666;** www.trenalasnubes.com.ar). The train operates from April to November and departs from Salta's General Belgrano Station.

Tickets cost $120, including breakfast and lunch, and can be purchased at any of Salta's conventional travel agencies.

Hertz, Caseros 374 (✆ **387/421-6785**; www.hertz.com), and the airport (✆ **387/24-0113**); **Avis,** Caseros 420 (✆ **387/421-2181**; www.avis.com), and at the airport (✆ **387/424-2289**); and **Budget,** Caseros 421 (✆ **387/421-1953;** www.budget.com.ar). Rates range from $45 to $90 per day.

WHAT TO SEE & DO

Most museums in the Northwest don't have formal admission fees; instead, they request small contributions, usually A$4 or less. In general, they are open Tuesday through Sunday from 9am to 1pm and 5pm to 8pm.

Salta's cultural center **Casa de la Cultura,** Caseros 460 (✆ **387/421-5763;** www.culturasalta.gov.ar), is a hive of activity, staging art exhibitions, dance performances, music recitals, and theater plays. **El Cabildo/Museo Histórico del Norte,** Caseros 54 (✆ **387/421-5340;** www.museonor.gov.ar) was first erected in 1582 when the city was founded and has since reinvented itself a number of times. The latest town hall was completed in 1783 and houses the Museo Histórico del Norte (Historical Museum of the North), with 15 exhibition halls. **Iglesia San Francisco (San Francisco Church)** ★★, Córdoba and Caseros (no phone) is Salta's most prominent postcard image. The terracotta facade, with its 53m (174-ft.) tower and tiered white pillars, holds the Campana de la Patria, a bronze bell made from the cannons used in the War of Independence's Battle of Salta.

Museo de Arqueológia de Alta Montaña ★★★, Mitre 77 (✆ **387/437-0499;** www.maam.org.ar) is a beautifully restored historic building that houses a good collection of Andean textiles and three mountain mummies, the perfectly preserved remains of three Inca children sacrificed to the gods. The Andean mummies (over 500 years old) were found in 1999 by a *National Geographic* team of archaeologists. **Museo Histórico**

José Evaristo Uriburu ★ Caseros 479 (✆ **387/421-5340**) is a simple adobe house with a roof of reeds and curved tiles with exhibits that include period furniture and costumes. **Museo Pajarito Velarde,** Pueyrredon 106 (✆ **387/421-2921**) once belonged to Guillermo Velarde Mors, one of Salta's most famous bohemians. The quaint little corner cottage is now an interesting museum crammed with musical instruments, Bolivian Carnaval masks, vinyl records, and Independence-era weaponry. **Museo Provincial de Bellas Artes de Salta** ★, Florida 20 (✆ **387/421-4714**) has colorfully decorated tapestries and other regional works in an 18th-century Spanish house. There is a permanent collection of colonial art upstairs, and religious and contemporary art downstairs.

Salta Cathedral, España 558 (no phone) has a corn-yellow facade that dominates the central plaza. Inside you'll find beautiful interiors of ocher, blue, green, and gold and a pantheon of Salta's luminaries, including local freedom fighter and strongman Martín Miguel de Güemes. **San Bernardo Convent** ★★, Caseros near Santa Fe (no phone) is Salta's oldest religious building and was declared a Historical National Monument in 1941. It's worthy of a walk by (only Carmelite nuns are allowed to enter) to admire the city's most impressive example of colonial and indigenous art. Indigenous craftsmen carved the entrance from a carob tree in 1762. **Teleférico (Salta Cable Car)** ★, at the intersection of avs. H. Yrigoyen and San Martín. (✆ **387/431-0641;** telerificosalta@salta.gov.ar) is a Swiss-made, well-maintained cable car that has been in operation since 1987, ferrying tourists to the top of San Bernardo Hill, 300m (984 ft.) over Salta. At the top there is a set of gardens, artificial waterfalls, and a panoramic view of the Lerma valley.

OUTDOOR ACTIVITIES & TOUR OPERATORS

The city is a good base to go farther and explore the eerie salt plains, known as Salinas, and the multicolored mountain ranges of Humahuaca, in Jujuy province to the north. **Volcan Higueras,** Mendoza 453, Salta (✆ **387/431-9175;** www.volcanhigueras.com.ar), and **Silvia Magno,** San Juan 2399 (✆ **387/434-1468;** silviamagnovyt@aol.com), conduct 1-day excursions to both places. **Agencia del Peregrino,** Alvarado 351 (✆ **387/422-9440;** www.agenciadelperegrino.com.ar), specializes in tours of the beautiful hilltop villages of Cachi and Purmamarca.

One- to 4-day safaris and bird-watching expeditions are organized by **Clark Expediciones,** Caseros 121, Salta (✆ **387/421-5390;** www.clarkexpediciones.com), an excellent local outfitter. **Finca Lesser** (✆ **387/155-827-332;** www.redsalta.com/fincalesser) is a private nature reserve 15km (9 miles) from the city center. **Los Amigos,** Quebrado de San Lorenzo (✆ **387/492-7033**), organizes horseback riding in the hills of San Lorenzo overlooking the city. **Sayta** (✆ **387/156-836-565;** www.sayta.com.ar) organizes 1-day excursions to a ranch 40km (25 miles) south of the city, costing A$270, including lunch and transfer.

Salta Rafting, Buenos Aires 88, Local 14 (✆ **387/401-0301;** www.saltarafting.com), takes you in a 4WD to a mountaintop 3,600m (9,843 ft.) high, where you start an exhilarating 45km (28-mile) descent on a mountain bike. **MTB Salta,** Gral. Güemes 569 (✆ **387/422-8317;** www.mtbsalta.com), also organizes mountain bike excursions, as well as canoe trips on Campo Alegre dam. **Amazing Mountains,** Juramento 466, Salta (✆ **387/422-3179**), has paragliding trips that jump off San Lorenzo hill and kite buggying journeys on Salinas salt plains for A$130 and A$300 a day, respectively. **Mandes Travel Europe,** Leguizamón 1308, Salta (✆ **387/422-7873;** www.andesmoto.com), organizes 1-day trekking and motorbike excursions from Salta. **Turismo San Lorenzo,** J.C. Dávalos 960, San Lorenzo (✆ **387/492-1757;** www.turismosanlorenzo.com), organizes treks through San Lorenzo, starting at A$230 per day.

Rafting and windsurfing are popular in the Dique Cabra Corral, 70km (43 miles) south of Salta. For more information, contact **Salta Rafting,** Buenos Aires 88, Local 14 (✆ **387/401-0301;** www.saltarafting.com), and **Active Argentina,** Zuviria 982, Salta (✆ **387/431-1868**).

SHOPPING

Salta province's secretary of tourism does a great job controlling their handmade products—from textiles to bamboo and wood ornaments. After certification, they're sold only at the **Mercado Artesanal★★**, San Martín 2555 (✆ **387/434-2808**), open from 9am to 9pm daily. Here in a beautifully restored millhouse 23 blocks from the central plaza, you'll find authentic products—from leather goods to candles—made throughout Salta Province by local artisans.

Casa de Antigüedades, Caseros 332 (✆ **387/421-1911**), is a rambling antiques store jammed with everything from period furniture and local art. It's open Monday to Saturday 9am to 1:30pm and 4 to 9:30pm; ring the bell and one of the owners from the Perez family will happily look after you. **La Casa del Arte,** Buenos Aires 25 (✆ **387/431-0050**), is a small store crammed with some beautiful art and jewelry, as is **Puestos del Marqués,** Buenos Aires 68 (✆ **387/422-0899**).

Amankay, Pueblo Chico, Balcarce 999 (✆ **387/431-0335**), and **Inyás Artisanías,** España 375 (✆ **387/436-0260;** www.artesaniasinyas.com.ar), both specialize in original handicrafts and precious stones. For alpaca goods and silverware, try **Ambay,** Caseros 376 (✆ **387/431-7182**), and **Suyay,** Caseros 525 (✆ **387/431-5961**). For all things leather, go to **Torcivia,** Buenos Aires 28 (✆ **387/422-7097**), or **Decuero,** Mitre 291 (✆ **387/422-4166**).

WHERE TO STAY

Salta has a wealth of accommodations, and prices are still reasonable in comparison with other parts of the country. Options are good both inside and outside the city center. Staying in the city center gives you a chance to walk everywhere. If you're after some peace and quiet, though, consider staying in the nearby village of San Lorenzo.

Very Expensive

Alejandro Primero ★★★ Value Salta's second five-star hotel beats the Sheraton for color and charm. Two gauchos greet you as you enter an 11-story glass vaulted building of Andean chic. Carpets are adorned with miniature designs of *guanacos* (llamas), ostriches, and cacti. Corridors are enlivened with leather wall hangings, indigenous art, and the occasional ceramic pot. Rooms are spacious with panoramic views, and double-glazing ensures the noisy downtown location does not intrude on your *tranquilidad.*

Balcarce 252. ✆ **387/400-0000.** www.alejandro1hotel.com.ar. 167 units. From $109 double; from $219 suite. Rates include buffet breakfast. AE, DC, MC, V. Free parking. **Amenities:** Restaurant; bar; lounge; exercise room; free high-speed Internet; indoor pool; room service; sauna. *In room:* A/C, TV, hair dryer, minibar.

Hotel Solar de la Plaza ★★★ Finds This absolutely charming hotel used to be the residence of one of Salta's well-known families, Patron Costas. The four rooms in the older part of the building were the actual bedrooms of the family members. They have been meticulously transformed into comfortable hotel rooms while retaining their old-world feel—hardwood floors, Jacuzzi tubs, and wrought-iron floor lamps (handmade in Salta). The rooms in the newer wing sport the same decor, but with a slightly more modern feel.

 Juan M. Leguizamon 669. ✆/fax **387/431-5111.** www.solardelaplaza.com.ar. 30 units. From $125 double; from $197 suite. Rates include continental breakfast. AE, DC, MC, V. Free parking. **Amenities:** Restaurant; bar; lounge; exercise room; small outdoor pool; room service; sauna; Wi-Fi. *In room:* A/C, TV, minibar.

The Sheraton Salta's first five-star hotel lacks imagination but has a winning location. The design could be described as very Sheraton-esque—bland but luxurious. A plain, cream-colored facade hangs over a dark lobby of stone walls, corduroy seating, and cobbled stones. Bright, terra-cotta hallways lead to an anticlimax, as the spacious rooms are somewhat colorless and sterile. Nevertheless, they have all the creature comforts expected of a Sheraton.

Av. Ejercito del Norte 330. ✆ **387/432-3000.** www.starwoodhotels.com. 145 units. $170 double; from $291 suite. Rates include buffet breakfast. AE, DC, MC, V. Free parking. **Amenities:** Restaurant; bar; lounge; casino; exercise room; Jacuzzi; outdoor pool; room service; sauna; Wi-Fi. *In room:* A/C, TV, hair dryer, minibar.

Expensive

Casa Real Hotel & Spa ★★ Value Rooms at the Casa Real are spacious and comfortable, with big picture windows (some overlooking the mountains), large-screen TVs, and firm, comfortable beds. Bathrooms are also large and very clean. The hotel boasts a decent-size exercise room and a good-size indoor pool, as well as an attractive restaurant and bar. The staff is friendly and can help arrange transportation and tours.

Mitre 669. ✆ **387/421-5675.** www.casarealsalta.com.ar. 80 units. $122 double; from $144 suite. Rates include buffet breakfast. AE, DC, MC, V. Free parking. **Amenities:** Restaurant; bar; lounge; exercise room; free high-speed Internet; indoor pool; room service; sauna. *In room:* A/C, TV, hair dryer, minibar.

Gran Hotel Presidente ★ This contemporary hotel has attractive guest rooms splashed in rose and apple green, with sparkling white-tile bathrooms. The chic lobby features black-and-white marble with Art Deco furniture and leopard-skin upholstery. The pleasant international restaurant is located on the upstairs mezzanine, and there's a spa with a heated indoor pool, a sauna, a fitness room, and a solarium.

Av. de Belgrano 353. ✆/fax **387/431-2022.** www.granhotelpresidente.com. 96 units. $90 double; $115 suite. Rates include buffet breakfast. AE, DC, MC, V. Free parking. **Amenities:** Restaurant; exercise room; small indoor pool; room service; sauna; Wi-Fi. *In room:* A/C, TV, hair dryer, minibar.

Moderate

Bloomers Small and quirky, Bloomers is a unique and charming place to stay in the city center. This is not called a bed-and-breakfast but a "bed and brunch," indicating the somewhat colorful, bohemian aspect of this boutique hotel. Wacky rugs and arty lamps adorn the five rooms, along with huge ceramic urns and luminous, cube-shaped bean-bag-type chairs.

Vicente Lopez 129. ✆/fax **387/422-7449.** www.bloomers-salta.com.ar. 5 units. From $70 double. Rates include breakfast. AE, DC, MC, V. Free parking. **Amenities:** Kitchen. *In room:* A/C, TV.

Hotel Almería ★ This new hotel has an old-fashioned efficiency about it. The deceptively mediocre white facade, complete with flagpoles, leads to a spacious marble lobby with a gold-trimmed elevator. Plush, upholstered hallways lead to modern, well-fitted rooms that have dark-wood furniture and custom-made headboards with inset light switches.

Vicente Lopez 146. ✆ **387/431-4848.** www.hotelalmeria.com.ar. 64 units. From $97 double; $145–$161 suite. Rates include buffet breakfast. AE, DC, MC, V. Free parking. **Amenities:** Restaurant; bar; Jacuzzi; outdoor pool; room service; solarium. *In room:* TV, hair dryer, minibar.

Hotel Salta ★ Moments Popular with Europeans, this neoclassical hotel sits in the heart of Salta—facing Plaza 9 de Julio—and makes an excellent base from which to explore the city. Opened in 1890, these are hardly the most modern accommodations you'll find, but the hotel's wood balconies and arabesque carvings, peaceful courtyard, refreshing pool, and beautiful dining room overlooking the plaza considerably heighten its appeal.

Buenos Aires 1. ✆/fax **387/431-0740.** www.hotelsalta.com. 99 units. From $93 double; from $160 suite. Rates include buffet breakfast. AE, DC, MC, V. Free parking. **Amenities:** Restaurant; bar; pool; room service; sauna. *In room:* A/C, TV, minibar.

Posada del Angel This is a tidy little boutique hotel located in the heart of the city. It has a homey, villa feel with parquet floors and small courtyard. The brass beds are a little on the small side and the curtains a little loud, but, in general, rooms have a very cool ambience.

Pueyreddon 25. ✆ **387/431-8223.** www.hotelposadadelangel.com.ar. 7 units. From $69 double. Rates include breakfast. AE, DC, MC, V. Free parking. **Amenities:** Library; Wi-Fi. *In room:* A/C, TV.

Inexpensive

Hotel del Antiguo Convento ★★ Finds The humble colonial entrance to this budget hotel might make you think it is a little too budget. But you will be pleasantly surprised as the modern reception area opens out into three courtyards and a garden pool, all decorated with flowers, pots, and flagstones. The surrounding rooms are midsize, with air-conditioning and TV. The bathrooms are small but sparkling clean and perfectly adequate.

Caseros 113. ✆/fax **387/422-7267.** www.hoteldelconvento.com.ar. 25 units. From $60 double. Rates include breakfast. AE, DC, MC, V. $5 parking. **Amenities:** Outdoor pool; Wi-Fi. *In room:* A/C, TV.

Los Cardones Youth Hostel If you want to meet people and be close to the nightlife action on Balcarce, this pleasant town house is not a bad choice. An attractive common room with comfy sofas leads to clean, simple rooms with bright blue walls and simple beds.

Entre Rios 454. ✆ **387/431-4026.** www.loscardones.todowebsalta.com.ar. 12 units. From $23 double with shared bathrooms; dorm bed $9 per person. Rates include breakfast. No credit cards. No parking. **Amenities:** Bar; communal TV/DVD player w/DVD library; high-speed Internet.

Victoria Plaza If you're in Salta to sightsee rather than to loll around in sumptuous hotel rooms, then the Victoria Plaza should do just fine. Rooms are stark and simple, but they're clean, comfortable, and cheerfully maintained.

Zuviría 16. ✆/fax **387/431-8500.** www.hotelvictoriaplaza.com.ar. 96 units. From $75 double. Rates include buffet breakfast. AE, DC, MC, V. Free parking. **Amenities:** Tiny exercise room; sauna; Wi-Fi. *In room:* A/C, TV, fridge.

WHERE TO DINE

The Northwest has its own cuisine influenced by indigenous cooking. *Locro* (a corn-and-bean soup), *humitas* (a sort of corn-and–goat cheese soufflé), tamales (meat and potatoes in a ground corn shell), empanadas (a turnover filled with potatoes, meat, and vegetables), *lechón* (suckling pig), and *cabrito* (goat) occupy most menus. In addition to the locations listed below, the **Mercado Central,** at Florida and San Martín, has a number of inexpensive eateries serving regional food.

Casa Moderna, España 674 (✆ **387/422-0066**), is a delicatessen/winebar located 2 blocks from the central plaza, and has a warm, genuine, old-world feel. You can dine in a lovely small courtyard or the adjacent black-framed sun house. Indoors, ham hangs from the ceiling over shelves crammed with wine, chocolates, cheese, and whiskey. The owners have opened a second branch several blocks away at Vte. Lopez 423. **El Solar del Convento,** Caseros 444 (✆ **387/439-3666**), is Salta's best "typical" restaurant. This former Jesuit convent has long been an outstanding *parrilla* (grill), serving quality steaks and regional specialties such as empanadas, tamales, and *humitas.* **José Balcarce ★★★**, Necochea 590 (✆ **387/421-1628**), is one of the most talked-about dining establishments in northwestern Argentina. Here's where you can try roasted llama meat served with Andean potatoes or quinoa, or llama medallions with prickly pear sauce. Order a well-chilled Torrontes white wine to round out your meal.

Malandrino, Balcarce 892 (✆ **387/154-767653**), is a bright arty restaurant with a nice fusion of old and new. Enjoy llama meat stirred in a wok, Andean cereal quinoa, and giant portions of *milanesa* (breaded meats). **Santana,** Mendoza 208 (✆ **387/432-0941**), is one of the few international restaurants in Salta with a classic rather than rustic style. The enticing menu features chicken with white-wine cream sauce, lobster with *chimichurri* sauce, and homemade ravioli with various cheeses.

SALTA AFTER DARK

BARS & NIGHTCLUBS Night owls will find plenty to occupy themselves, whether it's around the late-night eateries close to the plaza or the pleasant stretch of bars, restaurants, and nightclubs along the nighttime parade known as Calle Balcarce, close to the train station. **Goblin Irish Pub,** Caseros 445 (✆ **387/401-0886**), is a handsome bar that draws an expat crowd eager to speak English. Drinks are pricey, however, compared to other places. **Wasabi,** Balcarce 938 (✆ **387/421-6575**), is a trendy sushi bar and disco, open Tuesday to Sunday 9pm to 2am. **Uno,** Balcarce 926 (✆ **387/422-9120**), is a slick establishment that attracts a young crowd. **Club Nueve,** Balcarce 907 (✆ **387/155-323-009**), is a nightclub specializing in electronic music.

PEÑAS A trip to Salta would not be complete without a night spent tapping along to a singing gaucho dressed up in billowing pants and knee-high leather boots. Traditional music bars (known as *peñas*) are dotted all around the city, but are particularly numerous on Balcarce Street. **Café de Tiempo ★**, Balcarce 901 (✆ **387/432-0771**), is one of the most famous, with a colorful, old-world interior. **La Vieja Estacion,** Balcarce 885 (✆ **387/421-7727**), and **La Peña del Chaqueno,** Balcarce 935 (✆ **387/421-7727**), are both big and popular—with handkerchief-waving maidens dancing until late—and serve traditional food. **Peña Gauchos de Güemes,** Av. Uruguay 750 (✆ **387/421-7007;** www.gauchosdesalta.com.ar), takes it a little more seriously, and the adobe-style venue has been declared a Salta heritage site. It is located 13 blocks from the plaza, close to Alto Noa shopping mall.

A SIDE TRIP TO THE CALCHAQULES VALLEY VIA CACHI & CAFAYATE

With green rolling hills, lush jungle, and multicolored rock, the landscape surrounding Salta has it all. Tobacco, tropical fruits, and sugar cane are the main agricultural products here, and you will see tobacco "ovens" off the side of the road. Heading south from Salta on RN 68 for 38km (24 miles), you'll reach **El Carril,** a typical small town of the valley, with a central plaza and botanical garden displaying 70% of the region's flora.

Although you can reach **Cafayate** more quickly by continuing south on RN 68, it is far more interesting to go west on Ruta 33 for a longer, more rugged circuit that will require you to stop overnight. Travel 2.7km (1¾ miles) after El Carril to **Cabaña de Cabras,** in La Flor del Pago (✆ **387/499-1093**), one of the principal goat farms and cheese factories in Argentina. Ducks, geese, and hundreds of goats roam the scenic property, and you can sample the delicious *chivo* (goat) in the small dining room and cheese shop in the proprietors' home. A bread and jam snack costs only A$11; a cheese sandwich is A$18; and a glass of local wine is A$10.

Dense vegetation covers the region surrounding El Carril, but the land quickly dries out as you climb RP 33 toward **Piedra del Molino (Mill Rock).** The road narrows from pavement to dirt 10km (6¼ miles) west of El Carril—watch closely for oncoming cars. A small shrine to Saint Raphael (a patron saint of travelers) indicates your arrival at Mill Rock (3,620m/11,874 ft. elevation) and the entrance to **Parque Nacional los Cardones,** a semiarid landscape filled with cacti, sage, and limestone rock formations.

Ten kilometers (6¼ miles) before Cachi lies **Payogasta,** an ancient Indian town on the path of the Inca Road that once connected an empire stretching from Peru to northern Argentina. **Cachi** ★ is another precolonial village worth a visit for its Indian ruins and lovely chapel. From Cachi, take RN 40 south past Brealito to Molinos, a 17th-century town of adobe homes and dusty streets virtually unchanged from how it must have appeared 350 years ago. Here you will find the famous winery and wine lodge **Colomé.** Continuing south, consider stopping 9km (5½ miles) before Angastaco at the **Estancia Carmen** (✆ **387/1568-01322**), which boasts spectacular views of the Calchaquíes Valley and its long mountain canyon. Between 9am and 6pm, you can visit the ranch's Inca ruins, rent horses, and peek inside the private church in back, where two 300-year-old mummies rest in peace.

Continue south on RN 40 to **Angastaco,** which may be a good place to spend the night. **Hostería Angastaco,** Avenida Libertad (✆ **3868/497-700**), 1km (about ½ mile) west of the village, is popular with European travelers. Rooms start at $18. From Angastaco to San Carlos, you will pass the **Quebrada de las Flechas (Arrows Ravine),** with its stunning rock formations. **Cafayate** (see below) marks the southern end of this circuit.

Return to Salta along RN 68 heading north, which takes you through the **Río Calchaquíes Valley** and on to the **Quebrada del Río de las Conchas (Canyon of the River of Shells).** Salta is 194km (120 miles) from Cafayate, along RN 68, and it shouldn't take more than a few hours to drive.

Cafayate ★★★

The wine town of Cafayate has its own distinct colors—pink dust, red hills, and olive-green mountains. Corn-yellow sand gathers along the curbstones of this sun-kissed village, while donkeys graze on the central plaza, and heaps of unlocked bicycles stand outside schools and the coffee-colored cathedral. Add to this some pretty, palatial-style wineries, luxury lodges, excellent arts and crafts, and stunning vineyard country producing the aromatic white Torrontes grape, and you can see why this whole area is becoming known as the Tuscany of Argentina.

GETTING THERE Cafayate lies 194km (120 miles) southwest of Salta, on RN 68. **Empresa El Indio** (✆ **387/432-0846**) offers three buses daily from Salta; the trip takes 3½ hours and costs about A$35.

VISITOR INFORMATION The **tourist office** (✆ **3868/421470**) is located on the main plaza and provides maps, bus schedules, and lodging recommendations. Open hours are Monday through Saturday from 10am to 6pm.

Quilmes Ruins

The fascinating ruins of **Quilmes** ★, located on Route 40, approximately halfway between Cafayate and the green enclave of Tafi de Valle to the south, is one of Argentina's most fascinating pre-Columbian ruins. A field of giant cacti leads to an impressive hillside town with stone foundations—the remains of a thriving settlement built in A.D. 800 that once held 5,000 people. The ruins are open for visits, however, from 8am to 7pm daily. Admission is A$6 with an obligatory Spanish-speaking guide of dubious quality (✆ **381/1562-72329**).

Visiting the Wineries★

There are approximately 25 wineries to visit in the area, some palatial-style villas, others rustic boutique garages. All are within easy reach of the town and can be visited by bicycle or taxi. Most wineries are open Monday to Saturday.

Bodegas Etchart, Finca La Rosa, 3km (1¾ miles) from Cafayate, on RN 40 (✆ **3868/421310;** www.bodegasetchart.com), is owned by the French wine giant Pernod-Ricard and is one of the region's most important. **Finca Las Nubes,** El Divisadero, Alto Valle de Cafayate, 5km (3 miles) from Cafayate (✆ **3868/422129;** www.bodegamounier.com), is one of Argentina's smallest vineyards and is family-run, producing some young but excellent wines. The rustic facility is a few kilometers up a dirt road from the center of town and provides lunches with reservations. **Michel Torino,** Finca La Rosa, 3km (1¾ miles) from Cafayate, on RN 40 (✆ **3868/155-66019;** www.micheltorino.com.ar), is a beautiful, hacienda-style complex that houses the luxury wine lodge Patios de Cafayate.

The winery known as **Bodega El Esteco. Bodegas El Porvenir de los Andes** ★★, Córdoba 32, Cafayate (✆ **3868/422007;** www.bodegaselporvenir.com), is one of my favorites, producing rich, concentrated reds. The winery boasts a handsome town house with courtyard, located 2 blocks from the plaza. **San Pedro de Yacochuya** ★, RP 2, RN 40 (✆ **3868/421233;** www.sanpedrodeyacochuya.com.ar), is a boutique operation started by the Etchart family when they sold their larger winery. It is basically a tidy shed at the end of a dirt road lined by cactus 3km (2 miles) from the town. Reservations are required, and opening hours can be erratic. **Bodega Nanni,** Silverio Chavarria 151 (✆ **3868/421527;** www.bodegananni.com), is a traditional winery located in town, 2 blocks from the plaza. **Bodega Domingo Hermanos,** Nuestra Señora del Rosario s/n, Cafayate (✆ **3868/421225;** www.domingohermanos.com), is a famous local producer located .5km (⅓ mile) from the plaza. **Vasija Secreta,** RN 40 (✆ **3868/421850**), is a large *bodega* that also houses a small but interesting museum.

Museums & Workshops

Artesanías Víctor Cristófani, RN 40 at Arrollo Don Lelio (no phone), is a pottery workshop that provides an entertaining and fascinating tour. Owner Ana María wallops giant urns with a metal bar to demonstrate their strength. Huge clay ovens belch wood smoke while pots and urns and mud clay lie around in different stages of development. Visits are in the morning only. **Arte en Telar,** Colon 71 (no phone; rteentelar@hotmail.com), is a textile workshop that offers a fascinating look into the local tradition of hand weaving. It's open Monday to Saturday 10am to 2pm and 4 to 10pm. **Museo de Vitivinicultura,** RN 40 at Avenida General Guemes (✆ **3868/421-125**), tells the story of grape-growing and winemaking in and around Cafayate. It's open Monday to Friday 10am to 1pm and 5 to 9pm. **Museo Regional y Arqueológico Rodolfo Bravo,** Colon 191 (✆ **3868/421-054**), displays indigenous ceramics, textiles, and metal objects discovered over a 66-year period by Rodolfo Bravo. The museum is open Monday to Friday 11am to 9pm. On weekends hours vary.

Where to Stay

Cafayate has seen a surge in luxury accommodations, mostly of the wine lodge variety. Many are within easy walking distance of the village. **Killa Cafayate ★★**, Colón 47, 4427 Cafayate (✆ **3868/422254;** www.killacafayate.com.ar), has a long, rambling courtyard of whitewashed walls, terra-cotta tiles, wind chimes, and chunky wooden staircases. The 16 rooms are decked out with local stone, windowed wardrobes, and indigenous art, and start at $102 for a double. **Villa Vicuña,** Belgrano 76, 4427 Cafayate (✆ **3868/422145;** www.villavicuna.com.ar), has a shaded courtyard, surrounded by 12 simple but well-appointed rooms ($50 for a double) in a modern building with some colonial touches, such as an arched entrance and street balcony.

Hotel Gran Real Cafayate, Av. General Güemes 128, 4427 Cafayate (✆ **3868/421231;** fax 3868/421016; www.granrealcafayate.com.ar), is a modest hotel with quiet rooms and very simple furnishings. Rates start at $50 for a double.

La Casa de la Bodega ★, RP 68 Km 18, Valle de Cafayate (✆ **3868/421888;** www.lacasadelabodega.com.ar), is a 20km (12-mile) drive from town through a desert of pink sand and cactus sentinels. The eight luxurious rooms are large, with stone headboards, and cost from $137 for a double. **Patios de Cafayate Hotel & Spa,** RN 40, at RP 68 (part of El Esteco winery), 4427 Cafayate (✆ **3868/421747;** www.luxurycollection.com/cafayate), is a series of leafy, flower-adorned courtyards in a beautiful palatial-style villa with a cold and corporate atmosphere and staff who are not very engaging. Rooms start at $240. **Viñas de Cafayate Wine Resort ★★**, 25 de Mayo, Camino al Divisadero, Cafayate (✆ **3868/422272;** www.cafayatewineresort.com), is a beautiful, simply designed wine lodge with a commanding view of the valley situated 3km (2 miles) outside the town in the mountain foothills. The 12 rooms are big, with minimal decor, and cost from $125.

Where to Dine

El Rancho, Vicario Toscano 4 (✆ **3868/421256**), is the best restaurant on the main plaza, serving freshly made empanadas, *humitas,* tamales, and oven-baked *cabrito* (young goat) with roasted potatoes. Main courses vary from A$20 to A$35. **La Carreta de Don Olegario,** Av. General Güemes 20 (✆ **3868/421004**), lacks elegance but serves an authentic selection of regional dishes, including *cabritos.* **Machacha ★★**, Güemes 28 (✆ **3868/422319**), is Cafayate's only gourmet restaurant, offering dishes such as llama meat and duck. Platters of smoked cheese and cold meats compete with rabbit for your attention. Main courses vary from A$70 to A$110.

A SIDE TRIP TO QUEBRADA DE HUMAHUACA ★★★

Quebrada de Humahuaca is a 150km (93-mile) strip of land that brings you dangerously close to Bolivia, both in body and spirit. The fiery red ridges and copper-green plateaus hide timeless villages with genuine indigenous charm and picturesque architecture, and the whole area has been declared a UNESCO World Heritage Site. The area is a must-see, with 1-day excursions possible from Salta to the cobbled streets and low colonial buildings of **Tilcara ★★**. This lovely town is gaining a reputation, becoming a

The Dinosaur Parks of La Rioja and San Juan

Parque Nacional Talampaya ★★, RP 26, Villa Union, La Rioja (✆ **3825/470356;** www.talampaya.gov.ar; admission A$25; daily 9am–6pm), is one of Argentina's most amazing national parks, showcasing a 200-million-year-old era that first saw the emergence of reptiles and flowering plants that are caught now in a perfect geological etching. The UNESCO World Heritage Site also makes for some pretty spectacular scenery as it covers more than 215,000 hectares (a half-million acres) and has 150m-high (492-ft.) red sandstone walls that are as sharp as diamond-cut marble. The 1,800-year-old rock paintings here display birdlife and guanacos.

Parque Triásico Ischigualasto/Valle de la Luna ★★★, Los Baldecitos (no phone; 25 de Mayo and Las Heras, San Juan; ✆ **2646/420104;** www.ischigualasto.org; admission A$40), is 80km (50 miles) away and more famous for its dinosaur fossils, some of which are the oldest in the world. The 50,000-hectare (120,000-acre) site of yellow mushroom-shaped rocks and red cliffs is home to the bones of giant reptiles that are constantly surprising paleontologists who, every year, find new species. The entire evolutionary period of these grizzly dragons can be seen here, stretching over 255 million years, up until when they died out, approximately 65 million years ago.

There is no public transport to either park, so a taxi or tour company must be used from La Rioja (which has an airport connecting to Buenos Aires) 2½ hours away from the parks, or from the small towns Villa Union or Valle Fertil in San Juan province.

thriving tourist town and the center of operations for those who want to explore the area further.

Essentials

GETTING THERE There are regular buses that leave from **Salta Terminal de Omnibus,** at Avenida H. Yrigoyen and Abraham Cornejo, Salta (✆ **387/401-1143**), to Tilcara. The journey takes 4 hours and costs A$39. Travel agencies **Volcán Higueras,** Mendoza 453, Salta (✆ **387/431-9175;** www.volcanhigueras.com.ar), and **Silvia Magno,** San Juan 2399, Salta (✆ **387/434-1468;** silviamagnovyt@aol.com), offer 1-day excursions from Salta to Tilcara and beyond.

What to See & Do

Pucará is a reconstructed hilltop fort overlooking Tilcara town, first built 900 years ago by the Diaguita tribe. There is a pyramid-shaped monument at the summit and the entire site covers 8 hectares (20 acres), including a high-altitude botanical garden. The site is open daily from 9am to 12:30pm and 2 to 6pm. **Museo Arqueológico Eduardo Casanova,** Belgrano 445 (✆ **388/495-5006**), displays carved standing stones and other pre-Columbian artifacts. It is open every day from 9am to 12:30pm and 2 to 6pm; the admission is A$10. **Museo Regional de Pintura Jose A. Terry,** Rivadavia 459 (✆ **388/495-5005**), displays works by the area's most famous painter. It's open Tuesday to Sunday from 9am to 7pm. Lying 20km (13 miles) south of Tilcara is the small colonial hamlet of **Purmamarca ★★★**. **Cerro de los Siete Colores (Hill of the Seven Colors)** dominates the village, reflecting its startling red and purple colors onto the pueblo's quiet streets and dusty adobe homes. Try to arrive early—9am is best—when the morning sun shines brightly on the hill's facade and reveals its tapestry of colors. In front of the plaza, you cannot miss the 400-year-old **Iglesia de Santa Rosa,** one of the country's oldest and most beautiful churches. Continue west on RN 16 for 73km (45 miles), and you reach the surreal landscape known as **Salinas Grandes ★**, a dazzling salt plain that stretches for miles.

8 THE ARGENTINE LAKE DISTRICT ★★★

With its rolling forests, imposing peaks, and mirrorlike waters, the Argentine Lake District is one of the world's most spectacular mountain playgrounds. You'll find alpine adventures, aquatic sports, fabulous wine and cuisine, and cozy chalets and hotels. Although it is considered part of Patagonia, the Lake District is very different than the southern region of Patagonia, which is covered on p. 158.

Argentines flock here during their twice-annual holidays—to ski in July and August, and to raft in the lakes and hike the mountains in January. The rest of the year, it's *tranquilísimo.* I suggest you schedule your visit when the locals are back at work, during the shoulder-season months of November (spring) and March (autumn)—my favorite time to visit here. The region's principal destinations are San Carlos de Bariloche and San Martín de los Andes, but Villa La Angostura, El Bolsón, and Junín de los Andes are also popular stops (see the box "More Lake District Towns and Lakes" below for info). The area also includes numerous national parks, and you should not miss the chance to stay in either a rustic high-mountain hut, a fly-fishing lodge, or a simple tent, after you've taken in the scenery on horseback.

SAN CARLOS DE BARILOCHE ★★

1,621km (1,005 miles) SW of Buenos Aires; 180km (112 miles) S of San Martín de los Andes

Bariloche is blessed with a strategic geographic position. With the rugged plains of the Patagonian Steppe to the east, the towering snowy peaks of the Andes to the west, and the glistening and grand Nahuel Huapi Lake in front, opportunities for adventure are abundant. Even if you're not much of an adventurer, you'll still find plenty of pleasant sightseeing tours, boat trips, boutiques, driving excursions, and fine dining to keep you busy. Or just park yourself wherever the view is good and soak it all in.

The city itself embodies a strange juxtaposition: an urban city plopped down in the middle of beautiful wilderness. Unfortunately, Argentine migrants fleeing Buenos Aires, an ever-growing tourism industry, and 2 decades of unchecked development have left a cluttered mess in what was once an idyllic mountain town. Bits and pieces of the charming architecture influenced by German, Swiss, and English immigration are still in evidence, but *"el centro"* of Bariloche can be tacky and chaotic. Visitors to Bariloche are sometimes overwhelmed by its hodgepodge of ugly apartment buildings and clamorous discos, and the crowds that descend on this area from mid-December until the end of February and again during ski season in July. A visit to Bariloche, however, does not necessarily mean staying in (or spending hardly any time) in the city's core. Your best bet is to spend less time in town, and more on the lake or in the mountains. Drive 10 minutes outside town, and you'll be surrounded again by thick forests, rippling lakes, and snowcapped peaks that rival the Alps.

Getting There

BY PLANE The **Aeropuerto Bariloche** (airport code BRC; ✆ **02944/426162**) is 13km (8 miles) from downtown. Buses to the city center line up outside the arrival area; they're roughly scheduled to coordinate with flight arrivals. A taxi to the center costs about A$50—a bargain if you have a group of two or three people. **Aerolíneas Argentinas,** Mitre 185 (✆ **02944/422548;** www.aerolineas.com.ar), runs at least three daily flights from Buenos Aires; in summer, it operates two daily flights from El Calafate as well. **LAN,** Mitre 534 (✆ **800/999-9526;** www.lan.com), runs two or three flights a day from Buenos Aires. **Lineas Aéreas del Estado,** Quaglia 238, no. 8 (✆ **02944/423562;** www.lade.com.ar), serves small destinations in the area such as Neuquén and Esquel. It's nearly impossible to make it to Bariloche from North America or Europe in a day, as you must change airports in Buenos Aires. The Brazilian airline **TAM** (✆ **888/235-9826;** www.tam.com.br) has twice-weekly flights from Sao Paolo.

BY BUS The **Terminal de Omnibus** (✆ **02944/432860**) is at Av. 12 de Octubre 2400; a dozen companies serve most major destinations in Argentina and Chile. **Via TAC** (✆ **02944/434727**) schedules three daily arrivals from Buenos Aires and daily service from El Bolsón, Esquel, Mendoza, and Córdoba. **Vía Bariloche** (✆ **02944/432444**) has eight daily arrivals from Buenos Aires (the trip lasts about 20 hr.) and one daily trip from Mar del Plata. **Andesmar** (✆ **02944/430211**) has service from Mendoza, Río Gallegos, and Neuquén, and service from Osorno, Valdivia, and Puerto Montt in Chile. For long trips, opt for the slightly more expensive (usually A$60) *coche cama* or *supercama* for chairs that practically become beds. In addition, there are a few daily buses from San Martín de los Andes via the scenic Siete Lagos (Seven Lakes) route (only during the summer); from Villa La Angostura, try **Ko-Ko** (✆ **02944/431135**).

BY CAR Motorists can reach Bariloche from San Martín via several picturesque routes. The 200km (124-mile) scenic **Siete Lagos route,** from San Martín de los Andes, follows rutas 234, 231, and 237 (avoid this route when it's raining, as the dirt roads turn to mud). The 160km (99-mile) **Paso Córdoba** follows rutas 234, 63, and 237. The safest route for night driving or crummy weather, the **Collón Curá** runs 260km (161 miles) along rutas 234, 40, and 237; it's the longest route, but it's entirely paved. To get to El Bolsón, follow RN 258 south; continue down 40 to get to Esquel. To cross into Chile, take the Puyehue Pass via RN 231 (through Villa La Angostura); during periods of heavy snowfall, chains are required. The drive from Buenos Aires will take you upwards of 20 hours, and there are few pit stops en route. Driving here from Buenos Aires, or similarly far destinations such as El Calafate and Mendoza, is not recommended.

BY BOAT **Cruce Andino** (✆ **02944/425444** or 02944/426228; www.cruceandino.com) run a spectacular lake-crossing journey from Bariloche over the border (and the Andes Mountains) to the Chilean Lake District. It's a boat-and-bus combination that terminates in Lago Todos los Santos, near Ensenada and Puerto Varas, although it can also be done in reverse, from Chile to Bariloche. The 1-day trip costs $230 per person for the boat trip (including lunch).

Getting Around

BY FOOT The city is compact enough to explore on foot. The main streets for shopping and tourist agencies are Mitre and San Martín/Moreno. The center of town is the scenic Centro Cívico (Civic Center) plaza. While you may be tempted to try to walk into

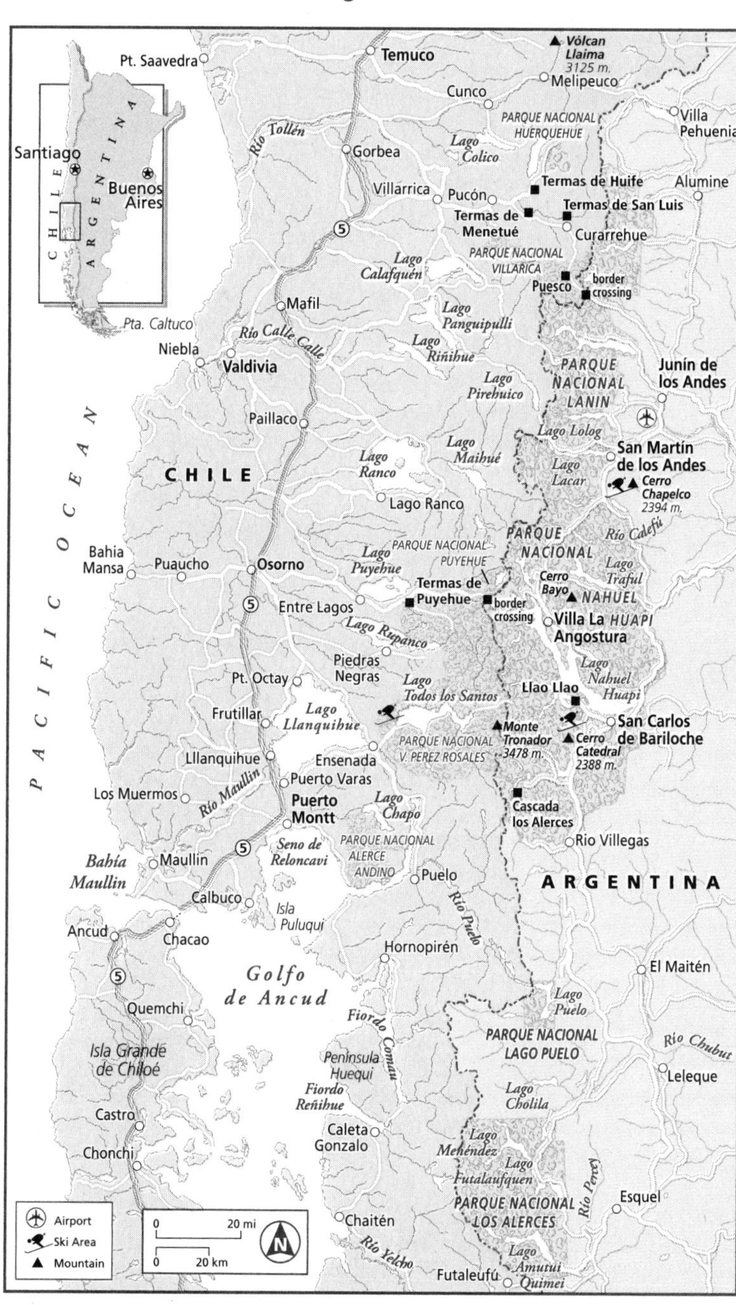
Temuco
Vólcan Llaima 3125 m.
Melipeuco
Pt. Saavedra
Cunco
Villa Pehuenia
PARQUE NACIONAL HUERQUEHUE
Río Tollén
Lago Colico
Gorbea
Termas de Huife
Alumine
Villarrica
Pucón
Termas de Menetué
Termas de San Luis
Curarrehue
Lago Calafquén
PARQUE NACIONAL VILLARICA
Puesco
border crossing
Mafil
Lago Panguipulli
Pta. Caltuco
Río Calle Calle
Lago Riñihue
Niebla
Valdivia
PARQUE NACIONAL LANIN
Junín de los Andes
Lago Pirehuico
Paillaco
Lago Lolog
Lago Maihué
San Martín de los Andes
Lago Ranco
Lago Lacar
Cerro Chapelco 2394 m.
CHILE
Lago Ranco
PACIFIC OCEAN
PARQUE NACIONAL NAHUEL HUAPI
Río Calefú
Lago Puyehue
PARQUE NACIONAL PUYEHUE
Bahia Mansa
Puaucho
Osorno
Lago Traful
Termas de Puyehue
Cerro Bayo
border crossing
Entre Lagos
Villa La Angostura
Lago Rupanco
Piedras Negras
Lago Nahuel Huapi
Pt. Octay
Lago Todos los Santos
Llao Llao
Frutillar
Lago Llanquihue
Monte Tronador 3478 m.
San Carlos de Bariloche
Cerro Catedral 2388 m.
PARQUE NACIONAL V. PEREZ ROSALES
Llanquihue
Ensenada
Puerto Varas
Los Muermos
Río Maullín
Puerto Montt
Lago Chapo
Cascada los Alerces
Rio Villegas
Seno de Reloncaví
PARQUE NACIONAL ALERCE ANDINO
Bahía Maullin
Maullin
Puelo
ARGENTINA
Calbuco
Isla Puluqui
Río Puelo
Ancud
Chacao
Hornopirén
El Maitén
Golfo de Ancud
Lago Puelo
Quemchi
Fiordo Comau
PARQUE NACIONAL LAGO PUELO
Río Chubut
Isla Grande de Chiloé
Península Huequi
Leleque
Fiordo Reñihue
Lago Cholila
Castro
Caleta Gonzalo
Chonchi
Lago Menéndez
Lago Futalaufquen
Río Percey
PARQUE NACIONAL LOS ALERCES
Esquel
Chaitén
Río Yelcho
Lago Amutui Quimei
Futaleufú
Airport
Ski Area
Mountain
0 20 mi
0 20 km
N
Santiago
Buenos Aires
CHILE
ARGENTINA

town along the lakeside road, it's a very busy street that isn't very enjoyable for walking; it's better to hop in a taxi or take the bus.

BY CAR Most savvy travelers rent a car to visit this area. You'll need wheels if you're staying outside the city center or planning to explore the sinuous roads that pass through exceptionally scenic landscapes, such as the Circuito Chico. All travel agencies offer bus excursions to these areas, which is another way to see them if you don't drive. Rental agencies, such as Budget, Dollar, Hertz, and Avis, have kiosks at the airport as well as a number of downtown offices: **Budget,** Mitre 106 (✆ 02944/422482); **AI Rent a Car,** Av. San Martín 127 (✆ 02944/436041); **Dollar,** Villegas 282 (✆ 02944/430333); **Hertz,** Quaglia 165 (✆ 02944/423457); **Bariloche Rent a Car,** Moreno 115 (✆ 02944/427638); and **Localiza,** V.A. O'Connor 602 (✆ 02944/435374). Rates are reasonable, starting at around $55 per day. Driving west of town, you have two options: the direct **Pioneros** road that locals use, a few blocks uphill from the lake, or **Bustillo,** the lakeside road.

BY BUS Bariloche's public bus system is cheap and efficient, whether you're heading to the Cerro Catedral ski resort or exploring the lakeside route of the Circuito Chico. Regular buses depart from Calle San Martín, just in front of the National Park headquarters, or from Moreno and Palacios. Bus no. 20 follows the shores of Lago Nahuel Huapi past the Campanario chairlift to the Llao Llao Hotel and Resort. Bus no. 10 does the same route, but continues past the village at Colonia Suiza. Bus no. 50 will take you directly to Cerro Catedral, and snowboards and skis are allowed onboard. Rides cost less than A$6 (just ask the driver for the exact price).

When navigating the streets of Bariloche, be aware that two streets have similar names, though they are distinct routes: V.A. O'Connor runs parallel to the Costanera, and J. O'Connor bisects it.

Visitor Information

The **Secretaría de Turismo,** in the stone-and-wood Civic Center complex between calles Urquiza and Panzoni (✆ **02944/429850;** secturismo@bariloche.com.ar), has general information about Bariloche and is an indispensable resource for accommodations listings, especially during the high season. They also operate an information stand in the bus terminal, open Monday through Friday from 8am to 9pm, and Saturday and Sunday from 9am to 9pm. Useful tourism information, as well as the best maps and local books, are available at an information kiosk at the corner of Villegas and Moreno, next to the Artisan Market (no phone). Good websites for all sorts of up-to-date travel information include **www.bariloche.org** and **www.interpatagonia.com**.

The **Club Andino Bariloche,** Av. 20 de Febrero 30 (✆ **02944/422266;** fax 02944/424579; www.clubandino.com.ar), provides excellent information about hiking, backpacking, and mountaineering in the area. They sell maps and provide treks and mountain ascents led by guides from the Club Andino; they are open daily from 9am to 1pm and 6 to 9pm during the winter, and daily from 8:30am to 3pm and 5 to 9pm during the summer. For general information about **Nahuel Huapi National Park,** head to the park's headquarters across the street from the Civic Center (✆ **02944/423111**), open Monday through Friday from 8:30am to 12:30pm.

FAST FACTS Most banks exchange currency, including **Banco de Galicia,** Moreno and Quaglia (✆ **2944/427125**), and **Banco Frances,** San Martín 332 (✆ **2944/430315**). Also try **Cambio Sudamérica,** Mitre 63 (✆ **2944/434555**).

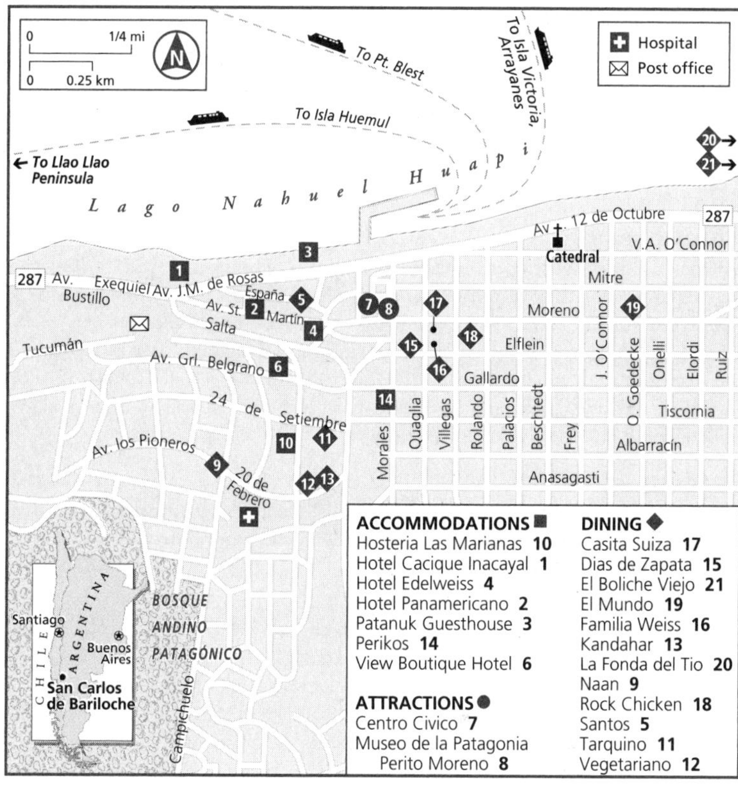

For **emergencies,** dial **101.** For other matters, call ✆ **2944/423434.** For medical assistance, your best bet is **Hospital Privado Regional,** 20 de Febrero 594 (✆ **2944/423074**).

Internet cafes are on just about every corner—and almost every hotel has Internet access, which is usually free for guests. There are two reliable laundromats here: **Mileo,** at Villegas 145 (✆ **2944/422331**), and **Lavadero Huemul,** on Juramento 36 (✆ **2944/522067**). The central **post office** (no phone) is in the Civic Center, next to the tourist office.

What to See & Do in & Around Bariloche

In Bariloche's **Centro Civico (Civic Center),** you'll find the **Museo de la Patagonia Perito Moreno** (✆ **2944/422309;** www.bariloche.com.ar/museo), open Tuesday through Friday from 10am to 12:30pm and 2 to 7pm, Saturday from 10am to 5pm. Exhibits include stuffed pumas and condors, as well as old Mapuche Indian artifacts, such as weapons, art, and jewelry. Admission is A$10.

Parque Nacional Nahuel Huapi ★★

Nahuel Huapi is Argentina's oldest and most popular national park, with a range of activities for any fitness level. It stretches from the Seven Lakes Road in the north to the Manso River in the south. The park also surrounds the city of Bariloche, and its headquarters are downtown in the Civic Center (see "Visitor Information," above).

Tour Operators

A plethora of travel agencies offer everything under the sun along the streets of Bariloche. The best of the lot includes **Travelideas,** Villegas 316 (✆ **02944/424659;** www.travelideas.com.ar), and **Limay Travel,** V.A. O'Connor 710 (✆ **02944/420268;** www.limaytravel.com.ar). Both offer a wide variety of land excursions to El Bolsón, Cerro Tronador, and circuit sightseeing routes. **Huala Adventure Tourism,** San Martín 86 (✆ **02944/522438;** www.huala.com.ar), specializes in adventure sports such as white-water rafting, trekking, and horseback riding.

Outdoor Activities

BIKING Mountain bike rental and information about bike trails are available from **Bike Way,** V.A. O'Connor 867 (✆ **02944/425616**), and **Dirty Bikes,** V. A. O'Connor 681 (✆ **02944/425616**).

FISHING This region provides anglers with excellent fly-fishing on the Manso, Limay, Traful, and Machico rivers. Fishermen also troll on Lake Nahuel Huapi for introduced species such as brown trout, rainbow trout, and landlocked salmon. The fishing season opens in November and runs through April. You can pick up information and fishing licenses at the **Baruzzi Fly Shop,** Urquiza 250 (✆ **02944/424922**), or the office of the Parque Nacional Nahuel Huapi in the Civic Center. Recommended outfitters are Nico Martin at **Bariloche Anglers** (✆ **02944/462102;** www.barilocheanglers.com.ar) or **Ricigliano Fly Fishing** (✆ **02944/420368;** www.riciglianoflyfishing.com). Trolling and spinning are also available. Tour agencies such as **Huala Adventure Tourism,** San Martín 86 (✆ **02944/522438;** www.huala.com.ar), offer half-day and full-day fly-casting and trolling excursions.

GOLF There are three golf courses in the Bariloche area. The crème de la crème is the par-70 18-hole course at the **Llao Llao Resort** (✆ **02944/448530**). Above the shores of Lago Gutierrez, the **Arelauquen Golf Resort** (✆ **02944/431111**) is the newest 18-hole course in the area. There are 9 holes at the **Pinares Golf Club** (✆ **02944/476122**) on the road to the Llao Llao.

HIKING The Nahuel Huapi National Park has a well-developed trail system for day hikes, multiple-day hikes, and loops that connect several backcountry *refugios,* some of which offer rustic lodging. The national park office in the Civic Center provides detailed maps and guides to the difficulty level of each trail. An excellent multilingual local hiking guide and naturalist is **Max Schoffel** (✆ **02944/15-669669;** www.patagoniatravelco.com). Another great source for information is the **Club Andino,** Av. 20 de Febrero 30 (✆ **02944/422266;** www.clubandino.com.ar).

More Lake District Towns & Lakes

Filled with magical forests with sculpted tree trunks, emerald lakes, waterfalls, riverside beaches, and trail heads that lead to glaciers, the Lake District is made for those who want to get off the beaten track and experience rugged nature. Amidst the smorgasbord of mountains and lakes are some beautiful towns worth visiting. **El Bolsón** (131km/81 miles south of Bariloche) is a lovely hamlet of 11,000 people set amid a lush valley famous for its warm climate and artisan's fair, where organic fruit, wool sweaters, homemade jams, and microbrewed beer are sold. Fifteen kilometers (9⅓ miles) south of El Bolsón is **Lago Puelo National Park,** where visitors can swim, boat, hike, camp, and fish.

Villa La Angostura (81km/50 miles north of Bariloche) is a lovely mountain village set on a slender isthmus that connects the town's center with the **Quetrihué Peninsula.** Once a quiet farming community, it is now an upscale getaway for the rich and famous, with shops and restaurants to suit that crowd.

The main attraction in the tiny town of **Junín de los Andes** (40km/25 miles north of San Martín de los Andes) is world class fly-fishing. This fertile little oasis along the shore of the **Río Chimehuín** is surrounded by dry pampa and a stunning setting that offers other outdoor sports such as hiking and boating. There are some lovely nearby ranches that may appeal to those searching for a rural getaway. Whatever you decide to do in this hiker's paradise, don't miss the chance to sleep in the backcountry—whether it's in a rustic high-mountain hut, a fly-fishing lodge, or a simple tent.

HORSEBACK RIDING Horseback rides in various areas of the park are offered by **Tom Wesley Viajes de Aventura,** Bustillo Km 15.5 (✆ **02944/448193**), which also has a kid-friendly adventure camp. Just east of town, visit the **Estancia Fortín Chacabuco** (✆ **02944/554148;** www.estanciaspatagonicas.com) and ride with local gauchos. For overnight or multiday horseback riding trips, contact **Gatomancha** (✆ **02944/15-593157;** www.gatomancha.com).

KAYAK TOURING Recently, the many fiords of Nahuel Huapi Lake have been tempting visitors to explore in sea kayaks, or touring kayaks. It's a lovely outing that's possible in a variety of weather conditions. Operators such as **Senza Limiti,** Julio Cortazar 5050 (✆ **02944/520597;** www.slimiti.com), also offer overnight tours, often year-round.

MOUNTAINEERING Experienced climbers, and those looking for a taste of the high peaks, have plenty of options in Bariloche, including the challenging 3-day climb of Mt. Tronador. Contact **Andes Cross** (✆ **02944/15-633581;** www.andescross.com) for guiding services.

RAFTING Various companies offer river rafting on the Río Manso in both Class III and Class IV sections, on full-day trips. The Rafting Frontera trip takes you to the Chilean border and is thrilling. The two best local rafting companies are **Patagonia Rafting,** San Martín 86 (✆ **02944/522438**), and **Extremo Sur,** Morales 765 (✆ **02944/427301**).

SKIING & SNOWBOARDING Bariloche's main winter draw is the ski resort at Cerro Catedral, perhaps South America's greatest ski hill, with stunning scenery. The season usually runs from June through October, with mid-August being the busiest time (when all Argentines have their 2-week winter holidays). Nonskiers can also enjoy the scene thanks to pedestrian lifts, open daily, that ferry passengers to the top. Every July or August, Catedral hosts the **National Snow Party,** with torchlight parades and other events. The bustling Villa Catedral is at the base of the resorts, with a jumble of shops, rental stores, and several lodging options. The nicest ski-in, ski-out hotel is **Pire-Hue Hotel and Resort** (✆ **2944/460040;** www.pire-hue.com.ar). **Sudbruck Hostería** has a handful of spacious rooms decorated with rustic cypress wood (✆ **2944/460156;** www.sudbruck.com). Rooms start at about $70 per night for a double. **Cabañas Antu Pukem** has cabins for six to eight guests; consult them directly for prices (✆ **2944/460035**).

Where to Stay Within the City Center

If you're looking for luxury, you'll find the most options along Avenida Bustillo, the main road outside town that runs parallel to the lake and leads to the Llao Llao Peninsula. The larger hotels in the city (such as the Panamericano; see below) tend to cater to tour groups or students and aren't especially luxurious or service-oriented.

During the high season (mid-Dec to Feb and Easter week), prices double. Many hotels consider the winter months of July and August to be a second high season, with prices to match. Rates listed here are generally for high season.

Expensive

Hotel Cacique Inacayal, Juan M. de Rosas 625 (✆ **02944/433888;** www.hotelinacayal.com.ar), is a new hotel right on the water downtown. It has an efficient atrium-view elevator and a fancy restaurant with bow-tied waiters. All rooms have great views, and the bottom-floor rooms include terraces. Decor is standard, with a dash of modernity. Lacquered wood, wicker, and wool predominate. Rates start at $185 for a double. **Hotel Edelweiss** ★, Av. San Martín 202 (✆ **02944/445510;** fax 02944/445520; www.edelweiss.com.ar), has reliable service and huge double bedrooms and is a solid choice in downtown Bariloche in this price category; just don't come expecting luxury. It's the most similar to a Holiday Inn–style hotel in town. Double superiors have two full-size beds, bay windows, and lake views, as do the suites. Standard doubles are smaller but just as comfortable and $10 cheaper. Rates start at $182.

Hotel Panamericano, Av. San Martín 536, San Carlos de Bariloche (✆/fax **02944/425846;** www.panamericanobariloche.com), is the biggest hotel in Patagonia and is undergoing a badly needed facelift. For the price, it offers none of the warmth, natural setting, or style of the Llao Llao (see below), for example. Rooms are spacious and comfortable but many still have old and used bathrooms, stuffy curtains, and dated carpets. Hallways are particularly dark and dreary. The spa is the finest in town however, with a lovely top-floor pool and deck. The hotel has another 100 or so rooms and a casino on the other side of the street, connected by an aerial walkway. Double rooms start at $160.

Moderate

Hostería Las Marianas ★★, 24 de Septiembre 218 (✆/fax **2944/439876;** www.hosterialasmarianas.com.ar), is a lovely, cozy inn just a few blocks from the Centro Cívico. It's a renovated, old Swiss-style mansion, and the beds have luxurious down comforters. Doubles start at $89. **View Boutique Hotel,** Tucumán 221, San Carlos de Bariloche (✆/fax **02944/522221;** www.viewhotel.com.ar), is practical, comfortable, modern, and friendly. This boutique-style hotel has a large, bright lobby and smallish rooms with dark wood and cream walls, cozy chocolate-colored fleece blankets, and lots of closet space. Doubles start at $75.

Inexpensive

Patanuk Guesthouse, Juan Manuel de Rosas 585, San Carlos de Bariloche (© **02944/434991;** www.patanuk.com), has a hostel vibe and an awesome location right on the lake. The style is loftlike, and the doubles and twins with private bathrooms here are good value. In the evenings, the garden opens up into a funky bar. Doubles start at $50.

Perikos, Morales 555 (© **2944/522326**; www.perikos.com), is the friendliest hostel in town and is a great choice for any traveler on a budget. Perikos has 10 rooms ranging from $12 for a shared room to $42 for a private double room, with breakfast included.

Where to Stay Outside the City Center

The southern shoreline of Nahuel Huapi Lake is dotted with cabin complexes for visitors. Some have only one or two cabanas for rent, while other have up to a dozen. They're a nice way to be self-sufficient, prepare your own meals, and make yourself at home. Some can be very affordable, especially outside the high-season months of January and August. Bungalows and apart-hotels are similar options. Try the fun **El Bosque de los Elfos,** Avenida Bustillo, Km 5 (© **02944/443079;** www.bungalowsdeloselfos.com.ar), or the upscale lakefront **Puerto Pireo,** Bustillo Km 17.1 (© **02944/448484;** www.puertopireo.com.ar). **Patagonia Vista,** Bustillo Km 21.85 (© **02944/448735;** www.patagoniavista.com.ar), is a new complex also right on the lake, with lake houses available.

Very Expensive

El Casco Art Hotel ★★★, Avenida Bustillo, Km 11.5, San Carlos de Bariloche (© **02944/462929;** www.hotelelcasco.com), is exclusive and elegant and located midway between Bariloche and the Llao Llao. It has remarkable services and amenities for an inn with only 33 rooms, not to mention a lovely lakeside setting. Highbrow artwork adorns palatial rooms. Plush marble bathrooms are slick and have separated tubs and a shower. Room rates vary from $360 to $600. **Hostería Isla Victoria Lodge ★★**, Nahuel Huapi National Park (© **02944/448088;** www.islavictoria.com), is a remote lodge on an island in the middle of the massive Nahuel Huapi Lake, and makes a divine upscale getaway. The views are truly stunning, with gourmet food, talented guides, and superb all-inclusive packages to match. Spacious, comfortable rooms are perched atop a cliff and the island is excellent for exploring on foot, horseback, bike, or kayak. Two-night packages start at $688 per person per double, including transfers, boat crossing, lodging, full board, and excursions.

The internationally renowned **Llao Llao Hotel & Resort ★★**, Avenida Bustillo, Km 25, San Carlos de Bariloche (© **02944/448530,** or 11/4311-3434 in Buenos Aires; www.llaollao.com), is one of the finest hotels in Latin America. Situated on a grassy crest of the Llao Llao Peninsula, and framed by rugged peaks, this five-star hotel is reminiscent of Canadian mountain lodges, with cypress and pine-log walls, stone fireplaces, antler chandeliers, and barn-size salons. Maintaining very high standards and offering a slew of amenities and activities, this is *the* place to spend the night if you're willing to splurge for a special evening. Doubles range from $450 to $700.

Expensive

Aldebaran ★, Península San Pedro, Avenida Bustillo, Km 20.4, San Carlos de Bariloche (© **02944/465143;** www.aldebaranpatagonia.com), is a remote, 10-room lakeside lodge with thick Mediterranean-style walls, curved ceilings, and dark hallways. Rooms are large, with earth-toned blankets, cozy nooks, and a blend of modern and recycled furniture. Rustic bathrooms have large tubs and spotlights. All have either a balcony or a patio. Aldebaran is a compelling hideaway, but media junkies be warned: Rooms don't have TV. Rates start at $254 for a double. **Design Suites ★**, Avenida Bustillo, Km 2.5, San Carlos de Bariloche (✆ **02944/457000;** www.designsuites.com), caters to stylish young couples who like interior design that is contemporary and minimalist, with local materials such as wood, stone, and glass enhanced by a revolving display of local art. Rooms are among the largest in town, with light hardwood floors, crisp cream walls, plenty of shelving, and small patios. Rates start at $330.

Where to Dine Within the City Center

Bariloche is full of restaurants and cafes, especially on Avenida San Martín and the side streets leading to it. As with its accommodations, Bariloche's best restaurants are outside the city center. In addition to the restaurants listed below, the **Familia Weiss,** at the corner of Palacios and V. A. O'Connor (✆ **2944/435789;** daily 11:30am–1am), and the **Casita Suiza,** Quaglia 342 (✆ **2944/435963;** daily 8pm–midnight), are solid choices for lunch and dinner.

Expensive

Kandahar, 20 de Febrero 628 (✆ **2944/424702;** Mon–Sat 8pm–midnight), is one of the best restaurants in town. In this funky and colorful old house with cozy nooks, the food is creative and fresh. For main dishes, try homemade pastas such as gnocchi with olives, trout with spinach, rabbit with quince sauce, or peppered tenderloin. Main courses start at A$55. **Naan,** Campichuelo 568 (✆ **2944/421785;** daily 8pm–midnight during the high season [Jan–Feb and July–Sep]; closed Mon during the rest of the year), is a revelation in Patagonia. Starters range from Italian and Middle Eastern dishes to Vietnamese and French specialties. Main courses, which include a lamb curry and a coconut chicken and prawns, costs between A$55 and A$75. **Santos ★★**, España 268 (✆ **02944/425942;** daily 8–1pm), is currently the best restaurant in the center of Bariloche. It's a hip, fun, stylish place, with a menu based on simple, fresh Italian food that is remarkably flavorful. Entrees include superb sirloin-stuffed panzottis with spinach and cream sauce. Main courses range between A$35 and A$60.

Moderate

Días de Zapata, Morales 362 (✆ **2944/423128;** daily noon–3:30pm and 7pm–midnight), is Bariloche's best Mexican restaurant and a nice change of pace from *parrillas.* You'll find the usual tacos, fajitas, and nachos on the menu, but you'll also find more uncommon Mexican dishes such as chicken *mole,* Veracruz conger eel, and spicy enchiladas. Happy hour is from 7 to 9pm. Main courses cost A$30 to A$60. **El Boliche Viejo ★**, Ruta 237, at Limay River bridge (✆ **02944/468452;** daily noon–4pm), is set in a country store dating back more than a century. Little has changed since the days when Butch Cassidy and the Sundance Kid purportedly stopped in for a meal. It's northeast of Bariloche, on the road to Villa La Angostura, past the airport turnoff and the town of Dina Huapi. The menu is pure Patagonian, including lamb slow-grilled on a spit and every cut of beef you could imagine, from T-bone to tongue. Main courses start at A$45. **Tarquino,** 24 de Septiembre and Saavedra (✆ **02944/434774;** daily noon–3pm and 8pm–midnight), is worth visiting for the architecture alone—it boasts a storybook treehouse vibe. There are standard grill selections, such as *bife de chorizo,* pork tenderloin, or grilled trout with almond sauce. Main courses start at A$40.

Inexpensive

El Mundo, Mitre 759 (✆ **2944/423461;** daily noon–3pm and 8pm–midnight), serves up crispy pizza in more than 100 varieties, as well as empanadas, pastas, and salads. **La**

Fonda del Tío, Mitre 1130 (✆ **02944/435011;** daily noon–midnight), is a good place to try real Argentine cooking such as *milanesas* (breaded veal cutlets) with cheese, jam, tomato sauce, or hard-boiled eggs, and take a break from the tourist scene. **Rock Chicken,** Rolando 245 (✆ **02944/435669;** daily 10am–4pm), is a local fast-food staple and a great place to grab a quick and cheap snack, such as *choripán* (chorizo sausage on a bun), *milanesa,* grilled chicken, or a slice of sirloin. **Vegetariano** ★, 20 de Febrero 730 (✆ **02944/421820;** Mon–Sat noon–3pm, Mon–Fri 8–11pm), is an unpretentious, cozy restaurant with homemade recipes.

Where to Dine Outside the City Center

Note that the majority of the restaurants outside downtown do not accept credit cards. **Butterfly** ★★★, Hua Huan 7831, at Bustillo, Km 7.9, Playa Bonita (✆ **02944/461441;** www.butterflypatagonia.com.ar), has a lovely location just above Bariloche's popular Playa Bonita. Local ingredients, from rabbit and duck to leeks and berries, are sourced daily and presented in an impeccably intricate seven-course menu. On summer days, lunch and dinner are served on the outdoor patio. The seven-course set menu costs A$180. **Cassis** ★, Ruta 82, on Lago Gutierrez, 1km (⅔ mile) past the entrance to the Coihues neighborhood (✆ **02944/476167**), is nestled on a cliff overlooking Lago Gutierrez, just to the south of Bariloche. There are usually three to five fixed four-course menus to choose from, and prices vary from A$170 to A$260. Warm shrimps with gin and lemon act as an appetizer, followed by sweetbreads in a pecan panzotti, and then a slow-cooked salmon or a lamb strudel in sauvignon blanc reduction.

Il Gabbiano ★★, Avenida Bustillo, Km 24.3 (✆ **02944/448346;** Wed–Mon 7:30pm–midnight), is an outstanding Italian restaurant close to the Llao Llao. The menu is authentic *Italiano.* Antipasti include bruschetta and salmon with grapefruit. Delicate homemade pastas are varied and fresh. Main entrees include *osso buco,* rabbit with garlic and rosemary, and a simple trout with lemon. Main courses start at A$60.

Bariloche After Dark

Bariloche is home to a handful of discos catering to the 16- to 30-year-old crowd. These discos adhere to Buenos Aires nightlife hours, beginning around midnight or 12:30am, with the evening peaking at about 3 or 4am. The cover charge is usually A$60 to A$85 per person, and women often enter for free. Also try **Roket,** J.M. de Rosas 424 (✆ **02944/431940**), or **Cerebro,** J.M. de Rosas 405 (✆ **02944/424948**).

Earlier in the evening, locals gather at the **Roxvury,** San Martín 490 (✆ **02944/400451**), for funky music and big-screen light shows. There are a number of local pubs, including **Wilkenny,** San Martín 435 (✆ **02944/424444**), and **Pilgrim,** Palacios 167 (✆ **02944/421686**). Microbrew pubs are also popular in Bariloche. Downtown, try **Antares,** Elflein 47 (✆ **02944/431454**), and **Cervecería Blest,** Avenida Bustillo, Km 11.5 (✆ **02944/461026**), the oldest microbrewery in Argentina. Next door, **Berlina,** Avenida Bustillo, Km 11.75 (✆ **02944/523336**), is hip and fresh.

SAN MARTIN DE LOS ANDES ★★

1,640km (1,017 miles) SW of Buenos Aires; 200km (124 miles) N of San Carlos de Bariloche

San Martín de los Andes, a charming mountain town of 35,000 inhabitants, is nestled on the tip of Lago Lácar between high peaks. The town is considered the tourism capital of the Neuquén province, a claim that's hard to negate, considering the copious arts-and-crafts shops, gear-rental shops, restaurants, and hotels that constitute much of downtown. The town is quieter than Bariloche and decidedly more picturesque, thanks to its timber-heavy architecture and Swiss Alpine influence. San Martín overflows with activities, including biking, hiking, boating, and skiing. The town is also very popular for hunting and fishing. The tourism infrastructure here is excellent, with every lodging option imaginable and plenty of great restaurants.

Essentials

Getting There

BY PLANE **Aeropuerto Internacional Chapelco** (airport code CPC; ✆ **02972/428388**) sits halfway between San Martín and Junín de los Andes (see later in this chapter) and, therefore, serves both destinations. **Aerolíneas Argentinas/Austral,** Capitán Drury 876 (✆ **02972/427871;** www.aerolineas.com.ar), flies from Buenos Aires. A new airline, **SUR Líneas Aéreas** (✆ **11/5278-6367** in Buenos Aires; www.surla.com.ar), began twice-weekly service in 2009. A taxi to San Martín costs about A$70; transfer services are also available at the airport for A$35 per person. A taxi to Junín de los Andes costs A$98. **By Mich Rent a Car** (✆ **0810/22-43789**) and **Avis** (✆ **02972/411141**) both have auto rental kiosks at the airport.

BY BUS The **Terminal de Omnibus** is at Villegas and Juez del Valle (✆ 02972/427044). **Via Bariloche** (✆ 02972/422800) runs daily bus service to San Martín de los Andes from Buenos Aires (a 19-hr. trip). **Ko-Ko Chevalier** (✆ 02972/411295) also offers service to and from Buenos Aires, and serves Villa La Angostura and Bariloche by the paved or by the scenic Siete Lagos route. **Centenario** (✆ 02972/427294) has service to Chile and also offers daily service to Buenos Aires; Villarrica- and Pucón-bound buses leave Monday through Saturday, and those for Puerto Montt depart Tuesday through Thursday. **Albus** (✆ 02972/423808 or 02944/423552) has trips to Bariloche via the Siete Lagos route (about 3 hr.).

BY CAR San Martín de los Andes can be reached from San Carlos de Bariloche following one of three routes: the popular 200km (124-mile) Siete Lagos route; the 160km (99-mile) Paso Córdoba route; and the longest, the entirely paved 260km (161-mile) Collón Curá route. If driving at night, take the paved route.

Getting Around

San Martín is compact enough to explore by foot. For outlying excursions, tour companies can arrange transportation. **El Sol Rent a Car,** Av. San Martín 461 (✆ **02944/421870**), will drop a car off in Junín de los Andes. **Hertz Rent a Car** is at Av. San Martín 831 (✆ **02972/430280**), and **Nieves Rent-A-Car** is at Villegas 668 (✆ **02972/428684**).

Note that two main streets in town have similar names and can be confusing: Perito Moreno and Mariano Moreno.

Visitor Information

San Martín's excellent **Oficina de Turismo** (✆/fax **02972/427347** or 02972/427695) offers comprehensive accommodations listings with prices and other tourism-related information, and the staff is friendly and eager to make your stay pleasurable. The office is open daily from 8am to 8pm, at Rosas and Avenida San Martín, on the main plaza. The **Asociación Hotelero y Gastronomía,** San Martín 1234 (✆ **02972/427166**), also offers lodging information, including photographs of each establishment, though service is not as efficient as it is at the Oficina de Turismo. During the off season, it's open daily from 9am to 1pm and 3 to 7pm; during high season, it's open daily from 9am to 10pm.

For information on Parque Nacional Lanín, drop by the park's information center, open daily from 9am to noon only, or visit **www.parquenacionallanin.gov.ar**.

A website chock-full of valuable information is **www.smandes.gov.ar**.

What to See & Do

San Martín de los Andes's heritage is in agriculture, cattle, and logging, all of which are carefully displayed at the **Museo de los Primeros Pobladores,** J. M. Rosas 750 (no phone), open on Tuesday and Friday afternoons only. Now San Martín is heavily geared toward tourism; accordingly, its streets are lined with shops selling arts and crafts, wonderful regional specialties such as smoked meats and cheeses, outdoor gear, books, and more. A lovely crafts market is open most afternoons in the central plaza.

San Martín is a mountain town geared toward outdoor activities. If you're not up to a lot of physical exertion, take a stroll down to the lake and kick back on the beach. Alternatively, rent a bike and take a slow pedal around town. Pack a picnic lunch and head to Hua Hum.

The vast **Parque Nacional Lanín,** founded in 1937, is the third-largest national park in the country. It has 35 lakes, as well as thick forests, abundant wildlife, and an extinct volcano. The park is still home to more than 50 native Mapuche communities.

Just up the hill above town, the quaint and cozy **Arrayán Tea House** ★, Circuito Arrayán, Km 4 (✆ **02972/425570**), has the area's best view. Built at a clearing in a cypress forest in 1938 by Renee Dickenson, a spirited young British woman, the house today maintains the same style that first charmed local residents. The **Red Bus** (✆ **02972/421185**) runs city tours on a double-decker bus that helps orient visitors and gives a glimpse into the town's history. Tours depart daily at 10:30am and 4:30pm from the Plaza San Martín. The tour costs A$30.

Tour Operators & Travel Agencies

Both **Huemul Turismo,** Av. San Martín 881 (✆ **02972/422903;** www.huemulturismo.com.ar), and **Pucará,** Av. San Martín 941 (✆ **02972/427218;** pucara@smandes.com.ar), offer similar tours and prices, and also operate as travel agencies for booking plane tickets. Popular excursions include day trips to the village Quila Quina, via a sinuous road that offers dramatic views of Lago Lácar, and the hot springs Termas de Lahuenco. Try to do the gorgeous circuit trip to Volcán Lanín and Lago Huechulafquén.

Outdoor Activities

BIKING San Martín is well suited for biking, and shops offer directions and maps. Bike rentals and tours are available at **Andes Bike,** at Avenida Costanera and Villegas (✆ **02972/15-552475**). You can also rent a bike from **Mountain Snow Shop,** Av. San Martín 861 (✆ **02972/427728**).

BIRD-WATCHING Horacio Matarasso is a passionate birder who hosts great bird-watching trips out of San Martín. Contact him at **Aves Patagonia** (✆ **02972/15-568427**; www.avespatagonia.com.ar).

BOATING **Naviera Lácar & Nonthué** (✆ **02972/427380**), at the Costanera and main pier, offers year-round boat excursions on Lago Lácar. A full-day excursion to Hua Hum includes a short navigation through Lago Nonthué. Naviera also operates three daily ferry services to the beautiful beaches of Quila Quina (which are packed in the summer).

 FISHING INFORMATION & LICENSES **Jorge Trucco,** Ten. Col. Perez 662 (✆ **02972/429561;** www.jorgetrucco.com), organizes day and overnight fishing expeditions to the Meliquina, Chimehuín, and Malleo rivers, among other areas. The other local fishing expert is **Alberto Cordero** (✆ **02972/421453;** www.ffandes.com), who will arrange fishing expeditions around the area.

GOLF The new 18-hole golf course at the **Chapelco Golf & Resort** (✆ **02972/427713;** www.chapelcogolf.com), just north of San Martín, was designed by Jack Nicklaus and his son.

HORSEBACK RIDING Take a trip with some local gauchos at the **Estancia Chapelco** (✆ **02972/411253;** www.chapelcogolf.com).

KAYAKING The dozens of lakes near San Martín practically call out for kayakers. **Paralelo 40 Expediciones** (✆ **02972/428213;** www.paralelo40.com.ar) organizes full-day and half-day outings in touring or sea kayaks.

MOUNTAINEERING The guides at **Lanín Expedition** (✆ **02972/429799;** www.laninexpediciones.com) have decades of experience and offer climbing and orientation courses; ascents of Volcán Lanín and Volcán Domuyo; and treks, climbs, and overnight trips in Lanín and Nahuel Huapi national parks.

SKIING The principal winter draw for San Martín de los Andes is **Cerro Chapelco,** one of the premier ski resorts in South America. Just 20km (12 miles) outside town, Cerro Chapelco is known for its plentiful, varying terrain and great amenities. Although popular, the resort isn't as swamped with skiers as Bariloche is.

To drive to the resort from town, follow Route 234 south along Lago Lácar; it's paved except for the last 5km (3 miles). During the summer, the resort is open for hiking and sightseeing, with lift access. For more information, call ✆ **02972/427460** or visit **www.sanmartindelosandes.com**.

Where to Stay

If you arrive in town without a reservation, your first stop should be the Oficina de Turismo (see above), next to the main plaza, which has an updated list of availabilities and prices. Rates almost double in most places from mid-December through February. For more information, go to **www.sanmartindelosandes.gov.ar**.

Expensive

Loi Suites Chapelco ★, Ruta 234, Km 57.5, San Martín de los Andes (✆ **02972/410304,** or 11/5777-8950 in Buenos Aires; www.loisuites.com.ar), is the first five-star hotel in San Martín. Rooms have Asian-inspired details, particularly in the modern, massive bathrooms. Furniture is chunky and heavy, and wool, leather, and hide predominate in accents. Rates start at $196 for a double. **Rio Hermoso Lodge** ★★, Ruta 63, Km 67, Paraje Rio Hermoso (25km/15.5 miles south of San Martín; ✆ **02972/410485;** www.riohermoso.com), is a delightful mountain lodge on the Seven Lakes Road south of San Martín de los Andes. It's natural without being rustic and rooms have giant windows overlooking the greenery. Bathrooms are a mixture of wood and stone, with large windows. Rates start at $370. **Ten Rivers and Ten Lakes Lodge** ★, Cerro Diaz, Ruta de los Arrayanes (✆ **011/5917-7710** in Buenos Aires; www.tenriverstenlakes.com), has undoubtedly the best view in all of San Martín, Located next to the lovely Arrayán Tea

House, this log-and-stone lodge originally opened as a lodge for fly-fishers. They still have excellent fishing packages, but anyone is welcome to spend a few nights in the four rooms. A double costs $230.

Moderate

Hostería La Casa de Eugenia ★ Colonel Díaz 1186 (✆ **02972/427206;** www.lacasadeeugenia.com.ar), is a lovely old building with bright blue trim that now functions as a bed-and-breakfast. The charming living room with its large fireplace, piano, and colorful sofas leads to nine bedrooms, named by color. Rooms range from $110 to $180. **Hostería Monte Verde,** Rivadavia 1165 (✆ **02972/410129;** www.hosteriamonteverde.com.ar), is a simple and clean *hostería.* The lobby is sparsely furnished with a giant stone fireplace. Rooms are large and comfortable, with new beds, and some rooms have Jacuzzi tubs and fireplaces. Rates range from $80 to $120.

Inexpensive

Hostería Anay, Capitán Drury 841, San Martín de los Andes (✆/fax **02972/427514;** www.interpatagonia.com/anay), has a convenient location, economical price, and simple yet comfortable accommodations. The rooms come with a double bed or two twins, and triples and apartments are available for four and five guests. Rates start at $61.

Where to Dine

San Martín has several excellent restaurants. For sandwiches and quick meals, try **Peuma Café,** Av. San Martín 851 (✆ **02972/428289**); for afternoon tea and delicious cakes and pastries, try **Unser Traum,** General Roca 868 (✆ **02972/422319**). Food is generally more affordable here than in Bariloche.

Expensive

La Tasca ★ Mariano Moreno 866 (✆ **02972/428663;** daily noon–3:30pm and 7pm–1am), is a solid choice for its fresh, high-quality cuisine and extensive wine offerings. Regional specialties are the focus, such as venison flambéed in cognac and blueberries, saffron trout, and ravioli stuffed with wild boar. The cozy restaurant is festooned with hanging hams, bordered with racks of wine bottles, and warmed by a few potbellied iron stoves. Main courses start at A$60.

Moderate

La Fondue de Betty ★ Villegas 586 (✆ **02972/422522;** daily 7pm–midnight), is a San Martín classic. Betty's friendly service and bubbling fondue pots make it an enchanting place for dinner, especially if you are with friends. A local favorite is *bagna cauda,* a Northern Italian fondue of anchovies, garlic, and cream, in which you dip vegetables. The menu also includes some nonfondue dishes. Main courses go from A$50 to A$80. **La Reserva** ★ Belgrano 940 (✆ **02972/428734;** daily noon–3pm and 7:30pm–midnight), is one of the most romantic restaurants in Patagonia, with a stone fireplace, elegant cloth-covered tables, soothing music, and superb service. On the menu is grilled trout, tender venison with fresh berry sauce, or chicken breast stuffed with feta cheese and herbs. A main course should not cost more than A$65.

Inexpensive

La Nonna Pizzería, Capitán Drury 857 (✆ **02972/422223;** daily noon–3pm and 8pm–12:30am), offers specialty regional pizzas with trout, wild boar, and deer. Calzone fillings include chicken, mozzarella, and bell pepper. Pizzas start at A$25.

9 SOUTHERN PATAGONIA & TIERRA DEL FUEGO ★★★

When the explorer Ferdinand Magellan sailed by the vast plateau we now call Patagonia, he called it the "land of giants." He was not exaggerating. This huge, remote region has some of the most beautiful natural attractions in the world, and they all come in a large scale. The granite towers of Torres del Paine and Los Glaciares national parks (though the former is found across the Chilean border), the Southern and Northern ice fields with their colossal glaciers, the rolling Alpine forests of the Lake District in northern Patagonia (see above), and the flat pampa broken by multicolored bluffs have captivated the imagination of explorers and travelers alike for 4 centuries.

A traveler can drive for days without seeing another soul on the immense Patagonian pampa. What seduces people to travel to Patagonia is the idea of the "remote"—indeed, the very notion of traveling to the end of the world in Tierra del Fuego. The people who live in this region (Chileans and Argentines, as well as some Welsh) are hardy survivors who live in a harsh climate. Such isolation is attracting more and more visitors, yet it is one destination that will never suffer overcrowding.

EL CALAFATE ★★

222km (138 miles) S of El Chaltén; 2,727km (1,691 miles) SW of Buenos Aires

El Calafate is a tourist-oriented town that has seen phenomenal growth in the past decade. It's best known for being the base from which to see the spectacular Perito Moreno Glacier. The town hugs the shore of turquoise Lago Argentino, and this location, combined with the town's leafy streets, gives it the feel of an oasis in the desert steppe. The town's population has grown from 5,000 in 1996 to 30,000 in 2009, and it's heavily dependent on its neighboring natural wonder, Perito Moreno Glacier, as well as the nine daily flights that arrive at the El Calafate International Airport packed with foreign and national tourists. Thousands of visitors come for the chance to stand face to face with this tremendous wall of ice, which is one of the few glaciers in the ice field that isn't retreating (scientists say it is "in balance," meaning it shrinks and grows constantly).

Essentials

Getting There

BY PLANE El Calafate's **Aeropuerto Internacional de El Calafate** (airport code FTE; **© 2902/491220**) is a modern complex that was built in 2000. Service is from Argentine destinations only: **Aerolíneas Argentinas/Austral** (**© 11/4340-3777** in Buenos Aires; www.aerolineas.com.ar) has daily flights from Buenos Aires and flights from Bariloche, Trelew, and Ushuaia several times a week. A daily 747 flight also arrives directly from Ezeiza International Airport in Buenos Aires during high season. **LAN** (**© 0810/999-9526**; www.lan.com) has three flights per week from Buenos Aires, and it's planning to

It's "Chile" in Patagonia

For information on traveling on the Chilean side of Patagonia, see chapter 7.

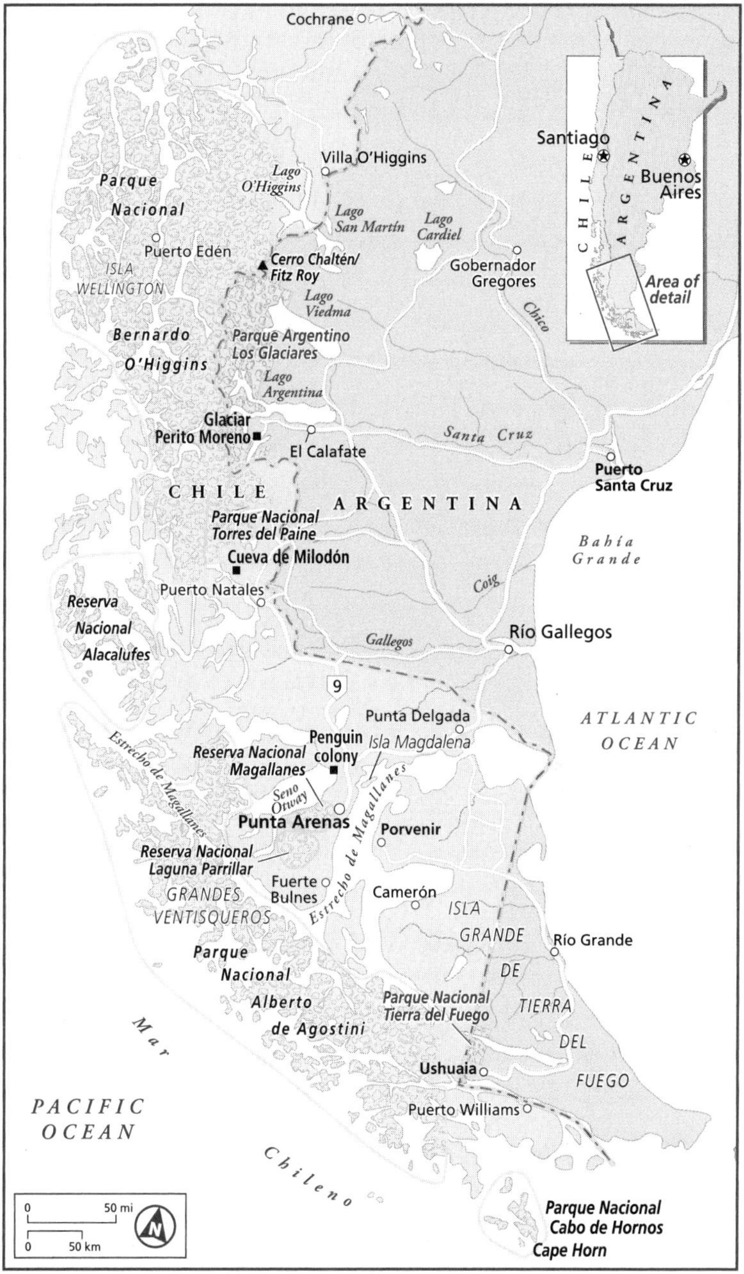

Cochrane
Villa O'Higgins
Lago O'Higgins
Parque Nacional Bernardo O'Higgins
Lago San Martín
Lago Cardiel
Santiago
Buenos Aires
CHILE
ARGENTINA
Area of detail
Puerto Edén
ISLA WELLINGTON
Cerro Chaltén/ Fitz Roy
Gobernador Gregores
Lago Viedma
Chico
Parque Argentino Los Glaciares
Lago Argentina
Glaciar Perito Moreno
El Calafate
Santa Cruz
Puerto Santa Cruz
CHILE
ARGENTINA
Parque Nacional Torres del Paine
Cueva de Milodón
Bahía Grande
Coig
Puerto Natales
Reserva Nacional Alacalufes
Río Gallegos
Gallegos
9
Punta Delgada
ATLANTIC OCEAN
Estrecho de Magallanes
Penguin colony
Isla Magdalena
Reserva Nacional Magallanes
Seno Otway
Punta Arenas
Porvenir
Estrecho de Magallanes
Reserva Nacional Laguna Parrillar
Fuerte Bulnes
Camerón
GRANDES VENTISQUEROS
ISLA GRANDE DE TIERRA DEL FUEGO
Río Grande
Parque Nacional Alberto de Agostini
Parque Nacional Tierra del Fuego
Ushuaia
Mar Chileno
PACIFIC OCEAN
Puerto Williams
0 50 mi
0 50 km
N
Parque Nacional Cabo de Hornos
Cape Horn

offer more in the future. **LADE (Líneas Areas del Estado; ✆ 0810/810-5233;** www.lade.com.ar) has a weekly flight from Buenos Aires and weekly connections to Puerto Madryn, Ushuaia, and Bariloche.

The airport is 23km (14 miles) from the center of town, which seems like a long way in the wide openness of Patagonia. From the airport, **Aerobús** (**✆ 2902/494355**) operates a bus to all the hotels in town for A$26; they can also pick you up for your return trip if you call 24 hours ahead. A taxi into town should cost no more than A$70 to A$80 for up to four people. There's also a Hertz rental-car desk (**✆ 2902/492525;** www.hertz.com) at the airport. Please note that upon exiting this airport, all car-rental travelers are required to pay an airport exit tax of 10% of the daily rate.

BY BUS El Calafate has a bus terminal on Julio A. Roca, reached via the stairs up from the main street, Avenida del Libertador. To and from Puerto Natales, Chile, **Turismo Zaahj** (**✆ 2902/491631;** www.turismozaahj.co.cl) has six weekly trips leaving at 1pm. **Cootra** (**✆ 2902/491144**) leaves at 8am. The trip takes 5 to 6 hours, depending on how long it takes to get through border-crossing procedures. To get to El Chaltén, three operators have departures at 6am, 1pm, and 6pm. The best is **Chaltén Travel** (**✆ 2902/491833**); also try **Caltur** (**✆ 2902/491842**) or **Interlagos Turismo** (**✆ 2902/491179**). The trip takes approximately 3 hours. Buy all bus tickets the day before, at least, to ensure you'll get a seat.

BY CAR Ruta 5, followed by Ruta 11, is paved entirely from Río Gallegos to El Calafate. From Puerto Natales, cross through the border at Cerro Castillo, which will lead you to the famous RN 40 and up to the paved portion of Ruta 11. The drive from Puerto Natales is roughly 5 hours, not including time spent at the border checkpoint.

Getting Around

For information about transportation to and from Perito Moreno Glacier, see "Parque Nacional Los Glaciares & the Perito Moreno Glacier," below. If you'd like to rent a car, there's a **Hertz** rental-car desk (**✆ 2902/492525;** www.hertz.com) at the airport. Rates begin at $76 per day, including insurance and taxes. To reach El Calafate via other Patagonian destinations, such as Puerto Madryn, via rental car, try **Fiorasi Rentacar,** Av. del Libertador 1341 (**✆ 02902/495330**). Most roads here are unpaved.

The town can be easily explored on foot, although many new hotels are either up a good-size hill or well out of town, so make sure your hotel offers a shuttle. Taxis in El Calafate are reasonably priced.

Visitor Information

The city's **visitor information kiosk** is inside the bus terminal. They offer an ample amount of printed material and can assist in planning a trip to Perito Moreno Glacier; the office is open daily October through April from 8am to 11pm, and daily May through September from 8am to 8pm (**✆ 2902/491090**). All other spots that look like information centers are travel agencies trying to sell tours. Two good websites for impartial information are **www.elcalafate.com.ar** or the municipal government's site at **www.elcalafate.gov.ar**.

What to See & Do in El Calafate

El Calafate is mostly a service town for visitors on their way to the glaciers (see "Parque Nacional Los Glaciares & the Perito Moreno Glacier," below), but it does have a pleasant main avenue for a stroll. As expected, there are lots of souvenir stores, bookstores, and crafts shops to keep you occupied. Heading out of town on Avenida del Libertador, you'll pass the **Museo Municipal,** Calle G. Bonarelli s/n (✆ **2902/492799;** free admission), open Monday through Friday from 10am to 9pm, with a collection of farming and ranching implements, Indian artifacts, and historical and ethnographical displays. It's worth a stop if you have the time. The **Los Glaciares National Park Headquarters,** Av. del Libertador 1302 (✆ **2902/491755**), has a good visitor information center and a lovely garden. If you are interested in bird-watching, you could take a short walk to the Bahía Redonda at the shore of Lago Argentino to view upland geese, black-necked swans, and flamingos. Scheduled to open in late 2010 is the **Glaciarium: Museum of Patagonian Ice** (www.glaciarium.com). Located 3km (2 miles) from town, its exhibits will focus on the ancient ices of Los Glaciares National Park, with a 3-D theater, interactive exhibits, and a thorough catalog of the planet's glaciers.

Attractions & Excursions Around El Calafate

For information about visiting the glaciers and the national park, see "Parque Nacional Los Glaciares & the Perito Moreno Glacier," below. Other typical excursions include the famous peaks of Cerro Torre and Mt. Fitzroy, or visiting Chile's Torres del Paine National Park. For either of these, try **Patagonia Extrema,** Av. del Libertador 1341 (✆ **2902/492393;** www.southroad.com.ar), or **Los Glaciares Turismo,** Brown 1188 (✆ **02902/498320**).

FISHING **Calafate Fishing,** Av. del Libertador 1826 (✆ **02902/496545;** www.calafatefishing.com), has half- and full-day fishing (mainly fly-fishing) trips in remote areas of Los Glaciares National Park, in search of brown, rainbow, and brook trout.

HORSEBACK RIDING Try to avoid tours that depart directly from El Calafate. A company called **02902 Cerro Frias,** Av. del Libertador 1857 (✆ **2902/492808;** www.cerrofrias.com), offers half-day horseback riding trips in the wide-open plains of Patagonia that take you up to a gorgeous viewpoint. **Cabalgata en Patagonia,** Av. del Libertador 4315 (✆ **02902/493278;** cabalgataenpatagonia@cotecal.com.ar), offers a 2-hour ride to Bahía Redonda for a panoramic view of El Calafate.

OFF-ROADING **Mil Outdoor Adventure,** Av. del Libertador 1029 (✆ **2902/491437**), takes you across rivers, over boulders, along ridges, and up to the El Calafate Balcony for a panoramic view. There are also fossils and rock mazes en route.

VISITING AN ESTANCIA An excellent day trip takes you to one of the several *estancias,* or ranches, that have opened their doors to the public. They typically run day activities and restaurant services, and some even offer lodging, should you opt to spend the night. They're a lovely way to experience the local history, immerse yourself in the wild landscapes, and experience Patagonia as authentically as possible. All of the following *estancias* offer meals, excursions such as horseback riding and trekking, and transportation from El Calafate. Close to town, **El Galpón del Glaciar** (✆ **2902/491793;** www.elgalpondelglaciar.com.ar) adds traditional *estancia* activities such as sheep shearing. Perhaps the most exclusive ranch in the area is the **Estancia Helsingfors,** open from October to March, on the shore of Lago Viedma about 150km (93 miles) from El Calafate. Helsingfors offers lodging, horseback riding, overflights, bird-watching, boat trips, and fine dining. For more information, contact their offices in Buenos Aires, Av Córdoba 827, 11A (✆/fax **11/4315-1222;** www.helsingfors.com.ar).

Estancia Cristina ★★ is situated at the end of the remote north arm of Lago Argentino. You take a spectacular 4-hour boat trip to get there, sailing past floating icebergs and the enormous Upsala Glacier. Contact their office in El Calafate at 9 de Julio 57, Local 10 (✆ **2902/491133;** www.estanciacristina.com).

The meticulously maintained **Estancia Alta Vista** (✆ **2902/491247;** altavista@cotecal.com.ar), 33km (20 miles) from El Calafate on the dirt road RP 15 near the beautiful area of Lago Roca, is open October through March and offers ranch activities and fishing. **Estancia Nibepo Aike** (✆ **2902/492797;** http://nibepoaike.com.ar) is picturesquely nestled on the southeast edge of the national park, about 60km (37 miles) from El Calafate. Closer to town, **Parque De La Bahía,** Padre Agostini and Avenida Costanera (✆ **2902/496555**), has a nightly shearing show and in-depth presentation on all things wool and sheep related.

Where to Stay

New hotels and *hosterías* are opening up every month in El Calafate. The bulk of them are 15-room inns on the outskirts of town. Really good value is hard to find here; most places capitalize on the short tourist season. Prices soar from December through February, making October to November and March to April the most economical time to visit.

Expensive

Esplendor El Calafate ★, Pte. Perón 1143 (✆ **2902/492454,** or 11/5217-5700 for reservations in Buenos Aires; www.esplendorelcalafate.com), is creative and modern, and exudes a warm and cozy feeling. This former white elephant was transformed in 2006 into a sleek new multistory hotel with a unique earthy style and stunning windows. The suites, for around $63 more, are a real bargain: They have step-in rounded tubs, a living room, and plenty of windows. Doubles start at $149. **Hotel Edenia** ★, Punta Soberana, Manzana 642 (✆ **02902/497021;** www.edeniahoteles.com.ar), is a very comfortable and functional new hotel on the outskirts of town. Rooms are similar to what you'd find in a classy business hotel and the friendly, multilingual staff welcome you with a glass of champagne. Doubles start at $109. **Kau Yatún Hotel de Campo** ★, Estancia 25 de Mayo (✆ **02902/491059,** or 11/4523-5894 in Buenos Aires; www.kauyatun.com), is a country inn located on the Estancia 25 de Mayo, only 5 blocks from El Calafate's main drag. It has a lovely rural charm and rooms are very large, with thick walls and ceilings. Bathrooms, likewise, are very large but somewhat dated. The hallway can be noisy and the restaurant and bar are both pricey. Doubles range in price from $150 to $190.

Moderate

Hostería Lupama, Calle 992 no. 19, Villa Parque Los Glaciares (✆ **2902/491110;** www.lupama.com), is compact in size but big in heart. This charming inn has towering windows and lovely wood architecture. The feeling inside is simple but rustic, with touches of wood and stone, and the spacious rooms upstairs have nice views. Doubles start at $90 to $110. **Kau Kaleshen,** Gobernador Gregores 1256 (✆ **2902/491188;** www.losglaciares.com/kaukaleshen), is a simple and charming inn with a central location. It's been around long enough to feel warm and authentic. Double rooms cost $75 and are all located around the tranquil garden out back. There is a lovely teahouse out front where breakfast is served, and where nonguests and guests alike can enjoy a A$20 *té completo*—afternoon tea with homemade pastries. **Patagonia Rebelde** José R. Haro 442, esq. Jean Mermoz (✆ **02902/494495;** www.patagoniarebelde.com) is a train-themed tin-walled *hostería* on the hill above town. The main room floors are recycled from a Buenos Aires *conventillo* (tenement house), furniture is from auctions, and even the key chains are from old train cars. Rooms are small but bright, with yellow walls and refurbished bureaus. All have showers only. Rates start at $110 for a double.

Inexpensive

America del Sur Hostel, Puerto Deseado 151 (© **2902/493523;** www.americahostel.com.ar), is the best hostel in town with dorms starting at $16 per person and double rooms at $65. Casa de Grillos, Los Condores 1215, esq. Las Bandurrias (© **2902/491160;** www.casadegrillos.com.ar), is the best bed-and-breakfast, with rooms starting at $60.

Where to Dine

A number of cafes and espresso bars are along the main drag, Libertador, and its side streets. Try **Elba'r,** in the De los Pajaros plaza at 9 de Julio 57 (© **2902/493594**), or the interesting **Borges & Alvarez Libro-Bar,** Av. del Libertador 1015 (© **2902/491464**), which has a fantastic selection of books to peruse while you sip a *café con leche.* For a light snack, try **Almacenes Patagónicos,** at Av. del Libertador 1044 (© **2902/491042**).

Moderate

Casimiro Biguá ★ Moments ARGENTINE This sleek wine bar is the best restaurant in El Calafate. The chic and modern black-and-white decor, thick tablecloths, flickering candles on every table, and young and energetic waitstaff make this place a winner. You can sample one of the many wines while enjoying an appetizer platter of regional Patagonian specialties such as smoked trout, smoked wild boar, and a variety of cheeses.

Av. del Libertador 963. © **2902/492590.** www.casimirobigua.com. Reservations recommended. Main courses A$55–A$80. AE, MC, V. Daily 10am–1am.

La Posta ★★ ARGENTINE This has long been considered El Calafate's most upscale restaurant, serving great cuisine and choice wines in a formal, candlelit environment. The menu blends Argentine and international-flavored fare, such as filet mignon in a puff pastry with rosemary-roasted potatoes, king crab ravioli, almond trout, or curried crayfish. Desserts are superb.

Gobernador Moyano and Bustillo. © **2902/491144.** Reservations recommended in high season. Main courses A$50–A$80. AE, DC, MC, V. Daily 7pm–midnight.

Inexpensive

Viva la Pepa ★, Emilio Amado 833 (© **02902/491880**), has fun vibes and healthy options such as crepes (both savory and sweet), salads, and sandwiches. Lots of juices, and a hearty breakfast, are also available. Hang out in the afternoon on the outdoor patio, or indoors with a sweet treat. **La Tablita,** Coronel Rosales 24 (© **2902/491065**), is all about meat, and it's one of the local favorites in town for its heaping platters and giant *parrilladas* (mixed grills) that come sizzling to your table on their own minibarbecues.

El Calafate After Dark

El Calafate's rapid expansion has brought with it some rustic watering holes for the tired hiker and climber. Nevertheless, its night scene remains quite subdued, with little in the way of nightclubs and late-night dancing. **La Toderia,** Av. del Libertador 1177 (no phone), serves fast food during the day and funky music at night. **Humus,** Gobernador Moyano and Bustillo (© **02902/491144**), is a very popular wine bar at the Posada los Alamos. **Don Diego de la Noche,** Avenida del Libertador and 17 de Octubre (© **02902/493270**), remains the town's most happening late-night pub.

PARQUE NACIONAL LOS GLACIARES & THE PERITO MORENO GLACIER ★★★

The Los Glaciares National Park covers 600,000 hectares (1,482,000 acres) of rugged land that stretches vertically along the crest of the Andes and spills east into flat pampa. Most of Los Glaciares is inaccessible to visitors except for the park's two dramatic highlights: the granite needles, such as Fitzroy near El Chaltén (see "El Chaltén & the Fitzroy Area," below), and this region's magnificent Perito Moreno Glacier. The park is also home to thundering rivers, blue lakes, and thick beech forest. Los Glaciares National Park was formed in 1937 as a means of protecting this unique wilderness, notable for its landscape carved and sculpted by ice-age and present-day glaciation.

If you don't get a chance to visit Glacier Grey in Torres del Paine, the Perito Moreno is a must-see. Few natural wonders in South America are as spectacular or as easily accessed as this glacier, and unlike the hundreds of glaciers that drain from the Southern Ice Field, the Perito Moreno is one of the few that is not receding. What impresses visitors most is the glacier's sheer size; it's a wall of jagged blue ice measuring 4,500m (14,760 ft.) across and soaring 60m (200 ft.) above the channel. From the parking lot on the Península Magallanes, a series of vista-point walkways descends, which take visitors to the glacier's face.

There are other magnificent glaciers in the national park; all are much harder to access than Perito Moreno but equally stunning. The Upsala Glacier is the largest in South America, and the Spegazzini Glacier has the largest snout of all the glaciers in the park. Onelli, Seco, and Agassiz are also gorgeous. All can be seen as part of the **All Glaciers Tour** organized by René Fernández Campbell, whose main office is at Av. del Libertador 867 (✆ **2902/492340**).

Getting There & Getting Around

Forty-nine kilometers (30 miles) from El Calafate, you'll pass through the park's entrance, where there's an information booth with erratic hours (no phone; www.calafate.com). The entrance fee is A$60 per person.

BY CAR Following Avenida del Libertador west out of town, the route turns into a well-maintained road that is almost completely paved. From here, it's 80km (50 miles) to the glacier.

BY TAXI OR REMISE If you want to see the glacier at your own pace, hire a taxi or *remise.* The cost averages A$300 (for up to four people), although many taxi companies will negotiate. Be sure to agree on an estimated amount of time spent at the glacier, and remember that the park entrance fee of A$60 per person is not included.

BY BUS **Cal-Tur** buses, Av. del Libertador 1080 (✆ **2902/491368**), leave downtown El Calafate twice a day (8am and 3pm, returning from the glacier at 1 and 8pm), allowing you to explore the glacier lookout area on your own. The bus ride costs a very reasonable A$80, plus the A$60 per person park entrance fee. Other buses leave on a similar schedule for similar prices from the bus terminal.

BY ORGANIZED TOUR Several companies offer transportation to and from the glacier, such as **Gigantes Patagones,** Av. Del Libertador 1315, Loc. 3 (✆ **02902/495525;** www.gigantespatagones.com.ar); **Caltur,** Av. del Libertador 1080 (✆ **02902/491368;** www.caltur.com.ar); and **Los Glaciares Turismo,** Av. Almirante Brown 1188 (✆ **02902/491159**). These minivan and bus services provide bilingual guides and leave around 9am and again at around 2:30pm, spending an average of 4 hours at the peninsula. For a more personalized tour—a private car with driver and a bilingual, licensed guide—contact **SurTurismo,** Av. Del Libertador 1226 (✆ **02902/491266;** suring@cotecal.com.ar).

Outdoor Activities

You can see the Perito Moreno glacier close up on your own in a half-day's outing by taxi or bus. But several exciting activities in the Perito Moreno region afford a more in-depth and thrilling experience. **"Minitrekking"** takes guests of all ages and abilities for a walk upon the glacier. More experienced, fit, and adventurous visitors can opt for the **"Big Ice"** ★★ option, which has a more technical approach. Both are organized exclusively by **Hielo y Aventura,** Av. del Libertador 935 (✆ **2902/492205;** www.hieloyaventura.com). **Solo Patagonia,** Av. del Libertador 963 (✆ **02902/491298;** www.solopatagonia.com.ar), offers visitors navigation trips through the Brazo Rico to the face of Perito Moreno, including treks to the base of Cerro Negro with a view of Glacier Negro.

Where to Stay Near the Glacier

Los Notros ★★★ **Moments** Few hotels in Argentina boast as spectacular and breathtaking a view as Los Notros. This luxury lodge sits high on a slope looking out at Perito Moreno Glacier, and all common areas and rooms have been fitted with picture windows to let guests soak up the marvelous sight. Although the wood-hewn exteriors give the hotel the feel of a mountain lodge, the interior decor is contemporary. Inside the main building is a large, chic, and expansive restaurant. Guests at the Los Notros must opt for one of the multiday packages that include airport transfers, meals, box lunches for expeditions, guided trekking, boat excursions, and ice walks. The guides are great, but hotel service is a bit spotty, and the restaurant is definitely understaffed. Note that prices jump substantially during Christmas, New Year's, and Easter week.

Main office in Buenos Aires: Arenales 1457, 7th floor. ✆ **11/4814-3934.** Fax 11/4815-7645. www.losnotros.com. 32 units. $480 double. $1,029 per person for 2-night package Cascada bungalow; $1,401 per person for 2-night package in double superior; $1,643 per person for 2-night package in double premium. Rates include all meals and transfers. Room-only rates available by request, depending on availability. AE, DC, MC, V. **Amenities:** Restaurant; bar; lounge; room service. *In room:* Minibar.

EL CHALTEN & THE FITZROY AREA ★

222km (138 miles) N of El Calafate

El Chaltén is a tiny village of about 500 residents whose lifeblood, like El Calafate's, is the throng of visitors who come each summer. In the world of mountaineering, the sheer and ice-encrusted peaks of Mt. Fitzroy, Cerro Torre, and their neighbors are considered some of the most formidable challenges in the world, and they draw hundreds of climbers here every year. El Chaltén is known as the "trekking capital of Argentina." Fitzroy's rugged beauty and great hiking opportunities have recently created somewhat of a boomtown effect for El Chaltén. The town sits nestled in a circular rock outcrop at the base of Mt. Fitzroy, and it's fronted by the vast, dry Patagonian Steppe. It's a wild and windy setting, and the town has a ramshackle feel. El Chaltén has definitely taken a turn upscale over the past few years, first with the Los Cerros hotel, and now with the planned arrival of two more luxury lodges.

Populated by folks with a pioneering spirit, this rough-around-the-edges town has the feeling of a place on the fringe of modernity. The town's layout is somewhat haphazard; the central Avenida Libertador (the main thoroughfare) is lined with stores, but the surrounding streets are unpaved and lead to open fields. Güemes and San Martín are the main drags; most hotels and restaurants don't have street numbers.

Getting There

BY PLANE All transportation to El Chaltén originates from El Calafate, which has daily plane service from Ushuaia and Buenos Aires. From El Calafate, you need to take a bus or rent a car; the trip takes from 2 to 2½ hours.

BY CAR From El Calafate, take RN 11 west for 30km (19 miles) and turn left on RN 40 north. Turn again, heading northwest, on RP 23 to El Chaltén. The only place for a midtrip pit stop is the rustic Estancia La Leona, where you can grab a snack and a coffee. The route is now almost entirely paved.

BY BUS Buses from El Calafate cost about $30 round-trip. A giant new bus terminal is being built in El Chaltén at the entrance to town. In the meantime, buses continue to use their normal drop-off/pickup locations listed here. **Chaltén Travel,** with offices in El Chaltén at Avenida Güemes and Lago del Desierto (✆ **02962/493092;** www.chaltentravel.com), leaves El Calafate daily at 8am, 1pm (Jan–Feb only), and 6:30pm, and El Chaltén at 7:30am, 1pm (Jan–Feb only), and 6pm, departing from the Rancho Grande hostel. **Caltur,** which leaves from El Chaltén's Hostería Fitz Roy, at Av. San Martín 520 (✆ **02962/493062;** www.caltur.com.ar), leaves El Calafate daily at 7:30am and 6:30pm, and leaves El Chaltén at 3pm.

Visitor Information

There is no admission fee to enter the park. El Chaltén also has a well-organized visitor center at the town's entrance—the **Comisión de Fomento,** Perito Moreno and Avenida Güemes (✆ **2962/493011**), open daily from 8am to 8pm. In El Calafate, the **APN Intendencia** (park service) has its offices at Av. del Libertador 1302. Its visitor center is open daily from 9am to 3pm (✆ **02962/493004**). There are ATMs at **Banco de la Nacion**, Avenida Libertador 1133 and **Banco Santa Cruz**, Avenida Libertador 1285. ***Note***: Many inns, restaurants, and stores in town don't take credit cards.

Outdoor Activities

Fitz Roy Expediciones ★★, Av. San Martín 5 (✆/fax **2962/493017;** www.fitzroyexpediciones.com.ar), offers a variety of trekking excursions.

GLACIER TREKS Similar to the minitreks on the Perito Moreno Glacier, but with less than half the people, you can strap on some crampons and explore the nearby Viedma Glacier from El Chaltén. **PatagoniaAventura ★** (✆ **02962/493110;** www.patagonia-aventura.com) conducts such tours.

HIKING & CAMPING The best guides can be found at **Mountaineering Patagonia,** whose office is at E. Brenner 88 (✆ **2962/493915;** www.mountaineeringpatagonia.com). Also try Manuel Quiroga at **El Chaltén Mountain Guides** (✆ **2962/493267**; www.ecmg.com.ar).

HORSEBACK RIDING There's nothing like horseback riding in Patagonia, and the gauchos at **El Relincho,** Avenida del Libertador (✆ **02962/493007**), have been leading rides from their stables in "downtown" El Chaltén for years.

Where to Stay

As the distances from El Calafate shrink, thanks to road improvements, El Chaltén is becoming more upscale. Formerly a destination for backpackers and hostelgoers, it now affords interesting new lodging options.

Very Expensive

Los Cerros Del Chaltén ★★ Los Cerros is by far the most luxurious place in town. The common spaces have a new cottage feel, with comfy sofas and tall ceilings. The rooms, on either side of green hallways, are large and open to fabulous views stretching above the village and across the valley. The restaurant is excellent, serving scrumptious baked goods. However, the all-inclusive nature of most packages keeps you from discovering the surprisingly fun and funky restaurants of El Chaltén.

San Martín s/n, El Chaltén. ✆ **2962/491185.** www.loscerrosdelchalten.com. 44 units. $328–$494 double; $836–$1,422 2-night all-inclusive double per person. All-inclusive packages include meals, transfers, and select excursions. Room and half-board-only options are also available. AE, MC, V. **Amenities:** Restaurant; lounge; Internet point (in lobby); library; minicinema; room service; small spa. *In room:* Hair dryer, no phone.

Expensive

Hostería El Pilar Seventeen kilometers (10 miles) from El Chaltén, Hostería El Pilar is a yellow-walled, red-roofed, former *estancia;* now it's tastefully and artistically decorated without distracting you from the outdoors. The lounge has a few couches and a fireplace, and it's a comfy spot in which to hang out and read a book. Rooms are simple but attractive, with peach walls and comfortable beds. Superior rooms are all doubles and have bigger bathrooms.

Ruta Provincial 23, 17km (10 miles) from El Chaltén. ✆/fax **2962/493002.** 10 units. A$470 double. No credit cards. Open Oct–Apr; rest of the year with a reservation. **Amenities:** Restaurant; bar; lounge; bus stop transfers.

Moderate

El Puma A mainstay that has played host to many mountaineers over the years, El Puma offers comfortable accommodations and friendly service. Inside, warm beige walls and wooden beams interplay with brick, offset with soft cotton curtains and ironwork. Although the common areas have terra-cotta ceramic floors, all rooms are carpeted. The rooms are well designed and spacious; the lounge has a few chairs that face a roaring fire.

Lionel Terray 512, El Chaltén. ✆/fax **2962/493095.** www.hosteriaelpuma.com.ar. 12 units. $160 double. Rates include buffet breakfast and transfers from the bus stop. MC, V. Closed Apr–Oct. **Amenities:** Restaurant; bar; excursions and transfers; lunch catering.

Kaulem Hosteria ★ (Finds) If you are looking for peace and quiet, very personalized service, and comfortable rooms with a great view, this charming (albeit tiny) B&B may be just right. Dark woods and natural colors fill up the two-story main room, where Fitzroy is on display. Rooms are simple, with more natural coloring, and are perhaps too simple for the price; the upstairs ones have superb views.

Av. Antonio Rojo and Comandante Arrua, El Chaltén. ✆/fax **02962/493251.** www.kaulem.com.ar. 4 units. $160 double. Rates include breakfast and transfers from bus stop. MC, V. **Amenities:** Lounge.

Inexpensive

In-Land-Sis ★ (Value) Run by two funky young mountain lovers, In-Land-Sis is just a small step up from a hostel and particularly appealing to young couples on a budget. There are eight doubles, each with a private bathroom. Four have queen-sized beds, and four have bunk beds squished in. All have views of the peaks; room no. 6 has a great view of Fitzroy.

Lago del Desierto 480, El Chaltén. ✆ **02962/493276.** www.inlandsis.com.ar. 8 units. $55 double with queen-size bed; $42 double with bunk. AE, MC, V. **Amenities:** Small restaurant.

Where to Dine

For a casual town where everyone wears hiking boots, El Chaltén has surprisingly good dining options. Climbers gather during a stormy day at **Patagonicus,** Güemes at Andreas Madsen (✆ **02962/493025**). Patagonicus serves mostly pizza and enormous salads in a woodsy dining area with fair prices; no credit cards are accepted. It's a good spot for an afternoon coffee. **Fuegia** ★, San Martín 342 (✆ **02962/493243**), has an eclectic, global menu including coconut chicken with cashews, and vegetarian items like excellent salads.

In a ramshackle old house loaded with character, **Ruca Mahuida** ★★, at Lionel Terray 55 (✆ **02962/493018**), has the feel of an old Alpine hut. The food is pure Patagonian, with stews, trout, and hearty pastas to fill you up after a day on the trail. Diners gather around a handful of tables, making this a great spot to make new friends. Reservations are recommended. For a funky scene with cool music and creative food, head to **Estepa,** at the corner of Cerro Solo and Antonio Rojo (✆ **02962/493069**). The lamb in soft mint sauce, pizzas, and pumpkin sorrentinos are superb. The restaurant at the **Senderos Hostería** ★★, within the national park (✆ **02962/493336**), is also excellent, and often offers wine-tasting evenings.

USHUAIA ★★

461km (286 miles) SW of Punta Arenas; 594km (368 miles) S of Río Gallegos

The windswept island of Tierra del Fuego has witnessed a rich history of shipwrecks, penal colonies, gold prospectors, and missionaries. Its capital, Ushuaia, is pinned snugly in a U-shaped cove facing the Beagle Channel. It is a substantial metropolis of 70,000 people with colorful clapboard houses, rickety staircases, and corrugated roofs set at impossible angles with a backdrop of beech trees and spirelike mountain summits. Not only is it the southernmost city in the world (Chilean Puerto Williams is actually lower but hardly qualifies as a city), it also has the distinction of being the only Argentine city on the other side of the Andes. What you find is a frontier town with lots of character and a surprisingly cosmopolitan feel. One hundred years ago the only people crazy enough to live here were convicts in chains. Indeed the city owes its existence to the prison, as its inmates built its railway, hospital, and port. Now it attracts Argentines from all over the country who come for tax breaks and plentiful jobs. Visitors find lots to do, whether it is visit that same prison (now a fascinating museum), explore the many attractions of the Beagle Channel, or use it as the last port of call before exploring Antarctica.

Essentials

Getting There

BY PLANE The **International Airport Malvinas Argentinas** is 5km (3 miles) from the city (airport code USH; ✆ **2901/431232**). There is no bus service to town, but cab fares are only about A$15. Always ask for a quote before accepting a ride. **Aerolíneas Argentinas/Austral** (✆ **0800/22286527** or 2901/437265; www.aerolineas.com.ar), operates eight or nine daily flights to Buenos Aires, one of which leaves from Ezeiza and stops in El Calafate. The average round-trip fare is $500. Frequency increases from November to March, when there's also a daily flight from Río Gallegos and twice-weekly flights from Trelew. **LAN** (✆ **0810/9999526** or 2901/424244; www.lan.com) operates from Buenos Aires once a day, Monday, Wednesday, and Saturday. They also fly from Santiago de Chile. Tuesday and Thursday, **Aerovías DAP,** Deloqui 575, Fourth Floor (✆ **2901/431110;** www.aeroviasdap.cl), operates charter flights from Punta Arenas and over Cape Horn. It costs around $3,000 for a group of seven people (round-trip), leaving whenever you want.

BY BUS There is no bus station in the city. Buses usually stop at the port (Maipú and Fadul). The service from Punta Arenas, Chile, costs $35 and takes about 12 hours. **Tecni Austral** (✆ **2901/431408** in Ushuaia, or 61/613423 in Punta Arenas) leaves Mondays, Wednesdays, and Fridays at 5:30am; tickets are sold in Ushuaia from the Tolkar office at Roca 157, and in Punta Arenas at Lautaro Navarro 975. **Tolkeyen,** San Martín 1267 (✆ **2901/437073;** ventas@tolkeyenpatagonia.com), works with the Chilean company Pacheco for trips to Punta Arenas, leaving on Monday, Wednesday, and Friday at 8am; it costs $54. To go to Río Grande, try **Lider LTD, Transporte Montiel,** or **Tecni Austral.** They offer eight daily departures, and the $18 trip takes around 4 hours.

BY BOAT The company **Crucero Australis** (✆ **56/2442-3115;** www.australis.com) operates a cruise to Ushuaia from Punta Arenas, and vice versa, aboard its ship the M/V *Mare Australis.* If you have the time, this is a recommended journey for any age.

Getting Around

BY CAR Everything in and around Ushuaia is easily accessible via bus or taxi or by using an inexpensive shuttle or tour service. Ushuaia's taxi drivers—seemingly the friendliest in Argentina—are fonts of information about the area. As there are a multitude of tourist excursions available (the best being by boat), renting a car is not necessary unless you want to explore the north of the island. Rentals, however, are very reasonable, from $55 to $75 per day. ***Note:*** It's worth the extra cost for enhanced insurance as basic insurance requires you to pay up to $1,000 for initial damage in even a minor accident. **Avis,** Godoy 46, drops its prices for multiday rentals (✆ **2901/436665;** www.avis.com); **Cardos Rent A Car** is at Av. San Martín 845 (✆ **2901/436388**); **Dollar Rent A Car** is on Belgrano 58 (✆ **2901/437203;** www.dollar.com); and **Localiza Rent A Car** is on Sarmiento 81 (✆ **2901/437780**). Most of them rent 4×4 jeeps with unlimited mileage. If you wish to cross into Chile at San Sebastián, you will have to acquire a special permission document costing $50.

Visitor Information

The **Subsecretaría de Turismo** has two very helpful and well-stocked offices, one at San Martín 674 (✆ **2901/432001**) and the other at the tourism pier, Maipú 505 (✆ **2901/437666;** www.e-ushuaia.com). They also have a counter at the airport. From November to March, the offices are open daily from 8am to 10pm. The rest of the year they are open Monday through Friday from 8am to 9pm and on Saturdays, Sundays, and holidays from 9am to 8pm. The national park administration office can be found on Av. San Martín 1395 (✆ **2901/421315;** Mon–Fri 9am–3pm).

FAST FACTS **Banco Patagonia,** Avenida San Martín and Godoy (✆ **2901/432080**), and **Banco Nación,** Av. San Martín 190 (✆ **2901/422086**), both exchange currency and have 24-hour ATMs. For laundry services, try **Los Tres Angeles,** Rosas 139, open Monday through Saturday from 9am to 8pm. **Andina,** Av. San Martín 638 (✆ **2901/423431**), is your best bet for a pharmacy.

Correo Argentino, at Avenida San Martín and Godoy (✆ **2901/421347**), is open Monday through Friday from 9am to 7pm, and Saturday from 9am to 1pm; the private postal company **OCA** is at Maipú and Avenida 9 de Julio (✆ **2901/424729**), and is open Monday through Saturday from 9am to 6pm. American Express travel and credit card services are provided by **All Patagonia,** Juana Fadul 48 (✆ **2901/433622**).

What to See & Do in & Around Town

An in-town walk can be taken to the city park and **Punto Panorámico,** which takes visitors up to a lookout point with good views of the city and the channel. It can be reached at the southwest terminus of Avenida del Libertador and is free.

Glacier Martial/Aerosilla ★, Avenida Luis Fernando Martial, is 7km (4¼ miles) from town. This is where you'll find a chairlift (A$50) that takes visitors to the small Glacier Martial. It's a long walk up the road, and no buses can take you there. Visitors usually hire a taxi for A$45 and walk all the way back down. At the base of the chairlift, don't miss **La Cabaña ★** (✆ **2901/424257**), an excellent teahouse.

Back in town, the **Museo del Fin de Mundo,** Maipú 175 (✆ **2901/421863;** www.museodelfindelmundo.org.ar), has an assortment of Indian hunting tools and colonial maritime instruments as well as a natural history display of stuffed birds. There is also an excellent bookstore. Admission is A$20 (with the ticket you can also visit the old Casa de Gobierno 1 block away) and it is open every day from 10am to 1pm and 3 to 7:30pm.

Museo Marítimo y Presidio de Ushuaia, Yaganes and Gobernador Paz (✆ **2901/437481;** www.museomaritimo.com), is sort of Ushuaia's Alcatraz, offering a fascinating look into prisoners and prison workers' lives during that time (early 20th century) through interpretive displays and artifacts, including the wool, striped prison uniforms that the prisoners were forced to wear. The complex also holds a number of art galleries and frequently hosts theater shows. Admission is A$50 and it is open every day from 9am to 8pm.

Outdoor Activities

BOATING The best way to explore the Beagle Channel is by boat, and numerous companies offer a variety of trips, usually in modern catamarans with excellent guides. Most companies visit the teeming penguin colony and pull the boats up to the shore, where you can get very close and watch these marvelous animals. The most popular excursion is a half-day trip cruising the Beagle Channel to view sea lions, penguins, and more. You'll find a cluster of kiosks near the pier offering a variety of excursions. **Motonave Barracuda** (✆ **2901/437606**) leaves twice daily for its 3-hour trip around the channel for A$170 per person, visiting Isla de Lobos, Isla de Pájaros, and a lighthouse. **Motovelero Tres Marías** (✆ **2901/436416**) also leaves twice daily and sails to the same location. The cost is around A$200 (including a bird and sea lion viewing and a 1-hour walk over Isla Hache). **Pira Tur,** B. Yaganes Casa 127 (✆ **2901/15604646**), offers walking tours onto the colony with controlled groups. **Motovelero Patagonia Adventure** (✆ **2901/15465842**) has an 18-passenger maximum for its daily tours.

FISHING For a fishing license and information, go the **Club de Pesca y Caza** at Av. del Libertador 818 (✆ **2901/423168**). The cost is A$75 per day.

SKIING Ushuaia's ski resort, **Cerro Castor** (✆ **2901/499302;** www.cerrocastor.com), is surprisingly good, with more than 400 skiable hectares (988 acres), 15 runs, 3 quad chairs and 1 double, a lodge/restaurant, and a slope-side bar. The resort is open from June 15 to October 15. To get there, take the shuttle bus **Pasarela** (✆ **2901/433712**); the fare is A$45.

Tour Operators

All Patagonia Viajes y Turismo, Juana Fadul 48 (✆ **2901/433622;** www.allpatagonia.com), is the local American Express travel representative and certainly one of the better agencies in town. It acts as a clearinghouse for everything. All Patagonia offers three glacier walks for those in physically good shape and impressive scenic flights over Tierra del Fuego. The cost is A$345 per person or A$270 per person for a party of two. The excursion takes 30 minutes and departs from an air club near the marina. They also arrange a bus and boat trip to Harberton and the penguin colony (A$310 per person), and they are one of the few agencies to operate afternoon tours of the national park. **Canal Fun & Nature,** Rivadavia 82 (✆ **2901/437395;** www.canalfun.com), specializes in "unconventional tourism" and is a great company to choose if you want some hair-raising adventure. The company does 4×4 trips, kayaking, and nighttime beaver watching, and they'll custom-build trips.

PARQUE NACIONAL TIERRA DEL FUEGO ★

Parque Nacional Tierra del Fuego was created in 1960 to protect a 63,000-hectare (155,610-acre) chunk of wilderness that includes mighty peaks, crystalline rivers, blackwater swamps, and forests of *lenga,* or deciduous beech. Only 2,000 hectares (4,940 acres) are designated as recreation areas, part of which offer a chance to view the prolific dam building carried out by beavers introduced to Tierra del Fuego in the 1950s with disastrous consequences. Another surprising feature of the park is its rampant rabbit population.

Chances are this park won't blow you away, however. Much of the landscape is identical to the thousands of kilometers of mountainous terrain in Patagonia, and there really isn't any special "thing" to see. Instead, it offers easy and medium day hikes, fresh air, boat rides, and bird-watching. Anglers can fish for trout in the park, but must first pick up a license at the **National Park Administration** office at Av. del Libertador 1395 (✆ **2901/421315;** Mon–Fri 9am–3pm) in Ushuaia. The Park Service issues maps at the park entrance showing the walking trails here, ranging from 300m (980 ft.) to 8km (5 miles); admission into the park is A$50. Parque Nacional Tierra del Fuego is located 11km (7 miles) west of Ushuaia on Ruta Nacional 3. Camping in the park is free, and although there are no services, potable water is available. At the end of the road to Lago Roca, there is a snack bar/restaurant. All tour companies offer guided trips to the park, but if you just need transportation there, call these shuttle bus companies: **Pasarela** (✆ **2901/433712**) or **Patagonia Transfers** (✆ **2901/445486**).

Where to Stay

Accommodations are not cheap in Ushuaia, and quality is often not on a par with price. For all hotels, parking is free or street parking is plentiful. The chain hotels are slowly moving in and a new Sheraton will have opened in November 2010.

Expensive

Cumbres del Martial ★★★ Finds Cumbres del Martial must be the most romantic and charming hotel in Ushuaia. Situated at the entrance to the Martial Glaciar, the complex of pristine, immaculate wood cabins form a leafy view of the bay with the relaxing tinkle of a mountain stream in the background. Long, white Georgian windows illuminate spacious, well-upholstered luxury rooms. There are two larger cabins with chunky, log walls, stone floors, and large Jacuzzis; but if you want charm and character and utter indulgence, I highly recommend the smaller cabins. This place is perfect for honeymooners, old romantics, and armchair tourists.

Luis Fernando 3560, Ushuaia. ✆ **2901/424779.** www.cumbresdelmartial.com.ar. 7 units. $210 double; large cabins $280. AE, MC, V. **Amenities:** Teahouse; bar; spa. *In room:* TV.

Las Hayas Resort Hotel ★★ Finds Ushuaia's most traditional hotel is located on the road to Glacier Martial, and sits nestled in a forest of beech, a location that gives sweeping views of the town and the Beagle Channel. The sumptuous lounge stretches the length of the building; here you'll find a clubby bar, formal restaurant, and fireside sitting area. The rooms are decorated with rich tapestries, upholstered walls, and bathrooms that are big and bright. The ultracomfortable beds with thick linens invite a good night's sleep. The hotel's gourmet restaurant is one of the best in Ushuaia.

Av. Luis Fernando Martial 1650, Ushuaia. ✆ **2901/430710.** Fax 2901/430719. www.lashayas.com.ar. 102 units. $298 double; $398–$598 suites. Rates include buffet breakfast. AE, DC, MC, V. **Amenities:** 2 restaurants; bar; lounge; concierge; exercise room; Jacuzzi; indoor pool; room service; sauna. *In room:* TV, hair dryer.

Tierra de Leyendas ★★ This delightful establishment has quickly gained a reputation as one of the best boutique hotels in Argentina, if not South America. A wooden mansion glows with warm, welcoming colors. The entire bottom floor is an open plan and is composed of a lounge room, restaurant, and reception area with huge windows overlooking the bay. The five rooms are all named after a local fable. Ask for the *Los Yamanas* with its stunning view and relaxing, giant hot tub. The small restaurant is open to the public Monday to Saturday so if you do decide to stay elsewhere, take advantage and book a table. The hotel is on the outskirts of the city in an upscale residential zone of rolling hills and huge mansions known as Río Pipo.

Calle Sin Nombre 2387, Ushuaia. ✆ **2901/443565.** www.tierradeleyendas.com.ar. 5 units. $195 double. AE, MC, V. **Amenities:** Restaurant; bar; room service. *In room:* TV/DVD, Jacuzzi.

Moderate

Hostal del Bosque Apart Hotel, Magallanes 709 (✆/fax **2901/430777;** www.hostaldelbosque.com.ar), gives guests a huge amount of space, including a separate living/dining area and a small kitchenette. The 40 guest rooms are spread out, much like a condominium complex. The exteriors and the decor are pretty bland, but very clean. Prices start at $120. **Hotel Lennox,** San Martín 776 (✆/fax **2901/436430;** www.lennoxhotel.com.ar), must be the hippest hotel in town, exuding style and modernity. In the lobby, modish sofas look out onto busy San Martín. The rooms are small but adequate and some of the sparkling bathrooms have a Jacuzzi. Be sure to ask for a room at the back facing the bay. Doubles start at $219. **Macondo,** Gobernador Paz 1410 (✆/fax **2901/437576;** www.macondohouse.com), is a green-roofed boutique hotel with a young, bohemian feel, mixed with style and elegance. The common room is surrounded by wall-to-wall Georgian windows, a black stone floor, and colorful, cubed armchairs. The spacious bedrooms have a loft-house ambience with red roof beams and rafters. The seven rooms start at $115.

Inexpensive

Hostal Yaktemi, San Martín 626 (✆ **2901/437437;** www.yaktemihostal.com.ar), is a decent budget option, though lacking charm and character. Situated above some stores on San Martín, the hotel's wooden staircase leads to fair size rooms with basic furnishings. Since they're centrally heated, the 13 rooms can get a little too warm and the bathrooms can be oppressively hot. Prices start at $95 for a double. **Galeazzi-Basily B&B,** Valdez 323 (✆ **2901/423213;** www.avesdelsur.com.ar), offers lodging in a family home and some well-appointed cabins out back. The house rooms are small and basic and a little gloomy; the cabins are much more spacious with lots more light. The Galeazzi-Basily family all speak perfect English and are very engaging and helpful. The kitchen is accessible as is the living room sofa and TV, and there is free Internet. Doubles start at $52.

Where to Dine

A dozen *confiterías* and cafes can be found on Avenida Magallanes between Godoy and Rosas, all of which offer inexpensive sandwiches and quick meals of varying quality. Two of the best restaurants in town are at Las Hayas Resort Hotel and the Tierra de Leyendas lodge, mentioned above.

Chez Manu ★ Finds SEAFOOD/FRENCH Chez Manu offers French-style cooking that uses fresh local ingredients. Dishes include black hake cooked with anise and herbs, or Fueguian lamb. Before taking your order, the owner/chef will describe the catch of the day, usually a cold-water fish from the bay such as abejado or a merluza from Chile. The side dishes include a delicious eggplant ratatouille, made with extra-virgin olive oil and herbs of Provence.

Av. Luis Fernando Martial 2135. ✆ **2901/432253.** www.chezmanu.com. Main courses A$60–A$90. AE, MC, V. Daily noon–3pm and 8pm–midnight.

El Almacén de Ramos GeneralCOFFEEHOUSE This 100-year-old general store has an appealing, relaxing ambience. The principal room is large and atmospheric with shelves on either side and a long, low shop counter. The classic emporium-like space is filled with old toys, fabrics, tools, and clothes all displayed from floor to ceiling. Situated in front of the port, the restaurant's menu offers items like cheese platters, generous king crab salads, and a good if very strong-smelling toasted brie sandwich. El Almacén makes for the perfect midmorning coffee stop while you're tramping the wet streets of Ushuaia.

Maipú 749. ✆ **2901/424317.** Main courses A$36–A$70. AE, MC, V. Daily 9:30am–12:30am.

Gustino ★★ Finds SEAFOOD/ARGENTINE This attractive, modern restaurant in the Albatros Hotel has all-glass walls overlooking the bay. The furnishings are clean cut and simple, with soft orange undertones and the occasional wood panel wall or rock pillar. The menu includes homemade lamb pâté and local lamb marinated in syrah wine. The steaming starter of mussels is so tasty you want to chew on the shells. The highlight of the menu is lasagna made from pastry layers and smoked salmon. The salmon dish itself comes in a huge slab the size of a sirloin steak. The restaurant—open all day, every day—is also a good place to stop for a coffee or milkshake.

Maipú 505. ✆ **2901/430003.** Main courses A$40–A$80. AE, MC, V. Daily 8am–midnight.

Kapué Restaurant ★ARGENTINE Kapué is owned and operated by the friendly, gracious Vivian family. The menu is brief, but the offerings are delicious. Don't start your meal without ordering a sumptuous appetizer of king crab wrapped in a crepe and bathed in saffron sauce. Main courses include seafood, beef, and chicken; sample items include tenderloin beef in a plum sauce or a subtly flavored sea bass steamed in parchment paper.

Roca 470. ✆ **02901/422704.** www.kaupe.com.ar. Reservations recommended on weekends. Main courses A$150–A$200. AE, MC, V. Mid-Nov to mid-Apr daily noon–2pm and 6–11pm; rest of the year dinner only 7–11pm.

Ushuaia After Dark

Nocturnal activities are somewhat sedate in this city, but a handful of good bars can help you wash down your king crab dinner with some locally brewed beer. Two to try are **Dreamland,** 9 de Julio and Deloqui (✆ **2901/421246**), and **Dublin Irish Pub,** 9 de Julio 168 (✆ **2901/430744**). Or try the more avant-garde **Kuar,** Ave. Perito Moreno 2232 (✆ **2901/437396**), with a cushioned miniamphitheater facing a giant, shoreline view of the bay. The bar brews its own beer and fermenting tanks can be spied through a glass panel beneath the dining room. It is 2km (1¼ miles) east of the city center and is open Tuesday through Sunday from 5pm to 2am.

Bolivia

by Nicholas Gill

Bolivia will take your breath away—and not just because of its bracing altitude. It may have the highest capital city in the world, and the highest lake, but what really makes it so fascinating are the incredible range of habitats and the rich indigenous culture.

Bolivia is a vast, landlocked plateau of barren plains, lush jungle, and fertile highland valleys. It has the largest salt flats in the world, where the earth mirrors the sky and flamingos drink from crimson lakes. Elsewhere, daredevil roads and dinosaur footprints lead to gilded colonial cities and windswept mining towns. Here dynamite and coca leaf are sold, and you can trace the final, tragic steps of Che Guevara. You can visit the birthplace of the Inca gods, dance with Carnaval devils, fish for piranha, or swim with jungle dolphins.

Bolivia's population is a teeming mass in petticoats and ponchos and jaunty bowler hats. Their country is the poorest in South America, yet the richest in natural wealth. Their politics and history are tumultuous and tragic, but their culture has changed little over the centuries. One might say that Bolivia is the most Andean of the Andean countries, the most South American in all of South America.

1 THE REGIONS IN BRIEF

Bolivia sits practically in the middle of South America, sharing its borders with Peru, Chile, Argentina, Paraguay, and Brazil. Landlocked since losing access to a seacoast during the Pacific War (1879–84), Bolivia still maintains a navy to protect the sacred Lake Titicaca, which it shares with Peru. Much of Bolivia is defined by the Andes Mountains. The range is at its widest in Bolivia and consists of two parallel chains here, separated by the Altiplano (high plain), the most densely populated area of the country. As you move farther east, the Andes give way to the jungle and tropical landscapes.

Because Bolivia is so vast, it's difficult to get a good feeling for the country if you have only 1 week to spend here. But you will have enough time to see all the highlights of La Paz, take a day trip to Tiwanaku, visit Lake Titicaca, and view Inca ruins on Isla del Sol (Island of the Sun) and in Copacabana. If you have 2 weeks, you can also explore Sucre, tour the mines at Potosí, and relax in Santa Cruz. The more physically adventurous traveler might consider sea kayaking on Lake Titicaca, climbing Huayna Potosí, trekking around the Illampu circuit, or taking a 4-day journey through the salt flats and desert near Salar de Uyuni.

LA PAZ La Paz is the administrative capital of Bolivia. From here, you can easily travel to **Lake Titicaca,** which is considered to be the birthplace of the Incas. The impressive pre-Inca archaeological site, **Tiwanaku,** is also only 2 hours away. Drive 3 hours to the east, and you will descend into the tropical area known as **Los Yungas.**

SOUTHERN ALTIPLANO This area made its mark on the world in the 16th, 17th, and 18th centuries, when **Potosí** was one of the great silver mining centers and consequently one of the wealthiest cities in the world. Today, highlights of the region include Potosí and **Sucre,** both of which are historical gems.

CENTRAL BOLIVIA The area of central Bolivia extends from the pleasant town of **Cochabamba,** at the foothills of the Andes, all the way east to **Santa Cruz.** Cochabamba is one of the commercial centers of Bolivia, with several major industry headquarters here, including chicken farms, airlines, and shoe companies. Some of the most colorful markets in Bolivia take place in the rural areas outside the city. The dusty city of Santa Cruz is a good base to explore Amboró National Park, the Inca ruins of Samaipata, Jesuit missions, and the town where Che Guevara made his last stand.

2 THE BEST OF BOLIVIA IN 2 WEEKS

Vertigo and claustrophobia are unwelcome conditions in a country where altitude is measured in gasps of air and your bus seat might be a stranger's lap. Fear of flying will disappear once you experience the kamikaze road network of potholes and deep ravines. Indeed, it's best to fly to get the most from your time here, but make sure you always reconfirm your flight, as schedules sometimes change.

Days ❶–❷: Arrive in La Paz ★

Soak up the atmosphere (and frequent rain showers) of a bustling market city lost in time. Mingle with the throngs of Indians in bowler hats and petticoats as you browse for something exotic at the **Witches' Market** (p. 194). Next, stop off at the **Museo de la Coca** (p. 191) and chew the infamous cud. Stay at the well-located **Hotel Europa** (p. 194), but dine at the Hotel Presidente; its restaurant, **La Bella Vista** (p. 196), has a bird's-eye view of this chaotic city. The next day explore the historical Plaza Murillo and the fascinating textile exhibit at the **Museo Nacional de Etnografía y Folklore** (p. 191). Catch some live music and dance at a *peña* such as **Casa de Corregidor (the House of Corrections;** p. 197).

Day ❸: A Daredevil Mountain Ride ★★★

Bike down the most dangerous road in the world from La Paz to Coroico, or if that's too dramatic, just watch the beautiful scenery from the security of a tour bus (not much safer!) See p. 193.

Day ❹: Tiwanaku ★

This pre-Inca city of monoliths and underground temples is a day trip from La Paz and well worth the journey. See p. 198.

Day ❺: Copacabana & Lake Titicaca ★★★

Take a taxi to the highest navigable lake in the world. Relax on Bolivia's only beach before visiting **Copacabana Cathedral** (p. 202). Here you can see a colorful procession of new cars, trucks, and buses getting blessed with beer and holy water (Sat–Sun only). Lunch on fresh trout at **La Orilla** (p. 207) before taking a gentle hike to the Inca ruins of **Asiento del Inca** (p. 203). Relax in a hammock at the artfully laid-back **Hostal La Cúpula** (p. 205).

Days ❻–❼: Empire of the Sun ★★★

Catch a ferry to **Isla del Sol,** the dazzling birthplace of the Inca gods, and stay 2 nights at **Posada del Inca** (p. 206). Dip into the gentle rhythm of island life, exploring the many ruins and enjoying the spectacular sunsets.

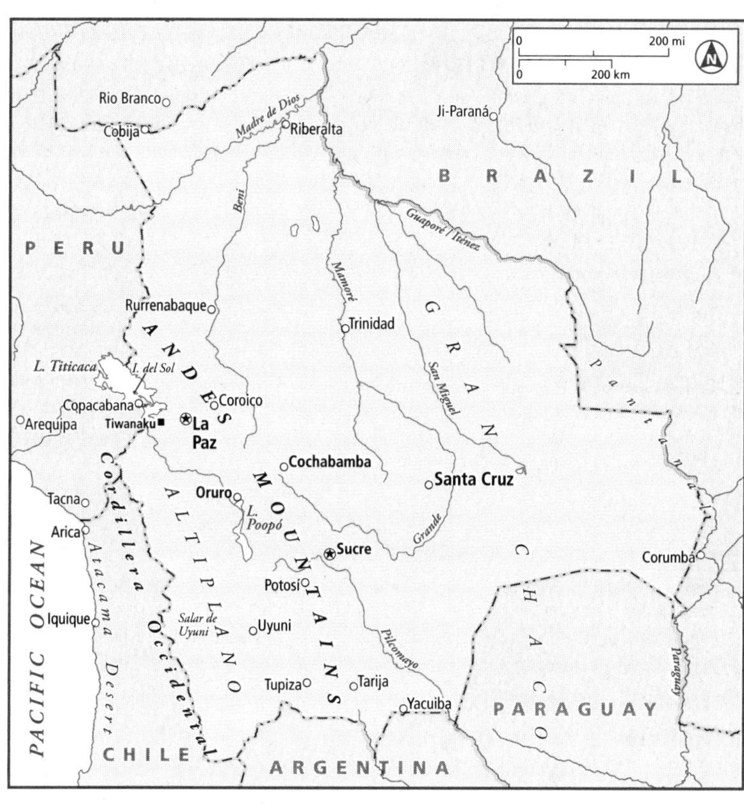

Days ❽–❿: Salar de Uyuni ★★★

Fly or catch an overnight bus from La Paz to **Uyuni,** adjacent to the largest salt lake in the world (p. 214). Visit a cactus island, green and red flamingo–filled lagoons, odd rock formations, geysers, and hot springs via the bumpy comfort of a Toyota Land Cruiser.

Days ⓫–⓭: Santa Cruz de la Sierra

Leave the Andes behind and descend into Bolivia's brand of brash *tropicalismo.* Stay at the very comfortable **Hotel Los Tajibos** (p. 225), but get out and explore the city's hinterland of Inca ruins, Jesuit missions, and subtropical woodlands. Bird-watching in **Amboro National Park** (p. 224) is highly recommended.

Day ⓮: Return to La Paz

Enjoy your final day shopping for genuine handicrafts at bargain prices on **Calle Sagárnaga** (p. 193). Have lunch at the colonial-style **Surucachi** restaurant (p. 197) before catching a flight from La Paz airport.

VISITOR INFORMATION

There are virtually no government-sponsored tourist offices outside Bolivia. The U.S.-based Embassy of Bolivia has a moderately useful website, **www.bolivia-usa.org**. For general travel information, you can also log onto **www.boliviaweb.com** or **www.bolivia bella.com**.

For more specific travel-related information, your best bet is to contact travel agencies that specialize in trips to Bolivia. Some of the best include:

- **Andean Summits,** Aranzaes 2974, Sopachi, La Paz (✆ **0102/2422-106;** fax 0102/2413-273; www.andeansummits.com). This Bolivia-based company specializes in active vacation packages, including sea-kayaking trips in Lake Titicaca and treks up Huayna Potosí.
- **Crillon Tours ★★**, 1450 S. Bayshore Dr., Suite 815, Miami, FL 33131 (✆ **888/TITICACA** [848-4222] or 305/358-5353; www.titicaca.com). Based in Miami, this company has a huge infrastructure in Bolivia and is the owner of several fantastic hotels in the Lake Titicaca area.
- **Explore Bolivia, Inc.,** 2510 N. 47th St., Suite 207, Boulder, CO 80301 (✆ **877/708-8810** or 303/545-5728; www.explorebolivia.com). This operation specializes in kayaking, trekking, and mountain-climbing packages.
- **Ruta Verde,** Calle 21 de Mayo 318, P.O. Box 4030, Santa Cruz de la Sierra (✆ **0103/339-6470;** www.rutaverdebolivia.com). This Dutch-owned operator runs highly regarded trips to off-the-beaten-track locations all over Bolivia, like Madidi National Park, the Jesuit missions near Santa Cruz, Amboro National Park, Noell Kempf Mercado National Park, and the Che Guevara trail.

In Bolivia

Although the **Viceministerio de Turismo** has an office in La Paz (✆ **02/2358-213**), the staff doesn't speak English, and the only resources on hand are some promotional brochures. You're much better off heading to the visitor information office on Plaza del Estudiante, where you can buy regional maps; see "Visitor Information" in "La Paz," later in this chapter.

ENTRY REQUIREMENTS

A valid passport is required to enter and depart Bolivia. In 2007, the Bolivian government announced that all U.S. citizens are also required to have a visa to enter the country, which can be purchased on arrival in the country for $135, and you must have a yellow fever vaccination. On rare occasions evidence of return flights, proof of funds, or hotel reservations are asked for. Visas, which last for 5 years, can also be applied for before your journey at the nearest Bolivian consulate. Visas are not required for stays of up to 30 days if you're a citizen of one of 44 designated countries, which include the United Kingdom, Canada, Australia, New Zealand, South Africa, France, Germany, and Switzerland. (Visit **www.bolivia-usa.org**, or check with your local embassy to determine whether you'll need a visa.) It's very easy to extend the visa for an additional 60 days by requesting one at a branch of the Oficina de Migración (Immigration Office). In La Paz, the office is located at Camacho 1433. It's open Monday through Friday from 9am to

Telephone Dialing Info at a Glance

- **To place a call from your home country to Bolivia,** dial the international access code (011 in the U.S. and Canada, 0011 in Australia, 0170 in New Zealand, 00 in the U.K.) plus the country code (591), plus the Bolivian area code minus the 010 (for example, La Paz 2, Santa Cruz 3, Cochabamba 4, Sucre 464, Potosí 262, Copacabana 2862), followed by the number. For example, a call from the United States to La Paz would be 011+591+2+0000+000.
- **To place a call within Bolivia,** you must use area codes if you're calling from one department (administrative district) to another. Note that for all calls within the country, area codes are preceded by 010 (for example, La Paz 0102, Santa Cruz 0103, Cochabamba 0104, Sucre 010464, Potosí 010262, Copacabana 0102862).
- **To place a direct international call from Bolivia,** dial the international access code (00), plus the country code of the place you are dialing, plus the area code and the local number.
- **To reach an international long-distance operator,** dial ✆ 35-67-00. Major long-distance company access codes are as follows: **AT&T** ✆ 0800-1111; **Bell Canada** ✆ 0800-0101; **British Telecom** ✆ 0800-0044; **MCI** ✆ 0800-2222; **Sprint** ✆ 0800-3333.

12:30pm and 3 to 6pm; it's best to go late in the afternoon. For more information, call ✆ **0800/10-3007.**

Bolivian Embassy & Consulate Locations

In Australia: The Consulate of the Republic of Bolivia is located at 74 Pitt St, Level 6, Sydney NSW 2000 (✆ **02/9235-1858**)

In Canada: 130 Albert St., Suite 416, Ottawa, ON K1P 5G4 (✆ **613/236-5730;** fax 613/236-8237)

In the U.K.: 106 Eaton Square, London SW1W 9AD (✆ **020/7235-4248** or 020/7235-2257; fax 020/7235-1286; embolivia-londres@rree.gov.bo)

In the U.S.: 3014 Massachusetts Ave. NW, Washington, DC 20008 (✆ **202/483-4410;** fax 202/328-3712; www.bolivia-usa.org)

CUSTOMS

Visitors to Bolivia are legally permitted to bring in up to $2,000 worth of items for personal use. If you bring in any new consumer goods with a value of more than $1,000, you must declare it at Customs.

There are very strict laws regarding removing national treasures. ***Beware:*** The Customs officials at the airports do search every person (for both drugs and national treasures) leaving the country.

MONEY

The Bolivian unit of currency is the **boliviano** (designated throughout this book as Bs). Besides coins with values of 1 and 2 bolivianos, all the currency is paper, in denominations of 2, 5, 10, 20, 50, and 100. It's very hard to make change, especially for a Bs100 note. If you are retrieving money from an ATM, be sure to request a denomination ending in 50. Restaurants seem to be the only places in the country capable of changing large bills.

CURRENCY EXCHANGE & RATES At press time, the boliviano was trading at a rate of **Bs707 to $1.** The boliviano has been relatively stable for the past few years. You should note, however, that Bolivia is the poorest country in South America, and it's hard to predict what will happen in the future.

When exchanging foreign currency in Bolivia, it's best to head to a *casa de cambio* (money-exchange house). Some banks will exchange American dollars and British pounds, but the lines are often long and the process can be chaotic. ***Note:*** U.S. dollars are widely accepted throughout Bolivia, especially at hotels and restaurants. **All hotel rates in this chapter, as well as some tours and airline fares, are quoted in U.S. dollars.**

ATMS ATMs are ubiquitous in Bolivia, except in small towns such as Coroico, Sorata, and Copacabana. Major banks include **Banco Santa Cruz** and **Banco de Crédito;** there are **Citibank** branches in both La Paz and Santa Cruz. Most ATMs accept cards on the **Cirrus** (✆ **800/424-7787**) and **PLUS** (✆ **800/843-7587**) networks; however, they can't deal with PINs that are more than four digits. Before you go to Bolivia, make sure that your PIN fits the bill.

TRAVELER'S CHECKS Citibank will exchange its own traveler's checks. But you can't change American Express traveler's checks at the American Express offices in Bolivia (sounds strange, but it's true). If you're traveling with traveler's checks, your best bet is to cash them at a *casa de cambio.* Most upscale hotels and restaurants in Bolivia will accept traveler's checks. For lost American Express traveler's checks, you must call collect to the United States at ✆ **801/964-6665.**

CREDIT CARDS MasterCard and Visa are accepted almost everywhere in Bolivia. American Express is less common, but it's still widely accepted. To report a lost or stolen **MasterCard,** call ✆ **0800-0172;** for **Visa,** call ✆ **0800-0188;** for **American Express,** call ✆ **800/327-1267** (via an AT&T operator).

WHEN TO GO

PEAK SEASON & CLIMATE The peak season for travelers in Bolivia is mid-June through early September, but this is only because most travelers come here when it's summer in the Northern Hemisphere. Ironically, this is the coldest time of year in Bolivia. Fortunately, it's also the dry season.

In the high plateau areas of Bolivia—La Paz, Lake Titicaca, and Potosí—it's generally always cold. The weather is only mildly more pleasant in the off season. La Paz has an average daytime high of 57°F (14°C) and an average nighttime low of 34°F (1°C). Santa Cruz has a tropical climate, although it can get chilly from June through September. Cochabamba has a pleasant springlike climate year-round.

PUBLIC HOLIDAYS Each city in Bolivia celebrates its own independence day, which always seems to correspond with a local festival. La Paz's independence day is July 16. The entire world seems to converge on Sucre on August 6, Bolivia's official independence day. In small towns throughout the country, you'll find colorful indigenous festivals on or near the summer solstice (June 21). National holidays include New Year's Day (Jan 1), Carnaval (dates vary), Good Friday, Labor Day (May 1), Corpus Christi (dates vary; usually in mid-June), Independence Day (Aug 6), All Saints' Day (Nov 1), and Christmas (Dec 25).

HEALTH CONCERNS

COMMON AILMENTS Travelers to Bolivia should be very careful about contracting **food-borne illnesses.** Always drink bottled water. Never drink beverages with ice, unless you are sure that the water for the ice has been previously boiled. Be very careful about eating food purchased from street vendors. I recommend taking a vitamin such as super bromelain, which helps aid in the digestion of parasites.

Because most of the popular tourist attractions in Bolivia are at an altitude of more than 2,500m (8,200 ft.), **altitude sickness** can be a serious problem. Common symptoms include headaches, nausea, sleeplessness, and a tendency to tire easily. The most common remedies include rest, abstaining from alcohol, drinking lots of bottled water, chewing coca leaves, or drinking coca tea. Coca leaves are readily available at street markets, and most restaurants offer some form of coca tea. To help alleviate the symptoms, you can also take the drug acetazolamide (Diamox); it's available by prescription only in the United States.

The **sun** can also be very dangerous in Bolivia, especially at high altitudes. Bring plenty of high-powered sunblock and a wide-brimmed hat. It gets very cold in cities such as La Paz and Potosí, but don't let this fool you into complacency—even when it's cold, the sun can inflict serious damage on your skin.

In general, the healthcare system in Bolivia is good enough to take care of mild illnesses. For a list of hospitals in La Paz, see "Hospitals" in "Fast Facts: Bolivia," below.

VACCINATIONS A yellow fever vaccination is required for U.S. travelers to enter the country, but otherwise no vaccines are required. If you're planning to visit the difficult-to-reach Pantanal in the far eastern end of Bolivia, a yellow fever vaccination certificate is recommended regardless of your nationality. Additionally, the Centers for Disease Control and Prevention (CDC) recommend that visitors to Bolivia vaccinate themselves against hepatitis A. Fortunately, since mosquitoes can't live in high altitudes, malaria is not a risk in the high plateau region of Bolivia, but there have been cases reported in rural parts of the Beni area and Santa Cruz.

GETTING THERE

By Plane

At 3,900m (just under 13,000 ft.), La Paz's **El Alto Airport** (airport code LPB; ✆ **0102/2810-122**) is one of the highest commercial airports in the world. Large planes, such as 747s, cannot land at such a high altitude; even smaller planes have to make sure that they have a light load before touching down. For this reason, very few international flights fly directly into La Paz and instead land in Santa Cruz. All international passengers leaving by air from Bolivia must pay a Bs170 departure tax.

FROM NORTH AMERICA **American Airlines** (✆ **800/100-229**, 0102/2372010; www.aa.com) offers nonstop flights from the United States (via Miami) to La Paz. **Aerosur** (✆ **0102/2817-281;** www.aerosur.com) offers nonstop flights from Miami to Santa Cruz, with connecting flights to La Paz. **Taca** (✆ **800/535-8780;** www.taca.com) offers flights from New York to La Paz, but you have to change planes both in San José, Costa

Rica, and Lima, Peru. Currently, there are no direct flights from Canada to Bolivia. Canadian travelers must catch a connecting flight in Miami. **LAN** (✆ **866/435-9526;** www.lan.com) offers flights to Miami and New York from Santa Cruz and La Paz, connecting in Lima.

FROM THE U.K. There are no direct flights from the United Kingdom to Bolivia. One good option is to connect with **Aerosur** (✆ **0102/2817-881;** www.aerosur.com) in Madrid and fly directly to Santa Cruz. You can fly **American Airlines** (✆ **020/8572-5555** in London, or 0102/2872-010 in La Paz; www.aa.com) direct from London to Miami, and then from Miami nonstop to La Paz. **LAN** (✆ **866/435-9526;** www.lan.com) flies from Madrid to Lima, with connecting flights to La Paz or Santa Cruz. Alternatively, **Gol Linhas Aeréas** (✆ **01080/0102-131**; www.voegol.com.br) offers direct flights from London to São Paulo, Brazil; from there, Gol offers a daily flight to Santa Cruz.

FROM AUSTRALIA Get ready for a long flight. The easiest way to get to Bolivia from Australia is to hop on an **Aerolíneas Argentinas** (✆ **800/222-215;** www.aerolineas.com.ar) flight from Sydney to Buenos Aires. From there, Aerolíneas Argentinas offers daily flights to Santa Cruz. **LAN** (✆ **866/435-9526;** www.lan.com) has a similar route from Sydney with stops in Santiago and Lima. Another route includes flying from Australia to Los Angeles to Miami and then on to La Paz. **Qantas** (✆ **13-13-13;** www.qantas.com.au) offers flights from Australia to Los Angeles—but from there, you must switch to American Airlines to Miami and then Bolivia.

By Bus

It is possible to travel by bus to Bolivia from Peru, Argentina, and Brazil. Usually, the bus routes end at the border, and you'll have to cross on your own and pick up another bus once you arrive in Bolivia. The most popular international route is from Puno, Peru, to Copacabana or La Paz. **Nuevo Continente,** Calle Sagárnaga 340 (between Illampu and Linares), La Paz (✆ **0102/2373-423**), can arrange trips from both La Paz and Copacabana to Puno and beyond.

GETTING AROUND

Getting around Bolivia is often unpleasant. Only about 5% of all the roads in the country are paved. Flying is a much better option, though expect delays and always reconfirm your reservations.

By Plane

Traveling by plane is my preferred method of travel in Bolivia. Flights aren't too expensive ($40–$100) and tickets can be bought at short notice with no rise in price. Because the roads are so bad in Bolivia, it's really worthwhile to spend the extra money to fly. Additionally, if you take a plane instead of a bus, you will save at least 12 hours in travel time. Air travel has improved immensely, but it is imperative that you reconfirm your flight, or you might miss it (and the next departing flight might not leave for another 27 hr.!). After check-in, make sure you pay the airport tax (see "Getting There"), known as *tasa.* Also, always hold onto your boarding card to prove luggage ownership at the other end.

Aero Sur, Av. 16 de Julio 1616, La Paz (✆ **0102/2312-244;** www.aerosur.com), is the largest airline in Bolivia, with a fleet of planes and routes to every major city. Other Bolivian airlines include **Amaszonas** (✆ **0102/2222-0848**; www.amaszonas.com.bo), which flies to jungle areas such as Rurrenbaque and Trinidad); **TAM** (© **0102/2268-1101**), which flies to major cities; and **BOA** (© **0102/4414-0873;** www.boa.bo), which flies to La Paz, Sucre, and Santa Cruz. I must warn you that these flights are not for the faint of heart. Delays are common and landings are harrowing, as the thin air and short runways usually dictate a fast approach.

By Bus

Traveling by bus in Bolivia has its charms, including economical bus fares and a chance to interact with "real" Bolivians. (You may even have the opportunity to sit next to live chickens.) But overall, buses are horribly slow and uncomfortable and have a terrible safety record. Most buses don't have bathrooms, and bus drivers don't like to stop along their route—some 12-hour bus rides will only make two bathroom stops during the entire journey. Buses are often crowded because most drivers will pick up anyone who needs a ride, regardless of how much space is left on the bus. Passengers sit on the floor, and then more passengers sit on their laps. Also, beware of strapping your bags to the top of buses since you might lose them along the way. Keep in mind, too, that 95% of the roads in Bolivia are unpaved, which means that 160km (100-mile) journeys can take more than 12 hours. In the rainy season, from October through April, some roads may become impassable.

Overall, if you have a lot of time and not much money, the buses in Bolivia are perfectly adequate. If you're traveling on an overnight bus, I highly recommend splurging for the *bus cama* (buses where the seats recline enough to almost resemble a bed). *Bus camas* usually only cost Bs20 to Bs30 more than the regular bus. Most bus companies offer very similar services. One of the most reputable companies is **Flota Copacabana** (© **0102/2281-596**). Always have loose change to tip the baggage handler if you're storing your baggage below. With the better companies, you will receive a security ticket to retrieve your luggage later. It is always wise to sit on the right of the bus to keep an eye on luggage as people board and alight during the journey. Be prepared to pay a small bus terminal tax as you board.

By Car

In Bolivia, there are 49,311km (30,573 miles) of highway. Guess how many of those are paved? A whopping 2,496km (1,548 miles). That's it. For the other 46,815km (29,025 miles), you're stuck on some of the bumpiest and most poorly maintained roads in the world. Additionally, there are no signs anywhere, so it's quite easy to get lost. If you decide to be adventurous and explore Bolivia by car, be sure to rent a 4×4. You'll definitely need it, especially in the rainy season (Oct–Apr), when most of the roads turn to mud.

Localiza Rent A Car (© **0800/2050;** www.localiza.com) is one of the largest car-rental companies in the country. **Hertz** has offices in La Paz (© **0102/2772-929**), Santa Cruz (© **0103/3336-010**), and Cochabamba (© **0104/4450-081**). **Avis** has offices at the La Paz (© **0102/2211-1870**) and Santa Cruz (© **0103/3343-3939**) airports. The rate for 4×4 vehicles ranges from Bs350 to Bs650 per day, including insurance. To rent a car in Bolivia, you must be at least 21 and have a valid driver's license and a passport.

TIPS ON ACCOMMODATIONS

Accommodations in Bolivia run the gamut in quality and expense. There are no world-renowned luxury hotels in Bolivia, but in both Santa Cruz and La Paz you will find some high-quality accommodations. Bolivia's specialty is historic hotels; in Sucre, you can stay in a 300-year-old mansion. Moderately priced hotels are usually spotless, with decent towels in the bathrooms. It's not uncommon to find hotels that only charge $5 a night—just don't expect anything other than a bed.

Most hotels, except for the very best ones, don't have heat. Some hotels have a limited number of space heaters *(estufas),* but you must specifically request one. Otherwise, be sure to bring warm pajamas. Also note that most showers are heated by electric power. Room availability is rarely an issue in Bolivia, except in Sucre on August 6, when rooms fill for Bolivia's independence day celebrations. Hotel rooms in this chapter fall under the price categories of **Very Expensive,** $185 and up; **Expensive,** $120 to $184; **Moderate,** $50 to $119; and **Inexpensive,** $49 and below.

TIPS ON DINING

The food is good in Bolivia—it's just not terribly varied. The diet here is rich in meat, corn, and potatoes. For breakfast, it's common to eat *salteñas* (either chicken or beef, spiced with onions and raisins, and wrapped up in a doughy pastry shell). In most towns, you'll find vendors selling them on nearly every street corner. It's also very easy to buy freshly squeezed orange juice on the street. Most typical Bolivian restaurants offer similar menus with local specialties such as *ají de lengua* (cow's tongue in a chili sauce); *picante surtido,* which consists of *sajta* (chicken in a chili sauce) and *saice* (chopped meat in a chili sauce); and *silpancho* (a very thin breaded piece of veal with two fried eggs, onions, and tomatoes). *Chuño putti* (dehydrated potatoes mixed together with milk and cheese) is a popular side dish. Usually, these restaurants also offer more international fare such as filet mignon, pineapple chicken, pasta, and omelets. In La Paz, there are a good variety of ethnic restaurants, including Japanese, Korean, French, German, and Italian. Outside La Paz, pizza and pasta are as international as it gets. To combat altitude sickness, many people drink *mate de coca,* which is tea made from coca leaves. *Tri-mate* tea, a combination of three herbal teas, is also a popular after-dinner drink. Fresh fruit is the most popular dessert. Flan (egg custard) is also available at many local restaurants. Meals in this chapter are listed according to **Very Expensive,** $20 and up; **Expensive,** $15 to $20; **Moderate,** $10 to $15; and **Inexpensive,** under $10. Prices shown don't include beverages or tax.

TIPS ON SHOPPING

Handicrafts are the name of the game in Bolivia. The country's indigenous people have been creating beautiful hand-woven goods for thousands of years. In La Paz, **Calle Sagárnaga** is shopper's central. Here you'll have the opportunity to browse in thousands of stores selling handmade goods, including alpaca sweaters, hats, gloves, leather bags, and textile products. Besides handicrafts, you can also buy folksy good-luck charms, from llama fetuses to miniature homes (supposedly, if you buy something in miniature, you'll soon have the *real* thing). Local markets are also a great place to find unique gifts. The **Sunday market in Tarabuco,** about an hour outside Sucre, is considered one of the best in Bolivia.

Bargaining is not part of Bolivian culture—for the most part, prices are fixed. If you play your cards right, you may be able to shave a few dollars off the asking price, but in general, most salespeople won't drop their prices significantly. Fortunately, prices are already rock bottom.

Bolivia

American Express There are two American Express travel offices in Bolivia, both run by Magri Turismo, but you can't exchange traveler's checks at either office. In La Paz, the office is on Calle Capitán Ravelo 2101 (✆ **0102/2442-727**). In Santa Cruz, the office is at the intersection of Calle Warnes and Calle Potosí (✆ **0103/3334-5663**).

Business Hours In general, business hours are Monday through Friday from 9am to 12:30pm and from 2:30 to 6:30pm. In smaller towns, such as Sucre and Potosí, *everything* closes down from noon until 3pm. In La Paz and Santa Cruz, most banks are open from about 9am to 4pm. Some banks do close in the middle of the day, so it's best to take care of your banking needs early in the morning. Most banks, museums, and stores are open on Saturday from 10am to noon. Everything is closed on Sunday.

Doctors & Hospitals **Clínica Cemes,** Av. 6 De Agosto 2881 (✆ **0102/2430-360**), and **Clínica del Sur** (✆ **0102/278-4001** or 278-4002), on Avenida Hernando Siles and the corner of Calle 7 in the Obrajes neighborhood, are the best hospitals in La Paz. These hospitals are also where you'll most likely find English-speaking doctors. For hospitals in other cities, see the "Fast Facts" for each individual city.

Drug Laws In Bolivia, it is legal to chew coca leaves and drink tea made from coca. (But note that it is illegal to bring these products into the U.S.) Cocaine, marijuana, and heroin are all highly illegal. Penalties are strongest for people caught selling drugs, but if you're caught buying or in possession, you're in for a lot of trouble.

Electricity The majority of outlets in Bolivia are 220 volts at 50 cycles. But in places such as La Paz and Potosí, it's common to see 110 volts at 50 cycles. To be on the safe side, always ask before plugging anything in.

Embassies & Consulates In La Paz, the embassies are: **Australia,** Av. Arce 2081, Edificio Montevideo (✆ **0102/2440-459**); Canada, Calle Victor Sanjínez 2678, Edificio Barcelona, 2nd Floor (✆ **0102/2415-021**); the **United Kingdom,** Av. Arce 2708 (✆ **0102/2433-424**); and the **United States,** Av. Arce 2780 (✆ **0102/2430-120**).

Emergencies Call ✆ **110** for the police or ✆ **118** for an ambulance.

Internet Access Internet service is available almost everywhere in Bolivia, with the possible exception of Isla del Sol on Lake Titicaca. Connections in major cities cost Bs3 per hour. In more faraway places, such as Sorata and Copacabana, connections can cost up to Bs10 an hour.

Language Spanish is the language most commonly used in business transactions. But indigenous languages, such as Quechua and Aymara, are also widely spoken throughout the country. It's best to come to Bolivia with a basic knowledge of Spanish. Outside of the major tourist sights, it's hard to find someone who speaks English.

Liquor Laws The official drinking age in Bolivia is 18. At clubs you often need to show a picture ID for admittance.

Newspapers & Magazines *La Razón* (published in La Paz) is one of the most popular Spanish-language newspapers in Bolivia. *El Nuevo Día* (in Santa Cruz) and *Los Tiempos* (in Cochabamba) also provide local news for their respective regions. If you're lucky, you may find English copies of *Time* or *Newsweek.*

Police Throughout Bolivia, you can reach the police by dialing ✆ **110.** The tourist police can also help sort out your problems in nonemergency situations. In La Paz, call ✆ **0102/2225-016,** and in Santa Cruz, ✆ **0103/3364-345.**

Post Offices & Mail Most post offices in Bolivia are open Monday through Friday from 8:30am to 8pm, Saturday from 8:30am to 6pm, and Sunday from 9am to noon. It costs Bs5 to mail a letter to the United States, Bs7 to Australia, and Bs6 to Europe. From time to time, you can buy stamps at kiosks and newspaper stands. There are no public mailboxes, so you'll have to mail your letter from the post office.

Restrooms The condition of public facilities is surprisingly good in Bolivia. In museums, the toilets are relatively clean, but they never have toilet paper. Note that most buses don't have toilet facilities, and on long-distance bus rides, the driver may only stop once or twice in a 12-hour stretch. And when they do stop, the facilities are often horrendous—usually smelly, squat toilets. It's always useful to have a roll of toilet paper handy.

Safety La Paz and Santa Cruz are the most dangerous cities in Bolivia. You'll need to beware of camera snatchers and be careful in crowded areas and hold on tightly to your personal belongings. Watch out for thieves who try to stain your bags (usually with mustard or peanut butter); they offer to help clean you off while cleaning you out. Taxis in La Paz can also be dangerous; never get in an unmarked taxi. Legitimate cabs have bright signs on top that illuminate their telephone numbers. Before you get in, be sure to write down the cab's number. If you're ever in doubt, ask a restaurant or hotel to call you a taxi. Report all problems to the tourist police (see "Police," above.)

Smoking There are no public bans on smoking in Bolivia; however, most hotels have some nonsmoking rooms.

Taxes While the Bolivian sales tax (IVA) is officially 13%, a tax is rarely charged since most transactions are informal. You'll likely only pay the tax if staying at a high end hotel or dining at a fancy restaurant.

Telephone & Fax Most high-end hotels in La Paz, Santa Cruz, and Cochabamba offer international direct-dial and long-distance service and in-house fax transmission. But these calls tend to be quite expensive, as hotels often levy a surcharge, even if you're calling a toll-free access number.

Practically every single town in Bolivia has an **Entel** office (almost always located in the main plaza). From here, you can make local, long-distance, and international calls. It's actually much more economical to make your international calls from an Entel office than to use an international calling card. For example, for calls to the United States, AT&T, MCI, and Sprint all charge about Bs70 for the first minute and Bs16 for each additional minute, plus a 10% surcharge. Entel charges Bs5 to Bs10 per minute.

To make local calls from a public phone, you need a phone card. You can buy them at any Entel office or any kiosk on the street. The average local call costs about Bs2 for 3 minutes.

For tips on dialing, see "Telephone Dialing Info at a Glance," on p. 179.

Time Zone Bolivia is 4 hours behind GMT (Greenwich Mean Time), except during daylight saving time, when it is 5 hours behind.

Tipping Restaurants in Bolivia never add a service charge. It's expected that you will add a 10% to 15% gratuity to the total bill. Taxi drivers don't expect tips. It's common to tip hotel porters about Bs4 to Bs8 per bag.

Water Always drink bottled water in Bolivia. Most hotels provide bottled water in the bathrooms, and you can buy bottles of water on practically any street corner. Small bottles cost about Bs1 to Bs2; large bottles cost just Bs3. Most restaurants use ice made from boiled water, but always ask to be sure.

4 LA PAZ ★★

The city of La Paz is nestled in a valley atop the Bolivian plateau, surrounded by snowy peaks and dominated by the white head of Illimani, the sacred mountain. The setting is sure to take your breath away (and if the setting doesn't, the 3,739m/12,264-ft. altitude will), but that's not what I love best about La Paz. The Paceños themselves, the city's inhabitants, are what make this place unforgettable. No other major South American city holds onto its past so firmly. Many of the women wear traditional clothing every day: colorful multilayered petticoats, fringed shawls, lace aprons, and (oddest of all) bowler hats, which look as if they came straight from a prewar London haberdashery. You'll see these women throughout the city—on the buses, in the churches, shopping, or perhaps setting up their own shops.

They probably won't be setting up shop inside, though—hardly anyone does in La Paz. The city is one giant street market. In stalls on the sidewalks or at street corners, you can buy not only batteries and chewing gum, but also dice and leather dice cups, socks, hats, sneakers, cameras, and telephones. In the Mercado Negro (Black Market) area of the city, computers, electric drills, bookcases, office supplies, and everything else you could think of are all displayed on the sidewalk. At the Mercado de los Brujos (Witches' Market), the discerning shopper can find the finest in good-luck statuettes and all the materials required for a proper offering to Pachamama, the Earth Mother, including baskets of dried llama fetuses. Perhaps *you* aren't in the market for such things, but just being in a place where people are is half the fun of La Paz.

ESSENTIALS

Getting There

Getting to La Paz is not an easy feat. For information on arriving by plane or bus, see "Getting There" in "Planning Your Trip to Bolivia," earlier in this chapter.

El Alto Airport (airport code LPB; ✆ **0102/2810-122**) is 25 minutes from the center of La Paz. A **taxi** ride to the city center should cost about Bs50. Most hotels will send a taxi to pick you up at the airport (when you arrive, a driver will be waiting for you with a welcome sign), but the taxi still costs about Bs55. Alternatively, you can take a minibus into the center of town. **GoTransTur buses** wait outside the airport (behind the taxis) and leave every 4 minutes daily from 6:15am to 9pm. The minibuses go past Plaza San Francisco and up Avenida 16 de Julio (La Paz's main street) to Plaza Isabel La Católica. The ride costs only Bs5, but the buses usually fill up, and it's hard to squeeze into the tight seats if you have luggage.

If you're arriving by bus, the main **bus terminal** is located on Plaza Antofagasta at the intersection of Avenida Uruguay, a short taxi ride (about 4 min.; Bs10) from the heart of town. You'll easily find a taxi outside the terminal.

Getting Around

BY TAXI You will never be at a loss for a taxi in La Paz. Because unemployment is so high in Bolivia, many people have converted their cars into taxis. ***But beware:*** You'll hear sketchy stories about these rogue taxi drivers. The most reliable taxi companies display brightly lit signs with their telephone numbers on top of their taxis. Drivers don't use meters, but fares are generally fixed. Rides within the center of town or to the Sopocachi neighborhood should only cost Bs7.

BY TRUFI The streets of La Paz are clogged with *trufis* (minibuses), which are always packed with locals. The routes are convoluted and confusing, except in the center of town (from Plaza San Francisco to Plaza del Estudiante), where *trufis* travel down one street without making any turns. So, if you're in the center of town and you're planning on going straight, flag down a *trufi.* There are no designated stops; drivers stop when they see prospective passengers. The fare is Bs2, payable to the driver at the end of your ride. To signal that you want to get off, simply shout *"Bajo"* or *"Me quedo aquí."*

BY FOOT It's hard to walk anywhere at an altitude of 3,739m (12,264 ft.) without feeling winded. But it's especially hard to walk around La Paz, where it feels as if all the streets have a steep uphill climb. After you spend a few days acclimating to the altitude, walking gets a little easier. Still, on streets such as Calle Sagárnaga, where the number of street-side vendors is roughly equivalent to the number of pedestrians, trying to fight your way through the throngs of people can be quite a challenge. I recommend walking around the center of town; it's fascinating to see the local people on the streets. But if you have to go a long distance—from one side of the city to another—it's much easier on the feet and the body to take a taxi or *trufi.*

Visitor Information

There are two very helpful government-run information offices in La Paz. The most centrally located office is at the end of El Prado (La Paz's main street) at Plaza del Estudiante; you can buy excellent maps here. The other office is just outside the main bus terminal. Both offices are open Monday through Friday from 9am to 6pm and Saturday from 10am to 12:30pm. Additionally, **Crillon Tours,** Av. Camacho 1233 (✆ **0102/2337-533,** or 305/358-5353 in the U.S.), is very helpful. The agents here can arrange city tours and trips throughout Bolivia.

FAST FACTS To exchange traveler's checks or foreign currency, your best bet is to head to one of the *casas de cambio* on Avenida Camacho. Two of the best are **Cambios "America,"** Av. Camacho 1233 near the corner of Ayacucho, and the **Casa de Cambio,** Av. Camacho 1311 at the corner of Colón. In general, Avenida Camacho is the banking center of La Paz—you'll find all types of ATMs here, as well as most Bolivian banks. **Citibank** is nearby at Av. 16 de Julio 1434 (✆ **0800/10-2000**); they exchange Citibank traveler's checks for free.

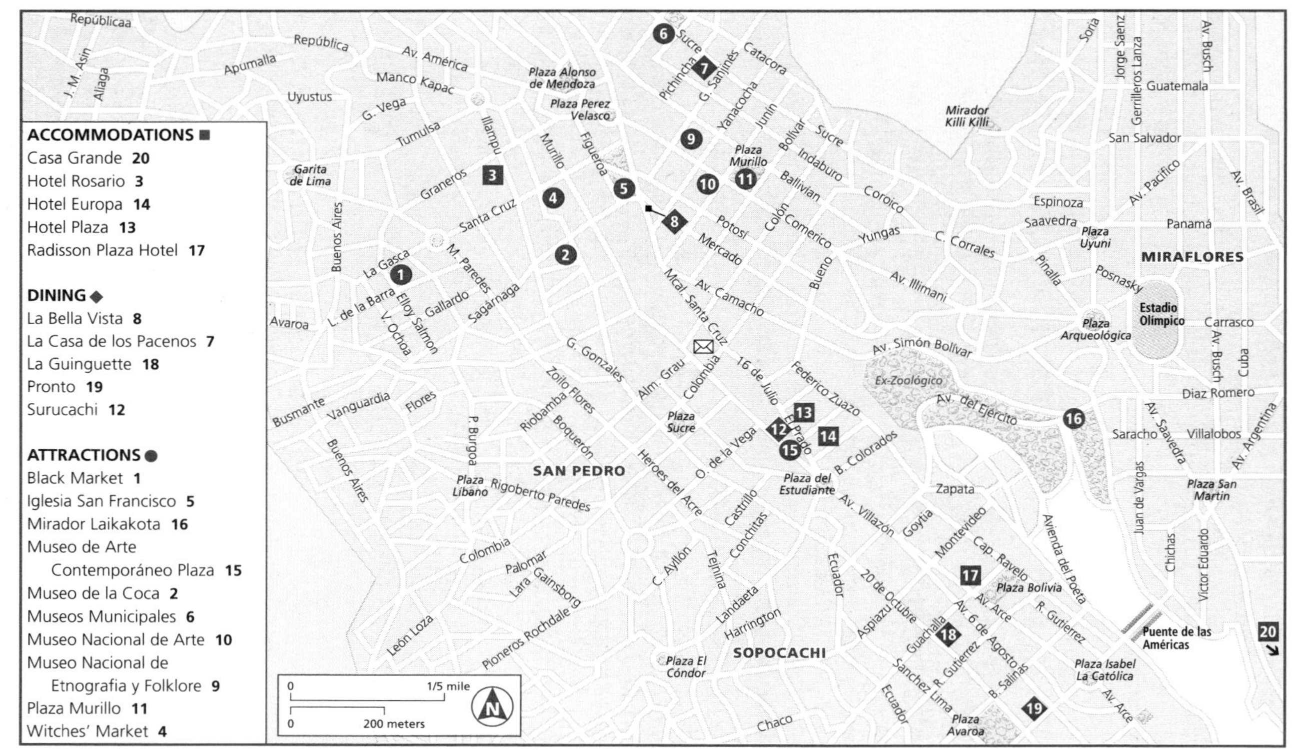
ACCOMMODATIONS ■
Casa Grande 20
Hotel Rosario 3
Hotel Europa 14
Hotel Plaza 13
Radisson Plaza Hotel 17
DINING ◆
La Bella Vista 8
La Casa de los Pacenos 7
La Guinguette 18
Pronto 19
Surucachi 12
ATTRACTIONS ●
Black Market 1
Iglesia San Francisco 5
Mirador Laikakota 16
Museo de Arte Contemporáneo Plaza 15
Museo de la Coca 2
Museos Municipales 6
Museo Nacional de Arte 10
Museo Nacional de Etnografia y Folklore 9
Plaza Murillo 11
Witches' Market 4
MIRAFLORES
SAN PEDRO
SOPOCACHI
Estadio Olímpico
Plaza Murillo
Plaza San Martin
Puente de las Américas
Mirador Killi Killi
Plaza Alonso de Mendoza
Plaza Perez Velasco
Garita de Lima
Plaza Uyuni
Plaza Arqueológica
Ex-Zoológico
Plaza Sucre
Plaza del Estudiante
Plaza Libano
Plaza Bolivia
Plaza Isabel La Católica
Plaza El Cóndor
Plaza Avaroa
0 1/5 mile
0 200 meters

In case of an **emergency,** call ✆ **110** for the regular police. For the **tourist police,** call ✆ 0102/2225-016. For an **ambulance,** call ✆ **118** or 0107/1268-502. If you need medical attention, the two best hospitals in La Paz are **Clínica Cemes,** Av. 6 De Agosto 2881 (✆ 0102/2430-360), and **Clínica del Sur,** at Avenida Hernando Siles and the corner of Calle 7 in the Obrajes neighborhood (✆ 0102/2784-001). **Farmacia Red Bolivia,** 16 de Julio 1473 (✆ 0102/2331-838), is probably the most centrally located 24-hour pharmacy in La Paz. If you need a delivery, try calling **Farmacia La Paz** at ✆ 0102/2371-828.

There is no lack of Internet cafes in La Paz, especially on Avenida 16 de Julio. The average cost is Bs7 an hour. You'll find the fastest Internet connections at **WeBolivia,** Av. 16 de Julio 1764; **Punto Entel,** Av. 16 de Julio 1473; and **Pl@net,** Calle Sagárnaga 213 at the corner of Murillo.

The main **post office** is in a large building on the corner of Avenida Mariscal Santa Cruz and Oruro. The post office is open Monday through Friday from 8:30am to 8:30pm, Saturday from 8:30am to 6pm, and Sunday from 9am to noon.

Punto Entel is the main telephone provider in La Paz. There are two offices on El Prado: one at Mariscal Santa Cruz 1287, the other at Av. 15 de Julio 1473. You can make local, long-distance, and international calls from these offices. It costs about Bs8 per minute to call the United States—a bargain compared to what most international companies charge. You can also buy phone cards here or at local kiosks to use the pay phones located throughout the city.

WHAT TO SEE & DO

Iglesia de San Francisco ★ The intricately stone-carved facade of the San Francisco church is one of the finest examples of baroque-mestizo architecture in the Americas. Look closely and you'll see a wealth of indigenous symbols—from masked figures to snakes, dragons, and tropical birds. The cornerstone for the original San Francisco church was placed in this spot in 1548, 1 year before the founding of La Paz. The church standing here today is not the original; it was completed in 1784. Once inside, the baroque influence seems to disappear. The small cedar altars with gold-leaf designs are much more typical of the neoclassical era.

Plaza San Francisco, at the north end of Av. Mariscal Santa Cruz. Free admission. Mon–Sat 4–6pm.

Mirador Laikakota From the lower points of La Paz, you may have noticed that, in the near distance, there is a large hill with a funky blue tower on top of it. This is the Mirador Laikakota, a good lookout point, offering a 360-degree view of La Paz. The Mirador isn't simply a *mirador* (view point)—it's also a very large children's park with rides, playgrounds, and food stands. To enjoy the best views, walk past all the playgrounds to the far end of the park. This is a good spot for a photo of the mighty snow-covered Illimani.

Av. del Ejército near the corner of Díaz Romero, Miraflores. Admission Bs7. Daily 8:30am–7pm.

Museo de Arte Contemporáneo Plaza ★★ The powerful art in this museum does an excellent job of conveying the issues that affect modern-day Bolivians. Notable permanent pieces include a collection of plaster sculptures by the museum's owner, Herman Plaza, called *Cuando los Hijos se Van (When the Kids Leave),* a very real depiction of young people who are leaving Bolivia for the United States; and paintings by José Rodríguez-Sánchez, who comes from Cochabamba, where the U.S.-directed program to eradicate coca growing in the region has wreaked havoc on the local people. The museum also houses the work of some well-known international artists. Occasionally, there is a Spanish-speaking guide who can take you on a 30-minute tour of the museum.

Even if there were no art here, it still would be worth a visit to see the interior of the 126-year-old mansion that houses the museum. This building and the bus station are the only structures in Bolivia that were designed by Señor Eiffel, of Eiffel Tower fame.

Av. 16 de Julio 1698 (near Plaza del Estudiante). ✆ **0102/2335-905.** Admission Bs15. Daily 9am–9pm.

Museo de la Coca Moments This museum provides visitors with a true "only in Bolivia" experience. Coca leaves have been an important part of Bolivian culture for thousands of years, and this tiny museum is dedicated solely to the coca leaf and its history. You'll learn tons of interesting facts about the coca leaf's healing properties, its nutritional value, and how it's transformed into cocaine. However, the real highlight is learning the proper way to chew coca leaves. Apparently, you must chew the bitter leaves for several minutes on one side of your mouth; once you've mashed up the leaves, the museum's owner will give you a pasty but sweet coca substance to add to the mix. Goodbye, altitude sickness! Set aside about an hour for your visit here.

Linares 906 (near Calle Sagárnaga). ✆ **5912/2311-998.** www.cocamuseum.com. Admission Bs10. Daily 10am–7pm.

Museo Nacional de Arte In the 17th and 18th centuries, Potosí may have been the mining center of the world. However, it was also a thriving cultural center and the home of some of the most famous colonial artists in the Americas. This museum is a treasure trove of colonial art, and it displays some of the most famous works of these artists. One of the most impressive is Gaspar Miguel de Berrio's two-paneled *Adoración de los Reyes y Adoración de los Pastores,* which is one of the few Bolivian colonial paintings with an African figure in it. There is an entire room dedicated to Melchor Pérez Holguín, who was actually a mestizo; if you look carefully at his work, you can see some indigenous influences. There are also several galleries dedicated to contemporary Bolivian art. The building dates from 1775. Plan on spending about an hour and a half here.

On the corner of Comercio and Socabaya (off Plaza Murillo). ✆ **0102/2408-600.** www.mna.org.bo. Admission Bs10. Tues–Sat 9:30am–12:30pm and 3–7pm; Sun 9am–12:30pm.

Museo Nacional de Etnografía y Folklore This museum is dedicated to the rich local culture in Bolivia. There are exhibits dedicated to specific tribes, including the URKU, who live near Lake Titicaca, as well as art that relates to the Casa de la Moneda (the Royal Mint) in Potosí. The real star here, however, is the *Tres Milenios de Tejidos (3,000 Years of Textiles)* exhibit, a varied collection of richly colored ponchos, skirts, and blankets that women use to carry their children. When you see all of them together, you really begin to understand that these aren't simply ponchos, skirts, or blankets—rather, these are works of art and self-expression. Plan on spending about 45 minutes here.

Ingavi 916 (at the corner of Genaro Sanjinés). ✆ **591/22408-640.** www.musef.org.bo. Free admission. Mon–Sat 9am–12:30pm and 3–7pm; Sun 9am–12:30pm.

Museos Municipales The Museos Municipales is actually a collection of four museums all located on the beautiful Spanish-style Calle Jaén. One ticket—purchased from the Museo Costumbrista Juan de Vargas (see below)—will allow you to gain access to all of them. Visiting four museums sounds like a lot, but they are all small, and it only takes about an hour to see everything. ***Note:*** There are very few explanations in English at the museums, and the ones in Spanish aren't especially descriptive.

If you only have time (or patience) for one museum, I recommend visiting the **Museo de Metales Preciosos** ★, Calle Jaén 777, where you'll see interesting gold and silver belts, necklaces, bowls, crowns, and bracelets from both the Inca and Tiwanaku cultures, as well as a Tiwanaku monolith. The courtyard here is also quite interesting: If you look closely at the ground, you can see the remains of sheep bones, which the Spanish used as home decorations during the colonial era.

The **Museo Costumbrista Juan de Vargas,** Calle Jaén on the corner of Calle Sucre, specializes in the early-20th-century history of La Paz. Some amazing photographs are on display, as well as old pianos and phonographs and many modern figurines depicting all styles of life and clothing in La Paz.

The **Museo del Litoral Boliviano,** Calle Jaén 789, is the least interesting of the bunch. It's tiny, and it houses relics from the Pacific War (1879–84), when Bolivia lost its access to the sea. On display are portraits of Bolivian generals, uniforms, guns, gun cases, and information about Ignacia Zeballos (one of the founders of the Red Cross, who was from Santa Cruz, Bolivia).

The **Museo Casa de Murillo,** Calle Jaén 790, is a beautiful old mansion dating from the 18th century. Inside, you will find baroque-style carved-wood furniture, including intricate picture frames. The house itself is also historically significant—the home of General Murillo, a prominent player in Bolivia's independence movement, is where the revolutionary leaders drew up Bolivia's declaration of independence.

Calle Jaén (near Calle Sucre). ✆ **591/22280-553.** Admission Bs4 adults, free for students and seniors over 65. Tues–Fri 9:30am–12:30pm and 3–7pm; Sat–Sun 9am–1pm.

Plaza Murillo Plaza Murillo is the historical center of La Paz. During colonial times, Plaza Murillo was on the Spanish side of the Prado, and it became the center of the action because it was the main water source in town. In its glory days, the plaza was surrounded by eucalyptus trees and a statue of Neptune. In 1900, the plaza was officially named Plaza Murillo after General Murillo, one of the heroes of the Bolivian independence movement.

On one side of the plaza, you'll find the neoclassical **cathedral,** which took 152 years to build (1835–1987). The towers are the newest part—they were constructed for the arrival of Pope John Paul II in 1989. If you want to visit the inside of the cathedral, it's open Monday to Friday from 3:30 to 7pm and in the mornings on Saturday and Sunday.

Next to the cathedral is the colonial **Government Palace,** also known as the Palacio Quemado (Burned Palace). Originally La Paz's City Hall and now the office of Bolivia's president, the building has been burned eight times. Every Thursday at 9am, you can take 15-minute guided tours in Spanish. Outside the Government Palace, you will probably notice guards in red uniforms. During the Pacific War (1879–84), when Bolivia lost its sea coast to Chile, the soldiers wore red uniforms. Today, these uniforms send the message that Chile must return that land to Bolivia.

Across from the palace is the **Congress** building, which has a long history: It was a convent, a jail, and a university before a 1904 renovation to house Bolivia's congress. Standing opposite the cathedral and the Government Palace is the 1911 **Grand Hotel París,** the first movie house in Bolivia.

To get here from El Prado, walk 3 blocks on Calle Ayacucho or Calle Socabaya.

Sports & Outdoor Activities

Bolivia is a haven for outdoor enthusiasts. It's nice to spend a few days in La Paz, but the surrounding mountains are truly spectacular and mighty enticing. Nearby you have the opportunity to climb some of the highest peaks in the world, bike down one of the most dangerous roads in the world, golf in one of the highest courses in the world, or ski down one of the highest slopes in the world.

CLIMBING, HIKING & TREKKING If you're serious about climbing, you should check out **Club Andino** on Calle México 1638 (✆ **0102/2312-875** or 0102/2324-682; Mon–Fri 9:30am–12:30pm and 3–7pm). The staff here can help arrange treks and climbs as well as recommend the best outfitters and guides.

Bolivian Journeys ★, Sagárnaga 363 between Linares and Illampu (✆ **0102/2357-848;** www.bolivianjourneys.org), is one of the most experienced climbing and hiking outfitters and organizes trips up the 5,990m (19,647-ft.) **Huayna Potosí.** Also try **Alberth Bolivia Tours** (✆**591/2245-8018;** www.hikingbolivia.com).

FUTBOL (SOCCER) Four teams play year-round at **Estadio Hernando Siles** in Miraflores. There are games most every week on Tuesday, Wednesday, and Sunday. You can buy tickets on game day at the stadium. Prices range from Bs10 to Bs25. To get here, just hop on any *trufi* with a sign marked ESTADIO in the front window, or take a taxi.

GOLF The 18-hole, 6,900-yard **Mallasilla La Paz Golf Club** (✆ **0102/2745-462**), about 15 minutes outside of La Paz, is considered to be one of the highest golf clubs in the world. Greens fees are Bs550 per person plus Bs80 for equipment and Bs80 for a caddie. **Crillon Tours,** Av. Camacho 1233 (✆ **0102/2337-533,** or 305/358-5353 in the U.S.), can arrange golf packages.

MOUNTAIN BIKING **Gravity Assisted Mountain Biking** ★★★, Av. 16 de Julio 1490 (✆ **0102/2313-849;** www.gravitybolivia.com), is by far the best biking outfitter in Bolivia. They specialize in the 64km (40-mile) descent from La Paz to Coroico along the most dangerous road in the world. The road is narrow, unpaved, crowded with trucks, and carved out of a cliff. ***Be careful:*** In 2001, a woman died here when her brakes snapped. Make sure your bike is in good condition. Gravity Assisted Mountain Biking also arranges rides to Sorata and the Zongo Valley.

WRESTLING ★★ **Las Cholitas Luchadores,** or the Fighting Cholitas, are a WWE-style wrestling organization that operates in a small stadium in El Alto. In the approximately 2½-hour "show," you'll see half a dozen matches between men and between women and men. The men's costumes are outlandish, while the women perform in traditional Andean dress. It's a fun Sunday afternoon, and lasts from approximately 5 to 7pm. You can book through **Andean Secrets** (✆ **591/2249-0160**; www.cholitaswrestling.com) or hostels such as **Adventure Brew** (www.theadventurebrewhostel.com). The price tag of Bs80 includes transport, entrance, front-row seating, snack, bathroom tickets, and a small souvenir.

Shopping

At times, it feels as though La Paz is one big shopping center. The streets teem with vendors peddling everything you can imagine. The city is a mecca for handmade arts-and-crafts products. **Calle Sagárnaga** is shopper's central, with thousands of stores all packed to the gills with local handicrafts. In general, most of the quality is mediocre, but the variety and uniqueness of the goods sold here is impressive. Some of the more popular items include alpaca sweaters (usually about Bs62–Bs77 each), hand-woven shoulder bags, leather bags, wool hats, textiles, and gloves. **ComArt,** Calle Linares 958, is the only association of organized workers in La Paz. When you buy something here, your money goes directly to the workers, not the shopkeepers. If you're trying to find some differences between all the stores in the area, here's a tip: The best quality alpaca sweaters in town can be found at **Walisuma,** Av. Mariscal Santa Cruz 938. On the other side of town, you'll find beautiful silver jewelry at **Kuka Pradel,** Av. 6 de Agosto 2190. For highly intricate handcrafted Andean festival masks, don't miss **Mama Coca,** Pasaje Jimenez 872, between Santa Cruz and Linares. For maps of every type—city, hiking, trekking, and road maps—hit up the **Way Maker Map Shop,** Calle Illampu 897 near Sagarnaga. The city's **Black Market** is a few blocks uphill from the heart of Sagárnaga, past Max Paredes; you'll find a lot of action around Calle La Gasca and Eloy Salmón.

THE WITCHES' MARKET ★★ Venture off Calle Sagárnaga onto Calle Linares and you'll find yourself in the appropriately named Witches' Market, which runs during daylight hours. Here, you can buy a ghoulish variety of charms, spices, and magic potions to help cast a positive spell on your future. Llama fetuses are one of the most popular items for sale here. If you're looking for luck, here's a list to help you decode the meaning of all the amulets on display: Frogs are said to bring good fortune; turtles are the symbol of long life; owls bring knowledge; snakes are a sign of progression (or moving in the right direction); koa—a dried plant made with molasses—is supposed to help your harvest; and pumas will help you achieve victory over your enemy.

WHERE TO STAY

Expensive

Casa Grande ★★ Though it is quite far from the center of town—10 minutes by taxi and 400m (1312 ft.) lower in altitude—this newcomer apart-hotel is one of the best options in La Paz, particularly for longer stays. Each contemporary room has a small kitchentte and dining table, as well as modern extras like iPod speakers and LCD TVs. Service is superb all around. Guests get free access to the large Go Fitness and Spa across the street and to the world's highest golf course. Weekend and long-term rates drop the price considerably.

Calle 17 No. 1000, Calacoto and Ballivian Av., Calacot, La Paz. ✆ **591/2279-5511.** www.casa-grande.com.bo. 36 units. $158–$208 double. Rates include free breakfast and airport transfers for international flights. AE, MC, V. **Amenities:** Restaurant; bar; fitness center; oxygen service; room service. *In room:* A/C, TV, hair dryer, kitchen, minibar, Wi-Fi.

Hotel Europa ★★★ Located on a quiet street just off the Prado, the Hotel Europa is an island of calm in this city of chaos. It is undoubtedly the best hotel in La Paz and resembles more an upscale business-style American hotel than anything from the old continent. The large, cream-colored rooms have fancy green and white carpets, built-in desks, and fresh plants. Mattresses are firm and all beds come with luxurious down comforters. The spacious bathrooms have white tiles and marble sinks. The Hotel Europa is the only hotel in Bolivia to have "floor heating" and a state-of-the-art air-circulation system. The suites are all full apartments with kitchenettes; some even have Jacuzzis. Opened in 1998, it is still relatively new by Bolivian standards but could definitely do with a makeover. The staff are very friendly and helpful, but service can be patchy. Expect your first shot of coca tea when you arrive.

Calle Tiwanaku 64 (between El Prado and F. Zuazo), La Paz. ✆ **0102/2315-656.** Fax 0102/2315-656. www.summithotels.com. 110 units. $149–$175 double; $200–$370 suite. AE, MC, V. **Amenities:** 2 restaurants; bar; babysitting; concierge; tiny exercise room; largest indoor pool in La Paz; room service; sauna; smoke-free rooms. *In room:* A/C, TV, fax and kitchenette in suites, hair dryer, minibar, Wi-Fi.

Radisson Plaza Hotel ★ Kids You can expect all the amenities of an exclusive business hotel here, but compared to the modern, sexy Hotel Europa (see above), it feels more like a comfortable old shoe. The lobby looks fantastic, but the rooms are disappointing and rather worn. Although the Radisson's rooms have enough space for two double beds, a large dresser, and two chairs, its decor is very dated and there are perpetual problems with temperature control—it's either too cold or too stuffy. Huge picture windows used to offer great views of the city, but unfortunately a high-rise went up right in front and ruined it for many. The sleek **Aransaya Restaurant,** which has outstanding views, is undoubtedly the hotel's best asset. This is also one of the only hotels in La Paz that offers a free airport shuttle. Be sure to ask for the "Super Saver" rates that sometimes shave almost 30% off the regular prices.

Av. Arce 2177 (corner of F. Guachalla), La Paz. ✆ **800/333-3333** in the U.S., or 0102/2441-111. Fax 0102/2440-402. www.radisson.com/lapazbo. 239 units. $119–$144 double; $254–$294 suite. Rates include breakfast. AE, MC, V. **Amenities:** 2 restaurants; bar; babysitting; exercise room; Jacuzzi; small indoor pool; room service; sauna; smoke-free rooms. *In room:* A/C, TV, hair dryer, minibar.

Moderate

Hotel Plaza ★ Hotel Plaza has an airy, expansive lobby with colorful modern art. All rooms are spacious, recently remodeled, and with so-so modern furnishings, and those on the seventh floor and above come with wonderful views of the city and mountains. You can even open the windows here, a rarity in the city's high-rise hotels. The marble bathrooms are small but clean, with big mirrors. There's a formal restaurant on the top floor with amazing views, and an informal coffee shop (adjacent to the lobby) that serves an excellent buffet lunch. The Plaza has the best hotel gym in La Paz, but the pool area is not very attractive. Rooms can be cold and the staff could be more helpful. Hot water could also be hotter and more plentiful. All in all, this is a good value if you score a good rate, but if you're paying full price, choose the Hotel Europa (see above).

Paseo del Prado, La Paz. ✆ **0102/2378-311.** Fax 0102/2378-318. www.plazabolivia.com.bo. 147 units. $80–$115 double; $150 suite. Rates include breakfast. AE, MC, V. **Amenities:** 2 restaurants; bar; concierge; large exercise room; Jacuzzi; small indoor pool; room service; sauna; smoke-free rooms. *In room:* A/C, TV, hair dryer, minibar.

Hostal Rosario ★ Hostal Rosario is a converted colonial mansion with two peaceful colonial-style courtyards. The rooms are small but cozy in a charming way, with parquet floors and bright Andean-style bedspreads. The bathrooms aren't big, either, but they do have bright, spotless tiles. The owners are constantly making improvements, so although the hotel is old, it feels new. If you're traveling in a group, request the suite, which has great views and sleeps up to six people. The hotel is close to the Witches' Market and all the handicrafts stores on Calle Sagárnaga. Be aware that the rooms out front can be noisy at night if it is Carnaval time. There is an excellent upscale restaurant and recommended tour agency on the premises.

Av. Illampu 704 (between Graneros and Santa Cruz), La Paz. ✆ **0102/2451-658.** Fax 0102/2451-991. www.hotelrosario.com. 45 units (3 with shared bathroom, most with shower only). $50–$65 double; $70 triple; $85 suite. Rates include continental breakfast. AE, MC, V. **Amenities:** Restaurant; bar; room service. *In room:* TV, Wi-Fi.

WHERE TO DINE

While other South American cities such as Lima, Bogotá, and Buenos Aires are undergoing a gastronomic revolution, La Paz is well behind. There are just a few high-end eateries, mostly in the ritzier Zona Sur. Street food in La Paz is good, found everywhere, and relatively safe. Look for *salteñas* (baked turnovers filled with chicken or beef and egg and onion), which can also be found in specialty shops all over the city. For coffee, try

Alexander Coffee, at Av. 20 de Octubre 2463, or **Café Blueberries,** at Av. 20 de Octubre 2475, both in Sopacachi.

Moderate

La Bella Vista ★★★ Moments BOLIVIAN/INTERNATIONAL The aliens have landed! No one knows what happened to the aliens themselves, but they left behind their spaceship right here in La Paz, on top of the Hotel Presidente, and it's been converted into an excellent restaurant with spectacular views of the city. This restaurant—hands down the best in the city—really feels like something from outer space, with an unbeatable 360-degree view of La Paz at night. The food, which includes homemade pasta, lamb kabobs, grilled chicken, and seafood, is out of this world as well. If you like fish, you must order the grilled trout—I've never eaten a more succulent piece of fish. The *parrilla mixta* (assorted cuts of grilled meat for two people) is also excellent.

In the Hotel Presidente, Calle Potosí 920 (at the corner of Genaro Sanjinés). ✆ **0102/2406-666.** Reservations recommended Thurs–Fri. Main courses Bs45–Bs117. AE, MC, V. Daily 11am–3pm and 7–11pm.

La Guinguette ★ Value FRENCH/BISTRO This intimate little French bistro under the Alianza Francesa in Sopacachi is an unbelievable value, not to mention a clean, modern dining and bar area. The three-course lunch menus are a steal, or you can order high-quality stand-alone French standards like steak frites, a croque monsieur sandwich, or trout meunière. It's popular with the after-work crowd for cocktails.

Guachalla and 20 de Octubre, Sopacachi. ✆ **0102/7307-3785.** Main courses Bs25–Bs45. MC, V. Mon–Sat 9am–11pm.

Pronto ★★ Moments NOVO ANDINO/INTERNATIONAL This "dalicatessen"—Salvador Dalí posters and statues are all over the restaurant—is one of the more creative eateries in La Paz. The menu slants towards *novo andino* cuisine and tries to incorporate Andean grains like quinoa and lake fish such as ispi, though there are standard steaks and pastas, too. For something light to pair with their decent list of Chilean and Argentine wines, try the llama carpaccio or perhaps some Thai basil fried rice. My favorite dish is the alpaca filet, which is served in an earthy *ají* (pepper) sauce with spaghetti made from coca flour.

Pasaje Jauregui 2248, Sopacachi. ✆ **0102/244-1369.** www.restaurantpronto.com. Reservations recommended Thurs–Sat. Main courses Bs48–Bs75. AE, MC, V. Mon–Sat 7–11pm.

Inexpensive

La Casa de los Paceños ★★ BOLIVIAN This charming restaurant is housed in an old colonial building, and it doesn't look as if much has changed in this dining room since colonial times. Traditional Bolivian food is the specialty here. For example, you can order *ají de lengua* (cow's tongue in a chili sauce) or, if you're feeling adventurous, *picante surtido,* which consists of *sajta* (chicken in a chili sauce), *saice* (chopped meat in a chili sauce), *ranga* (cow's stomach), *fritanga* (pork), and *charquekán* (shredded alpaca meat in chili sauce). More timid eaters should opt for the *pollo dorado* (chicken grilled in olive oil). If you're looking for Bolivian food in a livelier atmosphere, you should head to La Casa de los Paceños in the Zona Sur, Av. Fuerza Naval 275, between 18th and 19th streets (✆ **0102/2794-629**), where there is outdoor seating and live music on the weekends. A taxi from the center should cost no more than Bs30.

Av. Sucre 856 (between Genaro Sanjinés and Pichincha). ✆ **0102/2280-955.** Main courses Bs22–Bs33. AE, MC, V. Tues–Fri 11:30am–4pm and 6–10pm; Sat–Sun 11:30am–4pm.

Surucachi *Finds* BOLIVIAN You may have noticed that between 12:30 and 2:30pm, the streets of La Paz become mighty quiet. That's probably because everyone and his mother is eating lunch here at Surucachi. The food is pure Bolivian—*milanesas* (fried chicken or veal cutlets), *pejerrey* (kingfish from Lake Titicaca), and *picante mixto* (tongue, chicken, and chopped meat all in a spicy chili sauce). The *almuerzo del día* (lunch special), which includes a salad, soup, a main course, and dessert, is only Bs20. Add a colonial building with fancy gold-leaf moldings and huge picture windows to the mix, and you've got yourself the most popular lunch spot in town.

Av. 16 de Julio 1598. No phone. Lunch special Bs20; a la carte main courses Bs25–Bs40. No credit cards. Daily 9am–10pm.

LA PAZ AFTER DARK

Once the sun sets in La Paz, the temperature drops dramatically. Instead of going home (often to unheated apartments), many locals seek the warmth of bars and pubs. The nightlife scene in La Paz can hardly compare to New York or even Buenos Aires, but there are some funky places in the heart of the city where you can relax and kick back with a few drinks. ***Peñas,*** bars with live music, provide a place for visitors to experience traditional folk music and dance, although they tend to be very touristy. ***Note:*** Most bars (except in hotels) are open only Wednesday through Saturday.

BARS & PUBS The best hotel bar in La Paz is at the **Radisson** (p. 194); they have a happy hour nightly from 6:30 to 8:30pm offering two-for-one drinks, and it's very popular with expatriates and tourists alike. One of the most popular British-style watering holes in the city is **Mongo's** ★★, Hermanos Manchego 2444 (near the corner of Pedro Salazar, half a block up from Av. 6 de Agosto). It has a cozy feel and a wood-burning fireplace. Get here early, as the place fills up late at night; the food here is also surprisingly good. **Diesel Nacional** ★, Av. 20 de Octubre 2271, is a self-proclaimed industrial pub, which means the decor is on par with a junkyard: recycled car parts, railroad ties, and transmissions. Surprisingly, it lures a trendier-than-average crowd.

DANCE CLUBS **Pa'Goza** (✆ **0102/2342-787**), down from 6 de Agosto on Rosendo Gutiérrez, is one of the best dance clubs in La Paz; salsa is the specialty here. Also popular are **Forum,** Sanjinés 2908, with eclectic music but a strict dress code and Bs40 cover charge (which includes drink coupons), and **Ram Jam** on Calle Medina 2421. In general, the cover charge for clubs in La Paz is about Bs10.

PENAS & LIVE MUSIC These days, it's hard to find an authentic *peña* that caters to locals. Fortunately, for the most part, you'll hear authentic Andean music and watch folk dancers wearing unique but traditional costumes. **Restaurant Peña Marka Tambo,** Calle Jaén 710 near the corner of Indaburo, puts on a good show Thursday through Saturday nights. The cover is Bs25. The show starts at 9:30pm. **Casa de Corregidor,** Calle Murillo 1040 (✆ **0102/2363-633**), is a similar venue—it has typical Bolivian food and music but feels a bit more laid back than Marka Tambo. **Boca y Sapo,** Indaburo 654 (corner of Jaén), attracts locals as well as tourists; there's no dinner here, only live music, which makes it feel a bit more authentic.

For live jazz, try **Thelonious Jazz Bar,** Av. 20 de Octubre 2172. A lot of the bands that play here are from the United States.

Tiwanaku ★

A visit to Tiwanaku will take you back in time to an impressive city built by an extremely technologically advanced pre-Inca society. The Tiwanaku culture is believed to have lasted for 28 centuries, from 1600 B.C. to A.D. 1200. In this time, they created some of the most impressive stone monoliths in the world, developed a sophisticated irrigation system, and gained an advanced understanding of astronomy and the workings of the sun. Their territory spread from northern Argentina and Chile through Bolivia to the south of Peru. These people never came into contact with the Incas. By the time the Incas made it to Peru, a 100-year drought had ravaged the Titicaca area. The Tiwanaku people had long ago left the region in small groups and moved to different areas in the Altiplano or valleys.

Stop in at the museum before you visit the site. The Incas and the Spaniards destroyed the site while searching for gold and silver, and even the most respected archaeologists disagree on the meanings of the monoliths and the sun gate. But when you actually see these impressive structures firsthand, you can't help but stand in awe and wonderment of the amazing achievements of this pre-Columbian society. You gain a deep insight into the daily life and rituals of the people who inhabited this area for thousands of years. Highlights of the site include the **Semi-Underground Temple** ★, the **Kalassaya** ★, and the **Akapana (pyramid).** The museum and the archaeological site are open daily from 9am to 4:30pm. Admission is Bs15.

GETTING THERE Tiwanaku is located 1½ hours outside La Paz. I strongly recommend coming here on a guided tour. **Diana Tours,** Sagárnaga 326 (✆ **0102/2350-252**), organizes English-speaking tours to Tiwanaku for only Bs70, not including the Bs15 site admission fee. **Crillon Tours,** Av. Camacho 1233 (✆ **0102/2337-533**), also arranges tours to the area. If you prefer to visit on your own, **Trans Tours Tiwanaku,** Calle José Aliaga, operates buses that stop at Tiwanaku. The buses leave from the Cementerio District every half-hour from 8am to 4:30pm. The ride costs Bs8.

Madidi National Park ★★

Ranging from 180 to 5,600m (590–18,368 ft.) and covering nearly 19,000 sq. km (7,410 sq. miles), Madidi National Park is one of the most diverse ecosystems on earth. Connecting with the Tambopata National Reserve (p. 693) across the border in Peru, the park hosts approximately 900 species of birds, 156 species of mammals, 71 species of reptiles, and thousands of rare plants. There's a healthy jaguar population and the park is also home to the spectacled bear, numerous monkey species, and harpy eagles. The best accommodation is at **Chalalan Ecolodge,** 89 Sagarnaga St., Shopping Dorian, 2nd Floor, no. 22 in La Paz (✆ **0102/2311-451;** www.chalalan.com), 5 hours up the Tuichi River. The lodge is completely owned and operated by the Quechua-Tacana indigenous group and in 2009 was called one of *National Geographic Adventure's* Top 50 eco-lodges. The 13 Tacana-style thatched cabins are rustic yet comfortable with private bathrooms, verandas with hammocks, and mosquito nets. A 4-day/3-night package, which includes 1 night in Ruurenabaque, transport to the lodge, activities, English-speaking guides, and all meals, runs $350 per person. It does not include transportation to Rurrenbaque. There's a Bs125 entrance fee to enter the national park.

GETTING THERE Madidi is the most accessible of Bolivia's Amazon regions. Most trips start in the town of Rurrenabaque, accessible by either flight or road from La Paz. **Amaszonas** (✆ **0102/2222-0848**; www.amaszonas.com) offers several daily flights from La Paz ($150 round-trip), though these are frequently delayed and canceled due to rain. You can go by bus or taxi from La Paz (10 hr.) and most tourist offices in La Paz can arrange the trip.

The Best of Los Yungas: Coroico

Coroico makes a popular side trip for visitors to La Paz, but you'll probably remember the journey better than the destination. The road to Coroico narrows to one unpaved lane twisting down through the mountains. To one side is the mountain, to the other, a sheer drop of often hundreds of feet to the lush valley below. There will be times when the passage is tight and your vehicle is only an inch or two from the edge; there will be other times when you round a blind curve and your driver, confronted by oncoming traffic, has to slam on the brakes.

When the ride is over and your heart rate has returned to normal, you may be surprised at the tranquillity of Coroico. The views of the surrounding hills are lovely, the nearby hiking trails are picturesque, the bars and restaurants in town are pleasant, and there are some worthwhile excursions; but there's really nothing here to take your breath away. Nonetheless, Coroico makes a wonderful contrast to La Paz. Here in this tropical town, you'll find fruit orchards, twittering birds, coca fields, endless greenery, oxygen-rich air, warm weather, and friendly locals. The climate here seems to put everyone in a better mood.

The town of Coroico itself isn't anything special, but it's a lot of fun to explore the lush, colorful surrounding area. You can take a half-day tour of **Tocaña**★, a small Afro-Bolivian community about 7km (4⅓ miles) downhill from Coroico. It feels as if not much has changed over the past few hundred years in this farming village, where the locals survive mainly by growing coca. Also nearby are the **Vagante River Springs.** Here you can swim under a waterfall and in beautiful pools of water. **Vagantes Ecoaventuras,** at the kiosk in the Coroico main plaza, provides guides (not always English speaking) and jeeps to Tocaña and Vagante River Springs. Note that the jeeps are open and the roads aren't paved, so you will get extremely dirty.

In the dry season, the rivers in the Coroico area become low and unsuitable for **rafting.** However, in January through March, the Coroico River runs wild. River levels range from Class III to Class V. **Vagantes Ecoaventuras** (at the kiosk in Coroico's main plaza, by Heroes del Chaco) organizes rafting and kayaking tours in the area.

GETTING THERE **Buses** for Coroico leave La Paz on a frequent schedule from the Villa Fátima neighborhood, which is about 15 minutes by taxi from the center of La Paz (it costs about Bs9 for the cab ride to the station). Most of the bus companies are on Calle Yanacachi. One of the best is **Yungueña** (✆ **0102/2213-513;** call ahead for the schedule); the ride costs Bs15 each way. I recommend leaving around 10am—this way, you'll arrive in Coroico for lunch and then have the rest of the afternoon to walk around town or hang out by a pool. Buses depart less frequently in the afternoon (the last one leaves at about 4pm), but it's much nicer to travel during daylight and enjoy the view. ***Tip:*** Try to get a seat on the left side of the bus for the best views.

For information about **trekking** or **biking** to Coroico, see "Sports & Outdoor Activities," earlier in this section.

5 LAKE TITICACA ★★★

Copacabana: 151km (94 miles) NW of La Paz, 8km (5 miles) N of Kasani (the border of Peru)

Still, serene, and spiritual, this vast lake of blinding light and calm water is the birthplace of one of the greatest empires in history. At Lake Titicaca the children of the Sun stepped forth from the sacred rock that still stands near the northwest tip of the Isla del Sol (the Sun Island), and the Inca culture began.

The rugged, snow-covered peaks of the Cordillera Real loom over the shores of the lake, but its waters are calm and relaxing to the eye. They're disturbed only by the operators of a few tour boats, launches, and hydrofoils, and by local fishermen searching for trout, often in wooden sailboats or rowboats. Even the most primitive of these vessels are relative newcomers. The swaying reeds on the water's shore provided the material for the first boats on Lake Titicaca, and today there are still a few craftsmen who remember how to make boats from reeds, as their ancestors did.

Besides the lake itself, and the Isla del Sol within it, the highlight of the region is the picturesque lakeshore town of Copacabana, allegedly established by the Inca Tupac Yupanqui. Copacabana has a number of small but important Inca ruins, but all of them are overshadowed by the town's main attraction, the Virgin of Copacabana. Pilgrims travel from all over South America for the Virgin's blessing. If you're here on a Sunday, you'll notice many car and truck drivers, who come to have their vehicles blessed by one of the local priests in a ceremony that involves lots of garlands. On Sundays, locals celebrate by shaking and spraying fizzy drinks, and, of course, making a small donation to the church. Nobody seems to mind paying.

ESSENTIALS

Getting There

BY BUS Buses from La Paz to Copacabana leave from the Cementerio District, not from the main terminal; it costs about Bs15 to get here by taxi from the center of La Paz. **Trans "6 de Junio,"** Plaza Tupac Katari no. 55 (✆ **0102/2455-258**), is one of the most reliable bus companies. A one-way ticket costs Bs15; buses depart at 9:30 and 10:30am; noon; and 2:30, 5, 6, 7:30, and 8:30pm. The ride takes 3 hours, including a 3-minute ferry ride (Bs2) across the Straits of Tiquina. Here, you must disembark from the bus and take a ferry across to the other side. The bus is carried over on a separate boat. From the border, frequent service runs to Puno, Peru (Bs10; 2½ hours).

BY GUIDED TOUR **Crillon Tours,** Av. Camacho 1233 (✆ **0102/2337-533,** or 305/358-5353 in the U.S.; www.titicaca.com), specializes in tours to the Lake Titicaca area. The company owns two of the best hotels in the area—Inca Utama Hotel & Spa in Huatajata (p. 206) and La Posada del Inca hotel on the Sun Island (p. 206)—and is the only company that operates hydrofoils on the lake. Because of a business deal meant to protect local businesses, you can't stay at these hotels or use the hydrofoil if you're traveling independently. Crillon's tours are really the best way to see the area; they include excellent English-speaking guides and all transportation.

Getting Around

Copacabana, the largest city in the Lake Titicaca area, is where you'll find the best hotels and travel agencies, as well as some Inca ruins and the famous statue of the Virgen de Copacabana. From here, you can easily take a day trip to the Isla del Sol. **Huatajata** isn't

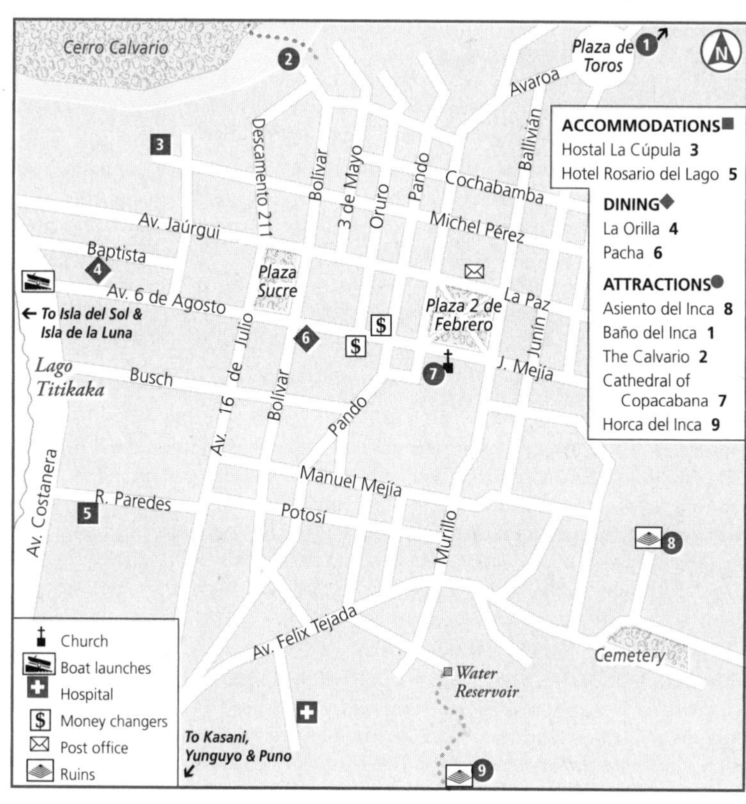

much of a town—its only attraction is Inca Utama Hotel & Spa—but it's only 1½ hours by car from La Paz. So instead of traveling 3 hours to Copacabana, you can spend the night here, and then hop on the hydrofoil for a quick jaunt over to the Sun Island. The hydrofoil also makes stops in Copacabana.

The only way to go from Copacabana or Huatajata to the Sun Island is by **boat.** From Huatajata, you can also take a hydrofoil to Copacabana or the Sun Island; contact **Crillon Tours** (✆ **0102/2337-533** or 305/358-5353 in the U.S.; www.titicaca.com) for more information. From Copacabana, nonhydrofoil boats leave around 8:15am and arrive at the Sun Island at 10:30am. The boat returns to pick you up at 4pm. If you want to walk from one side of the island to the other, the ride costs Bs35; if you want the boat to take you around the island, the whole trip will set you back Bs40. If you plan on spending the night on the Isla del Sol, you can catch a boat back to Copacabana at 10:30am. Both **Grace Tours,** Av. 6 de Agosto 200 (✆ **0102/862-2160**), and **Titicaca Tours,** at the dock at the end of Avenida 6 de Agosto (✆ **0102/862-2060**), are recommended tour agencies.

Transturin, on Avenida 6 de Agosto, about half a block up from the beach (✆ **0102/242-2222;** www.turismobolivia.com), organizes cruises to the Isla del Sol and to Puno on the Peruvian side of the lake. Day trips to both the Sun Island and Puno cost Bs500. You can also sleep on the boat; overnight trips to the Sun Island cost Bs620 per person.

Visitor Information

The main tourist office is on Plaza 2 de Febrero at the corner of Ballivián and La Paz in Copacabana. The office doesn't have a phone, the hours of operation are sporadic, there are no maps available, and, in general, the staff is of limited help.

FAST FACTS: COPACABANA There are several **banks** on Avenida 6 de Agosto; note that none of them exchange traveler's checks or have ATMs. You'll find a **pharmacy** on Plaza Tito Yupanqui right across from the Entel office behind the basilica. The **post office** is on La Paz near the corner of Ballivián. You can take care of all your **laundry** needs at Hostal Sucre, Murillo 228, near the corner of José P. Mejía. For Internet cafes, try **ALF@Net,** Av. 6 de Agosto 100, at the corner of Avenida 10 de Julio, and **Alcadi,** beside the post office in front of the cathedral. Rates are about Bs10 per hour.

WHAT TO SEE & DO

In Copacabana

Copacabana was an important religious site way before the Spanish realized that the world was round. Lake Titicaca is believed to be the birthplace of the Incas, and for many years, this city was one of the holiest of the Inca empire. These days, pilgrims come from far and wide to visit the Cathedral of Copacabana to pay homage to the Virgin of Copacabana (also known as the Queen of Bolivia and the Virgin of Candelaria), who has supposedly bestowed many miracles upon her true believers. She is the most venerated Virgin in all of Bolivia. In addition to visiting the most important Catholic icon in Bolivia, you can also explore some important Inca ruins.

THE CATHEDRAL OF COPACABANA In 1580, the Virgin of Copacabana appeared in a dream to Tito Yupanqui. He was so taken by this vision that he set out to Potosí (then one of the most important art centers in the world) to learn to sculpt. With his new skill, he hand-carved the Virgin from the wood of a maguey cactus. He then carried her, by foot, from Potosí to Copacabana (a journey of more than 640km/400 miles), where she was placed in an adobe chapel in 1583. Immediately afterwards, the crops of those who doubted her power were mysteriously destroyed. The Spanish, smitten with the Virgin, completed this Moorish-style cathedral for her in 1617. The Virgin stands in a majestic mechanical altar. On weekends, the priests rotate the Virgin so that she faces the main chapel; on weekdays, when there are fewer pilgrims here, they spin her around so that she looks over a smaller chapel on the other side. The silver ship at the bottom of the altar represents the moon, while the gold statue above the Virgin's head is believed to symbolize the power of the sun. Believers have bestowed millions of dollars worth of gifts upon the Virgin. In 1879, the government of Bolivia sold some of her jewelry to finance the War of the Pacific against Chile. The cathedral is open daily from 11am to noon and from 2 to 6pm; admission is free.

THE CALVARIO In the 1950s the Stations of the Cross were built on a hill overlooking the lake. The strenuous uphill walk takes more than 30 minutes, but the views of the lake are worth the effort. At the very bottom of the stairs, there is a man who can divine your future by dropping lead into a boiling pot of water. About halfway up, you will find native priests burning candles and working with coca leaves. If you're so inclined, this is a good place to stop and learn about the ancient rituals of fortunetelling. For the trip down, there are two options: You can return the way you came up, or you can take a rocky path that will lead you to the shores of the lake. Note that the winding path can get steep and narrow—it's best to descend it only if you're wearing a good pair of hiking shoes.

INCA RUINS Within Copacabana, there are three interesting archaeological sites. They are open Tuesday through Sunday from 9am to noon and from 2 to 5pm; admission to all three costs Bs10. The **Asiento del Inca (Seat of the Inca)** ★★ is my favorite of the three sites. No one knows the actual purpose of the stone carvings here, but some archaeologists speculate that this may have been a meeting point for Inca priests. The carvings are called Asiento del Inca because the huge indentations in the rocks resemble thrones. The rock carvings span different levels and what appear to be different rooms, and the "seats" don't all face the same direction. It's fun to sit on one of the thronelike rocks and dream about what may have happened here. To get here, walk from Plaza 2 de Febrero along Calle Murillo for 4 blocks until you reach the road to La Paz, where you should take a left. Walk 3 blocks uphill to the cemetery. The Asiento del Inca is about 90m (300 ft.) from the cemetery.

A bit farther outside of town is the **Horca del Inca,** a three-rock structure that resembles a gallows (hence the name). In actuality, it's believed that the Incas used these rocks as a tool to observe the sun and stars. If you happen to be here during one of the equinoxes, you can actually observe the sun as it reflects off the boulders. Unfortunately, the Spanish destroyed much of the site because they thought gold might be hidden inside some of the rocks. Of course, they found nothing. To get here, walk straight on Calle Murillo from the plaza until the road ends; here, you will see a rocky hill. About halfway up the hill, you'll find the Horca del Inca. The walk up to the actual site is steep and the terrain is rough. You should only head up here if you have good walking shoes and lots of energy. Young boys hanging around the area will offer to show you the way to the site for about Bs8. I recommend taking them up on their offer, because the climb is tricky.

At the **Baño del Inca,** about 30 minutes outside town, you'll find a small museum dedicated to some archaeological finds in the area. Behind the museum, there's a pretty little spring, which is said to have mystical powers. Baño del Inca is a nice peaceful spot outside of the city—great for a romantic picnic. To get here, start at Plaza 2 de Febrero and walk straight down Ballivián to Plaza de Toros. From Plaza de Toros, walk straight for about 20 minutes, until you see a green house. Take a right here and walk uphill for about 10 minutes. The Baño del Inca is on the right-hand side across from a church. There is no sign, but it's right behind a small farm.

Isla del Sol ★★★, Isla de la Luna & Isla de los Uros

Welcome to the birthplace of the Incas. The **Isla del Sol,** measuring only 9km (5½ miles) long by 6km (3¾ miles) wide, is one of the most spectacular places in all of Bolivia. On the north end are Challapampa and some fascinating Inca ruins. Yumani, on the south end, is the largest town on the island and also the site of the Inca steps.

Most tour operators run a day trip from Copacabana to the Sun Island, with a quick stop at the Isla de la Luna (Moon Island). You'll leave Copacabana at 8:15am and arrive at Challapampa around 10:30am. Here you pay a Bs15 entry fee, and a Spanish-speaking guide will show you around Chinkana (see "Challapamba," below, for more information). If you're feeling ambitious, you can walk from here all the way to the Fuente del Inca on the southern end of the island. I highly recommend this long and hilly hike. Along the way, you'll come across wild llamas, herds of sheep, and some of the most breathtaking vistas in the world. But keep in mind that the hike is difficult and more than 4 hours long, so you won't have time to sit and eat a proper lunch. If you have a hard time walking, you might not make it to the other side in time for the last boat to Copacabana at 4pm.

If you don't want to walk, the boat will then drop you off for a quick stop at the **Isla de la Luna.** During the time of the Incas, this island was used to house "chosen" women. The island was similar to a convent. The women here wove garments by hand with alpaca wool and performed special ceremonies dedicated to the sun. Unfortunately, most of the structures here have been destroyed. From the 1930s to the 1960s, this island became a political prison. In the 1960s, when some archaeologists got wind of what had become of the island, the prisoners were ordered to rebuild the main palace, which has 35 rooms around a courtyard. This is historically significant because the Aymara culture—not the Incas—used constructions with courtyards, thus proving that Moon Island was used by pre-Inca cultures. However, most of the remaining doors are trapezoidal shaped, which is very typical of the Incas. As you first walk onto the island, keep an eye out for the polished stones. These stones are similar to what you'd find in Machu Picchu, and they allow you to understand how the Incas used hinges to hold rocks together.

Note: When your boat driver forces you to choose between visiting Moon Island and walking across Sun Island, I recommend opting for the walk on Sun Island. You won't miss much if you don't stop off at Moon Island, and the setting of the sun on Sun Island is much more spectacular.

CHALLAPAMPA ★★ A visit to Challapampa will be the highlight of your visit to the Sun Island. Here, you will find the ruins of **Chinkana (the labyrinth).** It's a huge stone complex full of mazes, believed to be a seminary for Inca priests. The construction is actually a bit sloppy, which is very uncharacteristic of the Incas; some archaeologists theorize that the Incas must have been in a rush when they built it. A natural spring here runs under the island and appears again in a sacred stone fountain in Yumani (see below). On the path back to the town of Challapampa, about 100m (328 ft.) from Chinkana, you will pass by the **sacred rock,** carved in the shape of a puma. As you continue along this path toward Challapampa, look down: You will soon see two very large footprints, said to have been created when the Sun dropped down to Earth to give birth to Manco Capac and Mama Ocllo, the Adam and Eve of the Incas.

YUMANI/INCA STEPS If you arrive by boat to Yumani, you will have to walk up 206 steps to reach the main part of the town here. These steps are original Inca constructions, and they lead up to a sacred stone fountain with three separate springs, which are said to be a fountain of youth.

PILKOKAYNA There is a half-mile path from the top of the Inca Steps down to Pilkokayna (which literally means "where birds sleep"). This 14-room structure may have been used as a fortress to guard the Virgins of the Sun, who were living nearby on Moon Island. From here, you have a very clear view of Moon Island. The structure does have trapezoidal doors, which means that it was used by the Incas. However, some archaeologists speculate that the buildings here date back to the Classic Age of the Tiwanaku period (A.D. 100–900). One of the most impressive features is the remains of the original stone roof.

ISLAS DE LOS UROS ★★ Though they're much smaller than their counterparts in Peru, it is hard not to be enchanted by a visit to these floating islands made of totora reeds, about 20 minutes by boat from Huatajata. The initial purpose of the islands was for defense. The islanders actually live on dry land, but when danger was nearby they

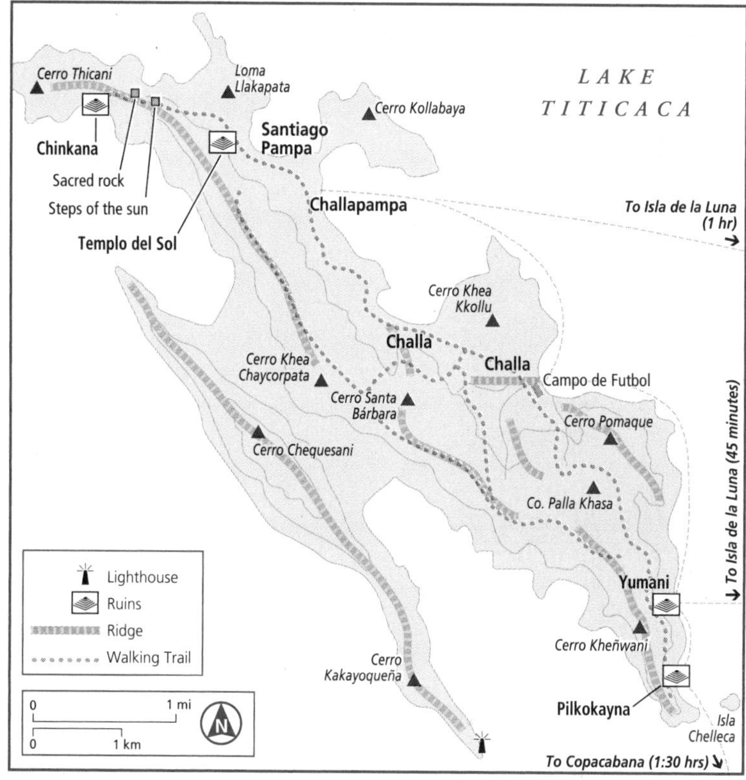

would retreat to their tortora islands and hide amidst the reeds or float down the Desaguadero River. Today the few dozen islanders survive on fishing, hunting birds, selling handicrafts, and the little money they receive from tour groups. Trips to the islands are best arranged as an excursion ($25 per person) while staying at the Inca Utama Hotel & Spa, though you may also arrange trips in Huatajata.

WHERE TO STAY

In Copacabana

Hostal La Cúpula *Finds* The owner of La Cúpula is a sculptor, and the beautiful garden areas and rooms here are filled with delightful pieces of artwork. Some of the rooms have lake views, while others look out onto the surrounding mountainside. All are bright, with big windows and funky bamboo furniture; some even have lofts, so you really feel as though you're staying in an artist's studio. Only seven of the rooms here have private shower-only bathrooms, but the public facilities are immaculate. The hotel is a 10-minute walk uphill from the heart of Copacabana, but it's not much of a problem. After eating at the excellent restaurant (or cooking your own meal in the public kitchen), you can relax in the cozy library or play one of many board games here. It can be cold in the winter months, so come prepared. Each room has a heater and hot-water bottles are provided.

Calle Michel Pérez 1–3, Copacabana. ✆ **0102/862-2029.** www.hotelcupula.com. 17 units (7 with private bathroom, shower only). $16–$36 double; $24–$36 triple. MC, V. **Amenities:** Restaurant. *In room:* No phone.

Hotel Rosario del Lago ★ The design of this lakeside hotel blends in perfectly with its surroundings. From the outside, the bright yellow stucco building looks like an old Spanish colonial–style castle. Inside, the brick tiles and earthy tones envelop you in a soothing way. In every room, there is a cozy sitting area with large bay windows, where you can gaze out over the shores of Lake Titicaca. The rooms aren't fancy, but with their shiny hardwood floors and dark-red bedspreads, they certainly have tons of charm. The bathrooms are small, but the rooms are so cute, it doesn't really matter. Families should try to request the suite—it feels like a small apartment, complete with two bedrooms, a refrigerator, and a separate living room and dining area. If you're sensitive to noise, make sure that your room is toward the back of the hotel; the rooms close to reception tend to be quite loud.

Rigoberto Paredes and Av. Costanera, Copacabana. ✆ **0102/862-2141.** Fax 0102/862-2140. www.hotelrosario.com/lago. 32 units (shower only). $56–$63 double; $74–$80 triple. Rates include breakfast. AE, MC, V. **Amenities:** Restaurant; room service. *In room:* TV, Wi-Fi.

On the Isla del Sol

Most of the accommodations on the Sun Island are, to put it kindly, rustic. Very few rooms have private bathrooms, and it's almost impossible to find a hot shower here. But once all the day-trippers leave, you will have the island to yourself. I think it's worth it to stay here just to feel the magic of the island. There is one exception to the rule, however: Crillon Tours' **La Posada del Inca ★★** is probably one of the best hotels in all of Bolivia. By Sun Island standards, it's luxurious—all rooms come with private bathrooms, hot showers, and electric blankets (a nice touch on freezing nights). The Spanish-style adobe hotel feels like an old farm. The rooms are cute, with handmade bamboo beds and Andean area rugs. Overall, the hotel is unbelievably charming. To book a room, you must reserve in advance with **Crillon Tours,** Av. Camacho 1233, La Paz (✆ **0102/2337-533,** or 305/358-5353 in the U.S.; www.titicaca.com).

In Huatajata

Inca Utama Hotel & Spa ★ Owned by Crillon Tours, this hotel and cultural complex is just 1½ hours from La Paz. The eco-friendly lakeside complex has two restaurants, a spa with Jacuzzi and sauna, and two towers of guest rooms (which are basically the same). Each room offers a fine view of the lake, Aymara decor, heated blankets, and clean, tiled bathrooms. This is by far the most modern hotel on the Bolivian side of the lake.

The highlight of the resort is the **Andean Roots Cultural Complex.** Essentially, it's the "colonial Williamsburg" of Lake Titicaca. The **Andean Eco Village** recreates an historic Andean village, with buildings and farms typical of this area: People here work exactly the same way their ancestors did—taking care of llamas and vicuñas, raising guinea pigs, storing corn, cooking traditional food, and weaving alpaca shawls. In the Andean Village, there is also a full-size reproduction of the reed boat, the *RA II,* used by Thor Heyerdahl to cross the Atlantic and designed by the local Limachi brothers, who work here building new reed boats. The small **Altiplano Museum** has exhibits about the history of Bolivia, with an emphasis on the Tiwanaku and Inca cultures. The **Kallawaya**

Museum ★★ is one of the most interesting museums in Bolivia. At the start of the museum, you'll learn about the healing powers of local herbs, plants, fruits, and vegetables. When you reach the end, you will enter a small brick room, brightened only by the warm glow of candles. Here a Kallawaya natural medicine doctor will bless you and, with the help of some coca leaves, tell you about your future. Finally, there is an observatory (with the second-most powerful telescope in Bolivia), where you can learn about all the constellations in the Southern Hemisphere.

Huatajata. ✆ **0102/2337-533,** or 305/358-5353 in the U.S. www.titicaca.com. 70 units. $80–$100 double. Rates include breakfast and admission to the museums. AE, MC, V. **Amenities:** 2 restaurants; spa; Wi-Fi in lobby. *In room:* Electric blankets, space heater.

WHERE TO DINE

Copacabana is the culinary capital of Lake Titicaca. Almost every restaurant here specializes in preparing trout fresh from the lake. The best restaurants are on Avenida 6 de Agosto. They all have pretty much the same menu, which consists of trout, pasta, and pizza. But **La Orilla,** Av. 6 de Agosto, about 20m (66 ft.) from the beach, has a terrace that overlooks the lake. In the evening, the lights go dim, and the dining room feels like a romantic hideaway. The trout curry is highly recommended. Other excellent options include a vegetable stir-fry, fajitas, and spring rolls. On the weekends, live bands sometimes perform here. Another good restaurant for trout is **Pacha,** Bolívar and Avenida 6 de Agosto (✆ **0102/8622-497**). An excellent coffee stop with English breakfasts and fruit juices is **Café Bistrot,** Avenida Costanera and Tito Yupanqui (✆ **0102/8622-497** or 0107/1518310).

On Sun Island there are a few small restaurants, such as **Inti Sol** (on the main path not far from the church), which is by far the best islander-run restaurant. None have names or addresses, but they all have similar menus, including fresh trout and grilled chicken. Your best bet is to ask your hotel for a recommendation.

LAKE TITICACA AFTER DARK

Don't expect to find a wild nightlife scene anywhere near Lake Titicaca. In Copacabana, **Akwaaba,** Avenida 6 de Augosto, is one of the hippest places in town. Live bands sometimes play here, but it's still a fairly laid-back place.

6 SUCRE ★★

701km (435 miles) SE of La Paz; 366km (227 miles) SE of Cochabamba; 612km (379 miles) SW of Santa Cruz; 162km (100 miles) NE of Potosí

During Bolivia's glory days, when Sucre—or, as it was known then, Chuquisaca—existed solely for the purpose of administering the silver mines in nearby Potosí, the wealthy locals here would often brag, "My mines are in Potosí, but I live in Chuquisaca." For those who could afford it, it made sense to live 162km (100 miles) down the road from Potosí in the relative lowlands (2,706m/8,876 ft.) of Sucre, which is blessed with a mild climate and a much cheerier disposition. Gradually, Sucre became a city of understated prestige. It's been called the Paris of South America because the wealth here attracted some of the finest arts and culture from all over the world. It's also been known as the Athens of South America because it's home to the continent's second-oldest and most prestigious university, San Francisco Xavier University, which dates to 1624 and has educated presidents of Argentina, Paraguay, Chile, Uruguay, and, of course, Bolivia.

(Today, out of a total pop. of about 200,000, over 30,000 are students, many of them studying medicine or law.)

For a city like Sucre, money, prestige, and knowledge weren't enough. It also had to have a place in the history books. In 1825, some of the most important South American revolutionaries converged upon the city and signed the country's declaration of independence. Sucre then became the capital of the new republic. These days, Sucre is the capital of Bolivia in name only—both the executive and legislative branches of the government left long ago for La Paz. The silver in nearby Potosí has pretty much run out, and the high culture has returned to Paris. Nevertheless, the city remains one of the most colorful and interesting places in Bolivia. Visitors can sit in the room where the Bolivian declaration of independence was signed, tour churches and museums that still have impressive collections of colonial art, and view the dinosaur tracks that archaeologists recently discovered right in Sucre's backyard.

ESSENTIALS

Getting There

BY PLANE **Aero Sur** (✆ **0103/3364-446** in Santa Cruz, or 0104/6462-141 in Sucre; www.aerosur.com) offers daily flights to Sucre from La Paz, Cochabamba, and Santa Cruz. One-way tickets cost about Bs500 each. **TAM** (✆ **0102/2268-1101**) also has daily flights to La Paz and Santa Cruz that usually costs slightly less. All planes arrive at the **Juana Azurduy de Padilla Airport** (airport code SRE), which is only a few miles outside town. Taxis from the airport to the center of town cost Bs25. The airport tax upon departure is Bs10.

BY BUS The Sucre bus terminal is about 1.5km (1 mile) northeast of the center of town at the corner of Alfredo Ostria Gutiérrez and Bustillos. See "Getting Around: By Bus" in "Planning Your Trip to Bolivia," earlier in this chapter, for bus company information. The 14-hour ride from La Paz costs Bs75 for a normal bus, and Bs100 for a *bus cama.* Buses from Cochabamba take about 12 hours and cost Bs30 for a normal bus, or Bs50 for a *bus cama.* Buses from Santa Cruz take 12 hours and cost Bs70for a normal bus, or Bs90 for a *bus cama.* Buses from Potosí leave in the morning, midafternoon, and early evening (around 5pm). The 2½- to 3-hour ride costs Bs20.

BY TAXI You can take a taxi from Potosí to Sucre for Bs200 for four people. I recommend using **Expreso Infinito** (✆ **0104/6422-277**).

Getting Around

Most of the banks, travel agencies, hotels, and attractions in Sucre are within easy walking distance of Plaza 25 de Mayo, the commercial heart of the city. If you want to get a bit off of the beaten path, the best option is to take a taxi. It's easy to hail one right off the street, but your hotel can also call one for you.

Visitor Information

The main tourist office is on Estudiantes 35. There aren't any maps available here, but the staff is knowledgeable and helpful. The office is open daily from 8:30am to 12:30pm and 2:30 to 6:30pm. The very friendly staff at **Candelaria Tours** ★★, off the central square at Audiencia 1 (✆ **0104/6461-661;** www.candelariatours.com), can also answer any questions you may have about the sights in the city or nearby attractions (including Potosí).

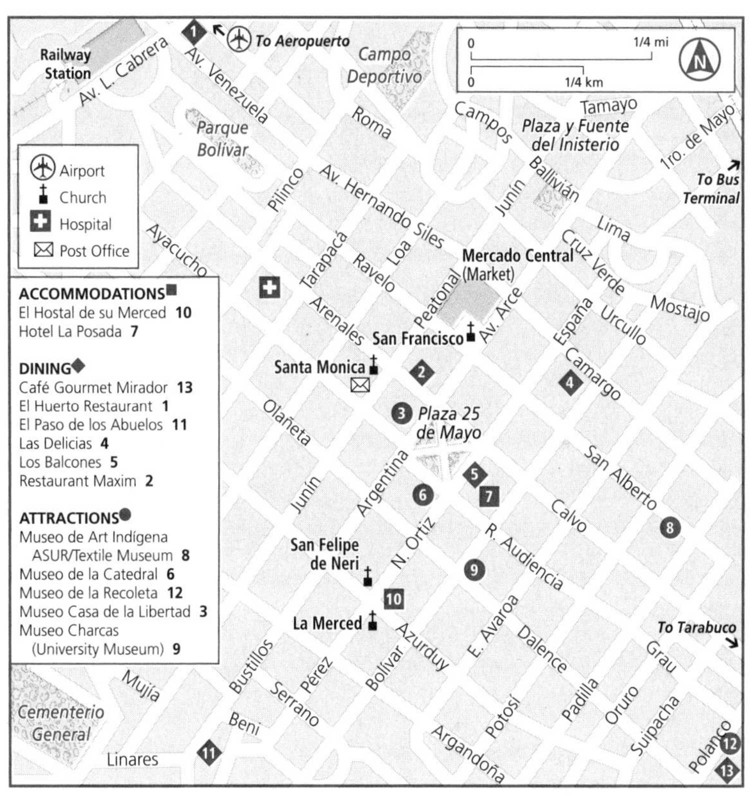

FAST FACTS You can exchange money and traveler's checks at **Cambios "El Arca,"** on España 134, or **Casa de Cambio Ambar,** on Ravelo 7 at the corner of Arce. You'll find ATMs on Calle España and all around the main Plaza. **Hospital Santa Bárbara,** Destacamento 111 at the corner of Arenales (✆ **0104/6460-133**), and **Hospital Gastroenterológico,** Avenida Colón between El Villar and Japón (✆ **0104/6454-700**), are the two best hospitals in Sucre. The **post office** is on Junín and the corner of Ayacucho. You can take care of all your laundry needs at **LaveRap,** Calle Bolívar 617 between Olañeta and Azurday. It's one of the few laundromats in all of Bolivia that is open on Sundays (only until 1pm). You'll find Internet cafes on all the side streets that lead off the plaza.

WHAT TO SEE & DO

Museums

Museo Casa de la Libertad ★ The United States has Liberty Hall in Philadelphia; Bolivia has the equivalent in Museo Casa de la Libertad. On August 6, 1825, the freedom fighters of Bolivia assembled here to declare independence from Spain. You can visit the exact room where the liberators met. Now known as the Salón de la Independencia, it's filled with portraits of the great liberators and baroque-style wood chairs painted in gold leaf. The portrait here of Simón Bolívar is believed to be the most lifelike reproduction of the great independence hero.

The museum complex was originally part of a Jesuit university that dates from 1624 (one of the oldest in Bolivia). In addition to the Salón de la Independencia, there are several galleries here dedicated to the history of Bolivia. Items on display include the first Argentine flag (the Bolivians refuse to return it to Argentina, saying "We are all the same"), a copy of the Bolivian declaration of independence, and paintings of the city of Sucre in the independence era. There's also a room dedicated to Mariscal Sucre, the first president of Bolivia. Plan on spending about 45 minutes here.

Plaza 25 de Mayo 25. ✆ **0104/6454-200.** Admission Bs10. Tues–Sat 9–11:15am; Sun 9am–2pm.

Museo Charcas (University Museum Colonial & Anthropological) This museum, which is housed in a 17th-century mansion, consists of three different mini-museums: colonial art, an ethnography and folk collection, and modern art. Overall, the museum provides a comprehensive look at the wide breadth of art forms—both indigenous and European—in Bolivia. In the Colonial Museum, most of the art dates from the 16th and 17th centuries. The museum houses paintings by the half-indigenous Melchor Pérez Holguín, including his most famous work, *San Juan de Dios,* which has an almost perfect depiction of human hands. You'll also find a collection of beautiful antique furniture on display. In the Ethnographic and Folkloric Museum, you can learn about local rituals and view a collection of mummified bodies that provide insight on local death rituals. Also on display is a good collection of pottery from the Yampara culture. Its pottery is some of the most beautiful and technically advanced of all pre-Columbian cultures—you can see tears on the faces and evidence of ponchos. The pieces in the Modern Art Gallery reflect contemporary Bolivian artists' focus on poverty and the back-breaking labor involved in working in the mines. Set aside at least 1½ hours to visit the entire collection.

Bolívar 698 (near the corner of Olañeta). ✆ **0104/6453-285.** Admission Bs10. Mon–Sat 8:30am–noon and 2:30–6pm.

Museo de Arte Indígena ASUR/Textile Museum ★★ ASUR is an acronym for Anthropologists of the Andean South, who are trying to recover the lost artesian techniques of the local population. This museum does an excellent job of displaying some magnificent pieces of art, mainly in the form of textiles that provide a real insight into these local cultures. For example, the Inca culture had three commandments: Don't be a thief, don't be a liar, and don't be lazy. Apparently, the indigenous people would create big intricate textiles as proof that they weren't being lazy. In the collection from the Tarabuco culture, the artists would only weave images of what they knew—people plowing the land, dancers, and horses. In addition to viewing textiles, you can also see artists hard at work using ancient techniques of weaving, washing, and spinning the wool. It's amazing to witness the intense work that goes into creating these unique forms of art. There is also a wonderful gift shop here that supports local communities. Plan on spending at least 2 hours here.

San Alberto 413 (near the corner of Potosí). ✆ **0104/6453-841.** Admission Bs16. Mon–Fri 8.30am–noon and 2:30–6pm; Sat 9:30am–noon. Closed Sat Oct–May.

Museo de la Catedral ★★ The Museo de la Catedral houses an excellent collection of colonial art and silver religious relics, but the **Chapel of the Virgin of Guadalupe ★★** is the star of the show here (and will probably be the highlight of your visit to

Moments **Take a Walk**

Be sure to set aside some time to stroll around Sucre's main Plaza 25 de Mayo. This is the largest and most beautiful square in all of Bolivia, ringed with palm and jacaranda trees.

Sucre). Fray Diego de Ocaña painted the original *Virgen de Guadalupe* in 1601. Today, you can see some remains of this oil painting and the canvas, but mostly it has been destroyed by the thousands of pounds of jewelry that the faithful have offered the Virgin over the past 400 years. The weight of the jewels (and 40,000 emeralds can certainly do a lot of damage) have torn the canvas to bits. All that survive are her face, her hands, and the face of the baby—the rest is pure gemstones. In addition to the Chapel of the Virgin, you can also visit the cathedral, which dates from 1559 but is purely neoclassical. After independence from Spain in 1825, the liberators tried to erase all colonial influences from the churches in the area. Instead of seeing the elaborate baroque designs from the colonial period, you'll find that this cathedral is very simple and understated.

Calle Nicolás Ortiz 61 (around the corner from Plaza 25 de Mayo). ✆ **0104/6452-257.** Admission Bs15. Mon–Fri 10am–noon and 3–5pm; Sat 10am–noon.

Museo de la Recoleta ★★ Moments This museum is housed in a convent that dates from the year 1600. Inside, you will find an excellent collection of colonial art and a courtyard that offers an incredible bird's-eye view of Sucre. Plus, you'll get a glimpse of what it must have been like to live and work here in the 17th century. For example, you can visit a recreated priest's room, very basic accommodations with only one blanket and a whip (used for self-flagellation). The **Courtyard of the Orange Trees ★★** is the most impressive part of the museum, featuring an orange tree that is said to be more than 1,000 years old. Before the Spanish arrived, the indigenous people used this tree as a totem pole. The museum also houses works by colonial painter Melchor Pérez de Holguín, pieces from the Cusqueña school, and an interesting painting of Jesus with an exaggerated flagellation scene, said to justify all the abuse being committed at that time. As you walk around the museum, you may notice that the walls are crooked. This is intentional—it protects the building from the destructive powers of earthquakes. It'll take you about an hour to visit the museum and courtyard.

Polano 162 (right in front of Plaza Anzures). Admission Bs10. Mon–Fri 9:30–11:30am and 2:30–4:30pm; Sat 3–4:30pm.

Attractions Outside Town

The most popular day trip from Sucre is the 2-hour ride to Tarabuco, home to one of the most colorful indigenous markets in Bolivia (see below).

Cal Orck'o (Dinosaur Tracks) ★★ Moments This is definitely one of the most unique attractions in Bolivia. At first glance, the dinosaur tracks look like simple holes in rocks. But after your eyes adjust, you'll start to see distinct patterns of movement. All of a sudden, it's very easy to envision dinosaurs slopping through the mud, trying to escape from their enemies, and searching for water. It's believed that the rocks in the area date back some 68 million years—well before the Andes were formed. Supposedly, there was a lake here surrounded by a forest. Dinosaurs trudged through the mud in the forest toward the lake in search of water. Before the footprints had a chance to disappear (about a 2-week time period), they would be covered by sediment, which settled over the mud and preserved the prints. The bilingual guides will be able to tell you their theories about which dinosaurs were doing what when they walked through this area 68 million years ago. I recommend taking the Dino-Truck to get here—you'll ride in the back of a pickup through the outskirts of Sucre and along roads with beautiful vistas. If you choose to take a taxi, it will cost you about Bs30. The tour lasts about 1½ hours.

About 20 min. outside Sucre on the road to Cochabamba. ✆ **0104/6451-863.** Take the Dino-Truck, which leaves daily from the cathedral on Plaza 25 de Mayo at 9:30am, noon, and 2:30pm. Dino-Truck and admission is Bs30. Admission without transportation is Bs20. Guided tours daily 10 and 11:30am, and 12:30, 2, and 3pm.

Shopping

Sucre and the surrounding area are famous for handicrafts. If you happen to be in town on a Sunday and you're looking for handicrafts, you should head to the market in **Tarabuco** ★ (about 56km/35 miles from Sucre). Here, you will find thousands of different textiles, hats, gloves, bags, and other hand-woven goodies. The market is one of the best in Bolivia. On Sunday mornings, buses leave from Sucre for Tarabuco from 7 to 9am at the corner of Avenida de la Américas and Manco Capac. The 1½-hour ride costs Bs15 each way. **Candelaria Tours** ★★, right off the central square at Audiencia 1 (✆ **0104/6461-661;** www.candelariatours.com), also organizes day trips to the market and the surrounding area for Bs150 per person.

The gift shop at the **Museo de Arte Indígena ASUR/Textile Museum,** on San Alberto 413 (near the corner of Potosí), offers the best selection of textiles and handmade crafts in Sucre. **Artesanías Sucre,** Calle Olañeta 42 at Plazuela Zudáñez, and **Artesanías Tesoros del Inca,** Calle Camargo 514, also sell local handicrafts. You'll find everything under the sun at the unique **Central Market** on the corner of Junín and Ravelo. I recommend heading up to the second floor to try the local *tojorí* drink (boiled corn, cinnamon, and sugar) for breakfast; because of its high protein content, it's called "the cornflakes of the Andes." **Para Ti** ★★ on Arenales (about a third of a block in from the plaza) sells delicious handmade chocolate that come in cute little bamboo or banana tree bark boxes. Some bars include quinoa, while others have Brazil nuts or macadamia nuts.

WHERE TO STAY

El Hostal de Su Merced ★★★ (Finds) Once you've stayed at this hotel, housed in a magnificent converted mansion from the 18th century, you can rest assured that you've slept in the best small hotel in Bolivia. What it lacks in luxury, it makes up for in charm and character. All the rooms are unique, with thick white adobe walls and antique furniture (some is original to this house). Room no. 7 is a junior suite with a separate sitting area with large antique chairs and a hand-embroidered ottoman, hand-carved wooden doors, lace curtains, a brass bed, and the aura of true elegance. All rooms have similar personal touches—including crystal chandeliers, brick floors, adorable basket-weave bins, sloped ceilings, and antiques galore. If you plan on staying here for a while, try room no. 16. It's very private, and it has its own quiet patio. The beautiful rooftop terrace has awesome views of the cathedral.

Calle Azurduy 16 (between N. Ortiz and Bolívar), Sucre. ✆ **0104/6442-706.** Fax 0104/6912-078. www.desumerced.com. 16 units. $52 double; $70 triple; $70 junior suite. Rates include breakfast. AE, MC, V. **Amenities:** Restaurant; room service. *In room:* TV, minibar in junior suites.

Hotel La Posada ★★ (Value) If you can't stay at the Hostal de su Merced, this hotel is an excellent second choice, especially if you're looking for the best bargain in Sucre.

Opened in 2003 in a renovated old house, La Posada's rooms overlook a lovely courtyard with mature trees and colorful plants; they all have tile floors, colorful blue-and-yellow bedspreads, and wrought-iron lamps. Rooms on the second floor have wood-beamed ceilings and are slightly more spacious than those on the ground floor. Bathrooms are nicely tiled and sparkling, if a bit small. The Posada's restaurant is excellent, serving a daily three-course menu for lunch and dinner priced at Bs20; in warm weather, you can dine outside under elegant parasols. If you're looking for the best deal in town with a healthy dose of charm, then this is it.

Calle Audiencia 92, Sucre. ✆ **0104/6460-101.** Fax 0104/6913-427. www.laposadahostal.com. 9 units. $55 double; $90 suite. Rates include breakfast. MC, V. **Amenities:** Restaurant; room service. *In room:* TV.

WHERE TO DINE

You'll dine really well in Sucre; this city has tons of interesting and delicious eateries. In addition to the restaurants listed below, here are some other good choices: The most delicious *salteñas* in town can be found at **El Paso de los Abuelos,** Bustillo 216 (✆ **0104/6455-173**); they're open daily from 8am to 1pm. For a simple but exquisite local experience, visit **Las Delicias ★**, Estudiantes 50 (✆ **0104/6442-502**). Here, owner (and baker) Dorly Fernández de Toro serves her amazing pastries; some are very unusual but delicious, such as the *sonso,* made from mashed yucas. There's also a good selection of yummy empanadas and *humitas* (a Bolivian version of the tamale). Las Delicias is open only Tuesday through Saturday from 4 to 8pm; come early as this place fills up fast. The best place for lunch with a terrific view is the **Café Gourmet Mirador,** Plaza Anzures, across from the Recoleta (✆ **0104/6440-299**). You'll dine outside under lovely bamboo umbrellas with Sucre stretched at your feet; the specialty here is crepes. They're open daily until 6pm. Also, try **Los Balcones,** 25 de Mayo 34, sitting right above the main plaza, which has a full Bolivian and international menu.

El Huerto Restaurant ★★ Moments BOLIVIAN In Spanish, *el huerto* means "the orchard," and that's exactly where you'll feel like you are when you dine outside in the lovely garden area of this popular lunch spot. Your fellow diners will probably be some of Sucre's biggest bigwigs, who come here for the relaxed atmosphere and excellent food. This is a great place to try some of Sucre's local specialties, such as *chorizos chuquisaqueños especiales* (a spicy pork sausage). You can also order more international fare, including filet mignon, pineapple chicken, and omelets. For dessert, I highly recommend the homemade ice cream.

Ladislao Cabrera 86 (it's a bit outside of town, so take a taxi). ✆ **0104/6451-538.** Main courses Bs39–Bs60. V. Sun–Wed noon–3pm; Thurs–Sat noon–9pm.

Restaurant Maxim ★ BOLIVIAN/FRENCH This restaurant feels very formal in a European way. The walls are covered with fancy lace French-style wallpaper, crystal chandeliers hang from the ceiling, and the tablecloths have hand-embroidered paisley designs. The waiters wear white tuxes and cater to your every need. The food here also has its own special flair. For an appetizer, order the tasty *ceviche de pejerrey* (raw kingfish marinated in a tangy lemon juice and served in an oyster shell). The *pollo Maxim* (chicken filled with ham and cheese) is one of the house specialties, and you can order local dishes such as *chorizos chuquisaqueños.* In a nod to French cooking, almost all of the dishes come bathed in a cream sauce, except for the *chuletas de cerdo glaseados* (pork chops in a red-wine sauce with a touch of sugar).

Arenales 19, 2nd floor (half a block from the main plaza). ✆ **0104/6451-798.** Reservations recommended on weekends. Main courses Bs30–Bs50. MC, V. Mon–Sat 7–11pm.

SUCRE AFTER DARK

Because Sucre is crawling with young university students, there are tons of charming bars near Plaza 25 de Mayo, especially on Calle N. Ortiz leading away from the square. I recommend the **Joy Ride Café & Bar,** Calle N. Ortiz 14 (© **0104/6425-544;** www.joyridebol.com), owned by an Italian guy and serving good beer and excellent light meals. This is where many gringos spend the evening and sign up for one of their biking or hiking tours. Next door, **Picadilly** is another popular bar that also serves Indonesian food. If you fancy mojitos with a Bolivian twist—coca leaf—go to **Locots,** Bolívar 465 (© **0104/6915-958**). Another good bar with both locals and foreigners is **Kultur Café Berlin,** Calle Avaroa 326 (© **0104/642-4521**). If you're looking to dance, try **Florín,** at Bolívar 567, which is the new "it" spot. They have a traditional bar with tables where they serve their own microbrewed beer, as well as a connecting dance hall that pumps out house music to a mixed crowd. Note that almost everything is eerily quiet during the week; the above bars and clubs, with the exception of Joy Ride, are open only Wednesday through Saturday.

A SIDE TRIP TO SALAR DE UYUNI ★★★

Salar de Uyuni, the largest salt lake in the world, is quickly becoming one of Bolivia's star attractions, along with the eerie desert that it connects with. You can visit the Salar in a single day, but to see the entire area, you'll need at least 3 days and 2 nights, usually ending with a connection to San Pedro de Atacama, Chile (though you can also return to Uyuni). There are no paved roads in these parts, so all the agencies use Toyota Land Cruisers to transport you through the desert with all necessary food, gear, and luggage attached to the top. The trip can be rough, especially on your bottom. But the desert landscape, with its volcanoes in the background and bizarre rock formations, is truly surreal. Some of the highlights of the trip include a stop at the **salt lake** itself; the oddly shaped **Isla del Pescado,** which is covered with cacti; and the **Laguna Colorado,** whose blood-red mineral-soaked waters are quite a sight. You'll see large herds of vicuñas, the occasional fox, and thousands upon thousands of flamingoes. My favorite stop on the tour is the **Sol de la Mañana,** where you can see geysers, fumaroles, and mud boiling in the earth. It's called Sol de la Mañana because it's best seen early in the morning. At the **Laguna Verde** (in the farthest southwest corner of Bolivia), be sure to hold on tightly to your hat, because the wind here is vicious. The emerald green Laguna Verde sits right below the Lincancabur Volcano (5,835m/19,139 ft.) and makes for a fantastic photograph.

Most tour operators in Bolivia run a bare-bones budget trip for $125 per person with shared transportation and simple lodging, though in the past several years new semiluxurious hotels such as the three Tayka properties (www.taykahoteles.com) and tour operators such as Adventure Associates (www.adventure-associates.com) have made this trip considerably easier, though they have the price tags to go with it. Regardless of where you stay, bring tons of warm clothing because the temperature can drop below freezing, and the budget places have no heat.

The town of Uyuni is located at the lake's edge. The best of the many hotels here is **Los Girasoles** (© **0102/6933-323;** www.girasoles-hotel.com). At Calle Santa Cruz 155, the hotel boasts simple, clean rooms with private bathrooms, heating, and 24-hour hot water. Doubles cost $65 to $75, including breakfast. You can also try the **Hotel Cristal Samaña** (© **0102/7644-2585;** www.hotelcristalsamana.com), a coca-leaf-shaped salt hotel, right at the edge of the Salar near the village of Colchani, which is designed with

Fun Facts The Next Great Bolivian Export

Southwest Bolivia is home to nearly half of the world's lithium reserves, an important component of the batteries of hybrid cars.

feng shui principles in mind. There's a small spa on-site, as well as a game room, yoga classes, cinema, and astronomical observatory. Doubles run $100 per night and include breakfast. Another option is **Hotel Luna Salada** (✆ **0102/7242-9716;** www.lunasaladahotel.com.bo), which has doubles from $110.

GETTING THERE There are several companies, such as **Todo Turismo** (Bs175) and **Trans Omar** (Bs105), that have transportation from La Paz departing at either 7 or 9pm for the 12-hour ride, just in time to depart on the 10am tours. Buses leave Potosí daily at 11:30am, 11:45am, and 6:30pm from the small bus terminal on Avenida Universitaria at the intersection of Sevilla. (They leave Uyuni for Potosí at 10am and 7pm.) The 5-hour ride costs Bs25. ***Note:*** A small airport was in construction at press time and should be running daily flights to La Paz by late 2010.

If you want a **guided tour,** it's not easy to find a reputable company. I suggest contacting **Mariana Tours,** Olaneta 101 A, Sucre (✆ **0104/6429-329;** mtours@cotes.net.bo); ask to speak to the manager, Rodrigo Garron, and he'll arrange the highest-quality trip for you. Their tours are tailor-made to fit your needs and leave from either Sucre or Potosí. Another well-known operator is **Andes Salt Expeditions,** 3 Alonso de Ibanez, Potosí (✆ **0102/6225-175;** www.andes-salt-uyuni.com.bo).

A SIDE TRIP TO POTOSI

You might find it hard to believe that bleak, wet, and windy Potosí was once one of the richest cities in the world. It's been said that enough silver was pulled from the bowels of nearby Cerro Rico to build a bridge from Potosí all the way to Madrid—and enough people died inside the mines to build a bridge of bones all the way back.

Nowadays, visitors can still see the two disparate sides of the city. Seven thousand workers still eke out a living from a mine where millions died. You can take tours there that'll bring you face to face with these miners and the dreary conditions in which they work. In contrast, you can then tour the sights that evoke the city's former glory. Potosí is not a heartwarming place. At more than 3,900m (12,800 ft.), it's one of the highest cities in the world. Even when the sun is shining bright, there is always a bitter chill in the air. It's painful to visit the mines and learn about the past exploitation of these workers, but it's also fascinating to see the remains of a place that was once the home of some of the wealthiest people in the world.

Getting There

The Potosí bus station is on the edge of town at the end of Avenida Universitaria (near the intersection of Av. Sevilla). Buses from Santa Cruz go through Cochabamba or Sucre. The 6-hour ride from Cochabamba costs Bs40. Buses depart from Sucre in the morning, midafternoon, and early evening (around 5pm). The 2½- to 3-hour ride costs Bs20. Buses depart from Uyuni at 10am and 7pm. The 6-hour ride costs Bs35. You can also take a taxi from Sucre for Bs200 for four people; contact **Auto Expreso** (✆ **0104/6422-277**).

What to See & Do

The main tourist office is in a kiosk on Plaza 6 de Agosto. No maps are available here, but the staff is knowledgeable and helpful. I recommend making a quick stop at the **Museo Sacro Jerusalén,** on Avenida Camacho at the corner of Avenida del Maestro. The church here dates from 1708. To really understand the history of Potosí, you have to visit **Casa Nacional de la Moneda,** Calle Ayacucho between Quijarro and Bustillos (© **0102/6223-986**), once the biggest building in the Americas. This former Spanish royal mint is now dedicated to Bolivian weapons, modern art, minerals, and archaeology. **Convento Museo Santa Teresa,** Calle Santa Teresa 15 and Calle Ayacucho (© **0102/6223-847**), was a working convent from 1691 through 1976 (nowadays, the sisters live next door). Here, the nuns were separated from their callers by a dark screened wall. They weren't allowed to touch or see their guests; they could only exchange words. You can visit the impressive church and countless galleries full of colonial art, antiques, Murano glass, and hand-painted porcelain dishes.

Visiting the Mines ★

The history of Potosí is inextricably linked to Cerro Rico. Taking a tour of the mines will open your eyes to a different side of Potosí, to the world of the people who actually work here. Let me warn you beforehand that it's not a pretty picture. Not much has changed here over the past few hundred years. Fortunately, the miners now work in cooperatives, and they do earn a percentage of what they find. The average salary here is equivalent to about $100 a month.

You'll see workers igniting dynamite to open new areas, shoveling rocks, and carrying heavy loads, all in one of the most abysmal work environments that you could ever imagine. These miners often spend 24-hour stretches in utter darkness, with cigarettes, soda, and coca leaves as their only form of sustenance. There are no proper stairways with handrails and the paths are narrow and very steep; and there is mud everywhere, which makes walking treacherous. Expect to get dirty. I would recommend that anyone with heart problems or claustrophobia skip the trip.

There are several companies in Potosí that offer mine tours. The best ones use guides who are former miners. Overall, however, the quality of the tours is horrendous: The equipment (hard hats, waterproof clothing, gloves, boots, lamps, surgical masks) is often in poor condition, and the guides can be unreliable. **Koala Tours,** Ayacucho 5 in front of Casa de la Moneda (© **0102/6222-092**), and **Banoa Tours,** at Ayacucho 17 (© **0102/622-8249**), are two of the more reputable companies. Tours leave Monday through Saturday, but it's best to go on a weekday because the mines are quiet on weekends. The 5-hour tour costs Bs80 per person; a percentage of the profits is donated to the cooperatives working in the mines.

Where to Stay & Dine

Most visitors come to Potosí on a day trip from Sucre or Cochamaba; accommodations here are nothing special and many don't have heat (it gets really cold at night). **Hotel Cima Argentum,** Av. Villazon 239 (© **0102/6229-538;** fax 0102/6122-603; www.hca-potosi.com), is situated about 6 blocks from the center of town, but it's worth the walk. Rooms are modern with colorful bedspreads; dark, clean carpets; and wood furniture. **Hostal Santa Teresa,** Calle Ayacucho 43 (© **0102/2622-5270;** www.hotelsantateresa.com.bo), offers somewhat worn modern rooms with Wi-Fi right near the plaza. **Hostal Colonial,** Calle Hoyos 8 (© **0102/6224-809;** fax 0102/6227-146; hcolonial_potosi@hotmail.com), is one of the best hotels in Potosí, but don't expect anything extraordinary.

The best restaurant in Potosí is **El Fogón,** Frías 58 (✆ **0102/622-4969;** www.elfogon.com.bo), a corner bar and grill serving massive portions of steaks, pasta, and regional plates. For something lighter, stop in at **Café la Plata,** right on the plaza.

7 COCHABAMBA

385km (239 miles) SE of La Paz; 473km (293 miles) W of Santa Cruz; 366km (227 miles) NW of Sucre

Cochabambinos are famous for their love of the good life. Their sun-bleached city is settled in a dusty hollow at the very center of Bolivia. The quiet plazas invite you to linger, and the year-round springlike climate encourages you to stroll along the quaint streets. Overlooking all this is the largest statue of Christ in the world, the 33m (108-ft.) *Cristo de la Concordia.* There's something very welcoming about Cochabamba: There may not be much to see and do in the city itself except eat and drink to your heart's content, but Cochabamba is a great place to relax and get to know the people of Bolivia. Or you can travel to the small towns in the nearby valleys and visit some of the most colorful local markets in the country.

ESSENTIALS

Getting There

BY PLANE **Aero Sur** (✆ **0103/3364-446** in Santa Cruz, or 0104/400-912 in Cochabamba; www.aerosur.com) and **BOA** (✆ **0102/4414-0873;** www.boa.bo) offers daily flights to Cochabamba from La Paz, Santa Cruz, Sucre, and Tarija. One-way tickets cost about Bs350 to Bs500 each. All planes arrive at the very modern **Aeropuerto Internacional Jorge Wilstermann** (airport code CBB; ✆ **0104/412-0400**). Taxis from the airport to the center of town cost about Bs25.

BY BUS The Cochabamba **bus terminal,** at Avenida Ayacucho and Avenida Aroma, is probably the nicest bus station in all of Bolivia. Buses from La Paz arrive almost every half-hour. The 8-hour journey costs Bs35 for a regular bus, or Bs50 for a *bus cama.* Buses from Santa Cruz take 11 hours and cost Bs35 for a normal bus, or Bs60 for a *bus cama.* Buses from Sucre take 11 hours and cost Bs30 for a normal bus, or Bs50 for a *bus cama.* See "Getting Around: By Bus" in "Planning Your Trip to Bolivia," earlier in this chapter, for bus company information.

Getting Around

Cochabamba is an extremely walkable city. For the most part, the city is compact. The streets Ayacucho and Las Heroínas are the center of Cochabamba. From Ayacucho the streets are labeled north and south. From Las Heroínas, the streets are numbered east to west. The best restaurants and hotels are in the upscale residential neighborhood known as Recoleta; it's best to take a taxi, which only costs about Bs8 from the center of town. To reach the statue of Christ, you can walk east 15 minutes from the center of town, or take a taxi for about Bs20 round-trip. *Trufis* are available throughout the city for Bs1.50; numbers are clearly marked on the front of the vans.

Visitor Information

The tourist information office is on General Acha and Calle Bautista; it's open Monday through Friday from 8:30am to 4:30pm. But unless you speak Spanish and have a very specific question, the tourist office is virtually useless.

Ranabol Expeditions, Av. Ayacucho 112 (✆ **0104/4583-039**), can help you find your bearings with their organized city tours and trips to the valley, Tunari, and the Chapare area. They have trips ranging from 1 to 20 days with experienced guides, camping equipment, and sleeping bags. If you're looking for an English-speaking tour guide, I highly recommend **Tim Johnson;** contact him at tim@bolivia.com. The organization **Sustainable Bolivia** (✆ **0104/423-3786;** www.sustainablebolivia.org) is an excellent source for arranging volunteer opportunities, language studies, homestays, and general tourism in and around Cochabamba.

FAST FACTS To change traveler's checks or exchange money, you should head to the travel agency **Exprintbol S.R.L,** Plaza 14 de Septiembre 242 (✆ **0104/4255-834**). **Hospital Belga** (✆ **0104/4251-579**), on Antezana between Paxxieri and Venezuela, is the best hospital in town. Pharmacies abound in Cochabamba. **Farmacia Boliviana** on 14 de Septiembre E-0202 was the first pharmacy in Cochabamba; **Farmacia San Mateo** on Las Heroínas E-0323 (between España and 25 de Mayo) is a bit more modern. The **post office** is on the corner of Las Heroínas and Ayacucho; the entrance is on Ayacucho. The best Internet cafe is **Black Cat Internet,** which is on General Acha, just half a block off the Plaza de 14 Septiembre. **Entelnet** on the Prado, Av. Ballivián 539 adjacent to Plaza Colón, is also reliable for Internet use.

WHAT TO SEE & DO

In addition to the sights listed below, you can also visit the **Capilla Cristo de las Lágrimas de San Pedro,** a chapel where there is a sculpture of Christ that allegedly cries tears of human blood every Good Friday. There are pictures of what this particular sculpture looked like when it was new (much less blood). The chapel, on the corner of Belzu and Las Heroínas, is open Monday and Wednesday through Saturday from 3 to 6pm.

The **Casona Santiváñez,** at 158 Calle Santiváñez, is also worth a stop if you're downtown. This old house, restored in 2001 by the municipality of Cochabamba, is now a cultural center. It's home to the **Museo de Fotografía Antigua,** which has some interesting old photographs of the city. There's also a room devoted to writers, the **Museo de Escritores,** with letters and photos from Latin American writers. The salons upstairs are worth a peek if they're open (official city functions are held here); they are grand with old colonial furniture. Admission is free and the center is open Monday through Friday from 9am to noon and 2:30 to 6pm.

Centro Simón I Patiño/Palacio Portales Ironically, the tin baron Simón Patiño never lived in this palace—he suffered a heart attack during its construction, and his heart condition prevented his return to his native country. In fact, Charles de Gaulle is the only person who has ever spent the night in the house. What a pity, because this mansion is a real beaut. Patiño was originally from the Cochabamba area, but he discovered an enormous tin deposit near the mining town of Oruro. By the turn of the 20th century, he controlled 10% of the world's tin. He commissioned a French architect to design and build the house from 1915 to 1927 while he was living in Europe. You enter the house through a round, neoclassical entrance. Inside, your guide will take you to several different rooms which speak of the opulence of that time period. The walls are covered with silk wallpaper; crystal chandeliers from Venice hang from the rafters; and green-and-white marble fireplaces were built to keep the house warm. Each room has its own unique floor design. Thanks to the dry climate of Cochabamba, everything here has been impeccably preserved. Today, the house is used as a cultural center. After the tour, you can walk through the beautiful Japanese gardens or visit the Contemporary Art Center (Mon–Fri 3–9pm; admission is Bs3). Plan on spending about an hour here.

Av. Potosí 1450 (near the intersection of Av. Portales). Admission Bs10. Tours in English Mon–Fri at 5:30pm and Sat at 11am. Take *trufi* no. 10 north from the corner of San Martín and Bolívar.

Cristo de la Concordia ★ **Moments** This steel-and-cement sculpture is believed to be the largest statue of Christ in the world. Because Christ died when he was 33 years old, it measures 33m (108 ft.). I recommend riding the cable car to the top, but if you're feeling energetic, you can climb the 2,000 litter-strewn steps. However you reach the summit, you will be rewarded with lovely views of the area. Christ faces the lower valley area of Cochabamba. From here, you can see Tunari—at 4,800m (15,744 ft.), these are the highest twin peaks in the area. The Christ the Redeemer statue in Rio de Janeiro is the model for Cristo de la Concordia, but the locals like to think that this one is more loving—the face has more human features and, unlike its counterpart in Rio, its hands seem to be in a welcoming embrace. There is an outdoor Mass here every Sunday morning. Set aside at least 2 hours for your visit, and do *not* go late at night.

Located at the far eastern end of Av. Las Heroínas. Cable car fare Bs3 each way. Tues–Sat 10am–7pm; Sun 9am–8pm.

Historic Churches & Plazas

Cochabamba was founded in 1574. By walking around the city's plazas and visiting the historic churches, you can travel back in time and feel what it must have been like to live here hundreds of years ago. In **Plaza San Sebastián,** you can see one of the first houses ever built in Cochabamba. Nearby is the first railroad station built in Bolivia. **Plaza 14 de Septiembre** is the historic heart of Cochabamba. September 14 is known as Cochabamba Day, when Cochabamba formally became a city. The plaza dates from 1571, and it is most remarkable because it has preserved its colonial archways on all four sides (very few plazas in South America can boast that the buildings on all four sides are original). On this plaza, you can visit the **cathedral,** which was the first church of Cochabamba. It still has its original baroque facade, and there's a good collection of colonial art inside. Nearby on Ayacucho and Santiváñez is **Santo Domingo,** which is one of my favorite churches. It's very simple inside (unlike the cathedral), which gives it a majestic air. The wooden doors are from 1612.

Shopping

Cochabamba and the surrounding area are famous for their colorful markets. If you happen to be in town on a Wednesday or Saturday, you must stop in at **La Cancha,** Avenida San Martín between Tarata and Pulacayo, a huge market where you can find handicrafts, fresh produce, herbs, and just about anything else you could ever want. In the valleys outside Cochabamba, there are also several towns that have authentic markets. **Caixa Tours,** Esteban Arze S-0563 (✆ **0104/4250-937**), organizes day trips to these market towns. **Tarata,** in the Upper Valley, is a lovely historic village about 1 hour from Cochabamba; market day is Thursday. The market in **Punata** (about 1½ hr. from Cochabamba) is considered to be one of the best and biggest in Bolivia. It's also one of the least touristy. On Sunday, you should head to **Cliza** for a taste of real Bolivian cooking. One of the specialties here is baked pigeon. Minibuses to these towns leave from the corner of Avenida Barrientos and Avenida 6 de Agosto; the trip costs Bs7.

Shopping at the local markets can be chaotic. If you're looking for something more tranquil, you should stop by **Vicuñita Handicrafts,** on Av. Rafael Pabón 777 (✆ **0104/4255-615**). Here you can shop for leather goods, tapestries, bags, and ceramic figurines (all handmade!) in the comfort of a private, uncrowded warehouse. For alpaca sweaters, I recommend **Casa Fisher** on Calle Ramorán Rivero 204.

Anteus Apart Hotel *Value* This attractive budget hotel in the upscale Recoleta residential neighborhood is Cochabamba's best value. A rather plain three-story building overlooks a nice garden in the back and the eastern range of the Andes in the distance. Rooms are bright and cheerful, with large windows and simple, modern furnishings. The 10 apartments come with a fully equipped kitchen and separate living area. Also, free transportation is offered from and to the airport. You can walk from here to several good restaurants, bars, and a huge grocery store.

Av. Potosí 1365, Cochabamba. ✆ **0104/4245-067.** Fax 0104/4320-166. www.hotelanteus.com. 24 units (shower only). $30 double; $40 triple; $50 quad; $40 apt for 2; $50 apt for 3. Additional person $10. MC, V. **Amenities:** Restaurant. *In room:* TV.

Gran Hotel Cochabamba ★ After a recent round of renovations, the Gran Hotel has become the best hotel near Cochabamba's center. It's located in the ritzy Recoleta residential neighborhood, surrounded by the city's most popular restaurants and bars. Though it's still relatively unluxurious, they've updated the decor and added LCD TVs, DVD players, and Wi-Fi throughout the hotel. On my last visit, some rooms, particularly those towards the ends, were in various states of renovation, so be sure to see a few rooms before settling. El Carrillón restaurant offers a full Bolivian and international menu, and the prices are quite reasonable.

Plaza Ubaldo Anze, Cochabamba. ✆ **0104/448-9520.** www.granhotelcochabamba.com. 43 units. $85 double; $95 suite. Rates include breakfast buffet. AE, MC, V. **Amenities:** Restaurant; bar; pool; room service; tennis court. *In room:* A/C, TV, DVD player, hair dryer, minibar, Wi-Fi.

Hotel Aranjuez ★★ *Finds* This is the most atmospheric hotel in town. Ignore the peeling paint outside—inside you'll find an elegant lobby of black sofas and wooden floors that lead to a charming courtyard with a fountain. It is a rambling family mansion of open fireplaces, gold-gilded mirrors, and hidden nooks and crannies. On top there is a beautiful rooftop terrace. The rooms are worn but have nice details such as arched door frames and walk-in wardrobes. Hugo Chávez and his entourage regularly take it over whenever there's a summit in town. The hotel is family run with extremely helpful staff. It is located on a quiet residential street in the Recoleta area.

Av. Buenos Aires E-0563 Cochabamba. ✆ **0104/4240-158.** www.aranjuezhotel.com. 30 units. $69 double; includes breakfast buffet. MC, V. **Amenities:** Restaurant; small pool. *In room:* TV, Wi-Fi.

A Hotel Outside Town

Hacienda De Kaluyo Resort ★★★ *Finds* For the ultimate escape, stay 30 minutes outside town at the most interesting resort in all of Bolivia. A grand private driveway leads to a beautiful hacienda built next to a 19th-century chapel (where weddings are frequently held). The vistas are beautiful, the swimming pool is incredibly serene, and the outdoor restaurant overlooks the endless fields leading down to a large lake. Rooms are in a two-story building, separate from the pool and restaurant area, so guests won't be disturbed when events are in progress. Every piece of furniture in the rooms was designed and built in Bolivia—from the lovely wooden beds to the delicate wrought-iron lamps and ceramic sconces. The bathrooms are spacious and sparkling. There are also two large cabins with their own private garages and kitchenettes; these cabins are very cozy and rustic, with wood-beam ceilings and exposed brick. There are hiking trails all around the property, a lovely open-air gym, a soccer field, and a basketball court. If you ask the friendly owners, they will arrange a water-skiing excursion for you; mountain bikes are also available.

Camino La Angostura (at the intersection of the old highway to Santa Cruz), Tarata. ✆ **0104/4576-593.** Fax 0104/4451-662. www.kaluyo.com. 17 units. $60 double; $120 cabin for 4 people. Rates include breakfast. AE, MC, V. **Amenities:** 2 restaurants; bar; lounge; outdoor exercise room; outdoor pool w/magnificent vistas; tennis court; limited watersports equipment rental. *In room:* TV, kitchenette in cabins.

WHERE TO DINE

Salteñería "Los Castores" ★, Av. Ballivián 790, at the corner of Oruro (✆ **0104/4259-585**), specializes in *salteñas.* There's no menu here; you can only order *salteñas de pollo* (chicken) or *salteñas de carne* (beef). They cost Bs3.50 each, and they are out of this world. You can do as the Bolivians do and eat breakfast here, but the place is open until 2pm.

Casa de Campo ★ Finds BOLIVIAN Cochabamba's best Bolivian restaurant is enormous. On weekends the place is filled to the brim with locals enjoying traditional cuisine. It's an unassuming place, but the food is divine. Come here to sample real Cochabamban dishes such as the *chanka de pollo* (chicken soup with beans) or the spicy *pique lobo* soup. If you're feeling adventurous, try one of the local sausages—chorizo or *chuleta.* For the main course, there are several stews; the most popular is the *picante de pollo* (a bit spicy with a locally grown green pepper). If you're in the mood for meat, the Lapping is excellent. It's a very thin (although sometimes not very tender) steak, grilled and served with broad beans, tomatoes, and sliced onion. (It seems to be a big mystery to everyone why it's called lapping.) This place gets busy after 9pm on Friday and Saturday, when there's a long wait for tables, so arrive early.

Av. Uyuni 618. ✆ **0104/4243-937.** Main courses Bs26–Bs45. MC, V. Daily noon–midnight (till 1am Fri–Sat).

La Cantonata ITALIAN This is one of the most romantic restaurants in town, with fancy tablecloths, formal place settings, and flickering candles. You can also relax by the cozy fireplace and gaze through the huge picture windows. For a few hours, you might forget that you're in Bolivia; it's easy to imagine that you're in your local Italian restaurant. All the pasta, except the spaghetti, is homemade. Choices include ravioli Bolognese and *pasta al pesto.* Besides pasta, there is a good selection of pizzas, meat, and fish, including several different types of steak. I recommend the *surubí alla Cantonata* (an Amazonian fish with oysters, white wine, and lemon sauce).

Calle Mayor Rocha 409 (corner of España). ✆ **0104/4259-222.** Main courses Bs31–Bs84. AE, MC, V. Daily noon–2:30pm and 6:30–11:30pm.

COCHABAMBA AFTER DARK

Cochabamba is a university town with more than 27,000 students. On Friday and Saturday nights, this town is hopping. Most of the trendy bars and cafes are clustered around Avenida España between Colombia and Ecuador. Two of the more happening are **Metrópolis** on the corner of España and Ecuador and **Na Cúnna Irish Pub** at Av. Salamanca 577. In Recoleta, there are several bars and nightclubs on Avenida Uyuni, close to La Estancia restaurant. Also, locals come out in droves on the weekends to sip beer and watch the action on the Prado—there are tons of cafes and places on Avenida Ballivián (Paseo el Prado).

8 SANTA CRUZ DE LA SIERRA

858km (532 miles) SE of La Paz; 473km (293 miles) E of Cochabamba; 612km (379 miles) NE of Sucre

Santa Cruz (also known as Santa Cruz de la Sierra) is undergoing a renaissance. Often dismissed as the brash oil capital of Bolivia, the city is asserting itself and increasingly attracting visitors. Traditionally it was a major railroad hub, with oil refining as its main industry. People came to Santa Cruz to make money and to escape their past. Here, SUVs outnumber *trufis* and the flat roads seem terribly out of place in a country of mountains and peaks. Compared to the cold nights and thin air so characteristic of the high plateau area, the tropical heat and humidity might feel a bit oppressive. Surprisingly for a new city, its streets are lined with low pillared buildings and tiled roofs. A visionary mayor has cleaned up the center and made the plaza one of the prettiest in Bolivia. Tourists are finally coming to Santa Cruz, using it as a base to explore a wealth of attractions—Inca ruins, historic Jesuit missions, and a unique national park, all only a few hours away from this booming metropolis.

ESSENTIALS

Getting There

BY PLANE **Aero Sur** (✆ **0103/3364-446** in Santa Cruz; www.aerosur.com), **TAM** (✆ **0102/2268-1101**), and **BOA** (✆ **0102/4414-0873;** www.boa.bo) offer daily flights to Santa Cruz from La Paz, Cochabamba, and Sucre. One-way tickets cost between Bs350 and Bs870 each. Additionally, both **Aero Sur** and **American Airlines** (✆ **0102/237-2010;** www.aaa.com) use Santa Cruz as their main hub for international flights to Miami and Madrid, so it may well be your first city when arriving to Bolivia. **LAN, Taca, Gol,** and **Copa** also fly to Santa Cruz from other South American destinations.

Most planes arrive at the modern **Viru Viru Airport** (airport code VVI; ✆ **0103/338-5000**), which is about 16km (10 miles) outside town. Taxis from the airport to the center of town cost between Bs50 and Bs60. There's also an airport bus, which leaves the airport about every 20 minutes and drops passengers off at the bus terminal and in nearby neighborhoods. The ride costs Bs8. Some national flights with TAM and Aero Sur land at **El Trompillo airport** (airport code SRZ; no phone), just outside the center. A taxi there from the center costs between BS15 and Bs25. There are free shuttle transfers between the airports every 30 minutes or so.

BY BUS The **Santa Cruz bus terminal** on Avenida Cañoto and Avenida Irala is a truly mad scene. Thousands of people crowd the station at all times of the day, and there's no central information office, so you have to figure out on your own where the bus you want is leaving from. Plus, not all the buses leave from the terminal—many buses depart from offices across the street from the terminal. Many bus companies have offices outside the terminal on Avenida Irala. Buses from La Paz usually arrive in the morning. The 14-hour journey costs Bs120. Buses from Cochabamba take 10 hours and cost Bs50 for a normal bus, or Bs80 for a *bus cama.* Buses from Sucre take a grueling 12 hours and cost Bs60 for a normal bus, or Bs80 for a *bus cama.* See p. 183.

Getting Around

A map of Santa Cruz resembles a large pizza. It is a circular city, with each neighborhood known as a "ring" *(anillo).* The first ring is the first circle around the city; as you move farther from the center, you reach the second and third *anillos.* Santa Cruz is quickly becoming a prime example of urban sprawl. The center of the city is getting smaller, while the outskirts of town keep moving farther and farther away. Taxis are, by far, the easiest way to get around. From the center of town to the hotels and restaurants in the nearby suburbs, a taxi should cost Bs15 to Bs25. Plaza 24 de Septiembre is the commercial heart of Santa Cruz; from here, you can walk to all the banks, travel agencies, and centrally located hotels. For a car rental, try **A. Barrons Renta Car,** Av. Alemana 50 (✆ **0103/342-0160;** www.rentacarbolivia.com). They also have offices in Cochabamba and Tarija.

Visitor Information

You'll find the **tourist information** office on the north side of the main plaza (✆ **0103/334-6776**), housed in a beautiful neocolonial building. It's open daily until 8pm. Beside the cathedral there is a space called **Manzana 1,** housing a gallery and exhibition center. An open-top city bus leaves from here on 3-hour tours of the city. For information about this and nearby attractions (the Jesuit missions, the Inca ruins of Samaipata, and Amboró National Park), your best bet is to contact **Rosario Tours** ★, Arenales 193 between Beni and Murillo (✆ **0103/3369-656;** www.rosariotours.com). Another excellent tour operator is Dutch-owned **Ruta Verde** ★ (✆ **0103/339-6470;** www.rutaverdebolivia.com). They offer a good variety of tours, including trips to the Jesuit missions, Amboro National Park, Noell Kempf Mercado National Park, and the town where Che Guevara made his last stand.

FAST FACTS **Magri Turismo,** Calle Warnes and the corner of Potosí (✆ **0103/345-663;** www.magriturismo.com), is the American Express representative in Santa Cruz. Unfortunately, you can't change traveler's checks here. If you need to change traveler's checks or exchange money, you should head to **Cambio Alemán Transatlántico,** on Calle 24 de Septiembre in the main plaza. There is also a **Citibank** on Avenida Mons Rivero at the corner of Asunción. **Hospital Universitario Japonés** (✆ **0103/462-032**), on Avenida Japón in the *tercer anillo* (third ring), is the best hospital in town. In an emergency, call ✆ **0103/462-031.** If you need a **pharmacy,** try **Farmacia Gutiérrez** at 21 de Mayo 26; for deliveries, call ✆ **0103/361-777.** Also nearby is **Farmacia Santa María,** on the corner of 21 de Mayo and Junín. The **post office** is at Junín 150 between Plaza 24 de Septiembre and 21 de Mayo. You can take care of all your laundry needs at **Lavandería España** on Calle España 160. The best Internet cafe is **Full Internet,** Ayacucho 208, on the corner of Velasco; the entrance is on the second floor, so look for the stairs on Ayacucho.

WHAT TO SEE & DO

The city's main attraction is the central plaza, where brass bands play beneath palm trees and there are frequent street events. As traffic is cut off at both ends, the square is a tranquil retreat from what is a chaotic city. The **Museo Etnofolklórico Municipal,** in Parque Arenal, has an interesting display of tools, baskets, and musical instruments used by indigenous groups of Bolivia. The museum is open Monday through Friday from 8:30am to noon and 2:30 to 6:30pm; admission is Bs5. Next door, explore **Parque Arenal,** where you can rent paddleboats for Bs8 per half-hour. The **cathedral** on Plaza 24 de Septiembre houses a small religious museum that's open on Tuesday and Thursday from 10am to noon and 4 to 6pm, and on Sunday from 10am to noon and 6 to 8pm. The **Museo de Historia y Archivo Regional de Santa Cruz de la Sierra,** Junín 151, offers a host of exhibits ranging from ceramics to photography; it's open Monday to Friday from 8am to noon and 3 to 6:30pm. Admission is free. **Casa de Cultura Franco Aleman,** 24 de Septiembre 36 (✆ **0103/333-3392;** www.ccfrancoaleman.org), is a beautifully restored colonial building facing the main plaza. It houses an exhibition room, small cinema, and theater. There's a small zoo on the third *anillo* and Avenida Redentor, but the animals are kept in rather poor conditions, so I don't recommend a visit.

Samaipata

Samaipata is a charming mountain town located about 2 hours southwest of Santa Cruz. The main attraction here is the Inca ruins known as **El Fuerte.** The ruins are a huge mysterious complex, much of it unexcavated. From what remains, it's hard to envision the site's former glory. The most impressive structure is the **Chinkana** ★, also known as the Labyrinth. It consists mainly of a hole that was originally 30m (9 ft.) deep. From the top of El Fuerte, you have great views of the surrounding mountains and perfect sight-lines of other Inca sites. Most scientists believe that the Incas built these villages in a pattern. At this site, you will also see what are believed to be amphitheaters and temples for religious ceremonies. The site is open daily from 9am to 5pm, and admission is Bs20.

GETTING THERE To understand Samaipata and the ruins of El Fuerte, you really need an experienced guide. **Rosario Tours** ★, Arenales 193 between Beni and Murillo (✆ **0103/369-977;** www.rosariotours.com), organizes day trips here with English-speaking guides. **Michael Blendinger Nature Tours** (✆ **0103/9446-227;** www.discoveringbolivia.com) also arranges trips to El Fuerte and nature hikes through the area. His office is in Samaipata, but he can arrange transportation from Santa Cruz. You can also arrange your own private taxi to Samaipata by contacting **Expreso Samaipata** (✆ **0102/2335-067**). In Santa Cruz, the taxis leave from the Residencial Señor de Los Milagros on Avenida Omar Chávez Ortiz.

Amboro National Park

Amboró, one of the most pristine national parks in all of Bolivia, is only 3 hours west of Santa Cruz. The park covers more than 600,000 hectares (1.5 million acres) and encompasses four different biodiversity zones: the Amazon basin, subtropical forests, temperate woodlands, and the cool mountainous terrain of the Andes. More than 700 species of birds have been seen in the area. Some of the rarer species include the red-fronted macaw, Bolivian recurvebill, and rufous-faced antpitta. You'll also have the opportunity to see monkeys here. There are some fantastic hiking trails that will take you to caves and waterfalls. Accommodations are mostly rustic campgrounds, though tour operators offer alternatives with the renowned bird-watching hangout **Refugio Los Volcanes** or the eco-friendly **Mataracú Tent Camp.**

GETTING THERE The roads to Amboró can be rough. I highly recommend taking a trip here with a guided tour. **Rosario Tours** (see above), organizes overnight bird-watching trips. **Michael Blendinger Nature Tours** (see above) also arranges excursions into the park, as does **Ruta Verde** (✆ **0103/339-6470;** www.rutaverdebolivia.com).

The Jesuit Missions ★

In the late 16th century, the Jesuits set out to the hinterlands of Bolivia and developed thriving cultural and religious centers for the local people. Victims of their own success, they were expelled from South America in 1773. Today, you can visit some of these missions, which have been amazingly preserved and restored. **San Javier** and **Concepción** are the two closest and most accessible missions from Santa Cruz. The 5-hour drive to San Javier is a sight itself: Along the way, you'll pass through Mennonite communities and see the landscape change from lush green farmland to tropical shrubbery. The road is paved, but it can be a bit rough.

San Javier was founded in 1691 and at its height included about 3,000 people. The remarkable church was constructed entirely of local wood. The ornate woodcarvings painted with local dyes are quite spectacular; the gold-colored interior is just as impressive. The road to Concepción from San Javier is mostly unpaved. You will find a similarly ornate wood church (with a silver altar), cloisters, and a historic main plaza. In the workshops adjacent to the church, you can observe local artisans restoring statues and creating new ones. These two missions are the most impressive of the six Jesuit missions in the Santa Cruz area and the most accessible.

GETTING THERE It's difficult to arrange public transportation to the Jesuit missions. Your best bet is to arrange a trip through a travel agency. I recommend using **Rosario Tours** (see above). The trip includes an English-speaking guide, transportation, and all meals. The price varies depending on how many people are on the trip. **Ruta Verde** (see above) also travels to the missions.

Shopping in Santa Cruz

Because Santa Cruz is one of the largest and wealthiest cities in Bolivia, you'll find many trendy boutiques and international retailers here. If you're looking for unique gifts typical of the area, you should buy jewelry or handicrafts. For jewelry, I recommend **Joyería Andrea,** at Junín 177. This store specializes in a stone called the Bolivian, a mix of amethyst and citrine. For high-quality handicrafts, your best option is **ARTECAMPO,** at Mons Salvatierra 407 (near the corner of Vallegrande). This beautiful store is an association of artists from the countryside—all the money you spend here will go directly to them.

WHERE TO STAY

If you're in town for the International Trade Fair (held annually in late Sept), you won't find a better place than **Buganvillas** ★, Av. Roca Coronado 901 (✆ **0103/551-212;** www.hotelbuganvillas.com). The hotel complex is right next to the convention center (although it is about a 15-min. ride from the center of the city). The beautiful rooms actually are all fully equipped apartments. The complex has three pools, a spa, several restaurants, and a minimart. Rates range from $109 for a one-bedroom apartment to $199 for a five-bedroom apartment.

If you're looking for budget accommodations, I recommend **La Siesta Hotel,** Calle Vallegrande 17, near the corner of Ayacucho (✆ **0103/3330-146;** lasiesta@infonet.com.bo). The rooms aren't fancy ($35 for a double), but they have cable TV and air-conditioning. Plus, when it gets hot here, you can relax by the pool.

The stunning **Senses Hotel Boutique** ★★, Plaza 24 de Septiembre and Sucre (✆ **0103/339-6666;** www.senseshotelboutique.com), opened at the end of 2009 in the all-brick La Pascana center across from the Catedral. It's the first true boutique hotel in Bolivia, with 49 design suites and a room personalized with your preferences in fragrances and music. Rooms start at $220 for doubles.

The best hotel in all of Santa Cruz, however, is **Hotel Los Tajibos** ★★, Av. San Martín 455 (✆ **0103/3421-000;** www.lostajiboshotel.com), which is a 10-minute taxi ride from the center of town. If you stay here, you can walk to the many bars and restaurants on Avenida San Martín and take advantage of its lush pool area and first-rate restaurants. Rooms run from $144 to $160 for doubles, $235 for suites.

WHERE TO DINE

If you need a break while wandering downtown, stop in at the **La Pascana Center,** which opened in late 2009. It has several restaurants, including **Ikirau** (an international café) and **Lyambae** (a place specializing in molecular gastronomy). On the opposing corner is **Café 24,** Calle René Moreno and Sucre (✆ **0103/330-4228**), a laid-back restaurant and cafe that comes alive at night with bands and young clientele, and **Lorca** (✆ **0103/334-0562;** www.lorcasantacruz.org), on the second level, which has one of the more eclectic menus in Santa Cruz—there's even a degustation menu.

For truly authentic Bolivian cuisine, visit **Casa del Camba ★★★**, Av. Cristóbal de Mendoza 539 (✆ **0103/427-864**), which boasts nightly entertainment by local singers and dancers, and a beautiful alfresco dining area where large cuts of beef and other Bolivian dishes are served. It's open daily from noon to 4pm and 6pm to 2am.

SANTA CRUZ AFTER DARK

The **Irish Pub,** on Calle 24 de Septiembre, right on the main plaza and also between the 3rd *anillo* interior (the inner part of the third ring road) and the zoo (*zoologico*), is a popular watering hole for foreigners. **Avenida San Martín** in Barrio Equipetrol, in the second ring, is lined with outdoor cafes, bars, and pubs. For something more central, try the **La Pascana Center** in the plaza, which has a lounge with live music on weekend nights, and **Sky Bar,** a rooftop bar with 360-degree views of the city.

6

Brazil

by Shawn Blore & Alexandra de Vries

There's a joke Brazilians like to tell: When the world was created, one of the archangels peered over God's shoulder at the work in progress and couldn't help noticing that one country had been especially favored. "You've given everything to Brazil," the archangel said. "It has the longest beaches, the largest river, the biggest forest, the best soil. The weather's always warm and sunny, with no floods, hurricanes, or natural disasters at all. Don't you think that's a little unfair?" "Ah," God replied, "just wait until you see the people I'm putting there."

Accuracy rarely comes with a punch line, but there's a significant grain of truth in that tale. Brazil as a nation *is* unusually blessed. Over 8,000km (5,000 miles) of coastline—some of it packed with cafes and partygoers, but long stretches blissfully empty. Rainforests and wetlands teem with exotic critters. Some of the oldest cities and civic architecture in the New World (and one of the newest cities in the entire world) are here. Restaurants match the snobbiest standards, with regional cuisines that have yet to be discovered in culinary capitals like New York or L.A. Music lovers could make Brazil a lifetime study. And let's not forget a little thing called Carnaval.

And about those Brazilians: They work as hard as anyone in the First World, and many a good deal harder. In recent years, Brazil has devoted time and resources to improving its tourism infrastructure, reflected in the new airports, hotels, and inns that have sprung up around the country. Yet no one could accuse Brazilians of worshiping efficiency. They'd much rather get along than get things done; the goal is, above all, harmony. Harmony can mean an entire Sunday spent watching soccer or afternoons off for quality time with your buddies at the beach. It can mean countless hours of effort for a single night's party. But above all, harmony mandates never taking anything all that seriously. And at this, Brazilians excel.

1 THE REGIONS IN BRIEF

Brazil's 170 million citizens inhabit the fifth-largest country in the world, a nation about 10% larger than the continental United States. The **Amazon** dominates the northern third of the country—a vast tropical rainforest with the river at its heart. The country's central interior is dominated by the ***planalto,*** a high dry plateau covered in ***cerrado,*** a type of dry savanna reminiscent of that of southern Africa. The chief city in this region is the planned federal capital Brasilia. West of the *planalto* but south of the Amazon rainforest you find the **Pantanal,** a wetland the size of France that is one of the best places to see wildlife in the whole of South America. Brazil's **Northeast** is a land apart. Running roughly from São Luis to Salvador, the coast is dominated by midsize cities and sugar cane, the culture strongly Afro-Brazilian, while on the dry interior plateau those Nordestinos who haven't yet fled to the cities eke out a bare living on the land. Brazil's two chief cities, **Rio de Janeiro** and **São Paulo,** stand within a few hundred miles of each other

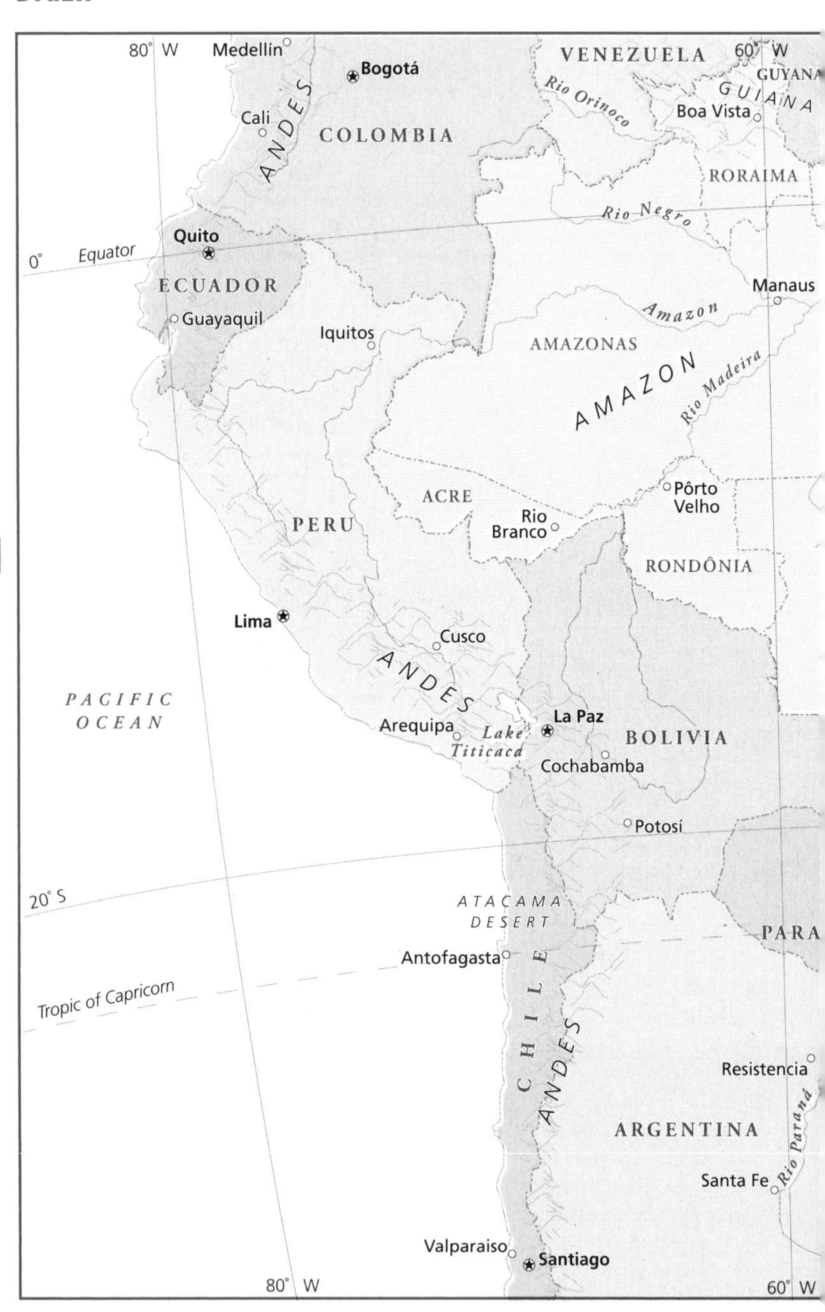
80° W
Medellín
Bogotá
ANDES
Cali
COLOMBIA
VENEZUELA
60° W
GUYANA
GUIANA
Rio Orinoco
Boa Vista
RORAIMA
Rio Negro
Quito
0°
Equator
ECUADOR
Guayaquil
Iquitos
Manaus
Amazon
AMAZONAS
AMAZON
Rio Madeira
ACRE
Pôrto Velho
Rio Branco
PERU
RONDÔNIA
Lima
Cusco
ANDES
PACIFIC OCEAN
Arequipa
Lake Titicaca
La Paz
BOLIVIA
Cochabamba
Potosí
20° S
ATACAMA DESERT
PARA
Antofagasta
Tropic of Capricorn
CHILE
ANDES
Resistencia
ARGENTINA
Rio Paraná
Santa Fe
Valparaiso
Santiago
80° W
60° W

Cayenne
SURINAME
FRENCH GUIANA (FRANCE)
HIGHLANDS
AMAPÁ
Macapá
BASIN
Equator 0°
40° W
ATLANTIC OCEAN
Belém
Alcântara
São Luís
Parque Nacional dos Lençóis Maranhenses
Santarém
Rio Xingu
Rio Tocantins
Rio Tapajós
Fortaleza
PARÁ
MARANHÃO
Teresina
CEARÁ
Fernando de Noronha
RIO GRANDE DO NORTE
Natal
PARAÍBA
João Pessoa
PIAUÍ
Recife
PERNAMBUCO
Rio São Francisco
Maceió
ALAGOAS
TOCANTINS
SERGIPE
Aracaju
BAHIA
MATO GROSSO
Salvador
R. Paraguai
BRAZILIAN HIGHLANDS
Cuiabá
Cáceres
GOIÁS
Goiânia
Brasilia
PANTANAL
MINAS GERAIS
Corumbá
Uberlândia
Campo Grande
Belo Horizonte
ESPÍRITO SANTO
MATO GROSSO DO SUL
Rio Paraná
SÃO PAULO
Vitória
20° S
RIO DE JANEIRO
GUAY
São Paulo
Rio de Janeiro
PARANÁ
Santos
Tropic of Capricorn
Asunción
Foz do Iguaçu
Curitiba
SANTA CATARINA
Florianópolis
ATLANTIC OCEAN
RIO GRANDE DO SUL
Pôrto Alegre
Rio Grande
URUGUAY
Buenos Aires
Montevideo
40° W
0
400 mi
0
400 km
N

close to the country's south coast. São Paulo is the larger and more important of the two, but Rio, the former capital and *cidade maravilhosa* (marvelous city), is by far the more interesting. The small southern tip of the country is inhabited largely by descendants of European immigrants. It's the most densely settled and best-organized part of Brazil. The area has the astonishing natural wonder of **Iguaçu Falls,** for many visitors a must-see. The island of Santa Catarina, also known as **Florianópolis,** has over 40 beaches and is the favorite summer destination in the south.

RIO DE JANEIRO Few cities are as striking as Rio. The city folds itself into the narrow bits of land between tropical beaches and mountains that leap to 750m (2,500-ft.) heights (one of these is crowned by the city's landmark statue of Christ). The city offers much in the way of sightseeing, from nature to sunbathing to museums and historic neighborhoods. The culture, perhaps best expressed in music and nightlife, is just as appealing. Samba is alive and well, augmented by many vibrant newer forms of distinctly Brazilian music. The event of the year is **Carnaval,** the biggest party of the world. And believe me when I say that Cariocas—as Rio residents are known—know how to throw a party.

SÃO PAULO Some 25 million people live in and around São Paulo, the largest city not only in Brazil but in all of South America. São Paulo is Brazil's New York. It's the melting pot that attracts the best and brightest to make their fortune. The city overflows with restaurants, including the best fine dining in Brazil. São Paulo has emerged as the cultural capital of Brazil, rich with art galleries and strong in new theater. And it's the best place in Brazil to shop.

THE NORTHEAST Even in a country with such strong regional distinctions, Brazil's Northeast (Nordeste) stands apart. Roughly speaking, the Nordeste encompasses the area from Salvador to São Luis, including cities such as Recife, Natal, and Fortaleza. Everything Nordeste is different: the food richer, the cities more historic, the beaches longer and whiter, the music more vibrant, the politics more Byzantine—and traditionally more corrupt. This was the first part of Brazil to be settled, the area where sugar cane and slavery dominated economy and society for more than 3 centuries. The downturn in the sugar economy left the area a backwater, and only with the recent advent of tourism have Nordeste fortunes really begun to pick up. For visitors the Northeast offers a year-round tropical climate with long white-sandy beaches, historic cities, and a vibrant Afro-Brazilian culture, which is reflected in the cuisine, the festivals, and, especially, the music and dance. Olinda is a quiet colonial gem of a city, while Salvador's 16th-century colonial core has been transformed into a stroller's dream.

THE AMAZON The largest rainforest in the world is so vast it defies easy description: All of western Europe would fit comfortably with room to spare beneath its leafy canopy. Thanks in large part to media coverage of the many threats to this region, interest in ecotourism and visits to the Amazon have skyrocketed. The main staging ground for trips to the Brazilian Amazon is the city of Manaus, located where the Rio Negro joins the Rio Solimões to form the Amazon. Manaus itself is surprisingly modern. Moderately interesting in itself, its real interest is as the starting point for expeditions into the rainforest. Options include everything from day trips on the Amazon to multiday trips to virgin rainforest where one can catch sight of countless unique plants and animals. In contrast to Manaus, the city of Belém, located at the mouth of the Amazon, is an old and settled city, with numerous churches and a historic downtown, and the incredible Ver-o-Peso market, where the entire produce of the Amazon is bought and sold. Close to Belém in the mouth of the Amazon river is Marajó, an island larger than Switzerland, dotted with buffalo ranches and rich with birdlife. Halfway between Manaus and Belém there is Santarem, and the astonishing white-sand beaches of Alter do Chão.

THE CENTER WEST Brazil's center west is a broad flat plain, dotted here and there with craggy highlands, and populated chiefly by ranchers, cowhands, and increasingly by large commercial farms. It was in the midst of this vast and not especially intriguing region that nearly 50 years ago Brazil erected its striking modernist capital, Brasilia. While the capital may be the region's man-made wonder, the natural wonder is the Pantanal. A wetland the size of France, the Pantanal has traditionally been overlooked in favor of the Amazon, but that's changing as people become increasingly aware of the incredible wildlife-viewing opportunities the area offers. More than 600 bird species, anacondas, jaguars, caiman, giant otters, and anteaters are just some of the animals found in the wetlands. As this area lacks the dense foliage of the Amazon, the animals are much easier to spot.

THE SOUTH The southern part of Brazil, made up of the states of Paraná, Santa Catarina, and Rio Grande do Sul, has a temperate climate and good soil, attributes that long attracted large numbers of European immigrants. It's a settled, well-organized region. The prime beach destination in the south is Florianópolis, a large island with over 40 beaches, clean waters, and excellent restaurants and nightlife. The Iguaçu Falls, a UNESCO World Heritage Site, are located on the border of Brazil, Argentina, and Paraguay. This spectacular site is made up of 275 falls that cascade from 72m (240 ft.) down a 2.5km-wide (1½-mile) precipice in a fabulous jungle setting.

2 THE BEST OF BRAZIL IN 2 WEEKS

In 2 weeks, you can get a good taste of Brazil at a pace that won't leave you with post-holiday stress disorder. The route below takes you to Rio de Janeiro and the historic city of Salvador. You then have the option of spending time in the Amazon or on a beautiful Bahian beach. The Amazon is fascinating, but it requires both money and travel time. This route includes Iguaçu Falls and a brief taste of the urban sophistication that is São Paulo.

Days ❶–❸: Rio de Janeiro ★★★

To get into the Brazilian spirit, start off your trip in **Rio de Janeiro.** After getting settled in your hotel, head for the beach. Enjoy the scene, tan a bit (but don't overdo it). Watch the sunset from **Arpoador** (p. 257). You'll be tired from the flight, so take it easy with a good dinner in one of the top restaurants of **Ipanema** or **Leblon.** On Day 2 get out and see the mountains. Take a tram up to the **Corcovado** (p. 254), or take a jeep tour up through **Tijuca Forest.** Stop by **Cinelândia** in Rio's Centro in the afternoon. That night, discover the late-night Carioca lifestyle. Have dinner around 11pm, then catch some samba, played live in **Lapa.** You'll be sleeping late the next day, so spend some more time at the beach, or take a trolley up to explore the hillside neighborhood of **Santa Teresa.** All this should acclimatize you to the Brazilian way before you set off to explore the rest of the country.

Days ❹–❻: Salvador ★★★

Early on Day 4, catch a flight for **Salvador.** This is the city where the country's

African roots are strongest. Stay in one of the lovely pousadas in **Pelourinho,** or pamper yourself with a stay in the restored 17th-century **Convento do Carmo** (p. 313). Wander through Pelourinho's 17th-century streets. In the evening, try some Bahian cuisine, then go out and enjoy the music in Pelourinho after dark. Next day, take the boat tour of the **Bay of All Saints,** or head out to the church of **Bonfim.** On your third day, dig deeper into this city's treasures at a leisurely pace; tour the lovely **Museu de Arte Sacra** (p. 288) or see the lighthouse and beaches of **Barra.**

Days ❼–⓫: The Amazon ★★★

Catch an early flight to **Manaus** (p. 338). It's time to experience a bit of the largest standing rainforest on earth, the Amazon. On your first day you should have time to see the highlights of Manaus, including the famous **Opera House.** The next morning, set off early for a jungle lodge (or better yet, if you have more time, go kayaking through the forest with **Amazon Mystery Tours** (p. 347). Choose a smaller lodge farther from the city. Don't go to the Ariaú. Although the area around Manaus is hardly unexplored, a few days will allow you to experience the fauna and flora of a tropical rainforest. Enjoy the trees, the monkeys, the caiman, and the bright pink dolphins.

Day ⓬: Transit

It's going to take a day of taxis, boats, and airplanes to get you to your next destination, Iguaçu.

Days ⓭ & ⓮: Iguaçu Falls ★★★

A final must-see—one of the most awe-inspiring natural wonders of the world—**Iguaçu Falls.** The early flight from Salvador should get you to Iguaçu before 2pm. Store your stuff and go see the falls. Stick to the Brazilian side today and perhaps take the **Macuco Boat Safari** (p. 357). The next day, go explore the falls from the Argentine side. You can catch an early flight to São Paulo and spend the next day exploring, or you can dawdle by the hotel pool in Iguaçu (or go see the **Bird Park,** p. 357), before catching a later flight to São Paulo and connecting to your evening flight home.

3 PLANNING YOUR TRIP TO BRAZIL

VISITOR INFORMATION

Travelers planning their trip to Brazil can browse the site of the Brazilian national tourism agency, **Embratur** at **www.embratur.gov.br**. The **Brazilian Embassy** in the U.K. has an outstanding website including links to all the state and many city tourism websites: **www.brazil.org.uk**. Visitors to Rio de Janeiro can get in touch with the city's tourist agency, **Riotur** (✆ **021/2271-7000;** www.riodejaneiro-turismo.com.br). Other useful websites include the following:

- **www.brazilnuts.com**: For information on packages and tours of Brazil.
- **www.naturesafaris.com.br**: A commercial site with good, basic natural history of the Amazon.
- **www.saltur.salvador.ba.gov.br**: Salvador's good official tourism agency.
- **www.infobrasilia.com.br**: For great info on Brasilia's architecture and design.
- **http://iguassu.com.br**: Iguaçu's very good official site.

In Brazil

Within Brazil, you'll have to rely on each city's tourist office, varying in quality from the extremely helpful ones in Rio, Salvador, Recife, and Manaus to the more indifferent one

Telephone Dialing Info at a Glance

- **To place a call from your home country to Brazil,** dial the international access code (0011 in Australia, 011 in the U.S. and Canada, 0170 in New Zealand, 00 in the U.K.), plus the country code (55), plus the Brazilian area code, followed by the number. For example, a call from the United States to Rio would be 011+55+21+0000+0000.
- **To place a local call within Brazil,** you must use the access code of a *prestadora* (service provider). The only code that works in all of Brazil (and the only *prestadora* code you need to remember) is the one for **Embratel**—21 (which also happens to be the area code of Rio). So, if you were dialing long distance to a number in Rio, you would dial 0-21 (selecting Embratel as your provider), 21 (Rio's area code), and 5555-5555 (the number).
- **To place a direct international call from Brazil,** dial the international access code (021), plus the country code of the place you are dialing, plus the area code and the local number.
- **To reach an international operator,** dial ✆ **000-111.** Major long-distance company access codes are as follows: **AT&T** ✆ 0800/890-0288; **MCI** ✆ 0800/890-0012; **Sprint** ✆ 0800/888-8000; and **Canada Direct** ✆ 0800/890-0014.

in São Paulo. ***Tip:*** Good countrywide or regional maps are almost nonexistent in Brazil. It's best to bring a good map with you.

ENTRY REQUIREMENTS

Nationals of the United States, Canada, and Australia require a visa to visit Brazil. **British nationals** (and holders of an E.U. passport) and **New Zealand** passport holders do not require a visa, but do need a passport valid for at least 6 months and a return ticket. A number of visa types are available; cost, processing time, and documentation requirements vary. Visas for **Australians** cost A$90, plus local handling fees, and again take about 2 weeks to process. For **Canadians** a similar visa costs C$72 and takes about the same processing time. **U.S. citizens** pay $100 for a standard single-entry tourist visa valid for 90 days (add another $10 for handling fees, passport photos, and courier costs if you don't live near a consulate). Count on at least 2 weeks of processing time.

Upon arrival in Brazil, visitors will receive a 90-day entry stamp in their passport and a stamped entry card. Hang on to the card for dear life, as losing it will result in a possible fine and a certain major hassle when you leave. If necessary, the visa can be renewed once for another 90 days. **Visa renewals** are obtained through the local Policia Federal. This is best done in large cities where the staff has experience with tourists. It's a good idea to print and fill in a copy of the requisite form, available at the following website: www.dpf.gov.br/web/formulario/form_cgpi/requerimento_de_prorrogacao_de_prazo.htm.

Shortly after the United States began fingerprinting Brazilian visitors, Brazil in a tit-for-tat bit of retaliation implemented its own fingerprint program for U.S. visitors. In its

Don't Leave Home Without a Picture ID

Bring an alternative picture ID, like a driver's license or student ID. You are required to carry ID in Brazil, and it's sometimes requested when entering office buildings or even tourist sites. Your passport is safer in the hotel safe and not required except for official transactions.

first few months the system caused numerous long delays; nowadays the fingerprint requirement is fulfilled with a quick and efficient digital reading of a single thumb digit.

For more information regarding visas and to obtain application details:

Australians can call ✆ **02/6273-2372** (in Australia) or log on to www.brazil.org.au.

Canadians can apply through **Toronto**'s Brazilian consulate (✆ **416/922-2503;** www.consbrastoronto.org).

In **New Zealand** inquiries can be made in Wellington at ✆ **04/473-3516,** or check www.brazil.org.nz.

In the **U.K.,** more information is available at ✆ **020/7399-9000** (in the U.K.), or www.brazil.org.uk.

U.S. citizens can contact the Brazilian consulate in **New York** (✆ **917/777-7791;** www.brazilny.org); **Los Angeles** (✆ **323/651-2664;** www.brazilian-consulate.org); or **Miami** (✆ **305/285-6200;** www.brazilmiami.org). Links will connect you to the consulate closest to you.

CUSTOMS

As a visitor you are unlikely to be scrutinized very closely by Brazilian Customs; however, there are random checks, and your luggage may be thoroughly inspected. Visitors are allowed to bring in whatever they need for personal use on their trip, including electronics such as a camera and laptop. If you are bringing in new electronic items you may be asked to register the item to ensure that you will take it with you when you leave. Gifts purchased abroad worth more than $500 must be declared and are subject to duties for the value over $500. Merchandise for sale or samples should also be declared upon arrival.

MONEY

The official unit of currency in Brazil is the **Real** (R$; pronounced Ray-*all;* the plural is **Reais,** pronounced Ray-*eyes*), which the Brazilian government introduced in 1994 in an attempt to control inflation. The U.S. dollar has been on a steady decline to its current level around **R$1.70 to the dollar.** For travelers this means that Brazil is still affordable, though not the bargain it was in years past. Throughout this chapter, the prices of some hotels, tours, and transportation options are listed in U.S. dollars.

Tip: When exchanging money, be it cash or traveler's checks, always keep the receipt. You will need it in case you want to change back any unused Reais at the end of your trip. See **www.xe.com** online for an easy currency converter.

Here's a general idea of what things cost in Rio: a beer on the beach, R$2; a night in a midrange hotel, R$150; midrange three-course dinner for two, no booze, R$130.

THE U.S. DOLLAR Up until 2004, many businesses based their rates on the U.S. dollar. With the dollar's fall, some businesses have lowered their Real prices to keep a steady dollar price, others have increased the Real rate, and still others have switched over to accounting in euros. For U.S. travelers, it means that Brazil has gotten a little bit more expensive. When prices are listed in U.S. dollars only, it's because these companies quote their prices directly in dollars. If in doubt, ask. And though it's a bad idea to carry large wads of cash, it can be helpful to bring a small amount of U.S. cash ($10s or $20s only, no $100s) as an emergency supply in case that ATM is broken or your credit card isn't working. Even in the smallest towns people will know the exchange rate, and someone will be happy to take the U.S. dollars off your hands.

ATMS Brazil's financial infrastructure is very sophisticated, and ATMs are common here, even in the smallest towns. The only trick is finding one that works with your card. ATMs are linked to a network that most likely includes your bank at home. **Cirrus** (✆ **800/424-7787;** www.mastercard.com) and **PLUS** (✆ **800/843-7587;** www.visa.com) are the two most popular networks in the U.S.; call or check online for ATM locations at your destination. You need to have a four-digit PIN to be able to access ATMs in Brazil. For most ATMs the limit is R$1,000 per transaction, but depending on the machine these amounts may be lower. R$1,000 is also the maximum that can be withdrawn each calendar day.

The vast majority of travelers find they are able to use the HSBC and Banco do Brasil ATMs bearing a PLUS/Visa and Cirrus/MasterCard logo. Almost all Brazilian airports have HSBC and Banco do Brasil ATMs. However, it's not a bad idea to bring two different cards to increase your access options with other banks. (Small towns normally only have one ATM. It will be PLUS/Visa or Cirrus/MasterCard, but not always both.) Bradesco, Banco 24 Horas, and Citibank ATMs are often compatible with PLUS/Visa. If in doubt, check with your bank to find out which Brazilian bank networks are compatible with your card. Also, plan ahead to ensure that you have enough cash; for safety reasons many ATMs do not operate 24 hours. Often they will close after 10pm or only allow a small amount of cash to be withdrawn during the off-hours. Your best bets for late-night withdrawals are airports, malls, or gas stations.

Finally, make sure that during New Year's and Carnaval you get enough cash ahead of time, as machines often run out of money by the end of the holidays.

CREDIT CARDS The best exchange rates can be obtained through credit cards, which are accepted at most Brazilian shops and hotels and restaurants. Just keep in mind that you are sometimes able to negotiate a better discount on a room or in a store if you pay cash. The most commonly accepted cards are Visa and MasterCard. American Express and Diners Club are also often accepted. It's a good idea to have at least two cards, as some stores and restaurants may only accept one card (usually Visa or MasterCard; Diners and Amex are less common, especially in small towns). Keep in mind that many banks now assess a 1% to 3% "transaction fee" on all charges you incur abroad (whether you're using the local currency or U.S. dollars). But credit cards still may be the smart way to go when you factor in things like exorbitant ATM fees and the higher exchange rates and service fees you'll pay with traveler's checks.

TRAVELER'S CHECKS Traveler's checks aren't a very good idea in Brazil. Most shops won't accept them, hotels give a miserable exchange rate (if they cash them at all), and many banks have a strange policy that they will not cash your traveler's checks unless you have an account at that branch of that bank. The Banco do Brasil is the only bank that will cash them with a minimum of hassle, but it will charge a $20 service fee.

WHEN TO GO

PEAK SEASON High season in Brazil lasts from the week before Christmas until Carnaval (which falls sometime in Feb or early Mar, depending on the year). Flights and accommodations are more expensive and more likely to be full during this period. Book well ahead of time for accommodations during New Year's and Carnaval. This is the most fun time to travel—towns and resorts are bustling as many Brazilians take their summer vacations, the weather's warm, and New Year's and Carnaval are fabulously entertaining. If you want to spend New Year's in Brazil, it's best to arrive after Christmas. The 25th is really a family affair, and most restaurants and shops will be closed.

Other busy times of the year include Easter week and the months of July, when Brazilian schools and universities take their winter break, and August, when most Europeans and North Americans visit during the summer vacation. This is probably the worst time of year to travel; prices go up significantly, and except for in the north and parts of the Northeast, the weather can be iffy and downright chilly from Rio de Janeiro southward. One year in Rio, I suffered through 4 straight weeks of rain, and temperatures as low as the 40s and 50s Fahrenheit (5°C–10°C) are not unheard of in the south. If you want to take advantage of the best deals and still have good weather, consider visiting Brazil in September or October. The spring weather means warm days in São Paulo, Iguaçu, and Rio, and tropical heat everywhere else; in the Amazon and the Pantanal, you'll be there just before the wet season starts. As an added bonus, in Rio you'll be able to attend some of the samba school rehearsals as they get ready for Carnaval (yes, they start 4 months early). Another good period for a visit is after Carnaval (early to mid-Mar, depending on the dates) through May, when you can take advantage of low-season prices, particularly in hotels, while still enjoying good weather.

CLIMATE As Brazil lies in the Southern Hemisphere, its seasons are the exact opposite of what Northern Hemisphere residents are used to: **summer is December through March,** and **winter, June through September.** Within the country the climate varies considerably from region to region. In most of Brazil the summers are very hot. Temperatures can rise to 110°F (43°C) with high humidity. The **Northeast** (from Salvador north) is warm year-round, often with a pleasant breeze coming off the ocean. Temperatures hover between the low 80s and mid-90s Fahrenheit (upper 20s to mid-30s Celsius). The winter months (June–July) are slightly wetter, but even then the amount of rain is limited—a quick shower that cools things down briefly before giving way to more sunshine.

As befits a rainforest, the **Amazon** is also hot and humid year-round, with temperatures hovering around the mid-90s to low 100s Fahrenheit (mid- to high 30s Celsius). The dry season lasts from June to December and is often called "summer" by the locals, as it is hot and sunny. As the rivers recede, beaches and islands reappear. The wet season typically runs from December to May and is referred to as "winter." The humidity is higher in the rainy season, building up over the course of the day to produce a heavy downfall almost every afternoon. Even then, however, mornings and early afternoons can be clear and sunny.

The **Pantanal** is very hot in the rainy season, with temperatures climbing over 100°F (the low 40s Celsius). Most of the rain falls December through March. The driest time of the year is May through October. In these winter months things cool down considerably, though nighttime temperatures will seldom drop below 68°F (20°C). **Rio** has very hot and humid summers—100°F (38°C) and 98% humidity are not uncommon. Rio winters are quite mild, with nighttime temperatures dropping as low as 66°F (19°C), and daytime temperatures climbing to the pleasant and sunny 86°F (30°C). Cariocas themselves find this lack of heat appalling, and will often throw on a coat or heavy sweater when the temperature drops below 70°F (21°C). In their defense, I should note that most houses and apartments are completely without heat, and many restaurants and stores lack windows or doors, so it can feel quite cool.

São Paulo has a similar climate to Rio's, hot in the summer and mild in winter. As São Paulo sits atop a plateau at approximately 700m (2,300 ft.) of elevation, it can sometimes get downright chilly, with daytime lows June through September sometimes reaching 54°F (12°C). **South of São Paulo,** things get even colder in the winter. In Florianópolis, many restaurants and even some hotels and pousadas shut down for the winter season. Also, in the mountain resort of **Petrópolis** and the historic towns of **Ouro Preto** and **Tiradentes,** it often gets cold enough to see your breath (41°F/5°C) in the fall and winter, and Brazilians will travel here to experience winter.

PUBLIC HOLIDAYS The following holidays are observed in Brazil: New Year's Day (Jan 1), Carnaval (March 5–8, 2011, and Feb 18–21, 2012), Easter (Apr 4, 2010, and Apr 24, 2011), Tiradentes Day (Apr 21), Labor Day (May 1), Corpus Christi (June 3, 2010, and June 23, 2011), Independence Day (Sept 7), Our Lady of Apparition (Oct 12), All Souls' Day (Nov 2), Proclamation of the Republic (Nov 15), and Christmas Day (Dec 25). On these days banks, schools, and government institutions will be closed, and some stores may be closed as well.

HEALTH CONCERNS

Standards for hygiene and public health in Brazil are generally high. Before leaving, however, check with your doctor or with the Centers for Disease Control (www.cdc.gov) for specific advisories. Use common sense when eating on the street or in restaurants.

COMMON AILMENTS **Dengue fever** is a viral infection transmitted by mosquitoes. It's unfortunately common in Rio de Janeiro. It's characterized by sudden onset high fever, severe headaches, joint and muscle pain, nausea/vomiting, and rash. (The rash may not appear until 3–4 days after the fever.) Proper diagnosis requires a blood test. The illness may last up to 10 days, but complete recovery can take 2 to 4 weeks. Dengue is rarely fatal.

The risk for dengue fever is highest during periods of heat and rain, where stagnant pools of water allow mosquitoes to breed. Though it strikes most often in poorer communities, the disease has infiltrated Rio's more affluent neighborhoods. There is no vaccine for dengue fever. Symptoms can be treated with bed rest, fluids, and medications to reduce fever, such as acetaminophen (Tylenol); aspirin should be avoided. The most important precaution a traveler can take is to avoid mosquito bites in dengue-prone areas. Try to remain in well-screened or air-conditioned areas, use mosquito repellents (preferably those containing DEET) on skin and clothing, and sleep with bed nets. For up-to-date information on the status of dengue fever in Brazil, consult the Centers for Disease Control website (www.cdc.gov) before departing.

Malaria is endemic to the Amazon or the Pantanal, though it's not very common. Still, a malaria prophylaxis (usually pills that you take daily) may be recommended.

According to recent UN statistics, Brazil has the dubious honor of ranking third in the world for total number of people with **HIV** infections. Though condom usage is becoming more accepted—thanks in part to the examples shown in popular nighttime soaps on TV—the reality is that some people still won't use them, and AIDS and other STDs are still being spread. So be careful and be safe—always insist on using a condom. Though condoms are readily available in Brazilian pharmacies, it's best to bring your own; brands are more reliable in North America and Europe. To purchase condoms in Brazil ask for a *preservativo* or a *camisinha* (kah-mee-*zeen*-ya), literally a small shirt; the latter word is the commonly used term for condom.

VACCINATIONS Before going, check your vaccinations and get booster shots for tetanus and polio if required. Children ages 3 months to 6 years may be required to show proof of polio vaccination. One vaccination that is definitely recommended—and sometimes mandatory—for Brazil is **yellow fever.** Outbreaks are sometimes reported in the Amazon, the Pantanal, Brasilia, or even Minas Gerais. Make sure you get an international certificate of vaccination, as Brazilian authorities sometimes require proof of vaccination for people going to or coming from an affected area. Travelers who have been to Colombia, Bolivia, Ecuador, French Guyana, Peru, or Venezuela within 90 days prior to their arrival in Brazil **must** show proof of yellow fever vaccination. Keep in mind that the vaccine takes 10 days to take effect.

HEALTH PRECAUTIONS If you do wind up with traveler's tummy or some other ailment (upset stomach, diarrhea, sunburn, or rash), **Brazilian pharmacies** are a wonder. Each has a licensed pharmacist who is trained to deal with small medical emergencies and can make recommendations for treatment. The service is free and medication is fairly inexpensive. If you take medication that may need replacement while in Brazil, ask your doctor to write out the active ingredients of the prescription, as many drugs are sold under different trade names in Brazil. Many drugs available by prescription only in the U.S. and Canada are available over the counter in Brazil.

GETTING THERE

By Plane

The major international gateway to Brazil is São Paulo's **Guarulhos International Airport** (airport code GRU). Most international airways have flights to Guarulhos, and it is possible to connect to all other cities in Brazil. The other major gateway is Rio de Janeiro's **Galeão International Airport** (airport code GIG). Though a modern international airport, Galeão has fewer direct flights to other Brazilian cities; you may have to connect through São Paulo or Brasilia.

The two big Brazilian airlines—**Gol/Varig** and **TAM**—also operate a number of international flights. **TAM** (✆ **888/2FLY-TAM** [235-9826] in the U.S. and Canada, 020/8897-0005 in the U.K., or 0800/570-5700 in Brazil; www.tam.com.br) has the most international connections to North America, Europe, Asia, and the rest of South America. Relative newcomer, low-budget carrier **Gol** (✆ **0300/115-2121** in Brazil; www.voegol.com.br), now offers service to a number of South American destinations (Argentina, Chile, Peru, and Bolivia), a good alternative for those traveling within South America.

By Package Tour

Many travel agencies offer package tours to Brazil, but few have the knowledge to effectively customize your trip or make interesting recommendations. To book a package with Brazil travel experts, contact **Brazil Nuts,** 1854 Trade Center Way, Suite 101A, Naples, FL 34109 (✆ **800/553-9959** or 914/593-0266; www.brazilnuts.com). The owners and staff are indeed nuts about Brazil and possess a vast amount of knowledge about the country and its attractions. Depending on your needs you can book just a flight and hotels, or you can add one or more group excursions in more inaccessible places such as the Amazon. Their website is a fount of information, and staff can answer any questions you may have about Brazil. Another excellent resource on Brazil and South America travel in general is **South America Travel** (✆ **800/747-4540;** www.southamerica.travel). South America Travel offers packages customizable to whatever level you're comfortable with. A number of interesting add-ons are available—outdoors lovers will be pleased to see some great hiking and camping options.

Travelers planning a trip beyond Brazil, to Argentina and Chile, may want to consult with **Borello Travel & Tours,** 7 Park Ave., Suite 21, New York, NY 10016 (✆ **800/405-3072** or 212/686-4911; www.borellotravel.com). This travel agency specializes in the Southern Cone and can help you plan a great itinerary to make the most of the region.

A good agency to book your ticket through is **Santini Tours,** 6575 Shattuck Ave., Oakland, CA 94609 (✆ **800/769-9669** or 510/652-8600; www.santours.com). The owner, as well as many of the travel agents, are Brazilian and can give you many useful suggestions on air pass routings and answer any questions you have about your itinerary. In addition to selling tickets and air passes, Santini can also arrange customized tours, including everything from airport transfers to guided tours.

GETTING AROUND

By Plane

The sheer vastness of Brazil (and the absence of rail travel) makes air travel the only viable option for those who want to visit a variety of cities and regions. However, the Brazilian airlinc industry has been experiencing turbulent times of late. The last 6 years has seen the bankruptcy of two Brazilian carriers, Transbrasil and Vasp, followed by the effective demise of the country's flagship carrier Varig. (A new, smaller Varig flew out of bankruptcy protection, only to merge with low-cost carrier Gol.) Disruptions by air-traffic controllers and delays at domestic airports lead the president to sack the head of the civilian air agency in mid-2007, and the new chief seems to be bringing order back to the skies. However, travelers should stock up on patience before entering a Brazilian airport. (It may well not be required, but you never know.) During peak travel times (holidays, high season) long delays are a not unlikely occurrence.

For those traveling larger distances in Brazil there is also the option of purchasing an **air pass** with TAM (much to the envy of Brazilians, this pass is available to foreigners only). The pass offers travelers four flights within a 21-day period. Air passes need to be purchased and booked outside of Brazil. Only limited changes are allowed once you arrive in the country. Also, it's a good idea to read the small print before choosing your pass. Often flights between Rio and São Paulo's downtown airports are excluded (meaning you have to use the international airports) and the pass does not allow returns on the same stretch.

TAM (✆ **0800/123-100** in Brazil; www.tam.com.br) offers four segments for $551 if you arrive on an international TAM flight (otherwise the pass costs $635). The pass is valid for 21 days. Check TAM's special English-language site for more details on the air pass (www.tamairlines.com). If you're traveling to only one or two destinations within Brazil, it can be cheaper to skip the pass and buy a separate ticket.

The big winner from much of the air chaos has been **Gol** (✆ **0300/789-2121** in Brazil; www.voegol.com.br). This airline has modeled itself after American discount carriers like Southwest Airlines—quick bookings online and no-frills flights, now between nearly every significant city in Brazil. Tickets can be purchased online—but only if you have an American Express card—or at the airport. The company flies brand-new Boeing 737s and provides friendly and efficient service.

In the past couple of years a number of lower-cost airlines have sprung up, offering competitive and often cheaper fares between Brazilian cities. These newcomers include **Azul** (✆ **011/3003-2985;** http://viajemais.voeazul.com.br); **Ocean Air** (✆ **0300/789-8160;** www.oceanair.com.br); **TRIP** (✆ **011/3003-8747;** www.voetrip.com.br); and **Webjet** (✆ **0300/210-1234;** www.webjet.com.br).

Domestic departure tax is around R$21 at most airports, and international departures are a hefty R$108. Payment can only be made in cash with U.S. dollars or Brazilian currency but not in a combination of both.

By Bus

Bus travel in Brazil is comfortable, efficient, and affordable. The only problem is, it's a long way from anywhere to anywhere else. A trip from Rio to São Paulo takes 6 to 8 hours; from Rio to Brasilia, it's closer to 20 hours. There are a vast number of bus companies, serving various regional routes. Unlike in North America, there is no nationwide bus company. To find out which bus company travels to your desired destination, you contact the bus station in your city of origin, and they pass on the number of the appropriate company. This can be tricky if you don't speak Portuguese. Fortunately, however, the bus stations in major cities now have websites, which allow you to select your destination from a drop-down menu, and then provide the departure times, price, and the name of the bus company. You can often also purchase tickets online. Tickets can be purchased ahead of time with reserved seats. All buses are nonsmoking. On many popular routes travelers can opt for a deluxe coach with air-conditioning and *leito* (seats that recline almost flat).

By Car

Car rentals are expensive, and the distances are huge. Car rental in Brazil is more expensive than in North America. A two-door compact (Fiat Palio, Ford Ka) with air-conditioning and unlimited mileage costs about R$100 per day, plus some R$20 to R$30 for insurance. Most rental cars in Brazil will work on either unleaded gasoline, gasohol, or pure alcohol (ethanol). Gasoline costs about R$2.70 per liter. Ethanol costs significantly less, about R$1.70 per liter, but burns more quickly. Still, ethanol winds up being cheaper overall. The following agencies have bureaus in most airports and major cities in Brazil: **Avis** (✆ **0800/725-2847;** www.avis.com.br); **Hertz** (✆ **0800/701-7300;** www.hertz.com.br); **Localiza** (✆ **0800/979-2000;** www.localiza.com); and **Unidas** (✆ **0800/121-121;** www.unidas.com.br). To rent a car you need a passport and valid driver's license. An international license is not required.

TIPS ON ACCOMMODATIONS

Brazil offers a wide range of accommodations. In the large cities there are modern high-rise hotels as well as apartment hotels (or rental flats, for you Brits) known in Brazil as apart-hotels. The apart-hotels are often a better deal than regular hotel rooms, offering both cheaper rates and more space.

Outside of the large cities you will often find pousadas, essentially our equivalent of a bed-and-breakfast or small inn. Accommodations prices fluctuate widely. The rates posted at the front desk—the rack rate, or *tarifa balcão*—are just a guideline. Outside of high season and on weekends you can almost always negotiate significant (20%–30%) discounts. High season is from mid-December to Carnaval (mid- to late Feb), Easter week, long weekends (see "Holidays," earlier in this chapter, for Brazilian holidays), and July (winter vacation). Notable exceptions are Brasilia and São Paulo, where business just dies during high season, and weekends, and rooms are heavily discounted.

Tip: Always check the quotes you have obtained from a hotel with a travel agency such as Brazil Nuts or South America Travel, as many hotels will give their best rates to travel agents and stick it to individual travelers or those who book via the Internet. The Copacabana Palace quoted us a price of $220 to $450 for a room, whereas Brazil Nuts can sell you that same room for $150.

Unlike North American hotels, Brazilian hotel rooms do not feature coffeemakers, irons, or ironing boards, although the latter can sometimes be delivered to your room upon request. Even in luxury hotels, the complimentary toiletries are usually very basic, so pack your own. On the other hand, **breakfast *(café de manha)*** at Brazilian hotels is almost always included in the room price, and at most places includes a nice buffet-style spread including bread, meats, cheeses, fruits, eggs (sometimes), and *café com leite,* strong coffee served with hot milk. In recent years a few of the more expensive hotels have taken to charging for *café de manha;* if this is the case it's noted in the review.

Throughout this chapter, hotel listings have been separated into several broad categories: **Very Expensive,** R$400 and up; **Expensive,** R$250 to R$400; **Moderate,** R$150 to R$250; and **Inexpensive,** under R$150 for a double. Accommodations **taxes** range from nothing to 15%, varying from city to city and hotel to hotel. Always check in advance.

TIPS ON DINING

Brazilians love to eat out. There is no shortage of eateries, from beach vendors selling grilled cheese and sweets, to lunch bars serving pastries and cold beers, to fine French cuisine complete with the elegance and pretensions of Paris. Most Brazilians eat a very small breakfast at home—usually cafe au lait and some bread—then go out for lunch. Traditionally, these lunches are full hot meals, but these days you can also find North American–style sandwiches and salads as a lighter alternative. Dinner is eaten late, especially when dining out. Most restaurants don't get busy until 9 or 10pm and will often serve dinner until 1 or 2am. The trick to lasting that long without fainting is to have a *lanche* or light meal—often a fruit juice and a pastry—around 5 or 6 pm.

In Brazil, portions often serve two people, especially in more casual restaurants. Always ask or you may well end up with an extraordinary amount of food. In Portuguese ask, *"Serve para dois?"* (pronounced *Sir*-vay p'ra doysh—"Does it serve two?").

The standard Brazilian menu comes close to what some restaurants label as international cuisine: pasta, seafood, beef, and chicken. Except in Brazil, these are served with a local or regional twist. The pasta may be stuffed with *catupiry* cheese and *abôbora* (a kind of pumpkin); the chicken could have *maracujá* (passion fruit) sauce. Brazilian beef comes from cows just like in the rest of the world, but in Brazil the cows are open range and grass fed, making for a very lean beef which comes in uniquely Brazilian cuts such as *picanha* (tender rump steak), *fraldinha* (bottom sirloin), or *alcatra* (top sirloin). And of course, for side dishes no Brazilian meal is complete without *farofa* and rice or black beans.

These days you will find more and more **kilo** (*quilo* in Portuguese) restaurants. The food is laid out in a large buffet, and at the better ones there's a grill at the back serving freshly cooked steaks, chicken, and sausage. Kilos aren't all-you-can-eat. Rather, you pay by weight (but the quality is *much* better than at American lunch buffets). If you're not familiar with Brazilian food, it's a great way to see all the dishes laid out in front of you; you can try as little or as much as you like. Even better, they often have a variety of salads and vegetables that are often hard to come by elsewhere in Brazil. The system works as follows: When you enter the restaurant, you're given a piece of paper on which all your orders are recorded. Don't lose this slip or you'll have to pay a ridiculously high penalty. You grab a plate, wander by the buffet and grill, filling up on whatever catches your eye (all items have the same per-kilogram cost, which is usually advertised both outside and inside the restaurant), and then take the plate to the scale to be weighed. The weigher records the charges on your bill, after which you find a table. Normally a waiter will then come by and take your drink order, adding these charges to your tally. On your way out the cashier sums it all up. ***Tip:*** Small cups of strong dark coffee (called *cafézinhos*) are usually served free by the cashier or exit. Look for a thermos and a stack of little plastic cups.

A **churrascaria** is a steakhouse that operates on the *rodízio* system, essentially all you can eat—though you'll pay extra for drinks and dessert. The set price buys you unlimited access to a massive salad bar buffet, often also including fish and sushi, and the attention of an army of waiters all offering different cuts of meat, sliced directly onto your plate. All the typical and unique Brazilian cuts of beef are on offer, as well as chicken breast, chicken hearts, sausage, and on and on and on.

We have separated restaurant listings into three price categories, based on the average cost of a meal per person, including tip: **Expensive,** over R$80; **Moderate,** R$40 to R$80; and **Inexpensive,** less than R$40. Note that prices given for entrees and main courses do not include service taxes.

TIPS ON SHOPPING

Brazil offers excellent shopping opportunities, particularly for precious stones; leather goods such as shoes, belts, purses, and wallets; and Brazilian music and musical instruments. Clothing is also very affordable and often of good quality. Rio and São Paulo are the best cities for buying fashionable clothes and shoes. If you plan on visiting Petrôpolis, do so early in your trip and stock up on inexpensive clothes. Styles follow the opposite seasonal calendar, so those visiting Brazil during the Northern Hemisphere winter can stock up on an excellent summer wardrobe. Sizes follow the European numbering system (36, 38, 40, and so on) or are marked P (*pequeno,* small), M (*medio,* medium), and G (*grande,* large).

Expect to haggle with street vendors. Even in stores, you can ask for a discount when buying more than one item or when paying cash. Shops will often advertise prices *"a vista"*—this means cash purchases only, and they can be 10% to 20% cheaper than paying by credit card.

Each region has its own crafts traditions. In the Amazon and Pantanal, good buys include Indian carvings and hammocks. The Northeast is particularly well known for its lovely linen and woodcarvings. Throughout Brazil, there are plenty of opportunities to shop for semiprecious stones, although the largest collections can be found in Rio and São Paulo jewelry stores.

Fast Facts Brazil

Addresses When writing addresses in Brazil, the street number follows the name of the street ("Av. Atlântica 2000" would roughly translate as "2000 Atlantic Ave."). Often in smaller towns a street name will be followed by the abbreviation "s/n." This stands for *sem numero* (without number), and is used when a building sits on a street but has no identifying number. Other words you might come across are: *loja* (shop or unit), *bloco* (building or block), and *sala* (room or suite, often abbreviated "sl."). In mailing addresses, the postal code usually precedes the two-letter state abbreviation.

American Express In Rio de Janeiro, there is an office at Av. Atlantica 1702, Copacabana (next to the Copacabana Palace Hotel). In São Paulo the office is located at Rua Haddock Lobo 400, on the corner of the Avenida Paulista (inside the Conjunto São Luis). Both offices are open Monday to Friday 9am to 4pm. At the São Paulo International Airport (GRU) and Rio de Janeiro International Airport (GIG) you will find offices that are open daily from 7am to 10:30pm. The general information number for all currency exchange offices is ✆ **4004-2639.** To report a lost or stolen card or traveler's checks call ✆ **0800/891-2614.**

Business Hours Stores are usually open from 9am to 7pm weekdays, 9am to 2pm on Saturdays. Most places close on Sundays. Small stores may close for lunch. Shopping centers are open Monday through Saturday from 10am to 8pm most places, though in Rio de Janeiro and São Paulo they often stay open until 10pm. On Sundays many malls open the food court and movie theaters all day, but mall shops will only open from 2 to 8pm. Banks are open Monday through Friday either from 10am to 4pm or from 9am to 3pm.

Doctors & Hospitals For minor medical problems, pharmacies are good resources. Most major hotels will be able to refer you to an English-speaking doctor. Brazil has a free public healthcare system, but conditions at public hospitals and clinics vary and the wait can be long. Private hospitals and clinics are modern and top-notch, but they can be expensive, so always carry valid travel insurance.

Electricity Brazil's electric current varies from 100 to 240 volts, and from 50 to 60Hz; even within one city there can be variations, and power surges are not uncommon. For laptops or battery chargers, bring an adaptor that can handle the full range of voltage. Most hotels do a good job of labeling their outlets, but when in doubt check before plugging in! Brazilian plugs usually have three prongs: two round and one flat. Adapters for converting North American plugs are cheap (R$3) and widely available.

Embassies & Consulates All embassies are located in Brasilia, the capital. Australia, Canada, the United States, and Great Britain have consulates in both Rio and São Paulo. New Zealand has a consulate in São Paulo.

In Brasilia: **Australia,** SES, Quadra 801, Conjunto K, lote 7 (✆ 061/3226-3111; www.brazil.embassy.gov.au). **Canada,** SES Av. das Nações Quadra 803, lote 16 (✆ 061/3424-5400; www.canada.org.br). **Great Britain,** SES Av. das Nações Quadra 801, lote 8 (✆ 061/3329-2300; www.uk.org.br). **New Zealand,** SHIS QI 09, Conj. 16, casa 01 (✆ 061/3248-9900; www.nzembassy.com/home.cfm?c=44). **United States,** SES Av. das Nações Quadra 801, lote 03 (✆ 061/3312-7000; www.embaixada-americana.org.br).

In Rio de Janeiro: **Australia,** Av. Presidente Wilson 231, Suite 23, Centro (✆ 021/3824-4624). **Canada,** Av. Atlântica 1130, Fifth Floor, Copacabana (✆ 021/2543-3004). **Great Britain,** Praia do Flamengo 284, Flamengo (✆ 021/2555-9600). **United States,** Av. Presidente Wilson 147, Centro (✆ 021/3823-2000).

In São Paulo: **Australia,** Alameda Santos 700, Ninth Floor, Jardim Paulista (✆ 011/3171 2889). **Canada,** Av. das Nações Unidas 12901, 19th Floor (✆ 011/5509-4321). **Great Britain,** Rua Ferreira de Araujo 741 (✆ 011/3094-2700). **New Zealand,** Av. Campinas 579, 15th Floor, Cerqueira Cesar (✆ 011/3148-0616). **United States,** Rua Henri Dunant 500, Chácara Santo Antonio (✆ 011/5186-7000).

Emergencies For police dial ✆ **190;** for ambulance or fire department dial ✆ **193.**

Gasoline (Petrol) Gasoline costs approximately R$2.80/liter. Most cars will also work on ethanol (alcohol), which costs only R$1.80 per liter. However, ethanol burns faster, so its effective cost works out to a bit more, close to R$2.20 per liter.

Internet Access Internet cafes (called *cyber cafés* in Brazil) are quite common everywhere in Brazil, from the Amazon to the big cities. Prices range from R$.57 to R$2 per hour; luxury hotels usually charge the most, anywhere up to R$30 per hour.

Language The language of Brazil is Portuguese. If you speak Spanish you will certainly have an easier time picking up words and phrases. In the large cities you will find people in the tourism industry who speak good English, but in smaller towns and resorts English is very limited. If you are picking up language books or tapes, make sure they are Brazilian Portuguese and not Portuguese from Portugal: big difference! A good pocket-size phrasebook is *Say It in Portuguese* (Brazilian usage) by Prista, Mickle, and Costa; or try *Conversational Brazilian Portuguese* by Cortina.

Liquor Laws Officially, the legal drinking age in Brazil is 18, but it's not often enforced. Beer, wine, and liquor can be bought on any day of the week from grocery stores and snack stands. Drinking is allowed in public places, and in motor vehicles. Drinking is now prohibited in most soccer stadiums. For drivers, the legal alcohol limit is 0.00—meaning even a single bottle of beer can put you over the limit. This is now strictly enforced.

Maps Good maps aren't Brazil's strong suit. Better to buy one before you come. In Brazil, your best bet for city maps is the ***Guia Quatro Rodas—Mapas das Capitais;*** this pocket book for sale at all newsstands (R$12) has indexed maps of all state capitals, including São Paulo, Rio, Salvador, Manaus, Brasilia, and Recife. Unfortunately it does not include any highways. The best highway map is sold with the ***Guia Quatro Rodas Brasil*** (for sale on newsstands for R$42), a Brazilian guidebook.

Newspapers & Magazines There are no English-language newspapers or magazines in Brazil. Foreign papers and magazines are only easily found in Rio and São Paulo. The most popular Brazilian newspapers are *O Globo* and *Jornal do Brasil,* published out of Rio, and *Folha de São Paulo,* the leading business paper published in São Paulo. The most popular current affairs magazine (the equivalent of *Newsweek*) is *Veja,* published weekly. In Rio and São Paulo, *Veja* magazine always includes an entertainment insert that provides a detailed listing of nightlife, restaurants, and events.

Post Offices & Mail Mail from Brazil is quick and efficient. Post offices *(correios)* are found everywhere, readily identifiable by the blue-and-yellow sign. A postcard or letter to Europe or North America costs R$1.80. Parcels can be sent through FedEx or regular mail (express or common); a small parcel—up to 2.5kg (5½ lb.)—costs about R$55 by common mail and takes about a week or two.

Restrooms Public toilets are rare in Brazil, except in shopping malls. You'll do better seeking out hotels and restaurants. Toilets in Brazil can be marked in a few different ways. Usually you will see *mulher* or an M for women and *homem* or an H for men. Sometimes it will read *damas* or D for ladies and *cavalheiros* or C for gentlemen. It's not a bad idea to carry some toilet paper with you as in many public restrooms, the toilet attendant doles out sheets only grudgingly.

Safety Sometime in the 1980s Brazil began developing a world reputation for violence and crime. Some of this was pure sensationalism, but there was a good measure of truth as well. Fortunately in the early '90s things began to turn around. Governments began putting money back into basic services, starting with policing. Though still not perfect by any means, Rio, São Paulo, and Brazil's other big cities have bounced back to the point where they're as safe as most large international cities. Statistically, of course, Rio and other big Brazilian cities still have very high crime rates. Most of that crime, however, takes place in the *favelas* and shantytowns of the far-off industrial outskirts. Avoid wandering in or near the hillside *favelas.* At night use taxis instead of public transportation, and stick to well-lit and well-traveled streets. Don't flash jewelry or wads of cash. And beware of pickpockets. Outside of the main cities, Brazil remains quite safe.

Smoking Smoking is prohibited on planes and long-distance buses. It is also prohibited in restaurants in Rio and São Paulo. Other Brazilian cities are expected to implement restaurant smoking bans in the near future.

Taxes There are no taxes added to goods purchased in Brazil. Restaurants and hotels normally add a 10% service tax. In Rio, the city also levies a 5% tax on hotels. All airports in Brazil charge departure taxes; this is usually included in the ticket price but it's wise to check. Domestic departures cost around R$21 at most airports, and international departures are a hefty R$108. Payment can only be made in cash with U.S. dollars or Brazilian currency, but not in a combination of both.

Time Zones Brazil has three time zones. The coast, including Rio de Janeiro, Salvador, and as far inland as São Paulo and Brasilia, is in one time zone. The ranching states of Mato Grosso and Mato Grosso do Sul, the Pantanal, and the Amazon around Manaus are in the second time zone, 1 hour behind Rio. The third time zone includes the state of Acre and the western part of the Amazon, 2 hours behind Rio. The time difference between cities in Brazil and North America varies by up to 2 hours over the course of the year as clocks spring forward and fall back for daylight saving time. From approximately March to September Rio de Janeiro is in the same time zone as New York City. From October to February, Rio is at least 1 and often 2 hours ahead of New York (for example, noon in New York City is 2pm in Rio).

Tipping A 10% service charge is automatically included on most restaurant and hotel bills and you are not expected to tip on top of this amount. If service has been particularly bad, you can request to have the 10% removed from your bill.

Taxi drivers do not get tipped; just round up the amount to facilitate change. Hairdressers and beauticians usually receive a 10% tip. Bellboys get tipped R$1 to R$2 per bag. Room service usually includes the 10% service charge on the bill.

Water The tap water in Brazil is increasingly safe to drink. However, as a result of the treatment process it still doesn't taste great. To be on the safe side, drink bottled or filtered water (most Brazilians do). All brands are reliable; ask for *agua sem gas* for still water and *agua com gas* for carbonated water. However, you can certainly shower, brush your teeth, or rinse an apple with tap water.

4 RIO DE JANEIRO

Say "Rio" and mental images explode: the glittering skimpy costumes of Carnaval; the statue of Christ, arms outspread on the mountaintop; the beach at Ipanema, crowded with women in minuscule bikinis; the rocky Sugarloaf; or the persistent rhythm of the samba.

Fortunately in Rio there's much more beyond the glitter: historic neighborhoods, compelling architecture, wildlife and nature, dining (fine and not so fine), nightspots, cafes, museums, and enclaves of rich and poor. In Rio, the more you explore, the more there is.

Stunning as the physical setting is—mountains tumbling down to sandy beaches and the sea—Rio was not always the *cidade maravilhosa* (marvelous city) it would become. The town grew up as a shipping center for gold and supplies during Brazil's 18th-century gold rush. In 1762, the colonial capital was transferred from Salvador to Rio, though the city remained a dusty colonial backwater.

In 1808, the Portuguese royal family fled Lisbon ahead of Napoleon's armies and moved court and the capital to Rio. Accustomed to the style of European capitals, the prince regent and the 12,000 nobles who accompanied him began to transform Rio into a city of ornate palaces and landscaped parks. High culture arrived in the form of a new library, an academy of arts and sciences, and the many glittering balls held by the imported elite. King João VI's son, Pedro, liked Rio so much that when the king returned to Lisbon, Pedro stayed on and declared Brazil independent.

Now the capital of a country larger and richer than many in Europe, Rio grew at a phenomenal pace; by the late 1800s it was one of the largest cities in the world. A sizable segment of the population were Brazilians of African descent who brought with them the musical traditions of Africa and the Brazilian Northeast.

A new distinctly Brazilian "popular culture" began to develop in the city's poorer neighborhoods. The high point of the year for both high and low cultures was the celebration of Carnaval. In palace ballrooms the elite held elaborate costume balls. In the streets, poorer residents staged their own all-night parades. Not until the 1920s did the two celebrations begin to merge. Low culture influenced composer Heitor Villa-Lobos, who incorporated Brazilian rhythms and sounds into his classical compositions. At about the same time, the first road was punched through to Copacabana, and Cariocas (as Rio residents are called) flocked to the new community by the beach.

In the years following World War II, São Paulo took over as Brazil's industrial leader; the federal capital moved inland to Brasilia in the early 1960s. By the 1980s, violence and

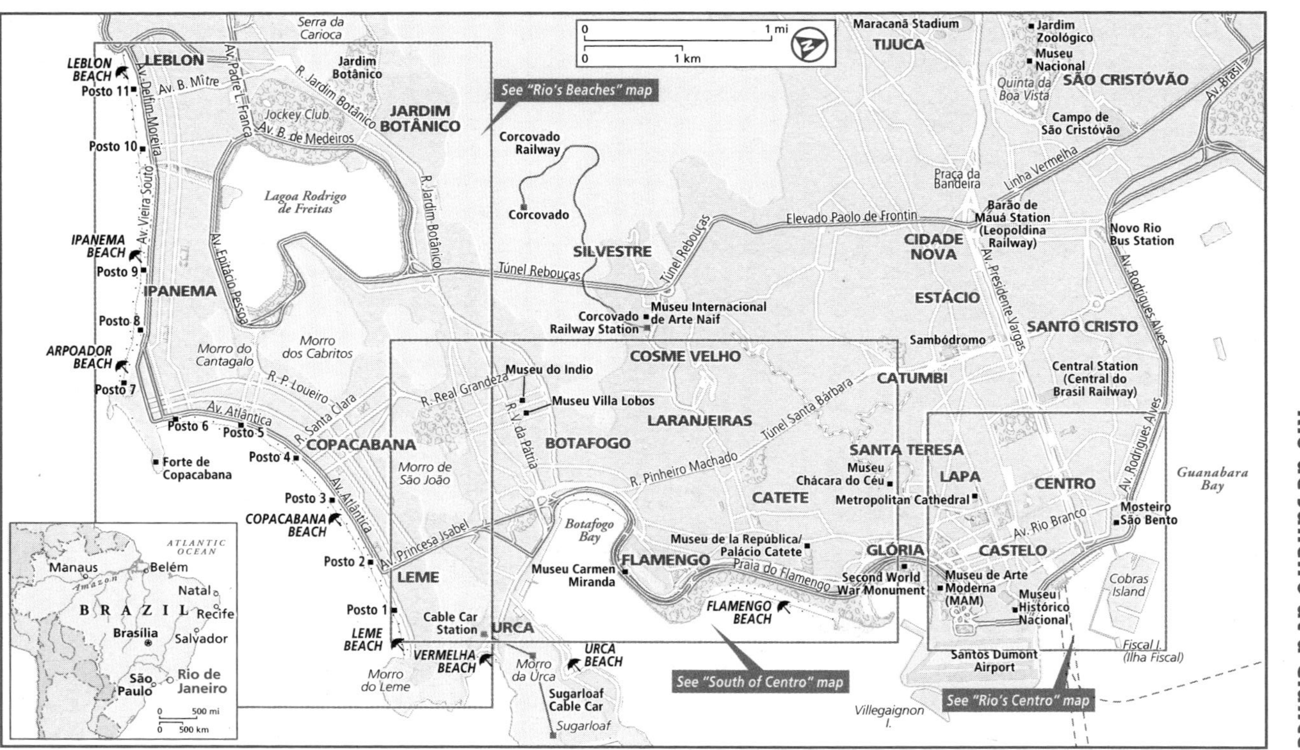

Serra da Carioca
0
1 mi
0
1 km
Maracanã Stadium
TIJUCA
Jardim Zoológico
Museu Nacional
Quinta da Boa Vista
SÃO CRISTÓVÃO
Av. Brasil
Campo de São Cristóvão
LEBLON BEACH
LEBLON
Posto 11
Av. B. Mitre
Av. Delfim Moreira
Av. Padre L. Franca
Jardim Botânico
R. Jardim Botânico
Jockey Club
Av. B. de Medeiros
JARDIM BOTÂNICO
See "Rio's Beaches" map
Corcovado Railway
Corcovado
Posto 10
Av. Vieira Souto
Lagoa Rodrigo de Freitas
R. Jardim Botânico
Praça da Bandeira
Linha Vermelha
Barão de Mauá Station (Leopoldina Railway)
Elevado Paolo de Frontin
Novo Rio Bus Station
IPANEMA BEACH
Posto 9
IPANEMA
Av. Epitácio Pessoa
Túnel Rebouças
SILVESTRE
CIDADE NOVA
Av. Presidente Vargas
Av. Rodrigues Alves
ESTÁCIO
Museu Internacional de Arte Naif
Corcovado Railway Station
Posto 8
Morro do Cantagalo
Morro dos Cabritos
Sambódromo
SANTO CRISTO
ARPOADOR BEACH
Posto 7
COSME VELHO
Museu do Indio
R. Real Grandeza
R. P. Loueiro
CATUMBI
Central Station (Central do Brasil Railway)
Museu Villa Lobos
R. V. da Pátria
Túnel Santa Bárbara
LARANJEIRAS
Av. Atlântica
R. Santa Clara
Posto 6
Posto 5
COPACABANA
BOTAFOGO
SANTA TERESA
Forte de Copacabana
Posto 4
Morro de São João
R. Pinheiro Machado
Museu Chácara do Céu
LAPA
CENTRO
Guanabara Bay
Posto 3
Av. Atlântica
CATETE
Metropolitan Cathedral
Mosteiro São Bento
COPACABANA BEACH
Botafogo Bay
Av. Rio Branco
Av. Princesa Isabel
Museu de la República/ Palácio Catete
GLÓRIA
CASTELO
ATLANTIC OCEAN
Manaus
Belém
Amazon
Natal
BRAZIL
Recife
Brasília
Salvador
São Paulo
Rio de Janeiro
500 mi
500 km
Posto 2
LEME
Museu Carmen Miranda
FLAMENGO
Praia do Flamengo
Second World War Monument
Museu de Arte Moderna (MAM)
Museu Histórico Nacional
Cobras Island
Posto 1
Cable Car Station
URCA
FLAMENGO BEACH
LEME BEACH
VERMELHA BEACH
Morro da Urca
URCA BEACH
Santos Dumont Airport
Fiscal I. (Ilha Fiscal)
Morro do Leme
Sugarloaf Cable Car
See "South of Centro" map
See "Rio's Centro" map
Villegaignon I.
Sugarloaf

crime plagued the country, and Rio was perceived as the sort of place where walking down the street was asking for a mugging. Fortunately, in the early 1990s, governments began putting money back into basic services. Public and private owners began renovating the many heritage buildings of the city's colonial core. Rio's youth rediscovered samba, returning to pack renovated clubs in the old bohemian enclave of Lapa. Rio began reaching out to the rest of the world, with successful bids to host the Pan-American games in 2007, followed by soccer's World Cup in 2014, capped off with the city's selection to host the 2016 Olympic Summer Games. A city of some seven million and growing, Rio remains one of Brazil's media capitals, an important business center, and Brazil's key tourist destination.

ESSENTIALS

Getting There

BY PLANE Most major airlines fly to Rio de Janeiro, sometimes with a stop or connection in São Paulo. International passengers arrive at **Antônio Carlos Jobim Airport** (✆ **021/3398-5050**), also known as **Galeão Airport,** 20km (12 miles) from downtown. Taxis at Galeão are a challenge. The safer but more expensive bet is to buy a prepaid fare at the **TransCoopass** desk in the arrivals hall (✆ **021/2209-1555;** www.transcoopass.com.br; all major credit cards accepted). Rates range from R$60 to Flamengo, and R$70 to R$80 to the beach hotels of Copacabana and Ipanema. These prepaid taxis are about 40% more expensive, but give you peace of mind. If you know what you're doing, you can hail a regular taxi out in front of the terminal. A ride to Copacabana should cost about R$45 in average traffic conditions. **Gray Line** (✆ **021/2512-9919;** www.grayline.com) offers a minibus transfer service from Galeão to the hotels of the Zona Sul or Barra. Cost is $21 (payable in advance online in U.S. dollars or in the equivalent value of Reais to the bus driver) one-way, with one bag free, extra bags R$5 (payable to the bus driver). Buses depart daily once an hour from 8am to 7pm. You meet the uniformed Gray Line driver by the RioTur booth in either Terminal 1 or Terminal 2. Transfers can be booked in advance on the Internet.

Rio's second airport, **Santos Dumont,** Praça Senador Salgado Filho (airport code SDU; ✆ **021/3814-7070**), is downtown and used primarily by TAM, Gol, Azul, Webjet, TRIP, and Ocean Air for Rio–São Paulo shuttles or domestic flights. Prepaid taxis are available from the TransCoopass (✆ **021/2209-1555;** www.transcoopass.com.br) booth in the arrivals hall, or hail a regular taxi outside. A metered taxi to Ipanema should cost around R$30.

BY BUS All long-distance buses arrive at the Novo Rio Rodoviaria, Av. Francisco Bicalho 1, Santo Cristo (✆ **021/3213-1800;** www.novorio.com.br), close to downtown near the old port. It's best to use a taxi traveling to or from the station.

BY CRUISE SHIP Cruise ships dock in the terminal almost opposite Praça Mauá. Downtown is an easy walk, and public transit is close by. If returning to the ship after dark, it's best to take a taxi. Praça Mauá becomes a somewhat seedy red-light district in the evening.

Orientation

Rio is normally divided into three zones: **North (Zona Norte), Center (Centro),** and **South (Zona Sul).** Largest and least interesting from a visitor's perspective, the **Zona Norte** stretches from a few blocks north of Avenida Presidente Vargas all the way to the city limits. With only a few bright exceptions—the Maracanã stadium, the Quinte de

Boa Vista gardens, the neighborhoods of Vila Isabel and Tijuca, and Galeão (Tom Jobim) airport—the region is a dull swath of port, lower-middle-class housing, industrial suburb, and *favelas.* After dark, it is definitely not the sort of place one should wander unaccompanied. The **Zona Sul** is the name given to the beach neighborhoods of **Copacabana, Ipanema, Leme, Lagoa,** and **São Conrado. Centro** is a bit more difficult to nail down. Defined narrowly, it's the old downtown and business section (described below). Used in a broader sense, Centro also includes older residential neighborhoods like **Santa Teresa, Catete,** and **Glória.**

Getting Around

The neighborhoods in which visitors spend most of their time are very easy to get around in. From Centro south to Leblon, the neighborhoods hang like beads on a string on the narrow strip of land between the ocean and the mountains. You can almost always see one or the other; with landmarks like that it's pretty hard to stray too far from where you want to go.

BY SUBWAY The easiest way to get around is by subway. There are only two lines: **Line 1** goes north from downtown—it's useful for going to the Maracanã and the Quinta da Boa Vista—while **Line 2** begins at the Central Station and goes south, covering most of Centro, then swinging thorough Glória, Catete, Flamengo, and Botafogo before ducking through the mountain to Copacabana and Ipanema. The trip takes about 20 minutes to move you from Centro to Copacabana. A single ride costs R$2.80.

The subway system has recently vastly expanded its integrated **Metrô/bus service.** New air-conditioned express buses feed into the Metrô system. The more popular routes include: Metrô/Ipanema and Metrô/Leblon or Gavea (transfer at Siqueira Campos); Metrô/Rodoviaria (to the main bus terminal; transfer at Largo do Machado); Metrô-Urca (to the Sugarloaf; transfer at Botafogo); and Metrô-Cosme Velho (to the Corcovado; transfer at Largo do Machado). The price is R$3.60. After you use the electronic ticket to enter the subway turnstile, the ticket is returned so that you can present it on the bus at the transfer station.

BY BUS Rio's buses follow direct, logical pathways, sticking to the main streets. The route number and final destination are displayed in big letters on the front of the bus. Smaller signs also list the intermediate stops. ***Tip:*** If you're going from Ipanema or Copacabana all the way to Centro (or vice versa), look for a bus that says VIA ATERRO in its smaller window sign. These buses get on the waterfront boulevard in Botafogo and don't stop until they reach downtown.

Have your bus money ready—R$2.50 to R$3.50—as you will go through a turnstile right away. There are no transfers. Buses are safe during the day. In the evening, it's better to take a taxi.

BY TAXI Regular yellow taxis are plentiful and can be hailed anywhere on the street. Radio taxis are about 20% more expensive, often work with a set fee per destination, and can be contacted by phone; try **Coopertramo** (**✆ 021/2209-9292**) or **Transcoopass** (**✆ 021/2209-1555**).

BY FERRY Rio has a number of ferries operated by **Barcas SA** (**✆ 0800/704-4113;** www.barcas-sa.com.br), departing from Praça XV downtown. The busiest routes link downtown Rio with downtown Niterói or Charitas (also in Niterói) across the bay. The service to Niterói runs daily from 6am to 11:30pm; to Charitas the service is Monday to Friday 6:50am to 9pm.

BY CAR A car is not required for exploring Rio, and the truth is, driving in this city is not for the weak of heart. Better to rent a car only if you're going out to destinations such as Petrópolis and the historic towns of the Minas Gerais region. To rent a car at the international airport, contact **Hertz** (✆ 021/3398-2379; www.hertz.com.br), **Localiza** (✆ 021/3398-5445; www.localiza.com), or **Unidas** (✆ 021/3398-2286; www.unidas.com.br). In Copacabana you will find **Hertz,** Av. Princesa Isabel 500 (✆ 021/2275-7440); Localiza, Av. Princesa Isabel 150 (✆ 021/2275-3340); and Unidas, Av. Princesa Isabel 166 (✆ 021/3873-2521). Rates start at R$100 per day for a compact car with air-conditioning. Insurance adds R$30 per day.

Visitor Information

Riotur (✆ 021/2271-7000; www.riodejaneiro-turismo.com.br) operates a number of offices and kiosks around town. At **Rio's international airport** booths in the international arrivals halls of both Terminal 1 (✆ 021/3398-4077) and Terminal 2 (✆ 021/3398-2245), plus the domestic arrivals hall (✆ 021/3398-3034), are all open daily 6am to midnight. The main **Riotur Information Center** (✆ 021/2541-7522) is on Av. Princesa Isabel 183, Copacabana. Open Monday to Friday 9am to 6pm, this office has the largest selection of brochures and information. Riotur also operates an information line, **Alô Rio** (✆ 021/2542-8080), with English-speaking staff, Monday to Friday from 9am to 6pm.

FAST FACTS Banco do Brasil has branches at Rua Joana Angelica, Ipanema (✆ 021/3544-9700), Av. N.S. de Copacabana 594, Copacabana (✆ 021/3816-5800), and **international airport, Terminal 1, third floor** (✆ 021/3398-3652); all have 24-hour ATMs. For currency exchange, try **Casa Aliança Cambio,** Rua Miguel Couto 35, Centro (✆ **021/2224-4617**), or **Casa Universal Cambio,** Av. N.S. Copacabana 371, loja E, Copcabana (✆ **021/2548-6696**).

In case of an emergency call the police at ✆ **190** or the fire brigade and ambulance ✆ **193;** English-speaking staff is available at the Tourist Police, Av. Afrânio de Melo Franco 159, Leblon (contact line ✆ **021/2332-2924,** 2332-2885, or 2332-2889).

For minor medical concerns, contact **Clinica Galdino Campos,** Av. N.S. de Copacabana 492, Copacabana (✆ **021/2548-9966**), offers 24-hour service, including house calls. English is spoken there. In case of major medical emergencies, public hospital emergency rooms can be found at Miguel Couto, Rua Bartolemeu Mitre 1108, Leblon (✆ **021/3111-3800**), or at Souza Aguiar, Praça da Republica 111, Centro (✆ **021/3111-2600**). The city's top private hospital is Copa D'or, Rua Figueiredo de Magalhães 875, Copacabana (✆ **021/2545-3600**).

WHAT TO SEE & DO

The Top Attractions

Centro

Ilha Fiscal ★ This little ceramic castle afloat on its own island in the bay off Praça XV looks like the dwelling of a fair elfin princess, but in fact was built as the headquarters for the Brazilian Custom Service. On the inside, alas, this Gothic Revival palace is mostly a small and rather boring museum on the Brazilian navy, which owns the island. The tour lasts about 2½ hours. On weekdays, the trip to the island is by boat, whereas on weekends it's by bus along a causeway.

Av. Alfredo Agache s/n, Centro (behind Praça XV). ✆ **021/2104-6992.** Admission R$10, R$5 children 12 and under. Guided tours only. Departures Wed–Sun at 1, 2:30, and 4pm. Bus: 415 (Praça XV).

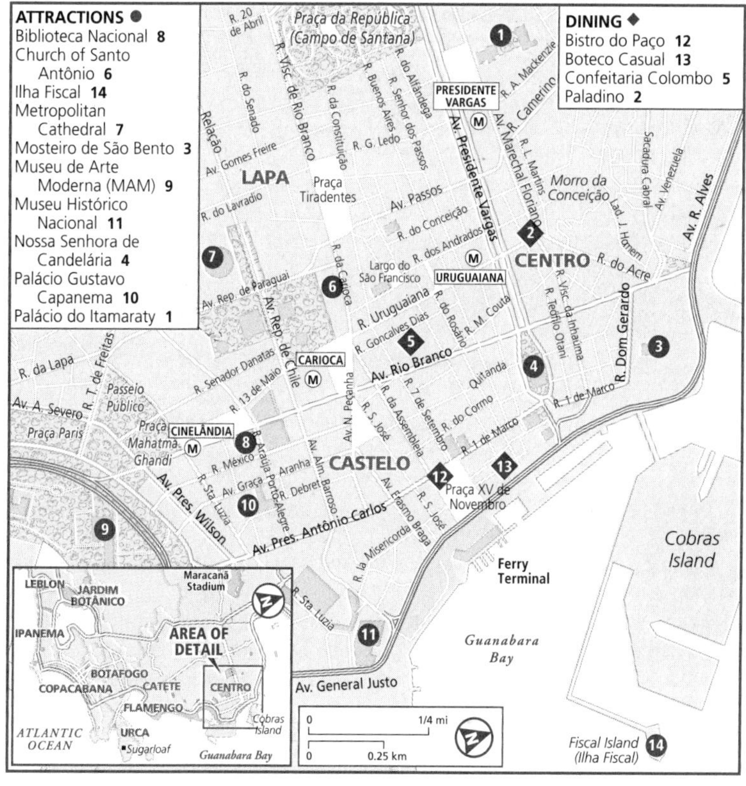

Museu de Arte Moderna (MAM) ★★ Located in the waterfront Flamengo park, the MAM is a long, rectangular building lofted off the ground by an arcade of concrete struts. Inside, the concrete struts do all the load-bearing work, allowing for walls of solid plate glass that welcome views of both city and sea. Displays change constantly, and include Brazilian art and international exhibitions—check the website to see what's on. Signage—a rare bonus—is in both English and Portuguese. The MAM also has a cafe, a bookstore, and a film archive containing over 20,000 Brazilian titles. Allow an hour to 90 minutes.

Av. Infante Dom Henrique 85, Parque do Flamengo (Aterro), Centro. ✆ **021/2240-4944.** www.mamrio.com.br. Admission R$8 adults, R$4 students and seniors, free for children 12 and under. Tues–Fri noon–6pm; Sat–Sun noon–7pm. Metrô: Cinelândia. Bus: 472 or 125 (get off at Av. Beira Mar by the museum's footbridge).

Museu Histórico Nacional ★★ The place for anyone looking for a good overview of Brazilian history from Cabral's arrival in 1500 to the present. Housed in the former national armory, the National History Museum features seven permanent exhibits on themes such as early exploration, coffee plantations, and modernism, each illustrated with abundant maps and artifacts. Better still, much of the Portuguese signage comes with often very opinionated English translation. Allow 2 hours.

Praça Marechal Âncora s/n. ✆ **021/2550-9224.** www.museuhistoriconacional.com.br. Admission R$6 adults, free children 5 and under; free for all Sun. Wed–Fri 10am–5:30pm; Sat–Sun 2–6pm. Bus: 119 or 415 (10-min. walk from the Praça XV).

Santa Teresa

Museu Chácara do Céu ★★ A wealthy man with eclectic tastes, Raymundo Castro Maya had this ultra-Modern mansion built in the hills of Santa Teresa, then filled it with all manner of paintings, engravings and drawings. The museum displays European painters (Monet, Matisse, Picasso, Dalí) and Brazilian art, particularly 19th-century landscapes. The house itself is a charmer, a stylish melding of hillside and structure that evokes Frank Lloyd Wright's work in the American West. The views from the garden are fabulous. ***Tip:*** Make sure to stop in at the **Ruin Park,** next to the Chácara do Céu, for fabulous views of the city and bay.

Rua Murtinho Nobre 93, Santa Teresa. ✆ **021/3970-1126.** www.museuscastromaya.com.br. Admission R$5 adults, free for children 11 and under; free for all Wed. Wed–Mon noon–5pm. Tram: Curvelo.

Catete

Museu da República—Palácio do Catete ★★ This gorgeous baroque palace served as the official residence of Brazilian presidents from 1897 to 1960. The more boring traditional displays preserve the air of the palace in its administrative days. The better exhibits try to engage visitors with the history and politics of the Brazilian republic. The best exhibit is the three-room hagiography of President Getulio Vargas. It even includes the pearl-handled Colt that Getulio used to kill himself with in 1954. The surrounding gardens include a small folklore museum, with free admission.

Rua do Catete 153, Catete. ✆ **021/3235-2650.** www.museudarepublica.org.br. Admission R$6 adults, free for children 10 and under; free for all Sun. Tues–Fri 10am–5pm; Sat–Sun 2–6pm. Metrô: Catete.

Urca

Sugarloaf (Pão de Açúcar) ★★★ The Sugarloaf remains one of the original and enduring Rio attractions. Deservedly so. Standing on its peak, the entire *cidade maravilhosa* lays at your feet: the beaches of Ipanema and Copacabana, the *favelas* of Babylonia, the Tijuca Forest, Christ the Redeemer on His mountain, the Bay of Guanabara, and the fortresses at the edge of far-off Niterói. It's a truly beautiful sight. The cable car leaves every half-hour from 8am to 10pm daily, more frequently if there are enough people waiting. ***Tip:*** If you're feeling active, hike up. You start just above the crashing waves, and the views just keep getting better as you go. See "Hiking" under "Sports & Outdoor Activities," below, for details.

Av. Pasteur 520, Urca. ✆ **021/2461-2700.** www.bondinho.com.br. Admission R$44 adults, R$22 children 6–12, free for children 5 and under. Daily 8am–9pm; last cable-car ride up at 8pm. Metrô: Botofogo, then catch the Integração bus marked Urca.

Lagoa

Jardim Botânico ★ In the 2 centuries since its founding by Emperor Dom João VI, the botanical garden has grown to 141 hectares (348 acres) and added 6,000 species of tropical plants and trees to its collection. Most visitors come to enjoy the peace and beauty, meandering along the many little paths and garden trails; the bromeliad and orchid greenhouses are especially nice. Free English-language guided tours are supposed to be available (call ahead or check in at the visitor center) but the service is sporadic and unreliable.

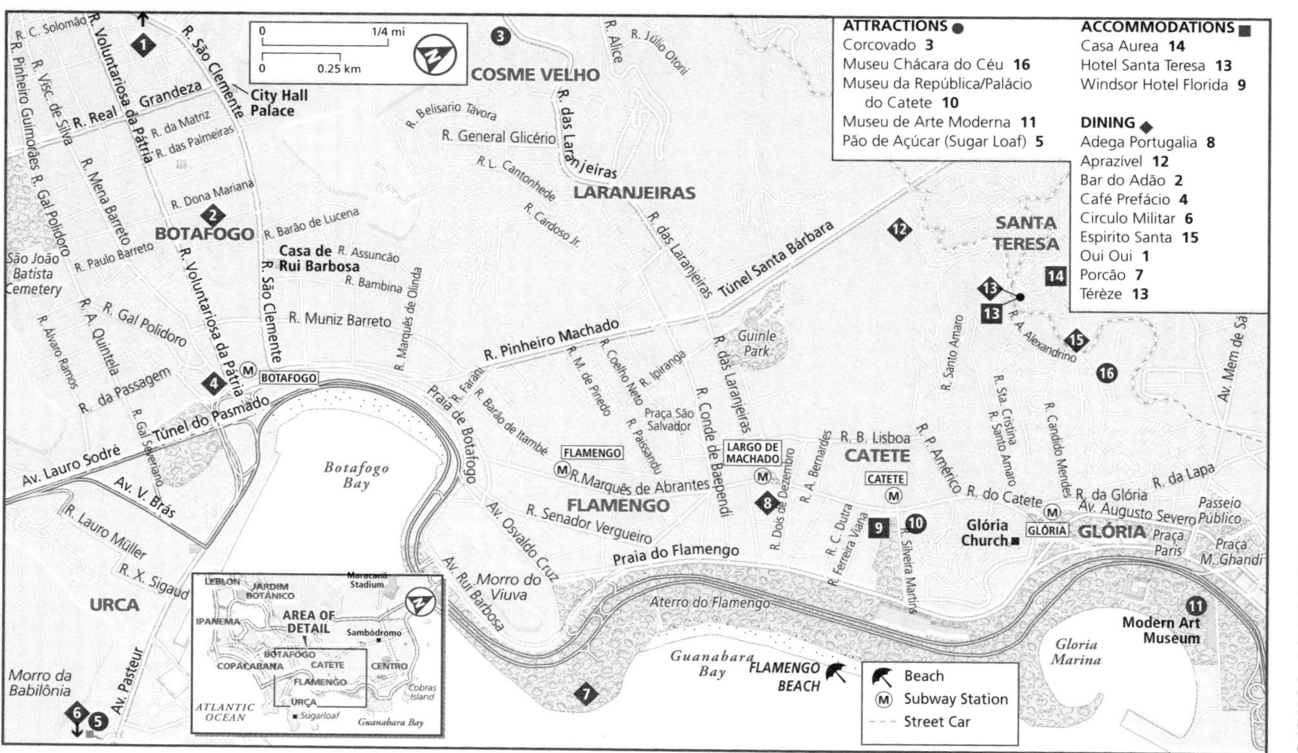

ATTRACTIONS ●
Corcovado 3
Museu Chácara do Céu 16
Museu da República/Palácio do Catete 10
Museu de Arte Moderna 11
Pão de Açúcar (Sugar Loaf) 5
ACCOMMODATIONS ■
Casa Aurea 14
Hotel Santa Teresa 13
Windsor Hotel Florida 9
DINING ◆
Adega Portugalia 8
Aprazível 12
Bar do Adão 2
Café Prefácio 4
Circulo Militar 6
Espirito Santa 15
Oui Oui 1
Porcão 7
Térèze 13
Beach
Subway Station
Street Car
0 1/4 mi
0 0.25 km
COSME VELHO
LARANJEIRAS
SANTA TERESA
CATETE
GLÓRIA
FLAMENGO
BOTAFOGO
URCA
LARGO DE MACHADO
FLAMENGO BEACH
Guanabara Bay
Botafogo Bay
Gloria Marina
Modern Art Museum
Glória Church
City Hall Palace
Casa de Rui Barbosa
Guinle Park
Túnel Santa Barbara
Túnel do Pasmado
Morro do Viúva
Morro da Babilônia
São João Batista Cemetery
Praia de Botafogo
Praia do Flamengo
Aterro do Flamengo
Av. Mem de Sá
Av. Augusto Severo
Av. Pasteur
Av. Rui Barbosa
Av. Osvaldo Cruz
Av. Lauro Sodré
Av. V. Brás
R. Pinheiro Machado
R. das Laranjeiras
R. Conde de Baependi
R. São Clemente
R. Voluntariosa da Pátria
R. Marquês de Abrantes
R. Senador Vergueiro
R. do Catete
R. da Glória
R. Candido Mendes
R. Santo Amaro
Passeio Público
Praça Paris
Praça M. Ghandi
AREA OF DETAIL
ATLANTIC OCEAN

 Rua Jardim Botânico 1008. ✆ **021/3874-1808.** www.jbrj.gov.br. Admission R$5 adults, free for children 7 and under. Daily 8am–5pm. Bus: Integração (Jardim Botanico) from Metrô Botafogo.

Leme

Forte do Leme ★★ Finds One of Rio's best-kept secrets. On the top of the 183m (600-ft.) granite rock you get a 360-degree view of Copacabana and Guanabara Bay. The main gate is toward the back of the square at the end of Leme beach. Once inside, you make your way up a cobblestone road that winds around the back of the hill. It's a 20-minute walk through lush forest to the top, where you'll be rewarded with a splendid view of Copacabana and beyond.

Praça Almirante Julio de Noronha s/n, Copacabana. ✆ **021/2275-7696.** Admission R$3. Sat–Sun 8am–4pm. Metrô: Cardeal Arcoverde/integração bus to Leme, or bus 472.

Cosme Velho

Corcovado ★★★ Kids The Corcovado was recently chosen as one of the new Seven Wonders of the World. The view from the toes of Rio's mountain-top Chirst is spectacular: the mountains, the bay, and the city all lay revealed beneath your (His?) feet. It's enough to give you a feeling of omniscience. The statue was intended to mark the 100th anniversary of Brazilian independence in 1922, but in true Carioca fashion it arrived a decade or so late in 1931. Access is via a steep narrow-gauge railway, followed by a pair of escalators that whisk you up to the base of the statue. Allow 2 hours round-trip.

Train Station address: Rua Cosme Velho 513, Cosme Velho. ✆ **021/2558-1329.** www.corcovado.com.br. Admission R$36, free for children 5 and under. Trains depart daily every 30 min. 8:30am–8pm. Bus: Cosme Velho Intergração from Metrô Largo do Machado.

Farther Afield

Museu de Arte Contemporânea—Niterói ★ Oscar Niemeyer's spaceship design for Niterói's new Contemporary Art Museum has done for this bedroom city what Gehry's Guggenheim did for Bilbao, Spain: put it on the map (at least in Brazil). As a gallery, however, the museum has serious drawbacks, not least that most of the construction funds were spent on the exterior. Curators bring in a constantly changing selection of Brazilian contemporary art (think abstract sculpture, textiles, and painting), but one can't help thinking the best piece of work on display is the building itself. Allow about an hour.

Mirante de Boa Viagem s/n, Niterói. ✆ **021/2620-2400.** www.macniteroi.com.br. Admission R$4, free for children 7 and under. Tues–Sun 10am–6pm. From Praça XV take the ferry to Niterói, then take a short taxi ride along Niterói's waterfront and up the hill to the museum.

Architectural Highlights

Historic Buildings & Monuments

For a city so blessed with mountains, ocean, and historical roots several centuries deep, Rio's movers and shakers have suffered from a striking sense of inferiority. As a result, various well-meaning Cariocas have since the early 1900s taken turns ripping out, blowing up, filling in, and generally reconfiguring huge swaths of their city in order to make Rio look more like Paris or Los Angeles or, lately, Miami Beach.

"Rio Civilizes Itself!" Armed with this slogan and a deep envy of what Baron Haussman had done in Paris, engineer-mayor **Pereiro Passos** set to work in 1903, ripping a large swath through Rio's Centro district to create the first of the city's grand boulevards, the **Avenida Central,** now renamed **Avenida Rio Branco.** It runs from **Praça Mauá** south past the grand neoclassical **Igreja de Nossa Senora da Candelária** to what was then the waterfront at the **Avenida Beira Mar.** The four-story Parisian structures that

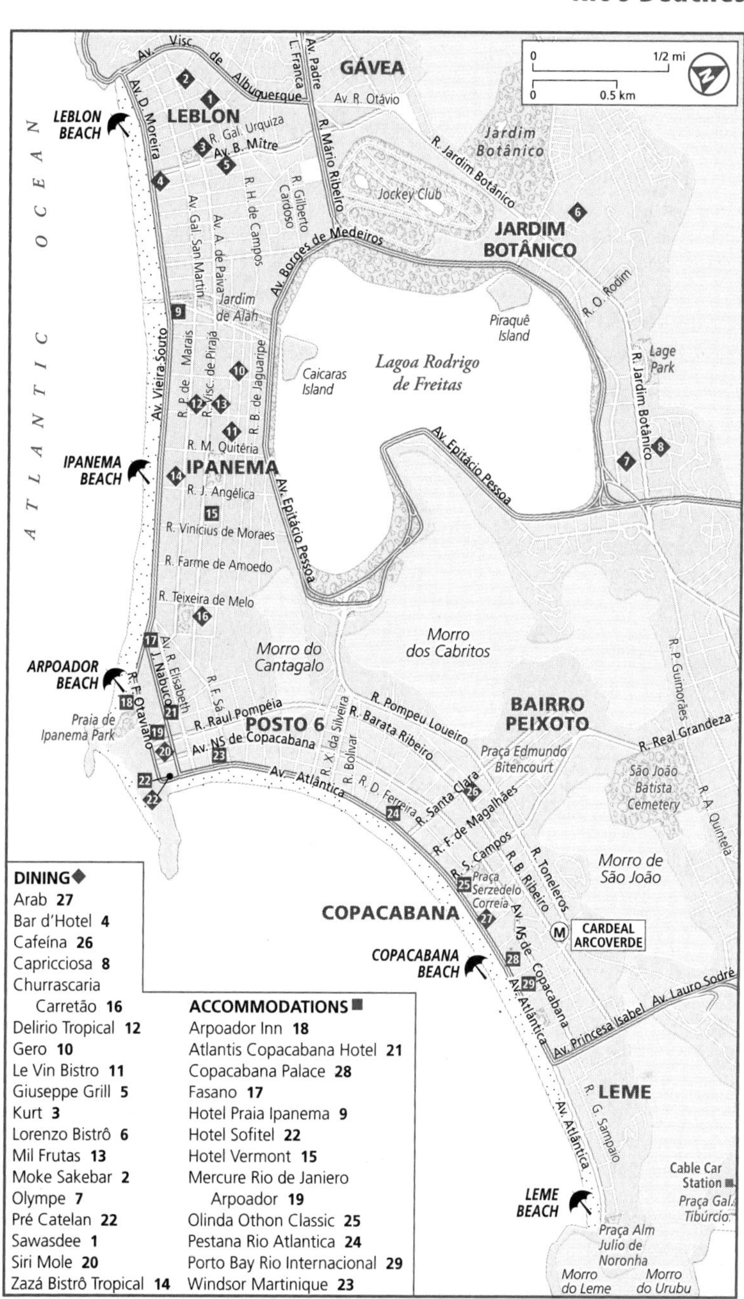

GÁVEA
LEBLON
LEBLON BEACH
ATLANTIC OCEAN
JARDIM BOTÂNICO
Jardim Botânico
Jockey Club
Lagoa Rodrigo de Freitas
Caicaras Island
Piraquê Island
Lage Park
Jardim de Alah
IPANEMA
IPANEMA BEACH
ARPOADOR BEACH
Praia de Ipanema Park
Morro do Cantagalo
Morro dos Cabritos
POSTO 6
BAIRRO PEIXOTO
Praça Edmundo Bitencourt
São João Batista Cemetery
Morro de São João
COPACABANA
COPACABANA BEACH
Praça Serzedelo Correia
CARDEAL ARCOVERDE
LEME
LEME BEACH
Cable Car Station
Praça Gal. Tibúrcio
Praça Alm Julio de Noronha
Morro do Leme
Morro do Urubu
Av. Visc. de Albuquerque
Av. D. Moreira
L. Franca
Av. Padre
Av. R. Otávio
R. Mário Ribeiro
R. Jardim Botânico
R. Gal. Urquiza
Av. B. Mítre
R. Gilberto Cardoso
R. H. de Campos
Av. A. de Paiva
Av. Gal. San Martin
Av. Borges de Medeiros
R. O. Rodim
Av. Vieira Souto
R. P. de Marais
R. Visc. de Pirajá
R. B. de Jaguaripe
R. M. Quitéria
Av. Epitácio Pessoa
R. J. Angélica
R. Vinícius de Moraes
R. Farme de Amoedo
R. Teixeira de Melo
R. F. Otaviano
Av. R. Elisabeth
J. Nabuco
R. F. Sá
R. Raul Pompéia
Av. NS de Copacabana
R. X. da Silveira
R. Bolivar
R. Pompeu Loureiro
R. Barata Ribeiro
Av. Atlântica
R. D. Ferreira
R. Santa Clara
R. F. de Magalhães
R. S. Campos
R. B. Ribeiro
R. Toneleros
R. P. Guimarães
R. Real Grandeza
R. A. Quintela
Av. Princesa Isabel
Av. Lauro Sodré
R. G. Sampaio
0 1/2 mi
0 0.5 km
DINING
Arab 27
Bar d'Hotel 4
Cafeína 26
Capricciosa 8
Churrascaria Carretão 16
Delirio Tropical 12
Gero 10
Le Vin Bistro 11
Giuseppe Grill 5
Kurt 3
Lorenzo Bistrô 6
Mil Frutas 13
Moke Sakebar 2
Olympe 7
Pré Catelan 22
Sawasdee 1
Siri Mole 20
Zazá Bistrô Tropical 14
ACCOMMODATIONS
Arpoador Inn 18
Atlantis Copacabana Hotel 21
Copacabana Palace 28
Fasano 17
Hotel Praia Ipanema 9
Hotel Sofitel 22
Hotel Vermont 15
Mercure Rio de Janiero Arpoador 19
Olinda Othon Classic 25
Pestana Rio Atlantica 24
Porto Bay Rio Internacional 29
Windsor Martinique 23

once lined the street are now found only on the **Praça Floriano,** better known as **Cinelândia.** Anchored at the north end by the extravagant Beaux Arts **Teatro Municipal,** and flanked by the equally ornate **Museu de Belas Artes** and neoclassical **Biblioteca Nacional,** the *praça* beautifully emulates the proportions, the monumentality, and the glorious detail of a classic Parisian square.

The next stage in urban reform came in the early '20s, when the 400-year-old castle (and the hill it stood on), south of Praça XV, was blown up and leveled. Starting in the early '30s, construction begun on a series of government office towers inspired by the modernist movement then sweeping Europe. The first of these—then the Ministry of Education and Health building but now known as the **Palácio Gustavo Capanema,** at Rua da Imprensa 16—listed among its architects nearly all the later greats of Brazilian architecture, including **Lucio Costa, Oscar Niemeyer,** and Roberto Burle Marx, with painter Candido Portinari thrown in for good measure. Knock-it-down Passos had nothing on Brazilian dictator Getulio Vargas. In 1940, on Vargas's personal order, a monster 12-lane boulevard was cut through the city fabric from the beautiful **N.S. de Candelária Church** out through the **Campo de Santana** park to the northern edges of downtown. Anchoring this new megaboulevard was the **Central Station,** a graceful Modern building with a 135m (443-ft.) clock tower that still stands overlooking the city, providing a much-needed reference point in the northern half of downtown. Vargas's plan called for the entire 4km (2½-mile) street to be lined with identical 22-story office blocks. However, only a few were ever built; they can be seen on the block crossed by Rua Uruguaiana.

The next great reconfiguration of Rio came 2 years after the federal capital fled inland to Brasilia. City designers took the huge high hill—**Morro Santo Antônio**—that once dominated the Largo da Carioca, scooped away the earth, and dumped it in the bay, creating a vast new waterfront park. On the rather raw spot where the hill once stood arose the innovative cone-shaped **Catedral Metropolitana,** and at the intersection of the new avenidas **República do Chile** and **República do Paraguai,** a trio of towering skyscrapers, the most interesting of which is the "hanging gardens" headquarters of Brazil's state oil company **Petrobras.** On the waterfront park—officially called Parque do Flamengo but most often referred to as Aterro, the Portuguese word for landfill—designers created new gardens and pathways, a new beach, and a pair of modernist monuments: the **MAM (Modern Art Museum)** and the impressive **Monument to the Dead of World War II.** Not incidentally, the park also bears two wide and fast roadways connecting Centro with the fashionable neighborhoods in the Zona Sul.

Churches & Temples

Rio is awash with churches, with some 20 in Centro alone. Likely the most impressive church in Rio is **Nossa Senhora de Candelária** ★★, set on a traffic island of its own at the head of Avenida Presidente Vargas (✆ **021/2233-2324**). The simple neoclassical design dates from a renovation begun in 1775. The church is open Monday to Friday from 8am to 4pm, and Saturday and Sunday from 9am to noon. More centrally located is the **Igreja da Ordem Terceira de São Francisco da Penitencia** ★, Largo da Carioca 5 (✆ **021/2262-0197**). On a hilltop overlooking Largo da Carioca, this and the Church of Santo Antônio next door form part of the large Franciscan complex in the city center. The São Francisco church is simply outstanding: Interior surfaces are filled with golden carvings and hung with censors of ornate silver. It's open Tuesday to Friday 9am to noon and 1 to 4pm.

Last and most innovative of Rio's significant churches is the **Catedral Metropolitana** ★★, Av. República de Chile 245 (✆ **021/2240-2669**). The form is modern; the feeling is soaring High Gothic.

Note: All attractions in Centro are best visited on weekdays. The area can be unsafe on weekends, when the streets are deserted.

Beaches, Parks & Plazas

BEACHES Beaches are to Rio what cafes are to Paris, and every Carioca has his or her favorite spot. The beaches facing Guanabara Bay (primarily **Flamengo** and **Botafogo**) are nearly always too polluted for swimming, but are great for an afternoon stroll. The first of the ocean beaches, **Copacabana** ★★ remains a favorite. The wide and beautifully landscaped Avenida Atlântica is a great place for a stroll.

Ipanema Beach ★★★ was famous among Brazilians even before Tom Jobim wrote his song about "his" tall and tan and young and lovely girl. Stretching almost 3km (2 miles) from the foot of the Pedra Dois Irmãos to the Ponta Arpoador, the beach at Ipanema is Rio in a (coco)nut shell; watch the Ipanema *garotas* (girls) or boys playing volleyball, *futvolei* (like volleyball, but no hands allowed), or beach soccer. The section just around the point from Copacabana—called **Praia do Arpoador**—is a prime surf spot. The area around Posto 8 (opposite Rua Farme Amoedo) is Ipanema's gay section.

Farther down into **Leblon** (still the same beach, just a different name once you cross the canal) you will find the **Baixo Baby,** an area with lots of playground equipment and beach toys.

PARKS & GARDENS On the waterfront near Centro there's **Flamengo Park,** a good place to stroll in the late afternoon if you're looking for a nice view of the Sugarloaf.

The **Parque Nacional da Tijuca (Tijuca National Park)** ★★ is the biggest urban forest in the world and one of the last remnants of Atlantic rainforest on Brazil's southern coast. It's a great place to go for a hike (see "Sports & Outdoor Activities" below) or admire the views.

SQUARES & PLAZAS Tucked away just a few hundred meters uphill along Rua Cosme Velho from the Corcovado Train Station is one of Rio's prettiest squares, the **Largo de Boticario** ★★. It's a gem of a spot, with five gaily painted colonial houses encircling a fountain in the middle of a flagstone square. It's well worth the 5-minute detour if you're going to the Corcovado anyway.

The **Largo de São Francisco de Paula** in Rio's old shopping district is well worth a visit. There's an outdoor market on one side of the square, and on the other the huge baroque-style **Igreja de São Francisco de Paula.**

Sports & Outdoor Activities

Adventure Sports Rio Hiking ★★ (✆ **021/9721-0594;** www.riohiking.com.br) is Rio's adventure-sport specialist, offering hiking, rock climbing, rafting, ocean kayaking, cycling, hang gliding, horseback riding, scuba diving, surfing (with lessons), and rappelling. Depending on the sport, half-day adventures cost from R$80 to R$150, full-day adventures from R$150 to R$250, with guides and transfer to and from your hotel included.

BICYCLING **Rio Hiking** offers two half-day guided bike tours of the city. The first involves an easy ride along the beach front of the Zona Sul. The second more challenging tour rides through the gorgeous rainforest of the Floresta da Tijuca. The tour costs R$150 per person.

GOLFING Rio's only public golf course is out in Barra da Tijuca. **Golden Green,** Av. Conde de Marapendi 2905 (✆ **021/2434-0696**), is a par-3, 6-hole course inside a private condominium but open to the public. The course is open Tuesday to Sunday from 7am to 10pm. Greens fees are R$60 Tuesday to Friday and R$75 on weekends and holidays.

HANG GLIDING For a bird's-eye view of Rio's beaches and mountains, check out **Just Fly Rio** ★★ (✆ **021/9985-7540** or 021/2268-0565; www.justfly.com.br). Experienced flight instructor Paulo Celani takes guests on a tandem flight. It's one of the most exciting things you can do in Rio, well worth the R$240 per flight (pickup and drop-off included). ***Tip:*** There's a 10% discount on the price if you call and book with Paulo directly.

HIKING **Rio Hiking** ★★ offers guided hiking trips to most of Rio's peaks. The 4-hour Sugarloaf trip, which includes a short stretch of rock climbing, costs R$150. The 6-hour Pedra da Gávea hike offers terrific views, a waterfall in the middle, and an ocean dip at the end. Cost is R$200. Less strenuous is the Tijuca Forest tour, which involves a tour of the forest, stops at a waterfall and a couple of lookouts, and a 2-hour hike to Pico de Tijuca. Cost is R$150, with the option of returning via the fascinating hilltop neighborhood of Santa Teresa.

SEA KAYAKING Get out onto Guanabara Bay. **Rio Hiking** organizes kayaking tours from Praia Vermelha at the foot of the Sugarloaf, traveling out to one of the small islands just off the coast for some snacks and snorkeling. Cost is R$160 for a half-day tour, including transfers, refreshments, and an English-speaking guide.

SURFING Rio has a number of good spots to catch the waves. The surfing beach closest to the main part of Rio is **Arpoador Beach** in Ipanema. Out in Barra de Tijuca the main surf beach is **Barra-Meio,** a 1km-long (½-mile) stretch in the middle of the beach (around Av. Sernambetiba 3100). Waves average around 2m (6 ft.). Continue another 6.5 to 8km (4–5 miles), and you come to **Macumba-Pontal,** a 2.5km (1½-mile) beach with waves up to 3m (10 ft.). If you need a board, **Hot Coast,** Galeria River, Rua Francisco Otaviano 67, loja 12, Ipanema (✆ **021/2287-9388**), rents short boards, fun boards, and long boards for R$60 a day. You need to book ahead if you want a board on the weekend.

If you're looking for **lessons, Rio Hiking** (✆ **021/9721-0594;** www.riohiking.com.br) offers the most hassle-free option, a half-day surf lesson with an English-speaking instructor, plus gear and transportation for R$200. For cheap transportation to the beaches in Barra and beyond, take the **surf bus.** It departs the Largo do Machado at 7am, 10am, 1pm, and 4pm and goes along Copacabana, Arpoador, São Conrado, and Barra de Tijuca as far as Prainha, past Recreio. Call to confirm departure times (✆ **021/2539-7555** or 021/8702-2837; www.surfbus.com.br); tickets cost R$4 each way.

Shopping

ARTS & CRAFTS **Brasil&Cia,** Rua Maria Quitéria 27, Ipanema (✆ **021/2267-46**), specializes in quality Brazilian arts and crafts made from wood, ceramics, paper, and fibers. A great little store in Santa Teresa, **Trilhos Urbanos,** Rua Almirante Alexandrino 402, Santa Teresa (✆ **021/2242-3632**), sells a variety of Brazilian artwork, including paintings, photographs, and crafts made out of tile, paper, and other materials. Every Sunday, there is the **Feira Hippie Ipanema,** Praça General Osorio (intersection of Rua Teixeira de Melo and Rua Visconde de Pirajá). This a fun, open-air market where you can browse for arts and crafts.

BEACHWEAR **Bum Bum,** Rua Vinicius de Morais 130, Ipanema (✆ **021/2521-1229**), is the place to shop for the infamous Rio bikini. For more sophisticated and stylish designs, head to **Blue Man,** Visconde de Pirajá 351, loja 308, Ipanema (✆ **021/2247-4905;** also in the Rio Sul mall). **Lenny Niemeyer,** Rua Garcia d'Avila 149, Ipanema (✆ **021/2227-5537;** one of several other stores), or simply Lenny, is quickly becoming one of Brazil's premier beachwear designers. Her recent collection was featured in *Vanity Fair.*

BOOKS Stock up on reading material at **Letras e Expressões,** Rua Visconde de Pirajá 276, Ipanema (✆ **021/2247-8737**). The store offers a wide selection of foreign magazines and newspapers, plus a number of excellent books on Rio, including some beautiful coffee-table books. Also worth browsing is **Livraria da Travessa,** Rua Visconde de Pirajá 462, Ipanema (✆ **021/3205-9002**). They have a good collection of English-language books, plus children's books and guidebooks.

CARNAVAL COSTUMES Founded in 1920, **Casa Turuna,** Rua Senhor dos Passos 77, Centro (✆ **021/2509-3908**), in Rio's downtown sells everything you can imagine: beads, feathers, sequins, fabric, headdresses, and so much more.

JEWELRY **Amsterdam Sauer,** Rua Visconde de Piraja 484, Ipanema (✆ **021/2279-6237**), is Brazil's best-known name for gems, jewelry, and semiprecious and precious stones. This location houses both a store and a museum with a display of Brazil's dazzling variety of gem stones. The other unavoidable name in jewelry is **H. Stern,** Rua Visconde de Pirajá 490, Ipanema (✆ **021/2274-3447**). Come within sniffing distance of a Rio hotel and you'll receive an invitation to visit an H. Stern store, transportation complimentary. The company specializes in precious and semiprecious stones.

SHOPPING CENTERS The **Rio Sul,** Rua Lauro Muller 116, Botafogo (✆ **021/2122-8070**), next to the tunnel to Copacabana, offers over 450 stores, a movie theater, and an excellent food court. **Shopping Leblon,** Rua Afrânio de Melo 290, Leblon (✆ **021/3138-8000**), attracts Rio's well-heeled fashionistas. The mall offers a good selection of upscale stores and designer labels.

MUSIC Music buffs will think they have died and gone to heaven at **Modern Sound,** Rua Barata Ribeiro 502, Copacabana (✆ **021/2548-5005**). This store houses an amazing collection of music. In the evenings, the store is often used as a small concert venue. For sheet music and musical instruments, visit **Musical Carioca,** Rua da Carioca 89 (✆ **021/3814-3400**), or **Casa Oliveira Musicais,** Rua da Carioca 70 (✆ **021/2252-5636**).

CARNAVAL

Ah, Carnaval. The name evokes explosive images of colorful costumes, lavish floats, swarming masses, and last-minute debauchery before the sober Lenten season begins. Although the religious aspect of the celebration faded some time ago, Carnaval's date is still determined by the ecclesiastical calendar, officially occupying only the 4 days immediately preceding Ash Wednesday. With typical ingenuity and panache, however, Cariocas have managed to stretch the party into an event lasting several months, culminating in the all-night feast of color and sound that is the Samba School Parade, where tens of thousands of costumed dancers, thousands of percussionists, and hundreds of gorgeous performers atop dozens of floats all move in choreographed harmony to the nonstop rhythm of samba.

If you're not able to attend Carnaval itself, **rehearsals**—which usually start in mid-September or early October—are a must, and the closest you'll get to the real thing.

In the weeks leading up to the big event, you'll begin to see the **blocos.** These are community groups—usually associated with a particular neighborhood or sometimes with a bar—who go around the neighborhood, playing music and singing and dancing through the streets.

Carnaval finally kicks off on the Friday before Ash Wednesday with an explosion of lavish **balls *(bailes).*** Originally the *bailes* were reserved for the elite, while the masses partied it up with vulgar splendor in the streets. Today, they're still a pricey affair and the **Grande Baile de Carnaval** at the Copacabana Palace remains *the* society event in Rio. The blocos also kick into high gear once Carnaval arrives, with several groups parading every day from Saturday through Tuesday.

Watching the Samba Parade

Then, there is the *pièce de résistance:* the **Samba School Parade,** the event that the samba schools work, plan, and sweat over for an entire year. Over two nights, the 12 top-ranked samba schools (community groups whose sole focus is the parade) compete for the honor of putting on the best show. The competition takes place in the **Sambodromo,** a 1.5km-long (1-mile) concrete parade ground built in the center of Rio for this once-a-year event. Each night over 60,000 spectators watch the contest live, while millions more tune in on TV to catch this feast for the senses.

On the day of each parade, the schools arrive outside the parade grounds to assemble their floats, props, and other gear. The streets around the Sambodromo, including Avenida Presidente Vargas, are closed for traffic; it's a great opportunity to take a close-up look at the floats, take pictures, and meet some of the people who put it all together.

The only way to get tickets for the event is through scalpers or travel agencies. Reputable travel agencies include **Blumar** (✆ **021/2142-9300;** www.blumar.com.br), **Rio Services Carnaval** (✆ **877/559-0088** in the U.S. and Canada; www.rio-carnival.net), and **BIT** (✆ **021/3208-9000;** www.bitourism.com), which sell good tickets at reasonable rates, but which often sell out early. If you've got your heart set on seeing the parade, buy your tickets by October or November at the latest. As a next to last resort, try your hotel, but expect to pay a hefty premium for this service.

Tickets for the bleachers begin at around R$110 for section 4, and rise to R$300 for section 7. Chairs in a front row box *(frisa)* start at R$3,000 in section 4 and R$4,800 in section 7. These are base prices. Many agencies charge much more.

Participating in the Parade

If you think watching the parade from up close sounds pretty amazing, imagine being in it. To raise funds, the samba schools open up some positions for outsiders to participate. To parade (*desfilar* in Portuguese) you need to buy a costume (about R$500–R$1,200), which you can often do online. Some sites are in English as well as Portuguese; if not, look under *fantasia* (costume). Depending on the school, they may courier the costume or arrange for a pickup downtown just before the parade, or you may have to make the trek out to wherever they are.

For an added charge, a number of agencies in Rio will organize it all for you, getting you in with a school and arranging the costume. **Blumar** or **Rio Services Carnaval** (see above) can organize the whole event for you for about R$1,000. Another agency is **Alô Rio** (✆ **0800/707-1888** or 021/2542-8080).

As a participant in the parade, you do not get a ticket to watch the parade. If you want to see the other schools you need to purchase a separate ticket.

Watching a Rehearsal

Every Saturday from September (or even as early as Aug) until Carnaval, each samba school holds a general samba rehearsal *(ensaio)* at its home base. The band and key people come out and practice their theme song over and over to perfection. It may sound a tad repetitious, but it's *really* a great party. People dance for hours, taking a break now and then for snacks and beer. The income generated goes toward the group's floats and costumes. (General rehearsals usually don't involve costumes or practicing dance routines.) In December and January, the schools also hold dress rehearsals and technical rehearsals at the Sambodromo. Check with Riotur for dates and times.

Most of the samba schools are based in the poorer and quite distant suburbs, but a number of schools—such as **Mangueira,** Rua Visconde de Niterói 1072, Mangueira (✆ **021/3872-6786;** www.mangueira.com.br); **Salgueiro,** Rua Silva Telles 104, Andaraí (✆ **021/2238-0389;** www.salgueiro.com.br); **Vila Isabel,** Boulevard 28 de Setembro 382, Vila Isabel (✆ **021/2578-0077;** www.gresunidosdevilaisabel.com.br); and **Rocinha,** Rua Bertha Lutz 80, São Conrado (✆ **021/3205-3318;** www.academicosdarocinha.com.br)—are very accessible and no more than an R$30 cab ride from Copacabana. Plan to arrive anytime after 11pm. When you are ready to leave there'll be lots of taxis around.

Hanging with the Blocos

To experience the real street Carnaval, don't miss the local blocos, groups of musicians and merrymakers that parade through the neighborhood. Everyone is welcome, and you don't need a costume, just comfortable clothes and shoes. Different blocos have certain styles or attract specific groups, so pick one that suits you and have fun. Riotur publishes an excellent brochure called *Bandas, Blocos and Ensaios,* available through Alô Rio (see above). In Portuguese, the website www.samba-choro.com.br provides a comprehensive list of blocos, including parade routes and starting times. The *O Globo* newspaper (www.oglobo.com.br) also provides a bloco listings page.

Some of the best blocos to look for are **Bloco Cacique de Ramos** and **Cordão do Bola Preta** in Centro; **Barbas** and **Bloco de Segunda** in Botafogo; **Bloco do Bip Bip** and **Banda Santa Clara** in Copacabana; **Bloco Meu Bem Volto Já** in Leme; and **Banda de Ipanema** and **Simpatia é Quase Amor** in Ipanema.

Bailes

More formal than the blocos, the samba *bailes* are where you go to see and be seen. Traditionally reserved for Rio's elite, some—such as the Copacabana Palace ball—remain the height of elegance, while others have become raunchy and risqué bacchanals. Numerous clubs around town host Carnaval balls. For more info contact **Alô Rio** (see above). Popular gay nightclub **Le Boy** (p. 277) organizes a differently themed ball every night during Carnaval, Friday through Tuesday included. These balls are gay-friendly but not gay only. Call ✆ **021/2240-3338.** The prime gay event—and one of Rio's most famous balls—is the Tuesday night **Gala Gay** at the Scala nightclub, Av. Afranio de Melo Franco 296, Leblon (✆ **021/2239-4448**). TV cameras vie for position by the red carpet, a la Oscar night.

The grand slam of all Carnaval balls is the Saturday night extravaganza at the Copacabana Palace Hotel, the **Grande Baile de Carnaval,** which plays host to the crème de la crème of Rio's high society. Tickets start at R$600 per person and sell out quickly. Call

New Year's Eve in Rio

Rio's annual New Year's Eve extravaganza unites millions of people on the beach for an all-night festival of music, food, and fun, punctuated by spectacular fireworks. At midnight, barges moored off Copacabana beach flood the sky with a shower of reds, greens, yellows, and golds. When the last whistling spark falls into the sea, bands fire up their instruments and welcome in the new year with a concert that goes on until wee hours.

✆ **021/2548-7070** for details. **Rio Services Carnaval** (✆ **877/559-0088** in the U.S. and Canada; www.rio-carnival.net) offers tickets to many of the balls listed above.

WHERE TO STAY

The only neighborhood to avoid hotel-wise is downtown Rio. The Praça Mauá hotels may look like a bargain, but this area transforms into a red-light district at night when the office workers have gone home.

Breakfast ***(café de manha)*** at Brazilian hotels is almost always included in the room price. In recent years a few of the more expensive hotels have taken to charging for *café de manha;* if this is the case it's noted in the review.

Ipanema

Very Expensive

Fasano ★★★ Overrated Overrated and three stars? Well, the design sense in this hotel is truly lovely. This first ever hotel designed inside and out by the famous *enfant terrible* of the design world, Phillippe Starck, the Fasano features wood-paneled hallways accented with big Dr. Seuss chairs, giving the hotel a James Bond/Austin Powers shaggalicious kind of feel. The rooftop pool is a thing of beauty. That said, though even the least expensive rooms (called Superior) come gussied up in high design, it doesn't change the fact that they are small, and very expensive, and lack both balcony and ocean view. If design is not your thing, you can get much more room for the money staying somewhere else. If you are in the mood to splurge, the deluxe oceanview rooms are sized much more comfortably. The quality of everything in all rooms—bedding, bathroom products, bathrobes—is top notch.

Av. Vieira Souto 88, Ipanema, Rio de Janeiro, 22420-000 RJ. ✆ **021/3202-4000.** Fax 021/3202-4010. www.fasano.com.br. 91 units. R$945 superior double; R$1,425 deluxe oceanview double; R$2,800 oceanview suite. Extra bed R$150. Children 12 and under stay free in parent's room. Inquire about seasonal discounts. AE, DC, MC, V. Valet parking. Metrô: General Osorio. **Amenities:** Restaurant; bar; babysitting; concierge; well-equipped fitness center; rooftop pool; room service; sauna; smoke-free floors; small spa. *In room:* A/C, TV, hair dryer, minibar, Wi-Fi.

Expensive

Hotel Praia Ipanema ★★★ Straddling the border between Ipanema and Leblon, the Praia Ipanema offers beachfront luxury accommodations, all within walking distance of Lagoa, the upscale shopping and restaurants of the Zona Sul, and the restaurants and bars of Leblon. All 105 units offer king-size beds and lovely bedding, plus balconies and ocean views. In the lowest category, Superior Master rooms offer either a front ocean view on a lower floor, or a side view from an upper floor. (As the side-view rooms are actually a bit larger than the front-views, an upper-floor side view may well be the best deal). One step up, the Deluxe *(luxo)* rooms offer a front view from a higher floor. Deluxe Master (*luxo* master) rooms offer the same front view from floors 10 and up—where views of sand and sea get ever more spectacular—plus extras like a DVD and flatscreen TV.

Av. Vieira Souto 706, Ipanema, Rio de Janeiro, 22420-000 RJ. ✆ **021/2540-4949.** Fax 021/2239-6889. www.praiaipanema.com. 101 units. R$500 Superior Master double; R$550 Deluxe double; R$580 Deluxe Master double; R$780 suite. AE, DC, MC, V. No parking. Bus: 474 or 404. **Amenities:** Restaurant; 2 bars; beach service; small gym; rooftop pool; room service. *In room:* A/C, TV, fridge, hair dryer, minibar, Wi-Fi.

Mercure Rio de Janeiro Arpoador ★★ Value An excellent value for money, and a location that lets you choose between Ipanema and Copacabana. All units in this flat hotel are small suites—bedrooms come with comfortable queen beds, the sitting rooms have a fold-out couch and sizable desk, and there's a small but fully equipped adjoining kitchen. Both bedroom and sitting room have a TV/DVD, and there's free Wi-Fi throughout. They're great for a family, or if you have work to do and are spending more time in Rio. Note that though the hotel backs onto the beach (rooms higher up on the back side get a beach view), to reach the beach you have to exit the hotel and walk a full 100m (328 ft.) or so on the street.

Rua Francisco Otaviano 61, Arpoador, Rio de Janeiro, 22080-060 RJ. ✆ **021/2113-8600.** www.accorhotels.com.br. 56 units. R$350 standard double. Up to 25% discount in low season and weekends. AE, DC, MC, V. Parking R$15. Bus: 474. **Amenities:** Beach service; outdoor pool; room service; sauna. *In room:* A/C, TV/DVD, kitchen, Wi-Fi.

Moderate

Arpoador Inn ★ Value The only moderately priced oceanfront hotel in Ipanema, the Arpoador Inn enjoys a privileged location on a quiet stretch of beach popular with the surf crowd, and just around the corner from Copacabana. Even better, the beach in front of the hotel is closed to cars and is therefore pleasantly quiet. The deluxe rooms all face the ocean. The furniture is simple but the rooms are bright and spotless. Obtaining these does require booking ahead; if they're full, the superior rooms, which look out over the street behind the beach, make an acceptable alternative. Avoid the standard rooms, which are small, dark, and look into an interior wall.

Rua Francisco Otaviano 177, Ipanema, Rio de Janeiro, 22080-040 RJ. ✆ **021/2523-0060.** Fax 021/2511-5094. www.arpoadorinn.com.br. 50 units. R$212 standard double; R$300 street-view superior double; R$440 deluxe ocean view. Extra person R$120. Children 6 and under stay free in parent's room. AE, DC, MC, V. No parking. Metrô: General Osorio. **Amenities:** Restaurant; room service. *In room:* A/C, TV, fridge.

Hotel Vermont ★ The Vermont sits smack in the middle of Ipanema's swankiest shopping district, and thanks to the rates at this small budget hotel, you'll have plenty of cash left for conspicuous consumption. All rooms have tile floors, new furniture, large mirrors, and clean, modern fixtures. Standard rooms face out the back and are simply furnished with two twins or a double bed, a closet, and a desk. Superior rooms are a little more spacious but they also get some street noise, although at night traffic slows down significantly. Most of the rooms have twin beds, so if you want a double it's best to reserve in advance. Note that the hotel is a bad choice for those with limited mobility—access to the hotel elevators is up one flight of stairs.

Rua Visconde de Pirajá 254, Ipanema, Rio de Janeiro, 22410-000 RJ. ✆ **021/3202-5500.** Fax 021/2267-7046. www.hotelvermont.com.br. 84 units. R$240 standard or superior double. Extra person R$90. Children 2 and under stay free in parent's room. AE, DC, MC, V. No parking. Bus: 415. *In room:* A/C, TV, minibar, Wi-Fi.

Copacabana

Very Expensive

The Copacabana Palace ★★ The spot where beachfront luxury in Rio began way back in the Jazz Age, the 86-year-old Palace is still the place to splurge. Don't bother with the city-view rooms and suites that face a busy street and offer no views. Better to simply stay elsewhere. Deluxe beach-view rooms do give you that coveted ocean view, but to get value for your money at the Palace it's really a case of go big or go home: The pool or ocean-view suites are spacious, elegant, and tastefully decorated, each with their own private veranda overlooking the pool and Copacabana beach. Now *that* is the life we were intended to live.

Av. Atlântica 1702, Copacabana, Rio de Janeiro, 22021-001 RJ. ✆ **0800/211-533** or 021/2548-7070. Fax 021/2235-7330. www.copacabanapalace.com. 225 units. R$960 deluxe city-view double; R$1,170 deluxe oceanview double; R$1,960 pool/oceanview suite double; penthouse suite R$3,580. Extra person about 25%. Children 12 and under stay free in parent's room. AE, DC, MC, V. Free parking. Metrô: Arcoverde. **Amenities:** 2 restaurants; bar; babysitting; concierge; executive-level rooms; health club; Jacuzzi; large outdoor pool; room service; sauna; rooftop tennis courts. *In room:* A/C, TV, hair dryer, minibar, Wi-Fi.

Hotel Sofitel ★★★ There may be newer, more trendy hotels in town, but when it comes to top-notch service and luxury accommodations, the Sofitel gets it right every time. "Standard" amenities in all rooms include elegant, modern furniture; efficient work spaces; a comfy lounge chair; top-notch lighting; flatscreen TVs; the Sofitel's signature mattresses and the finest linen; a pillow menu; fabulous showers; and luxurious l'Occitane amenities. But wait, there is more: two gorgeous swimming pools (one for the morning sun and the other for the afternoon rays), a state-of-the-art fitness center, a running kit for those who prefer to jog along the beach, and a killer oceanfront location with exclusive services for hotel guests. Sofitel also deserves kudos for offering the city's best rooms for disabled travelers. The hotel's **Pré Catelan** restaurant (p. 270) offers one of the best dining experiences in town.

Av. Atlântica 4240, Copacabana, Rio de Janeiro, 22070-002 RJ. ✆ **0800/241-232** or 021/2525-1232. Fax 021/2525-1200. www.accorhotels.com.br. 388 units. R$590 superior double; R$675 deluxe double; R$900 junior suite double. Children 12 and under stay free in parent's room. AE, DC, MC, V. Free parking. Bus: 474. **Amenities:** 2 restaurants; bar; babysitting; concierge; health club; 2 outdoor pools; room service; sauna; smoke-free floors. *In room:* A/C, TV, hair dryer, minibar, Wi-Fi.

Expensive

Olinda Othon Classic ★★ Value A lovely heritage building, the Olinda has finally gotten a much-needed makeover. The lobby has been transformed into an elegant salon with a restaurant and piano bar. Elevators have been upgraded to the 21st century, and all the rooms have been renovated, the dark colonial furniture replaced by lighter woods, soothing pale colors, and stylish furniture. You should still avoid the standard rooms, which are smaller and face the back of the building. The deluxe oceanview rooms *(luxo)* feature a king-size bed, elegant 1950s detailing, and a view of the ocean. The deluxe rooms with veranda are actually smaller, but that lovely little veranda for two affords a wonderful view out over the ocean.

Av. Atlântica 2230, Copacabana, 22041-001 RJ. ✆/fax **021/2545-9091.** www.hoteis-othon.com.br. 102 units. R$250 standard double; R$325 deluxe double; R$450 suite double. Extra person add 40%. Children 10 and under stay free in parent's room. AE, DC, MC, V. No parking. Metrô: Arcoverde. **Amenities:** Restaurant; bar; room service. *In room:* A/C, TV, minibar, Wi-Fi.

Pestana Rio Atlântica ★★★ Always one of the nicest hotels on the Avenida Atlântica, the Pestana looks brand new, thanks to a recent overhaul. The best rooms in the house are the Oceanica suites. These large rooms offer ocean views and large balconies, and come elegantly furnished with dark wooden furniture and splashes of yellow and beige. They are among the best in Copa, if you can afford the splurge. The standard and superior rooms are more plainly furnished, but still luxurious. Standard rooms look out over the buildings adjacent to the hotel. Superior rooms (on the 10th floor and higher) have a partial ocean view. There's a good fitness center and the rooftop pool area offers a massage room, sauna, and Jacuzzi. Breakfast costs R$36.

Av. Atlântica 2964, Copacabana, Rio de Janeiro, 22070-000 RJ. ✆ **021/2548-6332.** Fax 021/2255-6410. www.pestana.com. 216 units. R$400 standard double; R$450–R$550 superior double; R$750–R$950 Oceanica suite. Children 10 and under stay free in parent's room. AE, DC, MC, V. Valet parking. Metrô: Arcoverde. **Amenities:** Restaurant; bar; babysitting; concierge; health club; Jacuzzi; outdoor pool; room service; sauna; smoke-free rooms. *In room:* A/C, TV, hair dryer, Internet, minibar.

Porto Bay Rio Internacional Hotel ★★ The Porto Bay proves that you shouldn't judge a hotel by its cover. Behind the '80s-style black glass facade hides a remarkably pleasant hotel with friendly and attentive staff that welcome guests with a glass of champagne. A recent $4-million overhaul equipped all guest accommodations with new attractive furnishings, firm king- or queen-size beds, flatscreen TVs, and DVD and CD players. The prime rooms, the deluxe suites, have large panorama windows and a balcony—definitely worth the splurge. The hotel also has a lovely rooftop bar and swimming pool.

Av. Atlântica 1500, Copacabana, Rio de Janeiro, 22021-000 RJ. ✆ **0800/021-1559** or 021/2546-8000. Fax 021/2542-5443. www.portobay.com. 117 units. R$460 superior double; R$600 deluxe double. Children 10 and under stay free in parent's room. AE, DC, MC, V. Parking. Metrô: Cardeal Arcoverde. **Amenities:** Restaurant; bar; exercise room; rooftop pool; room service; smoke-free floors. *In room:* A/C, TV, DVD, CD player, hair dryer, minibar, Wi-Fi.

Moderate

Atlantis Copacabana Hotel ★ Located between Ipanema and Copacabana on a quiet residential street, the Atlantis Copacabana Hotel is perfect for those who like to keep their options open. Either beach is within minutes from your hotel, and shopping and restaurants are easily accessible. The hotel offers basic accommodations; all 87 rooms are standard, with only a small variation in size and layout; rooms ending in 07 and 08 (for example, nos. 107 and 108) are slightly larger. Rooms above the eighth floor that look out the back offer a view of Arpoador and Ipanema beach.

Rua Bulhões de Carvalho 61, Copacabana, Rio de Janeiro, RJ 22081-000. ✆ **021/2521-1142.** Fax 021/2287-8896. www.atlantishotel.com.br. 87 units. R$220–R$270 double. Extra person R$50. Children 5 and under stay free in parent's room. AE, DC, MC, V. Limited street parking. Bus: 128 or 474. **Amenities:** Concierge; rooftop pool; room service; sauna. *In room:* A/C, TV, fridge, minibar, Wi-Fi.

Windsor Martinique ★ Value Excellent value in a great location, only a half-block off the Avenida Atlântica and within easy walking distance of Ipanema. The best rooms are the superior ones that look out over the street. Corner rooms ending in -13 (such as 413 and 513, and so on) even have a partial ocean view. The standard rooms look out at adjacent buildings. All are pleasantly furnished in bright colors and have comfortable beds. Nice details at this price level include the hair dryer, electronic safe, and high-speed Internet in each room. Most rooms are a tad on the small side and accommodate two people only. There's even a rooftop pool and sun deck, but with the beach only 91m (300 ft.) away, you'd have to be pretty lazy not to make it out the door.

Rua Sá Ferreira 30, Copacabana, Rio de Janeiro, 22071-100 RJ. ✆ **021/2195-5200.** Fax 021/2195-5222. www.windsorhoteis.com. 116 units. R$220–R$275 double. Extra person 25%. Children 10 and under stay free in parent's room. AE, DC, MC, V. Metrô: Cantagalo. **Amenities:** Restaurant; concierge; cardio equipment; rooftop pool; room service; smoke-free floors. *In room:* A/C, TV, hair dryer, minibar.

Flamengo & Santa Teresa

Very Expensive

Hotel Santa Teresa ★★★ One of the most romantic small hotels in the whole city, the Hotel Santa Teresa offers infinitely more bang for your splurging buck. Rooms are tastefully decorated with hardwood floors, king-size four-poster beds, top-quality linen, and tasteful little touches of artwork and design. Deluxe rooms have a bit more space and better views of the city and surrounding hills. Suites are larger still, with sitting areas and designer bathrooms. The hotel spa features a variety of Amazon-themed treatments. The outdoor pool offers fabulous city views, as does the lounge bar. The hotel restaurant, **Térèze** (p. 268), is one of the city's best. The Largo dos Guimarães, Santa Teresa's main square and "restaurant row," is only a 5-minute walk away.

Rua Almirante Alexandrino 660, Santa Teresa, Rio de Janeiro, 20241-260 RJ. ✆ **021/2222-2755.** Fax 021/2221-1406. www.santateresahotel.com. 44 units. R$650–R$725 double; R$800–R$1,600 suite. Children 10 and under stay free in parent's room. AE, DC, MC, V. No parking. Bus: Silbestre. **Amenities:** Restaurant; outdoor pool; limited room service; spa. *In room:* A/C, TV, fridge, minibar, Wi-Fi.

Expensive

Windsor Hotel Florida ★★ *Finds* The Florida is popular with business travelers from São Paulo who know a good deal when they see it: On top of a reasonable room rate, the Florida offers free parking, free local calls, and free Internet access. Rooms are spacious and pleasant, and though furnishings are a bit dated, there are good queen beds, hardwood floors, and ample workspace. The standard rooms overlook the rear or the side of the building. Both the superior and deluxe rooms offer views and have bathrooms with whirlpool tubs. The nicest rooms are those overlooking the lush gardens of the Palácio do Catete, Brazil's former presidential palace. The hotel offers excellent discounts on weekends.

Rua Ferreira Viana 81, Flamengo, Rio de Janeiro, 22210-040 RJ. ✆ **021/2195-6800.** Fax 021/2285-5777. www.windsorhoteis.com. 312 units. R$275 standard double; R$275 superior double; R$325 deluxe double. Extra person add 25%. Children 10 and under stay free in parent's room. AE, DC, MC, V. Free parking. Metrô: Catete. **Amenities:** Restaurant; bar; concierge; rooftop pool; room service; sauna; smoke-free floors; weight room. *In room:* A/C, TV, fridge, hair dryer, minibar, Wi-Fi.

Moderate

Casa Aurea Only a short walk up the road from the main square in Santa Teresa, this affordable pousada is popular with sociable travelers and backpackers. Private rooms have en suite bathrooms, while other rooms share a bathroom down the hall. All are simply furnished but very clean and pleasant, with high ceilings and large windows with wooden shutters. The house has a gorgeous garden and patio, outdoor reading lounge, sitting room, and barbecue area, and is decorated with lovely artwork by some of the well-known artists from Santa Teresa.

Rua Aurea 80, Santa Teresa, Rio de Janeiro, 20240-210 RJ. ✆ **021/2242-5830.** www.casaaurea.com.br. 12 units. R$220–R$280 double; R$330–R$495 mini-apt double. Children 7 and under stay free in parent's room. No parking. **Amenities:** Bar; Wi-Fi. *In room:* Fan.

WHERE TO DINE

Centro

Expensive

Confeitaria Colombo ★★ BRAZILIAN/DESSERT This stunning Victorian tearoom hasn't changed much since it opened in 1894. The spacious room is divided into three sections. Two large counters at the entrance serve up sweets and snacks with coffee or other refreshments. The rest of the ground floor features an elegant tearoom, where a variety of teas, sandwiches, and sweets are served on fine china underneath a '20s stained-glass window. The upstairs is for full lunches—on Saturdays the *feijoada* (black beans and pork stew) is worth a trip downtown.

Rua Gonçalves Dias 32, Centro. ✆ **021/2505-1500.** www.confeitariacolombo.com.br. Tearoom snacks and lunches R$10–R$35; buffet lunch or Sat *feijoada* buffet R$55, including dessert. AE, DC, MC, V. Mon–Fri 8:30am–7pm; Sat 9am–5pm. Metrô: Carioca.

Moderate

Bistro do Paço ★ Finds BRAZILIAN Inside the historic Paço Imperial, the thick whitewashed walls keep out the bustle while you recharge your batteries in the cool shade of the inner courtyard. The restaurant serves mostly bistro fare, as well as a daily lunch special that will set you back R$15 to R$26 for a plate of roast beef with a side order of pasta, spinach and crepes with a ricotta-and-mushroom stuffing. Desserts are strictly European: Austrian *linzertortes,* German fruit strudels, and Black Forest chocolate cakes, all of which go so well with a Brazilian *cafezinho.*

Praça XV 48 (inside the Paço Imperial), Centro. ✆ **021/2262-3613.** Main courses R$18–R$35; sandwiches and quiches R$10–R$22. AE, DC, MC, V. Mon–Fri 10am–8pm; Sat noon–7pm. Bus: 415.

Boteco Casual BOTEQUIM In the heart of Rio's historic district just off Praça XV, this little bar-restaurant offers delicious cold beer and Portuguese specialties like stuffed octopus flavored with port, or salted grilled sardines. For dessert, try the *pastel de nata.* And if this little bar is packed, there's a bunch of others right alongside.

Rua do Ouvidor 26, Centro. ✆ **021/2232-0250.** R$10–R$25. AE, DC, MC, V. Mon–Fri 11am–2am. Sat 11am–6pm. Bus: 119 or 415 to Praça XV.

Inexpensive

Paladino ★ BRAZILIAN Is Paladino a deli, with racks of spices and jars of capers and artichoke hearts? Is it a liquor store, as the hundreds of glass bottles lined up in gleaming wooden cases seem to suggest? Or is it a bustling lunch bar with some of the best draft beer in town? Is an exact definition really important? What matters is that the atmosphere is that of Rio in the Belle Époque, the beer is cold, and waiters serve delicious sandwiches and snack plates loaded with sardines, olives, cheese, or great heaping stacks of smoked sausage.

Rua Uruguaiana 226, Centro. ✆ **021/2263-2094.** Reservations not accepted. Sandwiches and side dishes R$4–R$15. No credit cards. Mon–Fri 7am–8:30pm; Sat 8am–noon. Metrô: Uruguaiana.

Santa Teresa

Expensive

Aprazível ★ Finds BRAZILIAN Much of the charm of this Santa Teresa fixture comes from its setting in a hilltop mansion. Tables spill out over the gardens and patios, offering views of downtown Rio by day, and warm and exotic lighting in the evening. View junkies should ask for a table on the house veranda, or on the patio tables outside by the bar. The food, while good, doesn't quite rise to the same standard. The kitchen serves up intriguing variations on Brazilian cuisine, using many ingredients from the Nordeste region. Interesting starters include fresh grilled palm hearts, and pumpkin cream soup with prawns. The signature main is the *peixe tropical,* grilled fish in an orange sauce, served with coconut rice and baked banana.

 Rua Aprazível 62, Santa Teresa. ✆ **021/2508-9174.** www.aprazivel.com.br. Reservations recommended. Main courses R$38–R$55. AE, MC, V. Thurs 8pm–midnight; Fri–Sat noon–midnight; Sun 1–6pm. Taxi recommended.

Espirito Santa ★★ BRAZILIAN Espirito Santa proves there's no great secret to success—a cute restaurant, a great patio looking out over Santa Teresa, and excellent and inventive Brazilian cuisine. Chef Natacha Fink hails from the Amazon, and it shows in her menu. The signature starter is the *tambaqui* "ribs"—made of *tambaqui* (a popular Amazonian fish) lightly breaded and served with a pesto of *jambu* herbs. The *mujica de piranha* (piranha soup) is thick and tasty. For salads, there's one with toasted Brazil nuts and a passion fruit vinaigrette. The classic fish dish is a grilled *namorado* with a cashew crust, served on a bed of grilled fresh palm heart. Meat lovers should try the bacuri steak, grilled filet mignon served with a bacuri (Amazonian fruit) sauce and mashed sweet potatoes. For dessert, there's warm gâteau filled with guava cream and cheese, or ice cream of *cupuaçu* (fruit related to cacao).

Rua Almirante Alexandrino 264, Santa Teresa. ✆ **021/2508-7095.** www.espiritosanta.com.br. Main courses R$28–R$55. AE, DC, MC, V. Mon, Wed, and Sun noon–7pm; Thurs–Sat noon–midnight. Bus: 214, or take the tram, getting off just before the Largo dos Guimarães.

Térèze ★★ ASIAN/MEDITERANEAN Sophisticated dining on a hilltop in the heights of Rio's most historic neighborhood, with a view of treetops, colonial houses, and the city and bay below. The menu offers an upscale take on fusion, so miso-marinated lamb, grilled and served with wok-fried vegetables, *gyoza* with sweet-and-sour *maracujá* dipping sauce, or grilled *cherne* (sea bass) with cashew tapenade. Desserts can be equally creative, such as the macaroni-shaped chocolates with hazelnut *farofa* and vanilla ice cream. On Thursdays there's a tasting menu, featuring smaller portions and matched wines.

Rua Almirante Alexandrino 660 (in the Hotel Santa Teresa), Santa Teresa. ✆ **021/2222-2755.** www.tereze.com.br. Reservations recommended. Main courses R$38–R$65. AE, MC, V. Mon–Fri noon–5pm and 8pm–midnight; Sat noon–midnight; Sun noon–5pm. Taxi recommended.

Urca

Moderate

Bar Urca ★ BOTEQUIM This tiny botequim has one of the best views in the city—or does if you make like the locals, and drink your beer and munch from the delicious selection of *pastels* on the seawall overlooking Botafogo Bay. (Waiters used to cross the street and serve customers *in situ,* but due to a recent crackdown customers now have to order in the restaurant and carry their wares to the seawall themselves). If you do go inside, sit upstairs with a window view and order one of the delicious seafood stews—fish or prawns or octopus in a rich broth, with rice and *pirão* (fish gravy) on the side. Don't think of drinking anything but beer.

Rua Candido Gaffree 205, Urca. ✆ **021/2295-8744.** www.barurca.com.br. Main courses R$10–R$35. DC, MC, V. Daily 9am–11pm. Metrô: Integração from Botofogo.

Circulo Militar ★★ **Finds** BRAZILIAN Whenever we hanker for dinner and a view we head to the Circulo Militar. This fabulous view of the Sugarloaf and bay comes courtesy of the Brazilian armed forces. From the tree-shaded patio of a military club in Urca called the Circulo Militar, you look out across a tiny bay full of fishing boats to the sheer solid sides of the Sugarloaf. Civilians are completely welcome. The menu serves up standard Brazilian fare (the two stars are for the view, not for the food) such as the *churrasco* for two with beef, sausage, chicken, and pork served with fries and rice. In the evenings the kitchen fires up the wood-burning oven and turns out some decent pizzas. There's live music from 8pm onward, Tuesday through Sunday.

Praça General Tiburcio s/n, Praia Vermelha (on the far right, inside the military complex). ✆ **021/2275-7245.** www.cmpv.com.br. Main courses R$24–R$42. No credit cards. Daily noon–midnight. Bus: 107 from downtown, 512 from Ipanema and Copacabana.

Flamengo

Very Expensive

Porcão ★★ BRAZILIAN/STEAK A mass carnivorous orgy, Porcão is where you go not to sample or taste or nibble, but to munch and stuff and gorge yourself on some of the best beef the world has to offer—in this case served up with some of the best views in the world. Porcão is a churrascaria (a chain, in fact; there are several in Rio, but this one has the best view) operating on the *rodízio* system. It's one price for all you can eat (dessert and drinks are extra), and once you sit down, an onslaught of waiters comes bearing all manner of meat (steak cuts, roast cuts, filet mignon, chicken breast, chicken hearts, sausage, and much more), which they slice to perfection on your plate. Oh, and don't forget the nonmeat dishes: Included in your meal is a buffet with dozens of antipasto items, hot and cold seafood dishes, and at least 15 different kinds of salads and cheeses. Alas, no doggy bags allowed.

Av. Infante Dom Henrique s/n, Parque do Flamengo. ✆ **021/2554-8535.** www.porcao.com.br. Reservations accepted. R$75 per person all-you-can-eat meat and buffet. 50% discount for children 6–9, free for children 5 and under. AE, DC, MC, V. Daily 11:30am–1am. Taxi recommended.

Moderate

Adega Portugalia PORTUGUESE This simple little bar/restaurant looks out on the Largo do Machado, a graceful Rio urban square. Sample a plate of appetizers—cheese, olives, spiced potatoes, octopus—from the counter deli, order a portion of *frango a pasarinho* (garlic baked chicken wings), or sample a steak or Portuguesa pizza. Make sure to order a *chopp* (draft beer) to go with the munchies.

Largo do Machado 30, Flamengo. ✆ **021/2558-2821.** Reservations not accepted. R$15–R$30. MC, V, Mon–Sat 10am–midnight; Sun 10am–6pm. Metrô: Largo do Machado.

Botafogo

Expensive

Oui Oui ★★ FUSION Better late than never! Tapas has finally made it to Rio at Oui Oui, which has created a wonderful menu of 20 small dishes that can be combined into a very satisfying meal. Start off with a refreshing Moranguito cocktail (sparkling wine, strawberries, and mint) and a plate of spring rolls stuffed with fresh figs and shredded duck. Other interesting dishes include the vegetable risotto with mascarpone, spicy grilled beef with lemon grass, and the shrimp *moqueca* stew with cashew nuts and mango. The hands-down (and finger-licking) winner was the portion of caramelized spareribs served with a pumpkin-and–goat cheese purée, topped with toasted almonds. It probably violates the cardinal rule of tapas eating, but next time I am not sharing that dish! The wine list is a tad overpriced, but does contain a few good deals such as a South African Chenin blanc for R$64.

Rua Conde de Irajá 85, Humaitá. R$17–R$26. AE, DC, MC, V. Tues–Sun 7:30pm–1am. Metrô: Integração Botafogo.

Moderate

Café Prefácio CAFE Books. Wine. Food. Food. Books. Wine. No matter how you put the words together, it's a winning combination. This bookstore/cafe (or cafe/

bookstore) in the Botofogo cinema zone offers good coffee, wine by the glass, and a simple menu of delicious sandwiches and salads. Seating is at the coffee bar in the front, or the mezzanines above the bookshelves, or in the small dining room at the back. Browse the titles while awaiting your order (there's an English-language section, and a wide selection of art books), or order up a bottle of Argentine Malbec (R$40 or so) and stay the night.

Rua Voluntarios de Patria 39, Botafogo. ✆ **021/2527-5699.** www.prefaciolivrarias.com.br. Reservations not accepted. R$15–R$30. MC, V, Mon–Sat 9am–11pm; Sun 4:30–11pm. Metrô: Botafogo.

Inexpensive

Bar do Adão LIGHT FARE This lovely heritage house in Botafogo houses an excellent bar that serves up the best *pasteis* in town, or the second-best *pasteis,* as the original Bar do Adão in the Zona Norte neighborhood of Grajau first developed their recipe for success. Made out of light fluffy dough, the *pasteis* come in an amazing variety of fillings, are quickly deep-fried, and arrive piping hot at your table. The 60 different flavors include brie and apricot, Gorgonzola and sun-dried tomato, prawns and cream cheese, shiitake mushrooms, and more. On Tuesday nights it is two for one.

Rua Dona Mariana 81, Botafogo. ✆ **021/2535-4572.** www.bardoadao.com.br. Reservations not accepted. R$10–R$25. MC, V, Daily noon–midnight. Metrô: Botafogo.

Copacabana/Leme

Very Expensive

Le Pré Catelan ★★★ FRENCH Even after a decade as one of Rio's top celebrity chefs, Roland Villard still manages to offer diners a "wow" every time. His latest project is a 10-course menu of exclusively Amazonian dishes. Guests receive a booklet with pictures and descriptions of all the ingredients and dishes, such as the Tucanaré *brandade* (a purée made with fish, coconut milk, and olive oil), roasted tapioca stuffed with freshwater crustaceans, or Pirarucu fish with a cashew crust served in a mouth-tingling sauce made with the Amazonian jambu fruit. Other dishes include Tambaqui "cutlets" in a red wine *jus* and the outstanding sparerib confit in a sweet-tangy Jabuticaba sauce. Tropical fruit *granités* are served as palate cleansers between courses. Sommelier Jean Pierre pairs these fantastic flavors with some excellent wines. Guests can also order from the a la carte menu, but you would be foolish to miss this amazing Amazon dining experience!

Hotel Sofitel, Av. Atlântica 4240, Copacabana. ✆ **021/2525-1160.** Reservations required. Main courses R$88; Amazon 10-course tasting menu R$230. AE, DC, MC, V. Mon–Wed 7:30–11:30pm; Thurs–Sat 7:30pm–midnight. Bus: 415.

Expensive

Siri Mole ★★ BAHIAN This is one of the best Bahian restaurants in town, despite its uninspired location, on the corner of the busy Rua Francisco Otaviano. The *moquecas* are outstanding, perfectly balancing the mix of coconut milk, red dendê palm oil, and fresh cilantro that give this dish its signature flavor. Try a *moqueca* with prawns, octopus, fish, or langoustine. The grilled seafood dishes are also excellent. Portions are a reasonable size and can often be shared. During Saturday's lunch buffet (noon–5pm) the restaurant serves up a variety of delicacies (R$42 per person, all you can eat). Save room for dessert. There's *quindim,* a creamy coconut pudding, or *cocada,* pure coconut mixed with pure cane sugar—then wash it down with a hot and black *cafezinho. **Tip:*** For the same excellent food in a waterfront location, try the Sire Mole in one of the new kiosks on the Copacabana beachfront, opposite the Rua Bolívar: **Siri Mole Prai** (✆ **021/3684-6671;** www.sirimolepraia.com.br; Tues–Sun 9am–midnight).

Rua Francisco Otaviano 50, Copacabana. ✆ **021/2267-0894.** www.sirimole.com.br. Reservations accepted. Main courses R$60–R$95. AE, DC, MC, V. Mon 7pm–midnight; Tues–Sun noon–midnight. Bus: 415.

Moderate

Arab ★ MIDDLE EASTERN Arab has a terrific waterfront patio (on Copa beach) and delicious Middle Eastern cuisine. For lunch the kitchen puts on an excellent kilo buffet (R$42/kilo), great for trying a variety of dishes. Offerings include tasty salads with chickpeas, lentils, grilled vegetables, and outstanding main dishes such as the roasted chicken with apricots, couscous with cod, grilled lamb kabobs, and piping hot fresh pita breads. In the evenings, dishes are a la carte. Our favorites include the tray of *mezzes* (appetizer plates). Perfect for sharing, these plates come with enough munchies for three or four people and include hummus, baba ghanouj, savory pastries with ground beef or lamb, and other finger food.

Av. Atlântica 1936, Copacabana. ✆ **021/2235-6698.** www.restaurantearab.com.br. Main courses R$25–R$42. AE, DC, MC, V. Mon 5pm–1am; Tues–Sun 8am–1am. Metrô: Cardeal Arcoverde.

Churrascaria Carretão Kids Value BRAZILIAN/STEAK For a churrascaria meal without breaking the bank, try Carretão. It's an all-you-can-eat *rodízio* system: Meats are delivered to your table by a constant parade of waiters carrying a variety of cuts, and you can help yourself to a large buffet with a selection of 20 salads, sushi, and even grilled salmon or trout. Carretão also serves up a variety of pork, sausage, chicken, and turkey cuts. Children 4 and under eat free, while those ages 5 to 9 pay only half price. Just keep them away from the fruit smoothies and desserts so eagerly pushed by the waiters; these aren't included in the price, and jack up the bill pretty quickly.

Rua Visconde de Pirajá 112, Ipanema. ✆ **021/2267-3965.** Reservations accepted. R$35 all-you-can-eat; drinks and desserts extra. AE, DC, MC, V. Daily 11am–midnight. Bus: 404 or 474 (corner Teixeira de Melo). Also in Copacabana: Rua Ronald de Carvalho 55 (✆ **021/2543-2666**) and Rua Siqueira Campos 23 (✆ **021/2236-3435**).

Inexpensive

Cafeína CAFE/BREAKFAST There's excellent coffee and cappuccino here, homemade specialty breads, and a good selection of sandwiches, but what really draws folks in

Finds Where to Find the Finest Feijoada

For the best *feijoada* (black-bean stew) in town, try one of the following restaurants (on a Sat, of course—lunch only). **Confeitaria Colombo** serves an outstanding *feijoada* in the loveliest dining room in town, Rua Gonçalves Dias 32, Centro (✆ **021/2221-0107;** www.confeitariacolombo.com.br). **Galani,** on the 23rd floor of the plush Caesar Park Hotel, Av. Vieira Souto 460, Ipanema (✆ **021/2525-2525;** www.caesarpark-rio.com), is famous for its Saturday buffet. Even fancier is the spread at the Sheraton's **Mirador,** Avenida Niemeyer, São Conrado (✆ **021/2274-1122;** www.sheraton-rio.com). After lunch you'll welcome the 30-minute walk back to Leblon. The only restaurant specializing in *feijoada* every day of the week is the **Casa da Feijoada,** Rua Prudente de Moraes 10, Ipanema (✆ **021/2523-4994;** www.cozinhatipica.com.br). The full meal deal with all the trimmings, including a cup of bean soup to start with and a *batida de limão* (lime cocktail) to line your stomach, as the Brazilians would say, sets you back R$55.

is the breakfast menu: there are waffles with honey, whipped cream, or Nutella; delicious eggs and omelettes; or the classic breakfast for two—fresh OJ, a basket of breads with jam and honey and cheese, cold cuts, cakes, papayas, yogurt with granola, and, of course, coffee (R$47 for two).

Rua Barata Ribeiro 507, Copacabana. ✆ **021/2547-4390.** www.cafeina.biz. R$8–R$30. MC, V. Daily 8am–11pm.Metrô: Cardeal Arcoverde. Four other locations in Copacabana, Ipanema, and Leblon.

Ipanema

Very Expensive

Gero ★★ ITALIAN The Rio branch of a highly successful São Paulo restaurant brings the same sophisticated styling to the room and the same meticulous preparation to the meals. Signature dishes include rack of lamb with a black truffle and foie gras sauce, or *osso buco* with mushrooms. Pastas include gnocchi with squid, and a ravioli of veal with a mushroom sauce. The room is open but warm, with a hardwood floor and exposed brick walls. Wines lean to the higher end—avoid the overpriced token Brazilian vintages, and seek out the midpriced Chilean and Argentine vintages.

Rua Anibal de Mendonça 157, Ipanema. ✆ **021/2239-8158.** www.fasano.com.br. R$35–R$65. AE, DC, MC, V. Mon–Fri noon–4pm and 7pm–1am; Sat noon–2am; Sun noon–midnight. Bus: 415.

Expensive

Le Vin Bistro ★★ FRENCH Le Vin offers French bistro cuisine, though perhaps a tad higher end than is normal in Paris. For starters, try the half-dozen oysters, the *mouilles et frites* (mussels and french fries), or the obligatory escargots, served dripping in garlic and adorned with parsley. For a main course, try the lamb in a red-wine reduction, or steak in béarnaise sauce, with baked potatoes. The wine list has an extensive selection by the glass, a good way to mix and match reds and whites to every dish. For dessert, try the traditional profiterole or petit gateau. *Et voila.*

Rua Barão de Torre 490, Ipanema. ✆ **021/3502-1002.** www.levin.com.br. R$35–R$55. AE, DC, MC, V. Mon–Sat noon–midnight; Sun noon–11pm. Bus: 415.

Zazá Bistrô Tropical ★★ BRAZILIAN/FUSION Zazá is Rio's funkiest eatery, serving up a creative menu of South American cuisine fused with Oriental flavors. Everything about Zazá is fun, from the playful and eclectic decorations to the unique and excellent dishes. The menu offers plenty of choices. Appetizers include a deliciously grilled squid salad served on a bed of greens with an orange vinaigrette, or an order of mini-*acarajés* (deep-fried dumplings made of mashed beans and spicy shrimp) served with tomato chutney instead of the usual hot-pepper sauce. Main courses also mix up the flavors. Try the *namorado* fish filet served with a purée of banana and palm heart, or a prawn ravioli served with grilled salmon in a saffron sauce. For vegetarians there is always an intriguing daily special.

Rua Joana Angelica 40, Ipanema. ✆ **021/2247-9101.** www.zazabistro.com.br. R$28–R$45. AE, DC, MC, V. Sun–Thurs 7:30pm–1am; Fri–Sat 7:30pm–1:30am. Bus: 415.

Moderate

Delirio Tropical ★ BRAZILIAN Stop here for a lighter and healthier snack. The menu includes delicious fresh salads such as the caprese (a layered tower of sliced tomatoes, basil, and mozzarella), *salpição* (shredded chicken with carrots and corn), pasta salads, and at least six other salads. You can put together a meal with a selection of salads alone, or you can add some grilled meat, or make a choice from the daily hot dish specials, often stuffed cannelloni or roast beef. The sandwich bar serves made-to-order

Rio's Avenida Gourmet

We could probably fill half the Rio section with reviews of restaurants on the **Rua Dias Ferreira.** This windy street on the far edge of Leblon has become a one-stop shop for gourmands. Trendy vegetarians head straight for **O Celeiro,** at no. 199 (✆ **021/2274-7843**). You pay by the weight so help yourself to the delicious offerings and grab a spot on the large patio. To enjoy a stylish afternoon tea with all the trimmings, head over to **Eliane Carvalho,** no. 242 (✆ **021/2540-5438;** closed Mon). For pasta there's **Quadrucci,** no. 233 (✆ **021/2512-4551**), which is open for lunch and dinner and has a great patio.

For fine dining there are a number of options, mostly only open in the evenings. **Zuka,** no. 233 (✆ **021/3205-7154**) offers creative seafood dishes such as crab in filo pastry or grilled tuna in a cashew-nut crust. Farther down on the corner of Rua Rainha Guilhermina is the sushi hot spot of the city, **Sushi Leblon** (✆ **021/2512-7830**). Thursday through Saturday evenings the lines can be long, but most people don't seem to mind the wait. If you're up on who's who in the Brazilian entertainment world, you can pass the time spotting artists and actresses. If a smaller and intimate sushi venue is more your style, check out **Minimok,** no. 116 (✆ **021/2511-1476**). By the same owners as the **Moke Sakebar,** this very stylish hole in the wall serves up great variety of sushi, sashimi, tempura, and rolls.

sandwiches, with your choice of bread, filling, and salad. The service is cafeteria style; you choose your dishes, load up your tray, and find a seat. Perfect brunch spot!

Rua Garcia d'Avila 48, Ipanema. ✆ **021/3624-8164.** www.delirio.com.br. Main courses R$14–R$32. AE, MC, V. Daily 9am–9pm. Bus: 415.

Leblon

Very Expensive

Bar d'Hotel ★★ Finds CONTEMPORARY BRAZILIAN On the first floor of the Marina Hotel in Ipanema, this hip eatery overlooks the most famous beach in the world, yet doesn't even try to cash in on the view. Artists, actors, soccer players, designers, and others too cool to look at the ocean compete for each other's attention, all the while trying not to look like they're looking. Fortunately, the food is also great—the creations of chef Felipe Bronze—so we mere mortals can remain happily oblivious and just enjoy. Appetizers include mini lamb burgers with foie gras. For mains there's a rich stew of ginger-scented prawns with jasmine rice, or filet mignon with a crust of caramelized macadamia nuts. The restaurant is also a great place to just have a drink; the cocktail list is long and creative.

Av. Delfim Moreira 696, 2nd floor (inside the Marina All Suites Hotel), Leblon. ✆ **021/2540-4990.** Reservations recommended. Main courses R$24–R$48. MC, V. Daily noon–2am. Bus: 415.

Expensive

Giuseppe Grill ★★ STEAK With outstanding steak, an affordably priced wine list, and excellent and attentive service, what's not to recommend? The house specialty is beef. You can choose from grilled beef or slowly roasted beef on a charcoal grill. Both options include numerous cuts—prime rib, Argentine chorizo steak, filet mignon, and rump steak as well as beef ribs, pork, and chicken. Each main course comes with a side dish; you can choose from salads, rice, and potatoes served fried, roasted, baked, or sautéed. In addition, the restaurant also serves up outstanding fresh seafood.

Av. Bartolomeu Mitre 370, Leblon. ✆ **021/2249-3055.** www.bestfork.com.br. Main courses R$36–R$65. AE, DC, MC, V. Mon–Thurs noon–4pm and 7pm–midnight; Fri–Sat noon–1am; Sun noon–11pm. Bus: 415.

Moke Sakebar ★★★ JAPANESE To do this restaurant justice would require three reviews. First there is the sushi bar, run by talented chef Takashi Kawamura. Try the tuna marinated in green-apple wasabi, or the dragon roll with eel and shiitake mushrooms. Then there is the sake bar with an amazing selection of sake, including gold-flecked, bubbly, lime-flavored, or 30-year-old vintage sakes. No idea what to order? Try the sake sampler (three small shot glasses). As *pièce de résistance,* there is the restaurant itself, and the main courses created by French chef Pierre Landry, such as tender grilled duck breast or spicy seared tuna with avocado tempura. The perfect three-part harmony.

Rua Dias Ferreira 78, Leblon. ✆ **021/2512-6526.** www.moksushi.com.br. Main courses R$42–R$70. AE, V. Mon 7pm–1am; Tues–Thurs noon–3:30pm and 7pm–1am; Sat noon–1:30am; Sun 1–11pm. Bus: 415.

Sawasdee ★★ THAI Normally it's Rio restaurants that branch out, but in this case Búzios's best Thai restaurant made the trek in to the big city to set up shop in Leblon. The menu includes the tried and tested bestsellers, focusing on fresh, top-quality ingredients. Start off with the spicy chicken satay with peanut sauce, or salmon fishcakes with a tangy dipping sauce. For main courses, we highly recommend bringing friends, ordering a variety of dishes, and sharing. Try at least one of the salads, like the mango salad with shrimp, a noodle dish (the pad Thai is outstanding), and perhaps a traditional green or red curry. The kitchen also serves a large variety of vegetarian dishes and prepares several child-friendly versions of Thai classics.

Rua Dias Ferreira 771, Leblon. ✆ **021/2511-0057.** www.sawasdee.com.br. R$45–R$68. AE, MC, V. Tues–Thurs noon–midnight; Fri–Sat noon–1am; Sun noon–11pm. Bus: 415.

Inexpensive

KURT ★ Value DESSERT Even though German pastry maker Kurt passed away a few years ago, his legacy (and treats) live on in the hands of Kurt's grandsons. This tiny shop in Leblon remains one of the best places in town to go for an *apfel strude,* pecan pie, or apricot cake. A famous Kurt creation is the "bee sting" *(picada de abelha),* a chocolate cake, the recipe of which is a closely guarded family secret.

Rua General Urquiza 117 (corner of Rua Ataulfo de Paiva), Leblon. ✆ **021/2294-0599.** www.confeitariakurt.com.br. Everything under R$15. No credit cards. Mon–Fri 8am–7pm; Sat 8am–5pm. Bus: 415.

Mil Frutas ★ DESSERT One of the best ice-cream parlors in town, Mil Frutas offers a whole gamut of chocolate and fruit flavors, including some exotic ones from northern Brazil such as *açai, cupuaçu,* and *caja.* The staff is happy to give you a taste of several flavors before you decide on one, or two, or three.

Rua Garcia d'Avila 134, Ipanema. ✆ **021/2521-1584.** www.milfrutas.com.br. Everything under R$12. No credit cards. Daily 10:30am–1am. Bus: 415.

JARDIM BOTANICO/LAGOA

Very Expensive

Olympe ★★★ FRENCH You can tell from the Web address that chef Claude Troisgros doesn't exactly lack for ego, but then his restaurant and his recipes do regularly win awards for the best French cooking in the city and the country. His recipes combine a

French approach with ingredients drawn from Brazil. Thus, for appetizers there's Burgundy escargots with oven-roasted palm hearts. Mains include roast quail stuffed with *farofa* mixed with raisins and served with a sweet-and-sour *jabuticaba* sauce. Other chefs have tried this approach, of course; Troisgros just does it better. There are also more traditional French dishes: oven-roasted rabbit in red wine–and-chocolate sauce, coquilles St. Jacques with a caviar tapioca. The wine list is high end (nothing much under R$100) and drawn largely from France.

Rua Custódio Serrão 62, Jardim Botânico. © **021/2539-4542.** www.claudetroisgros.com.br. Reservations recommended. Main courses R$55–R$95. MC, V. Mon–Thurs 7:30pm–12:30am; Fri noon–4pm and 7:30pm–12:30am. Bus: 572 (from Leblon or Copacabana) or 170 (from downtown).

Expensive

Capricciosa ★ PIZZA One of Rio's trendiest pizza restaurants, Capricciosa features beautiful people at the tables and a wood-burning oven at the back. This turns out great-tasting pizzas and calzones, including the signature Capricciosa, with tomato, ham, artichoke, mushrooms, bacon, and egg. There's also a delicious cold cut and antipasto buffet, served with slices of homemade crusty bread, and a selection of pasta dishes. Those who prefer a more low-key and intimate setting can opt for the wine bar, to the left of the busy and bustling main dining room; the menus are the same. Note that a cheap meal this ain't . . . these prices would buy you a juicy steak elsewhere, but that is the price you pay to hobnob with the hip.

Rua Maria Angelica 37, Jardim Botânico. © **021/2527-2656.** www.capricciosa.com.br. Main courses R$28–R$42. AE, DC, MC, V. Daily 6pm–1am (later if it's busy). Bus: 572 (from Leblon or Copacabana) or 170 (from downtown).

Lorenzo Bistrô ★ FRENCH/ITALIAN Cute little bistros are hard to find in Rio and this is a real gem, tucked away in a Jardim Botânico side street. Grab a table on the pleasant sidewalk patio or find a spot in the cozy upstairs dining room. The menu offers satisfying French and Italian comfort food. No fussy, precious haute cuisine, but a decent steak *au poivre* or a traditional steak with *pommes frites* (make sure your fellow diners get a portion or they will steal yours!). Other dishes include *boeuf bourguignon,* a hearty *coq au vin,* or more Italian-inspired options such as risottos, fish, and pasta. Red wine drinkers will be pleased to find a number of good (and affordable) South American reds and whites.

Rua Visconde de Carandai 2, Jardim Botanico. © **021/2294-7830.** Main courses R$38–R$52. AE, MC, V. Mon–Thurs noon–11:30pm; Fri–Sat noon–12:30am; Sun 1–7:30pm. Bus:

RIO AFTER DARK

Rio has a lot to keep you busy at night. If you're in Rio between September and Carnaval, attending one of the **samba school rehearsals** (p. 261) on Saturday night is a must. Otherwise, on a Thursday night see who's playing at some of the hip samba spots in Lapa like the **Rio Scenarium, Carioca da Gema,** or the **Centro Cultural Carioca.** Or just enjoy the scene by the Arcos de Lapa on a Friday night. Of course, there are a number of discos and bars to choose from, and then there are always the botequins, Rio's neighborhood bars. For listings for arts and entertainment, pick up the Friday editions of the *O Globo* (www.oglobo.com.br), *O Dia* (www.odia.com.br), or *Jornal do Brasil* (http://jbonline.terra.com.br) newspapers. Under "Música" or "Show" you will find the listings for live music. Lovers of Brazilian music should look for anything under "Forró," "MPB" *(música popular brasileira)*, "Bossa Nova," "Choro," "Pagode," or "Samba." Listings under *Pista* refer to events at nightclubs or discos. The days of the week are given in abbreviations: *seg* or *2a* (Mon), *ter* or *3a* (Tues), *qua* or *4a* (Wed), *qui* or *5a* (Thurs), *sex* or *6a* (Fri), *sab* (Sat), and *dom* (Sun).

The Performing Arts

The performing-arts season in Brazil runs from early April until early December. The **Teatro Municipal,** Praça Marechal Floriano s/n, Centro (✆ **021/2332-9195;** www.theatromunicipal.rj.gov.br), is Brazil's prime venue for the performing arts. The elegant Parisian-style theater stages everything from opera to ballet to symphony concerts. The **Sala Cecelia Meireles,** Largo da Lapa 47, Centro (✆ **021/2224-3913;** www.salaceciliameireles.com.br), is a very popular venue for classical music, but there's also often more modern Brazilian rhythms such as bossa nova, jazz, and *choro.*

Live Music

If you're a fan of samba, check out the website **www.samba-choro.com.br** for weekly listings of all the clubs in Rio.

Carioca da Gema, Rua Mem de Sá 79, Lapa (✆ **021/2221-0043**), is one of the best little venues in town, offering excellent samba. Even on weeknights Carioca da Gema is often hopping. Another great live-music venue is the beautifully restored **Centro Cultural Carioca**★★, Rua do Teatro, Centro (✆ **021/2252-6468**). This cozy and intimate venue hosts local musicians and big names who specialize in samba, MPB, *choro,* and *gafieira.* Recently renovated, the small **Teatro Rival,** Rua Alvaro Alvim 33, Centro (✆ **021/2240-4469**), often hosts big names in Brazilian music. Ticket prices are quite reasonable. Just across the street from the Rio Sul Mall, the **Canecão,** Av. Venceslau Brás 215, Botafogo (✆ **021/2543-1241**), is the place to catch big Brazilian and international acts. **Estrela da Lapa,** Rua Mem de Sá 69 (✆ **021/2507-6686**), is proof that Lapa's appeal extends beyond the young and bohemian. This elegant star in the neighborhood caters to the moneyed 35-and-older Zona Sul crowd. Music varies from jazz to salsa, samba, swing, and even instrumental.

Dance Clubs

One of the most happening dance clubs in Rio, **Baronneti,** Rua Barão da Torre 354, Ipanema (✆ **021/2247-9100**), attracts a well-to-do and attractive crowd in their 20s to 40s. This upscale club offers two floors of fabulous dance music to dance the night away, plenty of couches, and a chill-out space. **Fosfobox,** Rua Siqueira Campos 143, 22A (in the basement), Copacabana (✆ **021/2548-7498**), is Copacabana's trendy *club du jour,* or rather *de nuit.* Nationally and internationally famous DJs spin rock, house, or techno. It's open Wednesday through Sunday. A lovely, upscale club in Lagoa, **Nuth,** Av. Epitacio Pessoa 1244, Lagoa (✆ **021/3575-6850**), has a small restaurant and dance floor featuring lounge music early on and dance beats as the night goes on.

Bars & Pubs

BOTEQUINS Tucked away in an alley just off Praça XV, the **Arco do Teles,** Travessa do Comércio, Arco do Teles (from the Praça XV, facing toward the bay, you will see the arch that marks the entrance to the alley on your left) looks like a movie set of old Rio. Perfectly preserved colonial two-stories are set on narrow cobblestone streets lined with restaurants and cafes. Prime time is after-work hours, especially on Thursday and Friday when office workers flock here to grab a few cold chopps and catch some music before heading home. An old-fashioned botequim with bright lights, dark-wood furniture, and tile floors, the **Belmonte,** Praia do Flamengo 300, Flamengo (✆ **021/2552-3349**), serves up great beer, sandwiches, and snacks. It's now a local chain with brand-new old-fashioned Belmonte's in Lagoa, Ipanema, and Copacabana, but the Flamengo Belmonte remains the best. **Jobi,** Av. Ataulfo de Paiva 1166, Leblon (✆ **021/2274-0547**), is busy any day of the week, but on Friday and Saturday a line is guaranteed. This botequim offers excellent beer, tasty snacks, and a great atmosphere. On top of that, Jobi stays open until 4:30am.

OTHER BARS & PUBS Fans of Brazilian *cachaça* will have a field day at the Academia da Cachaça, Rua Conde de Bernadotte 26, loja G, Leblon (✆ **021/2529-2680**). The variety of Brazil's traditional white-cane liquor on offer at the Academia is quite overwhelming, so don't be embarrassed to ask the bartenders for suggestions. Rio's most romantic patio bar, **Bar dos Descasados** ★★★, Rua Almirante Alexandrino 660, Santa Teresa (✆ **021/2222-2755**), sits tucked away inside the restored Hotel Santa Teresa. Order a caipirinha and enjoy the fabulous views of Santa Teresa and downtown. ***Tip:*** This is a prime sunset spot. **Venga,** Dias Ferreira 113, Leblon (✆ **021/2512-9826**), was Rio's first tapas bar and serves classic Spanish snacks and drinks. The bustling bar has a casual atmosphere, popular with Rio's 30-plus crowd.

Gay & Lesbian Nightlife

Rio's gay community is smaller than one would expect from a city of 10 million people. As lasciviously as heterosexual couples may behave in public, open displays of affection between same-sex couples are still not accepted in Brazil.

Currently, the most popular nightspot is in Ipanema around the Galeria Café on the Rua Teixeira de Melo. During the day the stretch of sand close to Posto 8 (opposite the Rua Farme de Amoedo) is also popular. Copacabana has a number of gay clubs and bars as well as a popular meeting place on the beach at Rainbow's, in front of the Copacabana Palace Hotel. A good resource to pick up is the latest edition of the *Gay Guide Brazil,* a small booklet available at some of the clubs and bookstores in Ipanema, or check http://riogayguide.com. The Brazilian term for gay-friendly is GLS, which stands for gay, lesbian, and sympathizers. Often you will see this abbreviation used in listings or restaurant and bar reviews.

After a day at the beach, go to **Bar Bofetada,** Rua Farme de Amoeda 87 (✆ **021/2227-6992**). Located just a few blocks from Ipanema's prime gay beach, this botequim is perfect for a beer, snack, and flirt with local guys.

Set in a small gallery stunningly decorated with a changing display of work by local artists, the **Galeria Café,** Rua Teixeira de Melo 31E, Ipanema (✆ **021/2523-8250;** www.galeriacafe.com.br), packs a gorgeous collection of men, shoulder to shoulder, bicep to bicep, into its combo art space, dance club, and bar. Those that can't fit—and there are many—just hang out in front. The Galeria really gets hopping, inside and out, after 1am. The cover charge is R$10 to R$25, open from Wednesday through Sunday.

Le Boy, Rua Raul Pompeia 102, Copacabana (✆ **021/2513-4993;** www.leboy.com.br), is glamorous, funky, and extremely spacious with a soaring four-story ceiling hovering somewhere above the dance floor. A range of special events attracts national and international celebrities and assorted (beautiful) hangers-on. Go after midnight, when things really start to hop. **La Girl** next door, Rua Raul Pompeia 102 (✆ **021/2247-8342;** www.lagirl.com.br), is Rio's first truly upscale nightclub for gay women with excellent DJs and go-go girl shows. La Girl is open Wednesday to Monday (men allowed Sun–Mon only).

The Week, Rua Sacadura Cabral 154, Saude (✆ **021/2253-1020;** www.theweek.com.br), is the new hottest gay dance club in town. This huge mega–dance club can hold 2,000 people and is packed every Saturday night. Famous national and international guest DJs and go-go boys keep the crowd going. The Week is open Saturdays at midnight, and often for events on Fridays and Wednesdays; check listings. In Centro, **Cine Ideal** (✆ **021/2221-1984;** www.cineideal.com.br), is a gay-friendly outpost of house, open every Friday and Saturday 11am to 6am. Cover is R$40.

SIDE TRIPS FROM RIO DE JANEIRO

On weekends and holidays, many Cariocas head to the beach resorts dotting the warm Atlantic coast. First and most famous of these is the town of **Búzios,** set on the tip of a long, beach-rich peninsula jutting out into the clear blue Atlantic.

Want some history served up with a splash of ocean? The perfect blend can be found in the former colonial port of **Paraty.** Explore the islands and beaches in the daytime and at night wander the cobblestone streets of this UNESCO World Heritage Site.

Búzios

Búzios is Rio's premier beach resort and a favorite haunt of Brazilian socialites and celebrities. The sheer number of beaches close to town makes it easy to experience Brazilian beach culture firsthand. Visitors can enjoy boat tours, diving, sailing, windsurfing, fine cuisine, and endless opportunities to shop. And at night, everyone comes to the busy bar- and cafe-lined **Rua das Pedras** to stroll, drink, and party.

Essentials

GETTING THERE **Malizia Tours** in Búzios (✆ **022/2623-1226** or 2623-2022; www.maliziatour.com.br) offers transfers to/from Rio by van and taxi. Cost in a 15-person air-conditioned minibus is R$50 per person one-way. Pickup can be at your hotel or from the airport. Bus company **Auto Viação 1001** (✆ **021/4004-5001;** www.autoviacao1001.com.br) has departures seven times a day from Rio's main bus station, **Novo Rio Rodoviaria,** Av. Francisco Bicalho 1, Santo Cristo (✆ **021/3849-5001**). Cost of the 3-hour trip is R$28. In Búzios, buses arrive (and depart) at the Búzios Bus Station on Estrada da Usina, at the corner of Rua Manoel de Carvalho (✆ **022/2623-2050**), a 10-minute walk from the center of town.

VISITOR INFORMATION The **Búzios Tourism Secretariat** operates an information kiosk on the downtown Praça Santos Dumont 111 (✆ **022/2633-6200;** daily 8am–10pm). Two good websites on Búzios are **www.buziosonline.com.br** and **www.buziosturismo.com**.

What to See & Do in Búzios

The charm of Búzios lies largely in its beaches, the 20 stretches of sand large and small within a few kilometers of the old town. Thanks to the irregular topography of this rugged little peninsula, each beach is set off from the other and has developed its own beach personality. Farthest from the old town is **Manguinhos** beach. Sheltered from the heavy surf, this gentle beach is where many learn to sail and windsurf. A short hop over the neck of the peninsula lies **Geribá** beach, a wonderful long stretch of sand facing out toward the open ocean. This is the beach for surfing, boogie boarding, and windsurfing. Closer to town is **Ferradura** or **Horseshoe** beach. On the calm inland side of the peninsula, **João Fernandes** and the pocket-size **João Fernandinho** beaches are busy, happening places lined with beachside cafes and full of people intent on getting and showing off their tans.

Outdoor Activities & Watersports

Most everything in the way of watersports equipment can be rented in Búzios, generally right on the beach. On **Ferradura** beach, **Happy Surf** (✆ **022/2623-3389**) rents **sailboards, lasers, Hobie Cats,** and **kayaks.** Happy Surf also gives courses. A 6-hour beginner's **sailboard** course costs R$150. More advanced students can choose from 1- and 2-hour courses costing from R$35 to R$60. Lasers rent for R$35 per half-hour, R$45 with instructor. Hobie Cats rent for R$25 per half-hour, R$40 with instructor. Kayaks rent for R$5 per half-hour.

On **Manguinhos** beach, **Búzios Vela Club,** Rua Maurício Dutra 303 (✆ **022/2623-0508**), rents windsurf equipment. A full day rental ranges from R$150 to R$210. Manguinhos is also a popular **kite-surfing** location. Intensive weekend courses are available for R$600, including gear and 6 hours of instruction. To book a lesson, call **Búzios Kite Surfing School** (✆ **022/2633-0396;** www.kitenews.com.br).

Schooner trips are a great way to spend a day in Búzios. A small fleet of converted fishing schooners makes a circuit of about eight of Búzios' beaches plus three offshore islands. One company is **Malizia Tour** (✆ **022/2623-1226**), but there's really no need to seek them out. Just walk along Rua das Pedras anywhere near the pier, and you're guaranteed to be approached by a schooner tout. The exact price depends on the time of year and how hard you negotiate, but competition between various schooner operators keeps things fairly competitive. Expect to pay from R$25 to R$45 for a half-day's cruise.

The islands just off Búzios are—along with Angra dos Reis and Arraial do Cabo—some of the best diving spots within a 1-day drive of Rio. Water temperature is normally around 72°F (22°C). Visibility ranges from 10 to 15m (30–50 ft.). Coral formations are fairly basic—mostly soft coral—but there are always lots of parrotfish, and there are often sea turtles (green and hawksbill) and stingrays of considerable size. **Casa Mar,** Rua das Pedras 242 (✆ **022/9817-6234;** www.casamar.com.br), offers a full range of services, including cylinder refill and courses all the way from basic to nitrox. For a certified diver, a two-dive excursion costs R$150, including all your gear. Nondivers who come on the boat pay R$80.

The **Búzios Golf Club & Resort** (✆ **022/2629-1240;** www.buziosgolf.com.br) is located just in from Manguinhos beach. Greens fees for this 18-hole course are R$165 per day for unlimited golf. Cart rental is R$100 for 18 holes and R$50 for 9 holes.

Where to Stay in Búzios

Búzios is known for its pousadas, similar to North American B&Bs. For more affordable rates, avoid high season (Dec–Mar and July) and weekends. However, except to pay more at a pousada in Búzios than you would anywhere else in Brazil.

Tucked away on Orla Bardot, **Pousada Casas Brancas**★★, Rua Alto do Humaitá 10 (✆ **022/2623-1458**), sits on a hill overlooking the ocean, yet is only a 5-minute walk from the nightlife and restaurants of the busy Rua das Pedras. This sprawling Greek villa–like hotel offers spacious, comfortable rooms decorated in a clean, modern style. Service is attentive and competent and the well-equipped spa offers a wide range of professional beauty treatments. High-season rates are R$550 to R$750 for a double; low season is R$420 to R$680. No children 4 and under are allowed.

At the beginning of João Fernandes Beach, **La Boheme**★, Praia de João Fernandes (✆ **022/2623-1744;** www.labohemehotel.com), offers spacious apartments, perfect for groups or families traveling with children. A few are split-level suites and sleep up to seven people. The pool area includes a great children's pool, and the beach, about 90m (300 ft.) below the hotel, is safe enough even for the little ones. The going rate is R$420 for a one-bedroom apartment that sleeps up to four people, and R$680 for an apartment that sleeps up to seven people.

The Búzios Internacional Apart Hotel, Estrada da Usina Velha 99 (✆ **022/2537-3876;** www.buziosbeach.com.br), is one of the few relatively inexpensive options in town. Just a few blocks from Rua das Pedras, the units are self-contained flats equipped with a living room with foldout couch, kitchen, and either one or two bedrooms. High-season (mid-Dec to Mar) double rates are R$260 to R$300, with prices dropping to R$160 to R$200 in low season.

Where to Dine in Búzios

One of the better kilo restaurants, **Buzin**, Rua Manoel Turibe de Farias 273 (✆ **022/2633-7051**), offers a large buffet of excellent salads, antipasto, and vegetables. The grill serves up a variety of cuts of steak, grilled to your preference. Of course, being right by the sea the restaurant also includes a daily selection of fresh seafood and fish in its offerings.

Estancia Don Juan, Rua das Pedras 178 (✆ **022/2623-2169**), specializes in tender Argentine steak. Side dishes such as broccoli, baked potatoes, or carrots must be ordered separately. You can eat your meat on a lovely flowered patio, or in a multilevel hacienda dripping with atmosphere. On Tuesday evenings at 9pm, there's a live tango show.

Chef Marcos Soudré and his wife Sandra have made **Sawasdee ★★★**, Av. José Bento Ribeiro Dantas 500 (Orla Bardot) (✆ **022/2623-4644**), into one of Brazil's finest Thai restaurants. Be adventurous and try the grilled fish with shiitake risotto and passion fruit curry, or grilled duck breast in tamarind sauce. The bar serves up creative concoctions like the Koh Thao (vodka, lychee, and orange juice) or the Mai Tai (a vodka cocktail with mint, ginger, and lemon grass).

Búzios After Dark

If you're looking for a night out, **Rua das Pedras** is the place to crawl. This 1,200m-long (4,000-ft.) street has pubs, bars, discos, and restaurants open on weekends until 5am. To simply sit, sip a drink, and check out the action, the place to be is the **Anexo Bar and Lounge,** overlooking the happening waterfront. If you prefer your entertainment live, there's **Patio Havana,** which features a nightly selection of jazz, blues, and MPB. Thursdays is salsa night. To dance until you drop, Búzios boasts two meganightclubs on the Orla Bardot, **Privilege** and **Pacha** (one of Ibiza's hottest clubs). These only operate on Saturdays, with additional nights in high season. But remember, don't bother showing up until 1 or 2am.

Paraty

Paraty has a gorgeous colonial center, surrounded by turquoise blue waters and flanked by the soaring rainforest-covered mountains of Rio de Janeiro's Costa Verde. Paraty first grew in importance in the 1800s when it became the main shipping port for the gold from the inland mines of Minas Gerais. Once gold became scarce, Paraty switched to coffee, but with the abolishment of slavery in 1888, that too dried up and Paraty faded to near oblivion; the population fell from 16,000 in its glory days to 600 in the early 1900s. From a heritage perspective it was the city's saving grace.

In 1966 the historic colonial center of Paraty was declared a UNESCO World Heritage Site and cars were banished from the old colonial core. The region surrounding the city adds much to Paraty's quiet beauty. The hills are still mostly covered in lush green coastal rainforest, and the waters around Paraty, dotted with 65 islands, are tropical turquoise, warm, and crystal clear.

Essentials

GETTING THERE From Rio de Janeiro, **Costa Verde** (✆ **024/3371-1326;** www.costaverdetransportes.com.br) has eight departures per day from Rio's main bus station (Novo Rio). Cost is R$49. The trip takes approximately 4 hours. From São Paulo, **Reunidas Paulista** (✆ **0300/210-3000;** www.reunidaspaulista.com.br) has six departures per day from the Tietê station. The trip takes about 6 hours and costs R$44.

Paraty Tours (✆ **024/3371-2651;** www.paratytours.com.br) offers private transfers from Rio de Janeiro with set times for a minimum of two people at 8:30am, 12:30pm, and 5pm; airport pickups are available anytime between 8:30am and 5pm. Rates per person R$145. For three people or more you can set your own pickup time.

VISITOR INFORMATION The official **Paraty Tourist Information,** Av. Roberto Silveira 1 on the corner of Rua Domingos Gonçalves de Abreu (✆ **024/3371-1897;** www.paraty.com.br), is open daily 9am to 9pm. **Paraty Tours** operates an information kiosk at Av. Roberto da Silveira 11 (✆ **024/3371-2651;** www.paratytours.com.br). They provide general tourist information as well as suggestions on hotels, tours, and excursions.

What to See & Do in Paraty

Start your exploration of Paraty at the main pier at the bottom of **Rua da Lapa.** Fishing boats come and go, as well as frequent schooner excursions. Turn and face the city and you will see the postcard-perfect vista of Paraty: the **Santa Rita** church framed by a background of lush green hills. The church was built by freed slaves in 1722, and despite its plain exterior displays some fine rococo artwork. The building just to the left of the church was once the town jail; now it's home to the city library and historical institute. Paraty's biggest and most ornate church, the **Igreja da Matriz,** stands on the Praça da Matriz, close to the River Perequê-Açu. What started with a small chapel in 1646 became a bigger church in 1712 and was finally replaced with the current large neoclassical building, completed in 1873. The **Casa da Cultura** (Rua Dona Geralda) was originally built in 1754 as a private residence and warehouse. Later it housed the town's public school. In the 1990s, the city restored it to serve as a cultural center and exhibit space.

Outdoor Activities

BIKING A mountain bike is the perfect way to reach some of the waterfalls in the surrounding hills or some of the beaches just a 10km (6½-mile) ride out of town. **Paraty Tours,** Av. Roberto da Silveira 11 (✆ **024/3371-1327**), rents bikes by the hour for R$10 or by the day for R$40. Maps are provided.

BOATING Just beyond the muddy Paraty waterfront, the coast is dotted with more than 60 islands, many lush and green, surrounded by turquoise water. Boats leave daily, weather permitting, and take you on a 5- to 6-hour tour, stopping several times for a swim or snorkel and a lunch break. **Paraty Tours** (see above) and **Saveiro Porto Seguro** (✆ **024/3371-1254**) are just two of several companies that have daily departures at 11am (in high season also at 10am and noon); the cost is R$35 for adults, R$15 for 5- to 10-year-olds.

DIVING The islands around Paraty have some decent diving. Dive companies in town include **Adrenalina,** Marina Farol de Paraty (✆ **024/3371-2991;** www.adrenalinamergulho.com.br), and **Una Tour e Dive,** Rua da Lapa 213 (✆ **024/3371-6188;** www.unatouredive.com.br). For a certified diver, a two-dive excursion costs approx. R$190, including full equipment rental.

HIKING **Paraty Tours** (see "Biking" above) offers a number of hikes, ranging from an easy 3-hour trek along the historic gold route (R$25 per person) to full-day hikes to the isolated beaches at Trinidade and Praia do Sono (R$35–R$45 per person).

Where to Stay in Paraty

Paraty's historic center is jampacked with charming bed-and-breakfasts in beautiful heritage buildings. **Pousada Arte Urquijo** ★★★, Rua Dona Geralda 79 (✆ **024/3371-1362**; www.urquijo.com.br), is a true labor of love by the owner, artist Luz Urquijo. Each of her six rooms is unique. Our favorite is the Sofia, which looks out over the rooftops toward the ocean and has a small deck. Probably the most unique room is Xul, decorated with a low Japanese bed, mats, and pillows. High season, expect to pay R$350 to R$390; low-season rates are R$330 to R$370. No children 11 and under are accepted.

A lovely sprawling colonial mansion, **Pousada da Marquesa** ★, Rua Dona Geralda 99 (✆ **024/3371-1263;** www.pousadamarquesa.com.br), offers affordable accommodations. All rooms are simply and nicely furnished and the common rooms have beautiful antiques. A swimming pool and garden offer a perfect refuge on hot summer days. Rates for a double room December to March are R$380, and April to November R$330.

One of the largest pousadas in the city center, **Pousada Porto Imperial,** Rua Tenente Francisco Antonio s/n (✆ **024/3371-2323;** www.portotel.com.br), still feels like a small inn. The decorations blend antique furniture with modern folk art and tropical colors. In contrast, the rooms are very simply decorated with plain wooden furniture and bedding. The inner courtyard hides a lovely garden and swimming pool as well as a sauna. Rates are R$400 for a standard, R$530 for a superior double (off season and weekdays 30% discount).

Where to Dine in Paraty

For your morning shot of caffeine or a sweet snack try **Café Pingado,** Rua Samuel Costa 11 (✆ **024/3371-8333**), which has great espressos and cappuccinos, and a good selection of sweet and savory snacks—only four tables, though, so order that coffee to go and take it for a stroll.

Beautiful little restaurant **Banana da Terra** ★★, Rua Dr. Samuel Costa 198 (✆ **024/3371-1725**), offers exotic combinations of seafood and tropical ingredients. *Ponta Negra* is a fabulous fish dish served in a coconut sauce with shrimp. Another seafood favorite is the risotto with squid, crab, and prawns spiced with ginger and chutney. Desserts include banana sweets or baked banana.

Restaurante Refúgio, Praça do Porto 1 (✆ **022/3371-2447**), is tucked away from the busy streets and offers a large patio overlooking Paraty's harbor. The specialty here is seafood. As an appetizer, try the *camarão casadinho* (a large deep-fried prawn stuffed with a spicy *farofa* and dried shrimp filling). For a main course, try the fish or seafood *moquecas* (stews with coconut milk and palm oil).

Paraty After Dark

Paraty is not a wild party town (that's Búzios). The crowd's a bit older, the nightlife more laid back. Enjoy some live music, have some drinks, and chat with the other folks who are quite likely visiting as well. One of the more popular live-music venues is the **Café Paraty,** Rua do Comércio 253 (✆ **024/3371-2600**). It bills itself as a restaurant—and the food is pretty decent—but the place really gets hopping later in the evening, after 10pm or so.

Another popular spot in the evenings is **Porto da Pinga,** Rua da Matriz 12 (✆ **024/9907-4370**). This bistro specializes in local *cachaças.* With live music nightly, it's a great spot to go and try some of the regionally produced firewater. Another restaurant doing double duty as a bar is the **Margarida Café,** Praça do Chafariz (✆ **024/3371-2441**). On weekends, there is always live Brazilian music, so it's a perfect spot to enjoy a nightcap after dinner.

5 SÃO PAULO

359km (223 miles) SW of Rio de Janeiro

The largest metropolis in South America—and, with 17 million people spread over 7,770 sq. km (3,000 sq. miles), the third-largest city in the world—São Paulo nevertheless sprang from humble beginnings. In 1554, Jesuit priests founded a mission on a small hill, strategically close to the River Tietê. The mission developed into a small trading post and then, in the 17th and early 18th century, into a jumping-off point for Bandeirante expeditions traveling into the interior. In 1711 the little market town was incorporated as the city of São Paulo. The seeds of its future prosperity showed up just 12 years later with the arrival of the first coffee plants in Brazil.

Prospective visitors often shy away from Brazil's big city, which is a shame. Visitors to São Paulo get all the benefits of a sophisticated, cosmopolitan city—they can eat at the finest restaurants in Brazil, shop at boutiques that even New York doesn't have, browse high-end art galleries, check out top-name Brazilian bands almost any night of the week, and take advantage of one of Brazil's most dynamic nightlife scenes to party until the wee-est of hours. And they can do all this without ever experiencing the big drawback to this city, which is traffic.

Time in São Paulo is a chance to get to know that subspecies of Brazilian known as the Paulista. They're proud of their work ethic and their "un-Brazilian" efficiency. Lacking beaches and mountains, Paulistas have devoted themselves entirely to urban pursuits. They dominate Brazilian politics. They run Brazilian business. Dining out is an almost religious observance. And in São Paulo, the music and nightlife never end.

ESSENTIALS

Getting There

BY PLANE Most international airlines fly through São Paulo. Even those heading for Rio often change planes or stop in São Paulo first. There are two main airports. International flights arrive at **Guarulhos Airport** (✆ **011/2445-2945**), 30km (19 miles) northeast of the city. From Guarulhos Airport to the city, travelers can either take a taxi or a bus. Prepaid taxi fares are available with **Taxi Guarucoop** (✆ **011/2440-7070;** www.guarucoop.com.br); sample fares are Congonhas Airport R$92, São Paulo Centro and Tietê R$75, and Jardins and Avenida Paulista R$85. There are regular metered taxis, which are cheaper when traffic is good. The **Airport Bus Service** (✆ **011/3775-3861**) operates six different shuttle bus routes to Congonhas Airport, to Praça da República, to Avenida Paulista (stopping at major hotels along the street), to Itaim Bibi, to the Rodoviario Tietê (bus station), and the Rodoviario Barra Funda. Cost is R$30, and each route takes about 50 minutes (if traffic is good). Shuttles depart daily every 30 minutes from 6am to 11pm, and then hourly overnight.

Congonhas Airport (✆ **011/5090-9000**), São Paulo's domestic airport, is within the city limits south of Centro. It is used by seven national airlines for their domestic flights. From Congonhas it is a 15- to 25-minute taxi ride to Jardins or Avenida Paulista. A taxi

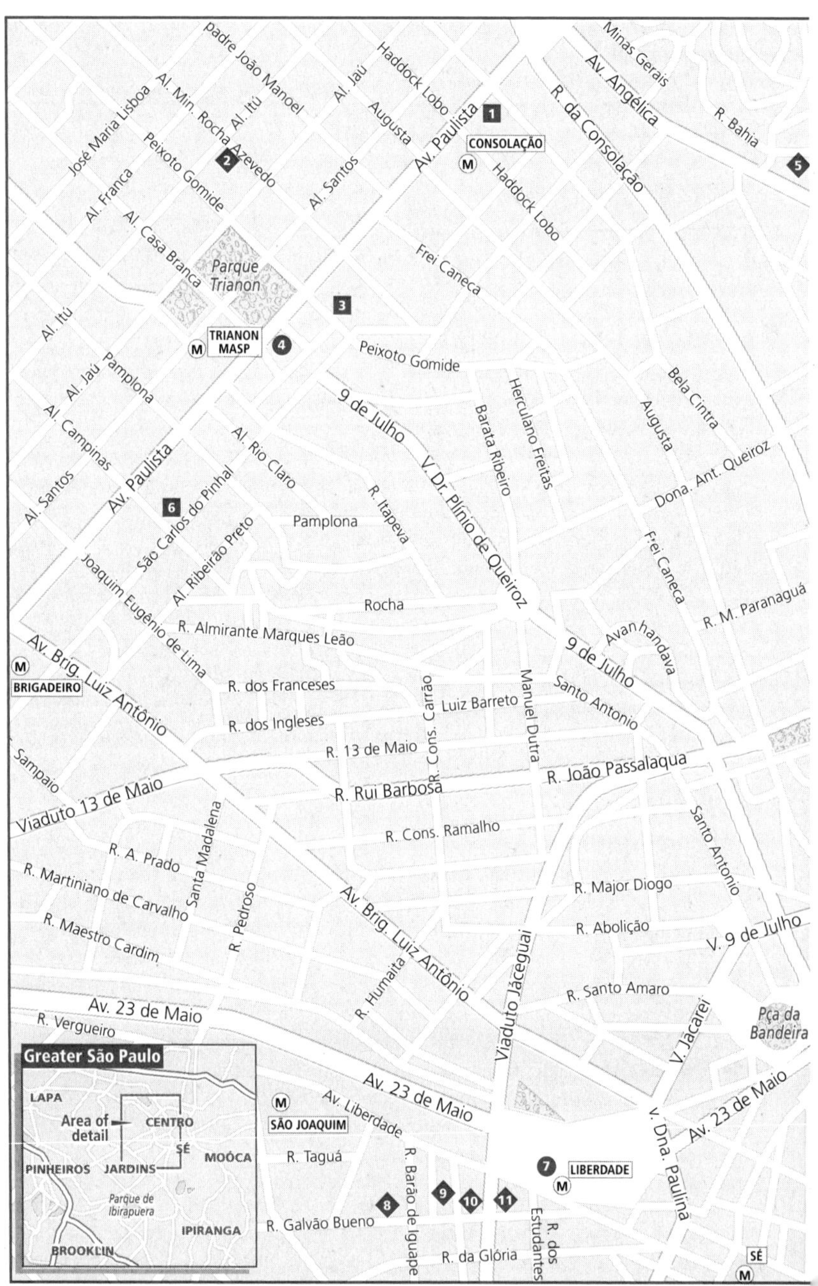
Padre João Manoel
Haddock Lobo
Minas Gerais
Av. Angélica
Al. Jaú
Al. Itú
Al. Min. Rocha Azevedo
José Maria Lisboa
Augusta
Av. Paulista
CONSOLAÇÃO
R. da Consolação
R. Bahia
Peixoto Gomide
Al. Santos
Al. Franca
Al. Casa Branca
Parque Trianon
Frei Caneca
TRIANON MASP
Al. Itú
Pamplona
Al. Jaú
Al. Campinas
9 de Julho
V. Dr. Plínio de Queiroz
Barata Ribeiro
Herculano Freitas
Bela Cintra
Augusta
Dona. Ant. Queiroz
Al. Rio Claro
R. Itapeva
Al. Santos
Av. Paulista
São Carlos do Pinhal
Al. Ribeirão Preto
Joaquim Eugênio de Lima
Frei Caneca
Rocha
R. Almirante Marques Leão
R. M. Paranaguá
Avanhandava
9 de Julho
Santo Antonio
Av. Brig. Luiz Antônio
BRIGADEIRO
R. dos Franceses
R. dos Ingleses
R. Cons. Carrão
Luiz Barreto
Manuel Dutra
R. 13 de Maio
Sampaio
Viaduto 13 de Maio
R. Rui Barbosa
R. João Passalaqua
R. Cons. Ramalho
Santo Antonio
R. A. Prado
Santa Madalena
R. Martiniano de Carvalho
R. Pedroso
Av. Brig. Luiz Antônio
R. Major Diogo
R. Abolição
V. 9 de Julho
R. Maestro Cardim
R. Humaitá
Viaduto Jacegüai
R. Santo Amaro
Av. 23 de Maio
R. Vergueiro
V. Jacareí
Pça da Bandeira
Greater São Paulo
LAPA
Area of detail
CENTRO
SÉ
PINHEIROS
JARDINS
MOÓCA
Parque de Ibirapuera
IPIRANGA
BROOKLIN
SÃO JOAQUIM
Av. Liberdade
Av. 23 de Maio
Av. 23 de Maio
V. Dna. Paulina
R. Taguá
R. Barão de Iguape
LIBERDADE
R. Galvão Bueno
R. dos Estudantes
R. da Glória
SÉ
1
2
3
4
5
6
7
8
9
10
11

BRAZIL 6 SÃO PAULO

ACCOMMODATIONS
Blue Tree Towers Paulista 3
L'Hotel Porto Bay São Paulo 6
Ibis São Paulo Paulista 1
DINING
La Brasserie Erick Jacquin 5
Capim Santo 2
Kaburá 8
Korea House 11
Shanghai 10
Sushi Yassu 9
ATTRACTIONS
Liberdade 7
MASP 4
Museu de Arte Sacra 13
Pinacoteca do Estado 12
0 1/4 mi
0 0.25 km
R. Ceará
R. Bahia
Sergipe
Alagoas
R. Piauí
R. Maranhão
Av. Higienópolis
R.DR. Veiga Filho
Albuquerque Lins
São Vicente de Paulo
Av. Angélica
Aureliano Coutinho
R. Itambé
Martinico Prado
Barão de Tatuí
Martim Francisco
Canuto do Val
Al. Barros
MAL DEODORO
R.Brig. Galvão
R. Dona Veridiana
R. das Palmeiras
Gen. J. M. Salgado
R. Maria Antônia
R. Major Sertório
Vl. Nova
Dr. Cesário Mota Jr.
STA. CECÍLIA
El. Costa e Silva
Eduardo Prado
Al. Ribeiro da Silva
Al. Nothmann
R. da Consolação
Amaral Gurgel
Sta. Isabel
Av. São João
R. Barão de Campinas
Al. Gilete
Pça. Roosevelt
R.Rego Freitas
R. Bento Freitas
Al. Barão de Limeira
R. Guaianazes
Av. Rio Branco
C. Nebias
R. Arouche
Vieira de Carvalho
Av. Duque de Caxias
Pça. Princesa Isabel
Barão Piracicaba
REPÚBLICA
Pça. da República
Av. São Luiz
Av. Ipiranga
R. dos Gusmões
R. Gen Osório
R. Helvetia
Al. Dino Bueno
Cel. Xavier Toledo
R. 7 de Abril
Br. Itapetininga
24 de Maio
R. Aurora
Av. Rio Branco
Al. Cleveland
R. Vitória
R. Sta. Efigênia
Cons. Crispiniano
Av. São João
ANHANGABAÚ
R. dos Andradas
R. José Paulino
Parque Anhangabaú
Pça. do Patriarca
V. Sta. Efigênia
R. Brig. Tobias
Av. Casper Líbero
LUZ
Jardim da Luz
Florêncio de Abreu
Av. Preses Maia
Metro Stop

 ride to Avenida Paulista or Jardins costs R$33 to R$38. The **Rádio Táxi Vermelho e Branco (Red and White Taxi Company; © 011/3146-4000;** www.radiotaxivermelhoebranco.com.br) charges about 15% more—R$38 to R$45—but has slightly larger, slightly nicer cars.

BY BUS São Paulo has three bus terminals *(rodoviaria).* All are connected to the Metrô system. **Barra Funda** (**© 011/3392-2110**), near the Barra Funda Metrô, serves buses to the interior of São Paulo, northern Paraná, Mato Grosso, and Minas Gerais. **Jabaquara** (**© 011/3235-0322**), next to the Jabaquara Metrô, provides transportation to Santos and the south coast. The **Rodoviaria Tietê** (**© 011/3235-0322**), for buses to Rio and connections to Paraguay, Uruguay, and Argentina, is by far the largest and most important bus station, located on the Tietê Metrô stop.

Orientation

The old heart of the city stands around **Praça da Sé,** atop what was once a small hill circled by a pair of small rivers. **Rua Direita,** São Paulo's original main street, leads through this maze to a viaduct crossing over a busy freeway that now occupies the Anhangabaú valley and goes into the "newer" section of the old town. This area, centered on leafy green **Praça República,** contains government buildings plus office buildings from the '20s to the '40s (and later). Back at the edge of the Anhangabaú valley stands the ornate **Teatro Municipal,** a Parisian-style opera house still used for concerts and theater.

Immediately west of Centro is one of São Paulo's original upscale suburbs, **Higienópolis.** Though long since swallowed up in the city, Higienópolis remains a green and leafy enclave with some good restaurants and the city's **Museum of Brazilian Art,** also known as **FAAP.**

Due south of Centro **is Liberdade,** said to have the largest Japanese population of any city outside Japan. The best way to experience the area is to get off at the Liberdade Metrô stop and take a stroll down Rua Galvão Bueno. The street has some great sushi restaurants (plus Chinese and Korean cuisine as an added bonus), knickknack shops, Asian grocery stores, and Japanese faces everywhere.

Set on a ridge, the **Avenida Paulista** has rank upon rank of skyscrapers, the headquarters of the city's banking and financial interests. On the adjacent side streets are numerous hotels catering to business travelers. Halfway along the street is São Paulo's top-notch **Museum of Art,** known by its Portuguese acronym as **MASP.** Avenida Paulista marks the border between the old working-class areas and the new middle-class neighborhoods.

Extending southwest from Avenida Paulista are a series of upscale neighborhoods (**Jardim Paulista, Jardim America, Cerqueira Cesar, Jardim Europa**)—Paulistas tend to refer to them collectively as **Jardins.** What these areas offer is a bit of calm, some terrific restaurants, and the best shopping in São Paulo. The few square blocks where **Rua Augusta** is intersected by **Alameda Lorena** and **Rua Oscar Freire** is the apex of the city's upscale shopping scene, São Paulo's Rodeo Drive.

Rua Augusta continues on straight through the Jardins, changing names as it goes to **Avenida Columbia** and then **Avenida Europa,** and finally **Avenida Cidade Jardim.** At this point it intersects with **Avenida Brigadeiro Faria Lima.** Though a much less fashionable street, Avenida Brig. Faria Lima is home to a number of large shopping malls. Following Avenida Brig. Faria Lima northwest leads to another Jardim-like area called **Pinheiros;** going the opposite direction leads to **Itaim Bibi** and then to a fun and slightly funky area of restaurants, clubs, and cafes called **Vila Olímpia.**

The last key element to São Paulo is a green space—**Ibirapuera Park.** Located immediately south of Jardim Paulista, Ibirapuera is to São Paulo what Central Park is to New York (see below).

Getting Around

ON FOOT Many São Paulo neighborhoods can easily be explored on foot. This is especially true of Centro, Higienópolis, Jardins, Vila Madalena, and Ibirapuera. In the evening avoid the quiet side streets of Centro, particularly around Praça Sé, Bexiga, and around Luz station.

BY SUBWAY This is the easiest and often fastest way to get around. There are three lines useful for tourists: the North-South line, East-West line, and the line that travels underneath the Avenida Paulista. It is usually a lot quicker to take the subway as close as possible to your destination—even if it means a bit of a walk or a short taxi ride—than taking the bus all the way. Tickets cost R$2.55.

BY BUS São Paulo buses are plentiful and frequent, but the city's sprawling layout and lack of landmarks can make the system confusing and hard to navigate. We recommend the subway/cab option. The routing information on the front and sides of the buses works the same as in Rio. Buses cost R$2.55, and you pay as you board through the front of the bus.

BY TAXI Taxis are an absolute must late at night and can be hailed anywhere on the street. To order a taxi at a specific time, call a radio taxi. **Rádio Táxi Vermelho e Branco (Red and White)** can be reached at ✆ **011/3146-4000** (www.radiotaxivermelhoebranco.com.br).

Visitor Information

The city and state tourist information services are next to useless. They are often closed and staff usually doesn't speak English. The state of São Paulo provides a tourist information service, **SELT** (✆ **011/6445-2380**), at Guarulhos airport both Terminal 1 and 2, supposedly open daily from 7am to 9pm (but don't be surprised if there's no one there). The only map/brochure worth looking for is the *Mapa das Artes São Paulo,* a clear and detailed city map showing the city's main attractions, its subway lines, and its art galleries (**www.mapadasartes.com.br**). The map is available, free of charge, at many city hotels and at the government tourist information booths.

FAST FACTS For your currency needs, you can go to **Banco do Brasil,** Av. Paulista 2163 (✆ **011/3066-9322**); Rua São Bento 483, Centro (✆ **011/3491-4008**); and Guarulhos International Airport, daily 6am to 10pm (✆ **011/6445-2223**). Other options are **Bank Boston,** Av. Paulista 800 (✆ **011/3171-0423;** Mon–Fri 11am–3pm), and **Citibank,** Av. Paulista 1111 (✆ **011/4009-2563;** Mon–Fri 11am–3pm).

For dental emergencies contact Portal do Sorriso (www.portaldosorriso.com; Mon–Sat 7am–9pm). The clinic has offices in Pinheiros (✆ **011/2626-0889**) and Morumbi (✆ **011/3772-5941**). For medical emergencies contact **Albert Einstein Hospital,** Av. Albert Einstein 627, Morumbi (✆ **011/2151-1233**), or **Hospital das Clinicas,** Av. Doutor Eneias de Carvalho Aguiar 255 (✆ **011/3069-6000**).

WHAT TO SEE & DO

The Top Attractions

Ibirapuera Park ★★ Blessed with over 2 sq. km (¾ sq. miles) of green space, São Paulo's version of Central Park offers quite a bit to see and do. Every Sunday morning there's a **free outdoor concert** in the park's Praça da Paz. In the corner near Gate 3 there's the **Museum of Modern Art.** Just nearby there's the excellent **Afro-Brazil Museum** and the **OCA Auditorium,** a flying saucer–shaped building that often hosts traveling art exhibits. Allow half a day. Saturday and Sundays are the busiest.

Administration ✆ **011/5574-5177.** www.parquedoibirapuera.com.br. Free admission. Daily 5am–midnight. Bus: 5185-10 (or taxi from Metrô Brigadeiro).

Mercado Municipal ★★ Built in the 1930s, this gorgeous market hall with its skylights and stained-glass windows is a fabulous setting for the city's largest food and produce market. Stand and gawk at fruit stands piled high with exotic tropical offerings, peruse the herbal remedies, or hang out by a deli stand sniffing the salamis and fondling the full round cheeses. Allow an hour, plus time for lunch.

Rua da Cantareira 306, Centro. ✆ **011/3326-3401.** Free admission. Mon–Sat 5am–4pm. Metrô: São Bento.

Museu Arte Brasileira/FAAP ★ This majestic and slightly pompous building (think Mussolini monumental) in quiet Higienópolis plays host to an ever-changing parade of international exhibits. Check the website before you go. If the exhibit interests you, the FAAP is a lovely space. Supposedly, the museum is also home to a number of works by Brazil's great painters—Portinari, Di Cavalcanti, and others—but in repeated visits over the years I've never seen these actually make it to the display floor. Allow 2 hours.

Rua Alagoas 903, Higienópolis. ✆ **011/3662-7200.** www.faap.br/museu. Admission varies from free to R$20 depending on exhibit. Tues–Fri 10am–8pm; Sat–Sun 1–5pm. Bus: 137T. Metrô: Consolação, then take a taxi.

Museu Arte São Paulo (MASP) ★★ São Pãulo's flagship art museum recently reorganized its galleries to give much more space to home-grown talent. The top floor contains the permanent collection, an excellent selection of Western art—Dutch Rembrandts, English Turners, Spanish El Grecos, French everythings (Rodin, Renoir, Degas, and Monet). However, several rooms on this floor are now dedicated to the Brazilian greats, among them Di Cavalcanti and Portinari. Allow 2 hours.

Av. Paulista 1578, Cerqueira César. ✆ **011/3251-5644.** www.masp.art.br. Admission R$15 adults, free for seniors and children 10 and under. Tues–Sun 11am–6pm; Wed 11am–8pm. Metrô: Trianon-MASP.

Museu da Imagen e do Som ★ **Finds** Recently reopened under new direction, the Museum of Image and Sound showcases the best Brazilian contemporary image-makers. Photographs in the changing exhibits are always compelling, beautifully displayed, and intelligently curated. The video lab offers installations and presentations of and about video art. Information on current, future, and past exhibits is available on the website. Allow 1 hour.

Av. Europa 158, Jardim Europa. ✆ **011/2117-4777.** www.mis-sp.gov.br. Admission R$4. Tues–Sat noon–10pm; Sun 11am–9pm. Bus: 373T.

Museu de Arte Sacra ★★ Sacred art refers to objects—chalices, crosses, statues, sculptures—created to adorn churches or for use in Catholic services. Built in 1774, the Mosteiro da Luz (still a working monastery) provides the perfect setting to view the large collection of ornate religious artifacts. Many of the silver objects sparkle in ostentatious testimony to the wealth of the Church. Older pieces include woodcarvings and clay statues of angels and saints. Portuguese and English texts explain the origins and name of each piece.

Av. Tiradentes 676, Luz. ✆ **011/3326-1373.** www.museuartesacra.org.br. Admission R$6 adults, free for seniors and children 5 and under. Wed–Sun 11am–7pm. Metrô: Luz.

Pinacoteca do Estado ★★★ The Pinacoteca is a sunlit joy to be in, and one of the best-curated art collections in the country. Though none of the signs are in English, the Pinacoteca does an excellent job of displaying some of the best Brazilian artists from the 19th and 20th centuries. The 20th-century work starts to break free of European influence and includes interesting examples of colorful Brazilian pieces bursting with energy. The Pinacoteca's sculpture collection includes a lovely statue by Raphael Galvez entitled *O Brasileiro,* as well as works by Alfredo Ceschiatti, the artist who designed many of the sculptures in Brasilia. Allow 2 hours.

Praça da Luz 2, Luz. ✆ **011/3324-1000.** www.pinacoteca.org.br. Admission R$6, free for children 10 and under; free for all Sat. Tues–Sun 10am–6pm. Metrô: Luz.

Shopping

Paulistas brag—correctly—that if you can't buy it in São Paulo, you can't buy it in Brazil. São Paulo has it all, from international boutiques to local crafts markets.

In terms of shopping areas, **Jardins** is known for its high-end fashion boutiques. The main shopping street is the **Rua Oscar Freire** and the parallel **Alameda Lorena,** and their cross streets the **Rua Augusta** and parallel **Rua Haddock Lobo** (this area is chic enough to have its own website—www.ruaoscarfreire.com.br).

In **Centro** (downtown São Paulo), **Rua 25 de Março** is the place where Paulistas rich and poor browse the market stalls and small shops for inexpensive items such as belts, buttons, small toys, gadgets, towels, textiles, and socks. Inexpensive lingerie is a specialty. Keep an eye on your purse in the busy, chaotic streets.

BOOKS/MUSIC The city's megabookstores are also the best place to find a wide variety of Brazilian music. **Livraria Cultura** (www.livrariacultura.com.br) has an extensive collection of CDs in its megastore in the Conjunto Nacional (✆ **11/3170-4033**). The **FNAC** flagship store, Av. Paulista 901 (✆ **11/2123-2000;** www.fnac.com.br), offers a whole floor of Brazilian and international CDs. Finally, in the Patio Paulista mall on the Av. Paulista is the **Saraiva Megastore,** Av. 13 de Maio 1947 (✆ **11/3171-3050;** www.livrariasaraiva.com.br).

FASHIONS The Jardins neighborhood is the place to find excellent Brazilian labels, including **Guaraná Brasil,** Alameda Lorena 1599 (✆ **011/3061-0182**); **Maria Bonita,** Rua Oscar Freire 705 (✆ **011/3063-3609**); and **Forum,** Rua Oscar Freire 916 (✆ **011/3085-6269**). For the latest beach styles check out **Rosa Chá,** Rua Oscar Freire 977 (✆ **011/3081-2793**). Shopping doesn't get any more decadent than at upscale **Daslu,** Av. Chedid Jafet 131, Vila Olímpia (✆ **011/3841-4000;** www.daslu.com.br). Uniformed staff guide you through the maze, while strategically placed espresso bars keep you energized with complimentary hits of caffeine. Daslu offers some of the best-known international designers, such as Prada, Dolce & Gabbana, Dior, Armani, and Gucci, as well as an array of Brazilian names.

MALLS One of the more elegant malls in town, **Shopping Iguatemi,** Av. Brigadeiro Faria Lima 2232, Jardim Paulistano (✆ **011/3816-6116;** www.iguatemisaopaulo.com.br), features high-end international and Brazilian brand names. On the top floor are a movie theater, a food court, and several full-service restaurants. **Shopping Pátio**

Paulista, Av. Paulista 52 (✆ **011/3145-8200**), is a small, pleasant mall featuring clothing, books, a cinema, cafes, and several restaurants. Built in 1999, **Shopping Patio Higienópolis,** Av. Higienópolis 618 (✆ **011/3823-2300**), offers no department stores or large chains; shops are mostly high-end boutiques. There's also a children's play area.

SHOES **Banana Price,** Alameda Lorena 1604 (✆ **011/3081-3460**), sells national and international designers at low prices, including heavily discounted collections from Nine West, Red's, Massimo, and Dilly. **Melissa,** Rua Oscar Freire 867, Jardins (✆ **011/3083-3613),** doesn't display any of its high-end shoe designs in their funky '60s Barbarella-style showroom. Instead, you scroll through the designs on offer on a video terminal, the pretty young clerks then bring you whatever catches your fancy.

WHERE TO STAY

As the financial and business hub of Brazil, São Paulo hotels fill up Monday through Friday with business travelers and then sit empty from Friday afternoon to Monday morning. This means great weekend discounts for tourists.

Avenida Paulista

Very Expensive

L'Hotel Porto Bay São Paulo ★★★ Just off the Avenida Paulista, L'Hotel is one of São Paulo's most elegant boutique hotels, offering luxury and friendly, attentive service. Rooms are luxuriously furnished with antique furniture, a queen- or king-size bed with top-quality linen, goose-down pillows, and a pleasant, well-lit work space. Bathrooms feature bathtubs and l'Occitane amenities. There's a small but well-designed fitness center, spa, small indoor pool, and business center. The prices listed are the high-season rack rates. Call or e-mail for discounts. Weekend packages can often be booked for as low as R$600 for 2 nights.

Alameda Campinas 266, Jardim Paulista, 01404-000 SP. ✆ **0800/130-080** or 011/2183-0500. Fax 011/2183-0505. www.lhotel.com.br. 75 units. R$750 double; R$1,100 suite. Children 12 and under stay free in parent's room. Extra person 25%. AE, DC, MC, V. Valet parking. Metrô: Brigadeiro. **Amenities:** Restaurant; bar; fitness center; small indoor pool; room service; smoke-free floors. *In room:* A/C, TV, hair dryer, minibar, MP3 dock, Wi-Fi.

Expensive

Blue Tree Towers Paulista ★★ A great location, friendly English-speaking staff, and comfortable rooms at a reasonable price. Rooms are clean and modern looking, with queen beds, high-quality linen, bright bathrooms with marble touches, and a good-size writing desk. Some floors feature carpeting, others tile flooring. The hotel is located just a few steps from the Avenida Paulista, the MASP, and the Metrô stop. On weekends, prices drop by 50% or more.

Rua Peixoto Gomide 707, Cerqueira César, 01409-001 SP. ✆ **011/3147-7000.** Fax 011/3147-7001. www.bluetree.com.br. 232 units. R$300 standard; R$375 superior; R$410 luxo. Children 12 and under stay free in parent's room. Extra person 25%. AE, DC, MC, V. Valet parking. Metrô: Trianon-MASP. **Amenities:** Restaurant; bar; fitness center; indoor pool; room service; sauna; smoke-free floors. *In room:* A/C, TV, minibar, Wi-Fi.

Moderate

Ibis São Paulo Paulista (Value) The Accor group's budget Ibis brand offers predictable but quality accommodations in the heart of the business district. All rooms are identically furnished with good firm double or twin beds, a desk, and a shower. Breakfast can be ordered for an extra R$9. This hotel is nonsmoking.

Av. Paulista 2355, Cerqueira Cesar, 01420-002 SP. ✆ **011/3523-3000.** Fax 011/3523-3030. www.accorhotels.com.br. 236 units. R$139 double. Children 12 and under stay free in parent's room. AE, DC, MC, V. Free parking. Metrô: Consolação. **Amenities:** Restaurant; limited room service. *In room:* A/C, TV, minibar, Wi-Fi.

Jardins

Very Expensive

Emiliano ★★★ The Emiliano offers the kind of five-star service that would cost far more in a place like New York or Paris. It's pampering all the way, from the welcome massage to the minibar stocked according to your preference, to the personalized selection of pillows, carefully fluffed and placed on your Egyptian cotton sheets. The fabulous rooms come with designer furniture and feature original artwork and the latest home entertainment electronics. The bed is king size and the bathroom is a minispa in itself; toiletries are customized to your skin type and you can relax in the claw-foot tub, maybe watch a little TV, or contemplate life on your heated toilet seat.

Rua Oscar Freire 384, Cerqueira César, 01426-000 SP. ✆ **011/3069-4399.** Fax 011/3728-2000. www.emiliano.com.br. 57 units. R$925 double; R$1,600 suite. Check the website for special packages. Extra person add 30%. Children 10 and under stay free in parent's room. AE, DC, MC, V. Free parking. **Amenities:** Restaurant; upscale lobby bar; babysitting; concierge; small exercise room; room service; smoke-free floors; outstanding spa. *In room:* A/C, TV/DVD, hair dryer, Internet, minibar.

Expensive

Quality Suites Imperial Hall ★★ The Imperial Hall sits in the heart of São Paulo's toniest neighborhood, surrounded by restaurants, designer boutiques, and trendy shops. Built with the business traveler in mind, the spacious rooms offer firm beds, large closets, a small kitchen, in-room Internet, and a large desk with easy access to lots of plugs. The Master rooms on the 13th to 19th floors feature balconies and perks like fluffy bathrobes. There's also a floor exclusively for women travelers.

Rua da Consolação 3555, Jardins, São Paulo, 01416-001 SP. ✆ **011/2137-4555.** Fax 011/2137-4560. www.atlanticahotels.com.br. 150 units. R$250 double; R$350 Master double. Extra person add 25%. Children 6 and under stay free in parent's room. AE, DC, MC, V. Free parking. **Amenities:** Restaurant; rooftop pool; room service; sauna; smoke-free rooms; spa; small weight room; women-only floor. *In room:* A/C, TV, kitchen, Wi-Fi.

Regent Park Suite Hotel ★ This small apart-hotel is only steps from the city's best shops and restaurants. The majority of units are one-bedroom suites, but two-bedroom suites are available as well. The furnishings are a little dated, with '80s rustic wood, but everything is very well maintained and clean, and all the suites have a full kitchen.

Rua Oscar Freire 533, Jardins, 01426-001. ✆ **011/3065-5555.** www.regent.com.br. 70 units. 1-bedroom R$270; 2-bedroom R$385. Weekend discounts available. Extra person R$40. Children 4 and under stay free in parent's room. AE, MC, V. Free parking. Bus: 702P. **Amenities:** Restaurant; concierge; outdoor rooftop pool; limited room service; sauna; smoke-free rooms; small weight room. *In room:* A/C, TV, fridge, Internet, kitchen, minibar.

Moderate

Transamerica Flat Opera Five Stars ★ Value Bargain of the century, Opera offers spacious flats, featuring a separate sitting room with comfy couch and TV and small dinette table, plus a good-size work desk with lamp and lots of plugs, plus a bedroom with firm queen-size bed and vast closets and full-length mirror, plus a kitchenette with stove and fridge—all for less than many hotels charge for just a bed. True, the furnishings are a tad dated (though nice, the rooms get nowhere near the five stars claimed in the name) but on the plus side, step out the door and you're in the heart of the Jardins shopping district.

Alameda Lorena 1748, Cerqueira César, 04003-010 SP. ✆ **011/3062-2666.** Fax 011/3062-2662. www.transamericaflats.com.br. 96 units. R$240 double. Discounts available on weekends. Children 10 and under stay free in parent's room. AE, DC, MC, V. Free parking. Metrô: Consolação. **Amenities:** Restaurant; bar; small gym; small indoor pool; room service; sauna; smoke-free floors. *In room:* A/C, TV, Internet, kitchenette, minibar.

Near Ibirapeura Park

Very Expensive

Unique ★★★ Unique truly is. In form this latest São Paulo design hotel is a teetering verdigris-colored disk, chopped off at the top to make a roof deck, and propped up at either end by pillars hanging down like unfurled banners. Paulistas call it the *melancia,* or watermelon. Inside it's all high design, from the lobby bar (named the Wall) to the rooms and suites that feature white-on-white decor, queen-size beds with luscious bedding, sparkling bathrooms with Jacuzzi tubs, clever desk space, and a plethora of room gadgets including electric blinds and 48-inch. TVs. Suites are all on the rim of the disk so their outer walls rise in one seamless curve from floor to ceiling. Views are excellent, but the ultimate view is from the rooftop pool and lounge, where you see both Ibirapuera Park and the ridgeline run of skyscrapers on Avenida Paulista.

Av. Brigadeiro Luis Antônio 4700, Jardim Paulista, 01402-002 SP. ✆ **011/3055-4700.** Fax 011/3889-8100. www.hotelunique.com.br. 95 units. R$850 double; R$1,800–R$2,000 suite. AE, DC, MC, V. Parking R$20 daily. Metrô: Brigadeiro. **Amenities:** Rooftop restaurant; bar; concierge; fitness center; rooftop pool and indoor pool; room service. *In room:* A/C, TV/DVD, stereo, fridge, Internet, minibar, whirlpool bathtub.

WHERE TO DINE

São Paulo is the gourmet capital of Brazil. The city's money attracts the country's best chefs, and with no beaches or mountains to play on, Paulistas amuse themselves by eating out. People dress up for dinner here (or more than they would elsewhere in the country) and usually go out around 9 or 10pm *at the earliest.* Though it's becoming more common for restaurants to accept reservations, many will do so only up to 9pm.

Liberdade

Expensive

Sushi Yassu ★★ JAPANESE The second-generation owners of this traditional Liberdade standard bearer have begun introducing some new dishes to the Paulista palate. Try the grilled white tuna or anchovy, in salt or with a sweetened soy sauce, or a steaming bowl of udon noodle soup with seafood or tempura vegetables. For traditionalists there's a large variety of sushi and sashimi, plus stir-fried teppanyaki and yakisoba noodles with meat and vegetables. On Sundays there can be a line.

Rua Tomas Gonzaga 98, Liberdade. ✆ **011/3209-6622.** Main courses R$20–R$66. AE, DC, MC, V. Tues–Fri 11:30am–3pm and 6–11pm; Sat noon–4pm and 6pm–midnight; Sun noon–10pm. Metrô: Liberdade.

Moderate

Kaburá JAPANESE Twenty years and still going strong, Kaburá offers late-night dining in the heart of São Paulo's little Japan. The restaurant serves up the usual Japanese faves—sushi, sashimi, donburi, and tempura—in generous portions at a reasonable price. For interesting appetizers try the sashimi made from Brazilian *picanha* beef, or the breaded and crunchy deep-fried oysters.

Rua Galvão Bueno 346, Liberdade. ✆ **011/3277-2918.** Reservations accepted. Main courses R$18–R$45. No credit cards. Mon–Sat 7pm–2am. Metrô: Liberdade.

Korea House KOREAN It's some of the best Korean food in the city, but finding it involves a journey—head down a long hallway, up the stairs and into a windowless room lit by fluorescent lights, with only the small BBQs built into every table to entice you into eating. Cuisine is a mix of Chinese and Korean, with both spicy dishes from the kitchen or Korean barbecue done in front of you at your table.

Rua Galvão Bueno 43, Liberdade. ✆ **011/3208-3052.** Reservations not accepted. Main courses R$15–R$45. MC, V. Mon–Sat 11am–10pm; Sun 11am–3pm and 6–10pm. Metrô: Liberdade.

Shanghai CHINESE Cheap and cheerful Chinese, in a busy room in the heart of São Paulo's Japan town. Order beef or chicken or vegetables, or splurge on one of the fish fresh from the entryway aquarium.

Rua Galvão Bueno 16, Liberdade. ✆ **011/3208-7914.** Reservations accepted. Main courses R$18–R$42 MC, V. Mon–Sat 11am–9pm; Sun 11am–3pm and 6–9pm. Metrô: Liberdade.

Jardins

Very Expensive

D.O.M. ★★★ CONTEMPORARY São Paulo's restaurant of the moment actually opened in 1999, when chef Alex Atala returned from years in Europe with a plan to showcase the best Brazilian ingredients, employing the most careful and innovative preparations in a custom-designed dining room. In the decade since, DOM has racked up every significant restaurant award in Brazil, culminating with its inscription in *Restaurant Magazine*'s list of the top 50 restaurants in the world. The menu changes constantly—ask about the specials—but may include favorites such as robalo with tucupi and manioc, or duck in red wine–and–golden banana sauce. Diners can also opt for a four- or eight-course tasting menu including fish, meat, and cheese. The wine list is extensive and expensive, but if you're dining here you expected that. Reserve at least a couple days in advance, or come prepared to wait: DOM is popular.

Rua Barão de Capanema 549, Jardim Paulista. ✆ **011/30898-0761.** www.domrestaurante.com.br. Reservations recommended. Tasting menus R$160–R$230. AE, MC, V. Daily 8am–7pm. Metrô: Liberdade.

Figueira Rubaiyat ★★★ BRAZILIAN/STEAK The most beautiful restaurant in the city, Figueira ("fig tree") Rubaiyat is built around the spreading limbs of a magnificent old fig tree. Seating can either be "outside" in the gazebo around the tree boughs or inside in the lovely restaurant. Rubaiyat's specialty is beef. Indeed, it serves the best prime beef in São Paulo, all of it raised with care at the owner's private cattle ranch. For the noncarnivorous, the Figueira also offers a wide variety of top-notch Mediterranean seafood dishes, such as paella, codfish, and grilled prawns.

Rua Haddock Lobo 1738, Cerqueira Cesar. ✆ **011/3063-3888.** www.rubaiyat.com.br. Main courses R$45–R$95. V. Daily noon–12:30am. Bus: 206E.

Expensive

Arabia ★★ MIDDLE EASTERN This spacious and modern restaurant serves up a range of favorites from Lebanon, including a regularly changing tasting menu. At R$38 it's a great way to sample some of the chef's best. The main menu includes Moroccan rice with roasted almonds and chicken, or the signature stuffed artichoke with ground beef. For a lighter meal, try the *mezze,* the Lebanese equivalent of tapas. Each tray comes with at least half a dozen tasters of the most popular dishes, including hummus, falafel, tabbouleh, and a generous serving of pita.

Rua Haddock Lobo 1397, Cerqueira Cesar. ✆ **011/3061-2203.** www.arabia.com.br. Main courses R$25–R$65. AE, DC, MC. Mon–Thurs noon–3:30pm and 7pm–midnight; Fri noon–3:30pm and 7pm–1am; Sat–Sun noon–midnight. Bus: 206E.

Brasil a Gosto ★★ BRAZILIAN Chef Ana Luiza Trajano made an extended culinary research tour through Brazil's vast hinterlands to come up with home-grown ingredients and recipes many Brazilians had never heard of. The result was a successful book and even more successful restaurant, which makes use of native ingredients—cane, cashew, *guarana, açaí,* sugar cane, manioc—to create innovative and delightful dishes: appetizers like pirarucu (Amazon fish) pastry, an entrée of pork cutlets with jabuticaba-berry sauce served with a side of grilled plantain, desserts of banana sweets with crushed Brazil nut–and-coconut topping, served with ice cream. For drinks, there's an extensive menu of home-made *cachaças.*

Rua Prof. Azevedo de Amaral 70, Jardim Paulista. ✆ **011/3086-3565.** www.brasilagosto.com.br. Main courses R$30–R$65. AE, DC, MC. Wed–Sat noon–4pm and 7pm–12:30am; Sun noon–6pm. Bus: 206E.

Capim Santo ★★ BRAZILIAN Set in a lovely garden with lush mango trees and plenty of outside tables, Capim Santo specializes in seafood. Try the robalo fish with a crust of cashew nuts and a side of *vatapá* shrimp stew, or the stew of prawns in coconut milk, served in a hollowed-out pumpkin. For a vegetarian option try the minicannelloni stuffed with asparagus, ricotta, and tomato confit. Desserts often feature a tropical twist, such as the guava crème brûlée or the tarte tartin with banana. The lunchtime buffet offers 15 salads and more than 10 hot dishes, including seafood, chicken, and pasta, for only R$36 (R$51 weekends), with dessert included.

Rua Ministro Rocha Azevedo 471, Cerqueira César. ✆ **011/3068-8486.** www.restaurantecapimsanto.com.br. Main courses R$26–R$49. AE. Tues–Sat noon–3pm and 7pm–midnight; Sun 12:30–4:30pm. Metrô: MASP.

Gero ★★ ITALIAN A modern masculine room in the heart of Jardims, distinguished from the surrounding boutiques by discreet doormen, valet parking, and lineup of clients waiting patiently for entry to this most successful of Italian establishments. Appetizers can be inventive, like the sliced and spiced fried pumpkin slivers, but the house forte is pasta, made fresh and served in intriguing combinations, like the signature duck-filled ravioli in orange sauce. Nonpasta options include some excellent risottos—including one made with red wine, white beans, and hearty Tuscan sausage. Steaks and poultry are on the menu, but if that's what you're hankering for you should really go elsewhere.

Rua Haddock Lobo 1629, Cerqueira Cesar. ✆ **011/3064-0005.** www.fasano.com.br. Main courses R$40–R$75. AE, DC, MC. Mon–Thurs noon–3pm and 7pm–1am; Fri–Sat noon–4pm and 7pm–1am; Sun noon–4:30pm and 7–11:30pm. Bus: 206E.

Moderate

Toro ★★ TAPAS Somewhat late, but very good, tapas have finally arrived in Brazil. This warm terra-cotta restaurant, rich with the look and scents of the owners native Andalusia, offers a wide variety of Spanish-style small plates—perfect for snacking and sharing over a glass of red from the substantial wine list. For those less inclined to sharing, there's excellent paella and lamb. All dishes, big and small, are served on hand-painted plates brought directly from Spain.

Rua Joaquim Antunes 224, Jardin Paulista. ✆ **011/3085-8485.** Reservations recommended. Tasting menus R$160–R$230. AE, MC, V. Daily 8am–7pm.

Vila Madalena

Expensive

Kabuki ★★ JAPANESE Romantic, chic, Japanese—not adjectives that usually go together (at least not in Brazil), but Kabuki's candlelit dining room, exposed brick, and wood accents make it an exception. For those who want to nibble there's a large menu of appetizers, including sautéed shitake or shimeji mushrooms, deep-fried prawn, and grilled skewers with meat, seafood, or vegetables. Main courses include a large variety of sushi and sashimi combos, tempuras, yakisoba noodles, and grilled meats. Interesting dessert options include the flambéed mango and banana or tempura ice cream, a wonderful sensation of a hot, crunchy crust and a soft, cold, creamy center.

Rua Girassol 384, Vila Madalena. ✆ **011/3814-5131.** www.kabuki.com.br. Reservations accepted. Main courses R$22–R$70. AE, DC, MC, V. Daily 7–11pm; Tues–Sun noon–3pm. Metrô: Vila Madalena.

Santa Gula ★★ Finds ITALIAN One of the quaintest restaurants in São Paulo, Santa Gula is reached via a fairy-tale lane lush with tropical plants, banana trees, and flickering candlelight. The lane leads to a dining room with the handmade furniture and rustic decor of a simple Tuscan villa. The kitchen serves up a mix of Italian and Brazilian flavors—think risotto with palm hearts or pasta stuffed with *carne seca* (a flavorful dried meat) and pumpkin purée. For meat lovers, the steaks arrive grilled to perfection. For dessert, don't pass up on the Brazil nut pie or the sweet coconut with tapioca mousse and tangerine sorbet.

Rua Fidalga 340, Vila Madalena. ✆ **011/3812-7815.** www.stagula.com.br. Reservations recommended. Main courses R$26–R$40. AE, DC, MC, V. Mon 8pm–midnight; Tues–Thurs noon–3pm and 8pm–1am; Fri–Sat noon–4pm and 8pm–2am; Sun noon–5pm. Metrô: Vila Madalena.

Inexpensive

Deliparis CAFE A combination of cafe and bakery, Deliparis has an excellent selection of freshly baked breads, including loaves made with olives, nuts, or multigrain. Clients linger in the cafe with a tea or cappuccino and some of the delicious fruit tarts, quiches, or brioches. Deliparis also bakes excellent pies and divine cakes: Think banana cake with almonds or creamy chocolate ganache.

Rua Harmonia 484, Vila Madalena. ✆ **011/3816-5911.** Everything under R$12. No credit cards. Daily 7am–10pm. Bus: 473T.

Higienópolis

Smack in the middle of Higienópolis, just behind the FAAP, sits the delightful **Praça Vila Boim.** A lovely three-sided square with beautiful trees, the *praça* offers great casual dining options covering most of the world's cuisines. Sushi lovers will be pleased to find **Sushi Papaia ★** (✆ **011/3666-2086;** www.sushipapaia.com.br). For pizza lovers there's **Piola ★** (✆ **011/3663-6539;** www.piola.it), famous almost as much for its edgy, industrial-chic decor as it is for its 30 pizza combinations. For a great burger and a heavy helping of nostalgia try the **Fifties** (✆ **011/5094-5454;** www.thefifties.com.br), an old-style diner offering burgers, chili dogs, shakes, and fries. If steak is on your mind, look no further than the **Empório Natan** (✆ **011/3828-1402**), which specializes in Argentine and Angus cuts. For Mexican lovers, there's **SiSenor** (✆ **011/3476-2538;** www.sisenor.com.br), with an excellent selection of tacos, enchiladas, and burritos.

Expensive

La Brasserie Erick Jacquin ★★ FRENCH Celebrity chefs have begun putting their names on their eateries in São Paulo, as this new high-end spot in Higienópolis bears witness. Decor is warm, clean and modern, with lots of leather and wood grain put to tasteful effect in both the airy front bar and restaurant area. Cuisine offers both traditional French—duck confit in peppercorn sauce—and French with a Brazilian touch—prawns Provençal, sliced duck in a passion fruit sauce. Wine list intelligently avoids overpriced French bottles for better value (and equivalent quality) from Chile and Argentina. Dessert features lots of Belgian chocolate. Enjoy!

Rua Bahia 683, Higienópolis. © **011/3826-5409.** www.brasserie.com.br. Main courses R$65–R$125. AE, DC, MC, V. Sun–Thurs noon–midnight; Fri–Sat noon–1am; Sun noon–5pm. Bus: 8107.

SÃO PAULO AFTER DARK

Even Cariocas will admit (albeit under their breath) that São Paulo's nightlife is the best in the country. Keep in mind that most Paulistas won't even *set foot* in a club until midnight. ***Veja*** magazine (Brazil's equivalent of *Newsweek*) comes out every week on Sunday and includes a separate entertainment guide called *Veja São Paulo;* many hotels provide this insert for free.

The Performing Arts

One of São Paulo's top venues is the **Estação Julio Prestes/Sala São Paulo,** Praça Julio Prestes s/n (© **011/3367-9500;** www.salasaopaulo.art.br). The soaring main hall of a former grand railway station is home to the **São Paulo Symphony Orchestra** (www.osesp.art.br). The elegant 19th-century **Theatro Municipal,** Praça Ramos de Azevedo s/n (© **011/3397-0327**), provides the perfect backdrop for any performance. São Paulo's city opera company, ballet company, and city symphonic orchestra all make their homes here.

Music & Dance Clubs

LIVE MUSIC **Black Bom Bom,** Rua Luis Murat 370, Vila Madalena (© **011/3813-3365;** www.blackbombom.com.br), specializes in rap, hip-hop, and Rio de Janeiro–style funk, sometimes with a DJ, but more often live. New venue **Bar Camará,** Rua Luís Murat 306, Vila Madalena (© **011/3816-6765;** www.barcamara.com.br), offers three spaces in one—a large indoor atrium graced with tall tropical trees, an upstairs terrace with a fine view of the city, and a second-floor bar with live music 7 nights a week. Clientele are upscale and in their late 20s to mid-30s. For 10 years and counting, **Grazie a Dio!,** Rua Girassol 67, Vila Madalena (© **011/3031-6568;** www.grazieadio.com.br), has been one of the best places in the city for live music almost any day of the week. Expect anything from pop to samba-rock to salsa. **HSBC Brasil,** Rua Bragança Paulista 1281, Chácara Santo Antonio (© **011/4003-1212;** www.hsbcbrasil.com.br), is one of the city's best midsize venues, dedicated to Brazilian MPB. The new custom-built complex hosts big names such as Gilberto Gil, Lulu Santos, and Jorge Ben.

DANCE CLUBS **Azucar,** Rua Mario Feraz 423, Itaim Bibi (© **011/3074-3737;** www.azucar.com.br), offers salsa and meringue most nights of the week, with free lessons Tuesday to Thursday. It attracts a more mature (30- to 45-year-old) and upscale crowd. **D-Edge,** Alameda Olga 170, Barra Funda (© **011/3667-8334;** www.d-edge.com.br), São Paulo's hottest club, features wall-long monster woofers, a *Saturday Night Fever* flashing disco floor, and some of the hottest heaviest funk beats this side of Birmingham. Once again, hip and trendy Rua Auguta features **Studio Roxy,** Rua Augusta 430 (© **011/7676-0622;** www.studioroxy.com.br). Open Friday and Saturday only, the club has two dance floors and excellent DJs. On the same street, there is also **Vegas,** Rua Augusta 765 (© **0911/3231-3705;** www.vegasclub.com.br), where some of the city's best DJs are invited to spin their stuff.

Bars & Pubs

One of São Paulo's happening nighttime neighborhoods for the young and pretty is currently Vila Olímpia. Many of the more popular bars are concentrated on the **Rua Prof. Atilio Innocenti. Bar Favela,** Prof. Atilio Innocenti 419 (✆ **011/3848-6988;** www.barfavela.com.br), is anything but downscale. This hip bar attracts a happening crowd who come to see and be seen. Also on the Atilio Innocenti is **Pennélope,** Rua Prof. Atilio Innocenti 380 (✆ **011/3842-3802**). Larger than some of the other bars, Pennélope has a small stage for live music and a couple of DJs who keep the crowd happy. A great place for a drink and a talk, **Filial,** Rua Fidalga 254, Vila Madalena (✆ **011/3813-9336**), features a vast collection of bottles lining the walls, intermingled with sports photos from the 1950s. Tables are occupied by youngish clientele quaffing draft beer and nibbling from the snacks menu. Since 1948, **Bar Brahma,** Av. São João 677, Centro (✆ **011/3333-0855;** www.barbrahmasp.com), has been the meeting place for intellectuals, musicians, politicians, and businessmen. Renovations have restored the original wooden and bronze furnishings, and the chandeliers once again illuminate the crowds that gather to chat and drink beer. **Bar Municipal,** Rua Aspicuelta 578, Vila Madalena (✆ **011/3812-0492;** www.barmunicipal.com.br), is the favorite haunt of the beautiful 25-to-35 crowd, who quaff chopp and sip delicately from long neck Stella Artois, while munching panini and calabresa. Weekends from 6 to 11pm there's live MPB and samba.

Gay & Lesbian Nightlife

On Friday and Saturday the GLS crowd flocks to **Studio Roxy,** Rua Augusta 430 (✆ **011/7676-0622;** www.studioroxy.com.br). The dance floors don't really fill up until after midnight. On the ground floor of a commercial building, the **Vermont Itaim,** Rua Pedroso Alvarenga 1192, Itaim Bibi (✆ **011/ 3071-1320**), offers live music and a young crowd most nights—MPB on Wednesdays, danceable pop Thursday though Saturdays. The boys predominate through the week and on Saturday, but Sundays the girls take over with a nine-woman samba band. Another popular venue for the ladies is **Farol Madalena,** Rua Jericó 179, Vila Madalena (✆ **011/3032-6470;** www.farolmadalena.com.br). The bar has live Brazilian music most evenings and is open Wednesday through Saturday 7pm to 1am, Sunday 4pm to midnight.

6 BRASILIA

924km (574 miles) NW of Rio de Janeiro, 870km (540 miles) N of São Pãulo

There are other planned cities in the world—Washington, D.C.; Chandigarh; Canberra—but none has the daring and sheer vision of Brasilia. In the 1950s, a country that had shucked off a failed monarchy, a corrupt republic, and a police-state dictatorship decided to make a clean break from the past by creating a brand-new space for politics.

The style of choice was Modernism; clean lines and honestly exposed structure, using new materials of glass and steel and concrete. The city plan was done by Lucio Costa. The buildings were designed by Oscar Niemeyer. The chosen site, on Brazil's high interior plateau, was nothing but *cerrado*—short scrubby forest, stretching thousands of miles in every direction. It was nearly 644km (400 miles) from the nearest paved road, over 120km (75 miles) from the nearest railroad, 193km (120 miles) from the nearest airport. Groundbreaking began in 1957. By April 21, 1960, there was enough of a city for a grand inauguration. Politicians and civil servants began the long shift inland.

In years since, Brasilia has been a source of controversy. Urbanists were beginning to doubt the rationality of rationalist planning. Cities, it was being discovered, were vital, growing entities, whose true complexity could never be encompassed in a single master plan. But if nothing else, Brasilia did succeed in shifting Brazil's focus from the coast to its vast interior. For visitors, the attractions here are purely architectural. Brazil's best designers, architects, and artists were commissioned to create the monuments and buildings and make them beautiful. A visit to Brasilia is a chance to see and judge their success.

ESSENTIALS

Getting There

Gol, TAM, and Webjet have several flights a day to Brasilia from major Brazilian cities. Brasilia's airport, **Aeroporto Internacional de Brasilia—Presidente Juscelino Kubitschek** (airport code BSB; ✆ **061/3364-9000**), is about 10km (6¼ miles) west of the Eixo Monumental. Taxis from the airport to the hotel zones cost about R$35.

Orientation

What makes Brasilia unique—besides its amazing architecture—is its layout. Two main traffic arteries divide the city. **Eixo Monumental** runs dead straight east-west; **Eixo Rodoviario** runs north-south, curving as it goes. Seen from above, the city resembles an airplane or an arrow notched into a partially bent bow. Where these two axes intersect is the city's central bus station. The other main distinguishing feature of the city plan is the strict separation of uses by zoning. All of the city's important government buildings are located at the "point" of the arrow—that is, on the eastern end of the Eixo Monumental. All of the city's hotels can be found in two hotel districts near the Rodoviaria. Similarly, the city's offices, shopping malls, theaters, and hospitals are in their individually designated clumps, usually close to where the "bow" meets the "arrow."

The Eixo Monumental (the east-west avenue) divides the city into two perfectly symmetric wings, the **Asa Norte,** or N (north wing), and **Asa Sul,** or S (south wing). Always check whether an address is in the south or north wing; otherwise, you could find yourself in the complete opposite part of town.

Getting Around

BY BUS Buses run from the tip of the south wing to the tip of the north wing, along W1 and W3 on the west side of the Eixo Rodoviario (the bow) and on L1 and L3 on the east side of the Eixo Rodoviario. To travel across town you catch a bus traveling to the opposite part of the city: From Asa Sul catch a bus that says ASA NORTE, or vice versa. On the Eixo Monumental you can catch buses labeled PLANO PILOTO CIRCULAR that just circle up and down this main boulevard. Many buses will go via the Rodoviaria, located in the center of town. These will get you pretty close to the main monuments, hotels, and malls along the Eixo Monumental. Bus tickets are R$1.85.

BY TOURIST BUS **Brasilia City Tour** (✆ **061/3356-1707** or 061/9298-9416; www.brasiliacitytour.com.br) offers a double-decker bus that covers the main tourist destinations along the Eixo Monumental. The bus operates Tuesday to Sunday, departing at 10 and 11:30am, and at 2, 3:30, and 5pm from the Torre da TV (TV tower). For R$20 (children 6–12 pay half price), you can get on and off wherever you like.

BY TAXI Taxis are plentiful and my preferred transportation method, especially if I can't easily figure out where I'm going. Just hand the address to the driver and he'll figure it out. From the hotel sector to the tip of the Asa Sul costs approximately R$25. For taxis call **Brasilia** (✆ **061/3344-1000**) or **Rádio Táxi** (✆ **061/3325-3030**).

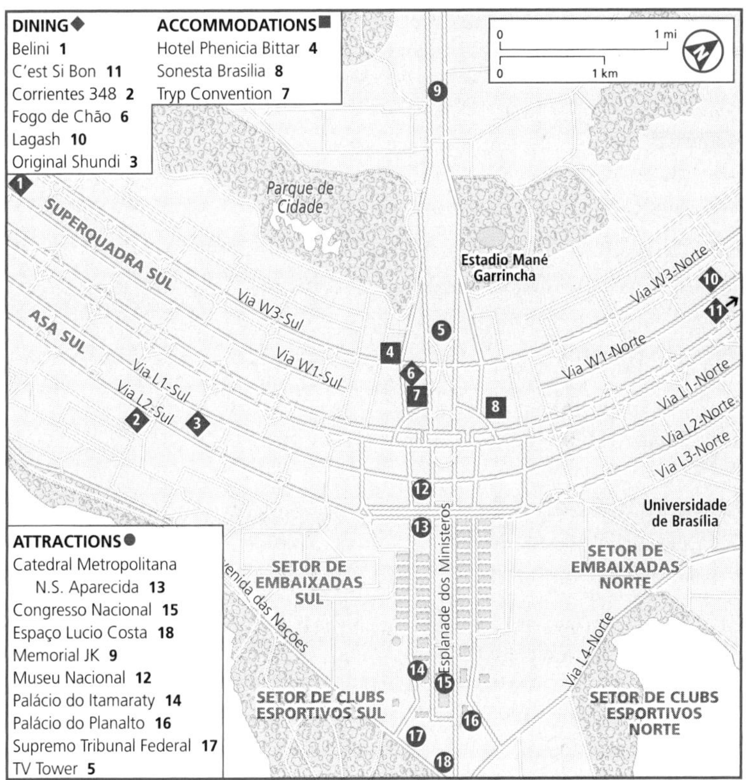

Visitor Information

The official government tourist agency **Setur** is reorganizing all of its information booths. The only information desk (Tues–Sun 9am–6pm) currently in operation is located on the ground floor of the Museu Nacional, the large white dome next to the cathedral.

FAST FACTS You can exchange money at **Air Brazil Turismo** (✆ **061/3321-2304**), in the National Hotel. The **Banco de Brasil** (✆ **061/3424-3000**), on the second floor of the Conjunto Nacional and in Brasilia Airport (✆ **061/3365-1183**), has 24-hour ATMs. ATMs are in all of the malls. All hospitals are in the Hospital section (SHLS and SHLN). For medical attention, try **Hospital Santa Lucia,** SHLS, Q. 76, conj. C (✆ **061/3445-0000;** www.santalucia.com.br).

WHAT TO SEE & DO

The Top Attractions

Catedral Metropolitana Nossa Senhora Aparecida ★★★ The cathedral is surprisingly small from the outside, but once you descend through the walkway, you emerge in the brightest and most spacious church you have ever seen. The floors and walls are made of white marble, with an expanse of glass overhead. Sculptor Alfredo Ceschiatti designed the statues of the four apostles in front of the cathedral, as well as the angels suspended from the ceiling.

Esplanada dos Ministerios. ✆ **061/3224-4073.** Daily 8am–5pm. Mass Mon–Fri 6:15pm; Tues–Fri 12:15pm; Sat 5pm; Sun 8:30am, 10:30am, and 6pm. No touring of the cathedral during Mass. No shorts or Bermudas. Bus: Rodoviaria (short walk to the cathedral) or the Plano Piloto Circular.

Memorial JK ★ This remarkable monument was built in 1980 by Niemeyer to honor the founder of Brasilia, Juscelino Kubitschek. Inside, the former president's remains rest beneath a skylight in a granite tomb. Upstairs, there's some interesting stuff on Brasilia, including photographs of the city being built, and copies of the designs that didn't get chosen.

Eixo Monumental Oeste. ✆ **061/3225-9451.** Admission R$4. Tues–Sun 9am–6pm. Bus: Plano Piloto Circular.

Museu Nacional ★ You can't miss the large white dome of the Museu Nacional, rising like a giant igloo from the barren concrete tundra. Built in 2006, the museum's pleasant interior space houses free changing exhibits.

Eixo Monumental Oeste. ✆ **061/3325-5220.** Free admission. Tues–Sun 9am–6:30pm. Bus: Plano Piloto Circular.

Palácio do Itamaraty ★★★ One of the most beautiful modernist structures, the Palácio do Itamaraty serves as a ceremonial reception hall for the Department of Foreign Affairs. The ultramodern structure—mostly open space inside—is decorated with rich antique furnishings of Persian carpets, hand-carved jacaranda-wood furniture, and 18th- and 19th-century paintings. Somehow it really works. Guided tours only. Call ahead to request an English-speaking guide.

Esplanada dos Ministerios. ✆ **061/3411-8051.** Free admission. Guided tours Mon–Fri 2 and 4:30pm; Sat–Sun 10am and 3:30pm; call to confirm. No shorts or tank tops allowed. Bus: Plano Piloto Circular.

TV Tower ★★★ Value The best view in town is free! Take the elevator up to the 72m-high (240-ft.) lookout, and Brasilia is laid out at your feet. You'll get the best perspective of the Eixo Monumental, with the ministry buildings lining the boulevard like dominos waiting to be knocked over. Time your visit towards day's end to take in the city with a fiery red Brasilia sunset.

Eixo Monumental (close to the bus station and malls). ✆ **061/3321-7944.** Free admission. Mon–Fri 9am–noon and 2–5:30pm; Sat–Sun 11am–5:30pm. Bus: Rodoviaria.

Architectural Highlights

To make the most of your visit to Brasilia it pays to hire a tour guide. Not only will it save you all the time and hassle of getting around but you will also gain a greater appreciation of the city's architecture and structure. **Roberto Torres** (✆ **061/9963-4732;** carneirotorres@msn.com) is an experienced licensed tour guide with architectural knowledge who speaks excellent English. Book in advance.

The signature buildings in Brasilia were all designed by architect **Oscar Niemeyer.** The strength of this Brazilian übermodernist has always been with form; his structures are often brilliant. His weakness has always been detailing, materials, and landscaping. Fortunately, in Brasilia Niemeyer was teamed up with Brazil's best landscape designer, **Roberto Burle Marx;** detailing- and materials-focused architects like **Milton Ramos;** and talented sculptors and artists like **Alfredo Ceschiatti.** Every building also had to conform to the overall plan of **Lucio Costa.** The result is a collection of buildings that has rightly been called the highest expression of architectural modernism on earth. Niemeyer's work is scattered far and wide throughout the city, but the best of the best is on the eastern portion of the Eixo Monumental, from the Rodoviario to the Praça dos Tres Poderes on the far side of the Congresso Nacional.

Behind the Congresso Nacional stands the wide, austere Praça dos Tres Poderes. On the north side of the square, the **Palácio do Planalto** is well worth a look. Visitors aren't allowed into this building, but can watch the not-very-exciting changing of the guard every 2 hours. Similar in form is the **Supremo Tribunal Federal,** the office of the Brazilian Supreme Court located on the other side of Three Power Plaza. The tribunal is open for guided visits, but only on weekends and holidays between 10am and 2pm.

Shopping

Shopping in Brasilia means malls. Close to the hotel district you find the **Patio Brasil,** SCS, Q. 7, Bl. A (✆ **061/2107-7400;** www.patiobrasil.com.br), located in the South Wing not far from the Meliá hotel. Near the hotel sector in the north wing, the **Brasilia Shopping,** SCN, Q. 5, lote 2 (✆ **061/3328-5259;** www.brasiliashopping.com.br), has a number of movie theaters and an excellent food court. Malls are open Monday through Saturday 10am to 10pm, Sunday 2 to 8pm.

WHERE TO STAY

The vast majority of hotels in Brasilia are located in one of the two hotel sectors: SHN (Setor Hoteleiro Norte, north hotel sector) or the SHS (Setor Hoteleiro Sul, south hotel sector). The areas are within a 10-minute walk of each other, and of the city's two shopping sectors. The only variety is the level of luxury and size of the building.

The majority of hotel guests in Brasilia are politicians and businesspeople. Demand for hotel rooms is thus huge on weekdays and almost nonexistent on weekends. It pays to schedule your visit to Brasilia on the weekend, as most hotels offer a decent discount.

Setor Hoteleiro Norte/Sul

Expensive

Sonesta Brasilia ★★ This 4-year-old hotel offers comfortable and pleasant accommodations in the heart of the hotel sector. The decorations are modern and bright and the rooms feature queen-size beds, a comfortable work desk, and free Internet. The deluxe rooms include a small sitting area with a sofa, while premium rooms come with a small kitchen. There's also an outdoor swimming pool, sauna, and small fitness center. Check the website for discounts and early booking specials.

SHN, Q. 5, Bl. B, Brasilia, 70705-000 DF. ✆ **061/3424-2500.** www.sonesta.com/brasilia. 159 units. R$280 deluxe (weekends and off season R$140); R$340 premium. AE, DC, MC, V. Free parking. **Amenities:** 2 restaurants; bar; outdoor pool; room service; sauna; smoke-free rooms. *In room:* A/C, TV, hair dryer, Internet, minibar.

Tryp Convention ★★ Inaugurated in 2009, the Tryp offers top-quality accommodations and the little extras business travelers need. Rooms are spacious, with queen-size beds, nice lighting, comfortable chairs, and a sofa. Desk space is more than adequate; amenities are excellent and include the use of a heated outdoor pool and full business center.

SHS, Q. 6, Bl. B Brasilia, 70316-000 DF. ✆ **0800/703-3399** or 061/3218-4700. Fax 061/3218-4703. www.solmelia.com. 150 units. R$250 standard; R$280 superior (weekends and off season R$130 standard, R$175 superior). AE, DC, MC, V. Free parking. **Amenities:** Restaurant; bar; gym; outdoor pool; room service; sauna; smoke-free rooms. *In room:* A/C, TV, hair dryer, Internet, minibar.

Moderate

Hotel Phenicia Bittar ★ This small Setor Sul hotel recently renovated its floors and rooms as part of a transformation into a boutique hotel. Renovated rooms have lovely hardwood floors or new carpets, double or twin beds, wood furniture, a sitting area, and brand-new beds. Even better are the stylish renovated suites, which feature a living room with a dining table, large desk, and a spacious bedroom with a second desk. A third bed can easily be added for those with children.

SHS, Q. 5, Bl. J, Brasilia, DF 70322-911. ✆ **061/3704-4000.** Fax 061/3225-1406. www.hoteisbittar.com.br. 130 units, shower only. R$240 double (weekends and low season R$150). AE, DC, MC, V. Free parking. **Amenities:** Restaurant; room service. *In room:* A/C, TV, Internet, minibar.

WHERE TO DINE

Brasilia has some outstanding restaurants; politicians and businesspeople prefer to eat well and having an expense account helps. Unfortunately, the fine-dining establishments are scattered throughout the residential wings, mostly in the Asa Sul.

Asa Sul

Belini ★ Finds ITALIAN This gourmet complex encompasses a deli, food store, restaurant, cafe, and cooking school. It's a great place to grab an espresso and some sweets, or buy some fresh bread and cold cuts for an impromptu picnic. The casual outdoor patio serves sandwiches (the pastrami, mortadella, and brie is good) for R$6 to R$14. For a more formal occasion, the restaurant upstairs serves fine Italian dishes, such as lamb filet with mint sauce and risotto, or large prawns in an apple-and-ginger sauce. The restaurant also serves breakfast and afternoon tea.

SCLS 113, Bl. D, loja 36. ✆ **061/3345-0777.** www.belini-gastronomia.com.br. Main courses R$14–R$40. MC, V. Restaurant Tues–Sat noon–3pm and 7:30pm–midnight; Sun noon–4pm. Bakery daily 6:30am–midnight. Bus: W3 Asa Sul.

Corrientes 348 ★★ Finds ARGENTINE/STEAK Here you'll find a large covered patio and some of the finest steaks in town. The menu offers classic Argentine appetizers, including grilled red peppers, stuffed empanadas, and grilled spicy sausage. Meat lovers will go ga-ga over the fine selection of prime Argentine steak, such as the *ojo de bife* (rib-eye) and *tapa de cuadril* (rump steak). Side dishes include salads, grilled vegetables, and rice.

SCLS 411, Bl. D, loja 36. ✆ **061/3345-1348.** www.restaurante348.com.br. Main courses R$49–R$89 for 2. AE, DC, MC, V. Mon–Thurs noon–3pm and 7pm–midnight; Fri–Sat 12:30pm–midnight; Sun noon–6pm. Bus: W3 Asa Sul.

Fogo de Chão ★★ STEAK One of the best all-you-can-eat steak restaurants in Brazil, Fogo de Chão serves high-quality cuts of meat. Start off with some delicious antipasto, grilled vegetables, or a salad, and then wait for the competent waiters to bring you cut after cut of fine beef, lamb, chicken or pork. As at most churrascarias, the drinks and desserts are not included in the price of the meal and tend to be on the pricey side, but the quality remains top notch.

SHS, Q. 5, Bl. E, Asa Sul. ✆ **061/3322-4666.** www.fogodechao.com.br. Main courses R$79. AE, DC, MC, V. Mon–Fri noon–4pm and 6pm–midnight; Sat noon–midnight; Sun noon–10pm.

Original Shundi ★★ JAPANESE This new Japanese restaurant makes a bold statement with its stunning red-and-black dining room, designed by Ruy Ohtake. Decoration aside, however, the food is the real star here. The best deal may be the all-you-can-eat lunch buffet (R$39), which includes creative sushi rolls, fresh sashimi, and several hot dishes. The a la carte menu goes way beyond the average list of sushi staples. Order one of the tasting menus and let the chef surprise you with dishes such as baby eel, mini octopus, or spring rolls with asparagus, mushrooms, and scallops.

SCLS 408, Bl. D, loja 35. ✆ **061/3244-5101.** Main courses R$36–R$64. AE, DC, MC, V. Mon–Fri noon–3pm and 8pm–1am; Sat noon–5pm and 8pm–1am; Sun noon–5pm and 8–11pm.

Asa Norte

C'Est Si Bon CREPES The place for an inexpensive snack or light meal. Owner and chef Sergio Quintiliano has created more than 50 different savory and sweet crepes. One recent addition is the Crepe Almodovar, stuffed with tender beef, mushrooms, and creamy catupiry cheese. There are now two locations; the Asa Sul location also features a lovely patio and Thursday evening jazz music.

Asa Norte: SCLN 213, Bl. A, loja 13, ✆ **061/3272-1005.** Asa Sul: SCLS 408, Bl. A, loja 5, ✆ **061/3244-6353.** www.cestsibon.com.br. Main courses R$12–R$20. MC, V. Daily noon–midnight.

Lagash ★★ MIDDLE EASTERN Lagash prepares the best Middle Eastern food in Brasilia. (Okay, there's not a lot of competition, but the quality here is excellent.) Appetizers include baba ghanouj, made with eggplant and tahini; hummus; and roasted *merguez* (lamb sausage). The most popular entree is the Moroccan lamb—tender pieces of boneless lamb cooked with nuts, scallions, onions, and rice. The wine list is heavy on the Italian and French reds to accompany the hearty and spicy dishes.

SCLN 308, Bl. B, loja 11. ✆ **061/3273-0098.** Main courses R$20–R$60. AE, DC, MC, V. Mon–Sat noon–4pm and 7pm–midnight; Sun noon–6pm. Bus: W3 Asa Norte.

BRASILIA AFTER DARK

There's a fair bit of stuff to do in Brasilia after dark, but there is no "scene" as such. Bars and cafes have sprung up in discrete, widely separate spots throughout the small commercial zones in the two residential wings. Most classical concerts and dance and theater performances in Brasilia take place in one of the three concert halls at the **Teatro Nacional,** Setor Cultural Norte (✆ **061/3325-6240**). For program information, phone the events calendar hot line at ✆ **061/3325-6239.**

Bars & Live Music

Armazém do Ferreira, CLN 202, Bl. A, loja 47, Asa Norte (✆ **061/3327-8342**), resembles a bustling Rio de Janeiro botequim, decorated with lovely 1950s photos of Brazil's former capital. The bar is a very popular happy hour destination for Brasilienses, especially on Fridays. Hidden in a basement on the Eixo Monumental, **Clube do Choro,** SDC, Eixo Monumental (✆ **061/3224-0599;** www.clubedochoro.com.br), specializes in *choro* and bossa nova. The crowd takes the music seriously, so this is not the place to catch up with old friends. Shows run Wednesday to Sunday. Restaurant **Feitiço Mineiro,** 306 Norte, Bl. B, loja 45 (✆ **061/3272-3032;** www.feiticomineiro.com.br), in the Asa Norte, has become one of the best places in town to catch well-known Brazilian acts, including samba, MPB, blues, and bossa nova. Shows usually take place Tuesdays through Saturdays and start around 10pm. **Gate's Pub,** SCLS 403, Bl. B, loja 34 (✆ **061/3225-4576**), offers great musical variety. On Friday and Saturday jazz, blues, rock, and MPB bands take the stage. Programming often includes new, upcoming bands. The rest of the week DJ's take care of the sound and keep the crowd moving.

7 SALVADOR

1,206km (749 miles) NE of Rio de Janeiro, 1,437km (893 miles) NE of São Paulo

The Italian navigator Amerigo Vespucci—the one who later gave his name to a pair of continents—was the first European to set eyes on the Baía de Todos os Santos, the beautiful bay around which Salvador now stands. He arrived in the service of the king of Portugal on November 1, 1501. By 1549, the new colony of Salvador was important enough that the Portuguese king had a royal governor and a small army to protect it from the French and Dutch.

The wealth of the new colony was not in silver or gold, but something almost as lucrative: sugar. Sugar cane thrived in the Northeast. As plantations grew, the Portuguese planters found themselves starved for labor, and so plunged headfirst into the slave trade. By the mid–19th century close to five million slaves had been taken from Africa to Brazil. The wealth earned by that trade is evident in the grand mansions and golden churches in Pelourinho. The legacy of the slave trade is also reflected in the population. Modern Salvador is a city of two million, and approximately 80% of its people are of Afro-Brazilian descent.

This heritage has had an enormous influence on Salvador's culture, food, religion, and especially its music. Even in a country as musical as Brazil, Bahia stands out. A new term has been coined to describe Bahia's Afro-Brazilian blend of upbeat dance music: *axé,* from the Yorubá word for energy. Over the past 2 decades, groups such as Olodum and Timbalada have blended complex African drumming rhythms with reggae melodies, while adding some social activism to the mix. Capoeira, the balletic mix of martial arts and dance, is on almost every Salvador street corner. The African religious practice of Candomblé is also emerging from generations in the shadows.

This past 20 years has seen the resurrection of Salvador's Pelourinho neighborhood. Derelict until as recently as the '80s, Pelourinho—the 16th-century heart of what was once the richest city on the Atlantic coast—has been painstakingly brought back to its former glory. And then there's Carnaval. Over a million people now come out to dance and revel their way through the city's streets. Salvador may soon claim to hold the biggest street party in the world.

ESSENTIALS

Getting There

BY PLANE **Gol** (✆ **0300/115-2121**), **TAM** (✆ **071/4002-5700**), and **TRIP** (✆ **071/3003-8747**) all fly from Rio, São Paulo, Recife, Brasilia, and other places with connections.

Salvador's modern **Aeroporto Deputado Luis Eduardo Magalhães** (airport code SSA; ✆ **071/3204-1010**) is 32km (20 miles) from downtown, and rides tend to be pricey. **Coometas** taxi (✆ **071/3244-4500**) offers prepaid fares; a trip to **Pelourinho** costs R$100, to **Ondina/Rio Vermelho** R$89, and to the northern beaches (such as **Itapuã**), R$50. Regular taxis are cheaper; on the meter a taxi from the airport to Pelourinho costs around R$65 to R$70.

BY BUS Long-distance buses arrive at **Terminal Rodoviaria de Salvador Armando Viana de Castro,** Av. ACM (Antônio Carlos Magalhães) 4362, Iguatemi (✆ **071/3460-8300**).

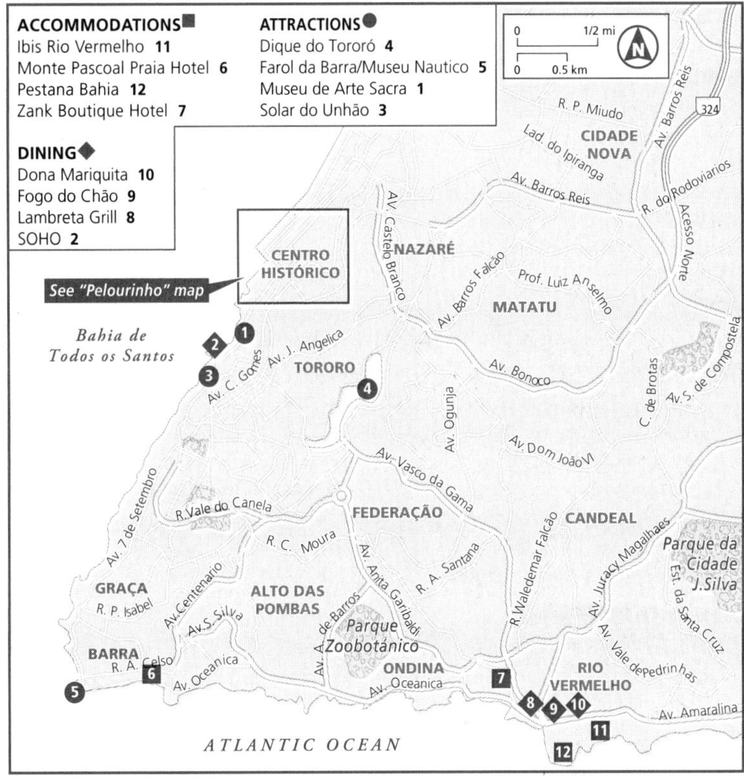

Orientation

Pelourinho, the historic old downtown, is perched on a high cliff overlooking the bay. This area is also sometimes referred to as the **centro histórico,** or as the **Cidade Alta,** the upper town. This is Salvador's chief area of interest. At the foot of the cliff lies **Comércio,** a modern area of commercial office towers. This area is also sometimes known as the **Cidade Baixa,** or lower town. Upper town and lower town are connected via a cliff-side elevator, the **Elevator Lacerda.** The point where All Saints Bay meets the Atlantic is marked by a tall white lighthouse, called the **Farol de Barra.** The strip of beach **(Praia da Barra)** that stretches beyond the lighthouse towards Ondina has seen better days, but is still one of the most popular gathering places during Carnaval.

The road running from the lighthouse out along the oceanside is called **Avenida Oceanica** and continues past a number of good hotels to the oceanside neighborhood of **Ondina.** From here, road names change frequently, and neighborhoods come thick and fast: **Rio Vermelho, Amaralina, Pituba, Costa Azul, Pituaçu, Piatã, Itapuã,** all the way to **Stella Maris** adjacent to the airport. There are pleasant **beaches** all along this stretch.

ON FOOT The old historic center, Pelourinho, is a stroller's dream. The narrow streets and cobblestone alleys open onto large squares with baroque churches; the stately mansions and homes now house shops, galleries, and wonderful little restaurants.

BY BUS Salvador buses are marked by name; the main buses going from any of the beach neighborhoods to downtown are marked PRAÇA DA SÉ for Pelourinho or COMÉRCIO for the lower town. To travel to the city's main bus station (or the large mall across from the bus station) take buses marked IGUATEMI. When leaving downtown for the beaches, take a bus that says VIA ORLA, which means along the coast, and make sure that the bus's final destination lies beyond the beach neighborhood you want to reach. Along the coast, you have the option of taking a regular bus (R$1.80) or an air-conditioned *frescão* bus (R$4–R$6).

BY TAXI Local taxis can be hailed on the street or from any taxi stand. To book a radio taxi, contact **Radiotaxi** (✆ **071/3243-4333**) or **LigueTaxi** (✆ **071/3357-7777**).

FAST FACTS To exchange money, go to the **Banco do Brasil,** Praça Padre Anchieta 11, Pelourinho (✆ **071/3321-9334**), or Rua Miguel Bournier 4, Barra Avenida, parallel to the Avenida Oceanica (✆ **071/3264-5099**). There is a **Citibank** branch at Rua Miguel Calmon 555, Comércio, close to the Mercado Modelo (✆ **071/3241-4745**).

In case of an emergency call the **police** at ✆ **190** and the **fire brigade and ambulance** at ✆ **193.** In case of a medical emergency contact the **Hospital Portugues,** Av. Princesa Isabel 2, Barra (✆ **071/3203-5700**) or **Hospital Aliança,** Av. Juracy Magalhães 2096, Rio Vermelho (✆ **071/3350-5600**).

Visitor Information

Bahiatursa, the state's tourist information service (www.bahia.com.br), has booths at the following locations: **Salvador International Airport** in the arrivals hall (✆ **071/3204-1244**), open daily from 7:30am to 11pm; **Rodoviaria** (✆ **071/3450-3871**), open daily from 7:30am to 9pm; **Mercado Modelo,** Praça Cayru 250, Cidade Baixa (✆ **071/3241-0242**), open Monday through Saturday 9am to 6pm and Sunday from 9am to 1:30pm; and **Pelourinho,** Rua das Laranjeiras 12 (✆ **071/3321-2463** or 3321-2133), open daily from 8:30am to 9pm. For quick questions and information, visitors can also call the 24-hour telephone service (in Portuguese, Spanish, and English), Disque Bahia Turismo (✆ **071/3103-3103**).

WHAT TO SEE & DO

Brazil's first capital city, Salvador serves simultaneously as the repository of the country's historical heritage and the source of much that is new and vibrant in its culture. Nothing symbolizes this dual role better than Pelourinho. The historic core of Salvador, Pelourinho is a perfectly preserved urban gem from the 16th and 17th centuries, with a wealth of richly decorated baroque churches, tiny squares, and fine old colonial mansions.

Tour operators around town operate a fairly standard package of tours. A reliable company is **Tatur** (✆ **071/3450-7216;** www.tatur.com.br). The half-day city tours include either a visit to Pelourinho or a more panoramic tour to the lighthouse and the beaches. They range from R$40 to R$60. Full-day schooner tours in the Bay of All Saints usually stop at Ilha dos Frades and Itaparica. Cost is about R$50 to R$70. This company also offers a number of interesting multiday customized excursions such as African-heritage tours, folklore, or even archaeological tours to Bahia's interior.

The Top Attractions

Pelourinho ★★★

Make your first stop the Bahiatursa office, located at Rua das Laranjeiras (✆ **071/3321-2133**) to pick up maps. In 1985 the historic core of colonial Salvador was designated a UNESCO World Heritage Site by the United Nations. It's well merited. One could spend years getting to know the history of the churches, squares, and colorful colonial mansions in this old part of the city. What follows is but a brief introduction.

Start a tour of Pelourinho in the main square, called the **Terreiro de Jesus.** Dominating the west end of the square is the 17th-century **Catedral Basílica.** The church was thoroughly restored in 1996 and features beautifully ornate altars made from cedar. Flanking the cathedral is the neoclassical **Antiga Faculdade de Medicina** (see listing for Museu Afro-Brasileiro/Faculdade de Medicina, below), now home to the excellent Afro-Brazilian Museum. Also on the north side of the square is the smaller baroque **Igreja São Pedro dos Clerigos** (Mon–Fri 1–5pm). Facing the cathedral at the far end of the *terreiro* is the **Igreja de Ordem Terceiro de São Domingos de Gusmão.** Built between 1713 and 1734, this baroque church suffered through an 1870s renovation that destroyed most of its fine interior painting and tile work. On the south side of this church there's a wide cobblestone street with a tall cross in the middle. This is the **Praça Anchieta.** The saint on the cross is São Francisco de Xavier, patron saint of Salvador. At the far end of this little *praça* stand two of the most impressive churches in the city. The large two-towered one on the right is the **Igreja de São Francisco** (see listing below); the central element is the surrounding **Convento de São Francisco.** Next to it is the **Igreja de Ordem Terceira de São Francisco** (Mon–Fri 8am–noon and 1–5pm), immediately recognizable by its ornately carved sandstone facade. Inside is a small green cloister, around the outside of which is some fine blue Portuguese tile.

Back at the Terreiro de Jesus, the two streets on either side of the Church of São Pedro (Rua Joao de Deus and Rua Alfredo de Brito) both run downhill to the **Largo Pelourinho.** This small, steeply sloping triangular square gets its name from the whipping post that used to stand at the top end. This was where slaves and criminals were flogged. The smaller building at the top of the square used to serve as the city's slave market, and now features the **Casa de Jorge Amado.** Unfortunately, there is very little to see in this museum set up in the former house of Brazil's most beloved writer. Looking downhill, on the right-hand side of the *largo* you'll find the blue-and–creamy yellow **Nossa Senora do Rosário dos Pretos** (Mon–Fri 7:30am–6pm; Sat–Sun 7:30am–noon). Literally translated as Our Lady of the Rosary of the Blacks, the high baroque structure was erected over the course of the 18th century by and for the African slaves who represented the backbone of Salvador's sugar economy. At the far end of the square is the tiny **Praça de Reggae.** At the lowest point of the Largo Pelourinho a narrow street leads steeply uphill to a trio of old baroque churches, the **Igreja de Carmo,** the **Igreja de Ordem Terceiro de Carmo,** and the **Igreja do Santissimo Santo do Passo.** Only the Ordem Terceiro is open to the public.

Igreja de São Francisco ★★★ At a time when Salvador was the biggest port in South America, the sugar barons of Salvador decided to show off their wealth by building this church in 1708. Completed in 1723, this high baroque church contains more than 100kg (220 lb.) of gold, slathered over every available knob and curlicue in the richly carved interior. On Monday, Wednesday, and Saturday, at 11:30am and 4pm, an impressive sound-and-light show takes place in the church.

 Largo Cruzeiro de S. Francisco s/n (off Terreiro de Jesus). ✆ **071/3322-6430.** Admission R$3. Mon–Sat 8am–5:30pm; Sun 7am–5pm. Bus: Praça de Sé.

Museu Afro-Brasileiro/Faculdade de Medicina ★ This fine old building (built in 1808) is now home to the Museu Afro-Brasileiro, which attempts to show the development of the Afro-Brazilian culture that arose as African slaves settled in Brazil. Particularly good is the large portion of the exhibit space dedicated to the Candomblé religion, explaining the meaning and characteristics of each god (Orixá) and the role it plays in the community. Make sure to ask for one of the English-language binders at the entrance—they contain translations of all of the displays. In the back room, 27 huge carved wood panels—the work of noted Bahian artist Carybé—portray the Orixás and the animal and symbol that goes with each. The museum staff can also provide information on Candomblé celebrations. Allow 30 to 45 minutes.

Antiga Faculdade de Medicina, Terreiro de Jesus s/n (just to the right of the basilica). ✆ **071/3321-2013.** Admission R$5. Mon–Fri 9am–6pm; Sat–Sun 10am–5pm. Bus: Praça da Sé.

Centro

Museu de Arte Sacra ★★★ This small but splendid museum displays one of Brazil's best collections of Catholic art. The artifacts are shown in the former Convent of Saint Teresa of Avila, a simple, beautiful building that is a work of art in itself. The collection includes oil paintings, oratorios (cabinets containing a crucifix), metalwork, and lots of wooden statues of saints. The jacaranda-wood oratorios are things of beauty, while the wooden saints seemed to have kept the same look of stunned piety through more than 2 centuries. If you're pressed for time, head for the two rooms of silver at the back.

Rua do Sodré 276. ✆ **071/3243-6310.** www.mas.ufba.br. Admission R$5 adults, R$3 students with valid ID, free for children 6 and under. Mon–Fri 11:30am–5pm. From Praça de Sé walk 10 min. south on Av. Carlos Gomes, turn right, and walk downhill on Ladeira Santa Teresa for 45m (150 ft.). Bus: Praça de Sé.

Cidade Baixa

Mercado Modelo ★ This former Customs building and slave warehouse burned to the ground in 1984 and was then rebuilt in its original 19th-century style. It houses just about everything Bahia has to offer in terms of arts, crafts, and souvenirs. Merchants invite you over for a closer look, press you if you seem interested, drop their prices if you hesitate (bargain hard in here!), and concede gracefully if you decline.

Praça Cayru (just across from the elevator). ✆ **071/3243-6543.** Mon–Sat 8am–7pm; Sun 8am–noon. Bus: Comércio.

Solar do Unhão ★★ An old sugar mill, the Solar consists of a number of beautifully preserved heritage buildings centered around a lovely stone courtyard that dates back to the 18th century. Half the fun is just to wander around and explore the various buildings set on the waterfront (the views are fabulous). The main building houses a small modern art museum; you'll find some works of Portinari and Di Cavalcanti on display. The path to the right of the main building leads to the sculpture garden with works by Caribé and Mario Cravo. Allow an hour. ***Tip***: On Saturdays at 6pm there is a live jazz performance, a great way to spend happy hour (R$4).

Av. do Contorno 8. ✆ **071/3329-0660.** Free admission. Tues–Sun 1–7pm. It is best to take a taxi from the Mercado Modelo or Pelourinho.

Barra

Museu Nautico da Bahia/Farol da Barra/Forte de Santo Antônio ★ The lighthouse, fort, and museum are mostly worth a visit for the views over the Bay of All

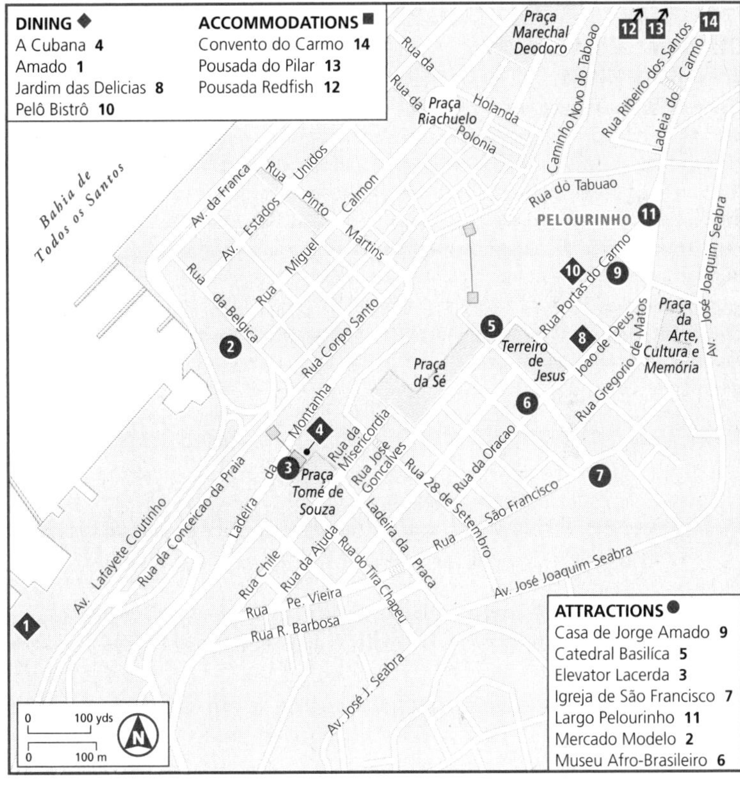

Saints. Erected in 1534, the Forte de Santo Antônio da Barra was the first and most important Portuguese fortress protecting Salvador. The museum inside the lighthouse contains a small collection of maps and charts, navigational instruments, and a number of archaeological finds from wrecks that the lighthouse obviously didn't help. Signage here is in English and Portuguese.

Farol da Barra, Praia da Barra s/n. ✆ **071/3264-3296.** Admission R$6. Mon 8:30am–noon; Tues–Sun 9am–7pm museum, 9am–10pm cafe. Bus: Barra or Via Orla.

Bonfim

Nosso Senhor do Bonfim ★★ Salvador's most famous church has a reputation for granting miracles, which explains why tourists and faithful alike flock to this relatively plain 18th-century church on a small peninsula just north of downtown. Don't miss the Room of Miracles at the back, where people give thanks for miracles by donating valuable or important objects. Definitely eye-catching are the numerous hanging body parts—models made of wood, plastic, even gold. This church also plays a very important role in the Candomblé religion and is dedicated to Oxalá, one of the highest deities. In January one of Salvador's most significant syncretist religious events takes place here, the famous washing of the steps.

 Largo do Bonfim. ✆ **071/3312-0196.** Free admission. Tues–Sun 6:30am–noon and 2–6pm. Located about 8km (5 miles)—or a R$20 taxi ride—north of Pelourinho on the Bonfim Peninsula. Bus: Catch a Bonfim bus at Praça de Sé or at the bottom of the Elevator Lacerda in Comércio.

Outdoor Activities

BEACHES & PARKS With over 48km (30 miles) of beaches within the city limits, finding a beach is much less trouble than deciding which one to go to. The beaches on the bay side of town (**Boa Viagem** and **Monte Serrat**) are not recommended for sunbathing but can be fun places to walk, watch a pickup soccer game, or have a beer. **Barra** is the closest clean beach area to downtown. Just around the bend you will come to **Praia de Ondina,** a narrow strip of beach cut off from Avenida Atlântica by shade-throwing hotel towers. **Praia de Amaralina** is as much known for the excellent food stalls as for the excellent surf and windsurfing conditions; the strong seas make it less ideal for swimming. **Praia dos Artistas** is highly recommended for swimmers and has waves gentle enough for children. **Praia de Piatã** has that tropical paradise look with lots of palm trees and kiosks offering cold drinks and perfect seafood snacks. One of the prettier beaches, **Itapuã,** has inspired many a song, including one by Vinicius de Moraes. The most recently trendy beaches are the ones the farthest from downtown; **Praia de Stella Maris** and **Flamengo** are where the young and beautiful gather on the weekends.

A number of the city parks provide plenty of recreational opportunities for kids and adults alike. In **Dique do Tororó Park,** Av. Marechal Costa e Silva s/n (✆ **071/3382-0847**), kayaks and paddleboats are available for rent. This pleasant park is also known for the set of 6m-tall (20-ft.) sculptures of eight Orixás in the middle of the lake. **Pituaçu Park,** Av. Otavio Mangabeira s/n, Pituaçu, across from Pituaçu beach (✆ **071/3231-2829**), contains a 2,500-hectare (1,000-acre-plus) reserve of Atlantic rainforest. This popular recreational park has 18km (11 miles) of cycle trails (plus bikes for rent) and a children's playground.

BOAT TOURS ★ Definitely worth the money, the schooner trips in the Bay of All Saints depart daily from the dock in Comércio. The city views from the water are fabulous, and the beaches at Ilha do Frade and Itaparica are quite refreshing. To book a schooner trip contact **Tatur** (✆ **071/3114-7900**). Prices range from R$50 to R$85, including pickup and drop-off at your hotel.

CAPOEIRA There are a few good schools in Pelourinho where you can either watch or learn capoeira. **Mestre Bimba's academy,** Rua das Laranjeiras 1, Pelourinho (✆ **071/3492-3197;** www.capoeiramestrebimba.com.br), is well set up to receive foreign students of all levels of experience. The academy offers 1-hour lessons for R$15 per person, no experience required (wear long comfortable pants and a T-shirt or tank top). Another popular school is the **Associação Brasileira de Capoeira Angola,** Rua Gregorio de Matos 38, Pelourinho (✆ **071/3321-3087**). Each class costs R$20, or you can purchase a package of six lessons for R$75. Contact the office for details.

DIVING The coast and bay around Salvador have some interesting dive spots, including reefs and shipwrecks. Trips and times vary according to the tides and weather conditions. Expect to pay around R$160 for a dive trip with two dives, including full equipment rental. Contact **Dive Bahia,** Av. Sete de Setembro 3809, Barra (✆ **071/3264-3820;** www.divebahia.com.br), for more information.

GOLF The closest golf course open to the general public can be found at the **Deville Salvador Hotel** (formerly the Sofitel). Greens fees are R$92 for 9 holes and R$145 to

Understanding Candomblé & the Terreiros

The religion of Candomblé is practiced throughout Brazil, but its roots are deepest in Salvador, where it forms an important part of community life. The practice originated with slaves brought to Brazil from West Africa; they believed in a pantheon of gods and goddesses (Orixás) who embodied natural forces such as wind, storm, ocean, and fire.

In Catholic Brazil, the practice of Candomblé was prohibited. Willing or no, Brazilian slaves were converted to Catholicism. By translating each of their gods into an equivalent saint, Candomblé followers found they could continue their native worship under the very noses of their Catholic priests and masters.

Oxalá, the creator and supreme ruler, thus became the Senhor do Bonfim; Iansã, the Orixá of wind and storms, resembled Santa Barbara; Yemanjá, the queen of the ocean and fresh water, seemed to have the same privileged position as Our Lady of Conception.

Actual Candomblé ceremonies are fun and fascinating—singing, chanting, and drumming, plus wonderful foods and perfumes are all used in order to please the Orixás and encourage them to come and possess some of the believers present.

Most *terreiros* (areas of worship) in Salvador will allow visitors, provided they follow a few basic rules: no revealing clothing (shorts and miniskirts are out); white clothing is preferred; no video or picture taking; visitors cannot participate but only observe. Real *terreiros* will not quote an admission price, but will appreciate a donation.

To attend a Candomblé session check with the Afro Brazilian Federation **(Federação Baiana de Culto Afro Brasileiro),** Rua Alfredo de Brito 39, 2nd Floor, Pelourinho (✆ **071/3321-1444**). Another good resource is the Afro-Brazilian museum in Pelourinho (✆ **071/3321-0383**), or contact **Tatur Turismo** (✆ **071/3450-7216;** www.tatur.com.br) to find out on which dates ceremonies take place.

Terreiros that accept visitors include **Menininha do Gantois,** Alto do Gantois 23, Federação (✆ **071/3331-9231;** service led by Mãe Carmem); **Ilê Axé Opô Afonjá,** Rua Direita de São Gonçalo do Retiro 245, Cabula (✆ **071/3384-6800;** especially popular with artists and visiting celebrities); and **Casa Branca,** Av. Vasco da Gama 463, Vasco da Gama (close to Rio Vermelho; ✆ **071/3334-2900**). Always take a taxi to the *terreiro;* some are in less safe neighborhoods, and addresses can be hard to find.

play the full 18-hole course; golf clubs rental R$40. Contact the hotel at ✆ **071/2106-8500** or the golf club directly at ✆ **071/2106-8522.**

Shopping

Salvador offers wonderful shopping and some of the best crafts in all of Brazil. The best buys include crafts made out of wood, ceramics, or leather; musical instruments; and CDs of *axé* music. Remember to always bargain. Pricey but unique pieces can be bought at the many galleries in Pelourinho. **Galeria 13,** Rua Santa Isabel 13 (✆ **071/3242-7783**), has a large exhibit space with regular showings of work by local artists. **Galeria de Arte Bel Borba,** Rua Luis Viana 14 (✆ **071/3243-9370**), specializes in the sculptures and paintings by Bel Borba; his work is colorful and fresh. For top-of-the-line names check out **Oxum Casa de Arte,** Rua Gregorio de Matos 18 (✆ **071/3321-0617**). The large collection of art includes work by Mario Cravo and Carybé, who did the large wood panels of the Orixás in the Afro-Brazilian museum. Founded by the government, the **Instituto de Artesanato Visconde de Mauá,** Rua Gregorio de Matos s/n, Pelourinho (✆ **071/3321-5638**), promotes and supports regional artists.

MUSIC/BOOKS To pick up the latest *axé* or Afro-reggae tunes, stop in at Aurisom, Praça da Sé 22, Pelourinho (✆ **071/3322-6893**). Small music store **Midialouca,** Rua da Fonte do Boi 81, Rio Vermelho (✆ **071/3334-2077**), offers a surprisingly large collection of Bahian and Brazilian music. In addition to DVDs and CDs, you will also find books on music and arts and songbooks. Bookstore **Tom do Saber,** Rua João Gomes 249, Rio Vermelho (✆ **071/3334-5677**), is hidden away in an odd pyramid-shaped building. You will find an excellent collection of art, travel and photo books of Salvador, Bahia, and Brazil as well as Brazilian literature (including translated versions), music CDs, and DVDs.

SHOPPING MALLS Salvador has a number of shopping malls outside of the downtown core. **Shopping Barra,** Av. Centenario 2992, Barra (✆ **071/3339-8222**), is just a few blocks from the Farol da Barra; it's open Monday through Friday from 10am to 10pm and Saturday from 9am to 8pm. Next to the bus station is one of the larger malls, **Shopping Iguatemi,** Av. Tancredo Neves 148, Pituba (✆ **071/3350-5060**), open Monday through Friday from 10am to 10pm and Saturday from 9am to 9pm.

SOUVENIRS For above-average souvenir T-shirts check out these stores: **Litoral Norte,** Rua Gregorio de Matos 30 (✆ **071/3322-3781**), which sells a beautiful collection of T-shirts and also has some lovely hand-painted hammocks; **Boutique Ilê Aiyê,** Rua Francisco Muniz Barreto 16 (✆ **071/3321-4193**), which sells CDs and T-shirts and other merchandise with the Ilê Aiyê band's logo, and part of the funds support the group's educational program; and **Projeto Axé,** Rua das Laranjeiras 9 (✆ **071/3321-7869**), a nonprofit organization that sells great skirts, shorts, kangas, blouses, and other clothing to raise funds to support projects for street children.

CARNAVAL IN SALVADOR

Carnaval is Salvador's biggest party. Over a million-and-a-half people (locals and tourists) join in to celebrate. In contrast to Rio's more spectator-oriented celebration, the focus in Salvador is on participation. The beat of choice is *axé* or Afro *axé,* the unique Bahian rhythm that combines African percussion with Caribbean reggae and Brazilian energy. The action is out on the streets with the blocos.

Salvador blocos have evolved into highly organized affairs that follow set routes. Many have corporate sponsorship; some even belong to production companies. Unavoidably, it also comes with a price tag.

The revelers that follow a bloco must buy a T-shirt *(abadá)* to identify themselves. In return they get to sing and dance behind the music truck in a large cordoned-off area, staffed by security guards who keep troublemakers out. If you follow the entire route you can expect to be on your feet for at least 6 hours. Most blocos parade 3 days in a row, and your *abadá* gives you the right to come all 3 days, if you've got the stamina. It is also possible to purchase an *abadá* for just 1 day.

Tips: Do not bring any valuables with you. Only bring as much money as you think you'll need. Don't dress up: For blocos just wear your *abadá,* shorts, and running shoes; otherwise shorts and a tank top will do just fine.

Blocos

Blocos all follow one of three set parade routes and start at designated times, taking 4 to 6 hours to complete the course. The blocos parade from Friday to Tuesday, some on 3 days, others on 4. Order and start times vary, so pick up an updated calendar just before Carnaval at one of the tourist offices.

The best resource for all Carnaval programming is the state tourism agency **Bahiatursa** (www.bahiatursa.ba.gov.br); they have information about all the parades and events taking place around town. To purchase an *abadá,* contact the **Central do Carnaval** (✆ **071/3372-6000;** www.centraldocarnaval.com.br); they represent at least a dozen of the most popular blocos. The prices for the *abadás* range from R$300 to R$900 for 2 or 3 days. The Central can also sell you an *abadá* for a day if you don't want to commit to the entire 3 days or want to try different blocos. Although trends change every year, some of the most popular blocos include **Camaleão;** its main attraction is Chiclete com Banana, one of the most popular Bahian bands. Brazilian superstar Ivete Sangalo has her own bloco, **Cerveja e Cia.** The followers of **Filhos de Ghandi** are instantly recognizable for the white Ghandi costumes worn by its 10,000 all-male followers. **Ilê Aiyê** is one of the most traditional Afro blocos. Only black participants are allowed to parade, but everyone is welcome to watch and cheer.

WHERE TO STAY

For visitors, it's really a choice of staying either in the heart of historic Pelourinho or in modern Rio Vermelho, close to the city's prime beaches. Pelourinho offers a number of comfortable pousadas, most of them located in restored historic buildings. Rio Vermelho, on the other hand, offers modern, comfortable hotels, beaches, and plenty of great restaurants and bars. Salvador's peak season ranges from mid-December to early March and maxes out during Carnaval. Most Carnaval packages start at R$1,500 and require a minimum 5-day stay. In the off season (Apr–June and Aug–Nov) some hotels give as much as a 50% discount, especially if you are staying a couple of nights.

Pelourinho

Very Expensive

Convento do Carmo ★★★ This former convent turned boutique hotel offers luxurious rooms with large comfy queen beds fitted out with softest of linens and piled high with a cornucopia of pillows. Little luxuries include free high-speed Internet and flatscreen TV. Bathrooms—converted monks cells, still with massive walls and thick wooden shutters—feature delightful rainfall showers. The conversion respected the original architecture as much as possible, and for that reason there is no standard room layout. The hotel's common areas are a delight; at night, subtle lighting is used to show off the convent to lovely effect.

Rua do Carmo 1, centro histórico, Salvador, 40030-170 BA. ✆/fax **0800/266-332** or 071/3327-8400. www.pousadas.pt. 79 units. R$450 double; R$650 luxury double. Extra person add R$50. Children 9 and under stay free in parent's room. AE, DC, MC, V. Parking R$25 daily. Bus: Praça de Sé. **Amenities:** Restaurant; bar; concierge; small health club; library; outdoor pool; room service; smoke-free rooms; spa. *In room:* A/C, TV, hair dryer, high-speed Internet, minibar.

Expensive

Pousada do Pilar ★★ This beautiful heritage building has been completely gutted and renovated, giving rooms a modern feel and bringing them up to modern standards. All 12 rooms are huge; seven have a veranda and face out over the port and ocean. The remaining five rooms have a small balcony (standing room only) and look onto the street. A wonderful breakfast with regional cakes is served on the rooftop patio overlooking Salvador's waterfront. Unlike most Pelourinho hotels, the Pousada do Pilar has an elevator.

Rua Direita de Santo Antônio 24, centro histórico, Salvador, 40301-280 BA. ✆ **071/3241-2033.** Fax 071/3241-3844. www.pousadadopilar.com. 12 units. City view R$230; ocean view and veranda R$270. Children 5 and under stay free in parent's room. Extra bed R$60. AE, DC, MC, V. Bus: Praça de Sé. **Amenities:** Room service. *In room:* A/C, TV, minibar, Wi-Fi.

Pousada Redfish ★★ Located in a gorgeous renovated colonial home, the Redfish features spacious rooms with high ceilings and tall windows. Standard rooms have two queen-size beds with firm mattresses, high ceilings, plus spacious bathrooms and a small balcony. (Avoid the two "garden" standard rooms that are just outside the breakfast area.) Room no. 6 is the largest standard room; no. 5 is the smallest. On the ground floor, a gallery features the artwork of the owner.

Ladeira do Boqueirão 1, centro histórico, Salvador, 40030-170 BA. ✆/fax **071/3241-0639.** www.hotelredfish.com. 8 units. R$240 standard double; R$300 luxury double. Extra person add R$45–R$60. Children 5 and under stay free in parent's room. MC, V. No parking. Bus: Praça de Sé. *In room:* A/C, minibar.

Barra

Barra offers sea and sun, but the area seems to have lost much of its previous charm. We recommend staying in Barra only during Carnaval, when the beachside boulevard transforms into one of the prime parade venues.

Expensive

Monte Pascoal Praia Hotel ★ Value Fabulously located across from Barra beach, the Monte Pascoal Praia offers great value. All rooms come with a king-size bed or two double beds—great for families traveling with young children. Every room has a balcony and at least a partial view of the ocean. This hotel is incredibly popular during Carnaval, as its pool deck overlooks the main parade route and the beach is just 45m (150 ft.) across the street.

Av. Oceanica 591, Barra, Salvador, 40170-010 BA. ✆ **071/2103-4000.** Fax 071/3245-4436. www.montepascoal.com.br. 83 units. R$185–R$235 double standard; R$250–R$300 double ocean view. Extra person R$60. Seasonal discounts available. Children 5 and under stay free in parent's room. AE, DC, MC, V. Parking R$12 per day. **Amenities:** Restaurant; bar; fitness room; outdoor pool; sauna. *In room:* A/C, TV, hair dryer, Internet, minibar.

Rio Vermelho

Very Expensive

Zank Boutique Hotel ★★★ Finds This is just what the (travel) doctor ordered, a stunningly beautiful, hip boutique hotel in the heart of Rio Vermelho. With only 20 rooms, Zank is an exclusive oasis on a hillside overlooking Rio Vermelho. To get the full experience, reserve one of the modern design rooms and let yourself be spoiled. The only "drawback" is that it will take a concerted effort to tear yourself away from your room, the roof top lounge, or the tropical garden patio.

Rua Almirante Barroso 161, Rio Vermelho, Salvador, 41950-350 BA. ✆/fax **071/3083-4000.** www.zankhotel.com.br. 20 units. R$530–R$700 double; R$630–R$850 deluxe double. AE, DC, MC, V. No children 13 and under allowed. **Amenities:** Restaurant; bar; concierge; outdoor pool; room service; smoke-free room; spa. *In room:* A/C, TV, hair dryer, minibar, Wi-Fi.

Expensive

Pestana Bahia ★★★ Set on an outcrop overlooking Rio Vermelho, the hotel's privileged location guarantees all 430 units an ocean view. Rooms on the 2nd through the 17th floors are superior, the ones on the 18th to the 22nd floors are deluxe. The difference is really in the small details; the deluxe rooms have bathtubs, 29-inch TVs, and a couch. Other than that the rooms are identical, very spacious with modern and funky decorations. The outdoor pool and sun deck overlook the beach; the Pestana's beach service includes towels, chairs, umbrellas, and drinks. A L'Occitane spa was inaugurated in 2009.

Rua Fonte do Boi, Rio Vermelho, Salvador, 41940-360 BA. ✆ **071/3453-8005.** Fax 071/3453-8066. www.pestanahotels.com.br. 430 units. R$240 superior double; R$320 deluxe double. Extra person add 30%. Children 12 and under stay free in parent's room. AE, DC, MC, V. Free parking. Bus: Rio Vermelho. **Amenities:** 3 restaurants; bar; concierge; small health club; large outdoor pool; smoke-free floors; spa. *In room:* A/C, TV, minibar, Wi-Fi.

Inexpensive

Ibis Rio Vermelho ★ The Ibis provides inexpensive no-frills accommodations in clean and plain rooms with quality basics such as firm beds with good linens, a desk or

A Glossary of Bahian Dishes

Rich with African influences, Bahian cuisine comes with its own ingredients and terminology. Here is a list of the most common dishes and ingredients:

abará (ah-bah-*rah*): Usually made by Baianas on the street, this is a tamale-like wrap made with bean paste, onions, and dendê oil, cooked in a banana leaf, and served with ginger and dried shrimp sauce.

acarajé (ah-kah-rah-*zhey*): Similar to the *abará* in that the dough is made with mashed beans, but the *acarajé* is deep-fried in dendê oil and stuffed with a shrimp sauce, hot peppers, and onion-tomato vinaigrette.

bobó de camarão (boh-*boh* dje cah-mah-*roun*): A stew made with shrimp, cassava paste, onion, tomato, cilantro, coconut milk, and dendê oil.

dendê oil (den-*de*): The key ingredient for Bahian food, this oil comes from the dendê palm tree and has a characteristic red color.

ensopado (en-so-*pah*-do): A lighter version of a *moqueca* made without the dendê oil.

moqueca (moo-*keck*-ah): Bahia's most popular dish, the ingredients include any kind of seafood stewed with coconut milk, lime juice, cilantro, onion, and tomato. Though the taste is similar, this stew is much thinner than a *bobó.*

vatapá (vah-tah-*pah*): One of the richest dishes, the *vatapá* is a stew made with fish, onion, tomato, cilantro, lime juice, dried shrimp, ground-up cashew nuts, peanuts, ginger, and coconut milk. The sauce is thickened with bread.

work table, and a hot shower. The hotel doesn't offer many services—no dry cleaning, gift shop, business center, buffet breakfast, or valet parking—but you do have the possibility of an ocean view at bargain rates. There is no price increase for rooms facing the ocean, so request one when you reserve or check in. Breakfast costs R$11. The Mercure hotel next door (owned by the same Accor group) offers pricier rooms with somewhat better amenities, but doesn't quite compare to the nearby Pestana.

Rua Fonte do Boi 215, Rio Vermelho, Salvador, 41940-360 BA. ✆ **071/3330-8300.** Fax 071/3330-8301. www.accorhotels.com.br. 252 units. R$115 double. Extra person add 30%. Children 12 and under stay free in parent's room. AE, DC, MC, V. Bus: Rio Vermelho. **Amenities:** Restaurant; bar; room service; smoke-free floors. *In room:* A/C, TV, minibar, Wi-Fi.

WHERE TO DINE

Pelourinho

Expensive

Pelô Bistrô ★★ BAHIAN This cute bistro goes far beyond the standard Bahian fare. The kitchen combines delicious local ingredients with a French flair, bringing a touch of sophistication to Pelourinho dining. Start with the grilled chicken saté with cashew sauce. Meat lovers may want to try the filet mignon with bacon and grainy mustard in an *açai* reduction. Lighter fare includes a prawn stir-fry with pineapple rice or a grilled fish with banana and Bahian *vatapá* stew.

Rua das portas do Carmo 6, Pelourinho. ✆ **071/3266-8550.** Main courses R$39–R$48. AE, DC, MC, V. Daily noon–10:30pm. Bus: Praça da Sé.

Moderate

Jardim das Delicias ★ Finds BRAZILIAN/CAFE Tucked away inside an antiques store on the ground floor of a colonial house in Pelourinho, this lovely courtyard restaurant is the perfect getaway from the bustle and crowds of Pelourinho. The restaurant serves a full Bahian menu, including *moquecas, bobô de camarão,* and even foods from the interior such as beans with smoked meat and sausage. However, the Jardim is also very nice for just a drink (the caipirinha made with cashew fruit is delicious) or a coffee and some sweets while you rest your feet.

Rua João de Deus 12, Pelourinho. ✆ **071/3321-1449.** Main courses R$40–R$70; the more expensive dishes serve 2. Sweets and desserts are all under R$15. AE, DC, MC, V. Daily noon–midnight. Bus: Praça da Sé.

Inexpensive

A Cubana ★ Finds DESSERT One of the oldest *sorveterias* (ice-cream parlors) in town, A Cubana can be found in the heart of Pelourinho. The menu is not huge, only 28 homemade flavors at any given time; the owners say they prefer quality to quantity. Try the unusual fruit flavors such as *jáca* (jack fruit) or *cupuaçu,* a fruit only found in the Northeast and the Amazon.

Rua das Portas do Carmo 12 (formerly known as Rua Alfredo de Brito), Pelourinho. A second A Cubana store is right next to the upper exit of the Lacerda elevator. ✆ **071/3321-6162.** Everything under R$12. No credit cards. Daily 8am–10pm. Bus: Praça da Sé.

Comércio

Very Expensive

Amado ★★ CONTEMPORARY BRAZILIAN Ultimately cool waterfront dining that combines traditional Bahian ingredients—manioc and seafood, principally—served in innovate ways. Try the giant squid stuffed with shrimp and leek in a Provençal sauce, the shrimp in a Gorgonzola-and-pistachio sauce, and a broiled *badejo* filet in a crust of cashews with an okra tapenade. For those not into fish, the menu has an equally intriguing array of chicken and beef creations. The wine list is on the pricey side. Service is young, pretty, and efficient.

Av. do Contorno 660, Comércio. ✆ **071/3322-3520.** www.amadobahia.com.br. Reservations recommended on weekends and in high season. Main courses R$36–R$54. AE, DC, MC, V. Mon–Sat noon–3pm and 7pm–midnight; Sun noon–4pm. Take a taxi. Even though it's not too far from the Mercado Modelo, the street is dark and very quiet at night.

Expensive

SOHO ★★★ JAPANESE Located inside the Bahia Marina, SOHO offers great waterfront seating and excellent dining. The large menu offers most of the usual Japanese suspects—sushis, sashimis, tempuras, yakisobas, and grilled meat teriyakis. But what earns this restaurant an above-average rating are intriguing local dishes such as the *shake lounge* (salmon sashimi with orange sauce, lime, and balsamic vinegar), the *uramaki shake* (salmon with green onion and sesame seeds), or the *marina maki* (a salmon-and-prawn roll flambéed in *cachaça*). Many of the hot dishes such as the yakisoba noodles are large enough to share, especially after a couple of the sashimi and sushi appetizers.

Av. do Contorno s/n, inside the Bahia Marina, Comércio. ✆ **071/3322-4554.** Reservations recommended. Main courses R$22–R$48. AE, DC, MC, V. Mon 7pm–midnight; Tues–Sun noon–3pm and 7pm–midnight. Take a taxi. Even though it is not too far from the Mercado Modelo, the street is dark and very quiet at night.

Rio Vermelho

Over the last few years, Rio Vermelho has grown into a bustling, lively restaurant destination. There are several excellent options, most centered on the main square, Praça Brigadeiro Farias Rocha.

Expensive

Fogo de Chão STEAK ★★ Even seafood lovers may crave a delicious piece of beef. This elegant all-you-can-eat steak restaurant serves up the finest beef in town. Cuts include all the Brazilian classics, such as *picanha, alcatra,* and *maminha,* as well as prime Argentine and Uruguayan beef. Makes sure you try the dessert of grilled mango and pineapple with a hint of brown sugar and a serving of fresh coconut ice cream.

Praça Colombo 4, Rio Vermelho. ✆ **071/3555-9292.** www.fogodechao.com.br. All-you-can-eat main course R$73 (doesn't include drinks or dessert); children 2 and under free, ages 3–7 R$24, and ages 8–11 R$48). AE, DC MC, V. Mon–Fri noon–4pm and 6pm–midnight; Sat noon–midnight; Sun noon–10pm. Bus: Rio Vermelho.

Moderate

Dona Mariquita BRAZILIAN Tucked away in a little laneway opposite the main square, Dona Mariquita serves great tasting Brazilian food. Start off with the *pastel,* puffy fried savory meat dumpling served with a hot pepper jam. Main courses include specialties from the coast (seafood and fish *moquecas* and *bobó*), as well as inland dishes such as a bean stew and *carne seca* (sun-dried beef). On Friday evenings there is live music. Instead of wine or beer, order a delicious caipirosca. We highly recommend the umbucaja, a combination of two typical Northeastern fruits with vodka.

Rua do Meio 178, Rio Vermelho. ✆ **071/3334-6947.** Main courses R$28–R$36 for 2. AE, V. Tues noon–3pm; Wed–Sat noon–3pm and 6pm–midnight. Bus: Rio Vermelho.

Lambreta Grill BRAZILIAN/SEAFOOD Japanese chef Fukino runs one of the most popular yet laid-back seafood restaurants in town. The decor is ultrabasic, but wait until you taste the food! Lambretas are small oysters; try them as an appetizer, grilled and topped with sun-dried tomato, curry sauce, garlic, or calabresa pepper. For the main course try the grilled seafood served on a piping-hot steel griddle, piled high with juicy and tender morsels of squid, prawns, mussels, and octopus, served with a side of potatoes and palm heart.

Rua Alexandre Gusmão 70, Rio Vermelho. ✆ **071/3335-0107.** Main courses R$35–R$50 for 2. AE, MC, V. Mon–Sat 6pm–2am. Bus: Rio Vermelho.

SALVADOR AFTER DARK

Night owls won't lack for options in Salvador. The old city center of Pelourinho hums with music, people, and a lively mix of activities that Brazilians call *movimento.* Farther out along the beaches, music venues are bigger and more geared toward the club crowd.

The Performing Arts

Home to the Bahian Symphony Orchestra and the Balé (ballet) de Castro Alves, the **Teatro Castro Alves,** Praça Dois de Julho s/n, Campo Grande (✆ **071/3339-8000;** www.tca.ba.gov.br), is your best bet for catching fine-arts performances. One of the best places to see contemporary bands is the **Teatro Sesi Rio Vermelho,** Rua Borges dos Reis 9, Rio Vermelho (✆ **071/3335-1529;** www.sesi.fieb.org.br/teatrosesi). Housed in a renovated heritage building, it hosts local and Brazilian acts, ranging from jazz to blues to MPB and even pop.

Music & Dance Clubs

In the evenings, Pelourinho often comes alive with music. Two of the most popular venues for concerts are the **Praça Quincas Berro D'Agua** and the **Largo Pedro Archanjo.** Check with the Bahiatursa office in Pelourinho or look in the newspaper for information on events (programming has become a bit spottier, alas, since a new state government cut back on cultural funding).

Groove Bar, Rua Almirante Marques de Leão 351, Barra (✆ **071/3267-5124;** www.groovebar.com.br), is the best place in town for live rock and blues. Thursdays and Fridays are reserved for excellent cover bands (think U2 and Pink Floyd), as well as original acts. Saturday's lineup is more pop and dance music, including classics from Michael Jackson and a range of Brazilian artists. **Olodum** started as a recreational group for residents of Pelourinho who had few options during Carnaval. More than 20 years later, Olodum has grown into a cultural phenomenon with international fame. The group's mandate is to preserve and value black culture and heritage. Every Tuesday night the group performs at the Praça Teresa Batista starting at 8pm. Contact the Olodum office at ✆ **071/3321-5010,** or log on to www.olodum.com.br for information on concerts and Carnaval rehearsals.

Salvador's current hottest dance club for lovers of house and electro is **Maddre,** Av. Otávio Mangabeira 2471, Pituba (✆ **071/3346-0012**). The beautifully designed space hosts a range of well-known national and international DJs. **Boomerangue,** Rua da Paciência 307, Rio Vermelho (✆ **071/3334-6640**), offers a great combination of dance club and live music venue, right in the heart of Rio Vermelho. It's usually open Thursday to Saturday.

Bars & Pubs

Close to centro, the **Bahia Café,** Quartel dos Aflitos s/n (the entrance is at the very end of the square, walk toward the viewpoint; ✆ **071/3328-1332**), offers spectacular views overlooking the bay. Built of glass and set at the very end of a long pier, the **Bar da Ponta,** Praça dos Tupinambas 2, Avenida Contorno (✆ **071/3326-2211**), is one of Salvador's prime sunset spots. The wine list and ultramodern decor attract a 30-something yuppie crowd who stay long after the sun goes down. No view in Salvador beats that of the **Café do Farol,** Praia da Barra s/n, Barra (✆ **071/3267-8881**), inside the lighthouse at Barra. To access the cafe you must pay admission to the museum (R$6). It's open Tuesday through Sunday 9am to 10pm.

Gay & Lesbian Bars

A great resource for gay travelers, the **Grupo Gay da Bahia,** Rua Frei Vicente 24, Pelourinho (✆ **071/3321-1848;** www.ggb.org.br), has information on tourism and recreational opportunities in Salvador, as well as on community activism.

The dance club at **Queens Clube,** Rua Teodoro Sampaio 160, just behind the Biblioteca Nacional (✆ **071/328-6220**), is open Friday and Saturday midnight to 6am. Also popular, **Off Club,** Rua Dias d'Avilla 33, Barra (✆ **071/3267-6215;** www.offclub.com.br), attracts a mixed crowd of both male and female clubbers. Doors don't open until 11:30pm. One of the more popular Carnaval blocos that counts on a huge gay following is the **Bloco dos Mascarados** (✆ **071/3237-0066**), led by Bahian singer Margaret Menezes. Check with the tourist office for the dates and locations of the Bloco rehearsals *(ensaios).*

A SIDE TRIP FROM SALVADOR

Morro de São Paulo ★★

To really get away from it all (as if the rest of Bahia wasn't relaxed enough), consider a beach holiday in Morro de São Paulo. Set on an island only accessible by boat or plane, this small beachside village is blissfully isolated—no cars, no lights, no motorcars, though luxuries abound. The main mode of transport is your feet; wheelbarrows double as taxis, transporting everything from luggage to food and drinks for the evening beach party. ***Tip:*** Plan your trip from April through June to take advantage of low season rates and enjoy peace and quiet.

Essentials

GETTING THERE The most direct route to Morro de São Paulo is via the catamaran departing from downtown Salvador; the Terminal Maritimo do Mercado Modelo is just across the street from the Mercado Modelo. There are several daily departures: 8:30 and 10:30am, Lancha Ilhabela (✆ **071/3326-7158** or 071/9195-6744); 1:30pm, Catamarã Farol do Morro (✆ **075/3652-1083**); and at 9am and 2pm, Catamarã Biotur (✆ **071/3326-7674**). Each way costs R$70 and takes about 2 hours.

The quickest way to get to Morro de São Paulo is to fly. Both **Addey** (✆ **071/3377-1993**) and **Aerostar** (✆ **071/3377-4406**) offers at least three flights a day, more on weekends and in high season; one-way fare is R$230, and flying time is 30 minutes. Flights depart and arrive at Salvador's international airport, making for convenient connections with onward flights.

VISITOR INFORMATION For visitor information stop by the **CIT (Central de Informações Turisticas),** Praça Aureliano Lima s/n (✆ **075/3652-1083**). This office can assist you with accommodations and transportation as well as book excursions. An excellent website on the area is www.morrodesaopaulo.com.br.

What to See & Do in Morro de São Paulo

The main attraction of Morro de São Paulo is the beach, or better, the beaches. Each has a unique flavor. **First Beach** is mostly residential; **Second Beach** has lots of pousadas and people. This is where you'll find vendors, watersports, and restaurants and nightlife after sundown. **Third Beach** is quite narrow; at high tide it almost disappears. It is much quieter, perfect for a stroll. **Fourth Beach** is the (almost) deserted island tropical beach—wide, white sand, palm trees, and a few small restaurants. The town itself consists of just a few streets and the main square. During the day it's pretty quiet, as most people hang out at the beach. In the evening, a crafts market starts up, attracting both locals and tourists to the main square. The restaurants surrounding the main square fill up with diners feasting on local seafood dishes. More active pursuits include boating, horseback riding, and hiking.

Outdoor Activities

Marlins, Rua da Prainha s/n (✆ **075/3652-1242**), the island's main tour operator, offers a number of trips. The most popular is the **8-hour boat trip** around the island, with plenty of stops for swimming or snorkeling. Another great boat tour goes out to **Ilha de Boibepa** (a small island off the main island). Tours cost R$50 per person, lunch not included. More active trips include **hikes** to waterfalls or a **walk** along the cliffs and beach to Gamboa for R$20 to R$30 per person.

Another operator that offers a number of interesting activities is **Rota Tropical,** Rua da Prainha 75, along the trail that connects Second and First beaches (✆ **075/3652-1151;** www.morrodesaopaulobrasil.com.br). The company covers practically every possible destination in the region. Full-day boat tours range from R$60 to R$80 per person (minimum of two). Other tours include horseback riding, various hikes, and boat tours. For scuba diving contact **Companhia do Mergulho,** Pousada Farol do Morro, Primeira Praia (✆ **075/3652-1200**). Conditions are best in the summer months (Dec–Jan); in the winter (June–Sept), when the rains are heavy, visibility can be poor. A double dive with all equipment included costs R$150. The dive store also rents out masks and snorkels for R$10 to R$15.

Where to Stay in Morro de São Paulo

In the heart of the village overlooking the main square, **Pousada o Casarão ★★**, Praça Aureliano Lima s/n (✆/fax **075/3652-1022;** www.ocasarao.net), offers pleasant rooms in the main heritage building. However, the best accommodations are the bungalows tucked away in the lush back garden, against the sloping hillside. Each is decorated in a different style—Indonesian, Japanese, Indian, African—with rich furnishings and artwork. Units in the main building cost R$125 to R$180 double; bungalows are R$160 to R$280 double.

Vila Guaiamú ★★★, Terceira Praia (✆ **075/3652-1035;** www.vilaguaiamu.com.br), is far enough from the village for total peace and quiet, yet close enough that within 10 minutes you can be dancing the night away. This lovely pousada consists of 24 cabins set among the lush green gardens. Cabins come in standard or deluxe, the only difference being the air-conditioning and television in the deluxe rooms. The pousada is located halfway down Terceira Praia, about a 20-minute walk from the village. High-season rates range from R$240 to R$340 for a double; low-season rates are R$160 to R$195. It's closed May to June.

The lovely **Anima** hotel, Praia do Encanto (✆ **075/3652-2077;** www.animahotel.com), sits in splendid isolation on the outer reaches of Fourth Beach. Accommodations are in self-contained bungalows. Some face the sea; others hide back in the coconut groves. All feature comfortable queen-size beds with top-quality linens, big windows, high ceilings, rattan chairs for relaxing, and hammocks on the balconies for relaxing even more. The only disadvantage to staying here is the long hike back to the village. High season, you'll pay R$250 to R$330 for a double; low-season rates drop to R$200 to R$240.

Where to Dine in Morro de São Paulo

Morro de São Paulo has a surprising number of excellent restaurants. The main street of the village, Broadway, is lined with eateries. **Sabor da Terra** (✆ **075/3652-1156**) is famous for its generous portions of outstanding *moquecas* and *bobó de camarão* (prawn stew). Meat eaters can order the *picanha na chapa,* tender steak served at your own table grill. The tables on the veranda (if you can snag one) offer great views of the main street. One of the prettiest viewpoints in town is that of **O Casarão** (✆ **075/3652-1022;** closed Sun), overlooking the main square. The menu offers a number of excellent fish and seafood dishes (portions serve two people), including *moquecas* and grilled fish. Located on the Fourth Beach (Quarta Praia), **Pimenta Rosa,** at Pousada Vila dos Corais (✆ **075/3652-1506;** daily 10am–6pm; closed May–June) is a great spot for a long leisurely lunch by the beach. Specialties include grilled fish and seafood stews.

8 RECIFE & OLINDA

1,874km (1,164 miles) NE of Rio de Janeiro, 2,121km (1,318 miles) NE of São Paulo, 682km (424 miles) NE of Salvador

Recife and Olinda stand within sight of each other on Brazil's Northeast coast, one city on a hilltop, the other on a river mouth, one founded by the Portuguese, the other by the Dutch. Recife is the second-largest city in Brazil's Northeast, and aside from a small but pretty historical core, it's not really worth a visit, at least not in comparison with Salvador or São Luis.

Then there's Olinda. Founded by the Portuguese in 1530 on a steep hill overlooking the harbor, Olinda grew rich and proud on sugar exports. The Dutch, keen to move in on the sugar business, took the Pernambuco capital in 1630. With the exception of a few churches, it was utterly destroyed. In need of a capital of their own, the Dutch set to work draining and diking the islands at the mouth of the harbor. Their new city of Mauritstad quickly turned into a bustling commercial center. When the Dutch were expelled in the 1654, the Portuguese rebuilt Olinda as a matter of pride, but the center of the region had shifted. The former Dutch city was renamed Recife. By the 19th century it had already far outgrown Olinda, still in its largely pristine 17th-century condition.

Restoration work began on Olinda in the 1970s. In 1982 its lovingly preserved historic core was declared a UNESCO World Heritage Site. Unlike Salvador's Pelourinho, however, Olinda feels very much lived in. Walk its streets and you'll come across kids playing soccer on a patch of hard-packed dirt, women carrying groceries, perhaps artists in courtyards carving interesting-looking woodwork. The city is hilly but distances are short, and with so much to capture your attention, it's a joy to explore.

ESSENTIALS

Getting There

BY PLANE **Azul, Gol, Ocean Air, TAM, TRIP,** and **Webjet** all fly into Recife's **Aeroporto Internacional dos Guararapes,** Praça Ministro Salgado Filho s/n, Boa Viagem (airport code REC; ✆ **081/3464-4188**), about 12km (7½ miles) south of the city center and just a few kilometers from the beachside hotels in Boa Viagem. A taxi to Boa Viagem costs R$18 to R$26 and to Olinda, R$45 to R$60.

BY BUS Buses arrive at Recife's **Terminal Integrado de Passageiros (TIP),** Rodovia BR-232, Km 15, Curado (✆ **081/3452-1999**), 14km (8½ miles) west of downtown. A

 Metrô connects the bus station to downtown Recife's station, Estação Central. ***Note:*** Buses from Recife to Olinda or to Porto de Galinhas leave from downtown and Boa Viagem, not from this station.

Getting Around

Downtown Recife consists of three main areas: **Bairro do Recife** (often called Recife Antigo, or Old Recife), **Santo Antônio,** and **Boa Vista/Santo Amaro.** Recife Antigo is the oldest part of the city, founded by the Dutch in the 1630s. An area of at least 15 city blocks centered on the Rua da Bom Jesus has been restored to its former glory. The best time to experience this area is during the weekends, when it is at its liveliest.

Three bridges connect Old Recife with Santo Antônio. It's one of Recife's main commercial areas, and the home of many of its most interesting sights. Narrow streets packed with shops and vendors surround beautiful baroque churches and plazas. The main beach and residential area of Recife starts just south of downtown and carries on uninterrupted for many miles. The first stretch, where Avenida Boa Viagem begins, is called Pina. The area around Polo Pina is a popular nightlife spot with some bars and restaurants. Farther along the beach the neighborhood name changes to Boa Viagem. This is the city's main hotel area. At low tide the reefs that lie just off the coast are easily visible in the perfectly clear blue water.

Olinda lies atop a hill, 7km (4¼ miles) north of downtown. Regular buses make the trip in about 30 minutes. You'll arrive at the Praça do Carmo bus station at the foot of Olinda. From there it's all uphill. The town is small enough that directions aren't really necessary. Keep strolling and you'll see everything.

BY BUS From Boa Viagem, regular buses run along Avenida Domingos Ferreira into downtown, about a 20-minute trip. Those marked CONDE DA BOA VISTA will loop through Boa Vista and into Santo Antônio via the Duarte Coelho Bridge, stopping at Praça da Independencia. Some of these buses continue across the Mauricio de Nassau bridge into Old Recife (ask the ticket seller). If not, it's only a 10-minute walk. Once downtown, all sights are easily reachable on foot.

From Boa Viagem, two regular buses travel directly to and from Olinda's Praça do Carmo bus station: SETUBAL-PRINCIPE and SETUBAL-CONDE DA BOA VISTA. The trip takes about 50 minutes. From Olinda, all buses depart from the bus station on Praça do Carmo.

BY TAXI Taxis are quick and reliable and can be hailed anywhere or booked by phone. **Coopseta Aeroporto** (✆ **081/3464-4153**) specializes in airport service. Both **Ligue-taxi** (✆ **081/3428-6830**) and **Tele-Taxi** (✆ **081/3429-4242**) can be booked ahead of time.

Visitor Information

Recife's airport has a **tourist information booth** at the arrivals level that's open daily from 8am to 6pm (✆ **081/3462-4960**). The best information booth is at Praça Boa Viagem, open daily from 8am to 8pm (✆ **081/3463-3621**). The staff is helpful and will provide an excellent free map of Recife.

In Olinda, the tourist information office is located near the Largo do Amparo on Rua do Bonsucesso 183 (✆ **081/3439-9434**), open daily from 9am to 6pm. There is also a kiosk at the Praça do Carmo, where the buses from Recife arrive.

FAST FACTS For a bank, go to **Banco do Brasil;** in Recife, you'll find a branch at Rua Barão De Souza Leão 440, Boa Viagem (✆ **081/3462-3777**), and in Olinda, at Av.

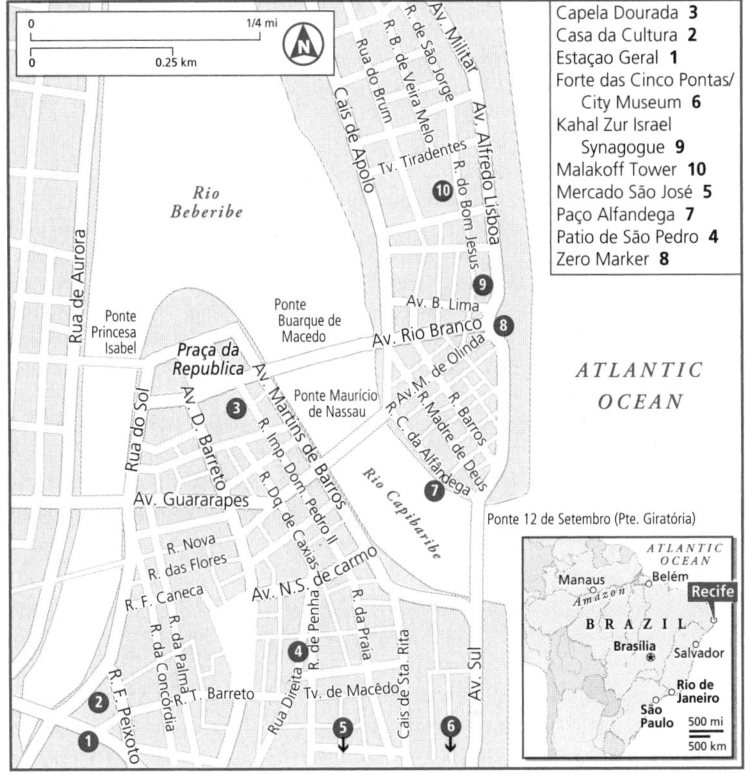

Getulio Vargas 1470, Bairro Novo (✆ **081/3439-1344**). To exchange currency, try **Monaco Cambio,** Praça Joaquim Nabuco 19, Santo Antônio (✆ **081/3424-3727**), or **Colmeia Cambio,** Rua dos Navegantes 783, Boa Viagem (✆ **081/3465-3822**).

In an emergency, dial ✆ **190** for police, ✆ **193** for fire and ambulance. You can also contact the **Tourist Police,** Praça Min. Salgado Filho s/n (at the airport; ✆ **081/3303-7217**). For medical attention, go to **Centro Hospitalar Albert Sabin,** Rua Senador José Henrique 141, Ilha do Leite (✆ **081/3421-5411**).

WHAT TO SEE & DO

The allure of both Olinda and Recife lies not so much in particular sights as in the urban fabric. In Olinda, while no particular church merits a special trip, the ensemble of 300- and 400-year-old architecture makes for a memorable stroll.

BUS TOURS **Luck Viagens** (✆ **081/3366-6222;** www.luckviagens.com.br) offers a range of bus tours, such as a 4-hour city tour that shows the highlights of Recife and Olinda (R$30). There's also a full-day tour to Itamaracá island (R$75), where the Dutch built Fort Orange in 1631, and day trips to Porto de Galinhas for the best beaches and snorkeling in the area.

ON FOOT The place to start a walking tour of Recife is at the **Zero Marker** in the heart of Old Recife. Gaze out toward the ocean from here, and about 90m (300 ft.) offshore you'll see the long low reef from which the city draws its name.

A block back from the Zero Marker is the **Rua do Bom Jesus.** The street and this whole island are the oldest part of Recife, founded by the Dutch. Take the Avenida Rio Branco and cross the Macedo bridge to **Santo Antônio.** This area, too, was the work of the Dutch. At the foot of the bridge is the **Praça da República**★, one of Recife's most graceful public areas.

Just behind the Beaux Arts **Palácio da Justiça** on Rua do Imperador Dom Pedro II, you pass by the aptly named **Capela Dourada (Golden Chapel),** Rua do Imperador Dom Pedro II 206. The altar is a two-story arch of jacaranda and cedar, gilt with gold. Christ hangs on a golden cross with gold and silver rays shining out behind his head.

Crossing Primeiro do Marco and sneaking south through the fun maze of narrow streets (parallel to but not on Av. Dantas Barreto), you will come—provided you find **Rua do Fogo** on the far side of **Avenida N.S. do Carmo**—to the **Pátio de São Pedro.** This broad cobblestone square is enclosed by dozens of small restored shops, all gaily painted in bright pinks, blues, and greens.

Crossing Avenida Dantas Barreto from here you come to the **N.S. do Carmo Basilica.** Continue for a few more blocks to reach the **Casa da Cultura**★, Rua Floriano Peixoto, Santo Antônio (✆ **081/3224-2850**). The cells of this former penitentiary are now occupied by souvenir shops. You'll find a good selection of local crafts: ceramics, woodcarvings, leather sandals, lace, and clothing.

Highlights of Recife

Centro Cultural Judaico de Pernambuco/Kahal Zur Israel Synagogue ★★

This reconstructed synagogue is built on the foundations of the original Kahal Zur Israel synagogue, founded in the 1640s when Recife was ruled by religiously tolerant Holland. With the end of Dutch rule in 1654 many of Recife's Jews fled to New Amsterdam (later New York), and evidence of the temple all but disappeared. In the late 1990s, traces of the old synagogue were discovered. The reconstructed building is not a replica of the original but a monument that honors the Jewish community in Recife.

Rua do Bom Jesus 197, Bairro do Recife. ✆ **081/3224-2128.** Admission R$4. Tues–Fri 9am–5pm; Sun 2–6pm. Bus: Conde de Boa Vista.

Forte das Cinco Pontas/City Museum ★★ Perhaps the most curious thing about the Fort of Five Points is that it only has four. The original Dutch fort built in 1630 had five, but the Portuguese leveled that fort and rebuilt in their traditional four-pointed style. The excellent city museum, which takes up two wings of the fort, has two rooms devoted to the Dutch period, including a wealth of maps and drawings of the early colony.

Largo dos Cinco Pontas, Bairro de São José. ✆ **081/3224-2812.** Admission R$3. Tues–Fri 9am–5pm; Sat–Sun 1–5pm. Bus: São Jose.

Oficina Cerâmica Francisco Brennand ★★★ The lifelong work of ceramic artist Francisco Brennand is on display at this sprawling estate/workshop. Although famous for some notorious giant phallic sculptures, his collection is so much more and includes thousands of sculptures, tiles, and pieces of ceramic art, as well as drawings. His work is beautifully displayed in several buildings as well as various outdoor settings. The Burle Marx garden was designed by the landscape artist himself and decorated with Brennand statues. ***Tip:*** The restaurant inside the gift shop serves excellent regional dishes and juices.

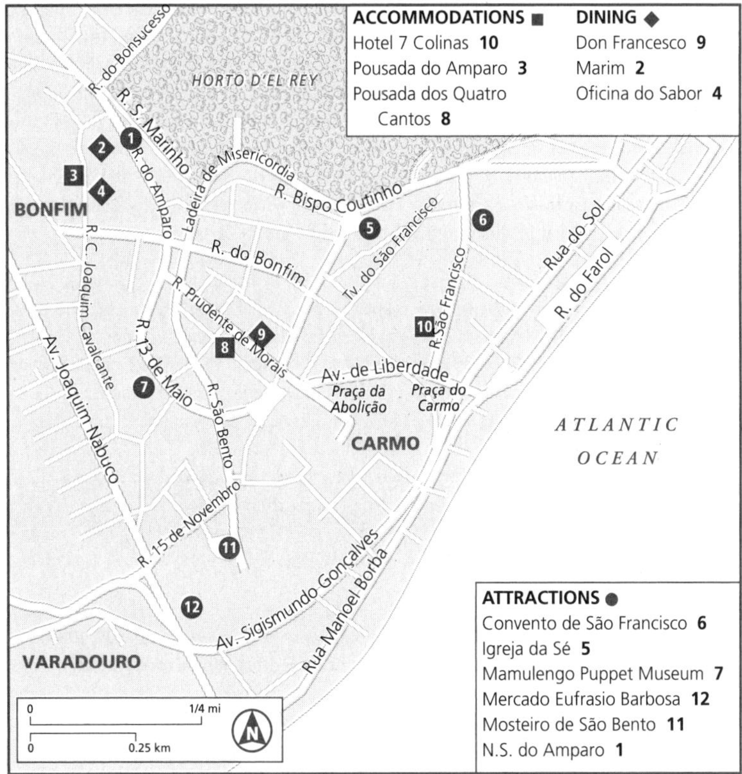

Propriedade Santos Cosme e Damião s/n, Várzea. ✆ **081/3271-2466.** www.brennand.com.br. Admission R$4. Mon–Thurs 8am–5pm; Fri 8am–4pm. Taxi recommended.

Highlights of Olinda

The only way to truly explore Olinda is by hitting the cobblestones and setting off on foot. Most attractions are open daily. Sunday and Monday are pretty quiet. If you like it more lively and bustling, visit on Friday and Saturday.

Buses from Recife will drop you off at the Praça do Carmo, dominated by the lovely **N.S. do Carmo church** ★. This more-than-400-year-old church has finally undergone a much-needed renovation. From N.S. do Carmo you can swing to your right on the Rua São Francisco, which leads to the **Convento de São Francisco** ★★ (closed Sat afternoon and all day Sun). Built in 1577, this was the first Franciscan monastery in Brazil. From the Convento São Francisco, the Travessia São Francisco leads up to the Ladeira de Sé and the **Igreja da Sé.** The square in front of the Igreja da Sé provides the best view in town. You see the red-tiled roofs and church towers of Olinda, and thick stands of tropical trees set against the sparkling blue ocean below. Farther south you get great views of Recife's skyline all the way to Boa Viagem. The very steep **Ladeira da Misericordia** leads down toward the **Rua do Amparo** ★★. This is one of Olinda's prettiest streets, featuring small, brightly colored colonial houses packed with galleries, restaurants, and shops. **Largo do Amparo★** has the feel of a little Mexican square.

Leaving the square and following Rua Amparo until it becomes Rua Treze de Maio, you come to the **Mamulengo Puppet Museum ★** (✆ **081/3429-6214;** Tues–Fri 10am–5pm, Sat–Sun 11am–5pm; free admission). The small three-floor museum assembles puppets used in Northeastern folk drama. Farther down, following Rua São Bento leads to the **Mosteiro de São Bento.** Built in 1582, this monastery is still home to 27 Benedictine monks, and only the church is open to the public. From the monastery, Rua XV de Novembro leads down to the **Largo do Varadouro;** the large crafts market, **Mercado Eufrasio Barbosa,** is worth a visit. Those returning to Recife can take a bus from this square instead of returning to the Praça do Carmo.

Outdoor Activities

Recife's location on a series of islands makes a boat tour a good way to see the town. **Catamaran Tours** (✆ **081/3424-2845;** www.catamarantours.com.br) offers sightseeing tours on broad, comfortable catamarans. Historic tours of 1½ hours take in the old city (R$25). Full-day tours head up the coast to visit Fort Orange and the beaches of Itamaracá (R$35). Tours depart from Avenida Sul, 50m (164 ft.) past the Forte Cinco Pontas. Exact departure times depend on the tide. Call ahead to confirm.

Wreck divers will be in heaven; at least 15 wrecks are diveable and within easy reach. For excursions contact **Projeto Mar,** Rua Bernardino Pessoa 410, Boa Viagem (✆ **081/3326-0162;** www.projetomar.com.br). Two dives including all the gear cost R$130; a nondiving companion pays R$30.

Shopping in Recife & Olinda

In Recife's downtown neighborhood of Santo Antônio, the streets around the **Pátio São Pedro** and in between **Avenida N.S. do Carmo** and **Rua Primeiro de Março** are all jampacked with little shops. Some of the alleys are so narrow that they resemble Asian street markets. The best time to explore is weekdays during office hours. The most beautiful mall is the **Shopping Paço Alfandega,** Cais da Alfandega 35, Recife Antigo (✆ **081/3419-7500**), housed in the restored 18th-century Customs building. Those who are staying in Boa Viagem can visit the large crafts market on the Praça Boa Viagem Monday through Friday 3 to 11pm and 8am to 11pm on weekends.

Olinda's historic downtown offers many art galleries and interesting shops. There are also two excellent markets for local handicrafts. **Mercado Eufrasio Barbosa** (also called Mercado Varadouro) is located in the former Customs house at Sigismundo Gonçalves s/n (closed Sun). Up the hill close to the Praça João Alfredo is the **Mercado Ribeira,** Bernardo Vieira de Melo s/n, open daily. The merchants there specialize in religious arts, paintings, woodcarvings, and regional crafts.

WHERE TO STAY

Recife/Boa Viagem

Just a 20-minute bus ride from downtown, the beach neighborhood of Boa Viagem offers a variety of hotels, some good restaurants, and a bit of nightlife, all within easy access of the beach.

Expensive

Beach Class Suites ★★★ The best option in Boa Viagem, the brand-new Beach Class Suites offers bright and spacious rooms at a lower rate than most five-star properties. All rooms are decorated with modern furniture, predominantly white with some splashes of colorful art. All rooms have balconies; some also have a small kitchen with a microwave and coffeemaker. A nice feature is the women's-only floor, ideal for women traveling alone. Internet rates offer as much as 50% savings.

Av. Boa Viagem 1906, Boa Viagem, Recife, 51011-000 PE. ✆ **0800/55-5855** or 081/2121-2626. www.beachclasssuites.com.br. 145 units. R$280–R$390 double (Internet special R$226–R$260). Extra person add 25%. Children 7 and under stay free in parent's room. AE, DC, MC, V. Free parking. Bus: Boa Viagem. **Amenities:** Restaurant; bar; exercise room; outdoor pool; room service; sauna; smoke-free rooms. *In room:* A/C, TV, hair dryer, Internet, minibar.

Moderate

Best Western Manibu ★ Kids Value The Best Western Manibu is one of the few hotels that easily accommodates three to four people in a room at a decent price, making it ideal for families or friends traveling together. The hotel offers affordable and comfortable rooms, pretty much what you would expect from a Best Western. Several floors, including all rooms in the green wing, have recently been renovated and are in tip-top shape. Being 2 blocks off the waterfront translates into significant savings. Senior travelers (over 55) are entitled to an addition 10% off. The leisure area has also been renovated and includes a pool, sauna, and small gym.

Av. Conselheiro Aguiar 919, Boa Viagem, Recife, 51011-031 PE. ✆ **081/3084-2811.** Fax 081/3084-2810. www.hotelmanibu.com.br. 156 units. R$175–R$220 double. Extra person add 20%. Children 12 and under stay free in parent's room. AE, DC, MC, V. Free parking. Bus: Boa Viagem. **Amenities:** Restaurant; bar; small outdoor pool; room service; smoke-free rooms; weight room. *In room:* A/C, TV, fridge, hair dryer, Internet.

Hotel Jangadeiro ★★ Value Overlooking Boa Viagem beach, Hotel Jangadeiro offers the best value for money in this upscale neighborhood. This small, pleasant hotel has been recently renovated and the rooms are spacious and bright. It's worth paying a little bit extra for the oceanview rooms; all come with balconies and offer stunning views of Boa Viagem beach. The standard rooms look out onto the neighboring buildings, or have a partial ocean view but lack the balcony.

Av. Boa Viagem 3114, Boa Viagem, Recife, 51020-001 PE. ✆ **081/3465-3544.** Fax 081/3466-5786. www.jangadeirohotel.com.br. 90 units. R$180 double; R$210–R$230 oceanview double. Children 7 and under stay free in parent's room; age 8 and over extra bed 25%. AE, MC, V. Free parking. **Amenities:** Restaurant; small rooftop pool; room service. *In room:* A/C, TV, minibar, Wi-Fi.

Olinda

Olinda's pousadas, located in the city's historic center, provide charming and comfortable accommodations in 200-year-old buildings.

Expensive

Hotel 7 Colinas ★★★ Kids Set on the grounds of a former sugar plantation, the hotel has beautiful lush gardens and the best leisure area of any hotel in the region. Rooms are spread out over a few low-rise buildings and all come with verandas that overlook the garden. The hotel's large outdoor pool is set in the lovely garden, with lots of space for kids to run and play, and there's a pleasant bar and restaurant.

Ladeira de São Francisco 307, Olinda 53020-170 PE. ✆/fax **081/3493-7766.** www.hotel7colinas.com.br. 45 units. R$270 double; R$350 deluxe double. Extra person add about 25%. Children 5 and under stay free in parent's room, children 6–12 pay 15%. AE, MC, V. Free parking. Bus: Rio Doce. **Amenities:** Restaurant; large outdoor pool; children's pool. *In room:* A/C, TV, minibar, Wi-Fi.

Pousada do Amparo ★★★ The most charming place to stay in all of greater Olinda is this concatenation of two 200-year-old colonial buildings in the heart of historic Olinda. Views down the hillside from the sumptuous back garden and pool deck are fabulous. Inside, tile floors, heavy ceiling beams, and lots of dark colonial furniture create a period feel. Rooms are furnished with a combination of antiques and modern artwork.

Rua do Amparo 199, Olinda, 53020-170 PE. ✆ **081/3439-1749.** Fax 081/3419-6889. www.pousadadoamparo.com.br. 18 units. R$260 double; R$360–R$520 deluxe double. Extra person add about 25%. Children 10 and under stay free in parent's room. V. Street parking. Bus: Rio Doce. **Amenities:** Restaurant; 2 pools (1 small, 1 children's); sauna. *In room:* A/C, TV, minibar.

Moderate

Pousada dos Quatro Cantos ★ A lovely large colonial building, this pousada takes up the entire block, hence the name (*quatro cantos* means "four corners"). The best rooms are the three deluxe ones that offer a view of the pool or the city. Also very nice are the newly upgraded deluxe superior rooms that have a jetted tub. The best room is the Veranda suite, a spacious chamber overlooking the garden. The two rooms on the ground floor lack air-conditioning and bathrooms, and they're next to the lobby. An annex across the garden contains five more rooms, which are comfortable but lack character.

Rua Prudente de Morais 441, Carmo, Olinda PE. ✆ **081/3429-0220.** www.pousada4cantos.com.br. 17 units (showers only). Annex room double, shared bathroom, no A/C, fan R$95; double R$140; deluxe and deluxe superior double R$170–R$230. Seasonal discounts up to 20%. Extra bed add 25%. Children 5 and under stay free in parent's room. MC, V. Street parking. Bus: Boa Viagem. **Amenities:** Small outdoor pool. *In room:* A/C, TV, fridge.

WHERE TO DINE

Recife/Boa Viagem

Expensive

Bargaço ★★ SEAFOOD A Recife institution, the Bargaço restaurant is *the* place in town for seafood. The menu includes such offerings as grilled fish and garlic-fried shrimp, but we recommend ordering those as an appetizer in order to save room for a *moqueca.* The menu features eight varieties, including lobster, octopus, shrimp, fish, or crab, but it's the Bahian *moqueca* dish that made this restaurant famous. If you can't decide, try the seafood combination *moqueca mixta.* These main courses are big enough for two. Your best bet for dessert is the *cocada,* a typical Bahian sweet made with sugar, more sugar, and coconut.

Av. Eng. Antonio de Gois 62, Pina. ✆ **081/3465-1847.** Reservations recommended on weekends. R$39–R$68 (most dishes serve 2). DC, MC, V. Sun–Thurs noon–midnight; Fri–Sat noon–1am.

É ★★ CONTEMPORARY BRAZILIAN Recife's best restaurant of the year takes you on a culinary tour of Vietnamese, Thai, Japanese, Italian, and French cuisine. Some interesting dishes you will find on the menu include *fillet ban chá* (grilled beef medallions served on pasta with a Dijon, miso, and green-tea sauce) and the Thai prawns (deep-fried and served with a sweet-and-sour honey sauce). The kitchen is open late, until 1:30am.

Rua do Atlântico 147, Boa Viagem. ✆ **081/3325-9323.** www.egastronomia.com.br. Reservations recommended on weekends. R$36–R$52. AE, DC, MC. Tues–Sat 8pm–1:30am. Bus: Boa Viagem.

Moderate

Alphaiate ★★ STEAK The Alphaiate is the perfect spot to take a break from eating fish and seafood. Located in Boa Viagem, the restaurant faces the ocean and offers indoor as well as covered alfresco dining. Even if you don't feel like a full meal, the Alphaiate is great for just a beer and snack. The beer list includes over 20 options, and a variety of the steaks come in appetizer format. Also good for nibbling are the pork spareribs, served with *farofa* and vinaigrette sauce. Main courses will often feed two people. The most popular dish is the *picanha* steak for two, served with a side of *farofa,* rice, and beans.

Rua Artur Muniz 82, Boa Viagem. ✆ **081/3465-7588.** R$16–R$46 (more expensive dishes serve 2). DC, MC, V. Sun–Wed 11:30am–1am; Thurs–Sat 11:30am–2am. Bus: Boa Viagem.

Olinda

Expensive

Oficina do Sabor ★★★ BRAZILIAN If you only have time for one meal in Olinda, make sure you reserve a table on the patio of Oficina do Sabor. The most popular dishes are the *jerimums,* a local variety of pumpkin. Bestsellers include the *jerimum recheado com camarão ao maracuja* (pumpkin filled with prawn and passion fruit sauce). Another popular dish is the *jerimum recheado com lagosta ao coco* (pumpkin filled with lobster in coconut milk).

Rua do Amparo 335, Olinda. ✆ **081/3429-3331.** www.oficinadosabor.com. Reservations recommended on weekends. R$34–R$60 (most dishes serve 2). AE, DC, MC, V. Tues–Fri noon–4pm and 6pm–midnight; Sat noon–1am; Sun noon–5pm.

Moderate

Don Francesco ★★★ Finds ITALIAN This little restaurant serves up some of the best Italian food in town. Many of the herbs and vegetables come from the owner's organic garden. The pastas are made from scratch by Francesco and served with simple sauces. The menu always includes a traditional and a vegetarian lasagna. All desserts, except for the ice cream, are also made in Don Francesco's kitchen.

Rua Prudente de Moraes 358, Olinda. ✆ **081/3429-3852.** R$18–R$32. M, V. Mon–Fri noon–3pm and 7–11pm; Sat 7pm–midnight.

Marim ★★ BRAZILIAN/SEAFOOD Not too far from the Oficina do Sabor is another great cozy restaurant where the lovely decorations aren't the only work of art. The kitchen serves some beautiful dishes, specializing in regional seafood such as prawns with mango sauce, grilled fish in banana leaf, or fish stuffed with spicy crabmeat. The atmosphere is bustling and pleasant, and the service is knowledgeable and friendly.

Rua do Amparo 157, Olinda. ✆ **081/3429-8762.** Reservations accepted. Main courses R$18–R$41. AE, DC, MC, V. Daily 11am–11pm. Bus: Rio Doce.

RECIFE & OLINDA AFTER DARK

Recife's historic downtown has undergone a complete face-lift, becoming a cultural and entertainment district. Activities center around the **Rua do Bom Jesus;** lined with at least 15 bars and restaurants, this is one of the best places in town Thursday through Saturday and Sunday afternoons. Free concerts add to the entertainment, and on Sunday there's a street market.

One of Old Recife's nicest bars is the **Arsenal do Chopp,** Praça Artur Oscar 59, at the corner of Rua do Bom Jesus (✆ **081/3224-6259**). Most tables are spread out over the sidewalk; for a quiet spot grab a table inside. Another great venue downtown is the **Patio de São Pedro.** Beautifully restored, this square hosts a variety of free outdoor music events. On Tuesday, locals gather for the Terça Negra, an event with *afoxé* music, a style with heavy African influences. On Saturday, a younger crowd gathers to dance to *maracatu, mangue beat,* and other regional tunes. Events start at 7 or 8pm.

In Boa Viagem, the favorite nightspot is **Polo Pina,** a few square blocks around Pina beach and Avenida Herculano Bandeira de Melo. Recently named the best bar in Recife, **Biruta Bar,** Rua Bem-te-Vi, Pina (✆ **081/3326-5151;** www.birutabar.com.br), features a large veranda looking out over the ocean, making it the perfect setting for a special date. ***Tip:*** This bar is not easy to find and the small detour cuts through a bit of a dark corner at the end of Pina. We recommend taking a taxi. **Boteco,** Av. Boa Viagem 1660, Boa Viagem (✆ **081/3325-1428**), is a popular destination almost any night of the week. Serving the best beer in town, the bar is often packed with locals stopping by for an ice-cold chopp.

Olinda is not known for its nightlife; most folks settle for wine and conversation over a late-night supper. One of the best spots for a drink or a stroll is the **Alto da Sé.** On weekends (Sun evening especially), locals flock to this prime view spot to grab a drink or some food from the many stalls and just hang out for an impromptu outdoor party. Olinda's cutest hole-in-the-wall spot is **Bodega de Veio,** Rua do Amparo 212 (✆ **081/3429-0185**). It's just a small bar/old-fashioned convenience store where people put their drinks on the counter or sit on the sidewalk.

A SIDE TRIP TO PORTO DE GALINHAS ★★★

Porto de Galinhas is one of the nicest beach destinations in all the Northeast. Known for its crystal-clear water, its lovely beaches, and the tidal pools that form in the nearby reefs, the region is a perfect water playground for adults and children. Development has been kept resolutely small scale. With no high-rises, the town is mostly small pousadas and low-rise hotels. The town has perhaps six streets: enough for a dozen restaurants, a bank, some surf shops, and some beachside bars. Colorful *jangadas* (one-sail fishing rafts) come and go all day, and the beachside restaurants and cafes are packed with people soaking up rays.

Essentials

GETTING THERE Porto de Galinhas is just 70km (43 miles) south of Recife, an hour by car. From Recife take BR-101 south until it connects with the PE-60, then look for the turnoff for the PE-38 that leads to Porto de Galinhas. Exits are well marked but the road has heavy traffic and is in very poor shape. If you are just going to Porto de Galinhas it's not worth renting a car.

Buses to Porto de Galinhas leave daily from 6:30am to 6:30pm every hour on the half-hour from the Avenida Dantas Barreto bus terminal in downtown Recife (across from N.S. do Carmo). Tickets are R$8 and the drive takes 2 hours. A number of these buses go through Boa Viagem and all stop at the airport on the way. From Porto de Galinhas to Recife, buses depart daily once an hour from 5:40am to 5:40pm.

A taxi from Recife airport or downtown will cost from R$80 to R$120 for up to four people and luggage. Agree on a price beforehand. Many hotels and pousadas can book a taxi service for you at a reasonable rate.

VISITOR INFORMATION The **tourist office** is at Rua da Esperança 188 (✆ **081/3552-1480;** www.portodegalinhas.com.br). Hours are Monday through Friday from 9am to 5pm, Saturday and Sunday from 9am to 3pm.

GETTING AROUND A minivan shuttle runs from the village to Pontal do Cupe and back, stopping by request at hotels and pousadas along the way. Departures are more or less half-hourly from the Petrobras station on Rua da Esperança (R$2).

There are taxi stands *(ponto de taxi)* for dune buggy taxis in the village and halfway down the beach in front of the Armação do Porto hotel. One-way fare is R$15 from the village to either Cupe or Maracaípi beach. If you're planning to spend time at Maracaípi beach, it's a good idea to set a pickup time with your driver, as it can be difficult to find a buggy to return. A full-day rental, including driver and up to four passengers, costs R$120 to R$150. In the unlikely event you can't find a buggy, contact **APCI Buggy** (✆ **081/3552-1930**).

FAST FACTS **Banco do Brasil,** Via Porto de Galinhas s/n (✆ **081/3552-1855**), has a 24-hour ATM. The bank is open Monday through Friday from 10am to 4pm. There is also a **Banco 24 Horas** ATM inside the Petrobras Gas Station, open from 7am to 10pm.

Exploring the Town

The main attraction at Porto de Galinhas is the beach, whether you swim, surf, snorkel, or snooze. **Cupe** beach stretches 4km (2½ miles) north from town; it's wide and warm, punctuated at either end by small coral reefs full of fish. Around the point in the other direction, **Maracaípi** beach regularly hosts national and international surfing competitions. And if the beach gets dull, you can take nature hikes, trips to nearby islands, or dive trips to offshore reefs.

Outdoor Activities & Adventure Sports

Porto de Galinhas is all about the sea, and the best way to explore the region is by boat.

BOAT TOURS **Cavalo Marinho** (✆ **081/3552-2180** or 081/8811-7393; www.catamaracavalomarinho.com.br) offers daily **catamaran tours** to offshore islands and isolated beaches, such as Ilha de Santo Aleixo and Praia dos Carneiros. Both are to the south of Porto de Galinhas and offer plenty of nice scenery, swimming, and snorkeling (R$90 per person; children 11 and under, R$60).

BUGGY TOURS The best way to see the local beaches is to head out in a buggy. The most popular tour is the "Ponta-a-Ponta," which takes you to four different beaches from the northern end of Porto de Galinhas to the southern end. A full-day trip costs R$120 to R$150, leaving from your hotel or from Avenida Beira Mar at the main square. Contact the buggy drivers at ✆ **081/9192-0280.** You can fit four in a buggy, but you'll likely have more fun with just two or three so that one person doesn't have to sit in the boring passenger seat.

DIVING Though most people opt for tide-pool snorkeling, a number of dive sites are in the surrounding area. Contact **Porto Point,** Praça Av. Beira Mar s/n (✆ **081/3552-1111**), for charters. Expect to pay R$90 to R$150 (no credit cards), including gear and two dives. Beginners can do an introductory lesson and dive for R$110.

SNORKELING The coast just off Porto de Galinhas is lined with coral reefs. At low tide they form natural pools that trap hundreds of tropical fish. With a mask and snorkel you just hop in and check out what's doing. Most pools are close enough that you could swim out, but another fun way of getting close is by taking a *jangada.* These one-sail fishing rafts are the boat of choice for local fishermen. For R$8 per person, local sailors will take you out to the best pools and provide you with a mask, snorkel, and some bread to lure in the fish. Check the tide tables at your hotel for low tide; early morning is best if you want to avoid crowds.

If you want to play in the water by yourself, you can rent a **mask/snorkel** combo for R$15 per day at **Porto Point** (see above).

Where to Stay

Porto de Galinhas is gloriously free of sun-blocking high-rises. Accommodations are mostly in small family-run pousadas and a few larger *cabaña*-style hotels. In high season, particularly on the weekend, reservations for accommodations are required.

In recent years, a number of bigger resorts have sprung up on the outskirts of Porto de Galinhas, but the only one worth the splurge is the Polynesian-style luxury **Nannai Beach Resort** ★★★, Muro Alto, Km 3 (✆ **081/3552-0100;** www.nannai.com.br). This exclusive resort consists of 49 bungalows set among lush tropical gardens. Each has a private swimming pool and beautiful rustic furnishings and decorations. The resort also offers a large sprawling pool complex and a host of activities such as tennis, pitch and putt golf, beach soccer and beach volleyball, snorkeling, sailing, kayaking, and children's activities. High-season rates are R$1,585 for a bungalow; in low season you'll pay R$1,170.

The **Tabapitanga** ★★★, Praia Pontal do Cupe (✆ **081/3552-1037;** www.tabapitanga.com.br), offers gorgeous accommodations on the beach just 5km (3 miles) from the village. Rooms are spacious and decorated with colorful artwork. Each room also comes with a veranda or deck with patio furniture and a hammock. High-season price is R$375 to R$430 for an oceanview double, and R$360 in low season.

Right on the beach, **Village Porto de Galinhas** ★★ Praia do Cupe Km 4.5 (✆ **081/3552-2945;** www.villageportodegalinhas.com.br), offers good value for families traveling with kids. The facilities have recently been renovated, and the swimming pools and leisure area have been expanded. All rooms are very spacious and, although not luxurious, pleasantly furnished with comfortable firm beds and splashes of color. Rates are R$425 in high season for a double and R$320 in low season.

Although just a 5-minute walk from the village, **Pousada Canto do Porto** ★★, Av. Beira Mar s/n (✆ **081/3552-2165;** www.pousadacantodoporto.com.br), is still on the beach. The nicest room is the deluxe oceanview panorama suite, with primo views, a king-size bed, and Jacuzzi. The more affordable master suites have a partial ocean view and a veranda. In high season, the cost is R$260 to R$290 for a deluxe or master double; low season, it falls to R$170 to R$190.

Where to Dine

One of the best restaurants in the region, **Beijupirá**, Rua Beijupirá s/n (✆ **081/3552-2354;** www.beijupira.com.br), is also one of the loveliest. Everything about this restaurant is creative and fun, from the funky decorations to the phenomenally inventive kitchen. The menu combines seafood and chicken with a range of interesting spices and flavors. Meat lovers can feast on delicious Brazilian *picanha* at **Picanha Tio Dadá**, Rua da Esperança 167 (✆ **081/3552-1319**). There are other cuts besides *picanha,* plus lamb, chicken, fish, and seafood. **Peixe na Telha,** Av. Beira Mar s/n (✆ **081/3552-18323**), offers one of the best patios in town, with a terrific view of the beach and fleet of *jangadas.* The menu offers regional fish and seafood dishes.

9 FORTALEZA

2,169km (1,348 miles) NE of Rio de Janeiro, 2,358km (1,465 miles) NE of São Paulo, 1,019km (633 miles) N of Salvador

The capital of the state of Ceará is best known for its beaches: glorious long stretches of sand interrupted by impressive red cliffs, palm trees, dunes, and lagoons that offer a true tropical playground. The most beautiful and isolated beach is the small settlement of Jericoacoara, a tiny coastal community with streets of sand, set by itself on the edge of its own tiny desert of Sahara-like dunes.

The first Portuguese settlers arrived in the area in 1603. Fortaleza remained a backwater until the 1820s, when Brazilian ports opened to foreign ships and the city began to grow into an important seaport, shipping cotton, cattle, and leather from the interior to England. In response to the resulting growth, city governors in 1875 commissioned a plan to transform Fortaleza into a tropical Paris, a city of broad boulevards overlaying a functional grid. Some of this early city planning can still be seen, but much was overwhelmed in the 1950s and 1960s as migrants from the state's dry and drought-stricken interior flocked into the city, practically doubling Fortaleza's population.

Now about two million strong, the city's major industries are cashews and tourism. What sets Fortaleza's beaches apart from Brazil's other 8,000km (4,960 miles) of coastline is the combination of colorful cliffs and huge sand dunes. For first-time visitors with limited amounts of time, the best plan of attack is to spend no more than a day in the city itself, then head out to explore the nearby beach communities, particularly the isolated Sahara-like dunes of Jericoacoara.

ESSENTIALS

Getting There

BY PLANE **Azul, Gol, TAM,** and **Webjet** have daily flights to most major cities in Brazil. Flights arrive at **Aeroporto Internacional Pinto Martins,** Av. Senador Carlos Jereissati 3000 (airport code FOR; ✆ **085/3392-1030**). Taxis cost about R$30 to the beaches or downtown.

BY BUS Long-distance buses arrive at the **Rodoviaria São Tomé,** Av. Borges de Melo 1630, Fatima (✆ **085/3256-2100**).

Visitor Information

Fortaleza's **airport** has a tourist information center (✆ **085/3477-1667**) in the arrivals hall, open daily 6am to 11pm, where you can pick up a good free map of the city. The **state tourist information center (Centro de Turismo do Ceará)** is downtown at Rua Senador Pompeu 350 (✆ **085/3101-5508**), open Monday through Saturday from 9am to 6pm, and Sunday 8am to noon.

Orientation

Located just east of the Ceará River, the commercial heart of Fortaleza—called **Centro**—is small and quite walkable, though the traffic and sidewalk vendors can make the area seem a little hectic. Starting from the waterfront **Fortaleza N.S. de Assunção,** Centro stretches inland in a grid pattern. Following the **Avenida General Sampaio** or **Rua Barão do Rio Branco** will lead you straight into Fortaleza's main shopping area, centered on a large city square, the **Praça José de Alencar.** Smaller but lovelier is the **Praça dos Leões,** just 1 block east of the Rua Barão do Rio Branco at the corner of **Rua São Paulo.**

An easy stroll to the east of Centro leads to the ocean-side neighborhood **Praia de Iracema,** the first of a long string of beaches that line the waterfront, linked together by the **Avenida Beira Mar.** (Unfortunately, none of the urban beaches is recommended for bathing.) Iracema isn't so much a beach as an ocean-side party place. You'll find lots of restaurants and bars along the seawall, and the **Rua Tabajaras** that runs parallel to the beach is packed with nightlife and restaurants. A kilometer or so east of Iracema, you come to the next beach neighborhood, **Meireles.** From here onward, the beachside boulevard becomes a pleasure to walk. The nightly **crafts market** always attracts large crowds. **Mucuripe** is the next neighborhood to the east of Meireles. At the end of

 Mucuripe beach there's a small colony of fishermen and a seafood market where the catch of the day is sold fresh off the boat.

Getting Around

Most visitors use the bus to go between the beach neighborhoods and Centro. In Meireles or Mucuripe you catch the bus on the street parallel to the beach (Av. Abolição). Look for buses marked MEIRELES, CAÇA E PESCA, or GRANDE CIRCULAR. Fare is R$1.80.

Taxis can be hailed almost anywhere. To order a taxi, call **Disk Rádio Táxi Ceará** (✆ **085/3243-8111**), **Taxi Fortaleza 24 Horas** (✆ **085/3254-5744**), or **Rádio Táxi Cooperativa** (✆ **085/3261-4181**). Fare from Meireles to Centro is about R$20, and from Mucuripe to Praia de Iracema about R$24.

FAST FACTS Currency exchange is available at **Banco do Brasil,** Rua Barão do Rio Branco 1515, Centro (✆ **085/3254-2122**), or at the **HSBC,** Av. Monsignor Tabosa 1200, Praia de Iracema (✆ **085/3219-2436**). For medical emergencies contact **Hospital Batista Memorial,** Av. Padre Antônio Tomás 256, Aldeota (✆ **085/3224-5417**).

WHAT TO SEE & DO

Fortaleza's main attractions are the beaches outside of the city, including **Morro Branco** with its multicolored cliffs, the sand dunes of **Canoa Quebrada,** and the idyllic and stunningly beautiful **Jericoacoara.** Fortaleza itself has a small **historic center** that's worth a visit if you have a day to spare, but it's certainly not worth the trip by itself. The **beaches** of Cumbuco, Canoa Quebrada, and Morro Branco make for a pleasant day tour. Only a short distance from Fortaleza, these beaches offer buggy tours, sand boarding, sand tobogganing, parasailing, boat rides—you name it and you can experience it, all under a hot tropical sun. But unless you are a kite surfer, these beaches also don't justify the trek to Fortaleza. What is worth the trip is Jericoacoara (see below), one of the jewels on the Brazilian coast. This isolated beach community features Sahara-like sand dunes, stunning white beaches, plus a steady wind that makes it Brazil's wind and kite surf capital.

The Top Attractions

Canoa Quebrada★★ offers miles of soft white sand and green-blue waters framed by low red cliffs. Locals offer **horseback riding** for R$30 per hour, **sand boarding** for R$3 per trip, and especially **buggy rides** either along the beach or into the vast sand dunes piled up behind the city. The full 2½-hour buggy tour, which includes a passage along the beach and up into the dunes, costs R$180 per buggy (buggies seat two or three comfortably, four if you squish). On the beach, *barracas* (stalls) rent out chairs and umbrellas, and food and drink is always close at hand, while local women offer scalp and shoulder massages for R$10. Canoa Quebrada is located 156km (97 miles) east of Fortaleza. The easiest way to visit is to book a day trip from Fortaleza. See "Tour Operators in Fortaleza," below.

Cumbuco★★, just a 45-minute drive from the city (37km/23 miles east), is where many Fortalezans come to spend a day at the beach. The big attraction? Beach and dunes. The main activity? The dune buggy ride. Drivers are able to take you on a roller-coaster ride over the shifting sands, dropping down steep inclines, swerving over piles of sand as if they were minor speed bumps, and skidding and sliding at almost vertical angles off the face of the taller dunes. **Buggy rides** cost R$100 per hour for a buggy that fits two or three people comfortably. Cumbuco is also one of the best places on the coast for **kite**

Tour Operators in Fortaleza

Several good tour operators are in Fortaleza, including **Ernanitur,** Av. Barão de Studart 1165 (✆ **085/3533-7700;** www.ernanitur.com.br), **Girafatur,** Rua Tenente Benévolo 13 (✆ **085/3219-3255;** www.girafatur.com.br), and **Hard Tour Ecotourism,** Rua Francisco Holanda 843 ap. 203 (✆ **085/3224-9300;** www.hardtour.com.br). All three offer transfers to Jericoacoara (prices range from R$50–R$100 each way) and tours to Cumbuco, Canoa Quebrada, Morro Branco, and Beach Park. Prices at all three are around R$40 for a city tour, R$50 for Cumbuco, R$25 for Beach Park (not including admission), R$40 for Morro Branco, and R$50 for Canoa Quebrada.

surfing. Optimal kite-surfing conditions occur from late June throughout November (check conditions on www.windfinder.com/forecast/cumbuco). The Dutch owners of **Windtown,** Rua das Cavalas 6 (✆ **085/8819-7887;** www.windtown.nl), have created a facility that offers top-notch windsurfing and kite-surfing lessons. To reach Cumbuco, follow the signs for CE-085. The turnoff for Cumbuco is 11km (7 miles) past Coité. For transfers to Cumbuco see "Tour Operators in Fortaleza," below.

Morro Branco★ offers visitors a maze of colored sand cliffs that line the beach. Local guides (who work for a donation, anything from R$5–R$10) will take you through the maze, showing off the spots with the best colors, ranging from almost pure white to yellow, gold, pink, orange, red, and purple. At the top of the cliffs there are usually artisans working on the region's best-known souvenir, sand-filled glass bottles with intricate designs of colored sands. The beach in itself is not significantly different from other beaches in the region. Allow an hour for a tour of the sand cliffs. Morro Branco is 85km (53 miles) east of Fortaleza. Take CE-040 to Beberibe, then take the turnoff for Morro Branco (it's approximately 4km/2½ miles from the main junction to the beach). For tours to Morro Branco see "Tour Operators in Fortaleza," above.

Downtown Fortaleza

Downtown Fortaleza has some worthwhile sights if you want to take a day off from the beach. Just a short stroll from the Praia de Iracema is the area that the locals call **Casario,** a lovely collection of restored 19th-century colonial buildings, primarily on the **Rua Dragão do Mar** and **Rua Almirante Tamandaré.** The area really comes to life at night, as most of the historic buildings house nightclubs or cafes. The centerpiece of this area—built in a contrasting but somehow complementary contemporary style—is the **Centro Cultural Dragão do Mar,** Rua Dragão do Mar 81 (✆ **085/3488-8600;** Tues–Fri 8:30am–9:30pm, Sat–Sun 2:30–9:30pm). This modern cultural center is built in the shape of a mosque with a white spiraling walkway that rests on an arcade over the historic buildings on the street below. Also downtown is the **Teatro José de Alencar,** Praça José de Alencar s/n (✆ **085/3101-2583**), open for visits Tuesday to Friday 8am to 5pm, Saturday 8 to 11:30am. At R$4, it's worth a peek. Built in 1908, the theater is a marvel of high-Victorian cast-iron construction, shipped in from Scotland. The gardens, added in 1974, were designed by Burle Marx.

Shopping in Fortaleza

Ceará is known for its quality handicrafts. The most famous souvenirs are the sand-filled glass bottles. Other excellent souvenirs include handmade cotton hammocks, lace, leather crafts and sweets. The **Mercado Central,** Rua Alberto Nepomuceno 199 (✆ **085/3454-8586;** Mon–Sat 9am–7pm, Sun 9am–noon), is one of the best crafts markets in the city. The large circular building houses over 500 stalls and small shops selling a variety of handicrafts, including hammocks, lace, T-shirts, leather products, and sweets. Another good place to browse for crafts is the **outdoor market** that takes place nightly from 5 to 10pm in **Meireles.**

WHERE TO STAY

Most people stay within walking distance of the city beaches. The boulevards are pleasant and there are plenty of restaurants and activity along the oceanfront. The best of the beach neighborhoods is **Meireles,** which has a wide, well-trod boulevard by the sand, dotted with pleasant little kiosks.

Expensive

Holiday Inn ★★ Deluxe accommodations on the waterfront, just a few minutes' walk from the nightlife attractions in Praia de Iracema. The rooms are divided into deluxe, superior deluxe, and suites. All are spacious and have ocean views; even the most basic room is large with a queen-size bed, big desk, a pullout couch, and a separate vanity area next to the bedroom. The superior deluxe rooms are larger and come with a veranda and a king-size bed. The furnishings are in great shape and the amenities are top notch—the pool is especially nice.

Av. Historiador Raimundo Girão 800, Praia de Iracema, Fortaleza 60165-050 CE. ✆ **085/3455-5000.** Fax 085/3455-5055. www.holidayfortaleza.com.br. 273 units. R$195–R$260. 20%–30% discounts in low season. Extra person 30% extra. Children 4 and under stay free in parent's room. AE, DC, MC, V. Free parking. **Amenities:** Restaurant; bar; outdoor pool; room service; sauna; smoke-free rooms. *In room:* A/C, TV, hair dryer, Internet, minibar.

Hotel Luzeiros ★★★ This is as hip as Fortaleza gets. Nearly all rooms have balconies; all have king-size beds and are elegantly furnished. White-tile floors, quality linens, and high-end finishes add an air of luxury to even the most basic rooms. The prime rooms have a full ocean view *(frente mar);* the standard rooms have partial views *(vista mar).* The swimming pool, business center, and fitness room are excellent.

Av. Beira Mar 2600, Meireles, Fortaleza 60165-121 CE. ✆ **085/3486-8585.** Fax 085/3486-8587. www.hotelluzeiros.com.br. 202 units. R$290 double, partial ocean view; R$360 double, full ocean view. Extra person add about 25%. Children 6 and under stay free in parent's room. AE, DC, MC, V. Free parking. **Amenities:** Restaurant; bar; outside pool; room service; smoke-free rooms. *In room:* A/C, TV, Internet, minibar.

Othon Palace Fortaleza ★★ Value Great location and even better value. The hotel's rooms are all beautifully furnished in blue and yellow tones and come with king-size beds; the bathrooms are done in beautiful marble. The smaller, standard rooms do not have balconies but do look out over the ocean. The deluxe rooms all have balconies and are spacious—definitely worth the price difference.

Av. Beira Mar 3470, Meireles, Fortaleza 60165-121 CE. ✆ **0800/725-0505** or 085/3466-5500. Fax 085/3466-5501. www.othonhotels.com. 110 units. R$214 standard double; R$260 deluxe double; R$430 executive suite double. Extra person add about 25%. Children 4 and under stay free in parent's room. AE, DC, MC, V. Free parking. **Amenities:** Restaurant; bar; fitness center; large outdoor pool; room service; sauna; smoke-free rooms. *In room:* A/C, TV, fridge, hair dryer, Internet, minibar.

Tips Good Eating at Aldeota

The restaurant neighborhood of Aldeota is becoming ever more popular with Fortalezan locals. Just a short taxi ride from the beach hotels, the area around the Shopping Buganvília mall off Rua Prof. Dias da Rocha has recently seen the opening of a number of outstanding restaurants. One of the most beautiful restaurants is **Lautrec,** Shopping Buganvília, Av. Dom Luis 1113 (✆ **085/3264-4020**), a small bistro offering outdoor dining and a menu of French and Italian seafood—think flambéed prawns with tarragon or grilled prawns with pesto and mozzarella. For sushi, there's **Ryori Sushi Lounge** (✆ **085/3224-9997;** www.ryori.com.br), inside the mall itself. For a more casual night out try **Zug Choperia,** Rua Prof. Dias da Rocha 579 (✆ **085/3224-4193;** www.zugchoperia.com.br), a lovely bar/restaurant with a large patio, live music, and fabulous appetizers, including a variety of *pasteis* or cold cut–and-cheese platters.

Moderate

Ibis Hotel Value Located a block off the water, the Ibis is the best value in Praia de Iracema. Like all Ibis hotels, the concept is basic: All rooms are identical and accommodations are comfortable but plain. Each room has a nice firm double bed, a desk, and closet space. Bathrooms are equally frill-free but are modern and spotless and come with showers only. The hotel amenities are kept to a minimum to reduce the operating costs. The optional breakfast is R$11.

Rua Dr. Atualpa Barbosa Lima 660, Praia de Iracema, Fortaleza 60060-370 CE. ✆ **0800/703-7000** or 085/3219-2121. Fax 085/3219-0000. www.accorhotels.com.br. 171 units. R$110 double. Extra person R$18. Children 4 and under stay free in parent's room. AE, DC, MC, V. Free parking. **Amenities:** Restaurant. *In room:* A/C, TV, fridge.

WHERE TO DINE

Fortaleza's restaurants are surprisingly excellent. There's fine dining, including outstanding seafood at surprisingly low prices. For a fun dining scene frequented mostly by Fortalezans, head to the ever-more-vibrant restaurant enclave of **Aldeota.**

Piaf ★★ FRENCH This small cozy bistro just a couple blocks off Meireles serves creative French cuisine at reasonable prices. Start off with some fresh oysters flown in from the Brazilian island of Florianopolis. Main courses include more traditional dishes, such as duck in orange sauce and exotic meats like ostrich served with risotto. For lunch the kitchen prepares excellent specials at R$19 a plate. Check the blackboard for the daily offerings. The wine list offers a decent selection from France, Italy, Portugal, Australia, and South America.

Rua Silva Jatahy 942, Aldeota. ✆ **085/3242-5079.** Main courses R$18–R$42. AE, DC, MC, V. Sun–Fri noon–4pm; Mon–Sat 6pm–midnight.

Pulcinella ★ ITALIAN Voted Fortaleza's best Italian year after year, this eatery features a traditional pasta menu just ever so slightly tilted toward the sea. Antipastos include sautéed shrimp and squid or salmon carpaccio. Mains include risottos and pastas with mussels, shrimp, and octopus. Stuffed ravioli dishes are more land based, including regional specialties such as sun-dried beef and locally made mozzarella, or chicken and catupiry cheese. The menu includes beef and chicken dishes for those not in the mood for pasta. The wine list includes a range of midpriced vintages from Brazil, South America, and Italy, with an added select few from Australia and France.

Rua Oswaldo Cruz 640, Aldeota. ✆ **085/3261-3411.** www.pulcinella.com.br. R$24–R$48. AE, DC, MC, V. Mon–Thurs noon–3pm and 6:30pm–1:30am; Sat noon–2am; Sun noon–1am.

FORTALEZA AFTER DARK

Performing Arts

The Victorian **Teatro José de Alencar,** Praça José de Alencar s/n, Centro (✆ **085/3101-2583**), is one of the loveliest venues in Fortaleza, with regular classical music performances by the Eleazar de Carvalho Chamber Orquestra. Call the box office or check out www.secult.ce.gov.br, under "programe-se" for schedules.

Clubs & Bars

Fortaleza is well known for its nightlife. The two most happening areas are **Praia de Iracema** and the **Casario,** the historic buildings around the **Centro Cultural do Dragão,** located at **Rua Dragão do Mar** and **Rua Alm. Tamandaré.** ***Note:*** The four bars at the intersection of Rua dos Tabajaras and Tr. Iracema (Cafe del Mar, Europa, Bikini, and Kapital) are patronized exclusively by working girls and their customers.

On Monday night, everybody heads down to **Pirata,** Rua dos Tabajaras 325, Praia de Iracema (✆ **085/4011-6161;** www.pirata.com.br). Doors open at 8pm, the band comes on at 1am, and the party continues until the wee hours. Tuesdays, the crowds leave the beach and head out to Varjota, to **Arre Égua,** Rua Delmiro Gouveia 420 (✆ **085/3267-5610;** www.arreegua.com.br), where things catch fire with the *nordeste* musical style known as *forró.*

On Thursday night, locals head out to **Praia do Futuro,** southwest of Mucuripe, for a traditional evening of crab eating *(caranguejada).* The place to be is **Chico do Caranguejo,** Av. Zéze Diogo 4930 (✆ **085/3262-0108;** www.chicodocaranguejo.com.br). Things warm up after 7pm. The band starts around 8:30pm. A taxi is recommended.

The historic downtown area around the **Centro Cultural do Dragão do Mar,** Rua Dragão do Mar 81 (✆ **985/3488-8600;** www.dragaodomar.org.br), features at least a dozen bars and nightclubs side by side. Many have live music and almost all have wonderful patios.

10 MANAUS & THE AMAZON

2,836km (1,762 miles) NW of Rio de Janeiro, 2,682km (1,666 miles) NW of São Paulo

It was a lost Spanish conquistador who gave a name to the largest river and rainforest on earth. In 1541, Francisco de Orellana returned after a year's absence with a tale of a vast new river, and of attacks by hostile Indians, some lead by bands of female warriors. In Europe, these women warriors were taken to be the last remaining members of the tribe whose queen Achilles slew at Troy. Land and river both were named for this likely mythical tribe—the Amazons.

Even today the Brazilian Amazon remains one of the most isolated, most sparsely populated regions on earth. Yet it is also home to more than four million people. Tarzan myths aside, most of them live not in the jungle, but in cities. Indeed, the state of Amazonas is one of the most urbanized in Brazil. On the surface, Manaus looks a lot like other Brazilian cities. The old downtown is shabby and bustling. Along the shoreline in the upscale Ponta Negra area you'll find the familiar beachside high-rises, wide streets,

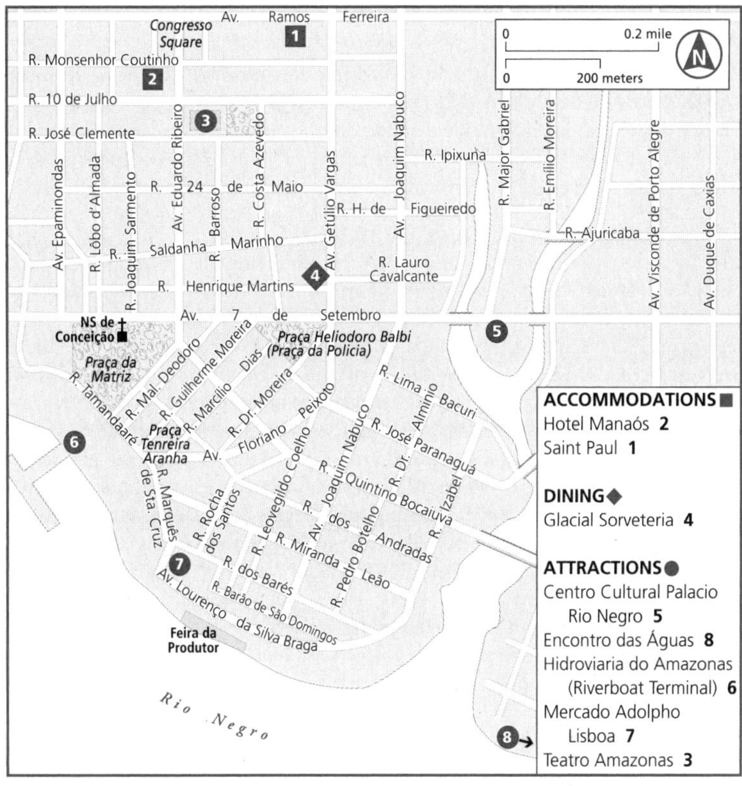

and waterfront kiosks. But stop for a moment and contemplate: You're in the middle of nowhere with 1,610km (1,000 miles) of forest in every direction.

Inhabitants of the largest city in the Amazon, Manaus's 1.6 million people live on the shores of the Rio Negro, just upstream from where it joins the Rio Solimões to become the Amazon. Though first settled in the 1600s, there's still a frontier feel to the place. Near the end of the 19th century, when the Amazon was the world's only rubber supplier, there was a 30-year boom in rubber and Manaus got rich indeed. Some of the city's finest buildings date back to this time, among them the Customs house and the famous Teatro Amazonas. The boom ended around 1910, after an enterprising Brit stole some Amazon rubber seeds and planted them in new plantations in Malaya (modern-day Malaysia). These days, foreigners come here to learn about the rainforest. Manaus is the main departure point for trips into the Amazon.

ESSENTIALS

Getting There

BY PLANE **Azul, Gol, TAM,** and **TRIP** have flights from major cities in Brazil. Flights from Rio or São Paulo take about 5 hours. TAM also has regular direct flights to Manaus from Miami. Manaus's international airport, **Eduardo Gomes,** Avenida Santos Dumont (airport code MAO; ✆ **092/3652-1212**), is 17km (10 miles) from downtown. A taxi to Manaus Centro will cost about R$45. You also have the option of taking a regular city bus, no. 306 to Centro, for R$1.80. Guests of the Tropical can take the Fontur shuttle, for R$24 per person.

BY BOAT Boats dock at the new Hidroviaria do Amazonas (Riverboat Terminal) (✆ **092/3621-4310**) in the middle of downtown at Rua Marquês de Santa Cruz 25. There is an information desk inside the front door where you can find out about arrival and departure times, and buy tickets. Boats for Belém normally depart Wednesday and Friday at noon. The trip downstream takes 4 days, while upstream travel takes 5 days.

Orientation

The city is the river. Downtown, all activity gravitates toward the waterfront on the Rio Negro, and it's there that you really feel the heart of the city. The **port** and the **municipal market (mercado municipal)** both face the river. The main attractions for visitors concentrate in a 20-block radius around the port and are easily accessible on foot. Close to the port is the newly renovated **Praça da Matriz.** To the east of the square are a number of narrow parallel streets, centered on **Rua Guilherme Moreira,** that form Manaus's main downtown **shopping district.** The busy east-west **Avenida Sete de Setembro** marks the end of the oldest section of downtown. From here north, the grid angles slightly, and things get less interesting. The only real sight of interest is the **Teatro Amazonas** (see below), 4 blocks farther north on **Rua Barroso.** From the downtown core, the city sprawls inland and along the river. **Ponta Negra Beach,** about 18km (11 miles) from downtown, is one of the more upscale neighborhoods where the beachfront has become a popular nightlife-and-entertainment area. This is also where you'll find the **Tropical Manaus** (p. 342). A good part of the beach disappears in the wet season (Jan–Apr), but the food stands and entertainment stay. In the dry season the beach is a great place to swim and suntan on the shores of the Rio Negro.

Getting Around

BY BUS From the Tropical Manaus to downtown, take bus no. 120 (R$2); the trip takes 35 to 40 minutes. The bus stops at the **Praça da Matriz,** which is within easy walking distance of all downtown attractions.

BY TAXI Taxis can be hailed on the street or reserved for a specific time by phoning ahead. For the airport contact **Coopertaxi** (✆ **092/3652-1544** or 3652-1568). In town, phone **Tele-Rádio Táxi** at ✆ **092/3633-3211.**

Visitor Information

The **Manaustur** tourism information desk at the airport is open daily from 7am to 11pm and located in the arrivals hall (✆ **092/3652-1120**). The State of Amazonas tourism agency, **AmazonasTur** (www.visitamazonas.am.gov.br), has an info center at the airport (✆ **092/3182-9850**), open 24 hours, and a downtown location close to the opera house, at Av. Eduardo Ribeiro 666 (✆ **092/3182-6250**), open Monday to Friday 8am to 5pm and Saturday till noon.

FAST FACTS For currency exchange try **Banco do Brasil,** Rua Guilherme Moreira 315, Centro (✆ **092/3621-5500**), or **Cortês Câmbio,** Av. Sete de Setembro 1199, Centro (✆ **092/3622-4222**). In case of a medical emergency, contact **Hospital dos Acidentados,** Av. Joaquim Nabuco 1755, Centro (✆ **092/3663-2200**).

EXPLORING MANAUS

The Top Attractions

The Meeting of the Waters (Encontro das Aguas) ★★ For more than 200 years tourists have been venturing out to see this remarkable sight: The dark slow waters of the Rio Negro meet the faster muddy brown waters from the Rio Solimões, and because of differences in velocity, temperature, and salinity, the two rivers carry on side-by-side for miles, with progressively less distinct whorls and eddies marking the interface between these two rivers. If you're booked at a lodge downstream of Manaus you'll pass through the Meeting of the Waters on the way there and back. If not, consider a day trip. This tour will usually include the main sights of Manaus, such as the public market, port, opera house, and a long stop at **Lago Janauary Ecological Park.** About an hour from Manaus, the Lago Janauary features some elevated boardwalks weaving through the trees and giant floating Vitoria Regia lily pads. ***Note:*** In the dry season (Aug–Dec), the trip through the Lago becomes impossible and tour operators take you to the Ilha da Terra Nova to see the rubber trees.

All Manaus agencies offer day tours for about R$110 per person. Try Viverde (✆ **092/3248-9988**).

Mercado Adolpho Lisboa ★ The Adolpho Lisboa is a beautiful iron-and-glass copy of the now-demolished market hall in Les Halles, Paris. It's a great place to see some of the local fish, fruits, and vegetables. The variety of fish is overwhelming. Not for the squeamish, the vendors cut and clean the fish on the spot; even chopped in half, some of the larger catfish still wriggle. The fruit and vegetable section is equally fascinating. Just in case you wanted to heal thyself, stop in at one of the herb stalls. A number of stalls have excellent indigenous handicrafts at reasonable prices.

Rua dos Barés 46, Centro. ✆ **092/3233-0469.** Daily 8am–6pm.

Teatro Amazonas ★★ This is one must-see that is actually worth seeing. This remarkable landmark was erected in the midst of the Amazon jungle in 1896, at the peak of the rubber boom. The half-hour guided tour shows off the lobby of marble and inlaid tropical hardwoods, the fine concert hall, and the romantic mural in the upstairs ballroom. Even better is to see a concert.

Praça São Sebastião. ✆ **092/3232-1768.** www.teatroamazonas.com.br. Guided 30-min. tours in English and Portuguese depart every 30 min. R$10. Mon–Sat 9am–5pm.

Organized Tours

Long the experts in deep Amazon exploration, **Amazon Mystery Tours** (✆ **092/3248-4258;** www.amazon-outdoor.com) has recently branched out into the city, offering innovative city tours. Canadian-born guide Jean Claude has developed a **Manaus by Night** series (R$90) which will take you out to a popular neighborhood to hang with locals, munch street food, and move to the sound of Manaus-based samba and *pagode*. The **Cultural Manaus** tours (R$90) offer visitors the chance to visit a kindergarten or spend a morning with Brazilian youth being shown their part of the city; there's also a tour that allows you to spend a night with a Brazilian family (R$150). And if all that's just too much culture, the company offers a day trip up to the waterfalls and caverns of **Presidente Figueiredo,** a beautiful highland area about 100km (62 miles) north of Manaus (R$250). Check the website for details on new tours being developed.

Shopping

Downtown Manaus is one big shopping area: Vendors hawk their wares, stalls clog up the sidewalks and squares, and the streets are jampacked with little stores. The main shopping streets run behind the **Praça Tenreiro Aranha, Rua Marcilio Dias, Rua Guilherme Moreira,** and **Rua Marechal Deodoro.** The streets around the market at **Rua dos Barés** sell more household goods and hammocks. The church square, **Praça da Matriz,** has a large market during weekdays selling everything from clothing to hair accessories and bags. The city's largest mall is **Shopping Amazonas,** Av. Djalma Batista 482, Parque 10 (✆ **092/3642-3555;** www.amazonasshopping.com.br). It's open Monday through Saturday from 10am to 10pm. Take bus no. 203, 209, or 214 from Praça da Matriz, Centro. The crafts market located on the Praça Tenreiro Aranha, Centro, sells a wide variety of Indian crafts, including necklaces, bracelets, woodcarvings, baskets, and handbags. It's open Monday through Saturday 8am to 6pm.

WHERE TO STAY

Centro

Expensive

Saint Paul ★ This hotel is convenient for those who are in town for a night before heading into the forest. The market, port, and opera house are all within walking distance. The area is not great at night when most of the businesses close, but a few restaurants are in the vicinity.

Rua Ramos Ferreira 1115, Centro, Manaus, 69020-080 AM. ✆ **092/2101-3800.** Fax 092/2101-3838. www.manaushoteis.tur.br. 70 apts. R$280 double. Children 5 and under stay free in parent's room. AE, DC, MC, V. Free parking. **Amenities:** Restaurant; bar; small outdoor pool; room service; sauna. *In room:* A/C, TV, Internet, minibar.

Moderate

Hotel Manaós Situated cater-corner from the Opera House, the Manaós provides something rare in the Amazon—basic clean accommodations at a moderate price. Rooms come in two flavors: two singles, or a double and a single. The price is the same for both. Bathrooms are extremely clean and bright. Best of all, room nos. 304 through 311 and 204 through 211 provide a fabulous view of the Opera House.

Av. Eduardo Ribeiro 881, Centro, Manaus, AM 69010-001. ✆ **092/3633-5744.** Fax 092/232-4443. www.hotelmanaos.com.br. 39 units. R$190 double. 10% discount for stays of more than 1 night. Children 6 and under stay free in parent's room. AE, DC, MC, V. Free parking. **Amenities:** Restaurant; room service. *In room:* A/C, TV, Internet, minibar.

Ponta Negra

Located 20km (12 miles) from downtown, the Tropical Manaus is the best place to stay in Manaus. Better yet, it's located on Ponta Negra Beach, a popular nightlife district on the banks of the Rio Negro.

Very Expensive

Tropical Manaus ★★★ After the Copacabana Palace, this is the most famous hotel in Brazil. Built on the shores of the Rio Negro, within its own little patch of rainforest, the Tropical is a destination in itself. Outside there's a vast pool, zoo, children's play area, archery range (lessons complimentary), a jogging trail, beach volleyball, soccer fields, horseback riding . . . the list goes on. Inside, the original wing of the hotel is referred to as *ala colonial,* in contrast to the more modern *ala moderna.* The colonial rooms have more character, with beautiful dark-wood furniture and hardwood floors, but they can also be a bit musty. The modern wing is pleasantly furnished with carpets and contemporary decor. All rooms are a good size with high ceilings and large windows, and the bathrooms are spacious and modern, with showers and bathtubs. A travel agent may get better rates than those listed below.

Av. Coronel Texeira 1320, Ponta Negra, Manaus, 69029-120 AM. ✆ **0800/701-2670** or 092/3659-5000. Fax 092/3658-5026. www.tropicalhotel.com.br. 601 units. Standard or superior double R$320–R$400; deluxe double R$475. There is often a 10%–30% discount on these rates. Extra person add 25%. Children 10 and under stay free in parent's room. AE, DC, MC, V. Bus: 120. **Amenities:** 3 restaurants, including Karu Grill (p. 344); 2 bars; children's program; disco; health club; large outdoor pool complex; room service; sauna; smoke-free floors; spa; tennis courts; watersports. *In room:* A/C, TV, hair dryer, Internet, minibar.

Tropical Manaus Business ★★★ Located on the shore of the Rio Negro, the Tropical Business is the newest addition to the Tropical complex. Bright and sleek, the hotel offers modern and spacious rooms with king-size beds, high-speed Internet, efficient air-conditioning and phone system, 21st-century plumbing, electronic safes, and fabulous views of the Rio Negro. The hotel has a large outdoor pool and sun deck overlooking the Rio Negro and a state-of-the-art fitness center. Guests may also use all facilities of the old Tropical.

Av. Coronel Texeira 1320, Ponta Negra, Manaus, 69037-000 AM. ✆ **0800/701-2670** or 092/2123-3000. Fax 092/2123-3021. www.tropicalhotel.com.br. 184 units. Standard R$290; suite R$350. Extra person add 25%. Children 10 and under stay free in parent's room. AE, DC, MC, V. Bus: 120. **Amenities:** Restaurant; 2 bars; concierge; health club; large outdoor pool; room service; sauna; smoke-free floors. *In room:* A/C, TV, hair dryer, minibar, Wi-Fi.

Elsewhere

Mango Guest House ★ The Mango is a nice small guesthouse, unfortunately located in a boring walled-off suburb about halfway between downtown and Ponta Negra. Rooms are simple, and pleasant, with firm single or double beds, and clean bathrooms with superhot showers. All rooms have a small veranda that looks out on a grassy courtyard and small pool, and the guesthouse has several nice lounges and sitting rooms and free Internet access. The Mango is perfect for those who just need to spend a night in Manaus before or after a jungle stay. All tours pick up and drop off, and the guesthouse will happily store your excess luggage while you are off in the rainforest. Tell taxi drivers the guesthouse is in Kissia Dois, off Rua Jacira Reis, which runs off Rua Darcy Vargas.

Rua Flavio Espirito Santo 1, Kissia II, 69040-250 AM. ✆ **092/3656-6033.** Fax 092/3656-6101. www.naturesafaris.com.br. 14 units. Standard R$100–R$150. Extra person add 25%. Credit cards only when booking online or via travel agency: AE, DC, MC, V. Bus 121. **Amenities:** Restaurant; outdoor pool; Wi-Fi. *In room:* A/C, fridge.

WHERE TO DINE

In the past year or so, the upscale neighborhood of Adrianópolis has emerged as Manaus's culinary hot spot. One of the city's best restaurants is the **Village,** Rua Mario Ypiranga Monteiro (formerly called Rua Recife) 948, Adrianópolis (✆ **092/3234-3296;** www.villagerestaurante.com.br). The menu covers a vast range, with seafood and fish dishes, risottos and pastas, meat, chicken, and lamb dishes all on offer. The chef's approach has a slight Italian tinge, while the use of Brazilian ingredients gives the dishes their local flavor. For more affordable Amazonian dishes there's **Choupana,** Rua Mario Ypiranga Monteiro 790 (✆ **092/3635-3878**). Even cheaper, and arguably more fun, is **Açaí e Companhia,** Rua Acre s/n, Adrianopolis (✆ **092/3653-3637;** daily noon–midnight), a kind of outdoor kiosk which specializes in local fish dishes such as *jambu* and *tambaqui.* On Friday and Saturday evening there's live music. Even if ice cream isn't a meal (although many kids will argue differently), it's one of the best ways to try the exotic fruits of the Amazon. **Glacial Sorveteria,** Av. Getulio Vargas 161, Centro (✆ **092/3233-7940**), serves up a great variety of flavors. Try the *cupuaçu, açai, jaca, taperaba,* or *graviola.*

The Lowdown on Amazonian Cuisine

Amazonian dishes mix a dollop of Portuguese and a dash of African flavors with native traditions and lots of local ingredients. The star attraction in most dishes is fish, fresh from the Amazon's many tributaries. Make sure you try at least the *tucunaré;* the meat is so tasty it's best served plainly grilled. *Pirarucú* is known as the codfish of the Amazon. It can be salted and used just like *bacalhau. Tambaqui* and *paçu* also have delicious firm flesh that works well in stews and broths. One popular stew is ***caldeirada.*** Often made with *tucanaré,* the rich broth is spiced with onion, tomato, peppers, and herbs.

The region is also rich in fruits, many of which can only be found in the Amazon, most of which do not even have English names. The citrus-like ***bacuri,*** with its soft spongelike skin and white flesh, is addictive; like Christmas mandarins, you can't eat just one. The most commonly eaten fruit is ***cupuaçu.*** This large round fruit, like a small pale coconut, has an odd sweet-and-sour taste at first bite, like it's almost *too* ripe. But you'll learn to savor it in desserts and juices. ***Tucumã*** is a small hard fruit similar to an unripe peach. Locals eat slices of it on bread. At lodges it's also a favorite of half-tame monkeys and parrots who will snag one whenever they get a chance. ***Açai*** is a popular fruit, but it can't be eaten raw; the berries are first soaked and then squashed to obtain the juice. You will find it in juices and ice cream.

Ponta Negra offers a number of nighttime dining options, none outstanding in terms of food, but most in very pleasant surroundings. On the waterfront, **Laranjinha** (✆ **092/3658-6666;** Mon–Sat 5pm–3am, Sun 5pm–5am) has a great patio and makes for fine people-watching. On a candlelit patio in the Tropical Manaus, the **Karu Grill** ★ (✆ **092/2123-5000**) offers a nightly buffet with excellent regional local fish, *macaxeira* (a local root that is often cooked like a potato), soups, or grilled steak.

EXPLORING THE AMAZON

There are many ways to explore the Amazon. What suits you depends on how much time you have and how comfortable you want to be. Most people choose to stay at a lodge. Most are land based, located within a few hours by boat from Manaus, and make excursions to the surrounding area. Lodges vary in luxury but the programs offered are similar. Another comfortable way of seeing the Amazon is by riverboat. These range from basic to air-conditioned and luxurious. The vessel serves as your home base; you take excursions in canoes up the smaller channels.

Specialized operators offer expedition-style trips where the emphasis is on truly experiencing the rainforest. You don't need to be in top shape for these; you just have to be able to hike or paddle a boat, and be willing to forego amenities like hot showers for a more hands-on jungle experience. One excellent outfitter is **Amazon Mystery Tours** (see "Deeper into the Amazon," below).

Lodges

You can contact lodges directly or contact a tour operator who can assist you in choosing the right package. In the U.S. or Canada, your best option is to contact the experts at

Brazil Nuts (✆ **800/553-9959;** www.brazilnuts.com). In Manaus, contact **Viverde,** Rua dos Cardeiros 26 (✆ **092/3248-9988**). They have an excellent English-language website (www.viverde.com.br) with detailed information on both tours and the Amazon in general.

Note: All prices are per person and include transportation, all meals, and basic excursions. Airport transfer is usually included in the price, but always check. The policies for children vary per lodge and per season; depending on occupancy you may have bargaining power. Ask when making reservations.

Lodges Close to Manaus

Amazon Ecopark Lodge ★★ The Amazon Ecopark is one of the better lodges close to Manaus, as long as you arrive with the right expectations. The lodge itself is about a 2-hour boat trip from Manaus and sits on a private reserve. The forest-clad river inlet, or *igarapé,* is of exclusive use to the lodge, which gives it a secluded feel. In the dry season there are several beaches right across from the lodge, and the vegetation is lush and beautiful. The lodge also has some natural pools for swimming, particularly nice for people who are never quite comfortable swimming in the dark waters of the Rio Negro. Most of the excursions take place in close proximity to the lodge and are done in non-motorized canoes. The lodge also houses a rehab for monkeys that are apprehended by Brazil's environmental agency, Ibama. The food is excellent and the guides speak excellent English.

Reservations office in Rio ✆ **021/2547-7742** or ✆/fax 021/2256-8083. www.amazonecopark.com.br. 64 units. 3-day package R$1,030 per person; 4-day package R$1,190 per person (both include a tour to the Meeting of the Waters). Children 6–12 pay 25%, ages 13–16 pay 50%. AE, DC, MC, V. **Amenities:** Restaurant; bar; outdoor pool. *In room:* A/C, fan, no phone.

Amazon Village Lodge ★ The Amazon Village is a well-run operation with its own small rainforest reserve, now alas being seriously encroached upon by ever-growing cattle operations and the beginnings of urban sprawl from the city. It's too bad, because the Amazon Village is a class act—owners treat guides well and do a good job presenting the rainforest. If at all possible, choose something farther from the city, but if you do for some reason have to be close, this would be a good option. The lodge buildings are attractively designed with local wood in the native *maloca* style, while rooms are small and clean with private toilets and showers. There is no hot water, and electricity is limited to the evening hours. The lodge doesn't have a swimming pool, but you can swim in the river.

Rua Ramos Ferreira 1189, sala 403, Manaus, AM 69010-120. ✆ **092/3633-1444.** Fax 092/3633-3217. www.amazon-village.com.br. 45 units. 3-day packages start at $440 per person. AE, DC, MC, V. **Amenities:** Restaurant; bar.

Lodges Farther from Manaus

Amazonat ★★ If you like space to move around, you will love the Amazonat, set on its own 900-hectare (2,223-acre) reserve of terra firma 160km (98 miles) east of Manaus. Amazonat is surrounded by extensive walking trails that you can roam at will. Though the lodge is not on a river, there is a lake with a beach for swimming and an orchid park with over 1,000 specimens to see and sniff and wonder at. The lodge itself is set in beautiful jungle gardens and the chalets are more than comfortable. There's also a variety of specialized programs for those who want to experience more of the jungle; the Jungle Trekker package includes a variety of longer hikes and two overnight stays at a jungle camp.

Caixa Postal 1273, Manaus, AM 69006-970. ✆ **092/3328-1183** (hotel) or ✆/fax 092/3652-1359 (reservations office). www.amazonat.com.br. 18 units. 4-day packages start at $550 per person; 5-day packages $660 per person. Children 6–12 pay 25%, ages 13–16 pay 50%. AE, DC, MC, V. **Amenities:** Restaurant; bar; outdoor pool. *In room:* Fan, minibar, no phone.

Amazon Eco Lodge ★★ Just a few kilometers from the Juma Lodge (see below), the Amazon Eco Lodge has the same excellent forest surroundings, and the same long trip from Manaus. The one thing the Eco Lodge has over the Juma is its fleet of small canoes, always at the ready should a guest feel like going off for a paddle. The Eco Lodge floats on the lake, on top of huge log rafts, which is really quite charming. It's also a great place for river swimming. The disadvantage is that accommodations are in fairly small rooms, built in wings with wooden walls; it can get noisy. Also, toilets and showers are shared, in a shower block near the center of the raft complex. Prices at the Juma and Eco Lodge are comparable, but for the money Juma provides better value.

Rua Flavio Espirito Santo 1, Kissia II, Manaus AM 69040-250. ✆ **092/3656-6033.** Fax 092/3656-6101. www.naturesafaris.com.br. 18 units (common bathrooms and showers). 4-day packages $599 per person. Policy for children negotiable. AE, DC, MC, V. **Amenities:** Restaurant; bar; Hobie Cat rentals; outdoor pool. *In room:* A/C, fridge, minibar, no phone.

Ariaú Amazon Towers (Overrated) Avoid this place. Just don't go. The Ariaú is all that is wrong with Amazon "ecotourism"; it is the Disneyland Ford Factory of jungle lodges. Marketing photos of treehouses and boardwalks may suggest a *Swiss Family Robinson* adventure, but what the Ariaú delivers is mass-market tourism. Although the Ariaú charges top price and has economies of scale on its side (it offers 300 rooms!), it has never seen fit to hire a lodge biologist (though there is a gym and spa, a helipad, and a jewelry boutique). Excursions are the usual, but at the Ariaú, group size runs up to 25. Trips are always in motorized canoes, equipped with noisy, fume-spewing two-stroke *rabete* motors.

Rua Leonardo Malcher 699, Manaus, AM 69010-040. ✆ **092/2121-5050,** or in Rio de Janeiro 021/2254-4507. Fax 092/3233-5615. www.ariautowers.com. 300 units. 3-day packages start at R$1,500 per person; 4-day packages start at R$1,900 per person. Children 6 and younger are free, ages 7–11 pay 50%. AE, DC, MC, V. **Amenities:** Restaurant; bar; gym; Internet (intermittent connection); outdoor pool; spa; TV room. *In room:* A/C, fridge, no phone.

Flotel Piranha ★★ The Flotel is unique among all the lodges in that it floats on varzea—flooded forest in the richer "white water" of the Solimões river system. White-water systems flow through younger, richer soils, and are thus richer in dissolved nutrients. White-water rivers support richer, denser populations of aquatic life—more fish, and consequently, more birds. The catch in all this, of course, is that the base of the food chain is also more abundant; white-water rivers are much richer in insect life, including mosquitoes.

To avoid mosquitoes, all other lodges are on black-water rivers, but the Piranha decided that the benefit was worth the cost. The lodge has good screens on the rooms and dining areas, and beds have mosquito nets. The benefit is you get to see and hear constant splashes from jumping fish, and see more and larger birdlife, particularly wading birds.

Rua Flavio Espirito Santo 1, Kissia II, Manaus AM 69040-250. ✆ **092/3656-6033.** Fax 092/3656-6101. www.naturesafaris.com.br. 20 units. 4-day, 3-night packages $649 per person. Policy for children negotiable. AE, DC, MC, V. **Amenities:** Restaurant; bar; swimming platform. *In room:* A/C, no phone.

Juma Lodge ★★★ One of the best of the lodges in the area, the Juma gets jungle points for its small size and its distance from Manaus. Rooms are all in comfortable small cabins built on stilts. The best rooms are the charming self-contained doubles (room nos. 9, 10, and 11) with a view out over the lake. From your veranda you can often see dolphins and caiman. Cabins are connected to the dining hall by elevated boardwalks. The Juma is located in the middle of a sizable private nature reserve, so the forest surroundings are quite well preserved. The lodge also has one dugout canoe that guests can borrow to paddle on their own. Note that the trip to the lodge from Manaus often takes longer than 3½ hours. It's not simply dead time, though. You see lots on the way out—from forest to birds to dolphins.

Lago do Juma (no mailing address). ✆ **092/3245-1177** (lodge) or 092/3232-2707 (reservations office). www.jumalodge.com.br. 23 units. 3-day, 2-night packages start at R$1,300 per person; 4-day packages start at R$1,600 per person. Children 6–12 pay 50% of rate. AE, MC, V. **Amenities:** Restaurant; bar. *In room:* Fan, fridge, no phone.

Boat Trips

On a boat-tour package, the experience is similar to that of a lodge; there are excursions on the small side channels, a sunset and sunrise tour, caiman spotting, piranha fishing, and a visit to a *caboclo* (river peasant) settlement. The difference is that in the time you're not on an excursion, you're moving on the river. There is always something to see, even if it's just the vastness of the river itself.

Viverde, Rua dos Cardeiros 26, Manaus (✆/fax **092/3248-9988;** www.viverde.com.br), can arrange boat voyages or charters. Their website has photos and descriptions of the better Manaus-based touring boats.

Amazon Clipper Cruises (✆ **092/3656-1246;** www.amazonastravel.com.br/amazon_clipper_i.html) has three old-style Amazon riverboats—the *Amazon Angler, Selly Clipper,* and *Selly Clipper II*—that make regular 3- and 4-day trips departing from the Tropical Manaus. The boats have cabins with bunk beds and private bathrooms, and in the evening the cabins have air-conditioning. The 3-day tour ($535) stays on the Amazonas River; the 4-day tour ($695) goes up the Rio Negro.

Swallows and Amazons ★, Rua Ramos Ferreira 922, Manaus (✆ **092/3622-1246;** www.swallowsandamazonstours.com), is run by New Englander Mark Aitchison and his Brazilian wife, Tania. The company's core trip is an 8-day adventure program that includes 2 nights in Manaus and then sets off up the Amazon and Rio Negro to explore the territory around the Anavilhanas Archipelago. Transportation is on company-owned traditional wooden riverboats, while exploration is done either on foot or by canoes. Accommodations are either on the riverboat (hammocks) or on a houseboat (with A/C and cabins). Prices range from $1,350 to $1,650 per person (includes all meals, transportation, and activities). These trips run year-round; check the website for timing and availability.

Deeper into the Amazon

Amazon Mystery Tours ★★★ (Value) If you want to really explore the jungle, this is the company to go with. Amazon Mystery has the skills and experience to bring you deep into the rainforest; make your time there safe, fun, and informative; and then get you back to town again. The company has core adventures in either a kayak or speedboat, descending the Amazon tributary rivers upstream of Manaus. For the kayak adventures, a typical day includes a few hours of paddling, followed by a delicious lunch of fresh fish, followed by a hike to a waterfall or hidden cavern that few have ever seen. At night, you head out with a spotlight to search for caiman or other jungle creatures. The company's regular guide is a Tucano Indian with an extensive traditional knowledge of Amazon plants and animals. Participants need a basic level of physical ability—for example, you should be able to hike and paddle a small boat—but no special skills. The camping is very comfortable and the food is excellent. You sleep in hammocks. At present, Amazon Mystery has 4- to 6-day descents on the Manacaparu river, 7-day descents of the Rio Urubu, and 10-day descents of the Jatapu river. The company also offers a 3-day adventure sports trip involving rappelling and white-water kayaking.

Av. Djalma Batista 385, sala 103, Manaus. ✆ **092/3248-4258.** www.amazon-outdoor.com. Prices average $190–$290 per person per day, which includes all airport transfers, accommodations in Manaus, equipment, drinks (alcoholic and non), meals, guides, and excursions.

Pousada Uakarí in the Mamiraua ★★★ The only place in the Brazilian Amazon practicing real ecotourism, the Uakarí pousada is part of the Mamiraua Sustainable Development Institute. Accommodations are in small but comfortable chalets, each with its own hot shower and veranda. Excursions completely break the pattern set in other lodges. In the wet season visitors get paddled through the forest in small canoes. In the dry season tours go on walking trails. Each trip goes to a different area, and the territory has very little human impact. Nighttime excursions aim not to capture a caiman, but to show off the nocturnal animals. A local guide is always present; normally there is a trained naturalist as well. Nature talks are a nightly occurrence. The researchers working in the area have dinner one evening with guests, and share their experience. For longer stays at certain times of year, guests can accompany researchers in the field. Good as all this sounds, there are disadvantages. Guides are local people being trained in tourism; they may not be as polished. It's a lot farther to go. The ecosystem is *varzea,* or clear-water Amazon, so there are more mosquitoes.

Getting to Tefe: Tefe lies some 200km (125 miles) upriver of Manaus. **TRIP** (✆ **0300-789-4747;** www.voetrip.com.br) has flights 6 days a week. The cost of a one-way ticket starts at R$349. There is also a fast ferry departing Manaus for Tefe at 7am every Wednesday and Saturday. The journey takes about 12 hours and costs R$190.

Av. Santos Dumont 1350, loja 16 (Manaus Airport), Manaus, AM 69049-000. ✆ **092/3652-1213** or (main ecotourism line) 097/3343-4160. Fax 097/3343-2967. www.mamiraua.org.br. 10 units. 4-day packages R$1,000; 5-day packages R$1,200 per person. Price does not include plane or boat fare to city of Tefe. AE, DC, MC, V. **Amenities:** Restaurant; bar.

11 THE PANTANAL

1,576km (979 miles) NW of Rio de Janeiro, 1,321km (815 miles) NW of São Paulo

The best place in South America to see wildlife is not the Amazon but the Pantanal, a Florida-size wetland on the far western edge of Brazil that bursts with animals—capybaras, caimans, jaguars, anacondas, giant otters, colorful hyacinth macaws, kites, hawks, and flocks of storks and herons hundreds strong.

The largest flood plain in the world, the Pantanal has a rhythm governed by its rivers. In the wet season (Nov–Apr), rivers swell and spill over to cover a vast alluvial plain for months. Millions of birds are attracted by this aquatic paradise, as mammals take refuge on the remaining few mounds of dry land. As the water drains (from May onward), the land dries up and the situation slowly reverses: Animals congregate around the few remaining water pools. Fish get trapped in these pools, and birds and mammals alike gather for water and food as they wait for the rains to start.

Few roads of any kind exist in the Pantanal; the best way to explore the area is to make like the locals and head out on horseback or boat. The best way to experience the

Pantanal and observe its amazing birds and wildlife is by staying at a small lodge; depending on the time of year you'll either head out in a four-wheel-drive, canoe, boat, on foot, on horseback, or a combination of these.

The Pantanal has three gateway cities: Cuiabá, which connects to the Transpantaneira Highway; Campo Grande, which leads in to the South Pantanal; and most isolated of all, Corumbá, which provides access to lodges in the southwest of the ecosystem. We recommend exploring the Northern Pantanal and the Transpantaneira Highway: The region abounds in wildlife, is very accessible, features excellent lodges, and has the most interesting landscape.

CUIABA & THE NORTH PANTANAL

The capital of Mato Grosso state, Cuiabá is a modern, pleasant town of 430,000 that sits in the middle of Brazilian cattle country. The city serves as the main gateway to the northern part of the Pantanal—the Transpantaneira Highway starts just 98km (61 miles) away—and as the jumping-off point to the Chapada dos Guimarães.

Getting There & Visitor Information

Flights to Cuiabá are available on **TAM, Gol,** and **TRIP,** landing at Cuiabá's **Aeroporto Marechal Rondon** (airport code CGB).

FAST FACTS Just outside the airport are 24-hour ATMs for all major banks that accept foreign cards. If you need to change money, you may want to do this before flying to Cuiabá—for example, at Rio or São Paulo's airport.

Yellow fever is endemic in this region of Brazil, so make sure you get a shot at least 10 days before you travel to the Pantanal. Make sure you bring your vaccination certificate.

Exploring the North Pantanal

Three days is the minimum reasonable itinerary for the Pantanal. With wildlife viewing, the longer you spend in an area, the better your chances of seeing animals.

After exploring the Pantanal, consider a 1-day or overnight trip to the **Chapada dos Guimarães** (below), the highlands to the north of Cuiabá. The beautiful red-rock formations, plateaus, and canyons offer excellent hiking and fabulous views, great waterfalls and swimming holes, and some excellent birdlife, including red macaws.

Tour Operators

The best tour operator is **Pantanal Explorer,** Av. Governador Ponce de Arruda 670, Varzea Grande (© **065/3682-2800;** fax 065/3682-1260; www.pantanalexplorer.com.br). Stays in the Pantanal are at the excellent Araras Eco Lodge. In addition, the company offers trips to the Chapada dos Guimarães and boat trips in the Pantanal, as well as ecotours to the Mato Grosso part of the Amazon rainforest (excellent if you do not have an opportunity to head up to the Amazon). Your package includes transportation from the airport to the lodge, accommodations, nature guide, activities, and all meals.

Driving the Transpantaneira

There are a couple of ironies about the Transpantaneira. Though the name implies that the road traverses the entire Pantanal, the highway stops in Porto Jofre, 144km (89 miles) from where it began, and at least that far from the opposite edge of the Pantanal. The other irony is that the project, which if completed would likely have destroyed the Pantanal (by skewing the ecosystem's drainage pattern), has instead, in its unfinished state, become one of the great wildlife-viewing areas of the world. Ditches on either side of the roadbed have become favorite feeding grounds for kingfishers, capybara, egrets, jabiru storks, giant river otters, and caiman by the dozen. Spend but a day on the Transpantaneira, and you'll see more wildlife than you'd see in a week in the Amazon.

Lodges in the North Pantanal

Araras Eco Lodge ★★★ Araras Lodge is the best spot for exploring the North Pantanal. The location by the Transpantaneira is excellent, and owner Andre Thuronyi has improved the local wildlife habitat. The lodge is pleasantly small and rustic. No fancy rooms or amenities here; each guest room comes with a private bathroom and a hammock on the veranda. The guides are usually knowledgeable. Activities include hikes along a rustic boardwalk through the flooded fields to the lodge's lookout tower. Other excursions include boat or canoe trips on a small local river known for large hawks and giant river otters (we saw both). On drives along the Transpantaneira, even in a 3-hour time span, you'll lose track of the number of birds you'll see. Fortunately, the guide always seems to remember their names. Horse lovers will be in heaven riding through the flooded fields. The food is delicious and plentiful, often including local fish. One of the most popular packages at Araras Eco Lodge offers a 3-night stay at the lodge and a 1-night stay in the Chapada dos Guimarães for some good hiking and swimming.

Transpantaneira Hwy. Reservation office: Av. Governador Ponce de Arruda 670, Varzea Grande, MT. ✆ **065/3682-2800.** Fax 065/3682-1260. www.araraslodge.com.br. 19 units (showers only). R$1,400–R$1,800 per person for a 3-day, 2-night package; 6-day package (including the Chapada Guimarães) R$3,000, including airport pickup and drop-off plus all meals and guided activities. Extra person add about 25%. Children 10 and under stay free in parent's room. AE, DC, MC, V. Free parking. **Amenities:** Restaurant; bar; outdoor pool. *In room:* A/C, no phone.

Jaguar Ecological Reserve ★★ Wildlife viewing is always a matter of luck and patience, particularly when it comes to large predators like jaguars, but at this private ecological reserve an astonishing one in four guests sees one of these huge South American cats. It's a long way (110km/68 miles) down the bumpy Transpantaneira, and the accommodations are expensive and only basic, but for a view of that big cat it may be worth it. For the 75% of guests who do not see jaguars, there is the usual vast array of caiman and colorful birds, so rare in the rest of the world, so common in the Pantanal. It's best to book your stay here through **Open Door Tours** (✆ **067/3321-8303;** www.opendoortur.com.br).

Transpantaneira Km 110, Poconé, MT. ✆ **065/3646-8557** (office) or 067/9919-5518 (lodge). www.jaguarreserve.com. 9 units. 4-day, 3-night package $750 per person, with accommodations, transfers, meals, and excursions. **Amenities:** Wildlife viewing. *In room:* No phone.

Pousada do Rio Mutum This pousada is highly recommended for those who enjoy fishing. The *pintado* catfish is a particularly prized catch, but anglers can also expect to hook *dourado, paçu,* or *piraputanga.* (The best months for fishing are Feb–Oct; there is no fishing Nov–Jan during spawning season.) For nonfishers there are tours of the Pantanal ecosystem by boat, foot, and canoe. Accommodations are in simply furnished rooms that come with private bathrooms and a veranda. All meals and activities are included. This region is a bit east of Poconé, and access is through the town of Barão de Melgaço.

Av. Isaac Póvoas 1177, Cuiabá, 78045-640 MT. ✆ **065/3052-7022.** www.pousadamutum.com.br. 22 units (showers only). 3-day, 2-night packages from $720 per person, including meals and pickup/drop-off at airport. MC, V. **Amenities:** Restaurant; bar; pool. *In room:* A/C, no phone.

CHAPADA DOS GUIMARÃES

In appearance, the Chapada dos Guimarães has much in common with the desert buttes of Arizona or Utah in the States—weird, wonderful formations of bright red rock, and

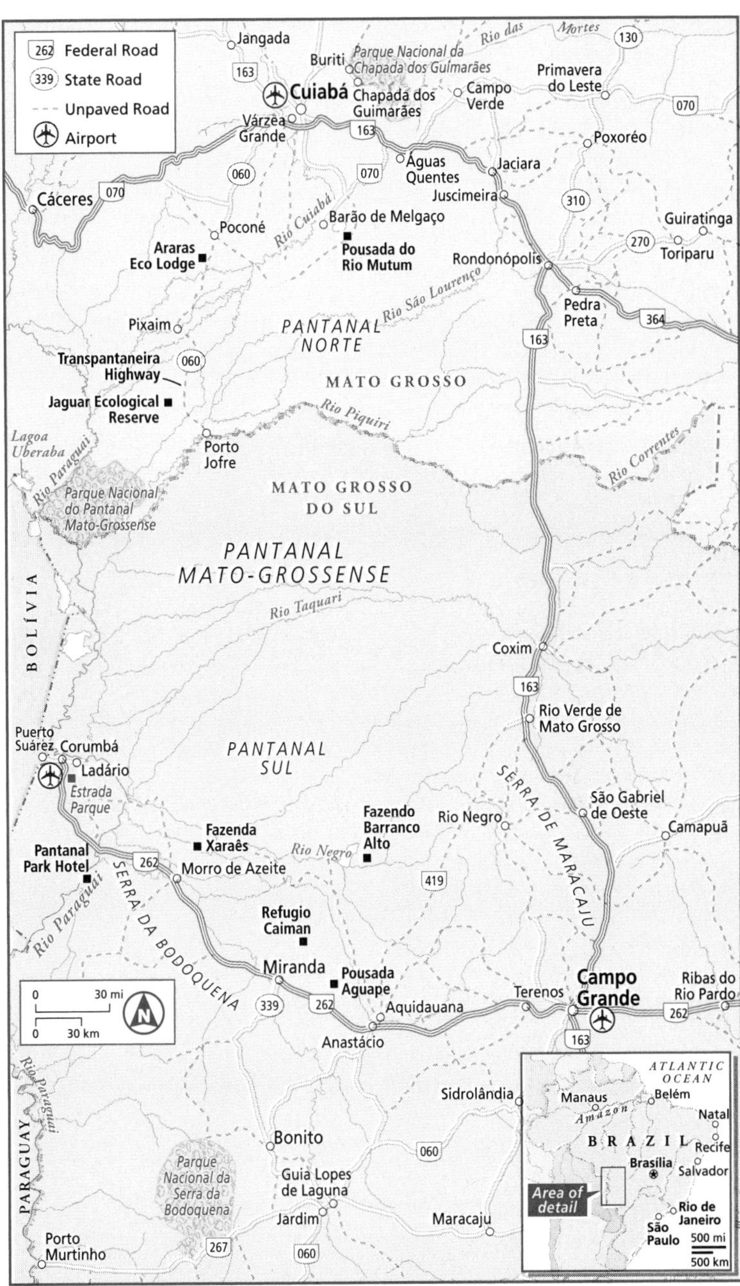
262 Federal Road
339 State Road
Unpaved Road
Airport
Jangada
Buriti
Parque Nacional da Chapada dos Guimarães
Rio das Mortes
Cuiabá
Chapada dos Guimarães
Campo Verde
Primavera do Leste
Várzea Grande
Poxoréo
Águas Quentes
Jaciara
Juscimeira
Cáceres
Poconé
Rio Cuiabá
Barão de Melgaço
Pousada do Rio Mutum
Guiratinga
Toriparu
Araras Eco Lodge
Rondonópolis
Rio São Lourenço
Pedra Preta
Pixaim
PANTANAL NORTE
Transpantaneira Highway
Jaguar Ecological Reserve
MATO GROSSO
Rio Piquiri
Lagoa Uberaba
Porto Jofre
Rio Correntes
Rio Paraguai
Parque Nacional do Pantanal Mato-Grossense
MATO GROSSO DO SUL
PANTANAL MATO-GROSSENSE
Rio Taquari
BOLÍVIA
Coxim
Rio Verde de Mato Grosso
Puerto Suárez
Corumbá
Ladário
Estrada Parque
PANTANAL SUL
SERRA DE MARACAJU
São Gabriel de Oeste
Fazendo Barranco Alto
Rio Negro
Camapuã
Fazenda Xaraês
Pantanal Park Hotel
Morro de Azeite
SERRA DA BODOQUENA
Refugio Caiman
Miranda
Pousada Aguape
Terenos
Campo Grande
Ribas do Rio Pardo
Aquidauana
Anastácio
0 30 mi
0 30 km
N
Sidrolândia
Bonito
Guia Lopes de Laguna
Jardim
Maracaju
Parque Nacional da Serra da Bodoquena
PARAGUAY
Porto Murtinho
ATLANTIC OCEAN
Manaus
Belém
Amazon
Natal
BRAZIL
Recife
Brasília
Salvador
Area of detail
Rio de Janeiro
São Paulo
500 mi
500 km

long beautiful canyons. Vegetation is dry and scrubby, except where the many river channels flow; then you get waterfalls streaming down into basins lush with tropical vegetation. Hiking nearby is excellent; most trails end at a viewpoint, a waterfall, or a natural pool (sometimes all three!).

Getting There

BY CAR The Chapada is 74km (46 miles) north of Cuiabá. Roads are excellent. Follow the MT-251 to the park and the town of Chapada dos Guimarães.

BY BUS Direct buses operated by **Viação Rubi** (✆ **065/3624-9044**) leave from Cuiabá's *rodoviaria* and take about 1 hour. Cost is R$8 and departures are daily at 9am, 10:30am, 2 and 6:30pm.

BY ORGANIZED TOUR For a hassle-free trip to the Chapada, reserve a tour with Pantanal Explorer (see "Tour Operators" above). They can put together a customized package in combination with the Panatanal. You will be accompanied by a private tour guide who can recommend the best hikes or sights, according to your interest and fitness level.

Visitor Information

The **tourist office** is at Rua Quinco Caldas s/n (✆ **065/3301-2045**). The park visitor center (✆ **065/3301-1133**) is located on highway MT-251 about 8km (5 miles) past the park entrance, and about 15km (9 miles) before the town of Chapada dos Guimarães.

Exploring the Park

Two days are plenty to explore the Chapada. Even if you have only a day, you can still see the "best of the Chapada"—take in the magnificent views, frolic in a few waterfalls, and get some hiking in, all before sunset.

Note: Due to park maintenance, some areas of the park are closed on Tuesdays and Wednesdays. Also, at the time this book went to press, trails to Cidade de Pedras were closed, but expected to reopen soon. Check with the park administration office (✆ **065/3301-1133**) or ask at your pousada.

The most popular hikes include **Cachoeira Veu de Noiva,** the tallest waterfall in the park. The trail head is at the park visitor's center, about 15km (9 miles) from the town of Chapada dos Guimarães. **Cidade de Pedras (City of Stones)** is named after the beautiful eroded rock formations that look like the ruins of buildings. A short hike takes you through these rocks to the edge of a canyon, where the sheer cliffs drop 350m (over 1,000 ft.) straight down. To reach the trail head, go west from town on MT-251 for about 2km (1¼ miles), turn right (there's a small sign), and follow the smaller, rougher blacktop road straight on for 13km (8 miles). A 20-minute hike takes you to **Paredão do Eco (Echo Cliff),** the edge of a mini–Grand Canyon. Steep cliff walls and eroded rocks in various shapes form an amazing pattern, and on the far side where the walls are the steepest and sheerest you can often spot scarlet red *araras* (macaws). To reach the trail head, follow the same directions for Cidade de Pedra, above. About 12km (7½ miles) along the blacktop road, take the left turn on a dirt road and follow it for 3km (2 miles).

Where to Stay

Pousada do Parque ★★★ (Kids) This pousada offers the best accommodations at a fabulous location, on the edge of a cliff looking out towards Morro São Jerônimo. The rooms are very comfortable and several have heaters, great for the chilly fall and winter days. Guests can also warm up in the fireplace lounge or enjoy a glass of wine and an outstanding meal by the wood-burning stove. The owners are avid hikers and birders with lots of tips to offer. ***Note:*** Access is via a dirt road at Km 52 of the Cuiabá–Chapada dos Guimarães highway. The gate is normally locked, so notify the staff of your expected time of arrival.

MT-251 Highway, Km 52 (15km/8 miles from the center of town), Chapada dos Guimarães, MT 78065-010. ✆ **065/3391-1346** or 065/3682-2800. www.pousadadoparque.com.br. 8 units. R$265 double. Seasonal discounts available. Children 5 and under stay free in parent's room. AE, DC, MC, V. Free parking. **Amenities:** Restaurant; bar; small outdoor pool; sauna. *In room:* A/C, no phone.

Where to Dine

The town of the Chapada dos Guimarães doesn't really stand out as a culinary destination. Perhaps most visitors are so tired after a day of hiking that they can't be bothered to go out and prefer to eat at their pousada.

An excellent lunch spot is **Morro dos Ventos,** Chacara Morro dos Ventos, via Estrada do Mirante Km 1 (✆ **065/3301-1030**). Perched on the edge of a cliff, the restaurant offers fabulous views. With luck you'll spot red macaws flying along the rock faces. The menu offers regional home cooking. Try the chicken stew with okra, served in a heavy cast-iron pot with generous side dishes of beans, salad, *farofa,* and rice. Other options include the *pintado* or *paçu* fish. It's open daily from 9am to 6pm.

12 FOZ DO IGUAÇU

1,093km (679 miles) SW of Rio de Janeiro, 847km (527 miles) SW of São Paulo

There are but three great waterfalls in the world, and curiously they seem to all fall on borders: Niagara Falls, on the border between the United States and Canada; Victoria Falls, between Zimbabwe and Zambia; and Iguaçu Falls, between Brazil and Argentina. Iguaçu is without doubt the most beautiful of the three; the water pours down over not one but some 275 different cataracts, spread over a precipice some 5km (3 miles) wide and 81m (266 ft.) high. The fine mist tossed up by all that falling water precipitates down and creates a microclimate of lush rainforest, with tropical birds and an abundant population of glorious butterflies.

Iguaçu has been attracting visitors since the first European explorer stumbled across the area in the 1540s. In the 1930s more than 400,000 hectares (1 million acres) on the Brazilian side was made into a national park, and in 1985 the falls were designated an UNESCO World Heritage Site. The falls are remote enough that a 1-day trip is, well, insane. With a Brazilian air pass, Iguaçu makes a perfect 2-day stopover.

ESSENTIALS

Getting There

Both **Gol** and **TAM** have daily flights, connecting through São Paulo or Curitiba. Book ahead in peak season; flights fill up quickly. The **Aeroporto Internacional Foz do Iguaçu** (airport code IGR; ✆ **045/3521-4200**) is on BR-469 halfway between downtown and the national park. The 13km (8-mile) taxi ride to downtown Iguaçu costs about R$50. Many of Iguaçu's hotels are on the highway into town, making taxi fare considerably less.

Orientation

A small, modern city of 250,000 people, **Foz do Iguaçu** (normally just called Iguaçu) is effectively located on a peninsula. West of the city is the **Rio Paraná** and, beyond that, Paraguay. North of the city lies **Lago de Itaipu,** a great man-made lake created by putting up the world's largest hydroelectric dam across the Rio Paraná. To the south of the city lies **Rio Iguaçu** and, beyond it, Argentina. The **falls** are upstream on this river, a 28km (18-mile) drive southeast from downtown. The city's downtown is small and easy to navigate, but offers few attractions. At the southern end of downtown, **Avenida das Cataratas** (BR-469) tracks southeast toward **Iguaçu National Park** and the falls. About 7km (4¼ miles) from downtown, there's a turnoff for the **Ponte Tancredo Neves,** which crosses into Argentina. Public buses take this route, and border formalities are minimal. The road to the falls, called **Rodovia das Cataratas,** continues past the airport turnoff until, at 17km (11 miles) from the city, it reaches the gates of **Iguaçu National Park.**

Getting Around

BY BUS City buses begin and end their routes at the **Terminal Urbana** on Avenida Juscelino Kubitschek (also called Av. J.K.—pronounced "zhota ka") at the corner of Avenida República Argentina. Buses for the falls run along Avenida J.K. and Avenida Jorge Schimmelpfeng to Avenida das Cataratas; they are marked CATARATAS or PARQUE NACIONAL. From the park gate, a free shuttle (departing every 20 min.) will take you the rest of the way to the falls.

BY TAXI Taxi *pontos* (stands) are throughout the city, or you can flag a taxi on the street. A trip across town costs around R$20. A trip from the city center to a hotel on the Avenida das Cataratas costs between R$25 and R$35; fare to the park gates costs R$45. **Coopertaxi** (✆ **0800/524-6464** or 045/3529-8821) has cabs available 24/7.

Visitor Information

Iguaçu's tourist bureau employs excellent English-speaking attendants who have up-to-date and accurate information at their fingertips. The main **tourist information center** is at Praça Getulio Vargas, Av. J.K. and Rua Rio Branco (✆ **045/3521-1455;** www.foz doiguacu.pr.gov.br; Mon–Fri 9am–5pm). There is also an information booth at the airport, or call the Iguaçu tourist information service, **Teletur** (✆ **0800/451-516** toll-free within Brazil). The service operates daily from 7am to 11pm.

FAST FACTS **Banco do Brasil,** Av. Brasil 1377 (✆ **045/3521-2525**), has a currency exchange and a 24-hour ATM. The **HSBC** branch is nearby at Av. Brasil 1151 (✆ **045/3523-1166**). In case of a medical emergency, contact **Hospital Internacional,** Av. Brasil 1637 (✆ **045/3523-1404**).

WHAT TO SEE & DO

GUIDED TOURS & TRANSFERS A number of tour operators organize transportation and guides for visits to the falls. For the visitor-friendly, easy-to-reach attractions on the Brazil side, it's a waste of money. However, we recommend booking a guided tour or transfer to visit the Argentine falls. This saves you the hassle of dealing with two different languages and currencies and saves time at the border. Reputable companies include **Conveniotur,** Rua Rui Barbosa 820 (✆ **045/3523-3500;** www.conveniotur.com.br), and **Loumar Tourismo** (✆ **045/3572-5005;** www.loumarturismo.com.br). Simple transfers start at R$60 per person.

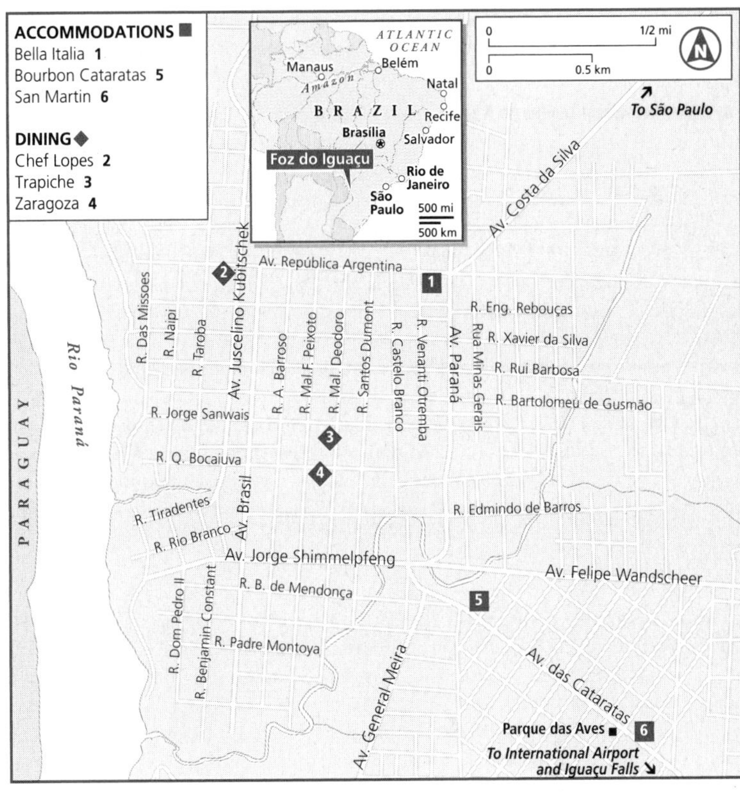

The Falls

Parque Nacional do Iguaçu (Brazilian Falls) ★★★ Start your tour at the **Park Visitor Center** to buy your entry tickets. The building has a gift shop and a small display area with some park history. From here, you board a shuttle bus and set off down the parkway for the falls. The bus will stop at the **Macuco Safari center** (from where rafting and zodiac trips depart, but do that after you've seen the falls), the pink **Hotel das Cataratas,** and then at **Canoas** restaurant before heading back to the visitor center. The hotel is the place to get off the bus. A small viewpoint at the foot of the hotel lawn is where you get your first magical view of the falls. From here, the pathway zigzags down the side of the gorge and trundles along the cliff face, providing views across the narrow gorge at water cascading down in a hundred different places. There are 275 separate waterfalls, with an average drop of around 60m (200 ft.). While you walk, you'll see colorful butterflies fluttering about the trail and grumbling coati (a larger relative of the raccoon) begging for food. At the end of the trail an elevator will lift you up to the restaurant by the edge of the falls. Before going up, take the elevated walkway leading out *in front* of one of the falls. The wind and spray coming off the falls are exhilarating and guaranteed to have you soaked in seconds. (You can buy a plastic coat from the souvenir stand for R$5.) Allow at least a half-day.

Rodovia dos Cataratas, Km 18. ✆ **045/3572-2261.** www.cataratasdoiguacu.com.br. Admission R$22 adults, R$7 children 2–6, includes transportation inside the park. Parking R$12. Daily 9am–5pm. Bus: Cataratas or Parque Nacional.

Parque Nacional Iguazú (Argentine Falls) ★★★ Visitors to the Argentine falls arrive at a brand-new complex, which consists mostly of restaurants and gift shops. Don't waste your time here; instead, head to the park's chief attraction, the **Devil's Throat walkway★★★**. To reach it, you take a free small-gauge railway, which departs every 30 minutes from 8am to 4pm, either from the visitor center station or from a second station located about 600m (2,000 ft.) down a paved walking trail. The train takes about 20 minutes to trundle the 3km (2 miles) up to the Devil's Throat station. From here it's about a 1km (.5-mile) walk along the steel catwalk to the viewpoint overlooking the falls. There is something both magical and awesome in that much water falling in one place; nothing people do seems to mar it. The return train leaves on the half-hour, with the last departure at 5:30pm.

There are several other trails in the park. The **Circuito Superior (Upper Trail)** loops around the top of the falls. The steep **Circuito Inferior (Lower Trail) ★★** leads down to the edge of the Iguazú River, offering some excellent views up toward the falls. It's the only way to reach **Isla San Martin★**, an island that's surrounded on all sides by falling water—well worth the short boat ride (currently free of charge). The last boat back leaves at 5pm.

To get to the falls from Foz do Iguaçu, take the bus designated PORTO IGUAZÚ from downtown. Customs formalities at the border are minimal. Stay on the bus, tell the Customs officer who boards that you're going to the Parque Nacional and—for citizens of the U.S., U.K., Canada, and Australia—you'll be waved through without even a stamp in your passport. The bus then goes to the main bus station in Puerto Iguazú. Go to stall no. 5, where a bus departs every hour between 7:40am and 7:40pm for the 20-minute trip to the park. Including connections, total trip time from Brazil will be at least an hour. The bus from Brazil to Argentina costs R$3, and the one from Puerto Iguazú to the falls costs R$5. A taxi to or from the Argentine side costs about R$80 each way. To get back, you can catch a bus from Parque Nacional to the Puerto Iguazú bus station hourly from 8am to 8pm. Once back at the bus station, go to stall no. 1 and catch the bus marked FOZ DO IGUAÇU back to Brazil.

Av. Victoria Aguirre 66, Puerto Iguazú, 3370 Misiones, Argentina. ✆ **03757/420-722.** www.iguazu argentina.com. Admission R$30 adults, R$15 children ages 6–11, free 5 and under. Oct–Mar daily 8am–7pm; April–Sept daily 8am–6pm.

Other Top Attractions

Canion Iguaçu (Rappel and Climbing Park) ★★ This company has converted a part of the park into a delightful adult playground. Very popular is the *arvorismo* (tree-climbing) trail, an obstacle course made out of ropes, wires, and platforms attached to the trees. For a greater thrill there is the 37m (120 ft.) rappel off a platform overlooking the falls. Maybe your thing is going up instead of down? The park offers a variety of climbing options. Beginners can try the artificial wall, while more experienced climbers can explore over 33 different routes on the basalt rock face. And last but not least, the company runs daily rafting trips over a 4km (2½-mile) stretch of the river. The run covers about 2km (1¼ miles) of rapids with a Class III+ rating; the rest is calmer water that gives you a chance to observe the forest and the river.

Parque Nacional do Iguaçu. ✆ **045/3529-6040.** www.campodedesafios.com.br. Rappel R$70; rafting R$90; tree climbing R$80 for the higher part, R$60 for lower part only; climbing R$50. Daily 9am–5:30pm. Bus: Parque Nacional or Cataratas.

Itaipu Dam ★★ The world's largest hydroelectric project stands 10km (6¼ miles) upriver from Foz do Iguaçu on the Rio Paraná. The project produces over 90 billion kilowatt hours per year, nearly 25% of Brazil's supply. Visitors are shown a 30-minute video on the dam's construction, featuring endless shots of frolicking children and nothing on the dam's environmental impact. Then you board a bus that crosses to an observation platform in the midpoint of the dam. For a much more in-depth look at the dam, including a visit to the production building and the central command post, book the "Special Tour." ***Note:*** No sandals, high heels, shorts, or miniskirts are allowed.

Av. Tancredo Neves 6702. ✆ **0800/645-4645.** www.itaipu.gov.br. Regular guided tour R$19. Daily hourly from 8:30am to 4:30pm. Special in-depth 2-hr. tours R$36. Daily every half hour from 8:30am to 11am, and 2, 2:30, 4, and 4:30pm. Call ahead to check times with English-speaking guide. Bus: 110 or 120.

Macuco Boat Safari ★★★ Niagara Falls has the *Maid of the Mist.* Iguaçu has *Macuco.* I know which one I'd choose. *Macuco* participants pile aboard 8m (25-ft.) zodiacs, the guide fires up twin 225-horsepower outboards, and you're off up the river, bouncing over wave trains, breaking eddy lines, powering your way up the surging current until the boat's in the gorge, advancing slowly toward one of the (smaller) falls. As the boat nears, the mist gets thicker, the roar louder, the passengers wetter and more and more thrilled (or terrified), until the zodiac peels away, slides downstream, and hides in an eddy until everyone's caught his or her breath. Then you do it all again. Allow 1 hour for the entire trip.

Parque Nacional do Iguaçu. ✆ **045/3523-6475.** www.macucosafari.com.br. R$170 per person, children 7–12 half price. Mon 1–5:30pm; Tues–Sun and holidays 9am–5:30pm. Bus: Parque Nacional or Cataratas.

Parque das Aves ★★ Set in 4.8 hectares (12 acres) of lush subtropical rainforest, the Bird Park offers the best bird-watching in Iguaçu. A large number of birds are in huge walk-through aviaries, some 24m (80 ft.) tall and at least 60m (200 ft.) long, allowing visitors to watch the birds interact as they go about their daily routines. Highlights include the toucans and multicolored tanagers as well as a Pantanal aviary with roseate spoonbills, herons, and egrets. Signage is in English. The best time to visit is early in the day when the birds are most active. Allow 2 hours.

Rodovia das Cataratas, Km 17, 300m (984 ft.) before the national park entrance. ✆ **045/3529-8282.** www.parquedasaves.com.br. Admission R$18, free for children 8 and under. Daily 8:30am–5:30pm. Bus: Parque Nacional or Cataratas.

WHERE TO STAY

Iguaçu has a variety of hotel options; more affordable options can be found in town and luxury accommodations on the park road. High season is from December to February and in July; outside of these months you can usually negotiate a discount of 20% to 40%.

Centro

Bella Italia (Value) Rooms at this midpriced hotel are pleasant enough—queen-size bed, writing desk, tub/shower combo in the bathroom, and a small balcony with a downtown view—but what makes the *Italia* so *bella* in terms of value is its packages. The "Iguassu Passport" package costs R$275 per person (based on double occupancy), and includes a night's accommodations with breakfast, plus the Macuco Safari boat ride, entrance to the Bird Park, lunch at Porto Canoas restaurant by the falls, and dinner at the hotel. Check the website for other packages and rates. The only real drawback to the hotel is the traffic noise. The best rooms and suites face downtown, and though the glass provides good sound insulation, there is still some traffic murmur, especially during rush hour. However, if you're up early and out sightseeing all day, this shouldn't be an issue.

Av. República Argentina 1700 (corner of Rua Venanti Otremba), Foz do Iguaçu, 85852-090 PR. ✆ **0800/45-4555** or 045/3521-5000. Fax 045/3521-5005. www.bellaitalia.tur.br. 135 units. R$155–R$250 suite. 20% discount for business travelers or in off season. Extra person add 30%. Children 7 and under stay free in parent's room, ages 8–12 R$30 extra. AE, DC, MC, V. Parking R$6 daily. **Amenities:** Restaurant; bar; 2 pools (small outdoor and children's); room service; smoke-free floors; small weight room; Wi-Fi. *In room:* A/C, TV, hair dryer, Internet, minibar.

On the Park Road

Bourbon Cataratas ★★★ Kids The real draw of the Bourbon is its leisure area. True, all the rooms are beautifully appointed. In the original wing, the standard rooms look out over the front of the hotel, whereas the superior rooms have a veranda and look over the pool. The new wing houses the master suites—really just a room, but with newer furnishings and huge windows providing lovely views. Out back, there's a 2km (1.25-mile) trail through orchards and lovely gardens; keep an eye out for toucans, parakeets, and colorful butterflies in the aviary. The vast pool complex includes three large pools, one especially for children. In high season, activity leaders organize all-day children's activities. But wait, there's more: a top-notch gym and indoor pool, a climbing wall and tennis courts, a soccer field, and a beach volleyball court. Brazil Nuts often has specials at a low R$250 a night.

Rodovia das Cataratas, Km 2.5, Foz do Iguaçu, 85853-000 PR. ✆ **0800/451-010** or 045/3521-3900. www.bourbon.com.br. 311 units. R$400–R$600 superior or master. Extra person R$140. AE, DC, MC, V. Free parking. Bus: Parque Nacional or Cataratas. **Amenities:** 3 restaurants; children's programs; huge pool complex (2 outdoor pools, 1 small indoor pool); room service; sauna (dry and steam); smoke-free rooms; outdoor lighted tennis courts. *In room:* A/C, TV, fridge, hair dryer, Internet, minibar.

Hotel das Cataratas ★★★ The only hotel inside the national park offers a variety of packages combining a 2-day stay with adventure sports or nature walks. Rooms have been recently renovated. Standard rooms are not overly large, but have nice hardwood floors and firm twin or double beds. The superior rooms are slightly larger. The deluxe rooms all have beautiful hardwood floors, dark-wood furniture, and bathrooms with large bathtubs; a few have balconies. Rooms are spread out over a number of wings, connected by spacious corridors. Guests also have use of a large pool complex and a forested area behind the hotel with nature trails to explore. And, of course, the falls are just on your doorstep. ***Tip:*** Check the website for Internet deals.

Parque Nacional do Iguaçu, Foz do Iguaçu, 85863-000 PR. ✆ **0800/726-4545** or 45/2102-7000. www.hoteldascataratas.com. 200 units. R$500 standard; R$580 superior; R$660 deluxe. Children 9 and under stay free in parent's room. AE, DC, MC, V. Free parking. Take the road to Iguaçu Falls and go straight toward the gate; do not turn left into the visitor's area. **Amenities:** 2 restaurants; bar; children's programs; large outdoor pool; room service; spa; tennis court. *In room:* A/C, TV, hair dryer, minibar, Wi-Fi.

San Martin ★ Kids San Martin is close to the Bird Park. The rooms are clean and pleasantly furnished and the rates are very affordable. Most of the superior rooms have been renovated and now feature hardwood floors and elegant, modern furnishings, quite an improvement from the '70s brown that still reigns in the standard rooms. The nicest rooms are the superior class rooms. These feature king-size beds and are much bigger than the standard rooms. For kids, the hotel's vast grounds offer several play areas, a soccer field, a swimming pool, and gardens.

Rodovia das Cataratas, Km 17, Foz do Iguaçu, 85853-000 PR. ✆ **0800/645-0045** or 045/3521-8088. www.hotelsanmartin.com.br. 135 units. R$180 standard; R$230 superior; R$320 family superior sleeping 4–6 people. AE, DC, MC, V. Free parking. Bus: Parque Nacional or Cataratas. **Amenities:** Restaurant; outdoor pool; room service; sauna; smoke-free rooms; tennis court; Wi-Fi. *In room:* A/C, TV, minibar.

WHERE TO DINE

Iguaçu is hardly a culinary experience, but expect excellent Brazilian (or Argentine) beef and fresh-caught fish from the Iguaçu or Paraná rivers. One restaurant that takes pride in serving local fish is **Trapiche,** Rua Marechal Deodoro 1087, Centro (✆ **045/3527-3951**). The large menu also includes high-end delicacies, such as lobster and oysters. Being just a hop and a skip from Argentina, it is not surprising that you would find excellent Argentine steak dishes in town. **Chef Lopes,** Av. República Argentina 632 (✆ **045/3028-3531;** www.cheflopes.com.br), woos guests with his fabulous juicy *bife de chorizo.* For something a little different, try Z**aragoza,** Rua Quintino Bocaiúva 882 (✆ **045/3574-3084;** www.restaurantezaragoza.com.br). The Spanish menu is particularly strong on seafood served grilled or broiled. On Sunday people come from far and wide to savor the paella for lunch.

7

Chile

by Christie Pashby

Sandwiched between the Andes and the Pacific Ocean, Chile's lengthy, serpentine shape at first glance seems preposterous: Nearly 4,830m (3,000 miles) of land stretches from Peru to Cape Horn (about the same distance as New York to Los Angeles), but the average width is just 185m (115 miles). Chile is a geographical extravaganza, encompassing such a breathtaking array of landscapes and climatic zones that it is difficult not to fall back on the old travel cliché "a country of contrasts"; but that is indeed what Chile is, and it is precisely what makes this South American country so unique. The north is home to the earth's driest desert, the Atacama; the Central Valley has a Mediterranean-like climate and a burgeoning wine and agricultural industry; farther south lie the volcanoes and forests of the Lake District; and at the very end are the vast plains, glaciers, and granite cathedrals of Patagonia. Chile also claims Easter and Robinson Crusoe islands in the Pacific Ocean, as well as a slice of Antarctica.

Travelers interested in nature and adventure will find much to keep themselves busy in Chile. The hundreds of rivers that descend from the Andes draw anglers from around the world for the phenomenal fly-fishing opportunities here, not to mention some of the planet's wildest white-water rafting. Snowy peaks and volcanoes provide excellent terrain for skiing and mountain climbing. The northern desert's eerie land formations and high-altitude salt flats are as easily explored by 4×4 as by mountain bike. The country's prize gem, the national park Torres del Paine, offers hiking, climbing, and backpacking. And there are kayak trips through remote sounds and slogs through exuberant temperate rainforest. There are plenty of low-key activities here as well, such as cruises through emerald fjords, soaks in hot springs, or just kicking back on a golden beach.

Best of all, Chile's strong economy and modern infrastructure promise high-quality amenities and services. Chile also boasts a solid reputation as the safest country in Latin America, and corruption is relatively absent. In addition, it is one of the most economically prosperous in Latin America, envied by its neighbors on all sides.

1 THE REGIONS IN BRIEF

Chile's enormous length makes traveling by air the fastest way to get around if you are planning to pack several destinations into one trip. The country has frequent air service and efficient transfers to get you from point A to B. If you have only a week to spare, you won't be able to visit more than two regions of the country. Visitors with 7 to 10 days who plan to visit Patagonia or a remote lodge with a long transfer time should be able to squeeze in a night or two in Santiago and maybe a quick day visit to the coast or the wine country, but little else. You may consider skipping more remote destinations like Patagonia or Easter Island to sample two widely different regions in Chile—for example, spend several days in the Atacama Desert, and then enjoy a few days in the Lake District. This

After the Earthquake

The catastrophic 8.8 magnitude earthquake that hit south-central Chile on February 27, 2010 was one of the strongest in recorded history. It resulted in more than approximately 450 deaths and severe damage to a number of cities and valleys. About 800,000 were left homeless and economists have pegged the reconstruction costs at upwards of $30 billion.

The hardest hit areas were around the city of Concepción, Chile's second-largest metropolis, about 564km (350 miles) south of Santiago. The majority of this area is far from the regular tourist path and isn't covered in this book. Tourist favorites, like Torres del Paine, the Atacama Desert, and the Lakes District were virtually unscathed.

The Chillán and Colchagua areas (p. 409) were also hit hard, but repairs began almost immediately, and most services were up and running within days. The Termas de Chillán ski resort, including all hotels and lifts, should be fully operational for the 2010 season. At presstime, repairs to roads, bridges, and wineries were expected to be fully completed by September 2010.

Likewise, the port at Valparaíso (p. 399) suffered damages, but they were fixed within a month of the quake. Finally, Santiago's Arturo Benitez International Airport suffered structural damages to its terminal but runways were unharmed.

would allow time for a day trip to the coast from Santiago. You might also consider a weeklong loop through the adjacent lake districts of both Chile and Argentina. (For information on Argentina's Lake District, see chapter 4.) Travelers with 2 to 3 weeks will have the freedom and the time to pick and choose destinations at will.

NORTHERN CHILE This region claims the world's driest desert, a pastel-colored "wasteland" set below a chain of rust-colored volcanoes and high-altitude salt flats. The sun-baked **San Pedro de Atacama,** a pueblo typical of the region, is the main oasis, and the best place to base your trip. Some of the finest lodges in the country are located here. Nearby are plentiful and well-preserved Indian ruin sites. The arid climate and the geological forces at work in this region have produced far-out land formations and superlatives such as the highest geyser field in the world.

SANTIAGO & CENTRAL CHILE The central region of Chile, including **Santiago** and its environs, features a mild, Mediterranean climate. This is Chile's breadbasket, with fertile valleys and rolling fields that harvest a large share of the country's fruit and vegetables; it is also Chile's main wine-producing region. Santiago's proximity to ski resorts, beach resorts, and the idyllic countryside, with its campestral and ranching traditions and colonial estates, offer plenty for the traveler to see and do. The sunny and character-rich port town of **Valparaíso,** an hour west of Santiago on the Pacific Coast, makes a fascinating base for your stay in the middle part of the country, an alternative to Santiago altogether. It's just south of the posh resort city of **Viña del Mar.**

LAKE DISTRICT Few destinations in the world rival the lush scenery of Chile's Lake District. This region is packed with a chain of conical, snowcapped volcanoes;

glacier-scoured valleys; several national parks; thick groves of native forest; hot springs; and, of course, many shimmering lakes. Temperatures during the summer are normally warm and pleasant, but winter is characterized by overcast days and drizzling rain. It's an outdoor lover and adventure seeker's paradise, especially in **Pucón** and **Puerto Varas.**

PATAGONIA Also known as the Magellanic Region, this part of the southern end of the continent has soared in popularity over the past 15 years, drawing visitors from all over the world to places such as **Torres del Paine National Park.** Chilean Patagonia officially begins in the south of the Lakes District, but the main area is the deep south of the country, a land characterized by vast, open steppe; the colossal Northern and Southern ice fields and the glaciers that descend from them; the rugged peaks of the Andes as they reach their terminus; a myriad of fjords and sounds that wind around thousands of uninhabited islands; and wind, wind, wind. Getting here is an adventure—it usually takes 24 hours if you're coming directly from the United States or Europe. But the long journey pays off in the beauty and singularity of the region.

2 THE BEST OF CHILE IN 2 WEEKS

This itinerary will take you from the windswept steppe and granite peaks of Patagonia, to the fertile valleys and the golden coast of central Chile, to the pastel-washed moonscape of the northern desert. Visitors with an eye toward relaxation might consider exchanging southern Patagonia for a Lake District destination such as Pucón, which has hot springs, a lakeshore for swimming and kicking back, and shopping, in addition to adventure sports. Travelers with less time will need to drop a destination all together, due to the country's enormous length and travel times.

Day ❶: Arrive & Tour Santiago ★★

Santiago, Chile's capital and home to nearly half the country's population, is not as culturally rich or exciting as Buenos Aires or Rio—however, there are plenty of top attractions to fill 1 day, including climbing **Cerro San Cristobal** (p. 379) for sweeping views of the city spread before the Andes, visiting the **historic downtown** and the **Museo Chileno de Arte Precolombino** (p. 376), and dining on the country's famed seafood in the **Mercado Central** (p. 379).

Day ❷: Sip Wine & See the Coast

Head west from the capital, stopping first for some wine tasting in the **Casablanca Valley** (p. 395). Then, continue on to colorful **Valparaíso** ★★ (p. 399) for lunch and a short walking tour of Chile's most storied port town. Finish the day with a pisco sour by the beach at **Viña del Mar** (p. 394). Return to Santiago, or spend the night at an oceanfront hotel in Viña or a cozy B&B in Valparaíso.

Day ❸: Head West

After breakfast by the sea, head to the Arturo Benítez Airport just west of Santiago and catch a midday flight south to **Punta Arenas** ★. Spend the late afternoon touring the city, including the Alice-in-Wonderland city cemetery, the port on the Strait of Magellan, and the **Museo Braun Menéndez** (p. 446) Or plan for a 5pm visit to a **penguin rookery** to watch the amusing birds waddle out to sea. In the evening, dine on the region's specialty, king crab. See section 8, "Southern Patagonia."

Days ❹–❽: Torres del Paine National Park ★★★

Head early from Punta Arenas to **Torres del Paine** (p. 454), Chile's breathtakingly

beautiful national park. Spend the following days hiking, horseback riding, or touring the park by van. Hotels, such as explora and Patagonia Camp, offer all-inclusive packages that include lodging, meals, and day tours with bilingual guides. Or plan to backpack the "W" trail, sleeping in tents or in comfortable *refugios* (shelters). Either way, don't miss **Glacier Grey** and, if you can hack it, the 6-hour **Towers hike** to the granite spires that give the park its name. Your final day is mostly spent driving back to Punta Arenas for an afternoon flight to Santiago, connecting to Calama. Arrive in **San Pedro de Atacama** ★ (p. 412) under the clear night sky.

Days ❾–⓭: Explore the Enigmatic Northern Desert ★★★

Wake up in the driest desert in the world. Spend the day lazily strolling the dirt streets of charming San Pedro de Atacama, and visit one of the best pre-Columbian museums in South America, the **Museo Arqueológico Padre le Paige** (p. 416). Book a nighttime astronomy tour; these are the some of the clearest skies in the world. During the next few days, hike or bike to **Atacaman Indian ruins**; visit the **Salt Lake** and take a dip; 4×4 to a lofty, turquoise Altiplanic lake; view the world's highest geyser field at sunrise; and finish the day with a soak in a hot spring. Book a midday flight back to the Santiago airport, spending the night in a different neighborhood than at the beginning of your trip. If you've been to Las Condes, try the gorgeous new **Aubrey hotel** (p. 384) in Bellavista.

Day 14: Back in the Capital

Spend the morning exploring **Bellavista,** shopping at Patio Bellavista, taking a tour of famed poet Pablo Neruda's house, **La Chascona** (p. 380), and having a last meal of *ceviche* at **Astrid y Gastón** (p. 389) in Providencia. After lunch, head to the airport for your international flight home.

3 PLANNING YOUR TRIP TO CHILE

VISITOR INFORMATION

You'll find a municipal tourism office in nearly every city and a **Sernatur (National Tourism Board)** office in major cities (www.sernatur.cl). The quality of service and availability of printed matter, such as maps and brochures, varies from office to office. Visitors are usually better off planning ahead via Internet research, booking a tour, or seeking the assistance of a hotel concierge rather than relying on the advice of a Sernatur clerk. **Turismo Chile,** which promotes tourism outside of Chile, has a useful website at www.turismochile.travel.

ENTRY REQUIREMENTS

Citizens of the United States, Canada, the United Kingdom, and Australia need only a valid passport to enter Chile. Visitors from New Zealand must apply for a tourist visa. Chile charges a **reciprocity fee** upon entry to citizens of the following countries: $131 for citizens of the U.S., $132 for Canadians, and $61 for Australians. Visitors from the U.K. and New Zealand do not pay a fee. Note that this fee is good for the life of a traveler's passport and is charged when entering through the **Santiago airport only.** Travelers crossing over land from Argentina, Peru, or Bolivia do not pay this fee. Before entering Chile, you'll need to fill out a tourist form that allows visitors to stay for 90 days. **Do not lose this form,** as you will need to present it to Customs when leaving the country. Also, many hotels waive Chile's 19% sales tax applied to rooms when guests show this form and pay with U.S. dollars. The easiest (and free) way to renew your 90-day stay is to cross the border and return. For $100, tourist forms can be renewed for another 90 days at the **Extranjería,** Agustinas 1235, Second Floor, in Santiago (✆ **2/550-2400**), open Monday to Friday 8:30am to 3:30pm (be prepared for excruciatingly long lines), or at any Gobernación Provincial office in the provinces. The extension must be applied for 1 month before the visa's expiration date. Bring the original form, your passport, and photocopies of the two.

Contact the Chilean consulate closest to you for information about children 17 and under traveling alone, with one parent, or with a third party, as departure Customs may demand written authorization by the absent parent(s) or legal guardian granting permission.

Lost Documents

Report lost tourist forms at the nearest police station or, in Santiago, at the **Policía Internacional,** Departamento Fronteras, General Borgoña 1052 (✆ **2/565-7863**), open Monday to Friday 9am to 5pm. If you lose your passport, contact your embassy for a

Telephone Dialing Info at a Glance

Kiosks and convenience stores sell phone cards with individual instructions on long-distance dialing, and phone booths at telephone centers will provide instructions on dialing according to the carrier they use. Visitors may rent **cellular phones** at the Santiago airport from the Entel desk near baggage claim or try the services of **ChileCellRent** (✆ **2/633-7600;** www.chilecellrent.com).

- **To place a call from your home country to Chile,** dial the international access code (011 in the U.S. and Canada, 0011 in Australia, 0170 in New Zealand, 00 in the U.K.), plus the country code (56), plus the Chilean area code, followed by the number. For example, a call from the United States to Santiago would be 011+56+2+000+0000. Cellphone numbers begin with a 9, 8, or 7. When dialing from outside Chile, dial the prefix 569 before the number; or from a land line within Chile dial 09 and then the number.
- **To place a call within Chile,** dial the area code, and then the number. (To place a collect call, dial 182 for an operator.)
- **To place a direct international call from Chile,** dial a carrier prefix followed by 0, and then the country code of the destination you are calling, plus the area code and the local number.
- To reach an English-speaking **international operator** from within Chile, dial ✆ **800/360-777** or 800/360-280. However, it is cheaper, and often easier, to simply go to one of many nearby *centros de llamadas* (call centers) for long-distance calling.

replacement. It is imperative that you carry a **photocopy of your passport** with you and another form of ID to facilitate the process.

Chilean Embassy Locations

In Australia: 10 Culgoa Circuit, O'Malley, ACT 2606 (✆ **02/6286-2098;** fax 02/6286-1289; http://chileabroad.gov.cl/australia).

In Canada: 1413-50 O'Connor St., Ottawa, ON K1P 6L2 (✆ **613/235-4402;** fax 613/235-1176; www.chile.ca).

In New Zealand: 19 Bolton St., Wellington (✆ **04/471-6270;** fax 04/472-5324; www.embchile.co.nz).

In the U.S.: 1732 Massachusetts Ave. NW, Washington, DC 20036 (✆ **202/785-1746;** fax 202/887-5579; www.chile-usa.org).

In the U.K.: 37–41 Old Queen St., London SW1H 9J1 (✆ **020/7222-2361;** fax 020/72220861; www.chileabroad.gov.cl/reino-unido).

CUSTOMS

Any travel-related merchandise brought into Chile, such as personal effects or clothing, is not taxed. Visitors entering Chile may also bring in no more than 400 cigarettes, 500 grams of pipe tobacco, or 50 cigars, and 2.5 liters of alcoholic beverages per adult.

MONEY

The unit of currency in Chile is the **peso**, denoted throughout this chapter with the abbreviation C$. The value of the peso has held steady at around **545 pesos to the dollar**, which is the rate used for prices listed in this book. Bills come in denominations of 1,000, 2,000, 5,000, 10,000, and 20,000 pesos. There are currently six coins in circulation, in denominations of 1, 5, 10, 50, 100, and 500 pesos; however, it's unusual to be issued 1 peso or even 5. In slang, Chileans commonly call 1,000 pesos a *luca.* ***Note:*** U.S. dollars are widely accepted throughout Chile, especially at hotels. Many hotel rates in this chapter, as well as some tours and airline fares, are quoted in U.S. dollars.

Chile levies a steep 19% **sales tax** called IVA (Impuesto al Valor Agregado) on all goods and services. Foreigners are exempt from the IVA tax when paying in U.S. dollars for hotel rooms and vacation packages; however, you might find this is not the case with low-budget hotels and hostels. Do a little math when you're offered a price in dollars, as the peso rate might be cheaper due to a proprietor's improper or inflated exchange rate.

A Chilean ATM is known as a "Redbanc," which is advertised on a maroon-and-white sticker. Redbancs are compatible with a variety of networks, including Cirrus (MasterCard) and PLUS (Visa). Most Chilean ATMs charge a minimal fee to use their ATMs. Your own institution might also charge you for foreign purchases or withdrawals, so check before you go. You'll find ATMs in banks, grocery stores, gas stations, and pharmacies.

Traveler's checks seem like an anachronism these days, given that 24-hour ATMs are ubiquitous and offer the best exchange rate. If you feel safer carrying a few traveler's checks just in case, **American Express** (✆ **800/221-7282**) offers denominations of $20, $50, $100, and $500, with a service charge of between 1% and 4% (unless you are a platinum or gold member). Traveler's checks, dollars, and euros can be exchanged at a ***casa de cambio*** (money-exchange house) for a small charge; *casas de cambio* are generally open Monday through Friday from 9am to 6pm (closed 1–3pm for lunch), and Saturday until 1pm.

Visa, MasterCard, and American Express are widely accepted throughout Chile, and Diner's Club isn't far behind. Many Chilean businesses are charged a 2% service fee and will pass that cost on to you, so expect cheaper deals with cash.

WHEN TO GO

PEAK SEASON High season for Chilean, Brazilian, and Argentine vacationers is during the summer from December 15 to the end of February, as well as the 2 middle weeks of July and Holy Week (Semana Santa), the week preceding Easter Sunday. These dates coincide with school vacations. Everybody, it seems, takes their vacation during these dates, and consequently the teeming masses seen in popular destinations such as Pucón or Viña del Mar during this time can be overwhelming. In spite of the fact that hotels double their prices during peak season, reservations sell out quickly, so book far in advance or come between late September (following the hectic national Independence Day holidays of Sept 18 and 19) and early December or March and mid-May. This "midseason" sees cheaper rates, pleasant weather, and uncrowded views. As well, the Desert North is scorching hot from November to February, and Patagonia typically experiences the strongest wind and its most capricious weather during the same period.

CLIMATE Chile's thin, drawn-out territory stretches over 38 degrees of latitude, encompassing every climate found in the world, except tropical. In many areas there are microclimates, pockets of localized weather that can completely alter the vegetation and landscape of a small area.

The northern region of Chile is so dry that some desert areas have never recorded rain. Summer temperatures from early December to late February in this region can top 100°F (38°C), and then drop dramatically at night to 30°F (–1°C). Winter days, from mid-June to late August, are crisp but sunny and pleasant, but as soon as the sun drops, it gets bitterly cold. Along the coast, the weather is mild and dry, ranging from 60°F to 90°F (16°C–32°C) during the summer.

The Santiago and Central Valley region features a Mediterranean climate, with rain during the winter only and temperatures that range from 32°F to 55°F (0°C–13°C) in the winter, and 60°F to 95°F (16°C–35°C) during the summer. Farther south, the Lake District and the Carretera Austral are home to sopping wet winters, and overcast days and rain are not uncommon during the summer, especially in the regions around Valdivia and Puerto Montt.

The Magellanic Region presents unpredictable weather patterns, especially during the summer, with extraordinary windstorms that can reach upwards of 120kmph (75 mph), and occasional rain. The windiest times are mid-November to February, but it can blow any time between October and April. Winters are calm, with irregular snowfall and temperatures that can dip to 5°F (–15°C).

PUBLIC HOLIDAYS Chile's national holidays are New Year's Day (Jan 1); Good Friday (late Mar or Apr); Labor Day (May 1); Remembrance of the War of the Pacific Victory (May 21); Corpus Christi (late May or early June); St. Peter & St. Paul Day (June 26); Asunción de la Virgen (Aug 15); Independence Day and Armed Forces Day, the major holiday of the year (Sept 18–19); The Meeting of Two Worlds Day (Oct 12); All Saint's Day (Nov 1); Feast of the Immaculate Conception (Dec 8); and Christmas (Dec 25).

Virtually every business in Chile shuts on public holidays, as is the case with national and local elections (from midnight to midnight). Alcohol is not sold on election days.

HEALTH CONCERNS

Chile poses few health risks to travelers, and no special vaccinations are required. In fact, there are no poisonous plants or animals in Chile, either. Nevertheless, standard wisdom says that travelers should get tetanus and hepatitis boosters.

Few visitors to Chile experience anything other than run-of-the-mill **traveler's stomach** in reaction to unfamiliar foods and any microorganisms in them. Chile's tap water is clean and generally safe to drink, though not particularly tasty. Bottled water is widely available throughout Chile. ***Warning:*** Do not, under any circumstances, drink tap water while in San Pedro de Atacama. It contains trace amounts of arsenic.

Altitude sickness, known as *soroche* or *puna,* is a temporary yet often debilitating affliction that affects about a quarter of travelers to the northern Altiplano, or the Andes at 2,400m (7,872 ft.) and up. Nausea, fatigue, headaches, shortness of breath, sleeplessness, and feeling "out of it" are the symptoms, which can last from 1 to 5 days. If affected, drink plenty of water, take aspirin or ibuprofen, and avoid alcohol and sleeping pills; or prevent the condition by breaking the climb to higher regions into segments.

The **thin ozone layer** in Patagonia and Tierra del Fuego is not to be taken lightly. During "red alert" days (typically Sept–Nov), fair-skinned visitors can burn within *10 minutes.* Protect yourself with sunblock, a long-sleeved shirt, a wide-brimmed hat, and sunglasses.

GETTING THERE

By Plane

Santiago's **Comodoro Arturo Merino Benítez Airport** (airport code SCL: ✆ **2/690-1900;** www.aeropuertosantiago.cl) is the international arrival point for Chile.

By Cruise Ship

South America is a hot cruise destination, and most companies now offer some version of the loop around Cape Horn. Journeys typically span 11 to 15 days and sail from Buenos Aires to Valparaíso, Chile, or vice versa, sometimes embarking in Florida or continuing on to the Panama Canal after Chile or Peru. Stops include Chile's Puerto Montt, Puerto Chacabuco, and Punta Arenas; and Argentina's Ushuaia, Puerto Madryn, Buenos Aires, and occasionally the Falkland Islands. It is a pity that cruisers get to spend so little time ashore; however, sailing through the southern region's fjords and around the Cape is truly remarkable. The following companies are best bets for sailing voyages; check for itineraries and prices: **Celebrity Cruises** (✆ **800/647-2251;** www.celebrity.com), **Crystal Cruises** (✆ **800/804-1500;** www.crystalcruises.com), **Holland America** (✆ **877-SAIL HAL** [724-5425]; www.hollandamerica.com), **Princess Cruises** (✆ **800/PRINCESS** [774-6237]; www.princesscruises.com), **Radisson Seven Seas** (✆ **877/505-5370;** www.rssc.com), and **Silversea** (✆ **877/760-9052;** www.silversea.com).

GETTING AROUND

By Plane

Travelers, especially those short on time, must fly if planning to visit several destinations. **LAN Airlines** (✆ **866/435-9526** in the U.S., or 600/526-2000 in Chile; www.lan.com) is the leader of the pack in terms of destinations, frequency, and quality of service. LAN serves Arica, Iquique, Calama, Antofagasta, Concepción, Temuco, Valdivia, Osorno, Pucón (Dec–Feb only), Puerto Montt, Coyhaique (Balmaceda), and Punta Arenas. **Sky Airline** (✆ **600/600-2828;** www.skyairline.cl) is another Chilean domestic carrier, with daily flights to all major destinations and service to smaller places like Puerto Natales and Copiapó.

By Bus

Chile has an efficient and inexpensive bus system, with three classes of service. Standard buses go by the name *clásico* or *pullman* (no relation to the giant bus company Pullman); an *ejecutivo* or *semicama* offers lots of legroom, and seats that recline; and the *salón cama* is fitted with seats that fold out into beds. Travelers seeking economical transportation to the Lake District or the Far North should consider a night bus on a *salón cama.* Short-haul coach rides to destinations such as Viña del Mar leave dozens of times a day; nevertheless it is a good idea to buy a round-trip ticket in advance during holidays and on weekends.

By Car

You won't need a vehicle for Santiago, but rentals do provide freedom to wander along the coast or sightsee in the Lake District. To make a reservation from the United States, call **Alamo** (✆ **800/GO-ALAMO** [462-5266]; www.alamo.com), **Avis** (✆ **800/230-4898;** www.avis.com), **Budget** (✆ **800/527-0700;** www.budget.com), **Dollar** (✆ **800/800-4000;** www.dollar.com), or **Hertz** (✆ **800/654-3001;** www.hertz.com). If renting once you're already in Chile, don't overlook a few of the local car-rental agencies for cheaper prices; you'll find their booths at major airports. Rental agencies at the Santiago airport now charge a small fee (around C$2725) for the Costanera Norte, a toll charged automatically to the vehicle when passing through the express tunnel from downtown to Las Condes, and Ruta 5 through the Santiago vicinity. You'll need special permission to take a Chilean rental car across the border into Argentina.

Save yourself a lot of frustration and avoid driving in Santiago if possible. Drivers here are aggressive, and it can be maddening to find your way around the labyrinth of one-way streets. Chile's modern and efficient four-lane Panamericana Highway spans the country, and charges tolls either at the on ramp or on the highway itself. Expect to pay between C$409 and C$2998 at a tollbooth. Car-rental agencies provide emergency road service. Be sure to obtain a 24-hour number before leaving with your rental vehicle.

By Ferry

Travelers concentrating on the Lake District and Patagonia regions might consider the 3-day journey aboard **Navimag** (✆ **61/411642;** www.navimag.com)**,** a passenger and cargo ferry that sails between Puerto Montt and Puerto Natales, introducing visitors to the remote, virgin fjordland that makes up the southern third of Chile. It is not a luxury liner, but some berths provide enough standard comfort for finicky travelers. **Transmarchilay** (✆ **65/270000**; www.transmarchilay.cl/) has cargo ferries (for vehicles) that link Puerto Montt and Chiloé with the Carretera Austral. The upscale **Skorpios** (p. 451) has 4- and 7-day cruises from Puerto Montt or Puerto Chacabuco, stopping at Chiloé before or after visiting the Laguna San Rafael Glacier. Skorpios has service from Puerto Natales that sails to the only advancing glacier, Pío XI. **Cruce Andino** (✆ **65/236150**; www.cruceandino.com) offers a land-and-lake crossing from Lago Todos los Santos in Vicente Pérez Rosales National Park near Puerto Varas, to Bariloche, Argentina. **Cruceros Australis** (✆ **2/4423115**; www.australis.com) offers memorable one-way and round-trip cruises from Punta Arenas to Ushuaia, sailing past Cape Horn.

TIPS ON ACCOMMODATIONS

It is imperative that travelers consider Chile's high season when considering accommodations, as prices soar and reservations are hard to come by without advance planning (See "When to Go" above). Chile's hotel rates, even for American chains, are lower than hotels of equivalent quality in the U.S. but generally much higher than in neighboring countries like Argentina and Bolivia. Comfy, midrange hotels and *cabañas* are plentiful—you can often find a terrific little place for $80 to $120 that is as good as an "expensive" hotel. The prices listed in this book are **rack rates,** but most hotels offer cheaper rates and promotional deals through their websites. And remember, if you are paying in US$ and have the entrance form from Customs, you'll save the 19% tax. ***Hotel tip:*** Don't be shy about negotiating a discount during the off season, as some hotel owners are willing to pass a travel agent's 10% to 20% commission on to you in the form of a discount. Hotels might charge a "midseason" rate during November and March. Price ranges listed in hotel write-ups reflect low to high season.

Price categories in this guide are listed according to **Very Expensive,** $255 and up; **Expensive,** $160 to $254; **Moderate,** $80 to $159; and **Inexpensive,** under $79. Prices shown reflect double occupancy; ask for details about a "single" rate, as single rooms are often small and come with a twin-size bed.

TIPS ON DINING

Chilean gastronomy is coming into its own, but for the most part you will not return from your trip raving about the country's cuisine. The focal point of Chilean *cocina de autor* (nouveau and fusion cuisine) is in Santiago; however, many restaurants in tourist-oriented destinations and most major hotels employ talented chefs and a long list of high-caliber wines. When ordering lunch, ask whether the restaurant has a *menú del día* or *menú ejecutivo,* a fixed-price lunch that typically includes an appetizer, main course, beverage or wine, coffee, and dessert. The lunch *menú* is normally a cheaper and fresher alternative to anything listed on the *carta* (menu). What beef is to Argentina, seafood is to Chile, and Chileans eat it all, from sole to sea urchin to conger eel. Price categories in this guide are listed according to **Expensive,** C$15,000; **Moderate,** C$7,000; and **Inexpensive,** under C$7,000.

TIPS ON SHOPPING

Bargaining for goods is accepted at stalls in central markets that sell arts and crafts and regional goods, but it is not a common practice. Chileans love to window-shop, and therefore malls heave with shoppers on weekends. The diverse regions of Chile produce their own specialties. The **Lake District** produces silver Mapuche Indian–influenced jewelry, smoked meats and seafood, cheeses, and sweet goodies such as marzipan and German cakes. **Chiloé** is known for its colorful woolen sweaters and scarves. The **Central Valley** specializes in wool ponchos and other Chilean cowboy gear, lapis lazuli jewelry (mostly Santiago), wine, and ceramic pottery (in Pomaire). One-stop shopping (a little of everything from Chile) is best at Los Dominicos or the Fería Santa Lucía in **Santiago**, or the markets in **Chillán** and **Puerto Montt.** Last-minute shoppers can pick up just about any curio, CD, book, or label of wine at the airport.

Fast Facts Chile

American Express The American Express office is at Av. Isidora Goyenechea 3621, Piso 10 (✆ **2/350-6855**). It's open Monday through Friday from 9am to 2pm and 3:30 to 5pm. The 24-hour customer service number in the U.S. is ✆ **800/545-1171,** although you will be charged for the call.

Business Hours Banks are open Monday to Friday from 9am to 2pm and are closed on Saturday and Sunday. Many commercial offices close for a long lunch hour, which can vary from business to business. Generally, hours are Monday through Friday from 10am to 7pm, closing for lunch around 1 or 1:30pm and reopening at 2:30 or 3pm.

Doctors & Hospitals *Clínicas* and private hospitals are always better than a town's general hospital. The cost of medicine and treatment can be expensive, but most hospitals and pharmacies accept credit cards. Many doctors, especially in Santiago, speak basic English; for a list of English-speaking doctors and medical specialists in Santiago, call your embassy. The best hospitals in Santiago are **Clínica Las Condes** at Lo Fontecilla 441 (✆ **2/210-4000**) and **Clínica Alemana** at Vitacura 5951 (✆ **2/210-1111**).

Drug Laws Possession and use of drugs and narcotics are subject to heavy fines and jail terms.

Electricity Chile's electricity standard is 220 volts/50Hz. Electrical sockets have two openings for tubular pins, not flat prongs; adapters are available from most travel stores.

Embassies & Consulates The **Australian Embassy** is at Isidora Goyenechea 3621, 13th Floor (✆ **2/550-3500;** http://chileabroad.gov.cl/australia). The **British Embassy** can be found at El Bosque Norte 0125 (✆ **2/370-4100;** www.britemb.cl). The **Canadian Embassy** is at Nuevo Tajamar 481, 12th Floor (✆ **2/652-3800;** www.dfait-maeci.gc.ca/chile). The **New Zealand Embassy** is at Av. Golf 99, no. 703 (✆ **2/290-9800;** www.nzembassy.com/chile).The only U.S. representative in Chile is the **U.S. Embassy** in Santiago, located at Av. Andrés Bello 2800 (✆ **2/232-2600;** www.chile.usembassy.govl).

Emergencies You'll want to contact the staff if something happens to you in your hotel. Otherwise, for a police emergency, call ✆ **133.** For fire, call ✆ **132.** To call an ambulance, dial ✆ **131.**

Internet Access No matter where you are in Chile, you should find an Internet station, either in a cafe or at telephone centers Telefónica or Entel. Most hotels, even hostels, have their own Internet service, and the majority now have wireless service. If they don't, the hotel staff can point out where to find one. Expect to pay C$600 to C$800 per hour.

Language Spanish is the official language of Chile. Many Chileans in the tourism industry and in major cities speak basic English, but don't count on it. Try to learn even a dozen basic Spanish phrases before arriving; *Frommer's Spanish Phrasefinder & Dictionary* will facilitate your trip tremendously.

Liquor Laws The legal drinking age in Chile is 18. Alcohol is sold every day of the year, except during elections.

Maps The best road maps for Chile come from Turistel guides, which are published twice a year and are sold at kiosks all over the country,

Newspapers & Magazines The major dailies are the conservative *El Mercurio* and the more moderate *La Tercera*. The English-language *Santiago Times* publishes online at www.santiagotimes.cl.

Police Police officers wear olive-green uniforms and are referred to as *carabineros,* or colloquially as *pacos.* Dial ✆ **133** for an emergency. Police officers in Chile are not corrupt and will not accept bribes on any occasion.

Post Offices/Mail The recently privatized **Correos Chile** (✆ **800/267736** or 2/956-0200; www.correoschile.cl) has post offices throughout the country, and has a decent international courier service. It costs C$400 to send a postcard to North America and C$470 to the rest of the world.

Restrooms Public restrooms in places like gas stations are generally clean, often attended by a employee who expects a small tip (C$200 is good) in exchange for toilet paper. Others won't have any toilet paper (or an employee) at all; it's a good idea to have your own supply.

Safety Serious violent crime is not unheard of, but it's not common either. Visitors should take measures against being pickpocketed, especially in crowded areas, and they should not leave valuables in a parked vehicle due to frequent break-ins. Santiago is probably the safest major city in South America.

Smoking Chile has strict anti-smoking laws that apply to restaurants (some of which still have a smoking section) and public spaces like airports and bus terminals. In general, fewer and fewer Chileans are smoking, although a post-meal cigarette is not uncommon. Most upscale and boutique hotels don't allow smoking.

Taxes Chile levies a steep 19% **sales tax,** called IVA (Impuesto al Valor Agregado), on all goods and services. Foreigners are exempt from the IVA tax when paying in U.S. dollars for hotel rooms and vacation packages; you'll often be required to present your entrance form from customs to save the 19%. Some low-budget hotels and hostels charge only in pesos, so this will not apply. Any travel-related merchandise brought into Chile, such as clothing, is not taxed.

Telephone For more information, see "Telephone Dialing Info at a Glance," earlier in this chapter. The country code for Chile is **56.** Telephone numbers in the Metropolitan Santiago area have 7 digits; elsewhere they have only 6. A local phone call requires C$100; phone cards sold in kiosks offer better rates.

Time Zone Chile is 4 hours behind Greenwich Mean Time (GMT) from the first Sunday in October until the second Sunday in March; the country is 6 hours behind during the rest of the year.

Tipping Diners leave a 10% tip in restaurants. In hotels, tipping is left to the guest's discretion. Don't tip taxi drivers.

4 SANTIAGO

Santiago, one of South America's most sophisticated cities, is a thriving metropolis that's home to five million people, or nearly 40% of Chile's entire population. Though it ranks third behind Miami and Sao Paulo for Latin American business travel, it is one of Chile's least popular tourist destinations, given the amount of travelers who use Santiago only as a jumping-off point to locations such as Patagonia or the Lake District. You won't find the wealth of things to do and see that defines such cities as Rio de Janeiro or Buenos Aires. But, that said, as the city booms economically and memories of the stifling Pinochet dictatorship fade, Santiago is reinventing itself, and the arts, nightlife, and restaurant scene have improved considerably as of late. As well, no other Latin American city has the proximity that Santiago has to such a diverse array of day attractions, including wineries, ski resorts, and beaches.

Santiago boasts a one-of-a-kind location sprawled below some of the highest peaks of the Andes range, providing a breathtaking city backdrop when the air is clear and the peaks are dusted with snow. Unfortunately, smog and dust particles in the air often shroud the view, especially during the winter months. From December to late February, when Santiaguinos abandon the city for summer vacation and the city is blessed with breezier days, the smog abates substantially. These are the most pleasant months to tour Santiago.

Architecturally, Santiago's city planners have shown indifference to continuity of design during the last century. Rather than look within for a style of their own, Chileans have instead copied the architecture of other continents: first Europe and now the U.S. Earthquakes and neglect eradicated most of Santiago's colonial-era buildings decades ago, and what 19th-century architecture remains is in danger of demolition to make way for yet another glitzy skyscraper or one of the ubiquitous and monotonous apartment buildings so popular with residents here.

ESSENTIALS

Getting There

BY PLANE Santiago's **Comodoro Arturo Merino Benítez Airport** (✆ **2/690-1900;** www.aeropuertosantiago.cl) is served by LAN and Sky Airline (formerly Aerolíneas del Sur), and most major international carriers. Within the Customs area is a **currency-exchange** kiosk. Men in olive jumpsuits at the arrival and the outdoor-departure curb work as airport bellhops, and they will assist you with your luggage for a C$500 or C$1,000 tip.

Depending on traffic, your Santiago destination, and how you get there, the city can be reached in 20 to 45 minutes. Most hotels offer a private car or van pickup for about $35. A **taxi** to Santiago costs between $30 and $35, depending on the area. ***Tip:*** Buy a taxi ride at the official counter to the right of the customs exit door to avoid getting ripped off. **TransVip** (✆ **2/677-3000**) and **Tur Transfer** (✆ **2/677-3600**) charge, per person, C$5,000 for downtown Santiago and C$6,100 to Las Condes. The drawback with this service is that you may stop at several other destinations before arriving at your own. The blue bus **Centropuerto** leaves every 10 minutes from 6am to 10:30pm and drops passengers at Los Héroes Metro station on the main avenue Alameda. **Tur Bus** leaves every 30 minutes from 6:30am to 9pm, dropping passengers off at Terminal Alameda at the Universidad de Santiago Metro station. The cost is C$1,750 one-way.

BY BUS There are three principal **bus stations** in Santiago. The station for international arrivals and departures to and from destinations in southern Chile is **Terminal Buses Estación Central,** formerly known as the Terminal Santiago and not to be confused with the actual Estación Central train station and Metro stop; it's located at Alameda 3850 (✆ **2/376-1755;** Metro: Universidad de Santiago). The **Terminal Alameda** next door at Alameda 3750 is the terminal for the Pullman and Tur Bus companies, two well-respected, high-quality services. For departures to northern and central Chile, you'll go to **Terminal San Borja,** Alameda 3250 (✆ **2/776-0645;** Metro: Estación Central). The smaller **Terminal Los Héroes,** Tucapel Jiménez 21 (✆ **2/423-9530;** Metro: Los Héroes), has service to a variety of destinations in both northern and southern Chile.

Orientation

Santiago incorporates 32 *comunas,* or neighborhoods, although most visitors will find they spend their time in just a few. **Downtown,** or *el centro,* is the political and historic center of Santiago and has a gritty feel. Most of the financial wealth has now relocated to **Providencia, Las Condes,** and the tiny area that separates the two, **El Golf** (also known as El Bosque, or colloquially as "San-hattan" in reference to its Wall Street–esque clout). These neighborhoods are impressively clean and modern, especially when compared to older, scruffier downtown or to other Latin American cities. **Vitacura,** separated from Las Condes by Avenida Kennedy, is home to Santiago's tony boutiques and several top restaurants. Santiago is bisected by the Río Mapocho; on the northern side rises Cerro San Cristóbal, a forested park and recreation area. Below this park is the artists' neighborhood **Bellavista,** with dozens of bars and restaurants.

Getting Around

Santiago is beset with traffic congestion during the day, making the Metro the fastest way to get around, especially from 4 to 7pm.

BY METRO Santiago's subway system, the Metro, is clean and efficient, but peak hours (7–10am and 5–8pm) can be packed; www.metrosantiago.cl). Line 1 runs from Las

Condes to downtown, following Avenida Alameda. This line will take you to most major attractions. Line 2 runs from Cal y Canto (near the Mercado Central) to Lo Ovalle (near the Palacio Cousiño). Lines 4 and 4a are residential lines connecting Avenida Alameda with La Reina. Line 5 runs from La Florida to Baquedano. There are two fares: 88¢ from 7 to 9am and 6 to 8pm; 72¢ from 6 to 7am, 9am to 6pm, and 8 to 11pm.

BY BUS The Santiago bus system has new gleaming white-and-green TransSantiago coaches, which you cannot ride without a "BIP" transit card. However, it is nearly impossible for a foreigner (or even a local) to find a BIP kiosk to buy one. In other words, city buses, or *micros,* are out of the question for travelers.

BY TAXI Taxis are reasonably priced and plentiful. They are identifiable by their black exterior and yellow roof; there's also a light in the corner of the windshield that displays a taxi's availability. Always check to see that the meter is in plain view, to avoid rip-offs. Drivers do not expect tips.

BY RENTAL CAR Do not rent a vehicle if staying within metropolitan Santiago, but consider doing so if you are an independent traveler seeking to visit the coast or wine country. Santiago's slick new Costanera Norte (an express transit tunnel that runs from La Dehesa and Las Condes to the Panamericana Highway and the airport) has entrances and exits along the River Mapocho, but finding one can be confusing (www.costanerannorte.cl). The city's new TAG system (an automatic toll charged electronically to the vehicle) is included in the rental price. Downtown Santiago, and the entire length of Avenida Alameda/Avenida Providencia are not recommended for timid drivers. Buses and other drivers steadfastly refuse to let other vehicles merge into their lane, so be prepared early to turn or exit a highway. Also, do not drive inside the yellow bus lanes unless preparing to turn.

At the airport you'll find most international rental agencies, such as **Alamo** (✆ 2/690-1370; www.alamochile.com), **Avis** (✆ 2/690-1382; www.avischile.cl), **Budget** (✆ 2/690-1233; www.budget.cl), **Dollar** (✆ 2/202-5510; www.dollar.com), and **Hertz** (✆ 2/601-0977; www.hertz.com), and local agency **Rosselot** (✆ 800/201298; www.rosselot.cl). All agencies have downtown or Providencia offices. Generally, Rosselot and Dollar are lower in cost.

Most hotels offer parking on their own property or in a nearby lot. Downtown street parking is virtually impossible except for Sundays. In Providencia, along Avenida Providencia, there is a series of underground lots; blue signs with a large white "E" point the way. Commercial and downtown streets are manned by meter maids. Chile is also home to the parking *cuidador,* where unofficial "caretakers" stake out individual blocks and "watch" your car for you. They are everywhere, even at grocery store lots, and they expect a small tip, about C$100 to C$200, when you leave. *Cuidadores* in busy commercial areas are very aggressive. ***Tip:*** Never leave valuable items in your vehicle when parking on the street due to frequent break-ins that occur throughout Santiago.

ON FOOT Santiago is not laid out on a perfect grid system; however, the neighborhoods most visitors stick to run along the length of the Mapocho River, and good paths through the riverside parks make for pleasant walking. Always carry a map with you. Saturday afternoons and Sundays are quieter days to explore neighborhoods such as downtown. Pedestrians should be alert at all times and never stand too close to sidewalk curbs due to buses that roar by dangerously close to sidewalks. Drivers do not always give the right of way to pedestrians, so cross streets quickly and carefully.

Visitor Information

The **National Tourism Service (Sernatur)** office is at Av. Providencia 1550 (✆ **600/SERNATUR** [600/731-8310]; www.sernatur.cl; Metro: Manuel Montt), and is open Monday through Friday from 9am to 6:30pm and Saturday from 9am to 2pm. Sernatur also has an information desk on the departure level of the airport open daily from 9am to 5pm (no phone). There's also an **Oficina de Turismo** downtown, inside the Casa Colorada at Merced 860 (✆ **2/632-7783**), with information about downtown Santiago attractions only. The **Yellow Pages** has detailed maps of the entire city of Santiago, or you can pick up a pocket guide to the city, called **"Map City"** (www.mapcity.cl), sold at newsstands and kiosks for C$4,000.

FAST FACTS **Banks** are open Monday through Friday from 9am to 2pm. ATMs are referred to as "RedBancs" and can be identified by a maroon-and-white logo sticker. Currency-exchange offices, called *casa de cambios,* are open from 9am to 7pm Monday to Friday, and 9am to 3pm Saturdays. On Sundays, currency can be exchanged at hotels or at an exchange house at Parque Arauco or Alto Las Condes malls. Exchange offices downtown are clustered at Paseo Huérfanos and Agustinas; in Providencia, at Avenida Pedro de Valdivia and Avenida Providencia.

For a **police emergency,** call ✆ **133.** For **fire,** call ✆ **132.** To call an **ambulance,** dial ✆ **131.** If you need medical attention, the American Embassy can provide a list of English-speaking medical specialists in Santiago. The best hospitals in Santiago are private: **Clínica Las Condes,** Lo Fontecilla 441 (✆ **2/210-4000**), **Clínica Alemana,** Vitacura 5951 (✆ **2/210-1111**), and **Clínica Indisa Santa María,** Santa María 1810 (✆ **2/362-5555**).

Every hotel has a computer with Internet connection for its guests, and most hotels now offer free Wi-Fi in guest rooms or public areas. Hours for phone centers and cafes are typically 9am to 10pm.

The main **post office** is on the Plaza de Armas (Mon–Fri 8:30am–7pm; Sat 8:30am–1pm). Branches are at Moneda 1155 in downtown and Av. 11 de Septiembre 2239. **FedEx** is at Av. Providencia 1951 and in the Dimacofi center at Moneda 792 (✆ **2/361-6000**).

WHAT TO SEE & DO

Even if you have just 1 day in Santiago, you should be able to pack in a sizable amount of the city's top attractions. It's a push, but nearly all attractions lie within a short walk or taxi ride from each other, which makes it easy to pick and choose according to your interests.

Downtown Historic & Civic Attractions

Begin your tour of Santiago at the historic heart of the city, the **Plaza de Armas** ★★★, which can be reached by taking the Metro to Estación Plaza de Armas. Chile's founder, Pedro de Valdivia, laid plans for the plaza in 1541 as the civic nucleus of the country and its importance was such that all distances to other parts of Chile were, and still are, measured from here. Take a seat and soak in the ambience of shoeshiners, religious fanatics, local artists, kissing couples, old men crouched over chessboards, and other colorful characters milling about. The **Basilica de la Merced**, Enrique MacIver 341, corner of Merced (✆ **2/633-0691**) is worth a stop to see a tiny piece of wood next to the collection box that is widely-believed to be a sliver from the actual cross of Christ. Inside is also the tomb of Inés de Suárez, the leading female conquistadora of Chile.

Casa Colorada & Museo de Santiago ★ Overrated Widely regarded as the best-preserved colonial structure in Santiago, the Casa Colorada, or Red House, was built between 1769 and 1779 as a residence for the first president of Chile, Mateo de Toro y Zambrano. Today, the Casa Colorada operates as the Santiago Museum, depicting the urban history of the city until the 19th century. The tiny museum, on the whole, is somewhat amateurish, seemingly directed at kids more than adults. A **visitor center** with information about downtown Santiago is also located in the Casa Colorada.

Merced 860. ✆ **2/633-0723.** Admission C$400. Tues–Fri 10am–6pm; Sat 10am–5pm; Sun 11am–2pm. Metro: Plaza de Armas.

Catedral Metropolitana & Museo de Arte Sagrado ★★ Santiago's grand cathedral spans a city block and is the fifth cathedral to have been erected at this site due to earthquake damage. The cathedral was also the subject of intrigue in 2005 when renovations unearthed the lost body of Diego Portales, the principal ideologist for the Chilean Constitution of 1833. The cathedral, designed by the Italian architect Joaquin Toesca in a neoclassical-baroque style, took nearly 30 years to complete, and was finished in 1780. Of most interest here are the hushed, cavernous cathedral interiors, with columns that soar high to arched ceilings, and an ornate alter made of marble, bronze, and lapis lazuli, and brought from Munich in 1912.

Paseo Ahumada, on the west side of the plaza. No phone. Free admission. Mon–Sat 9am–7pm; Sun 9am–noon. Metro: Plaza de Armas.

Museo Chileno de Arte Precolombino ★★★ Heading back on Merced and past the plaza to Bandera, you'll find the notable Chilean Museum of pre-Columbian Art, housed in the elegant 1807 ex-Royal Customs House. This is one of the better museums in Chile, both for its collection of pre-Columbian artifacts and its inviting design. There are more than 1,500 objects on display here, including textiles, metals, paintings, figurines, and ceramics spread throughout seven exhibition rooms. The collection is encompassing but not as extensive as, say, the Anthropological Museum of Mexico, but the exhibition does offer a vivid exhibition of indigenous life and culture before the arrival of the Spanish. There's also a well-stocked bookstore that sells music, videos, and reproductions of Indian art, textiles, and jewelry. Docents offer tours in English at 1 and 5pm Tuesday through Friday and at 10am and 2pm Saturday, but visitors must call ahead for a reservation. If you have time for one museum in Santiago, make it this one.

Bandera 361. ✆ **2/688-7348.** www.precolombino.cl. Admission C$3,000 adults, free for students; free for all Sun and holidays. Tues–Sun 10am–6pm. Metro: Plaza de Armas.

Palacio de la Real Audiencia/Museo Histórico Nacional ★★ This excellent museum is a must-see for history buffs and travelers seeking insight to Chile's past, from the conquest to present day, in a size and scope that doesn't feel overwhelming. The museum is housed in the elegant, lemon-colored Palacio de la Real, where Chile held its first congress following independence. The museum winds around a central courtyard, beginning with the Conquest, and finishing with a photo montage depicting modern political turmoil and literary and artistic accomplishment in Chile. Along the way, visitors can view weapons, agricultural tools, traditional costumes, household appliances, oil paintings depicting early Chile, and reproductions of home life during the 18th and 19th centuries. There are, unfortunately, no tours in English, and all interpretative information is in Spanish; however, most displays are self-explanatory. Plan to spend 30 minutes to 1 hour here.

Plaza de Armas 951. ✆ **2/411-7010.** www.museohistoriconacional.cl. Admission C$600 adults, C$300 seniors, free for children 17 and under; free for all Sun and holidays. Tues–Sun 10am–5:30pm. Metro: Plaza de Armas.

Plaza Constitucion & the Commerce Center

The Plaza Constitución, located between Agustinas, Morandé, Moneda, and Teatinos streets, is an expansive plaza used primarily as a pedestrian crossway and a venue for protests. It's also where you'll find the infamous **Palacio de la Moneda** ★★, the Government Palace and site of the September 11, 1973, coup d'état led by Augusto Pinochet to oust the socialist president Salvador Allende. The building, the largest erected by the Spanish government during the 18th century, was the focus of much criticism for being too ostentatious, but today it is considered one of the finest examples of neoclassical architecture in Latin America. This is the president of Chile's office. Depending on the daily activities of the president, visitors are often allowed to enter the courtyard and walk around after showing guards their passport. The **changing of the guard** ★★, when dozens of *carabineros* (police) march in step to the Chilean anthem in front of the palace, takes places every other day at 10am.

One block east from the plaza at Moneda and Bandera is the **Bolsa de Comercio** ★★ (✆ **2/399-3000;** www.bolsadesantiago.com), Santiago's stock market exchange, housed in an elegant, dome-roofed 1917 building and set amid some of downtown's more charming streets. Inside the Bolsa, traders group around La Rueda (the Wheel), a circular railing where they conduct hectic transactions—few people know that you can observe the action Monday to Friday from 9am to 5pm.

Centro Cultural Palacio La Moneda ★★ Chile's newest attraction hosts a revolving-door of exhibits ranging from modern art and literature to design and cultural heritage. The center is located underground before the Palacio (Citizen's Plaza) and can be accessed by walking down a ramp at either Teatinos or Morandé streets. The space is a sensational example of urban-contemporary design. The center also has an art-house cinema, library, educational center, and a sleek cafe. Check their website for upcoming exhibitions and events, and plan to spend about 30 minutes here.

Plaza de la Ciudadanía (underground). ✆ **2/355-6500.** www.ccplm.cl. Admission C$500 adults, C$300 students and seniors, children 4 and under free; Sun free for all. Daily 10am–7:30pm. Metro: La Moneda.

Attractions off the Alameda

In addition to the below attractions, the **Biblioteca Nacional** (Av. O'Higgins 651; ✆ **2/360-5259**; www.bndechile.cl) is a lovely, sprawling French neoclassically-styled building that houses the national map collection.

Barrio París-Londres ★★ This incongruous neighborhood is just a few blocks in diameter and was built between the 1920s and 1930s on the old gardens of the Monastery of San Francisco. The neighborhood oozes charm—it looks as if a chunk of Paris's Latin Quarter was airlifted and dropped down in the middle of downtown Santiago. The cobblestone streets of this neighborhood end at tacky, mismatched buildings on the neighborhood's outskirts. Safety is a concern here at nighttime.

The streets between Prat and Santa Rosa, walking south of Alameda O'Higgins. Metro: Universidad de Chile.

Calle Dieciocho (Overrated) **& Palacio Cousiño** ★ During the turn of the 20th century and before Santiago's elite packed it up and moved away from the downtown hubbub, Calle Dieciocho ranked as the city's toniest neighborhood. The tourism board touts Calle Dieciocho as a step back in time, but neglect has taken its toll, and the only site really worth visiting here is the **Palacio Cousiño Macul,** once the home of Chile's grandest entrepreneurial dynasties, the Goyenechea-Cousiño family. When finished in 1878, the palace dazzled society with its opulence: lavish parquet floors, Bohemian crystal chandeliers, Italian hand-painted ceramics, and French tapestries. A visit here not only provides an opportunity to view how Santiago's elite lived during the late 1800s, it also offers a chance to admire the most exquisite European craftsmanship available during that time. To get here, take a taxi or the Metro to Estación Toesca (turn left when leaving the station). Take a 10-minute detour around the corner (east on San Ignacio) to Parque Almagro, a scruffy park that nevertheless affords a view of the little-known, almost Gaudiesque **Basílica del Santísimo Sacramento,** constructed between 1919 and 1931 and modeled after the Sacre Coeur in Montmartre, Paris.

Dieciocho 438. ✆ **2/698-5063.** www.palaciocousino.co.cl. Admission C$3,000 adults, C$1,500 children 11 and under. Bilingual tours given Tues–Fri 10am–12:30pm and 2:30–4pm, Sat–Sun 10am–12:30pm. Metro: Toesca.

Iglesia, Convento, y Museo de San Francisco ★★ The Church of San Francisco is the oldest standing building in Santiago, and although this landmark has been renovated over the years, the main structure has miraculously survived three devastating earthquakes. The highlights are the museum and the convent, the latter with an idyllic patio planted with flora brought from destinations as near as the south of Chile and as far away as the Canary Islands. The garden, with its bubbling fountain and cooing white doves, is so peaceful, you'll find it hard to believe you're in downtown Santiago. The museum boasts 54 paintings depicting the life and death of San Francisco, one of the largest and best-conserved displays of 17th-century art in South America.

Londres and Alameda. ✆ **2/639-8737.** Admission to convent and museum C$1,250 adults. Tues–Sat 10am–1pm and 3–6pm; Sun and holidays 10am–2pm. Metro: Santa Lucía.

Cerro Santa Lucia

Materializing as if out of nowhere on the edge of the city's downtown limits, the **Cerro Santa Lucía ★★★** is a lavishly landscaped hilltop park and one of the more delightful attractions in Santiago. Native Mapuche Indians called this hill Huelén (Pain) until conqueror Pedro de Valdivia seized the property and planted the Spanish flag in 1570, thereby founding Santiago. In the late 1800s, Governor Benjamin Vicuña envisioned the hill as a recreation area and transformed Santa Lucía into an extravagant labyrinth of gardens, fountains, and flagstone promenades that gently spiral up to a 360-degree view of the city. The park is open daily September through March from 9am to 8pm, and April through August from 9am to 7pm; admission is free, though you'll be asked to sign a guest registry. The **Centro de Exposición de Arte** has indigenous crafts, clothing, and jewelry for sale, but you'll find better deals across the avenue at the **Centro Artesanal de Santa Lucía,** with handicrafts, T-shirts, and more.

Parque Forestal & Plaza Mulato Gil de Castro

Santiago's burgeoning arts and cafe scene centers around the tiny **Plaza Mulato Gil de Castro ★★**, located at José Victorino Lastarria and Rosal streets. The fine examples of early 1900s architecture at the plaza and many of the dozen streets that surround it provide visitors with a romantic step back into old Santiago. From Thursday to Sunday, antiques and book dealers line the plaza, but the highlights here are the **Museo de Artes Visuales (MAVI) ★★★** and the **Museo Arqueológico de Santiago (MAS) ★★** (✆ **2/638-3502;** www.mavi.cl; Tues–Sun 10:30am–6:30pm; C$1,000 adults, C$500 students; Sun free). Many of Chile's most promising contemporary artists exhibit their work at MAVI. The modern MAS offers archeological displays of artifacts produced by indigenous peoples throughout the length of Chile. The collection at MAS is extensive, but the museum is small and takes no more than 10 minutes to peruse. If you're short on time, skip the pre-Columbian museum and visit this one in tandem with the arts museum.

Parque Forestal is a slender, century-old park that skirts the perimeter of the Mapocho River from the Metro station Baquedano to the park's terminus at the Mapocho station. Lofty trees, soft grass, lovely fountains, and park benches provide a restful stop for the weary traveler. Nearby is the **Museo Nacional de Bellas Artes ★★**, José Miguel de la Barra and Ismael Valdés Vergara (✆ **2/633-0655;** www.mnba.cl; Tues–Sun 10am–6:50pm), housed in a regal, neoclassical, and Art Nouveau–style edifice built in 1910 to commemorate Chile's centennial. The museum's permanent collection showcases Chilean art from the colonial period to the 20th century only; international art expositions take place as temporary exhibits.

Mercado Central ★★★ (Kids) It's the quintessential tourist stop, but the colorful, chaotic Mercado Central is nevertheless a highlight for visitors to Santiago. Chile's economy depends on the exportation of natural products such as fruits, vegetables, and seafood, and the market here displays everything the country has to offer. Lively and staffed by pushy fishmongers who quickly and nimbly gut and fillet while you watch, the market displays every kind of fish and shellfish available along the Chilean coast. Depending on your perspective, the barking fishmongers and waitresses who harangue you to choose *their* zucchini, *their* sea bass, *their* restaurant can be entertaining or somewhat annoying. Either way, don't miss it, especially for the market's lofty, steel structure that was prefabricated in England and assembled here in 1868. You can also grab an affordable lunch at one of the exterior stalls. **Donde Augusto** is a good bet.

Vergara and Av. 21 de Mayo. No phone. Daily 7am–5pm (some stalls are open later). Metro: Cal y Canto.

Barrio Bellavista & Parque Metropolitano (Cerro San Cristobal)

The **Parque Metropolitano ★★★** is a 730-hectare (1,803-acre) park and recreation area with swimming pools, walking trails, a botanical garden, a zoo, picnic grounds, restaurants, and children's play areas. The park is divided into two sectors, Cumbre and Tupahue, both of which are accessed by car, cable car, funicular, or foot. On a clear day, the sweeping views of the city render this attraction as the best in the city, but it can be disappointing on a particularly smoggy day. To get here, head to the Plaza Caupolican at the end of Calle Pío Nono, where you'll encounter a 1925 **funicular** that lifts visitors up to a lookout point, open Monday from 1 to 6pm, and Tuesday through Sunday from 10am to 6:30pm; tickets cost C$1,700 adults, C$750 children ages 3 to 13. The lookout point is watched over by a 22m-high (72-ft.) statue of the **Virgen de la Inmaculada Concepción** a few dozens steps up. Along the way, the funicular stops at the **Jardín Zoológico ★★** (✆ **2/777-6666**), open Tuesday through Sunday from 10am to 6pm; tickets cost C$2,100 for adults, C$1,000 for children ages 3 to 13. This surprisingly diverse zoo features more than 200 species of mammals, reptiles, and birds, including native condors, pumas, and guanacos. Below the statue is the ***teleférico* (cable car)** that connects the two sections of the park, open Monday 1:30 to 5:30pm, and Tuesday through Sunday from 11:30am to 5:30pm. Tickets cost C$1,200 for adults and C$500 for children; ticket combinations with the funicular cost C$2,200 for adults, C$1,000 for children. The *teleférico* is a lot of fun, especially for kids, but it can be a roasting oven in the summertime heat. Admission for vehicles is C$1,200. It's also possible to take a taxi up, but you'll need to pay the park entrance fee as well as the fare. The Parque Metropolitano's hours are daily from 8:30am to 9pm, and cars run until 10pm.

Below the Cerro San Cristobál sits the bohemian neighborhood **Bellavista** ★★★. One of the more interesting neighborhoods in the city, its streets are lined with trees and colorful antique homes, many of which have been converted into restaurants and studios for artists and musicians. Come for shopping, an afternoon coffee break, or dinner (see later "Where to Dine"). In the evening, Bellavista pulses to the beat of music pouring from its many nightclubs and bars.

You might begin your visit with a trip to Bellavista's prime attraction, **La Chascona** ★★★, Fernando Márquez de la Plata 0192 (✆ **2/777-8741;** www.fundacion neruda.org). Located a block east of the Plaza Caupolican (entrance point to the Parque Metropolitano), this is one of three homes once owned by Chile's most famous literary artist, the Nobel Prize–winning poet Pablo Neruda. As with Neruda's other two homes, La Chascona is packed with quirky collections of antiques and whimsical curios collected during his travels. The home is headquarters for the Fundación Pablo Neruda, which provides guided tours. Admission is C$2,500 for adults for the Spanish tour, C$3,500 for the English tour; and it's open Tuesday through Sunday from 10am to 6pm. Call to make a reservation, or just show up and wait in the cafe until a guide frees up.

Especially for Kids

The Parque Metropolitano Zoo, the Mercado Central, and the aerial tram at Cerro San Cristobal described above are all kid-friendly. The prime kid attraction here is **Fantasilandia,** a modern amusement park (✆ **2/476-8600;** www.fantasilandia.cl); admission is C$6,500 for adults and C$3,200 for children. It's open April through November, Saturday, Sunday, and holidays only from noon to 7pm; December through March hours are Tuesday through Sunday from noon to 8pm. It's the largest amusement park in Chile, with four stomach-churning roller coasters, a toboggan ride, and haunted house. The **Museo Interactivo Mirador (MIM)** ★★★ and the **Santiago Aquarium** ★★ are neighbors within an 11-hectare (27-acre) park in the La Granja barrio (two entrances: Sebastopol 90 and Punta Arenas 6711; ✆ **2/280-7800;** www.mim.cl). Inaugurated in 2000, MIM dedicates itself to providing children with an introduction to the world of science and technology. The ultramodern museum has more than 300 exhibits, mostly interactive displays that cover the range of paleontology, computer animation, robotics, and 3-D cinema. You could spend nearly a full day here if you choose to check out the aquarium and its frolicking sea lion show. Buy a combo ticket for both if you have enough time. It's located fairly far from the city center; to get here, take the Metro Line 5 to the Mirador stop or take a taxi. Admission to the museum is C$4,000 for adults, C$2,500 for children; a combo ticket with the aquarium costs C$5,300 for adults, C$4,000 for children. For the aquarium only, it's C$2,500 for adults and children.

The **Parque Quinta Normal,** at 502 Av. Matucana, is also home to several museums ideally suited for kids. The **Museo Nacional de Historia Natural** ★ (✆ **2/680-4615;** www.mnhn.cl) displays native flora and fauna, and anthropological exhibits, and has an interactive area and fresh new design. Admission is C$600 for adults, C$500 for students; hours are Tuesday through Saturday 10am to 5:30pm, Sunday and holidays 11am to 5:30pm.

Organized Tours

Major hotels work with standard tour operators and can recommend a tour even at the last minute; however, you'd be better off planning ahead and reserving a tour with an operator or private guide who can show you the more interesting side of Santiago, or who is more attuned to foreign guests' desires or needs (i.e., a guide who is truly bilingual).

Santiago Adventures (© **2/244-2750;** www.santiagoadventures.com) offers a variety of set and custom-planned city tours and visits to attractions around the greater Central Valley region, including wine, hiking, and ski tours. The bicycle-based city tours run by **La Biclicleta Verde** (© **2/570-9338;** www.labicicletaverde.com) combine gentle and fun exercise with historical and cultural insights provided by excellent bilingual guides. **Slow Travel** (© **2/207-5372;** www.slowtravel.cl)focuses on wine, food, and nature, with journeys to neighboring wine and food regions outside of Santiago, and culinary tours within the city.

Spectator Sports & Recreation

FUTBOL (SOCCER) Top games are held at three stadiums: **Estadio Monumental,** Avenida Grecia and Marathón; **Universidad de Chile,** Camp de Deportes 565 (both are in the Ñuñoa neighborhood); and **Universidad Católica,** Andrés Bello 2782, in Providencia. The most popular teams, Colo Colo, Universidad Católica, and Universidad Chile, play at these stadiums. Check the sports pages of any local newspaper for game schedules. You can purchase tickets online at www.feriaticket.cl.

HORSE RACING Two racetracks hold events on either Saturday or Sunday throughout the year: the recommended **Club Hípico** at Blanco Encalada 2540 (© **2/683-9600**) and the **Hipódromo Chile** at Avenida Vivaceta in Independencia (© **2/270-9200**).

SWIMMING Your best bet for swimming are the public pools **Tupahue** and **Antilén,** atop Cerro San Cristóbal (© **2/777-6666**). Both are open November 15 to March 15 Tuesday to Sunday 10am to 6pm, and charge C$5,000 for adults, C$3,500 for children. You'll need a cab to Antilén, or you can walk northeast past the Camino Real to get here, about a 10-minute walk.

Shopping

Santiago is home to two American-style megamalls: **Parque Arauco,** Av. Kennedy 5413 (Mon–Sat 10am–9pm, Sun and holidays 11am–9pm), and **Alto Las Condes,** Av. Kennedy 9001 (Mon–Sun 10am–10pm). Public transportation is difficult, so take a cab.

The beautifully designed **Patio Bellavista** ★★, between Constitución and Pío Nono streets, a half-block from Dardignac (© **2/777-4766;** www.patiobellavista.cl), is a collection of shops hawking high-quality arts and crafts, jewelry, woolens, and woodwork, and centered around a cobblestone patio with a couple of cafes and outstanding restaurants. Patio Bellavista is open Wednesday through Sunday from 10am to 9pm, and Thursday though Saturday from 10am to 10pm. Farther away, but just as fun to visit, is **Los Domínicos** ★, Av. Apoquindo 9085 (no phone), open Tuesday through Sunday and holidays from 10:30am to 7pm. Los Domínicos is a folksy, mock colonial village with shops selling hand-knit sweaters, lapis lazuli, arts and crafts, antiques (expensive), and Chilean traditional wear such as ponchos. While it's a bit of a journey to get there, Los Domínicos is your best bet for good-quality traditional souvenirs.

Santiago's version of Rodeo Drive is Avenida Alonso de Cordoba in the Vitacura neighborhood, with upscale stores and brands such as Louis Vuitton. Supermarkets offer a wide selection of more traditional wines at cheaper prices than specialty shops. For those hard-to-get wines you won't find back in the U.S., try **El Mundo del Vino** at Av. Isidora Goyenechea 2931 (© **2/584-1172;** www.elmundodelvino.cl), open Monday through Wednesday 10:30am to 8:30pm, Thursday through Saturday 10am to 9pm, and Sunday 11am to 6pm. El Mundo del Vino has an extensive selection and knowledgeable

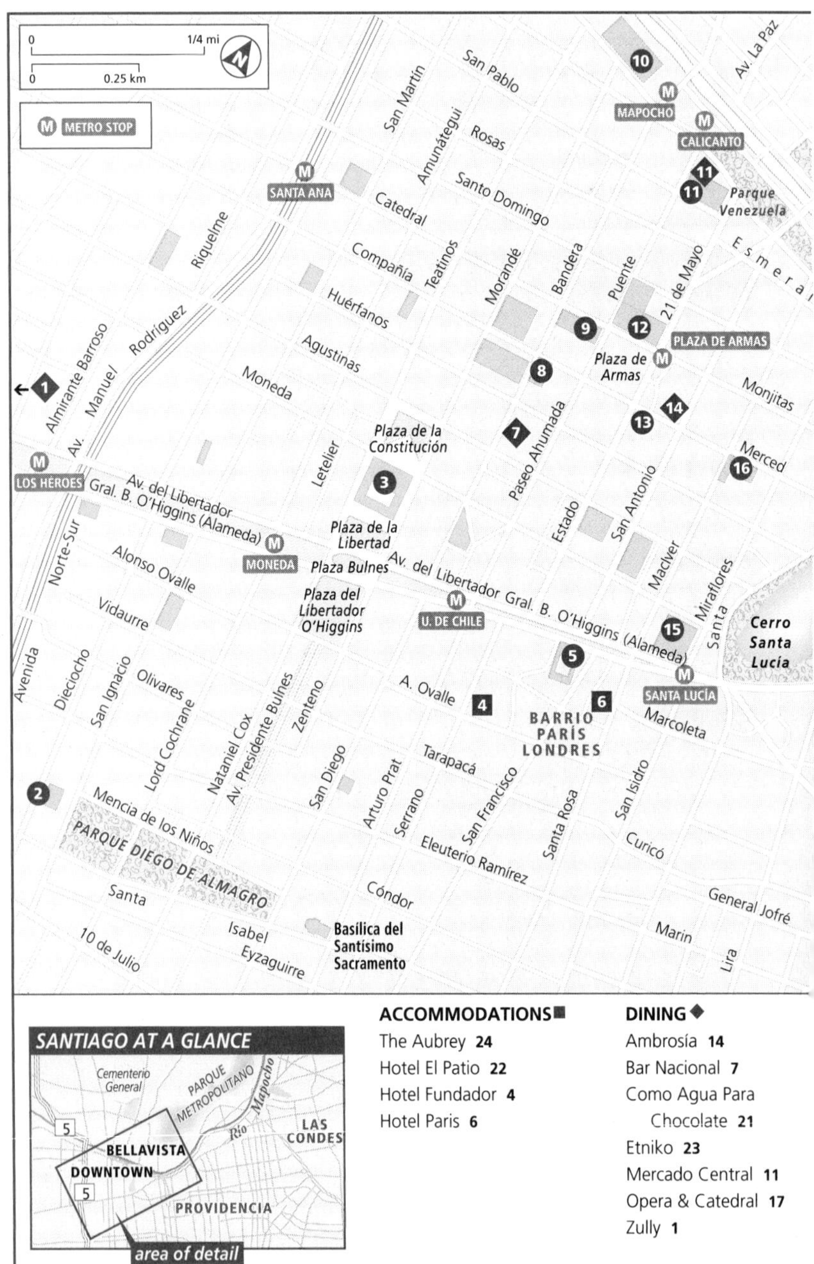

0 1/4 mi
0 0.25 km
N
METRO STOP
San Pablo
Rosas
Santo Domingo
Catedral
Compañía
Huérfanos
Agustinas
Moneda
San Martín
Amunátegui
Teatinos
Morandé
Bandera
Puente
21 de Mayo
Riquelme
Rodríguez
Av. Manuel
Almirante Barroso
Av. La Paz
MAPOCHO
CALICANTO
SANTA ANA
Parque Venezuela
Esmeral
PLAZA DE ARMAS
Plaza de Armas
Monjitas
Merced
Plaza de la Constitución
Paseo Ahumada
Estado
San Antonio
MacIver
Miraflores
Santa
Cerro Santa Lucía
LOS HÉROES
Av. del Libertador Gral. B. O'Higgins (Alameda)
MONEDA
Plaza de la Libertad
Plaza Bulnes
Plaza del Libertador O'Higgins
U. DE CHILE
Av. del Libertador Gral. B. O'Higgins (Alameda)
SANTA LUCÍA
Letelier
Norte-Sur
Alonso Ovalle
Vidaurre
Avenida
Dieciocho
San Ignacio
Olivares
Lord Cochrane
Nataniel Cox
Av. Presidente Bulnes
Zenteno
A. Ovalle
BARRIO PARÍS LONDRES
Marcoleta
Tarapacá
San Diego
Arturo Prat
Serrano
San Francisco
Santa Rosa
San Isidro
Curicó
Eleuterio Ramírez
Mencia de los Niños
PARQUE DIEGO DE ALMAGRO
Santa
Cóndor
General Jofré
Marín
Lira
10 de Julio
Isabel
Eyzaguirre
Basílica del Santísimo Sacramento
SANTIAGO AT A GLANCE
Cementerio General
PARQUE METROPOLITANO
Río Mapocho
5
LAS CONDES
BELLAVISTA
DOWNTOWN
5
PROVIDENCIA
area of detail
ACCOMMODATIONS
The Aubrey 24
Hotel El Patio 22
Hotel Fundador 4
Hotel Paris 6
DINING
Ambrosía 14
Bar Nacional 7
Como Agua Para Chocolate 21
Etniko 23
Mercado Central 11
Opera & Catedral 17
Zully 1

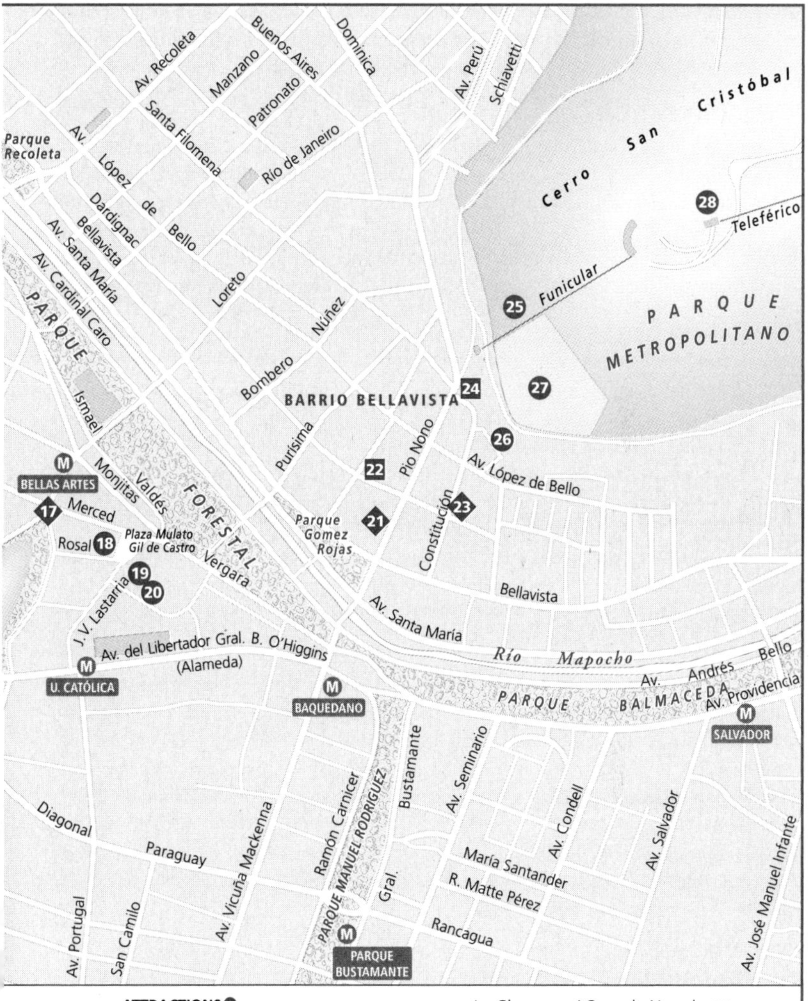

ATTRACTIONS ●

Basílica de la Merced **16**
Biblioteca Nacional **15**
Casa Colorado & Museo de Santiago **13**
Catedral Metropolitana & Museo de Arte Sagrado **9**
Centro Cultural Palacio de la Moneda **3**
Estación Mapocho **10**
Funicular **25**
Iglesia San Francisco **5**
Jardín Zoológico **27**
La Chascona / Casa de Neruda **26**
Museo Arqueológico de Santiago **19**
Museo de Artes Visuales (MAVI) **20**
Museo Nacional de Bellas Artes **18**
Mercado Central **11**
Museo Chileno de Arte Precolombino **8**
Palacio Cousiño **2**
Palacio de la Real Audencia / Museo Histórico Nacional **12**
Teleférico **28**

staff, but my pick for wine stores is undoubtedly **La Vinoteca,** Av. Isidora Goyenechea 3520 (✆ **2/334-1987**), open Monday through Friday from 10am to 9pm, Saturday 10am to 8pm. La Vinoteca's sales team really know their stuff, and the shop specializes in boutique and hard-to-find wines. Also, La Vinoteca has a shop in the airport; if you buy a case here, they'll wrap it up so you can check it like luggage.

WHERE TO STAY

Where you stay in Santiago will likely shape your opinion of the city. The cheapest accommodations are located in the downtown area, *el centro.* This neighborhood is congested and older. Historic city sights are concentrated in or near *el centro,* yet a Metro or taxi ride allows visitors staying in leafy Providencia or tony Las Condes to get here quickly. Parking is free unless otherwise indicated in the review. High season is generally October through March, yet many hotels offer cheaper deals in January and February.

Downtown Santiago

Expensive

Hotel Fundador Since being taken over by the Brazilian Blue Tree Hotels chain, this classic European-style hotel in the lovely Paris Londres neighborhood has stepped back into the spotlight. Its total renovation brought a flashy new style to the older part of the city. Rooms are still small, but the new decor (including hand-painted murals and wooden floors) brightens things up. It's popular with tour groups and the area in general can be noisy. Great deals can be found online at the hotel's website.

Paseo Serrano 34. ✆ **2/387-1200.** Fax 2/387-1300. www.fundador.cl. 147 units. $230–$290 double. AE, DC, MC, V. Metro: Universidad de Chile. **Amenities:** 2 restaurants; bar; concierge; health club; indoor pool; room service; sauna. *In room*: A/C, hair dryer, minibar, Wi-Fi (free).

Inexpensive

Hotel París ★ **Value** Stick with a room in the newer wing of this European-style budget hotel. Rooms in the older wing are resolutely for backpackers. The Hotel París is old and atmospheric, a mansion-turned-hotel with rooms of differing sizes and lots of winding stairs; some rooms feature Oriental rugs and mahogany molding. When booking, ask for a room with a terrace because they are the same price. Continental breakfast costs $4.

París 813. ✆ **2/664-0921.** Fax 2/639-4037. carbott@latinmail.com. 40 units. $45 double new wing; $35 double old wing. AE, DC, MC, V. Parking across the street $3–$5 per day. Metro: Universidad de Chile. **Amenities:** Cafe. *In room:* TV (in some rooms).

Bellavista

Very Expensive

The Aubrey ★★★ **Finds** Upping the wow factor with a trendy, tasteful tone, this new boutique hotel in the heart of Bellavista (it's right next to the funicular station) has finally brought some pizzazz to sedate Santiago. Two historic mansions were renovated as one to create the property. Every detail has been addressed, from the imported fixtures and safes big enough for a laptop to Italian ceramics and sommier beds. Top-floor doubles are tucked under the former attic; they're the most affordable of the rooms. The back terrace has a slick outdoor pool. Another major plus is the in-house restaurant, the Santiago home of Valparaíso's acclaimed Pasta E Vino (p. 404).

Constitución 317. ✆ **2/940-2800.** www.theaubrey.com. 15 units. $220–$450 double. AE, DC, MC, V. Parking. Metro: Baquedano. **Amenities:** Restaurant; lounge; concierge; outdoor heated pool; Wi-Fi. *In room*: A/C, TV, hair dryer, minibar, MP3 docking station, Wi-Fi.

Moderate

Hotel El Patio ★★ This boutique hotel marries an artistic flare with literary spirit in the heart of the bohemian Bellavista area. Occupying the creaky second floor of a 19th-century mansion, the property sports a design with stately and contemporary elements. The staff are courteous and knowledgeable, without being intrusive. A deliciously healthy continental breakfast is served on the rooftop terrace that overlooks the charming Patio de Bellavista outdoor gallery and mall. It makes for a lively social scene that could be rather intrusive to light sleepers. In fact all rooms now come with double-paneled windows and earplugs due to consistent noise problems. Those on their own or weary from travels would best go elsewhere. The physically challenged should also take note that there are plenty of stairs to negotiate.

Pio Nono 61. ✆ **2/732-7571.** www.hoteldelpatio.cl. 11 units. $120–$140 double. AE, MC, DC, V. Metro: Baquedano. **Amenities:** Restaurant; bar. *In room*: Fan, TV, hair dryer, Wi-Fi.

Providencia

Expensive

Radisson Hotel ★★ The Radisson Hotel is housed within the glitzy World Trade Center building in the area known as "San-hattan" for its financial clout. The location is very convenient for tourists and business travelers alike because it is close to Las Condes district businesses and the El Bosque restaurant row, and still just a few blocks from the heart of Providencia. Best of all, the guest rooms have a fresh and contemporary decor thanks to recent renovations. The gentlemany and plush lobby seems out of step with the hotel's glass high-rise exterior. Get a room that faces the Andes (seventh floor and up). The health club and small pool on the rooftop have panoramic views.

Av. Vitacura 2610. ✆ **800/333-3333** in the U.S., or 2/203-6000 in Santiago. www.radisson.cl. 159 units. $170 double. AE, DC, MC, V. Metro: Tobalaba. **Amenities:** Restaurant; 2 bars; babysitting; concierge; indoor pool; sauna; whirlpool. *In room:* A/C, TV, hair dryer, minibar.

Moderate

Hotel Orly ★★★ This European-style midrange hotel is close to absolutely everything and the staff really go above and beyond to welcome you. The Orly is housed in a renovated mansion with French-influenced architecture. The somewhat stuffy lobby has a few nooks for relaxing and a small, glass-roofed patio; there's also a bar and a dining area where the staff serves a hearty buffet breakfast and courtesy snacks throughout the day. The interiors are a restful white and decorated with country manor furnishings. Room sizes vary; doubles come with two twins or a full-size bed and are of average size; a few singles are decidedly not for the claustrophobic. About half the rooms are for smokers, so be sure to specify your preference.

Av. Pedro de Valdivia 027. ✆ **2/231-8947.** Fax 2/334-4403. www.hotelorly.cl. 28 units. $120–$130 double; $130–$140 junior suite. AE, DC, MC, V. Metro: Pedro de Valdivia. **Amenities:** Cafe; bar; room service. *In room:* A/C, TV, hair dryer, minibar.

Meridiano Sur Petit Hotel ★★ (Finds) What everybody loves about this new inn on a quiet street of Providencia is how well the vibe blends with what brings travelers to Chile in the first place: peace and nature. The innkeeper has roamed the country tip to tip, and provides personalized concierge services that hit traveler's needs head-on. This refurbished stucco home in Providencia has upscale touches, like mineral water on the bed stands, marble bathrooms, poetry painted on the walls, and artisanal weavings hanging in the hallways. The top floor loft sleeps up to five and is great for families. Standard rooms are smaller and below ground.

 Santa Beatriz 256. ✆ **2/235-3659.** www.meridianosur.cl. 8 rooms. $125–$135 double; $260 loft. AE, DC, MC, V. Metro: Manuel Montt. **Amenities:** Cafe; TV room; Wi-Fi. *In room*: A/C, TV.

Vilafranca Petit Hotel ★★★ Finds One of Santiago's original B&B-style hotels, the Vilafranca is housed in a superbly refurbished old mansion and provides travelers with a more personalized lodging option brimming with character and coziness, at a price that's reasonable. As with any B&B, the feeling that you're bunking in an old home is clearly evident, yet the interiors are bestowed with a French Provençal design, and lovely old antique armoires and nightstands, fresh white linens, and walls painted in soothing tones of ecru and decorated with dried sprigs of flowers and simple sketch art. It's great value for this neighborhood, but then many rooms are very small. Service is delightful. Common areas include a living room with overstuffed sofas and a cobblestone patio fringed in greenery.

Perez Valenzuela 1650. ✆ **2/232-1413.** www.vilafranca.cl. 8 units. $90 double AE, DC, MC, V. Metro: Manuel Montt. **Amenities:** Cafe. *In room:* A/C (some rooms), TV, hair dryer, Wi-Fi.

Las Condes

Very Expensive

Grand Hyatt Regency Santiago ★ The Grand Hyatt is a 24-story atrium tower with two adjacent wings and four glass elevators that whisk guests up to their split-level rooms and terraced suites. Inside it feels as spacious as an airport hanger, but it exudes a sense of glamour lacking in so many high-end hotels. What sets this hotel apart is the flawless service provided by the staff, amply spacious guest rooms with views of the Andes (rooms with an eastern orientation from the 10th floor up), a palm-and-fern-fringed pool, and the best gym/spa of any hotel in Santiago. Guests in suites enjoy their own 16th-floor private lounge for lingering over breakfast and soaking up the spectacular view. On the down side, you'll always need to take a taxi because the location at the head of a crazy traffic loop makes it difficult and too far away to walk anywhere from here. Cheaper deals can be found when booking on their website.

Av. Kennedy 4601. ✆ **2/950-1234.** Fax 2/950-3155. www.santiago.grand.hyatt.com. 310 units, 26 suites. $350 grand deluxe (double); $450 grand suite. AE, DC, MC, V. **Amenities:** 3 restaurants; bar; babysitting; concierge; gym; outdoor pool; room service; sauna; solarium; tennis courts; whirlpool. *In room:* A/C, TV, hair dryer, minibar, Wi-Fi.

Ritz-Carlton Santiago ★★ Expect to be pampered here. Though the exterior of the Ritz-Carlton is remarkably plain, it is one of Santiago's finest hotels. Not only are the interiors luxurious in the Ritz-Carlton fashion, the hotel has a fabulous rooftop health center with a glass-dome ceiling that provides a sweeping view of the city and the Andes. The Ritz is near restaurants and the thriving economic hub of Santiago, making this a more convenient choice than the Hyatt. But what really stands out here is the gracious, attentive service. The hotel's lobby, which has a two-story rotunda and floors made of imported marble, sets a plush, mature tone. In the spotless guest rooms, the beds are heavenly comfortable. Note that the Ritz in Santiago is more economically priced than many of their other hotels, and they offer special packages on their website.

El Alcalde 15. ✆ **800/241-3333** from the U.S., or 2/470-8500. Fax 2/470-8501. www.ritzcarlton.com. 205 units. $358 deluxe room; $390–$458 club room. AE, DC, MC, V. Metro: El Golf. **Amenities:** 3 restaurants; bar; babysitting; concierge; gym; indoor rooftop pool; room service; sauna; valet service; whirlpool. *In room:* A/C, TV, hair dryer, minibar.

W Hotel Santiago ★★★ Fashionistas now have somewhere to lay their heads in Santiago. The brand-new W has heaps more style than any other hotel in the city, and is

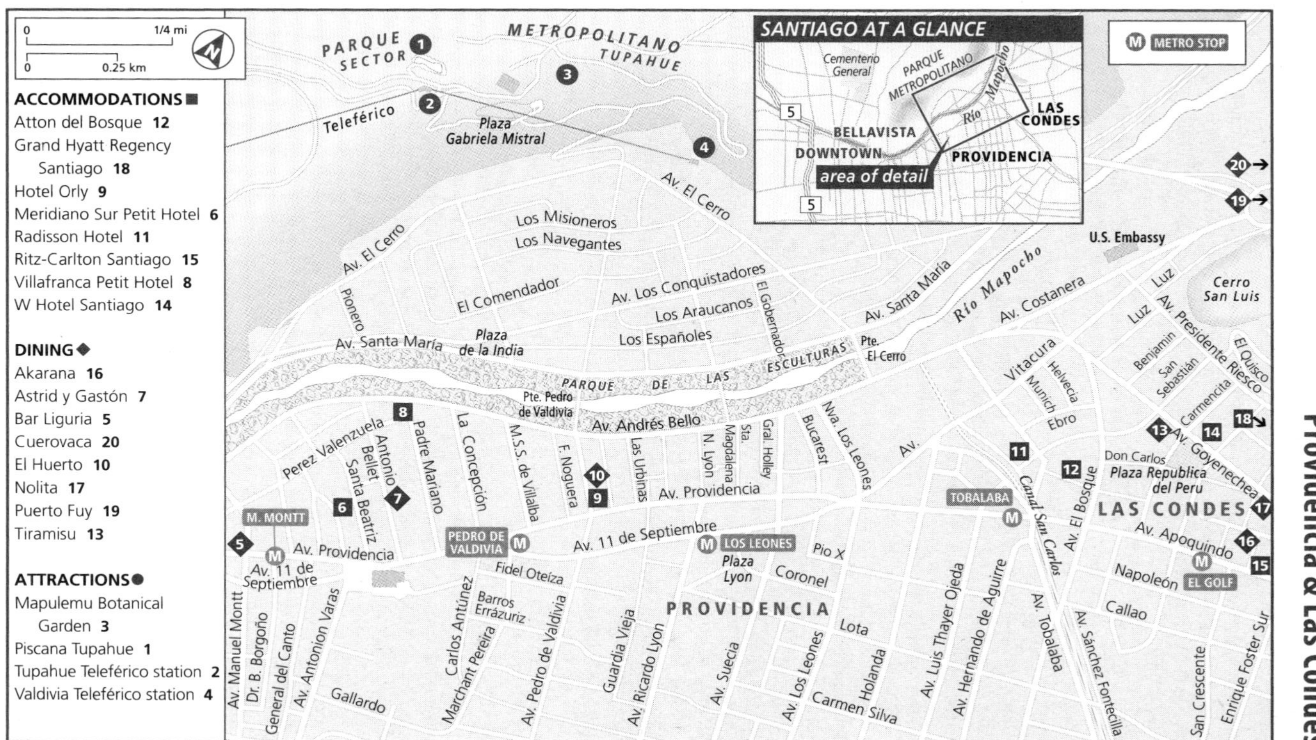

0 1/4 mi
0 0.25 km
ACCOMMODATIONS
Atton del Bosque 12
Grand Hyatt Regency Santiago 18
Hotel Orly 9
Meridiano Sur Petit Hotel 6
Radisson Hotel 11
Ritz-Carlton Santiago 15
Villafranca Petit Hotel 8
W Hotel Santiago 14
DINING
Akarana 16
Astrid y Gastón 7
Bar Liguria 5
Cuerovaca 20
El Huerto 10
Nolita 17
Puerto Fuy 19
Tiramisu 13
ATTRACTIONS
Mapulemu Botanical Garden 3
Piscana Tupahue 1
Tupahue Teleférico station 2
Valdivia Teleférico station 4
PARQUE METROPOLITANO
SECTOR TUPAHUE
Teleférico
Plaza Gabriela Mistral
SANTIAGO AT A GLANCE
Cementerio General
PARQUE METROPOLITANO
Río Mapocho
BELLAVISTA
DOWNTOWN
area of detail
PROVIDENCIA
LAS CONDES
METRO STOP
Av. El Cerro
Los Misioneros
Los Navegantes
El Comendador
Av. Los Conquistadores
Los Araucanos
Los Españoles
El Gobernador
Pionero
Av. Santa María
Plaza de la India
PARQUE DE LAS ESCULTURAS
Pte. El Cerro
Pte. Pedro de Valdivia
Río Mapocho
Av. Costanera
U.S. Embassy
Cerro San Luis
Luz
Av. Presidente Riesco
El Quisco
Benjamin
San Sebastián
Carmencita
Vitacura
Helvecia
Munich
Ebro
Av. Andrés Bello
Perez Valenzuela
Antonio Bellet
Santa Beatriz
Padre Mariano
La Concepción
M.S.S. de Villalba
F. Noguera
Las Urbinas
N. Lyon
Sta. Magdalena
Gral. Holley
Bucarest
Nva. Los Leones
Av. Providencia
Av. 11 de Septiembre
M. MONTT
PEDRO DE VALDIVIA
LOS LEONES
TOBALABA
EL GOLF
Plaza Lyon
Pio X
Coronel
Fidel Oteíza
Barros Errázuriz
PROVIDENCIA
Lota
Canal San Carlos
Av. El Bosque
Don Carlos
Plaza Republica del Peru
Av. Goyenechea
LAS CONDES
Av. Apoquindo
Napoleón
Callao
Av. Manuel Montt
Dr. B. Borgoño
General del Canto
Av. Antonion Varas
Gallardo
Carlos Antúnez
Marchant Pereira
Av. Pedro de Valdivia
Guardia Vieja
Av. Ricardo Lyon
Av. Suecia
Av. Los Leones
Holanda
Carmen Silva
Av. Luis Thayer Ojeda
Av. Hernando de Aguirre
Av. Tobalaba
Av. Sánchez Fontecilla
San Crescente
Enrique Foster Sur

located in the heart of the business area. The tone is set in the fourth-floor lobby and "Chilibary" with mirrors, funky music, fresh flowers, and aromatherapy. Even the vocabulary is a bit cheeky—the concierge is called "Whatever Wherever" and staff are known as "W insiders." All guest rooms are spacious and have floor-to-ceiling windows, and deluxe mattresses and sheets. The restaurants, from the covered terrace at Terraza to the Asian-Peruvian fusion at Osaka, are popular amongst the local Blackberry-and–high heels crowd.

Isidora Goyenechea 3000. ✆ **2/770-000.** Fax 2/770-0003. www.whotels.com. 196 units. $329–$429 double. AE, DC, MC, V. Metro: El Golf. **Amenities:** 3 restaurants; bar; concierge; gym; pool. *In room*: A/C, DVD player, hair dryer, minibar.

Moderate

Atton del Bosque ★ Value Just steps from the sidewalk cafes of El Bosque, this 3-year-old midrange hotel provides standard rooms at very good rates. In fact, it's the best priced in the area and appeals to many business travelers on more limited expense accounts. Rooms are decorated with earthy tones like rust and mustard yellow. All have plasma televisions and sterile bathrooms, which may remind you of a hospital. It may be a bit lackluster, but it's practical. This hotel is particularly friendly to those with mobility problems, from the rooms to the small wheelchair-accessible rooftop pool.

Roger de Flor 2770. ✆ **2/947-3682.** Fax 2/422-7906. www.atton.com. 240 units. $110–$150 double. AE, DC, MC, V. Metro: El Golf. **Amenities:** Restaurant; bar; small gym; pool. *In room:* A/C, hair dryer.

WHERE TO DINE

Santiago's gastronomic scene has undergone a culinary revolution during the past decade, with an influx of ethnic restaurants and trendy eateries serving fusion-style, creative cuisine commonly known as *cocina de autor.* Many restaurants are clustered along several streets in neighborhoods such as Bellavista, and along the streets Avenida El Bosque and Isabel Goyenechea—visitors might find it more adventurous to stroll around these neighborhoods until something takes their fancy.

Downtown

Most downtown eateries are open for lunch only and closed on Sunday. The only exception is the Lastarria Street/Plaza Mulato Gil de Castro neighborhood (located on the other side of Cerro St. Lucia), at the following restaurants: **La Pérgola de la Plaza**, Lastarría 321 (✆ **2/639-3604**), a bistro with a slightly expensive fixed-price lunch menu and outdoor seating; **"R,"** Lastarría 307 local 101 (✆ **2/664-9844**), a cozy spot for wine and conversation, although the food is overpriced and could be a lot tastier; and **Mosqueto Café,** at the corner of Villavicencio and Lastarría (✆ **2/639-1627**), which serves coffee, cakes, and sandwiches in a gorgeous, meticulously restored antique building.

Expensive

Zully ★★ Moments INTERNATIONAL Chic, yet true to the utterly charming, historical neighborhood in which it is located, Zully is a fun place to dine. The American-owned restaurant covers four floors of a lovingly restored old mansion and boasts a wine-tasting cellar, an interior patio, and trendily decorated dining rooms. For a memorable, even romantic, evening, you may sacrifice quality (especially considering the price). No matter, you won't be sorry you taxied over when you lay eyes on this architectural gem. It's best to take a taxi here at night; during the day you can take the Metro to the stop República, walk out the north exit and head east 1½ blocks to Calle Concha y Toro, and turn left.

Concha y Toro 34. ✆ **2/696-1378.** Reservations recommended for dinner. Main courses C$14,000–C$17,500. AE, DC, MC, V. Mon–Fri 1–4pm and 8pm–1am; Sat 8pm–2am (or when the last guest leaves). Metro: República.

Moderate

Ambrosía ★★ INTERNATIONAL Tucked behind the Casa Colorado Museum (enter the museum and cross the patio to get here), Ambrosía is a chic little eatery and quiet haven from the boisterous downtown street outside. The menu features an eclectic offering of Peruvian, French, and Italian dishes, each prepared by blending creative flavors and elements for a decidedly eclectic menu. Examples include panko-breaded shrimp in peanut sauce, beef tenderloin with candied carrots, and sea bass with port sauce and shiitake mushrooms. With its patio dining, this restaurant is ideal for summer days. Service is friendly, too, and attentive in a way common with family businesses.

Merced 838. ✆ **2/697-2023.** www.ambrosia.cl. Main courses C$5,800–C$7,000. AE, DC, MC, V. Mon–Fri 9am–6pm. Metro: Plaza de Armas.

Bar Nacional ★ CHILEAN These two traditional restaurants have been a hit with downtown workers for more than 50 years, serving honest Chilean food in a dinerlike atmosphere. On Calle Bandera and Paseo Huérfanos, both are relatively identical. This is where to try Chilean favorites such as empanadas, *cazuela* (a hearty chicken soup), *pastel de choclo* (a meat-and-corn casserole), and the cholesterol-boosting *lomo a lo pobre* (steak and fries topped with sautéed onions and a fried egg).

Bar Nacional 1 at Huérfanos 1151; ✆ **2/696-5986.** Bar Nacional 2 at Bandera 371; ✆ **2/695-3368.** Main courses C$4,000–C$6,000; sandwiches C$2,000–C$3,000. AE, DC, MC, V. Mon–Fri 7:30am–11pm; Sat 7:30am–4pm. Metro: Plaza de Armas.

Opera & Catedral ★★★ CONTEMPORARY FRENCH/CHILEAN These two eateries each have a sleek look that would fit in nicely in a city like New York or London, and accordingly, both are wildly popular with the young glitterati of Santiago, the arts scene, and discerning customers who enjoy a little more sophistication in their dining experience. Opera is a polished fine-dining establishment, with exposed brick walls and white-linen tablecloths. Upstairs at inexpensive Catedral, the look is minimalist, with gun-battle-gray walls, wicker chairs, and a couple of leather couches, and there is also an outdoor terrace for summer evenings. Cathedral serves modern takes on Chilean classics, with a few Asian-influenced dishes, gourmet sandwiches, and a very tasty *crudo,* or steak tartare.

Both located at the corner of Merced and José Miguel de la Barra. ✆ **2/664-3048.** www.operacatedral.cl. Reservations required at Opera; reservations not accepted at Catedral. AE, DC, MC, V. Opera: Main courses C$8,000–C$12,000. Mon–Fri 1–3:15pm and 8–10:30pm; Sat 8–10:30pm. Catedral: Main courses C$3,500–C$7,000. Mon–Wed 12:30pm–2am; Thurs–Sat 12:30pm–5am. Metro: Bellas Artes.

Bellavista & Providencia

Expensive

Astrid y Gastón ★★★ INTERNATIONAL If you're looking to blow your budget, this is your place. Peruvian celebrity chef Gastón, his wife Astrid, and his kitchen staff have created a wonderfully provocative menu filled with delicious flavor combinations using luxurious ingredients in unexpected ways. The ambience is brightly lit, elegant, and better for a meal among friends than a romantic date. The service at Astrid y Gastón is flawless, with a sommelier and one of the city's most interesting and varied wine lists. Try the fresh gooseliver, or my favorite, king crab ravioli. Dessert orders must be placed early so that the kitchen staff can make each one from scratch. If you are on a budget, come in for *ceviche* and a pisco sour.

Antonio Bellet 201. ✆ **2/650-9125.** Reservations required. Main courses C$7,500–C$10,000. AE, DC, MC, V. Mon–Fri 1–3pm and 8pm–midnight; Sat 8pm–midnight. Metro: Pedro de Valdivia.

Moderate

Como Agua Para Chocolate ★ NUEVO LATINO **Moments** Inspired by the romantic whimsy of the famous novel with the same name, this is not your average restaurant. The menu aims to spark passions, with aphrodisiac options like the Passion and Vigour Beef and a seafood sampler known as the Lover's Sigh. Lovers can also share the Diego (Rivera) and Frida (Kahlo) Stew. The decor is a dreamy renovation of two old homes. The food is not always as heart-throbbing, but the service is lovely and the entire experience fun and light-hearted.

Constitución 88. ✆ **2/777-8740.** www.comoaguaparachocolate.cl. Main courses C$6,500–C$8,000. AE, DC, MC, V. Reservations recommended. Tues–Sat 12:30–5pm and 8pm–1am; Sun 12:30–5pm and 8pm–midnight. Metro: Baquedano.

El Huerto ★★ VEGETARIAN Santiago's best-known vegetarian restaurant drags in even the most committed carnivore for creative, fresh, healthy meals in a warm and friendly sidewalk cafe. Daily lunch specials start with a hearty soup, then include some sort of a quiche, a colorful salad (the Flower Power salad has broccoli, peas, beets, alfafa sprouts, avocado, quinoa, and tofu) and usually a delicious panacotta dessert. There are regular items like burritos and Asian stir-fries. After eating, you can buy a pair of Birkenstocks or stock up on incense in the adjoining eco-products shop.

Orrego Luco 054. ✆ **2/233-2690.** www.elhuerto.cl. Main courses C$4,400–C$7,000. AE, DC, MC, V. Mon–Wed 8:30am–11:30pm; Thurs–Sat daily 8:30am–midnight; Sun 10am–4:30pm. Metro: Pedro de Valdivia.

Etniko ★★ ASIAN Etniko is one of Santiago's hippest restaurants, serving Asian-influenced cuisine to the modern beat of house music played by resident DJs. The place is trendy and sophisticated, and frequented by Santiago's stylish yuppies and expats. The menu offers a diverse selection, but the mainstay is the 16 varieties of sushi. Also on offer are Japanese tempura and Chinese and Vietnamese stir-fries. The bar is a lively, fun place for a cocktail, and there is an extensive wine and champagne menu. Don't expect the place to fill up until 9 or 10pm.

Constitución 172. ✆ **2/732-0119.** Main courses C$4,500–C$9,000. AE, DC, MC, V. Reservations recommended. Daily noon–4pm; Sun–Thurs 8pm–midnight; Fri–Sat 8pm–2am. Metro: Baquedano.

Inexpensive

Bar Liguria ★★★ **Moments** CHILEAN/BISTRO These bistro/bars are among my favorites in Santiago. Bar Liguria is vibrant, warm, and the "in" spot in Providencia for actors, writers, businesspeople, and just about everyone else who comes to soak up the kitschy, bohemian atmosphere. The Bar Liguria at Luis Thayer Ojeda Street has a large and lofty upstairs dining room that allows energy to simply radiate throughout the place, but I like the lively atmosphere at the Manuel Montt location better. The Liguria serves ample portions of emblematic Chilean dishes (and a few Italian dishes), as well as hefty sandwiches and salads that are reasonably priced. In the evening, the Bar Liguria is absolutely packed, and you might have to wait 10 to 15 minutes for a table; however, the bar makes a great hangout in the meantime.

Luis Thayer Ojeda 019: ✆ **2/231-1393.** Av. Providencia 1373: ✆ **2/235-7914.** Reservations not accepted. Main courses C$4,000–C$7,000. AE, DC, MC, V. Mon–Thurs noon–1am; Fri–Sat noon–3am. Metro: Los Leones (Ojeda branch), Manuel Montt (Providencia branch).

Las Condes (El Bosque Norte)/Vitacura

The street El Bosque has it all: Chilean, French, seafood, steakhouses, fast-food courts, and more. For American fare, there's a **T.G.I. Friday's** with the usual fattening menu at Goyenechea 3275 (✆ **2/234-4468;** Sun–Thurs noon–1:30am, Fri–Sat noon–2:30am). The best place for breakfast and lunch is **Cafe Melba,** Don Carlos 2898 (✆ **2/232-4546;** Mon–Fri 8am–3pm, Sat–Sun 8:30am–3:30pm).

You'll need a cab to reach restaurants in Vitacura, but they're well worth seeking out.

Expensive

Cuerovaca ★★★ STEAK Santiago's top steakhouse focuses on providing carnivores with the finest cuts of meat available in Santiago, including both Argentine and Chilean cuts of beef as well as *wagyu,* the Japanese-origin Kobe beef, Patagonian lamb, and locally produced Angus and Hereford beef. If you're not a beef eater, there are seafood dishes that specialize in Easter Island imports and locally produced salmon. Cuerovaca strives to educate diners and build a "culture" around the appreciation of fine beef, and they'll happily provide you with background information about your cut. The ambience is urban contemporary, with flagstone walls, wood, and glass, and they feature an outstanding wine list. Note that accompaniments and salads are an additional cost to prices listed below.

El Mañío 1659. ✆ **2/206-3911.** www.cuerovaca.cl. Reservations recommended. Beef cuts C$7,500–C$12,500; Kobe beef cuts average C$20,500; fish courses C$7,085–C$9,810. AE, DC, MC, V. Daily 1–4pm and 8–11:30pm.

Puerto Fuy ★★★ (Moments) SEAFOOD Fancy foodies not afraid of the price must make the trip out to this slick establishment, named for a remote outpost in the temperate rainforest of the Chilean Lake District. The stars here are Chilean fish and seafood, including a sesame tuna with puréed onions and an oh-so-modern foamed sea urchin. Both pair well with a sauvignon blanc from the 150-label thick wine list. A seven-step tasting menu, for a cost of C$29,000, starts with abalone carpaccio and ends with a lemon parfait, and may be the best splurge in town.

3969 Nueva Costanera. ✆ **2/208-8908.** Reservations highly recommended. Main courses C$12,500–C$13,000. AE, DC, MC, V. Mon–Sat 1–3:30pm and 8–11:20pm.

Moderate

Akarana ★★ (Finds) ASIAN FUSION I can't think of a more delightful place in Las Condes to dine alfresco than on this restaurant's wraparound patio, and Akarana's contemporary, all-white interiors are chic, fresh, and airy. Fusing Asian cuisine with New Zealand specialties, the chef here creates a wonderful feast for the palate, from grilled fresh tuna with chile and lime beurre blanc to good ol' fish and chips. This is an excellent place to enjoy well-prepared afternoon cocktails and a plate of appetizers, while listening to frequent live music.

Reyes Lavalle 3310. ✆ **2/231-9667.** Reservations recommended. Main courses C$8,000–C$10,500. AE, DC, MC, V. Daily noon–midnight. Metro: El Golf.

Nolita ★ ITALIAN/AMERICAN Taking its cue from Northern Italy and New York (yes, its name was borrowed from the NYC neighborhood), Nolita specializes in cuisine from the former and style from the latter. The El Bosque neighborhood is often referred to as "San-hattan," and so a restaurant like Nolita only makes sense with its cosmopolitan atmosphere, generous service, and refined cuisine created by a chef with roots in the U.S. What I like about Nolita is that the chef is adept at creating haute cuisine that isn't so haute that it leaves you yearning for comfort food. Try a rich pasta such as king crab cannelloni, or even better, their shellfish platter, a veritable Roman feast of smoked salmon, crab legs, scallops, shrimp, and ceviche, and save room for one of their delectable desserts. As prices shoot through the roof at other high-end eateries, Nolita remains reasonable for a restaurant of this caliber. You'll need reservations booked days in advance on weekends.

Isidora Goyenechea 3456. ✆ **2/232-6114.** Reservations recommended. Main courses C$6,000–C$12,500. AE, DC, MC, V. Daily 1–3:30pm; Mon–Thurs 8–11pm; Fri–Sat 8pm–midnight. Metro: El Golf.

Inexpensive

Tiramisu ★★ PIZZA/CAFE Kids This is a popular lunch spot during the weekdays, so come early or make a reservation. Tiramisu serves thin-crust pizzas (which are large enough for two when accompanied by a salad) baked in a stone oven and served in a delightful wood-and-checkered-tablecloth atmosphere. With dozens and dozens of combinations, from traditional tomato and basil to arugula with shaved Parmesan and artichokes, you'll have a hard time choosing. There are fresh, delicious salads, too, and desserts that of course include tiramisu. The dining area is mostly outdoor covered seating.

Av. Isidora Goyenechea 3141. ✆ **2/335-5135.** www.tiramisu.cl. Pizzas C$4,500–C$7,000; salads C$3,000–C$6,000. AE, DC, MC, V. Daily 1–4pm and 7pm–midnight. Metro: El Golf.

SANTIAGO AFTER DARK

There are plenty of theaters, nightclubs, and bars to keep your evenings busy in Santiago. Like Buenos Aires, Santiago adheres to a vampire's schedule, and people here dine as late as 10pm, arriving at a nightclub past midnight, and dive into bed just before the sun rises. It can take a little getting used to, but there are many early-hour nighttime attractions if you can't bear late nights. Several newspapers publish daily listings of movies, theater, and live music as well as Friday weekend-guide supplements such as *El Mercurio*'s "Wiken."

The Performing Arts

Santiago is known for its theater, from large-scale productions to one-person monologues at cafes. The following are some of the more well-established theaters in Santiago. I recommend two theaters in Bellavista that offer contemporary productions and comedies in an intimate setting: **Teatro Bellavista,** Dardignac 0110 (✆ **2/735-2395;** Metro: Salvador), and **Teatro San Ginés,** Mallinkrodt 76 (✆ **2/738-2159;** www.teatrosangines.cl; Metro: Salvador).

But let's be realistic. If you do not speak Spanish, even the city's hit production of the moment is going to be a waste of your time and money. Stick to something more accessible such as a symphony, ballet, or opera at the city's gorgeous, historic **Teatro Municipal,** downtown at Agustinas 749 (✆ **2/463-1000;** www.municipal.cl; Metro: Universidad de Chile). The National Chilean Ballet and invited guests hold productions from April to December, with contemporary and classic productions such as *The Nutcracker.* There are musical events and special productions throughout the year; the best way to find out what's on is to check the theater's website. You can even **reserve and buy tickets** on the site, and select a seat from a diagram and find out which seats have only a partial view. Tickets are also sold over the phone Monday through Friday from 10am to 6pm, or bought in person at the theater itself Monday through Friday from 10am to 7pm and Saturday and Sunday from 10am to 2pm. Tickets are sold beginning 1 month before the starting date.

Visiting orchestras, the Fundación Beethoven, and contemporary acts play at the **Teatro Oriente** at Av. Pedro de Valdivia 099 (✆ **2/334-2234**); buy tickets at the theater or from Ticketmaster. **Teatro Universidad de Chile,** at Av. Providencia 043 (✆ **2/634-5295;** http://teatro.uchile.cl), hosts ballet and symphony productions, both national and international, throughout the year. You may buy tickets at the theater near Plaza Italia or by phone. **Ticketmaster** sells tickets for nearly every act in Santiago, at CineHoyts cinemas, Falabella department stores, or by calling ✆ **2/690-2000** from 10am to 7pm daily.

The Live Music Scene

Crowd-pulling national and international megabands typically play in the **Estado Nacional,** the **Espacio Riesco,** or the **Estación Mapocho.** Espacio Riesco is on the road to the airport, about a 15-minute drive from Las Condes, and with no public transportation available you'll need a taxi. Both Espacio Riesco and Estación Mapocho are infamous for their tinny sound systems. You'll find listings for concerts in the daily newspaper or the *El Mercurio*'s website, **www.emol.com**, under "Tiempo Libre."

If you're looking for something mellower, Bellavista is a good bet for jazz, bolero, and folk music that is often performed Thursday through Saturday at venues such as **La Casa en el Aire** at Antonia López de Bello 0125 (✆ **2/735-6680;** www.lacasaenelaire.cl), with a cozy, candlelit ambience. Across the street at Antonia López de Bello 0126 is **El Perseguidor** (✆ **2/777-6763;** www.elperseguidor.cl), a happening jazz club with nightly performances starting around 11pm.

There are dozens of smaller music venues spread across the city, but the one that attracts the best bands and has the most variety is **La Batuta,** Jorge Washington 52 (✆ **2/274-7096;** www.batuta.cl), located in the Ñuñoa neighborhood, about a 10- to 15-minute taxi ride from downtown and Providencia. The atmosphere is underground, but the crowd profile depends on who's playing. The **Club de Jazz,** José Pedro Alessandri 85 (✆ **2/326-5065;** www.clubdejazz.cl), has been jamming since 1943, and it's one of the city's more traditional night spots. Louis Armstrong once played here, and the club continues to pull in talented acts from around Latin America and the world. Live music happens on Thursday, Friday, and Saturday beginning at 11pm.

The Bar & Club Scene

In Providencia, the wildly popular **Bar Liguria** ★★★, with two locations, Luis Thayer Ojeda 019 (✆ **2/231-1393**), and Av. Providencia 1373 (✆ **2/235-7914**), is without a doubt the best nightspot for visitors of any age; also see the review under "Where to Dine" earlier. The Ligurias are open until 2am Monday through Thursday and until 5am Friday and Saturday, and they serve food practically until closing time. Expats love to hang out at the American-owned **California Cantina and Sportsbar,** Las Urbinas 56 (✆ **2/361-1056**). **Bar Yellow,** General Flores 47 (✆ **2/946-5063**), is a hole in the wall where they shake up the city's best martinis and serve cocktails made from imported liquor—but they're not cheap.

Bellavista, long the hot spot for nightclubs mobbed by teens and university students, is now drawing in a more refined (and older) crowd with cosmopolitan bars, many of which are restaurants by day. **Santo Remedio,** Roman Díaz 152, provides one of the funkier atmospheres in Santiago, and it is the only bar open on Sunday nights (except for hotel bars). **Etniko** (p. 390) is a standby for a lively, sophisticated crowd, DJ music, a full bar, and an airy atrium that's ideal on a summer evening. Across the street at Constitución 187 is **Ozono** (✆ **2/735-3816**), a bar/restaurant within the old adobe walls of an antique *casona* (large house) that has all-white interiors, chill-out music, and outdoor seating. Around the corner, at Antonio López Bello 0135, is **Off the Record** (✆ **2/777-7710**), a bohemian pub/bar that attracts literary types and has interiors that hearken back to the early 1900s; the walls here are adorned with photos of famous Chilean artists, past and present.

Santiago's club scene caters to an 18- to 35-year-old crowd, and it all gets going pretty late, from midnight to 6am, on average. If you like electronica, you might check out "fiestas" publicized in the weekend entertainment sections of newspapers that list 1-night-only raves and live music, or, in Bellavista, try **La Feria** at Constitución 275, in an old theater, open Thursday through Saturday. **Blondie,** Alameda 2879 (✆ **2/681-7793;** www.blondie.cl), is a goth/'80s revival/electronic dance club, depending on the night. I recommend **Galpón 9** (no phone) for occasional live bands, a dance floor and bar, and music that ranges from hip-hop to pop to electronica. It's near the Pablo Neruda museum in Bellavista at Chucre Manzur 9; doors open at 11pm from Thursday to Saturday.

5 AROUND SANTIAGO & THE CENTRAL VALLEY

Santiaguinos and travelers agree that the best thing about Santiago is its proximity to a wealth of attractions such as beaches, nature preserves, hot springs, wineries, ski resorts, and more. These destinations are an alleviating escape when Santiago is smoggy; and all excursions are within 1 to 2 hours' drive from the city. Using Santiago as a base, it's possible to visit a few destinations listed in this chapter for the day, although I recommend spending a night or two at destinations such as Viña del Mar or Valparaíso. If you are an independent traveler and can afford a rental vehicle, get one; however you won't need one for ski resorts unless only visiting for the day (resorts are generally all inclusive, and include organized shuttles). You may consider renting a vehicle at the Santiago airport, driving to the coast or wine country, returning the vehicle and then taking a taxi into Santiago, or vice versa.

The following section proposes ideas for 1-day and multiple-day adventures outside Santiago. If you'd like a tour operator to plan a trip for you with a bilingual guide, transportation, and local know-how, try **Santiago Adventures** (✆ **2/244-2750** in Santiago, or 802/904-6798 in the U.S.; www.santiagoadventures.com).

VIÑA DEL MAR

Viña del Mar is the country's largest and best-known beach resort town, founded in 1874 as a weekend retreat for wealthy Santiaguinos and located 120km (74 miles) northwest of Santiago. It's less than a 1½-hour drive from the capital. Viña is made of manicured lawns, exuberant gardens, a bustling little downtown, and a waterfront lined with towering apartment buildings, restaurants, hotels, nightclubs, and a casino. Some refer to the town as Chile's Riviera, but most simply call it Viña—you'll call it chaos if you come during the high season between December and late February, when thousands of visitors arrive for summer vacation. There is, however, a heightened sense of excitement during these months, with so much activity happening in the area. Viña is also home to plenty of fine beaches, but the beach to see and be seen at is in Reñaca, about 6km (3¾ miles) north of Viña (see "Exploring Viña del Mar," below).

 **Wineries en Route to the Coast**

The main highway that connects Santiago with Valparaíso and Viña del Mar passes right through the renowned wine region of Casablanca. This valley is home to Chile's finest sauvignon blanc. Stop in for a visit at the biodynamic and organic **Viña Emiliana** (✆ **9/225-5679;** www.emiliana.cl) or at the traditional **Casa del Bosque** (✆ **2/377-9431;** www.casasdelbosque.cl). To really delve into the region's wines, spend the night at the luxurious **La Casona Inn at Matetic Vineyard** ★★★ (✆ **2/232-3134;** www.matetic.com).

Essentials

Getting There

BY BUS Both **Tur Bus** (✆ **600/660-6600;** www.turbus.cl) and **Pullman** (✆ **600/320-3200;** www.pullman.cl) offer service to Viña and Valparaíso (see below), leaving every 15 minutes from the Terminal Alameda (Metro: Universidad de Santiago). The fare averages C$12,000 one-way and takes about 1½ hours depending on traffic. Purchase a round-trip ticket on weekends and holidays if you can. Taxis are available at both bus stations and are a good idea at night.

BY CAR To get to Viña del Mar and Valparaíso from Santiago, take Avenida Alameda (Bernardo O'Higgins) west until it changes into Ruta Nacional 68. There are two toll-booths that charge between C$1,200 and C$3,000 on Ruta 68. Santiago's new Costanera tunnel is the speediest and easiest way to get out of the city; ask someone at your hotel to explain how to access the hard-to-find entrances tunnels, or check the map at **www.costaneranorte.cl**. Street parking is plentiful; in Valparaíso there is a central parking garage on Calle Errázuriz, across from the Plaza Sotomayor and near the visitor center.

Getting Around

A tour of Viña can be managed by foot, and there is a pleasant beachfront promenade for a stroll. The easiest way to travel between Viña and Valparaso is by **taxi** (about $22 one-way) or aboard the **Metrotren** (also known as the "Merval"; ✆ **32/238-1500;** www.merval.cl), an interurban train that leaves every 5 to 10 minutes from 7:30am to 10pm Monday through Friday, and every 15 to 20 minutes from 9:30am to 9pm on Saturdays, Sundays, and holidays. To ride the train, you must first make a one-time purchase: a rechargeable card for C$800 that you then charge with enough money to cover the cost of your trip (C$450–C$900, depending on the length of a one-way trip). If you're with friends or family, you need only purchase one card for your group. Viña has some great bike paths, and makes a nice place for a short bike tour. Contact **Bici en Viña** (✆ **32/8279-4741**) for 1- or 2-hour bike tours with bilingual guides.

Visitor Information

The **Oficina de Turismo de Viña** is located on Plaza Vergara, next to the post office near avenidas Libertad and Arlegui (✆ **800/800-830** toll-free in Chile; www.visitevinadel-mar.cl). The office is open year-round Saturday and Sunday from 10am to 7pm; Monday through Friday in summer, hours are from 9am to 9pm (10am to 7pm off season). The office closes 2 to 3pm daily all year. A helpful staff (a few speak basic English) can provide visitors with maps, events details, and accommodations information, including private cabin rentals.

FAST FACTS: VIÑA DEL MAR Most major **banks** can be found on Avenida Arlegui, open Monday through Friday from 9am to 2pm only; all have 24-hour ATMs (RedBancs), as do pharmacies and gas stations. *Casas de cambio* (money-exchange houses) are open in the summer Monday through Friday from 9am to 2pm and 3 to 8pm, Saturday from 9am to 2pm; in the winter, Monday through Friday from 9am to 2pm and 4 to 7pm, Saturday from 9am to 2pm. Several *cambios* can be found along Avenida Arlegui.

If you need to reach the **police** in an emergency, dial ✆ **133.** For **fire,** dial ✆ **132.** To call an **ambulance,** dial ✆ **131.** For **medical attention,** go to **Hospital Gustavo Fricke** on calles Alvarez and Simón Bolívar (✆ **32/675067,** or 32/652328 for emergencies).

Exploring Viña del Mar

BEACHES The **Playa Caleta Abarca** beach is located in a protected bay near the entrance to Viña del Mar, next to the oft-photographed flower clock and the Cerro Castillo—it is not the city's finest beach. Northeast and fronting the rows of terraced high-rise apartment buildings, you'll find **Playa Acapulco, Playa Mirasol,** and **Playa Las Salinas** (the latter is near the naval base). These beaches all see throngs of vacationers and families in the summer. The *in* spot for beaches is just north of Viña at **Reñaca**—it's close enough to take a taxi (about $7–$12 one-way), or grab a bus numbered 1, 10, or 111 at Avenida Libertad and Avenida 15 Norte.

Casino Municipal ★★ Built in 1930, the Casino Municipal was the most luxurious building in its day and is worth a visit even if you're not a gambler. The interior has been remodeled over time, but the facade has withstood the caprices of many a developer and is still as handsome as the day it opened. Semiformal attire (that is, no T-shirts, jeans, or sneakers) is required to enter the gaming room. Minimum bets of C$5,000 will deter budget travelers, but there are slot machines and video poker. The casino also holds temporary art exhibits on the second floor, and there are three bars. There is a kids' game room next door.

Plaza Colombia between Av. San Martín and Av. Perú. ✆ **32/250-0600.** www.hoteldelmar.cl. Hours vary, but generally in winter, gaming room Mon–Thurs noon–4am, Fri–Sun 24 hr.; in summer, daily 24 hr. Entrance fee of C$380 includes a drink. No one 18 and under allowed.

Museo de Arqueología e Historia Francisco Fonck ★★ Kids The natural history display at the Museo Fonck spans the entire second floor, but what really warrants a visit here is the museum's 1,400-piece collection of Rapa Nui (Easter Island) indigenous art and archaeological artifacts, including one of only six Moai sculptures found outside the island. Kids will love the mystery and grandeur of it. The display is more complete than the archaeological museum on Easter Island itself. Also on display are art and archaeological remnants of all cultures in Chile, and the size of the museum is just right to not grow tiresome—you'll need about 45 minutes here.

Av. 4 Norte 784. ✆ **32/268-6753.** www.museofonck.cl. Admission C$1,800 adults, C$300 children. Mon 10am–2pm and 3–6pm; Tues–Fri 10am–6pm; Sat, Sun, and holidays 10am–2pm (Oct–Mar Sat 10am–6pm).

Museo Palacio Rioja ★★ This enormous 1906 Belle Epoque stone mansion has been preserved in the architectural and decorative style of one of Viña's elite families in the early-20th-century elite. Built by Spaniard Fernando Rioja, a banker, and originally spanning 4 blocks, the palace took opulence to a new level, with a stone facade featuring Corinthian columns and a split double staircase. Interiors are made of oak and stone, with enough salons to fit a family of 10. Although a fraction of what it once was, the palm-fringed garden surrounding the house is idyllic for a quick stroll. Though much is self-explanatory, there are, unfortunately, no tours in English.

Quillota 214. ✆ **32/248-3664.** Admission C$650 adults, C$300 children. Tues–Sun 10am–1:30pm and 3–5:30pm.

Quinta Vergara Park/Museum of Fine Art ★★ A compact but absolutely lovely park, the Quinta Vergara pays homage to the future with its spaceshiplike music amphitheater, and to the past, with its converted 1910 Venetian-style palace, the former home of historical heavyweights the Alvarez/Vergara family, now transformed into a fine arts museum. Every February, this park fills with music lovers who come for the yearly Festival of Song; the rest of the year the park is an idyllic spot for a quiet stroll.

Near Plaza Parroquia. Park: Free admission. Daily 7am–6pm (until 7pm in summer). Museum: ✆ **32/226-9428.** Admission C$650 adults, C$200 children. Tues–Sun 10am–2pm and 3–6pm.

Where to Stay

Hotel del Mar ★★★ This is the icing on Viña's cake, a five-star hotel and casino in the heart of town overlooking the sea. Architects carefully adapted the style of the hotel to match the handsome, eggshell-colored casino, and the results are quite lovely. The central location near restaurants and fronting the beach is the best of any hotel in town. Guest rooms are contemporary and very spacious; most come with balconies that offer some of the best sea views in the area. The Salute Health Center and its infinity pool deserve special mention for their panoramic views, too. After a rough beginning, the hotel staff has streamlined its service and guests can now expect prompt, friendly assistance with whatever needs they may have. The hotel's restaurants (see p. 398 and p. 399) are some of the best in the area, and rooms include free entrance to the casino.

Av. San Martín 199. ✆ **32/250-0800.** Fax 32/250-0801. www.hoteldelmar.cl. 60 units. $247–$308 double; $395 suite. AE, DC, MC, V. Valet parking. **Amenities:** 4 restaurants; bar; art gallery; babysitting; cabaret shows; fitness center and spa; indoor pool; room service; solarium. *In room:* A/C, plasma TV/DVD w/pay-per-view movies, CD player, hair dryer, Wi-Fi.

Hotel Monterilla ★★ Finds This delightful, family-run boutique hotel, located near the beach and casino, is an excellent value and one of the best-kept secrets in Viña del Mar. Cheerful service and a central location are definite draws, but the hotel's contemporary decor is what really makes the Monterilla special. Chromatic furniture contrasted against white carpet, along with walls adorned with colorful postmodern art, provide crisp, eye-catching surroundings, and though the guest rooms are not huge, they're fresh and comfortable. There is one apartment with a kitchenette for four guests, but some doubles are on the small side. Centrally located yet quiet, the Monterrilla offers frequent promotions for parents with kids, and they have a special "Cruise Tourist" promotion that includes transportation from the Seaport in Valparaíso and from the hotel to the Santiago airport.

2 Norte 65, Plaza México, Viña del Mar. ✆ **32/297-6950.** Fax 32/268-3576. www.monterilla.cl. 24 units. $129 double; $188 suite. AE, DC, MC, V. **Amenities:** Cafeteria; bar. *In room:* Cable TV, hair dryer, minibar, Wi-Fi.

Miramar Sheraton ★★★ With the most stunning location of any hotel in Viña, this Sheraton offers sweeping ocean views, a state-of-the-art spa and fitness center, a delightful outdoor pool, and an endless range of high-end services. The hotel hugs the shore and is across from Viña's famous flower clock, about a 10-minute walk to beachfront restaurants. The Sheraton glitters in white-and-glass minimalism, yet the hotel's sleek packaging and voluminous public spaces accented with little or no furniture creates an air of emptiness. This is not a place where you will experience personalized service;

rather, it is difficult to shake the feeling that anyone knows you're there. The Sheraton's guest rooms are gorgeous and plush: every detail, from the silky cotton sheets to the marble inlaid bathrooms, is impeccable. All guest rooms come with ocean views, with small terraces. Listed rates include breakfast and access to all facilities, are for high season, and are supremely high, in my opinion.

Av. Marina 15. ✆ **32/238-8600.** www.starwoodhotels.com/sheraton. 142 units. $414–$484 double. Rates include breakfast. AE, DC, MC, V. Valet parking. **Amenities:** 2 restaurants; bar; babysitting; state-of-the-art fitness center and spa; indoor and outdoor pools; room service. *In room:* Plasma TV, hair dryer, minibar.

Offenbacher-hof Residencial ★ **Moments** Housed in a 100-year-old Victorian perched high atop Cerro Castillo, the Offenbacher has sweeping views of the city and the hills beyond, and a splendid glass-enclosed patio. It is by far one of the more interesting places to lodge, and its location on this historic hill puts you near some of the city's oldest homes—a delightful location, but guests must either grab a taxi to reach the beach, or hoof it. The mix-and-match decor is on the funky side, as if they purchased everything at a flea market, but it's hard to balk considering the panoramic views. But you can find better funky inns in Valparaíso. Superior rooms are worth the extra $10 for better views and substantially more space.

Balmaceda 102, Cerro Castillo, Viña del Mar. ✆ **32/621483.** Fax 32/662432. www.offenbacher-hof.cl. 15 units. $518–$660 double. AE, DC, MC, V. **Amenities:** Cafe; bar; tours and airport transfers; gym; sauna; solarium; whirlpool. *In room:* Cable TV, Wi-Fi.

Where to Dine

There are dozens of restaurants lining Avenida San Martín, including fast-food joints such as Pizza Hut and McDonald's, and in downtown Viña, along Avenida Valparaíso and around the plaza, visitors will find cheap eateries and sandwich shops. For afternoon tea, try **The Tea Pot,** 5 Norte 475 (✆ **32/268-7671;** Mon–Fri 10am–2pm and 4:30–9pm, Sat 10am–9pm), which offers more than 60 kinds of tea and delicious pastries. Along the beach there are several wood-and-glass concessions that serve sandwiches, drinks, coffee, and pastries. For nighttime cocktails and appetizers, try the slick **Barlovento,** 2 Norte 195 (✆ **32/297-7472**), a bar/restaurant with a second-floor lounge popular with young professionals.

Expensive

Savinya ★★★ INTERNATIONAL Savinya is part of the Hotel del Mar (see above) and known for its outstanding haute cuisine. It's Viña's most refined, and expensive, restaurant, and the place to go if you're looking to blow your budget on a special meal. Still, when compared to restaurants of the same caliber in the U.S., the prices at Savinya could be considered quite reasonable. The menu changes seasonally, but what doesn't change is the chef's impeccable technique and presentation of each dish, blending uncommon flavors and textures that work surprisingly well together, with a list of complementary palate-pleasing wines. Attentive, agreeable service comes with the price, as does an elegant-chic ambience and gigantic picture windows that offer a gorgeous view overlooking the ocean. The sommelier is one of the best in South America.

Av. Perú and Los Héroes. ✆ **32/250-0800.** www.hoteldelmar.cl. Reservations recommended for dinner. Main courses C$9,000–C$18,500. AE, DC, MC, V. Daily 12:30–3:30pm and 8pm–12:30am.

Moderate

Cap Ducal SEAFOOD This Viña del Mar institution is notable for one reason only: an intimate, candlelit dining experience with a view of the sparkling coastline and the crashing surf. The restaurant is designed to resemble a ship moored against the cliff, and it has been a fixture in the Viña dining scene since 1936. However, the ambience outshines the food, which is not bad but does lack creativity. The focus here is on Chilean cuisine and international-style seafood. Try the classic Chilean razor clams with Parmesan cheese.

Av. Marina 51. ✆ **32/262-6655.** www.capducal.cl. Main dishes C$4,800–C$7,000. AE, DC, MC, V. Daily 1pm–midnight.

Divino Pecado ★★ ITALIAN Cozy and centrally located, this chef-owned restaurant boasts delicious fresh pastas and other Italian dishes, as well as sharp service. For an aperitif, order a pisco sour—this restaurant is known for its delicious Peruvian variety. The menu features a build-your-own pasta section so that diners may invent their own concoction, or pick a pasta dish from their list of specialties, of which the standout is by far the "black" raviolis made with calamari ink and stuffed with curried shrimp. Divino Pecado specializes in "boutique" fish—that is, specialty fish such as sole, the delicate *mero* (grouper), and tuna, and they offer meats such as filet mignon.

Av. San Martín 180 (in front of casino). ✆ **32/297-5790.** divinopecado@terra.cl. Reservations recommended. Main courses C$8,000–C$9,000. AE, DC, MC, V. Daily 12:30–3:30pm; Mon–Fri 8–11pm; Sat–Sun 8pm–1am.

La Barquera ★★ INTERNATIONAL The best alfresco dining venue in Viña is at this open-air deck, with the sea breeze in your face and a cold glass of chardonnay in your hand. The restaurant is part of the Hotel del Mar (see above), but it is located across the street on the beach. The main courses strive for gourmet caliber, but never quite achieve that; instead, the best bet here is the pizza or salad bar. There are also sandwiches, burgers, and an ice-cream parlor. The restaurant is always open, from the early morning until the wee hours, and they host live music on weekends.

Av. Peru 100. ✆ **32/268-7755.** Main courses C$4,000–C$8,000. AE, DC, MC, V. Sun–Wed 7am–1am; Thurs–Sat 7am–3 or 4am.

VALPARAISO ★★

Just 15 minutes (8km/5 miles) south of Viña del Mar is one of Chile's most captivating cities, Valparaíso. The historic core, centered around Cerro Alegre and Cerro Concepción, was declared a UNESCO World Heritage Site in 2004. The historical importance of this city paired with its vibrant *porteño* culture make Valparaíso a far more interesting destination to visit and to spend the night than the Miami Beach–esque Viña, especially now that there are several boutique hotels and many outstanding restaurants. Its jumble of multicolored clapboard homes and weathered Victorian mansions that cling to sheer cliffs and other unusual spaces provide endless photo opportunities. You could spend days exploring the city's maze of narrow passageways and sinuous streets that snake their way down ravines and around hillsides. The city has a bohemian flair so lacking in overdeveloped coastal towns, but all its abandoned waterfront buildings and decrepit homes make it a little rough around the edges.

Essentials

Getting There & Getting Around

See "Viña del Mar" above for information on getting there. Walking and taking the *ascensores* (funiculars) is really the only way to get around Valparaíso. The main historic areas of Cerro Alegre and Cerro Concepción are off-limits to tour buses. For travel between Viña and Valparaíso, see above.

Visitor Information

There are two **tourist information kiosks,** one in the center at Plaza Sotomayor and another at Plaza Anibal Pinto in the business district (✆ **32/293-9669;** www.ciudaddevalparaiso.cl). Both are open Monday through Friday from 10am to 2pm and 3:30 to 5:30pm, and Saturdays and Sundays from 10:30am to 5:30pm.

Exploring Valparaíso

Cementerio 1, 2 & De Disidentes ★★ Featuring fascinating, baroque antique mausoleums, this museum offers stunning views and a walk through the past. Focus your visit on the Cemeterio de Disidentes; this is where the tombs of Protestant British and other European immigrants lie, having been shunned from the principal cemeteries for not being Catholic. This cemetery is by far more intriguing than the other two for its matter-of-fact gravestones spelling out often dramatic endings for (usually very young) adventurers who arrived during the 19th century. It's a short, but hearty, walk up Ecuador Street to get here.

Between Av. Ecuador and Cumming (Cerro Panteón). No phone. Free admission. Daily 10am–5pm (generally).

La Sebastiana ★★★ La Sebastiana is one of poet Pablo Neruda's three quirky homes that have been converted into museums honoring the distinguished Nobel laureate's work and life. Neruda is Chile's most beloved poet, and its most famous literary export. Even if you haven't familiarized yourself with Neruda's work, this museum is worth visiting to explore this eccentric home and view the whimsical knickknacks he relished collecting while traveling. There are self-guiding information sheets that explain the significance of important documents and items on display, and visitors are allowed to wander freely at their own pace—something you can't do at Neruda's other museums. The walk from Plaza Victoria is a hike, so you might want to take a taxi. From Plaza Ecuador, there's a bus, Verde "D," or the *colectivo* No. 39.

Calle Ferrari 692 (Cerro Bellavista). ✆ **32/225-6606.** www.fundacionneruda.org. Admission C$3,000 adults, C$1,500 students. Mar–Dec Tues–Sun 10am–6pm; Jan–Feb Tues–Sun 10:30am–6:50pm.

Museo Naval y Marítimo ★★ This museum merits a visit even if you do not particularly fancy naval and maritime-related artifacts and memorabilia. The museum is smartly designed and divided into four salons: the War of Independence, the War against the Peru–Bolivia Confederation, the War against Spain, and the War of the Pacific. Each salon holds antique documents, medals, uniforms, and war trophies. Of special note is the Arturo Prat room, with artifacts salvaged from the *Esmeralda,* a wooden ship that sank while valiantly defending Valparaíso during the War of the Pacific.

Paseo 21 de Mayo, Cerro Artillería. ✆ **32/228-3749.** www.museonaval.cl. Admission C$650 adults, C$409 children 11 and under. Tues–Sun 10am–5:30pm.

Walking Tours of Valparaíso

The Fundación Valparaíso has done an exceptional job of mapping out the Bicentennial Heritage Trail, a looping 30km (19-mile) walking tour divided into 15 thematic stages. I urge visitors to pick up a copy of the trail guide to supplement the walking tour described below; the guide can be found at the Gato Tuerto bookstore, located at Héctor Calvo 205 (Espíritu Santo Funicular), or other bookstores (if you are cruising, you may find the book at the Baron's Pier shopping gallery). Each stage takes approximately 90 minutes to 3 hours to walk, and the guide provides historical and architectural information, literary gossip, and fun anecdotes about the city. To help you navigate, the *fundación*

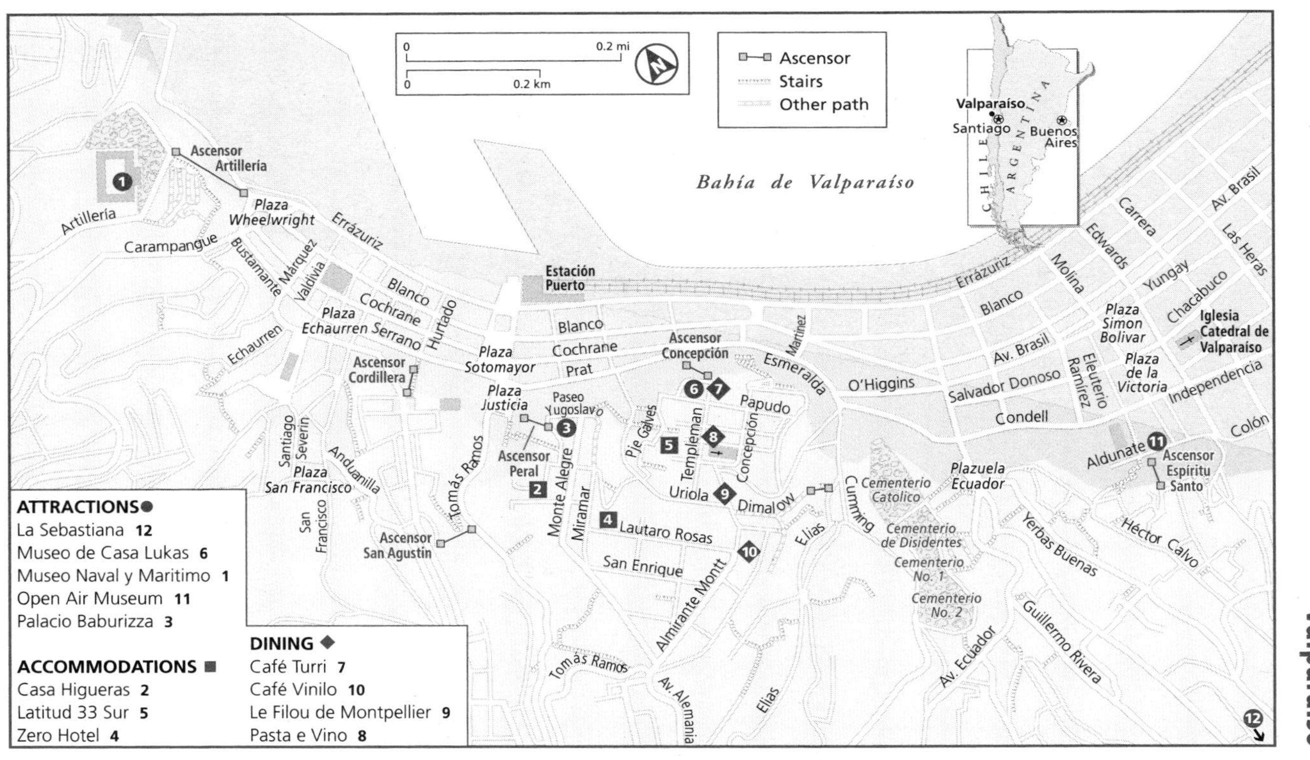
ATTRACTIONS
La Sebastiana 12
Museo de Casa Lukas 6
Museo Naval y Marítimo 1
Open Air Museum 11
Palacio Baburizza 3
ACCOMMODATIONS
Casa Higueras 2
Latitud 33 Sur 5
Zero Hotel 4
DINING
Café Turri 7
Café Vinilo 10
Le Filou de Montpellier 9
Pasta e Vino 8
Ascensor
Stairs
Other path
0 0.2 mi
0 0.2 km
Bahía de Valparaíso
Valparaíso
Santiago
Buenos Aires
CHILE
ARGENTINA
Estación Puerto
Iglesia Catedral de Valparaíso
Plaza Simon Bolivar
Plaza de la Victoria
Plazuela Ecuador
Cementerio Catolico
Cementerio de Disidentes
Cementerio No. 1
Cementerio No. 2
Ascensor Artillería
Ascensor Cordillera
Ascensor San Agustín
Ascensor Peral
Ascensor Concepción
Ascensor Espíritu Santo
Paseo Yugoslavo
Plaza Justicia
Plaza Sotomayor
Plaza Echaurren
Plaza Wheelwright
Plaza San Francisco
Av. Brasil
Las Heras
Carrera
Edwards
Molina
Yungay
Chacabuco
Independencia
Colón
Eleuterio Ramírez
Salvador Donoso
Condell
Aldunate
Héctor Calvo
Yerbas Buenas
Guillermo Rivera
Av. Ecuador
Errázuriz
Blanco
Cochrane
Prat
O'Higgins
Esmeralda
Martinez
Cumming
Papudo
Concepción
Templeman
Uriola
Dimalow
Elías
Almirante Montt
Av. Alemania
Lautaro Rosas
San Enrique
Pje Galves
Miramar
Monte Alegre
Tomás Ramos
Hurtado
Serrano
Anduanilla
Santiago Severín
San Francisco
Echaurren
Márquez
Valdivia
Bustamante
Carampangue
Artillería

has placed arrows on the street at various stages of the trail. For visitors with limited time in the city, the walking tour outlined below will take you to the city's finest viewpoints and top attractions. Walking tours led by excellent bilingual guides from the local agency **Guía-Tour** (✆ **9/876-3325;** http://guia-tour.com) are highly recommended and will really help you get the most out of your time in Valparaíso. These people are very passionate about their hometown.

With a city map in hand, head toward Plaza Sotomayor, Valparaíso's civic center until 1980. Here, you'll encounter the **Monument to the Heroes of Iquique,** under which the remains of Prat, Condell, and Serrano, heroes of the War of the Pacific, are buried. To the left of the plaza, next to the Palacio de Justicia, ride the Ascensor Peral (ca. 1902) for C$273 to the top of Cerro Alegre, and there you'll find the **Paseo Yugoslavo**—a terrace walkway built by Pascual Baburizza in 1929, whose **Palacio Baburizza** houses the Fine Arts Museum; delayed plans for renovations have stalled the reopening of the museum. As of press time, the museum was slated to open in late 2010. The walkway curves to the right around a tiny plaza; follow it until you reach Calle Alvaro Besa. Take the shortcut down **Pasaje Bavestrello,** a colorful cement stairway at the left. Continue until you reach Calle Urriola, which you'll cross, and then walk up to another stairway, Pasaje Gálvez. At Calle Papudo, climb the stairway and turn left into **Paseo Gervasoni,** lined with stately, 19th-century mansions. This street looks out onto the port of Valparaíso. Here, you'll also find the **Museo de Casa Lukas** (✆ **32/222-1344;** www.lukas.cl), an exhibition of illustrations made by cartoonist Renzo Pecchenino, who dedicated his career to sketching Valparaíso's eccentric characters; it's open Tuesday through Sunday from 11am to 8pm and admission is $500. After touring the museum, head up Calle Templeman to window-shop in the boutiques or pop in to one of the restaurants listed below. Then, continue around Gervasoni until you reach Papudo. At Paseo Atkinson, you'll find another pedestrian walkway, bordered by antique English homes. Continue down the pedestrian stairway until you reach Calle Esmeralda and the end of the walk. You can also descend by doubling back and riding the Ascensor Concepción to Calle Prat.

Other Short Walks

THE PORT NEIGHBORHOOD Begin at the **Aduana (Customs House),** the grand, colonial American–style building built in 1854 and located at the north of town at Plaza Wheelwright at the end of Cochrane and Calle Carampangue. To the right, you'll find the **Ascensor Artillería,** built in 1893; it costs C$273. The wobbly contraption is a delight, and it takes visitors to the most panoramic pedestrian walkway in Valparaíso, **Paseo 21 de Mayo.** This lovely promenade has a lookout gazebo from which it is possible to take in the town's bustling port activity. Follow the walkway until you reach the **Museo Naval y Marítimo** (see "Exploring Valparaíso," above). To return, double back and descend via the *ascensor,* or head down the walkway and take a left at Calle Carampangue.

PLAZA VICTORIA/MUSEO A CIELO ABIERTO/LA SEBASTIANA (PABLO NERUDA'S HOUSE) In the late 1880s, Plaza Victoria was the elegant center of society, as is evident by the grand trees, trickling fountain, and sculptures imported from Lima that recall that era's heyday. From the plaza, head south on Calle Molina to Alduante for the **Open Air Museum,** which features more than 20 murals painted on cement-retainer and building walls along winding streets. The project features murals conceived by well-known Chilean painters and carried out by students. Begin at the steep stairway at Calle Alduante and turn left at Pasaje Guimera, and left again at the balcony walkway that leads to **Ascensor Espíritu Santo.** (You can ride the funicular up and backtrack this route, walking down.) Continue along Calle Rudolph until you reach Calle Ferrari. Head down Ferrari all the way to Edwards and Colón. The Open Air Museum neighborhood has improved but is still grubby.

Where to Stay

Valparaíso is the epicenter of stylish boutique lodging, whereas Viña is known more for full-scale hotels and resorts with all the bells and whistles and beach access. You'll still spot a few *hostales* whose pretty, flower-boxed facades belie awful conditions within, but even these establishments are being bought up by hoteliers who see the potential in Valparaíso becoming the next hot tourism destination rather than just a character-rich—but down-at-the-heels—city suited only for a day visit. For longer stays, there are stylish lofts at **Casa Von Moltke** ★★ (✆ **32/3178849;** www.casavonmoltke.cl).

Casa Higueras ★★★ **Moments** If you've got the bucks and are looking for a luxurious and intimate hideaway, look no farther than this divine boutique hotel. A top Chilean interior designer took a more masculine, mature, 1930s-era approach with the renovation of this former mansion, using lots of dark-wood flooring and paneling, and minimal, but well-placed, designer furniture—a crystal chandelier here, a velvet pin-tuck couch there. The guest rooms have panoramic windows and amenities such as rich linens and plasma TV screens, and outside, the three-story hotel descends over a rectangular pool that is attractively landscaped into the hillside. There is also a minispa for unwinding after a day tromping up and down Valparaíso's hills. If you get bored of your balcony, and it's hard to imagine you would, you can kick back on their rooftop terrace or the hotel restaurant's patio.

Higueras 133, Cerro Alegre. ✆ **32/249-7900** (Valparaíso) or 2/657-3950 (Santiago). www.casahigueras.cl. 20 units. $248–$289 double; $334–$383 suite. AE, DC, MC, V. **Amenities:** Restaurant; Internet; outdoor pool; room service; sauna; whirlpool. *In room:* Plasma TV/DVD player, hair dryer, minibar, Wi-Fi.

Latitud 33 Sur ★★ **Kids** **Value** At the end of the delightful and brightly painted Calle Templeman row, steps from the best restaurants and the curving passageways, is another new boutique hotel inside a refurbished old home. That means it's a bit quirky and certainly not noise-proof. But it's loaded with charm, in clean, colorful rooms ranging from tight (room no. 5) to very spacious (room no. 7). Staff members are very helpful. One room is wheelchair-friendly, and two of the rooms on the top floor (including one with a bunk bed) share a bathroom, making it a good choice for families or groups. There's a cozy living room for mingling and relaxing.

Pasaje Templeman 183, Cerro Concepción. ✆ **32/211-7983.** www.hotellatitud33sur.cl. 10 units. $62 single; $92–$190 double; $124 triple. AE, MC, V. **Amenities:** Cafeteria; concierge; library. *In room:* TV, Wi-Fi.

Zero Hotel ★★★ **Finds** Relatively indistinguishable from its residential neighbors due to its tiny sign and soft lilac facade, this is another of Valparaíso's top lodging options—a boutique hotel that effectively blends a contemporary, whimsical decor with lovingly refurbished antique ceilings, wall panels, and parquet floors. The house overlooks a twisting road and, beyond that, wide views of the Valparaíso port, with outdoor terraces and a light and airy dining and lounge area. The location is ideal, close to restaurants. The rooms, like the Casa Higueras (see above), feature high-end amenities and Egyptian cotton sheets. But the style here is decidedly more young and funky than Casa Higueras. Rooms that face the hillside are considerably cheaper than rooms with a port view, so if you're not planning to spend a lot of time in your room, the views from the terrace will suffice.

 Lautaro Rosas 343, Valparaíso. ✆ **32/211-3114.** www.zerohotel.com. 9 units. $230–$320 double. AE, DC, MC, V. **Amenities:** Cafe. *In room:* TV, hair dryer, Wi-Fi.

Where to Dine

Valparaíso is the epicenter of hip new Chilean dining. New bistros are opening monthly, many with foreign chefs in the kitchen. Besides the spots listed below, you can dig into literary tendencies at **Café con Letras**, Almirante Montt 316 (✆ **32/223-5480**). For vegetarian food, try **epif**, Calle Dr. Grossi 268 (✆ **32/259-5630**; www.epif.cl). Grab an all-day breakfast and other homemade treats at **El Desayunador**, Almirante Montt 399 (✆ **32/236-5933**; www.eldesayunador.cl). All three are in the heart of the Cerro Concepción-Cerro Alegre neighborhoods.

Expensive

Pasta e Vino ★★★ CONTEMPORARY ITALIAN Pasta e Vino is one of the best restaurants in Chile. With a busy but hip staff supervised by a clever owner, and seriously spectacular pasta, the wait list to get in here is legendarily long. You'll need to make reservations days in advance. But it's worth all the hype. The last time I was here, we ate shrimp carpaccio, impeccably light artichoke-stuffed raviolis, and king crab gnocchis with caviar, with a crisp sauvignon blanc from their outstanding wine list. It was one of the best meals I've had in South America in more than a decade. The ambience is exposed brick walls and sophisticated chic, but wooden tables and a lively atmosphere keeps the restaurant down to earth. If you can't get in here, or if you can't get enough of it, the owners have recently opened a new restaurant in Santiago's Bellavista neighborhood, inside the chic new boutique hotel (p. 384).

Templeman 352. ✆ **32/249-6187.** www.pastaevinovalparaiso.cl. Reservations required. Main courses C$7,000–C$12,500. AE, DC, MC, V. Thurs–Sat 1–3:30pm; Tues–Fri 7pm–midnight; Sat 8pm–midnight.

Moderate

Café Turri ★★ (Moments) FRENCH/CHILEAN This restaurant has always reigned as the city's best spot for alfresco dining, and it's well located at the top of the La Concepción funicular and close to other points of interest. The owners (a French/Chilean pair) have preserved the restaurant's lovely antique interiors, but they've given them a contemporary update. They've also hired a cheery waitstaff and made a visitor-friendly menu full of the typical classics, with slight French influences. That said, while the food is night-and-day better than before, it still isn't as good as places like Pasta e Vino. For a primo table, book at least a day ahead on weekends. It's also a nice place for a pisco sour at sunset.

Calle Templeman 147 (Cerro Concepción; take the Concepción lift). ✆ **32/225-2091.** www.cafeturri.cl. Reservations recommended for outdoor seating. Main courses C$5,500–C$7,500. AE, DC, MC, V. Daily 10am–midnight (closed Mon Apr–Nov).

Café Vinilo ★ (Finds) CAFE/CHILEAN Boho hipsters congregate at this tiny bistro owned by a fashion designer (her work is on display throughout). It's the kind of place one imagines packed with intellectuals and poets, and the shared tables are conducive to mingling. The small menu suggests fusion-style Chilean dishes, like Pacific salmon in *lapsang souchong* tea sauce. The desserts don't make the menu, but are worth saving space for. Since it's open late, this also makes a great postdinner stop for coffee, sweets, or an artisanal beer.

Almirante Montt 448 (Cerro Alegre). ✆ **32/223-0665.** www.cafevinilo.cl. Main courses C$5,000–C$10,500. AE, DC, MC, V. Mon–Thurs 9am–1am; Fri–Sat 9am–2:30am; Sun 10am–10pm.

Le Filou de Montpellier ★★ Value FRENCH The first of the French chefs to put down roots in Valparaíso, Phillippe Grandgeorge arrived more than a decade ago. He serves authentic, exquisitely executed Gaelic cuisine at a great price. He may also be your waiter; take his suggestion for what to order. Fixed-price lunches are the best deal. The dining room is a cozy unpretentious bistro. It's open for dinner only on Fridays and Saturdays.

Almirante Montt 382, corner of Urriola. ✆ **32/2/222-4663.** www.lefiloudemontpellier.cl. Reservations recommended. Fixed-price lunch C$4,600; entrees C$4,500–C$6,200. No credit cards. Tues–Sun 1–4pm; Fri–Sat 8–11:30pm.

Valparaíso After Dark

Most restaurants and bars do not adhere to a set closing hour, but instead close "when the candles burn down." Try **Bar Cinzano** at Aníbal Pinto 1182 (✆ **32/221-3043**), which has been around for 110 years and spotlights tango crooners in a wonderful, early-20th-century ambience. **La Columbina** (✆ **32/223-6254**) is a cafe with a great view that is frequented by the 30-and-up crowd for its comfortable ambience, live jazz, and bolero music. **La Piedra Feliz,** Errázuriz 1054 (✆ **32/225-6788**), is a trendy bar inside the converted storehouse of an old shipping company, has a subterranean lounge with DJs (Thurs–Sat), and features two salons with tango and salsa lessons available. Twenty- and thirty-somethings sweat to electronic music at the ultracool **Mundo Pagano,** Blanco 236 (✆ **32/223-1118;** www.mundopagano.cl), which has nightly dance parties and occasionally live music.

CAJON DE MAIPO

Cajón de Maipo is a quick city escape that puts visitors in the middle of a rugged, alpine setting of towering peaks and freshly scented forest slopes along the Río Maipo. A highlight in this area is **El Morado National Monument** (see below), but it is certainly not a requisite destination. Cajón de Maipo offers a wide array of outdoor activities, such as rafting, horseback riding, hiking, climbing, and more, but it also offers a chance to linger over a good lunch or picnic, stroll around the area, and maybe even lay your head down for the night in one of the *cabañas* that line the valley. Take the Metro Line 4 toward Puente Alto and get off at the Las Mercedes station, for a *taxis colectivo,* which leaves every 10 minutes from 7am to 8pm and costs C$1,700 per person. Regular taxis (with a yellow roof) from the Mercedes Metro station can run anywhere from C$10,000 to C$12,500, depending on your destination in the Cajón. Always negotiate a price with the driver beforehand. It's relatively easy to access by car; ask for directions at your hotel and take a good map. Try to avoid coming on weekends when Santiago residents flee here to escape the smog.

Exploring the Area & Staying Active

EL MORADO NATIONAL MONUMENT This 3,000-hectare (7,410-acre) park is just 90km (56 miles) from Santiago, yet the dramatic, high-alpine landscape makes visitors here feel as if they are hundreds of miles away from the city. A great spot to take in all this beauty is the Tyrolean mountain lodge **Refugio Lo Valdés** (✆ **9/220-8525;** www.refugiolovaldes.com), a rustic "shelter" that serves a delicious, fixed-price lunch and dinner, where you can eat out on the deck while gazing at the snowcapped peaks. The owners of the historic Refugio also plan outdoor activities such as day hiking or overnight climbing trips, horseback riding, visits to the hot springs, and nature tours. There are clean, bunk-bed–style accommodations (there is one double room for couples), and a cozy dining area warmed by a huge woodstove. Rates are C$17,000 per adult, C$14,000 children 6 to 12, and C$10,000 kids 1 to 5; breakfast is included.

The Conaf park ranger hut is at the raggedy village of **Baños Morales.** The park is open daily October through April from 8:30am to 6pm and costs C$1,500 to enter. There is just one trail, an 8km (5-mile) easy-intermediate trail that borders an alpine lake and ends at a glacier, offering a profile view of the El Morado mountain (about 6 hr. round-trip). There are natural hot springs at **Termas de Colina,** in the form of clay pools descending a slope, jam-packed with Santiagueños on weekends. The expansive alpine setting adds a sense of grandeur to the experience. It takes time to get here due to the condition of the road; continue past Lo Valdés for 12km (7½ miles).

RAFTING Santiago is one of the only metropolitan cities in the world that offers Class III and IV rafting little more than half an hour from downtown. The season runs from September to April, but the river really gets going from November to February. Two reliable companies offer half-day rafting excursions: **Cascada de las Animas** (✆ **2/861-1303;** www.cascadadelasanimas.cl) arranges rafting trips from its tourism complex (see below) in San Alfonso, but it's best to reserve beforehand. Another highly respected outfitter is **Altué Expediciones,** in Santiago, Encomenderos 83 (✆ **2/232-1103;** www.altue.com). Both charge C$70,000.

HORSEBACK RIDING Visitors to El Morado can rent horses with a guide at Baños Morales or Termas de Colina for about C$15,000 to C$80,000 per person, depending on group size and duration. Cascada de las Animas has horseback riding through its own private chunk of the Andes and El Morado park, as does Altué Expediciones. The horseback rides are suitable for families.

Where to Stay & Dine in Cajón de Maipo

Cascada de las Animas ★★, Camino al Volcán, is a tourism center that's run by long-time residents who own a tremendous amount of acreage outside San Alfonso, part of which is used for excursions and 80 campground and picnic sites scattered about a lovely, wooded hillside (✆ **2/861-1303;** www.cascadadelasanimas.cl; from $88 *cabaña* for two). The complex includes nine rustic yet enchanting log cabins with fully equipped kitchens and wood-burning stoves, and the tiny **Hostal La Casa Grande** in San Alfonso, 4 blocks from the entrance to their complex, a hostel housed in a renovated 1930s home and surrounded by greenery. Cascada offers a swimming pool, kayaking, rafting, and horseback-riding excursions, as well as meditation sessions and a women's spiritual retreat. There is a full-service restaurant that looks out over the river, with excruciatingly slow service.

The gorgeous eight-room **Hotel Altiplanico San Alfonso ★★**, Camino al Volcán, (✆ **2/861-2078;** www.altiplanico.com) is the valley's upscale option, with shingled exteriors, an artsy decor, and flagstone floors; it also has a swimming pool, horseback riding, and wine trips to the Maipo Valley. Rates include lodging and meals, and cost $115 per person based on double occupancy.

Trattoria Calypso ★★ serves fresh, homemade pasta and, Saturday and Sunday only, stone oven–baked pizzas (Camino el Volcán 9831; ✆ **2/871-1498;** Thurs–Sat 12:30–10pm, Sun 12:30–6pm). Everything is made using organic and local farm ingredients, and there's outdoor seating. If you don't eat at **Casa Bosque ★**, stop here anyway to admire the fabulously outlandish architecture: polished, raw tree trunks left in their natural shapes form zany door frames, ceiling beams, and pillars. Casa Bosque is a *parrilla* serving barbecued meats paired with fresh salads and other accompaniments. It has good food and a great atmosphere, but service is slow and inattentive (Camino el Volcán

16829; ✆ **2/871-1570;** www.casabosque.cl; Mon–Thurs 12:30–6pm, Fri–Sat 12:30pm–midnight). **La Petite France** ★ serves Alsatian bistro classics and Chilean and international dishes, as well as incredible pastries (Camino el Volcán 16096; ✆ **2/861-1967;** www.lapetitefrance.cl; Tues–Sun noon–midnight). This is a good place to enjoy outdoor seating and afternoon tea.

Skiing & Snowboarding the Andes

It's no longer just a summer getaway for skiing fanatics searching for the endless winter; these days it seems everyone in the know is heading south for a summer ski vacation. Skiers have discovered that the Andean terrain is world class, with easy groomers and spine-tingling steeps, and with so few people on the slopes here, powder lasts for days, not hours. There are few lift lines, and the ambience is relaxed and conducive to making friends and waking up late. For families, the kids are on vacation, and most resorts offer reduced rates or free stays for kids 11 and under.

Resorts centered on the Farallones area, such as Valle Nevado, La Parva, and El Colorado, can be reached in a 1- to 2-hour drive from Santiago or the airport. The all-inclusive and venerable Portillo is a little over 2 hours from Santiago; Termas de Chillán is a short flight and a 1-hour transfer shuttle away, or a 5-hour train ride, offering tree skiing, a casino, and an extensive spa.

GETTING TO THE RESORTS You do not need to rent a vehicle if you are planning to spend the night at any of the resorts listed in this section. Portillo organizes transfers through its own company; **Ski Total** (✆ **2/246-0156;** www.skitotal.cl) has transfer shuttles to Valle Nevado for $33 round-trip per person, and El Colorado and La Parva for $18 round-trip per person. The shuttles leave at 8:30am from their offices at Av. Apoquindo 4900, no. 42 (in the Omnium shopping mall in Las Condes—there's no Metro station nearby, so take a taxi) and three other stops in the Las Condes area, and no reservation for these shuttles is required. Round-trip transportation with hotel pickup costs $33 to $40 per person and requires a reservation made 24 hours in advance; pickup time for this service is 8am.

Ski Portillo ★★★ **Kids** Internationally famous, Portillo is South America's oldest resort and one of the more singular ski destinations in the world. The resort is set high in the Andes on the shore of Lake Inca, and unlike most ski resorts, there is no town at Portillo, just one sunflower-yellow lodge and two more economical annexes. Although open to the public for day skiing, Portillo really operates as a weeklong, package-driven resort that includes lodging, ski tickets, all meals, and use of its plentiful amenities. The ski area is smaller than Valle Nevado and Termas de Chillán; however, Portillo offers steeper terrain and fewer crowds. Portillo is billed as a "boutique resort" with a maximum of 450 people, giving visitors the sensation of skiing in their own private resort. Nonskiers will be very bored here.

Intermediate skiers are strongly urged to take advantage of Portillo's top-rated ski school and use the week as a "training camp." Rooms are on the small side but entirely comfortable; the best rooms are on the sixth floor. The Octagon annex has shared rooms with four bunks and a private bathroom; the Inca annex is for backpackers and has tiny, shared rooms with a common bathroom. Dining takes place in the hotel's main restaurant, the cafeteria, or their mountainside restaurant. On certain nights, the party can really ignite with live music in the hotel bar, a thumping nightclub, and an off-site *cantina.*

There are 13 lifts, including five chairs, five T-bars, and three "slingshot" lifts that leave skiers at the top of vertiginous chutes. The terrain is 43% beginner and intermediate, 57% advanced and expert.

Hotel Portillo's 7-day packages include lodging, lift tickets, four meals per day, and use of all facilities. Per person rates are as follows: double with lake view $1,705 to $3,180; suites $2,200 to $4,015; family apartments (minimum four people) $1,320 to $2,365. One child 11 or under per family stays free in a parent's room and skis for free; additional kids 4 to 11 pay half price; and kids 12 to 17 are charged about 25% less than the adult rate. The **Octagon Lodge** includes the same amenities as above for $980 to $1,530. The **Inca Lodge** charges $650 to $770; meals for guests of the Inca Lodge are taken in the cafeteria.

Renato Sánchez 4270, Santiago. ✆ **800/829-5325** in the U.S., 800/514-2579 in Canada, or 2/263-0606. Fax 2/263-0595. www.skiportillo.com. AE, DC, MC, V. **Amenities:** Restaurant; cafeteria; bar; club; child-care center; cybercare; fitness center; full-court gymnasium; outdoor heated pool; sauna; ski tuning and repair; ski rental; theater.

Valle Nevado ★★ (Kids) Valle Nevado sits high above Santiago, near (and above) El Colorado and La Parva resorts, and it is the only resort in this "Three Valleys" area that offers a full-service tourism infrastructure. The resort complex is not a town, but there are clothing, gear, and souvenir shops, a variety of excellent restaurants, and a full-service spa, making Valle a good destination for nonskiing guests accompanying their family or friends. The French-designed resort is Chile's answer to Les Arcs, with three hotels and two condominium buildings that straddle a ridge line. The terrain is large enough to entertain skiers for days, and they can purchase an interconnect ticket and traverse over to La Parva and El Colorado. The steeper runs are at Portillo, yet Valle is larger and the runs longer. Of all the resorts in Chile, Valle is the most snowboard-friendly, offering a terrain park and monster half-pipe, and the resort hosts the Nokia Snowboarding World Cup every year. Many Santiaguinos visit Valle Nevado on weekends, and traffic up the winding mountain road can back up for hours if there has been a recent snowfall. Saturdays and Sundays bring long lift lines and crowded slopes. The terrain is 15% expert, 30% advanced, 40% intermediate, and 15% beginner.

Valle Nevado offers all-inclusive packages that include lodging, ski tickets, breakfast, and dinner, which can be taken in any one of the resort's restaurants. Prices are per person, double occupancy, and the range reflects low to high season. The five-star **Hotel Valle Nevado** (elegant, though closer to a four-star) is, per night, $244 to $438 per person based on double occupancy, and $288 to $538 per person in a suite. The mid-range **Hotel Puerta del Sol,** which is popular with families, is $181 to $371 a night per person in a double, and $193 to $295 per person a night for a suite. **Hotel Tres Puntas** has rooms with either two twins or four-bed bunks which are great values for their private bathrooms. The hotel is popular with younger guests and families; rates are $130 to $238 per person per night.

Office at Av. Vitacura 5250, no. 304, Santiago. ✆ **2/477-7700.** Fax 2/477-7736. www.vallenevado.com. Lift tickets C$24,000–C$32,000 adults, C$17,000–C$22,000 children 12 and under. AE, DC, MC, V. **Amenities:** Club; child-care center; cinema; full-court gymnasium; outdoor heated pool; room service; sauna; full-service spa w/fitness gym; whirlpool. *In room:* TV, minibar.

La Parva ★★ La Parva caters to Santiago's well-heeled skiers and snowboarders, many of whom own condos or chalets here. Apart from a condominium complex with independent units, there are few services for the ordinary tourist. La Parva offers good off-piste skiing conditions and the steepest inbounds terrain of the resorts in the area (however, an interconnect ticket means skiers can traverse to La Parva from Valle Nevado). The resort's terrain breaks down into 15% expert, 30% intermediate, 40% advanced, and 15% beginner. They offer 4 chairs and 10 surface lift runs, such as T-bars. Dining options here include **La Marmita de Pericles** for fondue, **El Piuquén Pub** for après ski and nightlife, and the **St. Tropez** for Italian food and breakfast. There is also a dance club, with a happy hour from 10pm to midnight.

Condominium lodging is the only option at La Parva, and during the high season in July they must be rented for 7 nights from Friday to Friday (call for shorter, last-minute stays). Standard condos for five to six people are $1,800 to $2,830; and superior apartments, for seven to eight people, are $2,750 to $3,650. Maid service is an additional $22 per day.

Av. Isidora Goyenechea 2939, no. 303, Santiago. ✆ **2/431-0420** in Santiago, or 2/220-9530 direct. Fax 2/431-0458. www.laparva.cl. Lift tickets low to high season: C$23,500–C$30,000 adults, C$18,000–C$20,500 children 5–12 and seniors, C$7,000 children 4 and under.

El Colorado/Farallones ★ Farallones is a collection of chalets and mom-and-pop shops sprawled across a ridge a little lower than the ski area El Colorado. Of the three resorts, El Colorado is the blue-collar brother, an older, more economical option that sees more Chileans than foreigners and is popular with beginning skiers, nonskiers who come to throw snowballs and take part in tubing, and so on. There is an ample variety of terrain and fewer skiers and snowboarders on the slopes than the neighboring resorts, but the lift system is dated. If you're looking for cheaper lodging at the Three Valleys area, this is where you'll find it. The 1,000-hectare (2,470-acre) resort has 5 chairlifts and 17 surface lifts, such as T-bars. There's a bit of off-piste skiing, and there are 22 runs: 4 expert, 3 advanced, 4 intermediate, and 11 beginner. El Colorado is also snowboard-friendly, and they have a snow park and half-pipe. The El Colorado Apart-Hotel is modern and clean, with two- and three-bedroom units with kitchenettes for $163 to $205 per person, double occupancy.

Apoquindo 4900, no. 47–48 (Edificio Omnium). ✆ **2/246-3344.** Fax 2/206-4078. www.elcolorado.cl. Lift tickets low to high season: C$21,000–C$30,000 adults, C$16,000–C$20,000 children 5–12, C$7,000 seniors and children 4 and under. Ski rental available.

Ski Arpa ★★ Moments Ski Arpa is Chile's only Sno-Cat operation, offering outstanding off-piste powder skiing and snowboarding, tremendous views, and more vertical for a much lower price than heliskiing. Ski Arpa covers 4,000 hectares (10,000 acres) of terrain located close to the town of Los Andes, fairly close to Portillo. The road to Ski Arpa is not paved and 4×4 vehicles are almost always necessary. There are two Sno-Cats that take skiers up about 3,500m (11,480 ft.) to an awesome, direct view of the 6,962m (22,835-ft.) peak Aconcagua, the highest in the Western Hemisphere. Ski Arpa arranges packages that include lodging in a 19th-century hacienda (the lovingly restored Casa St. Regis) and visits to top local wineries and hot springs, providing foreigners with a more "authentic" Chilean experience than any of Chile's resorts—it's a great place for 2 days of skiing before or after heading to Portillo or Valle Nevado.

Campos de Ahumada s/n. ✆ **802/904-6798** in the U.S., or 2/415-0667 in Santiago. Fax 2/234-9783. www.skiarpa.com. Prices approximately $165–$195 for 4 rooms.

COLCHAGUA & CHILLAN

Just outside the city limits of Santiago, the scenery opens into a patchwork of poplar-lined agricultural fields and grapevines, and tiny towns hearken back to a quieter, colonial era where it is common to see weathered adobe homes, horse-driven carts, and dirt roads. This is Chile's breadbasket, a region that boasts a mild, Mediterranean climate, fertile soil, and plenty of irrigation thanks to the Andes; proof of this natural bounty can be seen at the myriad of roadside stands hawking fresh fruit and vegetables at unbelievably cheap prices. Beyond the central valley is one of Chile's largest and most deluxe ski and summer resorts, Termas de Chillán.

The up-and-coming wine touring area with the most developed infrastructure is **Colchagua,** centered on the town of Santa Cruz, about a 2-hour drive from Santiago. Chile's best museum is here, the **Museo de Colchagua** ★★★ (✆ **72/821050;** www.museocolchagua.cl; daily 10am–6pm; admission C$4,000). The diverse collection here includes pre-Columbian archeological artifacts, Spanish conquest–era helmets and artillery, immigrant household items, carriages, collections of *huaso* and indigenous arts and clothing, farm machinery, and more. There is so much to see here you'll want to plan on spending 1 to 2 hours.

The way to see the valley is by contacting the **Ruta del Vino,** Plaza de Armas 298, Santa Cruz (✆ **72/823199;** www.colchaguavalley.cl), which offers half-day and full-day tours to some of Chile's most important wineries, such as **Viña Montes, Viu Manent, Casa Silva, Montgras,** and **Casa Lapostolle's Clos Apalta.** Reservations are required.

Casa Lapostolle ★★★ (Moments) The Colchagua Valley's most luxurious and exclusive lodging option is one of the most special places to stay in Chile. Clos Apalta has four *casitas,* or small individual units, nestled on a hillside near their winery. The guest rooms are elegantly appointed and modern in decor, with lots of dark wood, white and ecru-colored fabrics, freshly cut flowers, plush separated bathrooms, and wooden decks that afford truly magnificent, wide-open views of the Apalta Valley. Come for romance and indulgence.

Hijuela Villa Eloisa, Camino San Fernando a Pichilemu, Km 36. ✆ **72/953360.** www.casalapostolle.com. $900 for 2, all inclusive. AE, MC, V. **Amenities:** Gourmet restaurant; outdoor pool; wine tours. *In room:* Wi-Fi.

Hotel Santa Cruz Plaza (Overrated) This hotel's handy setting on the main plaza is convenient, but the hotel itself has grown too big, losing its charm in the process. There are now a spa, casino, two restaurants, a swim-up bar, a museum, more than 110 rooms, and endless meeting space. The guest rooms and bathrooms are not large, but they offer enough space for comfort and are decorated in a terra cotta–colored country style, featuring antiques and decorations found throughout the Santa Cruz area. Be sure to ask for a plaza view when booking (the best rates are online).

Plaza de Armas 286, Santa Cruz. ✆/fax **72/821010.** www.hotelsantacruzplaza.cl. 113 doubles, 14 suites. $325 double; $386–$506 suite. Rates include breakfast. AE, DC, MC, V. **Amenities:** Restaurant; babysitting; casino; museum; outdoor pool; sauna; spa. *In room:* A/C, TV.

Hotel Terravina ★ (Finds) Blending seamlessly with the vineyards that surround it, this new white-washed midlevel lodge is a great value. All rooms are tastefully decorated, with a small balcony facing out onto the boutique vineyard next door. Bathrooms are compact but tidy, with colorful tiles. There's a nice pool in the garden, and one of the best breakfasts in Chile is offered. The inn is close enough to walk to town, and to nearby wineries. It's run by a European-Chilean couple who are more than happy to help you sort out wine tour options.

Camino Los Boldos s/n, Barreales, Santa Cruz. ✆ **72/824696.** www.terravina.cl. 18 doubles, 1 suite. $140 double; $250 master suite. **Amenities**: Restaurant; outdoor pool. *In room:* A/C, TV.

A Visit to Chile's Oldest Hotel

Hacienda Los Lingues Overrated About 125km (78 miles) south of Santiago and nestled among poplar-lined country fields and rolling hills is the Hacienda Los Lingues, one of the oldest and best-preserved haciendas in Chile that is now run as a hotel, although it's better suited to visit as a pseudo-museum or for an afternoon coffee. The estate has remained in the same family for 400 years, though most of the buildings were built around 250 years ago. From the ruby-red French salon to the formal sitting room, every room is jam-packed with antiques and brimming with family photos, collector's items, and fascinating odds and ends that you could spend hours observing and admiring (and must take weeks to clean!). Some of the guest rooms are cleaner and cozier, but many are musty, cluttered, and uncomfortable.

Reservations in Santiago: Av. Providencia 1100, no. 205. ✆ **2/431-0510.** Fax 2/431-0501. www.loslingues.com. 19 units, 2 suites. $225 double; $330 suite. AE, DC, MC, V. **Amenities:** Outdoor pool; room service; clay tennis court.

Chillán & Termas de Chillan Resort

Chillán is a midsize city located 406km (252 miles) south of Santiago, and it is the gateway to the popular **Termas de Chillán,** one of South America's largest and most complete ski and summer resorts. A tidy city of 145,000, with five spruce plazas and hodgepodge, tasteless architecture, bustling streets, and street dogs, Chillán looks like any other Chilean city in the Central Valley. There is really only one reason to stop here, the **Feria de Chillán** ★★★, one of the largest and most colorful markets in Chile. The Feria is located between Maipón, Arturo Prat, 5 de Abril, and Isabel Riquelme streets; across Maipón Street is the food market, with everything from pickled vegetables to dried fruit to Chillán's famous sausages. The Feria is open every day, roughly from 11am to 7pm, with longer hours in summertime.

Essentials

GETTING THERE **By Air** Chillán is served by the **Aeropuerto Carriel Sur** in Concepción, about an hour away. There are direct flights here from Santiago several times daily from **LAN** (✆ **600/526-2000;** www.lan.com), and **Sky Airline** (✆ **600/600-2828;** www.skyairline.cl) airlines. If you've made hotel reservations at Termas de Chillán, their transfer service will pick you up and take you directly there. If not, you must take a taxi to the bus terminal, where buses for Chillán leave every 20 minutes.

By Bus **Buses Nilahue**, Av O'Higgins 010 (✆ **42/270569**) and **TurBus**, Av. Libertad 764 (✆**42/228699**) offer daily service from most major cities, including Santiago. The trip from Santiago takes about 5 to 6 hours and costs C$7,500 one-way. The bus terminal in Chillán is at Av. O'Higgins 010, and from there you can grab a bus for the Termas.

By Train **EFE** (Terrasur) offers a highly recommended 5-hour train trip from Santiago, leaving from the Estación Central and arriving in Chillán at the station at Calle Brasil (✆ **2/585-5000;** www.efe.cl). The per-person cost is C$7,650 for regular to C$16,650 for first class.

Termas de Chillan

Termas de Chillán ★★ Kids About 80km (50 miles) from the city is Termas de Chillán, a full-season resort that is principally known for skiing, but offers great hiking, biking, and horseback riding opportunities in the summer. The resort is nestled in a forested valley under the shadow of the double-peaked 3,212m (10,535-ft.) Chillán Volcano. The resort has 28 runs, 4 chairlifts, and 5 T-bars, as well as heliskiing, dog

Tips Get Your Funds in Order Before You Arrive

There are no ATMs or gas stations in Termas de Chillán, so do your banking beforehand and fill up at the last Copec on the road from Chillán to Termas de Chillán.

sledding, an international ski school, equipment rental, and restaurants. Many of the lifts are old and slow-going (though Termas was recently bought by new owners who have big plans to modernize the resort); Termas is notoriously anti-snowboard, and they will not allow snowboarders on certain poma lifts. Nevertheless, the off-piste terrain is excellent for snowboarding and skiing. The lava flows off the volcano have created natural half-pipes that snowboarders and free skiers will love. Termas is also known for its spa facilities and outdoor hot springs, produced by the natural geothermal fissures in the area. The spa offers hydrotherapy, aromatherapy, mud baths, and massages.

There are two hotels at the base of the lifts: the five-star **Gran Hotel Termas de Chillán,** with 120 rooms priced between $180 to $275 a night, and the three-star **Hotel Shangri-La,** with 48 rooms. Rates include breakfast and dinner, ski tickets, and spa facilities. There are other accommodation options in Las Trancas lower down the valley, including the **Hotel Pirmahuida** with doubles running $84 to $95 (with transportation available to and from the resort) and the French-owned skier-friendly **Mission Impossible Lodge** with doubles from $60. Rooms are also available weekly.

San Pío X 2460, no. 508 (Santiago). ✆ **42/434200** (in Chillán) or 2/233-1313 (in Santiago). www.termaschillan.cl. Average lift tickets C$18,000 adults, C$12,500 children. AE, DC, MC, V. **Amenities:** Restaurant; bar; child-care center; gym; room service; state-of-the-art spa; squash court. *In room:* TV, hair dryer, Wi-Fi.

6 THE DESERT NORTH

SAN PEDRO DE ATACAMA ★

Quaint, unhurried, and built of adobe brick, San Pedro de Atacama sits in the driest desert in the world 1,674km (1,038 miles) north of Santiago, a region replete with bizarre land formations including giant sand dunes, jagged canyons, salt pillars, boiling geysers, and a smoking volcano. Better to call it a moonscape than a landscape. For adventure seekers, a wealth of activities is available to participate in, including hiking, mountain biking, and horseback riding—or you can just sightsee with a tour van. Either way, the idea is to lose yourself in the landscape. This region was the principal center of the Atacamanian Indian culture, and relics such as Tulor, an ancient village estimated to have been built in 800 B.C., still survive. There's also a superb archaeology museum that boasts hundreds of artifacts that have been well preserved by the desert's arid climate. This is one of the top stargazing areas in the world; once you leave the village and are enveloped by a thick blanket of twinkling lights, you'd be forgiven for feeling that the galaxy was not so far, far away after all. The town has fomented somewhat of a bohemian ambience, but with the variety of activities and several outstanding lodging options, the region appeals to just about everyone. To visit the major sites here, you'll need 3 or 4 days, a few more to see everything including the outlying villages or the Chuquicamata

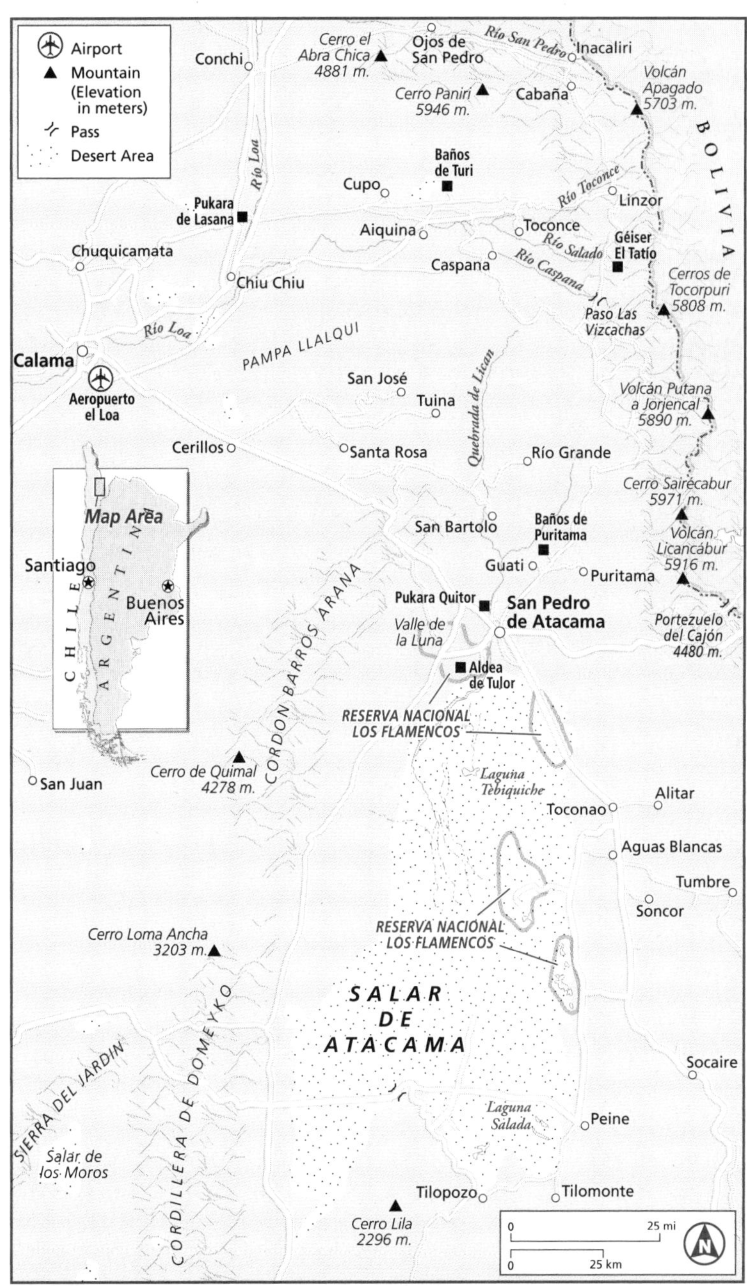
Airport
Mountain (Elevation in meters)
Pass
Desert Area
Conchi
Cerro el Abra Chica 4881 m.
Ojos de San Pedro
Río San Pedro
Inacaliri
Cerro Paniri 5946 m.
Cabaña
Volcán Apagado 5703 m.
BOLIVIA
Río Loa
Baños de Turi
Cupo
Río Toconce
Linzor
Pukara de Lasana
Aiquina
Toconce
Río Salado
Géiser El Tatío
Chuquicamata
Caspana
Río Caspana
Chiu Chiu
Cerros de Tocorpuri 5808 m.
Paso Las Vizcachas
Río Loa
PAMPA LLALQUI
Calama
Aeropuerto el Loa
Quebrada de Lican
San José
Tuina
Volcán Putana a Jorjencal 5890 m.
Cerillos
Santa Rosa
Río Grande
Cerro Sairécabur 5971 m.
Map Area
San Bartolo
Baños de Puritama
Volcán Licancábur 5916 m.
Santiago
CHILE
ARGENTINA
Buenos Aires
Guati
Puritama
Pukara Quitor
San Pedro de Atacama
Valle de la Luna
Portezuelo del Cajón 4480 m.
CORDON BARROS ARANA
Aldea de Tulor
RESERVA NACIONAL LOS FLAMENCOS
Cerro de Quimal 4278 m.
San Juan
Laguna Tebiquiche
Alitar
Toconao
Aguas Blancas
Tumbre
Soncor
RESERVA NACIONAL LOS FLAMENCOS
Cerro Loma Ancha 3203 m.
SALAR DE ATACAMA
CORDILLERA DE DOMEYKO
SIERRA DEL JARDIN
Socaire
Laguna Salada
Peine
Salar de los Moros
Tilopozo
Tilomonte
Cerro Lila 2296 m.
0 25 mi
0 25 km
N

Tips Important Info to Know Before Arriving in San Pedro

The altitude may slow you down at first, though few visitors are gravely affected by it. Don't undertake any grand expeditions to extreme altitudes during your first 2 days in San Pedro. The town has a small medical clinic, but no hospital. Don't drink tap water here, as the local supply contains trace amounts of arsenic. Bring a flashlight, too; the streets off the main drag are not lit and even a 2-block walk can be difficult to navigate.

mine. Outside of the May to July season, rooms can book up as far as 6 months ahead of time, so plan ahead.

Essentials

Getting There

Calama, a city of 120,000, is the gateway to San Pedro, 98 km (61 miles) to the west. The city depends on the mining industry, and like most boomtowns, it is ugly and hodgepodge, and reports of petty crime have soared here. Most travelers pass right through, although some spend the night only to see the Chuquicamata Copper Mine. The Indian ruins, **Pukará de Lasana,** and the colonial village, **Chiu Chiu,** are also close to Calama, although they can be visited on the way back to Calama from San Pedro via the Tatío Geysers on a very long day trip.

BY PLANE Calama's **Aeropuerto El Loa** (airport code CJC; ✆ **55/361956**) is served by **LAN Airlines** ✆ **600/526-2000;** www.lan.com), and **Sky Airline** (✆ **600/600-2828;** www.skyairline.cl). LAN has up to six daily flights from Santiago on weekdays and four on weekends; Sky has two daily flights. To get to San Pedro de Atacama, **Transfer Licancabur** (✆ **55/334194**) offers transfer services from 7am to 7:30pm for $30 per person one-way for a minimum of five people, or for $40 after 7:30pm. They'll drop you off at your hotel. Try to make friends on your flight to get a group of five or more. A taxi will cost about C$43,000—be sure to fix a price before leaving the airport.

BY BUS Direct luxury buses connect San Pedro de Atacama with Santiago, a 20-hour trip. Companies include **Tur Bus** (✆ **600/660-6600** or 2/490-7500; www.turbus.cl) and **Pullman** (✆ **600/320-3200;** www.pullman.cl). Prices range from C$34,000 to C$41,000, depending on the type of bus.

BY CAR Rental cars are available at the Calama airport. A word of caution, however, if you choose to rent. This is a vast desert and most areas are fairly isolated; roadside service is available from rental agencies, but without any services or phones on most roads, you will have to flag someone down for help—if someone comes along, that is. If you stay to main routes you should have no problem, but outside of that, be prepared for the worst, and bring extra water, food, and warm clothes in case you must spend the night on the road. A 4×4 is unnecessary unless you plan an expedition along poorly maintained roads. Most of the top hotels have all-inclusive packages that make having your own vehicle completely unnecessary. The airport has rental kiosks for **Avis** (✆ **600/601-9966** or 55/363325; www.avischile.cl), **Budget** (✆ **2/362-3200;** www.budget.cl), and **Hertz** (✆ **2/420-5222** or 55/341380; www.hertz.cl). Rates include insurance. **Alamo** (✆ **800/462-5266** or 2/225-3061; www.alamochile.com) is the cheapest, but you may want to check with a local agency when you arrive at the airport for deals. ***Tip:*** Fill the tank in Calama. The sole pump in San Pedro charges at least 30% more.

Visitor Information

Sernatur operates a small visitor center at the plaza on the corner of Antofagasta and Toconao (no phone). Hours are Saturday through Thursday from 9:30am to 1:30pm and 3 to 7pm. The best site for information is **www.sanpedroatacama.com**; its information is listed in English and Spanish.

Attractions Near Calama

CHUQUICAMATA COPPER MINE Ghost towns dot the northern desert from Chile's nitrate-mining days, but the copper-mining industry is alive and well, as is evident by Calama's **Chuquicamata mine.** This is the largest open-pit mine in the world at 4km (2½ miles) across and more than half a kilometer (⅓ mile) deep—everything at its bottom looks Lilliputian. The mine is owned by Codelco and yields more than 600,000 tons of copper per year, or 25% of Chile's export income. Few man-made wonders in the world provoke the visual awe of Chuquicamata; however, the tour will not appeal to travelers who have no interest of the inner workings of Chile's industrialization, or those with little time.

Tours run every weekday, except holidays, from 2 to 3pm; you must present yourself at the Chuquicamata office at the mine (Av. Tocopilla and José Miguel Carrera) at 1:30pm. For reservations, call ✆ **55/322122** or 55/345345, or e-mail visitas@codelco.cl. To get to the office, take an all-yellow *colectivo* taxi signed CALAMA CHUQUI from the corner of Ramirez and Aboroa in the plaza, or hire a regular taxi for about C$4,500 one-way. The mine tour is free, but donations to a foundation for underprivileged kids are encouraged. For safety reasons, wear trousers, long-sleeved shirts, and closed shoes.

COLONIAL VILLAGES & PUKARÁS Travelers interested in archeology and seeking an excursion with little physical exertion will enjoy the attractions listed below.

Chiu Chiu ★ was founded by the Spanish in the early 17th century as part of an extensive trading route that included Brazil. This speck of a village is known for the **Iglesia San Francisco** ★, the most picturesque church in the north. The whitewashed adobe walls of this weather-beaten structure are 120cm (47-in.) thick, and its doors are made of cedar and bordered with cactus, displaying a singular, Atacamanian style.

But it is more fascinating to explore the ruins of the National Monument **Pukará de Lasana** ★★, a 12th-century Atacama Indian fort influenced by the Incas, abandoned after the Spanish occupation and restored in 1951. You'll want to spend at least a half-hour wandering the labyrinthine streets that wind around the remains of 110 two- to five-story buildings.

North of Chiu Chiu is the engaging village of **Caspana,** surrounded by a fertile valley cultivated in a terraced formation like a sunken amphitheater. The village is characterized by its rock-wall and thatched-roof architecture. In the center, a tiny museum is dedicated to the culture of the area and there's an artisan shop selling textiles made from alpaca. Caspana also boasts a colonial-era church, the **Iglesia de San Lucas,** built in 1641 of stone, cactus, and mortar and covered in adobe.

Near Caspana is another National Monument, the **Pukará de Turi** ★★, the largest fortified city of the Atacama culture, built in the 12th century, and widely believed to be an Inca administrative center. The size of these ruins, with their circular towers and wide streets, is impressive, and you'll need about a half-hour to soak it all in.

Museo Arqueológico Padre le Paige ★★ This museum near the plaza displays one of South America's most fascinating collections of pre-Columbian artifacts, gathered by Padre Gustavo le Paige, a Belgian missionary. The Atacama Desert is so arid that most artifacts are notably well preserved, including hundreds of ceramics, textiles, tablets used for the inhalation of hallucinogens, tools, and more, all displayed according to time period. The museum's famous mummies and deformed craniums have been taken out in respect for the indigenous community, which was, for many, the highlight of a visit here, so plan on taking just 30 minutes to see everything.

Toconao and Padre Le Paige. ✆ **55/851002.** Admission C$1,500 adults, C$750 children. Jan–Feb daily 10am–1pm and 3–7pm; Mar–Dec Mon–Fri 9am–noon and 2–6pm, Sat–Sun 10am–noon and 2–6pm.

What to See & Do

OUTDOOR ACTIVITIES Excursions in the area either fall into preplanned trips (all-inclusive hotels), preplanned tours (made ahead of time with your travel agent), or locally owned operations. If you can afford it, I strongly recommend hiring a private guide. A private guide will take you on uncommon tours, such as backcountry roads to high-altitude salt lakes, and can adapt to your whims. For traditional tours (Valle de la Luna, the Salar de Atacama, Tatio Geysers, and archaeological tours), the following are tried and true: **Desert Adventure,** corner of Tocopilla and Caracoles (✆/fax **55/851067;** www.desertadventure.cl); **Cosmo Andino Expediciones,** Caracoles s/n (✆ **55/851069**; www.cosmoandino-expediciones.cl); or **Atacama Connection,** Caracoles and Toconao (✆/fax **55/851421;** www.atacamaconnection.com). Average prices are Valle de la Luna, C$6,000; Tatio Geysers, C$24,000; Salt Flat and altiplanic lakes, C$27,000.

The Atacama Desert is the apex of **stargazing** in the world, due to a lack of moisture in the air, low light pollution, and the high altitude. Marvel at the clear night skies with **Celestial Explorations,** Caracoles 166 (✆ **55/851935;** www.spaceobs.com), which gives amateur astronomers an opportunity to view constellations visible only in the Southern Hemisphere. The 3-hour tour leaves nightly except for evenings around a full moon and costs C$15,000, which includes transportation, use of powerful telescopes, and an easy-to-understand interpretation of the stars by a trilingual astronomer.

The **Atacama Salt Flat ★★**, a gigantic mineralized lake that is covered in many parts by a weird, putty-colored crust, is home to a **flamingo reserve.** There's also an interpretive center (no phone); it's open September through May daily from 8:30am to 8pm, and June through August daily from 8:30am to 7pm. A local favorite here is **Laguna Sejar ★**, 19km (12 miles) from San Pedro. This emerald lagoon is encircled by white salt encrustations that resemble and feel like coral reef—so bring flip-flops. Sejar affords a remarkable swimming experience, floating in water so saline it renders you virtually unsinkable.

A highlight in the Atacama Desert is the **Geysers del Tatio ★★★**; this excursion is not the easiest, as tours leave at 4 or 5am (the geysers are most active around 6–8am). These are the highest geysers in the world, and it is a marvelous spectacle to watch thick plumes of steam blow from holes in such a windswept, arid land. Interspersed between the geysers, bubbling pools encrusted with colorful minerals splash and splutter—but exercise extreme caution when walking near thin crust; careless visitors burn themselves frequently. I strongly recommend against travelers driving here—even habitual drivers to the geysers can get lost in the dark morning. If you insist, buy a map in San Pedro and get an experienced driver to run you through details of the route, or hire a day guide. If you take a day tour, make certain it stops at **Baños de Puritama ★★**, a hot springs oasis composed of rock pools that descend down a gorge, about 60km (37 miles) from the geysers (or 28km/17 miles from San Pedro, heading out on the road that borders the cemetery). Hotel explora (see "Where to Stay in San Pedro," below) runs the hot springs and charges C$10,000 to enter, but it is worth it, and the funds go to the local communities. You may want to tote a snack and a bottle of wine to enjoy while there. Changing rooms and bathrooms are available.

Two interesting archaeological sites are near town: the 12th-century, pre-Inca defensive fort **Pukará de Quitor** ★★ and the **Aldea de Tulor** ★★, the Atacama's oldest pueblo (dating from 800 B.C.). The Quitor is about 3km (2 miles) from San Pedro; to get there, walk, bike, or drive west up Calle Tocopilla and continue along the river until you see Quitor at your left. The Aldea de Tulor is a 9km (5½-mile) bike ride or drive southwest of San Pedro.

Sports Activities

BIKING The Atacama region offers excellent terrain for mountain-bike riding, including the Quebrada del Diablo (Devil's Gorge) and Valle de la Muerte (Death Valley); however, it is also enjoyable to ride across the flat desert to visit sites such as Tulor. Bike rental shops can be found along Caracoles, and they all are the same in terms of quality and charge about C$10,000 per day.

HORSEBACK RIDING Horseback riding is a quiet, relaxing way to experience the Atacama and view Indian ruins that are inaccessible by bike. If you are adept at galloping, fulfill your Lawrence of Arabia fantasies and race across a sand dune. **Rancho Cactus,** Toconao 568 (✆ **55/851506;** www.rancho-cactus.cl), and **La Herradura,** Tocopilla s/n (✆ **55/851087;** laherraduraatacama@hotmail.com), offer short and full-day rides to a variety of destinations for an average of C$7,500 per hour.

SANDBOARDING Sandboarding is the sand-dune version of snowboarding. Several places in San Pedro rent boards, and the place to head is Valle de la Muerte. It's best to go by bike or car. The more similar the bindings on your board are to snowboard bindings, the easier it will be to keep your balance. Also, take the more tapered, slightly longer boards instead of those short, wheel-less skateboards some places offer. No ski lifts are here—don't forget to take water and sunblock on this excursion, as you'll spend lots of time climbing back up the steep dunes in the heat.

VOLCANO ASCENTS Climbing one of the four volcanoes in the area requires total altitude acclimatization and being in good physical condition. It is a heart-pounding hike up, but if you can hack it, the sweeping views and the experience in itself are exhilarating. The most popular ascent is up the active Volcano Láscar to 5,400m (17,712 ft.), about a 4-hour climb, and leaves San Pedro before sunup. However, recent activity means this climb may not be available. Volcano Lincancabúr is also popular, but it requires an overnight stay at a rustic *refugio* just across the border and a Bolivian guide. Many tour companies offer these excursions; among the best is **Azimut 360,** Caracoles s/n (✆ **55/851-468** or 2/235-1519; www.azimut.cl).

Where to Stay in San Pedro

Very Expensive

Awasi ★★★ The Awasi is an award-winning inn that is one of the finest in Latin America, and wins raves from just about anyone with the money to step inside. It is luxury at its finest, with eight elegantly designed guest rooms centered on an open-air common area featuring a bar, restaurant, and pool. As boutique hotels go, the Awasi is small, and with a staff to guest ratio of two to one, this is definitely a hotel for those seeking intimacy and attentive service. Guests get a private driver, and food from the top chef in the area. The stylish decor uses high-quality materials and features top amenities. Guest rooms are referred to as cottages, with lots of space.

Tocopilla 4, San Pedro de Atacama. ✆ **888/880-3219** from North America, or 55/851460 local. www.awasi.com. 8 units. All-inclusive rates, double occupancy, per person: 2 nights $1,280; 4 nights $2,370. AE, DC, MC, V. **Amenities:** Restaurant; bar; horseback riding; outdoor pool. *In room:* Hair dryer.

Hotel explora ★★★ Moments The internationally acclaimed Hotel explora may be eclipsed by Awasi in terms of luxury, but it offers more to active travelers, and has a more friendly, unpretentious vibe. Explora is an all-inclusive hotel with an outstanding on-site restaurant, and this, coupled with a 3-block, dusty walk to San Pedro, means guests often spend little time in town. The exteriors are plain, but the enormous lounge and guest rooms are decorated with local art and painted in quiet, pastel tones. Guest rooms have ultracomfortable beds with crisp linens and fluffy down comforters. Slatted boardwalks lead guests around the property to a sybaritic, adobe-walled massage salon, a barbecue *quincho* (hut), and four irrigation-style pools. New this year is an astronomical observatory. Explora's excursions seek to introduce guests to the unknown, those off-the-beaten places where few others go. Packages include lodging, all excursions, meals, airport transfers, and an open bar. Check their website for information about new add-on trips to Bolivia and Argentina.

Domingo Atienza s/n, San Pedro de Atacama (main office: Américo Vespucio Sur 80, Piso 5, Santiago). ✆ **866/750-6699** in the U.S. and 55/851110 local, or 2/206-6060 in Santiago (reservations). Fax 2/228-4655; toll-free fax 800/858-0855 (U.S.), 800/275-1129 (Canada). www.explora.com. 52 units, 4 suites. All-inclusive rates, double occupancy, per person: 3 nights $1,920–$2,895; 4 nights $2,560–$3,860. Reduced rates available for children and teens. AE, DC, MC, V. **Amenities:** Restaurant; bar; babysitting; bikes; horseback riding; observatory; 4 outdoor pools; sauna; TV room. *In room:* Hair dryer.

Expensive

Altiplánico ★★ The hotel sits just outside of town, on the road to the Pukará de Quitor, and is a hot and dusty 10-minute walk to town. Like that of its predecessors, the striking architecture stays true to the style of the zone: river rock patios, adobe walls, peaked straw roofs, and tree trunks left in their spindly, natural state. It is quite an attractive hotel and a lower-cost option than explora (see above), and it is located on a spacious property with open views. Service can be slow and distant. Rooms are very comfortable, and the pool is delightful. This is a good hotel for a group, as it has a barbecue area near the pool for private parties.

Domingo Atienza 282, San Pedro de Atacama. ✆ **55/851212.** Fax 55/851238. www.altiplanico.com. 29 units. $200 double. AE, DC, MC, V. **Amenities:** Cafeteria; bar; bikes; large outdoor pool; room service. *In room:* No phone.

Hotel Kimal ★★ Finds The Hotel Kimal is one of my favorites in San Pedro. It doesn't have the same prestige as explora, but it offers a little slice of tranquillity for travelers. The location is central, the guest rooms are handsome, and the beds are heavenly soft. The rooms are softly lit by skylights and are fringed outside by pimiento trees and stone walkways, and most rooms have a little seating area outside. The restaurant is principally outdoors, and its proximity to the circular pool makes it a refreshing place to sit on a hot day. Consult their website for adventure-travel and relaxation-oriented packages.

Domingo Atienza 452 (at Caracoles), San Pedro de Atacama. ✆ **55/851152.** Fax 55/851030. www.kimal.cl. 19 units. $165 single; $185 double. AE, DC, MC, V. **Amenities:** Restaurant; bar; Internet; Jacuzzi; outdoor pool; room service. *In room:* Minibar.

Inexpensive

Hotel Tambillo ★ The Tambillo is the best option in this price range. The 15 units here are lined along both sides of a narrow, attractive pathway inlaid with stone. Units have arched windows and doors, and no decoration other than a light, but it's not unappealing—on the contrary, the atmosphere is fresh and clean. There's also a large restaurant and a tiny sheltered patio. It's a 4-block walk to the main street.

Gustavo (Padre) Le Paige 159, San Pedro de Atacama. ✆/fax **55/851078.** www.hoteltambillo.cl. 15 units. $70 double. No credit cards. **Amenities:** Cafeteria. *In room:* No phone.

Where to Dine in San Pedro

Many restaurants fill up after 8:30pm, so arrive early or consider making a reservation if the restaurant accepts them. Competition has drawn waiters onto the street to harangue for business; check out each restaurant's fixed-price menu, as it is often an excellent value. If you're looking for a quick, light lunch of empanadas or pizza, try **Petro Pizza,** at Toconao 447 (✆ **09/851827;** pizzas C$2,000–C$4,500); for dessert lovers, **Las Delicias de Carmen,** Gustavo (Padre) Le Paige 370 (✆ **9/089-5673**), offers apple and lemon pie, walnut tarts, strudel, and several kinds of cakes made to order or to try there at the restaurant. **Café Tierra ★★**, at Caracoles 271 (✆ **55/851585;** daily 9am–10:30pm), has vegetarian, whole-meal empanadas made from scratch while you wait, as well as sandwiches and breakfast.

Café Adobe ★★ CONTEMPORARY CHILEAN Adobe is one of the most enjoyable and cozy places to both dine and unwind in town. The blazing bonfire and thatched roof set the mood. Their best meals are satisfying meat dishes served *a la pobre* style (in olive oil with garlic), with huge hunks of beef or chicken served on a pile of fries and topped by a fried egg. Breakfasts are also good. Live music often takes place here, and though the Adobe serves dinner until 11:30pm only, the restaurant converts into a bar serving light snacks thereafter.

Caracoles 211. ✆ **55/851132.** www.cafeadobe.cl. Main courses C$3,500–C$6,000. AE, DC, MC, V. Daily 8am–1am.

Encanto ★ CHILEAN Encanto is one of the newest eateries on the scene, with a menu that highlights local Atacaman dishes and products such as *sopa de gigote* (poor man's stew), and dishes with the local grain *quinoa.* The ambience is fresh and clean, with molded adobe booths and soft light. Outside, an outdoor seating area with a fire pit makes for a pleasant place to dine. It's a good choice if you'd like to taste a few local items, and has a solid wine list, too.

Caracoles 195. ✆ **55/851939.** Main courses C$3,000–C$5,000. No credit cards. Daily 9am–1am.

La Casona ★★ CHILEAN La Casona is restaurant/bar housed in an old colonial building with soaring ceilings. Candlelit, wooden tables adorned with a few sprigs of flowers and a crackling fireplace set a quieter ambience. There's also daytime outdoor seating, a pub, and an outdoor bar in the back warmed by a blazing fire, and though it isn't the hot spot it once was with locals, it can get lively at night nevertheless. La Casona serves predominately Chilean specialties, in a slightly updated style, and delicious breakfasts. Don't miss their outstanding wine shop; it is really the only place to buy a decent bottle of wine in town.

Caracoles 195. ✆ **55/851004.** Reservations accepted. Main courses C$4,000–C$12,500. AE, DC, MC, V. Daily 8am–11pm.

Restaurant Blanco ★★ CHILEAN/INTERNATIONAL Restaurant Blanco is perhaps the most modern place on the San Pedro restaurant scene, brought to you by the owners of Adobe and La Estaka. True to its name, the atmosphere is almost entirely white and minimalist, a simple backdrop for its hallmark cuisine. The food is also modern in a chic (for these parts) fusion style. You shouldn't miss the quinoa canneloni, but the caramel ginger salmon and impressive wine list are also standouts.

Caracoles 195. ✆ **55/851164.** www.blancorestaurant.cl. Main courses C$6,500–C$8,500. AE, DC, MC, V. Daily 7–11pm.

7 THE CHILEAN LAKE DISTRICT ★★★

The region south of the Río BíoBío to Puerto Montt is collectively known as the Lake District, a fairy-tale land of emerald forests, snowcapped volcanoes, frothing waterfalls, and hundreds of lakes and lagoons that give the region its name. It is one of the most popular destinations in Chile, not only for its beauty, but for the diverse outdoor activities available and a well-organized tourism infrastructure that allows travelers to pack in a lot of action and yet rest, well fed and comfortable, in the evening.

Summers are usually balmy, but the rest of the year this region is very wet and impermeable clothing is essential, especially if you're planning on being outdoors.

EXPLORING THE REGION

The Lake District is composed of the **Región de la Araucania,** which includes the city **Temuco** and the resort area **Pucón,** and the **Región de los Lagos,** home to the port cities **Valdivia** and **Puerto Montt,** the lakefront towns of **Puerto Varas** and **Frutillar,** and the island **Chiloé.** There's plenty more to see and do outside these principal destinations, including hot springs, boat rides, adventure sports, and miles of bumpy dirt roads that make for picturesque drives through enchanting landscapes. Towns such as Puerto Varas and Pucón are excellent bases from which to take part in all of these activities. Most visitors will find they need 3 to 4 days to explore each destination, more if planning to backpack, fish, or really get out and see everything. You may consider crossing into the equally beautiful Argentine Lake District, which can be done by vehicle from Pucón or Osorno, or by boat from Puerto Varas.

TEMUCO

677km (420 miles) S of Santiago; 112km (69 miles) NW of Pucon

Temuco is the third-largest city in Chile, and its airport serves as the gateway to Pucón except for January and February when LAN Airlines offers direct service to Pucón. Temuco is home to a regional highlight, the **Mercado Municipal** ★★, a vibrant, crafts-filled market. If you've already done your souvenir shopping in Pucón (and there's a lot on offer there), skip Temuco. For information about getting to Temuco, see "Getting There" under "Pucón," below.

The Mercado can be found at Portales and Aldunate and is open Monday through Saturday from 8am to 8pm, Sunday and holidays from 8:30am to 3pm; from April to September, the market closes at 6pm Monday through Saturday. Rows of stalls sell everything from high-quality woven ponchos, knitwear, textiles, woodwork, hats, and silver Mapuche jewelry, to assorted arts and crafts.

PUCON ★

789km (489 miles) S of Santiago, 25km (16 miles) E of Temuco

Nationally and internationally known as the **"Adventure Capital of Chile,"** Pucón offers every outdoor activity imaginable: fly-fishing, rafting the Río Trancura, hiking Huerquehue and Villarrica national parks, and skiing the slopes of Volcán Villarrica—or even climbing to its bubbling crater. Yet there's also an abundance of low-key activities, such as hot-spring spas and scenic drives through landscapes that seem to have been the inspiration for every fairy tale written. You could just hang out on the beach and sun yourself, as hundreds do during the summer. Pucón is almost entirely dependent on tourism, and during the summer season, particularly December 15 to the end of February, as well as Easter week, the town teems with throngs of tourists. Hotel and business owners take advantage of this and jack up their prices, sometimes doubling their rates.

Essentials

Getting There

BY PLANE Visitors normally fly into Temuco's **Manquehue Airport** (airport code ZCO; ✆ **45/554801**) and then arrange transportation for the 1- to 1½-hour ride into Villarrica or Pucón. Most hotels will arrange transportation for you, although it's usually at an additional cost. **Transfer Temuco** (✆ **45/334-033;** www.transfertemuco.cl), a minivan service at the airport, will take a maximum of 10 guests (minimum of 4) to Pucón for C$27,500. Pucón's airport is equipped to handle jets, but for the time being, only two flights a week (on Fri and Sun) touch down here from Santiago, and only during the highest season, from mid-December to late February. Additional service is expected as demand continues to increase; for fares and up-to-the-minute schedule information, contact **LAN** (✆ **600/526-2000;** www.lan.com) and **Sky Airline** (✆ **600/600-2828;** www.skyairline.cl).

BY CAR From the Pan-American Highway south of Temuco, follow the signs for Villarrica onto Ruta 199. The road is well marked and easy to follow. If coming from Valdivia, take Ruta 205 to the Carretera Panamericana Norte (Hwy. 5). Just past Loncoche, continue east, following signs for Villarrica and Pucón.

BY BUS **Tur Bus** (✆ **600/660-6600** toll-free, or 2/270-7510; www.turbus.cl) offers service to Pucón from destinations such as Santiago, stopping first in Temuco and Villarrica. The trip is about 9 to 11 hours and generally a night journey; the cost is about C$18,000 for an economy seat and C$27,500 for an executive seat. **Buses JAC** (in Santiago, Av. Providencia 1072; ✆ **2/235-2484**) has service from Santiago to Pucón every half-hour from its Santiago terminal at Balmaceda and Aldunate (✆ **45/231330**).

VISITOR INFORMATION The local tourism board has an office at the corner of Brasil and Caupolicán streets; it's open daily from 9am to 8pm December through March and from 10am to 6:30pm April through November (✆ **45/441671**). The staff does not speak English very well. The website www.pucon.com is a corporate site listing loads of lodging options...

Outdoor Activities

With so many outdoor adventures available here, it's no wonder there's a surplus of outfitters eager to meet the demand. When choosing an outfitter in Pucón, remember that you get what you pay for, and be wary of those that treat you like just another nameless tourist. You want an experience to be memorable for the fun you've had, not for the mishaps and accidents. Most outfitters include insurance in the cost of a trip, but verify what their policy covers.

For more things to see and do in this area, see "Hot Springs Outside of Pucón" and "Natural Attractions Outside of Pucón," later.

TOUR OPERATORS Pucón's main street, O'Higgins, is chock-a-block with outdoor tour operators. Ask for guide credentials and language ability before booking. **Politur,** O'Higgins 635 (✆ **45/441373;** www.politur.com), is a well-respected tour company that offers fishing expeditions, Mapuche-themed tours, and sightseeing trips around the Seven Lakes area, in addition to volcano ascents. They're slightly more expensive than other agencies but are worth it. **Aguaventura,** Palguín 336 (✆ **45/444246;** www.aguaventura.com), is run by a dynamic French group, and their main focus is snowboarding in the winter with a shop that sells and rents boards, boots, and clothing; they also do volcano ascents with ski/snowboard descents, and rafting and kayaking, and they offer a half-day canyoneering and rappelling excursion. **Sol y Nieve,** O'Higgins and Lincoyán (✆ **45/463860;** www.solynievepucon.cl), has been on the scene for quite a while, offering rafting and volcano ascents as well as fishing, airport transfers, and excursions in other destinations around Chile. **Trancura,** O'Higgins 211-C (✆ **45/498575;** www.trancura.com), sells cheap trips to the masses, and they are best known for their rafting excursions, which they've been doing forever. Beyond that, I do not recommend any other trips with this company because of their yearly roster of inexperienced guides hired on the cheap. They do have ski and bike rentals, however, with low prices.

BIKING Several outfitters on the main street, O'Higgins, rent bicycles by the hour and provide trail information and guided tours. Bicycle rentals run an average of C$6,000 for a half-day. You can also just pedal around town, or take a pleasant, easy ride around the wooded peninsula. **Roncotrack,** O'Higgins 615 (✆ **45/441801;** www.roncotrack.cl), offers 3- and 4-hour medium-difficulty bike tours to the Ojos de Caburgua.

CANOPY TOURS ★★ The newest available adventure for thrill seekers, a canopy tour is much like a "flying fox," a swing through the treetops suspended by a cable and secured by a harness. Anybody can do this, and it is a great half-day adventure. Book your trip at **Aguaventura,** Palguin 336 (✆ **45/444246;** www.aguaventura.com).

CLIMBING THE VOLCANO ★★★ An ascent of Volcán Villarrica is perhaps the most thrilling excursion available here—there's nothing like peering into this percolating, fuming crater—but you've got to be in decent shape to tackle it. The excursion begins early in the morning, and the long climb requires crampons and ice axes, and also requires that you hire a mountain guide. It's an extremely popular excursion, drawing travelers from around the world by the dozen each day, weather permiting. Volcán Villarrica is perpetually on the verge of exploding, and sometimes trips are called off until the rumbling quiets down. Tour companies that offer this climb are **Politur** and **Sol y Nieve** (see above). Contract the services of a mountain guide directly at **Backpackers Pucón,** Palguin 695 (✆ **45/441417**), or try **Claudio Retamal** (✆ **9/927705974;** claudioreta@gmail.com). The average cost is $140 to $250, depending on group size, and includes transfers, entrance fee, insurance, equipment, and guides, but not lunch.

FISHING ★ You can pick up your fishing license at the visitor center at Caupolicán and Brasil. Guided fishing expeditions typically go to the Trancura River or the Liucura River. See a list of outfitters above for information, or try Mario at **FlyFishing Pucón,** O'Higgins 590 (✆ **45/09-760-7280;** www.flyfishingpucon.com).

GOLFING ★ Pucón's private 18-hole **Península de Pucón** golf course is open to the playing public. For information, call ✆ **45/443965,** ext 409. The cost is $52 for 18 holes. This is really the only way to get onto the private—and exclusive—peninsula that juts into the lake, by the way.

HIKING ★★ The two national parks, Villarrica and Huerquehue, and the Cañi nature reserve offer hiking trails that run from easy to difficult. An average excursion with an outfitter to Huerquehue, including transportation and a guided hike, costs about $32 per person. By far the best short-haul day hikes in the area are at Huerquehue and the Cañi nature reserve.

HORSEBACK RIDING ★ Half- and full-day horseback rides are offered throughout the area, including in the Villarrica National Park and the Liucura Valley. The **Centro de Turismo Huepilmalal** (✆ **9/643-2673**) offers day and multiday horseback rides from a small ranch about a half-hour from Pucón; you'll need to make a reservation beforehand. Tour agencies will also organize rides that leave from the **Rancho de Caballos** (✆ **45/441575**), near the Palguín thermal baths. If you're driving, the Rancho is at 30km (19 miles) on the Ruta International toward Argentina.

RAFTING ★ Rafting season runs from September to April, although some areas might be safe to descend only from December to March. The two classic descents in the area are the 14km (8¾-mile) Trancura Alto, rated at Class III to IV, and the somewhat gentler Trancura Bajo, rated at Class II to III. Both trips are very popular and can get crowded in the summer. The rafting outfitter **Trancura** (see above) also offers an excursion rafting the more technical Maichin River, which includes a barbecue lunch. **Sol y Nieve** also offers rafting. The 3-hour rafting trip on the Trancura Alto costs an average of $36; the 3-hour Trancura Bajo costs an average of $22.

SKIING The **Centro Esquí Villarrica** gives skiers the opportunity to schuss down a smoking volcano—not something you can do every day. There's a sizable amount of terrain here, and it's all open-field skiing, but, regrettably, the owners rarely open more than two of the five chairs, due to both consistently socked-in weather and a dose of laziness. You'll need to take a chairlift to the main lodge, which means that nonskiers, too, can enjoy the lovely views from the lodge's outdoor deck. There's a restaurant, child-care center, and store. The Centro has a ski school and ski equipment rental; there are slightly cheaper rentals from **Aguaventura, Sol y Nieve,** and **Trancura,** among other businesses along O'Higgins. Lift ticket prices vary but average about C$21,000. Most tour companies offer transport to and from the resort. For more information, contact one of the tour operators above.

Where to Stay

Pucón is chock-full of lodging options, including many *cabañas* (see below for info), and hostels for backpackers. Reservations are essential if visiting during the high season from December to the end of February; prices during this period nearly double at some hotels, so price-conscious travelers would be wise to visit outside these dates. Private parking or ample street parking is available and free for all hotels. Please note that the Hotel del Lago, the town's five-star hotel, burned to the ground in 2007, and the owners plan to rebuild and open it again in 2011.

Travelers spending a few days or more, or who have children or wish to cook occasionally, will find this region's *cabañas* (cabins with a kitchen or kitchenette) a tempting option. Monte Verde and Refugio Peninsula (see above) both have nice *cabañas.* **Cabañas Ruca Malal ★** at O'Higgins 770 (✆/fax **45/442297;** www.rucamalal.cl) are custom-made, cozy cabins within walking distance to shops and restaurants, and they have an outdoor pool and sauna. **Almoni del Lago Resort ★★** has a superb location on the lapping shore of Lake Villarrica, at Camino Villarrica-Pucón, Km 19 (✆ **45/442304;** www.almoni.cl). The *cabañas* are a 5-minute drive from town and come with an outdoor pool, tennis courts, and barbecues; each one sleeps two and runs from $47 to $94.

Expensive

Hotel Antumalal ★★★ Finds Perhaps it's the Antumalal's Bauhaus design and the lush gardens that reach down to a private beach, or perhaps it's the sumptuous view of the sunset on Lake Villarrica seen nightly through the hotel's picture windows or from its wisteria-roofed deck. Either way, this is simply one of the most lovely and unique hotels in Chile. Low slung and literally built into a rocky slope, the Antumalal was designed more than 50 years ago to blend with its natural environment. The lounge features walls made of glass and slabs of araucaria wood, goat skin rugs, and tree-trunk lamps. It's retro-chic, and the friendly, personal attention provided by the staff heightens a sense of intimacy with your surroundings. The rooms are all the same size, and they are very comfortable, with panoramic windows that look out onto the same gorgeous view, as well as honey-wood (very thin) walls, a fireplace, and a big, comfortable bed. The hotel's restaurant (see below) serves some of the best cuisine in Pucón.

Camino Pucón-Villarrica, Km 2. ✆ **45/441011.** Fax 45/441013. www.antumalal.com. 16 units. $239–$308 double. Rates include full breakfast. AE, DC, MC, V. **Amenities:** Restaurant; bar; outdoor pool; room service; tennis court. *In room:* Hair dryer.

Villarrica Park Lake Hotel ★★ Luxurious and expansive, this property strives to be the best in southern Chile. It has only 70 rooms, but it feels like a big corporate hotel, with its large lobby and aloof but polite staff. Extrawide doors made of local wood lead into comfortable and spacious modern rooms, all with sliding French doors that open up onto a balcony with a view of the lake. The marble bathrooms come with tub/shower combinations and heated towel racks. The spa has an exquisite selection of facials and body-work offerings. This is an excellent base for travelers who prefer large, full-service hotels, although you'd be well advised to book way in advance, as it occasionally fills up with corporate retreat groups for days at a time. Always request promotional rates when making your reservations.

Camino Pucón-Villarrica, Km 13. ✆ **45/450000.** Fax 45/450202. www.villarricaparklakehotel.cl. 70 units. $255 double; from $355 suite. AE, DC, MC, V. **Amenities:** Restaurant; bar; lounge; concierge; health club and spa; heated indoor pool; room service; limited watersports equipment. *In room:* TV, fax, hair dryer, high-speed Internet, minibar.

Moderate

La Casona de Pucón ★★ Finds A refurbished home overlooking the main square, La Casona offers tasteful and cozy lodging in a superb location. The main room includes a glorious fireplace. Rooms are decorated with a simple and natural country charm; wooden-framed beds are topped with puffy duvets. Three upstairs doubles have terraces overlooking the plaza. Ground-floor rooms can sleep up to four. Like any old house, the floors are a bit squeaky.

Lincoyán 48. ✆ **45/443179.** www.lacasonadepucon.cl 8 units. $76–$107 double. Rates include breakfast. AE, DC, MC, V. In room: TV.

Monte Verde Hotel & Cabañas ★★ Kids Built in 2003 and tastefully designed using nearly every kind of wood available in the area (including recycled alerce), this six-room hotel is about 6km (3¾ miles) from Pucón, meaning you'll need a taxi or rental car to get here. The hotel and *cabañas* are perched on a hill to afford views of the volcano and the lake. The distance from town means no summer crowds from December to February. All rooms are decorated differently; four have king-size beds, and all but one have private balconies with lake views. The bathrooms are decorated with old-fashioned sinks and bathtubs obtained from a turn-of-the-20th-century hotel in Villarrica. Attentive service and a complimentary bottle of red wine upon arrival are welcoming touches. There is also a cozy lounge with wood-burning fireplace and board games; during the high season, there are kayaks and boats available for guest use at the beach below and an outdoor pool, whirlpool, and hot tub.

Camino Pucón-Villarrica, Km 18. ✆ **45/442042.** Fax 45/443132. www.monteverdepucon.cl. 16 units, 14 *cabañas.* $67–$110 double; $85–$190 *cabaña.* Rates include buffet breakfast. AE, DC, MC, V. **Amenities:** Lounge; hot tub; pool; room service. *In room:* TV, kitchenette.

Inexpensive

For inexpensive lodging, the following hostels are pleasant and more "adult" than "youth" oriented. **¡école!** ★ at General Urrutia 592 (✆/fax **45/441675;** www.ecole.cl), has small but clean shared and private rooms, with beds blanketed with goose-down comforters for $16 to $66 for a double; they also have a restaurant (see below) with excellent breakfasts. The showers are so-so, but the price is nice and the vibe is eco- and traveler-friendly. **Refugio Peninsula Bed & Breakfast** ★, at Clemente Holazpfel 11 (✆ **45/443398;** www.refugiopeninsula.cl), is a hostal with a central location near the beach and restaurants, shared rooms with private bathrooms ($30 per person), and two doubles for $70 per night.

Where to Dine

Patagonia, Fresia 223 (✆ **45/443165**), is a good spot for a hot chocolate and a piece of cake on a rainy day or an ice cream in the summer. **Latitude 39** ★★, Alderete 324 (✆ **743/00016;** www.latitude39chile.com), is run by a couple from California and has the best breakfast, burgers, and espresso in town. **Café de la "P,"** Lincoyán 395 (✆ **45/442018;** www.cafedelap.com), has a menu with sandwiches, cakes, coffee drinks, and cocktails. It's a nice place to unwind with a drink in the evening and is open until 4am in the summer.

Antumalal ★★ **(Moments)** INTERNATIONAL The Hotel Antumalal's restaurant serves some of the most flavorful cuisine in Pucón, with creative dishes that are well prepared and seasoned with herbs from an extensive garden. In fact, most of the vegetables used here are local and organic; the milk comes from the family's own dairy farm. Try a thinly sliced beef carpaccio followed by chicken stuffed with smoked salmon, grilled local trout, or any one of the pastas. There's a good selection of wine and an ultracool cocktail lounge for an after-dinner drink (but it's tiny and not a "happening" spot). It's worth a visit for the view of Lake Villarrica alone.

Camino Pucón-Villarrica, Km 2. ✆ **45/441011.** Fax 45/441013. Reservations recommended. Main courses C$6,500–C$9,000. AE, DC, MC, V. Daily noon–4pm and 8–10pm.

¡école! ★ **(Value)** VEGETARIAN This is a predominantly vegetarian restaurant serving calzones, quiche, pizza, burritos, chop suey, and more. Sandwiches come on homemade bread, and breakfast is very good and inexpensive, featuring American breakfast as well as Mexican and Chilean. There are also fresh salads, and a lovely outdoor patio where you can dine under the grapevine in good weather. They have some of the best

Chilean *pebre* (a salsa served with bread as an appetizer) anywhere. The service is slow and disorganized, and they usually offer a shorter menu during the winter.

General Urrutia 592. ✆/fax **45/441675.** Main courses C$4,000–C$6,500. MC, V. Daily 8am–11pm.

La Maga ★★ URUGUAYAN/STEAK La Maga is undoubtedly the best *parrilla* (steakhouse) in town. The restaurant originated in the beach town of Punta del Este, Uruguay, and the food is excellent, especially the meat, chicken, and fish grilled on the giant barbecue on the patio. Order a bottle of wine and a large fresh salad and people-watch through large picture windows overlooking the street. Try the grilled salmon with capers if you're in the mood for fish. But, really, the best cuts here are the beef filets, known as *lomos,* served with mushrooms, Roquefort, or pepper sauce. The *bife de chorizo* (sirloin) is thick and tender. For dessert, the flan here stands out.

Fresia 125. ✆ **45/444277.** Main courses C$6,000–C$8,000. AE, MC, V. Daily noon–4pm and 7pm–midnight.

Viva Perú! ★ Kids PERUVIAN This Peruvian restaurant is a favorite hangout for locals, offering warm, personalized service and tasty cuisine. For solo travelers, there is bar seating, and there is a patio with a volcano view. The restaurant specializes in *ceviche* and seafood *picoteos* (appetizer platters), which are an excellent accompaniment to a frosty pisco sour. Daily fixed-price lunch specials include a mixed salad, entree (steamed or grilled fish, pork loin, or chicken), and coffee for about $8. The restaurant offers one of the few kids' menus in the area. Try the sugary-sweet *suspiro limeño,* a creamy Peruvian traditional dessert.

Lincoyan 372. ✆/fax **45/444025.** Main courses C$6,000–C$7,500. AE, DC, MC, V. Daily noon–2am.

Pucon After Dark

A fire completely gutted the Hotel del Lago and casino in 2007. Plans for reconstruction are moving slowly; the new casino is currently open at Clemente Holzapfel 190. For bars, **El Bosque,** 524 O'Higgins (✆/fax **45/444025**), is a popular local hangout open from 6pm until around 3am Tuesday through Sunday; it has Internet and a good fusion cuisine menu. **Mamas & Tapas,** at O'Higgins 597 (✆/fax **45/449002**), has long been one of the most popular bars in Pucón. It gets packed in the summer and has excellent music, even with DJs during peak season.

HOT SPRINGS OUTSIDE OF PUCON

All the volcanic activity in the region means there are plenty of *baños termales,* or hot springs, that range from rustic rock pools to full-service spas with massage and saunas. The two spas below are my favorites.

Termas de Huife ★ Nestled in a narrow valley on the shore of the Liucura River, Huife operates as a full-service health spa for day visitors, and there are attractive cabins for overnight stays. The complex features two large, soothing outdoor thermal pools and a cold-water pool, as well as private thermal bathtubs, individual whirlpools, and massage salons. There are two- and four-person *cabañas* with wood-burning stoves and Japanese-style, sunken showers and baths that run thermal water—but the price is expensive for Chilean cabin lodging. Because these *termales* are closer to Pucón, they receive many visitors during the summer.

Road to Huife, 33km (20 miles) east of Pucón. ✆/fax **45/441222.** www.termashuife.cl. 10 units. $230 double. Day-use fee C$10,500 adults, children 3–10 C$6,000, children 2 and under free. AE, DC, MC, V. Thermal baths daily 9am–8pm year-round. **Amenities:** Restaurant; cafeteria; exercise room; Jacuzzi; 3 outdoor pools; sauna. *In room:* TV, minibar.

Termas Geométricas ★★★ Finds I can't stop raving about these hot springs. They are a 90-minute drive from Pucón (near Coñaripe), but if you have the time, put these *termas* on your itinerary because they are the best in Chile. Designed by the architect of the explora hotels, there are more than a dozen pools built of handsome gray slate tiles in a lush, jungle-draped ravine, each one linked by a winding, terra cotta–colored boardwalk. It's incredibly natural, especially compared to complexes like Huife (see above). The style is minimalist and decidedly Japanese, with touches such as sinks with stream-fed taps, and changing rooms with grass roofs—utterly relaxing and enjoyable day or night, winter or summer. A small cafe serves coffee and snacks; picnic lunches are allowed during the winter only, and alcohol is prohibited. It's not cheap ($28 to enter), but it's money well spent. Check their website for a map, or ask any tour company to take you here.

12km (7½ miles) from Coñaripe on the road to Palguín. ✆ **2/214-1214** or 9/442-5420. Fax 2/214-1147. www.termasgeometricas.cl. C$14,000 adults, C$6,000 children 14 and under. Rate includes towel. No credit cards. Thermal baths daily 10am–9pm summer, 11am–8pm rest of year. **Amenities:** Cafe.

NATURAL ATTRACTIONS OUTSIDE OF PUCON

Parque Nacional Huerquehue

Parque Nacional Huerquehue boasts the best short-haul hike in the area, the **Sendero Los Lagos.** This 12,500-hectare (30,875-acre) park opens as a steeply walled amphitheater draped in matted greenery and crowned by a forest of lanky araucaria trees. There are a handful of lakes here; the first you come upon is Lago Tinquilco, upon whose shore sits a tiny, ramshackle village built by German colonists in the early 1900s.

GETTING THERE & BASICS The park is 35km (22 miles) from Pucón. JAC buses have daily service to the park (several times per day depending on season), and most tour companies offer minivan transportation. If you're driving your own car, head out of Pucón on O'Higgins toward Lago Caburga until you see the sign for Huerquehue that branches off to the right. From here it's a rutted, dirt road that can be difficult to manage when muddy. Conaf charges C$2,500 for adults and C$500 for kids to enter, and is open daily from 8:30am to 6pm.

VALDIVIA ★★

839km (520 miles) S of Santiago

Valdivia is a university town on the edge of a river delta, about a 20-minute drive from the coast. It has more charm than Temuco or Puerto Montt, yet Valdivia receives mixed reviews from visitors. It makes a nice lunch stop during a driving tour, and an afternoon boat trip around the delta or a drive to the market and beach town of Niebla are particularly pleasant. Parts of Valdivia are indeed ugly, with a mess of architectural styles—yet many lovely, old German immigrant homes line the waterfront, and there's a lively market where visitors can watch fishmongers peddle their catch of the day while pelicans, cormorants, and gigantic sea lions beg for scraps. If you are in Pucón for several days, consider a quick visit here or an overnight stay. Or if you are driving from Pucón to Puerto Varas or Puerto Montt, this makes a good midway stop for lunch by the market.

Valdivia has suffered attacks, floods, fires, and the disastrous earthquake (the strongest ever recorded) and tsunami of 1960 that nearly drowned the city under 3m (10 ft.) of water. During World War II, Valdivia's German colonists were blacklisted, ruining the economy. So if Valdivia looks a little weary—well, it's understandable. There are tours here to visit the tiny towns and ancient forts at the mouth of the bay that protected the city from seafaring intruders.

Getting There

BY PLANE Valdivia's **Aeródromo Pichoy** (airport code ZAL; ✆ **63/272295**) is about 32km (20 miles) northeast of the city. **LAN** (✆ **600/526-2000;** www.lan.com) has two daily flights from Santiago, one daily flight to Concepción, two weekly flights to Temuco, and one weekly flight to Puerto Montt. A **taxi** to town costs about C$11,000, or you can catch a ride on one of **Transfer Valdivia**'s minibuses (✆ **63/225533**) for C$3,500.

BY BUS The bus terminal (✆ **63/212212**) is at Anwandter and Muñoz, and nearly every bus company passes through here; there are multiple daily trips from Pucón and Santiago. The average cost for a ticket from Santiago to Valdivia is C$24,000; from Pucón to Valdivia, it is C$6,000.

BY CAR From the Pan-American Highway, take Ruta 205 and follow the signs for Valdivia. A car is not really necessary in Valdivia, as most attractions can be reached by boat, foot, or taxi. It's about a 2-hour drive from Pucón, 1½ hours from Temuco, and 3 hours from Puerto Montt.

Special Events

The city hosts a grand yearly event, the **Verano en Valdivia,** with several weeks of festivities that begin in January, culminating with the **Noche Valdiviana** on the third Saturday in February. On this evening, hundreds of floating candles and festively decorated boats fill the Valdivia River, and there is a fireworks display. Valdivia is packed during this time, so hotel reservations are essential.

What to See & Do

Elisabeth Lajtonyi at **Outdoors Chile** (✆ **63/287833;** www.outdoors-chile.com) can plan your Valdivia itinerary, including hotels, transfers, and personalized sightseeing tours.

BOAT TRIPS Valdivia's myriad waterways make for an enjoyable way to explore the region, and there are a variety of destinations and boating options that leave from the pier Muelle Schuster at the waterfront, including yachts, catamarans, and an antique steamer. Tours are in full swing during the summer, and although there's limited service during the off season, it is possible for a group to hire a launch for a private trip. The most interesting journeys sail through the **Carlos Anwanter Nature Sanctuary** to the **San Luis de Alba de Cruces Fort** and to **Isla Mancera** and **Corral** to visit other 17th-century historic forts; both tours run about 5 to 6 hours round-trip and usually include meals.

Embarcaciones Bahía (✆ **63/348727;** sergiosalgado60@yahoo.es) operates throughout the year with quick trips around Isla Teja (C$5,000 per person; children 9 and under ride free), and tours to Isla Mancera and Corral can be arranged during the off season with a negotiated price or when there are enough passengers. Other trips to Isla Mancera and Corral are offered by **Orión III** (✆/fax **63/247896;** hetours@telsur.cl), which also includes a stop at the Isla Huapi Natural Park (www.islahuapi.cl); the price is C$14,000 for adults, C$7,500 for children ages 3 to 12. Prices include the trip, lunch on Isla Huapi, and afternoon tea on board. By far the most luxurious is the **Catamarán Marqués de Mancera** (✆ **63/249191;** www.marquesdemancera.cl), which offers Isla Mancera and Corral tours, with lunch and snacks included, and evening dinner cruises (only specially organized for large groups); both cost from C$10,000 per person.

Other Attractions

The bustling **Mercado Fluvial** ★★ at Muelle Schuster (Av. Prat at Maipú) is the principal attraction in Valdivia; kids especially love to see the array of fish spread out by fishmongers and watch lanky pelicans and enormous sea lions bark for handouts.

A block up from the waterfront, turn right on Yungay and head south until the street changes into **General Lagos** at San Carlos, where you'll find stately, historic homes built by German immigrants between 1840 and 1930. At General Lagos 733 is the **Centro Cultural El Austral** ★, commonly known as the Casa Hoffman, of the Thater-Hoffman family who occupied the home from 1870 until 1980. It's open Tuesday through Sunday from 10am to 1pm and 4 to 7pm; admission is free (✆ **63/213658**). The first floor of this handsome building has been furnished to re-create the interior as it would have looked during the 19th century. At the junction of General Lagos and Yerbas Buenas, you'll find the **Torreón Los Canelos,** a 1781 defensive tower built to protect the southern end of the city—but if you're strapped for time, forget it.

Across the bridge in the neighborhood known as Isla Teja, visitors will find the splendid history museum, the **Museo Histórico y Antropológico Mauricio van de Maele** ★★ (✆ **63/212872;** Dec 15–Mar 15 Mon–Sun 10am–1pm and 2–8pm; Mar 16–Dec 14 Tues–Sun 10am–1pm and 2–6pm; admission C$2,000 adults, C$400 children 12 and under). To get there, cross the Pedro de Valdivia bridge, walk up a block, turn left, and continue for half a block. The museum is housed in the grand family home of Karl Anwanter, brewery owner and vociferous supporter and leader of German immigrants. The museum is a collection of antiques, photos, letters, everyday objects, and more culled from local well-to-do families, historical figures, Mapuche Indians, and Spanish conquistadors. Next door is the **Museo de Arte Moderno** ★ (✆ **63/221968;** www.macvaldivia.uach.cl; Tues–Sun 10am–1pm and 4–7pm; admission C$1,200), one of Chile's most important modern art museums, with rotating displays. Leaving the museum, turn right and continue north on Los Laureles until you reach the **Universidad Austral de Chile.** Once inside the campus, the road veers right; follow it and the signs to the **Jardín Botánico** ★★, a lovely botanical garden created in 1957.

Where to Stay

Airesbuenos International Hostel ★ *Value* This beautiful house is a historical monument in Valdivia and dates back to 1890. The young and friendly owner, Lionel Brossi, has meticulously restored the entire house and oversees the day-to-day operation of the hostel. Special touches can be found everywhere, which is rare when it comes to budget accommodations. A vintage staircase leads to 11 rooms of varying sizes, all with beautiful (and original) hardwood floors. Some of the rooms have bunk beds for backpackers; the bathroom in the hallway is clean and spacious. The five rooms with private bathrooms are pleasant and bright; the front room even has a balcony with river views. The hotel is located about a 15-minute walk from the market and most restaurants. A common kitchen is available for cooking, and there's a book exchange.

General Lagos 1036, Valdivia. ✆/fax **63/206304.** www.airesbuenos.cl. 11 units. $14 per person in a shared room; $54 double with private bathroom. All rates include breakfast. AE, DC, MC, V. **Amenities:** Lounge; Internet.

Hotel Dreams Pedro de Valdivia ★ Opened in March 2009, this modern white eight-story hotel has completely changed the face of Valdivia's skyline. It's got a whopping 104 rooms, a casino, a large spa, and a larger convention center. Sophisticated rooms are a black-and-gray contrast of modern furniture and blistering views from large windows.

Some have terraces. Ask for a view overlooking the Calle Calle River. Bathrooms have separated showers. Part of a Chilean hotel chain, Dreams cuts corners in a few places, like in charging for Wi-Fi over 30 minutes. The hotel's Doña Inés grill restaurant is one of the best in town.

Carampague 190. ✆ **63/267000.** www.mundodreams.com. 104 units. $167–$210 double. AE, MC, DC, V. **Amenities**: 2 restaurants; rooftop lounge; casino; indoor pool; full-service spa; Wi-Fi. *In room*: Minibar.

Hotel Naguilán ★ **Moments** About a 20-minute walk from the edge of downtown, the Hotel Naguilán boasts a pretty riverfront location and attractive accommodations. The hotel is housed in a converted 1890 shipbuilding edifice. All rooms face the Río Valdivia and the evening sunset; from here it's possible to watch waterfowl and colorful tugs and fishing skiffs motor by. The rooms are divided into 15 newer (superior) units in a detached building and 17 (standard) units in an older wing with a more dated decor. The newer terrace units sit directly on the riverbank and feature contemporary floral design in rich colors, classic furniture, ample bathrooms, and a terrace patio. The hotel has a private dock for guests to board excursion boats, and the hotel restaurant, serving international cuisine, has picture windows with a view of the river.

General Lagos 1927, Valdivia. ✆ **63/212851.** Fax 63/219130. www.hotelnaguilan.com. 32 units. $98 standard double (older units); $132 double (newer units); from $178 suite. AE, DC, MC, V. **Amenities:** Restaurant; bar; concierge; outdoor pool; room service; Wi-Fi. *In room:* TV, minibar.

Where to Dine

For an inexpensive meal, the **Municipal Market** at the waterfront at Yungay and Libertad has several simple restaurants with fresh seafood and Chilean specialties. Valdivia's two traditional cafes, Café Haussman and Entre Lagos, are excellent spots for lunch. **Café Haussman,** O'Higgins 394 (✆ **63/202219;** Mon–Sat 8am–9pm), is a tiny, old-fashioned diner that serves *crudos* (steak tartare), beer on tap, and sandwiches amid local color. **Entre Lagos,** Pérez Rosales 640 (✆ **63/212039;** daily 9am–10pm), is famous in Chile for its chocolate and marzipan, but it also serves equally delicious crepes, juicy sandwiches, heavenly cakes, and cappuccinos.

La Calesa ★ **Finds** PERUVIAN/INTERNATIONAL Owned and operated by a Peruvian family, the cozy La Calesa features spicy cuisine served in the old Casa Kaheni, a gorgeous 19th-century home with high ceilings, wood floors, and antique furnishings. The menu features Peruvian fare along with several international dishes. Standouts include grilled beef tenderloin in a cilantro sauce; *ají de gallina,* a spicy chicken and garlic stew with rice; or any of the nightly specials. The pisco sours are very good, as is the wine selection.

Yungay 735. ✆ **63/225467.** Dinner reservations recommended. Main courses C$6,000–C$7,500. AE, DC, MC, V. Mon–Fri noon–4pm and 8pm–midnight; Sat 8pm–midnight.

New Orleans INTERNATIONAL This is Valdivia's most popular restaurant, tucked away on a side street a few streets in from the river, and it seems to always be busy. There's a pleasant, if crowded, patio and a charming dining room with more spacious seating. The food here is consistently good and fresh and the menu changes often. Main courses often include pastas, grilled salmon or tuna, chicken, and steak. This is a loud, boisterous place, often filled with families with children early in the evening. Later, the atmosphere is more publike.

Esmeralda 682. ✆ **63/218771.** Dinner reservations recommended. Main courses C$6,000–C$7,500. AE, DC, MC, V. Mon–Fri noon–4pm and 7pm–midnight; Sat 5pm–midnight.

FRUTILLAR ★★

58km (36 miles) S of Osorno, 46km (29 miles) N of Puerto Montt

Frutillar offers a rich example of the architecture popular with German immigrants to the Lago Llanquihue area, and it is situated to take advantage of the dynamite view of the Osorno and Calbuco volcanoes. The town is smaller and quieter than Puerto Varas, and is farther away from the national park, but all tour operators can plan excursions around the area from here (see "Outdoor Activities" under "Puerto Varas," below). Frutillar is divided into the rather scrappy "high" area, which you'll drive straight through, and the "low" area along the lakeshore, where visitors will find a good supply of attractive hotels and bed-and-breakfasts.

Essentials

Getting There

For general information, see "Puerto Varas," below. For local bus service, frequent, inexpensive buses leave from the bus terminal in Puerto Montt; from Puerto Varas, take one of the small buses labeled FRUTILLAR that leave from the corner of Walker Martínez and San Bernardo.

BY TAXI Taxis will take you to Frutillar for around C$14,000 to C$17,500, depending on whether you're coming from Puerto Varas, Puerto Montt, or the airport. Agree on a price with your driver before leaving.

BY CAR From Puerto Montt or Puerto Varas, head north on the Panamericana Highway and look for signs for Frutillar. Remember to continue down to Frutillar "Bajo" (along the lakeshore) instead of getting off at Frutillar "Alto."

Visitor Information

The **Oficina de Información Turística** is along the coast at Costanera Philippi (✆ **65/421080**); it's open January through March daily from 8:30am to 1pm and 2 to 9pm. The **Oficina de Turismo Municipal** is open year-round and can be found at Av. Bernardo Philippi 753 (✆ **65/421685;** daily 8am–1pm and 2–5:30pm).

Exploring Frutillar

The two most visited attractions in town are the **Museo de la Colonización Alemana de Frutillar ★★** and the **Reserva Forestal Edmundo Winkler.** The museum (✆ **65/421142**) is located where Arturo Prat dead-ends at Calle Vicente Pérez Rosales. Admission is C$2,000 adults, C$450 children 12 and under; it's open daily April to November from 10am to 1pm and 2 to 6pm, and December to March from 10am to 1pm and 3 to 8pm. It features a collection of 19th-century antiques, clothing, and artifacts gathered from various German immigrant families in the area. It's quite interesting if you have 30 minutes to spare.

The *reserva* is run by the University of Chile and features a trail winding through native forest, giving visitors an idea of what the region looked like before immigrants went timber-crazy and chopped down a sizable percentage of trees in this region. It's open year-round daily from 10am to 7pm; admission costs C$1,500 for adults and C$400 for kids. To get there, you'll have to walk 1km (a half-mile) up to the park from the entrance at Calle Caupolican at the northern end of Avenida Philippi.

Where to Stay

Private parking or ample street parking is available and free for all hotels. Hotels can arrange excursions in the area, or can put you in contact with a tour operator who does.

Hotel Ayacara ★★ (Finds) The Ayacara is a top choice in Frutillar, housed in a superbly renovated 1910 antique home on the coast of Lago Llanquihue. The interior of the hotel is made of light wood and this, coupled with large, plentiful windows, translates into bright accommodations. The rooms come with comfy beds, crisp linens, wood headboards, country furnishings, and antiques brought from Santiago and Chiloé. The Capitán room is the largest and has the best view. An attractive dining area serves seasonal meals during the summer, and there's a small, ground-level outdoor deck with beach access and a TV/video lounge. The staff can arrange excursions around the area; fly-fishing excursions are their specialty.

Av. Philippi 1215, Frutillar. ✆/fax **65/421550.** www.hotelayacara.cl. 8 units. $135–$165 double; $100–$130 Capitán double. Rates include breakfast. AE, DC, MC, V. **Amenities:** Restaurant; bar; Wi-Fi. *In room:* TV.

Hotel Elun ★★ This azure-colored hotel is a good bet for anyone seeking modern accommodations, a room with a view, and a quiet, forested location. The hotel is made almost entirely of light, polished wood and was designed to take full advantage of the views. The lounge, bar, and lobby sit under a slanted roof that ends with picture windows; there's also a deck outside. Double standard rooms are decently sized and feature berber carpets and clean white bathrooms. The superiors are very large. The hotel is attended by its owners, who will arrange excursions. A restaurant serves dinner during the summer, and breakfast can be ordered in your room.

200m (656 ft.) from start of Camino Punta Larga, at the southern end of Costanera Phillipi. ✆/fax **65/420055.** www.hotelelun.cl. 14 units. $80–$126 double. Rates include breakfast. DC, MC, V. **Amenities:** Restaurant (summer only); lounge; bikes; library; sauna; Wi-Fi. *In room:* TV.

Where to Dine

You'll find better restaurants in Puerto Varas, and that town's proximity makes it feasible to plan on dining there. The best dining in town is at the **Hotel Ayacara** (above). Otherwise, the traditional **Club Alemán** ★, San Martín 22 (✆ **65/421249;** daily noon–4pm and 8pm–midnight), serves Chilean and German specialties. For smoked meats, game, and standard Chilean fare, try **El Ciervo,** San Martín 64 (✆ **65/420185;** daily noon–10pm).

PUERTO VARAS ★

20km (12 miles) N of Puerto Montt; 996km (618 miles) S of Santiago

Puerto Varas is one of Chile's most charming villages, located on the shore of Lago Llanquihue. Like Pucón, it is an adventure travel hub, and it is also the gateway to the **Parque Nacional Vicente Pérez Rosales** (see "Parque Nacional Vicente Pérez Rosales & the Lake Crossing to Argentina," below). Unlike its neighbor Puerto Montt, 20 minutes away, it is a spruce little town, with wood-shingled homes, a rose-encircled plaza, a handsomely designed casino, and an excellent tourism infrastructure that provides all the necessary services for visitors without seeming too touristy. It can get crowded during the summer months, but not as busy as Pucón; seemingly because of its distance from Santiago. The city was built by the sweat and tenacity of German immigrants, and later it became a port for goods being shipped from the Lago Llanquihue area to Puerto Montt (mostly timber). Today most of the area's middle- and upper-middle-class residents call Puerto Varas home and commute to Puerto Montt and other surrounding places for work.

Essentials

Getting There

BY PLANE **El Tepual** airport (airport code PMC; ✆ **65/294161**) is almost equidistant from Puerto Montt and Puerto Varas; it's about 25km (16 miles) from the airport to Puerto Varas. A taxi from the airport costs between C$9,500 and C$14,000, or you can arrange a transfer with **Buses ETM,** by either calling ahead or approaching their booth at the airport (✆ **32/294294**). They charge C$15,000 for a car for a maximum of three people. There normally are a few people waiting for a transfer, so you can drop the price by traveling together into town. **LAN** (✆ **600/526-2000;** www.lan.com) serves the El Tepual airport with nine daily flights from Santiago. **Sky Airline** (✆ **600/600-2828;** www.skyairline.cl) also has one daily flight to the El Tepual airport. Ask your hotel about a transfer shuttle, as many include one in their price.

BY BUS **Buses Cruz del Sur,** San Francisco 1317 and Walker Martínez 239 (✆ **65/236969** or 65/231925), and **Buses Tas Choapa,** Walker Martínez 320 (✆ **65/233831**), offer service to and from major cities in southern Chile, including Santiago. **Tas Choapa** and the Argentine company **Andesmar,** Walker Martinez 320 (✆ **65/233831;** www.andesmar.com.ar), have service to Bariloche, Argentina (Tas Choapa Thurs–Sun; Andesmar on Mon, Wed, and Fri). **Bus Norte,** Walker Martínez 239 (✆ **65/236969**), has daily service to Bariloche.

BY CAR Puerto Varas is just 20km (12 miles) north of Puerto Montt and 88km (55 miles) south of Osorno via the Panamericana. There are two exits leading to Puerto Varas, and both deposit you downtown. To get to Frutillar, you need to get back on the Panamericana, go north, and take the exit for that town. There is about a C$450 toll to enter the off ramp, and another toll for about C$750 to enter Puerto Montt.

Getting Around

BY BUS **Buses Cruz del Sur** offers transportation to Chiloé and nearly 20 daily trips to Puerto Montt, leaving from an office in Puerto Varas, at Walker Martínez 239 (✆ **65/236969** or 65/231925). There are also cheap minibuses that leave frequently from the corner of Del Salvador and San Pedro across from the pet shop, leaving you at the bus terminal in Puerto Montt. You'll also find minibuses at San Bernardo and Walker Martínez that go to Ensenada, Petrohué, and Lago Todos los Santos every day at 9:15am, 11am, 2pm and 4pm.

BY CAR Renting a car is perhaps the most enjoyable way (but also the most expensive) to see the surrounding area. Try **Adriazola Turismo Expediciones,** Santa Rosa 340 (✆ **65/233477;** www.adriazolaflyfishing.com); **Hunter Rent a Car,** San José 130 (✆ **65/237950;** hunters@telsur.cl); or **Jardinsa,** Mirador 135 (✆/fax **65/235050;** www.jardinsa.cl).

Visitor Information

The **Casa del Turista** tourism office can be found at the pier on the shore (✆ **65/237956;** www.puertovaras.org) and is open daily from December to March from 9am to 10pm, and April to November from 9am to 1:30pm and 3 to 7pm.

A Walk Around Town

Puerto Varas is compact enough to explore by foot, which is really the best way to view the wood-shingled homes built by German immigrants from 1910 until the mid-1930s. Eight of these homes have been declared national monuments, yet there are dozens more clustered mostly around the old train tracks reached by walking west on Del Salvador (heading away from downtown).

Take a quick tour by walking up San Francisco from Del Salvador and turning right on María Brunn, to view the neo-Romantic **Iglesia del Sagrado Corazón de Jesús,** built between 1915 and 1918 and modeled after the Marienkirche in the Black Forest. Continue along María Brunn and turn right on Purísima, where you'll encounter the **Gasthof Haus** (1930), the **Casa Yunge** (1932), the **Casa Horn** (1925), and finally **Casa Kaschel** at Del Salvador. More homes are concentrated near Dr. Giesseler and San Ignacio streets, reached by heading left on Del Salvador. Follow the road that borders the train tracks north and then east until it ends; then turn right and then left on Klenner, and follow it to Turismo Street to view the town's grandest historical home, **Casa Kuschel** (1910), now owned by American ecologist/philanthropist Doug Tompkins. A pleasant, easy walk (or short drive) extends up a dirt road from Casa Kuschel to **Parque Phillippi,** a lookout point with a sweeping view of Puerto Varas, the lake, and Mt. Osorno. Pick up a map at the visitor center.

Outdoor Activities

TOUR OPERATORS & OUTFITTERS Tour companies and outfitters seem to pop up annually. Some, however, have enough experience to warrant my recommendation. **Aquamotion Expediciones,** San Pedro 422 (✆ **65/232747;** fax 65/235938; www.aquamotion.cl), is a professional, competent operation with a bilingual staff that can organize trekking, rafting on the Petrohué, horseback riding, canyoneering, photo safaris, journeys to Chiloé, and much more. They also custom plan excursions and offer packages that include accommodations; and they are better than their competition, CTS, across the street. **Puelo Adventure,** San Pedro 311 (✆ **65/9799192**), and Aquamotion Expediciones both offer ascents of Volcano Osorno, for about $180 for two, which includes gear, lunch, and transportation.

For city tours and sightseeing tours around the Lake District, including trips to Frutillar, Puyehue, and Chiloé, try **TurisTour,** San Juan 430 (✆ **65/437127;** fax 65/236151; www.turistour.cl). They can also arrange for boat excursions on Lago Todos los Santos and the Chilean leg of the lake crossing to Argentina (for information, see "Parque Nacional Vicente Pérez Rosales & the Lake Crossing to Argentina," below).

For trips to Bariloche via road, contact **LS Travel,** San José 130, Puerto Varas (✆ **65/232424;** www.lstravel.com).

BOATING From December to February, visitors may rent kayaks and canoes near the pier at the beach. For a sunset cruise on the lake, board the 20m (65-ft) wooden motorboat **Captain Haase** (✆ **65/235120**) or ask at the tourist office by the pier for more information.

FISHING Fly-fishing is one of the region's top outdoor activities, principally along the shores of Río Puelo, Río Maullín, and Río Petrohué. The most exclusive fishing expeditions are offered to guests at the Yan Kee Way Lodge (see "Where to Stay Near the Park," below). There's also **Gray's Fly-Fishing Supplies,** which has two shops, at San José 192 and San Francisco 447 (✆ **65/310734;** www.grayfly.com). Gray's is a central hub for information, gear, and fishing licenses, and they can arrange day trips for river and lake fishing. Another good option for day trips is **Adriazola Fly Fishing,** Santa Rosa 340 (✆ **65/233477;** www.adriazolaflyfishing.com). The owner, Adrian, will custom arrange any fly-fishing and trolling day tour with a bilingual guide. Both outfitters charge around $350 for a full day (for two guests, including transportation, boat, lunch, wine, and fishing guides).

The exclusive, full-service **Río Puelo Lodge** (✆ **2/229-8533** in Santiago; fax 2/201-8042; www.riopuelolodge.cl) caters to fly-fishermen and hunters, but also offers horseback riding, boat rides, water-skiing, and more. The stately wood-and-stone lodge is tucked well into the backcountry on the shore of Lago Tagua Tagua, and it caters mainly to groups of guys who come to have fun in the backcountry. Packages average around $350 per person per day, including meals, open bar, guide, boats, horseback riding, trekking, and heated pool. Ask about discounts for groups. Also see Yan Kee Way Lodge ("Where to Stay Near the Park," below).

HORSEBACK RIDING **Campo Aventura,** San Bernardo 318, Puerto Varas (✆ **65/232910;** www.campo-aventura.com), offers year-round horseback riding leaving from a camp in Valle Cochamó, south of the national park. Campo Aventura has day and multiday trips, and **Aquamotion** also has day trips within the national park. Horseback riding through a forested area is a good rainy-day activity—just throw on a waterproof jacket and pants and let the horse walk through the mud for you.

KAYAKING **Ko'Kayak,** a small outfit run by French kayak enthusiasts, is the best choice for kayaking both for the day and for multiday kayak/camping trips. They have a base in Ensenada at Km 40, but make a reservation at their main office at San José 320 (✆ **65/511648** or 9/310-5272; www.kokayak.com).

RAFTING Few rivers in the world provide rafters with such stunning scenery as the Río Petrohué, whose frothy green waters begin at Lago Todos los Santos and end at the Reloncaví Estuary. Rafters are treated to towering views of the volcanoes Osorno and Puntiagudo. The river is Class III and suitable for nearly everyone, but there are a few rapids to negotiate with sudden bursts of heavy paddling, so timid travelers might consult with their tour agency before signing up. For rafting, go to **AlSur Expediciones,** Del Salvador 100 (✆ **65/232300;** www.alsurexpeditions.com).

Where to Stay

Arrebol Patagonia ★★★ Moments Anyone with an eye for design and style won't find a more appealing hotel in the entire Lake District of Chile. The woodwork alone is truly stunning, from an ancient and giant treeroot that serves as the reception desk to recycled alerce-wood closets. In fact, all the wood is recycled and the inn also has geothermic heating. Contrasting with the wood are white walls, sheets, and ceilings, and touches of color. It's sophisticated and simple at once. This place is not for families, nor for anyone accustomed to spreading out and kicking back. Rooms, for example, have no TVs, but all have a terrace and Scandnavian-styled baths. Silence and reticence are priorities. Downstairs is one of the hippest bistros in the area, with an excellent wine bar. The owners, a local family, were also the designers and builders, and provide guests excellent service and tour options that are as unique as the hotel.

Camino Ensenada Km 2, Ruta 225. ✆ **65/564900.** www.arrebolpatagonia.com. 22 units. $240 double; $280 suite. AE, DC, MC, V. Rates include breakfast. **Amenities:** Restaurant; bar; library; spa.

Cabanas del Lago ★★ Recent renovations and sweeping views of Puerto Varas, the lake, and the volcano make this hotel consistently reliable. Rooms are either colossal in size (lakeview and park suites) or quite small (in the oldest part of the hotel). Be sure to ask for a lake view as they're usually quoted at the same price as a garden view. The hotel's prime location means its lounge, restaurant, and sun deck enjoy a lovely setting. The pool could be updated, but the beach is right below you.

Klenner 195, Puerto Varas. ✆ **65/232291.** Fax 65/232707. www.cabanasdellago.cl. 130 units, 5 cabins. $180 standard double; $210 superior double; $230 triple. Rates include buffet breakfast. AE, DC, MC, V. **Amenities:** Restaurant; bar; lounge; indoor heated pool; room service; sauna. *In room:* Hair dryer.

Cumbres Patagonicas ★★ The newest mainstream hotel in Puerto Varas blends the notable characteristics of the area (the incredible view and lots of local wood) with great service and extremely comfortable rooms. The hotel has a gorgeous lobby with a towering fireplace, giant leather sofas, and cathedral windows overlooking the lake. The rooms are equally plush, among the largest in Southern Chile, with small terraces, gentle wool blankets atop crisp white duvets, a small seating area, and separated bathrooms. There is a small rooftop spa and indoor pool. The excellent buffet breakfast has homemade pastries, granolas, and local jellies. Service is certainly above standard.

Imperial 561, Puerto Varas. ✆ **65/494000.** www.cumbrespatagonicas.cl. 92 units. $200–$245 double. AE, DC, MC, V. Rates include excellent buffet breakfast. **Amenities:** Restaurant; bar; lounge; spa; Wi-Fi. *In room:* A/C, hair dryer, minibar.

The Guest House ★★ (Finds Owned and operated by an American, this bed-and-breakfast is a more intimate lodging option, located in a quiet residential area about a 4-block walk from the plaza. The hotel is in a converted 1926 mansion, and like most bed-and-breakfast inns, the experience here is much like staying at a friend's home, with a comfy living area decorated with art that has been collected, not store bought, and a dining area with one long family-style table and a spacious kitchen (visitors have the opportunity to help out with the cooking, if they dine in). The rooms are not huge, but they have high ceilings, comfortable beds, and a simple, clean decor.

O'Higgins 608, Puerto Varas. ✆ **65/231521.** Fax 65/232240. www.vicki-johnson.com/guesthouse. 10 units. $80 double standard. Rates include continental breakfast. AE, MC, V. **Amenities:** Room service.

Where to Dine

Puerto Varas has many good restaurants, but service generally moves at a snail's pace, so have patience. For a casual meal, try **Pim's,** San Francisco 712 (✆ **65/233998**), a country western–style pub with burgers, sandwiches, American-style appetizers such as buffalo wings, and salads. It is popular with locals, and the nighttime ambience is very lively.

Another good spot for a drink at night is the **Barómetro,** San Pedro 418 (✆ **65/236371**), with a wood-hewn bar and tree-trunk tables, a cozy atmosphere, and snacks.

Café Dane's ★ (Value CHILEAN CAFE It's often hard to get a table during the lunch hour in this popular local restaurant. Dane's serves inexpensive, hearty food in good-size portions, plus mouthwatering desserts. The interior is simple and unassuming, and much of the food is standard Chilean fare, all of it good or very good. The fried empanadas, especially shellfish, deserve special mention. Dane's serves a daily set menu for C$6,500 from Monday through Saturday and C$7,000 on Sunday, as well as a special dish, or *plato del día,* for C$4,750. It's less busy before 1pm or after 3pm. You can also buy food to go from the front counter.

Del Salvador 441. ✆ **65/232371.** Main courses C$2,500–C$6,000; sandwiches C$2,000–C$3,750. No credit cards. Daily 7:45am–1am.

La Chamaca ★★ (Finds SEAFOOD If you're like most travelers, you'll want to eat lots of seafood while you are in Chile. The best can be found at this down-home spot on the side of the hill (across from the Santa Isabel supermarket) that's been serving locals for more than 25 years. Start with a sampler of oysters, surf clams, and abalone. Then choose either salmon or white sea bass. I suggest you order your fish *a la arriero,* with garlic and parsley. A salad of avocado and tomatoes and natural potatoes top things off.

Del Salvador s/n. ✆ **65/232876.** Main courses C$4,000–C$8,000. AE, MC, V. Daily 11am–midnight.

La Cucina d'Alessandro ★★ PIZZA/ITALIAN The authentic, fresh pastas and thin-crust pizzas at this restaurant are made by an Italian family who immigrated to Puerto Varas only a few years ago, bringing with them Italian gastronomy know-how. The pizzas are what really shine here, and their special two-for-one pizza offer from 4 to 8pm every day makes this restaurant a good value. It has a cozy atmosphere and is housed in a typical, shingled home across from the beach. There are a few wooden tables that are large enough for groups of six to eight diners. It's a 15-minute walk from downtown. Apart from pasta and pizza, La Cucina has good seafood dishes and is open all day. It's a tiny restaurant, so make reservations for dinner and come early for lunch.

Av. Costanera. ✆ **65/310583.** Main courses C$2,500–C$4,500. No credit cards. Daily noon–midnight.

Mediterráneo ★ (Moments) INTERNATIONAL Boasting an excellent location right on the Costanera, this restaurant has a glass-enclosed terrace with water views. The cheerful orange tablecloths add to its bright ambience, as does the pleasant waitstaff. Mediterráneo is known for its imaginative dishes (think Chilean-Mediterranean fusion) that change weekly. The owners use mostly local produce, including spices bought from Mapuche natives. Start with a pisco sour and perhaps one of the big fresh salads, which mix such ingredients as endives, Swiss cheese, anchovies, olives, and local mushrooms. For the main course, the venison here is excellent, and is served with a tasty zucchini gratin. For dessert, try one of the yummy fruit sorbets.

Santa Rosa 068, corner of Portales. ✆ **65/237268.** AE, DC, MC, V. Main courses C$8,000–C$12,500. Apr–Nov daily noon–3:30pm and 7:30–11pm; Dec–Mar daily 10am–2am.

PARQUE NACIONAL VICENTE PEREZ ROSALES & THE LAKE CROSSING TO ARGENTINA ★★

About 65km (40 miles) from Puerto Varas is Chile's oldest national park, Vicente Pérez Rosales, founded in 1926. It covers an area of 251,000 hectares (620,000 acres), incorporating the park's centerpiece, Lake Todos los Santos, and the Saltos de Petrohué cascades and three volcanoes: Osorno, Tronador, and Puntiagudo. The park is open daily from December to February 8:30am to 8pm, March to November 8:30am to 6:30pm; admission to the Saltos de Petrohué is C$2,200 adults and C$1,700 kids. Conaf's **information center** (✆ **65/486115**) can be found toward the end of the dirt road.

By far the most popular excursions here are boat rides across the absinthe-colored waters of **Lago Todos los Santos,** and there are several options. From Petrohué, you can book a day trip to the Margarita island in the middle of the lake or cross to Peulla, a 1¾-hour crossing that departs daily at 10:30am October through April and in July; the rest of the year, the ship doesn't cross on Sundays.

Travelers may then return or continue on to Bariloche with the company **Cruce Andino** (✆ **65/236160;** www.cruceandino.com; $230 per person for lake crossing, not including accommodations at either Hotel Natura or Hotel Puella). This is a very popular and very touristy journey; though the trip to Bariloche offers rugged, panoramic views, the trip is not worth the money on stormy days. Those doing the crossing in 1 day are herded quickly through gorgeous scenery; it can be heart-breaking not to have more time en route. Better to take the 2-day options and give yourself time to really soak up the magic. The ferry portions of this journey are broken up by short bus rides from one body of water to the other.

There are relatively few hiking trails here. A short, touristy trail to the **Saltos de Petrohué** (admission C$1,500) takes visitors along a walkway built above Río Petrohué to admire the foaming, inky-green water crash through lava channels formed after the 1850 eruption of Volcán Osorno. One of my favorite treks here is a 1-night/2-day trek to the **Termas del Callao** thermal baths, the trail head of which is accessible only by boat. You can hire one of the boats at the dock (six-person maximum for C$25,000), or arrange a trip with **Expediciones Petrohué**, Ruta 225 Km 64 (✆/fax **65/212025**; www.petrohue.com) for an all-inclusive package. A rustic cabin is at the hot springs; check with Expediciones for availability. If you're into backpacking, pick up a copy of the JLM map "Ruta de los Jesuitas" for a description of longer trails in the park.

Volcán Osorno Ski Resort ★ (✆ **65/233445;** www.volcanosorno.com) on the western slope of the volcano, with two basic chairlifts and a T-bar, is a small resort on the volcano of the same name. It has just 600 hectares (1,482 acres) of terrain, but there are sweeping views and runs apt for every level. This is not a ski resort that travelers head to Chile specifically for, such as Valle Nevado or Portillo; it's more of a novelty for those in the area during the mid-June to early October season. The snow can be armor piercing, as this side of the lake receives a lot of wind and all the terrain is above tree level. Lift prices run C$18,000 for a full day, C$13,500 for a half-day, and C$12,000 for students.

Where to Stay Near the Park

Private parking and ample street parking are available and free for all hotels.

Hotel Natura ★★ *Finds* Built in 2005 on the fringe of the forest and the floodplain near Peulla, this hotel is less of a lodge than its name suggests; in fact, the building is more of a traditional grand wood-and-stone style you see in hotels much, much older. Rooms are chic and large; the matrimonial suite features a king-size bed, chimney, flatscreen TV, and a Jacuzzi, along with a balcony. The hotel also has a two-room family apartment, and 23 doubles with king-size beds. Irrespective of its traditional looks, it offers plenty of modern outdoor activities: canopying 15m (49 ft.) in the air over a .8km (½-mile) span, riding, and fly-fishing. You can zoom down nearby rivers like the Río Negro on a jet boat, and wind down with one of the 85 wines on the restaurant's list.

Lago Todos los Santos. ✆ **65/560483.** www.hotelnatura.cl. 45 units. $184 double. AE, MC, DC, V. **Amenities:** Restaurant; bar; gym; sauna; watersports equipment; Wi-Fi. *In room:* TV, hair dryer, high-speed Internet.

Hotel Petrohué ★★ The Hotel Petrohué (built to replace the old lodge that had burned to the ground in 2002) puts travelers right where the outdoor action is, without having to commute from Puerto Varas every day to the park—and the hotel has an excursion outfitter with a range of daily activities. It sits perched above the shore of the Todos los Santos Lake and is surrounded by thick rainforest, a gorgeous location even on an overcast day. The hotel looks like a large Alpine chalet and is a tad austere given the absence of homey touches such as artwork or plants, but the contemporary design of its interiors (stone, heavy wood beams, fresh white couches) is attractive, and the rooms are comfortable, with crisp linens and panoramic windows. The hotel also has four cabins with kitchenettes and maid service.

Petrohué s/n Ruta 225, Km 64, Parque Nacional. ✆ **65/212025.** www.hotelpetrohue.cl. 13 units, 4 *cabañas.* $197 double; $208 double with half-board; $329 double with all meals and excursions included; $186 *cabaña* for 4; $253 *cabaña* for 8. AE, MC, V. **Amenities:** Restaurant; bar; lounge; outdoor pool; room service. *In room:* Kitchenette in *cabañas.*

Yan Kee Way Lodge ★★★ Kids Finds The name "Yan Kee Way" is a play on words, a gringo's pronunciation of Llanquihue, and coincidentally it's owned and managed by Americans, who could not have chosen a more picture-perfect site: nestled in a thick forest of *arrayán* trees on the shore of Lago Llanquihue, and facing an astounding view of Volcano Osorno directly in front of the lodge.

Besides the superb location, Yan Kee Way Lodge offers the best experiences in the area, from fly-fishing to hiking, rafting, and biking. The hotel complex has independent units in standard rooms, two-story bungalows, and apartments, the latter of which are spacious and good for a family or group of friends. Blending with the surroundings from the outside, the guest rooms are a letdown on the inside, with dated decor and '80s-style fixtures. Service is attentive and friendly. The lodge is definitely family-friendly, and also has the region's finest restaurant, Latitude 42.

Road to Ensenada east of Puerto Varas, Km 42. ✆ **65/212030.** Fax 65/212031. www.southernchilexp.com. 18 units. $270 double; $450 per person per day all-inclusive sport adventure package, which includes all meals, house wines with dinner, and choice of 20 activities. Fly-fishing $157 per person. AE, DC, MC, V. **Amenities:** Restaurant; bar; lounge; exercise room; free Internet; Jacuzzis; room service; sauna; spa; watersports equipment. *In room:* Fridge, hair dryer.

PUERTO MONTT

1,016km (630 miles) S of Santiago; 20km (12 miles) S of Puerto Varas

This port town of roughly 110,000 residents is the central hub for travelers headed to the Island of Chiloé, and the parks Alerce Andino and Pumalín. It is also a major docking zone for dozens of large cruise companies circumnavigating the southern cone of South America and several ferry companies with southern destinations to Laguna San Rafael National Park and Puerto Natales in Patagonia.

The town presents a convenient stopover point for travelers, but it is an ugly place when compared to Puerto Varas or Frutillar, due to its mishmash of office buildings and its scrappy industrial port. There is an extensive outdoor market here that sells Chilean handicrafts, clothing, and other tourist souvenirs. Unless you need to be at the port early, I suggest you stay in Puerto Varas instead.

Essentials

Getting There

BY PLANE Puerto Montt's **El Tepual** airport (p. 433) is currently served by **LAN** (✆ **600/526-2000;** www.lan.com) and **Sky Airline** (✆ **600/600-2828;** www.skyairline.cl), with multiple daily flights to Santiago, Punta Arenas, Balmaceda (Coyhaique), and Temuco. An **ETM bus** from the airport to the city's downtown bus terminal costs C$1,250 and a taxi costs C$8,000. Agree on the fare before getting into the cab. There are several **car-rental agencies** at the airport, including Hertz and Avis.

BY BUS Puerto Montt's main terminal is at the waterfront (Diego Portales s/n), a 10- to 15-minute walk from downtown, or there are taxis to transport you. Regular bus service to and from most major cities, including Santiago, is provided by **Cruz del Sur** (✆ **65/254731**), **Tur Bus** (✆ **65/253329**), **Tas Choapa** (✆ **65/254828**), and **Bus Norte** (✆ **65/252783**).

BY CAR The Pan-American Highway ends at Puerto Montt.

Getting Around

BY FOOT The city center is small enough to be seen on foot. The Angelmó Fish and Artisans Market is a 20-minute walk from the center, or you can take a cab.

BY BUS **Buses Cruz del Sur** (✆ **65/254731**) leaves for Puerto Varas 19 times daily from the bus terminal, and so do the independent white shuttle buses to the left of the coaches; look for the sign in the window that says PUERTO VARAS. Cruz del Sur also serves Chiloé, including Castro and Ancud, with 25 trips per day. **TransChiloé** (✆ **65/254934**) goes to Chiloé seven times per day from the terminal.

Visitor Information

The municipality has a small **tourist office** in the plaza at the corner of Antonio Varas and San Martín (✆ **65/261823**); it's open December through March daily from 9am to 9pm, and April through November Monday through Friday from 9am to 1pm and 2:30 to 7pm, Saturday and Sunday from 9am to 1pm. A largely unhelpful tourism kiosk is located in the main plaza (✆ **65/261808;** turismomontt@puertomonttchile.cl).

FAST FACTS For currency exchange, try **Trans Afex,** Av. Diego Portales 516; **Cambios Inter,** Paseo Talca 84 (✆ **64/343683**); **La Moneda de Oro,** in the bus terminal, Office no. 37; and **Eureka Tour,** Guillermo Gallardo 65. **Hospital de la Seguridad** is at Panamericana 400 (✆ **65/257333**). Get online at **Arroba Cibercafé,** Guillermo Gallardo 218 A, or **New Ciber,** San Martín 230. Cybercafes come and go, but most are on Urmenta Street. Internet service costs about $2 per hour, but many hotels have access for guests.

TOUR OPERATORS & TRAVEL AGENCIES **Ace Lagos Andinos,** Antonio Varas 445 (✆ **65/257686** or 9/707-9445; www.aceturismo.cl), offers just about everything you could want, including tours to Vicente Pérez National Park, the Termas de Puyehue, and Chiloé; sightseeing tours around the circumference of Lago Llanquihue; 2-night treks around Volcán Osorno with an overnight in a family home; and more.

Attractions in & Around Puerto Montt

Museo Juan Pablo II ★ This museum contains a medley of artifacts culled from this region, including historical photos and objects made by local Mapuche and Chilote Indians, as well as an interpretive exhibit of the Monte Verde archaeological dig that found bones estimated to be 12,000 years old. The museum is a good place to kill time or stop by if in the area; if not, forget it.

Av. Diego Portales 991. ✆ **65/344457.** Admission C$1,500. Mon–Fri 9am–7pm; Sat–Sun 10am–6pm.

Angelmó Fish and Artisan Market ★★ The long line of vendors here selling sweaters, baskets, ashtrays, and colorful knick-knacks along the road leading to the fish market are certainly worth a browse. But it's inside the fish market that one really gets a sense of the wide scope of seafood that is considered both edible and marketable in Southern Chile. It's a fascinating extravaganza, with characters as colorful as the ponchos sold outside. It's about a 20-minute walk from the main plaza downtown; just follow the coast west. There are also a few cafes inside and along the road.

2km (1¼ miles) west of Puerto Montt on the Costanera Rd. No phone. Free admission. Daily 9am–7pm (until 9pm in the summer).

Where to Stay

Private parking and ample street parking are available and free for all hotels.

Holiday Inn Express (Value) Yes, it's a Holiday Inn, but the location is excellent, the views outstanding, there are all the amenities you need, and this is the best hotel for business travelers in town. It opened in 2006 over the Paseo Costanera shopping center right on the waterfront. Big windows, about half of which look out onto the harbor, are the highlight of the otherwise average rooms, which feature standard Holiday Inn unadventurous beige walls, carpeting, and bedding. Although it's not exciting, it's very reliable and a good value.

Av. Costanera s/n, Puerto Montt. ✆ **65/566600.** www.hiexpress.com. 105 units. $90–$130 double. Rates include buffet breakfast. AE, DC, MC, V. **Amenities:** Restaurant; bar; exercise room; room service; Wi-Fi. *In room:* TV, hair dryer.

Hotel Gran Pacífico ★★ The Gran Pacífico, with a 10-story structure that towers over the waterfront, is the only hotel in the city that claims to be luxurious—I think it's more well appointed than luxurious, however. The Art Deco lobby is sleek and modern with lots of wood and marble. The rooms follow the same motif and are spacious, modern, and bright. They have wood headboards, off-yellow wallpaper, and large-screen TVs. Those overlooking the water have breathtaking views (request an upper-level oceanview floor when you check in). The marble bathrooms are a tad small, but the size of the bedroom makes up for it. For such a high-caliber hotel, the staff is not too efficient nor do they speak much English, so be patient.

Urmeneta 719, Puerto Montt. ✆ **65/482100.** Fax 65/292979. www.hotelgranpacifico.cl. 48 units. $92–$118 double. AE, DC, MC, V. **Amenities:** Restaurant; bar; lounge; exercise room; room service; sauna. *In room:* TV, minibar.

Where to Dine

Puerto Montt is Chile's **seafood capital,** offering the widest variety of shellfish and fish found anywhere in the country. It'd be a crime if you left here without sampling at least a few delicacies. And where better to see, smell, and taste these fruits of the sea than the **Angelmó Fish and Artisan Market** (see above), located at the end of Avenida Angelmó where the artisan market terminates; it's open daily from 9am to 7pm (9pm in summer). Like most fish markets, it's a little grungy, but a colorful stop nevertheless, and several restaurant stalls offer the freshest local specialties around.

Club de Yates ★ SEAFOOD The light-blue Club de Yates looks like a traditional seafood restaurant that sits out over the water like a pier. Inside, though, the atmosphere is white tablecloths, candlesticks, and sharp waiters in bow ties; it's one of the more elegant dining areas in town. This is a good place to come if you're looking for typical Chilean seafood dishes, such as razor clams broiled with Parmesan, or sea bass margarita, a creamy shellfish sauce. It has a great waterfront view and is located about 1km (½ mile) from the plaza toward Pelluco.

Av. Juan Soler Manfredini 200. ✆ **65/82810.** Main courses C$10,000–C$12,500. AE, DC, MC, V. Daily noon–4pm and 7:30pm–midnight.

Pazos CHILEAN This is the place to come if you're interested in sampling *curanto* but don't have time to make it to Chiloé. *Curanto* is that island's specialty, a mixture of mussels, clams, sausage, chicken, pork, beef, and a gooey pancake steamed in a large pot and served with a cup of broth. Pazos also serves a variety of other seafood items, such as sea urchin omelets and the shellfish cornucopia *sopa marina.* The restaurant is on the waterfront in Pelluco, in a 90-year-old home. It's very popular with summer visitors to Puerto Montt.

Av. General Juan Soler Manfredini s/n, Balneario Pelluco. ✆ **65/252552.** Main courses C$4,000–C$6,000. AE, DC, MC, V. Daily 12:15–3pm and 8:15–10pm.

8 SOUTHERN PATAGONIA ★★★

Few places in the world have captivated the imagination of explorers and travelers like Patagonia and Tierra del Fuego, the island at the far southern tip of South America. The region's harsh, wind-whipped climate and its geological curiosities have produced some of the most beautiful natural attractions in the world: the granite towers of Torres del Paine and Los Glaciares national parks, the Southern and Northern ice fields with their colossal glaciers, the flat steppe broken by multicolored sedimentary bluffs, and the emerald fjords and turquoise lakes. In the end, this is what compels most travelers to plan a trip down here, but Patagonia's seduction also lies in the "remote"—the very notion of traveling to "the end of the world."

EXPLORING THE REGION

For the region's tremendous size, Patagonia and Tierra del Fuego are surprisingly easy to travel, especially now that most destinations have opened airports. Travelers can plan a circuit that loops through, for example, Ushuaia, Punta Arenas, Torres del Paine, and then El Calafate and El Chaltén. If you're planning a trip to Chile or Argentina, you'll really want to include a visit to this region if possible—there's so much to see and do here, you'd be missing out if you went home without setting foot in this magical territory. Prices jump and crowds swell from early November to late March, and some businesses open during this time frame only. The busiest months are January and February, but these summer months are not necessarily the best months to visit Patagonia, as calmer weather prevails in October, and from mid-March to late April.

PUNTA ARENAS ★

Punta Arenas is the capital of the Magellanic and Antarctic Región XII, and it is Chilean Patagonia's most important city, with a population of 113,000. Upon arrival, it seems unbelievable that Punta Arenas is able to prosper as well as it does in such a forsaken location on the gusty shore of the Strait of Magellan, but its streets hum with activity and its airport and seaports bustle with traffic passing through the strait or in transit to Antarctica. Citizens from Punta Arenas consider themselves somewhat of an independent republic due to their isolation from the rest of Chile, and they are an indefatigable bunch who brace themselves every summer against the gales that blow through this town like a hurricane.

Punta Arenas's history, extreme climate, and position overlooking the renowned Strait of Magellan make it a fascinating place to explore. There's enough to do here to fill a day, and you'll want to plan on spending 1 night here, even if your plans are to head directly to Torres del Paine.

Argentine Patagonia

For coverage of destinations on the Argentine side of Patagonia and Tierra del Fuego, see chapter 4. For a complete map of southern Patagonia, please refer to p. 159 in chapter 4.

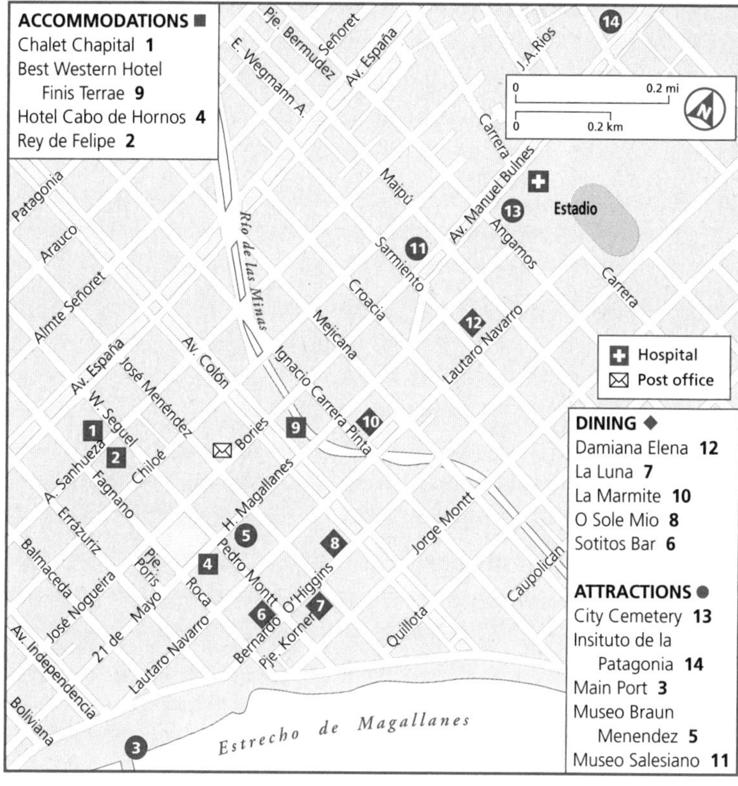

Essentials

Getting There

BY PLANE Punta Arenas's **Aeropuerto Presidente Ibáñez** (airport code PUQ; ✆ **61/ 218131**) is 20km (12 miles) north of town and, depending on the season, it's serviced with up to 10 flights per day from Santiago. **LAN,** Lautaro Navarro 999 (✆ **600/526-2000** or 61/241100; www.lan.com), has the most flights per day to both Puerto Montt and Santiago **Sky Airline,** Roca 935 (✆ **600/600-2828;** www.skyairline.cl), has one flight per day.

The regional **Aerovías DAP,** O'Higgins 891 (✆ **61/223340;** www.aeroviasdap.cl), has six weekly flights to Porvenir and to Puerto Williams. They also have charter flights to places like Ushuaia and Antarctica, and charter sightseeing flights to Cape Horn and Torres del Paine.

To get to Punta Arenas from the airport, hire a taxi for about C$6,000 or take one of the transfer services there (which can also arrange to take you back to the airport; their booths are at the baggage claim area). **Buses Transfer Austral** (✆ **61/229673;** www.transferaustral.com) has door-to-door service for C$3,500 per person.

Cruising from Punta Arenas to Ushuaia, Argentina

Crucero Australis runs an unforgettable journey between Punta Arenas and Ushuaia aboard its ships, the M/V *Mare Australis* and the M/V *Via Australis.* This cruise takes passengers to remote coves and narrow channels and fjords in Tierra del Fuego, and then heads into the Beagle Channel, ending at Ushuaia, Argentina. There's also a stop at the absolute end of the world, Cape Horn, although the chances that you will be able to get off the boat and touch *tierrafirma* there aren't likely due to notorious winds. The trip can be done as a 4-night one-way from Punta Arenas or a 3-night one-way journey from Ushuaia. I recommend that you take just the one-way journey, ideally departing Punta Arenas, leaving you to explore a new city and then travel by air or land from there. It's a fantastic way to link both countries and turn your Patagonian itinerary into a loop.

What is unique about this cruise is the intimacy of a smaller ship and its solitary route that takes passengers to places in Tierra del Fuego that few have a chance to see. Passengers are shuttled to shore via zodiacs (motorized inflatable boats) for two daily excursions that can include visits to glaciers or a penguin colony, or walks to view elaborate beaver dams and lookouts. There are several excellent bilingual guides who give daily talks about the region's flora, fauna, history, and geology. Service is stiff but professional, and the food is quite good. The accommodations are comfortable, ranging from suites to simple cabins. In 2011, the company will introduce a third ship, the M/V *Stella Australis.* All-inclusive, per-person prices (excluding cocktails) range from $1,550 to $4,390 one-way from Punta Arenas and $1,150 to $3,290 one-way from Ushuaia. It's not really worth it to pay extra for an upper deck; second-floor berths at the front of the ship are the most stable, quiet, and comfortable. This cruise operates from early October to late April. For reservations or information, contact their U.S. offices in Miami at 4014 Chase Ave., Suite 215 (✆ **305/695-9618;** fax 305/534-9276), or in Santiago at Av. El Bosque Norte 0440 (✆ **2/442-3110;** fax 2/203-5173); or visit www.australis.com.

BY BUS From Puerto Natales, **Bus Sur,** José Menéndez 565 (✆ **61/244464;** www.bus-sur.cl), has four daily trips; **Buses Fernández,** Armando Sanhueza 745 (✆ **61/221429;** www.busesfernandez.com), has seven daily trips; and **Buses Pacheco,** Av. Colón 900 (✆ **61/242174;** www.busespacheco.com), has five daily trips. The cost is about C$4,000 and the trip takes 3 to 4 hours.

To and from Ushuaia, Argentina, **Buses Tecni Austral,** Lautaro Navarro 975 (✆ **61/222078**), leaves Punta Arenas Tuesday, Thursday, and Saturday and returns from Ushuaia on Monday, Thursday, and Saturday, via Rio Grande. The direct trip to Ushuaia takes about 12 hours.

BY CAR Ruta 9 is a paved road between Punta Arenas and Puerto Natales. Strong winds often require that you exercise extreme caution when driving this route. To get to

Tierra del Fuego, there are two options: Cross by ferry from Punta Arenas to Porvenir, or drive east on Ruta 255 to Ruta 277 and Punta Delgada for the ferry crossing there.

International Rental Car, Waldo Seguel 443 (✆ **61/225323;** www.international-rac.com), is a helpful and locally owned agency with an office at the airport. You can drop your car off in Puerto Natales or Coyhaique for an extra fee. Another option is **Southland Rentacar,** General de Canto 010 (✆ **61/241143;** www.southlandrentacar.com).

Visitor Information

There's an excellent **Oficina de Turismo** (✆ **61/200610**) inside a glass gazebo in the Plaza de Armas. The staff is helpful, and they sell a wide range of historical and anthropological literature and postcards. The office is open from December to March Monday through Friday from 8am to 5:30pm, and Saturdays and Sundays from 9am to 2:30pm. From March through November, it's open weekdays only. **Sernatur**'s office at Lautoro Navarro 990 (✆ **61/225385;** www.sernatur.cl), on the other hand, is harried and inattentive; it's open Monday through Friday from 8:15am to 12:45pm and 2:30 to 7pm.

FAST FACTS Exchange money at **La Hermandad,** Lautaro Navarro 1099 (✆ 61/243991); **Cambio de Moneda STP,** José Nogueira 1168 (✆ 61/223334); or **Torres del Paine,** Lautaro Navarro 1013 (✆ **61/247675**). *Casas de cambio* are open Monday through Friday from 9am to 1pm and 3 to 7pm, and Saturday from 9am to 1pm.

For banks with 24-hour ATMs, go to **Banco Santander,** Magallanes 997 (✆ 61/201020); **Banco de Chile,** Roca 864 (✆ 61/735433); or **Banco Edwards,** Plaza Muñoz Gamero 1055 (✆ 61/241175). Banks are open Monday through Friday from 9am to 2pm.

For medical attention, go to **Hospital de las FF.AA. Cirujano Guzmán,** Avenida Manuel Bulnes and Guillermos (✆ **61/207500**), or the **Clínica Magallanes,** Av. Manuel Bulnes 1448 (✆ **61/211527**).

For Internet access, try **Telefónica,** Bories 798 (✆ **61/248230**).

The central **post office** is at José Menéndez and Bories (✆ **61/222210**); hours are Monday through Friday from 9am to 6pm and Saturday from 9am to 1pm.

Exploring Punta Arenas

Begin your tour of Punta Arenas in **Plaza Muñoz Gamero,** in whose center you'll find a bronze sculpture of Ferdinand Magellan, donated by José Menéndez on the 400-year anniversary of Magellan's discovery of the Strait of Magellan. From the plaza on Avenida 21 de Mayo, head north toward Avenida Colón for a look at the renovated Teatro Municipal, designed by the French architect Numa Mayer and modeled after the magnificent Teatro Colón in Buenos Aires. Head down to the waterfront and turn south toward the pier to watch the shipping action. At the pier is a 1913 clock imported from Germany that has complete meteorological instrumentation, hands showing the moon's phases, and a zodiac calendar.

City Cemetery ★★ They say you can't really understand a culture until you see where they bury their dead, and in the case of the cemetery of Punta Arenas, this edict certainly rings true. Inside this necropolis, opened in 1894, lies a veritable miniature city, with avenues that connect the magnificent tombs of the region's founding families, settlers, and civic workers, and a rather solemn tomb where lie the remains of the last Selk'nam Indians of Tierra del Fuego. The Alice in Wonderland bell-shaped cypress trees that line the tombs make for a surreal atmosphere. The cemetery is about a 15-minute walk from the plaza.

Av. Manuel Bulnes and Angamos. No phone. Free admission. Oct–Mar daily 7:30am–8pm; Apr–Sept daily 8am–6:30pm.

Instituto de la Patagonia/Museo del Recuerdo ★ The Instituto de Patagonia is an engaging exhibit of colonial artifacts called the Museum of Memories. Antique machinery and horse-drawn carts are displayed around the lawn and encircled by several colonial buildings that have been lifted and transported here from ranches around the area. One cabin shows visitors what home life was like for a ranch hand, another has been set up to resemble a typical dry goods store, another is a garage with a 1908 Peugeot, and another, a carpenter's workshop. There's a library on the premises with a collection of books and maps on display and for sale. The museum is about 4km (2½ miles) out of town, so you'll need to take a taxi.

Av. Manuel Bulnes 01890. ✆ **61/217173.** Admission C$400. Mon–Fri 8:30am–noon and 2:30–6pm; Sat 8:30am–noon; Sun hours vary (call ahead).

Museo Braun Menéndez ★★ (Moments This museum is testament to the staggering wealth produced by the region's large-scale, colonial-era sheep and cattle *estancias* (ranches). The museum is the former residence of the Braun Menéndez family, who believed that any far-flung, isolated locale could be tolerated if one were to "live splendidly and remain in constant contact with the outside world." The Museo Regional Braun Menéndez is the former residence of Mauricio Braun and Josefina Menéndez, a marriage that united the two largest fortunes in the Magellanic region.

If one wants European grandeur, one normally goes to Europe, not to Patagonia; still, the museum is impressive. The home is a national monument and has been preserved in its original state. European craftsmen were imported to craft marble fireplaces and hand-paint walls to resemble marble and leather. The interior fixtures and furniture include gold and crystal chandeliers, tapestries from Belgium, stained-glass cupolas, English and French furniture, hand-carved desks, and more. There is also a small ethnographic exhibit. Plan on 45 minutes to an hour to view the museum.

Museo Regional Braun Menéndez: Magallanes 949. ✆ **61/244216.** Admission C$1,000 adults, C$500 students and seniors 61 and older; Sun and holidays free. Oct–Apr Mon–Fri 3:30–8:30pm; Sun 11am–4pm.

Museo Salesiano Maggiorino Borgatello ★★ This mesmerizing museum offers an insight into the Magellanic region's history, anthropology, ecology, and industrial history. That said, the lobby-level floor is packed with a fusty collection of stuffed and mounted birds and mammals that at turns feels almost macabre, considering that many have lost their shape; nevertheless, it allows you to fully appreciate the tremendous size of the condor and the puma. Several rooms in the museum display Indian hunting tools, ritual garments, jewelry, an Alacalufe bark canoe, and colonial and ranching implements, as well as the religious artifacts from the Catholic missionaries who played such a controversial role in the native Indians' lives. Perhaps some of the most interesting items on view here are the black-and-white photos of the early missionary Alberto d'Agostini, who took most of the only photos available of the native people who have since disappeared from this region.

Av. Manuel Bulnes and Maipú. ✆ **61/221001.** Admission C$1,100. Tues–Sun 10am–12:30pm and 3–6pm.

Shopping

Punta Arenas is home to a duty-free shopping center called the **Zona Franca,** with several blocks of shops hawking supposedly cheaper electronics, imported foodstuffs, sporting goods, perfumes, clothing, booze, cigarettes, and more. It's a massive shopping mall, with big-box stores a la North America. The savings here are negligible, except for alcohol purchases, and the selection isn't what you'd hope for, although there certainly is a lot on offer. The Zona Franca is on Avenida Manuel Bulnes, just outside town. It's open Monday through Saturday from 10am to 12:30pm and 3 to 8pm, and is closed on holidays.

For regional crafts in town, try **Chile Típico,** Carrera Pinto 1015 (✆ **61/225827**), which has knitwear, carved-wood items, lapis lazuli, and more. For high-end, artsy-craftsy household items such as picture frames, candles, throws, curtains, and the like, try **Almacén Antaño,** Colón 100 (✆ **61/227283**).

Excursions Outside Punta Arenas

Tour Operators

Many tour operators run conventional city tours and trips to the penguin colonies, as well as short visits and trekking excursions to Torres del Paine National Park; however, I recommend one of the outfitters listed under tour operators in the Torres del Paine section for multiday excursions there (p. 452). A city tour here provides the historical background to this region and undoubtedly enriches a visitor's understanding of the hardship the immigrants and Native Indians faced during the past century.

Turismo Yamana, Errázuriz 932 (✆ **61/710567;** www.yamana.cl), offers full-day city tours (about $75 per person), penguin tours ($98 per person), and tours to Pali Aike National Park ($275 per person), as well as multiday kayaking and whale-watching expeditions. They also have an exhausting 14-hour "Torres del Paine in a Day" tour ($417 per person). Prices drop significantly for groups of four or more. The company also offers multiday trips to Lago Blanco in Tierra del Fuego for trekking, horseback riding, and fishing.

Turismo Comapa, Magallanes 990 (✆ **61/200200;** www.comapa.com), is the leader for conventional tours such as city tours and visits to the penguin colonies. Prices are similar to those of Turismo Yamana, above.

Fantastico Sur ★, José Menéndez 858 (✆ **61/615794;** www.fantasticosur.com), has naturalist tours, including a day-long bird-watching tour where you can spot condors, penguins, waders, and passerines. They also have multiday naturalist tours of Patagonia, and their guides are passionate, professional, and superb.

Penguin Colonies at Seno Otway & Isla Magdalena

If you have a day or a half-day to kill in Punta Arenas, from October through March, the most appealing activity is a visit to the Magellanic **penguin colonies** at either Seno Otway or Isla Magdalena. Both colonies allow visitors to get surprisingly close to the amusing Magellanic penguins at their nesting sites, whisking out sprays of sand or poking their heads out of their burrows. But this only happens during their natural nesting cycle from October to March—and even by early March they've all pretty much packed up and headed north. November to February provides the most active viewing. Isla Magdalena is the best colony to view the penguins (with an estimated 150,000, as compared to 3,000 at Seno Otway). But, the trip involves a ferry ride and will take up more of your time.

Seno Otway ★★ is accessible by road about 65km (40 miles) from Punta Arenas. A volunteer study group developed the site but now that the founder has passed away the site is run by the founder's family, who clearly care more about making a profit than carrying on the foundation's work. Most tour companies in town (see above) will provide transportation with daily departures in the afternoons, but if you have a rental car you can go on your own. The tickets now cost a whopping C$6,000 to C$7,500, plus a

C$4,500 entrance fee (kids 11 and under are free). Tours are offered in four languages, and there is an overpriced cafe here, too. Seno Otway is open from October 15 through March from 8am to 8pm. The best time to visit is between 9 and 10am and 5 and 7pm, when the majority of activity takes place (the crowds of visitors are thinner during the morning shift; ✆ **61/224454**). Take Ruta 9 toward Puerto Natales, and then turn left at the sign for Seno Otway—if you reach the police checkpoint you've gone too far.

The penguins at **Isla Magdalena** ★★★ are more timid than those at Seno Otway, but the sight of so many of these birds bustling to and fro is decidedly more impressive. To get here, you need to take a ferry, which makes for a pleasant half-day afternoon excursion. **Turismo Comapa,** Av. Magallanes 990 (✆ **61/200200;** www.comapa.com), puts this tour together. Its boat, the *Barcaza Melinka,* departs from the pier at 3:30pm and returns at 8:30pm on Tuesday, Thursday, and Saturday from mid-November to end of March ($50 for adults, $26 children 11 and under).

Estancia Lolita ★★ is a wildlife refuge and zoo for Patagonian fauna and the best place to view rarely seen species, 42km (16 miles) north of Punta Arenas. Josefina, a tame, rambunctious culpeo fox who loves to play with visitors, is one of the most charming living souls you'll meet in Patagonia. Guanacos, pumas, and other wild cats, and parrots and other endemic birds are among the denizens of the *estancia,* which has over 30 species in all (✆ **61/233057**; adults C$3,000, children C$2,000).

Where to Stay

In general, lodging in Punta Arenas is somewhat expensive for the caliber of accommodations available. Price ranges listed below reflects low to high season (high season is Oct 15–Apr 15). The newest spot in town is the massive **Dreams Hotel del Estrecho,** with a casino inside, on the waterfront (✆ **61/204500;** www.mundodreams.com; doubles from $210).

Expensive

Best Western Hotel Finis Terrae ★★ This hotel is very popular with foreigners, especially Americans. The well-lit accommodations and the hotel lobby are quite comfy; rooms have king-size beds in double rooms, and a softly hued decor in peach and beige. And although Richard Gere stayed here in 2002 (he chose the spacious fifth-floor suite with a whirlpool tub and minibar); the rooms are by no means luxurious. The singles are tiny, so be sure to ask for a larger double for the single price, which they will likely agree to, especially during slower months. The hotel's highlight is its panoramic penthouse restaurant that serves the best breakfast in Punta Arenas.

Av. Colón 766, Punta Arenas. ✆ **61/209100.** Fax 61/209121. www.hotelfinisterrae.com. 64 units. $185–$231 double. Rates include buffet breakfast. AE, DC, MC, V. **Amenities:** Restaurant; lounge; room service. *In room:* TV, hair dryer, minibar, Wi-Fi.

Hotel Cabo de Hornos ★★ Conveniently located on the northeast corner of the plaza, this traditional hotel has a modern feel and professional service. The Cabo de Hornos sports an impressive, elegant gray stone-clad reception and lounge area, very nicely decorated in a mixture of modern and rustic. A separate room, with a massive fireplace, is where stylish locals meet for a cocktail. The rooms don't quite match the wow factor of the ground floor, being just a little on the small size, but they are of decent quality and well suited for business travelers. Top-floor rooms have slanted ceilings and the best views.

Plaza Muñoz Gamero 1039, Punta Arenas. ✆ **61/715000.** www.hoteles-australis.com. 111 units. $124–$290 double. AE, DC, MC, V. **Amenities:** Restaurant; lounge; room service. *In room:* TV, high-speed Internet.

Rey de Felipe ★★★ (Finds Little known, off the beaten track, comfortable, and very quiet, this new hotel is cozy and private. There is an element of natural luxury here that stands out in Punta Arenas's hotel offerings. The spacious lobby has a giant fireplace and comfortable couches. Rooms are modern and plush, with natural colored carpets, and small details like old maps decorate the walls. All have deep bathtubs and wooden bathroom counters. Service is a bit stiff, but that may be due to the fact that there's hardly ever anybody at this hotel. Rooms vary in size; if you want to ensure a big room, be sure to ask. Located 3 blocks up the hill from the Plaza de Armas, it's farther from the water, so it's protected from the stormy weather.

Armando Sanhueza 965, Punta Arenas. ✆ **61/617500.** www.hotelreydonfelipe.com. 43 units. $145 single; $160 double; $210 suite. AE, DC, MC, V. **Amenities:** Restaurant; bar; gym; Wi-Fi. *In room:* TV, minibar.

Moderate

Chalet Chapital (Value A classic Punta Arenas mansion that was transformed into a simple, pleasant little inn, the best part of this hotel is the loving, friendly staff. Breakfasts, for example, are typically simple Chilean offerings. Rooms have comfortable beds, private bathrooms with hydro-massage showers, and nothing else fancy. There's a TV room downstairs. Like most small inns in town, it can be noisy when other guests get up early for excursions. This is a great midrange choice if you're not up for a hostel and your budget's not up for one of the hotels above.

Armando Sanhueza 974, Punta Arenas. ✆ **61/730100.** www.hotelchaletchapital.cl. 11 units. $85 double; $95 triple. AE, DC, MC, V. **Amenities:** TV room.

Where to Dine

Most of the restaurants in downtown Punta Arenas offer traditional fare and tourist-friendly local specialties like lamb, king crab, and shellfish. The best strip is along O'Higgins. For pastas at a good price, try **O Sole Mio,** O'Higgins 974 (✆ **61/242026**). The laid-back and friendly **La Luna,** O'Higgins 1017 (✆ **61/228555**), has a big menu and lively bar. Vegetarians will like the eclectic options at **La Marmite ★★**, Plaza Sampaio 678 (✆ **61/222056**).

Damiana Elena ★★ (Finds REGIONAL CHILEAN With a menu that changes so frequently it's not even printed, and a packed house most nights, this may be the best restaurant in Punta Arenas. There are eight daily specials, usually including seafood, fish, meat, and a pasta option. The chef's recommendation will be something like king crab canneloni with artichokes and fine herbs. They've recently moved into a larger location, in a refurbished old house in a residential area, far from the touristy strip on O'Higgins. The service (mostly bilingual!) is more youthful, relaxed, and friendly than in the other traditional restaurants in town. Upstairs is the nonsmoking section. There is also a large wine list, and a funky bar on the main floor.

Magallanes 341. ✆ **61/222818.** Main courses C$6,000–C$9,000. AE, DC, MC, V. Mon–Sat 8pm–12:30am. Reservations highly recommended.

Sotitos Bar ★★ CHILEAN Don't be fooled by the plain green front with the weathered sign: Sotitos has handsome semiformal interiors with brick walls and white-linen tablecloths. Sotitos also offers more than most Chilean restaurants, including steak and seafood, baked lamb, Valencia shellfish rice (which must be ordered ahead of time), pastas, and fresh salads. The fish is very fresh. The key is that everything is of high quality, regardless of how simple the dish. The service here is so-so. On Friday, Saturday, and Sunday they fire up their *parrilla* (grill) for barbecued meats.

O'Higgins 1138. ✆ **61/221061.** Main courses C$7,500–C$10,500. AE, DC, MC, V. Mon–Sat 11:30am–3pm and 7–11:45pm.

Punta Arenas After Dark

The city has a handful of good bars and pubs, including Sotitos Bar (see above). Another popular spot is the **Pub 1900,** at the corner of Avenida Colón and Bories (✆ **61/242759**). The **Cabo de Hornos Hotel,** on the plaza (✆ **61/242134**), has a chic yet more somber bar. The **Cine Estrella,** at Mejicana 777 (✆ **61/225630**), is the only cinema in town; call or check newspaper listings for what's playing.

PUERTO NATALES ★

Puerto Natales is a rambling town of 16,000, spread along the sloping coast of the Señoret Canal between the Ultima Esperanza Sound and the Almirante Montt Gulf. The setting has big mountains and wild sea. This is the jump-off point for trips to Torres del Paine, and most visitors find themselves spending at least 1 night here. The town itself has a frontier-town appeal. Within the ramshackled buildings are some truly cozy and delightful inns, cafes, and bistros. Along the Costanera, elegant black-necked swans drift along the rocky shore. From May to September, the town virtually goes into hibernation, but come October, the town's streets begin to fill with travelers decked out in parkas and hiking boots on their way to the park.

Essentials

Getting There & Getting Around

BY PLANE There is a tiny airport in Puerto Natales (airport code PNT; ✆ **61/411980**) that operates sporadically; many flights are canceled due to wind. **Sky Airline** (✆ **600/600-2828;** www.skyairline.cl) has scheduled flights from Santiago in January and February which stop here, conditions permiting, en route to Punta Arenas. The next closest airports are in El Calafate, Argentina (4–5 hr.) and Punta Arenas (3–4 hr.). A taxi from Puerto Natales to the airport costs C$3,000 and is only a 5-minute drive.

BY BUS Puerto Natales is the hub for bus service to Torres del Paine National Park and El Calafate, Argentina. For information about bus service to and from Torres del Paine, see "Parque Nacional Torres del Paine," later in this chapter. There are frequent daily trips between Punta Arenas and Puerto Natales. In Puerto Natales, each bus company leaves from its own office.

TO & FROM PUNTA ARENAS **Buses Fernández,** at Ramirez and Esmeralda streets (✆ **61/411111**), has seven daily trips; **Bus Sur,** Baquedano 668 (✆ **61/411859**), has two daily trips; **Buses Pacheco,** Baquedano 500 (✆ **61/414513**), has four daily trips (and the most comfortable buses); and **Transfer Austral,** Baquedano 414 (✆ **61/412616**), has two daily trips. The trip takes about 3 hours and the cost is about C$4,500 to C$6,000 one-way. Reserve early during the busy season, as tickets sell out fast. Round-trip fares to Punta Arenas are a little cheaper.

TO EL CALAFATE, ARGENTINA Options include **Buses Zaahj,** Arturo Prat 236 (✆ **61/412260;** www.turismozaahj.co.cl), departing at 8am on Tuesdays, Thursdays, and Saturdays; and **Cootra,** Baquedano 456 (✆ **61/412785**), which leaves at 7:30am daily. The cost is C$15,000 one-way. The trip takes 4 to 5 hours, depending on the traffic at the border crossing.

BY CAR Ruta 9 is a paved road that heads north from Punta Arenas. The drive is 254km (158 miles) and takes about 3 hours. If you're heading in from El Calafate, Argentina, you have your choice of two international borders: Cerro Castillo (otherwise known as Control Fronterizo Río Don Guillermo) or Río Turbio (otherwise known as Controles Fronterizos Dorotea y Laurita Casas Viejas). Both are the same in terms of road quality, but Río Turbio is busier, with Chileans heading to Argentina for cheaper goods and most of the bus traffic. Both are open 24 hours from September to May, and daily from 8am to 11pm the rest of the year. Gas is much cheaper in Argentina, so fill up there.

Car rentals in Puerto Natales are offered by **International Rental Car**, Waldo Seguel 443 (✆ **61/228323;** www.international-rac.com) and **Amazing Patagonia,** Baquedano 558 (✆ **61/414949;** www.amazingpatagonia.com), among several others.

All taxis charge a flat rate of C$1,200 for trips within the town limits.

BY BOAT **Navimag** runs a popular 3-night ferry trip between Puerto Natales and Puerto Montt, cruising through the southern fjords of Chile. This journey passes through breathtaking (though repetitive) scenery, and it makes for an interesting way to leave from or head to Chile's Lake District. Navimag leaves Puerto Montt heading south Friday afternoons and Puerto Natales heading north every Monday afternoon. Rates for a private berth start at $850 for a double. Its offices in Puerto Natales are at Pedro Montt 308 (✆ **61/411642;** www.navimag.com).

Visitor Information

Sernatur operates a well-stocked office on the Costanera at Pedro Montt and Philippi (✆ **61/412125;** www.sernatur.cl); it's open October through March Monday through Friday from 8:30am to 8pm, Saturday and Sunday from 9am to 1pm and 3 to 6pm; April through September, it's open Monday through Friday from 8:30am to 1pm and 3 to 6pm (closed holidays). Better yet is the **Municipal Tourism office,** tucked into a corner of the historical museum at Bulnes 285 (✆ **61/414808**), with a wealth of information on lodgings, restaurants, and day trips; the staff here is far more helpful than at Sernatur. It's closed on Sundays.

Sailing to Parque Nacional Bernardo O'Higgins ★

This national park, tremendous in its size, is largely unreachable except by boat tours to the glaciers Balmaceda and Serrano, tours that involve kayaking (for kayaking trips, contact **Bigfoot Expeditions** ✆ **61/414525**; www.bigfootpatagonia.com]), and the Skorpios journey to the grand Pio XI glacier (see below). A low-key, traditional day trip takes travelers to the Serrano and Balmeceda glaciers, with a stop at the Monte Balmaceda Hostel and a short walk along the glacier and its iceberg-studded bay. The trip is dull except for the glacier visits, and visitors are prone to being herded about.

Turismo 21 de Mayo, Eberhard 560 (✆ **61/411978;** www.turismo21demayo.cl), has a cutter and a yacht, and leaves daily (weather permitting) November through March and every Sunday from April to October (other days are dependent on demand). The trip leaves at 8:30am and returns at 5:30pm.

The luxury cruise company **Skorpios,** Augusto Leguia Norte 118 (✆ **2/477-1900,** or 305/484-5357 in North America; www.skorpios.cl), has an all-inclusive 6-day journey from Puerto Natales to Pio XI Glacier, the largest glacier in the Southern Hemisphere. The size of the Pio XI dwarfs other glaciers that descend from the Southern Ice Field, such as Glacier Grey in Torres del Paine, and thereby provides a truly awesome experience. This journey is recommended for travelers who are not very physically active and who wish to take a low-key yet special journey to an out-of-the-way destination few get the chance to see.

Tour Operators & Adventure Travel Outfitters

The many tour operators in Puerto Natales can be divided into two groups: conventional sightseeing day tours to Torres del Paine, Perito Moreno Glacier in Argentina's Los Glaciares National Park, the Cueva de Milodon, the Nordenskjöld Trail hike, and the icebergs at Lago Grey; and adventure travel outfitters that arrange multiday, all-inclusive excursions, including trekking the W or the Circuit and climbing in Torres del Paine, kayaking the Río Serrano in Parque Nacional Bernardo O'Higgins, and taking horseback trips. Keep in mind that it's quite easy to arrange your own trekking journey in Torres del Paine (especially with some help from companies below); the bonus with these outfitters is that they carry the tents (which they'll set up) and food (which they'll cook). They also will pick you up from the airport and provide guided information about the flora and fauna of the park.

CONVENTIONAL DAY TOURS These tours are for people with a limited amount of time in the area. Tours typically leave at 7:30am, return around 7:30pm, and cost about $65 per person, not including lunch or park entrance fees. For day tours, try **Turismo Comapa,** Manuel Bulnes 533 (✆ **61/414300**), or **Viaterra,** Bulnes 632 (✆ **61/410775;** www.viaterra.cl); Viaterra has transfers from Punta Arenas directly to the park on a charter basis. Probably the most interesting way to see the Cueva de Milodon is with **Estancia Travel** (✆ **61/412221;** www.estanciatravel.com), which offers a horseback-riding trip there for $108 per person, including transfers, equipment, a bilingual guide, lunch, and a horse you'll feel comfortable with.

ADVENTURE TRAVEL Dozens of international adventure travel companies run trips to Torres del Paine, and most work with a local operator. You can save money by going directly to the operator. Most of the following operators offer custom packages. **Indómita,** Bories 206 (✆ **61/414525;** www.indomitapatagonia.com), is one of the most respected local outfitters for climbing, mountaineering, and kayaking. One of their most popular trips is a 3-day kayak descent of the River Serrano, with a paddle around Serrano Glacier. Partner **Antares,** Barros Arana 111 (✆ **61/414611,** or ✆ 800/267-6129 for their U.S. office; www.antarespatagonia.com), focuses on the "softer" (meaning less strenuous and/or technical) side of adventure travel, with a variety of multiday trekking journeys that can include horseback riding, kayaking, and sailing. **Chile Nativo Expeditions** ★★, Eberhard 230 (✆ **800/649-8776** from the U.S. and Canada, or 61/411835; www.chilenativo.com), offers high-end trekking, bird-watching, and horseback-riding adventures outside of the more "touristy" areas. **Fantastico Sur** (✆ **61/615794;** www.fantasticosur.com) has wildlife-viewing tours, including a puma-watching tour that has a 70% guarantee of catching a glimpse of the elusive cat! **Onas,** Blanco Encalada and Eberhard (✆/fax **61/412707;** www.onaspatagonia.com), has a half-day zodiac trip down the Río Serrano.

Where to Stay

Many homes large enough to rent out a few rooms have hung an HOSPEDAJE sign above their door—these simple, inexpensive accommodations can be found everywhere, and quality is about the same. The high season in Puerto Natales runs from October to April, and the price range shown reflects this. For all hotels, parking is either free, or street parking is plentiful.

For inexpensive lodging, try **Amerindia Hostel** ★★ at Barros Arana 135 (✆ **61/411945;** www.hostelamerindia.com), which has doubles with private bathrooms for $70 and a friendly vibe. The popular **Casa Cecilia** ★ at Tomás Roger 60 (✆/fax **61/411797;** www.casaceciliahostal.com), has a kitchen, clean rooms, a tour desk, and equipment rental; a double room costs $47 to $60, or less for a shared bathroom.

Altiplánico Sur ★★ **Moments** One of several new options leaning heavily on contemporary style, the Altiplánico Sur is the southern brother of San Pedro's Altiplánico (p. 418). From the outside, it appears as a two-story building a bit reminiscent of a brick school, but on approach, you'll see much of it is in fact underground with grass-covered roofs, and the exterior walls are made of a dark, unpainted adobe-type material. Spacious on the inside, the ambience relies heavily on loft-style concrete, trimmed by zig-zagging wood and some metal decor. Views of the water, across the road, are lovely. Rooms, down the corridor, are good-size, comfortable, and come with warm touches like plushy sheepskins and bright cushions that offset other eye-catching but cooler materials. Bathrooms are similar—modern, functional, and elegant. Since they don't offer all-inclusive packages so popular in the region, this makes a good bet for independent travelers looking for a low profile.

Huerto Familiar 282, Puerto Natales. ✆ **61/412525.** www.altiplanico.cl. 22 units. $180 single; $220 double. AE, DC, MC, V. **Amenities:** Restaurant; bar; Jacuzzi; living room w/TV; room service; Wi-Fi.

Indigo ★★★ **Moments** The hip Concepto Indigo is Puerto Natales' only true boutique hotel., offering the finest views of the glaciers across the sound. It's a very cool spot. Rooms are in the multistory, red-and-black ship container-inspired cube that overshadows the shingled former hostel, now a restaurant on the ground floor and a lounge on the top floor where you can check your e-mail on iMacs. The hotel's top-level spa features heated whirlpools that overlook the sound. The airy, midsize rooms have comfy beds and good views and finishings. Concepto Indigo just slightly edges out Remota as the best place in town and will be preferred by more independent travelers; the eco-friendly property includes an advanced insulation system that requires no central heating for most of the spring and summer.

Ladrilleros 105, Puerto Natales. ✆ **61/413609.** www.indigopatagonia.com. 29 units. $290 double. AE, DC, MC, V. **Amenities:** Restaurant; bar; sauna; Wi-Fi. *In room:* Hair dryer.

Remota ★★★ **Moments** You will either love or hate this hotel. The architecture alone is provocative, alternately uncomfortable and brilliant. Built by a renowned Chilean architect (who designed the explora) it's a unique mix of a bunker with a greenhouse, inspired by the *estancias* of Patagonia. Black and a bit forbidding from the outside, the Remota's interiors couldn't be more different. Huge floor-to-ceiling windows flood the white walls and columns with light amid a generous lounge and dining areas. Rooftops are covered in grass, and a look around here will show you a gorgeous panorama across the bay. The beautiful black marble indoor pool reflects the sky and landscape from the outside. Their all-inclusive packages tend to focus on lesser traveled areas, and now include transfers from El Calafate, Argentina. Remota is the explora's top competition and is a decidedly sustainable property that features solar heating, energy-efficient lighting, and low-consumption water systems.

Huerto 279, 1.5km (less than a mile) north of Puerto Natales. ✆ **61/414040.** www.remota.cl. 77 units. 3-night package $1,548 per person double, $2,220 single. Rates include excursions, meals, spa, and transfers. AE, DC, MC, V. **Amenities:** Dining area; bar; bikes; indoor pool; Wi-Fi. *In room:* Hair dryer.

Afrigonia ★★ FUSION One of the most interesting dining experiences in all of Chile is this tiny, unassuming spot that surprisingly blends Chilean food with East African. Curries and tandooris have real spices, and the *ceviche* in coconut milk with mango may be the best *ceviche* you'll have in Chile. It's small and very popular, so reserve first.

Eberhard 343, ✆ **61/412232.** Reservations recommended. Main courses C$4,500–C$7,500. AE, DC, MC, V. Daily 7–11pm.

Cormoran de Las Rocas ★★ (Moments) SEAFOOD This is Puerto Natales' best seafood restaurant, and the top local choice for upscale dining. In a top-floor dining room designed to feel like a ship, the views are superb and the seafood-heavy menu large. Specialities include a king crab tart with four cheeses, rosemary octopus with a green-apple salad, and salmon or hake in coconut-and-saffron sauce. For dessert, try the cheesecake with calafate sauce. Service is very professional. The bar offers lighter tapas, and is open late.

Miguel Sanchez 72. ✆ **61/413723.** Main courses C$6,000–C$9,000. AE, DC, MC, V. Daily 12:30–3pm and 7:30–11pm.

El Living ★★ (Finds) CAFE/VEGETARIAN If you're looking for a friendly, comfortable place to spend the evening, then look no further. At El Living, run by a British expatriate couple who have lived in the area for more than a decade, you can lounge on a comfortable sofa with a pisco sour or have an excellent vegetarian dinner at one of their handmade wooden dining tables. The menu is simple and inexpensive but fresh and delicious. The Sweet and Sour Red Salad is a perfect mix of beetroot, red cabbage, kidney beans, and onion; the veggie burger is delicious and served on a whole-wheat baguette. This is one of the only places in Chile that serves a peanut-butter-and-jelly sandwich. There's also French toast with fried bananas, and a variety of cakes baked daily. A full bar and wine list round out this excellent place.

Arturo Prat 156. ✆ **61/411140.** Main courses C$4,500–C$7,500. No credit cards. Daily 11am–midnight.

PARQUE NACIONAL TORRES DEL PAINE ★★★

This is Chile's prized jewel, a national park so magnificent that few in the world can claim a rank in its class. The park is made of granite peaks and towers that soar from sea level to upward of 2,800m (9,200 ft.); golden pampas and steppes that are home to guanacos and more than 100 species of colorful birds, such as parakeets and flamingos; electric-blue icebergs that cleave from glaciers descending from the Southern Ice Field; and thick, virgin beech forest. The park is not something you visit; it is something you experience.

Although it sits next to the Andes, **Parque Nacional Torres del Paine** is a separate geologic formation created roughly 3 million years ago when bubbling magma pushed its way up, taking a thick sedimentary layer with it. Glaciation and severe climate weathered away the softer rock, leaving the spectacular Paine Massif whose prominent features are the *cuernos* (horns) and the one-of-a-kind Torres—three salmon-colored, spherical granite towers. *Paine* is the Tehuelche Indian word for "blue," and it brings to mind the varying shades found in the lakes that surround this massif—among them the milky, turquoise waters of lakes Nordenskjold and Pehoé.

This park is a backpacker's dream, but just as many visitors find pleasure staying in lodges here and taking day hikes and horseback rides—even those with a short amount of time are blown away by a 1-day visit. But come with your expectations in check—it's not uncommon to spend a week here and not see the towers even once due to bad weather. For more information, check out the website **www.torresdelpaine.com**.

When to Go & What to Bring

This is not the easiest of national parks to visit. The climate in the park can be abominable, with wind speeds that can peak at 161kmph (100 mph), and rain and snow even in the middle of summer. The period in which your chances are highest of avoiding wind and rain are October and mid-March to late April, but keep in mind that the only thing predictable here is the unpredictability of the weather. Spring is a beautiful time for budding flowers and birds; during the fall, the beech forests turn striking shades of crimson, orange, and yellow. The winter is very cold, with relatively few snowstorms and no wind—but short days. Summer is ironically the worst time to come, especially late December to mid-February, when the wind blows at full fury and crowds descend upon the park. When the wind blows it can make even a short walk a rather scary and often frustrating experience—just try to go with it and revel in the excitement of the extreme environment that makes Patagonia what it is.

It's imperative that you bring the right gear (especially waterproof hiking boots if you plan to do any trekking), including weatherproof outerwear and layers, even in the summer. The ozone problem is acute, so you'll need sunscreen, sunglasses, and a hat.

Getting There & Around

Many travelers are unaware of the enormous amount of time it takes to get to Torres del Paine. There are no direct transportation services from the airport in Punta Arenas to the park, except with package tours and hotels that have their own vehicles, or by chartering an auto or van (try **Viaterra** at ✆ **61/410775;** www.viaterra.cl). If you're relying on bus transportation (versus staying at an all-inclusive lodge), it's only logical that you will need to spend the night in Punta Arenas or Puerto Natales. Thanks to a new road, the west side of the park (where lodges like explora, Patagonia Camp, and Hosteria Lago Grey are) is now only 1 hour from Puerto Natales.

BY BUS Several companies offer daily service from October to April. During the low season, only **Bus Sur,** Baquedano 668 (✆ **61/614223**), offers service to the park. Buses to Torres del Paine enter through the Laguna Amarga ranger station, stop at the Pudeto catamaran dock, and terminate at the park administration center. If you're going directly to the Torres trail head at Hostería Las Torres, minivan transfers waiting at the Laguna Amarga station charge C$2,500 one-way. The return times given below are when the bus leaves from the park administration center; the bus will pass through the Laguna Amarga station about 45 minutes later.

Trans Via Paine, Bulnes 516 (✆ **61/413672**), leaves daily at 7:30am via Laguna Amarga. **Gomez,** Arturo Prat 234 (✆ **61/411971**), also leaves at 7:30am, returning from the administration building at 1pm. **Buses JB,** Arturo Prat 258 (✆ **61/410242**), also departs at 7:30am, returning at 1pm. The cost is around C$8,500 one-way.

BY CAR A new road linking Puerto Natales with Torres del Paine opened in 2007, and not only does it shave more than an hour off the trip to the park, it is also one of the most visually stunning drives in Chile. Head toward the park from Puerto Natales and turn left at the sign for the Milodon Cave; the road continues from here and enters near the administration center, about 80km (50 miles) along. The old road is 140km

(87 miles) from Puerto Natales and is best for backpackers interested in beginning their trek in the park with the Towers hike. When entering, follow the road toward the Laguna Amarga entrance.

CROSSING LAGO PEHOE BY CATAMARAN Day hikes to the Glacier Grey trail and backpackers taking the W or Circuit trails will need to cross Lake Pehoé at some point aboard a catamaran, about a 45-minute ride. The cost is C$12,500 one-way or C$21,000 round-trip. Buses from Puerto Natales are timed to drop off and pick up passengers in conjunction with the catamaran (Nov 15–Mar 15 leaving Pudeto at 9:30am, noon, and 6pm, and from Pehoé 10am, 12:30, and 6:30pm; ; Nov 1-14 and Mar 16–30 from Pudeto at noon and 6pm, and Pehoé at 12:30 and 6pm; in Oct and Apr, from Pudeto at noon, and Pehoé at 12:30pm). Hikers walking the entire round-trip Glacier Grey trail can do so only from December to March 15 by taking the 9:30am boat and returning at 6:30pm.

GETTING TO & FROM THE PARK BY BOAT Few are aware that they can leave or arrive by boat to or from Puerto Natales through the Ultima Esperanza Sound and up the Río Serrano. Visitors ride a zodiac inflatable boat along the Río Serrano and past the glaciers Tyndall and Geike, terminating at the Serrano Glacier. Here you disembark for a walk up to the ice, and then board another boat for a 3½-hour ride to Puerto Natales. The trip costs $85 depending on the season, and **Onas** (✆/fax **61/614300;** www.onaspatagonia.com) can make arrangements. Active travelers will be interested in following the same Río Serrano route but by **kayak,** about a 3-day journey. This trip is suitable for travelers on their way back to Puerto Natales, to take advantage of the river's downward current; at night, travelers camp out on shore. Check with **Indómita** (✆ **61/413247;** www.indomitapatagonia.com) on Bories 206 in Puerto Natales.

Where to Stay & Dine in Torres Del Paine

Hotels & Hosterías

In addition to the below properties, you might consider staying at **Estancia Cerro Guido** (✆ **61/411818;** www.cerroguido.cl.). This luxurious lodge may be a fair distance from the park proper, but it's the only top hotel with a view of the distinctive Torres, from its perspective due west across the plains. It's also one of the only properties by the park to offer an authentic *estancia* experience.

explora Patagonia ★★★ Moments Explora in Patagonia has garnered more fame than any other hotel in Chile, and deservedly so. Few hotels in the world offer as stunning a view as does explora, perched above the milky, turquoise waters of Lago Pehoé and facing the dramatic granite amphitheater of the Paine massif. It is terribly expensive, but worth the splurge if you can afford it. Explora's style is relaxed elegance: softly curving, blond-wood walls built entirely from native deciduous beech, a band of picture windows wrapping around the full front of the building, and large windows in each room. The smart guest rooms are accented with Spanish-made checkered linens, handsome slate-tiled bathrooms, and warming racks for drying gear. Explora, which now has 50 guest rooms—making it more of a hotel than a cozy mountain inn—is all inclusive, and offers outdoor excursions on regular 4-day rotations. At presstime, this property was midway through receiving prestigious LEED certification from the United States Green Building Council.

Office in Santiago, Américo Vespucio Sur 80, 5th floor. ✆ **866/750-6699** in the U.S., or 2/206-6060 in Santiago. Fax 2/228-4655. www.explora.com. 50 units. Packages per person, double occupancy; 4 nights from $2,260; 8 nights from $5,232. Rates include all meals, transportation, gear, excursions, and guides. AE, DC, MC, V. **Amenities:** Restaurant; bar; lounge; outdoor Jacuzzi; large indoor pool; sauna.

Hostería Las Torres ★ Kids This *hostería* sits at the trail head to the Torres on an *estancia* that still operates as a working cattle ranch. The complex includes a ranch-style hotel with a spa and other amenities, a large campground, and a hostel, meaning there's a lot of traffic coming in and out daily. The *hostería* is a decent value for its standard rooms, but their superior rooms are nothing special for the price and are relatively identical to standard rooms. Las Torres offers packages that include guided tours, meals, and transportation, much like explora, and off-season tours to little-explored areas—however, they are very pricey and the views and lodging facilities are a far cry from those at explora. The hotel has a delicious daily buffet dinner for $30 per person, not including drinks.

Office in Punta Arenas, Magallanes 960. ✆/fax **61/710050.** www.lastorres.com. 56 units. A 3-night/4-day package including meals, excursions, and airport transfers costs $1,270–$1,420 double occupancy. AE, DC, MC, V. **Amenities:** Restaurant; lounge; horseback riding; room service.

Patagonia Camp ★★ Kids Moments The most appealing new lodging option in the area is a camp for grown-ups. With a mountaineer's heart and a luxury bent, this is not a hotel, it's an experience in nature. Set on a slope above Lago del Toro, with stunning views of the Paine massif, the Patagonia Camp feels akin to safari camps found in the African savannah. There are 18 wood-framed yurts (Mongolian-inspired woodframed tents) situated along wooden walkways tucked inside a beech forest. Incredibly bright, cozy, and plush, the yurts have high-end touches like woven blankets, central heating, and deep tubs. But it's not a walk in the park: during storms, you may curse the tents that flap loudly and get wet just going from place to place. In the main lodge, meals (and pisco sours) are served. The all-inclusive packages mirror those of explora, but Patagonia Camp is much more quiet and intimate. The sustainable property features a gray-water treatment system and solar-powered lighting.

Office in Santiago Hernando de Aguirre 414. ✆ **2/335-6898.** www.patagoniacamp.com. 18 units. 3-night programs per person $2,110 single, $1,410 double. Rates include all meals, excursions, transfers in/out, guides. AE, DC, MC, V. **Amenities:** Restaurant; library.

Refugios & Albergues

Five cabinlike lodging units and one hostel, all with shared accommodation, are distributed along the park's Circuit and W trails, and they are moderately priced sleeping options for backpackers who are not interested in pitching a tent. Although most have bedding or sleeping bags for an expensive rental price, your best bet is to bring your own. The price, at $40 on average per night (about $63 for room and full board), may seem steep for a simple dorm bed (expect to pay $80 for full board); still, it is a far cry cheaper than many shared accommodations in national parks in the U.S. All come with hot showers, a simple cafe, and a common area for hiding out from bad weather. Meals served here are simply prepared but hearty, or alternatively, guests can bring their own food and cook for themselves. Each *refugio* has rooms with two to six bunks, which you'll have to share with strangers when they're full. During the high season, consider booking weeks in advance; although many visitors have reported luck when calling just a few days beforehand (due to cancellations). All agencies in Puerto Natales and Punta Arenas book reservations and issue vouchers, but your best bet is to call or e-mail. There is a scrappy *refugio* near the park administration center, with two rows of sleeping berths that I do not recommend except in an emergency situation. This *refugio* is on a first-come, first-served basis. The first three *refugios* are owned and operated by **Fantástico Sur,** a division of the Hostería las Torres. They can be booked by contacting ✆/fax **61/360361** or www.wcircuit.com.

- **Refugio Torres.** This *albergue* (lodge) is the largest and most full-service *refugio* in the park; it sits near the Hostería Las Torres. This is also the trail head for the W trail and the full Circuit trail. You may dine in the hotel or eat simple fare in the *refugio* itself. Horseback rides can be taken from here.
- **Refugio Los Cuernos.** This may be the park's loveliest *refugio,* at the base of the Cuernos. The wood structure (which miraculously holds up to some of the strongest winds in the park) has two walls of windows that look out onto Lago Nordenskjöld.

Both of the refugios below can be reserved at ✆ **61/412742** or booked online at www.verticepatagonia.cl.

- **Refugio Grey.** Tucked inside a forest on the shore of Lago Grey, this log-cabin *refugio* is a 10-minute walk to the lookout point for the glacier. It's a cold but refreshing setting, and it has a cozy fireside seating area. Spend a day here and take a walking tour on the glacier (see "Excursions Around Glacier Grey," below).
- **Refugio Dickson.** This is one of the loneliest *refugios,* due to its location well on the other side of the park (part of the Circuit trail). You can't beat the rugged location on a grassy glacial moraine, facing Dickson Glacier.
- **Lodge Paine Grande.** This hostel-like "lodge" replaces the old *refugio* Pehoé, at the busiest intersection in the park. It is the hub for several of the trail heads to the park administration center, Glacier Grey, and French Valley, as well as the docking site for the catamaran. Utilitarian in style, the hostel has 60 beds, two lounges, and a cafeteria that can serve 120 people. Day walks to Glacier Grey and French Valley can be taken from here.

Trails in Torres Del Paine

Torres del Paine has something for everyone, from easy, well-trammeled trails to remote walks through rough wilderness. If you have only a few days, stick to the major highlights. With 4 or 5 days, you can hike the ultraclassic W route. If you have a week or more, consider a backpacking trip around the Circuit or a walk to the Valle de Silencio beyond the Towers, or for easier excursions, a horseback ride to Mt. Donoso or a bird-watching trip to Valley Pingo (for bird-watching tours, try **Fantástico Sur,** ✆ **61/247194;** www.fantasticosur.com). Pick up a **JLM Torres del Paine map** or download a map from the website **www.torresdelpaine.com** to begin planning.

Day Hikes

The **Torres (Towers)** trail to view the granite formations that give the park its name is a classic hike, but certainly not the easiest. The 6-hour, moderate-to-difficult hike leaves from the Hostería Las Torres. The **Valle Francés (French Valley)** trail takes hikers into a granite amphitheater and past Paine Grande mountain and its hanging glacier. The 5-hour round-trip trail is moderate and can be reached from Refugio Los Cuernos or the Lodge Paine Grande (at Pehoé). The trail to the face of **Glacier Grey** is a moderate to difficult trail that takes about 3½ hours one-way. From the *refugio* just before the lookout, hikers may catch the catamaran to Hostería Grey (see below) rather than walk back along the same trail. The easiest walk in the park is also one of the most dramatic for the gigantic icebergs that rest along the shore of **Lago Grey.**

Excursions Around Glacier Grey

Glacier Grey has receded substantially over the past few years, and now the best way to get an up-close view is aboard the **Hostería Grey catamaran,** a half-day excursion that takes passengers to the glacier's blue walls and around floating icebergs. The round-trip journey leaves from the shore of Lake Grey; however, it is possible to take the early catamaran across Lake Pehoé, walk the approximately 4 hours to the Refugio Grey, and then return by the Lake Grey catamaran. You'll need to arrange transportation through your hotel; otherwise the Hostería leaves you at the administration center to catch a bus. The trip leaves a little after 8am and 2:30pm, and reservations are essential; contact the Hostería at ✆ **61/229512** (www.lagogrey.cl).

8

Colombia

by Jisel Perilla

If there's a country poised to be the next big ecotourism destination, it's Colombia—that is, so long as it can maintain the relative peace of the last few years. With an area equal to that of Spain, France, and Portugal combined, Colombia has coastlines on the Atlantic and Pacific oceans, thick Amazon jungle, immense flatlands evoking the American plains, scorching deserts, and snow-capped mountain peaks. All that plus 45 million residents means that Colombia is second only to Brazil in ecological and human diversity among South American countries.

Once considered the most dangerous country in the world, Colombia, having implemented security improvements over the last half decade, is slowly emerging from the internecine bloodshed of the 1980s and 1990s. Homicide rates in many Colombian cities, once among the highest in the world, have fallen to levels similar to those of U.S. cities such as Milwaukee and Philadelphia. Since President Alvaro Uribe took office in 2002, political kidnappings have decreased by over 70% and a strong military and police presence have made land transportation reasonably safe again. However, Uribe's popularity has decreased in the last year. No matter who takes office next, it's going to be a tough battle to maintain Colombia's delicate relative peace.

However, thanks to this improved security situation, Colombia is a country ripe for discovery by foreign tourists. Though politically one nation, it is made up of three distinct regions, each with its own customs and traditions. The Atlantic and Pacific coasts, inhabited mostly by descendents of African slaves, are culturally linked to the Caribbean, and rich in musical tradition and spectacular tropical scenery. The central and most densely populated portion of the country, crowned by the Andes Mountains, has managed to grow and prosper despite its unforgiving terrain. Dotted by most of Colombia's largest cities, it is the economic engine of the country. The eastern portion of Colombia is sparsely inhabited by tough, hard-working farmers and traditional indigenous tribes; it's a land of vast planes, thick jungle, unmatched natural beauty, and, unfortunately, high levels of guerilla activity and cocaine production.

Like most of the developing world, Colombia is a country of contradictions. Hip yuppies dress to the nines and sip $12 cocktails at über-upscale bars, while the poorest Colombians can barely afford life's necessities. Cosmopolitan cities offer luxury condos, theater, international cuisine, and all the amenities of the modern world, while many small *pueblos* seem stuck in the last century, stunted by high unemployment and old-fashioned attitudes. Despite all its woes—economic, social, and political—Colombia remains a fascinating country to visit.

1 THE REGIONS IN BRIEF

Colombia is a country with much to offer the adventurous tourist. Whether you want to enjoy the sophisticated city atmosphere of Bogotá or swim in the clear Caribbean waters of San Andrés or Providencia,, Colombia has what you're looking for.

BOGOTA Situated at more than 2,630m (8,600 ft.), and bordered by the Andes to the east, Bogotá is the third-highest capital in the world. Its nearly eight million residents make it Colombia's largest city by far, and one that has some of South America's best museums, universities, and restaurants. Bogotá is quickly taking on an international character as more and more multinationals invest in and set up headquarters there.

ANTIOQUIA & THE EJE CAFETERO Colombia's main coffee-growing region is blessed with magnificent mountain scenery, coffee-terraced slopes, and old-world small towns. But Antioquia and the Eje Cafetero aren't all country: Armenia, Manizales, and Pereira are thriving cities with a coffee-based economy and Medellín, Colombia's second-largest metropolis, is one of Latin America's most progressive and innovative cities.

SAN ANDRES, PROVIDENCIA & THE ATLANTIC COAST Some of the safest and most accessible travel experiences in the country are found here. San Andrés, long popular with Colombian tourists, has beautiful white-sand beaches and sprawling, all-inclusive resorts, while less developed Providencia is famous for its Caribbean-English architecture, dense jungle, and scuba diving. Cartagena, the pride and joy of Colombia, has the most impressive old city in the Americas, dating all the way back to the 16th century. Its many plazas and restaurants come alive at night and its colonial architecture is unmatched anywhere on the Western Hemisphere. North of Cartagena, check out the modern city of Santa Marta, a good base for exploring the Sierra Nevada Mountains and pristine jungles and beaches of Parque Tayrona.

THE SOUTHWEST & PACIFIC COAST Though still considered dangerous, this region has some accessible areas. Cali, the salsa-music capital of Colombia, claims to have the most beautiful women in Colombia, and its nightlife is unrivaled anywhere in the country. However, I recommend sticking to high-end areas and checking safety conditions before heading here. Popayán, second only to Cartagena in terms of colonial architecture, is a beautiful white-washed city with an active student and cafe life. The Pacific coast and El Chocó, inhabited almost exclusively by African descendants, is one of the wettest regions in the world, known for its dense jungles and unnavigable rivers. Unfortunately, much of this region is controlled by leftist guerillas or right-wing paramilitaries, but some intrepid travelers have visited the coast's pristine, virgin beaches. Nariño and its capital, Pasto, in many ways are culturally closer to Ecuador and Peru, and offer some of the highest peaks and best markets in the country. ***Warning:*** The Southwest and the Pacific Coast remain dangerous. If you're intent on going, fly to your destination and be sure to check security conditions first. Resources include the U.S. Department of State website (www.travel.state.gov), Colombian newspapers such as *El Tiempo* (www.eltiempo.com), and Colombians themselves.

THE EASTERN PLAINS & AMAZON JUNGLE Most of Colombia is composed of sparsely inhabited plains and jungle. Los Llanos, as they are known in Colombia, are physically similar to the American plains, and inhabitants have a definitively independent, relentless spirit. Los Llanos, Colombia's agricultural heartland, is known for its magnificent sunsets and beautiful *fincas* (farms), which fill up with tourists from Bogotá during

El Conflicto Armado: Who's Fighting Whom

Although security conditions have improved dramatically since conservative hard-liner Alvaro Uribe took office in 2002, Colombia can still be an unpredictable place, with flare-ups between guerilla and paramilitary factions. To understand the conflict, it's important to know the players. On the leftist, guerilla side is the **FARC (Revolutionary Armed Forces of Colombia),** the country's largest guerilla army, with about 12,000 members. The **ELN (National Liberation Army)** consists of about 5,000 people and is in on-and-off-again demobilization talks. The **M-19** was another deadly, mostly urban guerilla movement that demobilized in the late 1980s. On the far right are the **paramilitaries,** originally formed to combat the guerillas but now major players in the drug trade. **Las Aguilas Negras** are a relatively new group, composed mostly of so-called demobilized paramilitaries.

To make sense of all the acronyms and ideology, not to mention the corruption, consider reading one of the following books, all of which provide excellent background: *Killing Peace* (2002) by Gary Leech; *Walking Ghosts: Murder and Guerrilla Politics in Colombia* (2005) by Steven Dudley; and *More Terrible Than Death: Violence, Drugs, and America's War in Colombia* (2004) by Robin Kirk.

Although the modern Colombian conflict didn't technically start until 1964, when the FARC was founded, Colombia has had a bloody past almost as long as the country's history. The violence, always rooted in politics, pitted the Liberals against the Conservatives, resulting in both the Thousand Days War, from 1899 to 1902, and, later on, La Violencia of the 1940s and 1950s. Combined, these conflicts took the lives of almost half a million Colombians. After the relative peace of the 1960s and 1970s, violence flared up again during the '80s and '90s, mostly owing to the increased involvement of the guerillas and paramilitaries in the drug trade, as well as to Pablo Escobar, who had a hand in frequent bombings, assassinations, and campaigns of terror.

holiday weekends. The eastern plains have recently become safer, but there is still a strong guerilla presence here, and this is one of Colombia's main cocaine-producing regions.

The Amazon covers 33% of Colombia, but only 1% of the country's population, consisting mostly of traditional indigenous tribes. Except for Leticia and its surroundings, this area is inaccessible. ***Warning:*** The dense jungle make this region perfect for coca production as well as paramilitary and guerilla activity; do not venture here unless you're taking a direct flight to Leticia, which is considered very safe.

2 THE BEST OF COLOMBIA IN 2 WEEKS

Two weeks in Colombia should provide you with a good feel for the country and give you enough time to see some of the major sights and cities. Keep in mind that road conditions can be unpredictable, so it's best to fly between the far-flung destinations.

Unlike most Latin American movements, the FARC, paramilitaries, and other nongovernment armed forces have little backing among Colombia's poor, especially as these armed groups become more involved with narco trafficking, effectively disregarding their stated ideology. In fact, fighting for control of the lucrative cocaine trade appears to be the top priority for guerilla and paramilitary groups nowadays.

As a foreigner and a tourist, you are unlikely to face threats from any illegal groups, but it's still wise to avoid rural areas, city slums, and other "red zones"—so declared by the government depending on recent guerilla and paramilitary violence. Your best bet is to **stick to cities and heavily patrolled and visited destinations** such as the Eje Cafetero, the department of Boyacá, and most of the Atlantic coast. Unless for some reason you'll be traveling to guerilla- or paramilitary-controlled areas (where you absolutely don't want to talk about the conflict), you're fine to discuss the FARC, paramilitaries, or much-loved President Uribe with taxi drivers, waiters, receptionists, and other Colombians; everyone here seems to have an opinion, and this is a good way to interact with and learn about the locals and their country.

Keep tabs on the ever-changing situation by reading *El Tiempo* (www.eltiempo.com), Colombia's most important and popular newspaper, and by frequently checking the U.S Department of State website regarding travel warnings (http://travel.state.gov). You may also want to keep tabs on the growing tensions between President Alvaro Uribe and Venezuelan President Hugo Chávez, as this might result in further violence along the Colombia-Venezuela border. Although all this information may sound a bit ominous and discouraging, the bottom line is, unless you veer off the beaten path, you shouldn't face any problems.

Days ❶–❹: Bogotá

On your first day, arrive and get settled in the city. Stay at the amazing **Casa Medina** (p. 488) or **Hotel de la Opera** (p. 486) and eat at one of the many gourmet restaurants in Bogotá's "gourmet district." Spend your first full day in Colombia exploring **La Candelaria** and the historic center. Have breakfast at **La Puerta Falsa** (p. 491), Colombia's longest-running business and restaurant. Take the cable car up to Monserrate, Bogotá's highest peak, and admire the view of sprawling Bogotá. Stop at the **Museo del Oro** (p. 482) at Santander Square, and visit the **Museo Botero** (p. 481) for an overview of Colombia's most famous artist. Recharge your energy by having lunch at any of La Candelaria's quaint eateries, popular with college students. In the afternoon, head to **Plaza de Bolívar** to feed the pigeons and be awed by Bogotá's eclectic architecture.

On Day 3, if you're around on a weekend or holiday, hop on the **Turistren** (p. 484), the only remaining steam engine in Colombia, or visit a few more of Bogotá's 50-plus museums—those interested in Colombian history will enjoy the

Quinta de Bolívar (p. 482). Also explore some of the city's most popular parks, such as **Parque de la 93, Usaquén,** and **El Parque de Bolívar.**

Dedicate Day 4 to shopping. If you're around on a Sunday, head to **Usaquén** (p. 481). If you're looking for posh designer clothing, leather goods, or jewelry, head to one of the upscale malls in the city's northern districts. Also spend some time exploring some of the city's funkier neighborhoods, like **La Macarena,** home to some of the city's strangest (and most entertaining) bars and restaurants; **El Centro,** with its many universities and cafes, gallerias, and vibrant bar scene; or the **north,** home to the city's best malls and restaurants.

Days ❺–❼: Villa de Leyva

Take a 4-hour bus to the perfectly preserved town of Villa de Leyva, and spend Day 5 exploring the cobblestone streets and handicraft shops. Stay at the **Hospedería Duruelo** (p. 494) for a luxury experience, or **Hostal Renacer** (p. 494) if you want to get away from it all. On Day 6, learn a bit about the Colombian independence movement by visiting the **Museo de Antonio Nariño** (p. 493) and see one of Colombia's most complete collections of religious art at **El Museo de Arte Religioso** (p. 493). Spend the evening people-watching in the main plaza from one of the many open-air cafes bordering the plaza. Alternatively, book a tour with one of the numerous companies offering adventure and nature activities around Villa de Leyva. Go rock climbing, go horseback riding, visit a vineyard, hike in a nearby desert, or explore one of the many waterfalls around town.

Spend your last day in Villa de Leyva rapelling, hiking, mountain biking, or exploring the area's many natural attractions. Outdoor enthusiasts will enjoy horseback riding through the **Villa de Leyva desert** and visiting the area's many waterfalls and rivers.

Days ❽–❾: Medellín & Antioquia

Fly into Medellín and spend Day 8 exploring the city center. Hop on a Turibus to visit the **Catedral Metropolitana** (p. 498) and other major sites. In the early afternoon, take the free cable car up to the *comunas* (municipal districts) for great views of Medellín. For dinner, dine at one of the many classy restaurants around **Parque Lleras** before heading to **Vía de Las Palmas** for a night of dancing. For a change of pace, on Day 9, book a tour of the surrounding Antioquian countryside with **Aviatur** (p. 496).

Days ❿–⓭: The Atlantic Coast

Fly from Pereira, Armenia, or Manizales to the magical city of **Cartagena.** On Day 10, spend the morning sunbathing and swimming in the warm Caribbean waters. In the afternoon, book a *chiva* tour (p. 507) of the city for a brief history and overview of the city's major sights. At night, head to the **Club de Pesca** (p. 511) for a romantic seafood dinner overlooking Cartagena's yacht basin. Stay at the historic **Sofitel Santa Clara** (p. 510) in San Diego Square.

On Day 11, head to the **Old City** to explore its many plazas, museums, and shops. Have lunch in **Santo Domingo Square.** In the evening, book a spot on a ***rumba chiva*** (p. 507), a typical Colombia party bus, or, if you're feeling a bit more romantic, take your special someone on a carriage stroll through the Old Town.

Spend the next day in **Las Islas del Rosario.** Visit the Aquario de San Martín, and go snorkeling and swimming in the bright green waters of Isla de Barú, 45km (28 miles) from Cartagena. If you still have energy left, head to **Mr. Babilla** (p. 513), in Getsemaní, for a night of fun and dancing. On Day 13, depart Cartagena, flying either directly home from there or connecting in Bogotá.

3 PLANNING YOUR TRIP TO COLOMBIA

VISITOR INFORMATION

Because Colombia's tourism infrastructure is extremely underdeveloped, traveling here can be a bit tricky, especially if you don't speak Spanish. Except for Cartagena and some parts of the Atlantic Coast, many sections of Colombia have seen only a trickle of foreign visitors in the last few decades. Although tourists are generally treated formally and with polite curiosity, don't expect to find an overwhelming amount of tourist information. However, Colombians are generally friendly and your hotel staff will probably go out of their way to help you. Remember that a visit to Colombia requires patience and a sense of humor. One of the best ways to prepare for your trip to Colombia is on the Internet, where you will find plenty of useful information, especially from fellow travelers. The following websites contain useful information about Colombia.

- **www.iexplore.com/dmap/Colombia/Travel+and+Trips**: Dedicated to adventure travel, this site provides valuable country, etiquette, and excursion information.
- **poorbuthappy.com/colombia**: A great traveler-created site where you can find information, ask questions, and do research. Especially good for the younger, backpacker crowd.
- **www.roadjunky.com/guide/298/colombia-travel-guide-online**: An okay country guide with basic information.
- **www.colombiaemb.org**: Colombia's embassy in Washington. A good place to start exploring the country.

In Colombia

The Ministerio de Comercio, Industria y Turismo is Colombia's National Tourism Ministry. The main office is located at Calle 28 no. 13A–15 (✆ **1/606-7676** or 1/419-9450), but don't expect them to be very helpful or speak much English. In fact, good luck even getting into the building. But if you read Spanish, you may want to check out their website (www.mincomercio.gov.co/eContent/home.asp).

Colombia's most popular tourism agency, **Aviatur** (✆ **1/286-5555** or 1/234-7333; www.aviatur.com), will book tours all over Colombia, usually including transportation, lodging, and most meals. The main office in Bogotá is at Ave. 19 no. 4–62. There are offices throughout Bogotá and all large Colombian cities as well.

Tourism companies frequently come and go, so if you're looking for eco-adventure tours and travel, your best bet is your hotel which can give you information on local tours and tourism agencies, or at least provide some guidance.

ENTRY REQUIREMENTS

A valid passport is required to visit Colombia. Visas are not required if you are a citizen of Australia, Canada, France, Germany, New Zealand, South Africa, Switzerland, the United Kingdom, or the United States. You will automatically be granted permission to stay in the country for 60 days upon entering Colombia. If you plan to spend more than 60 days in the country, you will have to get permission from the Colombian Security Department (DAS) office in any departmental capital, though most tourists do so in Bogotá. To receive this 30- to 60-day extension, you will need to deposit COL$60,400 to Bancafé (account #056-99020-3, code 103), and then present your passport, your plane ticket (showing date of departure), four color passport pictures (3cm×4cm), two photocopies of your passport picture page, two copies of your passport entry stamp page, two copies of the Bancafé deposit slip, and two copies of your plane ticket. The process usually takes 1 to 2 hours, but you will be given the extension on the spot. You can repeat the process until you've been in the country 180 days. The **Bogotá DAS office,** at Calle 100 no. 11B–27, Edificio Platino (✆ **1/601-7200**), is open Monday through Thursday 7:30am to 4pm and Friday 7:30am to 3pm. If you stay in Colombia more than 60 days without a visa extension, you can be fined $60 to $1,600 (depending on how long you overstay).

Colombian Embassy Locations

In Australia: 161 London CCT, Level 2, CPA Bldg., ACT 2601 (✆ **02/6230-4203;** fax 02/6257-1448).

Telephone Dialing at a Glance

Colombia's phone system features a standardized system of seven-digit local numbers with one or two digit area codes.

- **To place a call from your home country to Colombia,** dial the international access code (0011 in Australia, 011 in the U.S and Canada, 0170 in New Zealand, and 00 in the U.K.), the country code (57), the one- or two-digit Colombian city code (Bogotá 1, Medellín 4, Cartagena 5, Pereira 61, Armenia 67, Manizales 69), plus the seven-digit local number.
- **To place a local call within Colombia,** dial the one- or two-digit city code followed by the seven-digit local number. To call within a city, you only need to dial the seven-digit number. If you're dialing from a cellphone to a land line, dial 031, the city code, then the seven digit number. To call a cellphone from a landline, dial the city code plus the 10 digit cell phone.
- **International operator info:** To reach an English-speaking **international operator** from within Colombia, dial ✆ **01/800-913-0110.**

In Canada: 360 Albert St., Ste 1002, Piso 10 K1R 7X7, Ottawa, ON (✆ **613/230-3760;** embajada@embajadacolombia.ca).

In New Zealand (consulate): PO Box 17072, Karori Wellington (✆ **644/4769-857;** fax 644/4769-779).

In the U.K.: 3 Hans Crescent, London, SW1X OLN (✆ **020/7589-9177;** fax 020/7581-1829; www.colombianembassy.co.uk).

In the U.S.: 2118 Leroy Place NW, Washington, DC 20008 (✆ **202/387-8338;** www.colombiaemb.org).

CUSTOMS

Upon entering Colombia, you will be asked to complete a Customs form detailing your personal effects. There is a regularly updated limit on cash and goods you may take out of the country. Because of strict drug-trafficking laws, *do not* try to take more money out of Colombia than you claim—at a minimum, this could result in heavy questioning. For more information regarding this limit, call ✆ **1/546-2200** or 1/457-8270. Usually, there's a limit of about US$10,000. When leaving the country, you must pay an airport departure tax of about COL$114,520, though this tax is often included in your airline ticket.

MONEY

The **Colombian peso (COL$)** is the official currency. Money is denominated in notes of 1,000, 2,000, 5,000, 10,000, 20,000, and 50,000, and coins of 20, 50, 100, 200, and 500 pesos. At press time, the exchange rate was about **COL$2,000 to US$1**. These rates can fluctuate somewhat, so it's important to check the latest exchange rate at **www.xe.com/ucc**.

CURRENCY EXCHANGE Unlike in other Latin-American countries, the U.S. dollar is not widely accepted in Colombia, except in a few super-high-end establishments. You can convert your currency in upscale hotels, at *casas de cambio* (money-exchange houses), at most banks, and at the airport. It's not recommended to bring traveler's checks to Colombia. They can be exchanged at some banks and used at high-end hotels, but usually they aren't accepted elsewhere. Make sure your bank or issuer has a representative in Colombia before purchasing traveler's checks.

ATMS Cash machines are easy to find in urban areas and most medium-to-large-size towns, though they are almost impossible to come across in rural areas. Withdrawing money from ATMs is preferable to exchanging money in banks, which charge a sometimes hefty transaction fee. ATMs also give you the most up-to-date rate of exchange. Thefts at ATMs have been reported, however, so if you are taking out large sums of money, be sure not to put all your cash in one place (spread the bills among your pockets). It's best to use ATM machines located inside a building, as these offer more security. ***Warning:*** If you are having trouble with an ATM, do not accept help from anyone, even if he or she seems friendly and honest. This is the easiest way to wipe out your bank account.

CREDIT CARDS Credit cards, particularly Visa and MasterCard, are generally accepted in midrange and upscale shops, as well as at upscale restaurants and hotels around the country. In rural areas and small towns, you are unlikely to find establishments that accept credit cards. When booking tours, you're likely to get a better deal when using cash.

WHEN TO GO

PEAK SEASON In the Andean region, the dry season falls between December and March and July and August. Christmas is a particularly festive time in Colombia, though prices often rise and hotel rooms fill up quickly in Cartagena and the Atlantic Coast, as well as in other popular tourist destinations. During the Christmas holiday, Easter, and summer vacation, you'll have to book hotels in advance and be prepared to pay a bit extra. If possible, avoid Colombia in October and November, as these are the rainiest months, and flooding and poor road conditions are common.

CLIMATE Because of its proximity to the Equator, Colombia's temperature varies according to altitude rather than season. In high altitudes, days are cool and nights can dip near the freezing mark. In lowlands, expect a tropical, humid climate with little difference between daytime and nighttime temperatures. As a general guide, the average temperature in Bogotá is 57°F (14°C), in Cartagena 87°F (31°C), and in Medellín 75°F (24°C). As stated above, the rainiest months are October and November.

PUBLIC HOLIDAYS Colombia has more public holidays than any other nation except Brazil. Usually, if a holiday falls on a Saturday or Sunday, it is celebrated the following Monday. Public holidays are New Year's Day (Jan 1); Epiphany (Jan 6); St. Joseph's Day (Mar 19); Maundy Thursday and Good Friday (Mar/Apr); Labor Day (May 1); Ascension (May); Corpus Christi (May/June); Sacred Heart (June); Day of St. Peter and St. Paul (June 29); Independence Day (Aug 7); Assumption (Aug 15); Discovery of America (Oct 12); All Saints' Day (Nov 1); Independence of Cartagena (Nov 11); Immaculate Conception (Dec 8); and Christmas (Dec 25). Bogotá and other major cities empty out during holiday weekends, and many businesses close early or don't open at all.

HEALTH CONCERNS

In major cities, you'll have little cause for worry. Water is generally fine to drink, though cautious travelers may want to stick to bottled water. The problem you're most likely to

Staying Safe

Colombia isn't the place to wander off the beaten path, not even in cities. Stick to neighborhoods you know are safe. The following advice is relevant, particularly in large cities.

- Never resist an attempted robbery—Colombian criminals can be armed and unpredictable. Carry at least a little cash on you to avoid angering thieves. There have been cases of tourists being killed for resisting robbery.
- Always call a cab at night, especially if you have been drinking or if you're traveling alone. If your Spanish skills are limited or you are a woman traveling alone, I advise you to always call a cab to avoid being taken on a long and expensive ride. Always make sure the cab door is locked to avoid an armed assailant hopping in at a stoplight. Calling a cab only costs a bit more, and since the cab number is registered by the company, the chances of something happening are much lower.
- Don't accept any drinks, drugs, or cigarettes from a stranger or someone you've just met; they could be laced with an odorless drug called scopolamine that makes you lose your will while you are robbed. Also, it's best not to pick up any papers or cash that someone walking ahead of you drops, as this can also be the same kind of trick. This is especially important for women. These types of crimes are rare but not unheard of, and can happen in taxis as well. If you start to feel dizzy or sick, get someone's attention.
- If you're a man out drinking or partying alone, be very cautious before going home with a Colombian woman or group of women. Although rare, there have been cases of foreigners and even Colombians being drugged with scopolamine and being robbed while under the influence. It's always best to go out with a group in Colombia, especially in big cities.
- Many travelers who come to Colombia do so because of the wide variety of drugs available. While you will probably see many locals smoking marijuana, getting high off of inhalants, and even smoking crack on the streets, particularly in Medellín, I strongly advise against buying or doing drugs in Colombia. You can easily be set up by the "seller," who then turns you in to the "police," who then extort significant sums of money from you. Also, penalties for buying drugs in Colombia are hefty, and the last thing you want to do is spend 10 years in a Colombian prison.
- If someone approaches you claiming to be a police officer and asks for your documents, go to the nearest police station; never give your money or documents to someone claiming to be an undercover officer.
- Women traveling alone may want to dress modestly to avoid unwanted attention from men. Colombia is still very much a "macho" country, and many men will think that a woman traveling alone, particularly one dressed provocatively, is fair game. In Bogotá, women tend to dress conservatively, and showing too much skin may attract unwanted attention. As an extra precaution, women should call for a taxi rather than hailing it on the street. (Though I have to admit, as a woman traveling alone, I have hailed taxis on the street throughout the country and always without incident.)

encounter is **traveler's diarrhea,** from inexpensive food. Use common sense—avoid eating unpeeled fruits and vegetables from street vendors, wash your hands frequently, and when trying a new fruit or vegetable, don't overdo it. Remember to wear sunscreen at all times, even in cool cities like Bogotá. You're closer to the sun, and you don't want to let **sunburn** ruin your vacation. In major cities, health care is adequate and professional, as long as you stick to private clinics. Public clinics tend to have long lines and are usually understaffed and underfunded.

If you are visiting the Andean region, **altitude sickness** is a possibility. Though it generally goes away after 2 to 5 days, it may be helpful to bring along Tylenol, Advil, or another over-the-counter painkiller. Symptoms include headache, shortness of breath, fatigue, nausea, and sleepiness. Try to take it easy the first day or two to avoid worsening your condition. You might experience altitude sickness in Bogotá or Tunja, or when hiking in the high Andes.

Though no vaccines are required to enter Colombia, it's a good idea to consider getting vaccinations for hepatitis A and B, typhoid, and yellow fever if you will be visiting the Atlantic or Pacific coasts, the Amazon region, or any other tropical region. (As a general rule, the more rural your location in the country's tropical regions, the higher your risk of contracting diseases such as **malaria, yellow fever,** or **cholera**). **Dengue fever** is another concern in the tropics, though unfortunately there is no preventative vaccine. You should also consider taking malaria pills if you will be visiting any of the above regions.

GETTING THERE

By Plane

Planes arrive at **El Dorado International Airport** (airport code BOG; ✆ **1/413-9053**), located about 13km (8 miles) from the city center. El Dorado handles most international arrivals and you'll likely fly into Bogotá. Upon exiting the country, there is a departure tax of $59 (payable in U.S. dollars or the peso equivalent), though all or at least part of this is usually included in your ticket. Other major international airports in Colombia include **Rio Negro International Airport** in Medellín and **Rafael Núñez International Airport** in Cartagena.

FROM THE U.S. There are direct flights from New York, Atlanta, Miami, and Washington D.C. **Avianca** (✆ 800/284-2622; www.avianca.com) has several daily flights to Bogotá, as well as one direct daily flight to Medellín and Cartagena. **American Airlines** (✆ 800/433-7300; www.aa.com) has three daily flights from Miami to Bogotá and two daily flights to Medellín. From JFK in New York, **Delta** (✆ 800/221-1212; www.delta.com) and Avianca each have one daily direct flight to Bogotá. From Atlanta, Delta and Avianca each offer one daily flight to Bogotá. **Continental** (✆ 800/944-0219; www.continental.com), **Copa** (✆ 800/550-7700; www.copaair.com), and **Taca** (✆ 800/535-8780; www.taca.com) also offer service to Bogotá, though you'll have to connect. **JetBlue** (✆ 800/538-2583; www.jetblue.com) flies direct from Orlando to Bogotá daily.

FROM CANADA **Air Canada** (✆ **888/247-2262;** www.aircanada.ca) offers a direct flight between Toronto and Bogotá several times a week. Otherwise, you'll have to connect in the U.S. using one of the carriers listed above, which might actually turn out to be a cheaper option.

FROM EUROPE & THE U.K. From Paris, **Air France** (✆ **0870/142-4343;** www.airfrance.co.uk) offers one daily direct flight to Bogotá. **Iberia** (✆ **0845/601-2854;** www.iberia.com) flies direct to Bogotá from Madrid. Avianca, American, Continental, and Air

France have flights from Madrid to Bogotá, connecting through Paris or in the U.S.; London, Rome, and Frankfurt offer similar options with one connection.

FROM AUSTRALIA & NEW ZEALAND You'll be connecting in the U.S, and possibly Central or South America as well. Your best bet from Australia is on American Airlines, connecting in Los Angeles en route to Bogotá. From New Zealand, some of your better options are **LAN** (✆ **800/221-572;** www.lan.com/index-en-un.html) and **Air New Zealand** (✆ **0800/737-000;** www.airnz.co.nz), though be prepared for at least two stops.

By Bus

Although you can technically enter Colombia via Venezuela to the east and Ecuador to the south, this is not your safest option. It's much safer than it was a few years ago, but flying is not only much more secure, it's quicker and definitely more comfortable. If you insist on traveling by bus, be sure to make your journey during the daytime, and keep an eye on worsening Colombia-Venezuela relations if you're crossing in from Venezuela. You'll probably have to transfer buses at the border.

By Boat

Unless you're going directly to Cartagena, you probably won't be arriving by boat. That said, Cartagena is now becoming a popular stop for Caribbean Cruise liners and private yacht owners. Private yacht and sailing companies also offer trips from the San Blas Islands in Panama to Cartagena, starting at $250 each way.

GETTING AROUND

By Plane

Flying is the fastest way to get around Colombia. Precipitous two-lane winding roads can make road travel long, tiring, and a bit nauseating. Distances by plane are usually short (between 30 min. and 1 hr.), though prices are relatively steep. Except to pay about COL$150,000 to COL$500,000 for a 30- to 60-minute flight between major cities. Colombian airline prices are generally fixed and unlikely to vary much between airline carriers. **Avianca/SAM** (✆ **018000/123-434;** www.avianca.com) is Colombia's largest and most extensive carrier, covering both domestic and international routes. That said, service is often inefficient and customer service is poor. **Aero República** (✆ **018000/917-766;** www.aerorepublica.com.co) covers much of the same territory as Avianca. **AIRES** (✆ **018000/524-737;** www.aires.com.co) services smaller cities and towns, and **SATENA** (✆ 01900/331-7100; www.satena.com) flies to difficult locations such as the Amazon, the Pacific coast, and dozens of other small towns and villages.

Tip: It's important to note that if you will be using an international (non-Colombian) credit card to purchase your airline ticket online, you will need to book your flight at least 3 days in advance, or through a non-Colombian search engine such as Expedia. Another choice if you are short on time is to buy your tickets at the airport, where you won't have any problems using your credit card. Unless you're traveling during Christmas, Easter, or a busy holiday weekend, you shouldn't have too much trouble purchasing last-minute Colombian tickets.

By Bus

Since President Uribe took office in 2002, road travel in Colombia has improved dramatically. Most routes between major cities and towns are safe, though southwest

Colombia can still be dangerous. As a woman traveling alone, I have taken buses throughout Colombia without incident, but every traveler's comfort level is different. It's a good idea to check security conditions before you board a long-distance night bus, especially if you'll be traveling through high-risk area. You can find a bus to almost any city or town in the country from the Bogotá bus terminal, Terminal de Buses. Bus routes from Medellín, Cali, and Barranquilla also cover much of the country. Road conditions are generally good, but it's important to remember that these are two-lane mountain roads, so if there is a back-up or accident, you're stuck in place for at least a couple of hours. Also during the wet season—particularly October and November—the rain can cause mudslides and unpredictable road conditions.

Unless you're taking a route with irregular departures, it's unnecessary to book in advance (the exception being if you are traveling during Christmas or a Puente weekend, both 3-day holiday weekends, when you might want to consider purchasing your ticket a day or two in advance). Bus travel isn't as cheap as in nearby Ecuador or Peru; expect to pay about COL$10,000 per 100km (62 miles), but buses are generally comfortable. ***Tip:*** Stick to large buses, since small *colectivos* are bumpy and uncomfortable. And avoid taking *corrientes,* which seem to stop every couple of meters. No matter what class of bus, be prepared for onboard entertainment of *vallenato* and *ranchera* tunes, as well as ultra-violent movies, at whatever volume your driver chooses.

By Car

Renting a car in Colombia is a bad idea. Car accidents are one of the top causes of death in Colombia. In urban areas, Colombians tend to be aggressive and careless behind the wheel, often neither following street signs or traffic lights nor giving pedestrians the right of way. On rural roads and mountain passes, winding roads and near head-on collisions with trucks, as well as the occasional livestock crossing, can be intimidating at best. Also, Colombian car-rental companies examine returned rentals extensively for the slightest dent and scratch. Public transportation options are safer and cheaper. Some upscale hotels offer a chauffeur/car service, which can be rented by the hour or by the day, but don't expect any great deals. If, after hearing all this, you are still determined to drive in Colombia, expect to pay at least COL$200,000 a day. Make sure you and the car are insured, and be aware that gas doesn't come cheap in Colombia—we're talking COL$7,158 a gallon. Some companies that rent cars in Colombia are: **Avis** (www.avis.com), **Hertz** (www.hertz.com), and **Budget** (www.budget.com).

TIPS ON ACCOMMODATIONS

Hotels in major cities tend to fill up on weekdays with business travelers and empty out on weekends, when you may be able to bargain up to a 50% discount. The reverse is true in small towns and in the countryside, where you'll pay up to 50% less during the week. One annoying thing about Colombian hotels is that many hotels won't take reservations during holiday weekends or festivals, meaning you'll have to arrive early to reserve a room. Hotels in city centers tend to be dodgier and lower quality than those in outer, more upscale neighborhoods, and many double as pay-by-the-hour establishments—you may want to keep this in mind when making your reservation. In this chapter, **Very Expensive** lodging options start at COL$450,000; **Expensive,** from COL$300,000 to COL$449,000; **Moderate** from COL$200,000 to COL$299,000; and **Inexpensive,** under COL$200,000.

TIPS ON DINING

You won't be hungry in Colombia. Though every region has its own specialties, you're never far from a plate of beans, beef, plantains, and rice. Food is good, hearty, and generally cheap, if not particularly varied. For gourmands, major cities such as Bogotá, Medellín, and Cartagena also offer a huge range of upscale, gourmet, and international options. Some typical dishes to look for on your menu include ***ajiaco*** (chicken soup with potatoes, avocado, corn, and capers), ***bandeja paisa*** (rice, avocado, salad), ***chicharrón*** (minced meat, egg, plantain, and yuca), ***sancocho*** (plantain, yuca, potato, and beef, chicken, or fish soup), ***lechona*** (stuffed baked pig), ***arepa*** (flat cornbread, often topped with cheese or butter), and **tamales** (corn dough, chicken, and vegetables cooked and served in plantain leaves).

Tinto, black coffee, is Colombia's most popular beverage and can be enjoyed at anytime, just about anywhere. Other popular drinks are beer, *aguardiente* (the licorice-flavored national liquor), hot chocolate, and soda products. Bottled water (or bagged) water can usually be found at most stores and street stands. Thanks to its tropical climate and fertile soil, Colombia has countless exotic fruit juices such as *guanábana* (soursop), *lulo, maracuyá* (passion fruit), and *tomate de árbol* (tree tomato). Wine is not particularly popular in Colombia, and Colombian wines on the whole leave a lot to be desired. However, upscale restaurants and grocery stores generally offer high-quality Argentine and Chilean varieties.

Dining categories in this chapter are as follows: **Very Expensive,** main courses from COL$30,000; **Expensive** from COL$22,000 to COL$29,000; **Moderate,** from COL$12,000 to COL$21,000; and **Inexpensive,** below COL$12,000.

TIPS ON SHOPPING

Handicrafts are relatively cheap and easy to find in Colombia, though the deals aren't as good as you get in Ecuador, Bolivia, and Peru. In urban areas, you're likely to find the best bargains in city centers; handicraft stores in upscale shopping malls charge at least double the price, though you're generally guaranteed quality. In small towns and rural areas, you can expect to find more authentic and regional crafts at fair prices. At markets and such, you may be able to bargain somewhat, though don't expect a price to drop more than a couple of thousand pesos.

Aside from handicrafts, Colombians are serious about clothing. Bogotá, Cartagena, and Cali are a shopaholic's dream come true. At shopping centers and boutiques in more upscale areas, clothing is generally high quality, albeit a bit expensive. In the most upscale city zones and shopping centers, you'll be greeted by the likes of Armani, Tommy Hilfiger, and other designers. Shoes and leather handbags, as well as gold and emerald jewelry, are popular buys and can be purchased at decent prices; it's best to ask around to find the spots with the best bargains.

Fast Facts Colombia

American Express To call American Express in Bogotá, dial ✆ **1/343-0000;** in Medellín, **1/510-9000;** in Cali, **1/554-0505;** and in Barranquilla, **1/361-8888.**

Business Hours Business hours vary significantly between urban and rural areas. In urban areas, businesses and banks are generally open between 8am and noon, and then again between 2 and 6pm. In Bogotá, banks are supposedly open all day between 8am and 4pm. Stores are generally open between 9am to 5pm, while department stores and large supermarkets generally stay open until around 9pm. In the countryside, businesses and stores are generally open fewer hours and don't necessarily stick to their posted schedules. Also, many businesses close down or reduce their hours on Sundays and holidays.

Doctors & Hospitals Some of the best hospitals in Bogotá are **Clínica Marly,** Calle 50, no. 9–67 (✆ **1/570-4424,** 1/572-5011, or 1/343-6600); **Fundación Santa Fe,** Calle 119, no. 9–02 (✆ **1/629-0766** or 629-0477); and **Clínica El Bosque,** Calle 134, no. 12–55 (✆ **1/274-0577,** 1/274-5445, or 1/649-9300).

Electricity Electric outlets accept U.S.-type plugs. Electricity in Colombia runs at 110 volts, so transformers are not necessary for tourists from the U.S. If you are planning to use anything with a three-prong plug, bring an adapter, as some establishments only have two-prong outlets.

Embassies & Consulates In Bogotá: **Australia** (consulate): Carrera 18 no. 90–38 (✆ **1/636-5247** or 1/530-1047); New Zealand (consulate): Diagonal 109 no. 1–39 Este, Apt. 401 (✆ **1/629-8524;** pearsona@cable.net.co); **United Kingdom:** Carrera 9 no. 76–49, Piso 9 (✆ **1/326-8300** or 1/317-6423 for visa information); **United States:** Calle 22, Bis. 47–51 (✆ **1/315-0811**); **Canada:** Carrera 7 no. 115–33, Piso 14 (✆ **1/657-9800**).

Emergencies In Bogotá, the police emergency number is ✆ **112.** Another emergency number that works throughout the country is **123.** Other good emergency numbers to know: the Security Police (DAS; ✆ **153/0180-0091-9622**); the Tourist Police (✆ **1/337-4413** or 1/243-1175); and the police station in Bogotá (✆ **156**). The fire department can be reached by calling 119, and information can be reached by dialing 113.

Internet Access You're never far from a cybercafe in Bogotá and other major urban centers. Small towns will also generally have at least one Internet cafe. In rural areas, Internet access is hard to come by. Connections are generally fast and cheap. Expect to pay about COL$1,500 to COL$2,500 per hour.

Language Except for a tiny percentage of rural indigenous communities, Spanish is universally spoken in Colombia. It's hard to find Colombians who speak English, even in Bogotá, so it's important to brush up on you skills before your trip. Outside of Bogotá and the major cities, you'll be hard-pressed to find any English speakers, which can make traveling in a nontouristy country quite difficult if you don't speak any Spanish.

Liquor Laws The legal drinking age in Colombia is 18, though laws are lenient. In urban areas such as Bogotá, Medellín, Cartagena, and Cali, you may be asked to show ID to get into upscale bars and clubs. There are no laws against drinking in public, so if you are low on funds, feel free to open up a bottle of *aguardiente* in the nearby park or plaza.

Maps Maps of Colombia and Bogotá can usually be found in tourist offices, though it's not uncommon for the tourist office to run out of maps. In Bogotá, you can also find high-quality maps in **La Panamericana** (www.panamericana.com.co) and most hotels. In fact, I recommend visiting the Panamericana (p. 480) for all your Colombia-related travel needs. They generally have more information than tourist offices, and sometimes offer English language guides.

Newspapers & Magazines National and local newspapers and magazines can be found in all cities and most towns. In Bogotá, look for ***El Tiempo*** and ***El Espectador;*** in Medellín look for ***El Mundo*** and ***El Colombiano;*** and in Cartagena, you'll find ***El Universal. Semana*** is the most popular weekly magazine. Unfortunately, there are few, if any, English-language publications in Colombia.

Post Offices & Mail The postal system in Colombia is relatively efficient in large cities, though the same can't be said for rural areas. Servientrega, DHL, FedEx, and DePrisa are available in Colombia for local and international shipping services, as is Avianca Airlines. While mail within Colombia is cheap, sending items abroad is extremely expensive.

Police See "Emergencies," above.

Restrooms Bathroom quality varies. Expensive hotels, restaurants, and shops generally have clean facilities and toilet paper. As long as you're polite, restaurant, hotel, and store owners won't mind if you use their facilities. It's a good idea to bring your own toilet paper and hand sanitizer wherever you go, as budget establishments rarely have these items. Usually, you'll have to pay a small fee (generally under CO$600) to use a public or restaurant restroom.

Safety Colombia is still far from being among the safest countries in the world. Much of the rural countryside is still tightly controlled by armed groups and is thus inaccessible to tourists. Travelers are advised to stick to well-touristed areas and keep up-to-date with the ever-changing political situation to avoid problems. But if you take adequate precautions, you're more likely to have a run-in with common street thieves than with guerilla or paramilitary factions. See the box "Staying Safe," earlier, for more tips on safety.

Smoking Colombians smoke less than Europeans but more than Americans. Most restaurants, hotels, shopping centers, bars, clubs, and other establishments have a no-smoking policy or a separate smoker's section. Make sure to ask if smoking is allowed before lighting up. Smoking is more prevalent in small towns than big cities.

Taxes There is a 10% tax on hotel rooms, and a 16% tax on food.

Telephone & Fax The best place to make calls and send faxes is in Internet cafes. Public phones are confusing (with instructions in Spanish). Street vendors offer minutes to cellphones and landlines for COL$200 to COL$400 per minute.

Time Zone All of Colombia is 5 hours behind Greenwich Mean Time. Colombia does not observe daylight saving time.

Tipping In midrange and expensive restaurants, there is usually a 10% tip included in the bill. It's not common to tip in budget restaurants or in taxis, so there's no need to do so unless you're feeling generous.

Water City water is usually safe to drink, but in nonurban areas it's best to stick to bottled water.

4 BOGOTA

At first sight, Bogotá may not impress you. The constant rain, chilliness, and ominous pine-forest mountains make London seem sunny. But give Bogotá time and you will discover a sophisticated city of skyscrapers, glitzy upscale shopping centers, restaurants to satisfy even the most discerning palettes, and a nightlife that will leave you needing a vacation from your vacation. Colombia's capital, and by far the country's largest city, Bogotá is a sprawling metropolis, home to eclectic, experimental architecture, a large bohemian university crowd, a lively cafe scene, and dozens of attractive city parks. It is a city bursting with energy and culture.

But it's not all good news. Bogotá is, more than anything, a city of contrasts. Class differences are still very much apparent, with the wealthy, modern northern section a world apart from the sprawling slums, poverty, and high crime rates of the southern part of the city. Though security has improved dramatically in the last few years, the city center can still be dangerous at night, so you're better off not wearing expensive-looking jewelry and clothing when visiting these areas. However, Bogotá is one of Latin America's safer cities, and it's unlikely you'll encounter any serious problems.

ESSENTIALS

Getting There

BY PLANE Planes arrive at **El Dorado International Airport** (airport code: BOG; **© 1/413-9053**), located about 13km (8 miles) from the city center. You can get to the city center by taxi or bus. Buses are parked next to the El Dorado Terminal and are marked AEROPUERTO—the last one each day leaves at 8pm. They drop you off at the city center, from which you will probably have to take a taxi to your hotel. If you have a lot of luggage and don't feel ready to deal with Colombian mass transit, your best bet is to take a taxi, which costs between COL$18,000 and COL$25,000 from the airport, depending on where you need to be dropped off. Make sure to obtain a computer-printed slip at the airport exit before getting into your taxi. Make a sharp right upon exiting the airport to obtain your computer-printed slip. This slip indicates how much your route will cost and prevents visitors from being ripped off by dishonest taxi drivers. You give this slip to the driver and pay upon arrival at your destination. Do not accept rides from solicitors at the airport exit; these drivers are not associated with the airport and you don't want to be the one to test their honesty. Getting to the city center or northern Bogotá from the airport should take about 20 to 45 minutes, depending on traffic.

BY BUS Buses arriving in Bogotá drop you off in the main bus terminal, **Terminal de Buses,** or at **El Portal del Norte,** depending on the bus company and where you are arriving from. Virtually every city and town has a bus service to Bogotá. From the terminal, you'll need to take a taxi to your hotel. It's important to obtain a computer-printed slip here as well and take a bus-terminal associated taxi.

Orientation

Although Bogotá is a massive, sprawling city covering over 1,555 sq. km (606 sq. miles), almost all tourist attractions are concentrated in the historic center and La Candelaria. Excellent transportation connects La Candelaria and El Centro to the northern section, where most of the city's best restaurants, hotels, and nightspots are located. Laid out in a grid, Bogotá can more or less be divided into three sections: **the north,** home to the city's top restaurants, hotels, shopping, and nightspots; **the center** (including La Candelaria), around which most tourist attractions are located; and **the south,** the poorest and least visited section of the city. *Carreras* run north to south, and *calles* run east to west. Streets and avenues are almost always referred to by number rather than by proper name. La Carrera Séptima is likely Bogotá's most important avenue, running the entire length of the city. If you're ever confused about whether you're heading east or west, remember the mountains are on the east of the city. Most tourists stick to the northeastern and central-eastern parts of the city.

Getting Around

BY TRANSMILENIO One of the fastest and cheapest ways to get around is the Transmilenio, Bogotá's decade-old bus system that runs on its own road lane. The Transmilenio runs weekdays and Saturdays between 5am and 11pm and Sundays and holidays 6am to 10pm. A single ticket will cost you COL$1,400. Some 882 buses cover 84km (52 miles) and move, on average, 1,250,000 people a day. You'll probably have to study the maps at each Transmilenio for quite a while to understand how the system works. If you speak some Spanish, you're best off asking one of the many Transmilenio workers, who can tell you what line and bus to take to your destination. Robberies are known to happen on the Transmilenio, so be sure to keep an eye on your personal belongings. ***Note:*** Supposedly, there's a metro system in the works, but it's unclear whether that project will be getting off the ground anytime soon.

BY BUS Hundreds, if not thousands, of buses service Bogotá. You'll pay a flat fare—usually about COL$1,100 to COL$1,300—no matter how far you're traveling. Get off and on buses as quickly as possible, as drivers are unlikely to be courteous enough to come to a complete stop or make sure you get off safely. When going from the north to La Candelaria, take buses marked GERMANIA. Don't take buses marked LA CANDELARIA, which will leave you in a bad part of town. When going to the north, buses that say UNICENTRO will generally drop you off a couple of blocks from where you want to go. Don't expect a bus to stop for you just because you're standing at a bus stop; you'll have to flag it down.

BY TAXI Perhaps the best way to get around the city, taxis are relatively inexpensive. Many foreigners choose to get around this way to avoid Bogotá's sometimes confusing bus and Transmilenio system. You can get from the north to the city center for about COL$8,000 to COL$14,000. It's wise to call a taxi from your hotel or restaurant, especially at night. Your biggest risk is that a taxi driver will take an out-of-the-way route to your destination and thus charge you an unfairly inflated fee. Make sure the driver turns on his meter. However, there have been cases of robbery, assault, and even rape reported involving taxi drivers, particularly at night. If you call a taxi, your driver is likely to charge COL$1,000 to COL$2,000 in addition to your fare. Recommended taxi companies include **Auto Taxi** (✆ 1/366-6666), **Radio Taxi** (✆ 1/288-8888), **Taxi Express** (✆ 1/411-1111), **Taxis Libres** (✆ 1/311-1111), and **Taxi Ya** (✆ 1/411-1112). If you're not used to getting around Latin American cities, I recommend you take taxis to avoid the hassle of the Transmilenio and buses.

BY CAR Driving in Bogotá is not for the faint of heart. Almost 50,000 Colombians a year are killed in traffic-related accidents, meaning your chances of being hurt or even killed in a car accident are far greater than your risk of being kidnapped or killed by guerillas or narco traffickers. Be prepared for honking cars weaving in and out of traffic,

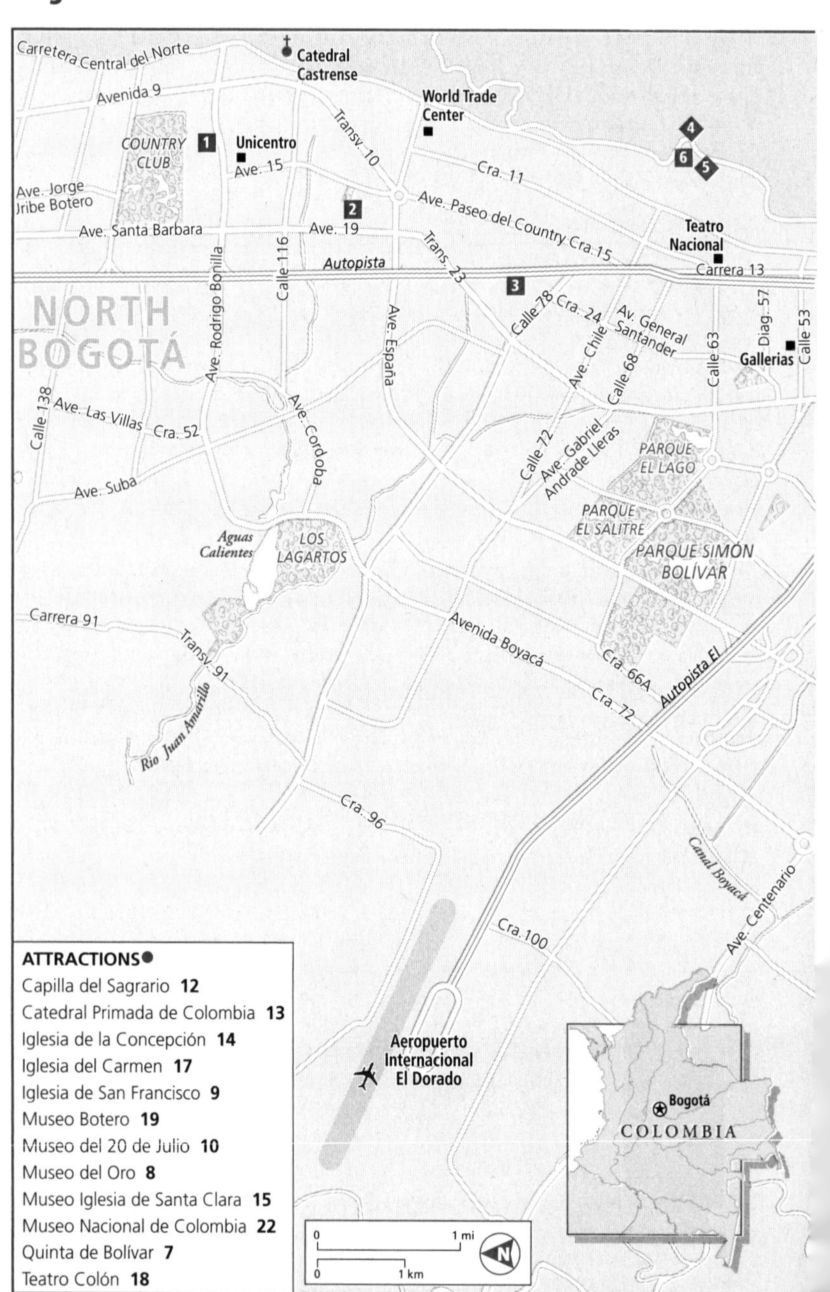
Carretera Central del Norte
Catedral Castrense
Avenida 9
World Trade Center
Transv. 10
COUNTRY CLUB
1
Unicentro
Ave. 15
Cra. 11
4
6
5
Ave. Jorge Uribe Botero
2
Ave. Paseo del Country Cra. 15
Ave. Santa Barbara
Ave. 19
Teatro Nacional
Trans. 23
Autopista
Carrera 13
3
NORTH BOGOTÁ
Ave. Rodrigo Bonilla
Calle 116
Ave. España
Calle 78 Cra. 24
Av. General Santander
Diag. 57
Calle 53
Ave. Chile
Calle 68
Calle 63
Gallerias
Calle 138
Ave. Las Villas Cra. 52
Ave. Cordoba
Calle 72
Ave. Gabriel Andrade Lleras
PARQUE EL LAGO
Ave. Suba
PARQUE EL SALITRE
Aguas Calientes
LOS LAGARTOS
PARQUE SIMÓN BOLÍVAR
Carrera 91
Avenida Boyacá
Transv. 91
Cra. 66A
Autopista El
Cra. 72
Rio Juan Amarillo
Cra. 96
Canal Boyacá
Ave. Centenario
Cra. 100
ATTRACTIONS
Capilla del Sagrario 12
Catedral Primada de Colombia 13
Iglesia de la Concepción 14
Iglesia del Carmen 17
Iglesia de San Francisco 9
Museo Botero 19
Museo del 20 de Julio 10
Museo del Oro 8
Museo Iglesia de Santa Clara 15
Museo Nacional de Colombia 22
Quinta de Bolívar 7
Teatro Colón 18
Aeropuerto Internacional El Dorado
Bogotá
COLOMBIA
0
1 mi
0
1 km
N

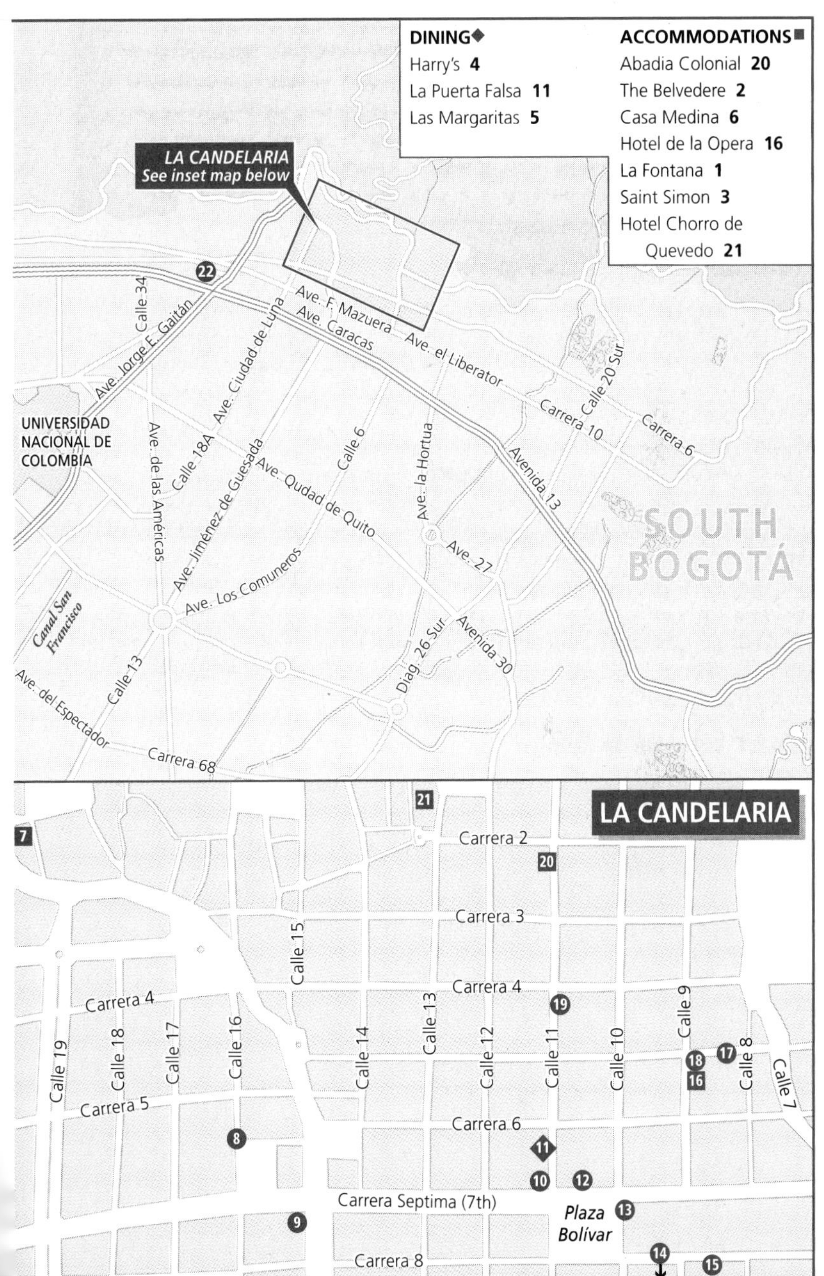
DINING◆
Harry's 4
La Puerta Falsa 11
Las Margaritas 5
ACCOMMODATIONS■
Abadia Colonial 20
The Belvedere 2
Casa Medina 6
Hotel de la Opera 16
La Fontana 1
Saint Simon 3
Hotel Chorro de Quevedo 21
LA CANDELARIA
See inset map below
Calle 34
Ave. Jorge E. Gaitán
Ave. Ciudad de Luna
Ave. F. Mazuera
Ave. Caracas
Ave. el Liberator
Carrera 10
Calle 20 Sur
Carrera 6
UNIVERSIDAD NACIONAL DE COLOMBIA
Calle 18A
Ave. de las Américas
Ave. Jiménez de Guesada
Ave. Qudad de Quito
Calle 6
Ave. la Hortua
Avenida 13
SOUTH BOGOTÁ
Ave. 27
Ave. Los Comuneros
Canal San Francisco
Calle 13
Diag. 26 Sur
Avenida 30
Ave. del Espectador
Carrera 68
LA CANDELARIA
Carrera 2
Carrera 3
Calle 15
Carrera 4
Calle 19
Calle 18
Calle 17
Calle 16
Calle 14
Calle 13
Calle 12
Calle 11
Calle 10
Calle 9
Calle 8
Calle 7
Carrera 5
Carrera 6
Carrera Septima (7th)
Plaza Bolívar
Carrera 8

reckless drivers, and many near collisions. Pedestrians often cross despite the presence of oncoming traffic, and vendors and beggars often congregate around traffic lights. If, after hearing this, you are still convinced you want to drive in Bogotá, you will need to present an international driver's license when renting your vehicle. See "Getting Around: By Car," in section 3.

BY FOOT La Candelaria and El Centro can be easily explored on foot. Usaquén, La Zona Rosa, and Parque de la 93 are other easy neighborhoods to explore on foot, though you'll have to get to these places by taxi, Transmilenio, or bus. Because Bogotá is essentially a grid, it's relatively easy to get from place to place on foot. Theoretically, you can get anywhere on Bogotá on foot, but long distances make taking a taxi more convenient.

Visitor Information

Tourist information in Bogotá is mediocre at best. Most of Bogotá's tourists are Colombians, so any brochures you manage to get will probably be in Spanish. The most helpful and informative tourist office is the **Instituto Distrital de Turismo y Cultura** (✆ **1/ 327-4916;** www.culturayturismo.gov.co), at Carrera 8 no. 9–83, right across from Plaza Bolívar. Unfortunately, they are often out of maps and brochures. The office is supposedly open daily between 8am and 6pm, but hours can be reduced, especially on Sunday. Other tourist offices can be found at **El Dorado Airport** (at both the national and international decks); **the main bus station,** Transversal 66 no. 35–11, Local Module 5–27; and the **International Center,** Carrera 13 no. 26–52. The bilingual ***Bogotá Turística*** is a decent city guide sold at **Panamericana** shops throughout the city. Your hotel should also be able to offer some information, maps, and a few pointers. Personally, I find Panamericana stores to be the best place to find tourist information, as they always have maps and sometimes sell English-language guides. Some popular Panamericanas are located on Carrera 15 no. 72–14; Unicentro mall; Calle 92 no. 15–37; Carrera 13 no. 59–69; and Carrera 7 no. 18–48.

WHAT TO SEE & DO

Neighborhoods to Explore

LA CANDELARIA Bogotá's semirestored colonial quarter is home to most of the city's tourist attractions. It was here that wealthy Spaniards founded the city. The sector has a definitively intellectual feel, being home to half a dozen universities, several museums, galleries, cafes, the famous Teatro Colón, and La Biblioteca Luis Angel Arango, once considered the most important library in the country. La Candelaria, with its many pedestrian-only stone-cobbled streets, is the perfect place to spend the morning or afternoon exploring, enjoying a leisurely lunch, taking in the colonial architecture and atmosphere, or visiting a museum or two. Most tourist and cultural attractions are between Calle 7 and Avenida Jiménez, and Circunvalar and Carrera 8. This sector has a long history with writers, artists, and journalists, and you'll probably spend most of your sightseeing time here.

PLAZA DE BOLIVAR Just South of La Candelaria, this is a great place to people-watch and admire examples of Bogotano architecture. Unfortunately, you have to keep an eye out for the thousands of pigeons that make the plaza their home. See p. 482.

DOWNTOWN & EL CENTRO INTERNACIONAL This is a chaotic, noisy, and vibrant area—not the kind of place you want to end up lost at night, but you should be all right during the day. Some of the city's best bargain shopping can be found here, particularly around Plaza San Vitorino, though you may feel a bit overwhelmed by the sheer number of shops and the somewhat seedy atmosphere. Be sure to stop in at the Cafeteria Florida for a Bogotá-style tamale and chocolate *con queso.* The international zone starts at Calle 30 and is home to many of Colombia's most important companies, high rises, restaurants, and cafes. Behind the Plaza de Toros between calles 22 to 26 and carreras 2 to 6, you will find the edgy, bohemian neighborhood of La Macarena, with its many cafes and bars. As one Colombian put it, La Macarena is the equivalent of New York City's East Village, on a much smaller scale.

USAQUEN Like La Candelaria, Usaquén is one of Bogotá's most picturesque neighborhoods. Home to a pleasant plaza, colonial-style church, and many restaurants and bars, Usaquén is also famous for its proximity to the Hacienda Santa Bárbara, a beautiful courtyard mall of upscale stores and boutiques that was once the home of a wealthy family. Usaquén really comes alive at night when the lively university and post-university crowd fills its restaurants and bars. This residential sector feels like a quaint small town and, in fact, it didn't become part of the city until 1954. Be sure to check out the impressive Sunday flea market, where you'll find everything from handmade clothes and one-of-a-kind jewelry to souvenir-style knick-knacks.

LA ZONA ROSA Located between carreras 11 and 15 and calles 79 and 85, near the upscale Andino mall, La Zona Rosa is Bogotá's most exclusive nightlife center. Home to many clubs, bars, and restaurants, La Zona Rosa is where you'll drop COL$10,000 to COL$30,000 for a cocktail or COL$100,000 for a bottle of rum. However, keep in mind that cocktails in La Zona T are two to three times bigger than what you get in North America. **La Zona T,** a cobblestone pedestrian walkway, makes for a pleasant night-time stroll. Just a few steps away, on Calle del Sol, you can window-shop at the stores of famous Colombian designers.

PARQUE DE LA 93 Located between calles 93A and 93B and carreras 11A and 13, Parque de la 93 is another exclusive area, popular with the city's worldly and elite. It's home to many international and gourmet restaurants as well as to several clubs, bars, and cafes; the park itself often hosts musical events and is beautifully decorated at Christmas time. During the day, families bring their children to the pleasant green park for ice cream and fresh air, and at night the area comes alive with music and energy. The bars and clubs here attract a slightly older crowd than those in La Zona T.

AVENIDA CHILE Also known as Calle 72, Avenida Chile occupies the city's former northernmost point. It was once home to Bogotá's wealthiest families, where they built their European-style mansions in the beginning of the 20th century. Over the years, the area has become a bustling, vibrant commercial area with dozens of skyscrapers and some of the city's top hotels. This is the city's most sophisticated cosmopolitan area, and its side streets are filled with English- and Swiss-style mansions.

LA ZONA G Also known as the Gourmet Zone, La Zona G is adjacent to the Centro Financiero and is home to the city's best restaurants. If you're looking for world-class dining, this is the place to come.

Museums

Bogotá has over 50 museums. In addition to the highlights below, try to visit **Museo de Trajes Regionales de Colombia,** Calle 10 no. 6–20 (✆ **1/282-6531;** www.uamerica.edu.co/museo/museo.html), the home of Simón Bolívar's lover, Manuelita Sáenz.

Museo Botero ★★ The Botero museum, which opened its doors in 2000, is housed in a restored colonial mansion. Fernando Botero, one of the world's most renowned painters, is famous for his voluptuous, over-the-top, Renaissance-inspired portraits. Love him or hate him, Botero is among Colombia's most famous exports, and you'll see his works all over Colombia. With over 120 sculptures, drawings, and paintings by the master himself, the permanent exhibition here, donated by Botero to the Banco de La República, is the largest permanent exhibition of his artwork in the world. The museum also houses over 80 works by other Colombian artists, as well as European masters such as Matisse, Renoir, and Picasso.

Calle 11 no. 4–21/93. ✆ **1/343-1212,** 343-1223, or 336-0200. Free admission. Mon–Sat 9am–7pm; Sun and holidays 10am–5pm. Transmilenio: Avenida Jiménez.

Museo del 20 de Julio Located on the northeast corner of Plaza Bolívar, the Museo del 20 de Julio, also known as La Casa del Florero (the House of the Vase), dates back to the late 16th century. It was here that a dispute over a vase, between Spaniard José González Llorente and Colombians Antonio and Francisco Morales, led to the War of Independence. The museum's 10 rooms, which feature independence memorabilia, are a fine example of early Colombian colonial architecture.

Calle 11 no. 6–94. ✆ **1/282-6647.** Admission COL$3,000. Tues–Fri 9am–4:30pm; Sat–Sun 10am–3:30pm. Transmilenio: Avenida Jiménez or Museo del Oro.

Museo del Oro ★★★ This is the pride and joy of Bogotá. It's home to one of the world's most impressive collections of its kind: more than 34,000 pieces of gold and 20,000 other pre-Columbian relics. The museum makes a great base from which to learn a bit about the pre-Columbian cultures that inhabited Colombia and South America before the Spanish conquest. Be prepared to be wowed by the top-floor, 8,000-piece "gold room." English-language tours are available at 11am and 3pm. If you can't make one of the guided tours, there are also English-language audio guides available—just ask at the front desk.

Corner of Calle 16 and Carrera 6. ✆ **1/343-2222** or 343-1424. www.banrep.gov.co/museo/esp/home.htm. Admission COL$2,600. Tues–Sat 9am–6pm; Sun 10am–4pm. Transmilenio: Museo del Oro.

Museo Nacional de Colombia Founded on June 28, 1823, this is Colombia's oldest and longest-functioning museum, providing a good overview of Colombian culture and history. It is currently home to over 20,000 historical and archeological items, dating from 10,000 B.C. to the modern era. Most impressive is the pre-Columbian exhibit of tools, handicrafts, and jewelry produced by Colombian indigenous communities before the Spanish conquest. You'll also find a modern-art collection here, as well as a pleasant cafe.

Carrera 7 no. 28–66. ✆ **1/334-8366.** www.museonacional.gov.co. Admission COL$3,000. Tues–Sat 10am–6pm; Sun 10am–5pm. Transmilenio: Estacion Calle 26.

Quinta de Bolívar This house was donated by the government of Nueva Granada to Simón Bolívar, in 1820, in gratitude for his quest for independence. The house was acquired and turned into a museum by the Colombian government in 1922. It was recently restored to its original state, when Bolívar and his lover, Manuelita Sáenz, lived in the house. Many of El Libertador's personal belongings can be found here.

Calle 20 no. 2–91. ✆ **1/336-6419** or 336-6410. www.quintadebolivar.gov.co. Admission COL$3,000. Tues–Fri 9am–5pm; Sat–Sun 10am–4pm. Transmilenio: Calle 22 or Calle 19.

Other Attractions

Created in 1539 by Bogotá's founder, Gonzalo Jiménez de Quesada, the **Plaza de Bolívar** has changed substantially over the last 5 centuries but has remained the sentimental center of Bogotá. The square was remodeled to its current appearance in 1960 as a tribute to 150 years of independence. Plaza de Bolívar provides a good insight into the eclectic architectural styles of Bogotá: Here you'll find the colonial-style Museo del 20 de Julio (see above); the 19th-century Catedral Primal, which evokes the Renaissance churches of Europe; the neoclassical Capitolio; and the palacelike Casa de Nariño. On the northern side, the Palacio de Justicia is an abrupt, monumental building with a tragic history: It has been burned down twice, first by a mob in 1948, and then by M-19 guerillas in 1985. The statue of Simón Bolívar in the middle of the square was the first public monument in Bogotá.

The majestic **Teatro Colón,** Calle 10 no. 5–32 (© **1/284-7420;** www1.mincultura.gov.co/nuevo/teatro_colon/index.php; Transmilenio: Museo del Oro), in the heart of La Candelaria, took its present form by 1895 under the direction of Italian architect Pietro Cantini. Check out the fresco-covered foyer; the wooden, beautifully engraved boxes; and the opulent chandelier marking the center of the theater. With a five-level, 938-person capacity, the theater is home to Bogotá's symphony orchestra and is still used for Bogotá's most important concerts, plays, ballets, and operas. For tickets, call © **1/341-0475.** Individual or group-guided visits are from Tuesday to Saturday between 10am to 5pm and Sunday from 1 to 5pm. Admission is COL$4,500, COL$8,000 for character/costume tour.

At an altitude of 3,048m (10,000 ft.), the **Cerro de Monserrate ★★** (www.cerromonserrate.com) offers spectacular views of Bogotá. It's also home to two excellent restaurants, the elegant **Restaurante San Isidro ★★**, serving perhaps Bogotá's best French cuisine, and **Casa Santa Clara,** a beautiful wooden building transported piece by piece from its original location in the Usaquén neighborhood. You'll also find decent souvenir shops here, as well as the **Santuario de Monserrate,** with its 17th-century figure of a fallen Christ, which attracts hundreds of pilgrims every weekend. You can see them climbing the slopes of Monserrate to pay their homage to the Fallen Christ. The top of Monserrate can be reached by cable car or funicular, beginning at Carrera 2E no. 21–48, Paseo Bolívar, Estación del Funicular (© **1/284-5700**). The funicular (train) costs COL$14,000 Monday to Saturday and COL$8,000 on Sundays; it runs 7:45am to 11:45pm on weekdays, 6am to 6:30pm Saturdays and Sundays. The *teleférico* (cable car) has the same price and runs from noon to midnight on Monday through Saturday and 9am to 5pm on Sunday.

Churches

Church lovers are in for a real treat in Bogotá. The city's colonial origin means that there are some excellent, fully preserved churches in La Candelaria and El Centro Histórico. Though Bogotá's many churches may be staid on the outside, their insides are often opulent examples of colonial religious art. Below is a list of some of the best churches. Except where noted, admission is free (though donations are accepted).

Capilla Del Sagrario Built between 1600 and 1700, and restored after the 1827 earthquake, the Capilla Del Sagrario is an excellent example of colonial architecture with Mannerist, Moorish, and even indigenous influences.

Carrera 7 between calles 10 and 11 in front of Plaza de Bolívar. © **1/212-6315.** Mon–Fri 7:30am–12:30pm and 3–5:30pm; Sun 4:30–5:30pm. Closed holidays. Transmilenio: Avenida Jiménez.

Catedral Primada de Colombia Finished in 1823, this cathedral stands in the same spot as the first church of Bogotá, which was finished in 1539. Inside are paintings

Bogotá Turistren

The Tren Turístico de la Sabana, as it's officially known, is Colombia's only remaining steam train and is a great way to see Bogotá's picturesque (if cloud-covered) countryside. The train departs from La Estación de la Sabana at 8:30am on Saturdays, Sundays, and holidays, or you can hop on board at the Usaquén train station at 9:20am. Passengers are dropped off at 4:30pm (Usaquén) and 5:30pm (Sabana). The train ride is popular with families, and on board you'll enjoy an authentic "papayera" band playing *vallenatos,* as well as an Andean band playing typical music from the Cundinamarca region. A small on-board restaurant serves typical Colombian fare such as hot chocolate accompanied by fresh cheese, tamales, and *aguapanela,* a sugar-cane-based hot beverage. You have the choice of disembarking at the salt mines of Zipaquira, where, for an extra fee, you can visit the famous, one-of-a-kind underground salt cathedral; or you can get off at Cajica, a typical Cundinamarca pueblo, with a pleasant plaza, cute stores, and tasty pastries. For more information about the Bogotá Turistren, visit **www.turistren.com.co.**

Note: To purchase tickets, go to the **Sabana station,** Calle 13 no. 18–24 (✆ **1/375-0557**), or the **Usaquén station,** Transversal 10 no. 110–8 (✆ **1/629-7407** or 629-7408). Tickets cost COL$32,000 for adults, COL$19,000 for children, and COL$25,000 seniors over 60.

and carvings dating from the 17th and 18th centuries, the tomb of Gonzalo Jiménez de Quesada (the founder of Bogotá), and one of the largest organs in all of Latin America.

Carrera 7 no. 10–11 (at Calle 11). ✆ **1/341-1954.** http://catedraldebogota.org . Mon–Sat 8:30am–1pm; Sun 8:30am–2pm.

Iglesia de la Concepción Construction on this church, began in 1583, making it one of the oldest in Bogotá. It is another good example of colonial and Moorish architecture.

Calle 10 no. 9–50. ✆ **1/284-6084.** Mon–Sat 7am–6:45pm; Sun and holidays 7am–1pm.

Iglesia del Carmen Built in 1938, my favorite church in the city looks like something out of a Candy Land game. The Iglesia also serves as a prestigious private school—you're best bet is to visit Sunday morning.

Carrera 5 no. 8–36. No phone. Transmilenio: Museo del Oro.

Iglesia de San Francisco This church once belonged to the Franciscans and was rebuilt after the 1785 earthquake. Check out its beautiful (and very gold) high altar, yet another excellent example of 17th-century church architecture.

Carrera 7 and Avenida Jiménez. ✆ **1/341-2357.** Mon–Fri 6am–7:45pm; Sat–Sun 6:30am–12:30pm and 4–7:45pm. Transmilenio: Avenida Jiménez.

Museo Iglesia de Santa Clara The single nave here is decorated entirely with painted motifs, and the monastery is considered the most architecturally rich in the country. The Museo Iglesia, built from 1629 to 1674, is one of the best examples of colonial church architecture in Bogotá.

Carrera 8 no. 8–91. ✆ **1/341-1009.** Admission COL$2,000; COL$1,000 for guided tour. Tues–Fri 9am–4:30pm; Sat–Sun 10am–3:30pm. Transmilenio: Avenida Jiménez.

Spectator Sports & Outdoor Activities

BIKING Bogotá is a biker's city, offering almost 300km (186 miles) of bike trails. On Sundays and holidays, the city hosts **Ciclovía,** an event where many roads are closed to automobiles and opened to bikers, walkers, and joggers; thousands of Bogotanos take to the streets between 7am and 2pm.

BULLFIGHTING Bullfighting season is in December, January, and February at La Plaza de Los Toros Santa María. A number of smaller events are held here throughout the year. For information about bullfighting, contact the **Corporación Taurina de Bogotá,** Calle 70A no. 6–24 (✆ **1/334-1628**), or **La Plaza de Toros,** Carrera 6 no. 26–50 (✆ **1/334-1482**).

FUTBOL (SOCCER) As in most of Latin America, soccer is popular in Bogotá. The two local teams are: **Los Millonarios,** Carrera 9 no.70–09 (✆ **1/347-7080**), and **Santa Fe,** Calle 64A no. 38–08 (✆ **1/544-6670**), both of which you can contact for tickets. Games take place at **El Estadio Nemesio Camacho El Campín,** Carrera 30 no. 57–60 (✆ **1/315-8726**).

TREKKING & ROCK CLIMBING Several trekking and adventure groups function in and around Bogotá. Try **Caminantes del Retorno** (contact Carlos Avellaneda at ✆ **1/285-5232** or 1/245-0518; www.caminantesdelretorno.com), **Clorofila Urbana** (✆ **1/616-8711;** www.clorofilaurbana.org), or **Colombia Ecoturística** (contact Arly Sarmiento at ✆ **1/286-3369**). For rock climbing, your best bet is **Roca Solida,** Av. 19 no. 133–23 (✆ **1/600-7480**), or **Rock Climbing,** Carrera 13A no. 35–66 (✆ **1/245-7284**).

SHOPPING

Shopping options in Bogotá are plentiful and varied. In the city center, look for bargains and handicrafts. In the north, you'll find upscale shopping malls and boutiques. Colombia is well known for its shoes, purses, emeralds, and gold. Good deals can be found on these items, but save your bargaining for El Centro; prices are fixed in more upscale northern Bogotá.

It almost seems as if there are more shops than people in Bogotá. The main shopping areas are in Usaquén, La Zona Rosa, Carrera 15, Avenida de Chile, Carrera 13, Calle 53, and the Chapinero neighborhood. Some popular shopping centers are the American-style **Atlantis Plaza,** Calle 81 no. 13–05; **Centro Commercial Andino,** Carrera 11 no. 83–71; **Unicentro,** Av. 15 no. 123–30; and **Hacienda Santa Bárabara,** Carrera 7 no. 115–60, which was once the property of a wealthy Bogotá family. The latter is a unique shopping center that has both a modern and colonial part built around a beautiful courtyard. Inside, you'll find high-quality boutique and jewelry stores.

For budget shopping, try **San Andresito,** at Carrera 38 and Calle 12, where you can find more or less anything you're looking for. The shopping centers and stores around **San Victorino Square,** Carrera 10 and Calle 10, in the center of the city are also very cheap, with a great assortment of clothing, handicrafts, and even electronics. However, the area can be a bit seedy, so try not to make your tourist status too obvious. ***Tip:*** Bargain hard around San Victorino, especially if it's obvious that you're not Colombian; otherwise you'll end up paying far too much.

A couple of good antiques stores are **Anticuarios Gilberto F. Hernández,** Calle 79B no. 7–48 (✆ **1/249-0041**), in the Zona T neighborhood, and **Almacén de Antigüedades Leonardo F,** at Carrera 4 no. 12–34 (✆ **1/334-8312**), in Candelaria. There are also several antique shops in **Usaquén.**

Most shops selling **emeralds** are located around Carrera 6 between calles 12 and 13, the Centro Internacional.

For **handicrafts,** try Carrera 15, between calles 74 and 77, the Centro Internacional (International Center), the Centro Histórico (Historic Center) and La Plaza de los Artesanos, located on Calle 63 at Carrera 50. Many handicrafts shops are found around La Candelaria and El Centro. **Artesanías de Colombia S.A.** has several locations throughout Bogotá, including at Carrera 11 no. 84–12 (✆ **1/218-0672**). Decent **flea markets** are held in Santander Square in the city center (daily 9am–6pm at Calle 24 and Carrera 7) and in Usaquén, on Saturday and Sunday, in the parking lot at Carrera 5 and Calle 119. My favorite spot for handicrafts is **Maku** ★, at Av. 19 no. 106–30 (✆ **1/620 8573**), in the Santa Bárbara neighborhood. While the prices are a bit higher than at stores in the city center, no one will hassle you, and goods are of decent quality.

For discount deals, head to the Restrepo neighborhood. Quality leather goods can also be found in upscale shopping centers. Good leather stores include **Mario Hernández,** which has several locations, including at Unicentro (✆ **1/213-0165**) and Carrera 68D no. 13–74 (✆ **1/292-6266**). Another good option is **Julia Rodríguez,** at Calle 81 no. 9–25 (✆ **1/249-5229**).

WHERE TO STAY

Most budget establishments are located in **La Candelaria** and **El Centro,** near the majority of the city's attractions. La Candelaria is relatively safe and a good place to stay if your budget is rock bottom and you want to save time and money on getting around. However, everything seems to close down when the sun sets; the nightlife that does exist here tends to be slightly bohemian and student-centered. You're best to avoid accommodations in El Centro, as this area can be loud and unpleasant at night. If you're intent on staying here, though, the **Tequendama Inter-Continental,** Carrera 10 no. 26–21 (✆ **1/382-2900** or 382-2929), is your best option in the city center.

Note: Colombian hotels use the New Year's holiday as an excuse to raise their rates by up to 10%.

In La Candelaria

You have a few decent budget options in La Candelaria. **Hotel Dorantes,** Calle 13 no. 5–07 (✆ **1/341-5365;** COL$50,000; AE, DC, MC, V), which could use a bit of renovating, offers 30 rooms ranging from tiny to large, some with good views of La Candelaria. All rooms have cable TV, rustic but clean bathrooms (with hot water), and old wooden furniture. Though not particularly attractive, rooms are clean and comfortable.

Expensive

Hotel de La Opera ★★★ The top spot to stay in La Candelaria, de La Opera is on a lovely cobblestone street adjacent to the Teatro Colón. Enjoy live-music shows on Friday and Saturday nights, as well as complimentary use of the pool, Jacuzzi, and sauna. The hotel is two restored colonial homes, and the results are impressive. The restorations give the buildings their original, colonial glory. All guest rooms are decorated Italian style. The spacious, beautifully decorated suites are well worth a splurge. The terrace restaurant, El Mirador, offers great views of La Candelaria, as do most of the hotel's rooms.

Calle 10 no. 5–72. ✆ **1/336-2066.** www.hotelopera.com.co. COL$258,000–COL$319,000 double; from COL$375,000 suite. Rates include continental breakfast. AE, DC, MC, V. Transmilenio: Museo del Oro. **Amenities:** Jacuzzi; pool; spa. *In room:* TV, hair dryer, minibar, Wi-Fi.

Moderate

Abadia Colonial Another good choice in La Candelaria, the Abadia Colonial has 12 rooms organized around three small courtyards and a pleasant dining area. The hotel is well maintained and spotless, with a fully restored Spanish-style exterior complete with wooden balcony. The simple but elegant guest rooms are comfortable, spacious, and tactfully decorated. Located right in the heart of La Candelaria, the hotel is close to the Museo Botero and dozens of cafes and restaurants.

Calle 11 no. 2–32. ✆ **1/341-1884.** www.abadiacolonial.com. 12 units. COL$150,000 double. Rates include breakfast. AE, DC, MC, V. Transmilenio: Museo del Oro or Las Aguas. **Amenities:** Restaurant. *In room:* TV, hair dryer, minibar.

Inexpensive

Hotel Chorro de Quevedo This brand-new hotel is owned and run by Massimo Gaudenzio, a friendly and helpful Italian. The hotel is set in a renovated colonial house where rooms range from cozy to large. The upstairs suites are a real bargain for families or those traveling in a large group. Though simple, rooms are tasteful, elegant, and, at this price, the best bang for your buck. Massimo can provide plenty of information about tourist sites, museums, and restaurants. The hotel is located in ultrabohemian Chorro de Quevedo, where plenty of cafes, restaurants, and bars are nearby, though you should be warned the plaza fills with hippie-esque bongo players all day and night Friday and Saturday, though the hotel rooms do a pretty good job of keeping the noise out.

Calle 13B no. 1–53 ✆ **1/342-6204.** www.hotelchorrodequevedo.com. 6 units. COL$60,000–COL$120,000. No credit cards. Transmilenio: Las Aguas or Museo del Oro. **Amenities:** Internet; room service; TV.

In North Bogotá

Ever since multinationals started moving in by the droves a few years ago, four- and five-star hotels in Bogotá are often booked at full capacity, and despite the seemingly endless selection of high-end lodging, finding a hotel in the northern part of town is no easy feat. I suggest booking at least 15 to 30 days in advance and calling a few days before arrival to confirm your reservation; guests have sometimes shown up only to discover the hotel is overbooked and they've been moved to another nearby hotel. ***Tip:*** Hotels in north Bogotá are business-oriented, so they often drop their rates (by as much as half) on weekends—be sure to ask about special deals.

Aside from the hotels listed below, **the Charleston,** Carrera 13 no. 85–46 (✆ **1/257-1100**), is a pleasant, modern, business-oriented choice in La Zona T. In the Centro Financiero, the **Rosales Plaza,** Calle 71A no. 5–47 (✆ **1/321-5917**), is a smart, bright hotel, and **Hoteles América,** Calle 6 no. 8–23 (✆ **1/249-4618**), which has an excellent location near the Centro Financiero and La Zona G, is currently being remodeled in order to obtain a four-star rating. Bogotá has plenty of upscale options and hostel options, but when it comes to midrange hotels, the options are lacking. However, **Hotel Casona del Patio Amarillo,** Carrera 8 no. 9–24 (✆ **1/212-8805;** www.lacasonadelpatio.net), is a pleasant bed-and-breakfast with rates starting at about COL$120,000 per night. Perhaps your cheapest option in the North is the Chapinorte Hostal, a 10-minute walk from the Zona T and about 15-minute taxi ride from the city center. The hostel is as plain as it gets: rooms are tiny, bathrooms are shared, and you'll have to rent a towel for COL$2,000, but singles start at COL$40,000 and the location is relatively safe.

Very Expensive

Casa Medina ★★ If you can afford it, this is the place to stay in Bogotá. Built in 1945 by the wealthy Don Santiago Medina, the well-located hotel has immaculately decorated rooms with classic furniture and all the modern amenities. The building was declared a national monument in 1985 for its unique Spanish- and French-inspired architectural style. All rooms are slightly different, but each has a spacious marble bathroom, a comfortable work area, and double-paned windows to keep out noise. Every floor has elegant sitting areas and balconies, and guests can enjoy a cup of coffee in any of the many terraces and courtyards that make the hotel feel more like a fantasy country-residence than an executive-style hotel. The reception staff is fluent in English, and the hotel offers chauffeur/car service by the hour or day. In this home away from home, you can dine in style in the intimate, atmospheric restaurant or on the beautiful rooftop terrace.

Carrera 7 no. 70A–22. ✆ **1/217-0288.** www.hoteles-charleston.com. 58 units. Superiors from COL$620,000; grand suites from COL$810,000. AE, DC, MC, V. Transmilenio: Calle 72 (about 3- to 4-block walk). **Amenities:** Restaurant; small gym; spa. *In room:* TV, CD player, hair dryer, minibar.

La Fontana Across the street from Unicentro, La Fontana is an elegant hotel popular with Brazilian, Argentinian, and American businesspeople. Accommodations range from comfortable standard rooms (though the bathrooms are a bit snug) to grandiose "special suites." Prices on the standards, juniors, and junior suites are cut in half on Fridays, Saturdays, and Sundays. La Fontana has a beautiful plant-filled courtyard where musical performances of salsa, tango, Chilean and Andean music, and more are held free on Sundays. If you stay here over the weekend, be sure not to miss the well-known Cremesse, La Fontana's Sunday artisan fair, where you'll find decently priced jewelry, clothing, and artwork. The reception staff speaks English and is generally helpful. La Fontana's impressive international restaurant, **El Cigarro,** is headed by Luis Ferrero, considered one of the top chefs in Colombia. If you plan to stay in Bogotá for an extended period of time, La Fontana also offers apartments.

Av. 127 no. 15A–10. ✆ **1/615-4400** (1/274-7868 for reservations). Fax 1/216-0449. www.hotelesestelar.com. 201 hotel units and 97 long-term apt units. COL$450,000 double; from COL$500,000 suite. Rates include breakfast. AE, DC, MC, V. Transmilenio: 127. **Amenities:** 2 restaurants; bar; concierge; gym. *In room:* TV, hair dryer, minibar, Wi-Fi (in suites).

Moderate

The Belvedere The recently remodeled Hotel Belvedere is well situated close to excellent restaurants and entertainment options, and walking distance to Parque de La 93. Rooms are standard with minibar, satellite TV, blackout curtains, work table, and comfortable bathrooms. The hotel is a good deal in comparison to its competition in the same sector. Located 4 blocks from the Transmilenio, the hotel is popular with national and international corporations, but is also well suited for tourists and families. Patrons can relax and dine on the attractive terrace, and the small but tasty restaurant serves both typical and international fare. The staff is professional and communicates well in English.

Carrera 17A no.100–16. ✆ **1/257-7700.** Fax 1/610-2468. www.ghlhoteles.com. 39 units. COL$200,000 double; COL$210,000 suite. Rates include breakfast (subject to change). AE, DC, MC, V. Transmilenio: 100 (a few blocks away). **Amenities:** Restaurant; bar; Wi-Fi. *In room:* TV, hair dryer, minibar.

Saint Simon This small European-style hotel in the heart of the Zona T is a good choice in northern Bogotá. The lobby is elegant and the reception staff is bilingual. The hotel's small size allows for personal attention and has many repeat customers. There is a tiny but pleasant dining area and rooms are fresh and comfortable. The hotel is popular with Colombian businesspeople and international solo tourists. There is a small but complete business center, and Wi-Fi is available for an extra fee. All rooms have a work area and small but comfortable bathrooms, and some have views of La Zona T and the mountains. Room size and layout vary, so ask to see a room before booking. As an added bonus, there is a small artisan fair in the plaza across from the hotel, where you can buy Colombian-style *mochilas* (backpacks), handicrafts, and clothing.

Carrera 14 no. 81–34. ✆ **1/621-8188.** Fax: 1/618-4279. http://saintsimonbogota.com/espanol.htm. 48 units, including 12 suites. COL$200,000 double; COL$400,000 suite. Discounts available on weekends. AE, DC, MC, V. Transmilenio: Los Héroes or Calle 76. **Amenities:** Restaurant; Wi-Fi (for a fee). *In room:* TV, fridge, hair dryer, minibar.

WHERE TO DINE

Even though Colombian food in itself is not exactly considered international fare, plenty of options in the city keep visitors happy. Bogotá is experiencing a culinary renaissance of sorts, with international and gourmet restaurants springing up all over the place, though there are still plenty of traditional (and cheap) joints where you can grab an *almojábana* (fried cheese-bread) or an empanada. Most exotic, innovative, and upscale restaurants are found in northern Bogotá, while hole-in-the wall eateries and set-menu spots are scattered throughout the center and La Candelaria. However, you will also find many atmospheric, bohemian restaurants in La Candelaria. For Bogotá's best restaurants, head to La Zona G, located between calles 69 and 72 and carreras 3 and 6. There are also excellent high-end choices in and around el Parque de la 93, La Zona T, and Usaquén. You can expect to pay COL$20,000 to COL$45,000 per plate at high-end restaurants, and COL$5,000 to COL$12,000 for set-price menus at budget restaurants.

Without exaggerating, Bogotá has tens of thousands of restaurants, so you can rest assured that you'll never be more than a few feet away from a local or gourmet eatery. However, because Bogotá restaurants open and close with great frequency, I've decided to include a few long-time staples below. In addition to those places, here are a few other good restaurant options. **Leo Cocina y Cava ★★★**, at Calle 27B no. 6–75 (✆ **1/286-7091**), is considered the top Caribbean-inspired restaurant in Bogotá. It's open Monday to Saturday noon to 4pm and 7:30pm to midnight. For the best Italian food in town, head to **Di Lucca,** an intimate, two-story house next to the Zona T at Calle 13 no. 85–32 (✆ **1/256-3019**). It's open Monday to Saturday 11am to midnight and Sunday noon to 10pm. For high-end Chinese food, head to **Zhangs,** in the Usaquén neighborhood, located at Calle 119 no. 7–08 (✆ **1/213-3979**), open daily noon to midnight. Of course, any review of Bogotá restaurants wouldn't be complete without mentioning **Crepes and Waffles,** perhaps Colombia's most famous restaurant chain. Started by a young university couple in the '80s, Crepes and Waffles serves up spicy curry crepes, as well as delicious desert waffles and crepes, and ice cream and hires only single mothers as servers. With over a dozen locations in Bogotá, the most convenient branches are in La Zona T, Usaquén, Parque de la 93, and Unicentro.

Expensive

Harry's PARRILLA/STEAK In 2005, brothers (and chefs) Jorge and Harry Sasson debuted this popular steakhouse in the heart of the Zona G, and it's been a hit ever since. With its extensive wine list and posh ambience, Harry's has become one of the hippest places in Bogotá to grab lunch, dinner, or an after-work cocktail. The steaks are excellent, as is the service, and the glass ceiling and windows let in plenty of natural light, creating an attractive, pleasant dining space. Note that diners are allowed to bring their own wine

Un Tinto (Y un biscocho), Por Favor

Colombia is one of the world's largest exporters of coffee, and its capital city makes New York's cafe scene look meager. Bogotanos love to take a break from their work day to enjoy a good cup of steaming coffee or hot chocolate, preferably with *queso fresco* or an *almojábana* (fried cheese-bread).

For one-of-a-kind cafes, head to La Candelaria, where the large student population drives the thriving cafe scene. **Café Del Sol,** Calle 14 no. 3–60 (✆ **315/335-8576;** daily 8am–8:30pm), has a laid-back, collegial atmosphere and plays mostly chill-out '60s and '70s Spanish music. Enjoy reading the many patron-written poems tacked on the wall while sipping a decent cup of cappuccino or *tinto*. For a truly unique experience, head to **Café de La Estación ★★**, Calle 14 no. 5–14 (✆ **1/562-4080;** Mon–Fri 7am–10pm, Sat 9am–8pm), a 120-year-old train car where everything but the wood floor is original. The wooden green windowpane, plaid curtain fringes, and many black-and-white pictures of turn-of-the-century Bogotá and Cartagena make you'll feel as if you've stepped back in time. (Though, unfortunately, one side of the cafe has views of an unattractive and definitively modern parking lot.) Café de La Estación is popular with businesspeople looking for an afternoon snack. Try the Chantilly hot chocolate or one of the delicious cheese platters while listening to tangos and old-time Colombian music. **El Duende Café Arte,** Carrera 3 no. 10–49 (✆ **1/281-8946;** Mon–Thurs noon–11pm, Fri–Sat noon–midnight), is rumored to be haunted by a ghost and offers an impressive variety of coffee drinks and light fare; there are musical acts on Friday nights. Finally, to sample the Starbucks of Colombia, head to **Juan Valdez,** which serves up a wide variety of gourmet coffees and cappuccinos. My favorite locations are in the Museo Botero (p. 481) and the Zona G, Calle 70 no. 6–80 (✆ **1/217-7501**). **Oma** is another popular coffee chain with great coffee, good food, and a pleasant ambience. Started by a *paisa* selling coffee on the street, several dozen Omas are now scattered throughout Bogotá (including the Zona T, Parque de la 93, Centro Andino, and Centro Internacional Baviaria).

and liquor, which can be stored in upstairs lockers and consumed on a subsequent visit. An added bonus: The restaurant will accept dollars if you're hard up for Colombian pesos.

Calle 70 no. 5–27. ✆ **1/321-3940.** Reservations recommended. Main courses COL$26,000–COL$80,000. AE, MC, V, DC. Mon–Sat noon–midnight; Sun noon–5pm. Closed holidays.

Moderate

Las Margaritas ★★ (Finds) COLOMBIAN At more than a century old, Las Margaritas has got to be doing something right. There's nothing pretentious or fancy about Las Margaritas, but it has a rustic charm that keeps customers coming back. In the historic Chapinero neighborhood, Las Margaritas offers more than a dining experience; it also gives guests a glimpse of Bogotá and Chapinero history and culture; friendly and bilingual owner and chef Julio Rios will be happy to tell you the restaurant's history. Start with a serving of empanadas with lemon and (spicy) *aji* (pepper), popularly considered the best empanadas in Bogotá (they account for 40% of the restaurant's earnings). Continue with *lengua en salsa* (tongue in sauce) served with salad, rice, and potatoes. Or try the roast beef or the *ajiaco,* a typical Bogotá chicken, corn, potato, and avocado soup. For dessert, ask for the *postre de natas,* a mouth-watering and artery-clogging pudding of sorts.

Calle 62 no. 7–77. ✆ **1/249-9468** or 1/217-0781. Main courses COL$14,000–COL$24,000. AE, DC, MC, V. Sat–Sun noon–4pm; Tues–Fri 8am–6pm.

Inexpensive

La Puerta Falsa *Finds* COLOMBIAN It may be unassuming, but La Puerta Falsa is as authentic as it gets in Bogotá. The quaint two-story eatery is housed in a 400-year-old building and is the best place to enjoy an old-fashioned Santa Fe tamale. Other popular choices are *salchichas* (sausages), eggs with bread, *agua panela* with *queso fresco,* and an assortment of typical Colombian pastries and desserts. Bogotá's oldest functioning restaurant, the family business has been passed down from generation to generation since 1816, preserving the consistency and quality of the food. The restaurant is popular with businesspeople and can fill up quickly around lunchtime. Its location, between La Candelaria and Plaza Bolívar, makes it a convenient breakfast or lunch choice, too.

Calle 11 no. 6–50. No phone. Reservations not accepted. Main courses COL$2,000–COL$4,000. No credit cards. Mon–Sat 7am–11pm.

BOGOTA AFTER DARK

Even though Bogotanos aren't known for their dancing abilities, they do enjoy an enviable nightlife. An active bar and club scene thrives in Usaquén, La Candelaria, La Zona Rosa, and Parque de la 93. Most bars and clubs get going around 11pm and close around 3am. In large clubs, you'll be expected to buy a bottle of liquor if you want to sit at a table; if you just want a shot or two, sit at the bar. Bogotanos dress up to go out, so make sure to look your best. An extensive listing of Bogotá clubs and bars can be found at www.bogota-dc.com/dir/rumba.html.

Andrés Carne De Res ★★★, at Calle 3 no. 11A–56 (no Transmilenio access), in Chia (✆ **1/863-7880;** www.andrescarnederes.com), is considered the king of Bogotá nightlife by most Bogotános (even though it's technically located in the municipality of Chia). It's the kind of place where young and old come to dance the night away. Ask any Bogotano where to party, and they'll say Andrés 99% of the time. The club doubles as a restaurant serving up excellent steaks and is decorated completely with second-hand items. The sprawling establishment plays mostly crossover music, and by the end of the night, everyone is on their feet—don't be surprised if you find yourself table dancing after several shots of *aguardiente.* Partying doesn't come cheap at Andrés Carne de Res, though: Expect to spend COL$100,000 to COL$200,000, not including the long taxi ride back to Bogotá. Cover is COL$10,000. The owner recently opened another Andrés in La Zona T divided into three floors (Heaven, Purgatory, and Hell), but a trip to the original Andrés is still definitely worth a visit.

At Parque de la 93, **Galeria Café Libro,** Calle 11A–93–42 (✆ **218-3435**), is one of my favorite salsa places in Bogotá and fills up Thursday to Saturday. They play only salsa here, so make sure you've polished up your moves. This *rumbero* caters to a 25-and-above crowd. Expect to be drenched in sweat upon leaving after a night of intense salsa dancing.

Punto G, at Calle 94 no. 11–46 (✆ **1/616-7046**), is another popular crossover club. It resembles a hotel reception hall and is popular with the over-30 crowd. There's live music Wednesday through Saturday (featuring reggae, rock *en español,* salsa, and traditional Colombian beats), as well as a decent food selection. A night of partying at Punto

G will also cost you: The average cocktail goes for COL$20,000, and a bottle of *aguardiente* costs about COL$90,000. Cover is COL$16,000 Thursday through Saturday.

The Bogotá Beer Company is popular with the post-university yuppie crowd. It plays '80s and '90s rock beats and serves several varieties of beer produced in a nearby Bogotá beer distillery. All locations are popular with Bogotanos, but some of my favorites are on Carrera 12 no. 83–33 (✆ **1/603-071**), Carrera 11A no. 93–94 (✆ **1/621-9914**), Av. 19 no. 120–76 (✆ **1/215-5150**), Carrera 6 no. 119–24 (✆ **1/620-8454**), Calle 85 no.13–06 (✆ **1/256-6950**), and the Usaquén location.

The always-popular **Irish Pub** in La Zona T caters to a diverse crowd of Bogotanos and foreigners. One of the few places you'll find quite a few foreigners, the mojitos are excellent—as they should be for COL$20,000 a pop—and the atmosphere is festive. This typical pub fills up early, so be sure to show up early if you want to get a much-coveted outside table. (Don't worry, there are heaters to warm you up on cold nights).

A SIDE TRIP FROM BOGOTA: VILLA DE LEYVA ★★★

The perfectly preserved colonial town of Villa de Leyva (pop. 12,000) was named a national heritage site by the Colombian government in 1954, and ever since, it has become a popular weekend hangout for Bogotanos looking for a break from hectic city life. The cobblestone streets, Spanish-style villas, and small-town pace give the town a charming, lost-in-time feel. Villa de Leyva and the surrounding countryside are among the safest places in Colombia to wonder off the beaten track and do a bit of exploring—and with multiple waterfalls, a nearby desert, adventure-sport opportunities, and even a couple of vineyards, there's plenty of exploring to do.

Even though the town's main sights can easily be explored in 1 day, most visitors end up staying at least 2 to 3 days, drawn in by the town's irresistible charm.

Essentials

GETTING THERE **Libertadores** (✆ **1/423-3600**) offers two direct daily buses from the Bogotá bus station to Villa de Leyva, at 4:30am and 2:20pm. Trip time is about 4 hours. Several other bus companies also offer direct routes, especially on weekends and holidays, but they often stop for passengers along the way, making for a long ride. If you can't make one of these two routes, take one of the buses to Tunja, which depart every 5 minutes or so, and from Tunja you can catch a 45-minute *colectivo* to Villa de Leyva. (At the Tunja station, head upstairs, and then outside and board any of the large vans labeled VILLA DE LEYVA.) In all, getting to Villa de Leyva should cost between COL$16,000 and COL$17,500. Take a taxi to the Bogotá terminal module 3, or head to the Portal del Norte, as buses headed for Boyacá and Villa de Leyva pick up passengers there, too. All buses and *colectivos* will drop you off 3 blocks from the main plaza in Villa de Leyva, walking distance from most hotels. If you have a lot of luggage, you may want to consider taking a short COL $4,000 taxi ride, especially if you're staying in one of the many farms or inns around town.

VISITOR INFORMATION The Villa de Leyva **tourist office** is located right off the main plaza at Carrera 9 no. 13–04 (✆ **8/732-0232;** www.villadeleyva.net) and is open daily from 8am to 5pm. If you plan to be in town for at least a couple of days, you might want to invest in the English/French *Villa de Leyva Tourist Guide,* available for COL$12,000 at the tourist office and in some hotels.

What to See & Do in Villa De Leyva

Villa de Leyva's main attraction is its large **cobblestone plaza ★★★**, supposedly the largest town plaza in Colombia. There are also a number of decent museums and sites in town worth seeing.

Located on the main plaza, the **Iglesia Parroquial De Villa de Leyva** was constructed in 1604, and it's here that independence hero Antonio Nariño lived from 1823 to 1846. Also located on the main plaza is the **Casa Museo Del Maestro Luis Alberto Acuña,** dedicated to the life and eclectic works of the eponymous artist; it's open daily 9am to 6pm. (If the museum appears closed, simply knock and someone will let you in.) Admission is COL$2,000 adults, COL$1,500 children.

In the **Casa Museo de Antonio Nariño,** Carrera 9 no. 10–21 (✆ **8/732-0342;** Thurs–Tues 8am–noon and 2–6pm; COL$3,000), you'll find documents and items belonging to Antonio Nariño. The house was built in 1600, and the independence hero spent a few years here prior to his death.

The **Museo de Arte Religioso,** Plazoleta del Carmen (✆ **8/732-0214;** Sat–Sun and holidays 10am–1pm and 2–5pm; COL$2,000), houses one of the country's best collections of religious art (17th–20th c.). At press time it was closed for renovation.

If you're in town on Saturday, be sure not to miss the **Saturday market,** when peasants from Villa de Leyva's rural sector come to town to sell their fruits and vegetables. The market is located 3 blocks from the main plaza, walking toward the Hospedería Duruelo (see below).

In addition to the sights listed below, walking tours and day-trips into the Boyacá countryside are available with tour companies. **Colombian Highlands,** Carrera 9 no. 11–02 (✆ **8/732-1379** or 311/308-3739; www.colombianhighlands.com), is run by bilingual biologist Oscar Gilede and offers many eco- and adventure tours that can be done by car or horse. He also runs the clean Renacer Guesthouse, a pleasant hostel about 1km (a half mile) from town. **Terra Touring,** Calle 13 no. 7–63 (✆ **8/732-0241**), provides tours in Spanish, French, and English. **Guías y Travesías,** Calle 11 no. 8A–50 (✆ **8/732-0742**), also provides excellent, relatively inexpensive day tours, as does **Aventourese** (✆ **311/877-4338**).

If you're looking for horseback-riding opportunities, contact **Hacienda Flamingo** (✆ **310/480-539;** ask for Rafael Orejuela or Patricia Delgado), **Criadero El Olivo** (✆ **315/324-9832;** elolivo@sinva.com.co), or **Yeguada Alcazaba Del Viento** (✆ **310/223-3955;** alcazabadelviento@hotmail.com). They all rent out horses by the hour or day. Your hotel should also be able to provide you with information.

Where to Stay

Villa de Leyva has about 150 lodging options. Unless you're going to be in town in December, January, or during a holiday weekend, it should be pretty easy to find a hotel room—though since Colombia seems to have more holidays than any other country, it's best to book in advance. It's imperative that you make advance reservations if you'll be here during the Astronomical Festival in the beginning of February, Holy Week in March or April, Villa de Leyva's anniversary on June 12, the Gastronomical Fair in July, the National Kite Festival in August, the National Tree Festival in September, or the Festival of Lights in December. Most hotels and *posadas* here are charming, colonial-style places, so it's hard to make a bad hotel choice. A good website to check out for Villa de Leyva lodging options is www.villadeleyva.net. Information is in English, Spanish, and French.

Pastries in Villa de Leyva

Villa de Leyva is well known for its charming, popular pastry shops. **La Galleta★**, Calle 13 no. 7–03 (✆ **8/732-1213**), is famous for its *milojas,* a typical Colombian dessert made with a cookie base, cream, and *arequipe.* This cozy little coffee-dessert shop plays jazz and blues and is open from noon to 7pm on Monday to Friday and 9am to 9pm on Saturday, Sunday, and holidays. The newly opened **Tortes y Tortas,** right off the plaza, is open Thursday to Tuesday from 10am to 8pm and makes low-fat, low-sugar desserts, in case you're watching your waistline. This comfortable pastry shop is owned by a friendly couple from Bogotá and specializes in Colombian desserts. Finally, **La Pastelaria Francesa,** Calle 10 no. 7–03 (no phone), owned by Frenchman Patrice Rio, bakes delicious bread and serves up a variety of quiches and European-style pastries, jams, and chocolates, and is always crowded on weekends.

The **Hospedería Duruelo,** Carrera 3 no. 12–88 (✆ **098/732-0222;** reservas@duruelo.com.co), is the poshest (and most expensive) place to stay in town, and it's easy to see why. The sprawling, 86-room Spanish-style residence is surrounded by beautiful, well-kept gardens and offers a gorgeous three-tiered pool, full spa service, and spectacular views of Villa de Leyva and the surrounding countryside. Guest rooms are standard, if not particularly impressive, though a splurge on one of the "Especial" rooms will get you a great view of the orange thatched roofs, unspoiled nature, and impressive mountains of Villa de Leyva. If you can't afford to stay at the Hospedería Duruelo but still want to be pampered like the rich and famous, the hotel offers day-use plans, which allow for use of the pool, bar, Jacuzzi, gym, sauna, and Turkish baths for COL$45,000 with lunch, COL$25,000 without lunch. In high season, a standard double will cost you COL$258,909. The hotel is a short but uphill walk from the main plaza.

For a truly unique lodging experience, head to the **Hostería Molino La Mesopotamia,** Calle del Silencio (ask for directions; ✆ **8/732-0235**), a more-than-4-centuries-old residence that once served as the town's grain mill. The mill was built in 1568, 4 years before Villa de Leyva itself was founded, and for the last 45 years, it's been a hotel. In high season, a double will cost you COL $150,000. The hotel is an easy 4-block walk from the main square. Note, however, that you shouldn't expect five-star comfort here, and there have been complaints that the hotel isn't being kept up as it should be, so pickier travelers may want to head elsewhere.

If you have a low budget, check out the ecofriendly **Hostal Renacer.** Run by biologist/environmentalist Oscar Gilede (who also runs Colombian Highlands), the hostal is about a kilometer from town and offers dorm and double rooms from COL$60,000 to COL$120,000 per room. The hostal is located in a beautiful, colonial-style farmhouse on a hill with beautiful views of the Villa de Leyva countryside. Breakfast is available for COL$5,000, and a kitchen and two common areas are available for guests. If you're traveling alone, Renacer is a good choice as you're likely to meet more solo travelers.

Where to Dine

For a small town, Villa de Leyva has a decent dining selection. Monday through Thursday, hours can be limited and many restaurants close down. When possible, call in advance to check hours. El Centro Gastronomico Casa La Quintera is located to the right side of the church on the main plaza and houses Villa de Leyva's best (and most upscale) restaurants. The restaurants on the plaza tend to be a bit more expensive (COL$10,000–COL$25,000); head to the side streets for better deals. For breakfast in town, head to **La Tienda de Teresa,** Carrera 10 no. 13–72, where you can have *arepas* with almost anything you can imagine—cheese, chicken, beans, and even hamburger. If you're here later in the day, try one of their great desserts, starting at COL$1,000. You can even leave your mark by signing the wall, as many visitors have.

A beautiful little restaurant, **Rincón del Bauchue,** at Carrera 9 no. 15A–05 (✆ **8/732-0884**), specializes in typical Boyacá dishes including *mazamorra chiquita* (well-cooked corn, often in a milky broth), *cuchuco de trigo con espinosa* (wheat/potato vegetable soup), and *cocido boyacense* (a sort of sampler platter that includes soup, potato, beef or pork, and rice). Rincón del Bauchue has its own minigreenhouse, a ceramics workshop, several dining rooms—including an outdoor eating area—and even offers guest rooms during high season.

5 MEDELLIN

233km (145 miles) NW of Bogotá, 473km (294 miles) SE of Cartagena

Fifteen years ago, few foreigners would have considered visiting Medellín. Once the most dangerous city in the world with a murder rate of 435 per 100,000 residents, all-too-frequent bombings, and deadly gang wars, Medellín was known as the murder capital of the world. But thanks to improvements in infrastructure and community planning, a new emphasis on education, and an increased police presence (not to mention the death of drug lord Pablo Escobar), Medellín is now considered a relatively safe large city with a homicide rate less than that of both Washington, D.C., and New Orleans. Medellín is now one of Colombia's wealthiest cities, and a model of excellent urban planning. However, travelers should note that the crime rate, particularly the murder rate, has spiked in the last year due mostly to gang activity in the *comunas.* However, because it's unlikely that foreigners will be spending much time in the *comunas,* normal city safety precautions should do.

A pleasant city with springlike weather year-round (daytime highs of 75°F–85°F/24°C–29°C) and a decent number of tourist and cultural sites, Medellín also makes a great base from which to explore the surrounding countryside and El Eje Cafetero.

ESSENTIALS

Getting There

BY PLANE You will most likely be arriving in Medellín's international airport, **José María Córdova** (airport code MDE; ✆ **4/601-212**), which lies about 45 minutes east of the city. Some smaller domestic flights land at **Olaya Herrera National Airport.** Several airlines provide service from the United States to Medellín, including **Avianca, Copa, Delta,** and **American Airlines** (see "Planning Your Trip to Colombia," earlier in this chapter, for contact information). Another option is to connect in Bogotá and take a flight to Medellín. Colombian airlines Avianca and Aires offer several dozen flights a day from Bogotá and about a dozen each from Cali and Cartagena, as well as a few flights from smaller cities such as Pereira, Manizales, and Armenia. To get from the José María

 Córdova airport to Medellín proper, you can take a taxi for COL$45,000 to COL$55,000, or you can take a COL$5,000 minibus, which will drop you off in the city center, the last stop being the Hotel Nutibara (see below). From the city center, you can take a much cheaper taxi to your hotel. Green minibuses are located at the exit of the airport and labeled MEDELLIN. If you arrive after 8pm, you'll have to take a taxi.

BY BUS You can get to Medellín from most major cities and large towns. The views are breathtaking, but it's not just because of the scenery: Mountain drop-offs and crazy Colombian drivers will try the nerves of even the most stoic travelers. Nervous travelers are encouraged to fly. Unlike most other Colombian cities, Medellín has two bus terminals, **El Terminal del Norte** and **El Terminal del Sur,** so check to see which end of town your hotel is closest to before booking your bus trip. ***Tip:*** If you will be staying in El Poblado, try to arrive at El Terminal de Sur to avoid a long and expensive ride to your hotel.

Getting Around

Most of Medellín's tourist attractions are within walking distance of the city center, but there is also a great Metro system (the only one in Colombia) covering 26km (16 miles) east to west and 6km (3¾ miles) north to south. Metro tickets cost COL$1,300 no matter where you go. A supplemental free cable car system moves about 27,000 people a day from the city center to the poorer *comunas* on the surrounding mountainsides. Taxis in Medellín are cheap and efficient. Even though I don't always take my own advice, I recommend solo (non-Colombian) travelers call a cab rather than hailing one on the street, especially if you look particularly foreign. At night it's always best to call a cab. A couple of taxi options include **Empresa de Taxis Super S.A.** (✆ **4/513-9700**) and **CityTaxi** (✆ **4/444-0002**).

Visitor Information

Getting to Medellín's tourism office feels a bit like entering a maximum-security prison. It's located in the **Palacio de Exposiciones,** at Calle 51 no. 55–80 (✆ **4/232-4022**), and you'll have to ring many bells and walk through many doors to find the office. As a bonus, though, it seems few tourists venture this way, so the office often gives away maps and activity guides (including a guide in English and Spanish). The office is supposedly open between 7:30am and 12:30pm and again between 1:30 and 5:30pm. There are also tourism offices located at **José María Córdova airport** (✆ **4/562-2885**) and **Olaya Herrera airport** (✆ **4/285-1048**). Keep in mind that foreign tourists are a relative novelty in Medellín, so the amount of information available is sometimes limited.

The best way to see the city is to take the **Turibus** (✆ **4/371-5054;** www.turibus colombia.com), which will drop you off at the city's major attractions as well as give you information about Medellín. Ask if a bilingual guide is available. You can catch the Turibus at Parque Del Poblado. The 4-hour tours are offered at 9am and 1pm. Tickets are COL$15,000 for adults and COL$7,500 for children. Turibus now also offers tours of the surrounding countryside and **El Circuito de Oriente** for COL$50,000 to COL$80,000 per person for all-day packages.

Another company that offers countryside tours is **Las Buseticas,** located on Carrera 43A no. 34–95 (✆ **4/262-7444;** www.lasbuseticas.com). The bigger your party, the better the prices. Las Buseticas also offers packaged tours of El Eje Cafetero and other Colombian destinations. Other bus and car companies offer day tours of the Circuito de Oriente; for more information, contact or visit the **Aviatur** office in Parque de Bolívar, at Carrera 49 no. 55–25, Edificio El Parque (✆ **4/576-5000** or 576-5002; www.aviatur.com). Your hotel should also be able to provide tour information.

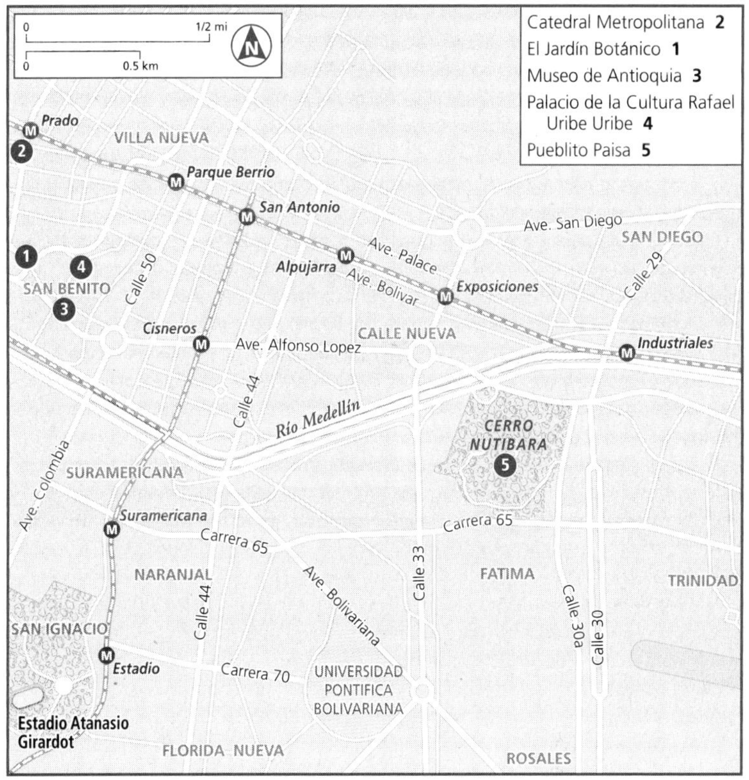

FAST FACTS You can change money at most banks, upscale hotels (though the rate is poor), and both of Medellín's airports. ATMs are scattered throughout the city, in malls, bus terminals, and in all EXITO stores. It's a bad idea to use ATMs in the city center, as robberies have been known to occur. Although Medellín is much safer than it was 15 years ago, you still want to take basic precautions. Don't carry large amounts of cash, and disperse it on your person, especially when in the city center, which can be a bit seedy. ***Tip:*** Try to withdraw money in the safer **Poblado** or **Laureles** neighborhoods.

If you have an emergency or need medical attention, try la **Clínica Medellín,** Calle 7 no. 39–290, in Poblado (✆ **4/511-6044**), or **Clínica de las Américas,** Diagonal 75B no. 2A–80 (✆ **4/342-1010**). Always head to private hospitals for the best care, especially if you have no cash or insurance card on you. Remember that in Colombia, *hospitales* are public, state-funded institutions and *clínicas* are private. Pharmacies are on nearly every corner of the city center.

To contact the metropolitan police, dial ✆ **112;** for medical and other emergencies dial ✆ **123.**

WHAT TO SEE & DO

If possible, try to visit Medellín in August, during **La Festival de Flores ★★★**, one of the most unique festivals in the world, when the *campesinos* from Antioquia come to the city to display their flower designs. The weeklong celebrations feature a number of events, including an antique car parade, horse parade, and the grand finale, the flower float parade, where young and old alike display their flower designs in a 3- or 4-hour parade, also featuring dancers, singers, and performers. Be sure to book your plane ticket far in advance if you'll be in Medellín during this time. Midrange and budget hotels sometimes won't take advance reservations, so you might need to arrive early in the morning or book a higher-end hotel.

Medellín is a city of parks and plazas. A great place to begin exploring is at **Parque Bolívar** (Metro: Prado), which admittedly is a popular hangout for bored old men, prostitutes, and drug addicts, even during the day. Avoid the park at night. Even so, this plaza is home to Medellín's largest church, the Romanesque-style **Catedral Metropolitana,** Carrera 48 no. 56–81 (✆ **4/513-2269**), made with over 1.2 million bricks, which, according to legend, were solidified with bulls' blood. The inside of the massive cathedral is rather dim and somber. The church closes at night, but generally remains open during the day.

To get to **Parque Berrío,** walk down **Avenida Junín**—a pleasant pedestrian promenade with many picturesque balcony-level restaurants and some decent shopping—or take the Metro to the Parque Berrío stop. From here, go to the **Museo de Antioquia,** Carrera 52 no. 52–43 (✆ **4/251-3636;** www.museodeantioquia.org), which features over 90 artworks donated by Medellín's native son, Fernando Botero. It's open Monday 9:30am to 5pm, and Friday to Sunday 10am to 4pm; admission is COL$8,000 adults, COL$3,000 students with college ID; children 11 and under are free. On the other side of the plaza is the **Palacio de La Cultura Rafael Uribe Uribe,** Carrera 51 no. 52–03 (✆ **4/251-1444**), a rather strange neoclassical cakelike palace-turned–art museum that features rotating exhibitions and workshops. It's open Monday to Friday 8am to 5pm.

If the Museo de Antioquia wasn't enough Botero for you, head to the **Plazoleta de las Esculturas,** where you can see (and be photographed with) his singular sculptures of *Adam and Eve* and the *Reclining Venus.*

Other parks worth checking out include **El Parque de Los Deseos,** a popular place for couples and movies on weekends; **El Parque de Los Pies Descalzos (Barefoot Park);** and **El Jardín Botánico,** Carrera 52 no. 73–182 (admission COL$3,000; Metro: Universidad).

The slightly cheesy but free **Pueblito Paisa,** Calle 30 no. 55–64 (✆ **4/235-8370;** daily 6am–midnight), is a miniature replica of a typical Antioquian town. It offers decent souvenir and handicraft shopping as well as an excellent *paisa* restaurant and great views overlooking Medellín. Take a taxi here—ideally on a weekday, when it's less busy. Do not attempt to climb up or down El Pueblito Paisa, as violent robberies have occurred here.

If you're interested in riding Medellín's cable-car system, take the Metro to the Acevedo station, from which you can board the cable car. You get great views of the city as you ascend—especially of the expansive *comunas*—and from the top, you'll have a great view of the Valle de Aburrá, in which Medellín's center was constructed. ***Tip:*** Avoid the cable-car system between the 4-to-6:30pm rush hour. If you don't want to get off at the top, you can stay in the cable car, which will take you directly back to the Acevedo Metro station. Make this trip during the day and don't stray far from the cable-car station at the top, particularly if you're taking pictures.

SHOPPING

Like most of Colombia, Medellín is a shopper's city. It's one of the largest textile producers in the country, and a fine place to go clothes shopping—in the city center, you will find inexpensive clothing and shoes. Although Medellín isn't particularly known for handicrafts, a couple of decent stores are around Plaza de Bolívar and on Avenida Junín. For extremely cheap (and possibly contraband) electronics, clothing, and home goods, head to **El Hueco,** Glorieta de San Juan and Avenida del Ferrocarril (✆ **4/512-7273**), but be sure to keep your guard up. It might be a good idea to hire a taxi driver for a few hours who can accompany you and offer some protection. For more traditional shopping, head to **Centro Comercial Vizcaya,** Calle 9 no. 30–382 (✆ **4/276-5194**); **Centro Comercial Oviedo,** Carrera 43A no. 6 Sur 15, off Avenida el Poblado (✆ **4/321-6116**); or the ultraupscale **Parque Comercial El Tesoro,** Carrera 25A 1ASur–45 (✆ **4/321-1010**). Your taxi driver will be familiar with any of these malls.

WHERE TO STAY

In general, upscale options are located in El Poblado, where you will be close to La Zona Rosa with its many restaurants and bars, as well as to Vía de las Palmas, Medellín's glitzy party avenue. A number of midrange establishments are around Carrera 70, near Medellín's stadium and with quick Metro access. Dozens of super budget options are in the city center, though it's important to note that this area is dodgier than Laureles or El Poblado, especially at night. Though the area isn't particularly *un*safe, it is home to most of the city's prostitutes, homeless, and drug addicts, and many of the hotels here double as pay-by-the-hour-type places. Upscale and midrange hotels in Medellín are generally a good deal and cheaper than those in Bogotá and Cartagena, so you may be able to splurge a bit here. Keep in mind that as in all of Colombia, hotel rates are negotiable and outside of holiday weekends and tourist season (Dec and Aug), you should be able to bargain the price down.

In addition to the hotels listed below, you might try the **Dann Carlton Medellín,** Carrera 43A no. 7–50 (✆ **4/444-5151;** www.danncarlton.com), considered the best hotel in Colombia and offering 200 rooms, 16 suites, and a rotating top-floor bar with excellent views of Medellín. Rooms here start from about COL$200,000 a night and go up from there.

Expensive

Inter-Continental (Kids) The sprawling 249-room Inter-Continental is a good, modern lodging option, close to some of Medellín's best restaurants and nightspots. Part of the large, international Inter-Continental chain, the hotel offers 12 meeting rooms, including one with capacity for 2,300 people, considered the largest dance hall in the city. Guest rooms are modern, airy, and comfortable. The Inter-Continental is a sport enthusiast's dream come true, with a great pool, a gym, spa, tennis courts, minigolf course, and even a bullring that doubles as a volleyball court. If you're really in the mood for a splurge—and we're talking COL$1,350,000—you can stay in the Presidential Suite, considered the best hotel suite in all of Colombia. Although the Inter-Continental caters to a mostly business crowd, it's one of the only hotels in this section of town—or in most of Medellín, for that matter—that makes a decent family hotel.

Calle 16 no. 28–51, Las Palmas. ✆ **4/315-4443.** Fax 4/415-4404. www.intercontinental.com/medellin. 249 units. COL$250,000 double; from COL$346,500 suite. Rates include breakfast. AE, DC, MC, V. No Metro access. **Amenities:** 2 bars; babysitting; pool; room service; sauna; spa. *In room:* TV, hair dryer, minibar, Wi-Fi.

Park 10 Hotel ★★ My favorite hotel in Medellín, this beautiful boutique hotel is just 3 blocks from Parque Lleras. The Park 10 offers 55 suites with top-notch modern amenities—some even come with an en suite Jacuzzi. The English-style hotel has a spectacular outdoor terrace, charming gardens, and fresh, spacious guest rooms, all with views of El Poblado. All rooms feature marble bathrooms, orthopedic mattresses, and stained-glass bathroom doors. For COL$60,000 more you might as well splurge on the two-level grand suite and indulge your taste for luxury. The hotel's policy against social events and its location in a residential neighborhood guarantee a quiet, good night's sleep. And if you're feeling a little out of breath, the small upstairs gym offers an oxygen bar as well as exercise equipment. As an added bonus, the hotel's restaurant, **La Fragata,** is considered one of the best seafood restaurants in the country.

Carrera 36B no. 11–12, El Poblado. ✆ **4/310-6060** or 4/312-7875. www.hotelpark10.com.co. 55 units. COL$220,000 standard suites; COL$320,000 grand suites. Rates include breakfast. AE, DC, MC, V. Free parking. Metro: 15-min. walk to El Poblado station. **Amenities:** Gym; room service; spa; free Wi-Fi (in common areas). *In room:* TV, hair dryer, minibar, Wi-Fi (for a fee).

Moderate

Hotel Florida The executive-style 50-room Hotel Florida is conveniently located a few blocks from the Metro, shopping centers, bars, clubs, and, in case you're in the mood to exercise, Medellín's stadium, *"el estadio."* There's nothing particularly memorable about Hotel Florida, but it's a good deal in this price category, and in a safe neighborhood. The 10-year-old hotel is a bit dark, but junior suites are spacious and have excellent lighting. The hotel is divided into two four-story towers, one with an elevator and one without.

Carrera 70 no. 44B–38. ✆ **4/260-0644** or 260-4900. www.hotelfloridamedellin.com/somos.html. 50 units. From COL$113,000 double; from COL$134,000 junior suite. Ask about discount rates on weekends. Rates include breakfast. AE, DC, MC, V. Free parking. Metro: Estadio. **Amenities:** Restaurant; free Wi-Fi. *In room:* A/C, TV, hair dryer, minibar.

Hotel Nutibara Though it may not be the grand hotel it was in days past, this 63-year-old hotel is still a decent midrange option. Centrally located 1 block from Parque Berrío, the Nutibara is walking distance from most of the city's main attractions. It was once the most modern and luxurious hotel in town, and while that's no longer true, it does still exude a certain charm. Rooms are standard, many with good views of Parque Berrío and the Palacio de Cultura, and there's an attractive open-air pool and bar area on the fifth floor. Most doubles fit up to five people. **La Orquídea,** the hotel's restaurant, serves up tasty *paisa* cuisine. Common areas and lobbies can be a bit dim, but the service is good, reception staff speaks English, and rooms are comfortable.

Plazuela Nutibara Calle 52A no. 50–46. ✆ **4/511-5111.** www.hotelnutibara.com. 140 units. From COL$100,000 double. Rates include breakfast. AE, DC, MC, V. Free parking. Metro: Parque Berrío. **Amenities:** Restaurant; bar; dance club; gym; Internet; massage; pool; room service; sauna; steam room. *In room:* A/C, TV, hair dryer, minibar.

Inexpensive

The Black Sheep Hostel Hidden in the leafy Patio Bonito neighborhood and just a short walk from trendy Parque Lleras, the Black Sheep is an excellent choice for solo travelers, and caters to the under-30 crowd. There's a fully equipped kitchen, a barbecue area, two TV rooms, and—most Colombian of all—a hammock-filled balcony. Opened in 2005 by New Zealander Kelvin Smith, the hostel has a laid-back, backpacker atmosphere and a bilingual daytime staff of informative, friendly university students. An added bonus you're unlikely to find in other budget options: extralong beds to accommodate tall foreigners. Units are spacious and comfortable, most featuring en suite bathrooms. The only downside is that the hostel isn't quite as clean as it could be. In high season, it's hard to get a single or a double unless you stick around for a couple of days, but dorm beds can usually be booked on the spot. There is a minimum 5-day stay during La Feria de las Flores.

Transversal 5A no. 45–133, Poblado. ✆ **4/311-1589** or 311-1379. www.blacksheepmedellin.com. 21 units. From COL$40,000 single; from COL$18,000 (per person) double. No credit cards. Metro: El Poblado. **Amenities:** TV lounge; Wi-Fi.

WHERE TO DINE

If you love *arepas* and beans, you're in luck. Food in Medellín is carb-based and filling, and you're never far from the famous *bandeja paisa,* a typical Antioquian plate featuring soup, rice, beans, avocado, salad, sausage, plantain, shredded beef, eggs, *arepa,* and *chicharrón* (pork rinds), which you can get for as little as COL$5,000. You can find plenty of small restaurants offering *almuerzos corrientes,* or set-price lunches, usually between COL$3,000 and COL$8,000. If you're looking for something a little more refined, head to La Calle de La Buena Mesa, Parque Lleras, or Vía de Las Palmas, where you'll find international and gourmet fare, a more exclusive atmosphere, and sometimes overpriced dishes.

For inexpensive eateries in El Poblado (where most Medellín tourists stay), check out Carrera 43B at Calle 8, right off Parque del Poblado. Try **Flor de Candela, Yulio's Restaurante, Menú Casero** (for typical fare), or **Picolo** (for Italian and pizza).

Expensive

Hato Viejo ★ COLOMBIAN/PAISA Hato Viejo is a great place to soak in the cowboy spirit that characterizes the people of Antioquia. Waiters dressed in typical 18th-century *paisa* attire provide attentive service and will be glad to share their version of the history of Colombia if you ask. (Just make sure you have a couple of free hours.) A typical Spanish courtyard and dozens of hanging flowers give the restaurant an intimate, elegant feel despite its 250-person capacity. For a crash-course introduction to the *paisa* diet, try the Plato Montanero, a typical Antioquian dish featuring ground beef, rice, avocado, *chicharrón,* sausage, egg, salad, beans, and fried *plátano.* Unless you're ravenous, ask for the *media porción* (half portion). For more privacy, ask for a table on one of the many balconies overlooking El Poblado.

Calle 16 no. 28–60, Vía de Las Palmas. ✆ **4/268-5412.** Dinner reservations recommended for parties of 4 or more. Main courses COL$16,000–COL$50,000. MC, DC, V. Daily noon–11pm (will sometimes stay open until midnight if business is good). No Metro access.

San Carbón GRILL/STEAKHOUSE My favorite Medellín grill and steakhouse, San Carbón has a covered terrace, wine, a chic bar, high ceilings, and an open-air kitchen, all of which make this a very pleasant and atmospheric place to enjoy the energy of Parque Lleras. Like almost all restaurants around Parque Lleras, San Carbón functions as a bar at night, popular with the city's young and hip. The steak and lobster are good, as are the Argentine and Chilean red wines. Call ahead and ask about live music.

Calle 9A no. 37A–13, Parque Lleras. ✆ **4/268-5570.** Main courses COL$23,000–COL$40,000. Daily noon–2am, though times vary depending on the crowd. AE, DC, MC, V. Metro: El Poblado.

Moderate

Ave María INTERNATIONAL An atmospheric and warm place with a bamboo ceiling and brick interior, Ave María is popular with Europeans and Americans, and is known for its international fare. Try the house specialty, *los lomitos Ave María* (beef tenderloin), or one of the other beef specialties. The restaurant, which overlooks Parque Lleras, also functions as a bar at night. It's a great place to enjoy a bottle of good wine, sit back, and take in the action of Parque Lleras on a Friday or Saturday, when it seems the cream of the crop of Medellín society comes to see and be seen. If you're low on funds, check out the special menu from noon to 6pm offering more economical options. Tuesday through Saturday, there's live music after 8pm.

Carrera 38 no. 9A–13. ✆ **4/311-5623.** www.avemaria.com.co. Main courses COL$12,000–COL$40,000. AE DC, MC, V. Mon–Wed noon–midnight; Thurs–Sun noon–2am. Metro: El Poblado.

Basílica SUSHI/PERUVIAN/GRILL Another good choice in Parque Lleras, Basílica offers an eclectic menu featuring sushi, Peruvian, and international fare. Though it might seem that every restaurant in Medellín is trying its hand at sushi, it's actually pretty good here. It's a great place to eat if everyone in your party wants something different. The metallic bars, high ceilings, and rustic dark-wood tables give the place a modern, urban feel. Try the tasty, if a bit small, *ceviche mixto,* or one of the many steak and beef plates the restaurant is well known for. The restaurant offers an excellent wine and cocktail list, and also functions as a bar at night.

Carrera 38 no. 8A–42. ✆ **4/311-7366** or 311-8527. Main courses COL$13,000–COL$30,000. AE, DC, MC, V. Daily noon–11pm (later Fri–Sat). Metro: El Poblado.

Inexpensive

If the restaurant reviewed below fills up, try **Los Monitos,** just opposite Maratial del Mar, which offers typical and international fare.

Marantial del Mar SEAFOOD This is my favorite place to eat in the city center. Among the loud, sometimes dingy hole-in-the wall establishments offering *almuerzo corriente* that characterize Medellín's city center, Marantial del Mar is a peaceful respite in the courtyard of the Villa Nueva shopping center, just 2 blocks from Parque de Bolívar. The beautiful building housing the shopping center used to serve as a cloister, and tables are arranged around a working fountain. The hanging flowers and balconies overlooking the courtyard add a touch of charm and make you forget you're in Medellín's chaotic core. The restaurant is popular with business folks who work in the area and specializes in seafood, but also offers typical fare. For a good deal, ask for the COL$6,000 *menú del día,* which generally includes soup, fruit juice, rice, beans, avocado, plantains, and some sort of meat.

Calle 57 no. 49–44 (Villa Nueva shopping center). ✆ **4/251-0365.** Reservations not accepted. Main courses COL$6,000–COL$20,000. No credit cards. Daily 8am–5pm. Metro: Prado.

MEDELLIN AFTER DARK

Years under the sway of drug cartels left their mark on Medellín, particularly on **Vía de Las Palmas,** Medellín's colorful, Las Vegas–style "party row." Medellinenses love to get their party on, and the city's beautiful women are famous throughout the country (as are their surgically enhanced faces and bodies). Medellín's best dance clubs are located on Vía de Las Palmas, popular with the area's famous as well as with foreigners. **La 70,** centered on Carrera 70 near the stadium (Metro: Stadio), is another popular party area featuring smaller, less glamorous clubs and bars. If you're not much of a dancer but enjoy downing a drink or two, head to **Parque Lleras** in La Zona Rosa, one of the most exclusive spots in town and a great place to people-watch. And if you're headed anywhere in La Zona

El Eje Cafetero ★★★

In a country of spectacular landscapes, El Eje Cafetero offers perhaps the most stunning scenery in Colombia. This verdant paradise, where orchids grow wild and coffee plants cover nearly every mountain slope, is quickly becoming one of Colombia's best spots. Here you can learn all about the coffee-making process in El Parque Nacional del Café, stay in a traditional farmhouse (blue pillars for Conservatives, red for Liberals), or simply lay back in a hammock, listening to the sounds of birds chirping and not much else.

This region was once a guerilla stronghold, but military action over the last few years has made the coffee-growing region safe again, and tourists are coming back in droves. The best and cheapest way to see the region is to book a tour through **Aviatur** (**1/286-5555** or 234-7333 in Bogotá; www.aviatur.com; in Medellín on Plaza de Bolívar) or another tourist agency. These tours can be booked in any major city, but because you'll be driving, you probably want to take off from Medellín, Cali, or Bogotá.

Rosa or La Vía de Las Palmas, make sure you go with a well-stocked wallet. Note, too, that most restaurants in La Zona Rosa turn into bars around 9 or 10pm.

I don't recommend partying in the bars and cantinas in the city center, as these can be a bit seedy, and inebriated foreigners may be targets of robbery and violence. I recommend going out in a group, so if you're traveling alone, try to meet people through your hostel or hotel. If you're headed to Vía de Las Palmas, be sure to dress appropriately: no flip-flops, sneakers, or ripped jeans. Using the foreigner excuse won't work—and an English friend I was traveling with was denied entry into a relatively casual rock club because of his "inappropriate" footwear. Medellín is one of the few places in Colombia that abides by the "must be 18 to party" rule; if you look young, bring a copy of your passport.

No trip to Medellín is complete without a visit to **Mangos,** Carrera 42 no. 67A–151 (✆ **4/277-6123**), Medellín's best-known nightspot (although it's technically located in the neighboring municipality of Itagüí). Mangos claims to be the largest dance club in Latin America; whether or not this is true, its crazy, over-the-top atmosphere, complete with costumed servers and frequent shows, are the reason why everyone flocks to Mangos. There is a strange American Old West theme (think lots of cowboy hats) as well as an "anything flies" attitude here—the kind of place to expect the unexpected. On weekends, the club stays open until 5am and there's usually a cover of about COL$20,000.

Palmitas, Carrera 38 no. 26–41, Km 2 (✆ **4/232-7199**), another glitzy crossover dance club, is located on Vía de Las Palmas and often puts on salsa, merengue, and even belly-dancing shows. Popular with foreigners out for a night of dancing and drinking, the club also doubles as a restaurant serving up international and traditional food, not to mention great views of Medellín. The cover charge varies here. Palmitas is open daily 11:30am to 3:30am (dance club opens at 8pm).

If you're a drinker but not a dancer, head to the Scottish-style and English-owned **Pub Escocia,** in Parque Lleras (✆ **4/311-5607**). The bar is open 10am to midnight (until 2am on weekends). Though it functions mostly as a nightspot, the bar also offers international and British-inspired food. And if you haven't quite taken a liking to Colombian beers, the pub offers a variety of European and Irish beers. In fact, Pub Escocia claims to have the largest selection of beer and whiskey in the country.

6 CARTAGENA & THE ATLANTIC COAST

473km (293 miles) NW of Medellín, 658km (408 miles) NW of Bogotá

Cartagena, a UNESCO World Heritage Site, is the Venice of Colombia and the country's most romantic city, with one of the most impressive old towns in the Western Hemisphere. With just the right mix of sun, sand, and colonial charm, it's likely to be the highlight of your trip. Cartagena's tourism infrastructure is more developed than anywhere else in the country, so unlike most Colombian destinations, it's a pretty easy place to visit. In fact, with the 300,000 cruise-liner passengers who stop in Cartagena, it might be the only city in Bogotá you actually see any foreigners. A walk through Cartagena's inner walled city feels a bit like stepping onto the set of a 16th-century *telenovela,* complete with cobblestone streets and grandiose balconies overflowing with flowers.

Whether you come to Cartagena to splurge on its many fine hotels and restaurants, to explore its 500 years of history, or to sunbathe on its popular beaches, you'll discover an enchanting place you're unlikely to forget. As Colombia's top honeymoon destination, the city is full of romance, five-star hotels, and excellent dining options. But all this ambience and charm comes with a price: Cartagena is by far Colombia's most expensive city for tourists and bargains are hard to come by, particularly during holiday weekends and Christmastime.

Note: One of the unpleasant effects of Cartagena's distinction as the tourism capital of Colombia is the presence of persistent beach vendors and Old Town musicians who can't seem to take "no" for an answer. And saying you don't speak Spanish won't help—these guys will talk to you in Hungarian, as long as they're selling you something. The best way to avoid unwanted solicitations or serenades is to say no firmly and avoid eye contact at all costs.

ESSENTIALS

Getting There

BY PLANE Cartagena's **Rafael Núñez Airport** (airport code CTG; ✆ **5/666-6610**) is about 3km (about 2 miles) from the historic Old Town and is serviced by national carriers **Avianca** and **Aero República** as well as by international carriers **Copa, Mexicana,** and **American Airlines** (see "Getting There," under "Planning Your Trip to Colombia," earlier in this chapter, for contact information). You pay a minimum COL$8,000 airport tariff for a taxi, though if you don't have too much luggage, you can ask to be dropped off at Avenida 4 and Calle 70 for half the price. You can also take a local bus to the city, but your best bet is to go by taxi.

BY BUS Buses arrive to the **Terminal de Buses,** on the eastern end of the city. From there, you're best off taking a taxi to your hotel. Remember that unless you're coming from somewhere else on the Atlantic coast, a bus trip to Cartagena is exceptionally long

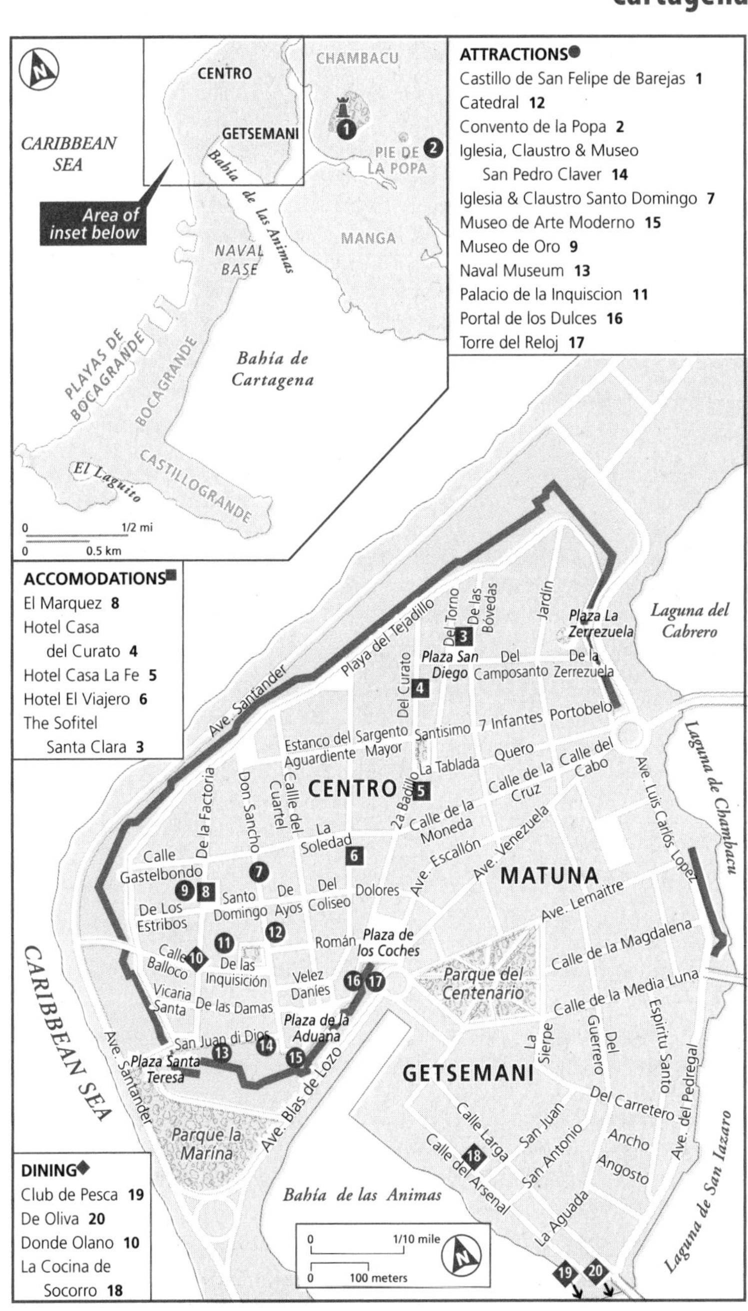
ATTRACTIONS
Castillo de San Felipe de Barejas 1
Catedral 12
Convento de la Popa 2
Iglesia, Claustro & Museo San Pedro Claver 14
Iglesia & Claustro Santo Domingo 7
Museo de Arte Moderno 15
Museo de Oro 9
Naval Museum 13
Palacio de la Inquiscion 11
Portal de los Dulces 16
Torre del Reloj 17
ACCOMODATIONS
El Marquez 8
Hotel Casa del Curato 4
Hotel Casa La Fe 5
Hotel El Viajero 6
The Sofitel Santa Clara 3
DINING
Club de Pesca 19
De Oliva 20
Donde Olano 10
La Cocina de Socorro 18
CARIBBEAN SEA
CENTRO
GETSEMANI
CHAMBACU
PIE DE LA POPA
MANGA
Area of inset below
NAVAL BASE
Bahía de las Animas
PLAYAS DE BOCAGRANDE
BOCAGRANDE
Bahía de Cartagena
El Laguito
CASTILLOGRANDE
0 1/2 mi
0 0.5 km
Laguna del Cabrero
Laguna de Chambacu
Laguna de San Lazaro
Plaza La Zerrezuela
Plaza San Diego
CENTRO
MATUNA
GETSEMANI
Parque del Centenario
Parque la Marina
Plaza Santa Teresa
Plaza de la Aduana
Plaza de los Coches
Ave. Santander
Playa del Tejadillo
Del Torno
De las Bóvedas
Jardín
Del Curato
Del Camposanto
De la Zerrezuela
Portobelo
7 Infantes
Santisimo
Estanco del Aguardiente
Sargento Mayor
La Tablada
Quero
Calle de la Cruz
Calle del Cabo
2a Badillo
Calle de la Moneda
Ave. Escallón
Ave. Venezuela
Ave. Luis Carlos Lopez
De la Factoria
Don Sancho
Calle del Cuartel
La Soledad
Calle Gastelbondo
Santo Domingo
De Ayos
Del Coliseo
Dolores
De Los Estribos
Román
Ave. Lemaitre
Calle Balloco
De las Inquisición
Velez Danies
Vicaria Santa
De las Damas
San Juan di Dios
Calle de la Magdalena
Calle de la Media Luna
Ave. Blas de Lozo
La Sierpe
Guerrero
Del Guerrero
Espiritu Santo
Ave. del Pedregal
Del Carretero
Ancho
Angosto
Calle Larga
San Juan
San Antonio
Calle del Arsenal
La Aguada
Bahía de las Animas
0 1/10 mile
0 100 meters

 (13 hr. from Medellín and 20 hr. from Bogotá), so I recommend that you splurge on a plane ticket.

Getting Around

You'll probably be spending most of your time in the small historic **Old Town,** where most tourist sites are located, or at the city's beaches. The modern part of the city has a Miami-style resort feel and consists of **Bocagrande, El Laguito,** and **Castillo Grande.** This is where you'll find modern high-rises, all inclusive resorts, many of the city's top-notch hotels, and some of Cartagena's better beaches. The outer walled city consists of the **Getsemaní** neighborhood, a poorer, less glamorous version of the inner walled city. However, foreigners are quickly buying and restoring properties in Getsemaní as prices in the Old City skyrocket. The exclusive neighborhood of **Manga,** about a 5-minute taxi ride from the Old Town, is home to Cartagena's yacht club.

BY FOOT This is the best way to explore the picturesque inner walled Old Town. You can stop and take in Cartagena's imposing churches, people-watch in its many plazas, and enjoy a bit of shopping.

BY TAXI Because Cartagena is so touristy, it's generally safe to hail taxis off the street. However, there is often a difference between what you should pay and what you will pay. Taxi drivers here are used to tourists and won't hesitate to rip you off, albeit usually by COL$1,000 to COL$2,000. As a general guide, a taxi from the airport to the Old Town should cost about COL$8,000, while a taxi to Bocagrande, Castillogrande, and El Laguito should cost COL$4,000. Before getting in your taxi, it's a good idea to ask how much the ride will cost to avoid unpleasant surprises at the end.

Visitor Information

In contrast with the rest of Colombia, you can actually get decent tourist information here. The city's best tourist office is located in **La Plaza de La Aduana,** Casa del Marqués del Premio Real (puntodeinformacion@turismocartagenadeindias.com; Mon–Sat 7am–7pm, Sun 9am–5pm), east of the Torre de Reloj. Here you can get a brochure (in both Spanish and imperfect English) with a map and descriptions of Cartagena's major sights. The office can also provide information about tours and excursions, and offers several interactive computers with information about Cartagena and Las Islas del Rosario. You'll also find small tourism offices at Plaza San Pedro Claver, Plaza de los Coches, and Centro de Convenciones de Cartagena, open Monday through Saturday 9am to 1pm and 4 to 8pm, and Sunday 9am to 5pm. Rafael Núñez International Airport also has tourism information. Additionally, hotels, whether luxury or budget, are also an excellent source of information.

FAST FACTS Call the police at ✆ **112.** The national emergency number, ✆ **123,** also works in Cartagena. For a medical emergency, head to **Hospital Bocagrande,** Calle 5 and Carrera 6 (✆ **5/665-5270**), or **Clínica A.M.I.S.A Centro Médico,** Carrera 30 no. 30–29. If you need to exchange money, head to one of several national banks to the right of **La Torre del Reloj,** immediately before you enter the Old Town (the side opposite the convention center). ATMs are abundant throughout Cartagena, however, so exchanging money shouldn't be difficult. Most midrange to high-end hotels should also be able to change your dollars.

WHAT TO SEE & DO

Cartagena, especially the inner walled Old Town, offers a wealth of colonial architectural gems and churches. There are also several excellent museums and 400-year-old plazas

A Wild Ride on the Chiva

A ***chiva*** ★ is a colorful bus made entirely of wood. *Chivas* have become a folkloric symbol of Colombia and are often decorated with festive designs, historical scenes, and even biblical imagery. In the past, *chivas* were used as a mode of transportation, but nowadays they're mostly used for city tours or as a nighttime bar on wheels. Riding a *chiva* is a must-do on a visit to Colombia—you'll see Colombians behaving their wildest.

that can't be missed. In fact, if it weren't for the motorcycles and taxis that whiz through the historic center, you'd think you were in a fantasy 16th-century Spanish town. I recommend just walking the many cobblestoned streets of Cartagena and entering whatever museums or cultural sites strike your fancy.

Much of the charm of Cartagena lies in strolling through its colonial streets; dining in one of its romantic, top-notch restaurants; and people-watching in one of its many plazas. Because some of the city's sites, such as the **Castillo de San Felipe de Barejas** and the **Convento de la Popa,** are a bit of a walk from the Old Town, you may want to take a *chiva* or carriage tour to get acquainted with the city. Your hotel will be able to provide (and even book) *chiva* and carriage tours, or you can inquire at the tourism office (see above). Daytime *chivas* should cost between COL$25,000 and COL$35,000, while a horse-drawn carriage tour should cost COL$35,000 to COL$45,000 depending on the length of your trip.

For a uniquely Colombian experience, try the *rumba chivas,* which depart at 8pm (they usually pick you up from your hotel), cost around COL$25,000, and will give you an oversight of Cartagena at night. In addition, you'll get an unlimited amount of national liquor (*aguardiente,* rum, and the like), a taste of typical Cartagena fried treats (yuca, plantain, *arepa*), and a demonstration of traditional Colombian folkloric dances. You'll be dropped off at a beachside nightclub around 10:30pm, where you can choose to stay or go back to your hotel at around midnight.

The Historic Old Town: the Top Attractions

In 1987, Cartagena's Old Town was declared a World Heritage Site by UNESCO, and its almost perfectly preserved colonial-era mansions, churches, and ornate balconies are the reason why. Where else in the Western Hemisphere can you sit in 16th-century plazas, walk along the walls of a 300-year-old fortress—one of the most impressive architectural feats of military history—and stay at a colonial-era hotel? Below are some of the city's most noteworthy sites.

Enter the city through the historic **Torre del Reloj,** one of Cartagena's most recognized architectural sites. From there, you'll find yourself in the **Plaza de los Coches,** where you can buy traditional Colombian and Cartagenian candy and sweets at the **Portal de Los Dulces.** Next head down Calle de la Amargura, past **La Plaza de La Aduana** (stop here if you're looking for tourist information), to La Plaza de San Pedro, where you can visit the **Iglesia/Claustro/Museo San Pedro Claver,** constructed in 1580, as well as the **Museo de Arte Moderno,** a decent modern-art museum right off the square. Walk down Calle San Juan de Dios to the Cartagena **Naval Museum,** where you can take in antique naval instruments and objects. Walk past La Plaza de Santa Teresa, up Calle de A. Ricaurte (which becomes Calle Santa Teresa) to Plaza de Bolívar, where you can visit the free **Museo del Oro,** as well as the **Palacio de La Inquisición** and **La Biblioteca Bartolomé Calvo,** once Cartagena's most important libraries. Be sure not to miss Cartagena's much photographed **Catedral,** built in 1586, destroyed by English pirate Francis Drake, and recently remodeled and opened to the public. Now walk up Calle Nuestra Señora del Carmen before arriving at the **Plaza de Santo Domingo,** one of Cartagena's most popular and vibrant plazas. Be sure to visit the **Iglesia/Claustro Santo Domingo,** a lovely 450-year-old church. Take a break at Plaza Santo Domingo for a light lunch or snack at one of the plaza's many outdoor cafes, where you can enjoy the colonial atmosphere.

With your energy restored, head north on Calle de la Iglesia (which becomes Calle de Don Sancocho), past El Teatro de Heredia and La Plaza del Merced, and turn right on Calle de la Merced (which becomes Calle Del Estanco del Aguardiente and Calle del Sargento Mayor). Next turn left on Calle Chochera del Hobo, where you'll find **La Plaza de San Diego,** with its many stores, restaurants, and the famous Hotel Santa Clara. A short walk up the Calle de las Bóvedas will take you to **Las Bóvedas,** a former jail, used during the independence period, that has been converted into 23 souvenir shops.

Other Tourist Sights

La Popa, Cartagena's highest point, is where you'll find the convent of Nuestra Señora de La Candelaria. ***Warning:*** If you decide not to take a *chiva* tour, be sure to come here by taxi; robberies and attacks have been reported for those who've tried to walk. **El Castillo de San Felipe de Borajas** is another Cartagena must-see, and one of the military wonders of the world. The castle/fort was built (1536–1657) to protect the city from attack. Be sure to check out its dark underground tunnels and peek through its many lookouts. Note that this site will be included in a *chiva* tour.

Las Islas del Rosario, a national park popular with tourists, is famous for its coral reefs, crystalline waters, and beautiful beaches. The islands are about 45km (28 miles) from the city and can only be reached by boat. You can arrange a trip to Las Islas del Rosario through your hotel or by heading to the Muelle Turístico, where you can buy tickets directly. Another option is to go through **Tesoro Tours,** Carrera 3 no. 6–153 (**© 5/665-4713;** www.tesorotours.com). Your hotel will also be able to arrange tours directly. Boat trips generally cost between COL$35,000 and COL$60,000, though you will also have to pay a national park tax of COL$9,400. Your boat will most likely take you to the **Acuario San Martín** on the **Isla San Martín de Pajarales,** where you can enjoy a dolphin show and observe other marine animals. Another choice on Isla San Martín de Pajarales is to go snorkeling. The island has excellent coral reefs, and if you've already seen your share of aquariums and dolphin shows, go for the snorkeling.

After visiting the aquarium, most boats will head to **Isla de Barú,** where you'll have a typical Cartagena-Caribbean lunch, complete with coconut rice, fried plantains, and a whole fish (eyes and all). Your tour will give you about 3 hours on Barú, where you can go swimming, sunbathe, or explore the island. Beware that beach vendors here are persistent, and the best way to be left alone is to get in the water as fast as possible.

If you don't have time to head to Las Islas del Rosario, visit Cartagena's main beaches—**Bocagrande, El Laguito,** and **Castillo Grande,** in the south, and, in the north, **La Boquilla** and **Marbella.** They aren't particularly breath-taking, but if you're just looking for a swim and a little sun and sand, they'll do.

SHOPPING

Prices on clothing, handicrafts, and emeralds tend to be higher in Cartagena than in other parts of the country. Plenty of attractive boutique shops are in the historic center, as well as shopping malls in El Laguito and Bocagrande.

If you are looking for handicrafts, head to Las Bóvedas—former jail cells turned souvenir shops. In the historic center are also plenty of high-end boutique shops selling Colombian designer clothing, leather goods, and emeralds. For discount shopping, head to Getsemaní, where you can buy cheap clothing, shoes, and just about anything else you can imagine; just don't count on top-notch quality. For a shopping mall, your best bet is **El Pueblito,** Carrera 2 no. 4, in Bocagrande, **La Matuna,** Carrera 8 no. 40, in El Centro, or **Pierino Gallo,** Calle 1L no. 1–12A, in El Laguito.

Tip: It seems everyone in Cartagena's Old Town wants to sell you emeralds; if you decide to purchase Colombia's favorite stone, do so because you love the look of emeralds, *not* because you think you're getting a good deal. Unless you're an expert, it's hard to know the quality of your purchase.

WHERE TO STAY

Most foreigners choose to stay in the historic Old Town. Midrange and expensive lodging options are found in the inner walled city, while the backpacker crowd heads to Getsemaní, the slightly dilapidated but much cheaper outer walled city. If you're looking for all-inclusive resorts, head to **Capilla del Mar,** Carrera 1 no. 8–12, Bocagrande (✆ **5/665-1140;** www.capilladelmar.com); **Americas Global Resort,** Anillo Vial Sector Cielo Mar (✆ **5/656-7222;** www.hotellasamericas.com.co); or the **Decameron,** Carrera 1 no. 10–80 Bocagrande (✆ **5/665-4400;** www.decameron.com).

Cartagena is jam-packed in December and January, with tourism slowly tapering off by April. July and August are busy again because of summer break. Throughout the year, various events, notably the Miss Colombia Pageant in November, fill the city. During these times, it's wise to book your hotel ahead of time. The city can also be pretty busy during mid-October, when students have a week off. You should note most Cartagena budget hotels don't usually have hot water. With the heat and humidity, though, this shouldn't be too much of a problem.

I recommend you avoid Cartagena from mid-October through the end of November; the city often floods then, making it difficult to sightsee or head to the beach.

Expensive

El Marqués El Marqués is Cartagena's best-known boutique hotel. Its lovely Asian-style gardens, multiple springs, and first-floor pool give the hotel a Zen-like quality. Antique wooden balconies overlook the courtyard, and modern artwork decorates the walls. The hotel has a long history in Cartagena, dating back to the 17th century, and is considered one of Cartagena's best and most established boutique hotels. But prestige doesn't come cheap: Don't expect to pay less than COL$500,000 a night. As an interesting side note, the hotel was home to American writer and painter Sam Green in the 1970s, where he entertained guests such as Greta Garbo and Yoko Ono. El Marqués also serves as a spa and sushi bar that's open to nonguests.

Calle de Nuestra Señora del Carmen no. 33–41, Centro Santo Domingo. ✆ **5/664-4438.** www.elmarqueshotelboutique.com. 8 units. COL$680,000 double; COL$780,000 suite; COL$980,000 presidential suite. AE, DC, MC, V. **Amenities:** Restaurant; pool; spa. *In room:* A/C, TV, minibar, Wi-Fi.

The Sofitel Santa Clara ★★★ The Sofitel Santa Clara is widely considered the top lodging option in Cartagena's historic center, close to some of Old City's best restaurants. The hotel has a history stretching as far back as 1617, when it served as the convent for the Clarisian nuns. In the late 1990s the building was restored and converted into a hotel, quickly becoming one of Colombia's best. Although the Santa Clara is an executive-style hotel, its amazing spa and rooms—with views of the ocean, the Old City, or the beautiful interior courtyards—make it a great choice for couples wanting a romantic getaway. The 102 Republican-style rooms and 17 colonial-style rooms have a chic "summer home" feel, complete with modern artwork, contemporary furniture, warm summer tones, and large windows. There's a great pool area and two excellent restaurants: **San Francisco,** which serves up Italian fare, and **El Refrectorio,** in a lovely courtyard that once was the Clarisian nuns' dining area.

Calle del Torno, Plaza San Diego. ✆ **5/664-6070.** www.hotelsantaclara.com. 119 units. COL$760,000 double; COL$1,000,000 colonial suite. Additional person (13 years old and over) COL$145,000. AE, DC, MC, V. Free parking. **Amenities:** 2 restaurants; gym; pool; room service; spa. *In room:* A/C, TV, minibar, Wi-Fi.

Moderate

Hotel Casa del Curato A delightful bed-and-breakfast, Casa del Curato dates back to the 18th century. A small, peaceful pool is in the first-floor courtyard and the stone-wall interior gives the hotel an enchanted ambience. The Casa del Curato served as a clergy house during the colonial period. The 11 uniquely decorated rooms range from typical Caribbean-contemporary all-white walls and sheets to Indian and indigenous-inspired decor—think textured walls, colorful tapestries, and carefully selected ethnic bedspreads. Suites have balconies. The upstairs terrace offers views of the Hotel Santa Clara and La Popa, and is a good place for an afternoon snack.

Calle del Curato no. 38–89, Centro. ✆ **5/664-3648.** www.casacurato.com. 11 units. COL$186,000–COL$208,000 double; COL$246,000 suite. AE, DC, MC, V. Rates include breakfast. **Amenities:** Pool. *In room:* A/C, TV, Internet, minibar.

Hotel Casa La Fe (Finds) This beautifully restored, English-owned bed-and-breakfast offers 11 cozy rooms, which are simple and minimalist. Dark-wood furnishings, pastel colors, and marble bathrooms make this a perfectly charming lodging option in the Old City, and a relatively good deal in this price range. There is an attractive downstairs sitting area, and breakfast is served daily in the lovely courtyard. The tropical vegetation gives the hotel a Caribbean feel. Unlike many of the city's historic buildings, 4-year-old Hotel Casa De La Fe dates back from the Republican rather than the colonial era. Be sure to check out the terrace, where you can cool off in the Jacuzzi-pool area or sunbathe under the hot Caribbean sun.

Calle Segunda de Badillo no. 36–125, Centro. ✆ **5/664-0306.** www.casalafe.com. 11 units. COL$220,000 1st-floor rooms; COL$264,000 2nd-floor rooms. AE, DC, MC, V. Rates include breakfast. **Amenities:** Pool; Jacuzzi. *In room:* A/C, ceiling fan, TV, minibar, Wi-Fi.

Inexpensive

In addition to the Hotel El Viajero (see below), several decent budget choices are in the Getsemaní neighborhood, the poorer, less glamorous part of Cartagena's Old Town. Even though this neighborhood isn't particularly picturesque and can get a bit seedy at night, it is popular with backpackers, and foreigners rarely encounter problems here. In addition, hotels in this area are only a 5-minute walk from the inner walled city. Don't expect hot water, however. One good option in Getsemaní is the lovely **Hostal Baluarte,** at Calle de la Media Luna no. 10–81 (✆ **5/664-2208**). The 24 rooms are small and plain, but each is clean and well kept, and comes with a TV. A double with air-conditioning costs COL$60,000, while rooms with only a fan go for COL$35,000. You might also consider the excellent **Hostal La Casona de Getsemaní,** at Calle Tripita y Media Carrera 10 no. 31–32 (✆ **5/664-1301**). All rooms come with en suite bathroom and cable TV, and some come with air-conditioning. Expect to pay COL$39,000 for a double without air-conditioning, COL$53,000 with air-conditioning. I prefer the hotels in this area because, compared to hotels in the inner walled and modern sections of town, you get more amenities for your money.

Hotel El Viajero All rooms face an unattractive courtyard, but the good news is that the 20-year-old hotel is undergoing an extensive restoration. Currently, rooms are small and clean and mattresses are a bit hard, and no hot water is available. Guests can use the kitchen facilities, and there is a pleasant dining area in case you feel inspired to try your skills at Cartagenan-Caribbean cooking. The pleasant social area has a TV, stereo, and sofas. The friendly hotel staff can arrange tours in and around Cartagena, as well as provide a map and useful information.

Calle del Provenir no. 35–68 (2nd floor). ✆ **5/664-3289.** 17 units. COL$65,000 double. Rates go up 20% in high season. No credit cards. **Amenities:** Kitchen facilities/dining area. *In room:* A/C, TV.

WHERE TO DINE

Seafood's the name of the game in Cartagena. In general, food is steeply overpriced in the inner walled city, but you'll find some of Colombia's most atmospheric and romantic restaurants here. In Getsemaní, you'll find many uncharming eateries offering cheap *almuerzo corriente,* while the modern city offers midrange and chain-restaurant options. During high season, it's smart to book ahead at Cartagena's more exclusive establishments, particularly at dinner time; during low season you may be the only diner present. Keep in mind that Cartagena restaurants are more expensive than anywhere else in Colombia, and choosing to dine in restaurants in one of the Cartagena's many plazas will likely cost you.

In addition to the places listed below, **La Vitrola,** Calle Baloco no. 33–201 (✆ **5/660-0711**), is one of Cartagena's most traditional restaurants, with nightly live Cuban music. **El Santísimo,** Calle del Santísimo no. 8–19 (✆ **5/660-1531**), specializing in fusion cuisine, is well known for its religious decorations. **San Pedro,** Centro Plaza de San Pedro Claver (✆ **5/664-5121**), also offers fusion cuisine, featuring sushi, Asian, and international dishes—be sure to make reservations here in high season.

Expensive

Club de Pesca ★★★ CARIBBEAN/SEAFOOD One of the most exclusive and romantic dining options in town, the Club de Pesca is one of my all-time favorite restaurants. In the 300-year-old Fuerte de San Sebastián Pastelillo, the restaurant overlooks Cartagena's marina. In fact, this is the only restaurant in town where you can arrive by land or by sea. The restaurant offers delicious Caribbean-inspired dishes, all with a contemporary touch. Start with the *langostinos portobello,* prawns marinated in orange and *maracuyá* juices and served with grilled portobello mushrooms. As your main dish, try *los mariscos a la Cartagenera* (Cartagena-style seafood) for an excellent sampling of different Cartagena dishes, including *ceviche,* shrimp cocktail, coconut rice, and fried plantains. The restaurant also offers an excellent variety of international wines and, for those feeling decadent, a cigar menu. Live music is on Thursday to Saturday, featuring mostly bossa nova, jazz, and flamenco.

 Manga, Fuerte de San Sabastián del Pastelillo. ✆ **5/660-5863.** www.clubdepesca.com. Reservations recommended in high season. Main courses COL$25,000–COL$55,000. AE, DC, MC, V. Daily noon–midnight.

Moderate

Donde Olano FRENCH/CREOLE This intimate, bistro-style French restaurant is an excellent dining option near la Plaza de Santo Domingo. The 10-year-old restaurant has classic-style artwork; a warm, cozy ambience; and a strong seafood influence. Try the *tentación de Zeus,* featuring lobster in white wine–and-cognac sauce, crab, shrimp marinated in sweet-and-sour *maracuyá* sauce, coconut rice, and wok-style vegetables. If you've had it with seafood, go for the *lomito de res creole,* featuring tender beef in a tomato-and-onion sauce with white rice. For dessert, try the *flan de café colombiano,* a unique, coffee-flavored flan.

Calle de Santo Domingo and Inquisión. ✆ **5/664-7099.** Reservations recommended in high season. www.dondeolano.com. Main courses COL$18,000–COL$45,000. No credit cards. Daily noon–11pm.

La Cocina de Socorro CARIBBEAN/SEAFOOD One of my favorite restaurants in town, La Cocina de Socorro has a 25-year history in Cartagena. The restaurant's style is somewhere between elegant and typical, with a modern waterfall, year-round Christmas lights, and traditional woven baskets hanging from the ceiling. A popular place for businessmen and tourists alike, La Cocina del Soccorro serves up one of the best, most generous, and cheapest *ceviche* dishes in town, and chef María Nelly del Socorro specializes in tasty Cartagena-inspired dishes. The restaurant has been visited by the likes of Colombia President Alvaro Uribe and soccer star Carlos Valderrama. Several restaurants have the word "Socorro" in their name on Calle del Arsenal, so make sure you make it to La Cocina del Socorro.

On Calle del Arsenal, near the Cartagena Convention Center in Getstemaní. ✆ **5/660-2044.** www.lacocinadesocorro.com. Main courses COL$20,000–COL$35,000. AE, DC, MC, V. Daily noon–11pm (later in high season, sometimes earlier in low season).

Inexpensive

De Oliva ARABIAN/MEDITERANNEAN This 1-year-old restaurant in the Manga area offers some of the best Arabian and Mediterranean food in town. Try the *langostinas al curry* (curried shrimp) or the *combo Arabe* (Arab combo), of almond rice, grape leaves, falafel, stuffed cabbage, and—to put a Latin twist on it—a spinach-and-tahini empanada. This fresh little restaurant is popular with Colombians of Arab descent and businesspeople on their lunch break. Considering the high quality of food here, De Oliva is one of the best restaurant deals in town.

Av. del Pastelillo no. 24–116. ✆ **5/660-6861.** Main courses COL$8,000–COL$20,000. AE, DC, MC, V. Daily noon–3pm and 6–10:30pm.

CARTAGENA AFTER DARK

Half the reason Cartagena is Colombia's top tourist destination is because of its vibrant nightlife. Cartagena's party scene is well developed with something for everyone—whether you want to sip cocktails on the beach, salsa dance Caribbean-style, or jam to '80s rock. Much of the nightlife is centered on Calle del Arsenal, in the Getsemaní neighborhood, though there are also several party options in the inner walled city.

San Andrés & Providencia

Only nominally part of Colombia, San Andrés and Providencia are culturally English-Caribbean, politically part of Colombia and geographically near Nicaragua. The islands are popular with Colombians in December and January, and during holiday weekends. Most people choose to visit San Andrés or Providencia as a 3- or 4-day all-inclusive package. San Andrés is more developed, with several top-notch hotels and resorts. Packages to San Andrés and Providencia often include airline tickets, hotel, and meals. In San Andrés, the **Decameron** (✆ **571/256-9800** in Bogotá, or 575/665-9800 in Cartagena) offers all-inclusive 4-day/3-night packages starting at around $400 per person (cheaper during low season). **Hotel Sol Caribe Campo** and **Hotel Sol Caribe Flowers** are two other pleasant options that are part of the Solar Hoteles and Resorts chain (✆ **574/448-0840;** reservas@solarhoteles.com) and start at about COL$150,000 per night per person. Both islands offer jungle backdrops, crystal clear waters, and excellent sunbathing and snorkeling opportunities. Contact **Aviatur** (✆ **571/382-1616** in Bogotá; www.aviatur.com) for more information on tour packages to Providencia. The Decameron and Hoteles Solarte also have resorts in Providencia.

San Andrés is small and Providencia is even smaller; you can easily get around by renting a moped or bike, which will also allow you to enjoy the lovely beaches and jungle scenery.

Mr. Babilla, Calle Arsenal no. 9B–137 (✆ **5/664-8616;** daily 8pm–4am), plays crossover music and is by far Cartagena's most famous nightclub. The eclectic decorations, tasty cocktails, and party-hard atmosphere bring in Colombia's cream of the crop and a large foreign clientele. **La Carbonera,** Av. del Arsenal no. 9A–47 (✆ **5/664-6237;** daily 9pm–4am), another popular nightclub in the Getsemaní neighborhood, plays a little bit of everything.

Café Havana★, Calle Media Luna and Calle del Guerrero (✆ **315/690-2566;** daily 7pm–4am), in the Getsemaní neighborhood, is dedicated to Cuban music. This place also offers decent sandwiches and light fare, and it's one of the more atmospheric places in town. There is often live music and the clientele tends to be foreigners.

9

Ecuador

by Eliot Greenspan

A small nation straddling the Equator, Ecuador likes to boast that it is, in fact, four distinct destinations: the Galápagos Islands, the Amazon basin, the Andean sierra, and the Pacific coast. Much of the country's attraction lies in its being small enough that you can see the best of everything in a relatively short time. From the high peaks and paramo of the Ecuadorian sierra, you can quickly descend and visit the rainforests of the Amazon basin. For those seeking more urban and urbane pleasures, Quito contains both the colonial and modern in a blend that is at once stark and stunning, while Cuenca is a compact colonial-era treasure, close to the ancient Inca ruins of Ingapirca, and Guayaquil is a major port city with a contemporary vibe and picturesque riverfront location.

Most visitors begin their journey in Quito, one of the oldest and best preserved cities in the Americas. Meticulously restored colonial-era churches, monasteries, and mansions abound along the cobblestone streets of the city's Old Town. Within a couple of hours of Quito, you can climb to the top of one of the highest active volcanoes in the world or shop for handicrafts in one of the largest and most colorful markets in South America.

Another option is to start your journey in Guayaquil, Ecuador's most populous city and the de facto gateway for all flights to the Galápagos, as well as to the most popular stretches of the country's Pacific coast. A booming metropolis, Guayaquil boasts a beautiful riverfront promenade, the Malecón Simón Bolívar, and a host of excellent hotels, restaurants, shops, clubs, and casinos.

Cuenca is arguably the country's most charming city. Before the Spanish arrived, this was the second-most important city in the Inca empire. And even before that it was settled and developed by the mysterious Cañari (also spelled Kañari) people. Today, the ruins and remnants of all three major colonizing civilizations are on display throughout the small city. Cuenca also boasts several excellent restaurants serving Ecuadorian specialties unique to this region.

Then there's the jungle. Early in the morning, you can watch parrots and macaws gather for breakfast. As you take canoe trips down the river, you might spot an anaconda curled up on the shores, waiting patiently for its prey, or perhaps catch a glimpse of playful freshwater dolphins frolicking in the river. You can also visit local villages, where people live very much the same way their ancestors did hundreds of years ago.

Finally, there's the Galápagos Islands, where you'll come as close as humanly possible to an astounding array of animals. A visit here is a once-in-a-lifetime experience and is sure to stay with you forever—as it did for Charles Darwin.

1 THE REGIONS IN BRIEF

The Republic of Ecuador sits near the northwestern corner of South America. It's bordered by Colombia to the north, Peru to the south and east, and the Pacific Ocean to the west. The Galápagos Islands, which straddle the Equator, are located about 1,000km (600 miles) to the west in the Pacific Ocean. The country covers an area of 272,046 sq. km (105,037 sq. miles), making it roughly the same size as Colorado.

QUITO Situated at some 2,850m (9,350 ft.) above sea level, Quito is the second-highest capital city in the world (after La Paz, Bolivia). Though it's the capital of Ecuador, Quito is actually the second-most populous city in the country (after Guayaquil). Still, Quito is a major transportation hub, and most visitors begin and end their trips to Ecuador here. Fortunately, Quito is one of the more charming cities in South America, and there's plenty here to see and do. Its **Old Town,** with its wonderfully preserved colonial-style buildings, was declared a World Heritage Site by UNESCO in 1978, the first city to ever earn the designation. The **New Town** is a lively cosmopolitan area, with all the modern amenities you would expect to find in a world-class destination.

THE NORTHERN SIERRA The Equator cuts across Ecuador just north of Quito. This invisible line also forms the border that roughly defines the country's Northern Sierra. **Imbabura Province** is the first province you hit, and one of the country's prime tourism destinations. In Imbabura, you can explore the colorful artisan's market of **Otavalo** and visit the small towns surrounding Otavalo, where you'll find the workshops and homes of many of the artisans who supply this fabulous market. In addition, this region is one of high volcanic mountains and crater lakes. There are great hiking opportunities, especially at such beautiful spots as **Cuicocha Lake** and **Mojanda Lakes.**

THE CENTRAL SIERRA The Central Sierra covers the area south of Quito. **Cotopaxi National Park** is a little more than an hour south of Quito, and it's one of the most popular attractions on mainland Ecuador. Active travelers can climb to the summit of the highest active volcano in the world, while anybody can marvel at its imposing beauty from the high-altitude paramo park that surrounds and contains it. All around the Central Sierra you will find isolated colonial-era haciendas that have been converted into fabulous boutique hotels, lodges, and spas. Most offer a variety of active tour options, with hiking and horseback riding being the mainstay at most of them.

CUENCA & THE SOUTHERN SIERRA **Cuenca** is the largest and most interesting city in the Southern Highlands. Like Quito, it was declared a World Heritage Site by UNESCO. Cuenca was the second-most important city in the Inca empire (after Cusco). Nearby, you can explore **Ingapirca,** an archaeological site with both Inca and pre-Inca ruins. Cajas National Park is located only an hour outside of the city.

GUAYAQUIL & THE SOUTHERN COAST **Guayaquil** is Ecuador's largest city. Historically a port and industrial city, Guayaquil has been reinventing itself at a dizzying pace. The city's attractive riverside walk, **Malecón Simón Bolívar** has served as the anchor for a minirenaissance. Guayaquil boasts several excellent museums, as well as top-notch hotels, restaurants, and bars. To the west of Guayaquil lies the Ruta del Sol (Route of the Sun), a string of beach resorts, small fishing villages, and isolated stretches of sand. At the north end of the Ruta del Sol sits **Machalilla National Park** as well as **Isla de la Plata,** which is home to a rich variety of wildlife and is often called the "Poor Person's Galápagos."

EL ORIENTE The eastern region of Ecuador, known as El Oriente, is a vast area of lowland tropical rainforests and wild jungle rivers. It is considered part of the Amazon basin, as the rivers here all feed and form the great Amazon river just a little farther downstream. The wildlife- and bird-watching here are phenomenal, with the chance to see hundreds of bird species, over a dozen monkey species, as well as anaconda, caiman, and freshwater dolphins. For the most part, the indigenous people in this region escaped domination by both the Incas and the Spanish, so they have been able to hold on to much of their ancient rituals and traditions. Most visitors explore this area by staying at a remote jungle lodge, some of which are surprisingly comfortable.

THE GALÁPAGOS ISLANDS The Galápagos Islands, located about 1,000km (600 miles) off the coast of Ecuador, are one of nature's most unique outdoor laboratories. The unusual wildlife here helped Charles Darwin formulate his theory of natural selection. Fortunately for modern-day visitors, not much has changed since Darwin's time, and the islands still offer visitors the chance to get up close and personal with a wide variety of unique and endemic species, including giant tortoises, marine iguanas, penguins, sea lions, albatrosses, boobies, and flightless cormorants. The most common way to explore the area is on a cruise ship or yacht. You should note, however, that this isn't your typical cruise destination—the trips involve packed days of tours and activities, some of them strenuous. A more relaxing option would be to base yourself at a hotel or resort on one of the main islands, taking day trips to other islands, snorkel sites, and wildlife-viewing spots.

2 THE BEST OF ECUADOR IN 2 WEEKS

If you want to visit the Galápagos, it's tough to see much of the rest of Ecuador in just 1 week. You have two options: You can spend your entire trip in the Galápagos on a 7-day tour, or you can see the highlights of the Galápagos on a 3- or 5-day tour and try to see some of the mainland in the few days you have left.

However, if you have 2 weeks, you'll be able to see much of the best that Ecuador has to offer. You'll be able to visit Quito and the highlands, the lovely colonial city of Cuenca, spend a full week in the enchanting Galápagos Islands, and have just enough time for an overnight in Guayaquil, one of South America's most up-and-coming cities. If you can tack on a few more days, then you'll have enough time to take a 3- or 4-day tour in El Oriente, Ecuador's lush Amazon region.

Days ❶–❷: Quito

Many international flights arrive in Quito in the late afternoon or early evening, so you'll need to check yourself into a hotel for 2 nights to enjoy 1 full day of sightseeing in the capital. Get to bed as early as possible so you can be rested and out the door early on Day 2. After breakfast at your hotel, spend the morning touring **Old Town.** Visit the magnificent **Iglesia de San Francisco** ★★ (p. 537), which dates back to 1535, and allow yourself a good 45 minutes to get a feel for the city's oldest church and its attached museum.

A few minutes' walk away, **La Compañía de Jesús** ★★★ (p. 538) Jesuit church features an incredibly ornate interior that shows baroque and Moorish influences. Nearby, **Casa Museo María Augusta Urrutia** ★ (p. 535) is a perfectly preserved 19th-century mansion worthy of at least a 45-minute visit. As the sun warms the cool

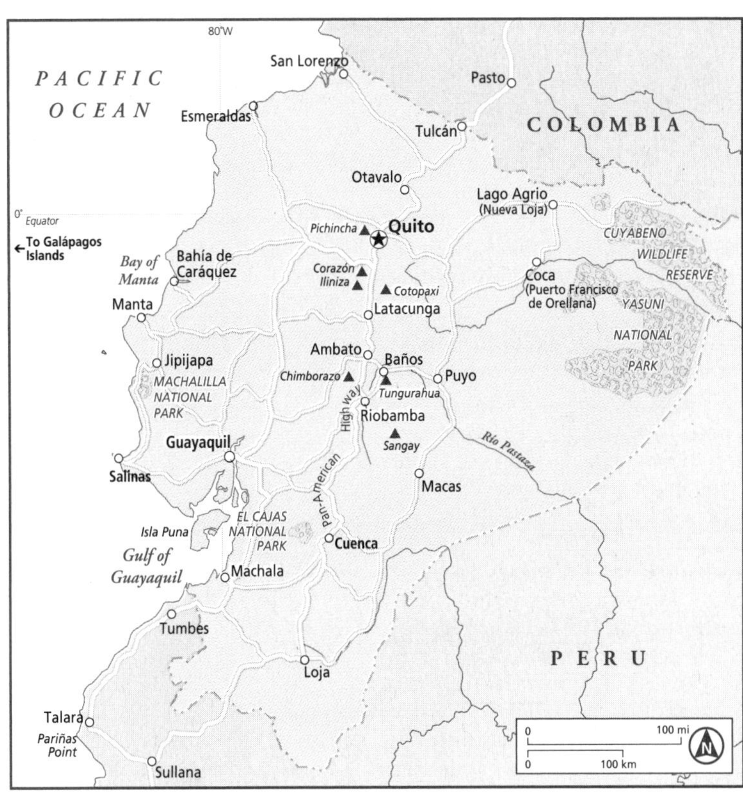

morning air, take some time to stroll around Old Town, ending up at **La Plaza de la Independencia** ★ (p. 538), which was the city's main square in the 16th century. Break for a cup of coffee at a sunny cafe on or around the plaza—there are plenty to choose from here.

Next, grab a taxi and head to **El Panecillo,** where you'll see the Virgin of Quito (p. 536). It's a 10-minute ride up a steep hill. From here, standing below the immense winged Virgin, you have a sweeping view of Old Town and the rest of the city. Right next to the monument is **PIM's Panecillo** (p. 549), a great place to enjoy local cuisine for lunch while you continue to enjoy the view. Remember to drink lots of bottled water, especially in the early afternoon, when the sun is at its highest and the atmosphere its driest.

After lunch, take a taxi to the **Fundación Guayasamín** ★★ (p. 548), named after the country's most famous and influential artist, Oswaldo Guayasamín. Expect to spend at least 2 hours here and at the nearby **Capilla del Hombre** ★. At both, you'll find original works by Guayasamín, as well as pieces from his personal collection.

You should be pretty beat by now, so head to Plaza Foch in the Mariscal district of **New Town** for a late-afternoon or early evening cup of coffee or a cocktail. If the weather is good, grab an outdoor table at one of the restaurants that line the plaza. If you're lucky, a jazz band or local indigenous *conjunto* (musical group) will be playing right in front of you.

For dinner, be sure to have reservations at **Zazu** ★★★ (p. 550), the best and hippest spot in Quito. You can end the meal with dessert or with a drink at their popular little laid-back bar. If you have the energy, pull out all the stops and head back to the Mariscal district's many bars and clubs to see where the night and your whims lead you.

Days ❸–❹: Otavalo & Imbabura Province ★★

After your grueling sightseeing day in Quito, it's time to leave the city behind and unwind in the highlands of the Northern Sierra for a couple of days. The roughly 2-hour drive is leisurely and scenic, and should include a stop at the **Quitsato Mitad del Mundo** (p. 557), where you can have your photo taken with one foot in each of the earth's hemispheres.

I recommend **Hacienda Cusín** ★★ (p. 562), a rambling, serene inn set amid 4 hectares (10 acres) of lush gardens, on the outskirts of **Otavalo.** In the distance, Volcán Imbabura makes for a breathtaking backdrop. Have lunch on the sun-splashed terrace and perhaps take a siesta afterward. In the afternoon, choose from a variety of activities, including horseback riding in the nearby hills, a Spanish lesson, or a meander in the lovely gardens. A candle-lit dinner is served in the cozy dining room, which makes for a perfect ending to a relaxing day. If you feel like going out for a gourmet dinner, make reservations at and take a taxi to **La Mirage Garden Hotel** ★★★ (p. 562), one of the finer restaurants in Ecuador. The drive takes about 20 minutes.

On Day 4, spend your morning perusing the artisans market at **Otavalo** ★★★ (p. 554), a 15-minute taxi ride away, and shop to your heart's content. Saturday is the main market day in Otavalo, but you'll find a permanent market set up on the town's main plaza every day of the week. Next, head to **Peguche** (p. 560) to visit some of the best weavers in Ecuador, before heading up to **Hacienda Pinsaquí** ★ (p. 563) for lunch at one of the region's most picturesque and historic old haciendas. If you have the energy after lunch, you can take a taxi up to **Cuicocha Lake** ★★ and hike around the rim of this beautiful volcanic-crater lake, or take a more relaxing boat ride on its waters.

In the evening, you can spend a quiet night at Hacienda Cusín or head back into Otavalo for dinner at **Hotel Ali Shungu** ★ (p. 564), and maybe catch some live music at one of the local *peña* bars. Whatever you choose, be sure to get a good night's rest, because you'll have to wake early in order to drive back to the Quito airport for your flight to Cuenca.

Day ❺: Cuenca ★★

Your 1-hour flight will bring you to **Cuenca,** one of Ecuador's most charming colonial cities. If you're seated on the left side of the plane, and if there's a break in the clouds, you'll probably get a great view of Volcán Cotopaxi on the way.

By the time you arrive and settle into your hotel, you should be ready for lunch. I recommend that you head to **El Maíz** ★ (p. 575), a lovely indoor-outdoor restaurant serving top-notch Ecuadorian cuisine. After lunch, visit the **Museo del Banco Central** ★★ (p. 570), just steps away from El Maíz. The museum contains an extensive art and archaeology collection, and is on the site of a major Cañari and Inca ceremonial center. After touring the museum, be sure to walk around the ruins and their botanical gardens.

From the museum, take a taxi to **Mirador de Turi,** a strategic lookout with a beautiful view of Cuenca and its broad valley. Be sure to combine a visit here with a stop at **Taller E. Vega** ★★ (p. 572), the gallery and workshop of one of the country's most prominent ceramic artists.

At some point during the day, be sure to sign up for a half-day tour to Ingapirca for the following day. Your hotel desk is probably your best bet. Otherwise, contact **Hualambari Tours★** (✆ **07/2830-037;** www.hualambari.com) or **TerraDiversa★** (✆ **07/2823-782;** www.terradiversa.com).

For dinner, you should splurge and head for the best restaurant in town, **Villa Rosa★★★** (p. 574), which serves creative takes on classic Ecuadorian dishes in a refined and elegant setting. If you have any energy left, have a nightcap at the **Wunderbar Café★** (p. 575).

Day 6: Ingapirca ★ & Colonial Cuenca ★★★

You'll probably leave just after breakfast for your trip to **Ingapirca,** the Machu Picchu of Ecuador. About a 2-hour drive north of Cuenca, Ingapirca is the largest and most significant archaeological site left by the Incas in Ecuador. It was built on the ruins of a Cañari settlement, and you will see evidence of their culture and architecture here as well. Your tour will likely include lunch, but you should be back in Cuenca with plenty of time to further explore its colonial core.

Start at the colorful **Flower Market** (p. 570), and continue from there to the main square, **Parque Calderón** (the heart of Cuenca). Be sure to visit the Gothic-Romanesque **Catedral Nueva★★** (p. 569), with its exquisite white-marble floors. Then catch a taxi from the square to the most interesting and best-known factory in the country. **Homero Ortega P. & Hijos★★★** (p. 572) makes some of the highest-quality Panama hats in the world. You'll get to see how they do it, as well as shop at slightly discounted prices in their showroom store.

For your last night, I recommend combining dinner and nightlife by heading to **Café Eucalyptus★★** (p. 574), where you can dine on a range of exotic tapas while mingling with the crème de la crème of Cuenca.

Days 7–13: The Galápagos Islands ★★★

Getting to the Galápagos from Cuenca will require an early morning departure with a change of planes in Guayaquil. The flight to Guayaquil is only 30 minutes, and from there to the Galápagos it's exactly 1½ hours. A 7-day cruise on one of the 100 or so vessels plying the waters of these magical islands is the best way to visit the Galápagos; the typical itinerary includes a visit to two islands a day—one in the morning and one in the afternoon.

Day 14: Guayaquil

Since all flights from the Galápagos first land in **Guayaquil**, spend your last night in Ecuador in this economically vibrant and up-and-coming city, the country's largest. Flights from the Galápagos arrive in the early afternoon, leaving you enough time to check into your hotel and stroll over to the **Malecón Simón Bolívar★★** (p. 578). You may want to visit the MAAC, the **Museo Antropológico y de Arte Contemporáneo★★ (Museum of Anthropology and Contemporary Art;** p. 580), or take a long walk in the interesting neighborhoods of **Cerro Santa Ana★★** and **Las Peñas★** (p. 580). Climb to the top for a sweeping view of the city.

For your last evening in Ecuador, head over to **Lo Nuestro★★** (p. 583), for some excellent traditional Ecuadorean fare in an elegant old home, or to **Sucre★★★** (p. 584), for top-notch fusion cuisine served up in a contemporary hip ambiance.

Day 15: Fly Home

It's unlikely you'll have much time during your last morning in Guayaquil, but if you do, head to **Parque Histórico Guayaquil★** (p. 581), a small theme-park with a re-creation of old colonial-era homes and haciendas, as well as lovely gardens.

VISITOR INFORMATION

The Ecuadorian Ministry of Tourism runs the website **www.ecuador.travel**, a pretty good all-purpose site, with loads of information.

Another excellent source of information on the web is the site run by the **Corporación Metropolitana de Turismo** (**Metropolitan Tourism Corporation;** www.quito.com.ec). These folks also hand out excellent city maps of Quito and the entire country at their various desks and offices, which includes those at both the major international airports in Quito and Guayaquil.

The most detailed map available is produced by **International Travel Maps** (www.itmb.com), available online from the website listed or from **www.amazon.com**.

For specific travel-related information, your best bet is to contact one of Ecuador's better travel agencies. Here is a list of some of my favorites:

- **Metropolitan Touring** ★★, De Las Palmeras Av. N45–74 and De Las Orquídeas, Quito (✆ **02/2988-200;** www.metropolitan-touring.com). This is certainly the largest and arguably best-established of the various full-service Ecuadorian travel agencies. They feature a vast selection of tour options, and their guides and customer service are top notch.
- **Safari Ecuador** ★, Av. Colón and Reina Victoria N25–33, Quito (✆ **02/2552-505;** www.safari.com.ec), offers various Galápagos cruises, an array of Amazon adventures, Andean camping safaris, and mountain climbing.
- **Surtrek** ★★, Av. Amazonas 897 and Wilson, Quito (✆ **866/978-7398** in the U.S. and Canada, or 02/2231-534 in Ecuador; www.surtrek.com), is a large in-country tour operator and wholesaler specializing in adventure tours. They offer everything from mountain-bike tours to white-water rafting, and can customize combination tours.

ENTRY REQUIREMENTS

A valid passport is required to enter and depart Ecuador. Visas are not required for citizens of the United States, the United Kingdom, Canada, Australia, New Zealand, South Africa, France, Germany, and Switzerland. Upon entry, you will automatically be granted permission to stay for up to 90 days. Technically, to enter the country you need a passport that is valid for more than 6 months, a return ticket, and proof of how you plan to support yourself while you're in Ecuador, but I've never seen a Customs official ask for the last two requirements. If you plan on spending more than 90 days here, you *will* need to apply for a visa at your local embassy (see "Ecuadorian Embassy Locations," below). Requirements include a passport valid for more than 6 months, a police certificate with criminal record from the state or province in which you currently live, a medical certificate, a return ticket, and two passport-size photographs.

Ecuadorian Embassy Locations

In Australia: 6 Pindari Crescent, O'Malley, ACT 2606 (✆ **628/64021;** fax 628/61231)

In Canada: 50 O'Connor St., Suite 316, Ottawa, ON K1P 6L2 (✆ **613/563-8206;** fax 613/235-5776)

Telephone Dialing Info at a Glance

- **To place a call from your home country to Ecuador:** Dial the international access code (011 in the U.S. and Canada, 0011 in Australia, 0170 in New Zealand, 00 in the U.K.), plus the country code (593), plus the Ecuadorian area code (for example, Quito 2, Cuenca 7, Guayaquil 4, the Galápagos 5, Otavalo 6), followed by the 7-digit number. For example, a call from the U.S. to Quito would be 011+593+2+0000+000.
- **To place a call within Ecuador:** If you are calling within the same area code inside Ecuador, you simply dial the 7-digit number. However, you must use area codes if you're calling from one area code to another. Note that for all calls within the country, area codes are preceded by a 0 (for example, Quito 02, Cuenca 07, Guayaquil 04, the Galápagos 05, Otavalo 06).
- **To place a direct international call from Ecuador,** dial the international access code (00), plus the country code of the place you are dialing, plus the area code and the local number.
- **To reach an international operator,** dial ✆ 116 or 117. Major long-distance company access codes are as follows: **AT&T** ✆ 1-999-119; **Bell Canada** ✆ 1-999-175; **British Telecom** ✆ 1-999-178; **MCI** ✆ 1-999-170; and **Sprint** ✆ 1-999-171.

In the U.S.: 2535 15th St. NW, Washington, DC 20009 (✆ **202/234-7200;** fax 202/667-3482)

In the U.K.: 3 Hans Crescent, Knightsbridge, London, SW1X OLS (✆ **020/7584-1367;** fax 020/7823-9701)

CUSTOMS

Visitors to Ecuador are legally permitted to bring in up to $1,250 worth of items for personal use, including cameras, portable typewriters, video cameras and accessories, tape recorders, personal computers, and CD players. You can also bring in up to 2 liters of alcoholic beverages and 200 cigarettes (one carton).

MONEY

Since 2000, the official unit of currency in Ecuador has been the **U.S. dollar.** You can use American or Ecuadorian coins, both of which come in denominations of 1¢, 5¢, 10¢, 25¢, and 50¢. Otherwise, all the currency is in the paper form of American dollars, in denominations of 1, 5, 10, 20, 50, and 100. It's very hard to make change, especially for any bill over $5 and especially in taxis. If you are retrieving money from an ATM, be sure to request a denomination ending in 1 or 5 (most ATMs will dispense money in multiples of $1) so that you won't have to worry about breaking a large bill. If you are stuck with big bills, try to use them in restaurants to make change.

ATMS ATMs are ubiquitous in Ecuador. You'll even find them in remote areas such as the Galápagos. Some of the major banks include **Banco de Guayaquil, Banco del Pichincha,** and **Banco del Pacífico.** Most ATMs accept cards from both the **Cirrus** and

 PLUS networks, but some can't deal with PINs that are more than four digits. Before you go to Ecuador, make sure that your PIN fits the bill. ***Tip:*** If you're unable to use ATMs for any reason, you can get a cash advance from inside the bank, although this might come with some hefty fees or be billed as a cash advance, which is hit with interest charges from the outset.

TRAVELER'S CHECKS Traveler's checks are seldom seen and frequently not accepted at most hotels in rural and remote areas of Ecuador. Given the fees you'll pay for ATM use at banks other than your own, however, you might be better off with traveler's checks if you're withdrawing money often.

If you do choose to carry traveler's checks, keep a record of their serial numbers separate from your checks in the event that they are stolen or lost. You'll get a refund faster if you know the numbers.

CREDIT CARDS MasterCard and Visa are accepted most everywhere. American Express and Diners Club are less common, but still widely accepted. To report lost or stolen credit cards, you can try the local numbers listed here, or call collect to the United States. For **American Express,** call ✆ **02/2560-488** in Ecuador, or 905/474-0870 collect in the U.S.; for **Diners Club,** call ✆ **02/2981-300** in Ecuador, or 303/799-1504 collect in the U.S., for **MasterCard,** call ✆ **636/722-7111** collect in the U.S.; and for **Visa,** call ✆ 410/581-9994 collect in the U.S.

WHEN TO GO

PEAK SEASON & CLIMATE The peak seasons for travelers in Ecuador last from mid-June to early September and from late December through early January, because most American and European visitors have vacation time during these months. Cruises in the Galápagos will be booked solid during these times of year. But since Ecuador is hardly Disney World, you'll always be able to find a room (or a berth on a ship), and the country never feels overcrowded. I find that Ecuador is great throughout the year, so whenever you visit, you won't be disappointed.

There are four distinct geographical zones in Ecuador that are all subject to their own weather patterns. In the Galápagos, from June through September, the air and water are chilly and the winds can be a bit rough. From October through May, the air and water temperatures are warmer, but you can expect periodic light rain almost daily. On the coast, the rainy season lasts from December through May; this season is marked by hot weather and humidity. The cooler air temperature from June through September attracts whales and dolphins to the waters off the coast. In Quito and the highlands, the weather is coolest from June through September (the dry season), but it's only a few degrees colder than the rest of the year. Keep in mind that although Quito is practically on the Equator, the temperature can get quite cool because it's at such a high altitude (more than 2,700m/8,800 ft. above sea level); the city has an average high of 67°F (19°C) and an average low of 50°F (10°C). In the jungle area, it rains year-round, but the rain is especially hard from December through April. The temperature in the jungle can reach 80°F to 90°F (27°C–32°C) during the day; it's a bit cooler at night.

PUBLIC HOLIDAYS Official holidays in Ecuador include New Year's Day (Jan 1), Easter, Labor Day (May 1), Simón Bolívar Day (July 24), National Independence Day (Aug 10), Guayaquil Independence Day (Oct 9), All Souls' Day (Nov 2), Cuenca Independence Day (Nov 3), and Christmas Day (Dec 25). The country also closes down on some nonofficial holidays, including Carnaval (Mon and Tues prior to Ash Wednesday),

Battle of Pichincha (May 24), Christmas Eve (Dec 24), and New Year's Eve (Dec 31). Foundation of Quito (Dec 6) is observed as a holiday only in Quito.

HEALTH CONCERNS

COMMON AILMENTS Travelers to Ecuador should be very careful about contracting **food-borne illnesses.** Always drink bottled water. Never drink beverages with ice unless you are sure that the water for the ice has been previously boiled. Be very careful about eating food purchased from street vendors. Some travelers swear by taking supplements such as super bromelain, which helps aid in the digestion of parasites; consult your doctor to find out whether this is a good option for you. In the event you experience any intestinal woe, staying well hydrated is the most important step. Be sure to drink plenty of bottled water, as well as some electrolyte-enhanced sports drinks, if possible.

If you plan on visiting the highlands of Ecuador, or the main cities and tourist destinations such as Quito, Otavalo, Baños, Cuenca, Guayaquil, and the Galápagos Islands, you don't have to worry about **malaria.** There have been reports of malaria in rural areas on the coast and in the jungle area. To prevent malaria, the U.S. Centers for Disease Control and Prevention (CDC) recommends taking the drugs mefloquine, doxycycline, or Malarone; consult your doctor for more information. Your best protection is to ward off bites with a mix of insect repellent and proper clothing.

Of concern in areas of high altitude (the sierra) is **altitude sickness.** Common symptoms include headaches, nausea, sleeplessness, and a tendency to tire easily. The most common remedies include taking it easy, abstaining from alcohol, and drinking lots of bottled water. To help alleviate these symptoms, you can also take the drug acetazolamide (Diamox); consult your doctor for more information.

The **sun** can also be very dangerous in Ecuador, especially at high altitudes. Be sure to bring plenty of high-powered sunblock and a wide-brimmed hat. It gets cold in Quito, but don't let this fool you into complacency—even when it's cold, the sun can inflict serious damage on your skin. In general, the healthcare system in Ecuador is good enough to take care of mild illnesses. For a list of hospitals in Quito, see "Hospitals" in "Fast Facts: Ecuador," below.

VACCINATIONS No inoculations or vaccines are required for visitors to Ecuador. The CDC recommends that visitors to Ecuador be vaccinated against hepatitis A and B. While not common, yellow fever has been reported in Ecuador's Amazon basin.

GETTING THERE

By Plane

There are two international airports in Ecuador. All flights into Quito land at the **Aeropuerto Internacional Mariscal Sucre** (✆ **02/2944-900;** www.quiport.com; airport code: UIO). Most international flights also touch down in Guayaquil's **José Joaquín de Olmedo International Airport** (✆ **04/2391-603;** airport code: GYE). If you plan to go to the Galápagos immediately after you arrive in Ecuador, it's best to fly into Guayaquil. All international passengers leaving by air from Ecuador must pay a departure tax, which is $26 from Guayaquil, and $42 from Quito. A new, modern, international airport is under construction some 24km (15 miles) east of the current facility. It is not expected to be operational until late 2010 or mid 2011; visit www.quiport.com for information.

FROM NORTH AMERICA **American Airlines, Continental Airlines, Delta, LAN, Taca,** and **Copa Airlines** all have regular flights from a variety of North American hub cities. Presently, there are no direct flights from Canada to Ecuador, so Canadians have to take a connecting flight via the United States.

FROM THE U.K. There are no direct flights from the United Kingdom to Ecuador. British travelers can fly to the United States (Atlanta, Miami, Houston, or New York) and then hook up with a direct flight (see "From North America," above). **Iberia** and **LAN** both offer daily nonstop service between Madrid and Ecuador; convenient daily connections are available from London and a plethora of other European cities, including Dublin, Paris, and Berlin. **KLM** offers service from many cities in England to both Guayaquil and Quito via Amsterdam and Bonaire. Otherwise, you will have to fly via a major U.S. hub city and connect with one of the airlines mentioned above.

FROM AUSTRALIA & NEW ZEALAND To get to Ecuador from Australia or New Zealand, you'll first have to fly to Los Angeles and then on to Miami or Houston, where you can connect with an American Airlines, Continental, or LAN flight to Ecuador. See "From North America," above, for more information.

By Bus

It is possible to travel by bus to Ecuador from Peru. From Colombia, the best border crossing is at the northern Ecuadorian town of Tulcán. The closest Colombian town to Tulcán is Ipiales, about 2km (1½ miles) north of the bridge that forms the actual border. Tulcán is approximately 5 hours by bus from Quito.

From Peru, the most popular border crossing is from Tumbes to Huaquillas in Ecuador. As you exit Peru, you will need to disembark from the bus and walk across the border. Peruvian buses don't usually cross into Ecuador, so to continue your journey, you will need to catch an Ecuadorian bus. Huaquillas is around 13 hours by bus from Quito, and 5 hours by bus from Guayaquil.

GETTING AROUND

Because Ecuador is one of the smallest countries in South America, traveling from one end of the country to another is not much of a challenge. The bus routes are comprehensive. However, the roads can be a bit rough, and the buses are often hot and crowded. If you're short on time, I really recommend flying, which is relatively cheap and efficient. If you're traveling only a short distance, however, say from Quito to Otavalo (a little more than 2 hr.) or Riobamba (almost 4 hr.), the bus is your best bet.

BY PLANE Most of Ecuador's major cities and tourist destinations are serviced by regular and reliable commuter air traffic. In some places, remote destinations can best be reached by charter flights, organized by the lodges themselves.

Aerogal (✆ **1-800/2376-425** toll-free nationwide; www.aerogal.com.ec), **Icaro** (✆ **1800/883-567** toll-free nationwide; www.icaro.aero), and **Tame** (✆ **02/3977-100;** www.tame.com.ec) are the main commuter airlines.

With the exception of the Galápagos, which is quite expensive, most flights cost between $50 and $90 for a one-way fare.

BY BUS In Ecuador, all roads lead to Quito. From Quito, you can find a bus to every corner of the country. But don't expect to get anywhere quickly. Locals seldom board buses at the actual bus terminals. Instead, buses often leave the station empty, and then drive very slowly through the outskirts of town, picking up passengers along the way. This adds at least an hour onto almost every bus ride. Still, for relatively short distances, buses are your best and cheapest option. The journeys between Quito and Riobamba,

Baños, Otavalo, and Cotopaxi are best served by bus, which leave frequently for these destinations. The road between Cuenca and Guayaquil is also a popular bus route.

BY CAR I don't recommend renting a car in Ecuador. For the most part, the roads are in bad condition, and since signs are nonexistent, it's very easy to get lost. For short-distance journeys, it's much more economical to take a bus, or even a taxi.

Nevertheless, if you're an adventurous type and you want to see the country from the privacy of your own car, you can certainly rent one. **Budget** (✆ **02/3300-979;** www.budget-ec.com) and **Hertz** (✆ **02/2254-257;** www.hertz.com) are the main rental-car agencies, with offices at both major international airports.

Because the roads are so poorly maintained, I recommend that you rent a 4WD. All the agencies listed above rent four-wheel drive vehicles. Rates run between $45 and $150 per day, with unlimited mileage and insurance, depending upon the type of vehicle you rent.

One very interesting option is to use **Rent 4WD.com** ★ (✆ **02/2544-719;** www.rent-4wd.com), which gets you a large, modern four-wheel drive vehicle, unlimited gas and mileage, and driver, for just $150 per day. They even cover the driver's lodging expenses.

BY TRAIN Once the principal means of long-haul transportation in Ecuador, trains were until recently on the verge of extinction in the country. However, efforts are underway to rehabilitate the nation's extensive rail system, and now several rail routes are open to tourists. The **Empresa de Ferrocarriles Ecuatorianos (Ecuadorean Railroad Company;** ✆ **1800/873-637;** www.efe.gov.ec) is behind these efforts. Although the information is in Spanish, itineraries, schedules, and fares are all listed on their site.

The most famous train ride in the country is the popular run from Riobamba to Alausí that travels along switchbacks known as the Nariz del Diablo (Devil's Nose). However, following a dual fatality, rooftop riding on the train ride has been suspended. The train still runs regularly, but the thrilling and chilling chance to make the trip atop the train is now prohibited. However, **Metropolitan Touring's Chiva Express** ★ (✆ **02/2988-200;** www.chivaexpress.com), which also makes this run, as well as several others, still offers open-air rooftop seating for this trip.

TIPS ON ACCOMMODATIONS

You'll find a whole range of accommodations in Ecuador. There are very few truly high-end luxury hotels and resorts. Most are in Quito or Guayaquil, and are geared toward business travelers. The country's strong suit is in elegant, midrange boutique hotels, many housed in old colonial-era homes or haciendas. The antique furnishings and cozy rooms will make you feel as though you are an Ecuadorian aristocrat living in the 18th century. In fact, throughout the Andean highlands, you will find a string of these lovely converted haciendas, which are among the best and most unique accommodations to be found. Some are in buildings over 200 years old.

On the other end of the spectrum are jungle lodges, usually built in the style typical to the Amazon basin (thatched roofs, bamboo walls, and so on). Accommodations are usually basic; the more expensive ones, such as **Kapawi Ecolodge & Reserve** (p. 566) and **Napo Wildlife Center** (p. 566), have private bathrooms, but hot showers are a rarity. In general, inexpensive accommodations are easy to find. In Quito, you can find a clean room with private bathroom and television for little more than $20; in smaller towns, you can often find a bed for as little as $10 a night.

Heads Up

When hotels quote prices, they rarely include the hefty tax. Unless otherwise noted, expect to pay an additional 22% in taxes on the prices quoted by hotels and listed throughout this chapter.

In the Galápagos, most visitors spend their nights sleeping on ships. The general rule is that if you don't pay a lot, you won't get a lot. The least expensive boats have dorm-style common sleeping rooms and one shower for everyone on board.

One good website and Ecuadorian travel operator, **Exclusive Hotels & Haciendas of Ecuador** (www.exclusivehotelshaciendasecuador.com), functions as a one-stop booking agent for various high-end boutique hotels and haciendas around the country.

Throughout this book, I separate hotel listings into several broad categories: **Very Expensive,** $200 and up; **Expensive,** $125 to $199; **Moderate,** $60 to $124; and **Inexpensive,** under $60 for a double.

TIPS ON DINING

In major cities such as Quito, Cuenca, Guayaquil, and Quito, you'll find tons of Ecuadorian restaurants, as well as an excellent selection of international cuisines. In Quito, there is everything from cutting-edge fusion cuisine to Thai food and sushi. Throughout the country, you'll also be able to find authentic pizza joints, as well as Chinese restaurants, known as *chifas.*

While you're in Ecuador, you should definitely try *comida típica* (typical food). *Ceviche de camarones* (shrimp cooked in a tangy lemon juice and served with onions and cilantro) is one of the most popular dishes in Ecuador—you'll find it on almost every menu. *Ceviche* is often served with a side of salty popcorn, fried corn, and fried plantains. The salt complements the tart lemon flavor. Other local specialties include *seco de chivo* (goat stew in a wine sauce), *empanadas de verde* (turnovers made with fried green bananas and filled with cheese), *tortillas de maíz* (small round corn pastries, served with avocado), and *humitas* (a sweet corn mush mixed with eggs, served in a corn husk). In the highlands area, where it can get very cold, locals often have a soup called *locro de papas* (a creamy potato soup with cheese). In Cuenca, *mote pillo con carne* (huge potato-like pieces of corn, mixed with onions and eggs, served with a fried piece of meat and *tortillas de papa*—the Ecuadorian version of potato pancakes) is one of the more popular local dishes.

Fixed-price lunches *(almuerzo del día)* are also common in smaller restaurants. For about $3 to $4, you will get soup, a main course, dessert, and fresh juice.

Prices on menus don't include tax or tip. Expect to pay an extra 22% in tax and service charges above the prices listed on menus and in this chapter. Although a 10% tip is typically included in the bill, if the service was particularly good and attentive, you should probably leave a little extra. I have separated restaurant listings throughout this book into three price categories, based on the average cost of a meal per person, including tax and service charge. The categories are **Expensive,** more than $25; **Moderate,** $10 to $25; and **Inexpensive,** less than $10. (Note, however, that prices in the listings—main courses, for instance—do not include sales or service taxes.)

TIPS ON SHOPPING

It's impossible to leave Ecuador empty-handed. Local artisan traditions have been thriving here for thousands of years. For any serious shopper, it's essential to take a trip up to the artisan's market in Otavalo, one of the best local handicraft markets in all of South America. Here you'll find an amazing array of hand-woven goods, including alpaca scarves, gloves, sweaters, colorful bags, tapestries, and ceramics. In the neighboring towns, you can buy leather goods and beautifully crafted hand-carved wood products. Keep in mind that Ecuadorians are not hagglers. At the markets, the prices are never fixed, but don't expect to spend hours negotiating. In the first few minutes, you can usually convince the seller to lower the price by a few dollars, but that's it. When vendors say that the price is final, it's usually not going to go any lower.

In Quito, you can find most everything from handcrafted silver jewelry to pre-Columbian masks. The Ecuadorian artists have done an excellent job of using traditional techniques to create products that appeal to modern-day tastes.

Cuenca is the largest producer of Panama hats in the world. These aren't your typical Panama Jack hats—these are stylish beauties worn by the likes of Danny Glover, Julia Roberts, and Queen Elizabeth. Ceramics are also a specialty in Cuenca.

Fast Facts Ecuador

American Express American Express has two travel offices in Ecuador—one in Quito, the other in Guayaquil—both run by **Global Tours** (www.globaltour.com.ec). In **Quito,** the office is located on Av. República El Salvador 309 and Calle Suiza (✆ **02/2265-222**). In **Guayaquil,** the office is located in the Edificio Las Cámaras, on Avenida Francisco de Orellana and Alcivar (✆ **04/2680-450**).

Business Hours In general, business hours are Monday to Friday from 9am to 1pm and 2:30 or 3 to 6:30pm. In Quito and Guayaquil, most banks stay open all day from about 9am to 5pm, but some still close in the middle of the day, so it's best to take care of your banking needs early in the morning. Most banks, museums, and stores are open on Saturday from 10am to noon. Everything closes down on Sunday.

Doctors & Hospitals If you need an English-speaking doctor, Quito is your best bet for finding one. Contact your embassy for information on doctors in Quito, or check out the Consular Section of the website of the U.S. Embassy in Quito (www.usembassy.org.ec), which has a list of recommended doctors and specialists. **Hospital Vozandes,** Villalengua 267 and 10 de Agosto (✆ **02/2262-142;** www.hospitalvozandes.org), and **Hospital Metropolitano,** Mariana de Jesús and Occidental (✆ **02/2261-520;** www.hospitalmetropolitano.org), are the two most modern and best equipped hospitals in Quito. Both have 24-hour emergency service and English-speaking doctors. For hospitals in other cities, see the "Fast Facts" for each individual city.

Drug Laws If you're caught possessing, using, or trafficking drugs in Ecuador, expect severe penalties, including long jail sentences and large fines. If you're arrested in Ecuador, you should also prepare yourself for a lengthy delay in prison before your case is tried before a judge. It's not uncommon to detain prisoners without bail.

Electricity The majority of outlets in Ecuador are standard U.S.-style two- and three-prong electric outlets with 110/120V AC (60 Hz) current.

Embassies & Consulates **United States,** in Quito: at the corner of Avenida 12 de Octubre and Avenida Patria, across from the Casa de la Cultura (✆ 02/2562-890, ext. 480), and in Guayaquil: Avenida 9 de Octubre and García Moreno (✆ 04/2323-570); **Canada,** in Quito: Avenida Amazonas and UNP 4153, Edificio Eurocenter, Third Floor (✆ 02/2455-499), and in Guayaquil: Avenida Juan Tanca Marengo and Orrantea (✆ 04/2296-837); and **United Kingdom** in Quito: Avenida Naciones Unidas and República de El Salvador, Edificio Citiplaza, 14th Floor (✆ 02/2970-800), and in Guayaquil: General Cordova 623 and Padre Solano (✆ 04/2560-400). There is no Australian Embassy in Ecuador, but there is an Australian Honorary Consul (✆ **04/6017-529**) in Guayaquil, on Rocafuerte 520 in the Fundacion Leonidas Ortega Building.

Emergencies In case of an emergency, call ✆ **911** or 101 for the police only.

Internet Access Internet service is available almost everywhere in Ecuador, including the Galápagos. However, don't expect to be able to surf the Web at any of the more remote jungle lodges. Connections in major cities cost 50¢ to $1 per hour. In smaller, more remote towns and the Galápagos, the connection can cost up to $3 per hour.

Language Spanish is the language most commonly used in business transactions. Indigenous languages such as Quichua are also widely spoken throughout the country. Shuar is common in the Amazon basin. It's best to come to Ecuador with a basic knowledge of Spanish. Outside of the major tourist sights, it's hard to find someone who speaks English.

Liquor Laws The official drinking age in Ecuador is 18. At nightclubs, you often need to show a picture ID for admittance.

Maps The **Corporación Metropolitana de Turismo** (**Metropolitan Tourism Corporation;** www.quito.com.ec) hands out excellent city maps of Quito and the entire country at all their desks, which includes those at both the major international airports in Quito and Guayaquil. The most detailed map available is produced by **International Travel Maps** (www.itmb.com), available online from the website listed or from www.amazon.com.

Newspapers & Magazines There are several Spanish-language daily papers in Ecuador. The most popular and prominent are *El Mercurio, El Universo,* and *El Comercio.*

At the airports in Quito and Guayaquil and at the high-end business hotels, you can usually find the latest edition of the *Miami Herald* or *New York Times* for around $1 to $3. English-language copies of *Time* or *Newsweek* are also available at some newsstands in the most touristy areas of Quito.

Police Throughout Ecuador, you can reach the police by dialing ✆ **101** in an emergency. The tourist police can also help sort out your problems. In Quito, the number for the tourist police is ✆ **02/2543-983.**

Post Offices & Mail A post office is called *correos* in Spanish. Most towns have a central post office, usually located right on the central park or plaza. In addition, most hotels will post letters and postcards for you. Most post offices in Ecuador are open Monday through Friday from 8am to 12:30pm and 2:30 to 6pm, and Saturday from 8am to 2pm. It costs 90¢ to mail a letter to the United States or Canada, and $1.20 to Australia and Europe. From time to time, you can buy stamps at kiosks and newsstands. But your best bet is to mail your letter and buy your stamps from the post office itself, especially since there are no public mailboxes.

However, it is best to send anything of value via an established international courier service. Most hotels, especially in major cities and tourist destinations, can arrange for express mail pickup. Alternately, you can contact **DHL** (✆ **02/3975-000;** www.dhl.com), **Fed Ex** (✆ **02/6017-818;** www.fedex.com), **EMS** (✆ **02/2561-962;** www.correosdelecuador.com.ec), or **UPS** (✆ **02/3960-000;** www.ups.com).

Restrooms The condition of public facilities is surprisingly good in Ecuador. In museums, the toilets are relatively clean, but they almost never have toilet paper. If you have an emergency, you can also use the restrooms in hotel lobbies without much of a problem. Note that most buses don't have toilet facilities, and when they stop at rest stops, the facilities are often horrendous—usually smelly squat toilets. It's always useful to have a roll of toilet paper handy.

Safety Pickpocketing is a problem in all large cities. But if you keep an eye on your belongings at all times, you should be fine. Never put anything valuable in your backpack. Also be especially careful on the buses and trolleys. At night, large cities can be dangerous, especially in the touristy areas—take a taxi, even if you're only going a short distance. Because the streets in Quito are often deserted at night, I recommend walking in the middle of them to prevent someone from jumping at you from a hidden doorway. Guayaquil used to hold the award for being the most dangerous city in Ecuador, but in recent years, the city has cleaned up its act. Cuenca is the safest large city in Ecuador and residents routinely walk around at night, especially on weekends. Report all problems to the tourist police (✆ **02/2543-983**).

Smoking By law, smoking is prohibited in all indoor public spaces, including restaurants, shops, cinemas, and offices. (Bars and discos are exempt.) That said, enforcement is virtually nonexistent. A large number of Ecuadorians smoke, and smoke-filled public spaces are common. Bars, discos, and clubs are often especially smoke-filled in Ecuador.

Taxes All goods and services are charged a 12% value-added tax. Hotels and restaurants also add on a 10% service charge, for a total of 22% more on your bill. There is an airport departure tax of $26 from Guayaquil, and $42 from Quito.

Telephone & Fax Most mid- to high-end hotels in Ecuador have international direct-dial and long-distance service, and in-house fax transmission. But these calls tend to be quite expensive, especially since hotels often levy a surcharge, even if you're calling a toll-free access number.

The least expensive way to make local phone calls is to go to one of many *cabinas telefónicas* offices found in every Ecuadorian town. There, you'll have a private booth where you can make all your calls and pay the attendant after you are done. These offices usually have a host of booths, with separate booths for calling numbers specific to each of the major phone companies in the country, thus reducing your calling cost.

You must pay in cash since most don't accept credit cards. It costs roughly 5¢ to 30¢ per minute for calls within Ecuador. Costs through these *cabinas telefónicas* average around 45¢ per minute to the U.S. and 60¢ to the U.K.

For tips on dialing, see "Telephone Dialing Info at a Glance," on p. 521.

Time Zone Mainland Ecuador is on Eastern Standard Time, 5 hours behind Greenwich Mean Time (GMT). The Galápagos Islands are on Central Standard Time, 6 hours behind GMT. Daylight saving time is not observed.

Tipping Restaurants in Ecuador add a 10% service charge to all checks. It's common to add 5% to 10% on top of this. Taxi drivers don't expect tips. Hotel porters are typically tipped 50¢ to $1 per bag.

Water Always drink bottled water in Ecuador. Most hotels provide bottled water in the bathroom. You can buy bottles of water on practically any street corner. Small bottles cost about 25¢. The better restaurants use ice made from boiled water, but always ask, to be on the safe side.

4 QUITO

Quito, Ecuador's capital, sits on a long, level plateau nestled between towering Andean peaks. It is a city of striking beauty and stark contrasts. Founded in 1534 by Sebastián de Benalcázar, many of the surviving colonial structures here have been magnificently preserved and restored. Quito was—and still is—a city of grand churches with detailed, hand-carved facades and altars. It is a place where 500-year-old buildings, which have survived earthquakes and volcanic eruptions, open onto medieval-style courtyards, complete with columned archways and stone fountains. In 1978, Quito was declared a UNESCO World Heritage Site, the first city to earn that designation.

But that's only one side of Quito. Quito is a place where you can travel to the past but still enjoy modern-day comforts. The living museum of Old Town nicely complements New Town's modern-art and archaeology museums, cosmopolitan restaurants, and hopping clubs. Spend a few days here and you can enjoy the best of both worlds. You can also travel to colorful indigenous markets, a unique cloud forest, or the world's highest active volcano—all within 2 hours of the city.

Remember that at 2,850m (9,348 ft.) above sea level, Quito is one of the highest capital cities in the world, and the air is much thinner here. Many visitors quickly feel the effects of the high altitude. Drink plenty of water and do not overdo it as your body acclimates.

ESSENTIALS

Getting There

For more information on arriving in Quito, see "Getting There" in "Planning Your Trip to Ecuador," earlier in this chapter.

BY PLANE All flights into Quito land at the **Aeropuerto Internacional Mariscal Sucre** (✆ **02/2944-900;** www.quiport.com; airport code: UIO). The airport is about 8km (5 miles) from the heart of New Town. Right before you exit the international terminal, you'll find several information desks. I recommend ordering and paying for your taxi here, then taking your receipt to one of the many taxis waiting outside the terminal. Taxis shouldn't cost more than $10. In fact, most rides to downtown hotels are around $7. You will find yellow taxis waiting as you exit anywhere in the airport.

BY BUS The municipal government of Quito is in the midst of transferring interprovincial bus offices and terminals from Quito's old main bus terminal, the **Terminal Terrestre Cumandá**, to two new terminals, the **Terminal Terrestre Quitumbe** (✆ **02/2286-866**), located on the southern end of the city, and the **Terminal Terrestre Carcelén** (✆ **02/3961-600** ext 6099), located on the city's northern outskirts.

However, the transition has been rocky. To date, the new terminals are not fully functioning, work has not been completed on the Carcelén terminal, and public transportation to the new terminals is still sketchy.

Eventually, both of the new stations will be serviced by the public bus and trolley system, with connections to all major points in downtown Quito. Ecovia's Rio Coca and Trolebus's Estacion Norte La Y station will have direct connections with the Carcelén station. Meanwhile, the new Quitumbe terminal will have direct bus connections with Trolebus's Estacion Sur station. In addition there will be a direct, nonstop bus connecting the two new stations. The Quitumbe terminal will service routes heading to provinces and cities to the south of Quito, while the Carcelén terminal will handle those buses serving routes to the north.

At press time, there were bus routes connecting the two separate stations with various points downtown. For current information on the situation, check out the "Getting Around" section at www.quito.com.ec.

Orientation

Quito is a long and thin city, set in a long and thin valley. It runs 35km (22 miles) from north to south and just 5km (3 miles) from east to west. If you were to combine the most visited areas, that area would measure only about 1.5km (1 mile). Most of the city's attractions are located in two main areas: the **Old Town** and the **New Town.** The Old Town, at the southern end of the city, is where you'll find most of the historic churches, museums, and colonial architecture. **Plaza de la Independencia** is in the heart of the Old Town. From here, you can walk to all the main attractions. **New Town** (also sometimes called the **Mariscal**), is north of Parque El Ejido. Most of the city's hotels are located here. You'll also find a host of good restaurants, Internet cafes, bars, and nightclubs in this part of town. New Town's main commercial street is **Avenida Amazonas,** where most of the banks and travel agencies are located.

All parts of Quito can be dangerous at night. Avoid dark and deserted areas, and take taxis, even when traveling relatively short distances.

Getting Around

BY TAXI The streets of Quito are swarming with yellow taxis, and they're my preferred means of transport here. Taxis are cheap, costing only $1 to $3 for a ride within the Old or New Town and $5 to $10 for longer distances. Drivers are required by law to use a meter, but it's obviously not a strict law because few taxis use them. Try to insist on the meter or negotiate a price with your driver before you take off for your destination. Since Quito can be dangerous at night, it's best to take a taxi wherever you go, no matter how short the distance. The staff at most restaurants, hotels, and bars will be happy to call a cab for you. In case you need to call one yourself, try **City Taxi** (✆ **02/2633-333**), **Taxi Amigo** (✆ **02/2222-222**), or **Taxi Express** (✆ **02/2500-600**).

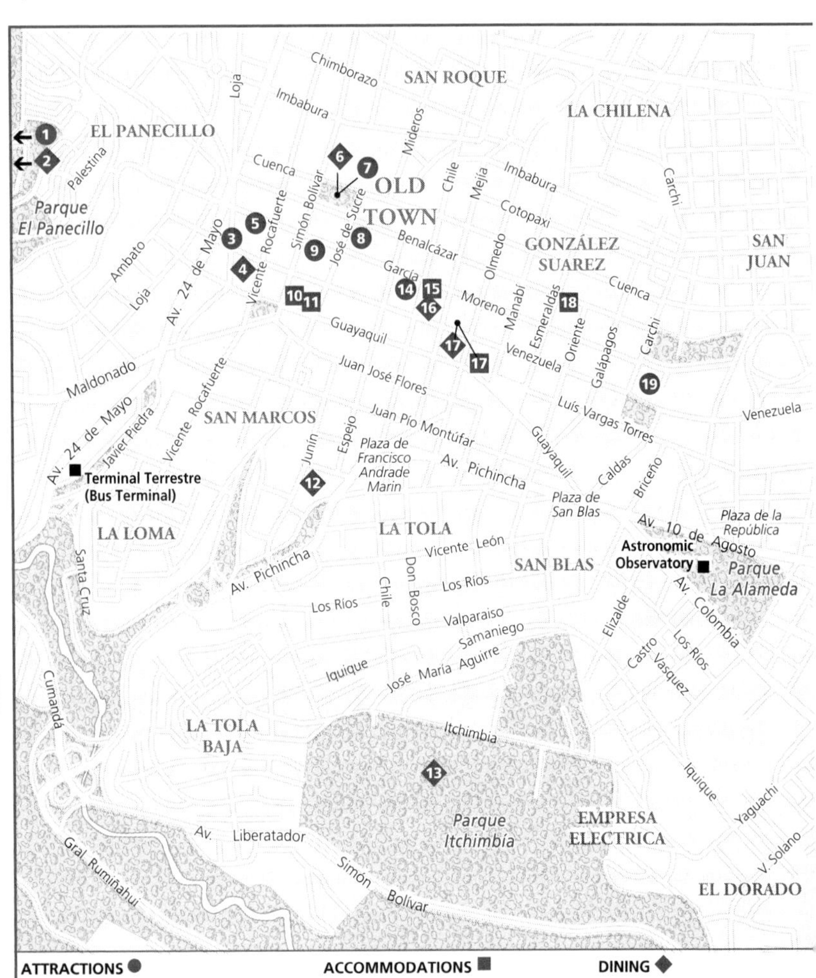

ATTRACTIONS ●
Calle La Ronda **3**
Capilla del Hombre **38**
Casa Museo María Augusta Urrutia **9**
El Panecillo **1**
Fundación Guayasamín **37**
Iglesia de San Francisco **7**
La Basílica del Voto Nacional **19**
La Compañía de Jesús **8**
La Plaza de la Independencia **14**
Museo de la Ciudad **5**
Museo Fray Pedro Gocial **7**
Museo Mindalae **34**
Museo Nacional del Banco
Central del Ecuador **20**

ACCOMMODATIONS ■
Crossroads Hostal **28**
Hotel Café Cultura **21**
Hotel Real Audiencia **10**
Hotel San Francisco de Quito **11**
Hotel Sebastián **33**
Hotel Sierra Madre **22**
JW Marriott Hotel **35**
La Posada del Maple **32**
Mansión del Angel **24**
Nu House **25**
Patio Andaluz **17**
Plaza Grande **15**
Villa Colonna **18**

DINING ◆
Azuca Latin Bistro **27**
Café Mosaico **13**
Chandani Tandoori **31**
El Atrio **26**
El Rincón del Catuña **17**
El Tianguiz **6**
La Casa de los Geráneos **4**
Las Redes **23**
The Magic Bean **29**
Mama Clorinda **30**
Mea Culpa **16**
Octava de Corpus **12**
PIM's Panecillo **2**
Zazu **36**

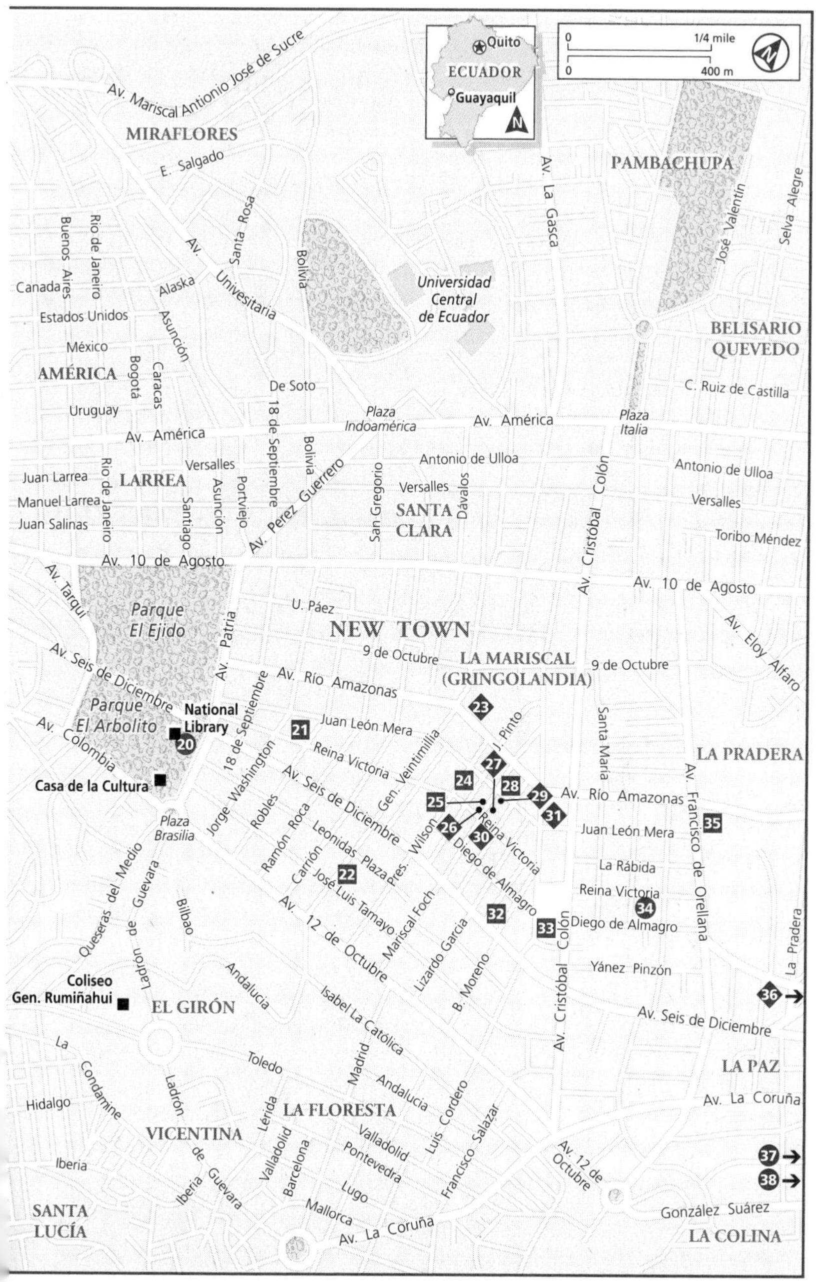
Quito
ECUADOR
Guayaquil
0 1/4 mile
0 400 m
MIRAFLORES
AMÉRICA
LARREA
SANTA CLARA
NEW TOWN
LA MARISCAL (GRINGOLANDIA)
PAMBACHUPA
BELISARIO QUEVEDO
LA PRADERA
EL GIRÓN
LA FLORESTA
VICENTINA
SANTA LUCÍA
LA PAZ
LA COLINA
Universidad Central de Ecuador
Plaza Indoamérica
Plaza Italia
Parque El Ejido
Parque El Arbolito
National Library
Casa de la Cultura
Plaza Brasilia
Coliseo Gen. Rumiñahui
Av. Mariscal Antonio José de Sucre
Av. Universitaria
Av. América
Av. 10 de Agosto
Av. Río Amazonas
Av. Seis de Diciembre
Av. 12 de Octubre
Av. La Coruña
Av. Cristóbal Colón
Av. La Gasca
Av. Francisco de Orellana
Av. Eloy Alfaro
Av. Perez Guerrero
Av. Patria
Av. Colombia
Av. Tarqui
Juan León Mera
Reina Victoria
Diego de Almagro
9 de Octubre
Antonio de Ulloa
Versalles
Toribo Méndez
C. Ruiz de Castilla
La Rábida
Yánez Pinzón
González Suárez
20
21
22
23
24
25
26
27
28
29
30
31
32
33
34
35
36
37
38

BY TROLLEY There are three electric trolley lines that wind their way through Quito, running north-south, and connecting the Old Town with the New Town. In the New Town, the **Trole** runs along Avenida 10 de Agosto, which is a few blocks west of Avenida Amazonas. When it reaches the Old Town, it travels along Avenida Guayaquil. To reach Plaza de la Independencia, be sure to get off at the Plaza Grande stop. The **Ecovía** is much more convenient if you want to start your journey in the New Town; it runs along Avenida 6 de Diciembre, which is one of the major streets. Unfortunately, when it reaches the Old Town, it stops several blocks east of the colonial core, and it's a bit of an uphill hike to the heart of the action. If you want to avoid this hike, transfer to the Trole at the Simón Bolívar stop. **Metrobus** runs along the western edge of town, along Avenida América. All three of these trolley lines cost 25¢ for a one-way trip. The turnstiles accept only exact change, but fortunately all stations have change machines. Trolleys run from around 5am until midnight. ***Warning:*** Pickpockets frequently operate on crowded trolleys and buses, so be careful.

BY BUS Quito has an extensive and very complicated system of city buses. In the New Town, buses run along Avenida Amazonas and Avenida 12 de Octubre. If you're only going a short distance along these streets, it's easy to hop on a bus (just flag it down). However, beware that once you pass Avenida Colón, the buses go off in many convoluted directions. Short rides cost 25¢, but overall, it's much easier to travel through Quito by taxi.

Visitor Information

The **Corporación Metropolitana de Turismo (Metropolitan Tourism Corporation;** ✆ **02/2959-505;** www.quito.com.ec) runs a few helpful information desks at strategic spots around Quito. You'll find one of their desks at the **Mariscal Sucre airport** (✆ **02/2300-163**), after you clear immigration and just before you exit Customs. This is a good place to pick up an excellent free map of Quito, as well as a host of promotional materials. Their **main office** (✆ **02/2570-786**) is in the Old Town, at the corner of García Moreno and Mejia (in the Palacio Municipal). These folks also have desks at the Museo Nacional del Banco Central and Telefériqo.

The nonprofit **South American Explorers** ★★, at Jorge Washington 311 and the corner of Leonidas Plaza (✆ **02/2225-228;** www.saexplorers.org), is perhaps the best source for visitor information and a great place to meet fellow travelers. The offices are staffed by native English speakers who seem to know everything about Ecuador. Membership costs $50 a year per person ($80 per couple). As a member, you will have access to trip reports (reviews of hotels, restaurants, and outfitters throughout Ecuador written by fellow travelers) and a trip counselor. If you aren't a member, the staff can give you basic information that will get you on your way.

Local travel agencies are excellent sources of information. **Metropolitan Touring** ★★ (✆ **02/2988-200;** www.metropolitan-touring.com), **Safari Ecuador** ★ (✆ **02/2552-505;** www.safari.com.ec), and **Surtrek** ★★ (✆ **866/978-7398** in the U.S. and Canada, or 02/2231-534 in Ecuador; www.surtrek.com) are some of the best and most helpful.

FAST FACTS In case of an **emergency,** call ✆ **911.** You can reach an **ambulance** at ✆ 09/2739-801 or 02/2442-974; for **police assistance** call ✆ **101.** For the **tourist police** call ✆ **02/2543-983;** the headquarters are located at Roca and Reina Victoria. You can reach the **Cruz Roja (Red Cross)** by dialing ✆ **131.**

Hospital Vozandes, Villalengua 267 and 10 de Agosto (✆ **02/2262-142;** www.hospitalvozandes.org), and **Hospital Metropolitano,** Mariana de Jesús and Occidental (✆ **02/2261-520;** www.hospitalmetropolitano.org), are the two most modern and best-equipped hospitals in Quito. Both have 24-hour emergency service and English-speaking doctors. **Fybeca** is the largest chain of pharmacies in Ecuador. You can call Fybeca's toll-free line (✆ **1800/2392-322**) 24 hours a day for delivery. The most centrally located Fybeca is at Avenida 6 de Diciembre and Cordero.

The **main post office** (✆ **02/2561-218**) is in New Town at Av. Eloy Alfaro 354 and 9 de Octubre. There's also a post office in Old Town (✆ **02/2959-875**) on Calle Espejo 935, between Guayaquil and Espejo. Perhaps the most conveniently located **post office** (✆ **02/2508-890**) is on the ground floor of the Torres de Almagro Building, on the corner of Avenida Cristóbal Colón and Reina Victoria.

WHAT TO SEE & DO

In Old Town

In addition to the places listed below, it's worth taking a walk along the restored **Calle La Ronda** ★. Once the city's "red light" district and home to its poets, painters, and troubadours, it now has a series of art galleries and functioning workshops. Stop in and see how the traditional ornate devotional candles are made. Calle La Ronda is located at the southern end of Old Town, running parallel and beside Avenida Morales, bounded by Avenida Maldonado to the east and García Moreno to the west. A good way to visit Calle La Ronda is to begin at the **Museo de la Ciudad** (✆ **02/2953-643;** www.museociudadquito.gov.ec) on García Moreno E1-47 at the western end of the street. The museum is housed in a meticulously restored old building, with several permanent historical exhibits, as well as a beautiful chapel, excavated catacombs, and regularly changing traveling or temporary shows and exhibits. Admission is $3 and it's open Tuesday to Sunday, from 9:30am to 5:30pm.

Tip: One of the best ways to tour Old Town is on a guided excursion led by a bilingual member of the **Metropolitan Police Force,** Palacio Municipal, on Venezuela at the corner of Espejo (✆ **02/2570-786**). Tours leave from the Plaza Grande daily at 10am and 2pm, and cost $12 for adults, $6 for children and seniors, including attraction entrance fees. Tours last for 2½ hours and take in many of the major sites, although a couple of different itineraries are offered, so check with them in advance. These folks also offer a night tour at 7pm, which costs $7.

Casa Museo María Augusta Urrutia ★ This museum is a nice change of pace, if you've been visiting churches all morning. It offers modern-day visitors a chance to envision what it must have been like to live in a 19th-century Spanish-style mansion in Old Town. When you enter the house, you immediately find yourself in a gorgeous courtyard. Not much has changed since Doña María Augusta Urrutia lived here, so the dramatic entry that you see is probably what the pope and many other world leaders also experienced when visiting this home. (Doña María devoted much of her life to philanthropy with a Catholic bent.) The house is surprisingly modern, with a full bathroom and modern kitchen appliances; but there are also a cold storage room, a wood-burning stove, and the oldest grain masher in Ecuador. The interior is gorgeous, featuring antique European furniture, a bed that belonged to General Sucre, hand-painted wallpaper, stained-glass windows, handcrafted moldings, murals on the walls, and Belgian tiles. There is also an incredible collection of Ecuadorian art, much of it by painter Victor Hideros. ***Note:*** Guided tours are available in English. Just ask for a guide when you enter. Most of the written display information is in both Spanish and English. Allow about 40 minutes to visit the whole house.

García Moreno N2-60, between Sucre and Bolívar. ✆ **02/2580-103.** Admission $2 adults; $1 students and seniors; 50¢ children 11 and under. Tues–Sat 10am–6pm; Sun 9:30am–5:30pm.

Getting High in Quito

One of the city's most popular attractions is **El Teleferiqo** ★, a cable car that transports you up the side of Volcán Pichincha to 4,050m (13,280 ft.). The quick climb over 1,000m (3,280 ft.) takes all of 8 minutes. At the top, you will have a magnificent view of the city and surrounding snow-covered mountain peaks. The air is thin up here, but don't worry: The ambitious and very modern complex includes an oxygen bar to replenish the weary traveler, along with several viewing platforms. You'll also find souvenir stands and shops, and a couple of restaurants and fast-food outlets.

If crowds bother you, avoid visiting here on weekends (and public holidays), when it's packed to the gills. That said, this attraction is enormously popular with Ecuadorian families and it's a wonderful cultural experience just to be out among the locals. People wait patiently in line just to get a glimpse of their city from an elevated perspective. You can escape the crowds by taking one of the marked paths on a stroll through the shrubby highlands. If you have kids in tow, you might want to return to the base of the mountain where you'll find an amusement park, **Vulqano Park,** complete with roller coasters, all kinds of rides, arcades, and video games.

The cable car operates daily from 10am to 8pm and Vulqano Park is open daily from 9am to 11pm. I strongly suggest you splurge for the Fast Pass ticket that will cut your wait time considerably. The cost for a regular ticket is $5 for adults and $3 for children; the Fast Pass ticket costs $8 for adults and $5 for children. Admission to Vulqano Park is free and prices for the rides average around 75¢ to $10.

To get here, take a 15-minute taxi ride from the center of Quito. The taxi ride should cost no more than $7. For more information, call ✆ **02/2222-996.**

El Panecillo & the Virgin Monument (Moments) From a distance, the hill that hosts a huge statue of the winged virgin does indeed look like a *panecillo* (small bread roll). Since it's directly south of the city, this hill was an ideal spot to construct the 45m-high (148-ft.) *La Virgen de Quito,* an enlarged copy of Bernardo de Lagarda's *La Virgen de Quito* sculpture that is on display on the main altar in the San Francisco church. The Panecillo stands at about 3,000m (9,840 ft.), so you can also see the sculpture from the center of Quito.

The significance of the Panecillo Hill dates back to Inca times, when it was known as Shungoloma (Hill of the Heart). Before the Spanish arrived, the Incas used this hill as a place to worship the sun. Later, from 1812 to 1815, the Spanish constructed a fortress, to control what was going on down below. These days, most people come up here for the 360-degree views of Quito. ***Tip:*** For the best vistas, try to get here early in the morning (around 10am), before the clouds settle in around the nearby mountains. On a clear day, you can see Cotopaxi in the distance. This is a relatively quick ride from Old Town, and a taxi should only cost about $3 each way. A half-hour is all you'll need to take in the sights.

Tips Touring Iglesia de San Francisco

The Iglesia de San Francisco closes at noon, earlier than most of the other churches in Old Town, and it doesn't open again until 3pm. So if you're trying to see everything in Old Town in one morning, be sure to visit San Francisco first. If you can't make it before 11:30am, you can visit Museo Fray Pedro Gocial, the museum connected to the church (see below).

El Panecillo, south of Old Town. Admission to grounds $1; admission to climb to the top of the monument $2. Mon–Fri 9am–6pm; Sat–Sun 9am–5pm.

Iglesia de San Francisco ★★ San Francisco was the first church built in Quito. Construction began in 1535, just 1 month after the Spanish arrived. (It took more than 100 years to finish.) You'll notice that Plaza San Francisco is distinctly sloped; for several hundred years, it was assumed that it followed the shape of the earth. However, a group of archaeologists discovered that San Francisco was built over an Inca temple, which is the reason the actual church is much higher than other structures in Quito. As you walk up the stairs from the plaza to the church, you can't help but realize how wide the stairs are. Supposedly, the architects designed the stairs this way so that as you approach the church, you have to keep your eyes on your feet to watch where you're going—in other words, you are forced to bow your head in respect.

Like La Compañía (see below), San Francisco is an important baroque church, but the latter is much larger and, for some reason, feels much more somber. The ceilings have a beautiful Moorish design. In the entryway, as in La Compañía, you will notice images of the sun, which were used to lure indigenous people to the Christian religion. Throughout the church are combinations of indigenous and Catholic symbols. For example, the interior is decorated with angels in the shape of the sun—and the faces of these angels have distinct Indian characteristics.

The baroque altar in the front of the church has three important sculptures: The top is *El Bautismo de Jesús (The Baptism of Jesus);* the bottom is a representation of *Jesús de Gran Poder (Almighty Jesus);* and the middle is probably one of the most important sculptures in Ecuador, the original *La Virgen de Quito (The Virgin of Quito),* designed by Bernardo de Legarda. (*La Virgen de Quito* was the model for the huge winged angel on the Panecillo; see above.)

When I last visited, in late 2009, the interior of the church was still in the midst of a major restoration and face-lift. Scaffolding had been erected throughout much of the interior, and much of the overhead artwork was covered up, or under repair. The full restoration may take another couple of years to complete. But there's still plenty to see, making this church worth a visit.

Plaza San Francisco. ✆ **02/2281-124.** Free admission. Mon–Sat 7am–noon and 3–5:30pm; Sun 7am–noon.

La Basílica del Voto Nacional Work on this basilica, which is modeled on Paris's Notre-Dame, began in 1883 and is still unfinished. Visitors are permitted inside the concrete marvel, however. The large central nave of this church feels cold, with so much unfinished concrete, but if you look up you'll see fabulous stained-glass works all around. Be sure to stop into the small side chapel, La Capilla de Sacramento, which features a mosaic tile floor, painted walls, columns, and a beautiful high altar of Mary. Yet most people come here for the spectacular aerial views of the Old City and to see the *La Virgin de Quito* in the distance. For the best views, you have to pay to take the elevator, or climb the 90m (300 ft.) to the top of the towers. ***Note:*** The elevators don't always work and the final "ladders" to the top are very narrow and quite steep. As you cross the bridge to enter the towers, look for the carved condors—the stonework is impressive and the condors look as though they are about to fly away. The basilica is also famous for its mystical gargoyles in the form of local Ecuadorian icons such as pumas, monkeys, penguins, tortoises, and condors that guard the outsides of the church. There is a cafe on the third floor—a good place to catch your breath after taking in the breathtaking views.

Carchi 122, at the corner of Calle Venezuela. ✆ **02/2289-428.** Admission $2 to the towers. Daily 9am–5pm.

La Compañía de Jesús ★★★ This Jesuit church is one of the great baroque masterpieces in South America. All the work took 160 years (1605–1765) to complete. The facade won't fail to impress you—the carvings are unbelievably detailed. Notice the Solomonic columns, which are symbolic of the Catholic doctrine that life's journey starts at the bottom (on earth), but by following the holy path, it ends at heaven.

Almost every inch of the interior has intricate decorations. When you enter La Compañía, look for the symbols of the sun in both the main door to the church and the ceiling. The sun was a very important Inca symbol, and the Spanish thought that if they decorated the entryway with indigenous symbols, it might encourage local people to join the church. The walls and ceilings of La Compañía are typical of Moorish design—you will only see geometric shapes but no human forms. The building has been under renovation for the past several years, and some of the gold leaf on the ceiling and walls has been restored to its original luster. Natural sunlight and candlelight really bring out an angelic brilliance.

Concerts are sometimes held inside this church, and the acoustics and setting are haunting. If you happen to be in Quito on November 1 (Day of the Dead), you can also visit the catacombs here.

On García Moreno near Sucre. ✆ **02/2584-175.** Admission $2. Mon–Fri 9:30am–5:30pm; Sat 9:30am–4pm; Sun 1:30–4:30pm.

La Plaza de la Independencia ★ Also called La Plaza Grande, this became the main square of Quito in the 16th century. The Spanish were afraid that the Incas might poison their water supply, so they set up their own protected well here, and this plaza subsequently became the social center of town. It also served as a central market and bullfighting area. Today, Old Town's main square is bordered by the Government Palace on the west, City Hall to the east, the Archbishop's Palace on the north, and the cathedral to the south.

The **Government Palace ★** is the most interesting building on the plaza. Don't be intimidated by the chain-link fence in front of the palace; everyone is welcome to walk inside the main area—just tell the guard that you're a curious tourist. Once you walk into the main entry area, you can get a sense of the Spanish/Moorish architecture. If you look straight ahead, you'll see the impressive 1966 mural by Guayasamín, of Orellana discovering the Amazon.

The **City Hall** is probably the least impressive structure on the plaza. It was built in 1952, in the Bauhaus style. The **Archbishop's Palace** was built in 1852; it was formerly the mayor's house. You can now walk inside and see the Andalusian- and Moorish-inspired courtyard; note that the floor of the courtyard is made from the spines of pigs.

This area is now an informal crafts market. The **cathedral** dates from the 16th century. Inside is a good collection of art from the Quito School, including works by Caspicara and Manuel Samaniego. You can visit the cathedral Monday through Saturday from 6 to 10am. The square is most beautiful at night, when all the buildings are lit up.

Bordered by Calle Venezuela to the east, García Moreno to the west, Chile to the north, and Espejo to the south. To get to the plaza from the Trole, get off at the Plaza Grande stop and walk 1 block on either Calle Espejo or Chile.

Museo Fray Pedro Gocial (San Francisco Museum and Convent) This museum, which is attached to the San Francisco church (see above), allows visitors to see the convent as well as the church's choir. Tour guides also will show you some of the pieces of the church's fantastic colonial art collection. I highly recommend a visit to the choir. Here you can see the church's original wood ceiling, as well as a beautiful wood inlaid "lyric box" that was used to hold up the music for the singers in the choir. You will also experience Manuel Chile Caspicara's famous crucifix, which dates back to 1650. It is said that Caspicara tied a model to a cross to learn how to realistically represent Christ's facial and body expressions; the glass eyes are piercing.

Plaza San Francisco, Cuenca 477 and Sucre. ✆ **02/2281-124.** Admission $2. Mon–Fri 9am–1pm and 2–6pm; Sat 9am--6pm; Sun 9am–1pm. Visits only by guided tour, which leave on an as-needed basis. English-language tours are available.

In New Town

Museo Mindalae ★★ This new and modern museum features five floors of displays dedicated to the traditional arts and crafts of Ecuador. Baskets, weavings, musical instruments, tools, weapons, pottery, clothing, and more are shown within their historical, geographical, and cultural contexts. A heavy emphasis is placed on works arising out of the Amazon basin tribes, although Andean and coastal communities are also represented. A central column of sunlight passes through the center of all five floors, through heavy clear Plexiglas inlays in the floor. On the top floor you'll find a representation of a shamanic ceremonial space. Most explanations are in English, Spanish, and French. The informative videos shown are available in English, but you may have to ask for them to switch languages. This museum has an excellent gift shop, where you can buy contemporary examples of many of the artifacts on display here.

Reina Victoria N26-166 and La Niña. ✆ **02/2230-609.** Admission $3 adults, $1.50 children. Mon–Sat 10am–5pm.

Museo Nacional del Banco Central del Ecuador ★★ Kids This huge and enormously rich museum offers visitors an opportunity to learn about the evolution of Ecuador—its human and natural history, as well as its art. When you see all the artifacts, archaeological finds, and works of art displayed chronologically, you get a profound sense of the country not commonly found in museums that focus on one era or type of exhibit. ***Tip:*** To see everything in this massive museum, you really need at least 4 hours; I recommend taking a guided tour. Most of the displays are in both Spanish and English.

If you visit the museum from beginning to end, you will start at the **Archaeological Gallery.** On display are artifacts dating from 11,000 B.C. Artifacts and dioramas explain the beliefs and lifestyle of a wide range of pre-Columbian and pre-Inca peoples. One of the most striking exhibits here is a Cañari mummy, though the **Golden Court ★★** is my favorite exhibit. Because many indigenous groups worshipped the sun, they used gold to create masks, chest decorations, and figurines to represent the sun. You can see the influence of the sun and the veneration of women in the work displayed in the **Colonial**

 Art Gallery, which contains pieces from 1534 to 1820. I find the colonial-era art is displayed better here—with better lighting and explanations—than at the Museo Fray Pedro Gocial (see above).

After independence from Spain, Ecuadorian artists began to eschew religious symbolism. In the **Republican Art Gallery,** you can see this transition. Instead of gory religious art and paintings of the Virgin, for example, you'll find lifelike portraits of Ecuador's independence heroes. One of my favorites is *Retrato de Simón Bolívar (Portrait of Simón Bolívar).*

On an entirely different plane is the **Contemporary Art Gallery.** Here you'll see everything from peaceful landscapes from the early 20th century to Oswaldo Guayasamín's tortured and angry portraits, as well as a wide range of modernist works by prominent Ecuadorian artists such as Pilar Bustos, Camilo Egas, Theo Constante, and Enrique Tabara. In addition to the above galleries, the museum also hosts temporary art exhibits. And in the same building, there is a **Museum of Musical Instruments,** which is a lot of fun if you're traveling with kids.

Av. Patria, between 6 de Diciembre and 12 de Octubre. ✆ **02/2223-258.** Adults $2, students and children $1. Mon–Fri 9am–5pm; Sat–Sun and holidays 10am–4pm. Free multilingual guided tours are available throughout the day.

North of New Town

The two nearby attractions described below are expected to one day be joined in a relatively massive museum, workshop, and cultural center.

Capilla del Hombre (Chapel of Mankind) ★ A few blocks from the Fundación Guayasamín (see below), this impressive structure is in many ways the culmination of the work and dreams of Ecuador's great modern artist, Oswaldo Guayasamín. Guayasamín, who died in 1999 at the age of 90, wanted to open the museum on the first day of the new century, but financial problems and construction delays postponed its opening until November 2002. Dedicated to "man's progress through art," the architecturally intriguing chapel houses many of the artist's paintings, murals, and sculptures, as well as parts of his personal collection of colonial art, archaeological finds, and contemporary art. Incan and indigenous mythological beliefs are incorporated into the design of the building, which is three levels and uses the number 3 for various motifs and architectural elements. The eternal flame in the chapel's altar is dedicated to those who died defending human rights (or the rights of man, which explains the name of the museum). Guayasamín himself is buried here, beneath a tree he planted, which has been renamed El Arbol de la Vida (the Tree of Life). Allot yourself 1 or 2 hours to view the museum.

Corner of Mariano Calvache and Lorenzo Chávez, Bellavista. ✆ **02/2448-492.** Admission $4, or $6 combined with the Fundación Guayasamín. Tues–Sun 10am–5:30pm.

Fundación Guayasamín ★★ This powerful museum displays the works and art collections of Oswaldo Guayasamín, one of Ecuador's most famous artists. The museum has three sections. **El Museo Arqueológico (Archaeology Museum)** houses Guayasamín's collection of pre-Columbian art. The artist once said, "I paint from 3,000 or 5,000 years ago." It's interesting to see both his collection and his inspiration. Keep an eye out for the sitting shamans and tribal chiefs, and the jugs with the intricately carved faces.

Across the courtyard is the **Museo de Arte Moderno (Museum of Modern Art) ★**, which displays Guayasamín's own work. Most impressive is his art from 1964 to 1984 entitled "La Edad de la Ira" (The Age of Anger), which represents his dismay over violence in the world, and in South America in particular. One of the most dramatic pieces is the three-paneled *Homenaje a Víctor Jara (Tribute to Víctor Jara).* Jara was a Chilean guitarist and Communist Party supporter who was tortured and killed by General Pinochet's army during the 1973 military junta. Military officers cut off his hands to try to stop his protest songs, but it took a machine gun to silence him. The images of a skeleton playing a guitar have a tremendous impact.

In the **Museo de Arte Colonial,** you can view Guayasamín's incredible collection of colonial art. The majority of the pieces are from the Quito School; they give viewers a good idea of the art created by the first inhabitants of Quito. The collection contains more than 80 crucifixes.

There is also a nice patio (with a great view) and a cafe on the premises. Plan on spending around 1½ hours enjoying the collections, and take a taxi (about $3 from the heart of New Town).

Calle José Bosmediano E 15-68 Bellavista (Batán). ✆ **02/2465-265.** Admission $4, or $6 combined with the Capilla del Hombre. Tues–Sun 10am–5pm.

SPORTS & OUTDOOR ACTIVITIES

Quito is a large sprawling city, so it's hard to do anything truly outdoorsy within the city limits. The large, central Parque La Carolina is the best spot for outdoor sports and activities. Your best bet, though, is to travel an hour or two outside the city, where you'll find an abundance of outdoor pursuits. These include hiking, climbing, trekking, whitewater rafting, mountain biking, and more.

CLIMBING, HIKING & TREKKING Quito is right in the heart of the "Avenue of the Volcanoes." Within an hour north or south of the city, hiking and trekking opportunities abound. One of the most exciting and rigorous treks is up the glacier-covered Cotopaxi Volcano (see "Cotopaxi National Park," p. 552). Other options abound, including nearby high Andean peaks and volcanoes around the popular tourist destinations of Mindo and Otavalo. **Moggely Climbing** ★ (✆ **02/2906-656;** www.moggely.com), **Safari Ecuador** ★ (✆ **02/2552-505;** www.safari.com.ec), and **Surtrek** ★★ (✆ **866/978-7398** in the U.S. and Canada, or 02/2231-534 in Ecuador; www.surtrek.com) all offer a range of hikes, climbs, and treks ranging from 1-day tours to multiday outings.

HORSEBACK RIDING The mountains and rolling paramo outside Quito are perfect for horseback riding. Although 1-day tours are available, I really recommend combining your equestrian adventure with a stay at a restored working hacienda. **Hacienda La Alegría** ★ (✆ **02/2462-319;** www.haciendalaalegria.com), **Hacienda Zuleta** ★★ (✆ **06/2662-182;** www.zuleta.com), and **San Jorge Eco-Lodge & Biological Reserve** ★ (✆ **877/565-2596** toll-free in the U.S. and Canada, or 02/2493-123 in Ecuador; www.eco-lodgesanjorge.com) are my top choices for horseback-based outings.

JOGGING The downtown Parque La Carolina is your best bet for jogging. This large, central city park has several jogging paths, and you'll usually find plenty of fellow joggers around. The much smaller Parque El Ejido is another option.

MOUNTAIN BIKING Biking down Cotopaxi from the *refugio* (not the summit) is one of the most popular biking trips in the area. Other routes include biking to Mindo (for bird-watching), Otavalo, or Papallacta Hot Spring. **Safari Ecuador** and **Surtrek** (see "Climbing, Hiking & Trekking," above) both offer a range of road and off-road biking options.

The Real Deal

If you're interested in contemporary Ecuadorian art, you can't do much better than a work by Osvaldo Guayasamin. The gift shops at both the **Fundación Guayasamín** (p. 540) and **Capilla del Hombre** (p. 540) both offer up a selection of original prints, silk screens, reproductions and other assorted items, at very reasonable prices.

SOCCER Soccer, or *fútbol*, is the principal spectator sport in Ecuador. Soccer season in Quito lasts March through December. Most important games take place at the **Estadio Olímpico Atahualpa** (✆ **02/2224-410**), on Avenida 6 de Diciembre and Avenida Naciones Unidas. Game day is usually Saturday or Sunday. General-admission seats cost $2; the good seats go for $10 to $15. You can buy tickets at the stadium on the day of the game. To get there, take the Ecovía trolley line to the Estadio stop.

TENNIS If you're not staying at a hotel with its own courts, the Parque La Carolina open-air public courts are your best bet. They are free of charge and awarded on a first-come, first-served basis. They fill up very fast on weekends and tend to be busy on weekdays as well.

WHITE-WATER RAFTING & KAYAKING The rivers near Quito are usually most rapid in October, November, and December, but it is possible to go white-water rafting year-round. **Ríos Ecuador**★★ (✆ **02/2904-054** in Quito, or 06/2886-727 in Tena; www.riosecuador.com) and **Yacu Amu Rafting** (✆ **02/2904-054;** www.raftingecuador.com) are two of the best outfitters with offices in Quito. You can arrange 1-day tours on the Toachi and Blanco rivers (Class III to III+) or the Quijos River (Class IV to IV+). Longer rafting trips in the jungle and other rivers are also available.

SHOPPING

As in the rest of the country, the shopping scene in Quito mainly consists of local handicrafts (alpaca sweaters, tapestries, figurines, pottery, hats, and jewelry) made by indigenous Ecuadorian artists. Some of the stuff you'll find is mass produced or of poor quality. But if you know where to go (see below), there are some great shops, which support local indigenous groups. You'll also find more high-end shops here than in other parts of the country.

MARKETS While nothing in Quito compares to the world-famous market in Otavalo (p. 554), a couple of Quito markets are worth visiting, especially if you can't visit Otavalo. In New Town, the **Mercado Artesanal La Mariscal (Mariscal Artisans Market)** is a tight warren of permanent booths selling all sorts of arts, crafts, and clothing. You should definitely be picky here—there are a lot of mass-produced and mediocre wares for sale. But if you shop carefully, you can find high-quality goods. You can bargain a little, but not too much. Located on Jorge Washington, between Reina Victoria and Juan León Mera, it's open daily from around 10am until 7pm. A similar option is available on weekends all along the north end of **Parque El Ejido.**

A note on store hours: Unless indicated below, all stores are open from 9am to 1:30pm and 3 to 7pm. Most stores close for a siesta from 1:30 to 3pm, and most are closed on Sunday.

Café Libro ★★ This is my favorite bookstore in Ecuador. It stocks an extensive collection of books in Spanish and English, with loads of books on natural history and tropical biology, as well as a fabulous collection of Ecuadorian and Latin American literature. Poetry readings, lectures, and concerts are often held here. Leonidas Plaza N23-56. ✆ **02/2234-265.** www.cafelibro.com.

Magic Hand Crafts ★ With an excellent selection of alpaca sweaters, this is the place to come if you're looking for something of better quality than that sold at the street markets. These folks work directly with weavers and producers, and have some unique designs you won't find elsewhere. Juan León Mera N24-237 and Cordero. ✆ **02/2542-345.**

Olga Fisch Folklore ★★ (Finds) Olga Fisch was a driving force in development and production of high-quality, locally made handicrafts. As an artist, Fisch had a keen eye and worked with indigenous groups to create carpets, figurines, jewelry, and decorative arts based on their traditional understanding of the arts. Her namesake store carries high-end art, crafts, and clothing, and the prices reflect the difference in quality that you'll find between the offerings here and those at street markets and run-of-the mill souvenir shops. A nonprofit museum here supports the development of these arts in indigenous communities. I suggest that you visit the museum first to get an idea of the local artisan traditions—it will help you understand what you are looking at in the showroom. In addition to the main shop, Olga Fisch has several other storefronts around Quito, including inside the Quicentro and San Marino malls, as well as at the **Patio Andaluz** (p. 546), and inside both the Guayaquil and Quito airports. Av. Colón E10-53 and Caamaño. ✆ **02/2541-315.** www.olgafisch.com.

Ortega P. & Hijos ★★★ This is the local outlet for renowned Cuenca hat manufacturer Ortega and Sons. If you aren't able to get to Cuenca, or to the other traditional Panama hat–making cities of Montecristi and Jipijapa, this is where you should pick up your own *super fino* (super fine) hat. If you really wait until the last minute, you can visit their outlet at the airport, but the selection there is reduced, and the prices slightly inflated. Isable La Católica N24-100 and Madrid. ✆ **02/2526-715.** www.homeroortega.com.

Tianguez ★★ Tianguez showcases products similar to those you'll find at Olga Fisch and Galería Latina, including masks, ceramics, and all sorts of pieces inspired by pre-Columbian artisan traditions. Tianguez means "market" in Quichua, and it's an especially appropriate name because the store is housed in a sprawling, mazelike old market in Old Town under the San Francisco church. It feels like the catacombs in Rome. A not-for-profit organization, Sinchi Sacha, runs Tianguez and supports indigenous and mestizo artisan groups. Plaza San Francisco. ✆ **02/2570-233.** www.sinchisacha.org.

WHERE TO STAY

In New Town

Expensive

JW Marriott Hotel ★★ (Kids) A luxurious and large hotel, the JW Marriott features some of the best rooms and facilities in town. Service is top-notch, the restaurants are excellent, and the large pool with its central Jacuzzi island and waterfalls makes you feel as if you've escaped to a tropical resort. Most rooms offer views of either the city or of the volcanoes. (If you can, opt for the volcano view; my least favorite rooms have views of the glass-enclosed lobby.) **La Hacienda restaurant** offers delicious local specialties in an elegant setting, while **Bistro Latino** is the hotel's buffet restaurant. The gym here is large and well equipped with a regular slate of classes and activities. The pool and outdoor patio area, safe neighborhood, and ample facilities make this a good choice for families.

Av. Orellana 1172 and Av. Amazonas, Quito. ✆ **888/236-2427** in the U.S. and Canada, or 02/2972-000 in Quito. Fax 02/2972-050. www.marriotthotels.com. 257 units. $149–$239 double; $249–$279 junior suite. AE, DC, MC, V. Free valet parking. **Amenities:** 3 restaurants; bar; babysitting; concierge; health club; Jacuzzi; large outdoor pool; room service; sauna; smoke-free floors; free Wi-Fi. *In room:* A/C, TV, hair dryer, Internet ($21 per day), minibar.

Nü House ★★ Finds This boutique hotel is stylish and chic—and it's hard to beat the location. The striking horizontal wood slat exterior of this joint has a commanding perch rising above the heart and soul of the Mariscal district, right on Plaza Foch. Room decor is decidedly contemporary, with wood floors, stone bathrooms, LCD televisions, and hip fixtures and furnishings—although the eclectic and minimalist design paradigm here might throw in a Victorian-style love seat where you least expect it. Suites all feature two small balconies, one overlooking Plaza Foch, and another off the master bedroom, as well as a deep two-person tub and separate shower. In addition to the hip "Q Restaurant" attached to the hotel, the owners here run several other excellent restaurants on the Plaza Foch and around the Mariscal district.

Foch E6-12 y Reina Victoria, Quito. ✆ **02/2557-845.** www.nuhousehotels.com. 59 units. $109–$119 double; $189 suite. Rates include breakfast. AE, DC, MC, V. Free parking. **Amenities:** Restaurant; bar; concierge; room service; smoke-free rooms. *In room:* A/C, TV, hair dryer, minibar, free Wi-Fi.

Moderate

Hotel Café Cultura ★★ Finds Housed in an old but beautifully renovated house, Café Cultura is one of the hippest hotels in the city. All the rooms have hand-painted designs on the walls and their own personal touches. For example, no. 25 has a tree growing through it; no. 1 has a fireplace, French doors, painted furniture, and a claw-foot tub. My favorite room, though, is no. 2, which has a beautiful sitting nook, with wraparound floor-to-ceiling windows. Several of the rooms have sloped wooden ceilings; most have been renovated in the past few years, and all the windows have been soundproofed. In general, the bathrooms are also excellent; although some are a bit small. The charming owner, Laszlo Karolyi, has done a great job of making this hotel feel like a real home. There's a lovely restaurant adjacent to the lobby, complete with hardwood floors, flickering candles, and a roaring fireplace.

Robles and Reina Victoria, Quito. ✆/fax **02/2224-271** or 02/2564-956. www.cafecultura.com. 26 units. $109 double; $119 triple and junior suite; $149 suite. AE, DC, MC, V. Free parking. **Amenities:** Restaurant; lounge; room service; all rooms smoke-free; free Wi-Fi.

Hotel Sebastián ★ Value This well-located business-class hotel offers tidy, well-maintained rooms, excellent service, and good value. All of the rooms feature carpeting and 29-inch flatscreen televisions. The decor is almost stately, with gold bedspreads and subdued colors on the walls. Free Wi-Fi reaches just about every nook and cranny in the hotel. Rooms on the higher floors have great views, especially those on the south side, from which you can see Volcán Cotopaxi on a clear day. With their own filtering system, this is one of the few hotels in Quito, or in the country for that matter, to offer safe drinking water straight from the tap. The small gym here is surprisingly well equipped.

Diego de Almagro 822 and Cordero, Quito. ✆/fax **02/2222-300** or 2222-400. Fax 02/2222-500. www.hotelsebastian.com. 55 units. $80 double; $100 junior suite. AE, DC, MC, V. Free parking. **Amenities:** Restaurant; bar; small gym; room service; free Wi-Fi. *In room:* TV, hair dryer.

Mansión del Angel ★★ Finds Mansión del Angel is an elegant and refined boutique hotel in the New Town. The sitting areas on the first floor are full of gorgeous antiques, handmade wood furniture, unique art, crystal chandeliers, and gilded mirrors. All the rooms have brass canopy beds, hand-carved moldings, Oriental carpets, and plush bedspreads. The bathrooms are not especially spacious; none have tubs, but they all have very large showers. The larger rooms, on the top floor, have a separate sitting area. Since the rooms in the back of the hotel don't face the street, they are a bit quieter, although I've never found noise to be a problem, even in the street-side rooms. The breakfast, served on the enclosed rooftop terrace, includes fresh-baked breads, and at night the smell of baking bread permeates the entire hotel. A formal English tea is served every afternoon, which is a good way to meet other guests.

Wilson E5-29 and Juan León Mera, Quito. ✆ **800/327-3573** in the U.S., or 02/2557-721. Fax 02/2237-819. www.mansiondelangel.com.ec. 11 units. $85–$135 double. Rates include full breakfast and tax. MC, V. Parking nearby. **Amenities:** Enclosed rooftop breakfast terrace; afternoon tea. *In room:* TV, hair dryer.

Inexpensive

In addition to the places below, **La Posada del Maple,** Juan Rodríguez E8-49 and 6 de Diciembre (✆ **02/2544-507;** www.posadadelmaple.com), is another top choice for backpackers and budget travelers.

Crossroads Hostal This centrally located Mariscal hostel is everything a hostel should be: friendly, busy, and funky. A shared kitchen and a large living area, with a television surrounded by bean-bag chairs and a couch, make up the communal space. One of the dorm rooms comes with a fireplace. Some of the rooms have wood floors, while others are carpeted. Nos. 16, 17, and 18 are my top choices; they're located in a quiet, newer section out back. Every guest gets a lock box in the office, but it's a bring-your-own-lock affair. This is a great place to meet and hook up with fellow travelers, and to arrange trips and adventure tours around the country. They offer free luggage storage, and you can leave some stuff here while you travel outside Quito.

Foch E5-23 and Juan León Mera, Quito. ✆ **02/2234-735** or 02/2545-514. www.crossroadshostal.com. 4 dorm rooms and 14 private rooms (9 with private bathroom). $7–$8 per person in dorm room; $20 double with shared bathroom; $26 double with private bathroom. MC, V. Parking nearby. **Amenities:** Restaurant; bar; lounge; free Wi-Fi. *In room:* No phone.

Hotel Sierra Madre ★ Value Just outside the central bustle of the Mariscal district, this hotel offers clean and cozy rooms in two separate three-story "towers" of an old restored building. Most of the rooms feature wood floors, colonial style furnishings, and original artworks. The best rooms in the house, nos. 11 and 12, are top-floor affairs with high ceilings and large private corner terraces, with great views. If you don't land one of these, you can still enjoy the hotel's common terrace areas. The staff and tour desk here are very helpful and friendly.

Veintimilla 464 and Luis Tamayo, Quito. ✆ **02/2505-687.** Fax 02/2505-715. www.hotelsierramadre.com. 21 units. $49–$57 double. AE, DC, MC, V. Free parking. **Amenities:** Restaurant; bar; free airport transfers; all rooms nonsmoking; room service; free Wi-Fi. *In room:* TV, hair dryer.

In Old Town

Quito's Old Town is in the midst of a major renaissance. Whereas just a few years ago I cautioned visitors against staying in this area, there are now several excellent hotel options in various price ranges, and the security situation has improved greatly. That said, you still need to be careful walking some of the streets around here at night, and taxis definitely should be used after nightfall.

Very Expensive

In addition to the places listed below, **Villa Colonna★★**, Benalcazar 1128 and Esmeraldas (✆ **02/2955-805;** www.villacolonna.ec), is a new six-room bed-and-breakfast housed in an old colonial manse, in the colonial core of the city.

Patio Andaluz ★★★ Finds This stately hotel is a fabulous option in the center of Quito's colonial core. Rooms are spread around the perimeters of two large central courtyard areas. The first courtyard houses the hotel's restaurant, while the second has a pretty garden bar. Rooms are all large and elegant, with wood floors, Persian rugs, antique-style furniture and beds, large desks, and flatscreen televisions. Only a handful of units have windows facing the street; most have windows opening onto one of the central courtyards. The suites are all two levels, with a bedroom on one level and sitting room on the other. My favorite room here is no. 401, which is a fourth-floor room with incredible 180-degree views of the basilica and Ichimbia hill. Patio Andaluz is certified by the Smart Voyager program and has a multipronged approach towards implementing sustainable practices into its business model.

Av. García Moreno N6-52, between Olmedo and Mejía, Quito. ✆ **02/2280-830.** Fax 02/2288-690. www.hotelpatioandaluz.com. 31 units. $200 double; $250 suite. Rates include breakfast buffet. AE, DC, MC, V. **Amenities:** Restaurant; bar; lounge; smoke-free rooms; free Wi-Fi. *In room:* TV.

Plaza Grande ★★ Finds Housed in the meticulously restored former home of one of Quito's founding fathers, this hotel fronts the Plaza de la Independencia (Plaza Grande), and is opulent and grand. All rooms are beautifully done and feature such perks as large flatscreen televisions, Jacuzzi tubs in large bathrooms with heated floors, and fine cotton linens and down comforters. The decor is refined, with plush furnishings, fine fabrics, and tasteful art and tapestries on the walls. The hotel's restaurants and wine cellar match the high standards set by the rooms, and the small but delightful spa is a great place to pamper yourself. Service is prompt, attentive, and friendly. Prices here are well above those at most other high-end hotels in Quito—in most cases more than two to three times as high as other upscale options. But no other Quito hotel can match the Plaza Grande in terms of intimacy, history, location, and luxury.

On the Plaza de la Independencia, Av. García Moreno N5-16, and Chile, Quito. ✆ **888/790-5264** in the U.S. and Canada, or 02/2510-777 in Ecuador. Fax 02/2510-800. www.plazagrandequito.com. 15 units. $550–$650 suite; $2,000 presidential suite. AE, DC, MC, V. Free valet parking. **Amenities:** 3 restaurants; cafe; bar; lounge; concierge; room service; sauna; small, well-equipped spa. *In room:* A/C, TV, hair dryer, minibar, free Wi-Fi.

Moderate

Hotel Real Audiencia This Old Town standby offers clean rooms at good prices. Still, the decor and furnishings are dated and dour, and in dire need of updating. The best rooms are spacious and come with views. No. 2A is a corner suite with a fabulous view of the Santo Domingo Plaza, while no. 301 is a floor higher up, with more panoramic views. The best feature of this hotel is its top-floor restaurant with wraparound picture windows and a view of Santo Domingo Plaza and El Panecillo. The owners aim to be socially and culturally conscious, with solar panels to heat their water, solid-waste recycling, and educational programs for local youths. You'll get a slight discount and free airport transfers if you book directly online with them. No. 2A, the Manuela Saenz suite, is a corner unit, with a fabulous view of the Santo Domingo Plaza.

Bolívar 220, at the corner of Guayaquil, Quito. ✆ **02/2952-711.** Fax 02/2580-213. www.realaudiencia.com. 32 units. $55 double; $66 junior suite; $90 Manuela Saenz suite. Rates include full breakfast and taxes. AE, DC, MC, V. **Amenities:** Restaurant; bar; free Wi-Fi. *In room:* TV.

Inexpensive

Hotel San Francisco de Quito *Value* This is my favorite budget option in Old Town. Housed in a 17th-century converted residence, the hotel's rooms are on the second, third, and fourth floors, which rise above a classic central stone courtyard with stone fountain. Rooms vary considerably in size, so try to see a few first if you can. Most have varnished wood floors, although a few are carpeted. No. 32 is the best room in the house. A large suite with fireplace and kitchenette, it's located on the fourth floor, and has excellent views in several directions.

Sucre 217, at the corner of Guayaquil, Quito. ✆ **02/2287-758** or 02/2951-241. www.sanfranciscodequito.com.ec. 32 units. $42 double; $48–$56 suite. Rates include breakfast and taxes. MC, V. **Amenities:** Restaurant; Jacuzzi; sauna; steam room; free Wi-Fi. *In room:* TV.

In the Foothills Overlooking Quito

Very Expensive

Hacienda Rumiloma ★★ *Finds* The views and accommodations at this rustically luxurious lodge—housed on the grounds of a colonial-era hacienda and nearby a volcano—are spectacular. Although just 10 minutes or less from downtown, this hotel feels worlds away. All of the rooms are large and unique, with extravagant and ornate decor. Adobe walls, red-tile floors, brass sinks, and exposed beam and brick ceilings are combined with an abundance of antiques, artworks, and eccentric design touches, including hand-painted ceramic toilets. The common areas are equally ornate and artistic, and the hacienda has almost 40 hectares (100 acres) of land, including both primary and secondary forest. The restaurant here is also excellent. You very well may never want to leave, but if you do, Quito's colonial splendor and modern Mariscal nightlife are really just a short taxi ride down the flanks of the Pichincha volcano.

Obispo de la Madrid, Quito. ✆ **02/2548-206** or 09/9703-130. www.haciendarumiloma.com. 8 units. $285 double; $325 superior suite. AE, DC, MC, V. Free parking. **Amenities:** Restaurant; bar; concierge; room service; smoke-free rooms. *In room:* No phone.

WHERE TO DINE

In New Town

In addition to the places listed below, a host of simple restaurants in town are geared toward the backpacker crowd. For tasty Indian food, try **Chandani Tandoori,** on Juan León Mera 1312, between Avenida Colón and Luis Cordero (✆ **02/2221-053**).

Expensive

El Atrio ★★★ *Finds* FUSION Located on the second floor of a building overlooking the Plaza Foch, this understated and elegant little restaurant is a hidden gem. The menu features a long list of creative dishes. I highly recommend the Ostrich San Luis, which is slow braised in a tamarind-and-cream sauce and served over egg noodles, as a sort of ostrich stroganoff. The Sea Bass Santa Maria is prepared in a ginger-and-coconut sauce, and served over quinoa. When the weather accommodates, I suggest grabbing one of the outdoor tables on the balcony overlooking the plaza, although you won't go wrong inside, where seating is available on a couple of levels, with soft lighting, plush furnishings and decor, and windows all around.

Reina Victoria N24-67 and Foch, on Plaza Foch. ✆ **02/2520-581.** Reservations recommended. Main courses $7.50–$15. AE, DC, MC, V. Daily 11am–midnight.

Moderate

Azuca Latin Bistro ★★ NUEVO LATINO Set right on the Plaza Foch, this joint is upbeat and chic, and a great spot for everything from drinks and appetizers to more filling fare—and it's open 24 hours daily. There's indoor seating, as well as a host of tables under shade umbrellas right on the plaza. Don't miss the appetizer of barbecue ribs in a tamarind-and-guava glaze. As a main dish, the traditional Cuban *ropa vieja,* a plate of seasoned shredded beef, is a standout. There's a long list of cocktails, with a variety of specialty mojitos offered. I recommend the *mojito apasionado,* which includes passion fruit juice. This place features live music or DJs Thursday to Saturday. On the second-floor you'll find the new Azuca Beach, which offers a similar party vibe, and serves up seafood and coastal cuisine.

Plaza Foch. ✆ **02/2907-164.** www.azucabistro.com. Main courses $7.50–$9.95. AE, DC, MC, V. Daily 24 hr.

Las Redes ★ SEAFOOD This place serves the best *ceviche* in Quito. You can order any type of *ceviche,* from clams to octopus to fish or shrimp. The chefs here also do an excellent job with all sorts of seafood. One of the specialties is the *gran mariscada,* an enormous, beautiful platter of assorted sizzling seafood. The *arroz con mariscos* (yellow rice with peppers, onions, mussels, clams, shrimp, calamari, octopus, and crayfish) is also delicious. Even though Las Redes is on one of the busiest streets of Quito, the simple wood tables and fishnets hanging from the ceilings make you feel as though you are at a local seafood joint on the coast.

Av. Amazonas 845 and Veintimilla. ✆ **02/2525-691.** Main courses $5.50–$12. AE, DC, MC, V. Mon–Sat 11am–11pm.

Inexpensive

The Magic Bean ★ Kids BREAKFAST/INTERNATIONAL The Magic Bean is a cozy cafe that would be right at home in any college town in the United States. It's not fancy, but it has a pleasant setting with a couple of small dining rooms and covered outdoor tables. The fare is typical cozy cafe food—pancakes, French toast, sandwiches, bagels, omelets, fresh fruit drinks, salads made with organic lettuce, and freshly brewed coffee. Overall, the food is quite good. Just beware: The pancakes are enormous! More hearty options range from grilled local trout to filet mignon. They do a lot of kabobs here, with everything from steak, chicken, and pork, to mahimahi and shrimp grilled on a spear. They even have a children's menu. If you've got a laptop or PDA, this is a good place to come for a free Wi-Fi fix. Though it's more popular as a restaurant, the Magic Bean also functions as a hostel.

Mariscal Foch 681 and Juan León Mera. ✆ **02/2566-181.** www.magicbeanquito.com. Sandwiches $4–$7; main courses $5–$12. AE, DC, MC, V. Daily 7am–10pm.

Mama Clorinda ECUADORIAN This enormously popular restaurant enjoys a loyal following—mostly of locals. Simplicity is the theme here; the food, not the atmosphere, is the attraction. The focus is on hearty and traditional recipes from the highlands, including *seco de chivo* (goat stew), *llapingachos* (cheese-filled potato patties), and *guatita* (beef, potato, and peanut stew). All varieties of grilled pork are also available, as well as roasted chicken served with *elote* (corn on the cob) and mashed potatoes. If you are a vegetarian, this is not a good place because even the mashed potatoes are cooked with pork fat (which is the traditional Ecuadorian way to cook them). Finish off your meal with a silky coconut flan or a fresh-fruit salad.

Reina Victoria 1144 and Calama. ✆ **02/2544-362.** Main courses $4–$7. MC, V. Daily noon–9pm.

In Old Town

In addition to the places listed below, you'll do well at the elegant courtyard restaurant **El Rincón de Cantuña** (✆ **02/2280-830**) inside the hotel Patio Andalúz (see above).

You might also try the **Octava de Corpus,** Calle Junín E2-167 (✆ **02/02/2952-989**), which is spread over several rooms in an old colonial home, with antiques and artworks everywhere and a great wine cellar; or **La Casa de los Geráneos,** Calle la Ronda OE 1-134 (✆ **02/2283-889**), which has lovely courtyard and indoor seating in an ancient home of the historic Calle la Ronda.

Two of the restaurants listed below, Café Mosaico and PIM's Panecillo, are actually located a little bit outside and above the center of Old Town, but for practical purposes—and for the views they provide of Old Town—they are included here. A taxi to either of these restaurants from Old Town should not cost more than $3.

Expensive

Mea Culpa ★ *Moments* INTERNATIONAL On the second floor of a building that overlooks the Plaza de la Independencia, Mea Culpa is one of the grandest restaurants in the entire city—so grand, in fact, that they require "business casual" attire. Sneakers and T-shirts are not allowed, although exceptions are sometimes made at lunch. Try to reserve a window table, if at all possible. You can start things off with a soup, or opt for salmon carpaccio, but I recommend their house specialty, the Frittata Mea Culpa (a crepe stuffed with octopus, shrimp, mussels, and calamari). Main courses include everything from simple pastas and steaks to pork tenderloin in a raspberry sauce or an ostrich filet flambéed in brandy and served with a maple-soy-apple reduction. The wine list leans heavily on Chilean and Argentine vineyards, but with some interesting and less common selections. Those looking to really splurge can drop a bundle on a bottle of Château Latour 1997.

2nd floor of the Palacio Arzobispal, on the Plaza de la Independencia, García Moreno and Chile. ✆ **02/2951-190.** www.meaculpa.com.ec. Reservations recommended. Main courses $12–$25. AE, DC, MC, V. Mon–Fri 12:30–3:30pm and 7–11pm; Sat 7–11pm.

Moderate

PIM's Panecillo *Moments* ECUADORIAN/INTERNATIONAL The food here is decidedly pedestrian, but, you're most likely coming here for the view. Located just off the *Virgen de Quito* monument, atop the Panecillo hill, the multileveled main dining room and heated outdoor areas offer up plenty of seating with a view. The menu is massive and ranges from hamburgers and sandwiches to a wide selection of meat, poultry, and seafood options. You can get a pepper steak or trout in almond sauce. There's a small children's menu, which includes chicken nuggets and minihamburgers. This is a popular tourist destination, and the place is often filled with tour bus groups. These folks have another branch, with an equally stunning view in the Centro Cultural Itchimbia, on the top of the Itchimbia hill.

Calle Melchor Aymerich, on top of the Panecillo. ✆ **02/2263-266.** www.grupopims.com. Reservations recommended. Main courses $7.50–$18. AE, DC, MC, V. Mon–Sat noon–midnight; Sun noon–6pm.

Inexpensive

Café Mosaico ★ *Finds* INTERNATIONAL Set high on a hill overlooking Old Town, Mosaico is run by an Ecuadorian-Greek-American family. The Greek moussaka is delicious, as is the souvlaki, and the vegetarian lasagna is excellent. Reservations are not accepted and this place fills up fast; be prepared to wait for a table. The best time to come here is late afternoons during the week, before the after-work crowd arrives. That way you'll score a table fast, get to see the place during the day, and also take in the incredible view as the city lights up after dark. The restaurant offers free Wi-Fi and a large telescope for stargazing at night and downtown spying during the day. A taxi here should cost under $5—just tell the driver to take you to Itchimbia.

 Manuel Samaniego N8-95 and Antepara, Itchimbia. ✆ **02/2542-871.** www.cafemosaico.com.ec. Reservations not accepted. Main courses $4–$12. MC, V. Daily 11am–10:30pm.

El Tianguez ★ Value ECUADORIAN This is the perfect place to grab a quick meal when you're spending the day in Old Town visiting the sights. Just below the Iglesia de San Francisco, the large outdoor cobblestone patio is set right on the Plaza de San Francisco. The indoor dining room is small and it can get a bit cramped when it's full; but the atmosphere is friendly and convivial and the staff works hard to keep everybody happy. Order a *plato típico* and you'll get a sampling of local specialties: empanadas, *humitas,* fried yuca, and fried pork. For something lighter, there's a good selection of large salads and sandwiches and fresh-squeezed fruit juices.

Below the Iglesia San Francisco, Plaza de San Francisco. ✆ **02/2570-233.** Main courses $3.60–$7.20. AE, DC, MC, V. Mon–Tues 9:30am–6:30pm; Wed–Sat 9:30am–midnight; Sun 9:30am–10pm.

North & East of New Town

Expensive

Hacienda Rumiloma ★★ Finds FUSION If you're not staying at this lovely mountain retreat, I highly recommend at least coming for dinner one night. The large dining room features heavy wood and stone-top tables, exposed wood beams, and a host of artworks and antiques. They actually have one of the original 18th-century wooden sculptures by Bernardo de Legarda, used as a model for the El Panecillo monument. The menu features a broad mix of creative contemporary concoctions, and it's hard to go wrong with any of them. You can start things off with a tuna carpaccio or some Ecuadorian stone crabs. For a main, I recommend the Lamb La Cantera, which is marinated for 3 days and then slow roasted. After dinner, savor a brandy while taking in the view, or head downstairs to the hotel's Irish-style pub for an aged single malt.

Obispo de la Madrid. ✆ **02/2548-206.** www.haciendarumiloma.com. Reservations recommended. Main courses $14–$34. AE, DC, MC, V. Tues–Sat 11am–11pm; Sun 10am–11pm.

Zazu ★★★ Finds FUSION Hip and eclectic, this restaurant gets just about everything right. The Peruvian-born chef, Alexander Lau, uses fresh, local ingredients whenever possible. Start things off with the *ceviche martini,* a relatively traditional *ceviche* of sole served in a martini glass, with a freshly shaken passion fruit martini poured over it as marinade. Don't miss the white-tuna appetizer, which comes baked in a delicate ginger and Peruvian hot chili broth, with bok choy and scallions. For a main dish, I recommend *langostinos Zazu,* which are first cooked tempura style and then served with a sauce made with six types of chilies and a side salad made from green mangos. Perhaps the best way to dine here, though, is to go with the chef's nightly tasting menu ($35–$40). Quito's hip crowd gathers at the bar here, which serves up a wide range of martinis and mixed drinks, including a couple of very tasty original concoctions.

Mariano Aguilera 331 and La Pradera. ✆ **02/2543-559.** www.zazuquito.com. Reservations recommended. Main courses $9–$21. AE, DC, MC, V. Mon–Fri 12:30–11:30pm; Sat 7–11:30pm.

QUITO AFTER DARK

From elegant opera performances to dirt-cheap all-you-can-drink bars, Quito offers a range of nocturnal activities for visitors and locals alike. The Mariscal sector, the hub for partying and dining out, has restaurants, pubs, and dance clubs pumping out popular salsa and infectious *reggaetón* beats until daybreak. To find out what's going on in Quito while you're in town, pick up a copy of ***Quito Cultura*** (www.quitocultura.com/alexis.swf), a monthly Spanish-language events guide that includes theater listings, concerts, and general cultural events.

Warning: Remember, at night, Quito can be quite dangerous, especially near the bars and clubs. Take a cab, even if it's only for a few blocks; bartenders can call a taxi for you. If you have a cellphone, call **Taxi Amigo** ✆ **02/2222-222** for a taxi 24 hours a day.

BARS & PUBS Quito's bar scene is extensive, offering options ranging from British-style beer pubs to sophisticated wine bars, and just about everything in between. The majority of places are situated in the Mariscal district. The Plaza Foch is generally targeted toward those in search of classier venues, while the majority of other bars, from funky cafes to laid-back bars, are located in and around the streets Calama, Reina Victoria, and Juan León Mera. With such a variety of bars and pubs in one area, the Mariscal is perfect for a pub crawl, although it can sometimes get a little dodgy after dark, so it's advisable not to go alone.

If you're looking to tap into Quito's happening bar scene, try **Bungalow Six** ★, at the corner of Calama and Diego de Almagro (✆ **08/5194-530**); **Naranjilla Mecánica** ★★, at Tamayo and Veintimilla (✆ **02/2526-468**); or **Sutra Lounge,** at Juan León Mera and Calama (✆ **02/2906-200**).

For a mellower time, try either **Reina Victoria** ★★, Reina Victoria 530 and Roca (✆ **02/2226-369**), or **Turtle's Head** ★, La Niña 626 and Juan León Mera (✆ **02/2565-544**), two British-style pubs with beer on tap, as well as pool tables, darts, and table soccer.

DANCE CLUBS On weekends, Quiteños get their dance grooves on to everything from salsa and merengue to hip-hop and house. Many clubs charge some sort of cover which can range from $5 to $10 on most nights, or as much as $15 to $20 for special events. For a contemporary scene, with plenty of electronic music, try **Acid Lounge** ★, Av. Orellana E9-26 and Pinzón (✆ **09/5834-262**), while for a more raucous vibe, with a wide range of music, you can try **La Bunga,** Francisco de Orellana 899 and Yánez Pinzón (✆ **02/2904-196**). I also like **No Bar** ★, Calama 380 and Juan León Mera (✆ **02/2545-145**), and **Macondo** ★★, Calama and Juan León Mera (✆ **02/2227-563;** www.macondoquito.com). For those looking to dance salsa, **Seseribó** ★, Veintimilla 352 and 12 de Octubre (✆ **02/2563-598**), is *the* place to go.

LIVE MUSIC Some live performances to watch out for are those by the jazz quartet **Plaza Foch** on Monday, Wednesday, and Saturday at **Coffee Tree,** Plaza Foch and Reina Victoria (✆ **02/2565-521**), and the Latin jazz band **Cabo Frío.** A good place to look for jazz is the restaurant and bar **El Pobre Diablo** ★, in La Floresta on Isabel La Católica E12-06 and Galavis (✆ **02/2235-194;** www.elpobrediablo.com). Other groups to watch out for at various venues are some of Ecuador's most influential bands: **NOTOKEN, Luis Rueda y el Feroz Tren Expreso, Sal y Mileto, Fausto Mino, Juan Fernando Velasco, Convicto, Muscaria,** and **Hector "El Napo" Napolitano.**

Blues, República 476 and Pradera (✆ **02/2223-206;** www.bluesestodo.com), is one of Quito's best and most dependable spots to find live music, particularly rock. On Thursday night, there's live Cuban music and dancing at **La Bodeguita de Cuba** ★ on Reina Victoria 1721 and La Pinta (✆ **02/2542-476**).

PERFORMING ARTS **The National Symphony** performs weekly in different venues around town, including some colonial churches; call ✆ **02/2256-5733** for up-to-date information. Every Wednesday at 7:30pm, the **Ballet Andino Humanizarte** (✆ **02/2226-116**) performs traditional Andean dances at the Fundación Cultural Humanizarte, on Leonidas Plaza N24-226 and Lizardo García. **The Ballet Folkórico Nacional Jacchigua** ★ (✆ **02/2952-025;** www.jacchiguaesecuador.com) performs traditional dances and songs on Wednesday and Friday nights at 7:30pm at the Teatro Aeropuerto. Tickets cost $12 to $14, and are often easiest to buy through **Metropolitan Touring** (✆ **02/2988-200;** www.metropolitan-touring.com) or through your hotel tour desk or concierge.

The restored **Teatro Nacional Sucre** ★★, in Old Town's Plaza del Teatro Manabí N8-131, between Guayaquil and Flores (✆ **02/2951-661;** www.teatrosucre.com), first opened its doors in 1867; it's Quito's most popular theater and offers a varied and exciting events program, including contemporary theater, ballet, electronic-music performances, and opera. Free concerts and street shows put on by the theater frequently take place just outside, on the Plaza del Teatro. Despite being almost completely destroyed by a fire in 1999, the restored neoclassic **Teatro Bolívar,** at Flores 421 and Junín (✆ **02/2582-486;** www.teatrobolivar.org), continues to host and produce a range of cultural events, including theater, dance, music, and Latin American cinema.

Another important outlet for the performing arts is the **Casa de la Cultura Ecuatoriana**, 6 de Diciembre N16-224 y Patria (✆ **02/2902-272;** www.cce.org.ec). Founded in the 1940s by writer, politician, and diplomat Benjamin Carrión ("If we can't be a military or economic power, we can, instead, be a cultural power fed by our rich traditions"), the Casa offers an extensive repertoire of events, including rock concerts, art exhibitions, and performances by the National Symphonic Orchestra.

The **Teatro del CCI,** at CCI Iñaquito, Avenida Amazonas and Nacionas Unidas (✆ **02/2921-308**), which opened its doors in January 2006, is a fine example of a modern theater with the latest technology in sound and lighting, offering up a mix of contemporary dance, theater, and music.

SIDE TRIPS FROM QUITO

Cotopaxi National Park ★★

At 5,897m (19,347 ft.), Cotopaxi is one of the world's highest continuously active volcanoes, and Ecuador's second-highest peak. Your first encounter with the almost perfectly cone-shaped and snow-covered Cotopaxi might be from overhead in a plane; I've been on planes that have flown terrifyingly close to the volcano, where I almost felt I could reach out and touch it. From above, it's hard to determine where the clouds end and where the glaciers begin. The snow glimmers in the sunlight and magically blends with the bright blue sky—and what a sight! On a clear day in Quito, even if you're not airborne, it's easy to see Cotopaxi rising high and mighty above the clouds.

Looking down from a plane at a volcano is one thing, but climbing it, camping on its flanks, riding a horse or mountain bike across the paramo, or hiking around it are much more rewarding. The high Andean paramo here features wild horses and llamas grazing. Below the volcano, the flat plains are peppered with volcanic boulders that give stark evidence of the power and fury of Cotopaxi's relatively recent eruptions. And everywhere you turn there are fantastic views of the snow-covered crater—that is, when it's not shrouded in low cloud cover.

Climbing to the summit is serious business, and not for those in merely average physical condition and with no experience at high altitudes. Nonetheless, every year, thousands of intrepid climbers take out their ice axes, strap on their crampons, and conquer the summit. An embarrassing admission: I've never done it. But according to those in the know, the climb is not terribly technical or difficult. On the other hand, I have met several experienced climbers who have been severely affected by the altitude and were forced to turn back early. Be sure to spend several days in Quito and at higher altitudes acclimating before you attempt to summit Cotopaxi. Even if you're feeling fine at 2,800m (9,000 ft.), remember that the air will feel a whole lot thinner at 5,000m (16,000 ft.), especially if you're exerting a lot of energy. You should also note that the climb typically starts at about 11pm to midnight and you will be going uphill on glaciers for about 8 continuous hours before you reach the top. This way, you reach the crater in the early morning light, before the clouds settle in.

Fortunately for the less adventurous and less fit, you really don't need to climb Cotopaxi to enjoy it. A host of outfitters in Quito, and all the hotels close to the volcano, organize day trips to the national park. Many day trips bring you to the small museum and visitor center, which has a somewhat sad collection of stuffed animals, including an Andean condor, as well as a relief map of the volcano and some explanatory materials. From here, these trips commonly take any number of short-to-midlength hikes around the park, most commonly to the Laguna de Limpiopungo. The museum is located at 4,500m (14,760 ft.) above sea level, and most of the hikes around the park take place at this general altitude—note that even at this altitude, the air is quite thin and it's not uncommon to feel lightheaded.

ORGANIZING A CLIMB TO THE TOP It's very important to make sure that you're climbing Cotopaxi with an experienced guide and good equipment. The best companies provide one guide for every two climbers. The finest and most experienced outfitters include **Moggely Climbing** ★ (✆ **02/2906-656;** www.moggely.com), **Safari Ecuador** ★ (✆ **02/2552-505;** www.safari.com.ec), and **Surtrek** ★★ (✆ **866/978-7398** in the U.S. and Canada, or 02/2231-534 in Ecuador; www.surtrek.com). Rates run $150 to $200 per person for a 2-day/1-night trip to the summit, depending upon the size of your group.

All the above companies also organize longer treks around the park and climbs to the summits of other nearby peaks, including Rumiñahui, Iliniza Norte, and Iliniza Sur, all of which are good practice climbs to tackle before attempting Cotopaxi.

VISITING AS PART OF A DAY TRIP Just about every tour desk and tour operator in Quito offers a day trip to Cotopaxi. The details may vary some, but most head first to the small museum and then spend anywhere from 1 to 3 hours hiking. In addition, most operators offer options for mountain biking or horseback riding.

The best general tour operators, in my opinion, are **Metropolitan Touring** ★ (✆ **02/2988-200;** www.metropolitan-touring.com) and **Surtrek** (see above). Day trips to Cotopaxi run $30 to $75, depending on the size of your group and whether lunch is included. The $10 national park entrance fee is rarely included.

Alternatively, you can organize a day trip to Cotopaxi on your own. You can hire a taxi in Quito for about $60 to $90 round-trip. The ride from Quito to the parking lot takes about 1½ hours. Once you reach the parking lot, you can then hike up to the *refugio* or glacier at your own pace while the taxi waits for you.

If you want to tour the park on a mountain bike, contact **Adventure Planet Ecuador** (✆ **02/2863-086;** www.adventureplanet-ecuador.com) or **Aries Bike Company** (✆ **02/2906-052;** www.ariesbikecompany.com).

For horseback-riding tours of Cotopaxi, I recommend **Ilalo Expeditions** ★ (✆ **09/7778-399** or 02/2484-219; www.ilaloexpeditions.com), **Hacienda El Porvenir** ★ (✆ **02/2231-806** or 09/4980-121; www.tierradelvolcan.com), or **Hacienda Hato Verde** ★ (✆/fax **03/2719-348** or 09/5978-016; www.haciendahatoverde.com).

Mountain-bike or horseback excursions to Cotopaxi run around $45 to $75 per person per day, depending upon the length of the ride and several other variables such as group size and equipment requirements.

La Mitad del Mundo (the Middle of the World)

One of the most common souvenir photos taken in Ecuador is that which has a visitor with one foot in either hemisphere, straddling the Equator. **Ciudad La Mitad del Mundo** (✆ **02/2396-871;** www.mitaddelmundo.com) is a tourist complex set up on the site where, in 1736, French explorer and scientist Charles-Marie de la Condamine made his final calculations to determine the precise Equatorial line. With modern GPS technology, we now know that de la Condamine was close, but erred by some 180m (600 ft.). For a more precise visit to the Equatorial line, I recommend visiting the **Quitsato Mitad del Mundo Monument,** which is on the road to Otavalo (see "En Route: Straddling Two Hemispheres," below).

The centerpiece of this attraction is a large, trapezoidal monument topped with a large globe. At the top of the monument is a viewing area, reached by an elevator, with great views of the surrounding mountains and countryside. My favorite attraction here is the large scale model of colonial-era Quito, called **Museo del Quito en Miniatura (Quito in Miniature).** This is a great way to get your bearings before touring around the colonial core. On the site, there's also a separate **Museo de Etnografía (Ethnographic Museum),** with displays about Ecuador's various indigenous tribes and peoples, as well as a small **planetarium.** All around are tourist shops and souvenir stands, snack bars, and restaurants. The whole place was built with a mock-colonial styling, sort of a miniature Epcot version of colonial Quito. Frequent shows of folkloric music and dance are performed. Quiteños flock here on Sunday.

Ciudad La Mitad del Mundo is open Monday to Thursday from 9am to 6pm, and Friday to Sunday from 9am to 7pm. Admission is $2. Admission to the Ethnographic Museum is an additional $3, while a visit to the planetarium will set you back another $1.50.

Separate from the main attraction, but just a few hundred yards away, is the **Museo Solar Intiñan ★ (Intiñan Solar Museum; ✆ 02/2395-122;** www.museointinan.com.ec). This interesting attraction has a series of exhibits and ongoing experiments relating to the geography, astrology, and natural sciences of the region. Try your hand at balancing an egg on its end, and watch how water flows down a drain on either side of the Equator. You can also test your accuracy with a blow gun. The museum is open daily from 9:30am to 5pm. Admission is $3.

GETTING THERE Located some 23km (14 miles) north of Quito, near San Antonio de Pichincha, Ciudad La Mitad del Mundo is connected to Quito by a well-paved road. Just about every tour agency and hotel desk in Quito offers a half-day tour here. Prices range from $9 to $30, depending on how exclusive the tour is, how many attractions it takes in, and whether or not lunch or admission fees are included in the price.

A taxi ride here from Quito should run about $12 to $15 each way. Regular buses, marked MITAD DEL MUNDO, leave from the Cotocallao stop of the Metrobus trolley line. The trolley costs 25¢, and the bus costs an extra 40¢. Be sure to stay on the bus until you reach the actual monument, its final stop.

Otavalo Market ★★★

Though Saturday is the main market day, most Quito-based operators offer daily excursions to nearby Otavalo, and there's plenty of good shopping in Otavalo any day of the week. There's also a lot to see and do around the town. Most tours last all day, with a stop at the artisans market as well as visits to any number of nearby attractions including Cuicocha Lake, Peguche Waterfall, Mojanda Lakes, and Condor Park. Most tours include lunch at one of the area's historic haciendas.

Guided tours to Otavalo run $30 to $75 per person. As with the tours to Cotopaxi, the price varies depending on group size, what's included, where you have lunch, the length of the tour, and other factors. For more information on Otavalo, the Otavalo market, and other attractions in the area, see below.

Mindo & Bellavista Cloud Forest Reserve ★★

Hiking through the cloud forests of Mindo and Bellavista is one of the most exciting and rewarding side trips you can take from Quito. Within 2 hours, you will escape the city and find yourself in a magical ecosystem where near-constant mist, as opposed to heavy rains, gives nourishment to a dense mix of trees, lichen, and epiphytes. Cloud forests are some of the most biologically diverse places on earth. Over 400 bird species have been recorded in the area, including the golden-headed quetzal, tanager finch and, my personal favorite, Chocó toucan. In addition, you will have the opportunity to hike to remote waterfalls, ride inner tubes on pristine rivers, take a zip-line canopy tour, and marvel at the rich array of orchids, butterflies, bromeliads, and flowers.

While the easy access makes this a potential (and popular) day-tour destination, I recommend spending at least a night or two. There are several lovely lodges in this region, with excellent naturalist guides, and a host of tour and activity options. In addition to bird- and wildlife-viewing, tour options include horseback riding, zip-line canopy excursions, mountain biking, and visits to local butterfly farms.

Much of the cloud forest around Mindo is protected in the **Bosque Protector Mindo-Nambillo (Mindo-Nambillo Protected Forest),** which is administered by **Amigos de la Naturaleza** (✆ **02/2765-463**). While most of the reserve is closed to the public, there are ample private reserves and publicly accessible trails through Mindo's cloud forests. The Mindo-Nambillo reserve was the source of controversy a few years ago, when the government ran an oil pipeline right through it, despite the objections of tourism and environmental groups. Today, the forest is recuperating and covering up much of the damage caused when the pipeline was pushed through.

Mindo is the more developed of these two cloud-forest destinations, with a host of hotels and lodges. The top hotel here is gorgeous **El Monte** ★ (✆ **09/3084-675** or 02/3900-402; www.ecuadorcloudforest.com). Accommodations are private, wood-and-thatch cabins set near the banks of the clear-flowing Río Mindo. This place is a couple of miles south of Mindo, and the final leg of your journey to the lodge is via a hand-cranked cable car over the river. Accommodations are $86 per person, for a 2-day/1-night stay, including three meals, guided hikes and activities, and taxes. A similar choice is the lovely **Casa Divina** (✆ **02/3900-457;** www.mindocasadivina.com), which has its own zip-line canopy tour, and **Tandayapa Bird Lodge** (✆ **02/2447-520;** www.tandayapa.com), which was built by and for bird-watchers, and is run by the folks behind **Tropical Birding** (www.tropicalbirding.com).

The 720-hectare (1,778-acre) **Bellavista Cloud Forest Reserve** (✆ **02/2116-232** or 09/9490-891; www.bellavistacloudforest.com) is privately owned and has a variety of accommodations options, from private cabins to dorm rooms in the top of a large geodesic dome. It's not a fancy place, but the views over the forest canopy are dramatic, the food is excellent, and the nature guides will open your eyes to a whole different world.

 Rates run $47 to $71 per person, including three meals, but a whole host of package options are available, including meals, tours, and transportation.

GETTING THERE If you're staying at a hotel here, you can usually arrange transportation with your hotel or lodge. Alternatively, a taxi from Quito should run around $40 to $60. Mindo is serviced by a couple of daily buses from Quito. **Cooperativa Flor de Valle** (✆ **02/2527-495**) has buses leaving Quito's northern bus terminal, Terminal de Norte La Ofelia, at 8:20am and 4pm, and returning at 6:30am and 2pm. On weekends and holidays there are additional buses and a slightly varied schedule. The ride takes around 2½ hours, and the fare is $3.

It's a little more complicated to travel to Bellavista on your own: You have to take the bus from Quito to the small town of Nanegalito, where you can arrange for a truck taxi to Bellavista. From Nanegalito, it's about a 45-minute ride to Bellavista. The ride should cost about $15 for the whole vehicle, which can hold up to six passengers. Any bus from Quito to Mindo, Puerto Quito, or San Miguel de los Bancos can drop you off in Nanegalito.

5 OTAVALO & IMBABURA PROVINCE ★★

Otavalo: 95km (59 miles) N of Quito, 515km (319 miles) NE of Guayaquil, 537km (333 miles) N of Cuenca

Otavalo is one of Ecuador's most popular destinations. The locals, known as Otavaleños, have been famous for their masterful craftsmanship for centuries, and the artisans market here is world renowned. Otavaleños still wear traditional clothing and cling to their heritage. Men wear their long straight black hair in distinctive ponytails, and women wear multistranded bead necklaces. Saturday is the main market day, when the impressive market spills out over much of this small city. Luckily for travelers with tight schedules, the market has become so popular that it now takes place on the other 6 days of the week, too, albeit on a smaller scale. In addition to shopping at Otavalo's market, you can explore the back roads of the province and visit local studios. Some of the smaller towns specialize in specific crafts: **Cotacachi,** for example, is known for leather work, **Peguche** for its weaving, and **San Antonio de Ibarra** for its age-old woodcarving techniques.

Even nonshoppers will love Otavalo and its surroundings. The town has an almost perfect setting. It's nestled in the Sunrise Valley in the shadow of two protective volcanoes, **Cotacachi** and **Imbabura.** According to local legend, Cotacachi is the area's symbolic mother, and Imbabura is the father standing watch. To feel the inspirational powers of Mother Nature, I recommend spending a few days exploring the area, breathing in the fresh air, gazing at the dark-blue waters of the local crater lakes, and standing in awe of the snow-covered volcanoes. Plus, after you find the perfect alpaca sweater, you can wear it as you stroll around **Cuicocha Lake** or hike in the mountains.

ESSENTIALS

Getting There

Every hotel desk and tour agency in Quito sells day tours to Otavalo and shuttle tickets aboard minivans and buses. The rate runs around $8 to $14 per person each way for just transportation, and around $30 to $75 for a day tour, including lunch. These shuttles and tours will pick you up at most hotels in Quito. If your hotel desk can't set one up for you, contact **Grayline Ecuador** (✆ **02/2907-577;** www.graylineecuador.com) or **Metropolitan Touring** ★ (✆ **02/2988-200;** www.metropolitan-touring.com). Alternately, a taxi holding up to four passengers should cost $45 to $60 from Quito to Otavalo.

En Route: Straddling Two Hemispheres

The Pan-American Highway north of Quito passes right through the Equator, close to Km 55. On your left, as you drive toward Otavalo, you'll see a cluster of souvenir stands and a small concrete globe allegedly sitting right on the Equatorial line. Avoid the temptation to pull over here, and head a few hundred feet farther to the **Quitsato Mitad del Mundo Monument** (✆ **09/9701-133;** www.quitsato.org), which is on the right-hand side of the road.

Opened in 2006, this attraction was built and is run by the folks at nearby Hacienda Guachala (discussed later). The centerpiece is a tall spire that works as one of the world's most accurate sundials. Stone inlays mark the cardinal directions, as well as the solstice limits and the exact Equatorial line. As far as I know, this is the most precise Mitad del Mundo (Middle of the World) attraction in Ecuador, and if you have a GPS, bring it to check. At noon, the spire casts absolutely no shadow in any direction, and on the equinox, the shadow falls exactly on the Equatorial line, which is the same width as the spire. The monument is open daily during daylight hours, and admission is free.

Buses leave Quito's **Terminal Terrestre Carcelén** (✆ **02/3961-600,** ext. 6099) roughly every 15 minutes between 5am and 10pm. The ride takes 2 to 2½ hours, and the fare is $2.50. Otavalo's main bus terminal, Terminal Terrestre, is on Quito and Atahualpa, about 8 blocks—or a 15-minute walk—from Plaza de los Ponchos.

Getting Around

It's easy to get around Otavalo and the surrounding area by taxi and local bus. Taxis are plentiful. A ride anywhere in the city of Otavalo itself should cost only $1.

If you're traveling farther afield and looking to explore Imbabura province, taxis can be hired for $6 to $10 per hour. A one-way taxi fare to Cotacachi or San Antonio de Ibarra should cost $5 to $7.

If you need a taxi, call **Taxis El Jordán** (✆ **06/2920-298**), **Taxi Copacabana** (✆ **06/2920-438**), or **Taxi Yamor** (✆ **06/2921-475**).

Most of the surrounding communities, towns, and cities are connected to Otavalo by **local bus service.** Buses leave Otavalo every 5 minutes or so for Ibarra. Other buses head to Intag, Cayambe, El Quinche, Peguche, and Cotacachi. Your best source of information is to simply head to the bus station on Quito and Atahualpa. Bus rides to nearby towns or villages run 15¢ to 50¢.

Visitor Information

The **Otavalo Chamber of Tourism** (**Cámara de Turismo de Otavalo;** ✆ **06/2921-994**) runs a helpful information office out of a third-floor office on Calle Sucre between Quiroga and Quito. You'll find another, similar office run by the **Municipal Tourism Office** (**Oficina Municipal de Turismo;** ✆ **06/2921-313**) on the corner of Quiroga and Modesto Jaramillo. Your best bet, though, is your hotel tour desk or a local tour agency. My favorite local agency is **Runa Tupari Native Travel** ★★, right on Plaza de los Ponchos, between Sucre and Quiroga (✆ **06/2925-985;** www.runatupari.com). They are not for profit and work to support rural indigenous communities.

FAST FACTS If you need to contact the **police,** dial ✆ **101,** or ✆ 06/2920-101. The main hospital in Otavalo, **Hospital San Luis** (✆ **06/2922-461** or 06/2920-600), is located on Sucre and Estados Unidos. The **post office** (✆ **06/2920-642** or 06/2923-520) is adjacent to Plaza de los Ponchos, on the corner of Sucre and Salinas; it's on the second floor. Yes, it looks as though the building has been condemned, but it hasn't, so head up the stairway and walk past the miniconstruction site to the post office.

Banks are abundant in Otavalo. There's a **Banco Pichincha** (✆ **06/2920-214**) on Bolívar 6164, near García Moreno, and a **Banco del Pacífico** (✆ **06/2923-300**) on the corner of Bolívar 4-86 and García Moreno. You'll find another branch of Banco Pichincha just north of Plaza de los Ponchos, on Sucre 413 between Quiroga and Quito.

Plenty of pharmacies are around downtown Otavalo. The **Farmacia Otavalo** (✆ **06/2920-716**), at Colón 510 between Sucre and Juan Jaramillo, is very helpful, as is **Sana Sana** (✆ **06/2924-944)** on Sucre and Pedraita. Pharmacies work on a *turno* system, which means that each pharmacy periodically takes responsibility for being open 24 hours.

It's easy to find an Internet cafe in Otavalo; there are over a half dozen within 2 blocks of the Plaza de los Ponchos. Fast connections can be found at **Mofuk CafeNet** (✆ **06/2926-000**) on Sucre 1205 and Morales. Rates run around $1 per hour.

WHAT TO SEE & DO

Aside from wandering around and shopping the outdoor markets (see below), there are few tourist attractions of note right in the town of Otavalo, although the surrounding towns, villages, and countryside are ripe with opportunities for sightseeing, shopping, and adventure activities.

In Town

If you tire of the hustle, bustle, and commerce of the artisans market on the Plaza de los Ponchos, head for the more peaceful Parque Bolívar. You can grab a bench in the gardens here, or venture into the city's main **Catholic church.** Although very plain from the outside, the church features an ornate gold-leaf and gold-painted altar, as well as a pretty tiled ceiling.

If you want to learn about the process of weaving used by the artisans in and around Otavalo, head to the **Museo de Tejidos El Obraje** (✆ **06/2920-261**), which was set up by Don Luis Maldonado and his wife, and has exhibits about the local weaving tools and techniques, as well as displays on the daily lives of the Otavaleños. This little museum is located on Calle Sucre 608, just across from the Sana Sana pharmacy. It is open Monday to Friday from 2 to 5pm and weekends from 9 to 11am. Admission is $2. They also offer classes on weaving.

OTAVALO MARKET ★★★ Because there are often several, simultaneous markets taking place, it's probably most accurate to talk about Otavalo's "markets" (not "market"). The artisans market presents some of the best bargains in Ecuador and, just as importantly, some of the best people-watching. On Saturday, almost the entire city becomes one big shopping area, and itinerant vendors set up stalls on every available speck of sidewalk and alleyway. It's not just for tourists, either; Ecuadorians come here from miles away, to peddle and buy high-quality, handmade goods. The Otavaleños are extremely friendly and helpful, and they wear beautiful traditional clothing. Overall, this is one of the most colorful markets in Ecuador, and the handicrafts are of excellent quality. Some of the best buys available here include handmade alpaca sweaters, soft alpaca scarves, wool fedoras, colorful straw bags, hand-embroidered blouses, musical instruments, ceramics, and large woven tapestries.

Though Saturday is market day, there is a relatively complete market every day in Plaza de los Ponchos. Whenever you visit, you'll find the same great crafts on sale here, and the same beautiful people selling them. ***Tip:*** I find that the Saturday market is a bit overwhelming; in fact, I prefer coming on a weekday, when I don't have to visit millions of stands to be sure that I have found the perfect bag or hat. You might also be able to bargain better on an off day, since fewer tourists mean less demand, and sellers are often a bit more flexible if they really want to make a sale.

Shoppers should expect to do some bargaining, but I've found that prices will only drop a dollar or two (or 20% at most). Don't worry—the asking price is usually quite low, and everything here is already a bargain.

Exploring the Area

Many of the textiles and crafts sold in Otavalo's markets are produced in the towns and villages nearby. Outside of Otavalo, you can visit weavers' studios in Peguche, leather shops in Cotacachi, and woodcarving workshops in San Antonio de Ibarra.

Nature lovers should also take note: With snow-covered Volcán Cayambe overhead and green mountains in the distance, Imbabura province is a place of stunning beauty. There are several excellent hiking possibilities in the area, including one from Otavalo to the Peguche waterfall, and a 4-hour hike around Cuicocha, a picturesque crater lake. All the travel agencies and tour desks in Otavalo can arrange hiking, trekking, and horseback-riding excursions to a range of beautiful and off-the-beaten-path spots in the area, as well as guided tours to the towns and artisans workshops all around outlying towns and villages.

Runa Tupari Native Travel ★★, right on Plaza de los Ponchos between Sucre and Quiroga (✆ **06/2925-985;** www.runatupari.com), and **Dicency Viajes,** on the corner of Sucre and Colón (✆ **06/2921-217**), are the two best agencies in town. Both offer a wide range of tours, hikes, and adventure activities around the area, including guided tours to all the sites and destinations listed below as well as organized climbs of Mount Cotacachi (4,939m/16,200 ft.).

CUICOCHA LAKE ★★ Cuicocha is a sparkling blue crater lake formed about 3,000 years ago, when the crater of the lake's namesake volcano collapsed during an eruption. The crater was covered with snow, which eventually melted and formed the lake. When the Incas came here, they thought that one of the islands in the middle looked like a *cuy* (guinea pig), hence the name Cuicocha (Guinea Pig Lake). You can take a motorized boat ride out and around the two islands in the middle of the lake, although you can't get off and hike on them. From the boat, along the shores and in the shallows, you will see *totora,* the reed used in this area for making baskets and floor coverings. A 20- to 40-minute boat ride should cost no more than $3 per person. Be sure to bring a warm sweater—the wind here can be vicious.

I prefer hiking here to riding around on a boat (although you can certainly do both). An 8km (5-mile) trail loops around the rim of the crater, which takes about 4 hours to circle. But even if you walk along it for only 5 or 10 minutes, you'll be able to see Otavalo, Cotacachi, Cayambe, and all the volcanoes of Imbabura province. The setting and views are consistently striking. There's a small visitor center, near the end of the road leading from Quiroga to Cuicocha, which has some basic exhibits on the geography, geology, and local history of the lake, and serves as the administration center for this entrance into the Cotacachi-Cayapas Ecological Reserve, of which Cuicocha is a part. Admission is $1 to visit the lake, $5 to visit other areas of the reserve.

Cuicocha Lake is about 16km (10 miles) west of the town of Cotacachi. Although a paved road leads almost to the crater's edge, no public transportation is available from Otavalo directly to Cuicocha.

Tip: I recommend taking a guided tour here, since robberies of unaccompanied tourists have been reported. If you're doing it on your own, it's best to hire a taxi in Otavalo for the full trip, or to take a bus from Otavalo to Cotacachi or Quiroga, and then hire a cab. If you hire a cab, be sure to either pay for the wait time, or designate a time for your return ride.

COTACACHI Cotacachi is a sleepy little pueblo with incredible vistas. From here, you can see snow-covered Volcán Cayambe and the lush green mountains in the distance. But no one comes here for the views, because Cuicocha, about 10 minutes up the road, offers much better views—perhaps the best in all of Imbabura province. People do, however, come here to shop. Cotacachi is famous for the leather stores that line Avenida 10 de Agosto. Offerings range from wallets and purses to shoes and clothing. Equestrian enthusiasts can shop for handmade saddles. The quality varies widely, but if you search hard enough you are bound to find some excellent work and great bargains. Cotacachi is about 15km (9½ miles), or 15 minutes, from Otavalo. You can easily take a public bus from the station in Otavalo, or hire a taxi for about $6 each way.

PEGUCHE Peguche is home to some of the best weavers in Ecuador. If you stop in the main square, you can start off by visiting the gallery and workshop of José Cotacachi, a master weaver. Peguche is also famous for its musical instruments. You'll find various shops that specialize in making single-reed flutes and *rondadores* (panpipes), as well as guitars and *charangos* (a mandolin-like instrument with five pairs of strings). Traditionally, the back of a *charango* is made from an armadillo shell. If you visit the town on a guided tour (which I highly recommend), you will explore the back streets of Peguche and visit the homes of some of the town's best weavers while learning about the old-fashioned process of spinning wool.

Just outside the town is **Peguche Waterfall** ★, a popular spot for tourists and locals alike. Peguche Waterfall is a tall and powerful torrent of water with lush vegetation on either side. Near the foot of the falls you'll find broad grassy areas with picnic tables and bench seating. Paths take you around the area, including one that goes to the top of the falls, with a sturdy wooden bridge taking you directly over the rushing water. The Peguche Waterfall plays an important role each year in the concurrent festivals of Inti Raymi and San Juan de Batista, which coincide with the summer solstice. Locals of both indigenous and Catholic faiths come to the falls for cleansing baths at this time of year. The tiny town is about 10 minutes by car from Otavalo. A taxi should cost $5 each way, and you can also walk to the falls from town in about 45 minutes. The route is well worn and popular—just ask one of the locals to point you in the right direction.

MOJANDA LAKES ★ After Cuicocha Lake, the Mojanda Lakes offer some of the best and most scenic hiking around Otavalo. The extinct volcano Fuya Fuya stands majestically above the three high mountain lakes, creating a beautiful setting. This is a great spot for bird-watching—more than 100 species of birds are found here, including the giant hummingbird and the endangered Andean condor. The Mojanda Lakes are about 30 minutes south of Otavalo. A taxi there costs about $12 each way.

PARQUE CONDOR (CONDOR PARK) Although you'll find Andean condors on display here, you'll find a whole host of other bird species as well. The emphasis is on raptors, with a variety of local raptor species represented, including various different owls. Several large birds are brought out by trainers and allowed to fly each day at 11:30am and 4:30pm. The park is set on a high hillside with a lovely view over Laguna San Pablo, the Otavalo Valley, and Volcán Imbabura. There's a small restaurant with great views, as well as a children's playground.

Parque Condor (✆ **06/2924-429;** www.parquecondor.org) is outside Otavalo near El Lechero and Peguche. It is open Tuesday through Sunday from 9:30am to 5pm. Admission is $2. A taxi ride here should cost no more than $4 each way.

SAN ANTONIO DE IBARRA Cedar wood is abundant in Imbabura province. Take a trip to the small town of San Antonio de Ibarra and you can see how local woodcarvers transform this raw wood into high art. The town is full of galleries selling wood figurines in almost every shape and size; all are beautifully hand painted. Many are religious themed, although there are plenty of artisans making secular decorative and functional pieces as well. The best stores are on the main street, 25 de Noviembre, and along Calle Ramón Teanga.

Tip: I recommend starting your tour of San Antonio de Ibarra near the church known locally as La Capilla del Barrio del Sur. This diminutive blue church is near the top of the beautifully restored section of Calle Ramón Teanga. Catty-corner to the church is **Escultura Cisneros** (✆ **06/2932-354**), the workshop of Saul and Alfonso Cisneros, two of the more prominent local sculptors. From here, walk downhill for several blocks, stopping in at shops as they strike your fancy, before jogging over toward the town's central plaza and the main avenue, 25 de Noviembre. Heading out of town on this avenue, be sure to stop at the **Asociación de Artesanos** (✆ **06/2933-538**). This large space exhibits works by a number of local artisans, and also has a large gallery area that often hosts traveling exhibitions. For a real treat, try calling on **Alcides Montesdeoca** (✆ **06/2932-106**), a renowned maker of large Virgin Mary sculptures used in prominent Holy Week processions around the world. Alcides can usually be found at his home workshop, on Calle Bolívar 5-38.

San Antonio de Ibarra is 5km (3 miles) south of Ibarra, just off the Pan-American Highway. Any bus from Ibarra to Quito or Otavalo will drop you off at the entrance to San Antonio de Ibarra, although it's 10 blocks or more uphill from here to the center of town, so be sure to hop on one of the similarly frequent direct buses to San Antonio proper. These leave roughly every 20 minutes from Ibarra's Terminal Terrestre throughout the day. The fare is 25¢. A taxi ride here should not cost over $5.

Outdoor Activities

Hiking trails abound here. One of my favorite hikes is the 4-hour trek around Cuicocha Lake. Keep in mind, however, that robberies have been reported in the area, so it's best to do the trail with a guide. You can also hike from Cuicocha to the Mojanda Lakes, up Volcán Cotacachi, or around the Mojanda Lakes and up Mount Fuya Fuya. Both **Dicency Viajes** (✆ **06/2921-217**) and **Runa Tupari Native Travel** ★★ (✆ **06/2925-985;** www.runatupari.com) can provide experienced guides and help organize your hiking excursions. Both of these tour agencies also offer **horseback-riding** trips. One of the most popular is the trail around Cuicocha Lake. A half-day trip costs $40 to $60 per person.

In Otavalo

Moderate

Hotel Ali Shungu ★ This popular hotel is a step up from most of the downtown options. The two-story building is built in a broad horseshoe around a large garden that attracts hummingbirds and other bird species. Ali Shungu translates as "good heart" in the native Quechua, and the owners are expatriated Americans who have put their hearts into this project and the area. The rooms are simple but comfortable, with firm beds and colorful art and handicrafts hanging from the walls. The two family suites are big, with two bedrooms and spacious living areas; they are located on the second floor and have large, inviting balconies. In addition to the rooms, all public indoor areas here are smoke-free. The **restaurant** here (see below) is one of the best in town, and they have a pretty little sister lodge in the mountains outside of town.

Calle Quito and Calle Migue Egas, Otavalo. ✆ **06/2920-750.** www.alishungu.com. 20 units. $55 double; $110–$150 apt. Rates include taxes. No credit cards. Parking nearby. **Amenities:** Restaurant; bar; all rooms smoke-free; free Wi-Fi. *In room:* No phone.

Inexpensive

Budget hotels and hostels abound in Otavalo; the one listed here is my favorite, but feel free to walk around the small town and check out a few for yourself before deciding.

Samay Inn ★ Finds This simple, budget hotel, centrally located on Calle Sucre, just a block from the Plaza de Ponchos, is a great choice in Otavalo. The rooms all have wood floors and faux-stucco walls painted with bold primary colors and an aged-wash effect. All come with flatscreen televisions. A relaxing interior courtyard lounge on the second floor is enclosed by a tall brick wall. Interior brick arches and other design touches give this place more charm and class than you'd expect at this price. Be careful, there are two Samay Inn sites in Otavalo—don't head to the one closer to the bus station.

Calle Sucre 1009 and Calle Colón, Otavalo. ✆ **06/2921-826.** samayinn@hotmail.com. 23 units. $20 double. Rates include taxes. DC, MC, V. Free parking. **Amenities:** Restaurant; bar. *In room:* TV.

Haciendas & Resorts Around Otavalo

Very Expensive

Hacienda Cusín ★★ Kids This 17th-century hacienda is a great choice in the Otavalo area, especially if you're looking for a mix of comfort, adventure and history. Cusín sits on over 4 hectares (10 acres) of lush gardens and cobblestone courtyards over-flowing with bougainvillea, orchids, and palm trees. Rooms are located in a mix of original and new constructions, scattered around the lush grounds, but all have a traditional feel and come with working fireplaces, and wood beds and armoires. The friendly staff can help you arrange activities, including the popular overnight horseback-riding trip to Volcán Imbabura. Spanish-language classes are also available. The restaurant serves a wonderful dinner by candlelight so there's no need to leave the property after dark. This hotel is closely tied into the local community and has implemented sustainable and conservation practices throughout its operation.

San Pablo del Lago, Otavalo. ✆ **06/2918-013.** Fax 06/2918-003. www.haciendacusin.com. 42 units. $120 double; $150 garden cottage; $220–$300 suite. Rates include breakfast; suite rates include dinner. AE, DC, MC, V. **Amenities:** Restaurant; bar. *In room:* No phone.

La Mirage Garden Hotel & Spa ★★★ If you're looking for luxury, you won't find a better hotel in the highlands than this member of the prestigious Relais & Châteaux.

All the rooms are essentially suites, with separate sitting areas and fireplaces. Just about every one of them could be featured in the pages of *House & Garden.* Some rooms have brass canopy beds; others have antique wood frames. Crystal chandeliers brighten the rooms, while plush Oriental carpets decorate the floors. The spacious bathrooms come with extralarge showers. Reina Sofía of Spain stayed in stately no. 114, and I'm sure she must have felt right at home. The spa here was the first one to open in Ecuador and it's a real classic. Indulge in clay baths and body massages, or treat yourself to a full-body purification performed by a local female shaman. The outdoor gardens are also magnificent, as is the fine-dining restaurant.

At the end of Calle 10 de Agosto, Cotacachi. ✆ **800/327-3573** in the U.S. and Canada, or 06/2915-237. Fax 02/2915-065. www.mirage.com.ec. 23 units. $300–$350 double; $350–$800 suite. Rates include breakfast and dinner. DC, MC, V. **Amenities:** Restaurant; bar; lounge; small exercise room; Jacuzzi; solar-heated indoor pool; room service; spa services; steam room; tennis court. *In room:* TV, hair dryer.

Expensive

Hacienda Pinsaquí ★ **Moments** The over-200-year-old Hacienda Pinsaquí is one of Ecuador's classic hotels—Simón Bolívar once stayed here. Pinsaquí immediately transports you back in time. The homey smell of well-worn fireplaces permeates the air. And the rooms are sumptuous; each one is unique, but all have a touch of old-fashioned country elegance. No. 8 has a magnificent canopy bed and beautiful antique furniture, as well as a separate sitting area where you can gaze out onto the property's wonderfully landscaped gardens. This room also has a sunken Jacuzzi tub set near a large window overlooking the gardens. Those in a newer wing were built to mimic the colonial-era style. Once you leave the comfort of your cozy room, you can walk around the property's gardens or explore the area by horseback—the hotel offers guided riding tours. Superb meals are served in an elegant dining room.

Pan-American Hwy., Km 5, Otavalo. ✆ **06/2946-116** or 09/9727-652. Fax 06/2946-117. www.hacienda pinsaqui.com. 20 units. $139 double. Rates include tax and breakfast. AE, DC, MC, V. **Amenities:** 2 restaurants; bar; room service. *In room:* No phone.

Inexpensive

Hacienda Guachala **Value** Dating to 1580, this claims to be the oldest hacienda in Ecuador. It was here that García Moreno, who lived in the hacienda for 7 years, planted the first eucalyptus trees in Ecuador, many of which still flourish on the grounds. Rooms are more rustic than those at most of the other converted haciendas, but then again, the prices are substantially lower. All feature wood floors, high ceilings, and rough wood beds and furnishings. Nos. 1 through 10 are slightly newer in feel and comfort. All but two of the rooms feature working fireplaces. There's a small pool under a greenhouse roof, with tropical fruits and flowers planted around it. The hacienda's large church has been converted into a small museum that contains historic photos and some pre-Inca pottery, including huge Cayambe pots.

Pan-American Hwy., Km 70, on the road to Cangahua, Cayambe. ✆ **02/2363-042** or 09/8146-688. Fax 02/2362-426. www.guachala.com. 31 units. $35–$50 double. AE, DC, MC, V. Free parking. **Amenities:** Restaurant; small, covered pool. *In room:* No phone.

An Isolated & Historic Hacienda

Hacienda Zuleta ★★ **Finds** This elegant old hacienda belonged to the former president and diplomat Galo Plaza. Rooms are quite plush. Many face an open-air courtyard or small garden. The Galo room, which is in the oldest part of the hacienda, features exposed beams that date back to 1691. Be sure to ask to visit Plaza's personal library, an impressive two-story room containing historic memorabilia, a massive book and art collection, and a portrait of the former president painted by Guayasamín. The hotel is actively involved with the local community and has implemented a range of sustainable practices. The farm here produces excellent cheeses, and local women produce renowned embroidery works that are sold here. Horseback riding is taken seriously—their horses are well trained and beautiful, and a wide range of tours are available. Zuleta oversees a condor recovery project, where injured condors are cared for, and where wild condors often visit.

Angochahua, Imbabura. ✆ **06/2662-182.** www.zuleta.com. 15 units. $155–$299 per person. Rates include 3 meals daily, nonalcoholic drinks, guided tours and activities around the hacienda, and taxes. Children 2 and under free; children 3–12 50% discount. Slight discounts for multiday stays. AE, DC, MC, V. Free parking. **Amenities:** Restaurant; lounge; free mountain bikes. *In room:* No phone.

WHERE TO DINE

In addition to the places listed below, you can treat yourself to some fine dining, with advance reservations, at the restaurant at **La Mirage** (see above) or **Hacienda Cusín** (see above).

If you're looking for somewhere with a view, I suggest dining at a restaurant overlooking Lago San Pablo, a beautiful little lake considered sacred by the local indigenous populations. The restaurant of the **Hostería Puerto Lago,** Lago San Pablo and Pan-American Highway, Km 5/12, Otavalo (✆ **06/2920-920**), sits right on the lake and serves delicious, fresh grilled trout in addition to the usual Ecuadorian and Continental offerings. Almost every table has a lake view with magnificent Volcán Imbabura in the background.

Hotel Ali Shungu ★★ ECUADORIAN/INTERNATIONAL The cozy restaurant of this popular hotel is one of the best in the city. Heavy wooden tables are spread around the large central dining room, which features terra-cotta tile floors and a fireplace. Local and regional art and handicrafts serve as decor, and there's a small bar in one corner. The restaurant uses locally grown organic produce whenever possible. The tomato-basil soup is a house specialty and delicious. For a main dish, I recommend the Indian lamb curry or the spinach cheese pie. For lunch you can get excellent sandwiches on homemade bread, or one of their massive hamburgers. Breakfasts are also superb and worth it if you want a change from traditional Ecuadorian morning fare; this is the only place around where you can get fresh waffles with homemade raspberry syrup.

Calles Quito and Miguel Egas. ✆ **06/2920-750.** www.alishungu.com. Reservations recommended. Sandwiches $4.50–$6, main courses $7–$9. No credit cards. Daily 7am–8:30pm.

Restaurante Mi Otavalito ★ Finds ECUADORIAN This lively and popular place is my favorite option for local cuisine. The menu features a wide range of fish, meat, poultry, and specialty items. I especially like the simple grilled trout. For a real value, order the three-course daily special, which costs around $3.50. Tables are spread throughout several rooms connected by arched brick doorways. Some of the walls feature a mix of wood and woven mat paneling. There's a small brick fireplace in the back. During lunch and dinner most days, local bands play Andean folk music—they're working for tips, so don't be stingy.

Calle Sucre 11-19, near Calle Morales. ✆ **06/2920-176.** Reservations recommended on weekends. Main courses $5–$7. No credit cards. Daily 9am–9pm.

6 EL ORIENTE ★★

Lago Agrio: 259km (161 miles) NE of Quito, 674km (418 miles) NE of Guayaquil, 700km (434 miles) NE of Cuenca

The vast territory of Ecuador that stretches from the eastern slopes of the Andes to the border with Peru is known as El Oriente, which means "the East." This area contains over 25% of the nation's territory and is commonly called the Amazon region (Las Amazonas) because the rivers here—created by melting snow from the Andes—flow into the Amazon. The rainforests of El Oriente have been home to Native Americans for thousands of years. Because of the natural barrier formed by the Andes, the people here have lived in almost complete isolation. Some tribes have only had contact with the "outside world" since the 1970s, when oil was discovered. Since then, development has increased dramatically with the construction of roads by the oil industry. Various tribes inhabit Ecuador's Amazon basin, including the Shuar, Cofán, Huaorani, and Quichua. Their languages and lifestyle are markedly different from that of Ecuadorians on the opposite side of the Andes. When you take a trip to this region, you'll have the opportunity to meet some of the indigenous people, who will share their land with you and teach you some of their age-old secrets, such as how to farm, fish, hunt, or use medicinal herbs and plants.

Fifty-seven percent of all mammals in Ecuador live in the Amazon basin, and more than 15,000 species of plants exist in Ecuador's rainforest. On a trip here, you'll have the chance to see more than 500 different species of tropical birds, as well as freshwater dolphins, monkeys, sloths, anacondas, boas, turtles, and, if you're extremely lucky, the rare and elusive jaguars.

A healthy ecotourism business has developed here over the past couple of decades. Several excellent jungle lodges were built to blend in with the natural environment. Naturalist guides from these lodges take visitors on all sorts of excursions: walks through the forest to learn about the medicinal properties of the local plants; fishing trips to catch piranhas; early morning bird-watching expeditions to see parrots, macaws, and other tropical species; visits to traditional villages; nighttime canoe rides in search of caimans; and outings where you can paddle downriver in an old-fashioned canoe.

ESSENTIALS

Getting There

All the jungle lodges listed below arrange their own transportation. Because many of these lodges are extremely isolated and difficult to find, I strongly encourage you to book your trip in advance. Depending on where you're staying, the journey usually involves a commercial flight to Coca, Lago Agrio, or a private landing strip. From there, your lodge will pick you up and take you the rest of the way in a motorized canoe.

Orientation

El Oriente consists of six different provinces, but it is generally divided up into two general areas: the **northern Oriente** and the **southern Oriente.** The geographic distinctions between northern and southern Oriente are of little consequence to most tourists. All the lodges listed below are found in areas of pristine beauty and biological abundance, and are safe for tourists.

Trips to the jungle usually last 4 or 5 days. In general, the 4-day trips leave on Friday and return on Monday. The 5-day trips run from Monday through Friday.

In addition to the lodges listed below, I also recommend **Cuyabeno Lodge★** (www.neotropicturis.com) and **Sacha Lodge★** (www.sachalodge.com). For a distinct take on this region, book a berth aboard the riverboat **Manatee Amazon Explorer★** (www.manateeamazonexplorer.com).

Kapawi Ecolodge & Reserve ★★ Kapawi is an excellent example of sustainable tourism in action. This lodge has been developed with the cooperation and participation of the local Achuar community, who took over complete ownership of the lodge in 2010. All the structures here were built using traditional methods and environmentally friendly technology. The 20 cabins, which are set on stilts over a black-water lagoon, are rustic but comfortable, with polished wood floors, thatched roofs, and bamboo walls. After a day of hiking or canoeing, you can relax in a hammock on your balcony as you gaze down at the lagoon. The bathrooms are small, but the showers have solar-heated hot water (a rarity in the jungle), and the food here is delicious. In addition to the cozy accommodations and remote jungle setting, the lodge offers well-organized hikes and excursions. To get you here, the lodge will arrange a private charter flight on a light propeller plane.

On the Río Pastaza, Pastaza province (mailing address: Mariscal Foch E7-38 and Reina Victoria, Edificio Reina Victoria, Quito). ✆ **02/6009-333** reservations office in Quito. Fax 02/6009-334. www.kapawi.com. 19 units. Double occupancy 4 days/3 nights $695 per person; 8 days/7 nights $1,395 per person. Round-trip airfare from Shell $174 per person. Rates include meals, nonalcoholic beverages, guide services, and daily excursions. Rates do not include taxes or a $10 one-time fee, plus $2.50 per person per day, given to the Achuar community. Half price for children 11 and under, accompanied by 2 adults. AE, DC, MC, V. **Amenities:** Restaurant; bar; library. *In room:* No phone.

Napo Wildlife Center ★★★ *Finds* This is perhaps the best-run, and most environmentally and socially conscious, of the area's lodges. A joint venture with the local Añangu Quichua community, the Napo Wildlife Center is actively involved in conservation efforts. The lodge consists of 12 lakefront bungalows, which are large and come with one king-size bed in the main living area and a twin-size bed in a small nook separated by a half wall. There's also a hammock hung on each bungalow's private balcony overlooking the lake. A favorite of bird-watchers, the grounds here are home to two parrot licks. No motorized vehicles are allowed anywhere near the lodge, which is located inside the Yasuni National Park. This means from Coca it's a 2-hour motorboat ride on the Río Napo, then either a 2-hour paddle or 2km (1.2-mile) hike to the lodge.

On Añangu Lake, off the Lower Río Napo, Coca (Quito office: Calle de las Magnolias 51 y Los Cristantemos, Cumbaya, Quito). ✆ **866/750-0830** in the U.S., or 02/6005-819 reservation office in Quito. www.napowildlifecenter.com. 12 units. 4-day/3-night tour $720 per person; 5-day/4-night tour $920 per person. Rates include round-trip transportation from and to Coca, all meals and nonalcoholic beverages, daily tours, and taxes. AE, DC, MC, V. **Amenities:** Restaurant; bar. *In room:* No phone.

7 CUENCA ★★

442km (274 miles) S of Quito, 250km (155 miles) SE of Guayaquil, 254km (157 miles) S of Riobamba

Cuenca is Ecuador's third-largest city, but it feels much more like a charming old-world town—with cobblestone streets and a rich collection of colonial-era churches, plazas, and buildings. Before the Spanish arrived here, Cuenca was the second-largest city in the Inca

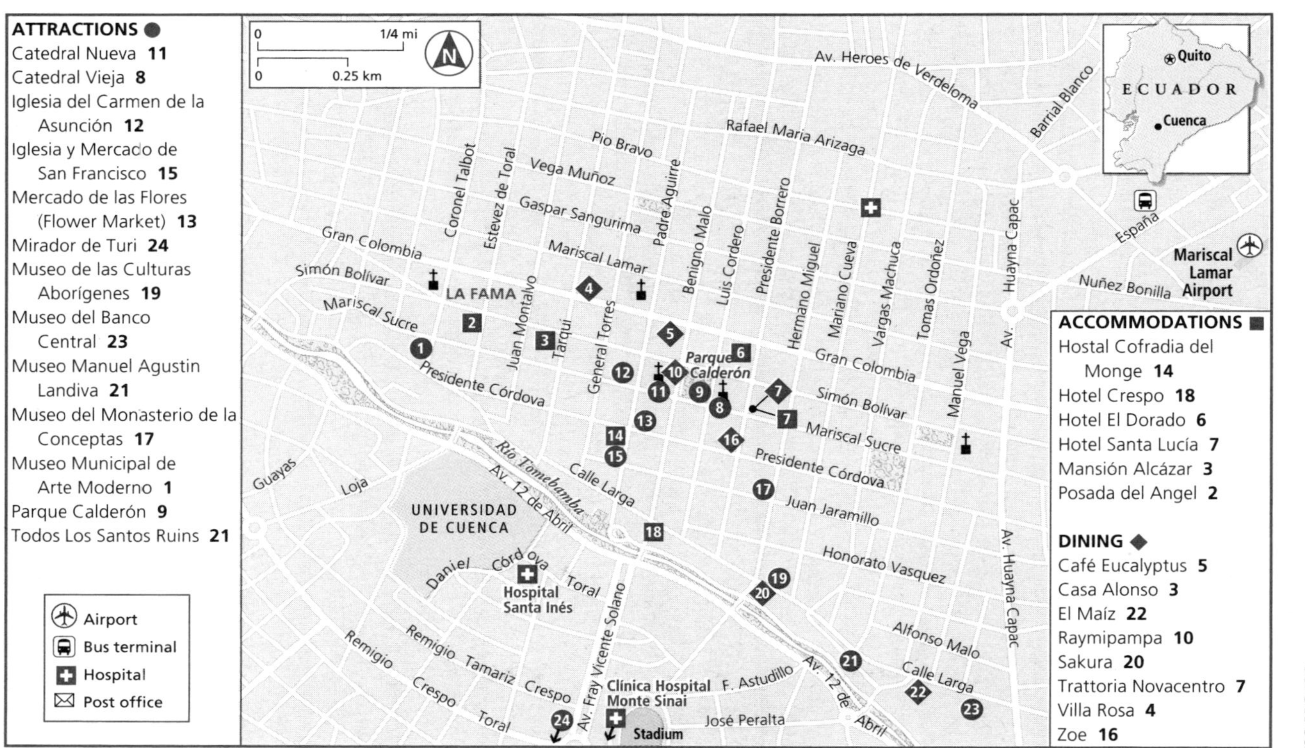
ATTRACTIONS
Catedral Nueva 11
Catedral Vieja 8
Iglesia del Carmen de la Asunción 12
Iglesia y Mercado de San Francisco 15
Mercado de las Flores (Flower Market) 13
Mirador de Turi 24
Museo de las Culturas Aborígenes 19
Museo del Banco Central 23
Museo Manuel Agustin Landiva 21
Museo del Monasterio de la Conceptas 17
Museo Municipal de Arte Moderno 1
Parque Calderón 9
Todos Los Santos Ruins 21
Airport
Bus terminal
Hospital
Post office
0 1/4 mi
0 0.25 km
N
ECUADOR
Quito
Cuenca
Av. Heroes de Verdeloma
Barrial Blanco
Rafael Maria Arizaga
Pio Bravo
Vega Muñoz
Gaspar Sangurima
Mariscal Lamar
Gran Colombia
Simón Bolívar
Mariscal Sucre
Presidente Córdova
Calle Larga
Juan Jaramillo
Honorato Vasquez
Alfonso Malo
Coronel Talbot
Estevez de Toral
Juan Montalvo
Tarqui
General Torres
Padre Aguirre
Benigno Malo
Luis Cordero
Presidente Borrero
Hermano Miguel
Mariano Cueva
Vargas Machuca
Tomas Ordoñez
Manuel Vega
Av. Huayna Capac
España
Nuñez Bonilla
Mariscal Lamar Airport
LA FAMA
Parque Calderón
Río Tomebamba
Av. 12 de Abril
UNIVERSIDAD DE CUENCA
Guayas
Loja
Daniel Córdova
Toral
Hospital Santa Inés
Remigio Tamariz Crespo
Remigio Crespo Toral
Av. Fray Vicente Solano
Clínica Hospital Monte Sinai
F. Astudillo
José Peralta
Stadium
ACCOMMODATIONS
Hostal Cofradia del Monge 14
Hotel Crespo 18
Hotel El Dorado 6
Hotel Santa Lucía 7
Mansión Alcázar 3
Posada del Angel 2
DINING
Café Eucalyptus 5
Casa Alonso 3
El Maíz 22
Raymipampa 10
Sakura 20
Trattoria Novacentro 7
Villa Rosa 4
Zoe 16

empire (after Cusco). In fact, when the Incas conquered the area, in the late 1400s, the Cañari had already been living here for centuries. The Incas—not unlike what the Spanish would eventually do—used stones from the Cañari structures to build their palaces. In time, these Incan palaces then became the foundations for the city's colonial-era churches and buildings. The **Museo del Banco Central** sits right next to the **Pumapungo** archaeological site, which was an Inca palace. A few blocks away, the **Todos Los Santos** archaeological site literally symbolizes the three layers of history—in one single area, you'll see structures built by Cañari, Incan, and Spanish settlers.

The mysterious Cañari (also spelled Kañari) people were the first known inhabitants of Cuenca, building a city here, around A.D. 500, called Guapondeleg. Their language and customs are largely a mystery, although several nearby villages do have names that end in *-deleg,* a common Cañari suffix. Around 1480 the Cañari were conquered by the Incas, who called the city Tomebamba, which is the current name of one of the rivers that runs through its center. Tomebamba was one of the preferred cities of Inca king Huayna Capac, who spent much time here. But the Incan reign was short-lived—they were vanquished by Pizarro and the Spanish conquistadors in 1534.

Outside Cuenca, there's also plenty to see and do. **Ingapirca,** for example, Ecuador's most impressive Inca ruins, are only 2 hours away; and **Cajas National Park,** which is full of scenic hiking trails and peaceful blue lagoons, is an hour north of the city. If you push yourself, you can visit Cuenca's top sites in just 1 day, but I recommend taking several days to really enjoy the city and its surrounding attractions.

ESSENTIALS

Getting There

BY PLANE **Tame** (✆ **02/3977-100** central reservation number, or 07/2889-581 in Cuenca; www.tame.com.ec) and **Aerogal** (✆ **1800/2376-425** toll-free nationwide; www.aerogal.com.ec) both offer daily flights to Cuenca from Quito and Guayaquil. **Icaro** (✆ **1800/883-567** toll-free nationwide; www.icaro.aero) has several daily flights between Quito and Cuenca. One-way tickets cost $50 to $70 to or from Guayaquil, and $60 to $90 to or from Quito. All planes arrive at the **Aeropuerto Mariscal LaMar** (✆ **07/2862-203;** airport code: CUE), which is located on Avenida España, about 1.6km (1 mile) northeast of downtown. Taxis are always waiting for incoming flights, and a ride from the airport to the center of town costs about $3.

BY BUS Cuenca is connected to the rest of Ecuador by frequent bus service. Several bus lines leave from Quito's **Terminal Terrestre Quitumbe** (✆ **02/2286-866**) at least every hour, around the clock, for the 8- to 10-hour ride. **Flota Imbabura** (✆ **02/2236-940** in Quito, or 07/2839-135 in Cuenca) and **Cooperativa Express Sucre** (✆ **02/2570-265**) are the main companies making this run. The fare runs around $10.

From Guayaquil, a cooperative of five different bus lines takes turns departing from the main bus terminal roughly every half-hour throughout the day. The buses use two different routes, alternating each departure either via Cajas or Cañar. The former route is faster, taking about 4 hours, while the latter route takes around 5 hours. The fare costs around $8.

The **Cuenca bus terminal** (✆ **07/2842-023**) is on Avenida España, about 1.6km (1 mile) northeast of the center of town, just before the airport. Taxis are always waiting here. A ride from the terminal to the center of town costs about $3.

Getting Around

Parque Calderón is the commercial and social heart of Cuenca. Most of Cuenca's sights are within walking distance of this main plaza. Still, taxis are abundant in Cuenca. A ride anywhere in town should cost no more than $2. If you can't flag one down, call **Radio Taxi Ejecutivo** (✆ **07/2809-605**).

Visitor Information

The main **tourist office** (✆ **07/2821-035**) is located on Mariscal Sucre on the south side of Parque Calderón. The friendly staff can give you maps and help you get your bearings. But for even better information, you should head to **TerraDiversa** ★, on Calle Hermano Miguel 5-42, 1½ blocks north of Calle Larga (✆ **07/2823-782;** www.terradiversa.com); or try **Hualambari Tours** ★, Av. Borrero 9-69, next to the post office (✆ **07/2830-037;** www.hualambari.com). The owners of TerraDiversa are former tour guides who know all of Ecuador like the backs of their hands, while Hualambari is the local representative of Grayline Tours. Both companies can provide a wealth of information and can arrange a wide variety of tours around Cuenca, the region, and the entire country.

FAST FACTS The main **police station** is located on Calle Luis Cordero, near Córdova (✆ **101**). The main office of the National Police is on Avenida Vallejo and Calle Espejo. You'll find the **post office** on the corner of Borrero and Gran Colombia (✆ **07/2838-111**). It's open Monday through Friday from 8am to 12:30pm and 2:30 to 6pm, and Saturday from 9am to noon. Banks and ATMs are ubiquitous in Cuenca; you'll find more than a half-dozen outlets within a block or two of Parque Calderón.

Clínica Hospital Monte Sinai, M. Cordero 6-111 and Avenida Solano (✆ **07/2885-595;** www.hospitalmontesinai.org), is the best hospital in Cuenca. **Fybeca** is a 24-hour pharmacy with several locations, including one at Bolívar 9-74 and Padre Aguire.

Internet cafes are abundant in Cuenca; two of my favorites are **Hol@net** (✆ **07/2843-126**), located at Borrero 5-90 and Juan Jaramillo, and **Cuenc@net Café** (✆ **07/2837-347**), on Calle Larga 602 and the corner of Hermano Miguel.

WHAT TO SEE & DO

Parque Calderon & Nearby Attractions

Parque Calderón is the historical heart of Cuenca and the center of the action. Here you'll find both the Catedral Nueva and the Catedral Vieja. The **Catedral Vieja (Old Cathedral)** ★, also known as the Iglesia del Sagrario, is the oldest structure in the city. Construction began in 1557 and utilized stones taken from the nearby Inca ruins of Pumapungo. Because cities can't have two cathedrals, once the Catedral Nueva opened in 1967, the old one went out of business, at least as a house of worship. Today, it houses a modest museum of religious art. The museum (no phone) is open Monday to Friday from 9am to 1pm and 2 to 6pm, and Saturday and Sunday from 10am to 1pm. Admission is $2.

Construction began on the **Catedral Nueva** ★★, also known as the Catedral de la Inmaculada Concepción, in 1885, but it wasn't completed for almost another 80 years. It has a mix of styles—Romanesque on the outside with Gothic windows—and is modeled on the Battistero (Baptistery) in Florence. The two massive blue domes are distinctive and visible from various vantage points around the city. The floors are made of white marble imported from Italy, while the stained-glass windows contain a mix of Catholic and indigenous symbols (the sun and the moon, for example). In 1985, when the pope visited this cathedral and saw the Renaissance-style main altar (which is modeled on the one in St. Peter's in Rome), he looked confused and asked, "Am I in Rome?"

Around the corner, on Padre Aguirre and Sucre, is the **Iglesia del Carmen de la Asunción.** The church is not open to the public, but from the outside you should take note of its unique stone entrance and neon-lit altar. The church sits on the delightful and colorful **Mercado de las Flores (Flower Market).** In the early part of the 20th century women weren't allowed to work. To create a diversion for them, the men of the city decided to set up this little market for the use of women only. Nowadays, anyone can wander around the fresh-smelling market. Ecuador is one of the world's largest exporters of flowers, and some beautiful varieties are found here. At the market, you'll find folk remedies for all sorts of illnesses, too. Nearby, on Presidente Córdova and Padre Aguirre, is the **Iglesia y Mercado de San Francisco.**

Museums & Other Points of Interest

In addition to the places mentioned below, if you're interested in archaeological finds, stop by the small **Todos Los Santos** archaeological site. Discovered in 1972, the short loop path here takes you through overlapping constructions by the Cañari, Inca, and Spanish cultures. As you walk the path, you will see the remains of massive Spanish milling stones, alongside an Inca-period wall with four of the style's classic trapezoidal niches, as well as pieces of wall that date to the era of the Cañari. The site is located at the intersection of Calle Large and Avenida Todos Los Santos (a few blocks down from the Museo del Banco Central). At the entrance to the site, you'll find the **Museo Manuel Agustin Landiva** (✆ **07/2842-586**), which has a small collection of archeological artifacts, and also serves as a gallery space for young Cuencan artists. The museum and archeological site are open Monday to Friday from 9am to 1pm and 3 to 6pm; and Saturdays from 9am to noon. Admission is $1.50.

For a bird's-eye view of Cuenca, take a taxi up to the **Mirador de Turi.** In Quichua, *turi* means twins, and from this sight you can see twin mountains in the distance. A taxi here should cost about $4 to $5 each way. You can—and really should—combine a visit here with a visit to the ceramic gallery **Taller E. Vega** (see below).

Museo de las Culturas Aborígenes ★ This amazing private collection includes more than 8,000 Ecuadorian archaeological pieces dating as far back as 500 B.C. Some of the most interesting are the pre-Inca urns that were used to bury the dead in an upright position, and the flutes made from the bones of different animals. The collection ranges far and wide, with works by the Valdivia, Machalilla, Tolita, Yasuni, and Quitis peoples. Near the entrance, there's an excellent gift shop and a pleasant little courtyard cafe and bakery.

Av. 10 de Agosto 4-70 and Rafael Torres Beltrán. ✆ **07/2839-181.** Admission $2. Mon–Fri 8:30am–noon and 1–6pm; Sat 9am–1pm.

Museo del Banco Central ★★ Kids This massive museum, archaeological site, small aviary, and botanical gardens is the pride and joy of Cuenca. The museum occupies several floors in a modern building next to the Central Bank building. Exhibits range from rooms filled with colonial and religious artwork, to walk-through re-creations of typical dwellings from the various regions of Ecuador, to an entire numismatic section that chronicles the country's currency from spondylus shells through the now-defunct sucre. The **Tomebamba Hall ★** is a highlight. The museum was constructed over the ruins of an Inca palace—Pumapungo—and in this room, you will learn the history of the Incas in Cuenca, as well as see archaeological artifacts found in the area. Afterwards, you can exit and walk behind the museum to see the actual archaeological site, which has a few llamas wandering around it. The complex is set on a high hillside, from which the views are wonderful. This museum complex is huge, and you really need 2 to 3 hours to see it. Groups of more than four people can ask for a free bilingual guide.

Calle Larga and Av. Huayna Capac. ✆ **07/2831-255.** Admission $3 adults, $1.50 children 6–18, children 5 and under free. Mon–Fri 9am–6pm; Sat 9am–1pm.

Museo del Monasterio de la Conceptas ★ This small museum was a former monastery. The nuns' rooms and common areas of the two-story adobe structure, which dates to the 17th century, are now all wonderfully curated art galleries; the theme is religious art. One of the highlights is an impressive collection of gruesome crucifixes by local artist Gaspar Sangurima. In one of these sculptures, you can see the carved heart through the gaping wounds in Christ's chest. The central courtyard is lushly planted and features a cherimoya tree that bears fruit each fall. Don't miss visiting the back patios, where you'll find the monastery's kitchen, as well as the old indoor cemetery with empty burial crypts.

Calle Hermano Miguel 6-33, between Presidente Córdova and Juan Jaramillo. ✆ **07/2830-625.** Admission $2.50, children 8–18 $1.50. Mon–Fri 9am–1pm and 3–5:30pm; Sat–Sun and holidays 10am–1pm.

Museo Municipal de Arte Moderno Art and sculpture adorn the many rooms and hallways of this old adobe home. It's hard to predict what type of art you'll see when you visit—there are no permanent exhibits. But the museum does display the best of Ecuadorian modern art—previous shows have included works by Guayasamín, Tábara, and Oswaldo Muñoz Mariño. The museum is also famous for hosting the Bienal Internacional de Pintura, a biannual exposition of Ecuadorian and American art. Even if you're not an art lover, it's nice to come here and relax in the peaceful colonial courtyard.

Calle Sucre 1527 and Coronel Tálbot. ✆ **07/2831-027.** Free admission. Mon–Fri 8:30am–1pm and 3–6:30pm; Sat 9am–1pm.

SPORTS & OUTDOOR ACTIVITIES

Cuenca may be Ecuador's third-largest city, but if you venture just a few miles outside the city center, you'll find yourself at one with nature. For the best hiking in the area, head to **Cajas National Park** (see "Side Trips from Cuenca," below). **Hualambari Tours ★** (✆ **07/2830-037;** www.hualambari.com) and **TerraDiversa ★** (✆ **07/2823-782;** www.terradiversa.com) both offer horseback-riding and mountain-biking expeditions through the outlying mountains and forests, stopping at small towns along the way. Day trips run $45 to $90 per person, including lunch, equipment, and transportation. Multiday trips and expeditions can also be arranged.

SHOPPING

Cuenca is a shopper's paradise. Ceramics and Panama hats are the best buys here, but, in general, you can find an excellent selection of folksy handicrafts, as well as some higher-end art and ceramic works.

ARTS & HANDICRAFTS Walk down any street in the center of Cuenca and you are sure to find scads of stores specializing in handmade crafts. I especially like **Arte con Sabor a Café ★** (✆ **07/2829-426**), a gallery, coffee shop, and bar with a good rotating selection of local art works and crafts; it's located on Paseo 3 de Bolívar 12-60 and Juan Montalvo. In the evenings, this place sometimes has live music.

CERAMICS For hundreds of years, Cuenca has been a center for ceramics. Walk into any museum in the area (see above), and you'll see examples of beautiful pre-Inca jugs and vases. **Artesa ★★**, at the corner of Gran Colombia and Luis Cordero (✆ **07/2842-647**), keeps the tradition alive. This is the best place in the city for hand-painted ceramics.

For a more personalized experience, I recommend visiting **Taller E. Vega ★★**, located just below the Mirador de Turi (✆ **07/2881-407;** www.eduardovega.com). Eduardo Vega is a ceramicist and one of Ecuador's most famous artists. Monumental ceramic sculptures and murals by Vega can be found around Cuenca, as well as in Quito. A visit to his hillside workshop and gallery is worthwhile just for the views, but you'll also have a chance to glimpse a bit of his production process, and to buy from his regularly changing collection of decorative and functional works, handicrafts, and wonderful jewelry. Most organized city tours stop here. If you're coming to Taller E. Vega on your own, I recommend calling in advance to be sure it's open.

PANAMA HATS You may be surprised to know that Panama hats have always been made in Ecuador: For generations, the people on the coast have been using local straw to create finely woven hats. The trade was moved inland, and Cuenca is now the major hub for the production of Panama hats. **Homero Ortega P. & Hijos ★★★** makes the highest-quality Panama hats in the world; patrons include the queen of England. You can visit the factory and learn how the hats are made, and afterwards you can browse in the elegant boutique. The store is located a few minutes outside the center of town, at Av. Gil Ramírez Dávalo 3-86 (✆ **07/2809-000;** www.homeroortega.com). **Sombreros Barranco,** at Calle Larga 10-41, between General Torres and Padre Aguirre (✆ **07/2831-569**), and **K. Dorfzaun ★**, Av. Gil Ramírez Cávalos 4-34 (✆ **07/2807-537;** www.kdorfzaun.com), also sell finely crafted hats. Panama hats in Cuenca vary greatly in price and quality, running from around $10 to $12 for a basic version, to around $150 to $250 for a *super fino.*

WHERE TO STAY

Expensive

Hotel El Dorado ★★ The El Dorado is bold and brash, and quite a contrast to the rest of colonial Cuenca. A glass-and-steel staircase leads up to the rooms, and several waterfalls are scattered around the building. The rooms—all spacious and well lit, have a clean and minimalist decor. The presidential suite is a two-room affair with a Jacuzzi tub, glass sinks, and elegant bathroom fixtures; a Zen-style water fountain on the writing desk; and a small Buddha sculpture on the bureau. Several floors have been designated smoke-free, and there's one very well-set-up room for travelers with disabilities. There's a small spa here, too, which covers the necessary bases, but isn't quite as large or well equipped as I would have expected. On the ground floor is a large, chic restaurant with nothing but full-length walls of glass separating it from the busy sidewalk outside.

Gran Colombia 7-87 and Luis Cordero, Cuenca. ✆ **07/2831-390.** Fax 07/2831-663. www.eldoradohotel.com.ec. 42 units. $100 double; $125 junior suite; $150 presidential suite. Rates include buffet breakfast. AE, DC MC, V. Free parking. **Amenities:** Restaurant; bar; babysitting; small, well-equipped health club; room service; sauna; smoke-free rooms; steam room. *In room:* TV, hair dryer, minibar, free Wi-Fi.

Mansión Alcázar ★★ This is an elegant oasis in the heart of Cuenca. A beautifully tiled enclosed courtyard with a fountain leads to plush accommodations on two floors. Each room is unique in size and decor, but they all have one thing in common: Every piece of furniture was made in Cuenca. Elegant antiques and fine objets d'art give the rooms that old colonial feel. The suites have wrought-iron four-poster beds; no. 207 has a mural of angels on its ceiling, but no. 202 is my favorite, with a view over the garden. Bathrooms boast Cuencan marble and each one has distinctly hand-painted walls. I think it's worth the splurge for one of the suites, as several of the standard rooms, especially those on the first floor, are quite small. The beautiful restaurant here (p. 574) overlooks the garden and there are a few tables outside for alfresco dining on warm days.

Calle Bolívar 12-55 and Tarqui, Cuenca. ✆ **800/327-3573** toll-free in the U.S. and Canada, or 07/2823-918 in Ecuador. Fax 07/2823-554. www.mansionalcazar.com. 14 units. $150 double; $200 suite. Rates include full breakfast and afternoon tea. AE, DC, MC, V. Free parking. **Amenities:** Restaurant; bar; lounge; room service; free Wi-Fi. *In room:* TV, hair dryer.

Moderate

Hotel Crespo The building housing this Cuenca hotel is more than 140 years old, and built on the steep hillside leading down to the Río Tomebamba. The rambling structure covers some five stories, and there's no elevator, so ask for a room close to the lobby if climbing several flights is a problem for you. The rooms have an old-fashioned charm, with wood paneling, dark furniture, and colorful hand-painted moldings and antique tin–like ceilings, although some feel a bit dated in their furnishings and decor. The bathrooms feature marble tiles, lots of counter space, and a second telephone. The best rooms have views of the river down below. Room no. 408 is my favorite—it has both river and mountain views. Overall, this is a good choice but not nearly as elegant or as intimate as Mansión Alcázar (see above) or the Santa Lucía (see below).

Calle Larga 7-93, Cuenca. ✆ **07/2842-571.** Fax 07/2839-473. www.hotel-crespo.com. 39 units. $89 double. Rates include full breakfast and airport transfers. AE, DC MC, V. **Amenities:** Restaurant; bar; room service; free Wi-Fi. *In room:* TV, hair dryer, minibar.

Hotel Santa Lucía ★★★ Finds The Hotel Santa Lucía is housed in a wonderfully restored downtown mansion that dates to 1859. Throughout, you'll enjoy the meticulous attention to detail—in both the decor and service. The large, enclosed courtyard, which contains a 100-year-old magnolia tree and beautiful baby palms, leads to spacious, comfortable accommodations. Rooms come with plasma-screen televisions, and the suites have sleeping lofts, hardwood floors, and Persian carpets. Room no. 212 has a view of the cathedral, and a small, private balcony overlooking the street. All but four of the spacious bathrooms have tubs, and many feature multiheaded spa showers. On the second floor, there's a huge salon with a fireplace for guests to gather around; antiques adorn the hallways and fresh flowers are arranged daily. The courtyard Trattoria Novacentro (see below) serves authentic Italian cuisine, while the cozy street-side **Bacchus Café** is very popular for its inexpensive Ecuadorian meals.

Antonio Borrero 8-44 and Sucre, Cuenca. ✆ **07/2828-000.** Fax 07/2842-443. www.santaluciahotel.com. 20 units. $99 double; $125 suite. Rates include full breakfast and tax. AE, DC, MC, V. Parking nearby. **Amenities:** 2 restaurants; lounge; room service. *In room:* TV, hair dryer, minibar, free Wi-Fi.

Inexpensive

In addition to the place listed below, the **Hostal Cofradia del Monge** (✆/fax **07/2831-251;** www.cofradiadelmonje.com) is an excellent boutique option just across from the Plaza San Francisco.

Posada del Angel Value The Posada del Angel is a whimsical, airy place. Bright yellow and blue are the themes here. You enter through a large enclosed courtyard, and most of the rooms, which come in all shapes and sizes, are found around the first two floors. All are simply furnished and very clean, and all but three have beautiful hardwood floors. Some rooms have wrought-iron lamps made in Cuenca and attractive wooden armoires. The tiled bathrooms are tiny but sparkling. If you're looking for some privacy, ask for one of the remote rooms located on the third or fourth floors. Free Internet access at a few computers is available for guests in the lobby. Several lounge areas and covered courtyards are spread around the rambling structure.

Bolívar 14-11 and Estévez de Toral, Cuenca. ✆ **07/2840-695.** ✆/fax 07/2821-360. www.hostalposadadelangel.com. 22 units. $42–$45 double. Rates include full breakfast. MC, V. Free parking. **Amenities:** Lounge; Wi-Fi. *In room:* TV.

WHERE TO DINE

Cuenca has excellent restaurants, inviting cafes, and wonderful bakeries so you'll eat well here. In addition to the places listed below, there's plenty of street food available all over town. You'll see *cuy* (guinea pig) and whole pigs on spits, or recently roasted, as well as empanadas and *llapingachos,* all for sale by street vendors. While not an option for those with sensitive stomachs, if you've got a sturdy intestinal tract, this is a tasty and inexpensive way to go.

Moderate

In addition to the places below, I enjoy the fine Italian cuisine served up at **Trattoria Novacentro** ★★ (✆ **07/2828-000**) in a refined and romantic setting inside the Hotel Santa Lucía (see above). Sushi lovers will want to head to **Sakura** (✆ **07/2827-740**) at the bottom of the stairway on Calle Larga at Hermano Miguel. The new hip restaurant and bar **Zoe,** at Borrero 7-61 between Sucre and Cordova (✆ **07/2841-005**), has been getting good reviews. Finally, for an elegant and refined meal, try **Casa Alonso** ★★ (✆ **07/2823-889**), which serves up classy old-world cuisine at the hotel Mansión Alcázar (see above).

Villa Rosa ★★★ Finds ECUADORIAN/INTERNATIONAL Cuenca's top restaurant is owned and managed by the friendly Berta Vintimilla. Set in the enclosed courtyard of an old Cuencan home, the creative cuisine here has its roots in Ecuador. Mrs. Vintimilla bakes the delicious empanadas herself, and they are excellent as an appetizer; the recipes for many of the Ecuadorian specials come from her family. Main courses include sea bass with crab sauce served with rice and vegetables, tenderloin of beef, jumbo langoustines with fennel, and a variety of daily specials. The service is excellent, the wine list is reasonable, and every ingredient used in the kitchen is of the highest quality. Note that the restaurant is closed on weekends, except for groups of a substantial size who have made prior reservations.

Gran Colombia 12-22 and Tarqui. ✆ **07/2837-944.** Reservations recommended. Main courses $6–$15. AE, DC, MC, V. Mon–Fri noon–3pm and 7–10:30pm.

Inexpensive

Café Eucalyptus ★★ Finds TAPAS/INTERNATIONAL This is Cuenca's most happening restaurant and bar. There's seating on two floors—head upstairs if you want to find a somewhat quieter table, or stick to the main floor and bar area to people-watch and mingle. The food here is tapas-style and tapas-size; most folks order several and share. Selections are truly international (more than 50 dishes from 20 countries) and include hot Cuban sandwiches, cheese quesadillas, pad Thai, and stuffed peppers with rice, raisins, and parsley. This is the only place in the city to offer sushi and sashimi, although the rest of their menu is much better. The liquor and wine selection is quite impressive, and there are a number of wine choices by the glass. Eucalyptus also has the only draft beer in the city, including Llama Negra, which is made in Quito and is a dark stout beer like a Guinness.

Gran Colombia 9-41 and Benigno Malo. ✆ **07/2849-157.** www.cafeeucalyptus.com. Tapas $4.50–$12. AE, DC, MC, V. Sun and Tues–Thurs 5–11pm; Fri–Sat 5pm–1am.

El Maíz ★ ECUADORIAN Set in a beautifully renovated old house, with a lovely outdoor patio for alfresco dining, this is a great place to come for local cooking. There are actually two outdoor seating areas: a lower patio, with colorful tiles, overlooking a courtyard full of plants, and an upper terrace with a lovely view of the green hills. The indoor dining room features wood floors and red tablecloths. Appetizers include the usual offerings of *humitas,* empanadas, and *locro de papas.* The main courses are terrific and unique. My favorites include the chicken in pumpkinseed-and–white wine sauce, beef medallions in a pear sauce, and *hornado cuencano* (roasted pork served with *llapingachos*). Rotating monthly specials are tied to national holidays and celebrations. For dessert, try the *almíbar de babaco* (a compote of a local fruit, tart and sweet).

Calle Larga 1-279 and Calle de los Molinos. ✆ **07/2840-224.** Main courses $4.50–$9. MC, V. Mon–Sat noon–9pm.

Raymipampa ★ Value ECUADORIAN/CUENCAN This popular local institution is located right next to the new cathedral. The cozy dining room features a loft area with tables under a low ceiling made of exposed log beams over much of the main dining area. The walls feature imitation baroque bas-reliefs. I like grabbing a table near the front windows, which have a view of Parque Calderón. The menu features a range of meat, poultry, and seafood. You can also get traditional Ecuadorian fare, such as *humitas* and *tamales de maíz.* I like the complete breakfast, which is an excellent deal at $2, including coffee, fresh juice, two eggs, two fresh-baked croissants, and local cheese. Broken plates and bent silverware have been fashioned into an interesting little sculpture hanging near the entrance.

Benigno Malo 8-59, between Sucre and Bolívar. ✆ **07/2834-159.** Reservations not accepted. Main courses $3.50–$6. MC, V. Daily 8:30am–11pm.

CUENCA AFTER DARK

Cuenca used to be a sleepy, provincial city, but local young folk and visiting tourists have turned this into a respectable little party city. For quiet drinking and conversation, **Wunderbar Café** ★, right off the stairs below Calle Larga and Hermano Miguel (✆ **07/2831-274**), and **La Parola** ★★, on Calle Larga and the Escalinata (✆ **09/9910-234**), are both popular spots. Early birds will appreciate the Wunderbar Café's happy hour, which begins at 11am and runs until 7pm, while you really can't beat the views from the open-air patio of La Parola. Cuenca's top bar and hangout is **Eucalyptus** ★★ (see above), which has a popular ladies' night every Wednesday and a rowdy salsa night every Saturday. Other good spots for mingling with the local crowd include **Tal Cual** (✆ **07/2801-459**) and **Sankt Florian** (✆ **07/2833-359**), both on Calle Larga, near the Hotel Crespo (p. 573), and **Tinku** ★ (✆ **07/2838-520**), on Calle Larga at the corner of Alfonso Jerves.

For live music, head to the **San Angel** ★, on Hermano Miguel at the corner of Presidente Córdova (✆ **07/2839-090**), or **Blanco & Tinto,** on Av. Jose Peralta 2-132 and Cordero (✆ **07/2455-196**). On any given night, both of these places might have anything from a folk singer or small combo to a DJ spinning electronic dance tunes.

If you're looking to go dancing, **La Mesa Salsoteca** ★, on Gran Colombia between Machuca and Ordóñez (✆ **07/2833-300**), is the best place in town, with a heavy mix of salsa, meringue, and other tropical rhythms.

Note: Many venues are only open Wednesday to Saturday. Sunday, Monday, and Tuesday are quiet nights in Cuenca and hardly anybody ventures out late. Covers are sometimes charged and usually range from $2 to $6, which may include a drink or two.

Hualambari Tours ★ (✆ **07/2830-037;** www.hualambari.com), **TerraDiversa** ★ (✆ **07/2823-782;** www.terradiversa.com), and **Metropolitan Touring** (✆ **07/2837-000;** www.metropolitan-touring.com) all offer a wide range of day trips out of Cuenca, including trips to the two attractions listed below.

Parque Nacional Cajas (Cajas National Park) ★★

After you've seen the museums and historic sights in Cuenca, it's great to get away from the city and immerse yourself in the area's natural wonders. Cajas is only about 32km (20 miles) west of the city (about a 1-hr. drive), but it feels worlds away. Covering about 29,000 hectares (71,660 acres), the park has 232 lakes. The terrain and ecosystems are varied here, allowing for an impressive variety of flora and fauna. In high-elevation cloud forests, bird species range from the masked trogon and gray-breasted mountain toucan, to the majestic Andean condor. The famed Inca Trail runs right through the park. One of my favorite hikes is up **Tres Cruces,** which offers spectacular views of the area and the opportunity to see the Continental Divide. I also recommend the hike around Laguna Quinoa Pato; the vistas of the lake are impressive, and as you walk on the trails you'll have a good chance of spotting ducks. From the main visitor center, you can explore the flora of the humid mountain-forest climate—mosses, orchids, fungi, and epiphytes are common. ***Note:*** It can get extremely cold here, so wear warm clothing.

GETTING THERE & VISITING THE PARK Cajas is huge, and much of its wildlife is elusive. I highly recommend exploring the park with a guide. Both Hualambari and Terra Diversa (p. 569) have excellent naturalist guides. If you want to go on your own, head to the main terminal in Cuenca and catch any Guayaquil-bound bus that takes the route via Molleturo and Cajas. These buses leave roughly every hour throughout the day. Ask to be dropped off at La Toreadora. Return buses run on a similar schedule and are easy to catch from the main road outside the visitor center. Admission to the park is $10 for adults and $5 for children 11 and under. If you have any questions, call the park office (✆ **07/2829-853**).

Ingapirca ★

Ingapirca is the largest pre-Columbian architectural complex in Ecuador. However, anyone familiar with the massive ruins of Machu Picchu or of the Mesoamerican Maya will find this site small and simple by comparison. The Incas arrived here around 1470. Before then, the Cañari people had inhabited the area. It's believed that both the Cañari and Incas used Ingapirca as a religious site. When the Incas conquered the area, they ordered all Cañari men to move to Cuzco. In the meantime, Inca men took up residence with Cañari women, as a means of imposing Inca beliefs on the local culture. In the end, Ingapirca shows a mix of Cañari and Inca influences. For example, many of the structures here are round or oval-shaped, which is very atypical of the Incas. In fact, Ingapirca is home to the only oval-shaped sacred Inca palace in the world.

Ingapirca means "the wall of the Inca," and you can see some fine examples of the famed Inca masonry here. The highlight of the site is **El Adoratorio/Castillo,** an elliptical structure which is believed to be a temple to the sun. Nearby are the **Aposentos,** rooms made with tight stonework, thought to have been used by the high priests. Most of the remains from the Cañari culture have been found at **Pilaloma,** at the south end of the site (near where you first enter). Pilaloma means "small hill," and some archaeologists surmise that this was a sacred spot, especially because it is the highest point in the area. Eleven bodies (most of them women) have been found here—perhaps the circle of stones was some sort of tomb. On a hill behind the entrance, near the parking area, is a small museum with a relief map of the site and a collection of artifacts and relics found here.

This site is administered and run by the local community. Llamas graze among the archaeological ruins. If you're lucky enough to visit before or after the large tour buses arrive, you'll find the place has a very peaceful vibe to it.

GETTING THERE The site (✆ **07/2215-115**) is open daily from 8am to 6pm; admission is $6. It's best to visit Ingapirca with an experienced guide because most of the resident guides here do not speak English, and all the explanations inside the museum are in Spanish only. A full-day trip to Ingapirca out of Cuenca, including transportation, lunch, and guided tour of the ruins, but not the admission fee, should cost $30 to $45. If you want to go to Ingapirca on your own, catch a bus from the main bus terminal in Cuenca. **Cooperativa Cañar** (✆ **07/2844-033**) operates buses that stop at the site; they depart at 9am and 1pm, and the 2-hour ride costs $3 each way. The return buses leave Ingapirca at 1 and 4pm. On weekends there's only the 9am bus, which returns at 1pm.

8 GUAYAQUIL

250km (155 miles) NW of Cuenca; 420km (260 miles) SW of Quito; 966km (618 miles) east of the Galápagos

Guayaquil is Ecuador's most populous and vibrant city. Still, many visitors to Ecuador only look upon Guayaquil as a necessary overnight stop on the way to the Galápagos Islands. But that is changing, and the city continues to reinvent itself at a dizzying pace. At the helm since 2000, Mayor Jaime Nebot has instituted a far-reaching urban renewal project that has already had impressive results. The **Malecón Simón Bolívar,** the city's main riverfront promenade, and the colorful neighborhoods of **Cerro Santa Ana (Santa Ana Hill)** and **Las Peñas** are emblematic of Nebot's plan. Whereas crime was once rampant and problematic, Guayaquil is now a relatively safe and tourist-friendly city. Perhaps the city's greatest challenge facing visitors is the sometimes oppressive heat and humidity. Nevertheless, if you avoid the midday heat, you'll find the early mornings, late afternoons, and evenings all very agreeable for taking in the city's pleasures.

Although Guayaquil was founded in 1537, it lacks the colonial architecture that you find in Quito and Cuenca. A devastating fire ravaged the city in 1896, almost completely leveling it. Virtually no buildings escaped the blaze, and today the city has a more modern and contemporary feel than any other major city in Ecuador.

ESSENTIALS

Getting There

BY PLANE All international and national flights arrive at the **José Joaquín de Olmedo International Airport** (✆ **04/2391-603;** airport code: GYE), which is located about 10 minutes north of downtown Guayaquil, just next door to the now-defunct Simón Bolívar International Airport. Many international flights to Quito first touch down in Guayaquil, and outgoing international flights also often stop in Guayaquil to pick up and discharge passengers.

Icaro (✆ **1800/883-567** toll-free nationwide; www.icaro.aero), **Tame** (✆ **02/3977-100** central reservations number in Quito, or 04/2310-305 in Guayaquil; www.tame.com.ec), and **Aerogal** (✆ **1800/2376-425** toll-free; www.aerogal.com.ec) all offer numerous daily flights between Guayaquil and Quito. Tame and Aerogal also offer a couple of daily flights between Guayaquil and Cuenca. One-way tickets range from $60 to $90 to or from Quito, and from $60 to $70 to or from Cuenca.

As you exit the Customs area in the international arrivals area, there is a desk with friendly staff who will arrange a taxi for you. You pay at the desk and receive a voucher, which you then present to a driver, who will be waiting for you once you exit the terminal. A taxi to the downtown area should cost no more than $9.

BY BUS The bus station, **Terminal Terrestre Jaime Roldos Aguilera** (✆ **04/2140-166**), is a few minutes north of the airport. From Quito, buses leave the **Terminal Terrestre Quitumbe** (✆ **02/2286-866**) at least every half-hour for Guayaquil; the 8-hour ride costs $10. Buses from Cuenca leave on a very frequent schedule as well; the 5-hour bus ride costs $8.

Getting Around

Guayaquil is a relatively compact city, and it's easy to walk most places around the downtown and Malecón Simón Bolívar. However, a fair amount of the hotels, shopping centers, and restaurants are outside of the downtown area. In Guayaquil, **taxis** are the cheapest and most efficient way to get around. It's easy to find them on any street corner. If you can't flag one down, call **Cooperativa de Taxis Bucaram** (✆ **04/2403-592**), **Cooperativa de Taxis Centro Cívico** (✆ **04/2450-145**), or **Cooperativa de Taxis Paraíso** (✆ **04/2201-877**). Rides within the center of the city cost only $2 to $6.

Visitor Information

The Guyas Province has a **tourist information office** (✆ **04/2684-274**) on the eighth floor of the Edificio Gobierno del Litoral, on Avenida Francisco de Orellana, out near the Hilton. The office is open Monday through Friday from 8:30am to 5pm, and provides a city map as well as other useful information on tours and attractions. There's also a helpful **information booth** beside the Museo Nahin Isaias in the center of town that is run by the municipality of Guayaquil, and is open Tuesday to Saturday from 9am to 5pm (no phone).

FAST FACTS In an emergency, dial ✆ **911.** To dial the police, call ✆ **101,** and for the Cruz Roja (Red Cross) ✆ **131.** The main **post office** is on Clemente Ballén and Pedro Carbo. Most banks in Guayaquil are clustered around the intersection of Pedro Icaza and General Córdova; you'll find branches of **Banco del Pichincha** and **Banco de Guayaquil** here. You'll also find ATMs all over the city and in all the modern malls and shopping centers.

The best hospital in Guayaquil is the **Hospital Clínica Kennedy** (✆ **04/2289-666;** www.hospikennedy.med.ec), which actually has three facilities in town. There are hundreds of other pharmacies around Guayaquil. The chain **Pharmacy's** (✆ **1800/9090-909**) has various outlets, is open 24 hours, and offers delivery.

There are scores of Internet cafes in Guayaquil. Rates run around 50¢ to $1.50 per hour.

WHAT TO SEE & DO

If you're short on time, it's still possible to get a feel for Guayaquil rather quickly, since the important attractions are quite close together (see "If You're Short on Time," below, for more information).

The **Malecón Simón Bolívar** ★★ is the shining star of the new and improved Guayaquil. Also sometimes called the Malecón 2000, it's impressive to enter from Avenida 9 de Octubre, where you are greeted by a 1937 statue of the independence heroes Simón Bolívar

and San Martín shaking hands. On either side of the statue, you can climb up lookout towers, which afford great views of the city and the river. Walk south and you'll hit the Moorish Clock Tower, Glorious Aurora's Obelisk, a McDonald's, a minimall, and tons of inexpensive food stalls. As you head in this direction, look across the street: You'll see the impressive neoclassical Palacio Municipal. If you walk north from the Bolívar-Martín statue, you'll come across a lively playground and an exercise course.

On the western end of Avenida 9 de Octubre is a separate, newer riverside promenade, along the narrow Estero Salado (Salt Water Estuary), known appropriately as the **Malecón del Estero Salado** ★. Like its more extravagant brethren, the Malecón here is a pleasant riverside pedestrian walkway sprinkled with little parks and plazas, benches for resting, and a few restaurants, shops, and food stands.

In addition to the Malecón Simón Bolívar, Malecón Salado, and attractions listed below, you can visit a few parks and an interesting cemetery. **Parque Seminario** ★ dates from 1880, and is adjacent to the city's principal church, a neo-Gothic cathedral whose most recent and primary construction dates from 1948. Parque Seminario is also called Iguana Park because a healthy population of these prehistoric-looking reptiles inhabit its trees and grounds. Much larger, **Parque Centenario** is in the middle of the city, bisected

If You're Short on Time

Many visitors find themselves with only a few hours in Guayaquil as they connect to or from the Galápagos. If you fall into that category, don't despair: You can still get a good feel for the city in just a few hours.

Grab a cab (or walk, if you're close) from your hotel to the **Malecón Simón Bolívar.** The Malecón area is ideally enjoyed on foot, so prepare yourself for a good 3.2km (2-mile) hike and bring protection from the sun. It's best to begin at the southern end, the corner of the Malecón and Avenida Olmedo. Here you can browse the shops selling local artifacts, and the boardwalk is breezy and airy on this end. As you walk north, you'll find many food shops (and more people). Take a break halfway; most of the food stalls here sell freshly squeezed juice that makes an excellent pick-me-up; small bottles of water are also readily available and there are impressively clean public restrooms here, too. At the end of the Malecón, just past the MAAC (see below), you'll find **Las Peñas** ★ neighborhood—a narrow street filled with art galleries and funky shops. After you walk around Las Peñas, climb to the top of **Cerro Santa Ana** ★★ to get a fantastic view of the entire city, the river, and the surrounding countryside. You'll find many places to eat and drink on the stairs leading up to the top. This is one of the city's safest areas, with specially trained tourist police patrolling the stairs day and night.

by Avenida 9 de Octubre. This park is a very popular lunchtime spot for downtown workers and is a pleasant place to relax and people-watch.

One good way to get a feel for the city is to hop on one of the red double-decker tourist buses run by **Guayaquil Vision** (✆ **04/2885-800**). These folks offer several options, including a 1½-hour loop around and through the city, passing its most important landmarks, as well as a 3-hour Gran Guayaquil tour, which makes three stops for visits at Las Peñas, Parque Seminario, and the handicraft market. Fares run around $5 per adult and $3 for children, students, and seniors for the basic loop trip; and $15 per adult, $12 for children, students, and seniors for the Gran Guayaquil tour.

Museo Antropológico y de Arte Contemporáneo (Museum of Anthropology and Contemporary Art) ★★ Commanding a spectacular location on the tip of the Malecón, this large and impressive museum is known locally as the MAAC. It focuses on the archaeological finds from around Ecuador (including some relatively recent discoveries from the coastal regions). However, one wing is dedicated to a large collection of Ecuadorian contemporary art, as well as to a smattering of international artists. Constantly changing temporary exhibits focus on local contemporary artists—usually accompanied by short films about those artists, which are quite interesting and worth your while. A library, a bookstore, and a pleasant cafe are also on-site. It will take you about 2 hours to visit the museum, though plan to spend a little longer if you are interested in the archaeological finds and the films about the artists.

Malecón Simón Bolívar and Calle Loja. ✆ **04/2309-383.** Admission $1.50; free Sun and holidays. Tues–Sat 10am–5:30pm; Sun and holidays 11am–5:30pm.

Museo Presley Norton (Presley Norton Museum) ★ This museum runs a close second to the MAAC as my favorite museum in Guayaquil. Like at the MAAC, *all* the exhibits here have explanations both in English and Spanish. Formerly called the Museo Archeologico del Banco del Pacifico and sporting a new location, this museum houses a small but excellent collection of archeological relics. The most interesting artifacts come from the Chorrera Period (1000–300 B.C.). Keep an eye out for the double-chambered whistling bottle and the descriptive figurines from this period.

Corner of Av. 9 de Octubre and Carchi. © **04/2293-423.** Free admission. Tues–Sat 10am–6pm.

Parque Histórico Guayaquil ★ (Kids) This historical theme park is a great place to spend a morning or afternoon, and to learn more about Guayaquil and Ecuador. You can walk along a raised pathway through several distinct ecosystems, with various native fauna and flora on display. You will also pass through rows of different banana plants (Ecuador is the world's largest banana exporter) and a tiny cacao plantation. Historic buildings and street scenes are recreated throughout the grounds. A traditional country house replicates how rural farmers lived and what farming utensils they used. In the courtyard of a beautiful old hacienda, plays, staged twice daily, depict life on a farm in the 19th century. The boardwalk here is dubbed Malecón 1900, and gives you a glimpse into how the city looked some 100 years ago. An old-fashioned bakery and cafe serves traditional dishes in a lovely outdoor setting. An old trolley completes the picture. I recommend coming here on a weekday if possible; weekends can be very crowded.

Vía Samborondón, between Av. Esmeraldas and Central. © **04/2832-958.** www.parquehistoricoguayaquil.com. Wed–Sat $3 adults; $1.50 children 6–12; children 5 and under free; Sun and holidays $4.50 adults, $3 children 6–12, children 5 and under free. Wed–Fri 9am–4:30pm; Sat–Sun and holidays 10am–5:30pm.

SHOPPING

The **Mercado Artesanal,** on Baquerizo Moreno, between calles Loja and Juan Montalvo (© **04/2306-266**), is the best place to buy local handicrafts. You'll find over 150 stalls and shops run by area businesspeople as well as by the artisans themselves. Everything from tagua nut—also called vegetable ivory—carvings to Otavaleño textiles to Panama hats and ceramics is available.

There's a similar, albeit much smaller, artisan's market at the southern end of the Malecón Simón Bolívar. I recommend you try to support the craft works of **Pro Pueblo** ★ (© **04/2683-598;** www.propueblo.com), a local, fair-trade cooperative of artisans from around the region. Their work is sold at shops at this artisans market, and at their large collection point in the coastal village of San Antonio, as well as online.

As a throbbing metropolis, Guayaquil is full of modern shopping malls that include the **San Marino Mall** (© **04/2083-180**), **Mall del Sur** (© **04/2085-110**), and **Mall del Sol** (© **04/2690-100**). Each has scores of shops, a couple of department stores, a food court and independent restaurants, and a multiplex cinema.

WHERE TO STAY

Very Expensive

If there's no space at the hotel below, the **Four Points Sheraton** ★★ (© **04/2691-888;** www.sheraton.com), and **Hotel Colón Guayaquil** ★★ (© **800/445-8667** in the U.S., or 04/2689-000 in Ecuador; www.guayaquil.hilton.com) are both good options.

Hotel Oro Verde Guayaquil ★★★ Extensive and comprehensive remodeling and upgrades have made this the top luxury hotel in Guayaquil. Rooms are spacious and have recessed lighting, laminated wood floors, and marble bathrooms. All the standard rooms are up to snuff, but try to land one of the corner units, which are a bit bigger and boast better views. Suites come with impressive bathrooms and large plasma televisions. Club Floor rooms come with a host of perks and particularly professional and personalized service. The public areas are stately and the restaurants are excellent. For anyone wanting to be downtown, the location is superb. For distraction, there's access to a health club and a pretty little outdoor pool, as well as a casino on-site. There's also an hourly complimentary shuttle to the airport. Despite being a downtown city hotel, the Oro Verde has earned ISO environmental practice awards and a Smart Voyager certificate for sustainable tourism practices.

Av. 9 de Octubre and García Moreno, Guayaquil. ✆ **04/2327-999.** Fax 04/2329-350. www.oroverdehotels.com. 230 units. $120–$360 double; $380–$430 suites; $1,100–$1,700 presidential or Oro Verde suite. AE, DC, MC, V. Free parking. **Amenities:** 4 restaurants; 2 bars; airport transfers; babysitting; casino; concierge; modern exercise room; Jacuzzi; small outdoor pool; room service; sauna; smoke-free floors; free Wi-Fi. *In room:* A/C, TV, hair dryer, minibar.

Expensive

UniPark Hotel ★ Value This large luxury hotel is located right downtown and connected to the UniPark mall, across from Parque Seminario and the cathedral and just 3 blocks from the Malecón. The rooms are everything you would want and expect in this category. The hotel lacks the pool and extensive facilities of some of the other upscale business hotels in town, but thanks to the local glut of rooms and competition, they've made up for this by dropping their rates substantially. The UniPark has several restaurants, including a sushi bar, and there are scores more in the adjacent mall.

Calle Clemente Ballén 406 and Calle Chimborazo, Guayaquil. ✆ **04/2327-100.** Fax 04/2328-352. www.uniparkhotel.com. 139 units. $80–$130 double. Rates include breakfast buffet and free airport shuttle. AE, DC, MC, V. Free parking. **Amenities:** 3 restaurants; 2 bars; concierge; small gym; room service; sauna; smoke-free rooms; free Wi-Fi. *In room:* A/C, TV, hair dryer, minibar.

Moderate

Apart Hotel Kennedy ★ Value Catering to business travelers, the Kennedy is located catty-corner to the much fancier Hilton Colón. Rooms are cool, sleek, and spacious. The large suites have separate sitting rooms and kitchenettes, which come in handy if you're here for several days. The decor aims to be elegant, but comes across as a bit kitschy. Still, this is a great value. The entire hotel features free wireless Internet for guests. ***Tip:*** The rates I list below are their "corporate" rates, which are less than their rack rates. That said, all you have to do is say you work for any company—heck, make one up—and they are usually more than happy to apply the corporate rate.

Calles Nahim Isaías and Vicente Norero, Kennedy Norte, Guayaquil. ✆ **04/2681-111.** Fax 04/2681-060. www.hotelkennedy.com.ec. 49 units. $80 double; $95 suite. Rates include buffet breakfast. AE, DC, MC, V. Free parking. **Amenities:** Restaurant; bar; room service; free Wi-Fi. *In room:* A/C, TV, fridge, hair dryer.

Inexpensive

There are plenty of run-down and seedy budget hotels in Guayaquil, but I really can't recommend any of them. Given the heat and humidity, I think it's worth the splurge for someplace with air-conditioning and a sense of style. If you're looking for a budget hotel, try the one below, as well as **Tangara Guest House** (✆ **04/2282-828;** www.tangara-ecuador.com) or the **Iguanazu Hostal** (✆ **04/2201-143** or 09/9867-968; www.iguanazuhostel.com).

Manso Boutique Hostal ★ Finds This place fills a much needed niche—a good boutique hotel right on the Malecón. The prize room here has A/C, a TV, and a balcony overlooking the Malecón and river beyond, although since it lets out on the street, it can be a bit noisy. They also have some shared bath private rooms, and two dorm rooms for real budget travelers in the back. The dorm rooms, which are gender specific, actually have private bathrooms. Throughout the decor is understated and artsy, and you'll often find the art and craft works of local artists on display or for sale here. The hotel's lovely garden includes a small restaurant specializing in creative contemporary cooking, using local organic ingredients whenever possible.

Malecón 1406 and Aguirre, Guayaquil. ✆/fax **09/6034-054.** www.manso.ec. 5 units (3 with private bath). $35 double shared bath; $50–$75 double. Rates include full breakfast. AE, MC, V. Parking nearby. **Amenities:** Restaurant; bar; free Wi-Fi. *In room:* No phone.

WHERE TO DINE

To a large extent, much of Guayaquil's dining scene can be found laid out along a stretch of Avenida Victor Emilio Estrada in the Urdesa neighborhood. Adventurous travelers could just hop a cab to Urdesa and walk around until something strikes their fancy.

In addition to the places listed below, you can get good sushi at **Sake** ★ on Victor Emilio Estrada and Circunvalacion Sur (✆ **04/2888-303**), and **Noe Sushi Bar** in the Centro Comercial San Marino (✆ **04/2083-389**). For a contemporary take on typical Ecuadorian fare, try **Olmedo** ★ on Las Monjas 120 and Circunvalacion (✆ **04/2389-973**). Finally, for fine Italian cooking in a refined environment, **Riviera** at Victor Emilio Estrada 707 and Calle Ficus (✆ **04/2883-790**) is also top notch.

Moderate

La Parrilla del Ñato ECUADORIAN/STEAKHOUSE This local minichain serves up excellent grilled meats in a lively setting. Portions are legendarily large, and easily shared. The dining room is also large and often as "loud" as the large neon signs out front. Still, the food is excellent. I'd stick to the simply grilled meats and seafood, though if you're feeling adventurous, you can order a dove breast; I don't know where they get their doves, but they're big. The *brocheta mixta* is a massive shish kabob with a couple of whole sausages and large cuts of meat interspersed with grilled onions and peppers. Avoid the pastas and pizzas, which are not the strong suit here. Other outlets around town can be found in Barrio Kennedy on Avenida Francisco de Orellana and Nahim Isaías (✆ **04/2682-338**), and at Km 2.5 on the road to Samborondón (✆ **04/2834-326**).

Av. Estrada 1219 and Laureles. ✆ **04/2387-098.** Main courses $6–$12. AE, DC, MC, V. Daily noon–midnight.

Lo Nuestro ★★ ECUADORIAN The best Ecuadorian restaurant in the city, located in the hip Urdesa restaurant district, is a small, elegant eatery whose walls are filled with historical photos of Guayaquil. Ask what the fresh fish is: Seafood reigns supreme here. *Ceviches* make for the best appetizers. The grilled sea bass with crab sauce is my favorite main course. There are myriad daily specials, but traditional favorites include homemade empanadas, *seco de chivo* (goat stew), and shrimp served several different ways. Everything is of the highest quality—and meticulously prepared. This is the kind of place where you enjoy a 3-hour meal and where the waiters wheel over a liquor tray to offer you an after-dinner drink. These folks also offer home delivery.

Av. Estrada 903 and Higueras. ✆ **04/2386-398.** Reservations recommended. Main courses $7–$25. MC, V. Mon–Thurs noon–3pm and 7pm–midnight; Fri–Sun noon–midnight.

Red Crab ★★ **Moments** SEAFOOD As the name implies, crabs are the star of the show here, and are served up in a variety of fashions. I recommend the Creole Crab,

An Alternative to the Galápagos

If you don't have the time or the money for a trip to the Galápagos Islands, you might consider visiting **Machalilla National Park.** At the park's main attraction, **Isla de la Plata** ★★★, which sits 37km (23 miles) off the coast, you will have the chance to see albatrosses; blue-footed, masked, and red-footed boobies; frigate birds; and sea lions, all of which also live in the Galápagos. There are also some colorful snorkeling spots here. From June through September, it's common to see whales as you make your way out to the island. But be careful—some of the boats are small and light, and the sea can be rough. If you're prone to seasickness, be sure to take some medication before you board the boat.

Isla de la Plata is the best-known attraction in Machalilla, but if you have a few days, you can also explore some archaeological sites (this area of the coast was home to a thriving pre-Columbian civilization) and hike along Los Frailes, a 3-hour trail that will reward you with breathtaking views of the coast.

All the tour agencies and hotels in town offer trips out to Isla de la Plata for around $30 to $40 including a guided hike, lunch, and snorkeling gear, plus an additional $15 national park fee.

Most visitors to Machalilla base themselves in Puerto López, a tiny little coastal town. Manta is the closest city with regular air and bus connections to Quito, although it's also quite common to visit Puerto López out of Guayaquil.

which is a large bowl of whole crabs boiled up with spices and accompanying chunks of tubers and corn. It comes with a large wooden mallet and plastic bib. For those looking for a less messy manner of digging in, you can order already shelled claws, in any number of sauces, or a wide range of other seafood dishes off the extensive menu. Heck, you could even get beef stroganoff or chicken cordon bleu here—but why would you? The decor is bright and gaudy, with porthole windows ringing the restaurant, neon blue lights embedded in the ceiling, and large fish tanks spread around. This place is very popular with locals, and has a loud, festive vibe. These folks also have branches in Quito and Cuenca.

At the corner of Victor Estrada and Laureles, Urdesa. ✆ **04/2380-512.** www.redcrab.com.ec. Reservations recommended. Main courses $7.75–$13. AE, MC, V. Daily 11am–midnight.

Sucre ★★★ *Finds* FUSION This chic restaurant serves up creative fusion cuisine in a stylish and relaxed ambience. The main dining room features wide wood floors, artistic lighting, and a whole wall of cushioned, built-in seating. Standout dishes include calamari in tempura batter with a mirin-chili dipping sauce, and the caramelized *osso buco* braised with apricots and served with a cheese ravioli with a hint of chocolate in the filling. The rest of the long menu is equally inspired, and presentations, while pretty, are far from ostentatious. Desserts are excellent, and the bar and wine list are top notch.

Centro Comercial La Piazza, Urdesa. ✆ **04/2838-068.** Reservations recommended. Main courses $6.70–$12. AE, MC, V. Sun–Fri noon–3:30pm and 7–11:30pm; Sat 7pm–midnight.

Inexpensive

Resaca ECUADORIAN/INTERNATIONAL There are scores of restaurants along the Malecón Simón Bolívar, but this is one of the only ones close enough to have a decent view. If the weather's nice, head straight upstairs for the second-floor, open-air patio and grab a seat close to the river. When it's too hot or windy or rainy, you can opt for a table near one of the large picture windows that ring the main dining room. The menu here leans heavily on bar-food staples, with nachos, fried calamari, *patacones* (fried plantains), and onion rings to choose from. You can also get main-course plates of fresh fish or grilled steaks and chicken. For lunch, try the three-course *menú ejecutivo* for $2.50. Weekend nights usually feature live bands. *Resaca* translates as "hangover," and the late-night scene here has certainly caused its fair share of them.

North end of Malecón Simón Bolívar, near Junín. ✆ **04/3000-805.** Reservations recommended. Main courses $4.50–$9. AE, DC, MC, V. Daily 11am–midnight.

GUAYAQUIL AFTER DARK

Guayaquil has made great strides in reducing crime and insecurity in recent years, and its nightlife has benefited greatly. Bars, cafes, and restaurants are sprouting like mushrooms around the **Zona Rosa** and **Cerro Santa Ana** (both toward the end of the Malecón). This is the best area to experience the city's nightlife. For more mellow options, you can stroll up the Cerro Santa Ana, where you'll find a plethora of bars and pubs flanking the steps leading to the top of the hill. Right at the foot of the steps is the always popular **Divina Nicotina** ★ (✆ **0409/9099-208**), while around the corner from the steps, in Las Peñas, is the boho standout **La Paleta** ★★ (✆ **04/2312-329**).

For dancing and a more lively time, try the Zona Rosa, a several-square-block area bordered by the Malecón to the east and Avenida Rocafuerte to the west, and by Calle Juan Montalvo to the north and Calle Manuel Luzarraga to the south. You'll find a score of bars here, and it's a relatively safe area to barhop. Down here, I like **Heineken Bar Music** ★, Rocafuerte and Padre Aguirre (✆ **08/5234-129**), which has atmospheric brick walls and often features live music; most Thursdays, this is a good place to find a local rock band playing.

Locals like to head to the handful of clubs and discos found in the neighborhood Kennedy Norte, at the **Mall Kennedy.** These clubs attract a broad mix of Guayaquil's young and restless. There's plenty to choose from, but if you want an all-out party, try **Ibiza Evolution** (✆ **09/7422-925**).

If you're in the mood for some gambling, there are large modern casinos at both the **Sheraton Four Points** and **Hilton Colón.**

9 THE GALAPAGOS ISLANDS ★★★

966km (600 miles) W of continental Ecuador

The Galápagos Islands offer some of the best wildlife viewing in the world, not only because the animals themselves are abundant, beautiful, and interesting, but because they are virtually fearless of humans. Through a quirk of evolution, large predators failed to evolve here, meaning, for example, that the famous blue-footed booby will perform its awkwardly elegant two-step mating dance right under your nose, oblivious to your camera. Sea lions will do figure eights to show off their swimming prowess as you snorkel among them. The local penguins are, admittedly, a bit aloof, but even they aren't above using a snorkeler as a human shield as they attempt to sneak up on schools of fish. In the Galápagos, you don't have to get downwind and peer through the bushes to glimpse the wildlife; you do, however, have to be careful not to step on sea lions sleeping on the beach as you position yourself to take a photo.

The islands' geographic isolation, over 960km (600 miles) off the continental coast, has led to the evolution of numerous endemic species here. This, combined with the animals' fearlessness of humans, played a key role in Charles Darwin's development of the theory of natural selection. The wildlife here, which so beguiled Charles Darwin, is no less astonishing now than it was when he visited. However, both the fragile ecosystems and wildlife are facing threats from overdevelopment, overfishing, and the increasing number of visiting tourists and introduced species. In 2007, UNESCO, which has declared the islands a World Heritage Site, announced that they were in serious danger of destruction. Although few formal measures have yet been adopted, the Ecuadorian government has vowed to take special steps to ensure that tourism and overall development on the Galápagos Islands is undertaken in a manner that will ensure the archipelago's survival and sustainability as an ecological wonder.

The best way to see the islands is to book a package tour out of Quito or Guayaquil. Most packages will include airfare and a berth on a local cruise ship, or a planned land-based itinerary. The ships that tour the islands vary widely in size and quality. My advice: Spend as much money as you can afford. But no matter what you can pay, you won't be disappointed.

The Galápagos Islands were formed over 5 million years ago by volcanic eruptions. These (and the ongoing formation and development of the islands) occur primarily over a relatively localized hot spot. However, due to continental drift, the islands are slowly but steadily migrating eastward. Today, the most active islands are Fernandina and Isabela, the westernmost islands, although several others have ongoing volcanic activity.

ESSENTIALS

Getting There

With very, very rare exceptions, travelers come by plane to the Galápagos Islands. **Tame** (✆ **02/3977-100;** www.tame.com.ec) and **Aerogal** (✆ **1-800/2376-425;** www.aerogal.com.ec) now offer daily flights to both **Baltra Airport** (✆ **05/2521-165;** airport code GPS), right off Santa Cruz island, and **Puerto Baquerizo Moreno** (✆ **05/2520-156;** airport code SCY), on San Cristóbal island. Note, however, that there are sometimes last-minute changes to flight schedules owing to inclement weather. Always check and double-check with your airline and the cruise company to confirm the airport that will be used for your particular itinerary. Round-trip fares run just under $400, including local taxes and airport fees. During the low season (mid-Sept through mid-Dec and mid-Jan through mid-June), flights are sometimes a bit less expensive.

Upon arrival you must pay a $100 fee to the **National Park** (www.galapagospark.org), which is good for the duration of your stay. This fee must be paid in cash, so be sure to plan ahead and have it ready. Children 11 and under pay $50. There is also a $10 "transit tax" that you must pay at a special booth in the airport before checking in and checking your bags for your flight to the Galápagos.

If you booked a boat tour before you arrived, the airfare and ticket booking should already be included. You can usually expect someone to pick you up at the airport and escort you through the logistics of arriving in the Galápagos and finding the way to your ship. If you're traveling on your own and you have a choice of flights (and airports), I

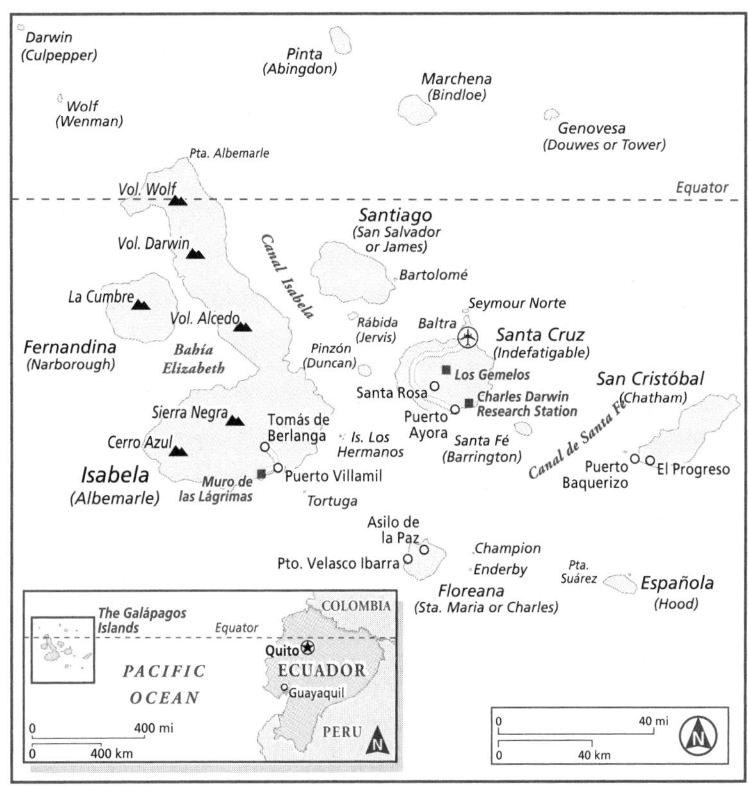

don't recommend flying into San Cristóbal; there is very little tourist infrastructure here. There are a handful of hotels on the island, and you can book last-minute tours and day trips from its port city of Puerto Baquerizo Moreno. But if you plan to base your touring out of a hotel on land, or if you're looking for a last-minute berth on a boat, the place to be is Puerto Ayora, on Santa Cruz, which is accessed from the Baltra airport.

All flights from the mainland originate in Quito and stop in Guayaquil. If you plan on flying to the Galápagos the day after you arrive in Ecuador, I recommend spending the night in Guayaquil. Most flights to the Galápagos leave Quito early in the morning and then stop for more than an hour to pick up passengers in Guayaquil. You gain precious sleep time if you board the plane there.

Getting Around

The Galápagos archipelago consists of 13 big islands, 6 small islands, and more than 40 islets. **Santa Cruz** is the most populated island; its main town, Puerto Ayora, is the major city in the Galápagos. From here, you can arrange last-minute tours around the islands, day trips, and scuba-diving excursions. Santa Cruz is also home to the Darwin Research

Tips Organizing a Last-Minute Trip to the Galápagos

There's no way around it—trips to the Galápagos are pretty expensive. But if you book a cruise at the last minute, you can sometimes save substantially off the regular rates. Most boats would rather sell a few spaces at steep discounts than send the ship out with empty staterooms. Unfortunately, it's not always easy to find a last-minute price, and you run the risk of not finding space. During the high season (June–Sept and late Dec to early Jan), you shouldn't even waste your time looking for one. Even during the low season, you shouldn't expect to come to Ecuador and immediately find a boat that's leaving the next day. In some cases, you may have to wait a week or more before you find an opening. The following info will help you plan a last-minute trip to the Galápagos.

Your best bet for finding a discount is to hit several of the budget-oriented travel agencies in the Mariscal district of Quito, or along Avenida Charles Darwin in Puerto Ayora. I've found the following agencies to be some of the best at arranging a last-minute cruise through the Galápagos.

In Quito

- **Ecoventura** ★ operates five ships and yachts in the Galápagos. Through the website (www.ecoventura.com) they sometimes offer last-minute deals at reduced rates. If there are no special discounts on the website, stop in or call their offices in Ecuador. These folks were pioneers in implementing sustainable tourism practices in Ecuador, and are a carbon-neutral company. In Quito they have an office at Almagro N31-80, Edificio Venecia (✆ **02/2907-396**); and in Guayaquil they have an office in the Edificio Samborondon Business Center, Torre A Piso 3 (✆ **04/2839-390**). At both offices, you can try to book a last-minute berth at last-minute prices.
- **Quasar Náutica** (✆ **800/247-2925** in the U.S. and Canada, 0800/883-0827 in the U.K., or 02/2446-996 in Ecuador; www.quasarnautica.com) is one of the larger cruise operators in the Galápagos, with a fleet of boats and a permanent office in Puerto Ayora.
- **Zenith Ecuador Travel** ★, Juan León Mera 453 and Roca (✆ **02/2529-993;** www.zenithecuador.com), has access to information about 100 boats that ply the waters around the Galápagos Islands. Give the staff your dates and your requirements, and they'll talk to their contacts and try to find you a special last-minute deal.

Station, where you can see giant land tortoises. **San Cristóbal** is the second-most populated island. Several tour boats begin their journeys from its port, Puerto Baquerizo Moreno. While serving as the official capital of Galápagos province, the town of Puerto Baquerizo Moreno is small. Moreover, there's not much to see on this island. **Isabela** is the largest island, but only the third-most populated. In general, most visitors only stop here on a guided tour.

To enjoy the best of what the Galápagos have to offer, I recommend exploring the islands by boat. However, if you're very prone to seasickness or uncomfortable sleeping on a boat, you can take a host of day trips out of Puerto Ayora.

Flights between the islands aren't frequent, but the local Galápagos airline **EMETEBE** (✆ **800/481-3163** in the U.S., or **05/2520-615;** www.emetebe.com) offers service on tiny propeller planes between Santa Cruz, San Cristóbal, and Isabela islands. Fares are $100 to $150 for each flight segment.

Visitor Information

There are only two substantial towns in the Galápagos Islands: **Puerto Ayora** on Santa Cruz island, and **Puerto Baquerizo Moreno** on San Cristóbal island. Both towns have banks, Internet cafes, a post office, pharmacies, and basic health clinics that serve as local hospitals.

In Puerto Ayora, there's a **tourist information office** (✆ **05/2526-613;** turismo@santacruz.gov.ec) on Avenida Charles Darwin, close to the corner of Charles Binford. It is open Monday through Friday from 8am to noon and 2 to 5:30pm. ***Note:*** The Galápagos Islands are 6 hours behind GMT, 1 hour earlier than mainland Ecuador.

EXPLORING THE GALAPAGOS

When to Go

There's never a bad time to visit the Galápagos. The peak season lasts from mid-June through early September and from mid-December through mid-January. It's almost impossible to find a last-minute deal at these times. The national park limits the number of visitors to each island and coordinates each ship's itinerary, so the Galápagos will never feel like Disney World. But if you visit in the summer, you are less likely to feel a sense of solitude and isolation. Below is a brief summary of the seasons to help you decide what time of year is best for you:

DECEMBER–MAY During these months, the water and the air are warmer, but this is the rainy season. It drizzles almost daily for a short period of time. Ironically, this is also the sunniest time of year. The end of December through the beginning of January is still the high season, so expect more crowds than during the rest of the year.

Because the water is warmer at this time, swimming and snorkeling are more enticing. On the flip side, there aren't as many fish to see as there are later in the year. This is the breeding season for land birds, so it's a good time to watch some unusual mating rituals. If you're into turtles, this is when you want to be here; you can watch sea turtles nesting on the beach, and March through May, you can often see land tortoises searching for mates around the lowland areas of the islands. Sea lions also mate in the rainy season—it's entertaining to watch as the males fight for the females. Around March and April, you'll see adorable newborn pups crawling around the islands.

In February, March, and April, as the rains dissipate, flowers start to blossom and the islands are awash in bright colors. Another benefit of traveling to the Galápagos at this time of year: The ocean is much calmer, so you'll have less chance of getting seasick.

JUNE–NOVEMBER June through November, the Humboldt Current makes its way up to the Galápagos from the southern end of South America. The current brings cold water and cold weather, but it also brings water rich in nutrients and plankton, which attracts fish and birds. During this season there always seem to be clouds in the air, but it rarely rains. It's also quite windy, and the seas tend to be rougher.

Tips Bring Your Own Gear & Wear Some Rubber

While most of the ships and boats and all of the dive shops in the Galápagos can provide snorkeling and diving gear, you might consider bringing your own. If nothing else, bring your own mask. A good, properly fitting mask is the single most important factor in predicting the success of a dive or snorkeling outing. Faces come in all sizes and shapes, and I really recommend finding a mask that gives you a perfect fit. If you plan on going out snorkeling or diving more than a few times, the investment will more than pay for itself. Fins are a lesser concern—most operators should have fins to fit your feet.

Even during the dry season, the waters of the Galápagos are much cooler than you'd expect this close to the Equator. Most scuba companies dive with full 6mm wet suits year-round. Even if you are snorkeling, a full or "shortie" wet suit will make the experience much more enjoyable, especially from June to November, when the Humboldt Current makes the water significantly colder. I highly recommend that you find out in advance if your ship or tour operator can provide or rent you a wet suit. If not, consider buying one.

Experienced divers claim that this is the best time of year to visit the Galápagos. Unfortunately, to see the wide variety of underwater marine life, you have to brave the cold water. Because there are more fish in the sea at this time of year, there are also more seabirds searching for these fish. Albatrosses arrive on Española in June and stay until December. Penguins also like the cold water and the abundance of fish, so you're more likely to see them here during this season. On Genovesa, the elusive owls mate in June and July, and you have the best chance of spotting one during this time. Blue-footed boobies also mate now, so it won't be difficult to witness their beautiful mating ritual known as the "sky point."

THE ISLANDS IN BRIEF

Every island in the Galápagos has its own allure. The more time you have, the richer your experience will be, but even if you have only a few days, with proper planning you'll come home with a lifetime of memories. When you're choosing a tour operator, you should always examine the itinerary. Note that 7-day trips often make frequent stops at Santa Cruz or San Cristóbal to collect and drop off passengers. The best trips head out to far-flung places, such as Genovesa, Española, and Fernandina, and spend only 1 day docked in Puerto Ayora, on Santa Cruz. To help you decide which trip might be best for you, here's a list of what each island has to offer.

Santa Cruz You will most likely begin and end your trip to the Galápagos on Santa Cruz. If you plan to arrange your trip on your own, you should use Santa Cruz as your base. The main city here, **Puerto Ayora,** is a bustling and attractive little burg, with a variety of small hotels, restaurants, gift shops, and tour operators. If you're looking for a luxury getaway, this island offers the only such choices, with both the Royal Palm Hotel (p. 595) and Finch Bay Hotel (p. 595). This island is also home to the **Charles Darwin Research Station,** where you can observe tortoises firsthand. Tours of the island include stops at **Los Gemelos (The Twins),** two sinkholes that stand side by side. As you walk around Los Gemelos, you will have a good chance of spotting the beautiful vermilion flycatcher. Some companies will take you to a farm in the highlands, where you can see tortoises in the wild. Most trips make a stop at the lava tubes, where you can wander though underground tunnels created by the movement of hot lava. On the north side of the island is **Cerro Dragon,** which is a great place to see the unique Galápagos land iguana.

Bartolomé Bartolomé (or Bartholomew) is famous for its dramatic vistas and barren volcanic landscape. The most common anchorage is near the oddly shaped **Pinnacle Rock.** From here, you can climb 372 steps of a wooden walkway to reach the top of an extinct volcano. The vigorous but technically easy climb is a lesson in volcano geography, with cooled-off lava flows and parasitic spatter cones clearly visible along the route to the main cone. On the way up, you will certainly see lava cactuses and lava lizards. The panoramic view from the lookout up top is beautiful, with Pinnacle Rock below you. Be sure to ask your guide to pick out a few of the lava rocks to show how light they are. This island has one of the larger colonies of Galápagos penguins, and many snorkelers have spotted penguins off this island.

San Cristóbal Most boats only stop on San Cristóbal to pick up and drop off passengers. The island's principal town, **Puerto Baquerizo Moreno,** features a pretty malecón, or seafront promenade, with a string of restaurants, cafes, and gift shops. The main attraction on the island is the **Centro de Interpretación (Interpretive Center),** a small museum with exhibits on the natural, human, and geological history of the island. If you spend any time on San Cristóbal, you will probably stop at **El Lobería,** a beach with sea lions, red crabs, and colorful lava gulls. It's also worth visiting **La Galapaguera de Cerro Colorado,** a natural giant-tortoise reserve. If you sail into or out of Puerto Baquerizo Moreno, you will pass through **Kicker Rock**—a unique rock formation set about 1.5km (1 mile) offshore. Take note of San Cristóbal's fishing and commuter craft; many are ringed with strands of barbed wire to keep off sea lions. Boats without the barbed wire almost always have one or two of these large sea mammals lounging around on the aft deck or sunning on the prow.

Santiago ★ Also called **James Island,** Santiago was a major base where early buccaneers and pirates stocked up on fresh water and food. Santiago is also a case study in the potential destruction caused by introduced species. Supposedly a couple of pairs of feral goats, left here as a future source of food by buccaneers in the 18th century, reproduced to the point where they numbered over 100,000. Efforts have greatly reduced the size of the herds of wild goats, but they are still wreaking havoc on certain native species, including giant tortoises. Most of the sea lions in the Galápagos are California sea lions. But on Santiago island, you will have the chance to see the only endemic species of sea lion in the Galápagos, which is incorrectly called the **Galápagos fur seal.** The island offers excellent snorkeling opportunities, and is also full of coastal birds such as great blue herons, lava herons, oystercatchers, and yellow-crowned night herons.

Española ★★ May through December, albatrosses settle down here to mate and take care of their young. In May and June, if you arrive early in the morning, you can witness the beak-cracking mating ritual of the albatross. Later in the season (Sept–Dec), you can see the little chicks. There must be some sort of avian aphrodisiac on this island because this is also a great place to see blue-footed boobies doing their mating dance, where the male extends his wings and lifts his beak at his prospective mate. If the female likes what she sees, she mimics her suitor.

Fernandina ★★ This is the westernmost island in the archipelago, and one of the best for wildlife encounters. The largest colony of marine iguanas live here. These cold-blooded animals hug and cuddle with each other to warm up after swimming. Flightless cormorants also inhabit the island; even though these birds can't fly (they are the only flightless cormorants in the world), they still dry their wings in the sun, just like their flying ancestors used to do millions of years ago. At something around 1 million years of age, Fernandina is the youngest of the Galápagos Islands, and one of the most volcanically active. Major eruptions here were recorded as recently as 1995.

Isabela Just to the east of Fernandina, this is the largest island in the Galápagos, formed by the volcanic activity and eventual joining of six different volcanoes—five of which are still active. Darwin's Lake provides an excellent backdrop for dramatic photos of the sea. The island is home to several different species of the giant Galápagos land tortoise, although you might not be able to see them in the wild. You should, however, be able to spot the land iguanas here, and you can take a long hike to a scenic point, from which you can see for miles. Isabela is particularly prized by bird-watchers; owing to its size, the island has a high species count. One of the common species here is the flamingo, found in its namesake **Pozo de los Flamingos (Flamingo Pond),** close to the main town of Puerto Villamil. Among the main attractions on Isabela is **El Muro de Lágrimas (The Wall of Tears),** a stone wall that was used as a torture mechanism for prisoners kept in a penal colony here during the mid–20th century. In town, you can also see graffiti that dates all the way back to 1836.

Rábida ★ Rábida, also known as **Jervis Island,** has a beautiful red-sand beach that is almost always heavily populated with sea lions. If you get too close to a female or child, the local bull male will probably make his presence known. Just behind the beach is a small saltwater lagoon that is a good place to see flamingos. A small loop trail leads to the top of a hill, with some good views of the island's coastline. In my opinion, the waters off Rábida offer the best snorkeling in the islands. I've found myself swimming simultaneously with sea lions and penguins here.

Genovesa (Tower) ★ Home to **Darwin Bay** and the popular hiking trail known as **"Prince Philip's Steps,"** Genovesa is on the far northeastern end of the archipelago. It's a long, often rough sail here, and only the longer tours include a visit to Genovesa. Almost every Galápagos tourist brochure has a picture of a frigate bird puffing up its red neck in an attempt to attract females; on Genovesa you'll have ample opportunities to see these birds in action. This island is also home to the largest colony of red-footed boobies on the archipelago. On another side of the island, you can see masked boobies and storm petrels. If you're lucky, you might spot the elusive short-eared owl—since these guys don't have predators, they are the only owls in the world that are diurnal. Genovese is also home to both sea lions and the endemic Galápagos fur seal.

Floreana ★ This small island, the first to be inhabited, is rich in lore and intrigue. Today, some 100 people live on Floreana, which is seldom visited by tourists. If you do come here, be sure to stop at **Post Office Bay,** where a barrel full of letters and postcards sits on the beach. It's a tradition begun by early whalers: If you see a letter or card addressed to someone in your town or country, you are supposed to carry it and post it from home. In exchange, feel free to leave a letter or postcard of your own for someone else to return the favor.

Choosing a Boat Tour

Hundreds of companies offer trips through the Galápagos, and trying to sift through all the tourist brochures is a daunting task. First and foremost, let me warn you that you tend to get what you pay for here. There are four classes of boats: economic, tourist class, first class, and luxury. The **economic boats** have shared dormitories and bathrooms, inexperienced (and non-English-speaking) guides, and mediocre food. On a **tourist-class boat** you may have your own private quarters, but expect them to be cramped. You probably won't have air-conditioning or hot water, and your guide might not have a good command of the English language. **First-class ships** have excellent guides, small but private cabins with hot water and air-conditioning, and passable food. The main difference between first-class and **luxury** service is the food; some luxury boats also have swimming pools or Jacuzzis, but the cabins are not necessarily much bigger.

Another word of caution: Don't expect your cruise in the Galápagos to be a typical pleasure cruise; the boats are used mainly for lodging and transportation purposes. During the day, small dinghies, known as *pangas,* will transport you to the actual islands. Once you're on land, the excursions often involve long, uphill hikes. The Galápagos are not a place for relaxing—expect to participate in strenuous activities. The larger ships, while very pleasant, accommodating, and efficient, definitely have a slight cattle-car feel. If you're looking for a more intimate experience, you'll want to book one of the smaller yachts.

Trips to the Galápagos venture out to the high seas, and the waters can be rough. Be sure to bring Dramamine or another antiseasickness medication with you. Candied ginger also helps settle small stomach upsets and is an alternative to medication. If you know that you are prone to sea sickness, you'll definitely want to book on one of the larger ships, which are much more stable and comfortable.

Recommended Boats & Operators

Galacruises Expeditions (©/fax **02/2509-007** in Ecuador; www.galacruises.com) runs four ships of their own and can book passage on a wide range of other boats and ships. Their boats range from tourist-class monohulls to modern luxury catamaran yachts. They do full-service tours around Ecuador and the region.

KLEIN Tours ★ (© **888/50-KLEIN** [505-5346] in the U.S., or 02/2430-345 in Ecuador; fax 02/2442-389; www.kleintours.com) is one of the oldest companies operating in the Galápagos, and their experience shows. The company maintains three first-class ships: the 20-passenger M/Y *Coral,* the 26-passenger M/Y *Coral II,* and the 110-passenger M/V *Galápagos Legend.* The *Coral* is the more deluxe option of the two smaller vessels, with a top-deck Jacuzzi and fine rooms. The *Legend* has large cabins, a swimming pool, massage service, a 24-hour coffee bar, and a jogging track. I prefer the intimate feel of the smaller boats, but on the *Legend,* you won't be lacking for any personal comforts.

Tips Scuba-Diving Trips

The waters surrounding the Galápagos offer some of **the best diving in the world ★★★**. If you want to dive here, you have two options: Book a tour on a dedicated dive boat—and dive every day—or take a nondiving cruise and then spend a couple of extra days in Puerto Ayora and arrange diving excursions from there. Two of the best diving outfitters in Puerto Ayora are SCUBA Iguana, at the end of Avenida Charles Darwin, right by the entrance to the Darwin Research Station (✆ 05/2526-497; www.scubaiguana.com); and **Sub-Aqua ★**, on Avenida Charles Darwin and Avenida 12 de Febrero (✆ **05/2526-633;** www.galapagos-sub-aqua.com). You can also dive out of Puerto Barquerizo Moreno on San Cristobal, or Puerto Villamil on Isabela.

Linblad Expeditions ★★ (✆ **800/397-3348** in the U.S. and Canada; www.expeditions.com) is another luxury-oriented tour agency with decades of experience in the Galápagos, and a particular commitment to protecting the environment and raising environmental awareness. The company operates three luxurious cruise ships here: the *National Geographic Explorer,* the *National Geographic Islander,* and the *National Geographic Polaris.*

Metropolitan Touring ★★★ (✆ **02/2988-200** in Ecuador; www.metropolitan-touring.com) runs three luxury ships (M/V *La Pinta,* M/V *Santa Cruz,* and M/V *Isabela II*) and one luxury hotel (Finch Bay Hotel), and is one of the largest and most professional tour agencies in Ecuador. Consider booking with them especially if you want to mix and match time on shore with time on a ship, or if you want to design a package that includes a Galápagos excursion as well as trips to other destinations in Ecuador. Their 32-passenger *La Pinta* combines the comforts and smooth ride of a large ship ride, with an intimate, small-group experience.

The **MV *Galápagos Explorer II* ★★** (✆ **04/2514-750;** www.galapagosexplorer.com) is one of the most luxurious ships in the Galápagos. The 100-passenger cruise ship offers all the amenities you could want: swimming pool, Jacuzzi, bars, first-class food, research center, nightly naturalist lectures, library, game room, and even a doctor on board. Most importantly, all the accommodations are exterior-facing suites, with small sitting areas, a minibar, and a TV/DVD.

Overseas Adventure Travel ★ (✆ **800/493-6824** in the U.S. and Canada; www.oattravel.com) offers good-value itineraries, often combining a Galápagos cruise with time in Ecuador's Amazon or a side trip to Machu Picchu. Tours are limited to 16 people and are guided by experienced naturalists.

SS *Mary Anne* ★★ (✆ **02/3237-186;** www.angermeyercruises.com) is the most unique vessel touring the Galápagos. The *Mary Anne* is a true three-masted square-rigged barkentine. Over 60m (200 ft.) long, including her bowsprit, she carries over 93 sq. m (1,000 sq. ft.) of sail, and a maximum of 16 passengers. That's a lot of ship for very few passengers. If you choose this vessel you'll truly feel transported back in time. The air-conditioned cabins aren't quite as large and luxurious as some of the other more modern luxury cruise ships listed here, but the *Mary Anne*'s food is good, and what you sacrifice in creature comforts you more than make up for in character and ambience. For a sailing vessel (with motor assist), the *Mary Anne* is surprisingly swift, and her itinerary is quite extensive and complete. These folks also run several other sail and motor vessels.

Quasar Náutica ★★ (✆ **800/247-2925** in the U.S. and Canada, 0800/883-0827 in the U.K., or 02/2446-996 in Ecuador; www.quasarnautica.com) operates five ships in the Galápagos, most of which are small and intimate. Their largest ship, the M/V *Evolution,* is a beautiful small cruise ship with 16 double staterooms. This vessel harkens back to the early 20th century, and features a wonderful aft-deck dining room. The M/S *Alta* is a regal three-masted motor ketch, while the M/V *Parranda* is an elegant 38m (125-ft.) classic motorized yacht. The M/V *Grace* is a classic and historic yacht that was actually the wedding present given by Aristotle Onasis to Prince Rainer and Grace Kelly—hence the name.

PUERTO AYORA

Puerto Ayora, the largest town in the Galápagos, is a good place to base yourself if you're traveling on your own. The **Moonrise Travel Agency** ★, Avenida Charles Darwin near the corner of Charles Binford (✆ **05/2526-589;** www.galapagosmoonrise.com), will be your best source of information. The staff is friendly and they can help you arrange a last-minute cruise of the Galápagos and independent tours around the islands.

Where to Stay

In addition to the luxury hotels listed below, the **Hotel Silberstein** (✆ **888/790-5264** in the U.S., 02/2269-626 reservations in Quito, or 05/2526-277 at the hotel; www.hotelsilberstein.com) and **Red Mangrove Adventure Inn** ★★ (✆ **888/254-3190** in the U.S. and Canada, or 05/2526-524 in Ecuador; www.redmangrove.com) are two excellent choices in downtown Puerto Ayora.

Finch Bay Hotel ★★★ *Moments* The only beachfront hotel in Santa Cruz is a 5-minute boat ride from Puerto Ayora. Secluded and serene among the mangroves with a magnificent pool and private beach, the Finch Bay has over 30 species of resident birds, including red-footed boobies. Rooms are tastefully decorated with yellow walls and attractive wooden blinds; bathrooms are large and have spacious showers with good water pressure (rare in the islands). The hotel prides itself on being environmentally friendly, with solar power and a conservation program. There's a Zen garden where yoga is offered in the mornings; bikes, kayaks, and snorkeling equipment are available for guests, too. When making your reservation, be sure to inquire about the all-inclusive packages, which include transfers from the airport, all meals, and daily tours on the hotel's fast, private yacht, the *Sea Finch.*

Punta Estrada, Isla Santa Cruz. ✆ **02/2988-200** reservations office in Quito, or 05/2526-297 at the hotel. Fax 02/3341-250. www.finchbayhotel.com. 21 units. $232 double. Rates include breakfast buffet and taxes. AE, DC, MC, V. **Amenities:** Restaurant; 2 bars; lounge; bikes; Jacuzzi; large outdoor pool; room service; smoke-free rooms; watersports equipment. *In room:* A/C, hair dryer.

Royal Palm Hotel ★★ *Finds* This exclusive resort sits on 200 lush hillside hectares (500 acres), a 20-minute drive from Puerto Ayora. There are 10 beautiful villas scattered on the hillside, four veranda studios, and three spectacular suites. The villas each have separate living/dining areas; bedrooms with king-size beds; and huge bathrooms with separate rooms featuring Jacuzzis. Windows face the serene countryside and the ocean at the bottom of the hill. The suites are all different from one another—the two-bedroom, two-bathroom Imperial comes with its own Jacuzzi hidden in a private garden, while the Prince of Wales suite has an indoor sauna. The studios are the simplest units but have charming patios with hammocks and spacious bathrooms with Jacuzzis. Service is exquisite, friendly, and not at all stuffy. In addition to working closely with the local community, the Royal Palm supports a program to promote the survival endemic species, while combating the impact of introduced species. Note that the hotel is more than a half-hour from the port.

Via Baltra, Km 18, Isla Santa Cruz. ✆ **05/2527-409.** Fax 05/2527-408. www.royalpalmgalapagos.com. 17 units. $375 studio; $500–$600 suite; $625 villa for 2; $875 Prince of Wales suite. Rates include American breakfast. AE, DC, MC, V. **Amenities:** Restaurant; bar; concierge; exercise room; outdoor swimming pool; room service; sauna; 2 outdoor tennis courts. *In room:* A/C, TV/DVD, hair dryer, minibar.

Where to Dine

The restaurants at the **Royal Palm Hotel** and **Finch Bay Hotel** (see above) are both excellent. In both cases, reservations are essential, and the food will be quite a bit more expensive than anything else you'll find around town. Another interesting option is the hip **Red Sushi** (✆ **05/2526-524**) at the Red Mangrove Adventure Inn.

Angermeyer Point Restaurant ★ Moments ECUADORIAN/SEAFOOD This restaurant gets my vote for the best-located and most atmospheric dining spot in Puerto Ayora. This old stone house, with a broad wraparound wooden deck, is set on a rocky promontory facing the bay. It was the former home of local legend and painter Karl Angermeyer, who arrived here in 1937. Weather permitting, you'll definitely want to grab one of the waterfront tables on the outdoor deck. You'll probably spend as much time enjoying the sight of sea lions, blue-footed boobies, and marine iguanas as you will enjoying your meal. In fact, this place is also known as La Casa de las Iguanas (the House of Iguanas), and there are always large groups of these remarkable reptiles here. The food is quite good; Friday is sushi night, although I prefer the sushi at Red Sushi (see above).

Angermeyer Point, Puerto Ayora. ✆ **05/2527-007.** Reservations recommended. Main courses $5–$20. DC, MC, V. Tues–Sun noon–9:30pm. Hire water taxi from main dock in Puerto Ayora for around $1 each way or call the restaurant to arrange transportation.

La Garrapata Restaurante ★ ECUADORIAN This place is where the expats eat—and it's also where all the foreign guides who work on cruise ships come to dine. There's a great selection of fresh juices and sandwiches. The open-air dining room features low wooden chairs and round tables with linen tablecloths. But there's nothing formal about either the vibe or service here. Main courses include a wide range of seafood and meat options, as well as some pastas. There's usually a *menú del día* (menu of the day) with soup, main course, and dessert for less than $5. They even have a pretty good wine list. On some weekends, there's live music.

Av. Charles Darwin and Charles Binford, Puerto Ayora. ✆ **05/2526-264.** Main courses $4–$16. AE, DC, MC, V. Mon–Sat 9am–4pm and 6:30–10pm.

Puerto Ayora After Dark

For such a seemingly sleepy little city, Puerto Ayora has a surprisingly lively, albeit limited, nightlife and bar scene. **Bongo Bar ★★** (✆ **05/2526-264**) is the most happening place in town at night. It's on a rooftop above and behind La Panga (see below). Bongo Bar opens at 4pm, but usually doesn't get busy until after 8pm. Across the street, the **Limón y Café** (✆ **05/2526-510**) is another downtown bar, which sometimes gets the crowds up and dancing. But if you're looking for the best dance club in town, head to **La Panga** (✆ **05/2527-199**). Finally, for a real local scene, head to **La Taberna del Duende ★** (✆ **05/2527-320**), which is located inland from the main tourist strip on Calle Juan Leon Mera and San Cristóbal.

10

Paraguay

by Charlie O'Malley

Paraguay is a mysterious enclave of rural plains and muddy rivers, bordered by pristine jungles and dotted with lichen-stained towns and cities. Tucked away in the tropical belly of South America, landlocked and dwarfed by Bolivia, Brazil, and Argentina, most travelers take its anonymity as a cue to skip it and continue on to more exotic places. If you do decide to go, you will be surprised to find a beautiful, humid, strikingly green countryside best explored by boat or on horseback.

Paraguay is a country that stands for paradox. The indigenous Guaraní people play sentimental European songs on giant harps. Huge Ciudad del Este shopping malls stand next to thundering, tropical waterfalls. Unpaved roads lead to a multi-billion-dollar dam called Itaipú. Asunción's squalor is punctuated by architectural jewels, while German Mennonite colonies scratch out a good living on the inhospitable Chaco. In the south, majestic Jesuit ruins in Encarnación hint at a lost utopia.

Paraguay's history is brutal and sad. Everywhere you go you will find references to the 19th-century War of the Triple Alliance, a lonely, ill-advised conflict against the combined might of Brazil, Argentina, and Uruguay that almost wiped out Paraguay's male population. Paraguay's isolation was compounded by a 20th century marked by military coups and long dictatorships. It is only recently that the country has opened up. Today, Paraguay is a destination for those who want the new and colorful and can tolerate the occasional discomfort. Its greatest assets are unexplored national parks with excellent wildlife, bird-watching, and unlimited potential for ecotourism.

1 THE REGIONS IN BRIEF

The south of the country is where everybody lives and thus is the most developed. The capital, **Asunción,** is the only major city in Paraguay and thus is its political and economic center. To the east and south of the capital are flat agricultural plains with sleepy colonial towns and the occasional lake or river resort. It is not unusual to hear the indigenous language, Guaraní, being spoken. The eastern border town of **Ciudad del Este** is a tax-free haven originally built to administer the nearby **Itaipú** hydroelectric dam. On the southern border with Argentina there is the modern town of **Encarnación,** famous for its nearby Jesuit ruins. The river Paraguay leads you north of Asunción to the town of **Concepción.** Indeed many people take the boat to visit there. Beyond is the Brazilian Pantanal and, to the northwest, the **Gran Chaco,** a vast territory of scrubland, savannah, and thorn forest. The border road to Bolivia has only recently been paved, and much of the area still requires 4×4 transport to explore. It is here that Mennonite communities chose to settle, and the area is famous for bird-watching.

2 THE BEST OF PARAGUAY IN 1 WEEK

Paraguay has so much to see and do that 1 week is not enough if you really want to get into the wilderness. That said, below is a 1-week itinerary designed as if treating Paraguay as a stepping stone between Argentina and Brazil. A second week gives you the opportunity to dwell a little longer and enjoy the Jesuit ruins of Encarnación and the country's untouched natural parks (see the box "Waterfalls & Jaguars" at the end of this chapter).

Days ❶–❸: Asunción & Environs

On your first day, fly into Paraguay's riverside capital, stay in the central **Crowne Plaza** (p. 608), and explore the city by foot and taxi, seeing firsthand the strong tribal heritage in the city's museums. Day 2 can be enjoyed in the leafy upscale suburb of Villa Mora and the nearby **Jardín Botánico** (p. 607). On your third day, take the rural tour called "Circuito de Oro" to visit the charming **Iglesia San Buenaventura** (p. 611) and the resort town of **San Bernardino** (p. 611) on Lago Ypacaraí or, if you have jungle fever, visit the pristine rainforest at **Parque Nacional Ybycui** (p. 615).

Day ❹: Ciudad del Este

You might hate it, but you'll certainly enjoy telling the folks back home of your time in this "Supermarket of South America." Revel in the gritty commercialism of the world's third-biggest tax-free zone by visiting its tacky stores and slick shopping malls. Spend the night in tropical splendor at the gorgeous **Las Ventanas** hotel (p. 614).

Days ❺–❼: Itaipú & the Border, then back to Asunción

On your last days in Paraguay, explore its less consumerist side. Start by visiting the engineering blockbuster that is **Itaipú** (p. 613) and the spectacular **Salto Monday falls** (p. 614). The next day, cross the massive **Friendship Bridge** (p. 613) and see the famous **Iguazú Falls** (p. 615) in Brazil and Argentina. Cross back over to Paraguay and spend your last night in the capital at the well-appointed **Sheraton Asunción** (p. 608).

3 PLANNING YOUR TRIP TO PARAGUAY

VISITOR INFORMATION

The tourism ministry, known as **Secretaría Nacional de Turismo,** has an informative website in Spanish and English at **www.senatur.gov.py** For cultural and historical information, head to **www.paraguay.com**. The website **www.yagua.com** has links to current affairs articles and weather reports.

ENTRY REQUIREMENTS & CUSTOMS

Citizens of the United States, Canada, New Zealand, and Australia need a visa to enter Paraguay. This must be obtained before your trip and costs $65.

Paraguayan Embassy Locations

In Canada: 151 Slater St., Suite 401, Ottawa, K1P 5H3 (✆ **613/567-1283;** fax 613/567-1679; www.embassyofparaguay.ca)

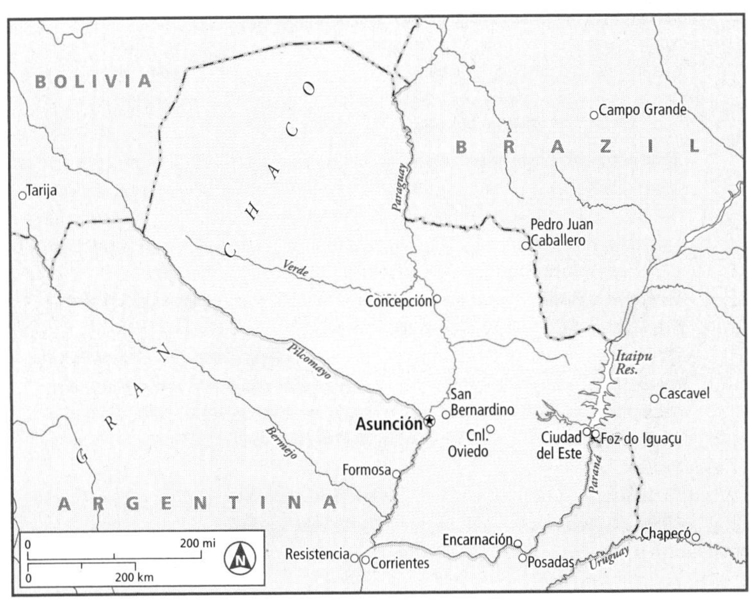

In the U.S.: 2400 Massachusetts Ave. NW, Washington, DC 20008 (✆ **202/483-6960;** fax 202/234-4508; www.embaparusa.gov.py)

In the U.K.: 344 Kensington High St., Third Floor, London W14 8NS (✆ **207/610-4180;** www.paraguayembassy.co.uk)

MONEY

Paraguay's currency is called the **guaraní** and is designated throughout this book with a G/. The exchange rate was $1 to 4,750 guaranís at press time. Guaranís are available in 1,000, 5,000, 10,000, 50,000, and 100,000 notes; coins come in 50, 100, and 500 guaranís. It is difficult to change this currency outside Paraguay, though you may have some luck in Buenos Aires and Montevideo. Dirty or torn U.S. dollars are difficult to change, though they can be replaced by better ones at some banks.

Note: Throughout this chapter, I list prices of hotels, tours and some transportation options in U.S. dollars.

Traveler's checks are accepted by most banks in Asunción but charge up to 5.5% commission. Currency-exchange houses may insist on seeing your purchase receipt before accepting. The most widely accepted **credit cards** are Visa and MasterCard; you'll have less luck with American Express and Diners Club. To report a lost or stolen credit card, call the following numbers: **American Express,** ✆ **0411/008-0071; MasterCard,** ✆ **636/722-7111** (collect call to the U.S.); and **Visa,** ✆ **0411/940-7915. ATMs** on the Cirrus and Visa/PLUS networks are widely available in Asunción and other large towns.

Telephone Dialing Info at a Glance

The national telephone company is called Copaco. Telephone centers are ubiquitous in every town and cards for phone boxes can be bought at most corner stores. Use **Hablemas phone cards** when making international calls.

- **To place a call from your home country to Paraguay,** dial the international access code (011 in the U.S., 0011 in Australia, 0170 in New Zealand, 00 in the U.K.), plus the country code (595), plus the city or region area code (for example, Asunción is 21), followed by the number. For example, a call from the United States to Asunción would be 011-595-21-XXX-XXX.
- **To place a domestic long-distance call within Paraguay,** dial a 0 before the area code, and then the local number.
- **To place a direct international call from Paraguay,** dial the international access code (00), plus the country code of the place you are dialing, plus the area code and the number. To make an international collect call, dial 0012. Calls cost G/1,853 per minute to the U.S. and G/2,850 per minute to Europe.
- **To reach an international long-distance operator,** dial ✆ 000-410 for **AT&T,** ✆ 000-412 for **MCI,** or ✆ 000-417 for **Sprint.**

WHEN TO GO

PEAK SEASON & CLIMATE With its subtropical climate, Paraguay is best to visit from May to September, though the weather can be very unreliable. The rainy season is from October to April when it rains 1 in 3 days, though it is not unknown to rain throughout the year. January is the hottest month, with average temperatures of 82°F (28°C), and July is the coolest month, with averages around 64°F (18 °C). Temperatures can drop as low as 40°F (5°C) in winter but rarely dip below freezing—which prevents snow.

PUBLIC HOLIDAYS National holidays include New Year's Day (Jan 1); San Blas Day (February 3); Memorial Day for former president Francisco Solana López (Mar 1); Holy Thursday and Good Friday (March or April); Labor Day (May 1, 14, and 15); Corpus Christi (May or June); Chaco Peace Day (June 12); the Battle of Acosta Ñu and Child's Day (Aug 15); Founding of Asuncion Day (Aug 25); Boqueron Victory Day (Sept 29); Immaculate Conception Day (Dec 8); and Christmas Day (Dec 25). On these holidays, all government offices are closed, but some museums remain open.

HEALTH CONCERNS

Mosquitoes are prevalent, and therefore dengue fever and malaria are endemic, especially in the east around Itaipú. The locally made repellent Repel and mosquito coils can keep the bugs at bay. Avoid tap water and salads, as dysentery is not unknown, and typhoid and tuberculosis are risks as well. Hookworm is common, and STDs are on the rise. Goiter and leprosy are also common ailments, but are unlikely to present a risk to travelers. Check the CDC's website at **www.cdc.gov** for the latest information before your trip.

GETTING THERE & GETTING AROUND

BY PLANE International flights land at **Silvio Pettirossi Airport** (airport code ASU; ✆ **021/645-600**), 15km (9 miles) northeast of the city. An airport tax of $25 is levied when leaving the country. A taxi to downtown costs about $17; to Villa Mora it's $11. Paraguay's main carrier is **TAM,** Oliva y Ayolas (✆ **021/465-600;** www.tamairlines.com), serving domestic and international destinations. There are no direct flights from Europe or North America. TAM flies via Sao Paulo to New York, Paris, Milan, and Miami. There are three daily flights to Buenos Aires and one a day to Cochabamba (Bolivia), Montevideo, Rio de Janeiro, Santa Cruz (Bolivia), and Santiago in Chile. **Gol** (www.voegol.com.br) has regular flights to Buenos Aires and Brazil. **United Airlines,** Mcal López 310 (✆ **021/213-019;** www.united.com), has offices in Asunción that can organize onward flights from Brazil.

BY BUS & BOAT See "Essentials" under "Asunción," below.

BY CAR A car is essential to visit many of the less accessible national parks, but be prepared for many annoying police stops between cities and the occasional solicitation of a bribe. **National Car Rental,** Ave. España 1009 (✆ **021/232-990;** www.national.com.py), offers small cars and SUVs. **Avis,** Eligio Ayala 695 (✆ **021/446-233;** www.avis-int.com), has offices in the Sheraton and in the airport. **American Rent a Car** (✆ **0991/761-632**) also has a location in the airport. Cars for the day start at $35. For roadside emergencies or general information on driving in Paraguay, contact the **Touring y Automóvil Club Paraguayo,** 25 de Mayo y Brasil (✆ **021/210-550;** www.tacpy.com.py). A reliable tow-truck service is **Allianza** (✆ **0971/262-529**).

TIPS ON ACCOMMODATIONS

The best hotels in the country are located in Asunción, though quality can vary greatly. The most upscale establishments cater mostly to business clientele, while most midrange places are in bad need of a makeover. Always try and get a room with A/C or at least one with windows facing a quiet street, or better still a leafy courtyard. Often the best bargains are small family-run establishments. There are very few hostels. Hotel rooms in this chapter fall under the price categories of **Very Expensive**, $200 and up; **Expensive**, $120 to $199; **Moderate**, $50 to $119; and **Inexpensive**, $49 and below.

TIPS ON DINING

Paraguay's enduring Guaraní heritage is most evident in its food, with subtropical *campesino* favorites such as maize and manioc (yuca) appearing in almost every dish. The national dish *sopa paraguaya* is in fact not a soup but cornbread and cheese. *Locro* is a type of maize stew and *mazzamorra* a corn mush. *Bori-bori* is a popular version of chicken soup, while *torta de almidos* is a pancake made from manioc flower. If you have had enough of tuberous root, you'll find plenty of *parrillas* (grill houses) serving steak and ribs, though the quality may not be as good as neighboring Argentina or Uruguay. A surprising variation is the quantity of Asian eateries offering Chinese, Korean, and Japanese food, the result of a wave of immigration in the 1980s. Like any poor country, there are plenty of food stalls in town centers offering everything from empanadas to *chipas* (cheese bread). More upscale restaurants are found in the well-to-do neighborhoods, and many offer excellent river fish such as *surubi.* Meals in this chapter are listed according to **Very Expensive**, G/71,250 and up; **Expensive**, G/47,500 to G/66,500; **Moderate**, G/33,250 to G/42,750; and **Inexpensive**, under G/33,250.

TIPS ON SHOPPING

Ñanduti lace and wood carvings (known as *palo santo*) are Paraguay's most famous handicrafts, made in some satellite towns of Asunción (see "Shopping" in the Asunción section on p. 607). The capital itself has the best selection of high-quality craft stores, while Ciudad del Este is the most famous place to buy cheap electronics. This tax-free zone is a magnet for bargain-hunting Argentines and Brazilians. Watch out for unscrupulous traders who specialize in counterfeit goods and phony packaging. It's best to stick with the more established malls while shopping in this chaotic border town, famed for its contraband.

Fast Facts Paraguay

American Express In Asunción, American Express is at InterExpress, Yegros 690 y Herrera (© **021/490-111;** iexpress@interexpress.com.py). Banespa, Independencia Nacional y Moreno (© **021/448-698**), changes traveler's checks but requires a purchase receipt. Money-exchange houses are on Palma and Estrella, but beware that their rates go up when banks are closed. Parapiti Cambios, Palma 449 (© **021/490-032**), will change traveler's checks for a small fee.

Business Hours In general, businesses stay open weekdays from 8am to 6:30 or 7pm, with a 2-hour break for lunch around noon. Retail outlets keep similar hours and are usually open a half-day on Saturday as well. Banks are open weekdays from 8:30am to 1:30pm.

Doctors & Hospitals The best private hospital is **Bautista,** Avenida Argentina and Cervera, Asunción (© **021/600-171**). The main public hospital is called **Emergencias Médicas,** Brasil and FR Moreno (© **021/204-800**).

Electricity Electricity in Paraguay runs on 220 volts, so bring a transformer and adapter along with any electrical appliances. Note that most laptops operate on both 110 and 220 volts. Some luxury hotels may supply transformers and adapters. Plugs have two pins.

Embassies & Consulates In Asunción: The **U.S. Consulate,** Av. Mcal López 1776 (© **021/213-715;** http://asuncion.usembassy.gov), is open Monday to Thursday from 7:30am to 5:30pm and Friday 7:30 to 11:30am. The **U.K. Consulate,** Eulogio Estigarribia 4846 (© **021/663-536**), is open Monday to Friday 8am to 1pm and 3 to 7pm; and the **Canada Consulate,** Prof. Ramirez 3, Office 102 (© **021/227-207**), is open Monday to Thursday 8am to 4pm and Friday 8am to noon.

Emergencies The general emergency number is © **911;** the fire department number is © **711.** For medical emergencies, call © **204-800.**

Internet Access Cybercafes are commonly found around Asunción and other Paraguayan cities. Many hotel business centers have Internet access, as do the guest rooms in high-end hotels. The average cost is $1 an hour.

Language Paraguay is a bilingual country, with Guaraní frequently spoken along with Spanish. Several other Indian languages are spoken to a much lesser extent, such as Aché, Nivaclé, and Lengua.

Liquor Laws The legal age for drinking in Paraguay is 20, but this is poorly enforced.

Police The main police station in Asunción is **Comisaria Tercera,** Chile y Colombia, Asunción. For emergencies, call 911.

Post Offices & Mail Post offices are generally open Monday through Friday from 8am to 6pm and Saturday from 8am to 1pm. You can buy stamps there or in mailing centers in shopping malls. The main post office is situated on Benjamin Constant and El Paraguayo Independiente (✆ **021/498-112**).

Restrooms There are very few public restrooms in the country's cities and towns, except in its large shopping malls. Restaurant owners will gladly oblige a nonpaying customer if you really need to go. In general, hygiene varies greatly, depending on the level of each establishment. Public buses have no restrooms and museums usually have a dark cubicle hidden away somewhere. It is always wise to carry your own toilet roll.

Safety Paraguay is a relatively safe country, but it is prudent to keep your eyes open and valuables hidden, especially in Ciudad del Este. Downtown Asunción is badly lit at night, but there are usually plenty of policemen out to prevent crime.

Smoking There is currently no smoking ban, though it is frowned upon to smoke on public buses.

Taxes Value-added tax is called IVA in Spanish. The standard rate in Paraguay is 10%.

Telephones See "Telephone Dialing Info at a Glance," above.

Time Zone Paraguay is 3 hours behind Greenwich Mean Time (GMT) and 4 hours behind during daylight saving time (Mar–Oct); Paraguay only sporadically observes daylight saving time.

Tipping A 10% to 15% tip is common in restaurants. For taxis, round up to the nearest 1,000 guaraní. Tips for porters and guides are discretionary.

Water You should drink only bottled water while in Paraguay, and avoid all salads and uncooked vegetables.

4 ASUNCION

Stand at the corner of Asunción's Plaza Independencia and Palacio Legislativo and you'll see urban South America in all its grisly glory. The peeling pink colonial palace is besieged on one side by a filthy ramshackle slum that tumbles down to the muddy shore of the Rio Paraguay. A stubbly football pitch lies in the distance and a stained cathedral sits on the other plaza corner, surrounded by potholed streets and vigilant policemen. Dirty buses rumble between whitewashed curbs, and a hodgepodge of decaying pastel-colored mansions stand squeezed between squalid concrete bunkers.

Asunción is glorious in the sun and miserable in the rain. Like most South American cities, the downtown area is poor, polluted, and neglected, yet alive with vendors, food stalls, and chaotic traffic. Here you'll find some interesting museums and monuments, and the shade they offer is a cool respite from the sweltering heat. The northeast of the city becomes decidedly tidier but characterless, with long avenues of car dealerships and shopping malls leading to upscale and leafy Villa Morra. Here you'll find some beautiful suburban streets and parks.

With a population of 1.2 million people, Asunción has the feel of a provincial city. Founded in 1557, the Spanish had big plans to make it the gateway to Peru. The vast, impenetrable Chaco soon stopped this idea in its tracks and the city lost its dominance to Buenos Aires and Salta. Thoughtless urban planning saw the destruction of many fine buildings, and what remains gives a sense of long-faded glory. Nevertheless, it is the political, economic, and cultural center of Paraguay, with most of the country's population living there or nearby. Those same people are very friendly and welcoming, unfamiliar with tourists, and anxious that you enjoy your stay.

ESSENTIALS

Getting There

BY PLANE To get to Asunción by plane, see "Getting There & Getting Around," above.

BY BOAT A ferry operates every 30 minutes from Itá Enramada to the Argentine side at Puerto Pilcomayo. The fare is G/2,375. Otherwise the only river route is to Concepción in the north. The *Cacique II* operates sailings to Concepción every Wednesday. The journey takes 27 to 30 hours. Another boat, called the *Guaraní,* sails every Friday morning. Times are flexible. It costs about $2 for first class, but be prepared for anything but first class. (Bring plenty of drinking water and toilet paper.) For something more upscale, try **Crucero Paraguay,** Edificio Mocipar, Third Floor, Office 302, Presidente Franco 982 (© **021/452-328;** www.cruceroparaguay.info). They conduct luxury 3-day cruises on the Rio Paraguay. The city port is behind the Customs office at the end of Calle Montevideo.

BY BUS **Terminal,** República Argentina y Fernando de La Mora (© **021/552-154** or 021/551-737), is Asunción's long-distance bus terminal and is 20 minutes south of the city center. It connects the capital with cities in Brazil, Argentina, Uruguay, and Bolivia. Buses take about 18 hours to Buenos Aires and 20 hours to Montevideo and cost $53 and $57 respectively. **Nuestra Señora de la Asunción** (© **021/289-1000;** www.nsa.com.py) is one of the main companies operating this route. Another is **Chevalier Paraguaya,** Mcal Estigarriba 767 (© **021/493-375**). Beware that local commuter buses crossing the border will not wait for you to go through formalities. You must wait for the next one, which will follow shortly. However, international express buses such as the companies mentioned here will wait. **Luma** (© **021/445-024**) operates a service to the Brazilian side of Iguazú (5–7 hr.: $8) and Sao Paolo (20 hr.: $30), as does **RYSA,** Eligio and Antequera, Asunción (© **021/444-244**).

Orientation

Asunción is settled on a bluff above the Rio Paraguay, though the river is hardly noticeable as you stroll around the central plazas. The city basically has two centers. One is the busy, polluted downtown with government buildings and grand plazas such as the Plaza de los Heroes. The other is leafy Villa Morra to the east and north, which is easier on the eye but very spread out and not suitable for exploring thoroughly on foot. Here you'll find the relaxing parkland of Jardín Botánico.

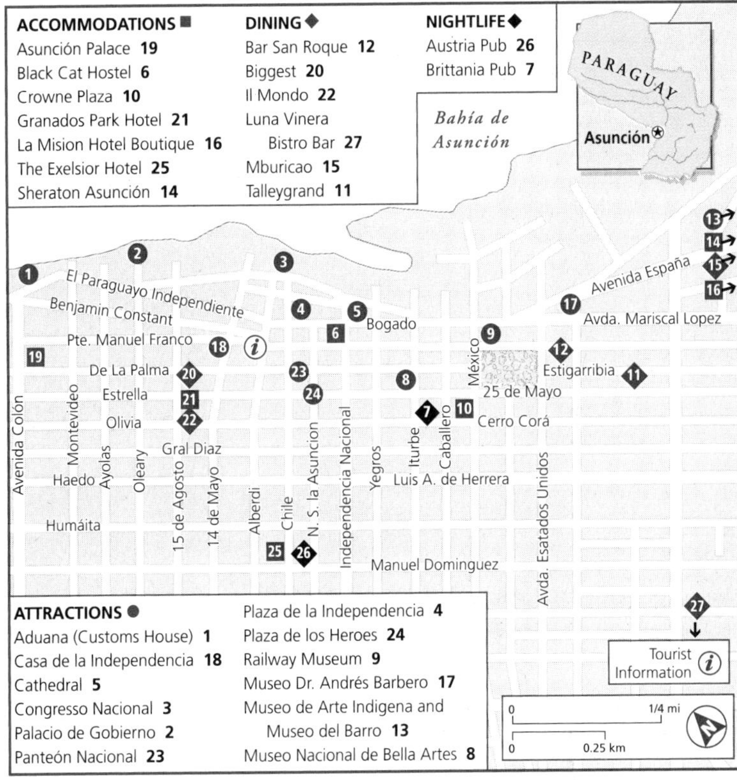

Getting Around

The downtown is relatively easy to walk around, though some streets toward the south have a steep incline. You will require patience while crossing at junctions, however, as there are no pedestrian crossings and drivers are oblivious to those on foot. Villa Morra is best explored by taxi, with many congregating around Plaza de Los Heroes. A ride should not cost more than $11, but beware there is a 15% surcharge on Saturdays, Sundays, and holidays. Old, noisy buses crisscross the city and cost G/2,375. They can be slow in rush hour. Numbers 28 and 31 leave for the terminal from Calle Cerro Corá. To get to Villa Mora, catch any bus going east on España.

Visitor Information

Paraguay's **Secretaria Nacional de Turismo** is on Palma 468 (✆ **021/494-110;** www.senatur.gov.py). It is open daily from 7am to 7pm. There's also a branch at the Airport. **Itra Travel,** Av. Venezuela 663 (✆ **021/200-190;** www.itra.com.py), provides good-quality tours of the surrounding area and farther afield to Itaipú and the Jesuit ruins near Encarnación. Another reliable operator is **Vips Tour,** México 782 (✆ **021/441-199;** www.vipstour.com.py).

WHAT TO SEE & DO

Take a walking tour of the city center, starting at the Customs house, locally known as the **Aduana,** at Avenida Colon and Paraguayo Independiente. Walk east to the **Palacio de Gobierno,** a beautiful Versailles-style palace. It was once decreed that if anybody so much as looked at this building they would be shot on sight. Gladly, this rule no longer applies and now the soldiers in front will only shoo you away, except on Sunday when the building is open to the public. Continue east onto **Plaza Independencia,** where you'll find a 19th-century building that houses the **Congresso Nacional.** The **Cathedral** on the far corner is entered from the side street Bogado.

Casa de la Independencia ★★ This quaint, low, white-washed building appears somewhat incongruous amidst the dirty, modern chaos of downtown Asunción. As you enter, two mannequins in full colonial regalia come alive and you realize they are actually two real men. Indeed, this museum is very much the real deal. It was here the idea of an independent Paraguay was first formed and the conspirators held clandestine meetings. Alongside is a preserved alleyway where the plotters sneaked in and out through stables and eventually left to march on the Spanish governor's house and declare independence. Inside you'll find the desk where the declaration was signed, as well as a mixture of domestic and historical memorabilia from the era, such as giant-size fans, old cannons, and marvelous Jesuit carvings. All are nicely arranged around a central courtyard. Ask for Maria, the English-speaking guide.

14 de Mayo y Pres Franco. ✆ **021/493 918.** www.casadelaindependencia.org.py. Free admission. Mon–Fri 7am–6:30pm; Sat 8am–noon.

Museo de Arte Indigena and Museo del Barro Located 5 blocks from the Sheraton in leafy suburbia, Museo del Barro is one of the more stylish and presentable museums in Asunción, though unfortunately it has limited opening hours. Here you'll find excellent indigenous art and handicrafts ranging from ceramic pots and figurines to wooden masks, crochet covers, and upholstered bags. Some of the most interesting exhibits are large urns with climbing children as handles and marvelous clay figurines with big hips and small heads. There is a gift store, bookstore, and an exhibition room displaying contemporary artists, including the charming, innocent religious art of Mabel Anconda.

Grabadores del Cabichuí, Isla de Francia. Admission G/12,000, free on Fri. ✆ **021/607-996.** www.museodelbarro.com. Thurs–Sat 3:30–8pm.

Museo Dr. Andrés Barbero ★★★ This is the best-stocked museum in town, with an amazing collection of indigenous objects, including tobacco-stained smoking pipes, brightly colored feather headdresses, giant bows and arrows, carved canoes, and fishing nets. Many of the exhibits were found buried with their Guaraní owners in ceramic funeral urns that also included food supplies and the tools of their trade, thus ensuring a successful reincarnation. Here you'll see clay bottles decorated with the maker's fingerprints and forbidding wooden masks with rattles and whistles. There is also a side corridor of sequenced photos displaying ancient initiation ceremonies. It's very much worth the visit and is 10 blocks west of downtown. Ring the bell to gain entrance.

España y Mompox. ✆ **021/441-696.** Free admission. Mon, Wed, and Fri 7–11am and 3–5pm; Tues 7–11am; Sun noon–6pm.

Museo Nacional de Bellas Artes This old, drafty building seems to have more pots catching leaks than actual exhibits. The bottom floor is a bare exhibition room, while up the dank marble stairs you'll find some faded colonial paintings, some nice miniatures, and a variety of busts and statues. The colorful Jesuit wood relief is about the best thing here. Located in the downtown area, it is worth a 5-minute visit to escape the rain.

Iturbe y Mcal Estigarribo. ✆ **021/447-716.** Free admission. Tues–Fri 7am–7pm; Sat 7am–noon.

Pantéon Nacional de los Heroes Located on the historic Plaza de los Heroes and inspired by Les Invalids in Paris, this monument contains the remains of Mariscal López and the unknown child soldier. It is a grand central dome over a round pit with flag-draped coffins and caskets below. Around it are various plaques and tributes with some nice stained-glass windows. Outside, it is in dire need of renovation, with peeling paint and decapitated statues.

Plaza de los Heroes. Palma y Chile. No telephone. Free admission. Daily 6am–6pm.

Other Attractions

You can catch some of Paraguay's former railway glory at the **Railway Museum,** Eligio Ayala and Mexico streets (✆ **021/447-848**), which is open daily 8am to 5pm and costs G/5,000. If the griminess of the city center gets overwhelming, go northwest on Avenida Ortigas 6km (3¾ miles) to the pastoral 250-hectare (618-acre) park **Jardín Botánico,** Avenida Ortigas and Primer Presidente (✆ **021/281-389**). It's open Monday to Friday from 7am to 6pm, Saturday from 7am to 5pm, and Sundays and holidays from 9am to 1pm. It also contains two natural history and indigenous museums. Admission into the park is G/950. One kilometer (about a half mile) south of the park is the beautiful and historical church **Santísima Trinidad,** Avenida Santísimo Sacramento and Santísima Trinidad. For something more somber, visit the burned-out shell of **Ycuá Bolaños Supermarket,** Santísima Trinidad and Estigarribia, the scene of a tragic fire in 2004 that killed 700 people. It is now a memorial site.

SHOPPING

For consumer goods, go to Ciudad del Este (p. 612). In Asunción you can come across some quality handicrafts, especially *Ñanduti* lace from the town of Itauguá. *Aó poí* is another famous product, a type of fine unbleached cotton. It and other textiles are made in the nearby town of Villarica. *Palo santo* are small items made from Paraguayan wood. You can find some of these items in the markets listed below or at roadside stores on the "Circuito de Oro" tour. A good quality store is **IPA,** Antequerra 241 (✆ **021/498-343;** www.artesania.gov.py). The products are certified and come straight from their creators. For textiles, check out **Taller Fábrica,** Mariscal Estigarribia 2174 (✆ **021/204-081**). For art, go to **Arte Latinoamericano,** Santa Rosa 586 (✆ **021/615-508**).

If you like air-conditioned shopping, there are plenty of upscale shopping malls, especially in the Villa Morra area. **Shopping del Sol,** Avenida Aviadores de Chaco and DF de Gonzalez (✆ **021/611-780;** www.shoppingdelsol.com.py), is the biggest in the country and is opposite the Sheraton. Close by is glitzy **Paseo Carmelitas,** Avenida España and Malutin (www.paseocarmelitas.com.py).

Markets

For handicrafts, go to Plaza de los Heroes. The biggest and liveliest market is **Mercado Cuatro,** Avenida Dr. Francia and Pettirossi. Vendors there sell everything from food to clothes; it's open daily from 6.30am to 6pm. On Saturday, **Plaza de la Independencia** has a morning market with handicrafts and souvenirs, and there is a small passageway with stalls selling similar items on Colon and Presidente Franco.

WHERE TO STAY

For a place with little tourism, the quality of accommodation in Asunción is surprisingly high. Most of the high-end hotels have business clientele and competition is fierce, so be sure to bargain. The more moderate hotels can vary greatly in quality, so thoroughly check the rooms before accepting. Watch out for noisy air-conditioners, as you can have a very uncomfortable night if the machine in the corner is making hissing or dripping sounds. Most hotels are in the claustrophobic center, but more and more are appearing in leafy Villa Morra.

Very Expensive

La Mision Hotel Boutique ★ Asunción's loveliest boutique hotel is an old mansion with a five-story redbrick annex. Immaculate rooms are decked out in a variety of tastes and styles but all are luminous and attractive, with lots of space and comfortable furnishings. The wood-paneled lounge emits a well-heeled ambience, and the pillared roof terrace is delightful. La Mision is located 15 minutes from the airport, close to Mariscal Lopez mall.

Eulogio Estigarribia and San Roque Gonzalez, Asunción. ✆ **021/621-800.** www.lamision.com.py. 26 units. $340 double. Rates include buffet breakfast. AE, DC, MC, V. Free parking. **Amenities:** Restaurant; bar; babysitting; concierge; pool. *In room:* A/C, TV, hair dryer, minibar, Wi-Fi.

Expensive

Granados Park Hotel (Value) One of Asunción´s best-located and well-established hotels is an old-fashioned establishment with a modern nod to luxury and style. Rooms are nicely sized with lovely, comfortable decor and lots of light. The TV has English channels and there are work desks with Internet access. Service can be a little slow but the facilities are excellent, including a decent restaurant, rooftop pool, and Jacuzzi.

15 de Agosto and Estrella, Asunción. ✆/fax **021/497-921.** www.granadospark.com.py. 62 units. $125 double. Rates include buffet breakfast. AE, DC, MC, V. Free parking. **Amenities:** Restaurant; bar; babysitting; concierge; deluxe health club w/fitness center; indoor pool; room service. *In room:* A/C, TV, hair dryer, minibar, Wi-Fi.

Sheraton Asunción ★★ (Kids) The Sheraton Asunción is a 10-story cream-colored building with an interior of bright wood paneling and frosted glass. It is undoubtedly one of the best, and most family-friendly, hotels in Asunción, with a modern, stylish ambience and courteous staff, many of whom speak English. The corridors are bright, with windows at either end, and walls decorated with abstract prints. Rooms are a good size, with a profusion of pneumatic pillows and wardrobes. The hotel's best asset is a fabulous rooftop restaurant right beside the pool, perfect for a cool beer in the early evening while watching the sunset. The hotel is 8km (5 miles) from the city center in upscale Villa Mora, in front of Paraguay's largest shopping mall and near some of Asunción's best restaurants. It is also convenient for the airport.

Aviadores del Chaco 2066. ✆ **021/617-7000.** Fax 021/617-7001. www.sheraton.com. 100 units. $159 double; from $210 suite. AE, DC, MC, V. Rates include breakfast. **Amenities:** 2 restaurants; bar; airport transfers; babysitting; small fitness center and sauna; rooftop pool; room service. *In room:* A/C, TV, hair dryer, minibar, Wi-Fi.

Moderate

Crowne Plaza ★ (Finds) A slick, modern hotel, the Crowne Plaza is on a busy, if somewhat seedy, street in the downtown area (though you could say this about all the streets in the city center). However, once you get past the revolving doors and into the expansive lobby with a fountain and zebra skin armchairs, the bustling city seems miles away. To the right is an all-glass facade that leads to a pleasant courtyard with a garden and chairs—a popular barbecue area on Sundays. A rust-colored partition separates the restaurant and leads to a small, modern bar with red-leather seating and high stools. The corridors are windowed on one side and thus have lots of light. The standard rooms are a good size with queen-size beds and a well-stocked, reasonably priced minibar. The bathrooms are immaculate.

Cero Cora 939, Asunción. ✆/fax **021/452-682.** www.crowneasuncion.com.py. 74 units. $114 double; from $125 suite. Rates include buffet breakfast. AE, DC, MC, V. Free parking. **Amenities:** Restaurant; bar; babysitting; concierge; deluxe health club w/fitness center; indoor pool; room service. *In room:* A/C, TV, hair dryer, minibar, Wi-Fi.

The Excelsior Hotel If there is one thing this old-fashioned hotel does not lack, it's space. Its dark, massive lobby of old-style wood paneling, chandeliers, and gold-gilded furniture seems to go on forever. The pride of the place is a somewhat tacky waterfall with plants. It's best to avoid the cheaper rooms, as they are on the noisy events floor. Go instead for the midrange rooms, which must be the biggest in Asunción—half a tennis court in size. If you don't mind clunky phones, outdated decor, and deep-pile carpets (there are some rooms with tiles), the hotel will do just fine. It's centrally located in front of a small shopping mall, the bathrooms are immaculate, and guests are welcomed with a complimentary caipirinha. Every night there's a traditional song and dance show at the main restaurant, and the second restaurant is an upscale Italian eatery.

Chile 980. ✆ **021/495-632.** Fax 021/496-748. www.excelsior.com.py. 116 units. $90–$110 double; from $120 suite. AE, DC, MC, V. **Amenities:** 2 restaurants; bar; airport transfer (sometimes included); concierge; room service. *In room:* A/C, TV, hair dryer, minibar.

Inexpensive

Asunción Palace Value The oldest hotel in Asunción is a cream-colored colonial building, three stories high and close to the river. It might lack the five-star sheen and luxury of other places, but it makes up for it with a very central location, helpful staff (led by the owners, two sisters named Graciela and Alicia), and an interesting history. It once belonged to President López's brother and was used as a hospital during the War of the Triple Alliance. Two balconies run around the entire building, offering good views of the city. The rooms are somewhat bare and old-fashioned, but there is lots of space in the midpriced range. The bathrooms are more modern, with powerful showers. Some rooms have private balconies and others have multiple beds. The continental breakfast includes delicious homemade cakes.

Colon 415. ✆ **021/492-151.** www.geocities.com/aphotel. 27 units. From $40 double. Rates include buffet breakfast. AE, DC, MC, V. Free parking. **Amenities:** Coffee shop; room service. *In room:* A/C, TV, hair dryer, minibar.

Black Cat Hostel The Black Cat is Asunción´s first youth hostel and lives up to its description with simple decor, narrow beds, and bare-bones dorms that sleep six. It is clean and relatively spacious with a pleasant courtyard and gallery.

President Franco 129, Asunción. ✆ **021/449-827.** www.blackcathostel.com. 3 units. $12 per bed. No credit cards. **Amenities:** Kitchen; TV room; bar. *In room:* A/C.

WHERE TO DINE

Asunción has plenty of street stalls and corner bars selling empanadas and *chipas* (a type of cheese bread made from yuca flour or cornflower). More upmarket restaurants offer the delicious river fish, *surubi,* in countless varieties. The downtown area does not have a great quantity of gourmet-style eateries. Instead, many are located in the Villa Morra district. *Parrillas* (grill houses) are plentiful, though the meat can vary in quality.

Expensive

Mburicao PARAGUAYAN On a quiet residential street in Villa Mora, Mburicao is where Asunción's illustrious come to dine. The large open dining area is attractive if a little uninteresting and lacking in character. That said, the food is great—including the best asparagus soup I've ever had, which comes with a mound of shredded carrot and onion and a sprinkling of Parmesan cheese. The *surubi* is crisp and succulent and presented on a bed of broad beans and tomatoes. Other standout items include tilapia in escargot sauce and filet steak with fresh mushroom and baby potatoes. My only complaint is the limited dessert menu, with only one dessert—a lonely strawberry cake with chocolate and custard. Recommended on the Chilean/Argentine wine list is the Ruca Malen Kinien.

Profesor Gonzalez Riobo 737. ✆ **021/660-048.** Main courses G/45,000–G/70,000. AE, DC, MC, V. Mon–Thurs noon–2:30pm and 8–11:30pm; Fri–Sat noon–2:30pm and 8pm–1:30am.

Moderate

Bar San Roque PARAGUAYAN/GERMAN This restaurant has an old-world feel, with its long, low counter bar with wood paneling, matching olive-green windows and ceiling fans, and black-and-white-tiled floor. It is popular with locals and has an easy, laid-back feel. The menu is meat based, with a variety of homemade pastas. There's a German connection, thus a good collection of beers and Liebfraumilch on the wine list. It's a good downtown choice.

Eligio Ayala 792. ✆ **021/446-015.** Main courses G/23,000–G/38,000. No credit cards. Daily 11:45am–3:30pm and 7:30pm–midnight.

Il Mondo ASIAN FUSION/PARAGUAYAN This is a good, high-end restaurant in the downtown area. The decor is Romanesque with a touch of the Far East. Togalike drapes hang from windows and walls, while a large urn sits on a grand central table surrounded by four templelike pillars. All is overlooked by a large wooden Buddha on the back wall. The menu is a 20-page extravaganza of seafood, river food, Far East stir fries, and meat (of course). I tried the pasta, which was excellent and came mixed with bacon, baby tomatoes, and a variety of nuts. The service was spot on, and the staff, though non-English speaking, were very friendly. Il Mondo is part of the Granado Park Hotel.

15 de Agosto y Estrella. ✆ **021/497-921.** Main courses G/38,000–G/57,000. AE, DC, MC, V. Daily noon–4pm and 7pm–1am.

Luna Vinera Bistro Bar PARAGUAYAN Tall arched doors lead to this stylish restaurant offering Paraguayan staples such as *surubi* and steak in a laid-back atmosphere. The space features occasional live performances of jazz and bossa nova.

Av. Ygatimi 250. ✆ **021/491-604.** www.lunavinera.com. Main courses G/40,000–G/50,000. No credit cards. Tues–Sun 7pm–late.

Talleygrand FRENCH/SPANISH The attractive, solid-white building of adobe walls and thick wooden beams gives assurance in a downtown area sorely lacking in good restaurants. The food is a mixture of French and Spanish, with a Paraguayan twist. This includes eight variations of the ubiquitous *surubi,* one of which is *surubi a la bonne* (*surubi,* done in white wine and mustard). The *festival de pasta* is a pasta party for two, with six types of sauce to choose from. There is rabbit with mushroom sauce, and good old-fashioned sirloin served with fried cassava. Out back is a small bar with a waiting area of embroidered curtains and cushions. The waiters are tall, dark, and very serious, but it's a popular place, with relaxing jazz playing in the background.

Mcal Estigarribia 441. ✆ **021/441-163.** Main courses G/38,000–G/50,000. MC, V. Daily noon–4pm and 8pm–1am.

Inexpensive

Biggest ★ (Value) PARAGUAYAN This corner diner lives up to its description with good size portions of burgers, fries, and pizza. Its location means it's perfect for a mid-morning coffee stop in a city that lacks coffee shops. Two matronly waitresses run the place with friendly efficiency.

Estrella and 15 de Agosto. ✆ **021/455-411.** Main courses G/12,000–G/23,000. No credit cards. Daily 11am–midnight.

ASUNCION AFTER DARK

Don't let its dark streets turn you off. There is a party going on somewhere in this city if you look hard enough. There are plenty of bars dotted all around the city, especially a few blocks east of Plaza Uruguaya. You'll also find some down-at-the-heel karaoke bars around Palma and Colon. The **Britannia Pub,** Cerro Cora 851 (✆ **021/901-2850**), is a British-style bar popular with locals and expats. In existence for over 20 years, it is still going strong, with good crowds drinking beer from huge tankards on any given night of the week (except Mon). Another favorite is **Austria Pub,** Austria 1783 y Vienna (✆ **021/604-662**), situated upstairs in a small shopping mall called Excelsior in the downtown area.

For something trendier and more upscale, you have to go to Villa Morra and its various glitzy shopping malls. **Kamastro** ★, Paseo Carmelitas, Avenida España and Senador Long (✆ **021/615-041**), is an interesting art-house bar with psychedelic guitars and naked body prints on the walls. Close by, you'll find **Kilkenny Irish Pub,** Malutin and Avenida España (✆ **021/672-768;** www.kilkenny.com.py). Across the road, in a smaller mall, is **Hooters,** Avenida España and Romulo Feliciangeli (✆ **021/665-215**), an American-based chain boasting cold beers and tasty chicken wings. Some of the best nightclubs are on the city outskirts. **Faces,** Mcal López 2585 (✆ **021/672-768**), and **Coyote,** Sucre 1655 (✆ **021/662-816;** www.coyote.com.py), are the biggest and best known. **Canvas,** Shopping del Sol ((✆ **021/622-875**), is a slick and happening night-spot with five dance floors pumping out electronica and bossa nova. The high-tech restaurant is worth a visit just to experience the touch-screen menus on each table.

A SIDE TRIP TO SAN BERNARDINO

54km (34 miles) SE of Asunción

San Bernardino is a small resort town on the eastern shore of Lago Ypacarai. A trip there makes for an interesting day tour (taking no more than 7 hr.) known as "Circuito de Oro." You leave Asunción via Avenida Mariscal López, a busy highway passing *Gone With the Wind*–style diplomatic mansions. Twelve kilometers (8 miles) away is the bustling satellite town of **San Lorenzo** with its gray neo-Gothic cathedral. On the open road, you will pass handicraft stores selling a variety of ceramics and basketware, much of it tacky. In the humble town of Yaguaron, be sure to visit **Iglesia San Buenaventura,** one of the most beautiful churches in Paraguay. Built in 1755, it is a small white-faced chapel with spectacular doors carved by indigenous artists. The inner pillars are brightly tinted with red, yellow, and green vegetable inks. The ceiling has 60 tiny individual portraits of the local craftsmen who worked on the church (their signatures) and the altar is a gold-painted spectacle with incredible detail. The church is open every day from 6am to 4pm, closing at midday from 11am to 1:30pm. It's open mornings only on Saturdays. The caretaker, Antolin Aleman, will also show you a small museum nearby. Be sure to leave a small donation, as the church is proudly cared for by the local community with little or no help from the authorities.

Back on the road, you'll notice the flatlands become gentle slopes with the occasional rocky cliff. You pass lemon groves, roadside stalls, and the occasional wandering farm fowl. Make sure to stop at **Fruteria Paraguan** (no phone). This large restaurant sells delicious, syrupy fruit salads. Nearby, in **Pararetá** and **Chololó,** are several beauty spots with small waterfalls and bathing areas popular in the summer. The town of **Pirebebuy** has another interesting colonial church and is infamous for a strong local brew called *caña.* The town was the site of a major battle in the War of the Triple Alliance. Here you are truly in the rural hinterland, surrounded by little more than stray cattle and road vendors selling bottles of dark honey. Next you arrive at **Caacupé,** the Lourdes of Paraguay. It is a major pilgrimage center, attracting thousands for the Immaculate Conception celebrations on December 8 each year, with fireworks, night processions, and displays of amazingly agile dancers balancing bottles on their heads. Finally, you reach **Ypacarai Lake** and the pleasant "beach" town of **San Bernardino.** In the summer, its bars, cafes, and shore are bustling with people enjoying the waterside atmosphere. Enjoy a late lunch at **Los Alpes** restaurant and hotel, Ruta General Morinigo, Km 46.5 (✆ **512/232-399;** www.hotellosalpes.com.py). It has a pretty flower-covered veranda and fountain with resident parrots. The restaurant does buffet-style lunches amid tropical decor. The direct route back to Asunción from here is 54km (35 miles).

5 CIUDAD DEL ESTE

327km (209 miles) E of Asunción

Prepare yourself for a city quite unlike any other; a dirty, sweltering warren of frenetic buying and selling, set beside a muddy river upon which thousands cross like ants carrying TVs, computers, even kitchen sinks! Ciudad del Este is the third-largest tax-free zone in the world and provides 60% of Paraguay's GDP. Here the currency is either dollars or Brazilian reals, and the nationalities are a melting pot of Taiwanese, Korean, Indian, Syrian, and Lebanese. Ciudad del Este gets a bad rap as South America's capital of contraband and piracy, where you can buy anything from AK47s to bales of marijuana to even babies (so one foreboding Argentine told me). Yet it is a modern frontier town (indeed, three frontiers), choked with billboards and vendors. Shoppers and porters hurriedly dodge money changers and dealers as motorcyclists weave between stalled cars and buses, all on a frantic break for the border. Stores vary from rickety stalls to giant luxury malls selling the real and the unreal. Ciudad del Este's existence began with the building of the impressive **Itaipú dam** and continues with the unchecked flood of Brazilian and Argentine bargain hunters. (It is linked to Brazil through a 500m/1,640 ft. rusting hulk called the **Friendship Bridge.**) It has some good hotels and is close to Iguazú Falls and its smaller counterpart, Monday Falls.

ESSENTIALS

Getting There

BY PLANE **Aeropuerto Guaraní** (airport code CDE; no phone) is 30km (19 miles) west of town. **TAM,** Curupayty 195 (✆ **064/420-843**), operates a daily service between Sao Paolo and Asunción.

BY BUS The **Terminal,** Chaco Boreal and Capitan del Puerto (✆ **061/510-421**) is on the southern outskirts of the city, beside a large soccer stadium. There are buses connecting in Asunción (4½ hr.) and Encarnación (3 hr.), costing $8 and $5. Local buses leave for Foz de Iguaçu every 15 minutes. **Nuestra Señora de la Asunción** (✆ **061/510-095;** www.nsa.com.py) operates a reliable service.

Getting Around

All the action takes place around the Microcentro and to the east towards **Puente de la Amistad,** the Friendship Bridge. It is often best to go everywhere on foot, as traffic is often at a standstill.

Border Crossing

The 500m-long (1,640-ft.) "Friendship Bridge" can be at times very informal, and chaotic—watch out for pickpockets, especially on Wednesdays and Sundays, which are the busiest days. Rush hour can be incredibly slow and it is often quicker to walk over the bridge than to take a bus or taxi. Pedestrians from Brazil walk on the northern side with goods-laden consumers exiting on the other side. If you are a U.S. or Canadian citizen (see "Entry Requirements & Customs," p. 598) you might be tempted to risk crossing without a visa, but be warned. If you're caught, it can mean the temporary confiscation of your passport until you pay a "fine." Local buses do not stop at the Customs offices, which are at either end of the bridge. You'll find a somewhat shabby but friendly and helpful **tourist office** (no phone) in the Paraguayan Customs building.

WHAT TO SEE & DO

Flora and Fauna Itaipú Binacional As a sop to the huge environmental damage caused by the dam, the builders were obliged to spend some money on remedial work such as relocation of wildlife and reforestation. One result is an interesting zoo with displaced jaguars and other animals. As part of this complex, you will also find two well-organized natural history and archaeological museums. It is located 2km (1¼ miles) from the Itaipú Visitors Center on the road back to Ciudad del Este.

Hernadarias. ✆ **061/599-8040.** Free admission. Mon–Sun 7:30am–1pm and 2–5pm.

Itaipú Dam The pride of Paraguay is one of the biggest hydroelectric projects in the world and actually produces 18 times more electricity than Paraguay needs (the remainder is sold to Brazil and Argentina). Although it has proved an economic boon to the area, it has an ambiguous past; its $25-billion price tag plunged all three border countries into debt and had a devastating effect on the surrounding environment. The submerged Sete Quedas falls were actually larger and more impressive than Iguazú. It has also proved a magnet for mosquitoes, boosting the risk of malaria in the area. Nevertheless, it is an engineering masterpiece, impressive in its size, volume, and ugliness. There are two types of tours. One is free via bus, where you cross the dam but see very little of the facility, and another costs $15, but is more technical and you get to disembark. This is recommended as you get to see the 1km-long (about a half mile) machine room. Tours also include a rather technical 30-minute film. On Fridays and Saturdays at 7pm, there is a nighttime illumination and fireworks display. The dam is 20km (12 miles) north of the city, near the town of Hernadarias. ***Don't forget:*** Bring your passport!

Visitor Center, Hernadarias. ✆ **061/599-8989.** www.itaipu.gov.py. Free admission. Mon–Sat tours 8am, 9:30am, 2pm, and 3pm; Fri–Sat 7pm; Sun and holidays 8am and 9:30am.

Salto Monday Anywhere else, this waterfall would be the star attraction, but when it's so close to the magnificence of Iguazú, Salto Monday's 80m-high (362-ft.) cascade takes on the role of a younger, neglected brother. Nearby you'll find a popular beach resort and nature reserve called Tati Yupi. The falls are located 10km (6 miles) south of the city, in the town of Puerto President Franco.

Puerto President Franco. ✆ **061/550-042.** Admission G/2,500. Mon–Sun 7am–4pm.

SHOPPING

Ciudad del Este is regarded as the cheapest place for electronic goods on the continent. Its shops and malls are plentiful and vary greatly in quality. The center is a maze of stores and stalls selling all types of cheap and tacky goods. Be careful of counterfeit products, near–name brands, and short-changing. Always haggle. If you get anything wrapped, make sure it is what you bought.

Some of the malls are more secure and certainly cleaner, such as **Mona Lisa,** Carlos A. Lopez 654 (✆ **061/513-622;** www.monalisa.com.py), which specializes in luxury goods. Casa China, Av. San Blas 206 (✆ **561/500-335;** www.casachina.net), sells everything from flowerpots to motorbike helmets.

WHERE TO STAY

Ciudad del Este goes dead after 5pm when the shopping frenzy ends and everybody crosses back over the border to Brazil. At night, the city has a dangerous reputation, which is not entirely unfounded, so be careful of where you choose to stay. The best hotels are situated outside the downtown area. **Las Ventanas,** Avenida Maria de los Angeles and Luis Bordon, Paraná Country Club (✆ **061/574-500;** www.lasventanas.com.py), is the newest and trendiest, with comfortable rooms and spacious balconies. Doubles start at $132.

Another excellent choice is the colonial **Casa Blanca,** Calle Botero Norte 69, Paraná Country Club (✆ **061/572-121;** www.casablancahotel.net), situated along the Paraná river. It is in an idyllic, tranquil setting and rooms come with a balcony overlooking a beautiful pool. Make sure you get a room in the original building, where rooms start at $140. A good city option is the **Panorama Inn,** Pampliega and Ayola (✆ **061/500-110;** www.hotelpanoramainn.com.py). It is not five-star but it is clean and modern, with an all-essential pool. Here room prices cost around $80. Another decent downtown hotel is **Hotel Austria,** E.R. Fernandez 165 (✆ **061/504-213;** www.hotelaustriarestaurante.com), a good value at $65 for a double room.

WHERE TO DINE

You'll find lots of cheap eateries on Garcia Street and in the marketplace. Main courses at more upscale restaurants range from G/30,000 to G/50,000. For more upscale, European cuisine, try the restaurant at **Hotel Austria,** E.R. Fernandez 165 (✆ **061/504-213**). An

Waterfalls & Jaguars

Paraguay has great potential regarding ecotourism. It has 11 national parks and 7 reserves offering diverse habitats. However, poor management and little infrastructure mean you really must make an effort to get there. Just be prepared to get your feet wet and your clothes dirty when you do so. For permits and information concerning all of Paraguay's parks, go to **Direccion de Parques Nacionales y Vida Silvestre,** Franco and Ayolas, Asunción (© **021/445-970**). Below are some of the best parks.

- **Parque Nacional Ybycui** is 5,000 hectares (12,350 acres) of rare rainforest, steep woodland, and idyllic waterfalls. It is the country's most accessible park and is famous for its partridges and multitudes of butterflies. It is only 120km (77 miles) south of Asunción and therefore can be crowded on weekends and holidays. On weekdays, its campsites and forest trails are deserted.
- **Parque Nacional Cerro Corrá** was the site of Mariscal López's last stand against his triple alliance enemies and is now a 22,000-hectare (54,340-acre) reserve of tropical forest and savannah grasslands. There are also caves, petroglyphs, and a small museum and information center. The town is 35km (22 miles) from the town of Pedro Juan Caballero, near the Brazilian border.
- **Parque Nacional Defensores del Chaco** is a 780,000-hectare (1.9-million acre) enclave of spectacular bird life, including 1.8m (6-ft.) storks called jabirus. Jaguars and pumas can be found lurking in the dense thorn forest. The park is 830km (515 miles) from Asunción and accessible only by 4×4. Permits are necessary and obtained in Asunción. It is highly recommended that you go with a guide.

excellent Brazilian-style churrascaria (grill house) is **Patussi Grill,** Avenida Monsignor Cedzich and Alejo Garcia (© **061/502-293**). **Belsit,** Avenida Boqueron (no phone), is a wonderful Italian restaurant, located away from the city center and close to El Lago de La Republica. For something completely different, try **New Tokyo,** Pampliega (© **061/514-379**), which, as the name implies, provides authentic Japanese food.

11

Peru

by Neil Edward Schlecht

When Francisco Pizarro, the Spanish conquistador, and his fortune-hunting cronies descended on Peru in 1528, they found the vast riches they were searching for, as well as an unexpectedly sophisticated culture. The Spaniards soon overpowered the awed and politically weakened Inca empire, but they didn't discover the Incas' greatest secret: the imperial city of Machu Picchu, hidden high in the Andes. Machu Picchu is acclaimed as the pinnacle achievement of the continent's pre-Columbian societies, yet it is only one of the exhilarating discoveries that await visitors to Peru.

Peru has a habit of turning virtually every visitor into an amateur archaeologist. Ruins fire the imagination and outstanding museum collections weave an intricate tale of complex cultures through ceramics, spectacular textiles, and remarkably preserved mummies. You can see the Lord of Sipán in all the glory of the jewels and rituals that accompanied his burial, as well as the frozen corpse of Juanita the Ice Maiden, an Inca princess sacrificed on a mountain ridge more than 500 years ago.

Peru has few peers when it comes to physical beauty and diversity. Its landscapes will delight anyone with an appreciation for the outdoors: the rugged, cloud-ringed Andes; the brilliant azure water of Lake Titicaca, the world's highest navigable body of water; great canyons graced by giant condors; and a teeming Amazon jungle that possesses one of the world's richest repositories of plant and animal life. Peru is fast becoming South America's top destination for mountain climbing, river rafting, bird-watching, river cruises, and rainforest treks. Urban Peru is a mix of laid-back and elegant colonial towns, a chaotic and cosmopolitan capital, and the surprisingly lively Cusco, a grand 16th-century city on Inca foundations that rocks to the beat of global backpackers.

Peru's history of suffering—political mayhem and corruption, surprise attacks from homegrown Maoist Shining Path terrorists, cocaine trafficking, and violent street crime—is well documented. In the late 1980s and early 1990s, Peruvians fled the capital and the countryside, and understandably, few travelers were brave enough to plan vacations in Peru. With the 2001 election of Alejandro Toledo, the nation's first president of native Indian origin, many Peruvians were hopeful that the country had finally turned a corner. Although the economy has grown at a rate of 7% to 8% annually for the past 6 years and Peru is safer and superficially more stable than before, widespread poverty, frequent strikes, and continued unease are still prevalent. One disgraced ex-president, Alberto Fujimori, returned from exile in Japan only to be jailed in Peru, while another, Alan García, surprisingly reappeared after his own exile abroad to recapture the presidency. Still, Peru is more welcoming than ever. Too many unfortunate years of corrupt politicians, lawlessness, and economic disarray clouded—but never succeeded in eclipsing—the resilient beauty of this fascinating Andean nation.

1 THE REGIONS IN BRIEF

Peru, which lies just below the Equator, is the third-largest country in South America, covering an area of nearly 1.3 million sq. km (507,000 sq. miles). Peru shares borders with Ecuador and Colombia to the north, Brazil and Bolivia to the east, and Chile to the south. Peruvians are fond of telling visitors that their country is in fact three countries (or at least three distinct geological components) in one: coast, sierra (highlands), and *selva* (jungle). Though Lima lies on the coast, the bold Andes Mountain range and Amazon rainforest, which makes up nearly two-thirds of Peru, dominate the country. Its considerable size, natural barriers, and a lack of efficient transportation options make Peru a somewhat difficult and time-consuming place in which to get around.

LIMA & THE CENTRAL COAST The Pacific coastal region is a narrow strip that runs from one end of the country to the other (a distance of some 2,254km/1,400 miles) and is almost entirely desert. Lima lies about halfway down the coast. To the south in one of the driest areas on earth are **Pisco, Ica,** and **Nazca,** cradle of several of Peru's most important ancient civilizations, as well as the famously mysterious **Nazca Lines** and the **Ballestas Islands,** promoted locally as "Peru's Galápagos" for their diverse indigenous fauna. In August 2007, a massive earthquake, which registered 7.9 on the Richter scale, devastated much of Pisco and Ica, killing more than 500 people and leaving nearly 100,000 homeless. The region will take years to rebuild, a factor travelers should keep in mind if they intend to travel to the area.

SOUTH CENTRAL PERU The dramatic Andes Mountains of the south, the focus of most first-time visitors to Peru, contain the country's most famous sights, including the former Inca capital of **Cusco** and scenic highland villages that run the length of the beautiful **Sacred Valley.** The valley is dotted with singularly impressive Inca ruins, of which **Machu Picchu** (and the **Inca Trail** leading to it) is undoubtedly the star.

SOUTHERN PERU Massive **Lake Titicaca,** shared with Bolivia, is the largest freshwater lake in South America and the world's highest navigable body of water. **Puno,** at the edge of Lake Titicaca, is a rough-and-tumble town that hosts some of Peru's liveliest festivals. The elegant colonial city of **Arequipa** is gorgeously situated at the base of three snowcapped volcanoes, and nearby is **Colca Canyon,** twice as deep as the Grand Canyon and perhaps the best place in South America to view the regal Andean condor.

NORTH CENTRAL HIGHLANDS The mountain ranges north of Lima are among the highest in Peru. Within **Huascarán National Park,** the Cordillera Blanca stretches for 200km (124 miles) and contains a dozen peaks over 5,000m (16,400 ft.) high. The region is a favorite of trekkers and outdoor adventure travelers. The main jumping-off point for these activities is the town of **Huaraz.** In valleys east of the capital is **Chavín de Huantar,** one of Peru's oldest archaeological sites.

NORTH COAST & NORTHERN HIGHLANDS Peru's north is much less visited than the south, even though it possesses some of the country's most outstanding archaeological sights. **Trujillo, Chiclayo,** and, particularly, **Cajamarca,** a lovely small city in the highlands, are the main colonial towns of interest. Near Trujillo and Chiclayo are **Chan Chan, Túcume,** and **Sipán,** extraordinary adobe cities, pyramids, and royal tombs and treasures that vastly predate the Incas.

Off the Beaten Path

Northern Peru is vastly underappreciated; in fact, most of the region is virtually unknown to foreigners who travel to Peru. The few travelers who get to know the north are mainly those with a specific interest in ancient Peruvian cultures or hikers and adventurous travelers looking to get out into the country, beyond the reach of the majority of gringos who trod well-beaten paths in the Andes and southern Peru. If you make it to this part of Peru, you may be in for the not-unwelcome treat of being one of the few.

You wouldn't know it from the paucity of foreign visitors, but the northern coastal desert of Peru holds some of the country's greatest archaeological treasures: **Chan Chan,** the great adobe city of the Chimú civilization; 1,500-year-old Moche temples; and the royal tomb that brought the great Lord of Sipán to the world's attention in 1987—Peru's very own King Tut. Northern beaches draw surfers to some of the best waves off South America, and nestled in the sierra is one of the country's most charming and beautiful mountain towns, **Cajamarca,** a mini-Cusco of the north.

Where gringos of a particular ilk and style of outdoor performance gear do make it in significant numbers is the **Cordillera Blanca,** home to some of the most beautiful peaks in South America and some of the finest trekking on the continent. Huaraz is the primary base for excursions into the valleys and mountain ranges of the northern Andes. For years, the destination has been favored principally by sports and adventure travelers, especially hard-core hikers, but the range of activities is opening up and appealing more and more to average travelers who also want a taste of Peru's great outdoors.

LAN (✆ 01/213-8200; www.lan.com) flies to Trujillo, Chiclayo, and Cajamarca from Lima, while sister company **LC Busre** (✆ 01/619-1313; www.lcbusre.com.pe) flies daily to Ayacucho and Cajamarca; **Star Perú** (✆ 01/705-9000; www.starperu.com) flies daily from Lima to Chiclayo, Trujillo, and Ayacucho. Agencies offering standard city and archaeological tours in Trujillo include **Guía Tours,** Jr. Independencia 580 (✆ 044/245-170); **Chacón Tours,** Av. España 106 (✆ 044/255-212); and **Trujillo Tours,** Diego de Almagro 301 (✆ 044/233-091). In Chiclayo, **Indiana Tours,** Colón 556 (✆ 074/222-991), offers a full range of northern archaeological tours.

Traveling by bus from Lima, or from other points along the north coast or the northern Andes, is the only way to get to Huaraz. For the 7- to 8-hour journey from Lima, major companies offering daily service are **CIVA** (**✆ 01/332-5236**), **Cruz del Sur** (**✆ 01/424-6158**), and **Móvil Tours** (**✆ 044/722-555** in Huaraz). For mountaineering and trekking information, consult the respected **Casa de Guías de Huaraz,** Parque Ginebra 28 (**✆ 044/721-811**).

THE AMAZON BASIN & THE JUNGLE Though about 60% of Peru is Amazon rainforest, only about 5% of the country's human inhabitants reside there. For the visitor, there are two primary jungle destinations. The northern jungle, of which **Iquitos** is the principal gateway, is the most explored and has the most facilities. Much less trafficked and more controlled is the Madre de Dios department (one of the administrative districts into which Peru is divided) in the south, which contains **Manu National Park** (and its Biosphere Reserve), **Puerto Maldonado,** and **Tambopata.**

2 THE BEST OF PERU IN 2 WEEKS

This itinerary will allow you to experience the greatest attractions of southern Peru, from its historic colonial cities to its natural wonders. First on everyone's list, of course, are the lively ancient Inca capital of Cusco and that empire's legendary lost city, Machu Picchu. But in a short amount of time, you can also delve into the dense Amazonian jungle; Lake Titicaca, the world's highest navigable body of water; and one of the world's deepest canyons, Cañón del Colca. Plenty of people linger, particularly in Cusco and the Sacred Valley of the Incas (especially if they want to hike the Inca Trail to Machu Picchu), or don't have a full 2 weeks for travel in Peru. In that case, it's probably best to concentrate on a particular region so that you don't lose too much time traveling. Of course, if your primary interest is wildlife viewing in the great Amazon, you'll want to plan everything around a 4- to 7-day jungle expedition deep into Tambopata National Reserve, Manu Biosphere Reserve, or the jungle around Iquitos in northern Peru.

Day ❶: Arrive in Lima ★

All international flights go into the chaotic capital, Lima, and even though most people are headed elsewhere, you may be obligated to spend at least a day in Lima. Make the most of it by touring the colonial quarter, or perhaps by visiting one of the country's great museums, such as the **Museo Arqueológico Rafael Larco Herrera** (p. 641) or **Museo de la Nación** (p. 641), and hitting either a great *cevichería* or a cutting-edge *novo andino* restaurant. Then get out of Lima on the way to Peru's greatest attractions. (If you're able to get an overnight flight that puts you into Lima early in the morning, you may want to consider flying immediately to Cusco.)

Days ❷–❸: On to Cusco & the Sacred Valley ★★★

The typical thing to do is hit Cusco running, but since the city's altitude, more than 3,600m (11,800 ft.), is daunting to most travelers, a great alternative is to head directly to the serene and beautiful (as well as lower-altitude) **Valle Sagrado de los Incas (Sacred Valley of the Incas).** Besides great Inca ruins in **Pisac** (p. 675) and **Ollantaytambo** (p. 679), you'll find excellent crafts markets, a wealth of outdoor activities such as trekking and white-water rafting, small rural villages, and a burgeoning roster of comfortable rustic lodgings. Relax, eat and sleep well, and get ready for Machu Picchu.

Day ❹: The Stuff of Legend: Machu Picchu ★★★

Take the morning train from Ollantaytambo to Aguas Calientes, which sits down below camouflaged **Machu Picchu** (p. 681), South America's number-one attraction. Spend the day exploring the ruins (hiking up to **Huayna Picchu** if you're in shape) and then spend the night either next to the ruins (if you've got deep pockets) or back down in Aguas Calientes (which is actually more fun). Hit the thermal baths and the bars to share stories with those who've hiked the Inca Trail.

Days ❺–❻: Back to Cusco ★★★

Now that you've acclimatized to the Andes Mountains and seen some of the greatest legacies of the Incas, head back by train to the old Inca capital, Cusco. Stroll around the hilly San Blas neighborhood, site of art galleries and shops; check out streets with foundations of Inca stone; and visit the **Cathedral, Plaza de Armas,** and stunning **Qoricancha (Temple of the Sun;** p. 657, 659, and 661). If you didn't catch an archaeology museum in Lima, or even if you did, check out the beautifully designed **Museo de Arte Precolombino** (p. 661). Enjoy some of the lively cafes, bars, and restaurants of Cusco. If you have time, catch a cab (or walk up to) the fantastic ruins, **Sacsayhuamán,** overlooking the city (p. 662).

Days ❼–❾: Into the Jungle ★★★

Take an early morning, half-hour flight from Cusco to **Puerto Maldonado,** the gateway to the southern Peruvian Amazon jungle of **Tambopata National Reserve** (p. 693). Board a boat on the way to a 3-day, 2-night adventure at a jungle lodge (either within 1 hr. of Puerto Maldonado, or 4–5 hr. along the Río Tambopata; if you're pressed for time, you can also do a 2-day, 1-night trip to one of the lodges along the Río Madre de Dios). On the third day, head back to Puerto and then catch a flight to Cusco. Spend the night in Cusco.

Day ❿: South to Lake Titicaca ★★★

From Cusco, take the extraordinarily scenic train to **Puno** and **Lake Titicaca** (p. 695); or, if you want to visit some of the Inca ruins en route, take one of the premium tour bus services that make a day of the journey. Spend the night in Puno and rest up (and get accustomed to the even higher altitude) for tomorrow's boat trip out on the lake.

Day ⓫: Lake Titicaca & Isla Taquile ★★★

While an overnight trip that allows you to spend a night with a family either on Isla Taquile or Amantaní is the best way to experience the people and customs of Titicaca, you can also do a 1-day trip that allows you to visit the **Uros floating islands** (p. 698) and the fascinating culture of **Isla Taquile** (p. 699).

Day ⓬: Arequipa ★★

Catch an early morning flight from Juliaca (the nearest airport, an hour from Puno) to Arequipa, the elegant southern city known as "La Ciudad Blanca" for its beautiful colonial buildings made of *sillar,* or white volcanic stone. Stay close to the gorgeous **Plaza de Armas** (p. 708) and spend the afternoon at the wondrous **Monasterio de Santa Catalina** (p. 707), one of the finest examples of colonial religious architecture in the Americas.

Days ⓭–⓮: Colca Valley ★★

If you're short on time, spend another day in Arequipa, shopping for alpaca garments and enjoying some of the finest cuisine in Peru. If you have an extra day, though, don't miss an overnight journey to **Colca Valley,** the site of **Colca Canyon** (twice as deep as the Grand Canyon) and the best spot in South America to observe giant Andean condors, which soar overhead at **Cruz del Cóndor** (p. 713). Spend your first night at a rustic hotel in Colca, and then head back to Arequipa.

Day ⓯: Morning in Arequipa, Then Back to Lima ★

If you were able to squeeze out the extra day, do a little shopping before flying to Lima, where you'll catch your flight back home.

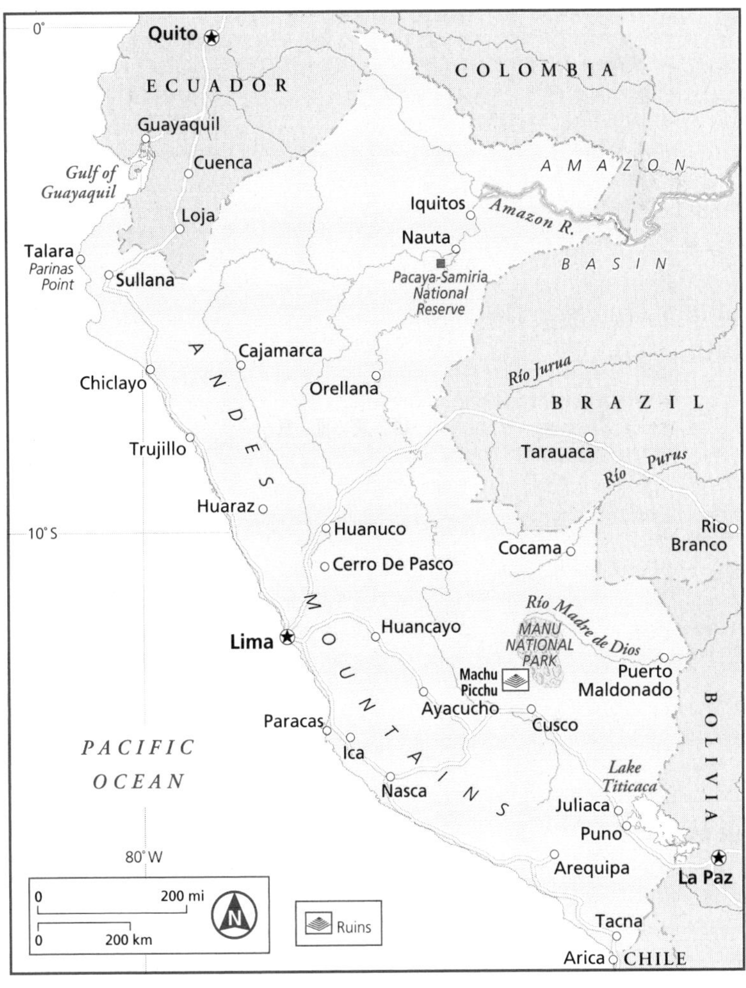

3 PLANNING YOUR TRIP TO PERU

VISITOR INFORMATION

Peru doesn't maintain national tourism offices abroad, so your best official source of information before you go is the **PromPerú (Commission for the Promotion of Peru)** website at **www.peru.info**. Peruvian embassies and consulates usually offer some brochures and other information on traveling to Peru, but it's probably best not to expect too much. Additional websites of interest include:

Telephone Dialing Info at a Glance

- **To place a call from your home country to Peru,** dial the international access code (0011 in Australia, 011 in the U.S. and Canada, 0170 in New Zealand, 00 in the U.K.), plus the country code (51), plus the Peruvian area code, followed by the number. For example, a call from the United States to Lima would be 011+51+1+000+0000.
- **To place a local call within Peru,** you do *not* need to dial the city area code (for example, 01 for Lima); dial only the number. To place a long-distance call within Peru, dial 0 plus the city code and the number. For information, dial ✆ 103.
- **To place a direct international call from Peru,** dial the international access code (00), plus the country code of the place you are dialing, plus the area code and the local number.
- **To reach an international operator,** dial ✆ 108. Major long-distance company access codes are as follows: **AT&T** ✆ 0800/50-888; **MCI** ✆ 0800/50-010; **Sprint** ✆ 0800/50-020.

- **www.peruvianembassy.us**: The official website for the Peruvian Embassy in Washington, D.C., with a roster of recent media articles about Peru and other news items.
- **www.perurail.com**, **www.incarail.com**, and **www.machupicchutrain.com**: the sites of the newly competitive rail carriers that travel from Cusco to the Sacred Valley and Machu Picchu (until recently, Peru Rail held a monopoly on these routes).
- **www.saexplorers.org**: The South American Explorers Club website, especially good for trekking and adventure travel.
- **www.traficoperu.com/english**: An online travel agency with information on flights, hotels, and special deals.

In Peru

Visitor information is not handled by a single, centralized government agency across Peru. PromPerú works alongside Mitinci (Ministry of Industry, Tourism & International Business Negotiation) and several private entities. The result is that tourism information is confusingly dispersed among sometimes poorly equipped small municipal offices and is often limited to regional or local information. Occasionally, private travel agencies are more adept at dispensing information, though their goal is, of course, to hawk their services.

PromPerú operates a 24-hour hotline (✆ **01/574-8000**), available from anywhere in the country. The **Tourist Protection Bureau (Indecopi)** operates a 24-hour traveler's assistance line that handles complaints and questions about consumer rights; call ✆ **01/224-7888** in Lima, or 0800/42-579 (toll-free) in other cities. The Tourist Protection Bureau's Lima office is at La Prosa 138, San Borja (✆ **01/224-8600**); for local branch numbers, see "Fast Facts" in the individual city sections in this chapter.

ENTRY REQUIREMENTS

Citizens of Australia, Canada, Great Britain, New Zealand, South Africa, and the United States require valid passports to enter Peru as tourists. Citizens of any of these countries conducting business or enrolled in formal educational programs in Peru also require visas.

Tourist (or landing) cards, distributed on arriving international flights or at border crossings, are good for stays of up to 90 days. Keep a copy of the tourist card for presentation upon departure from Peru. (If you lose it, you'll have to pay a $4 fine.) A maximum of three extensions of 30 days each, for a total of 180 days, is allowed.

Peruvian Embassy Locations

In Australia: 40 Brisbane Ave., Level 2, Barton, ACT 2600 (✆ **02/6273-7351;** www.embaperu.org.au)

In Canada: 130 Albert St., Suite 1901, Ottawa, Ontario K1P 5G4 (✆ **613/238-1777;** www.embassyofperu.ca)

In New Zealand: Cigna House, 40 Mercer St., Level 8, Wellington (✆ **04/499-8087;** www.embassyofperu.org.nz)

In the U.K.: 52 Sloane St., London SW1X 9SP (✆ **020/7235-1917;** www.peruembassy-uk.com)

In the U.S.: 1700 Massachusetts Ave. NW, Washington, DC 20036 (✆ **202/833-9860;** www.peruvianembassy.us)

CUSTOMS

You are allowed to bring 3 liters of alcohol and 400 cigarettes or 50 cigars into Peru duty-free. New items for personal use, including camera equipment and sports gear such as mountain bikes and kayaks, are allowed. Travelers may bring in up to $300 in varied gifts, as long as no individual item exceeds $100. To avoid the possibility of having to fill out forms or pay a bond, it's best not to draw attention to expensive, new-looking items that officials might believe you are intent on reselling. (In other words, take new items out of their original boxes.)

Exports of protected plant and endangered animal species—live or dead—are strictly prohibited by Peruvian law and should not be purchased. This includes headpieces and necklaces made with macaw feathers, and even common "rain sticks," unless authorized by the Natural Resources Institute (INRENA). Vendors in jungle cities and airports sell live animals and birds, as well as handicrafts made from insects, feathers, or other natural products. Travelers have been detained and arrested by the Ecology Police in Lima for carrying such items.

It is also illegal to take pre-Columbian archaeological items, antiques, and artifacts from precolonial civilizations (including ceramics and textiles), as well as colonial-era art, out of Peru. Reproductions of many such items are available, but even their export may cause difficulties at Customs or with overly cautious international courier services if you attempt to send them home. To be safe, look for the word REPRODUCCIÓN or an artist's name stamped on reproduction ceramics, and keep business cards and receipts from shops where you have purchased these items. Particularly fine items may require documentation from Peru's National Institute of Culture (INC) verifying that the object is a reproduction and may be exported. You may be able to obtain a certificate of authorization from the (only occasionally staffed) **INC kiosk** at Lima's Jorge Chávez International Airport or the **INC office** in Lima at the National Museum Building, 6th Floor, Av. Javier Prado Este 2465, San Borja (✆ **01/476-9900**).

MONEY

Peru's official currency is the **nuevo sol** (S/), divided into 100 centavos. Coins are issued in denominations of 5, 10, 20, and 50 centavos, and bank notes of S/10, 20, 50, 100, and 200. The U.S. dollar is the second currency; many hotels post their rates in dollars, and plenty of shops, taxi drivers, restaurants, and hotels across Peru accept U.S. dollars for payment. It is often difficult to pay with large bank notes (in either soles or dollars). Try to carry denominations of 50 and lower in both. ***Note:*** Throughout this chapter, I list prices of some hotels and tours in U.S. dollars as this is how they are typically listed within Peru.

Counterfeit bank notes and even coins are common, and merchants and consumers across Peru vigorously check the authenticity of money before accepting payment or change. (The simplest way: Hold the banknote up to the light to see the watermark.) Many people also refuse to accept bank notes that are not in good condition (including those with small tears, those that have been written on, and even those that are simply well worn) and visitors are wise to do the same when receiving change to avoid problems with other payments. Do not accept bills with tears (no matter how small), and refuse taped bills.

Here's an idea of what things cost in Peru: a short taxi ride, $2 to $3; coffee or bottle of water, $1; a movie, $3; lunch, $5 to $15; dinner, $20 to $40. (See "Tips on Accommodations," below, for general prices of hotel rooms.)

CURRENCY EXCHANGE & RATES At press time, the rate of exchange was approximately S/3.10 to the U.S. dollar. Rates are consistent across the country. If you pay in dollars, you will likely receive change in soles, so be aware of the correct exchange rate. Currencies other than U.S. dollars receive very poor exchange rates. Money can be exchanged at banks; with money changers (legal in Peru), often wearing colored smocks with "$" insignias, on the street; and at rarer *casas de cambio* (money-exchange houses). Money changers offer current rates of exchange, but you are advised to count your money carefully. You can simplify this by exchanging easily calculable amounts, such as $10 or $100 and make sure you have not received any counterfeit bills.

ATMS Peru is still, in many parts of the country, a cash society, though in larger tourist destinations you can expect to use credit cards at hotels and many restaurants. In villages and small towns, it may be impossible to cash traveler's checks or use credit cards. Make sure you have cash (in both soles and U.S. dollars) on hand. ATMs, which are the best way of getting cash in Peru, are found in most towns and cities, though certainly not on every street corner. Screen instructions are in English as well as Spanish. Some bank ATMs dispense money only to those who hold accounts there, and lines can be frustratingly long. Peruvian banks include Banco de Crédito, Banco Wiese, Interbank, Banco Central de Reserva, Banco de Comercio, and Banco Continental. Look for the symbols of major international networks, **PLUS** (✆ **800/843-7587**) and **Cirrus** (✆ **800/424-7787**). Your personal identification number (PIN) should contain four digits for most ATMs.

TRAVELER'S CHECKS Traveler's checks in Peru are exchanged at fewer places and at a considerably lower rate (often 2%) than cash. If you use traveler's checks, **American Express** is the brand most easily exchanged. Replacing traveler's checks outside of Lima can be very problematic, if not impossible. Keep a record of check numbers and the original bill of sale in a safe place. To report lost or stolen traveler's checks, call American Express at ✆ **01/330-4484.**

CREDIT CARDS Many establishments accept the major international credit cards, including **Visa, MasterCard, Diners Club,** and **American Express.** Visa is the most widely accepted card in Peru. However, some shops and restaurants charge the consumer an additional 10% for paying with a credit card; ask about this practice before you pay. (Offering to pay in cash rather than with a credit card can usually get you a 5%–10% discount.) When using a credit card, be careful to check the amount you are being charged. In rural areas and small towns, cash is essential for payment. At the very least, you should carry a supply of dollars in these areas.

To report lost or stolen credit cards, call Visa (collect) at ✆ **410/581-9994;** MasterCard at ✆ **800/307-7309;** American Express at ✆ **0800/51-531** or collect at **801/945-9450;** and Diners Club at ✆ **01/221-2050.**

WHEN TO GO

PEAK SEASON Peru's high season for travel coincides with the driest months: May through September, with the greatest number of visitors in July and August. May, September, and early October are particularly fine months to visit much of the country. Airlines and hotels also consider mid-December through mid-January to be peak season given the amount of holiday travel.

From June through September or October in the sierra, days are clear and often spectacularly sunny, with nights chilly or downright cold, especially at high elevations. For trekking in the mountains, including the Inca Trail, these are by far the best months. This is also the best time of the year to visit the Amazon basin: Mosquitoes are fewer, and many animals stay close to the rivers (although some people prefer to travel in the jungle during the wet season, when higher water levels allow more river penetration). Note that Peruvians travel in huge numbers around July 28, the national independence day, and finding accommodations in popular destinations can be difficult.

CLIMATE Generally speaking, May through early November is the dry season, and late November through April is the rainy season. The wettest months are January through April; in mountain areas, roads and trek paths may become impassable. Peru's climate, though, is markedly different among its three vastly different regions. The coast is predominantly arid and mild, the Andean region is temperate to cold, and the eastern lowlands are tropically warm and humid.

PUBLIC HOLIDAYS National public holidays in Peru include New Year's Day (Jan 1); Día de los Reyes (Jan 6); Maundy Thursday and Good Friday; Labor Day (May 1); Fiestas Patrias (Independence; July 28–29); Battle of Angamos (Oct 8); All Saints' Day (Nov 1); Feast of the Immaculate Conception (Dec 8); Christmas Eve (Dec 24); and Christmas (Dec 25).

HEALTH CONCERNS

COMMON AILMENTS As a tropical South American country, Peru presents certain health risks, but major concerns are limited to those traveling outside urban areas and to the Amazon jungle. The most common ailments for visitors to Peru are common **traveler's diarrhea** and altitude sickness, or **acute mountain sickness (AMS),** called *soroche* locally. Cusco sits at an elevation of about 3,400m (11,150 ft.), and Lake Titicaca, 3,830m (12,562 ft.). At these heights, shortness of breath and heart pounding are normal, given the paucity of oxygen. Some people may experience headaches, loss of appetite, extreme fatigue, and nausea. Most symptoms develop during the first day at high altitude, though occasionally travelers have delayed reactions. The best advice is to rest on your first day in the highlands and eat frugally. Drink plenty of liquids, including the local remedy *mate de coca,* or coca-leaf tea (perfectly legal), and avoid alcohol. Give yourself at least a day or two to acclimatize before launching into strenuous activities. Many hotels in Cusco offer oxygen for those severely affected with headaches and shortness of breath. If symptoms persist or become more severe, seek medical attention. People with heart or lung problems and persons with sickle cell anemia may develop serious health complications at high altitudes; consult your doctor before visiting Peru.

VACCINATIONS Though no vaccinations are required of travelers to Peru, it's wise to take certain precautions, especially if you are planning to travel to jungle regions. A yellow fever vaccine is strongly recommended for trips to the Amazon. The Pan American Health Organization last reported an outbreak in 2004, resulting in 52 total cases of yellow fever in Peru. Slightly more than half of those cases were fatal, though just two of those occurred in departments covered in this chapter, Loreto and Madre de Dios. The Centers for Disease Control and Prevention (CDC) warn that there is a risk of malaria and yellow fever in all departments except Arequipa, Moquegua, Puno, and Tacna, though Lima and the highland tourist areas (Cusco, Machu Picchu, and Lake Titicaca) are not at risk; consult your doctor about malaria prophylaxes and other preventative treatments.

The CDC also recommends hepatitis A or immune globulin (IG), hepatitis B, typhoid, and booster doses for tetanus-diphtheria and measles, though you may wish to weigh your potential exposure before getting all of these. For additional information on travel to tropical South America, see the CDC website at **wwwn.cdc.gov/travel/region tropicalsouthamerica.aspx** as well as the World Health Organization's website, **www.who.int**.

HEALTH PRECAUTIONS Other recommendations for safe and healthy travel in Peru: Drink only bottled or boiled water (and plenty of it, both at high altitudes and in hot and humid areas); eat only thoroughly cooked or boiled food or fruits and vegetables you have peeled yourself; avoid eating food from street vendors; bring insect repellent containing DEET (diethylmethyltoluamide) if you are traveling to the jungle; and avoid swimming in fresh water.

It is also advisable to get a thorough checkup and take out health insurance before your trip, and to bring along sufficient supplies of any required medicines.

GETTING THERE

By Plane

All flights from North America and Europe arrive at Lima's **Jorge Chávez International Airport** (© **01/511-6055;** www.lap.com.pe). International flights to Iquitos in the northern Amazon region may be resumed at some point in the near future.

The airport tax on domestic flights is $5.85; on international flights, it's $31. The tax must be paid in cash before boarding.

FROM NORTH AMERICA From the United States, direct flights connect Lima to Miami, New York, Newark, Houston, Dallas, and Atlanta. The major carriers are **American** (© **800/433-7300;** www.aa.com), **Continental** (© **800/231-0856;** www.continental.com), and **LAN** (© **866/435-9526;** www.lan.com).

From Canada, **American, Continental,** and **United** (© **800/864-8331;** www.united.com) all fly to Peru, making stops at their hubs in the United States first. **Air Canada** (© **888/247-2262;** www.aircanada.ca) makes connections with other carriers at U.S.

stops, usually Miami. **LAN** partners with other carriers to the United States, making stops in New York, Miami, or Los Angeles on the way to Lima.

FROM THE U.K. No direct flights connect Lima and London or any other part of the United Kingdom or Ireland; getting to Peru involves a layover in either another part of Europe or the United States. **American Airlines** (✆ **207/365-0777** in London, or 0845/778-9789) and **Continental** (✆ **0845/607-6760**) fly through their U.S. hubs (Dallas, Houston, and Miami) on the way to Lima. European carriers make stops in continental Europe; they include **Iberia** (✆ **870/609-0500;** www.iberia.com), **KLM** (✆ **08705/074-074;** www.klm.com), and **Lufthansa** (✆ **0845/7737-747;** www.lufthansa.com).

FROM AUSTRALIA & NEW ZEALAND You can fly to Buenos Aires on **Aerolíneas Argentinas** (✆ **612/9234-9000** in Australia or 649/379-3675 in New Zealand; www.aerolineas.com.au) and then connect to Lima, or you can go through Los Angeles or Buenos Aires on **Qantas** (✆ **13-13-13** in Australia or 800/808-767 in New Zealand; www.qantas.com) or **Air New Zealand** (✆ **0800/737-000;** www.airnz.co.nz). **LAN** (✆ **300/361-400** in Australia or 649/977-2233 in New Zealand; www.lanperu.com) also makes stops in Los Angeles on the way to Lima.

By Bus

You can travel overland to Peru through Ecuador, Bolivia, or Chile. Though the journey isn't short, Lima can be reached from major neighboring cities. If you're traveling from Quito or Guayaquil, you'll pass through the major northern coastal cities on the way to Lima. From Bolivia, there is frequent service from La Paz and Copacabana to Puno and then on to Cusco. From Chile, most travel from Arica to Tacna, making connections either to Arequipa or Lima.

GETTING AROUND

Because of its size and natural barriers, including difficult mountain terrain, long stretches of desert coast, and extensive rainforest, Peru is not easy to get around. Train service is limited, and many trips can take several days by land. Many visitors with limited time fly everywhere they can. Travel overland, though very inexpensive, can be extremely time consuming if not altogether uncomfortable. However, for certain routes, intercity buses are your only real option.

By Plane

Flying to major destinations within Peru is the only practical way around the country if you wish to see a large part of the country in a couple of weeks or less. Some places in the jungle can only be reached by airplane. Flying to major destinations, such as Cusco, Arequipa, Puerto Maldonado, and Iquitos in large part requires flying through Lima. Prices have increased dramatically in the last couple of years, and LAN now has a monopoly on many routes and has recently instituted a two-tier pricing system, with flights more expensive for foreigners not resident in Peru; round-trip flights to most destinations cost between $190 and $380. Puno (Lake Titicaca) requires passengers to fly into Juliaca, the nearest airport, before continuing by land the rest of the way (1 hr.). For many travelers, this makes the direct train from Cusco to Puno more appealing, if ultimately more time consuming.

Peru's domestic carriers include **LAN** (✆ **01/213-8200;** www.lan.com), **Taca** (✆ **01/511-8222;** www.taca.com), **LC Busre** (**01/619-1313;** www.lcbusre.com.pe), and **Star Perú** (✆ **01/705-9000;** www.starperu.com). LAN flies to most major destinations in

 Peru, often exclusively. Flight schedules and fares are apt to change frequently and without notice. Flights should be booked several days in advance, especially in high season, and it's very important to reconfirm airline tickets in advance (for local flights, reconfirm 48 hr. in advance; for international flights, 72 hr.). You should also make sure you get to the airport at least 45 minutes before your flight to avoid being bumped. In addition, every flight, whether domestic or international, requires payment of an airport tax before boarding.

By Train

Peru's national railway network was privatized in 1999, but the monopoly owned by Peru Rail has come to an end, and, as of late 2009, there are now two new options for traveling from Machu Picchu from the Sacred Valley (travel from Cusco is still available only on Peru Rail). The four tourist or passenger train routes operated by **Peru Rail,** owned by Orient Express (✆ **01/612-6700** in Lima or 84/581-414 in Cusco; www.perurail.com), are all very popular and scenic journeys. One is the **Cusco–Lake Titicaca Route** ($220 one-way). By far, the most popular train routes in Peru are the **Cusco–Machu Picchu** and **Sacred Valley–Machu Picchu** routes, which link Cusco and the Sacred Valley, traveling from the old Inca capital to Ollantaytambo and the world-famous ruins of Machu Picchu. From Cusco to Machu Picchu, there are three classes of service: the luxury Hiram Bingham, $307 to $334 one-way; Vistadome, $71 one-way; and Backpacker, $48 one-way. From Cusco to Ollantaytambo, prices are Vistadome, $43 to $60 one-way, and Backpacker, $31 to $43 one-way. On the new **Inca Rail,** Av. El Sol 611 in Cusco (✆ **084/233-030;** www.incarail.com), first-class travel from Ollantaytambo to Machu Picchu is $75; executive class is $50. On the similarly new **Andean Railways,** Av. El Sol 576 in Cusco (✆ **084/221-199;** www.machupicchutrain.com), full fare from Ollantaytambo to Machu Picchu is $59.

The **Ferrocarril Central Andino** (✆ **01/226-6363;** www.ferrocarrilcentral.com.pe), from Lima to Huancayo in the Central Highlands, is again operating after long periods of inactivity over the years. The incredibly scenic, 12-hour passenger train, which crosses 58 bridges and passes through 69 tunnels, runs once a month between July and November and costs S/165 to S/300 round-trip. Trains leave Lima from the **Estación Central de Desamparados.** Check for online updates before you arrive in Peru.

Luggage theft has long been a problem on Peruvian trains; if possible, purchase a premium-class ticket that limits access to ticketed passengers only.

By Bus

Buses are the cheapest and most popular form of transportation in Peru. A complex network of private bus companies crisscrosses Peru, with a number of competing lines covering the most popular routes. Many companies operate their own bus stations, and their locations, dispersed across many cities, can be endlessly frustrating to travelers. Theft of luggage is an issue on many buses, and passengers should keep a watchful eye on their carry-on items and pay close attention when bags are unloaded. Only a few long-distance buses have luxury buses comparable in comfort to European models (bathrooms, reclining seats, movies). These premium-class ("Royal" or "Imperial") buses cost up to twice as much as regular buses, though for many travelers the additional comfort and services are worth the difference in cost (which remains inexpensive). For many short distances (such as Cusco to Pisac), *colectivos* (smaller buses without assigned seats) are the fastest and cheapest option.

Ormeño (✆ **01/472-5000;** www.grupo-ormeno.com.pe) and **Cruz del Sur** (✆ **01/311-5050;** www.cruzdelsur.com.pe) are the top two bus companies with the best reputations for long-distance journeys and the most extensive coverage of Peru. **Civa** (✆ **01/418-1111;** www.civa.com.pe) and **Oltursa** (✆ **01/708-5000;** www.oltursa.com.pe) are also reputable companies with service to most parts of the country, though their buses are generally a notch down from Ormeño and Cruz del Sur. Given the mercurial and extremely confusing nature of bus companies, terminals, and destinations, it's always best to approach a local tourism information office or travel agency (most of which sell long-distance bus tickets) with a destination in mind and let them direct you to the terminal for the best service.

By Car

Getting around Peru by means of a rental car isn't the easiest or cheapest option for most travelers. Distances are long, roads are often not in very good condition, Peruvian drivers are aggressive, and accident rates are very high; the U.S. Department of State also warns against driving in Peru at night or alone on rural roads. A 4×4 vehicle would be the best option in many places, but trucks and jeeps are exceedingly expensive for most travelers. However, if you want maximum flexibility and independence in a particular region (say, to get around the Sacred Valley outside of Cusco, or to visit Colca Canyon beyond Arequipa) and have several people to share the cost, a rental car could be a decent option. By no means plan to rent a car in Lima and head off for the major sights across the country; you'll spend all your time in the car. It is much more feasible to fly or take a bus to a given destination and rent a car there.

The major international rental agencies are found at Lima's airport and around the city, and a handful of international and local companies operate in other cities, such as Cusco and Arequipa. Agencies in Lima include **Avis** (✆ 01/434-1111 or 434-1034; www.avis.com), **Budget** (✆ 01/442-8703; www.budget.com), **Dollar** (✆ 01/444-3050), **Hertz** (✆ 01/447-2129; www.hertz.com), **Inka's Rent A Car** (✆ 01/447-2129), and **Paz Rent A Car** (✆ 01/436-3941). An economy-size vehicle costs about $50 to $80 a day. To rent a car, you'll need to be at least 25 years old and have a valid driver's license and passport. Deposit by credit card is usually required. For mechanical assistance, contact the **Touring y Automóvil Club del Peru (Touring Club of Peru)** at ✆ 01/221-3225 in Lima, or 084/224-561 in Cusco.

TIPS ON ACCOMMODATIONS

A wide range of accommodations exists in Peru, including world-class luxury hotels, affordable small hotels in colonial houses, rustic rainforest lodges, and inexpensive budget inns. Midrange options have expanded in recent years, but the large majority of accommodations still court budget travelers and backpackers. Accommodations go by many names in Peru: "Hotel" generally refers to comfortable hotels with a range of services, but *hostal* is used for a wide variety of smaller hotels, inns, and pensions. At the lower end are mostly *hospedajes, pensiones,* and *residenciales.* However, these terms are often poor indicators of an establishment's quality or services. Luxury hotels are rare outside of Lima and Cusco; budget accommodations are plentiful, and many of them are quite good for the price.

Advance reservations are strongly recommended during high season (June–Oct) and at times of national holidays and important festivals. This is especially true of hotels in the middle and upper categories in popular places such as Cusco and Machu Picchu. **Many hotels quote their rates in U.S. dollars,** which is how I've listed them in this chapter. In general, **Very Expensive** hotels charge above $250 for a double; **Expensive,** $150 to $250; **Moderate,** $75 to $150; and **Inexpensive,** below $75. If you pay in cash, the price will be converted into soles at the going rate. Note that at most budget and many midrange hotels, credit cards are not accepted. Most published rates can be negotiated and travelers can often get greatly reduced rates outside of peak season simply by asking.

Hotel taxes and service charges are an issue that has caused some confusion in recent years. Most upper-level hotels add a 19% general sales tax (IGV) and a 10% service charge to the bill. However, foreigners who can demonstrate they live outside of Peru are not charged the 19% tax (although they are responsible for the 10% service charge). In practice, hotels sometimes mistakenly or purposely include the IGV on everyone's bill; presentation of a passport is sufficient to have the tax deducted from your tab. Many hotels—usually those at the midlevel and lower ranges—simplify matters by including the tax in their rates; at these establishments, you cannot expect to have the tax removed from your charges. At high-end hotels, be sure to review your bill and ask for an explanation of additional taxes and charges. Prices in this chapter do not include taxes and service charges unless otherwise noted.

Safety is an issue at many hotels, especially at the lower end, and extreme care should be taken with regard to personal belongings left in the hotel. Leaving valuables lying around is asking for trouble. Most hotels have safety-deposit boxes (only luxury hotels have room safes). Place your belongings in a carefully sealed envelope. Also, if you arrive in a town without previously arranged accommodations, you should be wary of taxi drivers and others who insist on showing you to a hotel. Occasionally, they will provide excellent tips, but in general they will merely be taking you to a place where they are confident they can earn a commission. A final precaution worth mentioning is the electric heater found on many shower heads: These can be dangerous, and touching them while they're functioning can prompt an unwelcome electric jolt.

TIPS ON DINING

Peruvian cuisine is among the best and most diverse cuisines found in Latin America, and it's one of the most important contributors to the wave of pan-Latino restaurants gaining popularity in many parts of the world. Peruvian cooking differs significantly by region, and subcategories mirror the country's geographical variety: coastal, highland, and tropical. The common denominator among them is a blend of indigenous and Spanish (or broader European) influences, which has evolved over the past 4 centuries. In addition to Peruvian cooking, visitors will also find plenty of international restaurants, including a particularly Peruvian variation: the *chifa* (Peruvian-influenced Chinese, developed by the large immigrant Chinese population), a mainstay among many non-Chinese Peruvians. *Chifas* are nearly as common as restaurants serving *pollo a la brasa* (spit-roasted chicken), which are everywhere in Peru.

Traditional Peruvian coastal cooking is often referred to as *comida criolla,* and it's found across Peru. The star dish is *ceviche,* a classic preparation of raw fish and shellfish marinated in lime or lemon juice and hot chili peppers, served with raw onion, sweet potato, and toasted corn. Coastal favorites also include *escabeche* (a tasty fish concoction served with peppers, eggs, olives, onions, and prawns), *conchitas* (scallops), and *corvina* (sea bass). Land-based favorites are *cabrito* (roast kid) and *ají de gallina* (a tangy creamed chicken-and-chili dish).

Highlanders favor a more substantial style of cooking. Meat, served with rice and potatoes, is a mainstay of the diet, as is *trucha* (trout). *Lomo saltado,* strips of beef mixed with onions, tomatoes, peppers, and french-fried potatoes and served with rice, seems to be on every menu. *Rocoto relleno,* a hot bell pepper stuffed with vegetables and meat; *papa rellena,* a potato stuffed with veggies and then fried; and *papa a la huancaína,* boiled potatoes served with a cheese sauce and garnished with hard-boiled eggs and a lettuce leaf, are just as common (but are occasionally extremely spicy). *Cuy* (guinea pig) is considered a delicacy in many parts of Peru; it comes roasted or fried, with head and feet upturned on the plate.

In the Amazon jungle regions, most people fish for their food, and their diets consist almost entirely of fish such as river trout and *paiche* (a huge river fish). Restaurants feature both of these, with accompaniments such as yuca (a root), *palmitos* (palm hearts) and *chonta* (palm-heart salad), bananas and plantains, and rice tamales known as *juanes.* Common menu items, such as chicken and game, are complemented by exotic fare: caiman, wild boar, turtle, monkey, and piranha.

Drinking is less of an event in Peru. Peruvian wines and beers can't compare with superior examples found elsewhere on the continent (though the selection of imported wines from Chile, Argentina, and Spain is improving, and top restaurants have good selections, though they're largely limited to those three wine-producing nations). One indigenous drink stands out: pisco, a powerful white-grape brandy. The pisco sour (a cocktail mixed with pisco, egg whites, lemon juice, sugar, and bitters) is Peru's margarita: tasty, refreshing, and ubiquitous. New-wave twists on pisco sours, such as *maracuyá* (passion fruit) sours, are popping up all over the country. Pisco is increasingly used to make local versions of standard cocktails from other lands (such as the *caipirpisco,* a Peruvian twist on a Brazilian classic). Peruvians everywhere drink *chicha,* a tangy, fermented brew made from maize and inherited from the Incas. Often served warm in huge glasses, it is unlikely to please the palates of most foreign visitors, though it's certainly worth a try if you come upon a small, informal place with the *chicha* flag flying (symbolizing something akin to "fresh *chicha* available inside") in a rural village. The potent *chicha* is not to be confused with another drink popular in Peru: *chicha morada,* a nonalcoholic refreshment made from blue corn.

Restaurants range from the rustic and incredibly inexpensive to polished places with impeccable service and international menus. Set three-course menus (*menú económico* or *menú ejecutivo*) can sometimes be had for as little as $2. In the sections that follow, restaurant prices are quoted in nuevo soles. **Very Expensive** restaurants are those charging above S/125 per person per meal (appetizer, main course, dessert, non-alcoholic drink); **Expensive,** S/75 to S/125; **Moderate,** S/35 to S/75; and **Inexpensive,** below S/35. In general, you should ask about the preparation of many Peruvian dishes, as many are quite spicy. Informal eateries serving Peruvian cooking are frequently called *picanterías* and *chicherías.* Very fancy restaurants may occasionally add service charges of 10% and an additional tax of up to 19%, as well as a *cubierto,* or cover charge, which is basically a small fee for bread and the privilege of sitting at a table. Less expensive restaurants usually charge either a 5% tax or no additional tax or service charge. At restaurants, tips normally range from 5% to 10%, whether or not a service charge is levied.

TIPS ON SHOPPING

Peru is one of the top shopping destinations in Latin America, with some of the finest and best-priced crafts anywhere. Its long traditions of textile weaving and colorful markets have produced a dazzling display of alpaca wool sweaters, blankets, ponchos, shawls, scarves, typical Peruvian hats, and other woven items. Peru's ancient indigenous civilizations were some of the world's greatest potters, and reproductions of Moche, Nazca, Paracas, and other ceramics are available.

Lima and Cusco have the lion's share of tourist-oriented shops and markets, but other places may be just as good for shopping. Locals in Puno and Taquile Island on Lake Titicaca produce spectacular textiles, and Arequipa is perhaps the best place in Peru to purchase very fine, extremely soft baby alpaca items. The Shipibo tribe of the northern Amazon produces excellent textiles and ceramics. You'll also see items in the jungle made from endangered species, including alligator skins and turtle shells, but purchasing these items is illegal.

Many tourist centers have *artesanía* shops, and prices may not be any higher than what you'd find at markets. At both stores and in open markets, bargaining—gentle, good-natured haggling over prices—is accepted and even expected. However, when it gets down to ridiculously small amounts of money, it's best to recognize that you are already getting a great deal on probably handmade goods (not to mention that a couple of soles here or there is likely to matter little to you and greatly to the seller) and relinquish the fight.

Fast Facts Peru

Addresses "Jr." doesn't mean "junior"; it is a designation meaning *jirón,* or street, just as "Av." (sometimes "Avda.") is an abbreviation for *avenida,* or avenue, and "Cdra." is an abbreviation for cuadra, or block. Perhaps the most confusing element in street addresses is "s/n," which frequently appears in place of a number after the name of the street. The designation "s/n" means *sin número,* or no number.

American Express The office in Lima, at Avenida Santa Cruz 621, Miraflores (✆ **01/710-3900**), is open Monday through Friday from 9am to 5pm. Other offices are at Jr. Rio de Janeiro 216, Miraflores, Lima (✆ **610-6000**); in Cusco, Av. del Sol 864 (✆ **84/243-918**); and in Arequipa, Santa Catalina 105B (✆ **54/281-800**). They will replace stolen or lost travelers' checks and sell American Express checks with an Amex card, but they do not cash their own checks.

Business Hours Most stores are open Monday through Friday from 9 or 10am to 12:30pm and from 3 to 5 or 8pm; banks are generally open Monday through Friday from 9:30am to 4pm, though some stay open until 6pm. In major cities, most banks are also open Saturday from 9:30am to 12:30pm.

Doctors & Hospitals Medical care is of a generally high standard in Lima and adequate in other major cities, where you are likely to find English-speaking doctors. Medical care is of a lesser standard in rural areas and small villages, and it's much less likely that you'll find an English-speaking physician in these locales. Many physicians and hospitals require immediate cash payment for health services, and they do not accept U.S. medical insurance (even if your policy applies overseas). That said, costs are reasonable, as compared to those in the U.S. You should check with your insurance company to see if your policy provides for overseas medical evacuation.

It's best to get vaccinations and obtain malaria pills before arriving in Peru, but if you decide at the last minute to go to the jungle and need to get a vaccine in the country, you may go to the following **Oficinas de Vacunación in Lima:**

Av. del Ejército 1756, San Isidro (✆ **01/264-6889**); Jorge Chávez International Airport, Second Floor; or the **International Vaccination Center,** Dos de Mayo National Hospital, Avenida Grau, Block 13 (✆ **01/517-1845**). You can also get a yellow fever shot at the airport in Puerto Maldonado before traveling to the Amazon jungle.

Drug Laws Cocaine and other illegal substances are not as ubiquitous in Peru as some might think, though in Lima and Cusco, they are commonly offered to foreigners. This is especially dangerous; many would-be dealers also operate as police informants, and some are said to be undercover narcotics officers. Penalties for possession and use of or trafficking in illegal drugs in Peru are strict; convicted offenders can expect long jail sentences and substantial fines. Peruvian police routinely detain drug smugglers at Lima's international airport and land border crossings. Since 1995, more than 40 U.S. citizens have been convicted of narcotics trafficking in Peru. If arrested on drug charges, you will face protracted pretrial detention in poor prison conditions.

Electricity All outlets are 220 volts, 60 cycles AC (except in Arequipa, which operates on 50 cycles), with two-prong outlets that accept both flat and round prongs. Some large hotels also have 110-volt outlets.

Embassies & Consulates In Lima: **Australia,** Victor A. Belaúnde 147/Vía Principal 155, Building 3, Office 1301, San Isidro (✆ 01/222-8281); **Canada,** Calle Bolognesi 228, Miraflores (✆ 01/ 319-3200); **United Kingdom** and **New Zealand,** Av. Jose Larco 1301, Floor 22, Miraflores (✆ 01/617-3000); **United States,** Av. La Encalada, Block 17, Surco (✆ 01/434-3000).

Emergencies In case of an emergency, call the 24-hour **traveler's hot line** (✆ **01/574-8000**) or the **tourist police (POLTUR;** ✆ **01/460-1060** in Lima, or 01/460-0965). The general **police** emergency number is ✆ **105.** The **INDECOPI** 24-hour hot line can also assist in contacting police to report a crime (✆ **01/224-7888** in Lima, 01/224-8600, or toll-free 0800/42579 from any private phone).

Guides Officially licensed guides are available at many archaeological sites and other places of interest to foreigners. They can be contracted directly (often for a tip), though you should verify their ability to speak English if you do not understand Spanish well. Establish a price beforehand. Many cities are battling a scourge of unlicensed and unscrupulous guides who provide inferior services or, worse, cheat visitors. As a general rule, do not accept unsolicited offers to arrange excursions, transportation, and hotel accommodations. For a full day's guide, tip $10.

Internet Access Public Internet booths, or *cabinas,* have proliferated throughout Peru, in major cities such as Lima, Cusco, and Arequipa as well as small towns. Most cities have several to choose from, but few are of the cybercafe variety. Most are simple cubicles with terminals; occasionally, printers are available. The average cost for 1 hour is less than $1. Many *cabinas* can now make very inexpensive international phone calls via the Internet.

Language Spanish is the official language of Peru. The Amerindian languages Quechua and Aymara are spoken primarily in the highlands. English is not widely spoken but is understood by those affiliated with the tourist industry in major cities and tourist destinations. Learning a few key phrases of Spanish will help immensely.

Liquor Laws A legal drinking age is not strictly enforced in Peru. Anyone over the age of 16 is unlikely to have any problems ordering liquor in any bar or other establishment. Wine, beer, and alcohol are widely available—sold daily at grocery stores, liquor stores, and in all cafes, bars, and restaurants—and consumed widely, especially in public during festivals. There appears to be very little taboo associated with public inebriation at festivals.

Maps Good topographical maps are available from the **Instituto Geográfico Nacional (IGN),** located at Av. Aramburú 1190, San Isidro, Lima (✆ **01/475-9960**). Hiking maps are available from the **South American Explorers Club,** Piura 135, Miraflores, Lima (✆ **01/445-3306**) and Choquechaca 188, Apto. 4, Cusco (✆ **084/245-484**).

Newspapers & Magazines If you read Spanish, *El Comercio* and *La República* are two of the best daily newspapers. Look for *Rumbos,* a glossy Peruvian travel magazine in English and Spanish with excellent photography. In Lima, you will find copies (although rarely same-day publications) of the *International Herald Tribune* and the *Miami Herald* as well as *Time, Newsweek,* and other special-interest publications. Outside of Lima, international newspapers and magazines are hard to come by.

Police Peru has special tourist police forces (Policía Nacional de Turismo) in all major tourist destinations, such as Lima, Cusco, Arequipa, and Puno, as well as a dozen other cities. You are more likely to get a satisfactory response, not to mention someone who speaks some English, from the tourist police, who are distinguished by their white shirts. See "Emergencies" above and "Fast Facts" in individual city sections for contact information.

Post Offices/Mail Peru's postal service is reasonably efficient, especially now that it is managed by a private company (Serpost S.A.). Post offices are generally open Monday through Saturday from 8am to 8pm; some are also open Sunday from 9am to 1pm. Letters and postcards to North America take between 10 days and 2 weeks to arrive. Postcards to North America or Europe cost S/5.50; a letter to North America, S/7.20; and a letter to Europe, S/7.80. If you are purchasing lots of textiles and other handicrafts, you can send packages home from post offices, but it's not inexpensive—more than $100 for 10 kilograms (22 lb.), similar to what it costs to use DHL, where you're likely to have an easier time communicating. UPS is found in several cities, but its courier services cost nearly three times as much as DHL.

Restrooms Public toilets are rarely available, except in railway stations, restaurants, and theaters. Peruvian men tend to urinate outside in full view; don't emulate them. Use the bathroom in a bar, cafe, or restaurant. Public restrooms are labeled WC (water closet), *damas* (ladies), and *caballeros* or *hombres* (men). Toilet paper is not always provided, and when it is, establishments ask patrons to throw it in the wastebasket rather than the toilet to avoid clogging.

Safety Most visitors travel freely throughout Peru without incident. However, in downtown Lima and the city's residential and hotel areas, the risk of street crime remains high. Carjackings, assaults, and armed robberies are not unheard of; occasional armed attacks at ATMs occur. Use ATMs during the day, with other people present. Street crime is prevalent in Cusco, Arequipa, and Puno, and pickpockets are known to patrol public markets. In Cusco, in particular, do not walk alone late at night on deserted streets.

In major cities, it's best to use telephone-dispatched radio taxis, especially at night. Travelers should exercise extreme caution on public city transportation, and on long-distance buses and trains (especially at night), where thieves employ any number of strategies to relieve passengers of their bags. Lock backpacks and suitcases to luggage racks.

In general, do not wear expensive jewelry; keep expensive camera equipment out of view as much as possible; use a money belt worn inside your pants or shirt to safeguard cash, credit cards, and passport. Wear your daypack on your chest rather than your back when walking in crowded areas. At airports, it's best to spend a little more for official airport taxis; if in doubt, request the driver's official ID. Don't venture beyond airport grounds for a street taxi.

Smoking Smoking is common in Peru, and it is rare to find a hotel, restaurant, or bar with nonsmoking rooms. However, there are now a few hotels (usually high end) and restaurants with nonsmoking rooms, and the trend is growing, albeit slowly. There are nonsmoking cars on trains, and most long-distance buses are also nonsmoking.

Taxes A general sales tax (IGV) is added automatically to most consumer bills (19%). In some upmarket hotels or restaurants, service charges of 10% are often added. At all airports, passengers must pay a $31 departure tax for international flights, $5.85 for domestic flights.

Telephone & Fax Peru's telephone system has been much improved since it was privatized and acquired by Spain's Telefónica in the mid-1990s. (There are now several additional players in the market, including BellSouth.) It's relatively simple to make local and long-distance domestic and international calls from pay phones, which accept coins and phone cards *(tarjetas telefónicas).* Most phone booths display country and city codes and contain instructions in English and Spanish.

You can also make international calls from Telefónica offices and hotels, though surcharges levied at the latter can be extraordinarily expensive. An inexpensive way to make international calls is through Internet software such as Skype or Net-2Phone, which more and more Internet booths in Peru are featuring. Rates are as low as 20¢ per minute to the United States. Reception, however, can be spotty.

Fax services are available at many hotels, but they are expensive, especially for international numbers ($3 per page and up).

Time Zone All of Peru is 5 hours behind GMT (Greenwich Mean Time). Peru does not observe daylight saving time.

Tipping Most people leave about a 10% tip for the waitstaff in restaurants. In nicer restaurants that add a 10% service charge (which your waiter is unlikely ever to see), many patrons tip an additional 5% or 10% for good service. Taxi drivers are not usually tipped unless they provide some additional service. Bilingual tour guides should be tipped $1 to $2 per person for a short visit, $5 per person or more for a full day. If you have a private guide, tip about $10.

Water Do not drink tap water, even in major hotels. Visitors should drink only bottled water, which is widely available. Try to avoid drinks with ice. *Agua con gas* is carbonated; *agua sin gas* is still.

4 LIMA

Lima was the richest and most important city in the Americas in the 17th century and was considered the most beautiful colonial settlement in the region. Today, the capital of Peru is a sprawling, chaotic, and mostly unlovely metropolis, and many visitors dart through it rather quickly or bypass it altogether. Peru's blistering poverty is more apparent here than perhaps anywhere else: Depressing shantytowns called *pueblos jóvenes* lacerate the outer rings of the city, and the despair of a large segment of the largely migrant and mestizo population contrasts uncomfortably with the ritzy apartment and office buildings in the residential suburbs. If that's not enough, for most of the year an unrelenting gray cloud called the *garúa* hangs heavy overhead, obscuring the coastline and dulling the city's appearance. The sun comes out in Lima only from December to April; the rest of the time, Lima makes London look almost like Lisbon.

With a population of more than eight million—about one-third of Peru's total population—and as the seat of the national government and headquarters of most industry, Lima thoroughly dominates Peru's political and commercial life. Lima demands some effort to sift beneath the soot and uncover the city's rewards, especially when such extraordinary treasures hover over the horizon in the Andes and the Amazon jungle. So why come to Lima except to beeline it to Cusco or elsewhere? If you skip Lima altogether, you'll miss a vital part of what is Peru today. Lima has calmed down since its days as a cauldron of chaos in the 1980s and 1990s. The country's finest museums are here, as are its fanciest and most creative restaurants and its most vibrant nightlife. Many of the classic colonial buildings in the old Lima Centro are being refurbished. But the city still feels schizophrenic; outer suburbs such as Barranco are relatively gentle oases, worlds removed from the congestion and grime of the rest of the city.

Even if you have only a day or two for Lima, the city's art and archaeology museums serve as perfect introductions to the rich history and culture you'll encounter elsewhere in the country. And the city's phenomenal restaurant scene draws travelers with a different agenda. If you also squeeze in a tour of colonial Lima, dine at a great *criollo* restaurant or *cevichería,* soak up some energetic nightlife, and browse the country's best shops, you may just come away from Lima pleasantly surprised, even if not wholly enamored of the city.

ESSENTIALS

Getting There

Lima is the gateway for most international arrivals to Peru; see "Getting There" in "Planning Your Trip to Peru," earlier in this chapter, for more detailed information.

BY PLANE All overseas flights from North America and Europe arrive at Lima's **Jorge Chávez International Airport** (airport code LIM). For flight information, call ✆ **01/511-6055.**

To get from the airport to Lima—either downtown, about 16km (10 miles) southwest of the airport, or to Miraflores, San Isidro, and Barranco (the major residential neighborhoods and sites of most tourist hotels), about 45 minutes away—you can take a taxi or private bus. **Taxis** inside the security area at the international arrivals terminal charge around $12 to downtown Lima (Lima Centro) and $15 to Miraflores. The **Urbanito Airport shuttle** service (✆ **99/573-238**) delivers passengers to the doors of their hotels. Stop by its desk in the international terminal; buses to downtown ($7) and Miraflores

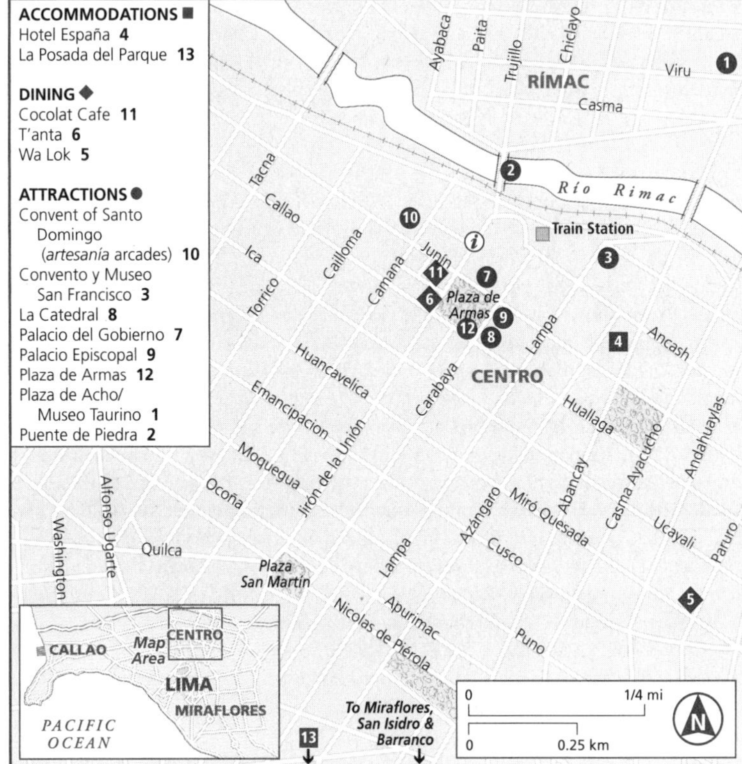

and San Isidro ($10) leave every half-hour or so. The shuttle stops by the hotel of each passenger; at peak hours, if there are many fellow passengers, this may not be the fastest way from the airport. Unless you're alone, it's also probably not the cheapest. Call a day ahead to arrange a pickup for your return to the airport (✆ **01/814-6932**). Private limousine taxis (*taxis ejecutivos* or *remises*) also have desks in the airport; their fares range from $40 to $60 round-trip. One is **MitsuTaxi** (✆ **01/349-7722**).

BY BUS The multitude of bus companies serving various regions of the country all have terminals in Lima. Many are located downtown, though several companies have their bases in the suburbs. Most bus terminals have nasty reputations for thievery and general unpleasantness; your best bet is to grab your things and hop into an airport shuttle or cab pronto.

Orientation

The city beyond central Lima **(Lima Centro)** is a warren of ill-defined neighborhoods; most visitors are likely to set foot into only a couple of them. Several of Lima's top museums are in **Pueblo Libre,** a couple of miles southwest of Lima Centro, while **San Borja,** a couple of miles directly south of Lima Centro, holds two of the finest art and archaeology collections in all of Peru. **San Isidro** and **Miraflores,** the most exclusive residential and commercial neighborhoods, and also where most tourist hotels are located, are farther south toward the coast. **Barranco,** a former seaside village now known primarily for its nightlife, is several miles farther out along the ocean, as is **Chorrillos,** a residential neighborhood known primarily for its Pantanos de Villa, or swamps that are rich with flora and fauna.

Getting Around

Navigating Lima is a complicated and time-consuming task, made difficult by the city's sprawling character (many of the best hotels and restaurants are far from downtown, spread among three or more residential neighborhoods), heavy traffic and pollution, and a chaotic network of confusing and crowded *colectivos* and unregulated taxis.

BY TAXI Taxis hailed on the street are a reasonable and relatively quick way to get around Lima. However, taxis are wholly unregulated by the government and do not use meters: All anyone has to do to become a taxi driver is get his hands on a vehicle—of any size and condition, though most are the tiny Daewoo "Ticos"—and plunk a cheap TAXI sticker inside the windshield. He is then free to charge whatever he thinks he can get—with no meters, no laws, and nobody to answer to besides the free market. I counsel visitors to be a bit wary taking taxis in Lima, though I personally have never had problems greater than a dispute over a fare. (If you're not fluent in Spanish, and even if you are but you have an obviously non-Peruvian appearance, be prepared to negotiate fares.) If the issue of getting into quasi-official cabs makes you nervous, by all means call a registered company from your hotel or restaurant—especially at night (even though the fare can be twice as much).

Registered, reputable taxi companies—the safest option—include **Taxi Amigo** (✆ **01/349-0177**), **Taxi Móvil** (✆ **01/422-6890**), and **Taxi Seguro** (✆ **01/275-2020**). Whether you call or hail a taxi, you'll need to establish a price beforehand—be prepared to bargain. Most fares range from $3 to $8.

BY BUS Local buses are of two types: *micros* (large buses) and *combis* (minibuses or vans). They're both quite crowded, with a reputation for pickpockets, and can be hailed at any place along the street without regard to bus stops. Routes are more or less identified by signs with street names placed in the windshield, making many trips confusing for those unfamiliar with Lima. Some do nothing more than race up and down long avenues. (For example: TODO AREQUIPA means it travels the length of Av. Arequipa.) For assistance, ask a local for help; most Limeños know the incredibly complex bus system surprisingly well. Because they make so many stops, trips from the outer suburbs to downtown can be quite slow. Most *micros* and *combis* cost S/2; it's slightly more after midnight and on Sunday and holidays. When you wish to get off, shout *"Baja"* (getting off) or *"Esquina"* (at the corner).

BY FOOT Lima can be navigated by foot only a neighborhood at a time. (And even then, congestion and pollution strongly discourage much walking.) Lima Centro and Barranco are best seen by foot, and, though large, parts of Miraflores are also walkable. Between neighborhoods, however, a taxi is essential.

Visitor Information

A 24-hour tourist information booth, **iperu** (✆ 01/574-8000), operates in the international terminal at the Jorge Chávez International Airport. The **Oficina de Información Turística** in Lima Centro is well located a block off the Plaza de Armas at Pasaje Los

Escribanos 145 (✆ 01/427-6080); it's open Monday through Friday from 9am to 6pm, Saturday and Sunday from 10am to 5pm. Perhaps the most helpful iperu office is in Miraflores, at the **Larcomar** shopping mall, Módulo 14, Av. Malecón de la Reserva 610 (✆ 01/445-9400); it's open Monday through Friday from 11am to 1pm and 2 to 8pm. One of the best private agencies for arrangements and city tours as well as general information is **Fertur Peru,** Jr. Junín 211, within the Hotel España (✆ 01/427-1958; www.fertur-travel.com) and Schell 485, Miraflores (✆ 01/445-1760). Also well worth a visit, especially for members, is the Lima office of the **South American Explorers Club,** Piura 135, Miraflores (✆ 01/445-3306; www.saexplorers.org).

FAST FACTS Peruvian and international **banks** with currency-exchange bureaus and ATMs are plentiful throughout central Lima and especially in the outer neighborhoods, such as Miraflores, San Isidro, and Barranco, which are full of shopping centers, hotels, and restaurants. Money changers, almost always wearing colored smocks (sometimes with obvious "$" insignias), patrol the main streets off Parque Central in Miraflores and Lima Centro with calculators and dollars in hand.

English-speaking medical personnel and 24-hour emergency service are available at the following hospitals and clinics in Lima: **Clínica Anglo-Americana,** Alfredo Salazar, Third Block, San Isidro (✆ 01/221-3656); **Clínica San Borja,** Guardia Civil 337, San Borja (✆ 01/475-4000); and **Maison de Sante,** Miguel Adgouin 208–222, near the Palacio de Justicia (✆ 01/428-3000, or emergency 01/427-2941). For an ambulance, call **Alerta Médica** (✆ 01/470-5000) or **San Cristóbal** (✆ 01/440-0200).

The **Policía Nacional de Turismo (National Tourism Police)** has an English-speaking staff and is specifically trained to handle needs of foreign visitors. The 24-hour tourist police line is ✆ **01/574-8000.** The main office in Lima is next to the Museo de la Nación at Av. Javier Prado Este 2465, Fifth Floor, San Borja (✆ **01/225-8698** or 01/476-9879).

Internet ***cabinas*** are everywhere in Lima. Rates are S/2 to S/3.50 per hour, and most are open daily from 9am to 10pm or later. Lima's main **post office (Central de Correos)** is located on the Plaza de Armas, Camaná 195 (✆ **01/427-0370**). The Miraflores branch is on Petit Thouars 5201 (✆ **01/445-0697**), the San Isidro branch, Calle Las Palmeras 205 (✆ **01/422-0981**). A **DHL/Western Union** office is located at Nicolás de Piérola 808 (✆ **01/424-5820**). The principal **Telefónica** office, where you can make long-distance and international calls, is on Plaza San Martín (Carabaya 937) in Lima Centro.

WHAT TO SEE & DO

Many visitors to Lima are merely on their way to other places in Peru. But, since everything goes through the capital, most people take advantage of layovers—or schedule a couple of days—to see what distinguishes Lima: its colonial old quarter, once the finest in the Americas, and several of the finest museums in Peru, all of which serve as magnificent introductions to Peruvian history and culture.

Much of the historic center has suffered from sad neglect; the municipal government is committed to restoring the aesthetic value, but with limited funds it faces a daunting task. Today, central Lima has a noticeable police presence and is considerably safer than it was just a few years ago. A full day in Lima Centro should suffice; depending on your interests, you could spend anywhere from a day to a week traipsing through Lima's many museum collections, many of which are dispersed in otherwise unremarkable neighborhoods. But for those with a couple extra days, more leisurely visits in neighborhoods like Miraflores and Barranco will likely greatly improve your impressions of the capital.

Lima Centro: Colonial Lima

Lima's grand **Plaza de Armas** ★ (also called the Plaza Mayor), the original center of the city and site where Francisco Pizarro founded the city in 1535, is essentially a modern reconstruction. The disastrous 1746 earthquake that initiated the city's decline leveled most of the 16th- and 17th-century buildings in the old center. The oldest surviving element of the square is the central bronze fountain, which dates from 1651. Today the square, while perhaps not the most beautiful or languid in South America, is still rather distinguished beneath a surface level of grime and bustle (and it has been named a UNESCO World Heritage Site). On the north side of the square is the early-20th-century **Palacio del Gobierno (Presidential Palace),** where a changing of the guard takes place daily at noon. The **Municipalidad de Lima (City Hall)** is on the west side of the plaza. Across the square is the **Catedral (Cathedral),** rebuilt after the earthquake, and the **Palacio Episcopal (Archbishop's Palace),** distinguished by an extraordinary wooden balcony next to it.

A block north of the Plaza de Armas, behind the Presidential Palace, is the Río Rímac and a 17th-century Roman-style bridge, the **Puente de Piedra** (literally, "stone bridge"). It leads to the once-fashionable **Rímac** district, today considerably less chic—some would say downright dangerous—though it is the location of a few of Lima's best *peñas,* or live *criollo* music clubs. The **Plaza de Acho** bullring, once the largest in the world, and decent **Museo Taurino (Bullfighting Museum)** are near the river at Hualgayoc 332 (✆ **01/482-3360**). The ring is in full swing during the Fiestas Patrias (national holidays) at the end of July; the regular season runs from October to December.

Five blocks southwest of Plaza de Armas is Lima Centro's other grand square, **Plaza de San Martín.** This stately square with handsome gardens, inaugurated in 1921, was recently renovated. At its center is a large monument to the South American liberator José de San Martín.

Lima's **Barrio Chino,** the largest Chinese community in South America (200,000 plus), is visited by most folks to get a taste of the Peruvian twist on traditional Chinese cooking at the neighborhood's *chifas.* The official boundary of Chinatown is the large gate, Portada China, on Jirón Ucayali.

Convento y Museo de San Francisco ★★ Probably the most spectacular of Lima's colonial-era churches, the Convent of St. Francis is a strikingly restored 17th-century complex that survived the massive earthquake in 1746. The facade is a favorite of thousands of pigeons, which rest on rows of ridges that rise up the towers—so much so that from a distance it looks like black spots, adding an unexpectedly funky flavor to this baroque church. Cloisters and interiors are lined with beautiful *azulejos* (glazed ceramic tiles) from Seville; carved *mudéjar* (Moorish-style) ceilings are overhead. The mandatory guided tour takes visitors past the cloisters to a fine museum of religious art, with beautifully carved saints and a series of portraits of the apostles by the studio of Francisco Zurbarán, the famed Spanish painter. For many, though, the most fascinating component of the visit is the descent into the catacombs, which were dug beginning in 1546 as a burial ground for priests and others. (As many as 75,000 bodies were interred here before the main cemetery was built.) Also of great interest are the church, outfitted with an impressive neoclassical altar, and a fantastic 17th-century library, which was the second-most important of its time in the Americas (after one in Quito) and holds 20,000 books (many date from the earliest years after Lima's foundation). A breathtaking carved Moorish ceiling over a staircase is a reconstruction of the original from 1625.

Ancash s/n (Plaza de San Francisco). ✆ **01/426-7377.** www.museocatacumbas.com. Admission S/5 adults, S/2.50 students. Guides available in English and Spanish. Daily 9am–6pm.

La Catedral ★ Lima's baroque cathedral, an enlargement of an earlier one from 1555, was completed in 1625. It suffered damage in earthquakes in 1687 and was decimated by the big one in 1746. The present building, though again damaged by tremors in 1940, is an 18th-century reconstruction of the early plans. Twin yellow towers sandwich an elaborate stone facade. Inside are several notable Churrigueresque altars and carved wooden choir stalls, but the cathedral is best known for the chapel where Francisco Pizarro lies. The founder of Lima and killer of Inca chieftain Atahualpa was himself assassinated in the Plaza de Armas in 1541, but his remains weren't brought to the cathedral until 1985. (They were discovered in a crypt in 1977.) Look closely at the mosaic on the far wall of the chapel; it depicts his coat of arms, Atahualpa reaching into his coffer to cough up a ransom in the hopes of attaining his release, and other symbols of Pizarro's life. The cathedral also houses the small **Museo de Arte Religioso,** which has a few fabulous painted glass mirrors from Cusco, a collection of unsigned paintings, and a seated sculpture of Jesus, with his chin resting pensively on his hand—it's as bloody a figure of Christ as you're likely to see.

Plaza de Armas. ✆ **01/427-5980.** Admission to cathedral and museum S/10 adults, S/5 students. Guides available in English and Spanish (tips accepted). Mon–Sat 10am–5pm.

The Top Museums

Museo Arqueológico Rafael Larco Herrera ★★ Founded in 1926, this is the largest private collection of pre-Columbian art in the world. It concentrates on the Moche dynasty, with an estimated 45,000 pieces—including incredibly fine textiles, jewelry, and stonework from several other ancient cultures—all housed in an 18th-century colonial building. Rafael Larco Hoyle, the author of the seminal study *Los Mochicas,* is considered the founder of Peruvian archaeology; he named the museum after his father. The Moche (A.D. 200–700), who lived along the northern coast in the large area near present-day Trujillo and Cajamarca, are credited with achieving one of the greatest artistic expressions of ancient Peru. The pottery gives clues to all elements of their society: diseases, curing practices, architecture, transportation, dance, agriculture, music, and religion. The Moche are also celebrated in the modern world for their erotic ceramics. The Sala Erótica is separated from the general collection, like the porn section in a video store. The Moche depicted sex in realistic, humorous, moralistic, and religious—but above all, explicit—terms. If you're traveling with kids, expect giggles or questions about the ancient Peruvians' mighty phalluses.

Av. Bolívar 1515, Pueblo Libre. ✆ **01/461-1312.** www.museolarco.org. Admission S/30 adults, S/25 seniors, S/15 students. Private guides available in English and Spanish (tip basis, minimum S/10). Daily 9am–6pm. Take a taxi or the Todo Brasil *colectivo* to Av. Brasil and then another to Av. Bolívar. If you're coming from the Museo Nacional de Arqueología, Antropología e Historia del Perú (below), walk along the blue path.

Museo de la Nación ★★ Kids Peru's ancient history is exceedingly complicated. Peru's pre-Columbian civilizations were among the most sophisticated of their time; when Egypt was building pyramids, Peruvians were constructing great cities. Lima's National Museum, the city's biggest and one of the most important in Peru, guides visitors through the highlights of overlapping and conquering cultures and their achievements, seen not only in architecture (including scale models of most major ruins in Peru) but also highly advanced ceramics and textiles. The exhibits, spread over three rambling floors, are ordered chronologically—very helpful for getting a grip on these many cultures dispersed across Peru. In case you aren't able to make it to the archaeology-rich north of Peru, pay special attention to the facsimile of the Lord of Sipán discovery, one of the most important in the world in recent years. Explanations accompanying the exhibits are usually in both Spanish and English. Allow 2 to 3 hours to see it all.

Av. Javier Prado Este 2465, San Borja. ✆ **01/476-9878.** Admission S/9 adults, S/3 seniors, S/1 students. Guides in several languages can be contracted. Tues–Sun 9am–6pm. You can get here by *colectivo* along Av. Prado from Av. Arequipa, but it is much simpler to take a taxi from Lima Centro or Miraflores/San Isidro.

Museo Nacional de Arqueología, Antropología e Historia del Perú ★ With such a mouthful of an official name, you might expect the National Museum of Archaeology, Anthropology, and History to be the Peruvian equivalent of New York's Met. It's not, but it's a worthwhile and enjoyable museum that covers Peruvian civilization from prehistoric times to the colonial and republican periods. There are ceramics, carved stone figures and obelisks, metalwork and jewelry, lovely textiles, and mummies in the fetal position wrapped in burial blankets. There's also a selection of erotic ceramics from the Moche culture, but not nearly as extensive as that of the Rafael Larco Herrera museum (see above). Individual rooms are dedicated to the Nazca, Paracas, and Moche and Chimú cultures. Toward the end of the exhibit, which wanders around the central courtyard of the handsome 19th-century Quinta de los Libertadores mansion (once the residence of South American independence heroes San Martín and Bolívar), is a large-scale model of Machu Picchu. Basic descriptions throughout the museum are mostly in Spanish, though some are also in English. Allow about an hour for your visit.

From the museum, you can follow a walking path along a painted blue line to the Rafael Larco Herrera museum. It's about 1.5km (1 mile), or 20 minutes, straight into traffic on Antonio de Sucre (make sure you turn at the Metro supermarket on Leguia Melendes).

Plaza Bolívar s/n, Pueblo Libre. ✆ **01/463-5070.** http://museonacional.perucultural.org.pe. Admission S/12 adults, S/3.50 seniors and students. Private guides available in English and Spanish (tip basis, minimum S/10). Tues–Sat 9am–5pm; Sun 10am–4pm. Take a taxi here, or take the Todo Brasil *colectivo* to Av. Vivanco and then take a 15-min. walk.

Shopping

Lima has the greatest variety of shopping in Peru, from tony boutiques to artisan and antiques shops. In Lima, you can find handicrafts from across Peru; prices are not usually much higher and the selection may be even better than in the regions where the items are made. One exception is alpaca goods, which are better purchased in the areas around Cusco, Puno, and Arequipa, both in terms of price and selection. Miraflores is where most shoppers congregate, though there are also several outlets in Lima Centro and elsewhere in the city.

LIMA CENTRO The best spot for handicrafts from around Peru is the **Santo Domingo *artesanía* arcades** across the street from the Santo Domingo convent on Conde de Superunda and Camaná. Lima Centro's crowded **Mercado Central** is south of the Plaza Mayor, at the edge of Chinatown (at the corner of Ayacucho and Ucayali). The **Feria Artesanal** on Avenida de la Marina in Pueblo Libre has a wide variety of handicrafts of varying quality but at lower prices than most tourist-oriented shops in Lima Centro or Miraflores. Haggling is a good idea.

SUBURBS Miraflores houses the lion's share of Lima's well-stocked shops overflowing in handicrafts from around Peru, including weavings, ceramics, and silver. Several of the largest malls are here, and several dozen large souvenir and handicrafts shops are clustered on and around Avenida Ricardo Palma (look for **Artesanías Miraflores,** no. 205) and Avenida Petit Thouars (try **Artesanía Expo Inti,** no. 5495). Other handicraft shops in Miraflores include **Agua y Tierra,** Diez Canseco 298 (✆ 01/445-6980), and **Silvania Prints,** Diez Canseco 378 (✆ 01/242-0667). Alpaca sweaters and other items can be had at **Alpaca 111,** Av. Larco 671 (✆ 01/447-1623); **Alpaca Perú,** Diez Canseco 315 (✆ 01/241-4175); **Mon Repos,** Tarata 288 (✆ 01/445-9740); and **All Alpaca,** Av. Schell 375 (✆ 01/427-4704). Look for silver jewelry and antiques along Avenida La Paz. *Platerías* and *joyerías* (silver and jewelry shops) worth a visit are **Ilaria,** Av. Larco 1325 (✆ 01/444-2347), and **El Tupo,** La Paz 553 (✆ 01/444-1511). Antiques shops include **El Almacén de Arte,** Francia 339 (✆ 01/445-6264), and **Porta 735,** Porta 735 (✆ 01/447-6158).

For fine *retablos* (gradines) and artisanship typical of Ayacucho (which produces some of Peru's most notable pieces), visit the **Museo-Galería Popular de Ayacucho,** Av. Pedro de Osma 116 (✆ **01/247-0599**), in Barranco. The finest upscale purveyor of crafts and home furnishings from across Peru is **Dédalo ★★**, Saenz Peña 295 (✆ **01/477-0562**), which also has a cafe and patio out back, in Barranco. Small handicrafts markets, open late to catch bar and post-dinner crowds, are in the main squares in both Miraflores and Barranco.

WHERE TO STAY

Lima Centro has its share of hotels and budget inns, but most people head out to Miraflores, San Isidro, and, to a lesser extent, Barranco. These barrios have little in the way of sights but are more convenient for nightlife and shopping and probably safer, if not necessarily much quieter, than Lima Centro.

Lima Centro

Inexpensive

Hotel España ★ Value Near the Convento de San Francisco and just 4 blocks from Plaza de Armas, this extremely popular budget hostel has a funky flair and communal atmosphere. If you're looking to hook up with backpackers from around the globe and set off to explore Peru, you can't do better than Hotel España. It occupies a rambling colonial building bursting with paintings, ceramics, faux Roman busts, plants, and even the occasional mummy and skull. A maze of rooms, most with shared bathrooms, are up a winding staircase. The rooms themselves are simple, with concrete floors but brightly colored walls; they're well kept, but with cheesy bedspreads. The leafy rooftop garden terrace, with views of San Francisco, is a good place to hang out and trade travel tales. Some complain that security is a little lax, so lock your stuff in the lockers. Hot water goes to the early bird. The place can be noisy, but that's part of its charm.

Azángaro 105, Lima. ✆/fax **01/428-5546.** www.hotelespanaperu.com. 30 units, 6 with private bathroom. $11 double without bathroom, $15 with bathroom. No credit cards. **Amenities:** Cafe. *In room:* No phone.

La Posada del Parque ★ Value Monica Moreno runs this safe, great-value, and delightful guesthouse, which occupies a lovely 1920s *casona* (large house) on what has to be one of the most peaceful streets—it's a long cul-de-sac lined with gardens and other stately homes—near the center of Lima. Her house, in the Santa Beatriz district, is stuffed with Peruvian popular art and offers unusual amenities at an economic rate, such as Internet access, satellite TV, and beer and homemade pizzas upon request. Monica is more than willing to help travelers with all their needs. The rooms are spacious and impeccable, with excellent bathrooms and hot water. The owner also has a one-bedroom suite (Suite del Parque) nearby, which is perfect for longer stays.

Parque Hernán Velarde 60 (off Av. Petit Thouars, Santa Beatriz), Lima. ✆ **01/433-2412.** Fax 01/332-6927. www.incacountry.com. 9 units. $45–$48 double (rates include taxes). No credit cards. No parking. **Amenities:** Communal TV room; Internet access. *In room:* No phone.

Miraflores

Expensive

Casa Andina Private Collection Miraflores ★★ Casa Andina, the fast-growing Peruvian hotel chain, took over this high-rise hotel, which had been Lima's first five-star hotel but was then abandoned for a number of years, and completely gutted it, turning it into its showcase property. The result is now a favorite of business travelers: It has all the amenities and services of the city's top luxury business hotels, but without the exorbitant prices of many of its competitors. The well-designed accommodations are sleeker and more luxurious than at most of the group's other hotels, and many feature nice views over the city. The chef from Casa Andina's top hotel in Cusco was brought in to oversee the modern restaurant here, and the spa and heated swimming pool are excellent bonuses.

Calle La Paz 463, Miraflores, Lima. ✆ **866/447-3270** in the U.S. and Canada, 01/213-9700, or 213-9739 for reservations. Fax 01/213-9790. www.casa-andina.com. 148 units. $190–$317 double; suites from $350. Rates include breakfast buffet. AE, DC, MC, V. **Amenities:** 2 restaurants; bar; babysitting; concierge; gym; heated swimming pool; room service; smoke-free rooms; spa. *In room:* A/C, TV, fridge, hair dryer, Wi-Fi.

Moderate

Casa Andina Classic Miraflores San Antonio ★ Value Well located and well executed, like all Casa Andina properties, this midsize hotel has ample, cheerfully decorated bedrooms with brightly striped bedspreads and sunburnt-yellow walls. Marble bathrooms are large, and the breakfast buffet is a winner. Casa Andina is perfect for the traveler who seeks comfort, good value, and no unpleasant surprises. A second Casa Andina Classic is located nearby, at Av. Petit Thouars 5444.

Av. 28 de Julio 1088, Miraflores, Lima. ✆ **01/241-4050**, or 01/213-9739 for reservations. Fax 01/241-4051. www.casa-andina.com. 49 units. $63–$97 double. Rates include breakfast buffet. AE, DC, MC, V. **Amenities:** Babysitting; concierge; room service; smoke-free rooms. *In room:* A/C, TV, fridge, hair dryer on request.

Hotel Antigua Miraflores ★ Finds This charming early-20th-century mansion, full of authentic Peruvian touches and color, calls itself "a hidden treasure in the heart of Miraflores." As many return visitors know, that's not just hype. The hotel is owned and operated by a North American who's a long-time Lima resident. The house is elegant and tasteful, lined with colonial Peruvian art and built around a leafy courtyard. The staff is exceptionally helpful and friendly. Rooms range from huge suites with large Jacuzzis and kitchenettes to comfortable double rooms with handcrafted furniture and good-quality beds. Most bathrooms are quite luxurious, with colonial tiles, brass fixtures, and bathtubs. The public rooms look more like an art gallery than a hotel lobby (the paintings are for sale).

Av. Grau 350, Miraflores, Lima. ✆ **01/241-6116.** Fax 01/241-6115. http://peru-hotels-inns.com. 35 units. $94–$109 double; $129 suite. Rates include taxes and a nice selection of breakfasts. AE, DC, MC, V. Free parking. **Amenities:** Restaurant; bar; exercise room; Jacuzzi; room service. *In room:* A/C, TV, hair dryer, minibar.

Inexpensive

Hostal El Patio Miraflores ★ *Finds* Set back from the street, behind an iron gate and built around a flower-filled Andalusian-style patio, this friendly, good-value inn has real personality. It's an unexpected but very welcome respite from the grime and chaos of Lima. The comfortable, if not luxurious, rooms in the rambling colonial mansion feature good natural light and are cozy and brightly colored. Though a relatively small hotel, it's run very efficiently, and the staff goes out of its way to help visitors find their way in Lima.

Calle Ernesto Diez Canseco 341, Miraflores, Lima. ✆ **01/444-2107.** Fax 01/444-1663. www.hostalelpatio.net. 25 units. S/150–S/180 double; S/195–S/225 suite. Rates include taxes and continental breakfast. AE, DC, MC, V. *In room:* A/C, TV, fridge, Wi-Fi.

San Isidro

Inexpensive

Casa Bella B&B ★ *Value* A very pleasant midrange choice in an area better known for its business-oriented luxury hotels, this safe and modern, exceptionally clean inn, 1 block from the swank Country Club, offers private and quiet accommodations. While a little larger than the typical B&B, with 12 rooms, this nicely furnished, slick contemporary home gives travelers a nice impression of staying at a friend's home. The spacious and airy nonsmoking rooms are attractively decorated, with good bedding, and several have backyard garden views. Whether for a few days or a longer stay, Casa Bella is tough to beat for the price.

Las Flores 459 San Isidro. ✆ **01/421-7354** or 720/470-7237 in the U.S. www.casabellaperu.net. 12 units. $65–$75 double; $85–$175 suite. Rates include continental breakfast. MC, V. Free parking. **Amenities:** Kitchen; smoke-free rooms. *In room:* Wi-Fi.

Barranco

Second Home Peru ★★★ Finds Lilian Delfín runs this extraordinary small inn in the home of her father, the Peruvian painter and sculptor Victor Delfín. Perfect for the relaxed and still slightly bohemian neighborhood of Barranco, this is no bland B&B; the idiosyncratic 1913 home is replete with artistic flavor—and works by Delfín, who continues to paint. Those interested in the arts or in spending a few days in town will find it a magical home away from home. It's one of the coolest and best-value places to stay in all of Peru. My large room had a beautiful wood floor and beams, a huge picture window framing the misty Pacific, deep claw-foot tub, and what felt like the most luxurious linens in Lima. Ask politely and Lilian may take you to visit her father's studio, where a giant puma-head fountain spouts water into the swimming pool (open to guests). At a minimum, you'll get to have breakfast at Delfín's Gaudí-style, neo-medieval kitchen.

Domeyer 366, Barranco, Lima. ✆ **01/247-5522.** Fax 01/247-1042. www.secondhomeperu.com. 5 units. $95–$100 double; $120 suite. Rates include taxes and breakfast. AE, DC, MC, V. *In room:* A/C, TV, hair dryer.

WHERE TO DINE

Lima offers the most cosmopolitan dining in Peru, with restaurants for all budgets serving a wide range of cuisines. Entire streets and neighborhoods specialize in a single type of food: In Lima Centro, you can visit the *chifas* of Chinatown, and in Miraflores, a pedestrian street off Parque Central, La Calle de las Pizzas, is lined with scores of look-alike pizzerias and quasi-Italian restaurants, which draw scores of tourists looking for cheap eats and plentiful beer. Lima is the top spot in the country to sample truly creative gastronomy, as well as the dish the city is known for: *ceviche.* Museumgoers-slash-foodies can kill two birds with one stone at the Museo Arqueológico Rafael Larco Herrera, which now features a handsome restaurant, Café del Museo, with a menu by Gastón Acurio, the celebrated chef and man behind the restaurants **Astrid y Gastón** (p. 647), **La Mar** (p. 647), and **T'anta** (p. 649).

Lima Centro

Moderate

El Rincón Que No Conoces ★★ Finds PERUVIAN/CREOLE Although stuck in a tourist no-man's land—at the edge of the Centro—this authentic, amiable, old-school Peruvian *criollo* restaurant is worth the trek. Doña Teresa has been cooking here for more than 30 years, and her neighborhood eatery may have gotten a little more polished and popular, but it hasn't deviated from its mission: classic Creole cooking. A good place to start is with a *causa* (a yellow potato torta stuffed with chicken, shrimp, or tuna), or perhaps a *palta rellena* (stuffed avocado). A similarly classic main dish is the *tacu-tacu* (rice and beans) with *asado a la tira* (short ribs). The menu is long, portions are large, and you can hardly take a wrong turn. With a name like "The Corner Joint You've Never

Heard of," one might expect this to be a modest little hut. Instead, it's a rather handsome and cozy two-story restaurant with high ceilings and a warm atmosphere—reflective of the woman in the kitchen.

Bernardo Alcedo 363 alt. cuadra 20 de Petit Thouars, Lince. ✆ **01/471-2171.** Reservations recommended. Main courses S/20–S/32. No credit cards. Tues–Sun noon–4:30pm.

Inexpensive

Cocolat Café BISTRO A good and quick spot for lunch or dinner, this simple little bistro rests on the popular pedestrian passageway near the Plaza de Armas. It serves sandwiches, salads, and sides such as empanadas. The midday menu is a good deal; it's just $5 for an appetizer and main course, or $7 for a full "chef's menu." It's also a good spot for breakfast. Whenever you visit, you'll want to top off your meal with a great selection of homemade chocolates and good coffee, and you might just want to linger for a while on the sidewalk terrace.

Pasaje Nicolás de Ribera El Viejo (Los Escribanos) 121. ✆ **01/427-4471.** Reservations not accepted. Main courses S/10–S/15; *menú del día* S/18–S/25. No credit cards. Mon–Sat 8am–6:30pm.

Miraflores & San Isidro

Very Expensive

Astrid y Gastón ★★★ PERUVIAN/INTERNATIONAL Hidden behind a nonchalant facade on a busy side street leading to Parque Central, this warm and chic modern colonial dining room and cozy bar continues to be my favorite restaurant in Peru. Gastón Acurio is the celebrity chef of the moment. His signature restaurant in the capital has high white peaked ceilings and orange walls decorated with colorful modern art. In back is an open kitchen, where Gastón can be seen cooking with his staff, and a secluded wine-salon dining room. The place is sophisticated and hip but low-key, a description that could fit most of its clients, who all seem to be regulars. The menu might be called *criollo*-Mediterranean: Peruvian with a light touch. Try spicy roasted kid or the excellent fish called *noble robado,* served in miso sauce with crunchy oysters. The list of desserts—the work of Astrid, the other half of the husband-wife team—is nearly as long as the main course menu, and they are spectacular.

Cantuarias 175, Miraflores. ✆ **01/444-1496.** www.astridygaston.com. Reservations recommended. Main courses S/38–S/79. AE, DC, MC, V. Mon–Sat 12:30–3:30pm and 7:30pm–midnight.

La Mar Cebichería ★★★ *CEVICHERIA*/SEAFOOD The restaurant everyone in Lima seems to be lining up to get in—no reservations are accepted, so get there early or sneak in late in the afternoon—is this upscale *cevichería,* courtesy of hot chef Gastón Acurio. Fashionable, stylishly designed, and moderately priced, it represents the best of traditional Limeño cooking, but with an edge. Some insist that you don't need to go to an expensive spot for *ceviche,* and while it's true that most authentic *ceviche* spots are no-frills neighborhood joints, there's nothing wrong with jazzing up the formula. The fish—choose from a couple dozen types of *ceviche,* as well as rice-based seafood dishes and whole fish—is always fresh and carefully prepared. Although La Mar is only open for lunch, it features a cool cocktail bar with great pisco-based drinks, such as the Cholopolitan.

Av. La Mar 770, Miraflores. ✆ **01/421-3365.** www.lamarcebicheria.com. Reservations not accepted. Main courses S/19–S/49. AE, DC, MC, V. Mon–Fri noon–5pm; Sat–Sun 11:30am–5:30pm.

Las Brujas de Cachiche ★★ PERUVIAN/*CRIOLLO* The Witches of Cachiche celebrates 2,000 years of local culture with a menu that's a tour of the "magical" cuisines of pre-Columbian Peru. The chef even uses ancient recipes and ingredients. The

Tips Peruvian Chifas

Chinatown (Barrio Chino), southeast of the Plaza de Armas and next to the Mercado Central (beyond the Chinese arch on Jirón Ucayali, a pedestrian mall that is lined with scores of *chifas*), is a good place to sample the Peruvian take on Chinese food. These *chifas,* inexpensive restaurants with similar menus, are everywhere in the small but dense neighborhood. Among those worth visiting (generally open daily 9am–10pm or later) are **Wa Lok** ★, Jr. Paruro 864 (✆ **01/427-2750;** www.walok.com), probably the best known (and most expensive) in the neighborhood; and **Salón China,** Jr. Ucayali 727 (✆ **01/428-8350**), which serves a good lunch buffet for S/35.

extensive menu includes classic Peruvian dishes, such as *ají de gallina* (creamed chicken with chilies), but concentrates on fresh fish and shellfish and fine cuts of meat with interesting twists and unusual accompaniments. Brujas de Cachiche sole, for instance, comes with Asian and *criollo* spices, plus peas and bell peppers sautéed in soybean sauce. Most of the excellent desserts continue the indigenous theme, such as *mazamorra morada* (purple corn pudding and dried fruit). The restaurant, in a sprawling old house with several warmly decorated dining rooms, is popular both night and day with well-heeled Limeños, expat businesspeople, foreign government officials, and tourists; it's exclusive and it's expensive, but it's worth the splurge. A lunch buffet is served Tuesday through Friday and Sunday from 11am to 4pm.

Jr. Bolognesi 460, Miraflores. ✆ **01/447-1883.** www.brujasdecachiche.com.pe. Reservations recommended. Main courses S/33–S/62; lunch buffet S/120, including 2 glasses of wine. AE, DC, MC, V. Mon 1pm–midnight; Tues–Sat 11am–midnight; Sun noon–5pm.

Restaurant Huaca Pucllana ★★ NOUVEAU PERUVIAN Located within the compound of a 1,500-year-old adobe pyramid built by the original inhabitants of Lima, this is one of the city's greatest dining surprises. This beautiful and serene upscale restaurant, with knockout views of the pyramid and secluded in the midst of Lima's chaotic jumble, makes for a remarkable night out. The low hump of adobe bricks and excavation walkways are illuminated at night, and diners can take a tour of the construction and digs after dinner. You can dine indoors or out, but the best spot is surely the covered terrace. The menu is creative Peruvian, with fusion touches spicing up classic *criollo* cooking. Excellent appetizers include *humitas verdes* (tamales) and *causitas pucllana* (balls of mashed potatoes with shrimp and avocado). Main courses are focused on meats, such as rack of lamb, but I had an excellent marinated grouper with an interesting Asian twist. Desserts are worth saving room for; the napoleon, with chocolate mousse and passion fruit sorbet between chocolate cookies, is heavenly.

General Borgoño, Block 8 (Huaca Pucllana), Miraflores. ✆ **01/445-4042.** Reservations recommended. Main courses S/28–S/60. AE, DC, MC, V. Mon–Sat 12:30pm–midnight; Sun 12:30–4pm.

Moderate

Segundo Muelle ★ Value SEAFOOD/CEVICHE This informal, lunch-only place in San Isidro, popular with local office workers, is one of the most reasonable options in Lima for excellent fresh fish and *ceviche* plates without any fuss. If you're new to *ceviche,* you can't go wrong with the *mixto* (white fish, octopus, prawns, snails, scallops, and squid). There is a long list of other fish dishes, including sole, salmon, and varied rice and seafood plates. Top off your meal with *chicha morada,* a sweet and delicious purple corn beverage made with pineapple and lemon. Kids' plates are available for S/12. A second branch in San Isidro is at Av. Conquistadores 490 (✆ **01/421-1206**).

Av. Canaval y Moreyra 605 (at the corner of Pablo Carriquirry), San Isidro. ✆ **01/224-3007.** www.segundomuelle.com. Reservations not accepted. Main courses S/18–S/38. MC, V. Daily noon–5pm.

T'anta ★ PERUVIAN/CAFE Like a Peruvian upscale deli/market, T'anta (which means "bread" in Quechua) serves delicious, casual eats in its cafe or prepared foods to go. It now has a complete menu, with a full range of creative snack foods and small meals, including classic Peruvian dishes. From fresh salads and panini to Peruvian sandwiches called *sánguches* and homemade pastas and terrific desserts, this stylish but informal place, the brainchild of Astrid (the dessert wizard of Astrid y Gastón fame) hits the spot no matter what you're in the mood for, or when. With its full list of cool cocktails (such as the *maricucha* or *aguaymanto* sour), it's also a great spot for drinks. You may come for a coffee or a cocktail, but I guarantee that you'll end up at least having dessert. One dessert that had me coming back for more was the *tartita de maracuyá* (passion fruit tart). There are now three other locations in Lima, including one in the Centro on Pasaje Nicolás de Rivera del Viejo 142.

Pancho Fierro 117, San Isidro. ✆ **01/421-9708.** Reservations not accepted. Main courses S/19–S/42. AE, DC, MC, V. Daily 8am–midnight.

Barranco

Expensive

Chala ★★★ Finds PERUVIAN/FUSION This sleek restaurant and lounge down by the "bridge of sighs" in Barranco is one of my newest faves in Lima. It delivers what it calls *"costa fusión,"* meaning adaptations of Peruvian coastal and Limeño dishes with largely Mediterranean influences. While the chic, colorful interior is coolly international, the gorgeous long deck outdoors, under an old wooden ceiling, tall trees, and squawking birds, has a great tropical, and sexy, feel. At a recent dinner, I started by sipping a *maracuyá* (passion fruit) sour and munching on banana chips, before moving on to an extremely fresh salad with mushrooms, avocado, and tomatoes. My entree was identified by the esoteric name "Oleaje Espirituoso," (spiritual swell) but it was a terrific dish of grouper served on a bed of zucchini gnocchi and a crème of *huacatay* (a local herb).

Bajada de Baños 343, Barranco. ✆ **01/252-8515.** www.chala.com.pe. Reservations recommended. Main courses S/28–S/55. AE, DC, MC, V. Tues–Sat noon–3pm and 5–11pm; Sun 11am–5pm.

Moderate

Antica Trattoria ★ Value ITALIAN This is a charming and laid-back Italian restaurant that perfectly suits the surrounding Barranco barrio. It has a number of small, separate dining rooms decorated with a rustic and minimalist masculinity: stucco walls, dark-wood-beamed ceilings, country-style wood tables, and simple, solid chairs. The house specialty is gourmet pizza from the wood-fired ovens, but the menu has several tempting ideas to lure you away from pizza, such as homemade pasta and *osso buco* or delicious *lomo fino a la tagliata,* beef tenderloin buried under a mound of arugula. The relaxed environment makes this a great date place, as well as the perfect spot for dinner before hitting one of Barranco's live music or dance clubs.

San Martín 201, Barranco. ✆ **01/247-5752.** Reservations recommended. Main courses S/21–S/39. AE, DC, MC, V. Daily noon–midnight.

Canta Rana ★★ *Finds* CEVICHE/SEAFOOD A relaxed and informal place (in local lingo, a *huarique*) that looks almost like the interior of a garage and is immensely popular with locals, the Singing Frog is the very definition of a neighborhood *cevichería.* You might not guess it from the outside, but it's one of the best spots in town for *ceviche* and fresh seafood in a classic coastal manner. The menu lists 15 types of sea bass, including one stuffed with langoustines, as well as infinite varieties of *ceviche.* The traditional *ceviche* (big enough for two) is served on a flat plate with heaps of purple onions, some *choclo* (maize), and a wedge of *camote* (sweet potato). The best way to wash it down is with a chilled pitcher of *chicha morada.* The shacklike interior is decorated with simple wood tables, and the walls are festooned with *fútbol* (soccer) paraphernalia. For a high dose of local color and excellent seafood, Canta Rana's a perfect lunch spot.

Génova 101, Barranco. ✆ **01/247-7274.** Reservations recommended. Main courses S/18–S/42. AE, MC, V. Tues–Sat 11am–11pm; Sun–Mon 11am–6pm.

LIMA AFTER DARK

As its largest city, Lima certainly has Peru's most varied nightlife scene. The best after-dark scenes are in Miraflores and particularly Barranco. Bars open in the early evening around 8pm, but dance clubs and live-music clubs generally don't get started until 10pm or later. Many are open very late, until 3 or 4am.

PEÑAS You should check out at least one *peña,* a *criollo*-music club that quite often inspires rousing participation. **Caballero de Fina Estampa** ★, Av. del Ejército 800, Miraflores (✆ **01/441-0552**), is one of the most chic, with a large colonial salon and balconies. **De Rompe y Raja** ★★, Manuel Segura 127, Barranco (✆ **01/247-3099;** www.derompeyraja.net), is a favorite of locals. Look for the popular Matices Negros (an Afro-Peruvian dance trio). **Las Guitarras,** Manuel Segura 295, Barranco (✆ **01/479-1874**), is a cool spot where locals go to play an active part in their *peña.* It's open Friday and Saturday only. **Brisas del Titicaca** ★★, Jr. Wukulski 168, at the first block of Avenida Brasil, Lima Centro (✆ **01/332-1901;** www.brisasdeltiticaca.com), is a cultural institution with *noches folklóricas* Thursday through Saturday and some of the best shows in Lima.

THE BAR & CLUB SCENE **Freiheit,** Lima 471, Miraflores (✆ **01/247-4630**), is a warmly decorated bar in the style of a German tavern. The dance floor is separate from the bar area. There's a drink minimum on weekends. **O'Murphy's Irish Pub,** Shell 627, Miraflores (✆ **01/242-1212**), is a longtime favorite drinking hole. Expect a pool table, darts, Guinness on tap, and Brits and Irish hoisting it. **Son de Cuba** ★, Bulevar San Ramón 277, Miraflores (✆ **01/445-1444**), is on the pedestrian street called "Little Italy" by locals, but the club focuses on the rhythms and drinks of the Caribbean from Tuesday through Sunday. **Ayahuasca** ★★, Prolongación San Martín 130, Barranco (✆ **01/9810-44745**), is a stylish bar in a stately colonial mansion with swank furnishings, art exhibits, and great cocktails, including an impressive array of pisco sours.

My vote for best live music club in Lima is **La Noche** ★★, Bolognesi 307, Barranco (✆ 01/247-1012; www.lanoche.com.pe); despite its prosaic name, this sprawling multi-level club feels like a swank treehouse, with a great stage and sound system and good bands every night of the week that run the gamut (though are frequently jazz), plus a hip mixed Limeño and international crowd. The Monday night jam sessions are particularly good and have no cover charge; otherwise, covers range from S/10 to S/20. There's now a new branch of La Noche in Lima Centro, at the corner of Quilca and Camaná, near

Plaza San Martín (✆ 01/423-0299). **El Ekeko,** Av. Grau 266, Barranco (✆ 01/247-3148), is a two-level place with live music Wednesday through Saturday; most acts fall within the Latin category, often Cuban. Covers range from S/12 to S/30. **La Estación de Barranco ★**, Pedro de Osma 112 (✆ 01/247-0344), is another nice place, with live music Tuesday through Saturday and a slightly more mature crowd. **Satchmo,** Av. La Paz 538, Miraflores (✆ 01/444-4957), is a sophisticated jazz joint with a variable roster of live bands; it's a good date spot. Covers are S/20 to S/45. Another very good jazz club, down a pedestrian-only walkway, is **Jazz Zone,** La Paz 646 (✆ 01/241-8139; www.jazzzoneperu.com), with a diverse program of live music, including Afro-Peruvian, Monday to Saturday.

Many of Lima's dance clubs are predominantly young and wild affairs. Two very chic and popular discotheques, **Gótica ★★** (✆ **01/445-6343;** www.gotica.com.pe) and **Aura ★★** (✆ **01/242-5516;** www.aura.com.pe) face each other in the Larcomar shopping center, Malecón de la Reserva 610, Miraflores, and feature interconnected open-air terraces, great sea views and dance music ranging from electronica to the Latin specialty, *pachanga.* Also check out **Deja-Vu Trattoria & Bar,** Av. Grau 294, Barranco (✆ **01/247-3742**), whose decor is based on TV commercials. The music trips from techno to trance; it's a dance fest Monday through Saturday. **Kitsch,** Bolognesi 743, Barranco (✆ **01/247-3325**), is one of Lima's hottest bars—literally, as it sometimes turns into a sweatbox—with over-the-top decor (flowery wallpaper and a fish tank in the floor) and recorded tunes that range from 1970s and 1980s pop to Latin and techno.

AN EXCURSION FROM LIMA: THE NAZCA LINES ★★

The unique Nazca Lines remain one of the great enigmas of the South American continent. The San José desert, bisected by the great Pan-American Highway that runs the length of Peru, is spectacularly marked by 70 giant plant and animal line drawings, as well as a warren of mysterious geometric lines, carved into the barren surface. Throughout the Nazca Valley, an area of nearly 1,000 sq. km (386 sq. miles), are at least 10,000 lines and 300 different figures. Most are found alongside a 50km (30-mile) stretch of the Pan-American Highway. Some of the biggest and best-known figures are about 21km (13 miles) north of the town of Nazca. Most experts believe they were constructed by the Nazca (pre-Inca) culture between 300 B.C. and A.D. 700, though predecessor and successor cultures—the Paracas and Huari—may have also contributed to the desert canvas. The lines were discovered in the 1920s when commercial airlines began flights over the Peruvian desert. From the sky, they appeared to be some sort of primitive landing strips.

As enigmatic as they are, the Nazca Lines are not some sort of desert-sands Rorschach inkblot; the figures are real and easily identifiable from the air. With the naked eye from the window of an airplane, you'll spot the outlines of a parrot, hummingbird, spider, condor, dog, whale, monkey with a tail wound like a top, giant spirals, huge trapezoids, and, perhaps oddest of all, a cartoonish anthropomorphic figure with its hand raised to the sky that has come to be known as the "Astronaut." Some figures are as much as 300m (1,000 ft.) long, while some lines are 30m (100 ft.) wide and stretch more than 9km (5½ miles).

Questions have long confounded observers. Who constructed these huge figures and lines and why? Apparently, the Nazca people, over many generations, removed hard stones turned dark by the sun to "draw" the lines in the fine, lighter colored sand. The incredibly dry desert conditions preserved the lines and figures for more than 1,000 years. Why the lines were constructed is more difficult to answer, especially considering that the authors were unable to see their work in its entirety without any sort of aerial perspective. A scientist who dedicated her life to study of the lines was a German mathematician, María Reiche. She concluded that the lines formed a giant astronomical calendar, crucial to calculating planting and harvest times. According to this theory, the Nazca were able to predict the arrival of rains, a valuable commodity in such barren territory. Other theories, though, abound. Nazca is a seismic zone, with 300 fault lines beneath the surface and hundreds of subterranean canals; an American scientist, David Johnson, proposed that the trapezoids held clues to subterranean water sources. Some suggest that the lines not only led to water sources, but that they were pilgrimage routes, part of the Nazca's ritual worship of water. Notions of extraterrestrials and the Nazca's ability to fly over the lines have been dismissed by most serious observers.

By far the most convenient—although certainly not the cheapest—way to see the lines is as part of a 1-day or overnight round-trip package from Lima with **AeroCondor's Nazca Conexxion,** Av. Aramburu 858, Surquillo (✆ **01/421-3105;** www.aerocondor.com.pe); **AeroIca,** Diez Canseco 480B, Miraflores (✆ **01/445-0859**; www.aeroica.net/icahomeing.html); or **Aeroparacas,** Av. Santa Fe 274 (✆ **01/265-8073;** www.aeroparacas.com), with packages ranging from $599 to $699 per person. Unfortunately, there are no independent flights from Lima to Nazca (or from any other city to Nazca), so you'll have to get there by bus—an 8-hour ride; programs with bus transportation from AeroCondor start at $130 per person.

Overflights organized in Nazca run around $75 per person (those originating in Ica run about $150–$180). The small aircraft seats between three and five passengers; if you're prone to airsickness, note that these flights take some stomach-turning dips and dives. (I once shared a plane with four French travelers who not 10 minutes into the flight were all tossing their *petits déjeuners* into the white plastic bags that had been thoughtfully provided.)

5 CUSCO ★★★

1,153km (715 miles) SE of Lima

As the storied capital of the Inca dynasty and the gateway to Machu Picchu, Cusco is one of the undisputed highlights of South America. Paved with stone streets and building foundations laid by the Incas more than 5 centuries ago, the town is far from a mere history lesson; it is also remarkably dynamic, enlivened by throngs of travelers who have transformed the center around the Plaza de Armas into a mecca for South American adventurers. Cusco is one of those rare places that seems able to preserve its unique character and enduring appeal despite its prominence on the international tourism radar.

Cusco looks and feels like the very definition of an Andean capital. It's a fascinating blend of pre-Columbian and colonial history and contemporary mestizo culture. Cusco's highlights include Inca ruins and colonial-era baroque and Renaissance churches and mansions. The heart of the historic center has suffered relatively few modern intrusions, and despite the staggering number of souvenir shops, travel agencies, hotels, and restaurants overflowing with visitors soaking up the flavor, it doesn't take an impossibly fertile imagination to conjure the magnificent capital of the 16th century.

Today, Cusco thrives as one of the most vibrant expressions of Amerindian and mestizo culture anywhere in the Americas. Every June, the city is packed during Inti Raymi, the celebration of the winter solstice and the sun god, a deeply religious festival that is also a magical display of pre-Columbian music and dance. Thousands trek out to Paucartambo for the riveting Virgen del Carmen festival in mid-July. Other traditional arts also flourish. Cusco is the handicrafts center of Peru, and its streets teem with merchants and their extraordinary textiles, many hand-woven using the exact techniques of their ancestors.

Spectacularly cradled by the southeastern Andes Mountains, Cusco sits at a daunting altitude of 3,400m (11,150 ft.). The air is noticeably thinner here than in almost any other city in South America, and the city, best explored on foot, demands arduous hiking up precipitous stone steps, leaving even the fittest of travelers gasping for breath. It takes a couple of days to get acclimatized before moving on from Cusco to explore the mountain villages of the Inca's Sacred Valley, the Amazon basin, and, of course, Machu Picchu, but many visitors find Cusco so seductive that they either delay plans to explore the surrounding region, or add a few days to their trip to allow more time in the city. Increasingly, travelers are basing themselves in one of the lower-altitude villages of the Sacred Valley, but there is so much to see and do in Cusco that an overnight stay is pretty much required of anyone who hasn't previously spent time in the area. The charms of Cusco become quickly addictive, and many travelers linger in the old Inca capital, even forsaking other travel plans in Peru.

ESSENTIALS

Getting There

BY PLANE Most visitors to Cusco arrive by plane from Lima (a 1-hr. flight). In high season, LAN, Taca, and other carriers' flights arrive by the dozens from Lima as well as Arequipa, Puerto Maldonado, and La Paz at **Aeropuerto Internacional Velasco Astete** (airport code CUZ; ✆ **084/222-611**). See "Getting Around" in "Planning Your Trip to Peru," earlier in this chapter, for more flight information. Flights are occasionally delayed by poor weather.

Transportation from the airport to downtown Cusco, about 20 minutes away, is by taxi or private hotel car. Taxis are plentiful and inexpensive. (A less convenient *combi,* or small bus, passes outside the airport parking lot and goes to Plaza San Francisco; unless you have almost no baggage and your hotel is right on that square, it's not worth the few soles you'll save to take a *combi.*) Most hotels, and even less expensive hostels, are happy to arrange airport pickup. If you take a taxi, note that the fare is likely to drop precipitously if you merely refuse the first offer you get (likely to be S/20). Taxi fare to Cusco is generally half that, S/10, from the airport to the center. If you have arranged for your hotel to pick you up, be certain that you are dealing with someone authorized by the hotel and who possesses your exact arrival information.

BY BUS Buses to Cusco arrive from Lima, Arequipa, Puno/Juliaca, and Puerto Maldonado in the Amazon basin. From Lima to Cusco is 26 hours by land; from Puno, 7 hours; and from Arequipa, 12 hours. There is no central bus terminal in Cusco. Buses arrive at either a terminal on Avenida Pachacutec or (more commonly) at the newer **Terminal Terrestre,** Av. Vellejos Santoni, Cdra. 2, Santiago (✆ **084/224-471;** several miles from the city center on the way to the airport). Buses to and from the Sacred Valley (Urubamba buses, which go through either Pisac or Chinchero) use small, makeshift terminals on Calle Puputi s/n, Cdra. 2 and Av. Grau s/n, and Cdra 1.

BY TRAIN There are two main Perurail train stations in Cusco. Trains from Puno and Arequipa arrive at **Estación de Huanchaq** (also spelled "Wanchac"), Av. Pachacútec s/n

A Safety Note

Over the years, Cusco has earned a reputation for being somewhat unsafe for foreign visitors, especially at night when violent muggings have been known to occur on empty streets. While I have never had a problem in the city in more than 20 years, it's advisable to take some precautions. Do not walk alone late at night, even in the town center; instead, have restaurant or bar staff call a taxi for you. Please refer to "Safety" in "Fast Facts: Peru" on p. 634 for more details.

(✆ **084/238-722** or 084/221-992; www.perurail.com), at the southeast end of Avenida El Sol. Trains from Ollantaytambo, Machu Picchu, and the Amazon jungle arrive at **Estación de San Pedro,** Calle Cascaparo s/n (✆ **084/221-352** or 221-313), southwest of the Plaza de Armas. Thieves operate in and around both stations, but visitors should be particularly cautious at San Pedro station, which is near the crowded Mercado Central.

Getting Around

Getting around Cusco is straightforward and relatively simple, especially since so many of the city sights are within walking distance of the Plaza de Armas in the historic center. You will mostly depend on leg power and inexpensive taxis to get around.

BY TAXI Unlike in Lima, taxis are regulated in Cusco and charge standard rates (although they do not have meters). Taxis are inexpensive (S/3–S/5 for any trip within the historic core during the day, S/3–S/8 at night) and are a good way to get around, especially at night. Hailing a cab in Cusco is considerably less daunting than in Lima, but you may still wish to call a registered taxi when traveling from your hotel to train or bus stations, going to the airport, and when returning to your hotel late at night. Licensed taxi companies include **Okarina** (✆ **084/247-080**) and **Aló Cusco** (✆ **084/222-222**). Taxis can be hired for return trips to nearby ruins or for half- or full days.

BY BUS Most buses—called variously *colectivos, micros,* and *combis*—cost S/2 or slightly more after midnight, on Sundays, and on holidays. You aren't likely to need buses often, or ever, within the city, though the *colectivos* that run up and down Avenida El Sol are also a useful option for some hotels, travel agencies, and shopping markets (taxis are much easier and not much more expensive). A bus departs from Plaza San Francisco to the airport, but it isn't very convenient.

BY CAR Renting a car in the Cusco region—more than likely to visit the beautiful Sacred Valley mountain villages—is a more practical idea than in most parts of Peru. Rental agencies include **Avis,** Av. El Sol 808 (✆ **084/248-800**), and **Localiza,** Av. Industrial J-3, Urbanización Huancaro (✆ **084/233-131**). Rates range from $50 per day for a standard four-door to $90 per day for a Jeep Cherokee 4×4. Check also with **4×4 Cusco,** Urb. San Borja, Huanchaq (✆ **084/227-730**), which has pickups and even Toyota Land Cruisers, though renters need to be at least 28 years old.

BY FOOT Most of Cusco is best navigated by foot, though because of the city's 3,400m (11,150 ft.) elevation and steep climbs, walking is demanding. Allow extra time to get around and carry a bottle of water. You can walk to the major ruins just beyond the city—Sacsayhuamán and Q'enko—but you should be fit to do so.

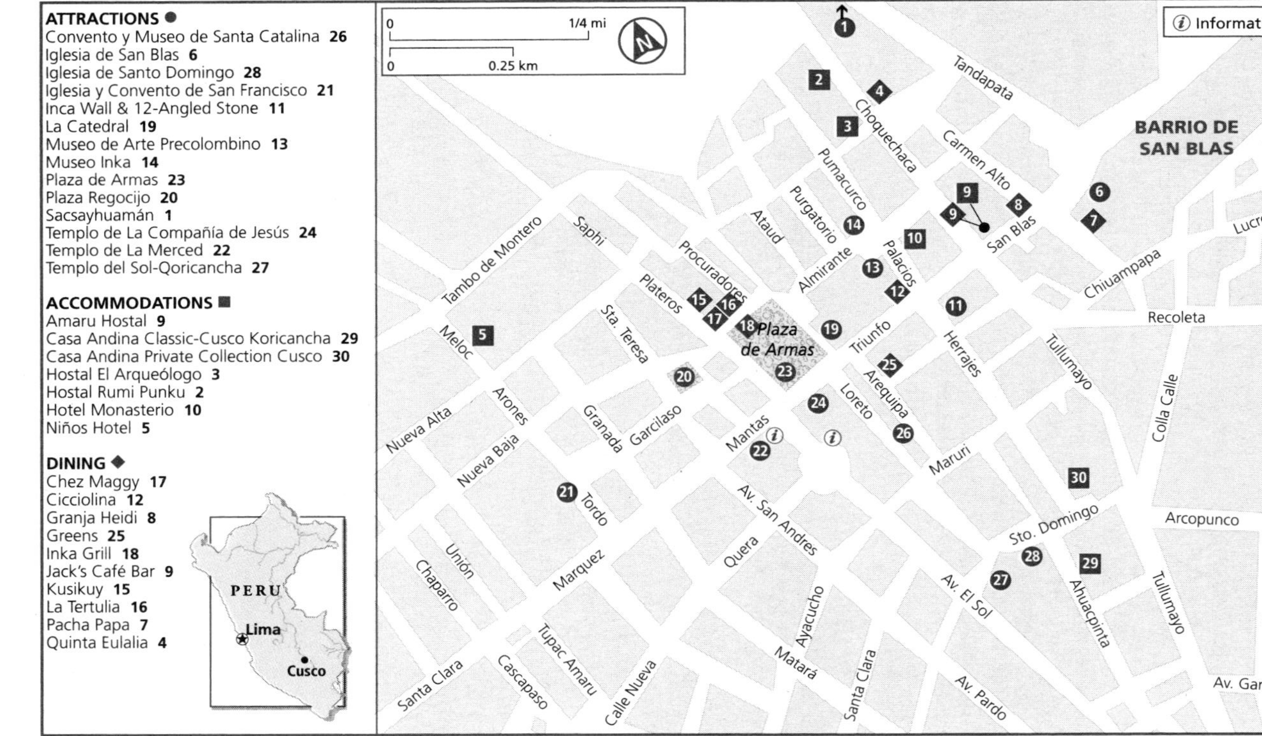
ATTRACTIONS ●
Convento y Museo de Santa Catalina 26
Iglesia de San Blas 6
Iglesia de Santo Domingo 28
Iglesia y Convento de San Francisco 21
Inca Wall & 12-Angled Stone 11
La Catedral 19
Museo de Arte Precolombino 13
Museo Inka 14
Plaza de Armas 23
Plaza Regocijo 20
Sacsayhuamán 1
Templo de La Compañía de Jesús 24
Templo de La Merced 22
Templo del Sol-Qoricancha 27
ACCOMMODATIONS ■
Amaru Hostal 9
Casa Andina Classic-Cusco Koricancha 29
Casa Andina Private Collection Cusco 30
Hostal El Arqueólogo 3
Hostal Rumi Punku 2
Hotel Monasterio 10
Niños Hotel 5
DINING ◆
Chez Maggy 17
Cicciolina 12
Granja Heidi 8
Greens 25
Inka Grill 18
Jack's Café Bar 9
Kusikuy 15
La Tertulia 16
Pacha Papa 7
Quinta Eulalia 4
PERU
Lima
Cusco
0
1/4 mi
0
0.25 km
Information
BARRIO DE SAN BLAS
Plaza de Armas
Tandapata
Choquechaca
Carmen Alto
San Blas
Lucrepata
Chiuampapa
Recoleta
Pumacurco
Purgatorio
Ataud
Almirante
Palacios
Procuradores
Plateros
Saphi
Tambo de Montero
Meloc
Sta. Teresa
Triunfo
Herrajes
Tullumayo
Colla Calle
Arequipa
Loreto
Mantas
Maruri
Garcilaso
Granada
Arones
Nueva Alta
Nueva Baja
Tordo
Av. San Andres
Quera
Sto. Domingo
Arcopunco
Ahuacpinta
Av. El Sol
Marquez
Unión
Chaparro
Ayacucho
Matará
Santa Clara
Tupac Amaru
Cascapaso
Calle Nueva
Av. Pardo
Huascar
Av. Garcilaso

Tips Altitude Acclimatization

You'll need to take it easy for the first few hours or even couple of days in Cusco—which sits at an altitude of just over 3,400m (11,150 ft.)—to adjust to the elevation. Pounding headaches and shortness of breath are the most common ailments, though some travelers are afflicted with nausea. Drink lots of water, avoid heavy meals, and do as the locals do: Drink *mate de coca,* or coca-leaf tea. (Don't worry, you won't get high or arrested, but you will adjust a little more smoothly to the thin air.) If that doesn't cure you, ask whether your hotel has an oxygen tank you can use for a few moments of assisted breathing. If you're really suffering, look for an over-the-counter medication in the pharmacy called "Sorojchi Pills." And if that doesn't do the trick, it may be time to seek medical assistance; see "Fast Facts," below. Those who think they may have an especially hard time with the altitude might consider staying the first couple of nights in the slightly lower Sacred Valley (near Urubamba, Yanahuara, or Ollantaytambo).

Visitor Information

As the top tourist destination in Peru, Cusco is well equipped with information outlets. A branch of the **Oficina de Información Turística** (✆ **084/237-364**) is at the Velasco Astete Airport in the arrivals terminal; it's open daily from 6:30am to 12:30pm. The principal **Oficina de Información Turística** is located on Mantas 117-A, a block from the Plaza de Armas (✆ **084/222-032**). It's open Monday through Saturday from 7am to 7pm and Sunday from 7am to noon. It's helpful and efficient, and it sells the essential *boleto turístico* (tourist ticket; see "Cusco's *Boleto Turístico*" below). However, the new **iperu office,** Av. El Sol 103, Of. 102 (✆ **084/252-974**), is better stocked with information and has been more helpful on recent visits; it's open daily from 8:30am to 7:30pm. Another information office is located in the **Terminal Terrestre de Huanchaq** train station, Av. Pachacútec s/n (✆ **084/238-722**); it's open Monday through Saturday from 8am to 6:30pm.

FAST FACTS Most Peruvian and international **banks** with money-exchange bureaus and ATMs are located along Avenida El Sol. A couple are also at entrances to stores and restaurants on the Plaza de Armas and at the Huanchaq train station. Money changers, usually wearing colored smocks, patrol the main streets off the Plaza de Armas.

In a **police emergency,** call ✆ **105.** The **National Tourist Police** are located at Saphy 510 (✆ 084/249-654). You can also try the **iperu/Tourist Protection Bureau,** Portal Carrizos 250, Plaza de Armas (✆ 084/252-974). If you have a medical emergency, contact **Tourist Medical Assistance** at Heladeros 157 (✆ 084/260-101). English-speaking medical personnel are available at the following hospitals and clinics: **Hospital Essalud,** Av. Anselmo Alvarez s/n (✆ 084/237-341); **Clínica Pardo,** Av. de la Cultura 710 (✆ 084/624-186); **Hospital Antonio Loren,** Plazoleta Belén 1358 (✆ 084/226-511); **Hospital Regional,** Av. de la Cultura s/n (✆ 084/223-691); and **Clínica Paredes,** Lechugal 405 (✆ 084/225-265).

Internet *cabinas* are everywhere in the old section of Cusco, and many permit cheap overseas Internet-based (Web2Phone) calls for as little as S/1 per minute. Rates are generally S/2 per hour. Most keep very late hours, opening at 9am and staying open until 11pm or midnight. Cusco's main **post office,** Av. El Sol 800 (✆ **084/224-212**), is open

Monday through Saturday from 7:30am to 7:30pm and Sunday from 7:30am to 2pm. A **DHL/Western Union** office is located at Av. El Sol 627-A (✆ **084/244-167**). The principal **Telefónica del Perú** office, for long-distance and international calls, is at Av. El Sol 382 (✆ **084/241-114**).

WHAT TO SEE & DO

The stately and lively **Plaza de Armas ★★**, lined by arcades and carved wooden balconies and framed by the Andes, is the focal point of Cusco. Next to Machu Picchu, it is one of the most familiar sights in Peru. You will cross it, relax on the benches in its center, and pass under the porticoes that line it with shops, restaurants, travel agencies, and bars innumerable times during your stay in Cusco. The plaza—which was twice its present size in Inca days—has two of Cusco's foremost churches and the remains of original Inca walls on the northwest side of the square, thought to be the foundation of the Inca Pachacutec's palace.

The Incas designed their capital in the shape of a puma, with the head at the north end, at Sacsayhuamán (even its zigzagged walls are said to have represented the animal's teeth). This is difficult to appreciate today; even though much of the original layout of the city remains, it has been engulfed by growth. Still, most of Cusco can be seen on foot, certainly the best way to appreciate this historic mountain town.

Many principal sights within the historic quarter of Cusco and beyond the city are included in the *boleto turístico* (see box, p. 658), but a few very worthwhile places of interest, including the Templo del Qoricancha (Temple of the Sun), are not.

Around the Plaza de Armas

Convento y Museo de Santa Catalina ★★ A small convent located a couple of blocks west of the Plaza de Armas, Santa Catalina was built between 1601 and 1610 on top of the Acllawasi, where the Inca king sequestered his chosen Virgins of the Sun. The convent contains a museum of colonial and religious art. The collection includes an excellent collection of Cusqueña School paintings, featuring some of the greatest works of Amerindian art—a combination of indigenous and typically Spanish styles—in Cusco. The interior of the monastery is quite beautiful, with painted arches and an interesting chapel with baroque frescoes of Inca vegetation. Other items of interest include very macabre statues of Jesus and an extraordinary trunk that, when opened, displays the life of Christ in 3-D figurines (it was employed by the Catholic Church's traveling salesmen, used to convert the natives in far-flung regions of Peru). The main altar of the convent church is tucked behind steel bars.

Santa Catalina Angosta s/n. ✆ **084/223-245.** Admission included in *boleto turístico.* Daily 8:30am–5:30pm.

Cusco = Cuzco = Q'osqo

Spanish and English spellings derived from the Quechua language are a little haphazard in Cusco, especially since there's been a linguistic movement to try to recuperate and value indigenous culture. For example, you may see *Inca* written *Inka; Cusco* written *Cuzco, Qosqo,* or *Q'osqo; Qoricancha* as *Coricancha* or *Koricancha; Wanchac* as *Huanchac* or *Huanchaq; Sacsayhuamán* as *Sacsaywaman;* and *Qenko* as *Kenko, Q'enko,* or *Qenqo.*

Cusco's Boleto Turístico

Cusco's municipal tourism office, at Calle Mantas 117-A, sells a tourist pass, or ***boleto turístico,*** that is virtually essential for visiting the city and surrounding areas. It is your admission to 16 of the most important places of interest in and around Cusco, including some of the major draws in the Sacred Valley. Though it has more than doubled in price in the last few years, the *boleto* is still a decent value, and you cannot get into a number of churches, museums, and ruins sites without it. The full ticket costs S/130 for adults and S/70 for students with ID and children; it's valid for 10 days and is available at the tourism office, open Monday through Friday from 8am to 6:30pm and Saturday from 8am to 2pm. The *boleto* allows admission to the following sights in Cusco: Convento y Museo de Santa Catalina, Museo Municipal de Arte Contemporáneo, Museo Histórico Regional, Museo de Sitio Qoricancha, Museo de Arte Popular, Centro Qosqo de Arte Nativo de Danzas Folklóricas, Monumento Pachacuteq, and Museo Palacio Municipal; as well as the Inca ruins just outside the city, Sacsayhuamán, Q'enko, Pukapukara, Tambomachay, Pikillacta, and Tipón; and the Valle Sagrado attractions of Pisac, Ollantaytambo, and Chinchero. La Catedral, the cathedral on the Plaza de Armas, formerly included in the *boleto,* now charges separate admission. Other principal attractions not covered by the *boleto* include the Templo Qoricancha, Museo Inca, and Iglesia de San Blas.

Not all of these attractions are indispensable, and you probably won't end up checking off absolutely everything on your color photo-coded *boleto,* but it remains the best admission ticket in Cusco. (You can also buy a partial ticket for S/70 that covers either attractions in the city, or ruins outside of Cusco.) Make sure you carry the ticket with you when you're planning to make visits (especially on day trips outside the city), as guards will demand to see it so that they can punch a hole alongside the corresponding picture. Students must also carry their International Student Identification Card (ISIC), as guards often demand to see that ID to prove that they didn't fraudulently obtain a student *boleto* and thus cheat the city out of 10 bucks.

In addition to the main Tourist Office, the *boleto* can be purchased at OFEC, Av. El Sol 103, Office 101 (Galerías Turísticas; ✆ **084/227-037;** Mon–Sat 8am–6pm); and Casa Garcilaso, at the corner of Garcilaso y Heladeros s/n (✆ **084/226-919**).

La Catedral ★★ Built on the site of the palace of the Inca Viracocha, Cusco's cathedral is a beautiful religious and artistic monument that dominates the Plaza de Armas. Completed in 1669 in the Renaissance style, the cathedral possesses some 400 canvases of the distinguished Cusqueña School, painted from the 16th to 18th centuries. There are also amazing woodcarvings, including the spectacular cedar choir stalls. The main altar—which weighs more than 400kg (882 lb.) and is fashioned from silver mined in Potosí, Bolivia—features the patron saints of Cusco. To the right of the altar is a particularly Peruvian painting of the Last Supper, with the apostles drinking *chicha* (fermented maize beer) and eating *cuy* (guinea pig). The **Capilla del Triunfo** (the first Christian church in Cusco) is next door, to the right of the main church. It holds a painting by Alonso Cortés de Monroy of the devastating earthquake of 1650 and an altar adorned by the locally famous "El Negrito" (El Señor de los Temblores, or Lord of the Earthquakes), a brown-skinned figure of Christ on the cross that was paraded around the city by frightened residents during the 1650 earthquake (which, miracle or not, ceased shortly thereafter).

The entrance to the cathedral and ticket office, where you can purchase the *boleto turístico,* is actually at the entrance to the **Capilla de la Sagrada Familia,** to the left of the main door and steps.

Plaza de Armas (north side). Admission not included in *boleto turístico;* S/25 adults, S/13 students and children. Mon–Sat 10am–6pm, Sun 2–6pm.

Museo Inka ★ Housed in the impressive Admirals Palace, this museum contains artifacts designed to trace Peruvian history from pre-Inca civilizations and Inca culture, including the impact of the conquest and colonial times on the culture. On view are ceramics, textiles, jewelry, mummies, architectural models, and an interesting collection (reputed to be the world's largest) of Inca drinking vessels *(qeros)* carved out of wood, many meticulously painted. The museum is a good introduction to Inca culture, and there are explanations in English. The palace itself is one of Cusco's finest colonial mansions, with a superbly ornate portal indicating the importance of its owner; the house was built on top of yet another Inca palace at the beginning of the 17th century. In the courtyard is a studio of women weaving traditional textiles.

Cuesta del Almirante 103 (corner of Ataúd and Tucumán). ✆ **084/237-380.** Admission not included in *boleto turístico;* S/10 adults, S/5 students. Mon–Sat 9am–5pm.

Templo de la Compañía de Jesús ★ Cater-cornered to the cathedral is this Jesuit church, which rivals the cathedral in grandeur and prominence on the square (an intentional move by the Jesuits, and one that had church diplomats running back and forth to the Vatican). Begun in the late 16th century, it was almost entirely demolished by the quake of 1650, rebuilt, and finally finished 18 years later. Like the cathedral, it was also built on the site of the Inca Huayna Capac (said to be the most beautiful of all the Inca rulers' palaces). Inside, it's rather gloomy, but the gilded altar is stunning, especially when illuminated. The church possesses several important works of art, including a picture of St. Ignatius de Loyola by the local painter Marcos Zapata, and the Cristo de Burgos crucifixion by the main altar. Also of note are the paintings to either side of the entrance, which depict the marriages of St. Ignatius's nephews; one is the very symbol of Peru's mestizo character, as the granddaughter of Manco Inca wed the man who captured the last Inca, Tupac Amaru, leader of an Indian uprising.

Plaza de Armas (southeast side). Admission not included in *boleto turístico;* S/10 adults, S/5 students. Mon–Sat 11am–noon and 3–4pm.

South & East of the Plaza de Armas

Barrio de San Blas ★★ Cusco's most atmospheric and picturesque neighborhood, San Blas, a short but increasingly steep walk from the Plaza de Armas, is lined with artists' studios and artisans' workshops, and stuffed with tourist haunts—many of the best bars and restaurants and a surfeit of hostels. It's a great area to wander around—many streets are pedestrian-only—though you should exercise caution with your belongings, especially at night. The neighborhood also affords some of the most spectacular panoramic vistas in the city. In the small plaza at the top and to the right of Cuesta San Blas is the

The Magic of Inca Stones: A Walking Tour ★★

The ancient streets of Cusco are lined by dramatic Inca walls, mammoth granite blocks so exquisitely carved that they fit together, without mortar, like jigsaw puzzle pieces. The Spaniards razed many Inca constructions but built others right on top of the original foundations. (Even hell-bent on destruction, they recognized the value of good engineering.) Colonial architecture has, in many cases, not stood up nearly as well as the Incas' bold structures, designed to withstand the immensity of seismic shifts common in this part of Peru.

Apart from the main attractions detailed in this section, a brief walking tour will take you past some of the finest Inca constructions that remain in the city. East of the Plaza de Armas, **Calle Loreto** is one of the best-known Inca thoroughfares. The massive wall on the left-hand side, composed of meticulously cut rectangular stones, was once part of the Acllahuasi, or the "House of the Chosen Maidens," the Incas' Virgins of the Sun. This is the oldest surviving Inca wall in Cusco, and one of the most distinguished. Northeast of the Plaza de Armas, off Calle Palacio, is **Hatunrumiyoc,** a cobbled street lined with impressive walls of polygonal stones. Past the Archbishop's Palace on the right side is the famed **12-angled stone** (now appropriated as the symbol of Cuzqueña beer and appearing on its labels), magnificently fitted into the wall. Originally, this wall belonged to the palace of the Inca Roca. Although this large stone is impressively cut, the Incas almost routinely fitted many-cornered stones (with as many as 32, as seen at Machu Picchu, or even 44 angles) into structures. From Hatunrumiyoc, make your first right down another pedestrian alleyway, Inca Roca; about halfway down on the right side is a series of stones said to form the shape of a **puma,** including head, large paws, and tail. It's not all that obvious, so if you see someone else studying the wall, ask him or her to point out the figure. Other streets with notable Inca foundations are Herrajes, Pasaje Arequipa, and Santa Catalina Angosta. Only a couple of genuine Inca **portals** remain; one is at Choquechaca 339 and another at Romeritos 402, near Qoricancha.

Not every impressive stone wall in Cusco is Inca in origin, however. Many are transitional period (postconquest) constructions, performed by local masons under the service of Spanish bosses. Peter Frost's *Exploring Cusco* (available in local bookstores, now in an updated edition) has a good explanation of what to look for in distinguishing an original from what amounts to a copy.

little white **Iglesia de San Blas** ★★, said to be the oldest parish church in Cusco (admission apart from *boleto turístico;* S/15 adults, S/7.50 students; Mon–Sat 2–5:30pm). Though a simple adobe structure, it contains a marvelously carved Churrigueresque cedar pulpit. It's carved from a single tree trunk; some have gone as far as proclaiming it the finest example of woodcarving in the world. The pulpit comes with an odd story, and it's difficult to determine whether it's fact or folklore: It is said that the carpenter who created it was rewarded by having his skull placed within his masterwork (at the top, beneath the feet of St. Paul) upon death. Also worth a look is the baroque gold-leaf main altar.

Museo de Arte Precolombino (MAP) ★★ A spectacular new addition to the Cusco cultural landscape is this archaeological museum run by and featuring part of the vast collection of pre-Columbian works, an outpost of the terrific Rafael Larco Herrera Museum in Lima. Housed in an erstwhile Inca ceremonial court and later mansion—now handsomely restored—of the Conquistador Alonso Díaz are 450 pieces (about 1% of the pieces in storage at the museum in Lima), dating from 1250 B.C. to A.D. 1532. Beautifully illuminated halls carefully exhibit gold and precious metal handicrafts, jewelry, and other artifacts depicting the rich traditions from the Nazca, Moche, Huari, Chimú, Chancay, and Inca cultures. The museum—which is open late and has one of the city's finest restaurants, in a contemporary glass box in the courtyard—is especially worthwhile for anyone unable to visit the major archaeological museums in Lima or any of the premier sites in northern Peru.

Plaza de las Nazarenas s/n, San Blas. ✆ **084/237-380.** Admission S/20 adults, S/10 students. Daily 9am–10pm.

Templo del Sol–Qoricancha (Temple of the Sun) & Iglesia de Santo Domingo ★★★ Qoricancha and Santo Domingo together form perhaps the most vivid illustration in Cusco of Andean culture's collision with western Europe. Like the Great Mosque in Córdoba, Spain—where Christians dared to build a massive church within the perfect Muslim shrine—the temple of one culture sits atop and encloses the other. The extraordinarily crafted Temple of the Sun was the most sumptuous temple in the Inca empire and the apogee of the Inca's naturalistic belief system. Some 4,000 of the highest-ranking priests and their attendants were housed here. Dedicated to worship of the sun, it was apparently a glittering palace straight out of El Dorado legend: Qoricancha means "golden courtyard" in Quechua, and in addition to hundreds of gold panels lining its walls, there were life-size gold figures, solid gold altars, and a huge golden sun disc. The sun disc reflected the sun and bathed the temple in light. During the summer solstice, the sun still shines directly into a niche where only the Inca chieftain was permitted to sit. Other temples and shrines existed for the worship of lesser natural gods: the Moon, Venus, Thunder, Lightning, and the Rainbow. Qoricancha was the main astronomical observatory for the Incas.

After the Spaniards ransacked the temple and emptied it of gold, the exquisite polished stone walls were employed as the foundations of the Convent of Santo Domingo, constructed in the 17th century. The baroque church pales next to the fine masonry of the Incas—and that's to say nothing about the original glory of the Sun Temple. Today all that remains is Inca stonework. Thankfully, a large section of the cloister has been removed, revealing four original chambers of the temple, all smoothly tapered examples of Inca trapezoidal architecture. Stand on the small platform in the first chamber and see the perfect symmetry of openings in the stone chambers. A series of Inca stones displayed reveals the fascinating concept of male and female blocks and how they fit together. The 6m (20-ft.) curved wall beneath the west end of the church, visible from the street, remains undamaged by repeated earthquakes and is perhaps the greatest example of Inca stonework. The curvature and fit of the massive stones is astounding.

After the Spaniards had taken Cusco, Juan Pizarro was given the eviscerated Temple of the Sun. He died soon after, though, at the battle at Sacsayhuamán, and he left the temple to the Dominicans, in whose hands it remains.

Plazoleta Santo Domingo. ✆ **084/222-071.** Admission not included in *boleto turístico;* S/10 adults, S/5 students. Mon–Sat 8:30am–6:30pm; Sun 2–5pm.

Southwest of the Plaza de Armas

Iglesia y Convento de San Francisco This large and austere 17th-century convent church extends the length of the plaza of the same name. It is best known for its collection of colonial artwork, including paintings by Marcos Zapata and Diego Quispe Tito, both of considerable local renown. A monumental canvas (12×9m/39×30 ft.) that details the genealogy of the Franciscan family (almost 700 individuals) is by Juan Espinoza de los Monteros. The Franciscans also decorated the convent with ceiling frescos and a number of displays of skulls and bones.

Plaza de San Francisco s/n. ✆ **084/221-361.** Admission S/5 adults, S/3 students. Mon–Sat 9am–4pm.

Templo de La Merced ★ Erected in 1536 and rebuilt after the great earthquake in the 17th century, La Merced ranks just below the cathedral and La Compañía in importance. It has a beautiful facade and lovely cloisters with a mural depicting the life of the Merced Order's founder. The sacristy contains a small museum of religious art, including a fantastic solid gold monstrance swathed in precious stones. In the vaults of the church are the remains of two famous conquistadors, Diego de Almagro and Gonzalo Pizarro.

Calle Mantas s/n. ✆ **084/231-821.** Admission S/5 adults. Mon–Sat 8:30am–noon and 2–5pm.

Inca Ruins Near Cusco

The best way to see the following set of Inca ruins just outside of Cusco is on a half-day tour. The hardy may want to approach it as an athletic archaeological expedition: If you've got 15km (9 miles) of walking and climbing at high altitude in you, it's a beautiful trek. Otherwise, you can walk to Sacsayhuamán and nearby Q'enko (the climb from the Plaza de Armas is strenuous and takes 30–45 min.) and take a *colectivo* or taxi to the other sites. Alternatively, you can take a Pisac/Urubamba minibus (leaving from the bus station at Calle Intiqhawarina, off Av. Tullumayo, or at Huáscar 128) and tell the driver you want to get off at the ruins farthest from Cusco, Tambomachay, and work your way back on foot. Some even make the rounds by horseback. (You can easily and cheaply contract a horse at Sacsayhuamán, but know that you'll walk to all the sites alongside a guide.) Visitors with less time in Cusco or interest in taxing themselves may wish to join a guided tour, probably the most popular and the easiest way of seeing the ruins. Virtually any of the scads of travel agencies and tour operators in the old center of Cusco offer them. Well-rated traditional agencies with a variety of city programs include **Milla Turismo,** Av. Pardo 689 (✆ **084/231-710;** www.millaturismo.com), and **SAS Travel,** Garcilaso 270, Plaza San Francisco (✆ **084/ 249-194;** www.sastravelperu.com).

Admission to the following sites is by *boleto turístico,* and they are all open daily from 7am to 6pm. Official and unofficial guides hover around the ruins; negotiate a price or decide on a proper tip. Even more Inca ruins are on the outskirts of Cusco, a couple of which even appear on the *boleto,* but the ones discussed below are the most interesting.

These sites are generally safe, but at certain times of day—usually dawn and dusk before and after tour groups' visits—several ruins are said to be favored by thieves. It's best to be alert and, if possible, go accompanied.

SACSAYHUAMAN ★★★ The greatest and nearest to Cusco of the ruins, Sacsayhuamán reveals some of the Incas' most extraordinary architecture and monumental stonework. Usually referred to as a garrison or fortress—it was constructed with forbidding, castlelike walls—it was probably a religious temple (though most experts also believe it had military significance). The festival Inti Raymi (June 24) is celebrated here annually, and it's a great spectacle.

The ruins cover a huge area, but they constitute perhaps one-quarter of the original complex. Surviving today are the astounding outer walls, constructed in a zigzag formation of three tiers. Many of the base stones employed are almost unimaginably massive; some are twice as tall as a 1.8m (6-ft.) man, and one is said to weigh 300 tons. Like all Inca constructions, the stones fit together perfectly without the aid of mortar. After victory here, the Spaniards made off with the more manageable blocks to build houses and other structures in Cusco. It's easy to see how hard it would have been to attack these ramparts; with 22 distinct zigzags, the design would automatically expose the flanks of an opponent.

Above the walls are the circular foundations of three towers—used for storage of provisions and water—that once stood here. The complex suffered such extensive destruction that little is known about the actual purpose Sacsayhuamán served. What is known is that it was the site of one of the bloodiest battles between the Spaniards and native Cusqueños. More than 2 years after the Spaniards initially marched on Cusco and installed a puppet government, the anointed Inca (Manco Inca) led a seditious campaign that took back Sacsayhuamán and nearly defeated the Spanish in a siege of the Inca capital. Juan Pizarro and his vastly outnumbered but superior armed forces stormed Sacsayhuamán in a horrific battle in 1536 that left thousands dead. Legend speaks of their remains as carrion for giant condors in the open fields here.

A flat, grassy esplanade separates the defense walls from a small hill where you'll find the Inca's Throne and large rocks with well-worn grooves, used by children (and, almost as frequently, adults) as slides. Nearby is a series of claustrophobia-inducing tunnels (pass through them if you dare).

Night visits to the ruins are now permitted from 8 to 10pm. Under a full moon in the huge star-lit Andean sky, Sacsayhuamán is so breathtaking that you'll instantly grasp the Incas' worship of the natural world, in which both the sun and moon were considered deities. If you go at night, take a flashlight and a few friends; security is a little lax, and assaults on foreigners have occurred.

If you're walking, it's a steep 2km (1¼-mile) walk from the center of Cusco. There are a couple of paths. Head northwest from the Plaza de Armas. You can take Palacio (behind the cathedral) until you reach stairs and signs to the ruins, or at the end of Suecia, climb either Huaynapata or Resbalosa (the name means "slippery") until you come to a curve and the old Inca road. Past the San Cristóbal church at the top, beyond a plaza with fruit-juice stands, are the ruins.

Q'ENKO ★ The road from Sacsayhuamán leads past fields—where Cusqueños play soccer and have cookouts on weekends—to the temple and amphitheater of Q'enko (*Ken*-koh); it's a distance of about 1km (a half mile). A large limestone outcrop was hollowed out by the Incas, and in the void they constructed a cavelike altar. (Some have claimed the smooth stone table inside was used for animal sacrifices.) You can also climb on the rock and see the many channels cut into the rock, where it is thought that either *chicha* or, more salaciously, sacrificial blood coursed during ceremonies.

PUCA PUCARA A small fortress (the name means "red fort") just off the main Cusco-Pisac road, this may have been some sort of storage facility or lodging. It is probably the least impressive of the sites, but it has nice views of the surrounding countryside.

TAMBOMACHAY ★ About 8km (5 miles) from Cusco on the way to Pisac (and a short, signposted walk off the main road) is this site, known as Los Baños del Inca (Inca Baths). Water still flows across a system of aqueducts and canals in the small complex of terraces and a pool, but these were not baths as we know them—they were most likely a place of water ceremonies and worship.

Can't Leave Well Enough Alone

The Peruvian authorities are notorious for messing with ruins, trying to rebuild them rather than letting them be what they are: ruins. You'll notice at Sacsayhuamán and other Inca sites that unnecessary and misleading restoration has been undertaken. The grotesque result is that small gaps where original stones are missing have been filled in with obviously new and misplaced garden rocks—a disgrace to the perfection pursued and achieved by Inca masons.

Shopping

Cusco is Peru's acknowledged center of handicraft production, especially of hand-woven textiles, and its premier shopping destination. Many Cusqueño artisans still employ ancient weaving techniques, and they produce some of the finest textiles in South America. From tiny one-person shops to large markets with dozens of stalls, there are few better places to shop than Cusco for excellent-value Andean handicrafts. Items to look for include alpaca wool sweaters, shawls, gloves, hats, scarves, blankets, and ponchos; antique blankets and textiles, beautiful but pricey; woodcarvings, especially nicely carved picture frames; fine ceramics and jewelry; and Cusqueña School reproduction paintings.

The barrio of **San Blas,** the streets right around the **Plaza de Armas** (particularly calles Plateros and Triunfo), and **Plaza Regocijo** are the best and most convenient haunts for shopping outings. You won't have to look hard for whatever it is that interests you, but a bit of price comparison is always helpful. If merchants think you've just arrived in Peru and don't know the real value of items, your price is guaranteed to be higher. Although bargaining is acceptable and almost expected, merchants in the center of Cusco are confident of a steady stream of buyers, and as a consequence are often less willing to negotiate than their counterparts in markets and more remote places in Peru. Most visitors will find prices delightfully affordable, though, and haggling beyond what you know is a fair price when the disparity of wealth is so great is generally viewed as bad form.

For a general selection of *artesanía,* **Galería Latina,** Calle San Agustín 427 (✆ **084/246-588**), has a wide range of top-end antique blankets, rugs, alpaca wool clothing, ceramics, jewelry, and handicrafts from the Amazon jungle in a large shop near the Hotel Libertador. About a block away from the Plaza de Armas on Plateros and also at Triunfo 393, you'll find good-size markets of crafts stalls. **Centro Artesanal Cusco,** at the end of Avenida El Sol, across from the large painted waterfall fountain and Hotel Savoy, is the largest indoor market of handicrafts stalls in Cusco, and many goods are slightly cheaper here than they are closer to the plaza. Especially noteworthy is the **Centro de Textiles Tradicionales del Cusco ★★**, Av. El Sol 603 (✆ **084/228-117;** www.textilescusco.org), an organization dedicated to fair-trade practices. It ensures that 70% of the sale price of the very fine textiles on display goes directly to the six communities and individual artisans it works with. On-site is an ongoing demonstration of weaving and a very good, informative textiles museum. Prices are a bit higher than what you may find in generic shops around town, though the textiles are also higher quality, and much more of your money will go to the women who work for days on individual pieces.

San Blas is swimming with art galleries, artisan workshops, and ceramics shops. You'll stumble upon many small shops dealing in reproduction Cusqueña School religious paintings and many workshops where you can watch artisans in action. Several of the best ceramics outlets are also here. Check out **Artesanías Mendivil,** Plazoleta San Blas 619 (✆ **084/233-247**), known for saint figures with elongated necks; the **Juan Garboza taller** (studio), Tandapata 676/Plazoleta San Blas (✆ **084/248-039**), which specializes in pre-Inca style ceramics; and **Artesanías Olave,** Triunfo 342 (✆ **084/252-935**), a high-quality crafts shop.

Several shops feature wool or alpaca *chompas,* or jackets, with Andean designs (often lifted directly from old blankets and weavings). For other upscale alpaca fashions—mostly sweaters and shawls—try **Alpaca 3,** Calle Ruinas 472 (✆ **084/226-101**); **Alpaca 111,** Herladeros 202 (✆ **084/243-233**); or **Royal Alpaca,** Santa Teresa 387 (✆ **084/252-346**). **Werner & Ana,** a Dutch-Peruvian design couple, sell stylish clothing in fine natural fabrics such as alpaca. They have a shop on Plaza San Francisco 295-A, at Calle Garcilaso (✆ **084/231-076**).

For jewelry, **Ilaria** deals in fine silver and unique Andean-style pieces and has two branches in Cusco: one at Hotel Monasterio, Calle Palacios 136 (✆ **084/221-192**), and another at Portal Carrizos 258, Plaza de Armas (✆ **084/246-253**). The contemporary jewelry designer **Carlos Chaquiras,** Triunfo 375 (✆ **084/227-470**), is an excellent craftsman; many of his pieces feature pre-Columbian designs. Lots of shops have hand-carved woodwork and frames, but the best spot for handmade baroque frames (perfect for your Cusqueña School reproduction or religious shrine) is **La Casa del Altar,** Mesa Redonda Lote A (✆ **084/244-712**), not far from the Plaza de Armas. In addition to frames, they make *retablos* and altars.

Cusco's famous, frenzied **Mercado Central** (near the San Pedro rail station) is shopping of a much different kind—almost more a top visitor's attraction than a shopping destination. Its array of products for sale—mostly produce, food, and household items—is dazzling, and even if you don't come to shop, this rich tapestry of modern and yet highly traditional Cusco still shouldn't be missed. Don't take valuables (or even your camera), though, and be on guard, as it is frequented by pickpockets on the lookout for tourists.

WHERE TO STAY

In recent years, the number of lodgings has skyrocketed in Cusco, now numbering in the hundreds (and the number of hotels continues to rise). Still, advance reservations in high season (June–Sept) in Cusco are essential, especially around the Inti Raymi and Fiestas Patrias festivals at the ends of June and July, respectively. Outside of high season, look for bargains, as hotel rates come down considerably. Most of the city's most desirable accommodations are very central, within walking distance of the Plaza de Armas. The San Blas neighborhood is also within walking distance, though many hotels and hostels in that district involve very steep climbs up the hillside. (The upside is that guests are rewarded with some of the finest views in the city.) Many hotels and inns will arrange free airport transfers if you communicate your arrival information to them in advance. Hot water is an issue at many hotels, even those that swear they offer 24-hour hot showers.

Several of the hostels below are cozy, family-run places, but travelers looking for even greater contact with a Peruvian family might want to check out the very inexpensive inns belonging to the **Asociación de Casas Familiares (Family Home Association),** which operates a website (www.cusco.net/familyhouse) with listings of guesthouses with one or more rooms available for short- or long-term stays.

Tips No Sleeping In

Most Cusco hotels have annoyingly early checkout times—often 9 or 9:30am—due to the deluge of early morning flight arrivals to the city. At least in high season, hotels are very serious about your need to rise and shine, but you can always store your bags until later.

Near the Plaza de Armas

Very Expensive

Hotel Monasterio ★★★ Peru's most extraordinary place to stay, this beautiful hotel occupies the San Antonio Abad monastery, constructed in 1592 on the foundations of an Inca palace. The Monasterio—converted into a hotel in 1995—exudes grace and luxury. While checking in, you relax in a lovely hall while sipping coca tea. As much a museum as a hotel, it has its own opulent, gilded chapel and 18th-century Cusqueña School art collection. The hotel makes fine use of two courtyards with stone arches; one is set up for lunch. Rooms are impeccably decorated in both colonial and modern styles; the accommodations off the first courtyard are more traditionally designed and authentic-feeling. The Tupay Restaurant is housed in the original vaulted refectory of the monastery; early risers enjoy a terrific buffet breakfast while being serenaded by Gregorian chants. If you're suffering from altitude sickness, the Monasterio is the only hotel in the world that can pipe oxygen into your room (for an additional $30 per day).

Calle Palacios 136 (Plazoleta Nazarenas), Cusco. ✆ **084/241-777.** Fax 084/246-983. http://monasterio.orient-express.com. 122 units. $399–$499 deluxe double; $580–$1,089 suite. Rates include buffet breakfast. AE, DC, MC, V. **Amenities:** 2 restaurants; cafe; bar; concierge; room service. *In room:* A/C, TV/VCR, fridge, hair dryer.

Expensive

Casa Andina Private Collection ★★ Value One of the newest upmarket hotels in Cusco inhabits one of the city's loveliest colonial structures, an 18th-century mansion on a small square in the heart of the old city. The hotel is like a budget version of the very elegant, and very expensive, Hotel Monasterio. For travelers looking for a bit of that hotel's ambience but not its elevated price tag, Casa Andina is among the best-value luxury options in town. Rooms are spacious and cleanly outfitted, with a minimalist take on Andean decor. While my favorites are the suites in the old section of the hotel, the newer rooms thankfully are not distractingly modern, and, tucked away as they are from the street, they're nice and quiet. The gorgeous, deep-red sitting room, with its massive, roaring fireplace, is the perfect place to sip a pisco sour or coca tea. And the gourmet restaurant features stone arches, strong colors, and Cusco-school paintings, as well as a very fine haute Andean menu, making it one of those all-too-rare hotel restaurants that merits staying in for the night.

Plazoleta de Limacpampa Chico 473, Cusco. ✆ **084/232-610;** reservations in the U.S. and Canada 866/447-3270, in Lima 01/446-8848 or 01/213-9739. Fax 084/232-629. www.casa-andina.com. 100 units. $124–$207 double; $279 suite. Rates include taxes and breakfast buffet. AE, DC, MC, V. **Amenities:** Restaurant; bar; babysitting; concierge. *In room:* TV, fridge, hair dryer, Wi-Fi.

Moderate

Casa Andina Classic-Cusco Koricancha ★ Value Similar in concept to the Sonesta Posadas del Inca, this very professionally run, midprice hotel belongs to the Peruvian

Casa Andina hotel chain. Visitors to Casa Andina know what to expect: excellent service and clean, ample rooms that are colorfully decorated. The hotel on San Agustín, 3 blocks from the main square, is built around a restful colonial courtyard and is in a somewhat quieter neighborhood, while two other, smaller chain locations are virtually on top of the Plaza de Armas. All have the same prices and same features (though the Cusco Catedral hotel has an Inca wall within the hotel).

San Agustín 371, Cusco. ✆ **084/252-633,** or 01/446-8848 or 01/213-9739 for reservations in Lima. Fax 084/222-908. www.casa-andina.com. 57 units. $99–$130 double. Rates include taxes and breakfast buffet. AE, DC, MC, V. **Amenities:** Babysitting; concierge. *In room:* TV, fridge, hair dryer on request.

Hostal El Arqueólogo (Kids) It takes a little bit of effort to uncover this hostel, named for the profession responsible for discovering so much of Peru's pre-Columbian past and owned by a Frenchman who's a longtime Cusco resident. Down a stone alleyway and tucked behind the unprepossessing facade of a late-19th-century house, it certainly doesn't jump out at you, but once inside, you'll find a lovely, sunny garden—with ample space for kids to play—and rooms that run along a corridor overlooking the patio. Rooms are simply furnished but comfortable and cozy. That said, prices have risen steadily, and the hostel is now overpriced, but promotional deals may be available online.

Pumacurco 408, Cusco. ✆ **084/232-569.** Fax 084/235-126. www.hotelarqueologo.com. 20 units. $99–$120 double; $120 suite. Rates include taxes and breakfast buffet. MC, V. **Amenities:** Restaurant; Internet access; room service. *In room:* TV, hair dryer, no phone.

Inexpensive

Hostal Rumi Punku ★ (Finds) A glance at the name or address of this idiosyncratic family-owned hostel will give you an indication of its strong connection to Cusco's Inca roots. The massive portal to the street is a fascinating original Inca construction of perfectly cut stones, once part of a sacred Inca temple. (The door is one of only three belonging to private houses in Cusco, and elderly residents of the city used to do the sign of the cross upon passing it.) Inside is a charming, flower-filled colonial courtyard with a cute little chapel and gardens along a large Inca wall. The clean bedrooms are ample, with hardwood floors and Norwegian thermal blankets. The top-floor dining room, where breakfast is served, has excellent panoramic views of Cusco's rooftops. The hostel is on the way up to Sacsayhuamán, but only a short walk from the Plaza de Armas. Rumi Punku, by the way, means "door of stone" in Quechua.

Choquechaca 339, Cusco. ✆ **084/221-102.** Fax 084/242-741. www.rumipunku.com. 30 units. $90 double. Rates include taxes and continental breakfast. AE, DC, MC, V. **Amenities:** Restaurant; Jacuzzi; sauna. *In room:* No phone.

Niños Hotel ★★★ (Kids) (Value) Jolanda van den Berg, in just 7 years in Peru, has mounted a small empire of goodwill through the Foundation Niños Unidos Peruanos: She adopted 12 Peruvian street children; constructed an extremely warm and inviting (not to mention great-value) hotel in the old section of Cusco that puts all its profits toward care for needy children; constructed a learning center and restaurant for 125 such kids; and created a second center with athletic facilities and additional medical attention for another 125 disadvantaged youth of Cusco.

The good news for travelers is that, should they be lucky enough to get a room here (reserve about 6 months in advance for high season), they won't have to suffer for their financial contribution to such an important cause. The main hotel, in a restored colonial house just 10 minutes from the Plaza de Armas, is one of the finest, cleanest, and most comfortable small inns in Peru. The large rooms—named for the couple's adopted children—are very nearly minimalist chic, with hardwood floors and quality beds, and they ring a lovely sunny courtyard, where breakfast is served. The ambitious Niños project has now added a second hotel, also of the same character in a historic building, and, incredibly, two more families (totaling 15 girls and another 2 boys). On the same street as the second hotel are four terrific apartments for longer stays, ideal for small families, in the first of the children's learning and day-care facilities.

Meloq 442, Cusco. ✆ **084/231-424.** www.ninoshotel.com. 20 units. $44 double with private bathroom; $40 double with shared bathroom. Apts $32 per person per day or $350 per month (2nd person an additional $130 per month). Rates include taxes. No credit cards. **Amenities:** Restaurant/cafe. *In room:* No phone.

San Blas & Beyond

Inexpensive

Amaru Hostal ★ Value Popular with legions of backpackers, this hostel, in a pretty colonial-republican house in the midst of the San Blas artist studios and shops, has a lovely balconied patio, with a very nice garden area (which tends to attract sunbathers) and good views of Cusco. Rooms are very comfortable, attractively decorated, and a good value. Several have colonial-style furnishings and lots of natural light. (Ask to see several rooms if you can.) This is a very friendly and relaxed place.

Cuesta San Blas 541, San Blas, Cusco. ✆/fax **084/225-933.** www.cusco.net/amaru. 16 units. $40–$48 double with bathroom; $23 double with shared bathroom. Rates include taxes, continental breakfast, and airport pickup. No credit cards. **Amenities:** Coffee shop. *In room:* No phone.

WHERE TO DINE

Visitors to Cusco have a huge array of restaurants and cafes at their disposal; eateries have sprouted up even faster than hostels and bars, and most are clustered around the main drags leading from Plaza de Armas. The large majority of them are economical, informal places favored by backpackers and adventure travelers—some offer midday three-course menus for as little as S/9—though there are now a greater number of upscale dining options than ever before, which for many travelers tend to be excellent values. Calle Procuradores, which leads off the Plaza de Armas across from the Compañía de Jesús church, is sometimes referred to as "Gringo Alley," but it could just as easily be called "Restaurant Row" for the cheap eateries that line both sides of the narrow passageway. Many are pizzerias, and Cusco has become known for its wood-fired, crispy-crusted pizzas.

Few restaurants in Cusco accept credit cards; many of those that do, especially the cheaper places, will charge a 10% surcharge to use plastic, so you're better off carrying cash (either soles or dollars). Top-flight restaurants often charge both a 10% service charge and 18% sales tax.

Expensive

Cicciolina ★★★ Finds MEDITERRANEAN/*NOVO ANDINO* This delightfully chic restaurant is probably the hottest and most stylish in Cusco. The restaurant looks ripped from the Tuscan countryside. The long and often boisterous country-elegant bar is decorated with bunches of garlic, peppers, and fresh-cut flowers and is a great spot for one of the excellent cocktails (such as a *maracuyá* sour), or dinner itself, especially if you're in the mood for creative tapas (which are served only in the bar). The menu focuses on unusual spices and accents, with a number of adventurous dishes. You might start with porcini mushroom soup (topped with a pisco froth) or spicy barbecued calamari, prawns, and scallops, which is served with a minty rice noodle salad. Main courses

Cusco's Quintas

When the day warms up under a huge blue sky in Cusco, you'll want to be outside. Cusco doesn't have many sidewalk cafes, but it does have *quintas,* traditional open-air restaurants that are most popular with locals on weekends. These are places to get large portions of good-quality Peruvian cooking at pretty reasonable prices. Among the dishes they all offer are tamales, *cuy chactado* (fried guinea pig) with potatoes, *chicharrón* (deep-fried pork, usually served with mint, onions, and corn), alpaca steak, *lechón* (suckling pig), and *costillas* (ribs). You can also get classics such as *rocoto relleno* (stuffed hot peppers) and *papa rellena* (potatoes stuffed with meat or vegetables). Vegetarian options include *sopa de quinoa* (grain soup), fried yuca, and *torta de papa* (potato omelet). *Quintas* are open only for lunch (noon–5 or 6pm), and most people make a visit their main meal of the day. Main courses cost between S/15 and S/45.

Quinta Eulalia ★, Choquechaca 384 (✆ **084/224-951**), is Cusco's oldest *quinta* (open since 1941). From a lovely colonial courtyard, there are views of the San Cristóbal district to the surrounding hills from the upper eating area. It's a great place on a sunny day, and the Andean specialties are reasonably priced. **Pacha Papa** ★, Plazoleta San Blas 120 (✆ **084/241-318**), is in a beautiful courtyard across from the small church in San Blas. In addition to Andean dishes, you'll find sandwiches. The house specialty, *cuy* (guinea pig), must be ordered 1 day in advance. Alpaca steak is served in several varieties, including alpaca goulash and alpaca kabob.

include large, superb salads (including a yummy mix of rare roast beef and vegetables), excellent homemade pastas, and alpaca filet.

Triunfo 393, 2nd Floor. ✆ **084/239-510.** Reservations recommended. Main courses S/28–S/48. AE, DC, MC, V. Daily 11am–midnight.

Greens ★★ (Value) INTERNATIONAL/NOVO ANDINO Having moved from its home in the bohemian heart of San Blas, Greens has gone upscale, on the second floor in an old building just off the Plaza de Armas. It remains one of Cusco's most stylish and intimate restaurants, though it is more sedate and less funky than its previous incarnation. The romantic space has just a handful of tables with candlelight and a soundtrack of laid-back dance beats. The creative organic and vegetarian menu features delicious salads, steaks, homemade pastas, and curries.

Santa Catalina Angosta 135. ✆ **084/243-579.** Reservations recommended. Main courses S/28–S/45. No credit cards. Daily 11am–11pm.

Inka Grill ★★ PERUVIAN/NOVO ANDINO A large and attractive modern two-level place right on the Plaza de Armas, the distinguished Inka Grill serves *novo andino* fare and is one of Cusco's best dining experiences. Start with a bowl of yummy *camote* (sweet potato) chips and green salsa. The best dishes are Peruvian standards such as sautéed alpaca tenderloin served over quinoa (a grain) and *ají de gallina* (shredded chicken with nuts, cheese, and chili peppers), and desserts such as coca-leaf crème brûlée. The extensive menu also features a wide range of international dishes, including pizza, pasta, and risotto.

Portal de Panes 115. ✆ **084/262-992.** Reservations recommended. Main courses S/24–S/55. AE, DC, MC, V. Mon–Sat 8am–midnight.

Moderate

Kusikuy *Finds* ANDEAN/INTERNATIONAL If you've resisted trying the Andean specialty that makes most foreigners recoil or at least raise an eyebrow, this could be the place to get adventurous. The restaurant's name in Quechua means "happy little guinea pig," so *cuy al horno* is, of course, the house dish. The rest of the menu focuses on other typical Peruvian dishes and adds stuff for gringos, such as pasta and basic chicken and meat dishes. It also serves a good-value lunch menu. The cozy and good-looking loftlike space, in a new location on a hilly street above the Plaza de Armas, is warmly decorated with hardwood tables, and a mix of antiques and musical instruments from the Amazon. With pillows and couches, it is also a cool, relaxed spot for a drink.

Suecia 339. ✆ **084/262-870.** Reservations not accepted. Main courses S/15–S/39. MC, V. Mon–Sat 8am–midnight.

Inexpensive

Chez Maggy ITALIAN/PERUVIAN This bustling little joint, which has been around for over 25 years and spawned a couple of branches in other parts of Peru, has a bit of everything, from trout and alpaca to homemade pasta to Mexican food, but most people jam their way in for the freshly baked pizza. Made in a traditional wood-burning brick oven, it's some of the best in Cusco. Chez Maggy is usually packed in the evenings, and there's often live *andina* music when roaming street musicians pop in to entertain diners. The restaurant is a long corridor with shared bench tables full of gringos—a good way to meet other travelers, since you'll be jockeying for elbow space with them. A second location is on Procuradores, better known as Gringo Alley. If you want a pizza on the terrace of your hostel, Chez Maggy will deliver for free.

Plateros 339. ✆ **084/234-861.** Reservations not accepted. Main courses S/12–S/32. MC, V. Daily 6–11pm.

Granja Heidi ★ *Finds* HEALTH FOOD/VEGETARIAN A healthy new addition to the Cusco dining scene is this cute upstairs place in San Blas serving great breakfasts and very good-value fixed-price menu meals. With a high ceiling and the airy, sun-filled look of an art studio, it's perfect for the neighborhood. Run by a German woman who also has a farm of the same name outside of Cusco, the restaurant features fresh ingredients and products, such as yogurt, cheese, and quiches, that taste like they came straight from the farm. The daily menu offers vegetarian and nonvegetarian choices, and might start with pumpkin soup, followed by lamb or a veggie stir-fry, fruit salad, and tea. Don't pass on dessert or you'll miss excellent home-baked cakes, such as the cheesecake or the irresistible Nelson Mandela chocolate cake.

Cuesta San Blas 525. ✆ **084/233-759.** Reservations not accepted. Main courses S/9–S/24; daily menu S/15. No credit cards. Daily 8am–9:30pm.

Jack's Café Bar ★★ CAFE/INTERNATIONAL One of the most popular gringo hangouts in Cusco, owned by the guy who runs a thriving Irish pub in town, this isn't just a spot to have a drink and check out some American and British magazines. It serves very fresh, very good meals throughout the day, and features enough variety that you wouldn't be the first to eat here several times during your stay. For breakfast, try scrumptious fluffy pancakes; at lunch, sample towering salads or creative gourmet sandwiches.

Finish with a dinner of "really hot" green chicken curry or a red wine, beef, and mushroom casserole. There are plenty of items for vegetarians, smoothies, wine, and beer, as well as great coffee drinks and hot chocolate (for those cool Andean nights). And it's a friendly place to linger and meet folks, to boot.

Choquechaca 509 (corner of Cuesta San Blas). ✆ **084/806-960.** Reservations not accepted. Main courses S/9–S/24. No credit cards. Daily 7am–10pm.

La Tertulia (Value) BREAKFAST/CAFE This little restaurant is a gringo hangout par excellence. The name means "discussion," which is fitting because people gather here to read newspapers and foreign magazines, and to exchange books and advice on hiking the Inca Trail and other far-flung adventures across South America. Many come to fuel up as early as 6:30am before setting out on one of those trips, and the superb breakfast buffet does the trick. It's all-you-can-eat eggs, fruit salads, granola, amazing homemade wholemeal bread, French toast, tamales, fresh juices, and coffee—truly the breakfast of champions and an excellent value. The breakfast menu also features 16 types of crepes. There is a fixed-price lunch deal and a nice salad bar, as well as pizza, sandwiches, and fondue. If you feel bad about stuffing yourself at breakfast, you can feel good about the fact that La Tertulia donates S/1 of each buffet to a Peruvian orphanage.

Procuradores 44, 2nd Floor. ✆ **084/241-422.** Reservations not accepted. Main courses S/9–S/20; buffet breakfast S/12. MC, V. Daily 6:30am–3pm and 5–11pm.

CUSCO AFTER DARK

Most first-time visitors to Cusco, discovering an Andean city with such a gentle, pervasive Amerindian influence and colonial feel, are surprised to find that it has such a rollicking nightlife. It's not as diverse as Lima's, true, but if you like your nights full of predominantly young and rowdy patrons in the latest trekking gear, Cusco's your kind of place. I have heard countless young backpackers from countries across the world exclaim, in universal MTV lingo and with pisco sour in hand, "Cusco rocks!" Perhaps the best part is that, even though the city is inundated with foreigners many months of the year, it isn't just gringoland in the bars. Locals (and Peruvians from other cities, principally Lima, and other South Americans) tend to make up a pretty healthy percentage of the clientele. Clubs are in close range of each other—in the streets just off the Plaza de Armas and to a lesser extent in San Blas—and virtually everyone seems to adopt a pub-crawl attitude, bopping from one bar or dance club to the next, often reconvening with friends in the plaza before picking up a "free drink ticket" and free admission card from any of the many girls on the square handing them out and moving on to the next club. It's rare that you'll have to pay a cover charge in Cusco.

For those who are saving their energy, there are less rowdy options, such as Andean music in restaurants, more sedate bars, and English-language movies every night of the week.

BARS & PUBS Bars are often very crowded, with gringos hoisting cheap drinks and trading information on the Inca Trail or latest jungle or rafting expedition. They're generally open from 11am or noon until 1 or 2am. Most have elongated or frequent happy hours with half-price drinks, making it absurdly cheap to tie one on. **Cross Keys** ★, Portal Confiturias 233, Plaza de Armas, Second Floor (✆ **084/229-227**), is one of the oldest pubs in town, owned by the English honorary consul and owner of Manu Expeditions. It's especially popular with Brits who can play darts or catch up on European soccer on satellite. **Los Perros** ★★, Tecsicocha 436 (✆ **084/241-447**), is one of the coolest bars in Cusco, a funky lounge with sofas, good food, and drinks (including hot wine), as well as live jazz on Sunday and Monday nights. A cool new wine bar, which also offers gourmet pizzas and munchies—owned by the same people behind the excellent restaurant Cicciolina—is **Baco ★**, Calle Ruinas 465 (✆ **084/242-808**). **Cicciolina** itself (p. 668 has a very appealing wine and cocktail bar, and it's a good place to begin or end the evening. **Norton Rat's Tavern,** Loreto 115, Plaza de Armas (✆ **084/246-204**), is American-owned and sometimes it can feel like you're in Ohio, hanging with bikers—there's pool and lots of sports on the tube. **Paddy Flaherty's,** Triunfo 124, Plaza de Armas (✆ **084/246-903**), is a cozy, relaxed, and often crowded Irish bar. **Rosie O'Grady's,** Santa Catalina Ancha 360, around the corner from the Plaza de Armas (✆ **084/247-935**), sports fancier digs in which to down your (canned) Guinness.

LIVE MUSIC Live music starts around 11pm in most clubs. By far the best place in Cusco for nightly live music is **Ukukus ★★**, Plateros 316, Second Floor (✆ **084/227-867**). The range of acts extends from bar rock to Afro-Peruvian, and the crowd jams the dance floor. Often the mix is half gringo, half Peruvian. It's open late nightly (until 4 or 5am), and there's pizza and 24-hour Internet. Pick up a pass for free entrance so you don't get stuck paying a cover. **Kamikase,** Plaza Regocijo 274, Second Floor (✆ **084/233-865**), is a two-level bar and a live music area with tables and funky decor. Music ranges from "rock en español" to reggae. **Rosie O'Grady's** (see "Bars & Pubs," above) also has live music on weekends (usually Peruvian, jazz, and blues).

DANCE CLUBS A young crowd of both backpackers and Peruvians is lured to the dance clubs by the free-drink cards handed out on the Plaza de Armas. Popular and often full and sweaty, **Mama Amérika,** at the corner of Calle Triunfo and Santa Catalina Angosta, just off the Plaza de Armas at Portal Belén 115, Second Floor (✆ **084/245-550**), spins a good international dance mix of Latin, reggae, rock, and techno, as does its spin-off, **Mama Africa,** Portal Harinas 191 (✆ **084/246-544**). Both are decent down-scale spots for cheap drinks. **Eko Club,** Plateros 334, Second Floor (no phone), remains the hottest dance club. It throbs with a variety of rock and techno; for those who need a break, there's a cool and laid-back lounge out back. With two bars and a fleet of what seems like dozens of young girls enticing visitors with free-drink cards, **Extrem,** Portal de Carnes 298 (✆ **084/240-901**), swarms with one of Cusco's youngest crowds.

TRADITIONAL PERUVIAN MUSIC You can catch Peruvian bands with a beat at Ukukus and Rosie O'Grady's (see "Live Music," above), but for a traditional folk music–and-dance show, you'll need to check out one of the restaurants featuring nightly entertainment. **Tunupa,** Portal de Confituria 233, Plaza de Armas (✆ **084/252-936**), has a pretty good traditional music and dance show.

MOVIES Probably the best selection of films, mostly American, shows at **the Film Movies & Lounge,** Procuradores 389, Second Floor (✆ **084/962-589**); it has a nice little bar and serves food. Other screens showing movies, usually daily, can be found at **Ukukus** (see above) and **Andes Grill,** Portal de Panes, Plaza de Armas (✆ **084/243-422**).

6 THE SACRED VALLEY OF THE INCAS

The Urubamba Valley, better known as the Valle Sagrado de los Incas, or Sacred Valley of the Incas, is a relaxed and extraordinarily picturesque stretch of villages and ancient ruins spread across a broad plain and the gentle mountain slopes northwest of Cusco.

Through the valley rolls the revered Río Urubamba, a pivotal religious feature of the Incas' cosmology. With the river as its source, the fertile valley was a major center of agricultural production for the Incas, who grew native Andean crops such as white corn, coca, and potatoes, and it continues to function as the region's breadbasket today. Along with Cusco and Machu Picchu, the Valle Sagrado ranks as one of the highlights of Peru—if you're visiting either of the former, it would be a shame not to spend at least a couple of days in the valley. The magnificent ruins found from Pisac to Ollantaytambo and beyond are testaments to the region's immense ceremonial importance. The Incas built several of the empire's greatest estates, temples, and royal palaces between the sacred centers of Cusco and Machu Picchu. Today, the rural villages of the Sacred Valley remain starkly, charmingly traditional. Quechua-speaking residents work the fields and harvest salt with methods unchanged since the days of the Incas, and market days—although now conducted to attract the tourist trade as well as intervillage commerce—remain important rituals.

The Sacred Valley is really taking off as a destination on its own, rather than just an add-on to Cusco or Machu Picchu. Seeing the valley's highlights on a daylong guided bus tour is certainly doable, but it can't compare to a leisurely pace that allows you an overnight stay and the chance to soak up the area's immense history, relaxed character, stunning scenery, and, in the dry season, equally gorgeous springlike weather. Not only that, the valley is about 500m (1,640 ft.) lower than Cusco, making it much more agreeable for those potentially afflicted with altitude-related health problems. If you have the time, a good way to explore the valley is to advance town by town toward Machu Picchu or vice versa, starting out from Machu Picchu and returning piecemeal towards Cusco. More and more visitors are now spending several days in the valley, choosing to base themselves at least initially in Pisac, Urubamba, or Ollantaytambo rather than the capital of the department, Cusco.

ESSENTIALS

Getting There & Getting Around

BY GUIDED TOUR Nearly every Cusco travel agency offers a 1-day Sacred Valley tour for as little as $25 per person, and most provide English-speaking guides. The tours tend to coincide with market days (Tues, Thurs, and Sun) and generally include Pisac, Ollantaytambo, and Chinchero. It's not enough time to explore the ruins, though a quickie tour gives at least a taste of the Valley's charms.

BY TRAIN The only spots in the Sacred Valley you can reach by train are Urubamba and Ollantaytambo, roughly midway on the Cusco–Machu Picchu route. All trains traveling from Cusco to Machu Picchu stop at Ollantaytambo. From Cusco to Machu Picchu are three classes of service on the longtime rail carrier, **Peru Rail** (✆ **01/612-6700** in Lima, or 084/581-414 in Cusco; www.perurail.com): the luxury Hiram Bingham, $307 to $334 one-way; Vistadome, $71 one-way; and Backpacker, $48 one-way. From Cusco to Ollantaytambo, prices are Vistadome $43 to $60 one-way and Backpacker $31 to $43 one-way. On the new **Inca Rail,** Av. El Sol 611 in Cusco (✆ **084/233-030;** www.incarail.com), first-class travel from Ollantaytambo to Machu Picchu is $70; executive class is $40. On the similarly new **Andean Railways,** Av. El Sol 576 in Cusco (✆ **084/221-199;** www.machupicchutrain.com), full fare from Ollantaytambo to Machu Picchu is $59.

Trains depart Cusco from **Estación San Pedro,** Calle Cascaparo s/n (✆ **084/221-352** or 221-313), and arrive in Ollantaytambo about 2 hours later. The train station in

Tips Boleto Turístico in the Valle Sagrado

The Cusco *boleto turístico* (tourist pass) is pretty much essential for visiting the Sacred Valley, in particular the ruins of Pisac and Ollantaytambo, as well as the market and town of Chinchero. You can purchase it in any of those places if you haven't already bought it in Cusco before traveling to the Valley. See p. 658 for more information.

Ollantaytambo is a long 15-minute walk from the main square. Besides the Inca Trail, the train is the only option for traveling from Ollantaytambo to Machu Picchu. For reservations, call ✆ **084/238-722.**

BY BUS Local buses (often small *combis* or *colectivos*) are the easiest and cheapest way to get around the Sacred Valley. They are often full of color if not comfort. (Tall people forced to stand will not find them much fun, however.) Buses to and from the Sacred Valley use terminals on Calle Huáscar and Calle Intiqhawarina, off Tullumayo, in Cusco. They leave regularly throughout the day, departing when full. Fares are S/3. The trip to Pisac takes about an hour; for Urubamba, just over 2 hours from Cusco, you can go via Pisac or via Chinchero. To travel to Ollantaytambo, you'll need to change buses at the terminal in Urubamba. The train is a simpler option if you don't plan on intermediate stops in the valley. Shared private cars *(autos)* to Urubamba leave from Calle Pavitos 567, with four passengers per car (they're generally station wagons with room for luggage in back and take just 50 min.) for just S/8 per person.

In **Pisac,** buses leave for Cusco and other parts of the valley from the main street just across the river (about 3 blocks west of the main square). In **Urubamba,** buses for Cusco and Chinchero leave from the Terminal Terrestre about 1km (a half mile) from town on the main road to Ollantaytambo (just beyond and across from the Incaland Hotel). *Combis* for other points in the valley and shared *autos* for Cusco depart from the intersection of the main road at Avenida Castilla. In **Ollantaytambo,** buses for Cusco depart from Avenida Estación, the main street leading away from the rail terminal.

BY TAXI You can easily hire a taxi for a daylong tour of the Sacred Valley or any of the valley towns; expect to pay about S/90. While a taxi to Pisac on your own may cost S/40, it is often possible to go by joining other travelers in a private car for as little as S/5 per person. Private taxis from Ollantaytambo or Urubamba to Cusco generally charge about S/80.

Visitor Information

You're best off getting information on the Sacred Valley before leaving Cusco at the helpful main Tourist Information Office (Oficina de Información Turística; see "Visitor Information" in section 5). Cusco's **South American Explorers Club,** Choquechaca 188, Apto. 4 (✆ **084/245-484;** www.saexplorers.org), is also an excellent source of information, particularly on the Inca Trail and other treks, mountaineering, and whitewater rafting in the valley. Inquire there about current conditions and updated transportation alternatives. In the valley itself, you may be able to scare up some limited assistance in Urubamba (Av. Cabo Conchatupa s/n) and Yucay (office of Turismo Participativo, Plaza Manco II 103; ✆ **084/201-099**). Aguas Calientes (at the foot of Machu Picchu) has an **iperu** office at Av. Pachacútec, Cdra. 1 s/n, Of. 4, in the INC building (✆ **084/211-104**). Beyond that, the best sources of local information are hotels.

FAST FACTS You can exchange dollars—in cash—with small shops in Pisac or Ollantaytambo; in Urubamba, there are ATMs on either side of the main road to Yucay, and there's an ATM on the Plaza de Armas in Pisac.

In a medical emergency, contact **Centro de Salud,** Av. Cabo Conchatupa s/n, Urubamba (✆ **084/201-334**), or **Hospital del Instituto Peruano de Seguridad Social,** Av. 9 de Noviembre s/n, Urubamba (✆ **084/201-032**). For the police, contact **Policía Nacional,** Palacio s/n, Urubamba (✆ **084/201-092**).

Urubamba has the best Internet *cabinas* in the region, with a good supply of machines and fast connections. **Academia Internet Urubamba,** begun with the help of an American exchange student, is 2 blocks northeast of the Plaza de Armas, on the corner of Jirón Belén and Jirón Grau. The **post office** in Pisac is on the corner of Comercio and Intihuatana, in Ollantaytambo and Urubamba on their respective Plazas de Armas.

PISAC ★★

The pretty Andean village of Pisac lies at the eastern end of the valley, 32km (20 miles) from Cusco. Though the town seems to be prized principally for its Sunday artisan market, Pisac should be more widely recognized for its splendid Inca ruins, which rival Machu Picchu. Perched high on a cliff is the largest fortress complex built by the Incas. The commanding distant views from atop the mountain, over a luxuriously long valley of green patchwork fields, are breathtaking.

Pisac's famed **market** draws hundreds of visitors on Sunday mornings in high season, when it is without doubt one of the liveliest in Peru. (There are slightly less popular markets on Tues and Thurs as well.) Hundreds of stalls crowd the central square and spill down side streets. Sellers come from many villages, many of them remote places high in the Andes, and wear the dress typical of their village. Dignitaries from the local villages usually lead processions after Mass (said in Quechua), dressed in their versions of Sunday finery. The goods for sale at the market—sweaters, ponchos, rugs—are familiar to anyone who's spent at least a day in Cusco, but prices are occasionally lower on selected goods such as ceramics. The market begins at around 9am and lasts until midafternoon.

The Pisac **ruins** ★★ are some of the finest in the entire valley. The best but most time-consuming way to see the ruins is to climb the hillside, where you'll encounter an extraordinary path and slice of local life. Trudging along steep mountain paths is still the way most Quechua descendants from remote villages get around these parts; many people you see at the Pisac market will have walked a couple of hours or more to get there. To reach the site on foot (about 5km/3 miles, or about 90 min.), you'll need to be pretty fit and/or willing to take it very slowly. Begin the ascent at the back of the main square, to the left of the church. The path bends to the right through agricultural terraces. There appear to be several competing paths; all of them lead up the mountain to the ruins. When you come to a section that rises straight up, choose the extremely steep stairs to the right (the path to the left is overgrown and poorly defined). If an arduous trek is more than you've bargained for, you can also hire a taxi in Pisac (easier on market days) to take you around the back way (about S/15). If you arrive by car or *colectivo* rather than by your own power, the ruins will be laid out the opposite of the way they are described below. The ruins are open daily from 7am to 5:30pm; admission is by *boleto turístico* (see "Cusco's *Boleto Turístico*" on p. 658).

From a semicircular terrace and fortified section at the top, called the **Quorihuayrachina,** the views south and west are spectacular. The Pisac nucleus was both a fortress and ceremonial center, and its delicately cut stones are some of the best found at

Extreme Sacred Valley

The Sacred Valley region is one of the best in South America for white-water rafting, mountain biking, trekking, hang gliding, and paragliding. River runs are extremely popular, and justifiably so: Peru has some of the world's wildest rivers. The most popular activity is, of course, hiking the Inca Trail to Machu Picchu, but there are plenty of other adventure opportunities. Many tour operators in Cusco organize adventure trips. Participants range from novices to hard-core adventure junkies; no experience is required for many trips, but make sure you sign up for a program appropriate for your level of interest and ability. Extreme sports being what they are, thoroughly check out potential agencies and speak directly to the guides, if possible. Hunting for bargains in this category is not advisable; quality equipment and good English-speaking guides are fundamental for safety considerations.

White-Water Rafting There are some terrific Andean river runs near Cusco, ranging from mild Class II to moderate and world Class IV and V. Recommended agencies include **Amazonas Explorer** ★★, Av. Collasuyo 910, Urb. Miravalle, Cusco (✆ 084/252846; www.amazonas-explorer.com); **Apumayo Expediciones,** Jr. Ricardo Palma N-5 Santa Monica, Wanchaq, Cusco (✆ 084/246-018; www.apumayo.com); **Eric Adventures** ★, Urb. Velasco Astete B-8-B (✆ 084/234-764; www.ericadventures.com); **Instinct Travel,** Av. de la Cultura No. 1318, Cusco (✆ 084/233-451; www.instinct-travel.com); **Loreto Tours,** Calle del Medio 111, Cusco (✆ 084/228-264; www.loretotours.com); and **Mayuc,** Portal Confiturías 211, Plaza de Armas, Cusco (✆ 084/ 242-824; www.mayuc.com).

any Inca site. The most important component of the complex is the **Templo del Sol (Temple of the Sun),** one of the Incas' most impressive examples of masonry, found on the upper section of the ruins. There you'll find the **Intiwatana,** the so-called "hitching post of the sun," which looks to be a sundial but, in fact, is an instrument that helped the Incas determine the arrival of important growing seasons. Nearby (just paces to the west) is another temple, thought to be the Temple of the Moon, and a ritual bathing complex fed by canals. Continuing north from this section, as you pass along the eastern edge of the cliff, you'll arrive at a tunnel, which leads to a summit lookout at 3,400m (11,150 ft.).

WHERE TO STAY **Paz y Luz** ★★, Ctra. Pisac Ruinas s/n (✆ **084/203-204;** www.pazyluzperu.com), about a 20-minute walk from the village along a road up to the Inca ruins, is a cool B&B and healing center run by a woman from New York, Diane Dunn. Rooms (S/160 double; S/220 suite including breakfast) are in comfortable bungalows with splendid views of the Pisac ruins and surrounding valley. Andean healing workshops and sacred-plant ceremonies are a good part of the attraction for guests interested in the Sacred Valley's spiritual offerings. The small, pleasant, and central **Hotel Pisaq** ★, Plaza Constitución 333 (✆ **084/203-062;** www.hotelpisaq.com), right on the main square, is a great place to stay in town. The cozy little inn, run by a Peruvian-American couple, has a stone-heated sauna and an attractive courtyard, as well as a good restaurant serving

Trekking In addition to the groups that organize Inca Trail hikes (see "Hiking the Inca Trail," p. 687), the following agencies handle a wide variety of trekking excursions: **Aventours,** Saphi 456, Cusco (© 084/224-050; http://ecoinka.com); **Manu Expeditions,** Calle Clorinda Matto de Turner 330, Urbanizacion Magisterial Primero Etapa, Cusco (© 084/225-990; www.manuexpeditions.com); **Mayuc,** Portal Confiturías 211, Plaza de Armas, Cusco (© 084/242-824; www.mayuc.com); and U.S.-based **Peruvian Andean Treks** (© 800/683-8148 or 617/924-1974 in the U.S.; www.andeantreks.com). **Peru Discovery** (see "Mountain Biking," below) also organizes excellent trekking expeditions. **Peru Uhupi,** Saguán del Cielo d-5, Urubamba (© 084/201-568; www.peru.uhupi.com), run by Chalo, the owner of cool, eco-styled lodge **Las Chullpas** in Urubamba (p. 678), leads small-group treks into nearby ranges.

Mountain Biking Mountain biking is really just beginning to catch on, and tour operators are rapidly expanding their services and equipment. **Peru Discovery,** Santa María F-3, San Sebastián, Cusco (© **054/274-541;** www.perudiscovery.com), is the top specialist, with a half-dozen bike trips that include hard-core excursions. **Ecomontana** (http://ecomontana.com), run by Omar Zarzar, rents mountain bikes and leads tours throughout the Sacred Valley. **Amazonas Explorer, Apumayo Expediciones, Eric Adventures, Instinct Travel** (see "White-Water Rafting," above), and **Manu Ecological Adventures** (© **084/261-640** or 213/283-6987 in the U.S. or Canada; www.manuadventures.com) offer 1- to 5-day organized mountain-biking excursions ranging from easy to rigorous.

wood-fired pizzas; the nicely decorated double rooms with private bathrooms cost $50 to $65 ($40–$45 with shared bath).

WHERE TO DINE A genial and inexpensive spot for any meal, from breakfast to hearty lunches and vegetarian options, is **Ulrike's Café** ★, Plaza de Armas 828 (© **084/203-195**). A relaxed cafe on the main square run by a German expat, Ulrike's can be counted on for a great-value lunch menu, homemade lasagna, omelets, salads, and great desserts (like Ulrike's famous strudel) and coffee. For very good trout dishes from the river, check out **Restaurant Valle Sagrado,** Amazonas 116 (© **084/436-915**). Another good bet is the excellent, unnamed **bakery** using traditional, wood-fired colonial ovens, on the corner of the main square next to Hotel Pisaq, and on Mariscal Castilla 372, a short walk from the plaza. The bakery serves excellent empanadas and breads; it is especially popular on market days.

URUBAMBA & ENVIRONS

Centrally located Urubamba (77km/48 miles northwest of Cusco) is the busiest of the Sacred Valley towns. Although the town itself doesn't have much more than magnificent mountain scenery and a popular main square to offer visitors, several of the best hotels in the region are located just south near Yucay, about 3km (1¾ miles) down the road, and north toward Ollantaytambo. Yucay is an attractive colonial village backed by a sophisticated system of agricultural terraces and irrigation canals. The area is a fine base from which to explore the Sacred Valley region.

The main square of Urubamba, the Plaza de Armas, is handsomely framed by a twin-towered colonial church and *pisonay* trees. Dozens of *mototaxis,* a funky form of local transportation not seen in other places in the valley, buzz around the plaza in search of passengers. Worth visiting in town is the beautiful home and workshop of **Pablo Seminario** ★, Berriozábal 111 (✆ **084/201-002;** www.ceramicaseminario.com), a ceramicist whose whimsical work features pre-Columbian motifs and is sold throughout Peru. The grounds are a minizoo, with llamas, parrots, nocturnal monkeys, falcons, rabbits, and more. Seminario now has shops in the Sonesta Posadas del Inca hotel in Yucay as well as Cusco.

About 6km (3½ miles) down the main road toward Ollantaytambo is the amazing sight of the **Salineras de Maras** ★★, thousands of individual ancient salt pans that form unique terraces in a hillside. The mines, small pools thickly coated with crystallized salt like dirty snow, have existed in the same spot since Inca days and are still operable. Families pass them down like deeds and continue the backbreaking and poorly remunerated tradition of salt extraction (crystallizing salt from subterranean spring water). To get to the salt pans, take a taxi to a point near the village of Tarabamba. (You can either have the taxi wait for you or hail a *combi* on the main road when you return.) From there, it's a lovely 45-minute walk along a footpath next to the river. There are no signs; cross the footbridge and bend right along the far side of the river and up through the mountains toward the salt pans. As you begin the gentle climb up the mountain, stick to the right to avoid the cliff-hugging, inches-wide trail that forks to the left. Another great walking route to the salt pans, more taxing but even more spectacular, is along a path from the town of Maras (90 minutes) or from the Inca agricultural site Moray (3 hours).

WHERE TO STAY One of the best hotels in the region is the handsome, ranch-style **Sonesta Posadas del Inca** ★★, Plaza Manco II de Yucay 123, Yucay (✆ **084/201-107;** fax 084/201-345; www.sonesta.com). Originally a monastery in the late 1600s (with a picturesque chapel to prove it) and then a hacienda, it is now a colonial villagelike complex with great character, great mountain views, and relaxed comfort. It recently added a nice spa with massages, yoga, a sauna, an outdoor Jacuzzi, and other treatments. Double rooms cost $110 to $140.

A funky place to stay is **Las Chullpas** ★ (✆ **084/201-568;** www.chullpas.uhupi.com), an "ecological guest house" that is more like something you'd find in the Amazon cloud forest rather than in the Sacred Valley. Run by a young Chilean and his German expat wife (a midwife who works with *campesina* women from the countryside), the nine rooms are connected huts that have the feel of tree forts, but with an abundance of style, including comfortable beds and hand-painted tiles in the bathrooms. Profits from the huge suite go toward Leonie's midwifery practice. Chalo prepares excellent organic and vegetarian meals in the cozy, fireplace-warmed dining room. Rates with breakfast are S/70 per person; the suite runs S/350 per night. In Huicho, 2km (1¼ miles) west of Urubamba, **Sol y Luna Lodge & Spa** ★★ (✆ **084/201-620;** fax 084/201-084; www.hotelsolyluna.com) is a French- and Swiss-owned cluster of 28 invitingly decorated, circular bungalow-style rooms (including four family bungalows) with private terraces, surrounded by beautifully landscaped gardens and gorgeous mountain views. The hotel has a nice (if small) pool, as well as a supersleek restaurant and pub (see below), appealing spa, and adventure club offering all sorts of outdoor activities (horseback riding, mountain biking, trekking, paragliding) in the region. Continually expanding, Sol y Luna is one of the nicest spots in the valley. Doubles cost $235.

In the hamlet of Yanahuara, on the way to Ollantaytambo, are two terrific new options in the burgeoning Sacred Valley. **Casa Andina Private Collection ★★**, Yanahuara (✆ **084/98476-5501,** or 01/213-9739 for reservations; fax 01/445-4775; www.casa-andina.com) is one of the group's few upscale offerings, a large (85-room), mountain-chalet-type hotel in a beautiful setting with large and handsomely decorated rooms with excellent views of the countryside. The hotel features an excellent, full-service spa, a good restaurant, and even a planetarium, making it popular with groups of diverse size. Two-story suites with balconies are especially alluring. Rates are $125 to $185 for doubles, $295 for suites.

WHERE TO DINE Many guests dine at their hotels, and the major ones above (Casa Andina, Libertador, and Sonesta) all have very good restaurants. The best restaurant in Urubamba is **El Huacatay ★★**, Jr. Arica 620 (✆ **084/201-790**), open Monday through Saturday from 2 to 10pm. Sit on the garden terrace or in the small, elegant dining room and enjoy local specialties such as alpaca lasagna. Sol y Luna's new and very sophisticated restaurant, **Wayra ★**, is probably the best of the hotel restaurants and is open for lunch and dinner (and serving a buffet lunch on Valley market days).

The Muse Too, Plaza de Armas, at the corner of Comercio and Grau (✆ **084/201-280**), the cutely named sister establishment of the Cusco bar/restaurant **the Muse,** is a funky two-story pub/restaurant that features tasty soups, sandwiches, and cocktails. At night, it is more music pub than restaurant.

OLLANTAYTAMBO ★★★

A tongue twister of a town—the last settlement in the valley before Agua Calientes and Machu Picchu—this historic and lovely little place 97km (60 miles) northwest of Cusco is affectionately called Ollanta (Oh-*yan*-tah) by locals. Plenty of outsiders who can't pronounce it fall in love with the town, too. The scenery around Ollantaytambo is some of the most stunning in the region. The snowcapped mountains that embrace the town frame a much narrower valley here than at Urubamba or Pisac, and both sides of the gorge are lined with Inca stone *andenes,* or agricultural terraces. Most extraordinary are the precipitous terraced ruins of a massive temple-fortress built by the Inca Pachacutec. Below the ruins, Ollantaytambo's old town is a splendid Inca grid of streets lined with adobe brick walls, blooming bougainvillea, and perfect canals, still carrying rushing water down from the mountains. Though Ollanta has exploded in popularity in just the last few years, except for the couple of hours a day when tour buses deposit large groups at the foot of the fortress (where a handicrafts market habitually breaks out to welcome them) and tourists overrun the main square, the town remains pretty quiet, a traditional and thoroughly charming Valle Sagrado village.

The Inca elite adopted Ollantaytambo, building irrigation systems and a crowning temple designed for worship and astronomical observation. The **temple ruins ★★** represent one of the Incas' most formidable feats of architecture—and are perhaps second only to Machu Picchu in their grandeur and harmony with the surrounding landscape. Rising above the valley and an ancient square (Plaza Mañaraki) are dozens of rows of stunningly steep stone terraces carved into the hillside. They appear both forbidding and admirably perfect. The Incas were able to successfully defend the site against the Spanish in 1537, protecting Manco Inca after his retreat here from defeat at Sacsayhuamán. The complex, in all probability, was more a temple than a citadel to the Incas. The upper section—reached after you've climbed 200 steps—contains typically masterful masonry of the kind that adorned great Inca temples. A massive and supremely elegant doorjamb—site of many a photo—indicates the principal entry to the temple; next to it is the **Temple of Ten Niches.** On the next level are six huge pink granite blocks, amazingly cut, polished, and fitted together, which appear to be parts of rooms never completed. This **Temple of the Sun** is one of the great stone masonry achievements of the Incas. On the stones, you can still make out faint, ancient symbolic markings in relief. Across the valley is the quarry that provided the stones for the structure; a great ramp descending from the hilltop ruins was the means by which the Incas transported the massive stones from several kilometers away. The ruins are open daily from 7am to 5:30pm; admission is by *boleto turístico* (see "Cusco's *Boleto Turístico*" on p. 658). To see the ruins in peace before the tour buses arrive, get there before 11am. Early morning is best of all, when the sun rises over mountains to the east and then quickly bathes the entire valley in light.

A footpath winds up the hill behind an outer wall of the ruins to a clearing and wall with niches that have led some to believe prisoners were tied up here—a theory that is unfounded. Regardless of the purpose, the views south over the Urubamba Valley and of the snowcapped peak of Verónica are outstanding. At the bottom of the terraces, next to the Patacancha River, are the **Baños de la Ñusta (Princess Baths),** a place of ceremonial bathing. Wedged into the mountains facing the baths are granaries built by the Incas. Locals like to point out the face of the Inca carved into the cliff high above the valley. (If you can't make it out, ask the guard at the entrance to the ruins for a little help.)

Ollantaytambo's outstanding **Old Town** ★★, below (or south of) the ruins and across the River Patacancha, is the finest extant example of the Incas' masterful urban planning. Many original residential *canchas,* or blocks, each inhabited by several families during the 15th century, are still present; each *cancha* had a single entrance opening onto a main courtyard. The finest streets of this stone village are directly behind the main square. Get a good glimpse of community life within a *cancha* by peeking in at Calle del Medio (Calle Chautik'ikllu), where a couple of neighboring houses have their ancestors' skulls displayed as shrines on the walls of their living quarters. The entire village retains a solid Amerindian air, unperturbed by the crowds of gringos who wander through, snapping photos of children and old women. It's a traditional place, largely populated by locals in colorful native dress and women who pace up and down the streets or through fields absentmindedly spinning the ancient spools used in making hand-woven textiles.

WHERE TO STAY **El Albergue** ★★, located next to the railway station platform in Ollantaytambo (✆/fax **084/204-014;** www.rumbosperu.com/elalbergue), is the best choice in town; it's an attractive and homey hostel owned by an American longtime resident of Ollantaytambo. With large, comfortable, and nicely—if austerely—furnished rooms, great gardens, a wood-fired sauna, three Labrador retrievers roaming the grounds, and a spot right next to the train to Machu Picchu, it's often full, even though prices have climbed steadily over the years. Double rooms with shared bathrooms cost $58 to $74. On the road from the train station to town, **Hotel Pakaritampu** ★, Av. Ferrocarril s/n, Ollantaytambo (✆ **084/204-020;** fax 084/204-105; www.pakaritampu.com), is surprisingly upscale for unassuming Ollantaytambo. Rooms are tasteful, with sturdy, comfortable furnishings, and there's a nice restaurant/bar. Double rooms cost S/396. Budget travelers gravitate toward **Hostal La Ñusta,** Carretera Ocobamba (✆ **084/204-032**), a clean and friendly place with good views from the balcony but small and plain rooms. Doubles with private bathrooms are $20.

WHERE TO DINE **Kusicoyllor,** Plaza Araccama s/n (✆ **084/204-103**), is a cool cafe/bar right next to ruins, so you might expect it to be a tad touristy and overpriced, which it is—but it's still nice. It serves standard Peruvian and predominantly Italian dishes and offers a fixed-price menu (S/24). Breakfast is especially good, making it a fine stop after an early morning tour of the ruins. Other cheap restaurants, principally pizzerias, such as **Bar Ollantay,** ring the main square in the Old Town. **Ganso,** Calle del Costado (no phone), is the swankest place in town for a drink.

MACHU PICCHU ★★★

The stunning and immaculately sited Machu Picchu, the fabled "lost city of the Incas," is South America's greatest attraction. The Incas hid Machu Picchu so high in the clouds that the empire-raiding Spaniards never found it. It is no longer lost, of course, and you can now zip there by high-speed train as well as by a more traditional 2- or 4-day trek, but Machu Picchu retains its great sense of mystery and magic. No longer overgrown with brush, as it was when it was discovered—with the aid of a local farmer who knew of its existence—by the Yale historian Hiram Bingham in 1911, it still cannot be seen from below. The majestic setting that the Incas chose for it remains unchanged. When the early morning sun rises over the peaks and methodically illuminates the ruins' granite stones row by row, Machu Picchu leaves visitors as awestruck as ever.

Machu Picchu's popularity continues to grow by leaps and bounds, straining both its infrastructure and the fragile surrounding ecosystem, forcing state officials to limit the number of visitors in high season. Indeed, a recent mudslide at Machu Picchu, in January 2010, killed five people (including two on the Inca trail) and stranded 2,000 tourists, who had to be evacuated by helicopter. Officials said the rains that swelled the Urubamba River were the heaviest in 15 years, and floods affected 80,000 people living in or near Aguas Calientes, leaving many homeless. Train service to Machu Picchu was not restored for more than a month. It was the latest in a series of catastrophic, rain-related events near the ancient ruins.

The great majority of visitors to Machu Picchu still do it as a day trip from Cusco, but many people feel that a few hurried hours to the ruins at peak hours, amid throngs of people following guided tours, simply do not suffice. By staying at least 1 night, either at the one upscale hotel just outside the grounds of Machu Picchu or down below in the town of Aguas Calientes (also called Machu Picchu Pueblo), you can remain at the ruins later in the afternoon after most of the tour groups have gone home, or get there for sunrise—a dramatic, unforgettable sight. Aguas Calientes is a small, ramshackle tourist trade town where weary backpackers rest up and celebrate their treks along the Inca Trail over cheap eats and cheaper beers. There are some additional good hikes in the area, but most people head back to Cusco after a couple of days in the area.

Getting to Machu Picchu

BY TRAIN The 112km (69-mile) train ride from Cusco to Machu Picchu is a truly spectacular journey. It zigzags up Huayna Picchu and then through lush valleys hugging the Río Urubamba, with views of snowcapped Andes peaks in the distance. **Peru Rail** (✆ **01/612-6700** in Lima, or 084/581-414 in Cusco; www.perurail.com) has three tourist trains from Cusco to Machu Picchu, taking just under 4 hours: the **Backpacker,** the slowest and least expensive; the **Vistadome,** the faster first-class service; and the top-of-the-line, newly inaugurated luxury line **Hiram Bingham** (named after the discoverer of Machu Picchu). Peru Rail's tourist trains depart from Cusco's **Estación Poroy,** a 15-minute taxi from Cusco, 6 days a week in high season (May–Oct) and 4 days a week in low season (Nov–Mar). Make your train reservations as early as possible; tickets can be purchased online or at **Estación Huanchaq** on Avenida Pachacútec (in cash, dollars, or soles) for tickets reserved in advance. It's open Monday through Friday from 8:30am to 5:30pm, Saturday and Sunday from 8:30am to 12:30pm. The Backpacker departs Cusco at 7am and arrives in Aguas Calientes at 10:10am; the Vistadome leaves at 6am and arrives at 9:40am; and the Hiram Bingham starts out at 9am and arrives at 12:30pm. Fares are $48 one-way for Backpacker; Vistadome, $71 one-way; and $307 to $334 one-way for Hiram Bingham (which includes brunch, afternoon tea, a guided tour of the ruins, and cocktails and dinner on the return trip). ***Tip:*** For the best views on the way to Machu Picchu, sit on the left side of the train.

Travelers based in the Urubamba Valley have additional options to travel by train to Machu Picchu, with two new rail lines challenging the decade-long monopoly held by Peru Rail. On the new **Inca Rail,** Av. El Sol 611 in Cusco (✆ **084/233-030**; www.incarail.com), first-class travel from Ollantaytambo to Machu Picchu is $70; executive class is $40. On the similarly new **Andean Railways,** Av. El Sol 576 in Cusco (✆ **084/221-199;** www.machupicchutrain.com), full fare from Ollantaytambo to Machu Picchu is $59. Peru Rail's Backpacker Cerrojo and Vistadome service originates in Ollantaytambo, leaving several times a day; the journey takes under 2 hours. The trip costs $31 to $43 each way in Backpacker class, $43 to $60 in Vistadome.

Train schedules and names and classes of service have changed frequently in the past few years, so verify hours and fares before you go. It's wise to make your reservation several days or a week in advance, if not more in high season. For the luxury service, reservations several weeks or more in advance are recommended.

BY BUS You can't travel from Cusco to Machu Picchu by bus, but if you walk the Inca Trail or ascend the slope to the ruins from the town of Aguas Calientes, you can take one of the frequent buses that depart from the railroad tracks. The buses wend their way up the mountain, performing exaggerated switchbacks for 15 minutes before suddenly depositing passengers at the entrance to the ruins. The cost is $14 round-trip. There's no need to reserve; just purchase your ticket at the little booth in front of the line of buses. Buses begin running at 6:30am and come down all day, with the last one descending at dusk. Some people choose to purchase a one-way ticket ($7) up and walk down (30–45 min.) to Aguas Calientes.

Tips Package Visits to Machu Picchu

One-day Machu Picchu tour packages that include a round-trip train ride from Cusco to Aguas Calientes (Machu Picchu Pueblo), a bus to the ruins, admission, a guided tour, and sometimes lunch at Machu Picchu Sanctuary Lodge, can be purchased from travel agencies in Cusco. Package deals generally start at around $140; it's worth shopping around for the best deal. Try **Milla Turismo,** Av. Pardo 689 (✆ **084/231-710;** www.millaturismo.com); **SAS Travel,** Calle Garcilaso 270, Plaza San Francisco (✆ **084/249-194;** www.sastravelperu.com); or any of the tour agencies that organize Inca Trail treks (see "Hiking the Inca Trail" on p. 687). Packages that include overnight accommodations can also be arranged.

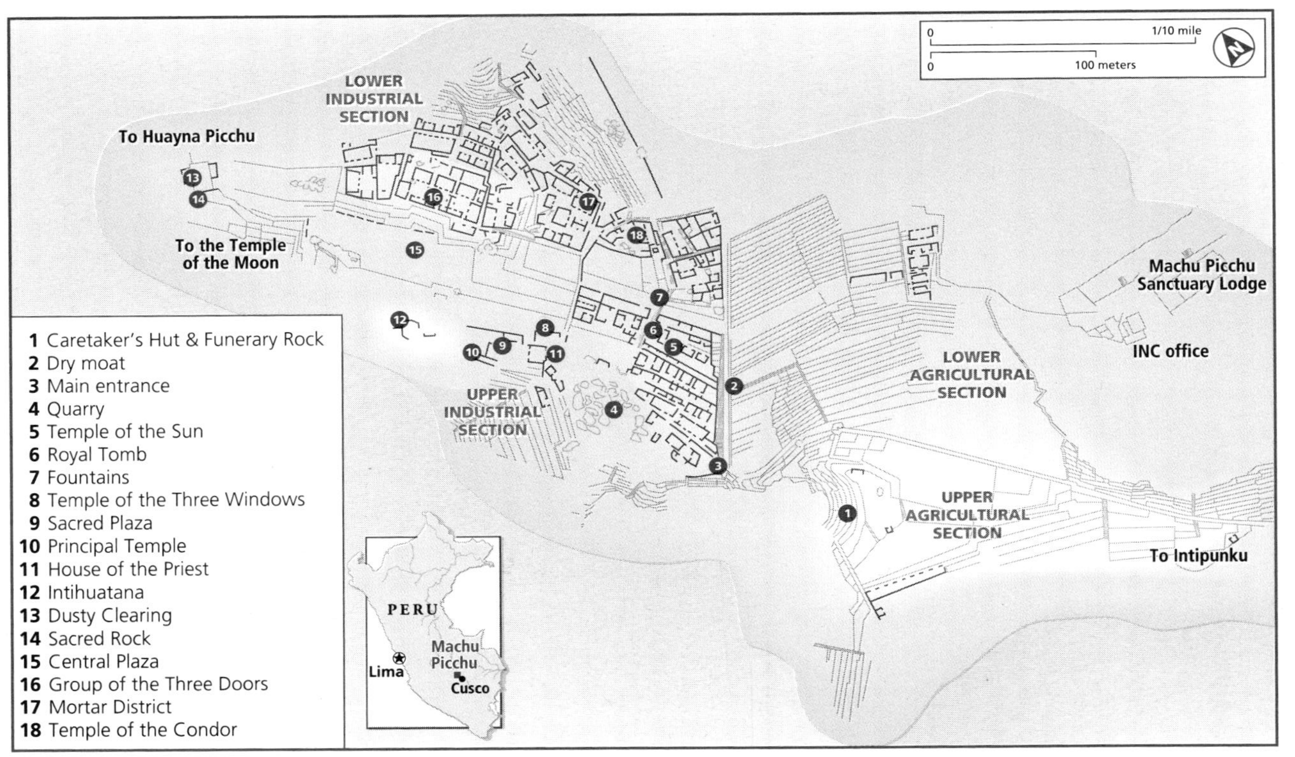
0
1/10 mile
0
100 meters
LOWER INDUSTRIAL SECTION
To Huayna Picchu
To the Temple of the Moon
UPPER INDUSTRIAL SECTION
LOWER AGRICULTURAL SECTION
UPPER AGRICULTURAL SECTION
Machu Picchu Sanctuary Lodge
INC office
To Intipunku
PERU
Lima
Machu Picchu
Cusco
1 Caretaker's Hut & Funerary Rock
2 Dry moat
3 Main entrance
4 Quarry
5 Temple of the Sun
6 Royal Tomb
7 Fountains
8 Temple of the Three Windows
9 Sacred Plaza
10 Principal Temple
11 House of the Priest
12 Intihuatana
13 Dusty Clearing
14 Sacred Rock
15 Central Plaza
16 Group of the Three Doors
17 Mortar District
18 Temple of the Condor

BY FOOT The celebrated **Inca Trail (Camino del Inca)** is almost as famous as the ruins themselves, and the trek is rightly viewed as an attraction in itself. See "Hiking the Inca Trail" on p. 687 for more details.

Exploring Machu Picchu

Since its initial exploration by American archaeologists from 1911 to 1915, Machu Picchu has resonated far beyond the status of a mere archaeological site. Reputed to be the legendary "lost city of the Incas," it is deeply steeped in mystery and folklore. The ruins of the complex—the only significant Inca site to escape the ravenous appetites of the conquistadors in the 16th century—rank as the top attraction in Peru, arguably the greatest in South America, and for my money, one of the world's most stunning sights. Countless glossy photographs of the ruins, gently positioned like a saddle between two massive peaks swathed in cottony clouds, can't do it justice.

Invisible from the Urubamba Valley below, Machu Picchu lay dormant for more than 4 centuries, nestled nearly 2,400m (7,872 ft.) above sea level under thick jungle and known only to a handful of Amerindian peasants. Never mentioned in the Spanish chronicles, it was seemingly lost in the collective memory of the Incas and their descendants. Its unearthing raised more questions than it answered, and experts still argue over its purpose. Was it a citadel? An agricultural site? An astronomical observatory? A ceremonial city or sacred retreat for the Inca emperor? Or some combination of all of these? Adding to the mystery, this complex city of exceedingly fine architecture and masonry was constructed, inhabited, and abandoned all in less than a century—a flash in the 4,000-year history of Andean Peru. It was very probably abandoned even before the arrival of the Spanish, perhaps a result of the Incas' civil war. Or perhaps it was drought that drove the Incas elsewhere.

Yale historian Hiram Bingham had thought Machu Picchu to be the lost city of Vilcabamba, the last refuge of the rebellious Manco Inca. Machu Picchu is not that lost city, which exists deeper in the jungle, at Espíritu Pampa. Most believe that the Inca Pachacutec, who founded the Inca empire, had Machu Picchu built sometime in the mid-1400s. It appears that the complex was both a ceremonial and agricultural center. Never looted by the Spanish, many of its architectural features remain in excellent condition—even if they do little to advance our understanding of the exact nature of Machu Picchu.

One thing is certain: Machu Picchu is one of the world's great examples of landscape art. The Incas revered nature, worshipping celestial bodies and more earthly streams and stones. The spectacular setting of Machu Picchu reveals just how much they reveled in their environment. Steep terraces, gardens, granite and limestone temples, staircases, and aqueducts seem to be carved directly out of the hillside. Forms echo the very shape of the surrounding mountains, and windows and instruments appear to have been constructed to track the sun during the June and December solstices. Machu Picchu lies 300m (1,000 ft.) lower than Cusco, but you'd imagine the exact opposite, so nestled are the ruins among mountaintops and clouds.

Appreciating Machu Picchu for its aesthetic qualities is no slight to its significance. The Incas obviously chose the site for the power of its natural beauty. They, like we, must have been in awe of the snowcapped peaks to the east; the rugged panorama of towering, forested mountains and the sacred cliff of Putukusi to the west; and the city sitting gracefully between two huge peaks. It remains one of the most thrilling sights in the world.

Visiting the Ruins

From May to September, as many as 2,500 visitors a day (the maximum allowed) visit the ruins. The place is large enough to escape most tour group bottlenecks, though people fearful of the crush should plan to arrive as early as possible in the morning, especially to see the sun rise, and climb Huayna Picchu (the peak directly behind the ruins, to which access is now limited to 400 athletic trekkers per day) and/or stay past 3pm. Perhaps the worst time to visit is from July 28 to August 10, when Peruvian national holidays bring untold numbers of school groups and families to Machu Picchu.

The ruins are open from dawn to dusk; the first visitors, usually those staying at the hotel next door or arriving from the Inca Trail, enter at 6am. Everyone is ushered out by 6pm. Tickets no longer can be purchased at the entrance; they must be purchased (take your passport) at the **Machu Picchu Cultural Center** in Aguas Calientes, Av. Pachacutec s/n (✆ **084/211-196**), near the main plaza. They may also be purchased at the **Instituto Nacional de Cultural (INC)** offices in Cusco, Calle San Bernardo, several blocks from the Plaza de Armas. The entrance fee has doubled to S/124 (students half price with an ISIC card; S/62 ages 8–21; free for children 7 and under). Many expect the entrance fee to increase again, perhaps dramatically, in the near future. Tickets are valid for 3 days from date of purchase, but are good for a single day's entrance only. You will be given a map of the ruins, which gives the names of the individual sections, but no detailed explanations. The numbers indicated in brackets below follow our own map on p. 683. For a detailed guide of the ruins and their history, Peter Frost's *Exploring Cusco,* available in Cusco bookstores, is quite excellent.

English-speaking guides can be independently arranged on-site. Most charge around $20 to $30 for a private 2-hour tour. You can also join a tour group for about $5 per person.

Inside the Ruins

After passing through the ticket booth, you can either head left and straight up the hill, or down to the right. (See "Machu Picchu" map, p. 683; its **bullets correlate to this section.**) The path up to the left takes you to the spot above the ruins, near the **Caretaker's Hut** and **Funerary Rock** (1), which affords the classic postcard overview of Machu Picchu. If you arrive early enough for sunrise (6:30–7:30am), by all means go here first. The hut overlooks rows and rows of steep agricultural terraces. From this vantage point, you can see clearly the full layout of Machu Picchu, which had clearly defined agricultural and urban zones; a long **dry moat** (2) separates the two sectors. A population of perhaps 1,000 lived here at the high point of Machu Picchu.

Head down into the main section of the ruins, past a series of burial grounds and dwellings and the **main entrance to the city** (3). A section of stones, likely a **quarry** (4), sits atop a clearing with occasionally great views of the snowcapped peaks (Cordillera Vilcabamba) to the southwest.

Down a steep series of stairs is one of the most famous Inca constructions, the **Temple of the Sun** (5) (also called the Torreón). The rounded, tapering tower has extraordinary stonework, the finest in Machu Picchu; its large stones fit together seamlessly. From the ledge above the temple, you can appreciate the window perfectly aligned for the June winter solstice, when the sun's rays come streaming through at dawn and illuminate the stone at the center of the temple. The temple is cordoned off, and entry is not permitted. Below the temple, a cave carved from the rock, is a section traditionally called the **Royal Tomb** (6), even though no human remains have been found there. Inside is a meticulously carved altar and series of niches that produce intricate morning shadows. To the

Tips Come Prepared

Take a bottle of water in a knapsack to Machu Picchu (not to mention a good sun hat and sunscreen), no matter how long you plan to stay. It gets very warm, the sun is incredibly strong at this elevation, and there's nowhere to go for refreshment (and few places to find shade) besides the hotel at the entrance.

north, just down the stairs that divide this section from a series of dwellings called the **Royal Sector,** is a still-functioning canal and series of interconnected **fountains** (7). The main fountain is distinguished both by its size and excellent stonework.

Back up the stairs to the high section of the ruins (north of the quarry) is the main ceremonial area. The **Temple of the Three Windows** (8), each a trapezoid extraordinarily cut with views of the Andes in the distance across the Urubamba gorge, is likely to be one of your lasting images of Machu Picchu. It fronts one side of the **Sacred Plaza** (9). To the left, if you're facing the Temple of the Three Windows, is the **Principal Temple** (10), which has masterful stonework in its three high walls. Directly opposite is the **House of the Priest** (11). Just behind the Principal Temple is a small cell, termed the **Sacristy** and renowned for its exquisite masonry. It's a good place to examine how amazingly these many-angled stones (one to the left of the doorjamb has 32 distinct angles) were fitted together by Inca stonemasons.

Up a short flight of stairs is the **Intihuatana** (12), popularly called the "hitching post of the sun." It looks to be a ritualistic carved rock or sort of sundial, and its shape echoes that of the sacred peak Huayna Picchu beyond the ruins. The stone almost certainly functioned as an astronomical and agricultural calendar. It appears to be powerfully connected to mountains in all directions. The Incas built similar monuments elsewhere across the empire, but most were destroyed by the Spanish (who surely thought them to be instruments of pagan worship). The one at Machu Picchu survived in perfect form until 2001, when authorities allowed the filming of a Cuzqueña beer commercial here and the crew sneaked in a 1,000-pound crane, which fell over and chipped off the top section of the Intihuatana. All to sell more beer!

Follow a trail down through terraces and past a small plaza to a **dusty clearing** (13) with covered stone benches on either side. Fronting the square is the massive sculpted **Sacred Rock** (14), whose shape mimics that of Putukusi, the sacred peak that looms due east across the valley. This area likely served as a communal area for meetings and perhaps performances.

To the left of the Sacred Rock, down a path, is the gateway to **Huayna Picchu ★★**, the huge outcrop that serves as a dramatic backdrop to Machu Picchu. Though it looks forbidding, it can be climbed by anyone in reasonable shape. Note, however, that only 400 people per day are permitted to make the climb; if you are keen on ascending Huyana Picchu for the views and exercise, arrive early. The steep path up takes most visitors about an hour or more, though some (including me) have ascended the peak in less than 25 minutes. Guards at a small booth require visitors to sign in and out; the path is open from 7am to 1pm and the first group of 200 must exit by 10am. The views from the very top, of Machu Picchu below and the panorama of forested mountains, are breathtaking. The climb is highly recommended for all energetic sorts, but young children are not allowed. (I've seen octogenarians climb the path at an enviable clip.) In wet weather, you may want to reconsider, as the stone steps can get very slippery and dangerous.

Returning back down the same path (frighteningly steep at a couple points) is a turn-off to the **Temple of the Moon,** usually visited only by Machu Picchu completists. Cleaved into the rock at a point midway down the peak, it almost surely was not a lunar observatory, but it is a strangely forlorn and mysterious place of caverns and niches and enigmatic portals. It has some terrific stonework. The path takes about an hour round-trip from the detour.

Continuing back into the complex, enter the lower section of the ruins, separated from the spiritually oriented upper section by a **Central Plaza** (15). The lower section was more prosaic in function (it was mostly residential and industrial). Eventually, you'll come to a series of cells and quarters, called the **Group of the Three Doors** (16) and the **Mortar District** or Industrial Sector (17). By far the most interesting part of this lower section is the **Temple of the Condor** (18). Said to be a carving of a giant condor, the rock above symbolizes the great bird's wings. You can actually crawl through the cave at the base of the rock.

Hiking the Inca Trail ★★★

The Incas conceived of both Machu Picchu and the great trail leading to it in grand artistic and spiritual terms. Hiking the Inca Trail—the ancient royal highway—is hands down the most authentic and scenic way to visit Machu Picchu and get a clear grasp of the Incas' overarching architectural concept and supreme regard for nature. As impressive as Machu Picchu itself, the trail traverses a 325-sq.-km (125-sq.-mile) national park designated the Machu Picchu Historical Sanctuary. The zone is replete with extraordinary natural and man-made sights: Inca ruins, exotic vegetation and animals, and dazzling vistas.

Visitors have two options when hiking to Machu Picchu: either along an arduous 4-day, 3-night path, or as part of a more recently opened 2-day, 1-night trail. You can hire porters to haul your packs or suck it up and do it the hard way, but **you must go as part of an organized group arranged by an officially sanctioned tour agency.** Independent trekking (without an official guide) on the Inca Trail has been prohibited since 2001. However, a couple or small number of people can organize their own group if they are willing to pay higher prices for the luxury of not having to join an ad-hoc group. The classic 4-day route is along hand-hewn stone stairs and through sumptuous mountain scenery, amazing forest, and dozens of Inca ruins. The zone is inhabited by rare orchids, 300-plus species of birds, and even the indigenous spectacled bear. The trek begins at Qorihuayrachina, more easily described as Km 88 of the railway to Aguas Calientes. The 43km (27-mile) route passes three steep mountain passes, including the dreaded "Dead Woman's Pass," to a maximum altitude of 4,200m (13,776 ft.). Virtually all groups enter the ruins of Machu Picchu at sunrise on the fourth day.

Others choose to take the 2-day trek, a reasonable alternative if time or fitness are lacking. This trail begins closer to Machu Picchu, at Km 104, and circumvents much of the finest mountain scenery and ruins. Groups spend the night near the ruins of Wiñay Wayna before arriving at Machu Picchu for sunrise on the second day. More and more people of all ages and athletic abilities are tackling the Inca Trail; the Peruvian government, in addition to adopting more stringent regulations governing its use, also placed flush toilets in campsites several years ago in an attempt to make the trail cleaner and more user-friendly.

Either way you go, it is advisable to give yourself a couple of days in Cusco or the Sacred Valley to acclimatize to the high elevation. Cold- and wet-weather technical gear, a solid backpack, and comfortable, sturdy hiking boots are musts (also needed: a sleeping bag, flashlight, and sunblock). Above all, respect the ancient trail and its environment. Whatever you pack in, you must also pack out. You must also choose your dates extremely carefully. The dry season (June–Sept) is the most crowded time on the trail but excellent in terms of weather. Shoulder seasons can be best of all, even with the threat of a bit of rain; May is perhaps the best of these, with good weather and low numbers of trekkers. Other months—especially December through March—are simply too wet for all but the hardest-core trail vets. The entire trail is now closed for maintenance and conservation during the month of February—which was one of the rainiest and least appealing months for trekking to Machu Picchu anyway. For the most popular months (May–Sept), early booking (4–6 months in advance) is essential.

The Peruvian government has sought to limit numbers of trekkers (now capped at 500 per day, including tourists and trek staff) on the Inca Trail but also to maximize revenue from one of its foremost attractions. Thus, the cost of hiking the trail has steadily climbed: It now costs at least three times what it did just a few years ago. Standard-class treks, the most common and economical service, cost between $450 and $550 per person, including entrance fees ($88 adults and $44 students) and return by tourist train. Independent trekkers generally join a mixed group of travelers; groups tend to be between 12 and 16 people with guaranteed daily departures. The cost includes a bus transfer to Km 88 to begin the trek, an English-speaking guide, tents, mattresses, three daily meals, and porters who carry all common equipment. Tips for porters or guides are extra. Personal porters, to carry your personal items, can be hired for about $130 for the 4 days. Premium-class services generally operate smaller group sizes (a maximum of 10 trekkers), and you often get an upgrade on the return train. Prices for premium group treks, organized for private groups, range from $750 to as much as $1,000 per person.

Prices vary for trail packages based on services and the quality and experience of the agency. In general, you get what you pay for. Rock-bottom prices will probably get you an inexperienced guide who speaks little English, food that is barely edible, camping equipment on its last legs, and a large, rowdy group (usually 16 young trekkers). Especially important is the ability of an agency to guarantee departure even if its desired target number of travelers is not filled. Never purchase Inca Trail (or, for that matter, any tour) packages from anyone other than officially licensed agencies, and be careful to make payments (and get official receipts) at the physical offices of the agencies. If you have questions about whether an agency is legitimate or is authorized to sell Inca Trail packages, ask for assistance at the main tourism information office in Cusco.

At least 160 tour operators have been granted government licenses to sell and operate Inca Trail treks. Recommended agencies (all based in Cusco) for organizing treks along the Inca Trail include **Andean Life,** Plateros 372 (✆ 084/249-491; www.andeanlifeperu.com); **Big Foot Tours,** Triunfo 392, 2nd level (✆ 084/238-568; www.bigfootcusco.com); **Explorandes,** Garcilaso 316-A (✆ 084/238-380; www.explorandes.com); **Q'Ente,** Garcilaso 210 (✆ 084/222-535; www.qente.com); **SAS Adventure Travel,** Garcilaso 270, Plaza San Francisco (✆ **084/249-194;** www.sastravelperu.com); and **United Mice,** Plateros 351 (✆ 084/221-139; www.unitedmice.com).

To guarantee a spot with an agency (which must request a trek permit for each trekker) it is imperative that you make a reservation and pay for your entrance fee at least 15 days in advance (although in practice, several months in advance if you plan to go during the peak months of May–Sept). Reservations can be made as much as a year in advance. Gone are the days when trekkers could simply show up in Cusco and organize a trek on the fly. Changing dates once you make a reservation is difficult if not impossible. If spots remain on agency rosters, they are offered on a first-come, first-served basis.

Where to Stay in Aguas Calientes

The **Machu Picchu Sanctuary Lodge** ★★ is a newly transformed, extraordinarily expensive luxury lodge next to the ruins (✆ **084/246-419;** www.orient-express.com). Rooms are not especially large, but they have a good deal of Peruvian character, and one-third of them have views of the ruins. Clearly, you are paying for the unique proposition of staying right next to Machu Picchu. Rooms cost a staggering $1,009 to $1,420 for a double, $1,584 for a suite (though rates *do* include three meals a day); even at those prices, you must reserve 3 months in advance during the high season of May to September. You must also hold a reservation in Cusco at the Hotel Monasterio. Easily the best place to stay if you can't get into the Machu Picchu Sanctuary Lodge (or are understandably scared off by its prices and restrictions) is the **Machu Picchu Pueblo Hotel** ★★★, Avenida Imperio de los Incas (✆ **800/442-5042** in the U.S. and Canada, or 084/211-122 for reservations; www.inkaterra.com). This rustic but upscale hotel, a compound of Spanish-colonial bungalows *(casitas),* has real flavor, though it too has gotten quite expensive. It is craftily set into lush gardens, and it offers orchid tours, bird-watching, and guided ecological hikes. The large, comfortable rooms (many with fireplaces) are $459 to $516 for a double, $569 to $960 for a suite. The newest upscale hotel in Aguas Calientes, **Sumaq Machu Picchu Hotel** ★, Av. Hermanos Ayar Mz 1 Lote 3 (✆ **084/211-05;** www.sumaqhotelperu.com), is perfect for someone who wants the comfort and services of Machu Picchu Pueblo Hotel but at a more accessible cost—$205 to $245 for a double, $315 for a suite. A sprawling, cantilevered structure—with stonework designed to echo Inca masonry—near the river and a 10-minute walk from the train station, it offers spacious tiled-floor rooms with excellent bedding, soft linens, and Andean motifs in bathrooms and on the headboards. Guests who are beat from scaling Machu Picchu will revel in the full-service on-premises Aqlla spa, where they can pick up a relaxing massage or indulge in the steam sauna. Quite a notch down in both price and comfort is **Gringo Bill's Hostal** ★, Colla Raymi 104, Plaza de Armas (✆/fax **084/211-046;** www.gringobills.com), which was started by an American expat and has been a backpacker's institution since the early 1980s, though lately it's gone quite a bit upscale. The comfortable and clean rooms have good beds, and many have great views of the Upper Amazon tropical rainforest. Double rooms with private bathrooms cost $75; suites range from $105 to $135. **Hostal Machupicchu,** Av. Imperio de los Incas s/n (✆ **888/790-5264** toll-free or 084/211-065; fax 084/212-034; www.hostalmachupicchu.com), is one of the best midrange options in Aguas Calientes. Restored and redecorated a few years ago, it has very clean, well-furnished, and airy rooms, some painted in funky colors. Double rooms with private bathrooms cost $65. One of the best of the inexpensive hostels along the main drag and railroad tracks, **Hostal Continental,** Av. Imperio de Los Incas 177 (✆ **084/211-034**), is very tidy, and you won't lack for hot water. Rooms aren't large, but the beds are pretty decent for a budget backpacker; $50 will get you a double with a private bathroom.

Where to Dine in Aguas Calientes

Scores of small and friendly restaurants line the only two streets in Aguas Calientes, Avenida Imperio de Los Incas and Avenida Pachacutec. Many are fairly generic, serving decent, cheap *menús* and pizza from wood-fired ovens. If you're just looking for pizza and a cold beer, **El Fogón de las Mestizas** and **Chez Maggy** (on Pachacutec) and **Incawasi, Inti Killa, Pizzería Su Chosa,** and **Pachamama** (all on Avenida Imperio de los Incas) are all dependable. Menu hawkers, often the kids of the cook or owner, will try to lure you in with very cheap menu deals. If you're just looking for lunch during visits to the ruins, you have two choices: the overpriced buffet lunch at Machu Picchu Sanctuary Lodge, or a sack lunch. I recommend the latter (pick one up at Gringo Bill's or assemble one from your hotel's buffet breakfast). The best restaurant in town is the friendly **Indio Feliz ★★**, Calle Lloque Yupanqui 112 (✆ **084/211-090**), serving Peruvian and French cuisine. Other good dining options include **Pueblo Viejo,** Av. Pachacutec s/n (✆ **084/211-193**), a simple and cozy restaurant specializing in grilled meats; **Toto's House ★**, Av. Imperio de los Incas s/n (✆ **084/211-020**), a large, airy place that sits overlooking the river and serves good Peruvian dishes, barbecue, and pizzas (often to the tune of Altiplano music); and **Restaurant Manu,** Av. Pachacutec 139 (✆ **084/211-101**), a relaxed and friendly spot featuring lots of international and Peruvian items, including pizza, homemade pasta, baked trout, and grilled chicken.

7 THE SOUTHERN AMAZON: MANU & TAMBOPATA ★★★

Puerto Maldonado: 500km (310 miles) NE of Cusco

Nearly two-thirds of Peru is Amazon rainforest, which thrives with some of the richest biodiversity on the planet. Not surprisingly, jungle ecotourism has exploded in Peru. The Amazonian regions are now more accessible, though some areas remain very complicated and time-consuming to get to, and there are more lodges and eco-options than ever.

Cusco is the gateway to the southeastern jungle and some of Peru's finest Amazon rainforest expeditions. Two of Peru's top three jungle sites—among the greatest not just in South America, but the world—are found in the southern Amazon. The region's two principal protected areas, the **Manu Biosphere Reserve** (which encompasses the Parque Nacional del Manu, or Manu National Park) and the **Tambopata National Reserve (Reserva Nacional de Tambopata),** differ in terms of remoteness and facilities. Manu, considered to be one of the most pristine jungle regions in the world, is complicated and expensive to visit; travel is possible only with one of eight officially sanctioned agencies. Most expeditions last a minimum of 5 days and involve both overland and air (not to mention extensive river) travel. The jungle frontier city of Puerto Maldonado, the unassuming capital of the region and a half-hour flight from Cusco, is the jumping-off point to explore more accessible Tambopata. Travelers without the time or budget to accommodate Manu often find Tambopata a worthy alternative.

Lodge visits include boat transportation and three meals daily, as well as guided visits and activities (some, such as canopy walks, entail additional fees). For both destinations, airfare from Cusco to Puerto Maldonado or Boca Manu (the gateway to the Manu Biosphere Reserve) is usually extra. Cheaper tours travel overland, stay at lesser lodges (or primarily at campsites), and may travel on riverboats without canopies. Independent travel to Tambopata and two-way overland travel to either are options only for those with a lot of time and patience on their hands. Organizing your trip with a specialized tour operator is highly recommended (and in the case of Manu, required). Most have fixed departure dates throughout the year. Do not purchase any jungle packages from salespeople on the streets of Cusco; their agencies may not be authorized to enter restricted zones, and last-minute "itinerary changes" are likely.

Dry season (May–Oct) is the best time for southern jungle expeditions; during the rainy season, rivers overflow and mosquitoes gobble up everything in sight. But intense heat and humidity are year-round constants in the jungle.

MANU BIOSPHERE RESERVE

Manu is the least accessible and explored jungle in Peru, and about as close as you're likely to come to virgin rainforest anywhere in the world. A UNESCO World Heritage Site and the largest protected area in Peru (and one of the largest in the world), Manu—about half the size of Switzerland—has a surface area of nearly 1.7 million hectares (4 million acres) of varied habitats, including Andes highlands, cloud forests, and lowland tropical rainforests. The Manu Biosphere Reserve comprises three zones: **Manu National Park,** an area of dedicated conservation reserved for scientific study; the **Reserve Zone,** up the River Manu northwest of Boca Manu, is by permit and accompanied by an authorized guide only for ecotourist activities; the Multi-Use or **Cultural Zone,** home to traditional nomadic groups and open to all visitors. The whole of Manu is unparalleled for its wealth of wildlife, which includes more than 1,000 species of birds, 1,200 butterfly species, 15,000 plants, 200 mammal species and 13 species of primates. Birdwatchers thrill at the prospect of glimpsing bird populations that account for 10% of the world's total, more than those found in all of Costa Rica. Other Manu fauna include jaguars, tapirs, spectacled bears, ocelots, and giant otters. Manu is also home to untold quantities of reptiles, amphibians, and insects, as well as dozens of native tribes, some of which have contact with the modern world.

Only a handful of travel agencies in Cusco are authorized to organize excursions to Manu. Getting to Manu is an eco-adventure in itself. Overland access to the Manu Reserve Zone from Cusco is a stunning 2-day journey through 4,000m (13,120-ft.) mountains and cloud forest before descending into lowland rainforest. Because the reserve is so isolated and access is so restricted, Manu visits are rather expensive, generally ranging from $700 to more than $2,500 per person for a 5- to 8-day trip.

Manu Tour Operators

Only eight tour companies are permitted to run organized expeditions to Manu (and they are limited to 30 travelers each per week). The best of the firms listed below are closely involved with conservation and local development programs.

- **InkaNatura ★★★**, Calle Ricardo Palma N° J1, Urb Santa Monica, Cusco (✆ **084/25-5255;** www.inkanatura.com). Perhaps the most serious and sophisticated outfit operating ecotourism trips in the Peruvian Amazon, InkaNatura, associated with the Peruvian conservation group PerúVerde and the American organization Tropical Nature, organizes stays at the famed **Manu Wildlife Center.** The lodge, opened in 1996, is located near the world's largest tapir clay lick, as well as the Blanquillo macaw clay lick, and it features 48km (30 miles) of nature trails and two canopy-viewing platforms. Accommodations are in 22 spacious, private bungalows with tiled bathrooms. Packages at Manu Wildlife Center range from 4 days, 3 nights for $1,285 to 5 days, 4 nights for $1,475. InkaNatura also operates shorter trips to the **Cock-of-the-Rock Lodge,** several lodges in Tambopata (see below), and multilodge sojourns that include Cusco and Machu Picchu. Outside Peru, trips can be organized through

Tips Wildlife Viewing

Peru's Amazon jungle regions have some of the greatest recorded biodiversity and species of plants and animals on earth. However, you may be disappointed if you go expecting a daily episode of *Wild Kingdom.* An expedition to the Amazon is not like a safari to the African savanna. Many mammals are extremely difficult to see in the thick jungle vegetation, and though the best tour operators employ guides skilled in ferreting them out, there are no guarantees. Even in the most virgin sections, after devoting several patient days to the exercise, you are unlikely to see a huge number of mammals, especially the rare large species such as tapirs, jaguars, and giant river otters. If you spot a single one of these prized mammals, your jungle expedition can be considered a roaring success. However, in both Manu and Tambopata you are very likely to see a wealth of jungle birds (including the region's famous macaws), several species of monkeys, black caimans, butterflies, and insects.

Tropical Nature Travel, P.O. Box 5276, Gainesville, FL 32627-5276 (✆ **877/827-8350** toll-free in the U.S.; www.tropicalnaturetravel.com).

- **Manu Expeditions ★★★**, Urbanización Magisterio, Segunda Etapa G-5, P.O. Box 606, Cusco (✆ **084/226-671;** www.manuexpeditions.com). One of the pioneering ecotourism operators in southern Peruvian Amazon, Manu Expeditions—run by an ornithologist who is the British consul in Cusco, has been organizing rainforest tours for more than 2 decades. Tours include stays at the **Manu Wildlife Center,** of which the group is part owner (see above), near the famed macaw clay lick, and a safari camp facility deep at Cocha Salvador within the Manu Biosphere Reserve. The Wildlife Center is considered the best lodge in Peru for birding. The longer tours include initial stays at the **Cock-of-the-Rock Lodge** in cloud forest. Four-, six-, and nine-day fixed-departure tours range from $1,180 to $1,895 per person.
- **Manu Nature Tours ★★★**, Av. Pardo 1046, Cusco (✆ **084/252-721;** www.manuperu.com). A highly professional, prize-winning outfit with 20 years' experience in Manu, it operates the well-known and comfortable **Manu Lodge,** situated next to a pristine lake and the only full-service lodge within Manu National Park itself (5-day, 4-night trips, $1,029–$1,500), and the excellent **Manu Cloud Forest Lodge,** the first of its kind in Peru, overlooking a waterfall (3-day, 2-night trips, $849). Add-on options include mountain biking, rafting, and tree canopy climbs. The company runs Manu Café & Restaurant in Cusco, next to its offices.
- **Pantiacolla ★**, Saphy 554, Cusco (✆ **084/238-323;** www.pantiacolla.com). An initiative of a Dutch biologist and Boca Manu-born conservationist, the agency operates the small **Pantiacolla Lodge,** with double rooms in bungalows, on bluffs overlooking the Madre de Dios River at the edge of Manu National Park. The organization also operates a community-based ecotourism project with the Yine Indians of the Manu rainforest, with a lodge that will be entirely turned over to the community in 2011. Pantiacolla is favored by eco-travelers on a budget, offering camping and lodge trips ranging from $990 for 5 days to $1,064 for 7 days for Reserve Zone tours.

Other reputable Manu tour companies, which run economical camping-based trips, include **Manu Ecological Adventures,** Plateros 356, Cusco (✆ **213/283-6987** in the U.S. and Canada, or **084/261-640;** www.manuadventures.com); and **SAS Travel,** Garcilaso 270, Plaza San Francisco (✆ **084/249-194;** www.sastravelperu.com), a well-run and popular all-purpose agency that offers varied programs to both Manu and Tambopata and stays at various lodges.

TAMBOPATA NATIONAL RESERVE

Accessible from Puerto Maldonado, jungle lodges in and around the Tambopata National Reserve—a massive tract of tropical rainforest in the department of Madre de Dios—are located either along the Tambopata or Madre de Dios Rivers. The National Reserve covers 275,000 hectares (nearly 700,000 acres), while the entire area, including the Bahuaja-Sonene National Park, encompasses some 1.5 million hectares (3.7 million acres) of Amazonian jungle. Visits to lodges here are considerably more accessible than those in Manu. Most trips involve flying a half-hour from Cusco and then boarding a boat and traveling by river for 45 minutes to up to 5 hours to reach a jungle lodge. Although man's imprints are more noticeable in the Tambopata region, the area remains one of superb environmental diversity, with a dozen different types of forest. Many environmentalists claim that Tambopata has one of the greatest diversities of wildlife recorded, owing to a location at the confluence of lowland Amazon forest with three other ecosystems. At least 13 endangered species are found in the region, including the jaguar, giant river otter, ocelot, harpy eagle, and giant armadillo. The farther one travels from Puerto Maldonado, the greater the chances of wildlife viewing. The famous **Macaw Clay Lick (Colpa de Guacamayos)** within Tambopata National Reserve is one of the largest natural clay licks in Peru and perhaps the wildlife highlight of the country. Thousands of brilliantly colored macaws and parrots arrive daily at the cliffs to feed on mineral salts.

Flights to Puerto Maldonado from Cusco are about $220 round-trip. (Flights are often included in packages.) Packages begin with 2-day, 1-night arrangements, but 3-day, 2-night packages are better. Lodge stays generally allow visitors to see a large variety of trees, plants, and birds, as well as caimans, but few wild mammals apart from monkeys. Rare species such as the jaguar or tapir are infrequently seen, though visitors to Lago Sandoval, an oxbow lake, have the exciting opportunity to see an extended family of resident giant river otters *(lobos de río)*. Lodges within an hour or so of Puerto Maldonado are generally cheaper, but because they are located in secondary jungle and are not nearly as remote, they best serve as introductory visits to the Amazon rainforest.

Tambopata Lodges

- **Explorer's Inn ★★★**, the only lodge located within the Tambopata National Reserve, is a comfortable 30-year-old lodge that hosts both ecotourists and scientists. It's a little over 3 hours upriver from Puerto Maldonado along the River Tambopata and is excellent for viewing fauna, including otters, monkeys, and particularly jungle birds. Accommodations are in rustic, thatched-roof bungalows. Trips are arranged through **Peruvian Safaris,** Alcanfores 459, Miraflores, Lima (✆ **01/447-8888;** www.explorersinn.com or www.peruviansafaris.com), at the edge of the Tambopata Reserve Zone, Prices range from $198 per person for 2 nights to $450 for a 4-night Macaw Clay Lick program.
- **Posada Amazonas ★**, about 2 hours up the Tambopata River from Puerto Maldonado, is owned jointly with the Infierno indigenous community and is quite good for

inexpensive, introductory nature tours. It has an eagle nest site and a canopy observation tower, and two parrot clay licks are within a kilometer of the lodge. The lodge, inaugurated in 1998, features 30 rustic rooms and a wall open to the forest. It is operated by award-winning **Rainforest Expeditions,** Av. Aramburú 166-4B, Miraflores, Lima (✆ **877/870-0578** toll-free in the U.S., or 01/421-8347; www.perunature.com). This veteran ecotourism company promotes tourism with environmental education, research, and conservation and operates two Tambopata lodges. The prices are $295 to $565 for 3- to 5-day trips. The 13-room **Tambopata Research Center ★★★** is more remote (8 hr. upriver from Puerto Maldonado), located just 500m (1,640 ft.) from the jungle's largest and most famous Macaw Clay Lick. Just one of three Peruvian lodges in a protected national nature reserve, it is the best lodge in Tambopata for in-depth tours and viewing wildlife, including several species of monkeys. It's certainly *the* place to see flocks of colorful macaws and parrots. Trips usually entail an overnight at Posada Amazonas before continuing on to the Research Center. Prices are $745 to $945 for 5- to 7-day trips and can be booked through Rainforest Expeditions.

- **Reserva Amazónica ★★** (✆ **01/610-0404** or 800/442-5042 toll-free in the U.S. and Canada; www.inkaterra.com) is less than an hour downriver by boat from Puerto Maldonado. This stylish, luxurious lodge is very professionally run and a great, and supremely comfortable, introduction to the Amazon. Operated by owners of the eco-friendly, upscale Machu Picchu Pueblo Hotel, Reserva Amazónica features the plushest private, African-style bungalow accommodations and coolest dining room and lounge, as well as the best food and wine, in the Peruvian jungle. It also offers massages and spa treatments. Though the immediate jungle in and around the lodge doesn't teem with wildlife (except for sonorous russet-backed Oropendula birds that make waking up a treat), the lodge offers a private monkey island of rescued spider, capuchin, and squirrel monkeys and a superb canopy walk, as well as visits to Sandoval Lake. If you're after creature comforts as well as a taste of nature, this is the best option. Rates range from $337 per night in a standard cabaña to $573 in a swank Amazonia suite (4-day, 3-night packages start at $1,290).
- **Sandoval Lake Lodge ★★**, Calle Ricardo Palma N°1, Urb Santa Monica, Cusco (✆ **01/440-2022** or 877/870-7378 in the U.S.; www.inkanatura.com), is relatively near to Puerto Maldonado—getting there involves a 45-minute boat ride downriver along the Madre de Dios, and then a 1-hour walk and a 30-minute paddle across Sandoval Lake—and is the best option for those hoping to see a good diversity of wildlife and scenery without venturing too deep into the jungle. Located on a bluff overlooking a beautiful oxbow lake ringed by palm trees, the lodge is rustic but comfortable, with two wings of connected rooms open at the ceiling. Wildlife-viewing centers on leisurely paddled catamaran and canoe trips on the lake; most visitors see not only a wealth of aquatic and jungle birds but several species of monkeys, caimans, and the elusive, highly prized community of giant river otters (a family of 10 resides in the lake). Prices range from $178 to $438 for 2- to 4-day stays. InkaNatura's newest lodge is the remote **Heath River Wildlife Center,** situated another 3 hours downriver near the Bolivian border, within easy reach of a large macaw clay lick and owned and staffed by the indigenous Ese'Eja Sonene people; it is possible to combine a couple of nights at either lodge. Heath River prices range from $575 for 4 days to $855 to 6 days. Outside Peru, trips can be organized through **Tropical Nature Travel,** P.O. Box 5276, Gainesville, FL 32627-5276 (✆ **877/827-8350** toll-free in the U.S. and Canada; www.tropicalnaturetravel.com).

8 PUNO & LAKE TITICACA

388km (241 miles) S of Cusco

Puno, founded in the late 17th century following the discovery of nearby silver mines, is a ramshackle town that draws numbers of visitors wholly disproportionate to its own innate attractions. A mostly unlovely city on a high plateau, it has one thing going for it that no other place on earth can claim: Puno hugs the shores of fabled Lake Titicaca, the world's highest navigable body of water, a sterling expanse of deep blue at 3,830m (12,562 ft.) above sea level. The magnificent lake straddles the border of Peru and Bolivia; many Andean travelers move on from Puno to La Paz, going around, or in some cases over, Titicaca. Before leaving Puno, though, almost everyone hops aboard a boat to visit at least one of several ancient island-dwelling peoples. A 2-day tour takes travelers to the Uros floating islands, where Indian communities consisting of just a few families construct tiny islands out of totora reeds; there are two inhabited natural islands, Amantani and Taquile.

Puno has one other thing in its favor. Though dry and often brutally cold, the city is celebrated for its spectacular festivals, veritable explosions of *cultura popular*. The unassuming town, where the people descended from the Aymara from the south and the Quechua from the north, reigns as the capital of Peruvian folklore. Its traditional fiestas, dances, and music—and consequent street partying—are without argument among the most vibrant and uninhibited in Peru. Among those worth planning your trip around are the **Festival de la Virgen de la Candelaria (Candlemas)** ★★★, February 2 to 15; San Juan de Dios, March 8; Fiesta de las Cruces Alasitas, May 8; San Juan, San Pedro, and San Pablo, June 24 to 29; Apóstol Santiago, July 25; and **Puno Week** ★★, celebrating the birth of the city and the Inca empire, November 1 to 7. Of these, Candlemas and Puno Week (especially Nov 5) are the most exceptional and attract the greatest number of visitors.

ESSENTIALS

Getting There

BY PLANE Puno does not have an airport; the nearest is **Aeropuerto Manco Capac** (✆ **054/322-905**) in Juliaca, 45km (28 miles), or about an hour, north of Puno. **LAN** flies daily from Lima and Arequipa to Juliaca. Flights from Lima or Arequipa start at about $280 round-trip. LAN flies from Cusco to Juliaca for similar fares. Tourist buses run from the Juliaca airport to Puno, depositing travelers on Jirón Tacna (S/15).

BY BUS Puno has a modern, safe bus station, **Terminal Terrestre** (✆ **051/364-733**), Jr. Primero de Mayo 703, Barrio Magistral. Road service from Cusco to Puno has greatly improved, and many more tourists now travel by bus, which is faster and cheaper than the train.

The trip between Puno and Arequipa by bus is no longer tortuous; the long-awaited highway between the cities has dramatically shortened travel time from 12 to just 5 hours. **Cruz del Sur** (✆ **01/311-5050;** www.cruzdelsur.com.pe) and **Ormeño** (✆ **01/472-5000;** www.grupo-ormeno.com.pe) make the trip for around S/40.

From Cusco, executive-, imperial-, or royal-class buses make the trip in less than 7 hours (though some services, such as Inka Express, make stop-offs at Inca ruins en route, extending the trip a couple of hours; this is highly recommended if you have the extra time) and cost $45. **Imexso** (✆ **084/240-801;** www.perucuzco.com/imexsotours), **Inka**

Take It Easy

Puno's elevation of 3,300m (10,824 ft.) is nearly as high as Cusco, and unless you've already spent time in the Andes, you'll almost certainly need to rest for at least a day to acclimatize. See "Health Concerns" in "Planning Your Trip to Peru," earlier in this chapter, for further information on how to address altitude sickness.

Express (© **084/247-887;** www.inkaexpress.com), and **Cruz del Sur** operate buses with videos and English-speaking tour guides. **Ormeño** has daily direct departures between Cusco and Puno (6 hr.).

Given the confusing number of bus companies and services, it's wise to make bus reservations with a travel agent. See "Puno Travel Agencies & Tour Operators" on p. 701.

BY TRAIN The Titicaca Route journey from Cusco to Puno, along tracks at an altitude of 3,500m (11,500 ft.), is one of the most scenic in Peru. Though it is slower (10 hr. and prone to late arrivals) and has experienced its share of onboard thievery, it is a favorite of travelers in Peru and preferable to the bus if you've got the time and money. ***Note:*** Keep a careful eye on your bags and, if possible, lock backpacks to the luggage rack. Also keep valuables close to your person.

Peru Rail's Andean Explorer trains (www.perurail.com) from Cusco to Puno depart from **Estación Huanchaq** (© **084/238-722**), at the end of Av. Sol. Service to Puno is Monday, Wednesday, and Saturday from November to March, with an additional run on Fridays from April to October, departing at 8am and arriving at 6pm. Fare is $220 one-way in swank coaches and includes lunch in luxurious dining cars. The Puno train station (© **051/351-041**) is located at Av. La Torre 224.

Getting Around

Few visitors spend more than a day or two in Puno, and get around by foot or taxi. Taxis are inexpensive and plentiful, are easily hailed on the street, and are best used at night and to get back and forth from the hotels out on the banks of Titicaca. Most trips in town cost no more than S/3. Taxis can also be hired for return trips to nearby ruins or for half- or full days. Visits to Lake Titicaca and its islands, as well as the ruins on the outskirts of town, are best done by organized tour; see "Puno Travel Agencies & Tour Operators" on p. 701.

Visitor Information

A small **tourist information office** is located at Pasaje Lima 549 (© **051/365-088**), the pedestrian-only main drag of Puno (at Jr. Deustua, just off the Plaza de Armas), though you're probably better off going to one of the travel agencies that organizes Titicaca and area trips, such as All Ways Travel or Edgar Adventures. See "Puno Travel Agencies & Tour Operators" on p. 701.

For those crossing into Bolivia who need visas or other information, the **Bolivian Consulate** is located at Jr. Arequipa 120 (© **051/351-251**). North Americans and Europeans do not need a visa to enter Bolivia, but the border is a historically problematic one (it was closed for more than a month in 2001 and again in 2005 during the widespread strikes that paralyzed parts of Bolivia), so you may need to check on the status of the crossing before traveling to Bolivia.

FAST FACTS You'll find **banks** and **ATMs** located along Jirón Lima (also called Pasaje Lima), just before the tourist information office. Money changers can generally be found along Jirón Tacna, where most bus stations are located, and the market near the railway and Avenida de los Incas.

For medical attention, go to **Clínica Puno,** Jr. Ramón Castilla 178–180 (✆ **051/368-835**), or **Hospital Nacional,** Av. El Sol 1022 (✆ **051/369-696**). The **tourist police** are located at Jr. Deustua 530 (✆ **051/353-988**).

Pretty fast Internet connections are available at **Qoll@internet,** Jr. Oquendo 340 (Parque Pino), where you can make inexpensive international calls. It's open Monday through Saturday from 8am to midnight and Sunday from 3 to 9pm; rates are S/2 per hour. Other Internet *cabinas* are located along Pasaje Lima. Puno's main **Serpost post office** (✆ **051/351-141**) is located at Moquegua 269; it's open Monday through Saturday from 8am to 8pm. The **Telefónica del Perú** office is on the corner of Moquegua and Arequipa.

WHAT TO SEE & DO IN PUNO

Most of the year, Puno itself is a rather unimpressive place if you don't take into account its enviable geography. The top attractions in Puno are outside the city: Lake Titicaca and the ancient Sillustaini ruins, and there's not much in Puno proper to delay most visitors more than a half-day or so. However, if you stumble upon one of Puno's famously colorful festivals—among the most spectacular in Peru—you may want to linger. (The big ones are worth planning your trip around, but make sure you make hotel and transportation reservations far in advance.)

The large **cathedral,** on the west side of the Plaza de Armas (at the end of Jr. Lima), is the focal point of downtown Puno. The 18th-century baroque church is big, but no great shakes; the elaborate exterior is much more impressive than the spartan, spacious, chilly interior. On the plaza is the 17th-century **La Casa del Corregidor** (✆ **051/351-921**), Deustua 576, purportedly Puno's oldest house, with an impressive Spanish balcony; it now houses a lovely "cultural" cafe and is the best spot in town for a breather. Nearby, the **Museo Municipal Carlos Dryer,** Conde de Lemos 289, is the town's principal (but small) museum. It has a decent selection of pre-Inca ceramics and textiles, as well as mummies with cranial deformations, but it's not very well illuminated. It's open Monday through Friday from 7:30am to 3:30pm; admission is S/5. For a superb view of Lake Titicaca and a vantage point that makes Puno look more attractive than it is, climb the steep hill to **Mirador Kuntur Wasi** and **Huajsapata Park,** about 10 minutes southwest of the main square. On top is a statue of Manco Capac, the first Inca.

Back down below, Jirón Lima is a pedestrianized mall, chock-full of shops, restaurants and bars, that runs from the Plaza de Armas to **Parque Pino,** a relaxed square populated by locals. Puno's seedy **central market** is 2 blocks east, and it spills across several streets. Although not attractive, it's a realistic look at the underbelly of the Peruvian economy. Beyond the railroad tracks is a **market** targeting tourists with all kinds of alpaca and woolen goods, often much cheaper than those found in Cusco and other cities.

LAKE TITICACA ★★★

South America's largest lake and the world's highest navigable body of water, Lake Titicaca has long been considered a sacred place among indigenous Andean peoples. According to Andean legend, Lake Titicaca—which straddles the modern border between Peru and Bolivia—was the birthplace of civilization. Viracocha, the creator deity, lightened a dark world by having the sun, moon, and stars rise from the lake and occupy their places in the sky. The people who live in and around the lake consider themselves descendants of Mama Qota (Sacred Mother), and they believe that powerful spirits live in the lake's depths.

Lake Titicaca is a dazzling sight, worthy of such mystical associations: Its deep azure waters seemingly extend forever across the Altiplano at more than 3,800m (12,540 ft.). The lake covers more than 8,500 sq. km (3,282 sq. miles); it is 176km (109 miles) long and 50km (31 miles) wide. The sun is extraordinarily intense at this altitude, scorching off 600 cubic m (21,000 cubic ft.) of water per second. Daybreak and sunset, as the sun sinks low into the horizon, are particularly stunning to witness.

Lake Titicaca has been inhabited for thousands of years. Totora reed boats roamed the lake as early as 2500 B.C. Titicaca's 16 islands—both man-made and natural—are home to several communities of Quechua and Aymara Indians, groups with remarkably different traditions and ways of life. Visiting them, and staying overnight on one of the islands if you can, is one of the highlights of Peru and one of the most unique experiences in South America.

The most convenient way to visit is by an inexpensive and well-run guided tour, arranged by one of several travel agencies in Puno; see "Puno Travel Agencies & Tour Operators" on p. 701. Although it is possible to arrange independent travel, the low cost and easy organization of a group don't encourage it. Even if you go on your own, you'll inevitably fall in with groups, and your experience won't differ radically. You can go on a half-day tour of the **Uros floating islands** or a full-day tour that combines **Taquile Island,** but the best way to experience Lake Titicaca's unique indigenous life is to stay at least 1 night on either Taquile or Amantani, preferably in the home of a local family. Those with more time and money to burn may want to explore the singular experience of staying on private **Isla Suasi,** home to little more than a solar-powered hotel and a dozen llamas and vicuñas.

Uros Floating Islands (Las Islas Flotantes) ★

As improbable as it sounds, the Uros Indians of Lake Titicaca live on floating "islands" made by hand from totora reeds that grow in abundance in the shallow waters of Lake Titicaca. This unique practice has endured since the time of the Incas, and today, there are some 45 floating islands in the Bay of Puno. The islands first came into contact with the modern world in the mid-1960s, and their inhabitants now live mostly off tourism. To some visitors, this obvious dependency is a little unseemly. Many visitors faced with this strange sight conclude that the impoverished islanders can't possibly still live on the islands, that it must be a show created for their benefit. True, they can seem to be little more than floating souvenir stands; the communities idly await the arrival of tourist boats and then seek to sell them handmade textiles and reed-crafted items while the gringos walk gingerly about the spongy islands—truly a strange sensation—photographing the Uros's houses and children.

But it's not just a show. A couple hundred Titicaca natives continue to live year-round on the islands, even if they venture to Puno for commercial transactions. The largest island, Huacavacani, has homes and a floating Seventh-day Adventist church, a candidate for one of the more bizarre scenes you're likely to find in Peru—or anywhere. Others islands have schools, a post office, a public telephone, and souvenir shops. Only a few islands are set up to receive tourists, though. The vast majority of the Uros people live in continued isolation and peace, away from curious onlookers and camera lenses.

Tips Traveling to Bolivia

Plenty of travelers continue on to Bolivia, which shares Lake Titicaca with Peru, from Puno; several travel agencies in Puno sell packages and bus tickets. The most common and scenic route is from Puno to La Paz via Yunguyo and Copacabana. The trip to La Paz takes 7 or 8 hours by bus. You can also go by a combination of overland travel and hydrofoil or catamaran, a unique but very time-consuming journey (13 hr.). At the border, visitors get an exit stamp from Peru and a tourist visa (30 days) from Bolivia. Foreigners are commonly tapped for phony departure and entry fees; resist the corrupt attempts. For more information on Bolivia, see chapter 5.

The Uros, who fled to the middle of the lake to escape conflicts with the Collas and Incas, long ago began intermarrying with the Aymara Indians, and many have now converted to Catholicism. Fishermen and birders, the Uros live grouped by family sectors, and entire families live in one-room, tentlike, thatched huts constructed on the shifting reed island that floats beneath. They build modest houses and boats with fanciful animal-head bows out of the reeds and continually replenish the fast-rotting mats that form their fragile islands. Visitors might be surprised, to say the least, to find some huts outfitted with TVs powered by solar panels (donated by the Fujimori administration after a presidential visit to the islands).

Inexpensive tours that go only to the Uros Islands last about 3 hours and include hotel pickup, an English-speaking guide, and motorboat transportation to the islands. Unless you're unusually pressed for time, it's much more enjoyable and informative to visit the Uros as a brief stop en route to the natural islands of Amantani or Taquile.

Taquile Island (Isla Taquile) ★★★

Taquile is a fascinating and stunningly beautiful island about 4 hours from Puno. The island is only 1km (a half mile) wide and about 6km (3¾ miles) long. It rises to a high point of 264m (870 ft.), and the hillsides are laced with formidable Inca stone agricultural terraces. The island is a rugged ruddy color, which contrasts spectacularly with the blue lake and sky. Taquile is littered with Inca and pre-Inca stone ruins.

The island is as serene as the views. Taquile has been inhabited for 10,000 years, and life remains starkly traditional; there are no vehicles and no electricity, and islanders (who number slightly more than 1,000) quietly go about their business. Taquile natives allow tourists to stay at private houses (in primitive but not uncomfortable conditions), and there are a number of simple restaurants near the central plaza. Though friendly to outsiders, the Quechua-speaking islanders remain a famously reserved and insular community. Their dress is equally famous—Taquile textiles are some of the finest in Peru. Men wear embroidered, woven red waistbands *(fajas),* and embroidered, wool stocking caps that indicate marital status: red for married men, red and white for bachelors. Women wear layered skirts and black shawls over their heads. Taquile textiles are much sought-after for their hand-woven quality, but they are considerably more expensive than mass-produced handicrafts in other parts of Peru. There's a cooperative shop on the main plaza, and stalls are set up during festivals. Locals are more reluctant to haggle than artisans in other parts of Peru.

If you are lucky enough to catch a festival on the island, you will be treated to a festive and traditional pageant of color, with picturesque dances and women twirling in circles, revealing as many as 16 layered, multicolored skirts. Easter, Fiesta de Santiago (July 25), August 1 and 2, and New Year's are the best celebrations. Any time on the island, though, is a splendid and unique experience—especially once the day-trippers have departed and you have the island and incomparable views and stars virtually to yourself. Taquile then seems about as far away from modernity and "civilization" as you can travel on this planet.

Access to the island from the boat dock is either by a long path that wends around the island or by an amazing 533-step stone staircase that climbs to the top, passing through two stone arches with astonishing views of the lake. Independent travelers sign in and pay a nominal fee. Those wishing to spend the night can arrange for a family-house stay; expect to rough it a bit without proper showers. Many islanders do not speak Spanish, and English is likely to be met with blank stares.

Most single-day tours of the Uros and Taquile islands depart early in the morning and stop at the islands of Uros for a half-hour en route. For most visitors, a day trip—which allows only 1 or 2 hours on the island and 8 hours of boat time—is too grueling and insufficient to appreciate the beauty and culture of Taquile Island.

Amantani Island (Isla Amantani) ★★

Amantani, a circular island about 4½ hours from Puno (and about 2 hr. from Taquile), is home to a very different but equally fascinating Titicaca community. Also handsomely terraced and home to farmers, fishers, and weavers, in many ways Amantani is even more rustic and unspoiled than Taquile. It is a beautiful place, with a handful of villages composed of about 800 families and ruins clinging to the island's two peaks, Pachatata and Pachamama (Father Earth and Mother Earth). The islanders, who for the most part understand Spanish, are more open and approachable than natives of Taquile.

Amantani is best visited on a tour that allows you to spend the night (visiting the Uros islands en route) and travel the next day to Taquile. Tour groups place groups of four or five travelers with local families for overnight stays. Not only will the family prepare your simple meals, you will be invited to a friendly dance in the village meeting place. Most families dress up their guests in local outfits—women in layered, multicolored, embroidered skirts and blouses, and the men in wool ponchos—for the event. Though the evening is obviously staged for tourists' benefit, it's low-key and charming rather than cheesy. It's a good idea to bring small gifts for your family on Amantani, since they make little from stays and must alternate with other families on the island. Pens, pencils, and batteries all make good gifts. The tour price normally includes accommodations, lunch and an evening meal on the first day, and breakfast the following morning.

SILLUSTANI RUINS ★

Just beyond Puno are mysterious pre-Inca ruins called *chullpas* (funeral towers). The finest sit on the windswept Altiplano on a peninsula in Lake Umayo at Sillustani, 32km (20 miles) from Puno. The Colla people—a warrior tribe who spoke Aymara—buried their elite in giant cylindrical tombs, some as tall as 12m (40 ft.). The Collas dominated the Titicaca region before the arrival of the Incas. After burying their dead along with foodstuffs, jewels, and other possessions, they sealed the towers. The stone masonry is exquisite; many archaeologists and historians find them more complex than and superior to Inca engineering. The structures form quite an impression on such a harsh landscape.

The best way to visit Sillustani is by guided tour, usually in the afternoon; see "Puno Travel Agencies & Tour Operators," below. Dress warmly, as the wind gets bitter here.

PUNO TRAVEL AGENCIES & TOUR OPERATORS

Most travel agencies in Puno handle the conventional tours of Lake Titicaca and Sillustani, along with a handful of other ruins programs. Two of the best agencies are All Ways Travel and Edgar Adventures. **All Ways Travel ★★**, Jr. Deustua 576 (in courtyard of La Casa del Corregidor; ✆ **051/353-979;** www.titicacaperu.com), and Jr. Tacna 234 (✆ **051/355-552**), is run by the very friendly and helpful Víctor Pauca and his daughter Eliana. They offer well thought-out, progressive cultural trips in addition to the standard tours. **Edgar Adventures,** Jr. Lima 328 (✆ **051/353-444;** www.edgaradventures.com), is run by a Peruvian husband-and-wife team. Both can arrange bus and air travel as well, including travel to Bolivia. Uros Islands group trips cost about $12 per person; full-day Uros Floating Reed Islands/Taquile Island trips are $25 per person; 2-day, 1-night Uros, Amantani, and Taquile islands trips are $30 to $35 per person; and 3-hour Sillustani tours are $12 per person.

WHERE TO STAY

Puno has grown rapidly as a tourist destination in the past few years, and its accommodations are no longer geared almost exclusively toward the backpacker crowd. A couple of good midrange options are in town, but if you don't mind relying on taxis to get back and forth, the best options are out on the banks of Lake Titicaca (about a 10-minute cab ride).

Expensive

Casa Andina Private Collection Puno ★★ Value This low-slung and attractively rustic place is perched over Titicaca and has marvelous lake views from its deck, dining room, and, especially, the single enormous suite, which has a large Jacuzzi and is the perfect place to splurge (a bit) and feel like a gazillionaire (a lot). Regular rooms are spacious but not pretentious and are decorated in a warm, Andean style. (Be sure to ask for a room with a lake view.) The gourmet restaurant, which concentrates on local ingredients and lake fish, is as good if not better than anything else in town. While Casa Andina is similar to the nearby Posada del Inca, it is considerably newer and has a couple of singular amenities, including a pier, with its own floating island a la Uros, extending over the lake, and a private train station—so that if you're coming from Cusco, you can get off right at the hotel without having to go into Puno. After a long train ride, that's a nice little bonus.

Av. Sesquicentenario 1970–72, Sector Huaje, Lake Titicaca (Puno). ✆ **051/363-992,** or 01/213-9739 for reservations; or 866/447-3270 toll-free in the U.S. and Canada. Fax 051/364-082. www.casa-andina.com. 46 units. $91–$186 double; $318 suite. Rates include breakfast buffet. AE, DC, MC, V. **Amenities:** Restaurant; bar; concierge; room service. *In room:* A/C, TV, fridge, hair dryer, Wi-Fi.

Sonesta Posadas del Inca ★★ Kids Value Posadas del Inca is perched on the shores of Titicaca, but it fits more sensitively into its enviable surroundings. Opened in 1999, it is imaginatively designed, with warm colors and Peruvian touches, including bright modern art and folk artifacts. Rooms are large and comfortable, and bathrooms are also large and nicely equipped. The restaurant and many rooms look over the lake; other rooms have views of the mountains. The relaxed lobby has a cozy fireplace. Service is friendly, and the staff can arrange visits to Titicaca's islands. Children will enjoy the miniversion of a floating lake community on the grounds by the lake.

Sesquicentenario 610, Sector Huaje, Lake Titicaca. ✆ **051/364-111** or 800/SONESTA (766-3782) in the U.S. and Canada. Fax 051/363-672. www.sonesta.com. 62 units. $99–$125 double. Children 7 and under stay free in parent's room. Rates include breakfast buffet. AE, DC, MC, V. **Amenities:** Restaurant; cocktail lounge; concierge; room service. *In room:* A/C, TV, fridge, hair dryer.

Moderate

Casa Andina Classic Puno Tikarani ★ Value This Peruvian chain of popular and comfortable midsize hotels, with good service and impeccable rooms, has two locations in downtown Puno; this branch, 4 blocks from the Plaza de Armas, is the larger and quieter of the two. (The other, Casa Andina Puno Plaza, on Jr. Grau 270, is just a short block from the square and one off the main pedestrian drag.) As always, the rooms are good-sized, extremely clean, and well equipped. Those on the second floor in the interior are quietest.

Jr. Independencia 185. ✆ **051/367-803,** or 01/213-9739 for reservations. Fax 051/365-333. www.casa-andina.com. 53 units. $65–$86 double. Rates include breakfast buffet. AE, DC, MC, V. **Amenities:** Concierge. *In room:* A/C, TV, fridge, hair dryer.

Inexpensive

Hostal Los Uros One of the most popular Puno hostels targeting backpackers, Los Uros represents a good value at the low end. The basic rooms are clean, beds are pretty decent, the place is quiet, and if you get chilly, the staff will dole out extra wool blankets. Rooms have either private or shared bathrooms. Your best bet for hot water is in the evening. Breakfast is available at the simple cafeteria.

Jr. Teodoro Valcarcel 135, Puno. ✆ **051/352-141.** Fax 051/367-016. 24 units. S/50 double with private bathroom; S/40 with shared bathroom. Rates include taxes. No credit cards. **Amenities:** Cafeteria. *In room:* No phone.

WHERE TO DINE

Most of Puno's more attractive restaurants, popular with gringos, are located on the pedestrian-only main drag, Jirón Lima. In addition to those listed below, check out the two restaurants at Hotel Colón Inn.

Moderate

Apu Salkantay PERUVIAN/INTERNATIONAL In a new, chic location on the same street, this restaurant, named for a Quechua mountain god, attracts plenty of people for drinks next to the fireplace-stove. But it's also a good place for Peruvian dishes, such as *cuy,* alpaca steak with quinoa, and alpaca *piqueo* with fries, onions, tomatoes, and peppers; and standard soups, pizza, pasta, and basic fish (king fish and trout). The daily *menú* includes a soft drink, bread, and main course.

Jr. Lima 425. ✆ **051/363-955.** Reservations not accepted. Main courses S/21–S/30; daily *menú* S/24. DC, MC, V. Daily 9am–10pm.

Incabar ★ NOVO ANDINO/INTERNATIONAL Awfully stylish and downright funky for rough-around-the-edges Puno, this lounge bar/restaurant aims high. The menu is much more creative and flavorful than other places in town (even if dishes don't always succeed), with interesting sauces for lake fish and alpaca steak, curried dishes, and artful presentations. For a recent meal, I had a spinach-and-tomato-cream soup and *atravezados de pollo*—chicken rolls marinated in sesame, ginger, and garlic and served with pineapple, peppers, and rice. Incabar is also a good place to hang out, have a beer or coffee, and write postcards—the back room has comfortable sofas. Breakfast is also served. Also check out the owners' other restaurant down the street, Colors Lounge, Lima 342.

Jr. Lima 356. ✆ **051/368-865.** Reservations recommended. Main courses S/22–S/35. AE, DC, MC, V. Daily 9am–10pm.

Ukuku's ★ PIZZA/PERUVIAN In a second-story space overlooking Jirón Lima, the main drag, this large, relaxed pizzeria has pizzas from a wood-burning oven, but also offers a full menu of Peruvian specialties, such as alpaca steak cooked in red wine, *ceviche,* and even *chifa* (Peruvian Chinese cooking). If that's not enough, you can also get a passable plate of pasta. A second location is at Libertad 216.

Jr. Grau 172 (at Jr. Lima). ✆ **051/367-373.** Reservations not accepted. Main courses S/12–S/27. MC, V. Daily 11am–10pm.

Inexpensive

Pizzería El Buho Value PIZZA/ITALIAN El Buho's new location is bigger and a bit less cozy, but its wood-burning oven/chimney still kicks out some of Puno's best pizzas. It's extremely popular with both gringos and locals. The menu also lists a good number of pastas and handful of soups, but I swear I've never seen anyone have anything other than pizza.

Jr. Lima 371. ✆ **051/363-955.** Reservations not accepted. Main courses S/12–S/28. DC, V. Daily 4:30–11pm.

9 AREQUIPA

1,020km (632 miles) SE of Lima; 521km (323 miles) S of Cusco; 297km (184 miles) SW of Puno

The southern city of Arequipa, the second largest in Peru, may well be the country's most handsome. Founded in 1540, it retains an elegant historic center constructed almost entirely of *sillar* (a porous, white volcanic stone), which gives the city its distinctive look and nickname *la ciudad blanca,* or the white city. Colonial churches and the sumptuous 16th-century Santa Catalina convent gleam beneath palm trees and a brilliant sun. Ringing the city, in full view, are three delightfully named snowcapped volcanic peaks: El Misti, Chachani, and Pichu Pichu, all of which hover around 6,000m (20,000 ft.).

Arequipa has emerged as a favorite of outdoors enthusiasts who come to climb volcanoes, raft on rivers, trek through the valleys, and above all, head out to Colca Canyon—twice as deep as the Grand Canyon and the best place in South America to see giant condors soar overhead. Suiting its reputation as an outdoor paradise, Arequipa enjoys weather that is Southern California perfect: more than 300 days a year of sunshine, huge blue skies, and low humidity. Arequipa looks very much the part of a desert oasis.

The commercial capital of the south, Arequipa not only looks different; it feels dissimilar from the rest of Peru. Arequipeños have earned a reputation as aloof and distrusting of the centralized power in Lima. Relatively wealthy and a place of prominent intellectuals, politicians, and industrialists, Arequipa has a haughty air about it—at least in the view of many Peruvians who hail from less distinguished places.

As beautiful and confident as it is, Arequipa has not escaped disaster. The most recent devastating earthquake (which registered 8.1 on the Richter scale) struck the city and other points farther south in June 2001. Though international reports at the time painted a picture of a city that had caved in on itself, thankfully, that wasn't the case. The colonial core of the city survived intact, as elegant as ever.

ESSENTIALS

Getting There

BY PLANE **Aeropuerto Rodríquez Ballón** (✆ **054/443-464** or 054/443-458), Av. Aviación s/n, Zamácola, Cerro Colorado, is about 7km (4 miles) northwest of the city. There are daily flights to and from Lima, Juliaca, and Cusco on **LAN** (✆ **01/213-8200;** www.lan.com).

From the airport, transportation is by taxi (about $5) or shared *colectivo* service (about $2 per person) to downtown hotels.

BY BUS The main **Terminal Terrestre** (✆ 054/427-798), Av. Andrés Avelino Cáceres, at Av. Arturo Ibáñez s/n, is about 4km (2½ miles) south of downtown Arequipa; nearby is a newer station, **Nuevo Terrapuerto** (✆ 054/348-810), Av. Arturo Ibáñez s/n. Both stations are on Av. Andrés Cáceres (Parque Industrial). A huge number of bus companies travel in and out of Peru's second city from across the country, and you'll need to ask if leaving Arequipa by bus whether it departs from Terminal or Terrapuerto. From Lima (16 hr.), recommended companies include **Ormeño** (✆ 01/472-5000; www.grupo-ormeno.com.pe), **Cruz del Sur** (✆ 01/311-5050; www.cruzdelsur.com.pe), **Civa** (✆ 01/418-1111; www.civa.com.pe), and **Oltursa** (✆ 01/708-5000; www.oltursa.com.pe); from Puno and Juliaca (5 hr.), **Civa, Cruz del Sur,** and **Julsa** (✆ 054/430-843); from Cusco (10–12 hr.), **Cruz del Sur**; and from Chivay/Colca Canyon (3–4 hr.), **Reyna** (✆ 054/426-549), and **Cristo Rey** (✆ 054/213-094).

Getting Around

Arequipa is compact, and most of its top attractions can easily be seen on foot. Taxis are inexpensive and plentiful, easily hailed on the street, and best used at night. Most trips in town cost no more than S/5. To call a taxi at night, try **Taxi Seguro** (✆ **054/450-250**), **Taxi Sur** (✆ **054/465-656**), **Master Taxi** (✆ **054/220-505**), or **Ideal Taxi** (✆ **054/288-888**).

A car isn't necessary in Arequipa unless you wish to explore the countryside, especially Colca and/or Cotahuasi canyons, independently. Try **Lucava Rent-A-Car,** Aeropuerto and Centro Comercial Cayma no. 10 (✆ **054/663-378**); or **Avis,** Aeropuerto (✆ **054/443-576**) and Palacio Viejo 214 (✆ **054/282-519**).

Visitor Information

There's a **tourist information booth** at the Aeropuerto Rodríquez Ballón, Calle Moral 316 (✆ **054/444-564**), open Monday through Friday from 9am to 4pm. There's also an office at Portal de la Municipalidad 112 (✆ **054/211-021**), on the Plaza de Armas across from the cathedral; it's open daily from 8am to 6pm. The best information office in town is in **Casona de Santa Catalina,** Santa Catalina 210 (across from the Convent; ✆ **054/221-227**); it's open daily from 9am to 9pm. The **tourist police,** Jerusalén 315 at the corner of Ugarte (✆ **054/201-258**), also give out maps and tourism information.

FAST FACTS You'll find ATMs in the courtyards of the historic Casa Ricketts, San Francisco 108, now the offices of **Banco Continental.** Other banks in the historic center include **Banco Latino** at San Juan de Dios 112 and **Banco de Crédito** at San Juan de

A Note of Caution

Arequipa's bus stations—as well as the buses themselves—are said to be notorious for attracting thieves (though I've never encountered any difficulties). Travelers are advised to pay very close attention to their belongings, even going so far as to lock them to luggage racks. The route between Arequipa and Puno especially has earned a bad reputation. It's best to opt for more exclusive and safer, as well as more expensive, first-class seats on the more upscale bus companies recommended above.

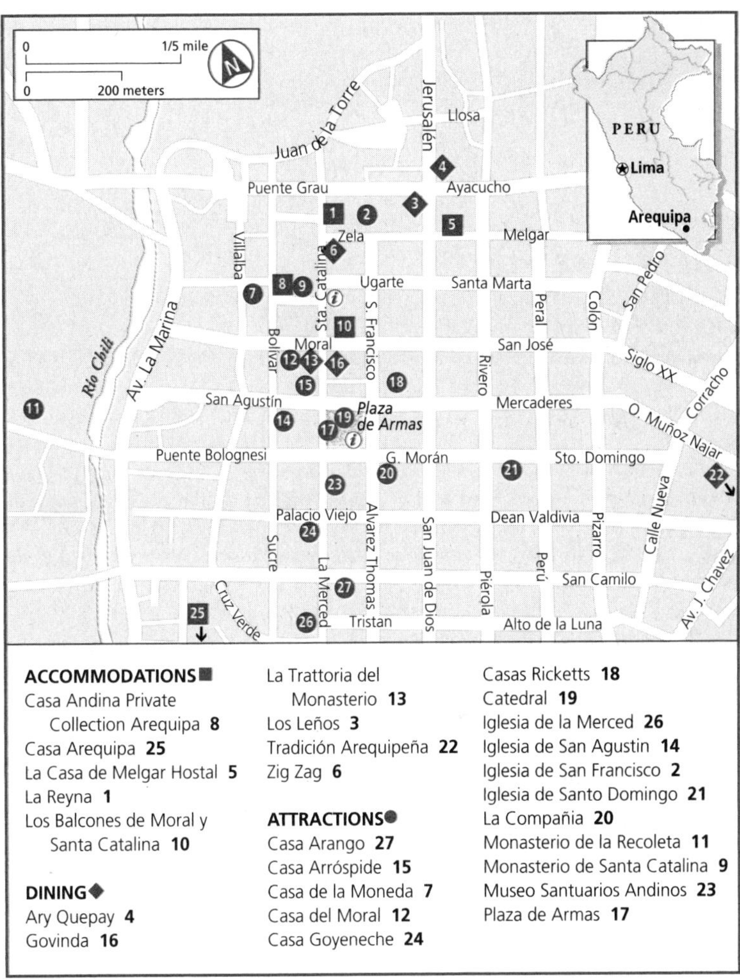

Dios and General Morán 101. Money changers can generally be found waving calculators and stacks of dollars on the Plaza de Armas and major streets leading off the main square. There are several *casas de cambio* (money-exchange houses) near the Plaza de Armas, and Global Net ATMs in several shops around the Plaza.

In an emergency, call **Policía Nacional** at ✆ **054/254-020** or **Policía de Turismo,** Jerusalén 315 at the corner of Ugarte, at ✆ **054/201-258.** For medical attention, go to **Clínica Arequipa,** Avenida Bolognesi at Puente Grau (✆ **054/253-416**), **Hospital Regional,** Av. Daniel Alcides Carrión s/n (✆ **054/231-818**), or **Hospital General,** Peral/Don Bosco (✆ **054/231-818**).

Arequipa has plenty of Internet *cabinas.* Two of the cheapest and fastest are **La Red,** Jerusalén 306B (✆ **054/286-700**), and **TravelNet,** Jerusalén 218 (✆ **054/205-548**). Another good spot is **Catedral Internet,** Pasaje Catedral 101 (✆ **054/282-074**), in the small passageway behind the cathedral. Most *cabinas* are open daily from 8am to 10pm, charge S/2 per hour, and have Net2Phone or other programs allowing very cheap Web-based international phone calls.

The main Serpost **post office** is located at Moral 118 (✆ **054/215-247**); it's open Monday through Saturday from 8am to 8pm and Sunday from 9am to 1pm. There's a **DHL** office at Santa Catalina 115 (✆ **054/220-045**). The **Telefónica del Perú** main offices are located at Av. Los Arces 200 B, Cayma district (✆ **054/252-020**).

WHAT TO SEE & DO

The Top Attractions

Casa del Moral ★ An extraordinary mestizo-baroque mansion, built in 1733 by a Spanish knight and nicely restored with period detail in 1994, Casa del Moral offers one of the best windows onto colonial times in Arequipa. Named for an ancient mulberry tree—the *moral* found in the courtyard—the home is also distinguished by a magnificent stone portal with heraldic emblems carved in *sillar.* Handsome furnishings, carved wooden doors, and Cusco School oil paintings decorate large salons, built around a beautiful courtyard in the largest of the colonial residences in the city. Look for 17th-century maps that depict the borders and shapes of countries quite differently from their usual representations today. A second courtyard, painted cobalt blue, was used as the summer patio. Climb to the rooftop for a great view of Arequipa and the surrounding volcanoes. Visits are by guided tour (at no extra cost).

Calle Moral 318 (at Bolívar). ✆ **054/210-084.** Admission S/5 adults, S/3 students. Mon–Sat 9am–5pm; Sun 9am–1pm.

Monasterio de la Recoleta ★ Across the Río Chili from the historic center of town, distinguished by its tall brick red-and-white steeple, is the Recoleta convent museum. It's only a 10-minute walk or short cab ride from the Plaza de Armas. Founded in 1648 and rebuilt after earthquakes, the peaceful Franciscan convent contains impressive cloisters with *sillar* columns and lovely gardens; today, just four of the original seven remain. The convent museum comprises several collections. In one room is a collection of pre-Inca culture artifacts, including funereal masks, textiles, and totems; in another are mummies and a series of paintings of the 12 Inca chieftains. At the rear of the convent is a small Amazonian museum, stocked with curious items collected by Franciscan missionaries in the Amazon basin. The missionaries were understandably fascinated by prehistoric-looking fish, crocodiles, and piranhas, and the clothing of indigenous communities. Those souvenirs pose an interesting contrast to the Dominicans' fine library containing some 20,000 volumes, including rare published texts from the 15th century. Guides (tip basis) are available for 1-hour tours in English, Spanish, and French.

Recoleta 117. ✆ **054/270-966.** Admission adults S/5, students S/3, free for seniors. Mon–Sat 9am–noon and 3–5pm.

Monasterio de Santa Catalina ★★★ Kids Arequipa's stellar and serene Convent of Santa Catalina, founded in 1579 under the Dominican order, is the most important and impressive religious monument in Peru. This is not just another church complex; it is more like a small, labyrinthine village, with narrow cobblestone streets, plant-lined passageways, pretty plazas and fountains, chapels, and cloisters. Tall, thick walls, painted sunburned orange, cobalt blue, and brick red, hide dozens of small cells where more than 200 sequestered nuns once lived. Built in 1569, the convent remained a mysterious world unto itself until 1970, when local authorities forced the sisters to install modern infrastructure, a requirement that led to opening the convent for tourism. Today, only a couple of dozen cloistered nuns remain, out of sight of the hundreds of tourists who arrive daily to explore the huge and curious complex.

Santa Catalina feels like a small village in Andalucía, Spain, with its predominantly *mudéjar* (Moorish-Christian) architecture, intense sunlight and shadows, and streets named for Spanish cities. In all, it contains 3 cloisters, 6 streets, 80 housing units, a square, an art gallery, and a cemetery. Though the nuns entered the convent having taken vows of poverty, they lived in relative luxury, having paid a dowry to live the monastic life amid servants (who outnumbered the nuns), well-equipped kitchens, and art collections. Today, the convent has been nicely restored, though it retains a rustic appeal. Visitors are advised to wait for an informative guided tour (in English and other languages, available for a tip), though it's also transfixing just to wander around, especially before the crowds arrive. Of particular note are the Orange Tree Cloister, with mural paintings over the arches; Calle Toledo, a long boulevard with a communal *lavandería* at its end, where the sisters washed their clothes in halved earthenware jugs; the 17th-century kitchen with charred walls; and the rooms belonging to Sor Ana, a 17th-century nun at the convent who was beatified by Pope John Paul II and is on her way to becoming a saint. Visitors can enter the choir room of the church, but it's difficult to get a good look at the main chapel and its marvelous painted cupola. To see the church, slip in during early morning mass (daily at 7:30am); the cloistered nuns remain secluded behind a wooden grille. Allow a couple of hours or more here.

Santa Catalina 301. ✆ **054/608-282.** www.santacatalina.org.pe. Admission S/30. Fri–Mon 9am–5pm; Tues–Thurs 8am–8pm.

Museo Santuarios Andinos ★★ Kids Now in a new location south of the Plaza de Armas, the Museum of Andean Sanctuaries features a small collection of fascinating exhibits, including mummies and artifacts from the Inca empire, but it is dominated by one tiny girl: Juanita, the Ice Maiden of Ampato. The victim of a ritualistic sacrifice by Inca priests high on the volcano Mount Ampato and buried in ice at 6,380m (20,926 ft.), Juanita—named after the leader of the expedition, Johan Rhinehard—was discovered in almost perfect condition in September 1995 after the eruption of the nearby Sabancay Volcano melted ice on the peak. Juanita had lain buried in the snow for more than 550 years. Only Inca priests were allowed to ascend to such a high point, where the gods were believed to have lived. Juanita, who became famous worldwide through a *National Geographic* report on the find, died from a violent blow to the head; she was 13 at the time of her death. Her remarkable preservation has allowed researchers to gain great insights into Inca culture by analyzing her DNA. Today, she is kept in a glass-walled freezer chamber here, less a mummy than a frozen body, in astoundingly good condition, nearly 600 years old. Displayed nearby and in adjacent rooms are some of the superb doll offerings and burial items found alongside Juanita's corpse and those of three other sacrificial victims also found on the mountain. Guided visits, which begin with a good *National Geographic* film, are mandatory. Allow about an hour for your visit.

La Merced 110. ✆ **054/200-345.** Admission S/15 adults, S/5 students, free for seniors. Mon–Sat 9am–6pm; Sun 9am–3pm.

Tips Arequipa's Colonial Churches

Arequipa has a wealth of colonial churches that are well worth a visit if you have the time. They include **Iglesia de San Francisco** (Zela 103), built of *sillar* and brick in the 16th century with an impressive all-silver altar and a beautiful vaulted ceiling; **Iglesia de San Agustín** (at the corner of San Agustín and Sucre), with a superbly stylized baroque facade, an excellent example of 16th- and 17th-century mestizo architecture (it was rebuilt in 1898 after earthquake damage and was restored, with an unfortunate new bell tower, again in October 2005); **Iglesia de Santo Domingo** (at Santo Domingo and Piérola), with a handsome 1734 cloisters, and **Iglesia de La Merced** (La Merced 303).

Plaza de Armas ★★★ Arequipa's grand Plaza de Armas, an elegant and symmetrical square of gardens and a central fountain lined by arcaded buildings on three sides, is the focus of the city's urban life. Dominated by the massive, 17th-century neoclassical **Catedral ★**, it is perhaps the loveliest main square in Peru, even though its profile suffered considerable damage when the great earthquake of 2001 felled one of the cathedral's two towers and whittled the other to a delicate pedestal. The cathedral, previously devastated by fire and other earthquakes, has now been fully restored to its original grandeur. The cathedral is open Monday to Saturday from 7 to 11:30am and 5 to 7:30pm, Sunday from 7am to 1pm and 5 to 7pm.

La Compañía ★★, just off the plaza at the corner of Alvarez Thomas and General Morán, opposite the cathedral, is a splendid 17th-century Jesuit church with an elaborate (plateresque) facade carved of *sillar* stone. The magnificent portal, one of the finest in Peru, shows the end date of the church's construction, 1698, more than a century after work began on it. The interior holds a handsome carved cedar main altar, bathed in gold leaf, and two impressive chapels: the Capilla de San Ignacio, which has a remarkable painted cupola, and the Capilla Real, or Royal Chapel. Next door to the church are the stately Jesuit cloisters, of stark *sillar* construction, now housing upscale boutiques (enter on Calle Morán). Climb to the top for good views of the city's rooftops and distant volcanoes. The church is open Monday through Saturday from 9 to 11am and 3 to 6pm.

Shopping

Arequipa is one of the best places in Peru to shop for top-quality baby alpaca, vicuña, and woolen goods. Many items are more expensive than the lesser-quality goods sold in other parts of Peru. In Arequipa, though, you'll find nicer designs and export-quality knit sweaters, shawls, blankets, and scarves. Arequipa also has good leather goods and several excellent antiques shops featuring colonial pieces and even older items (remember, though, that these antiques cannot legally be exported from Peru).

Three general areas are particularly good for alpaca items. One is the cloisters next to La Compañía church at General Morán and San Juan de Dios, housing several alpaca boutiques and outlets. Another is Pasaje Catedral, the pedestrian mall just behind the cathedral. A third is Calle Santa Catalina. Shops with fine alpaca items include **Millma's Baby Alpaca,** Pasaje Catedral 177 (**© 054/205-134**); **Baby Alpaca Boutique,** Santa

House Tour: Arequipa's Other Colonial Mansions

Arequipa possesses one of the most attractive and harmonious colonial nuclei in Peru. Several extraordinary seigniorial houses were constructed in white *sillar* stone. They are predominantly flat-roofed single-story structures, a design that has helped them withstand the effects of frequent earthquakes that would have toppled less solid buildings. Most of these houses have attractive interior patios and elaborately carved facades. Best equipped for visitors is the restored **Casa del Moral** (see above), but several others are worth a look, especially if you have an interest in colonial architecture.

Just off the main square, **Casa Ricketts** (also called **Casa Tristán del Pozo;** San Francisco 108), a former seminary and today the offices of Banco Continental, is one of the finest colonial homes in Arequipa. Built in the 1730s, its beautiful portal, perhaps Arequipa's finest expression of colonial civil architecture, has delicate representations of the life of Jesus. Inside are two large, beautiful courtyards with gargoyle drainage pipes. On the other side of the cathedral, **Casa Arróspide** (also called **Casa Iriberry;** at the corner of Santa Catalina 101 at San Agustín), built in the late 18th century, is one of the most distinguished *sillar* mansions in the city. Now the **Cultural Center of San Agustín University** (✆ **054/204-482**), it hosts temporary exhibits of contemporary art and photography; you'll also find an art shop and nice cafe with a terrace and great views over the top of the cathedral. Other colonial houses of interest include **Casa Arango** (Consuelo at La Merced), a squat and eclectic 17th-century home; **Casa Goyeneche** (La Merced 201), now the offices of Banco de Reserva; and **Casa de la Moneda** (Ugarte at Villaba).

About a 15-minute cab ride outside of town, in Huasacache, is the **Mansión del Fundador** (✆ **054/442-460**), one of the most important *sillar* mansions in Arequipa. Said to have been constructed by the founder of Arequipa, Manuel de Carbajal, for his son, it features terrific vaulted ceilings and a large interior patio. The house is open daily from 9am to 5pm; admission is S/10.

Catalina 208 (✆ **054/206-716**); **Anselmo's Souvenirs,** Pasaje Catedral 119 (no phone); and an outlet store of the chain **Alpaca 111,** Calle Zela 212 (✆ **054/223-238**).

For antiques, Calle Santa Catalina and nearby streets have several antiques shops. I found lots of items I wished I could have taken home at **Curiosidades,** Zela 207 (✆ **054/952-986**); **Alvaro Valdivia Montoya**'s two shops at Santa Catalina 204 and Santa Catalina 217 (✆ **054/229-103**); and **Arte Colonial,** Santa Catalina 312 (✆ **054/214-887**).

There is a general handicrafts market with dozens of stalls in the old town jail, next door to the Plazuela de San Francisco (between Zela and Puente Grau). For handmade leather goods, stroll along Puente Bolognesi, which leads west from the Plaza de Armas, and you'll find numerous small stores with handbags, shoes, and other items.

A very good bookstore with art books and English-language paperbacks is **Librería El Lector,** San Francisco 221 (✆ **054/288-677**).

WHERE TO STAY

Arequipa has an ample roster of hotels and hostels at all levels. Several occupy historic houses in the old quarter. The area north of the Plaza de Armas is nicer and less chaotic and commercial than the streets south of the square. If you hop in a taxi from the airport or bus or train station, insist on going to the hotel of your choice; taxi drivers will often claim that a particular hotel is closed in order to take you to one that will pay them a commission.

Expensive

Casa Andina Private Collection Arequipa ★★★ Inaugurated in 2008, this upscale midsize hotel, in one of Arequipa's emblematic colonial buildings, the storied Mint House—a national historic monument—is a terrific new addition to the city's few true luxury options. Just 3 blocks from the Plaza de Armas, around the corner from the Santa Catalina convent, it's ideally located. It features beautiful *sillar* walls, two lovely interior courtyards, an elegant gourmet restaurant, and even a small on-site museum on the minting of old coins. Accommodations in the modern wing are elegantly understated and spacious, with nice bathrooms, while the sprawling suites in the historic main house are downright sumptuous. Intimate, with a boutique feel but all the services of a larger luxury hotel, and prices that, while not inexpensive, seem merited, it has immediately become Arequipa's top place to stay, and one of the finest hotels in Peru.

Ugarte 403, Arequipa. ✆ **054/226-907** or 01/213-9739 for reservations; 866/477-3270 toll-free in the U.S. and Canada. Fax 054/226-908. www.casa-andina.com. 41 units. $124–$207 double; $263–$494 suite. Rates include taxes and breakfast buffet. AE, DC, MC, V. **Amenities:** Restaurant; bar; concierge; room service. *In room:* A/C, TV, fridge, hair dryer, Wi-Fi.

Moderate

Casa Arequipa ★★★ Value This surprising and outstanding inn, akin to a European boutique hotel—something very unusual for Peru—is one of the most luxurious places to stay in the country at bargain prices. A B&B in a beautifully restored, pink 1950s mansion in the quiet Vallecito residential district, just a short walk or cab ride from the Plaza de Armas, the inn features elegantly designed guest rooms, with nicely chosen antiques, comfortable beds, and the finest towels and bed linens you'll find in Peru. Photographs of the Andes, taken by the owner (who splits his time between Arequipa and Washington, D.C.), decorate the rooms, and fresh flowers are placed in every room and throughout the house. The excellent bathrooms, several of which have tubs, are of gleaming marble. The breakfast buffet and personal attention are worthy of a five-star hotel.

Av. Lima, Vallecito, Arequipa. ✆ **054/284-219,** or 202/332-1942 for reservations in U.S. Fax 054/253-343. www.arequipacasa.com. 10 units. $65–$99 double. Rates include taxes. AE, DC, MC, V. **Amenities:** Concierge; CD library. *In room:* A/C, TV, CD player.

La Casa de Melgar Hostal ★★ Value A spectacular colonial house made of white volcanic stone, this charming small hotel is one of the nicest and most relaxed in Peru, and one of the best values. Just 3 blocks from the Plaza de Armas, the lovingly restored 18th-century mansion—the former residence of the bishop of Arequipa—has massive, thick walls, and three interior courtyards. The decor echoes the rich, brick-red and royal-blue tones of the Santa Catalina Monastery, making it the perfect place to stay if you're a fan of colonial architecture. The ample rooms have good beds. Some rooms—especially those on the ground floor that have high vaulted brick ceilings—exude colonial character; ask to see these. A new wing of rooms, also in a colonial building, behind a garden and terrace are lovely; some have incredibly high ceilings. The staff is very friendly. Breakfast is served in the little cafe next door in one of the courtyards. Advance reservations are a must in high season.

Melgar 108, Cercado, Arequipa. ✆/fax **054/222-459,** or 01/446-8343 for reservations. www.lacasademelgar.com. 30 units. $50 double. Rates include taxes and breakfast. V. **Amenities:** Restaurant/bar. *In room:* No phone.

Inexpensive

La Reyna Value A popular backpacker inn, La Reyna is smack in the middle of the historic center, just a block from the famed Santa Catalina monastery and paces away from plenty of bars and restaurants. The hostel's many rooms feed off a labyrinth of narrow staircases that climb up three floors to a roof terrace, a popular spot to hang out. There are simple, rock-bottom dormitory rooms for zero-budget travelers and a couple of rooftop *casitas* that have private bathrooms and their own terraces with awesome views of the mountains and the monastery below—something akin to backpacker penthouse suites. Room no. 20 is worth reserving if you can. The hostel, though a little haphazardly run, organizes lots of canyon treks and volcano climbing tours, and even offers Spanish classes.

Zela 209, Arequipa. ✆/fax **054/286-578.** 20 units. $10 double without bathroom, $12 double with bathroom; $6 per person in shared rooms. Rates include taxes. No credit cards. *In room:* No phone.

Los Balcones de Moral y Santa Catalina ★ Value This inviting small hotel is very comfortable and decently furnished, a nice step up from budget hostels for not much more money. In the heart of the old quarter, it's only a couple of blocks from the Plaza de Armas. Half of the house is colonial (first floor); the other is republican, dating from the 1800s. The house is built around a colonial patio with a sunny terrace. Furnishings are modern, with wallpaper and firm beds. Eleven of the good-size rooms have hardwood floors and large balconies with nice views looking toward the back of the cathedral; the other rooms are carpeted and less desirable (though quieter). All have good, tiled bathrooms.

Moral 217, Arequipa. ✆/fax **054/201-291.** www.balconeshotel.com. 17 units. S/135 double. Rate includes taxes. MC, V. **Amenities:** Restaurant. *In room:* TV.

WHERE TO DINE

Arequipa is one of the finest cities in Peru for gastronomic adventures, and at very reasonable prices. Several restaurants in the historic quarter—the two streets leading north from the Plaza de Armas are the main hub of nighttime activity—specialize in traditional Arequipeña cooking, though two of the best are a short taxi ride beyond downtown.

Moderate

Ary Quepay ★ Value PERUVIAN/AREQUIPEÑA A relaxed and friendly, rustic restaurant with a gardenlike dining room under a bamboo roof and skylights, Ary Quepay, a longtime favorite of both locals and in-the-know visitors, specializes in traditional Peruvian cooking. It's less fancy than a couple of the better-known restaurants specializing in Arequipeña cooking in the city. Starters include *choclo con queso* (corn on the cob with cheese) and stuffed avocado. The main dishes are classic: *rocoto relleno* (stuffed peppers), *adobo* (pork stew with *ají*), and *escabeche de pescado* (spicy fish stew). There are a number of dishes for vegetarians, as well as good breakfasts, juices, and milkshakes. In the evenings, there's often live folkloric music.

Jerusalén 502. ✆ **054/672-922.** Main courses S/16–S/30. DC, MC, V. Daily 8am–10pm.

La Trattoria del Monasterio ★★ Value ITALIAN Cleaved into the outer *sillar* wall of the splendid Santa Catalina monastery, this chic but unassuming Italian restaurant—a new addition to the Arequipa dining scene—is an excellent spot to linger over an intimate dinner. It's considerably quieter than the hopping restaurant row just 1 block over on San Francisco. Spilling into three elegant, small, whitewashed dining rooms, it specializes in Italian favorites like risottos, lasagnas, ravioli, and *osso buco.* For cognoscenti, it features both long and short pastas. The menu was prepared by the hot chef of the moment in Peru, Gastón Acurio of Astrid & Gastón, La Mar, and other spots in Lima and up and down South America. You'll also find a good selection of wines, great desserts, and fine, attentive service.

Santa Catalina 309. ✆ **054/204-062.** Main courses S/20–S/39. AE, DC, MC, V. Mon–Sat noon–3pm and 7–11pm; Sunday noon–4pm.

Tradición Arequipeña ★★ Value PERUVIAN/AREQUIPEÑA It's a few miles outside of town in the Paucarpata district, so you'll need to grab a taxi to get to this classic open-air restaurant. Elegantly set amid beautiful gardens with stunning views of snowcapped El Misti from the upper deck, it's open only for lunch (although you could also squeeze in an early dinner at 5 or 6pm). Most encouraging is how popular it is among tourists and locals alike. It serves large portions of classic Peruvian and Arequipeña dishes, such as *cuy, adobo,* and *ceviche,* but they're more carefully prepared here than in many other *comida típica* restaurants. A good starter is the combination fried cheese and fried yuca with picante sauce and *salsa verde* (green sauce). Meals are very affordable for such a refined place, perfect for a leisurely lunch.

Av. Dolores 111, Paucarpata. ✆ **054/426-467.** Reservations recommended on weekends. Main courses S/15–S/45. AE, DC, MC, V. Daily noon–7pm.

Zig Zag ★★ SWISS/GRILLED MEAT This remains one of my favorite restaurants in Arequipa; it's chic enough to appeal to young people on dates and comfortable enough for families and small tourist groups. Zig Zag occupies a cool two-level, *sillar*-walled space with a fantastic, twisting iron staircase, and it recently expanded into the space next door. The house specialty is stone-grilled meats, including ostrich and alpaca. The owners like to educate their customers about these lean meats as a healthy alternative to other meats. Try the ostrich carpaccio in lemon or ostrich stone-grilled with Swiss-style hash browns. Big-time meat eaters should order the *piedra criolla* (stone-grilled *chorizo,* beef, lamb, pork, hearts, intestines, and gizzards with potatoes and *chimichurri* sauce). The two-level restaurant plays hip music and has attentive service. A couple of tables upstairs are perched on a ledge overlooking the attractive Plazuela San Francisco.

Zela 210. ✆ **054/206-020.** Reservations recommended. Main courses S/25–S/45. AE, DC, MC, V. Daily 6pm–midnight.

Inexpensive

Govinda INDIAN/VEGETARIAN A good all-around vegetarian restaurant, Govinda—part of a chain across Peru, with the original in London—has a pleasant outdoor garden dining area and good value dishes. It serves vegetarian Italian, Asian, and Peruvian items, as well as pizza, pasta, soup, salad, and yogurt dishes—a welcome reprieve from many travelers' overdose of chicken, pork, and alpaca in Peru. The daily fixed-price menus are very cheap, though the self-service buffet is not all-you-can-eat and its lineup of vegetarian dishes isn't the most creative you've ever seen. It's a good place for breakfast, with muesli, brown bread, fruit salad, and juice.

Santa Catalina 120. ✆ **054/285-540.** Reservations not accepted. Main courses S/6–S/20; *menú* S/8–S/15; buffet S/15. No credit cards. Daily 7am–9:30pm.

Los Leños Value PIZZERIA In this charming cave of a pizza place, diners share long wooden tables, and the footprints of many hundreds of travelers carry on in the graffiti that covers every square inch of stone walls up to a vaulted ceiling. The house specialty is pizza from the wood-fired oven; among the many varieties, the Leños house pizza is a standout, with cheese, sausage, bacon, ham, chicken, and mushrooms. Those who've had their fill of pizza can go for other standards, such as lasagna and a slew of other pastas. Los Leños opens early; you can choose from among 20 different "American breakfasts." Jerusalén 407. ✆ **054/289-179.** Reservations not accepted. Main courses S/6–S/18. No credit cards. Daily 7am–11pm.

AREQUIPA AFTER DARK

Arequipa has a pretty hopping nightlife in the old quarter, with plenty of bars, restaurants, and dance clubs catering both to gringos and locals. Sunday through Wednesday is usually pretty quiet, with things heating up on Thursday night. Virtually every bar in town advertises extended happy hours, with drinks going for as little as 3 for S/12. Calles San Francisco and Zela are the hot spots.

Las Quenas, Santa Catalina 302 (✆ **054/281-115**), is a *peña* bar and restaurant featuring live Andean music Monday through Saturday from 9pm to midnight and special dance performances on Friday and Saturday nights. There's a nominal cover charge of S/5. It's a cozy little place that serves pretty good Peruvian dishes. You can also catch *peña* music at **El Tuturutu,** Portal San Agustín 105 (✆ **054/201-842**), a restaurant on the main square. Another spot for folkloric music is **La Troica,** Jerusalén 522 (✆ **054/225-690**), a tourist-oriented restaurant in an old house.

As for pubs and bars, **Siwara,** Santa Catalina 210 (✆ **054/626-218**), is a great-looking beer tavern that spills into two patios in the building of the Santuarios Andinos museum, across from the Santa Catalina monastery. **Farrens Irish Pub,** Pasaje Catedral 107 (tel] **054/238-465**), which is very popular with visiting gringos, is a cool two-level joint with good drink specials and a rock and pop soundtrack. Another good spot for a drink is **Montreál Le Café Art,** Ugarte 210 (✆ **054/931-2796**), which features live music Wednesday through Saturday and has happy hours between 5 and 11pm. **La Casa de Klaus,** Zela 207 (✆ **054/203-711**), is a simple and brightly lit tavern popular with German, British, and local beer drinkers.

For a little more action, check out **Forum Rock Café,** San Francisco 317 (✆ **054/202-697**), a huge place that is equal parts restaurant, bar, disco, and concert hall. It sports a rainforest theme, with jungle vegetation and "canopy walkways" everywhere. Live bands (usually rock) take the stage Thursday through Saturday. Just down the street, **Déjà Vu,** San Francisco 319 (✆ **054/221-904**), has a good bar with a mix of locals and gringos, a lively dance floor, and English-language movies on a big screen every night at 8pm. **Kibosh,** Zela 205 (✆ **054/626-218**), is a chic, upscale pub with four bars, a dance floor, and live music (ranging from Latin to hard rock) Wednesday through Saturday.

AN EXCURSION FROM AREQUIPA: COLCA VALLEY

The primary day trips and overnight excursions from Arequipa are to Valle del Colca, site of Colca Canyon and **Cruz del Cóndor,** a lookout point where giant South American condors soar overhead; and trekking, rafting, and mountaineering expeditions through the valley. Tour agencies have mushroomed in Arequipa, and most offer very similar city, canyon, countryside *(campiña),* and adventure trips. Going with a tour operator is economical and by far the most convenient option—public transportation is poor and very time-consuming in these parts. Only a handful of tour operators in Arequipa are well run, however, and visitors need to be careful when signing up for guided tours to the canyon and valley. Avoid independent guides who don't have official accreditation. Adventure and sports enthusiasts should contact one of the specialist agencies listed later in this chapter. A minimum of 2 or 3 days is needed to see a significant part of the valley.

Colca Canyon ★★★

Mario Vargas Llosa, novelist and the most famous Arequipeño, described Colca as "The Valley of Wonders." That is no literary overstatement. Colca, located 165km (102 miles) north of Arequipa, is one of the most scenic regions in Peru, a land of imposing snow-capped volcanoes, artistically terraced agricultural slopes, narrow gorges, arid desert landscapes and vegetation, and remote traditional villages, many visibly scarred by seismic tremors common in southern Peru.

The Río Colca, the origin of the mighty Amazon, cuts through the canyon, which remained largely unexplored until the 1970s, when rafting expeditions descended to the bottom of the gorge. Reaching depths of 3,400m (11,152 ft.)—twice as deep as the Grand Canyon—the Cañón del Colca forms part of a volcanic mountain range more than 100km (62 miles) long. Among the great volcanoes, several of which are still active, are Mount Ampato, where a sacrificed Inca maiden was discovered frozen in 1995, and Mount Coropuna, Peru's second-highest peak at 6,425m (21,200 ft.).

Dispersed across the Colca Valley are 14 colonial-era villages that date from the 16th century, distinguished primarily by their small but often richly decorated churches. Local populations, descendants of the Collaguas and Cabanas, pre-Inca ethnic groups, preserve ancient customs and distinctive traditional dress. Ethnic groups can be distinguished by their hats; some women wear hats with colored ribbons; others have elaborately embroidered and sequined headgear. The valley's meticulous agricultural terracing, even more extensive than the terraces of the Sacred Valley, were first cultivated more than 1,000 years ago. Colca villages are celebrated for their vibrant festivals, as authentic as any in Peru, throughout the year.

Most organized tours of the region are very similar if not identical. The road that leads out of Arequipa and into the valley, bending around the Misti and Chachani volcanoes, is poor, long and unbearably dusty. It passes through the **Salinas and Aguada Blanca Nature Reserve,** where you'll usually have a chance to see vicuñas, llamas, and alpacas grazing from the road. The Altiplano landscape, especially outside the rainy season, is barren and bleak. Most tours stop at volcano and valley lookout points along the way before arriving in Chivay.

The gateway to the region is **Chivay,** the Colca's main town on the edge of the canyon, a little more than 3 hours from Arequipa. This easygoing market town lies at an altitude of 3,600m (11,800 ft.). From here, many organized tours embark on short treks in the valley and visit the wonderfully relaxing hot springs of **La Calera,** about 4km (2½ miles) from Chivay. Evening visits to the hot springs allow visitors to bathe in open-air pools beneath a huge, starry sky; artificial light in the valley is almost nonexistent. Charming colonial villages in the valley often visited by tours include Yanque, Coporaque, Maca, and Lari.

Most 2-day tours head out early the following morning for **Cruz del Cóndor,** a lookout point that has become famous throughout Peru; most mornings, it overflows with hundreds of binocular- and camera-toting tourists hoping to get close-up views of the mighty Andean condors. Beginning around 9am, Andean condors—the largest birds in the world, with wingspans of 3.5m (12 ft.)—begin to appear, circling far below in the gorge and gradually gaining altitude with each pass, until they soar silently above the heads of awestruck admirers. Condors are such immense creatures that they cannot lift off from the ground; instead, they take flight from cliff perches. Each morning, the condors glide and climb theatrically before heading out along the river in search of prey. To witness the condors' majestic flight up close is a mesmerizing sight, capable of producing goose bumps in even the most jaded travelers. The condors return late in the afternoon, but fewer people attend the show then. Recent reports of dwindling number of Andean condors in the canyon, perhaps due to continuing development in the region, are certainly cause for concern.

GETTING THERE The great majority of travelers to the Colca Valley visit on guided tours, arranged in Arequipa. Conventional travel agencies offer day trips to Cruz del Cóndor, leaving at 3 or 4am, with brief stops at Chivay before returning to Arequipa (about $20 per person)—it's an awful lot to pack into a single day, especially at high altitude. More relaxed two-day "pool" (group) tours ($30–$70 per person), including an overnight stay at a hotel—at a choice of backpacker inns and rustic upscale lodges—are much more enjoyable. Private tours to the valley, in chauffer-driven cars with guides, cost $150–$350 per person. The best all-purpose agencies in Arequipa are **Giardino Tours,** Calle Jerusalén 604-A (✆ **054/241-206**); **Santa Catalina Tours,** Santa Catalina 219 (✆ **054/216-994**); **Colonial Tours,** Santa Catalina 106 (✆ **054/286-868**); and **Illary Tours,** Santa Catalina 205 (✆ **054/220-844**).

The best hotels in Colca Valley are, at the very high end, **Las Casitas del Colca** ★★★ (✆ **01/242-3425;** www.lascasitasdelcolca.com), an Orient-Express hotel, and the more rustic **Colca Lodge** (✆ **054/531-191;** www.colca-lodge.com), which has its own thermal bath pools; and at the midrange **Casa Andina Colca** ★ (✆ **054/531-020;** www.casa-andina.com), which has a cool planetarium on-site, and **La Casa de Mamayacchi** (✆ **054/241-206;** www.lacasademamayacchi.com), owned by Giardino Tours. The small inns offered by tour operators at backpacker rates tend to be in the town of Chivay and are very basic, but acceptable. The **Inkari Eco Lodge** (✆ **054/284-292**), owned by Santa Catalina Tours is a little tacky, but it's comfortable and has bargain rates.

Local buses travel from Arequipa to Cabanaconde, near the Cruz del Cóndor, with stops in Chivay. **Reyna,** Terminal Terrestre (✆ **054/426-549**), and **Cristo Rey,** San Juan de Dios 510 (✆ **054/213-094**), make these runs.

Outdoor Adventures in Colca Valley

The countryside around Arequipa is some of the best in Peru for outdoor adventure travel. Trails crisscross the Colca Valley, crossing mountain ridges, agricultural terraces, and curious rock formations, and passing colonial towns and fields where llamas and vicuñas graze. The most common pursuits are river running, treks through the canyon valleys, and mountain climbing on the volcanoes just beyond the city. Many tour agencies in Arequipa offer 2- and 3-day visits to the Colca and Cotahuasi canyons, as well as longer, more strenuous treks through the valleys. (Some of the most interesting, but most time-consuming and difficult, expeditions combine rafting and trekking.) Your best bet for organizing any of these activities is with one of the tour operators below; several in Arequipa focus solely on eco- and adventure tourism.

Cusipata Viajes y Turismo ★, Jerusalén 408 (✆ **054/203-966;** www.cusipata.com), is the local specialist for Chili and Colca rafting and kayaking (including courses), and its guides frequently subcontract out to other agencies in Arequipa. **Ideal Tours** (✆ **054/244-433**) handles Chili and Majes rafting, as well as Colca and other standard tours. **Apumayo Expediciones** ★★, Garcilaso 265 Interior 3, Cusco (✆ **084/246-018;** www.apumayo.com), is very good for long trekking/rafting expeditions to Cotahuasi and Colca, as is **Amazonas Explorer,** Zela 212 (✆ **054/212-813;** www.amazonas-explorer.com), an international company that organizes hardy multisport trips to Cotahuasi and Colca (which can be combined with tours to Cusco, the Inca Trail, and Machu Picchu).

Colca Trek, Jerusalén 401-B (✆ **054/206-217;** www.colcatrek.com.pe), and **Peru Trekking,** Jerusalén 302-B (✆ **054/223-404**), are two other local outfits that offer canyon treks of 3 to 5 days or more and a number of other adventure activities, such as horseback riding, mountain biking, rafting, and climbing.

For mountain climbing, one agency stands out: **Zárate Aventuras** ★★, Santa Catalina 204, no. 3 (✆ **054/202-461;** fax 054/263-107; www.zarateadventures.com), which is run by Carlos Zárate, the top climbing guide in Arequipa (a title his dad held before him). He can arrange any area climb and has equipment rental and a 24-hour mountain rescue service. Climbing expedition costs (per person) are El Misti, $50; Chachani, $70; and Colca Canyon, $75. They also organize rafting and mountain biking adventures.

10 IQUITOS & THE NORTHERN AMAZON

1,860km (1,153 miles) NE of Lima

Iquitos, the gateway to the northern Amazon, is Peru's largest jungle town and the capital of its largest region, Loreto (which occupies nearly a third of the national territory). Though you must fly to get here—unless you have a full week to kill for hot and uncomfortable river travel—the pockets of jungle down- and upriver from Iquitos are among the most accessible of the Peruvian Amazon basin. Some of the best jungle lodges in the country are located just a few hours by boat from Iquitos. Because the region is the most trafficked and developed of the Peruvian Amazon, costs are lower for most jungle excursions than they are in the more exclusive Manu Biosphere Reserve in southeastern Peru.

Founded by Jesuits in the 1750s, Iquitos lies about 3,220km (2,000 miles) upriver from the mouth of the Amazon River. Its proximity to South America's greatest rainforest and its isolation from the rest of Peru have created a unique tropical atmosphere. In the late 1860s and 1870s, pioneering merchants got rich off the booming rubber trade and built ostentatious mansions along the river. Today, though, those great homes are faded monuments to the city's glory days, and just blocks from the main square lies the fascinating Belén district, where families live in a squalid pile of ramshackle wooden houses on the banks of the river. Some houses are propped up by spindly stilts, while others float, tethered to poles, when the river rises 6m (20 ft.) or more. Belén looks Far Eastern, and Iquitos seemingly has more in common with steamy tropical Asian cities than the highlands of Peru. Like a South American Saigon, the air is waterlogged, and the streets buzz with unrelenting waves of motorcycles and *motocarros* (or rickshaws). Locals speak a languid, mellifluous Spanish unmatched in other parts of the country, and they dress not in alpaca sweaters and shawls, but in flesh-baring tank tops and short skirts.

Iquitos has an intoxicating feel that's likely to detain you for at least a couple of days. But for most visitors, the lure of the Amazon rainforest is the primary attraction. Virgin

rainforest, though, is hard to find. To lay eyes on exotic wildlife, such as pink dolphins, caiman, and macaws, you have to get at least 80km (50 miles) away from Iquitos and onto secondary waterways. Options for rainforest excursions include lodge visits, river cruises, and independent guided treks.

ESSENTIALS

Getting There

BY PLANE Iquitos's **Aeropuerto Francisco Secada Vigneta,** Av. Abelardo Quiñones, Km 6 (✆ **065/260-147**), is several miles outside of town. **LAN** (✆ **01/213-8200;** www.lan.com) and **Star Perú** (✆ **01/705-9000;** www.starperu.com) fly daily from Lima and other cities in the Loreto department.

The airport is usually chaotic when flights arrive, with dozens of representatives of tour operators competing for your attention. Do not let anyone take your bags, and don't let anyone you don't know hop in a cab with you. To downtown Iquitos, an automobile taxi costs about S/12, by *motocarro* (rickshaw) costs S/8.

BY BOAT Arriving by boat is an option only for those with the luxury of ample time and patience; it takes about a week when the river is high (and 3–4 days in the dry season) to reach the capital city of Loreto upriver along the Amazon from Pucallpa or Yurimaguas. The Iquitos port, **Puerto Masusa,** is about 3km (2 miles) north of the Plaza de Armas. To travel to Colombia or Brazil by boat, your best bet is by river cruise (p. 721). Cruises to Manaus, Santarém, and Belém in Brazil are offered by Amazon Tours & Cruises. Direct service all the way to Manaus has been suspended.

Getting Around

BY TAXI/MOTOTAXI Motorcycle buggies or rickshaws *(motocarros)* are everywhere in Iquitos; if you don't mind the noise and wind in your face (and aren't worried about accidents), it's a great way to get around. In-town fares are S/2. Regular car taxis are only slightly less ubiquitous; most trips in town cost S/3.

BY BUS *Combis* (minivans) and *ómnibuses* (buses) travel principal routes, but are much less comfortable and not much less expensive than more convenient *motocarros.*

BY FOOT Though the city is spread over several square kilometers, the core of downtown Iquitos is compact and easy to get around on foot, and even the waterfront Belén district is easy to walk to. Some hostels and hotels are a distance from the main square, though, requiring the occasional use of inexpensive *motocarros.*

Visitor Information

A municipal **tourism information booth** is located in the arrivals terminal at the airport (✆ **065/260-251**). It maintains a chart of hotels and prices, and the staff is happy to dispense information about the various jungle tour and lodge operators. One of Peru's more helpful tourism information offices is at Napo 226 on the north side of the Plaza de Armas (✆ **065/236-144**). The English-speaking staff offers free maps and lists of all recommended hotels and tour operators (including photo albums of lodges) and will try to sort through the (often intentionally) confusing sales pitches of jungle-tour companies. The office is open Monday through Saturday from 8am to 8pm, as well as occasional Sunday mornings.

FAST FACTS Banks and ATMs are located along Putumayo and Próspero, on the south side of the Plaza de Armas. Two banks that exchange traveler's checks and cash are **Banco de Crédito,** Putumayo 201, and **Banco Continental,** Sargento Lores 171. Money changers can usually be found hanging about the Plaza de Armas and along Putumayo and Próspero, but figure the exchange beforehand and count your money carefully.

If you're planning to cross into Brazil or Colombia, I suggest you make contact with your embassy in Lima or even at home before traveling to Peru. For questions about border-crossing formalities for jungle travel to and from Brazil and Colombia (regulations have been known to change frequently), contact the **Migraciones** office at Malecón Tarapacá 382 (✆ **065/235-371**).

In a medical emergency, call **Cruz Roja (Red Cross)** at ✆ **065/241-072.** For medical attention, visit **Clínica Ana Stahl,** Av. la Marina 285 (✆ **065/252-535**); **Essalud,** Av. la Marina 2054 (✆ **065/250-333**); or **Hospital Regional de Loreto,** Av. 28 de Julio s/n, Punchana (✆ **065/252-004**). The **tourist police** office is located at Sargento Lores 834 (✆ **065/242-081**).

There are several **Internet *cabinas*** near the Plaza de Armas, particularly on Próspero and Putumayo. The one next to the entrance to the Casa de Fierro is pretty dependable. Most stay open late, and rates are about S/2 per hour. Iquitos's **post office** is located at Arica 402, at the corner of Morona (✆ **065/223-812**); it's open Monday through Saturday from 8am to 7:30pm. The **Telefónica del Perú** office is at Arica 276.

WHAT TO SEE & DO

In Iquitos

The Plaza de Armas, while perhaps not Peru's most distinguished, is marked by an early-20th-century, neo-Gothic **Iglesia Matriz** (parish church) and the **Casa de Fierro.** The walls, ceiling, and balcony of this Gustave Eiffel–designed house (for the 1889 Paris Exhibition) are plastered in rectangular sheets of iron. Said to be the first prefabricated house in the Americas, it was shipped unassembled from Europe and built on-site where it currently stands.

One block away from the plaza, facing the Amazon River, the riverfront promenade known as the **Malecón Tarapacá** was recently enlarged and improved with fountains, benches, and street lamps, making it the focus of Iquitos's urban life. It is lined with several exquisite 19th-century mansions; the most spectacular is probably **Casa Hernández,** no. 302–308. The **Museo Amazónico,** Malecón Tarapacá 386 (✆ **065/231-072**), has occasionally interesting exhibits of Amazon folklore and tribal art, as well as a curious collection of 76 Indian statues made of fiberglass but fashioned as if they were bronze. It's open Monday through Friday from 8am to 1pm and 3 to 7pm, Saturday from 9am to 1pm; admission is S/3. Other houses worth checking out are **Casa Fitzcarrald,** Napo 200–212, an adobe house belonging to a famed rubber baron; **Casa Cohen,** Próspero 401–437; **Casa Morey,** Brasil, first block; and the **Logia Unión Amazónica,** Nauta 262.

The waterfront **Barrio de Belén** ★, about a 15-minute walk south along the *malecón,* is Iquitos's most interesting quarter. Known for its sprawling and odiferous open-air market, where you'll find a bounty of strange and wonderful Amazon fish, fauna, and fruit, Belén's residential district is a seedy but endlessly fascinating shantytown. Houses are constructed above the waters of the Amazon, and when the river is high, the primary mode of transportation is by canoe. You are free to walk around in dry season (or take a locally arranged canoe trip during much of the year), but you should go in a group and only during the day.

Jungle Lodges & Tours

The giant Amazon River system just beyond the city holds a wealth of natural wonders: rustic jungle lodges, canopy walks, and opportunities for bird-watching, piranha fishing, visits to Indian villages, and wildlife-spotting (as well as less-standard activities, such as shaman consultations and *ayahuasca* drug ceremonies). The mighty Amazon reaches widths of about 4km (2½ miles) beyond Iquitos, and the river basin contains some 2,000 species of fish; 4,000 species of birds; native mammals such as anteaters, tapirs, marmosets, and pink dolphins; and 60 species of reptiles, including caiman and anacondas. Your options for exploring the jungle are lodge stays (which include jungle activities such as treks and canoe excursions), river cruises, or more adventurous guided camping treks. Don't expect to spend your time in the jungle checking off a lengthy list of wildlife sightings, though; no matter where you go, your opportunities for viewing more than a couple of these birds, fish, and mammals will be severely limited by their natural shyness and the density of the tropical vegetation. The northern Amazon basin within reach of Iquitos has been explored and popularly exploited far longer than the more remote southern jungle areas of Manu and Tambopata.

For a quick and simple experience, you can stay at a lodge only an hour or two by boat from Iquitos, in secondary jungle. You're likely to see more fauna and have a more authentic experience in primary rainforest, but you'll have to travel up to 4 hours by boat and pay quite a bit more for the privilege. Generally speaking, you'll have to trade comfort for authenticity. A true foray into virgin jungle, far from the heavy footsteps of thousands of guides and visitors, requires at least a week of demanding camping and trekking. Hard-core eco-types may wish to contract private guides to go deep into the *selva* and camp; ask at the tourism information office for a list of licensed, official guides. (They also have a list of blacklisted guides.)

Prices for lodges and tours vary tremendously. Costs are directly related to distance from Iquitos; the farther away, the more expensive they are. For conventional lodges contracted in Iquitos, lodge tours average around $50 to $60, going up to $175 or more per person per day for lodges located farthest from the city. Some budget lodges offer bargain rates, as little as $30 per day (in most cases, you get what you pay for), and independent guides may charge as little as $20 a day. Costs include transportation, lodging, buffet-style meals, and guided activities. (Beverages are extra.)

Beware: There are many look-alike lodges and tours. Hustlers and con artists abound in Iquitos, and you need to exercise a certain amount of caution before handing over your money for a promised itinerary. The local tourism office (© **065/260-251**) works hard to ferret out guides, tours, and lodges with bad reputations. If you're making a tour decision on the ground in Iquitos, it's a good idea to visit the office first for the most up-to-date information.

Jungle Lodges

Most jungle lodges have either individual thatched-roof bungalows or main buildings with individual rooms; communal dining areas; hammock lounges; covered plank walkways; toilets; and hot- or cold-water sinks and showers. A few lodges have extras such as swimming pools, lookout towers, canopy walkways, and electricity. Guests are taken on guided day- and nighttime excursions, including jungle walks, piranha fishing, and canoe and motorboat trips to spot birds, caimans, and dolphins. Many lodges offer cheesy visits with local Indian tribes, staged for your pleasure, and some host *ayahuasca* rituals (with the privilege of taking a natural hallucinogenic potion prepared by an "authentic" Indian shaman at $15 a shot—the local version of taking peyote with Don Juan).

The following tour operators and lodges have good reputations, though the list is not by any means exhaustive.

- **Explorama** ★, Av. la Marina 340 (© **065/252-530** or 800/707-5275 in the U.S. and Canada; www.explorama.com). The most established jungle tour company in Iquitos (now into its fifth decade) and owned by an American, Explorama operates three lodges and a campsite, ranging from 40km to 160km (25–100 miles) downriver from Iquitos. Near **Explornapo** (the lodge deepest in the jungle), there's a splendid canopy walkway high above the treetops. Explorama owns the jungle's most luxurious lodge, **Ceiba Tops,** a jungle resort hotel with air-conditioning, pool, and Jacuzzi. Prices range from $270 for a 2-day, 1-night trip to Ceiba Tops to $890 for a 5-day, 4-night trip to Explornapo. Web specials as well as special programs are frequently available.
- **Tahuayo Lodge** ★★★, Amazonia Expeditions, 10305 Riverburn Dr., Tampa, FL (© **800/262-9669** in the U.S.; www.perujungle.com). The finest lodge in the northern Amazon, this low-impact eco-property, associated with the Rainforest Conservation Fund, lies on the shores of the River Tahuayo, about 4 hours from Iquitos. *Outside* magazine has touted it as one of the top-10 travel finds in the world. It is the only lodge with access to the Tamshiyacu-Tahuayo Reserve, a splendid area for primate and other wildlife viewing (it counts 500 species of birds). Because of its remoteness, it recommends visits of at least a week; programs are individually tailored. The 15

Tips Eco-nomizing

You can almost certainly get a better deal by going door-to-door to the lodge and tour sales offices in Iquitos and comparing programs and prices than you would by contracting one in Lima or from your home country prior to stepping foot in Peru. However, you risk not getting the tour you want when you want it. For many travelers, the extra hassle and uncertainty may not be worth the dollars saved. Prices quoted on websites and through travel agents may be quite negotiable if you contact operators directly, depending on season and occupancy rates.

cabins are open year-round, and the lodge offers an excellent schedule of excursions ranging from the rugged (jungle survival training) to relaxed; most enticing are zip-line canopy ropes for tree-top viewing. An 8-day, 7-night trip is $1,295 per person (additional days $100).

- **Yarapa River Lodge** ★★★ (✆ **065/993-1172** or 315/952-6771 in the U.S. and Canada; www.yarapa.com). Associated with Cornell University (which built a field lab for students and faculty here), this attractive, conservation-minded lodge is 186km (110 miles) upriver on the Yarapa River, near the Reserva Nacional Pacaya-Samiria. Surrounded by pristine jungle and oxbow lakes, the handsome lodge features composting, full solar power, and flush toilets with a waste-management system. The lodge is a two-time winner of World Travel Awards' "Best Resort in Peru." A 4-day, 3-night trip (with private bathroom) runs $1,020 per person; a 7-day, 6-night trip is $1,575 per person. Travelers can opt for an overnight in the remote Pacaya-Samiria National Park Reserve, 4 hours away by boat.

Cruises

Riverboat cruises down the Amazon and along its tributaries don't allow you to see much in the way of fauna or pristine jungle, though you will likely spot lots of birds and dolphins. Cruises are best for people who don't want to rough it too much and like the romance of traveling the Amazon by boat. Many cruises stop off at reserves for jungle walks and visits to local villages.

- **GreenTracks Amazon Cruises** (✆ **065/231-611** or 800/892-1035 in the U.S. and Canada; www.amazontours.net). This American-owned company has been active in the northern Amazon for more than 4 decades. Its midlevel cruises are aboard older, air-conditioned fleets that aren't quite as nice or as expensive as those of Jungle Expeditions (see below). A 4-night riverboat cruise on the Delfin II is $1,808 per person in a double room; a 7-night cruise on a rubber boom-era riverboat to the Pacaya-Samiria National Reserve is $2,500 per person.
- **Jungle Expeditions** ★, Av. Quiñones 1980 (✆ **065/262-340;** www.junglex.com). This company offers luxury river cruises on a fleet of three elegant, 19th-century style boats, and cruises upriver along the Río Ucayali. Prices are about $2,700 for 7-day and $3,300 for 10-day expeditions. The company also accepts passengers through their Lima booking office (✆ **01/241-3232**) or **International Expeditions** (✆ **800/633-4734;** www.internationalexpeditions.com) in the United States, which offers air-inclusive packages and programs with Cusco and Machu Picchu extensions.

Shopping

The most intriguing shopping option in town is the Belén open-air market, though it's likely you'll find more to photograph and smell than actually buy. For local artisans' goods, there aren't many options; try the sparsely populated market downstairs from the *malecón.* **Centro Artesanal Anaconda,** Malecón Tarapacá-Boulevard, or the larger market, **Mercado Artesanal de San Juan,** with stalls selling hammocks, woodcarvings, and paintings on Avenida Quiñones 4.5km (3 miles), on the way out to the airport (about 3km/2 miles from downtown). Some of the best crafts, including textiles and pottery, come from the Shipibo Indian tribe.

WHERE TO STAY

Iquitos has fewer good hotels than its environs have attractive jungle lodges—which is perhaps logical, since the jungle is the primary attraction here. All but the cheapest will arrange for a free airport transfer if you pass on your arrival information ahead of time.

Expensive

El Dorado Plaza Hotel ★ With a privileged location on the Plaza de Armas, the El Dorado Plaza has filled a gaping hole in the Iquitos hotel scene—the city never before had a bona fide high-end hotel. A modern high-rise, with a soaring lobby, good restaurant, and bar, this is clearly the finest hotel in town. Rooms are large and nicely outfitted, if not quite at the upper-echelon levels found in Lima or Cusco. Guests have a view of either the main square or the pool. The hotel has quickly become popular with foreigners who come to Iquitos for top-of-the-line jungle tours. The staff is very friendly and helpful. Occasionally there are deals for as much as half the rack rate.

Napo 258 (Plaza de Armas), Iquitos. ✆ **065/222-555.** Fax 065/224-304. www.eldoradoplazahotel.com. 65 units. $242–$297 double; $385–$660 suite. Rate includes breakfast buffet. AE, DC, MC, V. **Amenities:** Restaurant; coffee shop; 2 bars; concierge; exercise room; Jacuzzi; excellent outdoor pool; room service; sauna. *In room:* A/C, TV, fridge, hair dryer.

Moderate

Victoria Regia (Value) An extremely comfortable and friendly midsize hotel, the Victoria Regia—named for the lily found throughout the Amazon—is a good choice for both independent travelers and business execs with long-term affairs to attend to in Iquitos. It's a modern block hotel on a busy residential street about 10 minutes from the main square. The rooms are built around an indoor pool and are just a notch below the El Dorado in terms of comfort, although they have air-conditioning that really cranks.

Av. Ricardo Palma 252, Iquitos. ✆/fax **065/231-983** or 01/442-4515 for reservations. www.victoriaregiahotel.com. 65 units. S/264 double; S/396–S/495 suite. Rates include breakfast buffet. AE, DC, MC, V. **Amenities:** Restaurant/bar; covered pool. *In room:* A/C, TV, fridge.

WHERE TO DINE

The relaxed restaurants in Iquitos are a good place to sample dishes straight out of the Amazon, such as turtle meat soup, *paiche* (a huge fish), heart of palm salad, and *juanes* (rice *tamales* made with chicken or fish). Although protected species are not supposed to appear on menus, they often do. If you venture into the Belén market, you'll see even more exotic foodstuffs, such as monkey and lizard meat.

Moderate

Antica Pizzeria ★ PIZZA/ITALIAN A sister to several popular branches in Lima's coolest neighborhoods, this stylish, modern Italian restaurant, a half-block from the Plaza de Armas, is a very welcome addition to Iquitos' more local dining scene. Though you can feast on very good thin-crust pizzas from the wood-burning stove or straightforward pastas, chef Juan Seminario's "fusioini" menu also includes more sophisticated fare, such as tuna tartare, octopus salad, and porcini mushroom risotto, as well as *maracuyá* (passion fruit) cheesecake for dessert. The place has a cool, relaxed atmosphere, with a reggae and pop soundtrack and young clientele.

Jr. Napo 159. ✆ **065/241-988.** Reservations recommended for groups. Main courses S/15–S/38. AE, MC, V. Daily noon–midnight.

Fitzcarraldo ★ INTERNATIONAL This popular joint right on the *malecón* has a diverse menu to appeal to tourists of all stripes and appetites. You can go light, choosing from a number of salads such as *chonta* with avocado and tomato, or opt for a regular dinner including *pescado a la Loretana,* or even turtle in ginger sauce with manioc. There are also excellent pizzas, sandwiches, and hamburgers, as well as large salads. The restaurant is a convivial, lively place in an open-air house with views of the Amazon, good music, sidewalk tables, and underpowered ceiling fans.

Napo 100 (at Malecón Tarapacá). ✆ **065/243-434.** Reservations recommended for groups. Main courses S/13–S/40. MC, V. Daily noon–midnight.

Regal (Casa de Fierro) INTERNATIONAL/PERUVIAN In the famed Iron House on the Plaza de Armas, this British pub and hangout is also a reputable restaurant exuding a desultory colonial atmosphere. There are great views from the wraparound iron balcony, with its slowly rotating old-style ceiling fans. It's a good place to try local dishes such as *paiche* (Amazon river fish), which is served any number of ways, or the house specialty, Regal *lomo fino* (beef tenderloin in port-wine sauce), served with salad, Greek rice, a peach stuffed with Russian salad, and french fries. Some find that the food suffers in comparison with the general ambience, so you might opt just to kick back with the expat Brits around the bar for a pint.

Putumayo 182, Plaza de Armas (2nd floor). ✆ **065/222-732.** Reservations recommended. Main courses S/18–S/36. AE, DC, MC, V. Daily noon–10pm.

IQUITOS AFTER DARK

More locals than gringos usually make it to the coolest spot in Iquitos, **Café-Teatro Amauta ★**, Nauta 250 (✆ **065/233-366**), a bar with great bohemian flavor, a romantic interior, and sidewalk tables. Calling itself El Rincón de los Artistas (The Artists' Corner), it supports live music of diverse types (Peruvian, Latino, and Amazon sounds) Monday through Saturday from 10pm until 3am. Along the *malecón* are a couple of lively bars with good views of the river. **Arandú Bar** (✆ **065/243-434**) is particularly hopping, and a good place for a pitcher of sangria. You can also grab a drink at **The Yellow Rose of Texas,** Putumayo 180 (✆ **065/241-010**), a spot owned by the former head of the local tourist office (a Texan). Locals hang out at **Noa-Noa** (✆ **065/232-902**), a rock bar near the Plaza de Armas at Pevas 298.

12

Uruguay

by Charlie O'Malley

A cosmopolitan capital, a jet-set beach scene, and a wild and majestic interior are just some of the draws to Uruguay. This nation of 3.2 million tea lovers, meat eaters, and African drummers is full of surprises. Hemmed in on both sides by Brazilians and Argentinians, Uruguayans will proudly tell you that they have the best beaches, the best meat, the best *fútbol,* the best wine, the best health service, and, perhaps most important, the least corrupt government in South America. It is no wonder its neighbors are fond of taking holidays here. Whether you are a day-tripper to unassuming Montevideo, a history buff in historical Colonia, or a night owl amid the glitzy bars and clubs of Punta del Este, you might come to look upon this, the smallest Spanish-speaking country on the continent, as also the most special.

1 THE REGIONS IN BRIEF

Uruguay's origins as a country rest firmly in Europe; the indigenous people inhabiting the region were displaced by the colonizing Portuguese and Spaniards in the late-17th and early-18th centuries. You will find the European influence most evident among the historic treasures of **Colonia,** where the Portuguese first entrenched themselves, and amid the rich architecture of **Montevideo,** where the Spaniards landed. Montevideo is the cultural heartland of the country, a place where you will discover the bold accomplishments of Uruguay in music, art, and literature. Among the several internationally accomplished artists are Pedro Figari, who inspired a school of painters; José Enrique Rodó, Uruguay's famed essayist from the early 20th century; and Mauricio Rosencof, the politically active playwright from recent decades. Outside the capital, miles of pastureland and rolling hills draw your attention away from the urban capital to a softer, quieter life. But this rural lifestyle stops at the coast, where world-class resorts centered on **Punta del Este** lure the continent's rich and famous.

2 THE BEST OF URUGUAY IN 1 WEEK

Most people arrive in Uruguay from Argentina, and the itinerary below is designed accordingly. If you're traveling with family, my advice is to go straight to the beach.

Days ❶–❷: Arrive in Colonia ★★★

Popular with day-trippers, **Colonia** deserves your attention and is worth an overnight stay to truly enjoy its old-time, otherworldly pace of life. Stay at the colonial-style Hotel Plaza Mayor, and explore the Barrio Histórico on foot or by scooter.

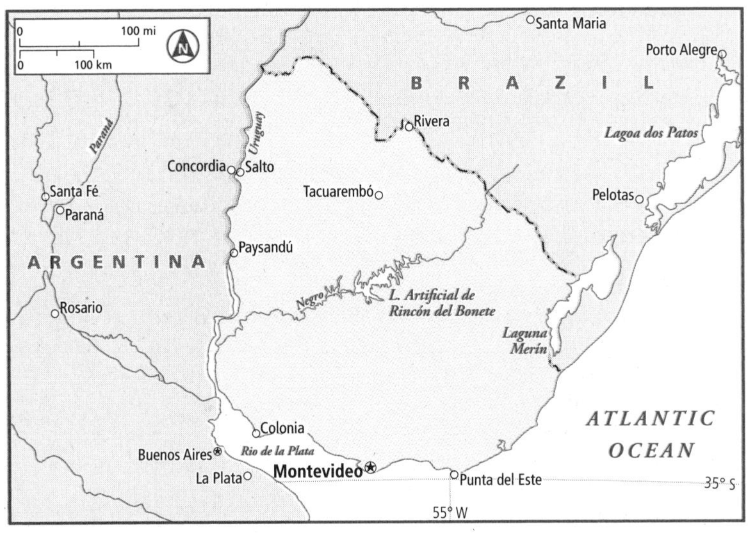

Day 3: Montevideo
Stay in the upscale neighborhood of Carrasco at the intimate **Belmont House** (p. 735). From here you can walk the coastal road, La Rambla, to the rundown but historical Old City, stopping off to enjoy the **Port Market** (p. 734). Dine at the very grand **Arcadia** restaurant (p. 737) atop the Plaza Victoria.

Days 4–7: Punta del Este
Pass most of your time on Uruguay's famous beaches and rub shoulders with the glitterati. If sunbathing is not your thing, you'll find plenty of outdoor activities such as horseback riding and watersports.

3 PLANNING YOUR TRIP TO URUGUAY

VISITOR INFORMATION

The Internet is an excellent source of information on Uruguay. Try **www.turismo.gub.uy** or **www.uruguaynatural.com** for official visitor information. Additional countrywide tourist information can be found at **www.visit-uruguay.com**. A bilingual magazine called ***Pasaporte Uruguay*** is distributed in all the tourist spots and can be seen at **www.pasaporteuruguay.com**.

ENTRY REQUIREMENTS & CUSTOMS

Citizens of the United States, the United Kingdom, Canada, and New Zealand need only a passport to enter Uruguay (for tourist stays of up to 90 days). Australian citizens must get a tourist visa before arrival.

Telephone Dialing Info at a Glance

Uruguay is in the middle of transforming its fixed-line numbers, with the object of having eight digits instead of seven or five. The process is taking longer than expected, but basically the idea is that every area code is joined with the local number. For example, a Montevideo number 02/123-4567 will become 21234567 or a Colonia number 042/12345 will become 4212345, with no need for local area codes. As no crossover date has been set, I have kept to the original format in this chapter. The changeover does not affect numbers dialed from outside Uruguay. Uruguay's national telephone company is called ANTEL. You can buy a telephone card from any kiosk or ANTEL *telecentro* location. You can also make domestic and international calls from *telecentro* offices—they are located every few blocks in major cities—but be warned that international calls are very expensive, especially during peak hours.

- **To place a call from your home country to Uruguay,** dial the international access code (011 in the U.S., 0011 in Australia, 0170 in New Zealand, 00 in the U.K.) plus the country code (598), plus the city or region area code (for example, Montevideo 2, Punta del Este 42, Colonia del Sacramento 11), followed by the number. For example, a call from the United States to Montevideo would be 011+598+2+000+0000.
- **To place a domestic long-distance call within Uruguay,** dial a 0 before the area code, and then the local number.
- **To place a direct international call from Uruguay,** dial the international access code (00), plus the country code of the place you are dialing, plus the area code and the number.
- **To reach an international long-distance operator,** dial ✆ 000-410 for **AT&T,** ✆ 000-412 for **MCI,** or ✆ 000-417 for **Sprint.**
- **While calling within the country,** you will notice some numbers with four-digit numbers. Sometimes these do not work properly, so be sure to try and get a conventional seven-digit land-line number as well. Cellphones have no area code but a three-digit beginning code, usually beginning with 9, followed by six digits.

Uruguayan Embassy Locations

In Australia: Ste. 2 Level 4, Commerce House, 24 Brisbane Ave., Barton ACT 2600, P.O Box 5058, Kingston ACT 2604 (✆ **2/6372-9100**)

In Canada: 130 Albert St., Suite 1905, Ottawa, ON K1P 5G4 (✆ **613/234-2727;** fax 613/233-4670; www.embassyofuruguay.ca)

In the U.K.: 125 Kensington High St., First Floor, London W8 5SF (✆ **207/937-4170**)

In the U.S.: 1913 I St. NW, Washington, DC 20006 (✆ **202/331-1313;** fax 202/331-8142; www.uruwashi.org)

MONEY

The official currency is the **Uruguayan peso** (designated NP$, U$, or simply $ throughout the country, and as U$ in this book); each peso comprises 100 **centavos.** Uruguayan pesos are available in $10, $20, $50, $100, $200, $500, $1,000, and $5,000 notes; coins come in 10, 20, and 50 centavos, and 1 and 2 pesos. The exchange rate as this book went to press was approximately **21 pesos to the U.S. dollar.**

Note: Throughout this chapter, I list prices of hotels, tours, and some transportation options in U.S. dollars.

Traveler's checks are accepted only at some currency-exchange houses. The most widely accepted **credit cards** are Visa and MasterCard; you'll have less luck with American Express and Diners Club. To report a lost or stolen credit card, call the following numbers: for **American Express, ✆ 0411/008-0071;** for **MasterCard, ✆ 636/722-7111** (collect call to the U.S.); and for **Visa, ✆ 0411/940-7915.**

ATMS ATMs on the Cirrus network are widely available in Montevideo and Punta del Este. If you travel to Colonia or elsewhere outside these cities, you should bring Uruguayan pesos.

WHEN TO GO

PEAK SEASON & CLIMATE The best time to visit Uruguay is October through March, when the sun shines and temperatures are mild. Punta del Este overflows with tourists from Argentina in summer; if you're seeking a more relaxed time to visit the beaches of the coast, consider going between October and December. Average temperatures are 62°F (17°C) in spring, 73°F (23°C) in summer, 64°F (18°C) in autumn, and 53°F (12°C) in winter.

PUBLIC HOLIDAYS National holidays include New Year's Day (Jan 1), Día de los Reyes (Jan 6), Carnaval (the days leading up to Ash Wednesday), Easter, Desembarco de los 33 Orientales (Apr 19), Labor Day (May 1), Batalla de las Piedras (May 18), Natalicio de José Gervasio Artigas (June 19), Jura de la Constitución (July 18), Independence Day (Aug 25), Día de la Raza (Oct 12), Día de los Difuntos (Nov 2), and Christmas (Dec 25).

HEALTH CONCERNS

There are no specific health concerns or vaccination requirements for travel to Uruguay.

GETTING THERE & GETTING AROUND

International flights land at **Carrasco International Airport** (✆ 02/604-0272), 19km (12 miles) from downtown Montevideo. A taxi to downtown costs about U$500. Uruguay's national carrier is **Pluna** (✆ 0800/112-910 or 02/902-1414; www.pluna.aero), serving domestic and international destinations. **American Airlines** (✆ 02/916-3929; www.aa.com) offers connecting service from the United States. **Aerolíneas Argentinas** (✆ 02/902-0828; www.aerolineas.com) connects Buenos Aires and Montevideo; the flight takes 50 minutes. **Varig** (✆ 0800/997-000 in the U.K.; www.voegol.com.br) offers flights from the U.K. or Europe. **LAN** (✆ 02/902-3881; www.lan.com) and Aerolíneas Argentinas connect Australia and New Zealand.

Argentina and Uruguay are in a long-term diplomatic dispute over a paper mill in Uruguay that is allegedly polluting the Río Uruguay, near the Argentine town of Gualeguaychú. Access to Uruguay, at times, is restricted because of ongoing protests, and extra security is sometimes in place at crossings, airline gates, and the Buquebús terminal. From Montevideo, the easiest way to reach Colonia and Punta del Este is by bus.

TIPS ON ACCOMMODATIONS

Accommodations in Uruguay run the full gamut from a booming hostel scene in the capital to a burgeoning *estancia* network in the countryside to a series of well-established beach resorts along the coast, in particular Punta del Este. In between you'll find well-run business hotels in Montevideo and small lodges, known as *posadas,* in Colonia. Prices can vary greatly depending on the time you go, with weekends usually more expensive throughout the year. Prices rise off the charts in the summer season, particularly along the coast, where a three-star establishment will charge five-star rates during the peak times at Christmas and January. In this chapter, I have classified any rates more than $300 as **Very Expensive;** between $175 and $300 as **Expensive;** between $100 and $175 as **Moderate;** and below $100 as **Inexpensive.** Hotel prices in Uruguay are quoted in U.S. dollars.

TIPS ON DINING

Strangely enough, you'll not find Uruguay's national drink, *mate* tea, on any restaurant menu. The locals prefer to drink it at home or in the park, and it is made to be shared, with several drinkers sharing the same cup. What you will find instead is lots of meat. Uruguayans are committed carnivores and *parrillas* (grill houses) dot the landscape, offering *asado de tira* (ribs) and *pulpo* (fillet steak) among many other cuts of the sacred cow. Thankfully, along the coast great seafood is available.

Pizza and pasta are also common and the steak sandwich, known as *chivito,* is the national snack. All menus offering lack spice, and vegetarian options are limited, though growing in the capital. There is, however, plenty for sweet tooths, with *dulce de leche* (caramelized milk) slathered across everything from croissants to meringue pie. Most upscale restaurants charge a flat fee of U$20 just to sit at the table. Restaurants that charge more than U$400 for a main dish are classified as **Expensive;** between U$200 and U$400 are **Moderate;** and any below U$200 are **Inexpensive.**

TIPS ON SHOPPING

Look out for **Manos del Uruguay** (www.manos.com.uy), a nationwide cooperative that specializes in handicrafts, particularly fine woolens. It has store branches in all the main tourist centers. Uruguay is also the place to stock up on gaucho paraphernalia, be it decorated knives, *mate* gourds, leather accessories, or silverware. Montevideo has some excellent open-air markets selling everything from books to jewelry and the occasional antique. Colonia displays a fine line in Portuguese ceramics, and Punta del Este has all the high-end stores you'd associate with a chic beach town—they stay open late so as not to disturb your tan time. The capital also has some excellent art stores displaying the country's vibrant art scene.

Fast Facts Uruguay

American Express In Montevideo, American Express Bank is located at Rincón 477, 8th Floor (✆ **02/916-0000**). Turisport Limitada, Calle San José 930 (✆ **02/902-0829;** fax 02/902-0852), acts as an agent of American Express Travel Services in Uruguay; hours are Monday through Friday from 9am to 5pm

Business Hours In general, businesses stay open weekdays from 9am to 6:30 or 7pm, with a 2-hour break for lunch around noon. Retail outlets keep similar hours and are usually open a half-day on Saturday as well. Banks are open weekdays from 1 to 5pm.

Electricity Electricity in Uruguay runs on 220 volts, so bring a transformer and adapter along with any electrical appliances. Note that most laptops operate on both 110 and 220 volts. Some luxury hotels may supply transformers and adapters.

Embassies & Consulates In Montevideo: **U.S.,** Lauro Muller 1776 (✆ **02/418-7777;** http://uruguay.usembassy.gov); **U.K.,** Marco Bruto 1073 (✆ **02/623-3630;** www.ukinuruguay.fco.gov.uk); **Canada,** Plaza Independencia 749, Office 102 (✆ **02/902-2030;** www.dfait-maeci.gc.ca/uruguay); and **Australia,** Cerro Largo 1000 (✆ **02/901-0743**).

Emergencies The general emergency number is ✆ **911.** Outside Montevideo, dial ✆ **02-911** to connect with Montevideo Central Emergency Authority. The following numbers also work: police ✆ **109;** ambulance ✆ **105;** and fire department ✆ **104.**

Hospital A colonial-style mansion houses the **British Hospital,** Av. Italia 2420 (✆ **02/487-1020**), which has emergency-room services.

Internet Access Cybercafes are commonly found around Montevideo and other Uruguayan cities. Many hotel business centers have Internet access, as do the guest rooms in high-end hotels.

Language Spanish is the universal tongue here and understood by everybody. Along the Brazilian border you'll find many people who can also speak Portuguese, with a local dialect known as Portuñol that mixes both languages together.

Liquor Laws The legal age for drinking is 18.

Newspapers & Magazines The three main newspapers in Uruguay are *El Pais* (www.elpais.com.uy), *El Observador* (www.observa.com.uy), and *La República* (www.diariolarepublica.com.uy). Well-known current affairs magazines are *Brecha* (www.brecha.com.uy) and *Comentario Nacional* (www.comentarionacional.com).

Police See "Emergencies," above.

Post Offices/Mail Post offices are generally open Monday through Friday from 8am to 6pm and Saturday from 8am to 1pm. You can buy stamps there or in mailing centers in shopping malls.

Restrooms It's permissible to use the toilets in restaurants and bars without patronizing the establishment; offer a nice smile on the way in. Nobody should bother you unless they're having a bad day.

Safety Uruguay is one of the world's safest countries, although petty crime in Montevideo has risen in recent years. Outside the capital, cities and beach resorts such as Punta del Este are considered safe. Travelers visiting Uruguay are nevertheless advised to take common-sense precautions.

Smoking Uruguay has one of the most strictly enforced smoking bans in the region, instituted by President Tabaré Vázquez—a practicing oncologist.

Taxes Value-added tax is called IVA in Spanish. IVA is 14% for hotels, 23% in restaurants, and 24% for general sales tax; the tax is almost always included in your bill. The departure tax when leaving the country is $31, paid before boarding your flight.

Telephone & Fax See "Telephone Dialing Info at a Glance," above.

Time Zone Uruguay is 1 hour ahead of Eastern Standard Time, although the country doesn't observe daylight saving time.

Tipping A 10% to 15% tip is common in restaurants. For taxis, round up to the nearest peso. Tip bellhops 50¢ per bag.

Water Locals swear that the drinking water in Uruguay is perfectly healthy; in fact, Uruguay was the only country in the Americas (along with the nations of the Caribbean) to escape the cholera pandemic of the early 1990s. If you are concerned, stick with bottled water *(agua mineral sin gas).*

4 MONTEVIDEO

Montevideo has all the variety, culture and architecture of Buenos Aires, but without the hordes of tourists and traffic—plus, everything is within walking distance. A wide, blustery waterfront with a backdrop of gray Soviet-style apartment blocks contrasts with handsome government buildings and crumbling mansions in the Ciudad Vieja. Karaoke sailor bars stand next to Art Deco diners, and fishermen tend their catches while elders sip *mate* (a tealike beverage and national obsession) in the city parks, all buffeted by a sea breeze that reveals this city, the southernmost capital on the continent, is in fact surrounded on three sides by water.

Montevideo is often regarded as a downsized Buenos Aires, but it has a discreet charm and compactness that its sister city lacks across the wide choppy waters of the Río de la Plata. Its colorful port area and market betrays its strong maritime past, first as a Spanish fort and then as a major port city. Rich European style architecture reveals a diverse immigrant population, and though this city may have seen better times, it makes for a relaxing stopover and an interesting destination to linger, stroll, and relax.

ESSENTIALS

Getting There

BY PLANE To get to Montevideo by plane, see "Getting There & Getting Around," above. A private, unmetered taxi or *remise* (radio taxi) from the airport to downtown costs about U$500 and takes 30 minutes.

BY BOAT OR HYDROFOIL **Buquebús,** Terminal Fluvio-Maritima de Montivideo (✆ **02/916-8801** or 130; www.buquebus.com), operates three to four hydrofoils per day between Montevideo and Buenos Aires; the trip takes about 3 hours and costs about $120 round-trip. Montevideo's port is just over 1.5km (1 mile) from downtown. Taxis from here to downtown cost about U$200 and take 7 minutes. If you have taken a ferry to Colonia, you can get connecting bus service to Montevideo; the bus terminal is near the port on Manuel de Lobos and Avenida Roosevelt. The trip takes 3 hours and costs U$176. Try **COT** (✆ **02/409-4949;** www.cot.com.uy).

BY BUS **Terminal Omnibus Tres Cruces,** General Artigas 1825 (© **02/409-7399** or 02/401-8998), is Montevideo's long-distance bus terminal, connecting the capital with cities in Uruguay and throughout South America. Buses to Buenos Aires take about 8 hours. **COT** (© **02/409-4949**) offers the best service to Punta del Este (U$142), Maldonado (U$137), and Colonia (U$176).

Orientation

The **Old City** begins near the western edge of Montevideo, found on the skinny portion of a peninsula between the **Rambla Gran Bretaña** and the city's main artery, **Avenida 18 de Julio.** Look for the **Plaza Independencia** and the **Plaza Constitución** to find the center of the district. Many of the city's museums, theaters, and hotels reside in this historic area, although a trip east on Avenida 18 de Julio reveals the more modern Montevideo, with its own share of hotels, markets, and monuments. Along the city's long southern coastline runs the Rambla Gran Bretaña, traveling 21km (13 miles) from the piers of the Old City past Parque Rodó and on to points south and east, passing fish stalls and street performers along the way.

Getting Around

It's easy to navigate around the center of Montevideo on foot or by bus. Safe, convenient buses crisscross Montevideo, making it easy to venture outside the city center, for U$15. Taxis are safe and relatively inexpensive, but it can be difficult to hail one during rush hour. I recommend calling **Remises Carrasco** (© **09/440-5473**). To rent a car, try **Thrifty** (© **02/481-8170;** www.thrifty.com.uy). Another reputable company based at the airport is **Europcar** (© **02/4010575;** www.europcar.com.uy). Cars start at $50. For roadside emergencies or general information on driving in Uruguay, contact the **Automóvil Club de Uruguay,** Av. Libertador 1532 (© **02/902-4792**), or the **Centro Automovilista del Uruguay,** E. V. Haedo 2378 (© **02/408-2091**).

Visitor Information

Uruguay's **Ministerio de Turismo** is at Av. Libertador 1409 and Colonia (© **02/908-9105**). It assists travelers with countrywide information and is open daily from 8am to 8pm in winter, and from 8am to 2pm in summer. There are also branches at Carrasco International Airport (© **02/604-0386**); at Tres Cruces bus station (© **02/409-7399**) and at the port where Buquebus docks, Rambla 25 de Agosto de 1825 and Yacaré (© **02/188-5100**). The **municipal tourist office,** Explanada Municipal (© **02/916-8434**), offers city maps and brochures of tourist activities and is open Monday to Friday from 10am to 4pm, Saturday and Sunday 10am to 6pm. It also organizes cultural city tours on weekends. In the event of an emergency, the **Tourist Police** can be reached at (© **0800-8226**), and their office is at Colonia 1021.

Tour Companies

Buemes Travel Services, Colonia 979, Montevideo (© **02/902-1050;** www.buemes.com.uy), is a large conventional agency which will help with everything from city tours to *estancia* stays. Another reputable company is **Cecilia Regules Viajes,** Bacacay 1334, Local C, Montevideo (© **02/916-3011;** www.ceciliaregulesviajes.com).

FAST FACTS To exchange money, try **Turisport Limitada** (the local Amex representative), San José 930 (© **02/902-0829;** www.turisport.com.uy); **Gales Casa Cambiaria,** Av. 18 de Julio 1046 (© **02/902-0229**); or one of the airport exchanges.

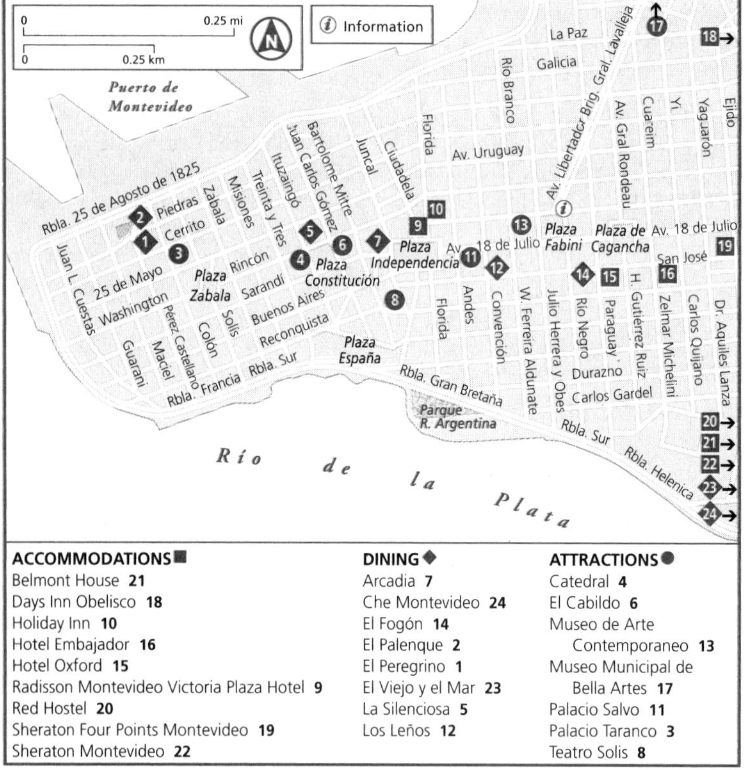

For medical attention, go to the **British Hospital,** at Av. Italia 2420 (✆ **02/487-1020**). Internet cafes appear and disappear faster than dance clubs, but you won't walk long before coming across one in the city center. Reliable cybercafes include **El Cybercafé,** Calle 25 de Mayo 568; **Arroba del Sur,** Guayabo 1858; and **El Cybercafé Softec,** Santiago de Chile 1286. The average cost is U$40 per hour of usage. The main **post office** is at Calle Buenos Aires 451 (✆ **0810/444-267736**), open weekdays from 9am to 6pm.

WHAT TO SEE & DO

Catedral ★ Also known as Iglesia Matriz (parish church), the cathedral was the city's first public building, erected in 1804. It houses the remains of some of Uruguay's most important political, religious, and economic figures, and is distinguished by its domed bell towers.

Calle Sarandí at Ituzaingó. Free admission. Mon–Fri 8am–8pm.

El Cabildo (Town Hall) ★ Uruguay's constitution was signed in the old town hall, which also served as the city's jailhouse in the 19th century. Now a museum, the Cabildo

Ranch Romance

Gaucho life is alive and well in Uruguay, and to experience some bucolic days on horseback in the vast rolling fields of the interior is something you are not likely to forget. The finer *estancias* now offer top-notch accommodation as well as day trips with lunch and activates included. The most famous and luxurious is **San Pedro de Timote,** Cerro Colorado, 160km (99 miles) northeast of Montevideo (✆ **0310/8086;** www.sanpedrodetimote.com.uy), a lovely property with a long history and the architecture to prove it, including a lovely white chapel. Another well-appointed farm offering cowboy chic is **Estancia La Paz,** Paysandu, 370km (230 miles) northwest of Montevideo (✆ **072/02272;** www.estancialapaz.com.uy). Just down river, close to the town of Mercedes, is **La Sirena** (✆ **02/606-2924;** www.lasirena.com.uy), a pastoral paradise with a gorgeous old ranch house and English-speaking owners. Access is a problem at most *estancias,* so it is often more convenient to arrange transfers directly with the lodges. For day tours contact tour operators that specialize in agrotourism, such as **Cecilia Regules Viajes,** Bacacay 1334, Local C, Montevideo (✆ **02/916-3011;** www.ceciliaregulesviajes.com), or **Lares,** WF Aldunate, Local 15, Montevideo (✆ **02/901-9120;** www.lares.com.uy).

houses the city's historic archives as well as maps and photos, antiques, costumes, and artwork.

Juan Carlos Gómez 1362. ✆ **02/915-9685.** Free admission. Tues–Sun 2:30–7pm.

Museo de Arte Contemporáneo ★ Opened in 1997, this museum is dedicated to contemporary Uruguayan art and exhibits the country's biggest names. To promote cultural exchange across the region, a section of the museum has been set aside for artists who hail from various South American countries. Allow an hour for your visit.

Av. 18 de Julio 965, 2nd floor. ✆ **02/900-6662.** Free admission. Daily noon–8pm.

Museo Municipal de Bellas Artes Juan Manuel Blanes ★ The national art history museum displays Uruguayan artistic styles from the beginning of the nation to the present day. Works include oils, engravings, drawings, sculptures, and documents. Among the great Uruguayan artists exhibited are Juan Manuel Blanes, Pedro Figari, Rafael Barradas, José Cúneo, and Carlos González. Plan to spend an hour here.

Av. Millán 4015. ✆ **02/336-2248.** Free admission. Tues–Sun noon–5:45pm.

Palacio Salvo Often referred to as the symbol of Montevideo, the Salvo Palace was once the tallest building in South America. Although its 26 stories might not impress you, it remains the city's highest structure. Unfortunately, its highest floors are not open to the public, though you can visit the lobby, which hosts frequent exhibitions.

Plaza Independencia and Av. 18 de Julio.

Palacio Taranco ★ Now the decorative arts museum, the Taranco Palace was built in the early 20th century and represents the trend toward French architecture during that

Safety Note

Although Montevideo remains very safe by big-city standards, street crime has risen in recent years. Travelers should avoid walking alone, particularly at night, in Ciudad Vieja, Avenida 18 de Julio, Plaza Independencia, and the vicinity around the port. Take a taxi instead.

period. The museum displays an assortment of Uruguayan furniture, draperies, clocks, paintings, and other cultural works. There is also a small section exhibiting Islamic art, including a collection of ancient Egyptian statuettes. An hour should give you enough time to see it all.

Calle 25 de Mayo 379. ✆ **02/915-6060.** Free admission. Tues–Sat 10am–6pm.

Plaza Independencia ★★ Originally the site of a Spanish citadel, Independence Square marks the beginning of the Old City and is a good point from which to begin your tour of Montevideo. An enormous statue of General José Gervasio Artigas, father of Uruguay and hero of its independent movement, stands in the center.

Bordered by Av. 18 de Julio, Florida, and Juncal.

Teatro Solís ★★ Montevideo's main theater and opera house, opened in 1852, underwent an extensive renovation in the late 1990s. It hosts Uruguay's most important cultural events. While the structure on its outside remains historical, the interior is a thoroughly modern contrast.

Calle Buenos Aires 652. ✆ **02/1950-1856.** www.teatrosolis.org.uy. Free admission. Museum Mon–Fri 2–6pm.

Shopping

Shopping in Montevideo is concentrated in a few downtown shops, markets, and in three major shopping centers. In Uruguayan stores, expect to find leather goods, jewelry, and local crafts and textiles—including sweaters, cardigan jackets, ponchos, coats, and tapestries made of high-quality wool (Uruguay is one of the world's largest exporters of wool). International stores carry American and European products. Montevideo's most fashionable mall is the **Punta Carretas Shopping Center,** Calle Ellauri and Solano, on the site of a former prison next to the Sheraton hotel. Downtown, the **Montevideo Shopping Center,** Av. Luis Alberto de Herrera 1290, is the city's original mall, with more than 180 stores and a 10-screen theater. **Portones de Carrasco,** avenidas Bolivia and Italia, is another recommended shopping center in the Carrasco neighborhood. **Tres Cruces Shopping Mall** is part of the bus terminal complex, with dozens of shops. It's at Avenida Serra with Acevedo Díaz (✆ **02/408 8710;** www.trescruces.com.uy). Leather goods at great prices are at **Casa Mario Leather Factory,** Piedras 641 at Bartolomo Mitre (✆ **02/916-2356;** www.casamarioleather.com).

MARKETS The **Villa Biarritz fair,** at Parque Zorilla de San Martín-Ellauri, takes place Saturday from 9:30am to 3pm and features handicrafts, antiques, books, fruit and vegetable vendors, flowers, and other goodies. The **Mercado del Puerto (Port Market) ★★** opens afternoons and weekends at Piedras and Yacaré, letting you sample the flavors of Uruguay, from small empanadas to enormous barbecued meats. Saturday is the best day

Carnaval Time in Montevideo

Catch the lively street party that takes the city by storm in late January and throughout February. Colorful half-naked dancers and noisy *candombe* percussion bands celebrate Uruguay's African slave heritage. On February 2, the crowds head for Playa Ramírez for a big beach party celebrating the sea goddess Yemanga. If your timing is wrong, you can still see an exhibition on the festival at the **Museo de Carnaval,** Rambla 25 de Agosto de 1825 no. 218, at Maciel (✆ **02/916-5493**), in the port area.

to visit, when cultural activities accompany the market. **Tristán Narvaja,** Avenida 18 de Julio in the Cordón neighborhood, is the city's Sunday flea market (6am–3pm), initiated more than 50 years ago by Italian immigrants. **De la Abundancia/Artesanos** is a combined food and handicrafts market. It takes place Monday through Saturday from 10am to 8pm at San José 1312.

WHERE TO STAY

Montevideo's hotel infrastructure is improving and foreigners no longer pay tax on the rates (unlike the locals). Prices are jacked up during Carnaval time in February and when major conventions come to town, however. Parking is included in the rates of most Uruguay hotels.

Expensive

Belmont House ★★ Finds A boutique hotel in Montevideo's peaceful Carrasco neighborhood, Belmont House offers its privileged guests intimacy and luxury. Small, elegant spaces with carefully chosen antiques and wood furnishings give this hotel the feeling of a wealthy private home. Beautiful guest rooms feature two- or four-poster beds; rich, colorful linens; and marble bathrooms with small details such as towel warmers and deluxe toiletries. Many of the rooms feature balconies overlooking the pretty courtyard and pool, and two of the rooms have Jacuzzis. Gourmands will find an excellent international restaurant, afternoon tea, and a *parrilla* open weekends next to the pool.

Av. Rivera 6512, 11500 Montevideo. ✆ **02/600-0430.** Fax 02/600-8609. www.belmonthouse.com.uy. 28 units. $220 double; from $255–$360 suite. Rates include gourmet breakfast. AE, DC, MC, V. **Amenities:** Restaurant; tearoom; bar; babysitting; small fitness center; beautiful outdoor pool; sauna; discounts for tennis and golf. *In room:* A/C, TV, hair dryer, minibar.

Radisson Montevideo Victoria Plaza Hotel ★★ The Victoria Plaza has long been one of Montevideo's top hotels. Standing in the heart of the financial district, this European-style hotel makes a good base, and there is lots of business and social activity. Ask for a room in the new tower, which houses spacious guest rooms and executive suites with classic French-style furnishings and panoramic city or river views. The busy hotel has a large multilingual staff that attends closely to guests' needs. Inquire about weekend spa packages. Plaza Victoria is famous for its casino, with French roulette tables, blackjack, baccarat, slot machines, horse races, and bingo. There are two lobby bars, in addition to the casino bars. **Arcadia** (p. 737), on the 25th floor, is the city's most elegant dining room.

 Plaza Independencia 759, 11100 Montevideo. ✆ **02/902-0111.** Fax 02/902-1628. www.radisson.com/montevideouy. 254 units. $209 double; from $229 suite. Rates include breakfast at rooftop restaurant. AE, DC, MC, V. **Amenities:** Restaurant; cafe; 2 bars; aerobics classes; concierge; executive floors; fitness center; excellent health club w/skylit indoor pool; high-speed Internet access; Jacuzzi; room service; sauna. *In room:* A/C, TV, hair dryer, Internet, minibar.

Sheraton Montevideo ★★ The Sheraton Montevideo is the city's most luxurious hotel. A walkway connects the hotel to the Punta Carretas Shopping Center, one of the city's best malls. Spacious guest rooms have imported furniture, king-size beds, sleeper chairs, marble bathrooms, 25-inch televisions, and works by Uruguayan artists. Rooms on the top two executive floors feature Jacuzzis and individual sound systems. Hotel service is excellent, particularly for guests with business needs. The main restaurant, Las Carretas, serves Continental cuisine with a Mediterranean flair. Don't miss the dining room's spectacular murals by contemporary Uruguayan artist Carlos Vilaró.

Calle Víctor Soliño 349, 11300 Montevideo. ✆ **02/710-2121.** Fax 02/712-1262. www.sheraton.com. 207 units. From $175 double; from $275 suite. Rates include buffet breakfast. AE, DC, MC, V. **Amenities:** Restaurant; bar; babysitting; concierge; executive floors; deluxe health club w/fitness center; emergency medical service; indoor pool; room service; sauna. *In room:* A/C, TV, hair dryer, Internet, minibar.

Moderate

Holiday Inn ★ This colorful Holiday Inn is actually one of the city's best hotels, popular both with tourists and business travelers. It's in the heart of downtown, next to Montevideo's main square. Bilingual staff members greet you in the marble lobby, which is attached to a good restaurant and bar. Guest rooms have simple, contemporary furnishings typical of an American chain. Because the hotel doubles as a convention center, it can become very busy. On the flip side, rooms are heavily discounted when the hotel is empty; be sure to ask for promotional rates, which can be as low as $70 per night.

Colonia 823, 11100 Montevideo. ✆ **02/902-0001.** Fax 02/902-1242. www.holidayinn.com.uy. 137 units. From $108 double. Rates include buffet breakfast. AE, DC, MC, V. **Amenities:** Restaurant; bar; fitness center; heated indoor pool; room service; sauna; Wi-Fi. *In room:* A/C, TV, Internet, minibar.

Sheraton Four Points Montevideo ★★ The Sheraton Four Points is considered a four-star property, but it falls somewhere between four and five, save for its smaller size. The lobby is stark and modern, with polished black-granite panels over white walls in the soaring atrium. Walkways open onto the atrium on each floor, all connected by a glass elevator. Rooms are on the dark side, with charcoal carpeting, dark woods, and rust-colored bedspreads. The bathrooms are spacious, however, and suite bathrooms have hydromassage bathtubs. All rooms have high-speed Internet access, at a charge of $16 a day. Wi-Fi access is also available, all at the same price as an in-room connection. The desks make a great work space.

Ejido 1275 at Soriano, across from the Intendencia or City Hall, 11000 Montevideo. ✆ **02/901-7000.** Fax 02/903-2247. www.fourpoints.com/montevideo. 135 units, including 18 suites. From $129 double; from $220 suite. AE, DC, MC, V. Free parking. **Amenities:** Restaurant; bar; babysitting; concierge; health club w/fitness center; indoor pool; room service; sauna. *In room:* A/C, TV, hair dryer, Internet, minibar.

Inexpensive

Days Inn Obelisco (Value) The modern Days Inn caters to business travelers looking for good-value accommodations. The hotel is next to the Tres Cruces bus station and not far from downtown or the airport. Rooms are comfortable and modern, if not overly spacious. Free local calls are permitted.

Acevedo Díaz 1821, 11800 Montevideo. ✆ **02/400-4840.** Fax 02/402-0229. www.daysinn.com. 60 units. From $95 double; from $120 suite. Rates include buffet breakfast. AE, DC, MC, V. Free parking. **Amenities:** Coffee shop; small health club; room service. *In room:* A/C, TV, hair dryer, minibar.

Hotel Embajador The Embajador is a good-value four-star option right in the heart of the city center. The room decor is a little dated, with small wooden headboards, bulky TVs, flowery sofas, and corduroy carpets. Yet everything is spick-and-span, including the bathrooms, which have all-glass shower partitions. Its biggest plus is a rooftop pool, gym, and seating area where you can enjoy the view.

San José 1212, 11100 Montevideo. ✆ **02/902-0012.** www.hotelembajador.com. 75 units. From $70 double. Rates include buffet breakfast. AE, DC, MC, V. **Amenities:** Restaurant; bar; fitness center; heated indoor pool; room service; sauna; Wi-Fi. *In room:* A/C, TV, Internet, minibar.

Hotel Oxford Seven blocks from the waterfront, the Hotel Oxford is very much like its name—old and reliable. The rooms are somewhat dinky and the decor is 1970s, but they have lots of light and everything is reasonably clean. The Oxford is an unremarkable but sufficient hotel in a good location and with a very good price.

Paraguay 1286, 11100 Montevideo. ✆ **02/902-0046.** www.hoteloxford.com.uy. 66 units. $80 double. AE, DC, MC, V. Free parking. **Amenities:** Cafe; bar; concierge; room service. *In room:* A/C, TV, minibar.

Red Hostel High ceilings, tall doors, and brightly colored walls make this hostel one of the more pleasant budget options in the city center. Rooms and hallways have lots of light, not least because of the handsome skylights with stained-glass trimmings. The communal areas are a little cramped and the dorms have their fair share of beds, but the private doubles are a bargain if you book in time.

San José 1406. ✆ **02/908-8514.** www.redhostel.com. 16 units. $50 double; $15 dormitory bed. No credit cards. **Amenities:** Cafe; bar; roof terrace; TV room. *In room:* A/C.

WHERE TO DINE

Restaurants in Montevideo serve steak—just as high quality as Argentine beef—and usually include a number of stews and seafood selections as well. You will find the native barbecue, in which beef and lamb are grilled on the fire, in any of the city's grill restaurants, referred to interchangeably in Spanish as *parrillas* or *parrilladas.* Sales tax on dining in Montevideo is a whopping 23%. There is usually a table cover charge, called the *cubierto,* as well—usually about U$25 per person.

Expensive

Arcadia ★★ (Moments) INTERNATIONAL This elegant restaurant is a 25-story-high paradise and one of the best places to eat in Montevideo. Tables are nestled in semiprivate nooks with floor-to-ceiling bay windows. The classic dining room is decorated with Italian curtains and crystal chandeliers; each table has a fresh rose and sterling-silver place settings. Creative plates such as terrine of pheasant marinated in cognac are followed by grilled rack of lamb glazed with mint and garlic, or duck confit served on a thin strudel pastry with red cabbage.

Plaza Independencia 759. ✆ **02/902-0111.** Main courses U$400–U$600. AE, DC, MC, V. Daily 7pm–midnight.

La Silenciosa FRENCH/INTERNATIONAL This lovely old building was once a Jesuit convent, and its colonial past is evident in the bare brick arches and pillars and whitewashed walls. The wine-colored awning out front matches the tablecloths inside, with rolled napkins and polished wine glasses emphasizing this is one of the best fine-dining options in the Ciudad Vieja. The menu is international with a French flavor, the highlights of which are the fresh salads and glazed-fruit deserts.

Ituzaingó 1426. ✆ **02/915-9409.** Main courses U$400–U$600. AE, DC, MC, V. Mon–Sat noon–3pm and Thurs–Sat 8:30pm–1am.

Moderate

Che Montevideo URUGUAYAN You cannot beat this warm, welcoming restaurant for location with an open-air deck overlooking the river. Inside you'll find a cozy arrangement of stone walls, thatched ceilings, and lots of windows to catch the view. The menu has a little of everything, including good seafood, pizza, and steak. Order a Picada Che, which is a giant platter of cheese and cold meats. Service is prompt and the ambience relaxing, though the flickering TV gives it away that this is just as much a casual stopover for a snack and drink as much as it is for an evening dinner beside the water. Look out for the live music on Friday nights.

Rambla Gandhi 630. ✆ **02/710-6941.** Main courses U$200–U$300. AE, DC, MC. Daily noon–3am.

El Fogón ★ URUGUAYAN/PARRILLADA This brightly lit *parrillada* and seafood restaurant is popular with Montevideo's late-night crowd. The extensive menu includes calamari, salmon, shrimp, and other fish, as well as generous steak and pasta dishes. Food here is priced well and prepared with care. The express lunch menu comes with steak or chicken, dessert, and a glass of wine.

San José 1080. ✆ **02/900-0900.** Main courses U$200–U$300. AE, DC, MC, V. Daily noon–4pm and 7pm–1am.

El Palenque ★ SEAFOOD/PARRILLADA Located in the Mercado del Puerto, this is one of the area's most popular restaurants, crowded with locals and tourists alike. It gets especially crowded when the cruise ships come in. It has been around since 1958. Fish is the highlight, but they also have tapas, pasta, paella, and lots of grilled meat. A specialty is the Paella Exotica, made with rabbit.

Pérez Castellano 1579 (at Rambla 25 de Agosto 400 in the Mercado del Puerto). ✆ **02/917-0190** or 02/915-4704. www.elpalenque.com.uy. Main courses U$300–U$600. AE, DC, MC, V. Mon–Sat noon–1am; Sun noon–5pm.

El Viejo y el Mar ★ SEAFOOD Resembling an old fishing club, El Viejo y el Mar is on the riverfront near the Sheraton. The bar is made from an abandoned boat, while the dining room is decorated with dock lines, sea lamps, and pictures of 19th-century regattas. You'll find every kind of fish and pasta on the menu, and the restaurant is equally popular for evening cocktails. The outdoor patio is open most of the year.

Rambla Gandhi 400. ✆ **02/710-5704.** Main courses U$300–U$600. MC, V. Daily noon–4pm and 8pm–1am.

Los Leños ★★ URUGUAYAN This casual *parrillada* resembles one you'd find in Buenos Aires—except that Los Leños also serves an outstanding range of *mariscos* (seafood), such as the Spanish paella or *lenguado Las Brasas* (a flathead fish) served with prawns, mushrooms, and mashed potatoes. From the grill, the *filet de lomo* is the best cut—order it with Roquefort, mustard, or black-pepper sauce. The restaurant's fresh produce is displayed in a case near the kitchen.

San José 909. ✆ **02/900-2285.** Main courses U$300–U$600. AE, DC, MC, V. Daily 11:45am–3:30pm and 7:30pm–midnight.

Inexpensive

El Peregrino ITALIAN/PARRILLADA This large, charming spot offers atmospheric dining with its rustic tables, brick and yellow walls, and numerous old photographs. They offer several fish dishes, Italian, and lots of beef, pork, and chicken dishes.

Pérez Castellano 1553, at Piedras (at the Mercado del Puerto). ✆ **02/916-4737.** Main courses U$200–U$300. AE, DC, MC, V. Daily noon–1am.

MONTEVIDEO AFTER DARK

As in Buenos Aires, nightlife in Montevideo means drinks after 10pm and dancing after midnight. For earlier entertainment, ask at your hotel or call the **Teatro Solís,** Calle Buenos Aires 652 (✆ **02/1950-1856:** www.teatrosolis.org.uy), the city's center for opera, theater, ballet, and symphonies. For up-to-date listings, try and get your hands on a copy of *Guía del Ocio* (www.guiadelocio.com.uy), which comes out every Friday and costs U$10. For hardcore clubbers, check out the website **www.aromperlanoche.com**.

Gamblers should head to the **Plaza Victoria Casino,** Plaza Independencia (✆ **02/902-0111**), a fashionable venue with French roulette tables, blackjack, baccarat, slot machines, horse races, and bingo. It opens at 2pm and keeps going through most of the night. **Mariachi,** Gabriel Pereira 2964 (✆ **02/709-1600**), is one of the city's top bars and dance clubs, with live bands or DJ music Wednesday to Sunday after 10pm. **Café Misterio,** Costa Rica 1700 (✆ **02/600-5999**), is another popular bar. The hottest clubs going to print are **W Lounge,** Rambla Wilson, Parque Rodo (✆ **02/712-2671**), and **Almodó Bar,** Rincón 626, Ciudad Vieja (✆ **02/916-6665**),

Tango & *Candombe*

Montevideo's best tango clubs are **La Casa de Becho,** Nueva York 1415 (✆ **02/400-2717;** Fri–Sat after 10:30pm), where composer Gerardo Mattos Rodríguez wrote the famous La Cumparsita, and **Cuareim,** Zelmar Michelini 1079 (no phone; Wed and Fri–Sat after 9pm), which offers both tango and *candombe,* a lively dance indigenous to the area, with roots in early slave culture. This samba-style drum performance is a sight (and sound) to behold, especially if you wander the neighborhood of Barrio Sur on a Sunday evening, when all the locals spill out onto the street to practice. **El Tartamudo Cafe,** 8 de Octubre 2543 (✆ **02/480-4332**), is one of the city's best-known small music venues, showcasing tango musicians as well as jazz and *candombe* performers. The tourist office can give you schedule information for Montevideo's other tango salons.

5 A SIDE TRIP TO COLONIA DEL SACRAMENTO

242km (150 miles) W of Montevideo

The tiny gem of Colonia del Sacramento, declared a World Heritage Site by UNESCO, appears untouched by time. Dating from the 17th century, the Old City has beautifully preserved colonial artistry down its dusty streets. A leisurely stroll from the Puerta de Campo into the **Barrio Histórico** (Old, or Historic, Neighborhood) leads under flower-laden windowsills to churches dating from the 1680s, past exquisite single-story homes from Colonia's time as a Portuguese settlement and on to local museums detailing the riches of the town's past. The Barrio Histórico contains brilliant examples of colonial wealth and many of Uruguay's oldest structures. Yet while the city resides happily in

Top up on Tannat

Uruguayan wine is catching up with is more famous regional cousins in Argentina and Chile. Likewise, the wineries, based around Colonia and Carmelo (77km/48 miles northwest of Colonia), are opening up to touring, where you can visit traditional style wineries and try the country's signature red Tannat. **Bodega Bernardi,** Ruta 1, Laguna de los Patos, Colonia (✆ **052/24752;** www.bodegabernardi.com), is a lovely old family-run operation that dates back to the 19th century. There, owner Roberto Bernardi will show you around and introduce you to the Uruguayan sparkling known as frizzante and the ubiquitous Tannat. No appointments are necessary unless you wish to have lunch there. The bodega is 7km (4 miles) from Colonia. A larger operation with lots of tradition is **Irurtia,** Ramal Ruta 97, Carmelo (✆ **0542/2323;** www.irurtia.com.uy), which has atmospheric brick-arched cellars and a 3-million-liter production that includes cabernet and pinot noir. Guide Maria-Noel Irurtia is part of the four generations of winemakers who run the place and gives visitors a very personal tour. A little more humble is **Zubizarreta,** Ruta 21, Camino de la Calera de las Huerfanas, Carmelo (✆ **0540/2677;** www.vinoszubizarreta.com.uy), a modern-warehouse-style winery producing merlot, cabernet sauvignon, and Tannat. As far as tour operators that will take you around the wineries, the best are **Lares,** WF Aldunate, Local 15, Montevideo (✆ **02/901-9120;** www.lares.com.uy), and **Robertson Tours,** the Penthouse 1202, 2865 Vázquez Ledesma, Villla Biarritz, Montevideo (✆ **02/7113032;** www.robertsonwinetours.com).

tradition, a mix of lovely shops, delicious cafes, and thoughtful museums make the town more than a history lesson.

ESSENTIALS

Getting There

The easiest way to reach Colonia from Buenos Aires is by ferry. **FerryLíneas** (✆ **02/900-6617;** www.ferryturismo.com.uy) runs a fast boat that arrives in 45 minutes (fare U$1,572) and a slower 3-hour ferry (U$1,000). **Buquebús** (✆ **02/916-1910;** www.buquebus.com) also offers two classes of service. Prices range from $40 to $70 each way. **Colonia Express** (✆ **54/11/4313-5100** in Buenos Aires, or 02/901-9597 in Montevideo; www.coloniaexpress.com) offers a similar ferryboat-and-bus combination to Montevideo but has a less frequent schedule. Colonia is a good stopping-off point if you're traveling between Buenos Aires and Montevideo. **COT** (✆ **02/409-4949** in Montevideo; www.cot.com.uy) offers **bus service** from Montevideo and from Punta del Este.

Visitor Information

The **Oficina de Turismo,** General Flores and Rivera (✆ **052/23700** or 26141), is open daily from 8am to 8pm. There is a smaller Oficina de Turismo on Calle Manuel Lobo 224, near the Barrio Historico (✆ **052/28506**) with similar opening hours. Speak with someone at the tourism office to arrange a guided tour of the town or contact the local guide association **AGDC** (✆ **052/22309;** asociacionguiascolonia@gmail.com). Websites www.colonia.gub.uy and www.guiacolonia.com.uy have info on the area, while ***Guear*** (www.guear.com) is a slick booklet specializing in the fine dining and nightlife around Colonia.

A WALK THROUGH COLONIA'S BARRIO HISTORICO

Concentrate in the **Barrio Histórico (Old Neighborhood),** on the coast at the far southwestern corner of town. The sights, which are all within a few blocks, can easily be visited on foot in a few hours. Museums and tourist sites are open Thursday to Tuesday from 11am to 5:45pm. For U$40, you can buy a pass at the Portuguese or Municipal museum that will get you into all the sights.

Start your tour at **Plaza Mayor,** the principal square that served as the center of the colonial establishment. To explore Colonia's Portuguese history, cross Calle Manuel Lobo on the southeastern side of the plaza and enter the **Museo Portugués.** Upon exiting the museum, turn left and walk to the **Iglesia Matriz,** among the oldest churches in the country and a good example of 17th-century architecture and design.

Next, exit the church and turn left to the **Ruinas Convento San Francisco.** Dating from 1696, the San Francisco convent was once inhabited by Jesuit and Franciscan monks. Continue up Calle San Francisco to the **Casa de Brown,** which houses the **Museo Municipal.** Here you will find an impressive collection of colonial documents and artifacts, a must-see for history buffs.

For those with a more artistic bent, turn left on Calle Misiones de los Tapes and walk 2 blocks to the **Museo del Azulejo,** a unique museum of 19th-century European and Uruguayan tiles housed in a gorgeous 300-year-old country house. Then stroll back into the center of town along Calle de la Playa, enjoying the shops and cafes along the way, until you come to the **Ruinas Casa del Gobernador.** The House of the Viceroy captures something of the glorious past of the city's 17th- and 18th-century magistrates, when the port was used for imports, exports, and smuggling. After exploring the opulent lifestyle of colonial leaders, complete your walk with a visit to the **UNESCO-Colonia** headquarters.

WHERE TO STAY & DINE

Few people stay in Colonia, preferring to make a day trip from Buenos Aires or stop along the way to Montevideo. If you'd rather get a hotel, however, your best bets are the colonial-style **Posada Plaza Mayor,** Calle del Comercio 111 (✆ **052/23193;** www.posadaplazamayor.com), and **Hotel La Misión,** Calle Misiones de los Tapes 171 (✆ **052/26767;** www.lamisionhotel.com), whose original building dates from 1762. Both hotels charge from $100 for a double. A small **Sheraton,** Continuación de la Rambla de Las Américas s/n (✆ **052/29000:** www.sheraton.com), is 10 minutes by car from Colonia. It offers doubles from $185 and has a spa and a golf course. The **Four Seasons,** Ruta 21, Km 262, Carmelo (✆ **0542/9000;** www.fourseasons.com/carmelo), operates a luxury resort in nearby Carmelo, about 45 minutes away. Rooms start at $350.

For dining, **Mesón de la Plaza,** Vasconcellos 153 (✆ **052/24807**), serves quality international and Uruguayan food in a colonial setting. **Pulpería de los Faroles,** Calle Misiones de los Tapes 101 (✆ **052/25399**), in front of Plaza Mayor, specializes in beef and bean dishes and homemade pasta, and has an elegant vibe with pastel tablecloths and well-dressed waiters. **Lobo,** Calle de Comercio, at La Playa (✆ **052/29254;** www.loborestaurante.com), offers creative dishes such as leek-and-bacon raviolis in an attractive setting with live music at weekends. **El Drugstore,** Vasconcellos 179, at Portugal (✆ **052/25241**), has decor as eclectic as its menu. Polka-dot tables and antique cars will catch your eyes, while Japanese sushi and steak compete for your stomach.

6 PUNTA DEL ESTE

140km (87 miles) E of Montevideo

Few resorts in South America rival Punta del Este for glamour. It might be geographically located in Uruguay, but it's where the glitterati and elite of Buenos Aires make their homes for the summer. As Mar del Plata's reputation downscales, this Uruguayan resort area has become a place to see and be seen

Punta is actually a reference to several towns on a small peninsula where the Río de la Plata meets the Atlantic Ocean. Together they have over 50km (31 miles) of waterfront. The majority of the city's major hotels are on the calmer river side. As a general rule, the farther you get from the center, the less crowded the beaches. Little of historical value is left anymore except a few buildings, such as the *faro* (lighthouse), churches, schoolhouses, and turn-of-the-20th-century buildings. The port is often jammed with yachts in the summer.

About 10km (6 miles) up from Punta del Este is the small town of **La Barra.** Many young beachgoers flock here, and it's never quiet in high season. Farther along Ruta 10 is the very exclusive **José Ignacio,** a small quiet community that's even more expensive than La Barra. Summer season lasts from October to March, but "the Season," as it is known in the area, is a very specific time; from a few days after Christmas through the first 2 weeks of January, the Punta, La Barra, and José Ignacio swell with movie stars and models.

ESSENTIALS

Getting There

BY PLANE Punta del Este has its own international airport, **Laguna del Sauce Airport** (airport code PDP; © **042/559777**), about 16km (10 miles) from the city center, which has direct flights from Buenos Aires's Jorge Newberry Airport. **Aerolíneas Argentinas** (© **000-4054-86527** in Punta, or 0810/222-86527 in Buenos Aires; www.aerolineas.com.ar) services the airports. **Pluna Airlines** is another carrier (© **042/492050** in Punta, or 11/4342-4420 in Buenos Aires; www.pluna.aero).

BY BUS The **Terminal de Buses Punta del Este,** Rambla Artigas and Calle Inzaurraga, has buses connecting to Montevideo, Colonia, and other cities throughout Uruguay. **COT** (© **042/486-810,** or 02/409-4949 in Montevideo; www.cot.com.uy) offers the best service to Montevideo. The trip takes 1½ to 2 hours and costs about U$284 round-trip.

BY CAR If you are driving from Montevideo, you can reach Punta in 1½ hours by taking Route 1 east past Atlántida and Piriápolis to the turnoff for Route 93.

Getting Around

If you're staying in Punta del Este itself, the beaches are just a quick walk over either the **Rambla Claudio Williman,** on the Río de la Plata side, or the **Rambla Lorenzo Batlle Pacheco,** on the Atlantic side. Although these two *ramblas* have different names, they are part of the same coastal highway, Ruta 10. The city's main shopping street is **Avenida Gorlero,** lined with stores and cafes. Another shopping street is **El Remanso,** 1 block parallel.

Many people hitchhike—it's not considered dangerous here. It's best to rent a car, though, if you want to do some exploring or head to La Barra or José Ignacio. Car rental can be expensive, however, starting at $90 a day in high season. **Europcar** is at Gorlero and Calle 20 (✆ **042/495017** or 042/445018; www.europcar.com.uy). **Dollar** is at Gorlero 961 (✆ **042/443444;** www.dollar.com.uy).

Taxis are hard to come by, especially in high season. Keep the following numbers handy: **Shopping** (✆ **042/484704**), **Parada 5** (✆ **042/490302**), and **Aeropuerto** (✆ **042/559100**). The bus company **COT** (✆ **042/486810:** www.cot.com.uy) runs a service up and down the coastal routes, connecting the various towns in the area. You may have to wait a long time for one to pass by, though.

Visitor Information

Punta del Este has several tourist information centers. Within the bus station **Terminal Punta Del Este** (✆ **042/494042**), there is a very small one with a very helpful staff. Overlooking the ocean at Parada 1 near Calle 21, the **Liga de Fomento** has a tourist information center (✆ **042/446519**). Another city office is at **Plaza Artigas,** on Gorlero between calles 25 and 23 (✆ **042/4465190**). The city's offices are open daily from 10am to 10pm. The government of Uruguay also maintains a tourist information office for the entire country at Gorlero 942 between calles 30 and 29 (✆ **042/441218**). The national office is open 10am to 7pm every day in the summer, and in winter daily from 10am to 5pm. The city government website (www.maldonado.gub.uy) has a section on tourist information; also visit **www.uruguaynatural.com**. Pick up ***Qué Hacemos Hoy*** (www.quehacemoshoy.com.uy), a free tourist publication, available throughout the city, with information on events around town.

Tour Companies

Take a break from such a hard life on the beach and take a 2-hour boat tour to a nearby island called Isla de Lobos. **Calypso Charter & Excursions,** Rambla Artigas and Calle 21, Punta del Este (✆ **042/446152;** www.calypso.com.uy), has a 17m-long (55-ft.) catamaran that lets you go in style. For city tours and a day visit to the beautiful Casapueblo, try **Novo Turismo,** Terminal de Omnibuses, Localo 4, Punta del Este (✆ **042/493154;** www.novoturismo.com).

WHAT TO SEE & DO

The main reason to visit Punta del Este is the beach, but you'll also find a few sights of interest. The symbol of Punta del Este is **La Mano,** a giant concrete hand sculpture rising out of the sands of the Atlantic, opposite the bus station. On the tip of the peninsula, **Puerto Punta del Este** is pleasant for strolling and watching the boats come in. A tranquil change of pace from the beach is the church **Nuestra Señora de la Candelaria,** at the corner of Calle 12 (or Virazon) and Calle 5 (or El Faro), a beautiful sky-blue-and-white Victorian structure. Across the street is the **Meteorological Station,** Calle 5 and Calle 10 (or Calle Dos de Febrero), a modern lookout tower built over a 100-year-old schoolhouse. Directly across the street is **Faro de Punta del Este,** the city's symbolic lighthouse, dating from 1860, at Calle 5 and Calle 10. **Plaza Artigas,** at Gorlero and Arrecifes, has a daily artist market with souvenirs and crafts. Along Ruta 10, just outside downtown La Barra, is the **Museo del Mar** ★★ (✆ **042/771-817;** www.museodelmar.com.uy), an interesting museum open daily in summer from 10:30am to 8:30pm, and in winter daily from 11am to 6pm. Admission is U$100 for adults and U$50 for children.

SHOPPING

The majority of shops run along Avenida Gorlero and Calle 20, also known as El Remanso, or the Little Paris. Many stores do not open until the evening. For leather goods, try **Leather Corner,** Calle 31 at Inzaurraga and Gorlero (✆ **042/441901**). **Duo,** Calle 20 at Calle 30 (✆ **042/447709**), is an upscale sportswear store for men and women. **100% Uruguayo,** Gorlero 883 at Calle 28 (✆ **042/446530**), has a large collection of handmade and distinctive locally produced goods; leather is the highlight. **Punta Shopping** is the main mall, Avenida Roosevelt at Parada 7 (✆ **042/489666;** www.puntashopping.com.uy). **Plaza Artigas,** at Gorlero and Arrecifes, has a daily artist market with souvenirs and crafts. The town of La Barra is better known for its art galleries, including the popular **Trench Gallery,** Ruta 10, Km 161, Parada 45 (✆ **042/771597**).

WHERE TO STAY

Unless otherwise indicated, prices listed below are for summer peak season and are often half that in the off season. **Christmas** and **New Year** is the busiest, most expensive time. Reserve well ahead.

Very Expensive

The Awa Hotel ★★ This small, well-designed boutique hotel has clean lines—a sort of 1950s interpretation of Alpine architecture, set on a landscaped hill with soaring pine trees. Rooms are a good size, set in pure radiant white, with African-made, wall-to-wall cotton carpeting in neutral tones. Bathrooms are large and the suites have hydromassage tubs. One of the most amazing things about the hotel is its theater. The hotel is a bit of a walk from the beach, but it's surrounded by several restaurants, and it's close to the Punta Shopping mall.

Pedragosa Sierra and San Ciro; CP 20100, Punta del Este. ✆ **042/499999.** www.awahotel.com. 48 units, including 4 suites and 8 executive corner oversize rooms. In low season from $110 double, from $210 suite; high season from $260 double, from $640 suite. Rates include buffet breakfast. AE, DC, MC, V. Free on-site parking. **Amenities:** Restaurant; concierge; small health club; minitheater; heated outdoor pool; room service; spa; Wi-Fi in lobby. *In room:* A/C, TV, hair dryer, minibar, Wi-Fi.

Casapueblo ★ To stay at this hillside hotel is like residing in a piece of art. Indeed, Uruguay's most distinctive property was designed and built by the artist Carlos Páez Vilaró. Its playful spires and domes and uneven walls have overtones of Gaudí with a Moorish brilliance. The location has stamped its character on the building, with the lobby at the top, and the rooms descending toward the sea, enclosing three gorgeous pools. Rooms are delightful and spacious, with pastel-blue wardrobe doors and white gauze hanging over the beds and windows. Unfortunately, the hotel's artistry does not extend to the staff's hospitality and efficiency, and its isolated location (10km/6 miles from Punta del Este) means you will definitely need a car. It's probably best to stay here for just for 1 night before throwing yourself into the party atmosphere farther down the peninsula.

Punta Ballena. ✆ **042/578611.** www.clubhotel.com.ar. 70 units. $460 double high season; $575 suite. AE, DC, MC, V. Free on-site parking. **Amenities:** Restaurant; concierge; small health club; minitheater; 3 pools (1 heated indoor); room service; spa. *In room:* A/C, TV, hair dryer, minibar, Wi-Fi.

The Conrad Resort & Casino ★★★ This 14-story complex, a blue streamlined structure, has became the de facto town center and is a hive of activity. Some rooms have a California vibe, with casual decor in terra cottas and neutral tones; others are modern and more severe; and still others have a tropical playfulness to them. All rooms facing the Río de la Plata have balconies, and the suites have balconies enormous enough for entertaining several guests, which is common in the summertime. There are several restaurants in the lobby and other areas of the hotel. The pool and spa complex is a combination of indoor and outdoor spaces, with a view to the Río de la Plata. There is also the children's complex, where you can leave your kids and gain some free time. The 24-hour casino has 450 slot machines and 63 gaming tables; it's definitely worth visiting even if you're not staying here.

Parada 4 on Rambla Claudio Williman (between Chivert and Biarritz on Playa Mansa), CP 20100, Punta del Este. ✆ **042/491111.** Fax 042/490803. www.conrad.com.uy. 302 units, including 24 suites. In low season from $200 double, from $400 suite; high season from $500 double, from $800 suite. Rates include luxurious buffet breakfast. AE, DC, MC, V. **Amenities:** 5 restaurants; several bars; babysitting; casino; children's center; concierge; large health club; indoor and outdoor heated pools; room service; spa; theater and show complex; Wi-Fi in lobby. *In room:* A/C, TV, hair dryer, high-speed Internet, kitchens in select suites, minibar.

L'Auberge ★★ Finds This exclusive boutique hotel lies in the quiet residential neighborhood of Parque de Golf and is 2 blocks from the beach. Formerly an 18th-century water tower, the hotel today houses beautiful guest rooms decorated with antiques and has a dedicated staff committed to warm, personalized service. The colorful gardens and pool will draw you outside, and the staff can help you arrange horseback riding, golf, tennis, or other outdoor sports in the surrounding parks. The sophisticated resort has an elegant European tearoom overlooking the gardens, famous for its homemade waffles. An evening barbecue is offered by the pool.

Barrio Parque del Golf, 20100 Punta del Este. ✆ **042/482-601.** Fax 042/483-408. www.laubergehotel.com. 40 units. From $300 double; from $610 suite. Rates include continental breakfast. AE, DC, MC, V. **Amenities:** Babysitting; concierge; fitness center; golf; outdoor pool; room service; spa; tennis court. *In room:* TV, hair dryer, minibar.

Moderate

Best Western La Foret ★ Kids La Foret offers spacious guest rooms 1 block from Playa Mansa. The amenities are extensive and the hotel is a nice option for families (children 11 and under stay free, and there are a children's playground and babysitting services). There's also a good international restaurant and coffee shop with a multilingual staff.

Calle La Foret, Parada 6, Playa Mansa, 20100 Punta del Este. ✆/fax **042/481-004.** www.bestwestern.com. 59 units. From $90 double. Rates include buffet breakfast. AE, DC, MC, V. **Amenities:** Restaurant; bar/lounge; babysitting; concierge; Jacuzzi; pool; sauna. *In room:* TV, hair dryer, Internet, minibar.

Days Inn Punta del Este ★★ Value This atypical Days Inn sits on the waterfront and offers excellent value for its location. It features simple but modern rooms, many with ocean views. The Conrad Resort & Casino is next door, along with restaurants, cinemas, and excellent beaches. This is the best midrange hotel in Punta.

Rambla Williman, Parada 3, Playa Mansa, 20100 Punta del Este. ✆ **042/484-353.** Fax 042/484-683. www.daysinn.com. 38 units. From $86 double. Rates include buffet breakfast. AE, DC, MC, V. **Amenities:** Bar/lounge; babysitting; indoor heated and outdoor pools; room service. *In room:* TV, hair dryer, Internet, minibar.

Inexpensive

1949 Hostel This modern corner house in the heart of town is about as cool as you can get without depending on a supermodel's salary to get you through a weekend in the Punta. Bright clean dorms and some private rooms have views of the water, while down below you can relax in hammocks or take a drink on the happening terrace bar. This place gets lively at night, so don't depend on getting too much sleep.

Calle 25 544, Punta del Este. ✆ **042/440-719.** www.1949hostel.com. 10 units. From $100 double with private bathroom; $18 dorm. No credit cards. **Amenities:** Bar/lounge; communal kitchen.

Manantiales Hostel This surf-style hostel is a bit of a hike from downtown Punta but worth the bother if you're looking for a lively party scene with lots of communal fun and games for the budget orientated. The cramped and somewhat rickety interiors are more than compensated by an expansive pool and garden area with deck, bar, and hammocks. What more could you ask for? Wait—the enticingly named Bikini Beach is just down the road. The hostel is closed from April to October, and with a capacity of only 60 people, it fills up with partying Brazilians over the New Year.

Ruta 10, Km 164. ✆ **042/774-427.** www.manantialeshostel.com. 20 units. $22 dorms. AE, DC, MC, V. **Amenities:** Bar/lounge; communal kitchen; outdoor pool.

WHERE TO DINE

Expensive

El Viejo Marino ★ SEAFOOD/PARRILLA This charming seafood restaurant and *parrilla* has a strong sailor theme. The smiling friendly waitresses all wear dresses inspired by sailor uniforms. The dark interior mimics a ship, with navy-blue walls, dark woods, rope-back chairs, and old marine equipment scattered about. The menu has interesting combinations, such as sole cooked with Roquefort or mozzarella, several varieties of salmon, and catches of the day, much of it from the Río de la Plata.

Calle 11 at Calle 14. ✆ **042/443565.** Main courses U$400–U$700. AE, MC, V. Daily noon–2am.

Lo de Tere ★ INTERNATIONAL Overlooking the yacht-filled port, this elegant but casual restaurant is a good choice. The menu includes fish, pasta, and sandwiches named for celebrities (including the hunky beef sandwich called the Brad Pitt).

Rambla de Puerto at Calle 21. ✆ **042/440492.** www.lodetere.com. Main courses U$300–U$800. AE, DC, MC, V. Thurs–Tues noon–4pm and 8pm–1 or 2am.

Moderate

La Fonda del Pesca SEAFOOD This tiny, kitsch restaurant is just 2 blocks from the rolling waves of Playa Brava. The maritime theme is very much in evidence on the colorful murals and even more so via the menu, which specializes in fresh fish, lightly battered and topped with melted cheese. The owner, Pesca, will engage you with conversation as he pulls down vegetables and spices from the packed shelves behind the tiny counter. La Fonda del Pesca is fun, casual, and very small, with only a handful of tables to dine upon, and all the more intimate for it.

Calle 29 and Calle 24. ✆ **042/ 449-165.** Main courses U$70–U$180. No credit cards. Daily noon–11pm.

Inexpensive

Chivitería Marcos URUGUAYAN This corner sandwich bar might not have the most salubrious location next to a gas station, and the specialty steak sandwiches are a heart attack on a plate. Yet the food is hard to beat for stomach-filling value and mouth-watering taste. This casual, all-glass restaurant offers a vast array of toppings and sauces to pile on Uruguay's national snack—the *chivito.*

Rambla Artigas and Calle 12. ✆ **042/449932.** Main courses U$120. No credit cards. Daily 11am–4pm year-round; also 8pm–late Dec–Feb.

Los Caracoles ★ Value URUGUAYAN The town's most recommended *parrillada* also serves excellent seafood, including Spanish-style paella. A good salad bar accompanies the hearty selection of meats and fish, and there are a number of homemade pastas to choose from as well. Packed with 70 tables, the rustic dining room is casual and boisterous.

Calle Gorlero 20. ✆ **042/440-912.** Main courses U$160–U$200. AE, DC, MC, V. Summer daily noon–6pm and 8pm–3am; winter daily noon–4pm and 7pm–1am.

PUNTA DEL ESTE AFTER DARK

The **Conrad Resort & Casino,** Parada 4, Playa Mansa (✆ **042/491-111**), is the focal point for evening entertainment in Punta, featuring Las Vegas–style reviews and other music, dance, and magic shows—sometimes around the torch-lit swimming pools. The enormous 24-hour casino has tables playing baccarat, roulette, blackjack, poker, dice, and a fortune wheel.

Bars and clubs come and go with frequency in Punta, often changing names. The best bar is **Moby Dick,** at Rambla de la Circunvalación (✆ **042/441-240**), near the yacht harbor. **Company Bar,** Calle 29 and Calle 18 (✆ **042/440-130**), is another popular downtown drinking spot and has live music at weekends. Punta's bronzed Latin bodies then make their way to **Gitane** and **La Plage** (✆ **042/484-869**), two nearby clubs on Rambla Brava, Parada 12. La Barra, 10km (6 miles) to the north, has become the main strip for bars and clubs that perennially change name and location.

13

Venezuela

by Eliot Greenspan

Venezuela is a vast and varied destination that remains largely undiscovered and undervisited by international tourists. From snowcapped Andean peaks to white-sand Caribbean beaches, from the Orinoco River to the skyscrapers of Caracas, there's an astounding range of places to see and things to do. Adventurous types can hike to the foot of Angel Falls, the tallest waterfall on the planet, or fish for piranha and wrangle anaconda on the flooded plains of Los Llanos.

Venezuela is exceptionally rich in biological diversity and pure natural beauty. With 43 national parks and a score of other natural monuments and protected areas, it's a fabulous destination for nature lovers, bird-watchers, and adventure travelers. There's great windsurfing, kite boarding, scuba diving, fishing, mountain biking, mountain climbing, hiking, trekking, and river rafting.

Venezuela has the richest oil reserves in the Western Hemisphere. Thanks to the oil, it is one of the most modern and industrialized countries in Latin America. Still, despite skyrocketing crude oil prices and over 11 years of rule under the charismatic and controversial President Hugo Chávez, nearly half of the population still lives below the poverty line. Widespread unemployment, underemployment, and crippling poverty spur high levels of crime and violence, especially in Caracas and other urban areas.

Venezuela, the closest South American country to the United States, has frequent and affordable air connections to both the U.S. and Europe, and is thus easily accessible to international tourists. Most of the country is connected by an excellent network of paved roads and a good internal commuter air system. This chapter covers the top tourist destinations—Caracas, Isla de Margarita, Los Llanos, Mérida and Los Andes, Los Roques, and Canaima and Angel Falls—and will guide you to some unforgettable experiences.

1 THE REGIONS IN BRIEF

Lying between 1° and 12° north latitude and rising from sea level to 5,007m (16,443 ft.), Venezuela has everything from steamy Equatorial jungles to perennially snowcapped mountains. There are dry barren deserts and lush tropical rainforests. More than 90% of the population lives in cities located in the northern part of this country, bordered by the Caribbean Sea, Colombia, Brazil, and Guyana.

Given the wide range of destinations, attractions, and adventures offered in Venezuela, the itinerary you choose will greatly depend on your particular interests and needs. Business travelers in Caracas with a free day or two should head to Los Roques for some fun in the sun, and a chance to go fishing or scuba diving. Adventure travelers should definitely visit Mérida and the Andes. Bird-watchers and nature lovers should not miss Los Llanos. Families looking for an all-inclusive resort vacation with plenty of activities to keep the kids busy should choose Isla de Margarita. And those seeking an adventurous tour through some of South America's most stunning scenery should head to Canaima and Angel Falls.

CARACAS Caracas is an overcrowded, inhospitable, and famously violent city. The city center occupies a flat valley surrounded by high mountains and hillsides. Urban sprawl has covered most of these hillsides with dense *ranchitos* (shantytowns). A total of some four million inhabitants, or Caraqueños, make up the greater metropolitan area. Despite the widespread poverty and overcrowding, Caracas is one of the more cosmopolitan and architecturally distinctive cities in Latin America, with a vibrant and active population.

THE URBAN BELT From Maracaibo in the west to Cumaná and Maturin in the east is a more or less linear belt of urban development, much of it based around major petroleum, mining, and agricultural centers, and most of it on or close to the Caribbean coast. Major cities include Maracaibo, Barquisimeto, Valencia, Maracay, and Caracas. An estimated 80% of the country's population lives within this relatively narrow urban belt. In fact, Venezuelans refer to almost all the rest of the country as "the interior."

THE CARIBBEAN COAST & THE ISLANDS Venezuela has 3,000km (1,860 miles) of coastline and hundreds of coastal islands, most of them uninhabited. The largest of the islands, **Isla de Margarita,** is Venezuela's most popular tourist destination. **Los Roques,** an archipelago of 42 named islands and 200 sand spits, mangrove islands, and tiny cays, is also very popular. The coastal region closest to Caracas, known as **El Litoral,** was devastated in 1999 by massive landslides and flooding, which left an estimated 20,000 dead and many more homeless. While this region has largely recovered, it still shows the effects of the disaster, and there are no beaches or tourist destinations of note here. The coastal areas farther east and west of El Litoral, however, offer scores of relatively undiscovered and undeveloped beaches for the more intrepid and independent travelers. The climate all along the coast and on the Caribbean islands is hot and tropical, and much drier than the rest of the country.

THE ANDES The great South American mountain chain, the Andes, runs through Venezuela from the Colombian border in a northeasterly direction through the states of Táchira, Mérida, and Trujillo. The mountains here, in three major spines—the Sierra Nevada, Sierra de La Culata, and Sierra de Santo Domingo—rise to more than 5,000m (16,400 ft.). The principal city here is **Mérida,** a picturesque and bustling college town nestled in a narrow valley. However, there are many small mountain towns, as well as some interesting indigenous villages, that are scattered about and worth exploring. This is a prime area for hiking, trekking, and a wide range of adventure sports.

LOS LLANOS Located on plains that roll on for hundreds of miles south and east of the Andes, **Los Llanos** is an area of flat, mostly open cattle ground, punctuated with some isolated stands of forest. During the latter part of the rainy season (July–Nov), the plains are almost entirely flooded, with only a few raised highways and service roads passable in anything that doesn't float. In the dry season, the land reemerges and wildlife congregates in dense herds and mixed flocks around the ponds and creeks that are left behind. The quantity and variety of wildlife visible at the nature lodges located in Los Llanos are truly phenomenal—anaconda, caiman, capybara, deer, and even wildcats are commonly sighted. This is one of the top spots on the planet for bird-watching.

SOUTHERN VENEZUELA & THE GRAN SABANA Southern Venezuela is a largely uninhabited and wild region of tropical forests and jungle rivers. The region is home to several ancient indigenous tribes, including the Piaroa, Pemón, and Yanomami, who still live an often-nomadic lifestyle based on hunting and gathering. This area is home to vast expanses of forest, including **Canaima National Park,** the largest national park in Venezuela and the sixth largest in the world; **Angel Falls,** the highest waterfall on the planet; and a series of stunning steep-walled mesas called ***tepuis.*** Much of this region is also known as the Gran Sabana (Great Plains), as it features large stretches of flat savanna broken up only by these imposing *tepuis.*

THE ORINOCO DELTA The eastern end of Venezuela comprises the largely uninhabited Orinoco Delta. Second in size and import to the Amazon (both as a river and a river basin), the Orinoco Delta is a vast area of shifting rivers, tributaries, mangroves, rainforests, and natural canals. The area is also known as the Delta Amacuro, after a smaller river that empties into the basin and forms part of the border with Guyana. This area is just starting to develop as a destination for naturalists and ecotourists.

2 THE BEST OF VENEZUELA IN 2 WEEKS

This itinerary will take you from the turquoise waters and white sands of Venezuela's Caribbean islands to the snowcapped peaks of Los Andes. In between you'll marvel at the amazing biological diversity of Los Llanos and swim at the foot of Angel Falls, the world's tallest waterfall. Some travelers opt to extend their time in any one of the destinations listed below, or have less than 2 weeks budgeted. If so, you'll have to make some tough choices, but you'll want to use this route as a reference point.

Day 1: Arrive & Head Immediately to Los Roques ★★★

Venezuela's principal airport is right on the Caribbean coast, in **Maiquetia.** Don't even leave the airport. You'll visit Caracas later. Instead, hook up with a local commuter flight to **Los Roques** and settle into your *posada* in time for a sunset cocktail overlooking the sea at **Bora El Mar.** See p. 792.

Day 2: Commandeer an Island for the Day ★★★

Have your *posada* arrange for a morning transfer to **your own private cay.** Be sure to bring plenty of water and sunscreen and a shade umbrella, in addition to your packed lunch. Spend the day beachcombing and snorkeling, until the motor launch comes to pick you up in the afternoon. See p. 790.

Day 3: Head to Canaima ★★

Fly from Los Roques down to **Canaima** and check in to **Jungle Rudy Campamento** (p. 806). You should have time to take an afternoon boat tour of **Canaima Lagoon,** with views of **Hacha, Golondrina,** and **Ucaima Falls.** Be sure also to allow time for a visit to **Makunaima Arte Indígena** (p. 806), an excellent gift shop filled with local and regional arts and crafts.

Day 4: Visit Angel Falls ★★★

This entire day will be devoted to visiting **Angel Falls** (p. 804). Be sure to insist on some good quality time at the foot of the falls, for bathing and soaking in the sights. On the return trip you'll probably visit **Sapo Falls.** Be prepared to get wet again on the hike behind and under the waterfall.

Days 5–6: Spot Anaconda, Caiman & Capybara in Los Llanos ★★

Take an early morning flight out of Canaima to Ciudad Bolívar or Puerto Ordaz and connect with a subsequent flight or land transfer to **Hato El Cedral** (p. 801). You should arrive in time for an

afternoon tour. If not, settle into your room and prepare to wake up early for a full day of intense wildlife viewing. In addition to the animals listed above, you'll see scores, or more, of bird species, and probably fish for **piranha.**

Days 7–10: Get High in Mérida & the Venezuelan Andes

Head from Los Llanos to **Mérida** either by land or air, and check in to **Posada Casa Sol** (p. 797). Spend your time here taking advantage of the high mountain scenery and numerous tour options. Those who are physically fit and adventurous should definitely take a canyoning trip with **Arassari Treks** (p. 795).

Days 11–12: Isla Margarita ★

You've earned a little more beach time, so take a commuter flight to **Isla Margarita** and decompress on the beaches of this Caribbean island. Be sure to reserve a table at **Casa Caranta** (p. 785) for dinner one night. On the other evening, have dinner at **Catabar** (p. 786), and afterwards have a nightcap at **Guayoyo Café** (p. 786).

Days 13–14: Caracas

Return to **Caracas** and take a crash course in this capital city. Visit the **Museo de Arte Contemporáneo** and the **Iglesia de San Francisco** (p. 767). Be sure to schedule a trip to **El Hatillo** (p. 776), which will include a shopping excursion to the **Hannsi Centro Artesanal** (p. 770). After dinner, be sure to cap everything off with a drink at **360°** (p. 775), taking in the view of the city from the uppermost rooftop bar here.

3 PLANNING YOUR TRIP TO VENEZUELA

VISITOR INFORMATION

Good tourist information on Venezuela is hard to come by. The country's **Ministry of Tourism** (**MINTUR; © 0800/887-4766;** www.mintur.gob.ve) offers precious little in the way of information or help geared toward individual travelers, and their website is entirely in Spanish. Your best bet is to search the Internet, or deal directly with hotels and tour operators working in Venezuela. The following websites contain useful information pertaining to the country.

- **http://lanic.utexas.edu/la/venezuela**: The University of Texas Latin American Studies Department's database features an extensive list of useful links.
- **www.embavenez-us.org**: The website for the embassy of Venezuela in the United States has current information and a small section of links.
- **http://english.eluniversal.com**: The English-language site of one of the country's main daily newspaper, *El Universal.*

In Venezuela

MINTUR (**© 0800/887-4766;** www.mintur.gob.ve) is the national tourism ministry. Its main office, located in Caracas at the intersection of avenidas Francisco de Miranda and Principal de La Floresta, is open weekdays during business hours. The staff can give you a basic map and some brochures for hotels and attractions; however, they are not really geared to serve as an information source for individual tourists.

For the best tourism information in the country, contact the established tourism agencies, including **Akanan Travel & Adventure** (**© 0212/715-5433** or 0414/116-0107; www.akanan.com), **Cacao Expeditions** (**© 0212/977-1234;** www.cacaotravel.com), **Lost World Adventures** (**© 800/999-0558** in the U.S. and Canada, or 0212/577-0303 in Caracas; www.lostworldadventures.com), and **Natoura Adventure Tours** (**© 303/800-4639** in the U.S. and Canada, or 0274/252-4216 in Venezuela; www.natoura.com). Most bookstores and many hotel gift shops around the country stock a small selection of maps and useful books (some in English) on Venezuelan history, culture, and tourism.

ENTRY REQUIREMENTS

You need a valid passport to enter Venezuela. Upon arrival, citizens and residents of Australia, Canada, Great Britain, New Zealand, and the United States who enter by air or cruise ship are issued a free general visa valid for 90 days.

If you plan to enter Venezuela by sea or land, it is advisable to try to obtain a visa in advance from your nearest Venezuelan embassy or consulate, although, in practice, this is usually not necessary. When applied for in advance through a Venezuelan embassy or consulate, the visa costs BsF65. However, you may be charged more depending on the processing fees and policies of your local embassy or consulate. I've heard reports that you may face an arbitrary charge of between BsF5 and BsF35 at some of the crossings along the borders with Colombia and Brazil.

Telephone Dialing Info at a Glance

Venezuela's phone system features a standardized system of seven-digit local numbers, with three-digit area codes. Note that you must add a zero before the three-digit area code when dialing from within Venezuela, but not when dialing to Venezuela from abroad.

- **To place a call from your home country to Venezuela,** dial the international access code (0011 in Australia, 011 in the U.S. and Canada, 0170 in New Zealand, 00 in the U.K.), plus the country code (58), plus the three-digit Venezuelan area code (Caracas 212, Isla de Margarita 295, Mérida 274), plus the seven-digit phone number.
- **To place a local call within Venezuela,** dial the seven-digit local number. To call another area within Venezuela, you must add a 0 before the three-digit area code. If you are calling from a cellphone, or between competing cellphone companies, you must also add the 0 before the three-digit area code. For information, dial ✆ **113;** to place national collect calls, dial ✆ **101.**
- Dial **113** for **directory assistance** (most operators will speak English) and **122** to reach an **international operator.**

Venezuela requires children 17 and under traveling alone, with one parent, or with a third party to present a copy of their birth certificate and written, notarized authorization by the absent parent(s) or legal guardian granting permission to travel alone, with one parent, or with a third party. For more details, contact your embassy or consulate.

Venezuelan Embassy Locations

In Australia & New Zealand: 7 Culgoa Circuit, O'Malley, Canberra, ACT 2606 (✆ **02/6290-2967;** fax 02/6290-2911; www.venezuela-emb.org.au)

In Canada: 32 Range Rd., Ottawa, ON KIN 8J4 (✆ **613/235-5151;** fax 613/235-3205; www.misionvenezuela.org)

In the U.K.: 1 Cromwell Rd., London SW7 2HW (✆ **020/7584-4206;** fax 44/020-7589-8887; http://venezuela.embassyhomepage.com)

In the U.S.: 1099 30th St. NW, Washington, DC 20007 (✆ **202/342-2214;** fax 202/342-6820; www.embavenez-us.org)

CUSTOMS

You may bring into Venezuela all reasonable manner of electronic devices and items for personal use (including cameras, personal stereos, and laptop computers). Officially, you may bring in up to $3,000 worth of miscellaneous merchandise—tobacco, liquor, chocolate, and the like. However, this is only loosely enforced. The guiding rule is to try to not attract the interest of immigration officials. Once their interest is piqued, they could decide to give you a hard time.

MONEY

In January 2008, Venezuela changed its unit of currency from the **bolívar (Bs)** to the **bolívar fuerte (BsF).** The change simply involves chopping three decimal points off of

Devaluation

In January 2010, President Chávez announced a two-tiered devaluation of the Venezuelan currency. So called *petrodólares* ("oil dollars") would be exchanged at the new official rate of BsF4.30 to the dollar, while certain basic goods, materials, and medical supplies would be imported at the exchange rate of BsF2.30 to the dollar. What this means for tourists and visitors is that all credit card purchases will be billed at the new rate of BsF4.30 to the dollar. A black market still exists for changing hard currency, both dollars and euros, at rates above the official rate. Note that all prices in this book were current at the time of research, which occurred prior to the devaluation, and any prices listed in dollars were converted at BsF2.15 to the dollar.

the severely devalued bolívar. So BsF1 is equivalent to the old 1,000 Bs. The bolívar fuerte comes in paper bills of 2, 5, 10, 20, and BsF50, while there are coins of BsF1, as well as 1, 5, 10, 12.5, 25, and 50 céntimos. There are 100 céntimos (cents) to each BsF. ***Tip:*** Many taxis, small shops, and restaurants are reluctant (and sometimes unable) to change larger denomination bills, so it's always good to try to keep a few smaller notes and coins on hand.

CURRENCY EXCHANGE & RATES At press time, the official exchange rate was **BsF4.30 to US$1.** However, the black-market exchange rate is radically different from the official rate. At press time, the unofficial exchange rate was approximately BsF6.40 to the dollar. The most common place to exchange hard currencies for bolívares fuertes at the black-market rate is the Simón Bolívar International airport. While this is technically illegal, and you should be careful about whom you deal with, it is very common. Note that if you are dealing with a Venezuelan-based tour agency, be sure to ask if they would be willing to buy your dollars, euros, or pounds at a more favorable rate. They usually are willing and able to exchange currency for you, and this takes some of the risk out of dealing with an unknown entity at the airport.

Many banks do not exchange foreign currencies, and those that do often make the process cumbersome and unpleasant. But there are currency-exchange offices in most major cities and tourist destinations, as well as 24-hour exchange offices in both the national and international airport terminals at the Simón Bolívar International Airport. While the official money-exchange bureaus at the airport and around Caracas exchange at the official rate, you may find money-exchange offices *(casas de cambio)* in outlying cities and tourist destinations that give a better rate. All credit card purchases and ATM withdrawals are charged at the official exchange rate.

ATMS ATMs are readily available in Caracas and most major cities and tourist destinations. **Cirrus** (**✆ 800/424-7787;** www.mastercard.com) and **PLUS** (**✆ 800/843-7587;** www.visa.com) are the two most popular networks; check the back of your ATM card to see which network your bank belongs to. Use the toll-free numbers to locate ATMs in your destination. It might take a few tries, but you should be able to find one connected to either, or both, of the PLUS and Cirrus systems that will allow you to withdraw bolívares against your home bank account. However, these will be sold to you at the official exchange rate.

TRAVELER'S CHECKS In an era of almost universally accepted bank and credit cards, traveler's checks are becoming less and less common. Most hotels, restaurants, and shops that cater to foreign tourists will still accept and cash traveler's checks—some will actually change them for you at or near the going black-market exchange rate—but most will only change them at the official exchange rate, and they often exact a surcharge as well. Money-exchange houses will only change traveler's checks at the official rate and usually charge an additional 1% to 5% fee.

To report lost or stolen traveler's checks, see "Credit Cards," below.

CREDIT CARDS Credit cards are widely accepted at most hotels, restaurants, shops, and attractions in all but the most remote destinations. American Express, MasterCard, and Visa have the greatest coverage, with a far smaller number of establishments accepting Diners Club. It is currently common practice to have to show a passport or photo ID when making a credit card purchase in Venezuela. Remember, credit card purchases are billed at the official exchange rate.

To report lost or stolen credit cards or traveler's checks, call the following numbers: **American Express,** call ✆ **0212/206-2796** or collect to ✆ 336/393-111; **Diners Club,** ✆ **0212/503-2461; MasterCard,** ✆ **0800/100-2902;** and **Visa,** ✆ **0800/100-2167** or 0212/285-2510.

WHEN TO GO

PEAK SEASON November through February, when it's cold and bleak in Europe and North America, is the peak season in Venezuela, but you can enjoy the country any time of year. Venezuelans travel a lot within the country on holidays and during the school break lasting from late July through early September. It is often difficult to find a hotel room or bus or airline seat during these holidays, as well as during Christmas and Easter vacations. April through June is a fabulous time to enjoy great deals, deserted beaches, and glorious solitude in the more popular destinations.

CLIMATE Venezuela has two distinct seasons: **rainy** (June–Oct) and **dry** (Nov–May). The rainy season is locally called *invierno* (winter), while the dry season is called *verano* (summer). However, temperatures vary principally according to altitude. Coastal and lowland areas are hot year-round, and temperatures drop as you rise in altitude.

Tips Getting the Most of Your Bolívares Fuertes

Exchanging your dollars, euros, or pounds at the black-market rate will more than double your buying power. Prices in this book are listed at the former official exchange rate of BsF2.15 to the dollar. Most restaurants, tour agencies, and attractions set their prices in bolívares fuertes. On the other hand, many hotel prices, particularly at the higher-end hotels, as well as tours, are quoted in and pegged to the U.S. dollar. These hotels and tour agencies then use the current black-market rate to arrive at a bolívar fuerte price. For example, if a hotel charges $100 per night, the price in BsF will be roughly BsF640, which then converts to $149 at the official exchange rate. The bottom line is that if you use dollars or dollars exchanged at the black-market rate, you pay roughly $100; if, however, you use a credit card or exchange money at a bank, you'll be charged $149.

Set at an altitude of some 1,000m (3,280 ft.), Caracas has an average temperature of 72°F (22°C), with little seasonal variation. Daytime highs can reach around 90°F (32°C) on clear sunny days. Nights get a little cooler, but you'll rarely need more than a light jacket or sweater.

PUBLIC HOLIDAYS Official public holidays celebrated in Venezuela include New Year's Day (Jan 1), Carnaval (the Mon and Tues before Ash Wednesday), Easter (Thurs and Fri of Holy Week are official holidays), Declaration of Independence (Apr 19), Labor Day (May 1), Battle of Carabobo (June 24), Independence Day (July 5), Birth of Simón Bolívar (July 24), Día de la Raza, or Discovery Day (Oct 12), and Christmas Day (Dec 25).

HEALTH CONCERNS

COMMON AILMENTS Your chances of contracting any serious tropical disease in Venezuela are slim, especially if you stick to the major tourist destinations. However, malaria, dengue fever, yellow fever, hepatitis, and leptospirosis all exist in Venezuela, so it's a good idea to be careful and consult your doctor before a trip here.

Yellow fever, while very rare, does exist in some remote areas of Venezuela. A yellow fever vaccine, though not required, is often recommended and is good for 10 years. If you do get a yellow fever vaccine, be sure to carry a copy of the proof of vaccination.

Malaria is found predominantly in the jungle areas of the Amazonas and Bolívar states, as well as in the Orinoco Delta. Malaria prophylaxes are often recommended, but several have side effects and others are of questionable effectiveness. Consult your doctor as to what is currently considered the best preventive treatment for malaria. Be sure to ask whether a recommended drug will cause hypersensitivity to the sun; it would be a shame to travel here for the beaches and then have to hide under an umbrella the entire time. If you are in a malarial area, wear long pants and long sleeves, use insect repellent, and either sleep under a mosquito net or burn mosquito coils (similar to incense but with a pesticide).

Of greater concern may be **dengue fever.** Dengue fever is similar to malaria and is spread by an aggressive daytime mosquito. This mosquito seems to be most common in lowland urban areas, although dengue cases have been reported throughout the country. Dengue is also known as "bone-break fever" because it is usually accompanied by severe body aches. The first infection with dengue fever will make you very sick but should cause no permanent damage. However, a second infection with a different strain of the dengue virus can lead to internal hemorrhaging and may be life threatening. Take the same precautions as you would against malaria.

The most common health concern for travelers to Venezuela is a touch of **diarrhea.** The best way to protect yourself from diarrhea is to avoid tap water and drinks or ice made from tap water. Those with really tender intestinal tracts should avoid uncooked fruits and vegetables likely to have been washed in tap water, unless you can peel and prepare them yourself.

VACCINATIONS No specific vaccinations are necessary for travel to Venezuela, although it is recommended that you be up-to-date on your tetanus, typhoid, and yellow-fever vaccines. It is also a good idea to get a vaccination for hepatitis A and B.

HEALTH PRECAUTIONS Staying healthy on a trip to Venezuela is predominantly a matter of being a little cautious about what you eat and drink, and using common sense. Know your physical limits and don't overexert yourself in the ocean, on hikes, or in athletic activities. Respect the tropical sun and protect yourself from it. Also try to protect yourself from biting insects, using a combination of repellent and light, loose long-sleeved clothing. I recommend buying and drinking bottled water or soft drinks, although the water in Caracas and in most of the major tourist destinations is reputed to be safe to drink.

GETTING THERE

By Plane

The **Simón Bolívar International Airport** (airport code CCS; ✆ **0212/303-1330;** www.aeropuerto-maiquetia.com.ve) in Maiquetía, 28km (17 miles) north of Caracas, is the gateway to Venezuela and the point of entry for most visitors to the country. There is a departure tax of BsF110 combined with an airport tax of BsF138. The airport tax is sometimes included in the airline ticket price, so be sure to ask before paying twice.

FROM AUSTRALIA & NEW ZEALAND To fly to Venezuela from either Australia or New Zealand, you will almost certainly have to connect via the United States.

FROM CANADA **Air Canada** (✆ **888/247-226;** www.aircanada.com) flies several times weekly between Toronto and Caracas. **American** (✆ **800/433-7300;** www.aa.com), **Continental** (✆ **800/525-0280;** www.continental.com), **Delta** (✆ **800/221-1212;** www.delta.com), and **Mexicana** (✆ **800/531-7921;** www.mexicana.com) have flights from Montreal, Toronto, and Vancouver to Caracas, connecting through Atlanta, Miami, Los Angeles, or New York.

Numerous charters fly from Toronto and Montreal to Isla de Margarita, particularly during the winter months. Ask your travel agent, check online, or look in the Sunday travel section of your local newspaper to find them.

FROM EUROPE & THE U.K. **Air Europa** (✆ 902/401-501 in Spain; www.air-europa.com) from Madrid, **Air France** (✆ 800/237-2747; www.airfrance.com) from Paris, **Alitalia** (✆ 800/223-5730; www.alitalia.com) from Rome and Milan, **Iberia** (✆ 800/772-4642; www.iberia.com) from Madrid, and **Lufthansa** (✆ 800/645-3880; www.lufthansa.com) from Frankfurt all offer regular service to Venezuela. **Santa Bárbara** (✆ 212/204-4000; www.sbairlines.com) flies direct from Madrid several times weekly.

FROM THE U.S. **American Airlines, Continental,** and **Delta Airlines** have regular direct service to Caracas from several different U.S. hub cities. Venezuelan airline **Santa Bárbara** also has one daily direct flight from Miami. **Mexicana** and **Taca** (✆ **800/400-8222;** www.taca.com) have flights connecting through Mexico City, Mexico, and San José, Costa Rica, respectively.

By Bus

Venezuela is serviced by international bus routes via Colombia to the west and Brazil to the south. In general, crossings from Colombia are considered dangerous, due to guerrilla and drug-cartel activity, and political tensions between the two countries. The only road route between Brazil and Venezuela connects Boa Vista, Brazil, and Santa Elena de Uairén, Venezuela. **Bus Ven** (✆ **0212/953-8441;** www.busven.com) is a reputable bus line for travel to and from Colombia. To travel to Brazil, you will first have to make your way south via local bus lines to Santa Elena.

By Boat

Ferry services run between several Caribbean islands and Isla de Margarita, Venezuela. Routes and schedules vary seasonally and change on short notice. Islands with the most consistent connections include Barbados, St. Vincent, and Trinidad and Tobago.

BY PLANE Because distances are relatively long and land travel time consuming, Venezuela has an excellent network of commuter airlines servicing the entire country and all major tourist destinations. Fares run around BsF150 to BsF600 each way, depending on destination, distance, availability, and demand. On any internal flight, you have to pay an airport tax of BsF10 to BsF38, depending on the local airport you are using. For the names and contact information of individual commuter airlines, see "Getting There," in each destination section in this chapter.

BY BUS Regular and inexpensive buses service all of terrestrial Venezuela. Most popular destinations are also serviced by *expreso* (express), *ejecutivo* (executive), and/or *de lujo* (luxury) buses. In most cases, it's worth the few extra dollars for these options. Two reputable luxury lines are **Aeroexpresos Ejecutivos** (✆ **0212/266-2321;** www.aeroexpresos.com.ve) and **Rodovías** (✆ **0212/577-6622**). There are two principal bus terminals in Caracas, Terminal La Bandera and Terminal del Oriente, although depending on the route, destination, and bus line, you may embark from either of these or a private terminal.

BY CAR I do not recommend a rental car as a means of exploring Venezuela. Many of the top destinations—Los Roques, Canaima, and Angel Falls, for example—are inaccessible by car. (***Note:*** The only two destinations included in this chapter where a car would come in handy are Isla de Margarita and Mérida. In both cases, you'd be better off flying to the destination and renting a car there for the duration of your stay.) Venezuelan drivers are aggressive and ignore most common traffic laws and general rules of road safety. Moreover, roads are not well marked, distances between destinations are considerable, and you run the risk of becoming a target for one of many robbery schemes. If you do decide to rent a car, many of the major international agencies operate in Venezuela, with offices in Caracas (often with a branch at the airport) and in most major cities and tourist destinations. Rates run BsF150 to BsF300 per day.

Your best bet for renting a car, both in terms of rates and reliability, is to choose one of the major international agencies and book in advance from your home country. **Avis** (✆ **800/331-1084** in the U.S., or 0800/227-7600 in Venezuela; www.avis.com), **Budget** (✆ **800/472-3325** in the U.S., or 0800/283-4381 in Venezuela; www.budget.com.ve), **Dollar** (✆ **800/800-3665** in the U.S., or 0212/993-8259 in Venezuela; www.dollar.com), **Hertz** (✆ **800/654-3001** in the U.S., or 0800/800-0000 in Venezuela; www.hertz.com), and **Thrifty** (✆ **800/847-4389** in the U.S., or 0800/250-8453 in Venezuela; www.thrifty.com) all have offices both in Caracas and at Simón Bolívar International Airport.

One upside of driving around Venezuela is that gas is amazingly cheap, around BsF .09 per liter, or BsF.35 per gallon.

BY ORGANIZED TOUR Considering the current state of affairs, organized tours are a reasonable way to go in Venezuela. The country is still a bit inhospitable and unused to freewheeling independent exploration. The tourism industry here was built top down, with lots of big hotels and big operations that almost seem to not want to waste their time on independent travelers. In many cases, tour operators and wholesalers are able to get better rates on rooms, tours, and transfers than you'd be able to find on your own. Many of them use the hotels and local tour operators recommended in this book.

Akanan Travel & Adventure ★★ (✆ **0212/715-5433** or 0414/116-0107; www.akanan.com) is one of my favorite operators on the ground in Caracas. It offers a wide range of tour options. **Lost World Adventures** ★★ (✆ **800/999-0558** in the U.S., or 0212/577-0303 in Caracas; www.lostworldadventures.com) is an excellent operator and a pioneer in Venezuelan travel. It offers a wide range of tour options and can customize a trip to your needs and specifications.

Geodyssey (✆ **020/7281-7788;** www.geodyssey.co.uk) is a British operator with a good amount of experience in Venezuela. **Journey Latin America** (✆ **020/8747-3108;** www.journeylatinamerica.co.uk) is a large British operator specializing in Latin American travel, that often has excellent deals on airfare.

TIPS ON ACCOMMODATIONS

You'll find hotel rooms in all price ranges, although in Caracas and on Isla Margarita, the offerings are skewed toward high-end business travelers—and rates tend to be high. A dozen or so large, all-inclusive resorts are on Isla de Margarita. However, in Mérida, Canaima, Los Roques, and Los Llanos, you can find delightful small hotels and isolated lodges. While Venezuelan tourism is relatively strong, very few foreign tourists visit Venezuela. Still, there is a major glut of hotel rooms throughout the country, and competition is often fierce. Few of the large hotels actually charge their published or advertised rack rate. You can get especially good deals in the off season and midweek. It always pays to bargain, especially if you book directly by phone, or the Internet. Finally, you can also save substantially if you pay in cash, especially if you exchange at the black-market rate.

Venezuela has a broad network of *posadas,* small inns, and lodges. If you're looking for a small, intimate hotel experience, your best bets are Mérida and Los Roques, where *posadas* abound.

When booking a room, if you ask for a double *(doble),* you may be given a room with two twin beds. If you want a double or queen-size bed, be specific and ask for a *cama matrimonial.*

Throughout this chapter, I separate hotel listings into several broad categories: **Very Expensive,** BsF450 and up; **Expensive,** BsF250 to BsF450; **Moderate,** BsF150 to BsF250; and **Inexpensive,** under BsF150 for a double. *Rates do not include the 15% goods and services sales tax, unless otherwise specified.*

TIPS ON DINING

Although both Caracas and Isla de Margarita have a wide range of restaurants serving a gamut of international cuisines, your choices will be much more limited throughout most of the rest of the country. Venezuelan cuisine is neither very distinctive nor noteworthy. Most meals consist of a meat or chicken dish (either fried, grilled, or in a stew), accompanied by some stewed vegetables, rice, and the ubiquitous *arepa,* the traditional cornmeal patty that's a kind of cross between a tortilla and a biscuit. Vegetarians may have a particularly hard time. If you are vegetarian, try to coordinate your meals in advance with hotels and tour agencies.

For those with a sweet tooth, be sure to try a piece of the national cake, *bienmesabe,* a soft sponge cake soaked in a sweet coconut-cream sauce. (Its name literally means "Tastes good to me!") Also be sure to sample some of the fresh fruit drinks, or *batidos.* These are made with whatever ripe tropical fruits are on hand. My favorite *batido* is made of mango, but *parchita,* or passion fruit, runs a close second.

I have separated restaurant listings into three price categories, based on the average cost of a meal per person, including tax and tip: **Expensive,** more than BsF150; **Moderate,** BsF60 to BsF150; and **Inexpensive,** less than BsF60. Note that prices given for entrees and main courses do not include sales or service taxes.

TIPS ON SHOPPING

Outside of the massive malls in Caracas, which have all the standard international designer stores you could ask for, shopping is far from rewarding in Venezuela. Your best bet is to look for and stick to local and indigenous arts and crafts. Masks are particularly attractive and varied. Keep an eye out for the local hammocks, called *chinchorros,* which are an intricate weave of thin strands of rough natural fibers. You'll also find a variety of woven baskets, hats, and handbags, as well as simple ceramic wares. Despite its duty-free status, Isla de Margarita is unlikely to be of much interest for international shoppers. Prices and selection are comparable to what most folks can find at home.

Outside of department stores, hotel gift shops, and malls, you should bargain. In many cases, street merchants and sellers at outdoor markets and souvenir shops can easily be bartered down by 25% to 30%.

Fast Facts Venezuela

American Express American Express is represented by the **Italcambio** (www.italcambio.com) chain of money-exchange houses and travel agencies with offices around Caracas and other parts of Venezuela. You'll find a convenient office in the Centro Comercial Lido shopping mall (✆ **0212/953-9901**); it's open Monday through Friday from 8am to 5pm, and Saturday from 9am to noon. For Global Assist, call ✆ **0212/206-0333.** To report a lost card, call ✆ **0212/206-2796,** or call collect 336/393-1111 in the United States.

Business Hours Most businesses open between 8am and 9am, and close between 5 and 6pm. Many businesses and stores close down for an hour or more for a lunch break between noon and 2:30pm. On Saturday, most shops are open and most businesses are closed. On Sunday, only shops in malls and major shopping districts are open. Most banks are open Monday to Friday from 8:30am to 4pm; however, banks and exchange houses in some of the major malls are open during shopping hours, which often include the early evenings and weekends.

Doctors & Dentists Medical and dental care generally ranges from acceptable to high quality in Venezuela. If you need care while in the country, contact your embassy, ask at your hotel, or look in the English-language *Daily Journal*. In the event of a medical emergency, contact one of the clinics listed under "Fast Facts" in "Caracas," later in this chapter.

Drug Laws Venezuelan drug laws are strict, and punishment, especially for foreigners, is severe. Do not try to smuggle, buy, or use illegal drugs in Venezuela.

Electricity Electric current is 110 volts AC (60 cycles). U.S.-style flat-prong plugs are used. However, three-prong grounded outlets are not universally available. It's helpful to bring a three-to-two prong adapter.

Embassies & Consulates In Caracas: **Canada,** avenidas Francisco de Miranda and Sur, Altamira (✆ **0212/600-3000;** www.canadainternational.gc.ca/venezuela); **United Kingdom,** Torre La Castellana, Avenida Principal La Castellana, Piso 11 (✆ **0212/263-8411;** http://ukinvenezuela.fco.gov.uk/en); and the **United States,** calles F and Suapure, Colinas de Valle Arriba (✆ **0212/975-6411;** http://caracas.usembassy.gov).

Australia and **New Zealand** do not have embassies in Venezuela. The Canadian and U.K. embassies (see above) will assist Australian and Kiwi travelers in most instances, except for the issuing of passports. The nearest Australian Embassy is in Brasilia, Brazil (✆ **55/61-3226-3111;** www.dfat.gov.au/geo/venezuela/index.html); the nearest New Zealand embassy is also in Brasilia (✆ **55/61-3248-9900;** www.nzembassy.com).

Emergencies Venezuela has an integrated emergency network (police, fire, ambulance). To reach it, dial ✆ **171.** You can dial 171 from any pay phone, without using a calling card. Don't expect the operator to speak English.

Internet Access There are Internet cafes all over Venezuela, particularly in tourist destinations. Rates run BsF1 to BsF10 per hour.

Language Spanish is the official language of Venezuela. Although most hotels and tourist destinations have staff and guides with at least some command of English, it is not widely spoken among the general population.

Liquor Laws The official drinking age in Venezuela is 18, although it is rarely enforced. At discos, however, you often need to show a picture ID for admittance.

Newspapers & Magazines There are around a dozen daily newspapers and tabloids. The main Spanish-language newspapers are *El Nacional* (http://el-nacional.com) and *El Universal* (www.el-universal.com).

Police Venezuela has a host of overlapping police departments but no specific tourist police. Depending on the circumstances, you may encounter metropolitan police *(policía metropolitana),* municipal police *(policía municipal),* investigative police *(policía técnica judicial),* the National Guard *(guardia nacional),* or transit police *(policía de tránsito).* Their uniforms and specific responsibilities vary. Corruption and indifference are widespread. Venezuela has an integrated emergency network (police, fire, ambulance). To reach it, just dial ✆ **171.** However, don't expect the operator to speak English.

Post Offices/Mail **Ipostel** (www.ipostel.gov.ve) is the national mail service. It is considered neither swift nor secure for international correspondence. Generally, a letter or postcard takes 10 to 20 days to reach most parts of the United States and Europe. There are branch post offices in most cities and tourist destinations, and some malls even have Ipostel offices. Still, your hotel is usually your best bet for buying stamps and mailing a letter. Feel free to mail home postcards and letters, but avoid using Ipostel for anything of value or importance.

In the event that you need to mail anything of value or personal import, call any of the following international courier services: **DHL** (✆ **0800/225-5345;** www.dhl.com), **FedEx** (✆ **0800/463-3399;** www.fedex.com), or **UPS** (✆ **0212/401-4900;** www.ups.com).

Restrooms There are few readily available public toilets in Venezuela. Your best bet is a restaurant, hotel, or service station. Some of these establishments (particularly service stations and roadside restaurants) will actually charge you a small fee for the use of the facilities. It's always a good idea to carry a small amount of toilet paper with you, especially on the road, as the facilities at many service stations—and at lower-end restaurants and hotels—might not have any.

Safety Venezuela has a well-deserved reputation for its violence and crime. Caraqueños talk about muggings, car thefts, and burglaries with amazing candidness and regularity. The greatest danger to travelers is theft. If you use common sense and standard precautions, you should have no problems. Keep a tab on your belongings, use hotel safes whenever possible, and don't carry large sums of money with you or wear obviously expensive clothing or jewelry. Stick to the well-worn tourist parts of Caracas and other major cities. Avoid the *ranchitos* (shantytowns) and poorer *barrios*. Take reputable taxis whenever possible and definitely avoid strolling around cities at night. If you have a rental car, always leave it in guarded parking and never leave anything of value inside.

Smoking Venezuela has very lax anti-smoking laws. Basically, smoking is prohibited only in public hospitals and clinics, elevators, and public transportation. A large number of Venezuelans smoke, and smoke-filled public spaces are common. Bars, discos, and clubs are often especially smoke filled.

Taxes There is a 15% sales tax on all purchases, including both goods and services.

Telephone & Fax There are public phones all around most cities and major tourist destinations. You'll even find public phones in places as remote as Canaima and Los Roques. Most work with magnetic-strip calling cards that are readily available in stores all over the country. Look for signs or stickers advertising CANTV calling cards. A local call costs just a few pennies per minute. Calls to cellphones or between competing phone companies can be much more expensive. Your hotel is usually your best bet for sending and receiving faxes, although they may charge exorbitant rates for international faxes. For tips on dialing, see "Telephone Dialing Info at a Glance," on p. 753.

Time Zone Venezuela is 4½ hours behind Greenwich Mean Time (GMT) and does not observe daylight saving time.

Tipping Most restaurants automatically add a 10% service charge. If you feel the service was particularly good, you should leave an additional 5% to 10%. If they don't add the service charge, tip as you would at home. Similarly, tip the hotel staff as you would at home. Since most taxi drivers do not use meters and are almost always overcharging foreigners, it is not customary to tip them. If you feel you are getting an extremely good deal or beyond-the-call-of-duty treatment, by all means, tip your driver.

Water Although the water is considered safe to drink in most urban areas, I recommend that visitors stick to bottled water to be on the safe side. Ask for *agua mineral sin gas* (noncarbonated mineral water).

4 CARACAS

With a well-deserved reputation for violence and danger, Caracas is a daunting city for many travelers. It is still one of the more cosmopolitan cities in Latin America, with vibrant business, social, and cultural scenes. Architecturally, Caracas is one of the most modern and distinctive cities in Latin America. Concrete and plate glass reign supreme, much of it showing the bold forms and sleek lines of the Art Deco and postmodern architectural currents of the last half of the 20th century. Aficionados will enjoy works of

Carlos Raúl Villanueva, a local architect who often integrated into his designs large kinetic sculptures by such renowned figures as Alexander Calder and Jesús Soto.

Caracas, and the international airport in Maiquetía, is the de facto hub for travel to and around Venezuela. If you plan on visiting several destinations in the country, you will be passing through Caracas as part of your itinerary. You can easily get a good feel for the city and its major attractions in a couple of days.

ESSENTIALS

Getting There

The **Simón Bolívar International Airport** (airport code CCS; © **0212/303-1330;** www.aeropuerto-maiquetia.com.ve) in Maiquetía, 28km (17 miles) north of Caracas, is the gateway to Venezuela and the point of entry for most visitors to the country. ***Note:*** The airport is most commonly referred to as the Maiquetía Airport by locals, travel agents, and taxi drivers. For information on arriving by plane, see "Getting There" in "Planning Your Trip to Venezuela," earlier in this chapter.

A taxi from the airport should cost between BsF80 and BsF150, depending on where in the city you are going. Official fares are slightly higher after 5pm. You will be immediately set upon by both official and informal or "pirate" *(pirata)* taxi drivers as soon as you exit Customs. Unless your hotel or tour agency sends a trusted driver, I recommend you use the official airport taxi company (© **0212/355-2770**). These folks have several kiosks spread throughout the airport and their official rates are posted. While you may be offered a slightly better fare by one of the *pirata* drivers, there have been reports of mistreatment and muggings of tourists by these operators.

Por puestos (private buses and vans) run between the airport and the Gato Negro Metro station. The fare is BsF5; however, note that you should not use this option at night or if you have much luggage. There are regular free shuttles between the national and international terminals at Maiquetía, although you can also hoof it.

Orientation

Of greatest interest to tourists are the **Capitolio** area around **Plaza Bolívar,** the historic center of Caracas, and **Parque Central,** a modern zone of high-rise office towers and home to several important museums and theaters. The **Sabana Grande** is an open-air pedestrian mall of small shops and street vendors that stretches on for nearly a mile, between the Plaza Venezuela and Plaza Chacaito. However, the Sabana Grande area has become increasingly seedy and dangerous, especially after dark. Today, shoppers and affluent Caraqueños tend to favor modern malls and the more exclusive areas of **Altamira, El Rosal,** and **Las Mercedes.** The latter three zones are the principal upscale residential, business, and shopping districts, respectively—they all have a mix of hotels, restaurants, cafes, shops, and private residences.

Getting Around

BY METRO Caracas has a clean, relatively safe, and efficient **Metro** system (www.metrodecaracas.com.ve). The main line of the system crosses the city from Palo Verde in the east to Propatria in the west.

Ticket prices are BsF0.50 for a one-way fare, and BsF0.90 for a two-trip ticket. You can buy a 10-trip ticket for BsF4.50. Even if you buy a one-way fare, keep your ticket handy because you have to pass it through the electronic turnstiles upon entering and again upon exiting at some stations. The Metro operates daily from 5:30am to 11pm.

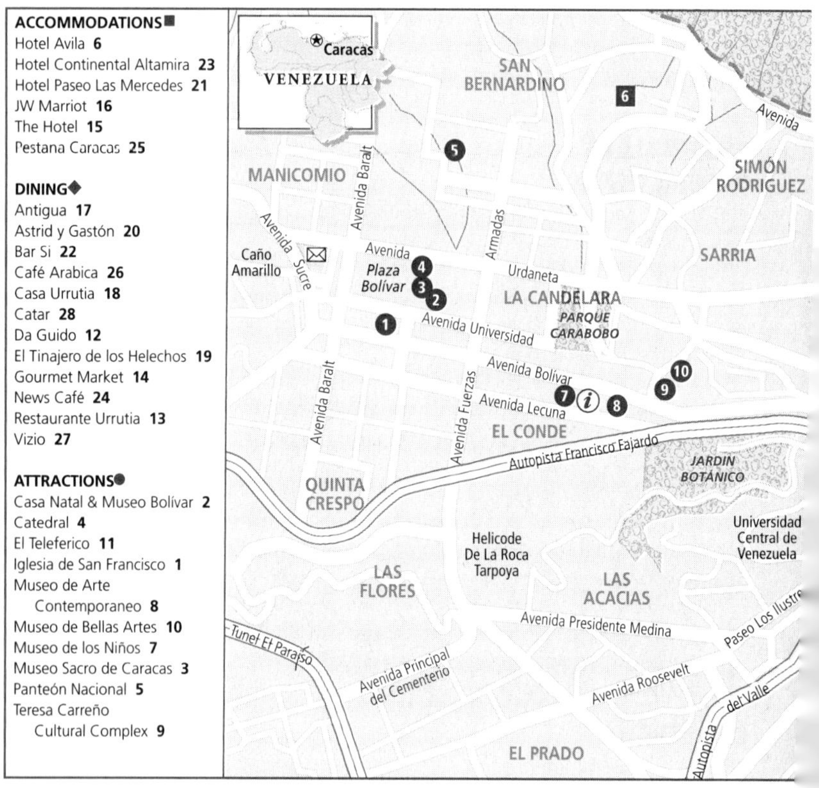

Although the Metro is generally safe, be wary of pickpockets and muggings at either very busy or very desolate times and stations.

BY BUS There are two parallel bus systems in Caracas. The **Metrobús** (www.metrodecaracas.com.ve) is a traditional urban bus system that, in theory, can be used in conjunction with the Metro. More common are the ***por puestos,*** private buses or vans running fixed routes servicing most of the metropolitan area. Fares on both systems are extremely inexpensive, but I don't recommend them as the transportation of choice because there's little rhyme or reason to the routes and, in the case of the *por puestos,* no readily available maps or guides. Moreover, crowded buses are prime haunts of pickpockets and petty thieves.

BY TAXI Taxis in Caracas generally do not have meters. Most rides within the city limits should cost you BsF15 and BsF30. There are a host of different taxi companies, some of which are based in certain zones, others at specific hotels and malls. In general, taxis based at a hotel or mall will charge more than a typical cab hailed on the street. However, given the current economic environment, the difference is often inconsequential. As a traveler, you will likely be a target for overcharging. Always try to ask hotel staff

or other locals what a specific ride should cost and negotiate in advance with the driver. Taxi drivers are legally allowed to charge an additional 20% after 6pm.

If you can't flag a cab in the street, try **Taxiven** (✆ **0212/985-5715**), **Taxitour** (✆ **0212/794-1264;** www.taxi-tour.com.ve), or **Taxco** (✆ **0212/576-8322;** www.taxco.com.ve).

BY FOOT Caracas is not particularly amenable to exploration by foot. Street crime is a real problem in all but a few neighborhoods. In fact, almost no place is absolutely safe. The safest neighborhoods to walk around are Las Mercedes, El Rosal, Los Palos Grandes, and Altamira. With care, you should also be fine during the daytime around the Capitolio, Sabana Grande, and Parque Central areas, although their popularity as tourist destinations attracts pickpockets.

Visitor Information

MINTUR (✆ **0212/208-4511;** www.mintur.gob.ve) is the national tourism ministry. Its main office, located at the intersection of avenidas Francisco de Miranda and Principal de La Floresta, is open weekdays 9am to 5pm. The staff can give you a basic map and

Tips Safety First

It's not just hype: Caracas is one of the most violent and dangerous cities in Latin America. Be very careful about where you walk, what you wear, and with whom you associate. Don't wear fancy jewelry or flash lots of cash, and keep close watch on your personal belongings. Take a well-marked taxi, or one called by your hotel, whenever possible. Be wary of unofficial cabs, or *piratas.* And, finally, don't get too adventurous at night.

some brochures for hotels and attractions; however, they are not truly geared towards attending to independent travelers.

A good alternative is to head to the offices of **Akanan Travel & Adventure** ★★ (✆ **0212/715-5433** or 0414/116-0107; www.akanan.com; Calle Bolívar, Edificio Grano de Oro, Chacao), one of my favorite operators in Caracas. Not only are they well located, close to the Altamira Metro stop, but they have a welcoming and informative staff, a small shop with adventure-travel supplies, and will usually allow travelers to check e-mail, chat, or make a VoIP call on one of their many computers.

Most bookstores around town and many hotel gift shops stock a small selection of maps to Caracas and the rest of the country. The best bookshop for English-language materials is the **American Book Shop,** Centro Plaza, Nivel Jardín, Avenida Francisco de Miranda, Los Palos Grandes (✆ **0212/285-8779**).

FAST FACTS A couple of currency-exchange offices, including an **Italcambio** branch, are at the airport, and scores of money-exchange houses are around town. Many hotels will change dollars and traveler's checks, although usually at or even slightly below the official exchange rate. Most banks won't change money, but they often have ATMs.

In the event that you need medical care, consult with your hotel first or head to the **Hospital de Clínicas de Caracas,** Avenida Panteón, San Bernardino (✆ **0212/508-6111**); the **Policlínica Las Mercedes,** Avenida Principal Las Mercedes and Calle Monterrey (✆ **0212/993-5944**); or the **Clínica El Avila,** Avenida San Juan Bosco and 6th Transversal, Altamira (✆ **0212/276-1111;** www.clinicaelavila.com).

Internet cafes are located all over town, and most hotels either have their own Internet cafe or can refer you to the closest option. Rates run BsF1 to BsF5 per hour.

The main **post office,** or *correo,* is located at Avenida Urdaneta and Norte 4 (✆ **0800/476-7835;** www.ipostel.gov.ve), near the Plaza Bolívar, and is open weekdays from 8am to 6pm, closing an hour earlier on weekends. Quite a few branch post offices are around town and in the suburbs, and several of the modern malls have Ipostel offices; many of these have a reduced schedule. Your hotel is usually your best bet for getting stamps and mailing a letter.

You'll find public phones all around Caracas. Most phones work with magnetic-strip calling cards that are readily available in stores and hotels all over the city. You can send and receive faxes and make credit card international calls from the **CANTV Centro Plaza** office, on Avenida Francisco Miranda in Los Palos Grandes, 2 blocks east of the Altamira Metro station (✆ **0212/285-6788;** fax 0212/286-2261; www.cantv.net). However, your best bet is to find one of the many Internet cafes around town that offer calling via Skype or some other VoIP service.

EXPLORING CARACAS

Plaza Bolívar & El Capitolio

Pigeons, pedestrians, park benches, and a towering bronze statue of El Libertador on his sturdy steed are the hallmarks of this square city block, which was once the heart of colonial Caracas. Within a 4- or 5-block radius, you will find several important museums and cathedrals, as well as the birthplace of Simón Bolívar, the national Congress (El Capitolio), and the **Panteón Nacional**, the country's most important mausoleum. This area is relatively safe to explore during the day, but I would definitely avoid it after dark.

Casa Natal & Museo Bolívar These side-by-side attractions, housed in two old colonial-era homes, make up the restored birthplace of Simón Bolívar and a modest museum of memorabilia and historic items related to El Libertador—his life, death, and military and political campaigns. A place of pilgrimage for many Venezuelans, the simple house where Bolívar was born on July 24, 1783, features a series of large oil paintings depicting important historical events, while the museum has exhibits of his clothing, battle gear, and writings. Give yourself about an hour to visit both sites.

Av. Universidad and Norte 1. ✆ **0212/541-2563.** Free admission. Tues–Sun 9am–noon and 2:30–5:30pm. Metro: Capitolio.

Catedral ★ Anchoring the eastern end of Plaza Bolívar, this is the national cathedral. The present-day church was built between 1665 and 1713, after the original building was destroyed in the 1641 earthquake. It's home to the personal Bolívar family chapel and features a painting by Rubens. Adjoining the cathedral is the **Museo Sacro de Caracas ★**, which has a good collection of religious art and sculpture, as well as colonial-era dress and relics and a delightful little cafe. Of ghoulish interest to many is the restored, yet still dank and dark, ecclesiastical prison once housed here. About half the museum exhibits here are in English.

Plaza Bolívar. Cathedral ✆ **0212/862-4963;** museum ✆ 0212/861-6562. Free admission to cathedral; admission to museum BsF2 adults, BsF0.50 children. Cathedral daily 7am–1pm and 3–6pm; museum Tues–Sun 10am–5pm. Metro: Capitolio.

Iglesia de San Francisco ★★ Not as large or ornate as the Catedral, this is the church where Bolívar was proclaimed El Libertador in 1813, and the site of his massive funeral in 1842—the year his remains were brought back from Colombia, some 12 years after his actual death. Begun in 1575, the church bears the architectural influences of various periods and styles but retains much of its colonial-era charm. The ornate gilded altars and religious paintings that line both of the long side walls are worthy of a stroll through the building.

Av. Universidad and Norte 2. ✆ **0212/484-2442.** Free admission. Mon–Fri 7am–noon and 2–5pm; Sat–Sun 10am–5pm. Metro: Capitolio.

Parque Central & Bellas Artes

Museo de Arte Contemporáneo ★★ The 13 rooms here form a minimaze covering several floors of the angular concrete architecture of Parque Central. The permanent collection features a good representation of the conceptual works of Venezuelan star Jesús Soto, as well as a small but high-quality collection of singular works by such modern masters as Picasso, Red Grooms, Henry Moore, Joan Miró, and Francis Bacon. The museum regularly hosts traveling exhibits of international stature. The small sculpture

Safety Advice

Although outwardly inviting, you should avoid El Calvario Park, which lies on the western end of the Capitolio area. This is a dangerous area, especially for tourists.

garden here is nowhere near as lovely as that found at the nearby Bellas Artes, but the elegant museum cafe is one of the nicer casual dining spots on this side of town.

Parque Central. ✆ **0212/573-8289.** Free admission. Daily 9am–5pm. Metro: Bellas Artes.

Museo de Bellas Artes ★ Taking up an area popularly known as the Plaza de los Museos, this museum houses a broad collection of Venezuelan art, ranging from the fine arts and modern masters to folk art and crafts, dating from the colonial period to the present. One of the nicer features here is the shady sculpture garden, which borders Parque Los Caobos. The Bellas Artes gift shop has a small, but worthwhile, selection of mostly high-end artworks and indigenous crafts.

Plaza Morelos, beside the Parque Los Caobos. ✆ **0212/578-0275.** www.fmn.gob.ve/fmn_gan.htm. Free admission. Mon–Fri 9am–4pm; Sat–Sun and holidays 10am–5pm. Metro: Bellas Artes.

Museo de los Niños (Children's Museum) Kids It's nothing truly spectacular, but this museum is a great place to pass a couple of hours if you've got children with you. A wide range of interactive and participatory exhibits cover the natural sciences, physics, medicine, and more. This place is often quite crowded with school groups during the week and families on weekends.

Av. Bolívar, between the 2 towers of Parque Central. ✆ **0212/575-3522.** www.maravillosarealidad.com. Admission BsF18 adults, BsF15 children. Mon–Fri 9am–5pm; Sat–Sun and holidays 10am–5pm. Metro: Bellas Artes.

Sports & Outdoor Activities

BASEBALL Baseball is the number-one sport in Venezuela. Venezuelans follow the sport with devotion and fervor. It's hard to find pickup games, but if you're in town for the season, you might want to catch a game. The local professional season runs October 20 through January 30 every year. As this is the off season for U.S. Major League Baseball, plenty of Venezuelan and international professional and minor-league players play here to stay in shape. Caracas has a couple of professional teams, as do most major cities around the country. The main Caracas team is Los Leones; another popular team (formerly of Caracas, but currently based out of Valencia) is Los Magallanes. The Leones-Magallanes rivalry is quite heated. You can get tickets to most games rather easily for BsF5 to BsF30. I'd recommend splurging for the more expensive seats, as they often provide protection from the sun, the rain, and the rowdier crowds. Los Leones play at the Estadio Universitario de Caracas (at the university). Tickets can be purchased in advance by calling ✆ **0212/762-1211,** although you can usually buy tickets the day of the game.

HIKING The place to go for hiking around Caracas is **Parque Nacional El Avila ★**, located on the northern edge of the city and encompassing some 82 hectares (203 acres) of the coastal mountain range separating the city from the Caribbean Sea. The park has dozens of trails as well as a well-developed network of restrooms, ranger stations, and campsites. The park and its trails get crowded on weekends. You should be able to reach

Pico El Avila (2,153m/7,062 ft.) in 2 to 4 hours of semistrenuous hiking, depending on the pace and route you choose. The highest peak here, **Pico Naiguatá,** rises to 2,765m (9,070 ft.). Be prepared for wide ranges in temperatures and the possibility of late-afternoon rains on the forested slopes of the park. It's best to hike in groups of at least four persons, as some robberies and muggings have been reported in the park. The most popular access to the park is from the northern end of the Altamira district, at the end of Avenida San Juan Bosco, and from all along Avenida Boyacá. You can take the Metro to the Altamira stop, although it's a steep 10-block walk uphill from both the Metro station and from the San Bernardino area to the entrance to the park. Admission to the park is free.

EL TELEFERICO ★ Another, much less strenuous, way to reach Pico El Avila is via the *teleférico.* This cable-car system stretches from the Maripérez station on the northern edge of the city to the top of El Avila mountain. The 3.4km (2-mile) ride to the top takes between 12 and 15 minutes, where you'll find a skating rink, rock-climbing wall, telescopes, simple restaurants, souvenir shops, snack stands, and the dormant 14-story Hotel Humbolt.

When the weather is clear, there are fabulous views over both Caracas and down the coastal mountains to the Caribbean sea. At the summit, you can also hire a taxi to take you to one of the dozen or so restaurants in and near the small mountain village of Galipán. These restaurants range from simple roadside shacks, to fine dining establishments serving everything from Mexican to French cuisine.

The *teleférico* (✆ **0800/887-4766**) is open Tuesday through Sunday from 10am to 8pm. The round-trip cost is BsF25 adults and BsF10 children 4 to 12. A light sweater or windbreaker is recommended, as it can get chilly up top. To get here, just ask a taxi to take you to *el terminal Maripérez del teleférico.*

JOGGING Joggers should definitely head to either **Parque del Este** for more or less flat terrain, or **Parque Nacional El Avila** (see "Hiking," above) for more challenging mountainous terrain.

Shopping

Venezuelans—and most visitors—tend to shop at one of the many modern malls that have been built around Caracas over the past 20 years. Of these, the **Centro Comercial Sambil ★**, Avenida Libertador (Metro: Chacao), is perhaps the most popular. Reputed to be the largest mall in South America, it features everything from a multiplex cinema to gourmet restaurants to a performing arts space to a mini–amusement park. Other

Finds Parque del Este

This large **urban oasis ★★** is a favorite spot for Caraqueños. Joggers, yoga and tai chi enthusiasts, tennis players, and people looking for pickup soccer and basketball games fill this park on most mornings and throughout the weekend. You can take part in any of the aforementioned activities or just stroll the paths, sit on a bench, or visit the tiny zoo. On weekends you can catch one of the shows at the Humbolt Planetarium here. The park is open Tuesday through Sunday from 5am to 5pm, Monday from 5 to 9am. Admission is free. Metro: Parque del Este.

prominent malls include the **Centro Comercial Ciudad Tamanaco (CCCT),** Autopista Francisco Fajardo and Calle La Estancia (no Metro); and the **Centro Lido,** Avenida Francisco de Miranda, El Rosal (Metro: Chacaito).

Las Mercedes ★★ is an upscale district of restaurants, shops, nightclubs, and art galleries, which makes it the choice spot for a leisurely afternoon of browsing and buying.

If you're looking for arts and crafts, you can head to the **Mercado Guajiro** ★, Paseo Las Flores near the western end of Plaza Chacaito, a collection of 30 shops featuring indigenous and other arts and crafts. However, perhaps the best shopping for Venezuelan arts and crafts is to be found in El Hatillo at the **Hannsi Centro Artesanal** ★★★, Calle Bolívar 12 (✆ **0212/963-7184;** www.hannsi.com.ve). This huge indoor bazaar has everything from indigenous masks to ceramic wares to woven baskets. The selection is broad and covers everything from trinkets to major pieces of fine craftsmanship.

WHERE TO STAY

Hotel rates in Caracas are crazy. Business travelers fill almost every room in the city Monday through Thursday, and hotels slash their rates on weekends. Moreover, the high occupancy and heavy corporate traffic have made rack rates at most Caracas hotels almost meaningless. Few hotels actually charge their published and advertised rack rate. It always pays to ask for a corporate or special rate, and if that fails, try to bargain at all but the truly top-end hotels.

Note: Most of the upscale hotels in Caracas either list their prices in dollars, or peg them to the dollar.

Very Expensive

In addition to the hotels mentioned below, the new **Pestana Caracas** ★★ (✆ **0212/202-1900;** www.pestana.com) is another excellent option in this category, with a luxurious rooftop pool and lounge area.

The Hotel ★★ This midsize boutique hotel offers a refreshing alternative to the large chain options that dominate here in Caracas. The Hotel is chic and modern. Flatscreen LCD and plasma TV screens are everywhere—in the lobby, lounge, restaurant, and even the elevators. Rooms are sleek and stylish, with marble or wood floors, thick down-feather bed cushions and comforters, and modern entertainment systems ready for you to plug in your laptop, iPod, or video camera. There's a range of suite categories, all of which come with Jacuzzi tubs, and some of which have private steam showers. The standards are quite acceptable, but lack these perks. All, except the larger suites are on the compact side, especially at these prices. All rooms are nonsmoking.

Calle Mohedano, El Rosal, Caracas. ✆ **0212/951-3275.** www.thehotel.com.ve. 63 units. BsF688 double; from BsF882 suite. AE, MC, V. Free valet parking. **Amenities:** Restaurant; bar; lounge; concierge; room service; small, well-equipped spa and exercise room. *In room:* A/C, TV, hair dryer, minibar, free Wi-Fi.

JW Marriott ★★★ This upscale hotel caters primarily to business travelers, though it works just as well for a casual traveler. The rooms are all very comfortable and spacious, with lush furnishings and decor, and sleek marble bathrooms. There are two towers here, and one contains suites entirely. The regular deluxe rooms all come with separate tubs and showers, although oddly some of the suites only have a tub/shower combo. The large "spa suites" come with a private Jacuzzi tub. Most rooms, particularly those on higher floors, have wonderful views, but the best view to be found is on the 17th-floor bridge connecting the two towers. Service is attentive and accommodating. Dining options include Sur, an excellent *nuevo Latino* restaurant, as well as a sushi bar.

Av. Venezuela and Calle Mohedano, El Rosal, Caracas. ✆ **888/236-2427** in the U.S. and Canada, or 0212/957-2222 in Venezuela. Fax 0212/957-1111. www.marriott.com. 269 units. BsF880 double; BsF944–BsF1,094 suite. AE, MC, V. Valet parking BsF11. **Amenities:** 2 restaurants; bar; coffee shop; concierge; small, well-equipped health club; outdoor pool; room service; smoke-free rooms. *In room:* A/C, TV, hair dryer, Internet (for a fee), minibar.

Expensive

In addition to the hotel listed in this section, the **Hotel Paseo Las Mercedes ★**, Centro Comercial Paseo Las Mercedes (✆ **0212/993-6644;** www.hotelpaseolasmercedes.com), is a business-class hotel located in the heart of the fashionable Las Mercedes shopping and dining district.

Hotel Continental Altamira ★ This hotel offers a great location, acceptable levels of comfort, and a good array of amenities. The high-rise building is located about a block and a half from the Altamira Metro station and the heart of the area's restaurants and shops. Most of the rooms are quite large and qualify as junior suites, although the bathrooms in most cases are disproportionately small. The nicest feature here is the shady outdoor terrace area surrounding the hotel's surprisingly inviting little pool. Maintenance and upkeep have historically been lax, and the hotel is in need of some upkeep and updating.

Av. San Juan Bosco, Altamira, Caracas. ✆ **0212/261-0644.** Fax 0212/261-0131. www.hotel-continental.org.ve. 82 units. BsF473–BsF731 double. AE, MC, V. Free valet parking. **Amenities:** Restaurant; bar; small outdoor pool; room service. *In room:* A/C, TV.

Moderate

Hotel Avila (Finds) The aged grande dame of Caracas hotels, this place is worth considering. Built by Nelson Rockefeller in 1942, the hotel is a quiet oasis located on the outskirts of downtown on the flanks of Mount Avila. The lush grounds and flowering gardens are a welcome change from the cold concrete and glass that characterize most of Caracas. The hotel definitely shows its age, and perennially feels as if it could use some major maintenance and upkeep. Yet, it retains a certain dignity and charm, if not glamour. Most of the rooms are spacious, with high ceilings, carpeting, and rattan furnishings, although most do not have air-conditioning. The suites are a mixed bag: Some are quite attractive, while others are less appealing than the standard rooms. The Tower and Executive suites are the best rooms in the house. A taxi from the hotel to downtown will cost you BsF20 to BsF25.

Av. Washington, San Bernardino, Caracas. ✆ **0212/555-3000.** Fax 0212/552-3021. www.hotelavila.com.ve. 113 units. BsF150–BsF250 double; BsF280 junior suite; BsF300–BsF350 suite. Rates include breakfast buffet. AE, MC, V. Free parking. **Amenities:** Restaurant; bar; lounge; concierge; small health club; small outdoor pool; room service; 6 lighted tennis courts. *In room:* TV.

WHERE TO STAY NEAR THE AIRPORT

If you're just looking for a quick overnight, are planning on heading straight to a beach, jungle or mountain destination, or simply have little use or interest in Caracas, you should consider staying near the airport.

In addition to the options listed below, the **Eurobuilding Express Hotel,** Av. La Armada, Urbanización 10 de Marzo, Maiquetía (✆ **0212/700-0700;** www.eurobuilding.com.ve), is located directly across from the Simón Bolívar International Airport. This business-class hotel offers little in the way of personality, but they do have a free shuttle to the airport, and if you arrive late and leave early the next morning, it's worth considering.

 If you're looking for a budget option in the area, try the **Buenavista Inn,** Av. el Hotel con Calle 4, Playa Grande, Catia La Mar (✆ **0212/352-9163;** www.buenavistainn.com.ve).

Very Expensive

Hotel Olé Caribe ★ A comfortable and well-maintained hotel, the Olé Caribe was my top choice in this area, until the Marriott (see below) opened. The rooms are all clean, bright, and well maintained, and feature a handful of amenities to be expected in this class. Most of the rooms have ocean views; those that don't face the coastal mountains behind the hotel. The Olé Caribe is a bit inland from the sea and there are no worthwhile beaches close by; however, the pool area and surrounding landscaped grounds are tropical and inviting. Located 15 minutes from the airport, this is a popular choice of local and international tour operators who are increasingly having their guests bypass Caracas altogether.

Av. Intercomunal, El Playón Macuto. ✆ **0212/620-200.** Fax 0212/620-2060. www.hotelolecaribe.com. 122 units. BsF473–BsF645 double; BsF1,204 suite. Rates include buffet breakfast. AE, MC, V. Free parking. **Amenities:** 3 restaurants; 2 bars; concierge; small gym; large outdoor pool w/unheated Jacuzzi and children's pool; room service; squash court; unlit tennis court. *In room:* A/C, TV, hair dryer, minibar, free Wi-Fi.

Marriott Playa Grande ★★ This new hotel ups the ante on the coast. Rooms are large, sparkling, and well equipped. Rooms on the higher floors have excellent views, and most of these overlook the Caribbean sea. The small health club and gym are top notch, and the common areas and restaurants are up to snuff. There's a small protected cove of a beach a block or so away, but it's far from spectacular, and I'd recommend you stick to the delightful pool. The hotel is only a few miles from the airport, but be forewarned: It's in a somewhat sketchy area, there's little to do or see nearby, and walking around on your own is discouraged.

Av. El Hotel, Playa Grande, Catia La Mar. ✆ **888/236-2427** in the U.S. and Canada, or 0212/535-2222 in Venezuela. Fax 0212/957-6333. www.marriott.com. 206 units. BsF649 double; BsF729 suite. AE, DC, DISC, MC, V. Valet parking BsF45. **Amenities:** 2 restaurants; bar; children's center; concierge; well-equipped health club; outdoor pool; room service; smoke-free rooms; Wi-Fi. *In room:* A/C, TV, hair dryer, Internet (for a fee).

WHERE TO DINE

Caracas has a lively restaurant scene. The local upper and middle classes support a host of fine restaurants and trendy joints. World and fusion cuisines are the rage, along with sushi bars and upscale steakhouses. New places open and close with the frequency and fanfare worthy of New York City. If you're serious about delving into the local restaurant scene, pick up a copy of the latest edition of Miro Popic's ***Guía Gastronómica de Caracas*** ★★ (www.miropopic.com), a comprehensive, accurate, and bilingual guide to metropolitan restaurants, cafes, and nightspots.

In addition to the places listed below, **Chez Wong,** Plaza La Castellana (✆ **0212/266-5015;** no Metro), is widely considered the best Chinese restaurant in town, while **Da Guido,** Avenida Francisco Solano, Sabana Grande (✆ **0212/763-0937;** Metro: Sabana Grande), and **Vizio ★**, Avenida Luis Rocha, bottom floor of the Casa Rómulo Gallegos, Altamira (✆ **0212/285-5675;** Metro: Altamira), are recommended for Italian cuisine.

On a more popular level, simple *arreperías* and informal *fuentes de soda,* the local equivalent of diners, are ubiquitous. Be sure to stop in to one or two of them for a light meal and a bit of local color. Given the prevalence and popularity of huge modern malls, you can usually count on finding a wide selection of restaurants, as well as an assortment of U.S.-based and -styled fast-food chains, in most of them.

Note: Though I've included Metro stops for the restaurants in this section, at press time Las Mercedes station was still under construction, tentatively scheduled to open sometime in 2010. Your best bet is, when possible, to take a taxi to and from restaurants.

Expensive

Check out the local branch of famed Peruvian restaurant **Astrid y Gastón**, Calle Londres, Las Mercedes (✆ **0212/993-1119;** Metro: Las Mercedes; see p. 389 for the review of the original restaurant).

Antigua ★★ ITALIAN This homey place serves up fine fare in a lively, eclectic ambience. The restaurant rambles through several rooms over two floors, and has a busy mix of antiques, potted plants, paintings, and sculptures for decor. My favorite spot is the second-floor balcony. The menu is heavy on pastas, risotto, and wood-oven pizzas, but also includes more substantial main courses and nightly specials. I highly recommend the sweet potato gnocchi served with caramelized onions, prosciutto, and a creamy nut sauce.

Calle Madrid, between Mucuchies and Monterrey, Las Mercedes. ✆ **0212/991-9056.** Reservations recommended. Main courses BsF54–BsF90; pizzas BsF30–BsF67. AE, MC, V. Mon–Sat noon–midnight; Sun 9am–11pm. Metro: Las Mercedes.

Bar Si ★★ PAN-ASIAN The menu here features a broad mix of various Asian classics and its modern offshoots, including some Peruvian-inspired fusions. There's a wide selection of Japanese dishes, including a small sushi bar. You can start things off with some sushi or one of the many *ceviche* choices. For a main dish, I always enjoy the Thai-inspired grouper in a coconut-milk curry with fresh mango, all served in a banana leaf. The low ceilings and low lighting give this place an intimate (though sometimes claustrophobic) feel. The bar here is extremely popular on weekends, and sometimes features live music or DJs. The food is expensive, but definitely top notch.

Calle Madrid, between Veraruz and Caroní, Las Mercedes. ✆ **0212/993-9124.** Reservations recommended. Main courses BsF35–BsF90. AE, MC, V. Mon–Wed noon–3pm and 7–11pm; Thurs–Sat noon–3pm and 7pm–midnight; Sun noon–3pm. Metro: Las Mercedes.

Gourmet Market ★★ INTERNATIONAL/SUSHI This casual and bustling joint covers a lot of bases. The sushi is very respectable, and features some interesting fusion options, like the tandoori roll, which has a filling of crab, salmon, and tempura shrimp dressed with a curry sauce and served with a raita. You can also get a generous cut of steak in a rosemary sauce served with roasted veggies, or a sweet-and-sour duck confit with fried rice. For lighter fare there are a range of sandwiches, pastas, salads, and carpaccios. Most of the seating is on an open-air wooden deck protected from the street by a thick wall of bamboo and potted plants.

Av. Principal Las Mercedes and the corner of Calle Guaicaipuro, El Rosal. ✆ **0212/951-5195.** Main courses BsF50–BsF79; sushi BsF13–BsF63. AE, MC, V. Daily 7am–11pm. Metro: Chacaito.

Restaurante Urrutia ★ SPANISH This has been one of the most popular restaurants in Caracas for more than 50 years. As befits a family-run institution, the place has an intimate feel, with low ceilings and dark-wood beams. Start with a carpaccio of beef or salmon, or a tapa of Spanish tortilla (a potato-and-egg omelet). Although everything's delicious, one specialty here is the *piquillo* peppers stuffed with your choice of grouper, squid, or *bacalao* (cod) in a tomato-based Vizcaina sauce. If you make it through the extensive menu with room to spare, try the homemade *membrillo* jam with Manchego cheese for dessert. They have another branch, **Casa Urrutia** (✆ **0212/993-9526;** Metro: Las Mercedes) in the Las Mercedes district, at Calle Madrid and Calle Monterrey.

Av. Francisco Solano and Los Manguitos, Sabana Grande. ✆ **0212/763-0448.** Reservations recommended. Main courses BsF35–BsF70. MC, V. Mon–Sat noon–11pm; Sun noon–5pm. Metro: Sabana Grande.

Moderate

Catar ★ INTERNATIONAL The outgrowth of a popular bakery and deli operation, this casual restaurant serves a wide range of fare, from simple pizzas and panini and ornate organic salads, to full meals. Everything is well prepared and tasty. For a main dish, I recommend the seared tuna in a soy-ginger sauce. There's an open kitchen and deli counter for take out, as well as two main dining rooms. Both feature walls of glass, and marble-topped tables. This place is housed in a small shopping center known as the Cuadro Gastrónomico (Gastronomic Block) and is surrounded by several other good restaurants.

6th Tranversal, between avs. 3 and 4, Los Palos Grandes. ✆ **0212/285-0649.** Reservations recommended. Main courses BsF35–BsF75; pizzas BsF25–BsF35. MC, V. Daily 11:30am–11pm. Metro: Los Palos Grandes.

El Tinajero de los Helechos VENEZUELAN Caracas has plenty of reputable steakhouses, but this is my favorite—as much for the casual vibe as for the fine meats and side dishes. There's an extensive selection of meat dishes, and nearly as many fish and chicken choices. The classic *pabellón criollo* and *asado negro* are both excellent. If you want something less traditional, try the chateaubriand or medallions of sirloin in a port sauce. A wide range of traditional Venezuelan appetizers and sides are available as well. The four rooms contain indigenous craftworks and plenty of ferns—*helecho* is Spanish for fern—which liven up the decor.

Av. Rio de Janeiro, between Caroní and New York, Las Mercedes. ✆ **0212/993-3581.** Reservations recommended. Main courses BsF30–BsF70. AE, DC, MC, V. Daily 11:30am–midnight. Metro: Las Mercedes.

News Café ★ Finds INTERNATIONAL This multifaceted joint tries to do it all and does a great job on all counts. Part bookstore, part cafe, part jazz club, and full-time restaurant, it serves breakfast, lunch, and dinner daily. There are several rooms and environments, including an open-air rooftop terrace with heavy marble tables under white-canvas umbrellas, a second-floor balcony space, and a vibrant main dining room with cracked-tile mosaic floors. The food is simple and straightforward, with a host of interesting sandwiches served on fresh-baked baguettes, mixed with a selection of salads, crepes, bruschettas, and pastas. More substantial entrees include medallions of beef in a white wine, porcini, and cream sauce, or, my favorite, Salmon al Matteotti, which is served in a champagne-and-almond reduction. There's live music most afternoons for lunch, as well as Thursday through Saturday evenings.

1st Transversal de los Palos Grandes and 1st Av. Quinta d'Casa. ✆ **0212/286-5096.** Reservations recommended for dinner. Sandwiches BsF12–BsF20; main courses BsF22–BsF45. AE, MC, V. Mon–Fri 10am–1am; Sat–Sun 8am–1am. Metro: Los Palos Grandes.

Inexpensive

El Fogón Finds VENEZUELAN Take a table on the second-floor open-air balcony of this popular local joint. Hanging ferns and wind chimes give the place an air of sophistication, but the food is as traditional as it comes. Order an *arepa* to start things off, or try a *cachapa*—a sweet corn pancake folded over your choice of filling. The *asado* here is excellent, and they almost always have *hallacas,* the local equivalent of tamales, cornmeal paste stuffed with chicken, pork, olives, raisins, boiled egg, and other goodies, wrapped in a banana leaf, and boiled or steamed. For dessert, have some fried *churros.*

Calle La Paz, El Hatillo. ✆ **0212/963-1068.** Reservations recommended on weekends. Main courses BsF10–BsF22. No credit cards. Tues–Fri 9am–8pm; Sat–Sun 8am–10pm. No Metro stop.

Snacks & Cafes

In addition to the News Café (see above), another nearby coffeehouse worth checking is the **Café Arábica** ★, Avenida Andres Bello between 1st Transversal and Avenida Francisco Miranda (✆ **0212/286-3636;** Metro: Los Palos Grandes), a trendy joint on the ground floor of the Multicentro Los Palos Grandes mall that roasts its own beans bought from local producers.

If you're hungry for a quick bite and there's a *fuente de soda* handy—the local equivalent of a diner or deli—you should definitely try an *arepa,* the traditional cornmeal patty that usually comes stuffed with meat, cheese, or chicken.

CARACAS AFTER DARK

Caracas is a big, cosmopolitan city, and your nighttime options are many and varied. It's advisable to stick to the more upscale and relatively safe neighborhoods such as Altamira, El Rosal, and Las Mercedes, or one of the popular malls.

In terms of malls, the **Centro Comercial San Ignacio** has emerged as a popular one-stop shop for young Caraqueños looking to party. However, my favorite bar in Caracas is located atop the Altamira Suites hotel. As its name implies, **360°** ★★, 1st Avenida Los Palos Grandes and 1st Tranversal (✆ **0212/284-1874**), offers up panoramic views from its rooftop perch. The bar actually starts out with a large indoor space on the 19th floor, with plush cushions, couches, and even hammocks for seating, and climbs two more stories outdoors with a handful of different open-air patios, bars, and seating areas.

The **Juan Sebastián Bar** ★★, Avenida Venezuela, El Rosal (✆ **0212/951-3750**), is a popular restaurant and bar—and the most consistent place in the city to catch live jazz. Rockers head to **Greenwich** ★, Avenida San Juan Bosco, Altamira (✆ **0212/267-1760**), a small place with live bands, or **Little Rock Café,** Avenida 6 between 3rd and 4th Transversal, Altamira (✆ **0212/267-8337**), a knock-off of the Hard Rock chain that also has live bands on most nights. And there's even an official franchise of the **Hard Rock Cafe** (✆ **0212/267-7662**) located in the huge Centro Comercial Sambil. **El Maní Es Así** ★, Avenida Francisco Solano and Calle El Cristo, Sabana Grande (✆ **0212/763-6671**), is one of the more popular salsa and Latin dance spots. Open Tuesday through Sunday from 5pm until around 5am, they charge no cover and always have a live band.

Located just across from the Caracas Hilton, the **Teresa Carreño Cultural Complex** (✆ **0500/673-7200** or 0212/576-6411; www.teatroteresacarreno.gob.ve) and the **Ateneo de Caracas** (✆ **0212/573-4799**) are the places to go for live performances. Top-notch popular and classical concerts take place in the Teresa Carreño, while film series and modern theater are often on tap at the Ateneo. The **Trasnocho Cultural** ★, Centro Comercial Paseo Las Mercedes (✆ **0212/993-1910;** www.trasnochocultural.com), is a popular option with a beautiful theater and a couple of cinemas offering a steady diet of live music, theater, and avant-garde cinema. They also have a hip little bar and cafe. Check the local papers or ask at your hotel for a performance schedule. Ticket prices range from BsF5 to BsF50.

Caracas-based tour companies offer a host of **tour options,** from guided city tours and adventure activities to longer excursions to destinations such as Los Roques and Angel Falls (see below). Some of the more popular day-tour options from Caracas include mountain-bike or jeep tours through Parque Nacional El Avila. Prices for day tours range from BsF95 to BsF250 per person. A half-day guided tour to El Hatillo usually runs around BsF75 per person.

Akanan Travel & Adventure ★★ (✆ **0212/715-5433** or 0414/116-0107; www.akanan.com) and **Cacao Expeditions** (✆ **0212/977-1234;** www.cacaotravel.com) are both reputable local operators offering a wide range of single and multiday options.

EL HATILLO ★★ This neocolonial town, located 15km (9 miles) southeast of downtown, is a great place to spend a few leisurely hours and grab a meal. You'll want to spend most of your time strolling around, but be prepared—it's hilly here. Moreover, the narrow streets have even narrower sidewalks, so beware of car traffic. Window-shop the many crafts and artisan jewelry stores and be sure to sample some homemade sweets at one of the many local pastry and candy shops. You'll find a good selection of restaurants, cafes, and bars here. Stop in for a coffee or a light bite at **Croquer,** Calle Bolívar 17 (✆ **0212/961-4269**). After admiring the memorabilia, try to grab one of the third-floor tables under canvas umbrellas on the terrace. A taxi to El Hatillo should cost around BsF40.

LOS ROQUES ★★ Perhaps the most popular excursions from Caracas are to Los Roques, a gorgeous archipelago of small islands around a calm saltwater lagoon in crystal-clear Caribbean waters. **Aerotuy** (✆ **0212/212-3110;** www.tuy.com) is by far the most established operator offering trips to Los Roques. The cost for a full-day trip is around BsF860 per person. Children's rates are roughly half price, and rates are slightly lower during the low season and midweek. For more information, see "Los Roques National Park," later in this chapter.

CANAIMA & ANGEL FALLS ★★ You may actually see advertisements for or be offered a day tour to Canaima and Angel Falls. However, given the distance, travel time, and outstanding natural beauty of the area, I highly recommend a longer trip. See "Canaima, Angel Falls & the Río Caura," later in this chapter, for more information.

5 ISLA DE MARGARITA ★

40km (25 miles) N of Cumaná

Known locally as La Perla del Caribe, or the Pearl of the Caribbean, Isla de Margarita is Venezuela's most popular tourist destination. Venezuelans come here in droves for weekend and holiday getaways, and to take advantage of the island's status as a duty-free port, while Canadian, European, and Latin American travelers come to enjoy the warm sun, white sands, and turquoise waters of this small Caribbean island. In many ways, the pleasures to be had on Isla de Margarita mirror and compete with those offered in Cancún, Punta Cana, Varadero, and other beach destinations around the Caribbean, although on a much smaller scale. And Margarita remains relatively undiscovered and unexplored by Americans. Columbus actually landed here, in 1498, on his third voyage, and named the island La Asunción. However, a year later it was rechristened La Margarita.

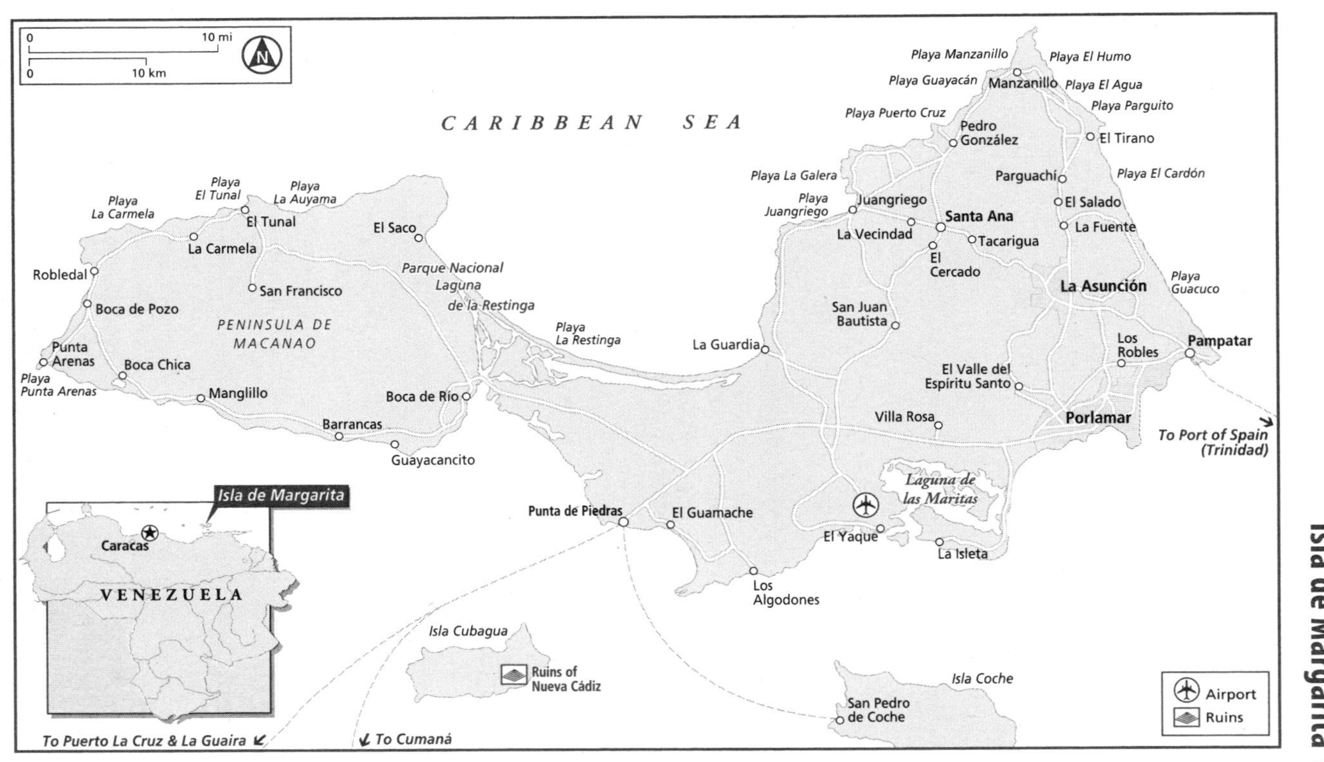
0
10 mi
0
10 km
N
CARIBBEAN SEA
Playa Manzanillo
Playa El Humo
Playa Guayacán
Manzanillo
Playa El Agua
Playa Parguito
Playa Puerto Cruz
Pedro González
El Tirano
Playa La Galera
Parguachí
Playa El Cardón
Playa Juangriego
Juangriego
El Salado
Santa Ana
La Fuente
La Vecindad
Tacarigua
El Cercado
La Asunción
Playa Guacuco
San Juan Bautista
Los Robles
Pampatar
La Guardia
El Valle del Espíritu Santo
Villa Rosa
Porlamar
To Port of Spain (Trinidad)
Laguna de las Maritas
El Yaque
La Isleta
Los Algodones
El Guamache
Punta de Piedras
Playa La Restinga
Parque Nacional Laguna de la Restinga
Playa La Carmela
Playa El Tunal
Playa La Auyama
El Tunal
El Saco
La Carmela
Robledal
San Francisco
Boca de Pozo
PENINSULA DE MACANAO
Punta Arenas
Boca Chica
Playa Punta Arenas
Manglillo
Boca de Río
Barrancas
Guayacancito
Isla de Margarita
Caracas
VENEZUELA
Isla Cubagua
Ruins of Nueva Cádiz
Isla Coche
San Pedro de Coche
Airport
Ruins
To Puerto La Cruz & La Guaira
To Cumaná

Margarita is really two islands joined in the middle by a stretch of sand, mangrove, and marsh that make up **La Restinga National Park.** The western side, called the **Peninsula de Macanao,** is largely undeveloped. It's an extremely arid and dry area, crisscrossed with rugged dirt roads and horse trails, and it's home to the endemic yellow-headed and yellow-shouldered Margaritan parrot. Almost all development is found on the larger, eastern side, which has three principal cities—**Porlamar, Pampatar,** and **La Asunción**—and a couple of dozen different beaches and resort areas. The island has two national parks and three nature reserves, as well as several colonial-era forts and churches.

Margarita's climate is hot and tropical, with ample sunshine and very little rainfall year-round. You're most likely to encounter some rain during the months of July and August and between November and January.

ESSENTIALS

Getting There

BY PLANE Several international airlines and dozens of charter carriers have service to Margarita's **Aeropuerto Internacional del Caribe Santiago Mariño** (airport code PMV; ✆ **0295/269-1081**) from major European cities, as well as from Toronto, Montreal, Miami, and New York. Many of these are sold as package tours.

From Caracas, a couple of dozen flights go to Margarita throughout the day. **Aeropostal** (✆ **0800/284-6637;** www.aeropostal.com), **Aserca** (✆ **0800/648-8356;** www.asercaairlines.com), **Conviasa** (✆ **0500/266-84272;** www.conviasa.aero), and **Laser** (✆ **0501/527-3700;** www.laser.com.ve) all fly between Caracas's Simón Bolívar International Airport and Isla de Margarita. Fares vary radically according to season and day of the week, ranging from BsF150 to BsF300 each way. Midweek and low-season fares are considerably less expensive. Conversely, seats sell out well in advance and at a premium on weekends and holidays and during the high season. Flight schedules and travel agents refer to the airport as Porlamar, although it is around 20km (13 miles) from the city, on the southern part of the island near the beach of El Yaque.

BY FERRY Although much more time consuming and not much less expensive, ferry service has and continues to be one of Margarita's principal links to the mainland. Visitors, residents, cars, buses, and much of the island's goods and merchandise travel by sea. The main ferry station is at Punta de Piedras on the southern end of the island. The main departure points for ferries to Margarita are Puerto La Cruz and Cumaná on the northern coast of Venezuela several hours east of Caracas. Numerous public buses throughout the day connect Caracas to both Puerto La Cruz and Cumaná. The bus trip runs about 5 hours from Caracas to Puerto La Cruz (fare BsF15–BsF30), and 7 to 8 hours to Cumaná (fare BsF18–BsF35). Several bus lines make this run. Or you can try the **Unión Conductores de Margarita,** Terminal Oriente, Caracas (✆ **0212/541-0035** or 0295/287-0931), which has a direct combined trip that costs around BsF70 each way.

Basically, there are two types of ferries running from Puerto La Cruz and Cumaná: the older regular ferries, which take between 3 and 4 hours each way, and the newer "express" ferries, which make the crossing in around 2 hours. Ferry schedules change drastically according to season and demand, and even the set schedules are sometimes somewhat flexible. For current ferry schedules and fares, contact **Conferry** (✆ **0501/266-33779;** www.conferry.com) or **Gran Cacique Express** (✆ **0501/693-3779** or 0295/264-1160; www.grancacique.com.ve).

It's recommended to try buying tickets in advance on weekends and during high season. Costs range from BsF35 to BsF134 per person, each way, and BsF75 to BsF135 per car. The cost difference for passengers is tied to the "class" of your ticket and speed of the boat. I recommend you splurge for the higher-class fares on the express ferries, which will get you a seat in an enclosed and air-conditioned lounge deck, and a quicker ride.

Getting Around

Renting a car is not essential, but it does make getting around Margarita easier. **Avis** (✆ **0800/227-7600;** www.avis.com); **Budget** (✆ **0800/472-3325;** www.budget.com.ve), **Hertz** (✆ **0800/800-0000;** www.hertz.com), and **Margarita Rentals** (✆ **0295/263-2711**) all have offices at the airport. It costs BsF180 to BsF300 per day to rent a car. Several outfits around the island rent scooters and mopeds for between BsF90 and BsF120 per day.

Por puesto buses service most of the island. They are a very inexpensive and reliable way to get around, although the going can be slow, as they often stop to pick up and discharge passengers at maddeningly short intervals. Typical service hours are daily from 6am to 8pm. Fares range from BsF0.50 to BsF2.

Taxis are also readily available. It will cost you around BsF70 to travel between the airport and Porlamar; BsF20 between Porlamar and Pampatar; BsF40 between Playa El Agua and either Porlamar or Pampatar; and BsF100 between Playa El Agua and the airport. If you can't flag one down on the street, you can order a cab by calling **Sam Mar Taxi** (✆ **0295/262-4733**) or **Taxis Unidos** (✆ **0295/263-2269**).

Visitor Information

There is a simple, very basic information desk at the airport in Porlamar. However, you're better off heading to one of the scores of tour agencies to be found around Porlamar and Pampatar and at most major hotels on the island.

FAST FACTS There are scores of **banks** on Isla de Margarita. They often have ATMs connected to PLUS or Cirrus systems that will advance you bolívares fuertes against your home account. You'll find ATMs in both Porlamar and Pampatar, as well as at all the large malls and some of the large resort hotels.

In case of any medical emergency, consult with your hotel first, or head to the **Luis Ortega Hospital** in Porlamar (✆ **0295/261-6508**).

Internet cafes are located in most malls and major resorts, as well as in Porlamar, in Pampatar, and along Playa El Agua. For regular mail, there are **Ipostel** offices in both Porlamar and Pampatar. Most hotels will also post mail for you.

EXPLORING ISLA DE MARGARITA

Cities & Towns

Porlamar is the largest city and the commercial hub of the island. Founded in 1536, Porlamar is not particularly attractive. The city center is a chaotic jumble of shops and small department stores. However, these days the majority of shoppers are heading to large, modern malls built on the outskirts of the city. Still, Porlamar has the highest concentration of shops, restaurants, bars, and dance clubs on Margarita.

Pampatar, about 10km (6 miles) northeast of Porlamar, is much more picturesque and calm. Founded in 1535 around the island's most protected deep-water harbor, Pampatar still retains much of its colonial-era flavor and architecture. The main attraction here is the **Castillo de San Carlos Borromeo ★**, a 17th-century fort that protected the town and harbor from foreign and pirate attacks. The fort's thick stone walls and bronze cannons still watch over the beach, harbor, and Caribbean Sea. The fort is open Monday through Saturday; admission is free. Across from the fort, you'll find the **Iglesia de Santísimo Cristo del Buen Viaje,** a church of great importance to the sailors and fishermen of Margarita. Legend has it that the crucifix here was left as a last resort, when the colonial-era vessel transporting it was unable, after repeated attempts, to leave the harbor. At the eastern end of the harbor are the ruins of the **Fortín de la Caranta,** which offers excellent views of the town and bay.

Located on a hillside, inland from Pampatar, **La Asunción** is the capital of the island and of the entire state of Nueva Esparta. The city's church, **La Catedral de Nuestra Señora de la Asunción★**, is said to be the oldest in Venezuela. A few minutes from the center of town is the **Castillo de Santa Rosa,** another of the island's historic and battle-worn forts.

In between Porlamar and Pampatar is the area known as **Los Robles.** Here, you'll find the colonial-era **Iglesia El Pilar de Los Robles,** whose statue of the Virgin Mary is reputed to be of solid gold.

On the road north of La Asunción is the town of **Santa Ana.** In 1816, Simón Bolívar signed the proclamation of the Third Republic in the small church here. It's now best known as the hub for a series of small artisan villages and roadside crafts shops.

Finally, on the northern coast of the island is the popular fishing village and bay of **Juangriego★**. This spot is becoming increasingly popular, particularly for **sunsets.** The small **Fortín La Galera★★**, on a bluff on the northern end of the bay, is probably the most sought-after spot for sunsets on the island. Arrive early if you want a prime table and viewing spot at one of the small open-air restaurants and bars here.

The Beaches ★★

Isla de Margarita is ringed with dozens of white-sand beaches. Some have huge modern resorts and facilities, others are home to a handful of fishermen and locals, and some are entirely undeveloped and deserted. Perhaps the most popular beach on the island is **Playa El Agua,** a long, broad, straight stretch of white sand with moderate surf, backed by palm trees and a broad selection of restaurants and shops. **Playa Parguito** has begun to rival El Agua in terms of popularity. Both of these beaches can get packed on weekends and during peak periods. To the south and north of Playa El Agua, you'll find beaches such as **Manzanillo★**, **El Tirano★**, **Cardón,** and **Guacuco.** Manzanillo and El Tirano are my favorites, because they are the least developed and often quite deserted. Manzanillo is a great place to watch sunsets. Playas Parguito and El Tirano are the best surf breaks on the island. Close to Porlamar, folks head to **Playa Bella Vista** and **Playa Morena,** although I'm not particularly taken by the vibe or water quality at either.

On the northern coast of Margarita you will find a string of excellent and less developed beaches, including **Playa Caribe★**, **Playa Pedro González,** and **Playa Puerto Viejo.** These are some of my favorite beaches on Margarita, and they are building up fast. Those looking for solitude should head to the still-undeveloped beaches that ring the Macanao Peninsula.

Although one of the least attractive beaches on the island, **Playa Pampatar** is nonetheless quite popular with locals. It is also lined with a string of simple restaurants set on the sand, just a few yards from the sea.

La Restinga National Park ★

This 10,700-hectare (26,429-acre) park encompasses a zone of mangroves, marshland, sandbar, and coral-sand beaches, making a natural land bridge between the two islands that today are Isla de Margarita. A visit to the park usually involves a boat tour through the mangroves, followed by some beach time on the 10km (6-mile) stretch of beach that forms the isthmus uniting the two sides of Margarita. You'll find some simple beachside restaurants and souvenir stands here. The bird-watching is excellent in the mangroves, and the park's beach is renowned for its supply of seashells. To reach La Restinga, take a taxi or the Línea La Restinga *por puesto* out of Porlamar. At the park entrance you'll have to pay a BsF1 entrance fee and then walk to the nearby pier, where scores of boats are waiting to take you on a tour. The boats charge BsF20 to BsF45 per person, depending on the size of your group. The trip through the mangroves usually lasts between 30 minutes and 1 hour, at which point you will be left at the beach. Have the boatman wait, or arrange a firm pickup time and place for your return to the pier.

Islas Coche & Cubagua

The entire state of Nueva Esparta is made up of Isla de Margarita and two much smaller neighboring islands, **Isla Coche** and **Isla Cubagua.** The pearl beds off these two islands were major sources of wealth during the colonial period. Both islands are popular destinations for day cruises, which bring folks to their pristine and nearly deserted beaches. Isla Coche has some development and rolling hills, while Isla Cubagua is mostly barren, flat, and undeveloped. One of the only attractions here is the ruins of Nueva Cádiz. Founded on Isla Cubagua in 1528, this was the first Spanish town formally established in the Americas. However, its heyday was short-lived: An earthquake and tidal wave destroyed the town in 1541.

Day tours by small cruise ships and converted fishing boats are common. The full-day tour usually includes round-trip transportation from your hotel to the marina, continental breakfast, a buffet lunch, an open bar, beach chairs, umbrellas, and organized activities on the island. Prices range from BsF75 to BsF150 per person. ***Be forewarned:*** There's a real cattle-car feel to most of these tours.

There's also a daily Conferry vessel leaving at 6:30am from the Punta de Piedras pier for Isla Coche and returning at 4pm. The cost is BsF17 per person, BsF38 per car, each way.

Outdoor Activities

In addition to the activities mentioned below, jet skis and WaveRunners are available at many beaches and resorts around the island, as are parasail flights.

AMUSEMENT PARKS **Parque El Agua,** Av. 31 de Julio, El Cardón, on the way to Playa El Agua (✆ **0295/263-0710;** www.parqueelagua.com), is a fairly extensive and well-maintained water park with an assortment of pools, slides, and rides. The park is open daily from 10am to 6pm. Admission is BsF75 for adults, BsF55 for children. During the low season, the park only opens Thursday through Sunday.

Diverland, Isla Aventura near Pampatar (✆ **0295/267-0571**), is a combination amusement park and water park, with a wide range of attractions and rides. You'll find typical amusement park rides, such as Ferris wheels and roller coasters, as well as go-karts, a petting zoo, and batting cages. They also have trained dolphin and seal shows, as well as a swim-with-the dolphins program. However, I find both the shows and the swim program rather sad and unfortunate for the animals. It's open from 10am to 11pm daily throughout the high season and most weekends the rest of the year. Operating days and hours are much more limited during the week and low season. Admission is BsF55 for adults and BsF35 for children for unlimited use of the rides and pools. Some features and exhibits, such as swimming with dolphins, have additional fees.

BIKING The stunning scenery and combination of off-road and paved highway possibilities make Margarita a good place to rent a bike for exploring. Be careful, though: The sun can be brutal, and the distances between towns and beaches can quickly become more daunting than you might expect. The best place for mountain biking is the Macanao Peninsula.

CRUISES & SAILBOAT CHARTERS The most popular day cruises from Margarita are to the islands of Coche, Cubagua, and Los Frailes. Trips cost from BsF100 to BsF200 per person for a full-day tour with lunch. See "Islas Coche & Cubagua," above, and "Scuba Diving & Snorkeling," below, for more information.

With the constant trade winds and translucent turquoise waters, Margarita is a great place to sail. A host of charter vessels anchor in the Pampatar harbor and other protected anchorages and bays around Margarita. The fleet fluctuates seasonally, but a sailboat is always available for a day cruise or multiday charter. Day tours cost from BsF90 to BsF200 per person. Rates for all-inclusive multiday charters range from BsF200 to BsF500 per person per day. Contact **Explore Yachts** (✆ **0212/635-2166** or 0414/287-7554; www.explore-yachts.com), which manages a fleet of vessels.

FISHING The waters off Isla de Margarita are excellent fishing grounds. A day's catch might include any combination of tuna, dorado, marlin, and sailfish. You can hire a guide and a boat for the day, with lunch and beverages, for between BsF700 and BsF2,500, depending on the size of the boat, number of fishermen, and game sought; check with your hotel or call **Explore Yachts** (see above).

GOLF There's only one working 18-hole course on the island. The **Isla Margarita Golf Club** (✆ **0295/265-7371**) at the Hesperia Isla Margarita is a 70-par links course. The course is fairly flat and open, with few trees, little rough, and very inconsistent groundskeeping. During the dry season, the course gets particularly brown and parched. This isn't a popular golf destination, so tee times generally aren't required, but it never hurts to make a reservation. Greens fees are free for guests at both Hesperia hotels on the island and BsF90 for visitors.

HORSEBACK RIDING Whether you fancy a ride on the beach, through the forested hills of the Cerro El Copey, or over the barren desertlike landscape of the Macanao Peninsula, there are great opportunities for horseback riding all over Margarita. Inquire at your hotel, or contact **Cabatucan Ranch** (✆ **0416/681-9348;** www.cabatucan.com), which specialize in tours of the Macanao Peninsula. A 2-hour ride, with transportation to and from your hotel, should run around BsF90 per person.

JEEP TOURS Small 4×4 jeeps are the ideal transport for a full-day tour taking in a wide range of the sights and scenery of Isla de Margarita. The tours usually include pickup at your hotel, a trip to the top of Cerro El Copey, visits to a couple of churches and forts, a boat ride through La Restinga, stops at several beaches, and lunch and an open bar. The prices range from BsF90 to BsF180 per person. Both **Highberg Tours** (✆ **0414/789-7000;** www.highbergtours.com) and **Walter's Tours** ★ (✆ **0295/274-1265** or 0416/696-2212; www.margaritaislandguide.com) offer this adventure outing.

KITESAILING & WINDSURFING Although you can rent a Windsurfer on many of the beaches on Margarita, **Playa El Yaque,** on the southern end of the island near the airport, is the place to be if you are a windsurfer or kitesailer. A handful of small hotels here cater specifically to windsurfers and kitesailers, usually with a wide selection of boards and sails for rent, and lesson options. **El Yaque Paradise** (✆ **0295/263-9418;**

www.hotelyaqueparadise.com) and **El Yaque Motion** (✆/fax **0295/263-9742;** www.elyaquemotion.com) are both excellent options.

SCUBA DIVING & SNORKELING As this is the Caribbean, count on some good snorkeling and scuba diving on and around Isla de Margarita. Conditions immediately around the island can be a little too rough and murky. Two of the more popular dive sites close to Margarita are **Los Frailes,** a group of small rock islands about 11km (7 miles) offshore that are good for both snorkeling and scuba, and the **Cueva el Bufón,** a small cave near Pampatar thought to be a hiding place for pirate loot that can only be visited with scuba gear. Off **Isla Cubagua,** you can dive the wreck of a sunken ferry, with intact cars still aboard.

Snorkel trips average between BsF90 to BsF180 per person for a full-day tour with lunch, and scuba tours cost around BsF205 for a two-tank dive trip. Contact **Ecobuzos** (✆ **0295/262-9811;** www.ecobuzos.com).

SURFING If the swell is right, you can find ridable surf on the island. **Playa Parguito,** just south of Playa El Agua, and **El Tirano,** a little farther south, are the principal breaks on Margarita.

Shopping

Venezuelans and visitors alike take advantage of the island's status as a duty-free port, although the fact is the deals and selection are not all that special. The downtown heart of Porlamar is a chaotic jumble of shops and small department stores selling everything from perfume to lingerie to electronics and appliances to liquor and foodstuffs. In 2002, the Puerto de la Mar pier was opened for cruise-ship traffic, allowing cruise passengers to disembark in downtown Porlamar, just blocks from the aforementioned jumble of shops and stores. However, as is the trend across Venezuela, large malls draw shoppers away from the downtown options. The biggest of the bunch is the **Centro Sambil Margarita,** Avenida Jovito Villalba, Pampatar. Other popular malls include the **Centro Comercial Rattan Plaza,** Avenida Jovito Villalba, Los Robles; and **Centro Comercial Jumbo,** Avenida 4 de Mayo.

At shops and roadside stands around the island, you will come across locally produced jewelry and ceramic wares of varying quality. Among the nicer and more readily available handicrafts for sale on Margarita are the local hammocks, or *chinchorros,* an intricate weave of thin strands of rough natural fibers. You'll also find woven baskets, hats, and handbags. The town of Santa Ana and the roads that form a triangle between Santa Ana, Pedro González, and Juangriego are prime hunting grounds for crafts shops and galleries.

WHERE TO STAY

Isla de Margarita has an oversupply of hotel rooms. Visions of a tourist mecca led to the construction of massive resorts in the style of Cancún and the Dominican Republic. The tourists never arrived in large enough numbers, and the current political climate has further affected the industry.

In general, all-inclusive packages here are a good bet and can often come quite cheap. Charter packages to Margarita from the United States, Canada, and even Europe, including round-trip airfare, can cost as little as $1,000 per person for a full week. Another alternative is to book your tour in bolívares fuertes through a Venezuelan-based tour agency. Margarita hotels do about 80% of their business with national tourists; competition is steep, and if you exchange money at the black-market rate, you can get a real bargain. Try **Akanan Travel & Adventure** (✆ **0212/715-5433** or 0414/116-0107; www.akanan.com) or **Natoura Adventure Tours** (✆ **303/800-4639** in the U.S., or 0274/252-4216 in Venezuela; www.natoura.com).

The prices listed below are the hotels' published rack rates. These tend to be the highest rate applicable, and as in Caracas, most hotels here sell very few rooms at the actual rack rate. Prices fluctuate radically according to season and demand. If you book direct, feel free to bargain—it may pay off with some deep discounts.

Very Expensive

In addition to the hotels reviewed below, you might also consider the **Dunes Hotel & Beach Resort** (✆ **0295/250-0000;** www.dunesmargarita.com), which is set on a gorgeous stretch of beach on the northern end of the island, near the Hesperia Isla Margarita.

Hesperia Isla Margarita ★ This luxury resort is located on the northern end of the island, near Pedro González. The hotel has the only operational 18-hole golf course on the island, a well-equipped and luxurious spa, and a lovely little section of semiprivate beach. The central lobby is a large hexagonal area heavily draped in ferns and tropical plants that reach up five stories to a skylight. The rooms are large, with dark-wood floors, high ceilings, rattan furnishings, and comfortable bathrooms. A large wall of windows lets in plenty of light. Around 70% of the rooms have an ocean view. The best are those that look out over the pool and golf course to the sea; those with the least impressive views face inland over a mostly barren landscape.

The hotel is about a 30- to 35-minute taxi ride from either Porlamar or the airport, although they do provide a twice-daily shuttle to Porlamar.

Playa Bonita, Pedro González, Isla de Margarita. ✆ **0295/400-7111.** Fax 0295/400-7150. www.hesperia.com. 312 units. BsF550–BsF800 double; BsF900–BsF1,500 suite. Rates are all inclusive. AE, DC, MC, V. Free self-parking. **Amenities:** 4 restaurants; 3 bars; 2 lounges; babysitting; children's programs; concierge; golf course and pro shop; well-equipped health club and spa; large pool w/children's pool; room service; smoke-free rooms; 2 lighted tennis courts; watersports. *In room:* A/C, TV, hair dryer, minibar.

Laguna Mar ★★ (Kids) This massive resort has the most extensive and impressive facilities on the island. From the wave pool to the water-slide pool to the private watersports lagoon, the installations here make it a great choice for families and anyone looking for constant activity. The rooms are spacious and cool, with plenty of light. Some rooms have private balconies, and the best of the lot have ocean views and balconies. All the bathrooms come with bidets, although some are quite cramped. The hotel is located on a long stretch of beautiful beach, which can get a bit rough at times. Free jitneys circulate constantly to take you around the extensive grounds. With a steady flow of European all-inclusive travelers, Laguna Mar's bars, dance club, and casino stay fairly lively. Most of the meals are served buffet style. Reserve early if you want to eat at one of the a la carte restaurants.

Pampatar, Isla de Margarita. ✆ **0295/400-4035.** Fax 0295/262-1445. www.lagunamar.com.ve. 409 units. BsF350–BsF550 standard; BsF525–BsF752 suite. Rates are per person, all inclusive. AE, DC, MC, V. Free self-parking. **Amenities:** 5 restaurants; snack bar; 4 bars; babysitting; midsize casino; children's programs; dance club; health club and spa; 3 Jacuzzis; 6 outdoor pools and several children's pools; room service; 9 lighted tennis courts; watersports. *In room:* A/C, TV, minibar.

Moderate

In addition to the hotels listed below, there is a growing range of small *posadas,* bed-and-breakfasts, and condo rentals, particularly at the popular beaches. Two of the best are

Casa Caracol (✆ **0295/416-8439;** www.caracolgroup.com) and **Posada Casa Mejillon** (✆ **0295/872-5518**; http://posadacasamejillon.jimdo.com).

Hesperia Playa Agua Value This all-inclusive resort has a bit of a small village feel to it, although it is rather large. Rooms are either in small duplex or triplex bungalows, or one of the hotel's four seven-story towers. All the rooms are clean, comfortable, and contemporary. Rooms in the towers have private balconies, some of which have ocean views. The hotel is located just across the street from the gorgeous central section of Playa El Agua. Buffet meals are served in the large, central dining area; at the beachside **Frailemar** restaurant; or around the main pool. There are nightly entertainment reviews and a variety of organized activities throughout the day. This hotel doesn't have near as many facilities as Laguna Mar or some of the other large all- inclusive resorts, but it does have a great location, plenty to keep you busy, and is less expensive.

Playa El Agua, Isla de Margarita. ✆ **0295/400-8111.** Fax 0295/400-8151. www.hesperia.com. 355 units. BsF420–BsF800 standard; BsF540–BsF1,200 suite. Rates are all –inclusive (for 2 people). AE, DC, MC, V. Free self-parking. **Amenities:** 2 restaurants; 3 bars; children's programs; 4 outdoor pools; 3 lighted tennis courts; watersports. *In room:* A/C, TV, fridge.

Hotel Costa Linda Beach Finds This friendly hotel is one of the better options on the island, especially if you want an alternative to the large all-inclusive resorts. The rooms are spacious and cool, with rustic red-tile floors and white stucco walls. Most have high ceilings with exposed wood beams. The best rooms are higher up and have a private balcony with a hammock. Everything is set around the small central pool area, which is planted with lush gardens. The hotel is located about 2 blocks inland from the central section of Playa El Agua, and they have an arrangement with one of the beach restaurants there that gets you free beach lounges and umbrellas, as well as use of their facilities.

Playa El Agua, Isla de Margarita. ✆ **0295/249-1303** or 0295/415-9961. Fax 0295/249-1229. www.hotelcostalinda.com. 40 units. BsF240–BsF420 double. Rates include buffet breakfast. MC, V. Free self-parking. **Amenities:** Restaurant; bar; small exercise room; outdoor pool; free Wi-Fi. *In room:* A/C, TV, hair dryer.

WHERE TO DINE

Despite the fact that most visitors to Isla de Margarita stay at all-inclusive resorts, there are a host of restaurants around the island. Many of the beaches have simple restaurants on or close to the sand; they're great options for a lunch of fresh fish, lobster, or *pabellón,* the Venezuelan national dish consisting of shredded beef, rice, beans, and fried plantains.

Tip: Even if you are staying at an all-inclusive resort, I recommend heading out on the town to any of the restaurants recommended below, at least once or twice during your stay.

In addition to the places listed below, **El Rancho de Pablo,** Avenida Raúl Leoni, Porlamar (✆ **0295/263-1121**), and **La Isla,** Bulevard Turístico, Playa El Agua (✆ **0295/249-0035**), are two excellent open-air waterfront restaurants specializing in fresh local seafood, while **Il Positano,** Calle Fermín and Calle Tubores, Porlamar (✆ **0295/264-1110**), is a good choice for Italian. Both El Rancho de Pablo and Il Positano have sister restaurants in the Sambil Mall.

Casa Caranta ★★★ Finds FUSION/SEAFOOD Housed in a beautifully restored colonial-era house in downtown Pampatar, this creative restaurant is a must-stop on any visit to Isla Margarita. Italy, Asia, and the Americas are the principal inspirations for the regularly changing menu, which is handwritten on a few large chalkboards and brought to your table. Options range from homemade pasta with shrimp and porcini mushrooms to fresh grouper in a green curry sauce. The excellent wine list is fairly priced. In fact, given the hefty size of the portions, this place is actually a bargain. With live music most nights, the joint really gets going after around 10pm each evening.

Pampatar. ✆ **0295/262-8610** or 0414/793-5248. Reservations recommended. Main courses BsF45–BsF95. MC, V. Daily 7pm–12:30am; closed Sun during the low season.

Catabar ★★ FUSION This refined restaurant offers up an interesting and adventurous menu in an elegant ambiance. The vibe here is much more formal and fancy than that found at nearby Casa Caranta. White linens and fancy flatware adorn the tables, while stone and stucco are artfully done on the walls. The menu ranges wildly, and features everything from Japanese scallops wrapped in bacon with a goat cheese sauce, to fresh grouper served in a Thai curry sauce. One of the more eclectic entrees is the Catabar Burger, which features a mix of ground beef and duck meat. In the back there's a relaxed bar and lounge for late-night lingering.

Pampatar. ✆ **0295/772-7589** or 0414/981-8121. Reservations recommended. Main courses BsF75–BsF180. MC, V. Daily 7pm–midnight.

El Pacífico VENEZUELAN/SEAFOOD This is the best of the bunch among the strip of beachside seafood joints lining Playa El Agua. Get a table near the large windows overlooking the sea, or live dangerously and dine at a table under one of the tall coconut palms. Start things off with the *plato de pescado ahumado* (plate of smoked fish) and follow it with the fresh grilled red snapper or *langostinos al parchita* (jumbo shrimp in passion fruit sauce). The elegant presentation of plates garnished with swirled sauces and parsley flakes contrasts nicely with the plastic lawn furniture and worn tablecloths.

Playa El Agua. ✆ **0295/249-0640.** www.restaurantelpacifico.com. Reservations recommended during high season. Main courses BsF50–BsF110. AE, MC, V. Daily 9am–11pm.

ISLA DE MARGARITA AFTER DARK

Given its status as a vacation getaway, Isla de Margarita has plenty of bars and nightclubs. Still, many visitors stick to their all-inclusive resort, which usually features a small collection of bars and a dance club and nightly entertainment revue. Others like to barhop sections of Avenida 4 de Mayo and Avenida Santiago Mariño.

The loudest and most happening scene can be found at **Kamy Beach,** on Playa Varadero, just outside Pampatar (✆ **0414/794-1188**). For a similar vibe, you can try **Beach Bar,** on Calle El Cristo in the La Caranta section of Pampatar (✆ **0295/267-2392**).

If you're looking for something somewhat familiar, **Señor Frogs** (✆ **0295/262-0451**), the popular Mexican chain, has a lively restaurant and bar in the Centro Comercial Costa Azul which turns into a raging dance club most evenings after 11pm, while over in the Sambil Mall, there's a local branch of the **Hard Rock Cafe** (✆ **0295/260-2400**).

For a mellower scene, with a lot more atmosphere, I recommend both **Guayoyo Café★** (✆ **0295/262-4514**) and **Mykonos Lounge** (✆ **0295/267-1850**), two side-by-side joints set on a steep cliff overlooking the ocean in Pampatar.

Casino gaming is an option on Margarita, with modern and well-fitted casinos at the Laguna Mar and Marina Bay hotels.

SIDE TRIPS FROM ISLA DE MARGARITA

Perhaps the most popular excursions from Margarita are to either **Los Roques** or **Canaima** and **Angel Falls.** By far the most established company making trips to both destinations is **Aerotuy** (✆ **0212/212-3110;** www.tuy.com), although there's often a cattle-car feel to their operation, and the price is hefty. The cost for the Los Roques day trip is BsF860 per person; to Canaima and Angel Falls, the cost is BsF1,716 per person. The fares for children are roughly half price, and rates are slightly lower during the low season and midweek. See the sections on each destination below for more information.

6 LOS ROQUES NATIONAL PARK ★★★

166km (103 miles) N of Caracas

Few island getaways are as remote, romantic, intimate, or idyllic as Los Roques. Hundreds of deserted little islands of soft white sand surrounded by crystal-clear turquoise waters and lively tropical reefs make Los Roques one of the prime vacation destinations in Venezuela. About 42 named islands—only a couple of which are inhabited—and 200-plus sand spits, mangrove islands, and tiny cays surround a 400-sq.-km (156-sq.-mile) central lagoon. The most popular activity here is getting dropped off on an isolated little island in the morning with a beach umbrella, some chaise longues, and a cooler full of food and drink, and getting picked up again in the late afternoon. You spend your day beachcombing, sunbathing, swimming, and snorkeling. Depending on your point of view, you can imagine yourself shipwrecked on a deserted island or the ruler of some new territory.

Declared a national park in 1972, Los Roques protects vast areas of sea-grass beds, mangroves, and coral reef. The park is an important sea-turtle nesting ground. Of the 92 recorded bird species here, you are likely to see brown- and red-footed boobies, as well as scores of pelicans, gulls, terns, and other assorted shorebirds. There's even a small flock of pink flamingos on one of the isolated cays. The barrier reefs that protect the archipelago's perimeter make this one of the premier dive spots in the country. Near-constant trade winds from the northeast also make this a great place to sail and windsurf.

Los Roques is not particularly geared toward independent travelers. Almost all visitors come as part of an organized tour or an all-inclusive stay at one of the *posadas* on Gran Roque. Given the isolation and limited number of hotel rooms, you should make firm reservations before arriving, particularly on weekends and during the high season.

Independent travelers can purchase, a la carte, all the typical tours and activities offered on the islands. Inquire at your hotel or at one of the small information/tour desks beside the airstrip.

ESSENTIALS

Getting There

BY GUIDED TOUR One of the most popular ways to visit Los Roques is on a day tour from Caracas or Isla de Margarita. These trips are sold by almost every travel agent and tour company in Caracas and are aggressively hawked at the airport. **Aerotuy** ★ (✆ **0212/212-3110;** www.tuy.com) is by far the most established operator on the archipelago, with a fleet of catamarans anchored at Gran Roque. The tour generally leaves between 6 and 8am, arriving on Gran Roque in less than an hour. Soon after arrival, you'll board one of the catamarans for a sail to one or more of the nearby cays, with one or more stops for beach time and snorkeling, as well as a buffet lunch onboard the vessel. You'll return to Gran Roque in the late afternoon for your flight back to Caracas. The cost is BsF860 per person. Although there is a cattle-car feel to the operation, organization is tight, and the bilingual guides tend to be helpful, knowledgeable, and cheerful.

However, Los Roques is so isolated and enchanting, you'll definitely wish you had spent the night . . . or two.

BY PLANE Several daily flights connect Los Roques to Caracas and Isla de Margarita, with extra scheduled and charter flights on weekends and during peak periods (although demand often outstrips supply, so I recommend reserving well in advance). **Aerotuy** (✆ **0212/212-3110;** www.tuy.com), **Blue Star Airline** (✆ **0412/310-1962;** www.bluestar.us), and **Rainbow Airlines** (✆ **0212/421-9191**), all offer regular service to Los Roques. Round-trip airfare from Caracas or Margarita costs from BsF600 to BsF1,050. Prices fluctuate a little seasonally, and you can sometimes get good deals midweek or on afternoon flights to Los Roques.

All visitors to Los Roques must pay a BsF46 one-time entrance fee for the national park, good for the duration of your stay.

Getting Around

There are no passenger cars on Gran Roque—just a garbage truck, a water truck, and a handful of golf carts. You can walk from one end of the town of Gran Roque to the other in less than 10 minutes; you can hike to the more distant spots on the island in under an hour.

The only permanent settlement is on the main island of Gran Roque. There are some private vacation homes and fishermen's shacks on some of the other islands, but for all intents and purposes, a visit to Los Roques implies a visit to Gran Roque.

Four crushed-coral-and-sand streets run lengthwise through the town, beginning at the airstrip on the eastern end of the island. The small Plaza Bolívar is just a block or so from the airstrip. The public dock is on the southern side of the island nearly smack-dab in the middle of town.

FAST FACTS There is actually a branch of the **Banesco** (✆ **0237/221-1265**), which has an ATM and will change money. Some hotels and shops are reluctant to change money, and quite a few do not accept credit cards. Many will accept dollars for payment. The local ATM may or may not be able to access funds in your home account, so it's always best to bring a sufficient supply of bolívares fuertes for your stay, although if you ask around you should be able to find someone who will change foreign currency at or near the going black-market rate.

If you have a **medical emergency,** you will have to be air evacuated on the next scheduled flight or special charter. Local dive shops often have dive masters and instructors schooled in first aid.

An **Internet cafe** is on the back street near Posada Guaripete. They charge BsF25 per hour and can get quite busy, as they are the only game in town. Also, note that there is **no Ipostel** office on the island—you'll have to mail your postcards and letters from the mainland. A handful of public phones operate on calling cards available at one of the few general stores on Gran Roque.

OUTDOOR ACTIVITIES

Most of the fun to be had here is either on or below the surface of the water. The most popular activity on Los Roques is to take a **day trip** to one of the nearby uninhabited cays. If your hotel doesn't include excursions to the outer islands and cays, you can hire a *peñero* (small boat) at the main docks for between BsF20 and BsF70 per person, depending on the distance to the cay chosen and the number of people in your party. You should pack a lunch, bring plenty of drinks, and try to secure a beach umbrella for shade. Make sure you firmly arrange a pickup time and place for your return to Gran Roque.

In addition to the activities discussed below, you should be able to find a Windsurfer, Hobie Cat, or kayak to rent for a few hours or for the day. Ask at your hotel or around town.

FISHING Bonefish *(pez ratón)* is the primary game fish here. They are stalked in the shallow waters and grass flats all over the archipelago. Offshore fishing options include tuna, dorado, marlin, and sailfish.

You can hire a guide and a boat for the day, with lunch and beverages, for between BsF500 and BsF1,200 for bonefishing, and up to BsF3,500 for offshore fishing, depending on the size of the boat, number of fishermen, and game sought. Most hotels either have their own fishing guides, or will hook you up with one. Alternately, you could look into working with a specialized fishing operation such as **Pez Ratón Fishing Lodge** ★ (✆ **800/245-1950** in the U.S., or 0414/257-0167; www.pezraton.com).

HIKING Two volcanic humps mark the western end of Gran Roque and give the archipelago its name. The tallest of these is just 130m (426 ft.) above sea level. An active lighthouse is on the farthest hump, as well as an abandoned lighthouse on a high hill toward the center of the island. Both make nice little hikes, providing wonderful views of the Caribbean Sea, turquoise lagoon, and surrounding islands.

SAILING A handful of charter vessels anchor in the Gran Roque harbor. With the constant trade winds and flat water, Los Roques is an ideal place to sail. The fleet fluctuates seasonally, but there's always a sailboat available for a day cruise or multiday charter. Rates range from BsF215 to BsF550 per person per day, all inclusive, for multiday charters with a minimum of four people. Day tours cost BsF95 to BsF215 per person. Ask at your hotel, or contact **TTM** (✆ **0212/978-4092;** www.roques.org) or **Explore Yachts** (✆ **0212/635-2166** or 0414/287-7554; www.explore-yachts.com), both of whom manage a fleet of vessels.

SNORKELING & DIVING The diving and snorkeling around Los Roques is some of the best in the Caribbean. Barrier reefs surround the archipelago, with sheer walls on the southern and eastern flanks dropping off steeply to depths of as much as 900m (2,952 ft.).

As part of their day tours to the outlying cays, almost all the hotels and local operators will include snorkel equipment (or help arrange rental); note, however, that I recommend bringing a mask from home that fits you well. A knowledgeable guide will be able to point you to many excellent shallow reefs for great snorkeling. ***Tip:*** Whenever you sign up for a snorkel trip, insist on being taken to a live and active reef. Many of the trips are more geared toward bringing guests to the nearest and most popular cayes, where the reefs may be dead, or unspectacular at best.

Ecobuzos (✆ **0295/262-9811;** www.ecobuzos.com) is the best and most established dive operation on Gran Roque. Rates run around BsF205 for a full day of diving (two tanks), including a guide and gear. Your hotel will most likely pack you a bag lunch. Ecobuzos also offers package tours and certification courses.

Scuba divers will have to pay a one-time BsF5 national park dive fee, in addition to the park's entrance fee paid upon arrival.

Given its status as a national park, building is extremely regulated and limited on Los Roques. The 50 or so *posadas* on Gran Roque are all small and usually have between 3 and 10 rooms. A great majority of the *posadas* are owned and managed by Italians, to the point that you might imagine you're in Sardinia. Rooms are at a premium, and the *posadas* fill up fast on weekends and during holiday periods.

Most of the *posadas* on Los Roques are all inclusive, which means they provide breakfast and dinner at the lodge, as well as a day trip to one of the outlying cays, with a packed lunch. In some cases, alcoholic beverages are included in the price; in others, they cost extra. Many *posadas* offer a 2-day/1-night package, taking advantage of the early flights in and late-afternoon departures out of Gran Roque. With this package, you'll get lunch and a tour on both days.

Note: While true for much of the country, prices in Los Roques are almost exclusively pegged to hard currencies, either dollars or euros, with the bolívar fuerte conversion done at black-market rates. For example, if a *posada* charges $100 per day, the price in BsF will be roughly BsF520, which then converts to $242 at the official exchange rate. The bottom line is that if you use dollars, you pay $100; if, however, you use a credit card, you'll be charged $242.

Very Expensive

Macanao Lodge ★ Rooms here have wood floors, heavy wood doors, and attractive latticework above the windows. All have high ceilings, ceiling fans, two twin beds, and mosquito netting over the beds, although no televisions or phones. Rooms numbered 8, 9, and 10 have ocean views. It's a pet peeve of mine, but I strongly prefer a real queen- or king-size bed over two twin beds pushed together, which is what you get in most of the rooms here. The large central courtyard, with its seagrape trees and fountains, is the nicest feature here. There's also a comfortable rooftop terrace for enjoying the sea views and sunsets. The restaurant serves a mix of Italian and Venezuelan cuisine.

Los Roques. ✆ **0237/221-1301.** Fax 0237/221-1040. www.macanaolodge.com. 8 units. BsF1,000–BsF1,400 per person per day, all inclusive. MC, V. **Amenities:** Restaurant; bar, lounge. *In room:* No phone.

Posada Albacora ★★ With just three rooms, this intimate Italian-run *posada* has some of the best equipped accommodations on the island, with quiet, modern air-conditioned units and satellite television. One room is a minisuite with the bedroom on a second floor and a living room and bathroom below. While a tad compact, the two standard rooms are plush and inviting, with understated yet tasteful decor and well-equipped bathrooms. Excellent meals are served on the rooftop terrace, and service is quite personable and attentive.

Los Roques. ✆ **0237/221-1305** or 0414/282-6131. www.albacora.com.ve. 3 units. BsF780–BsF1,144 per person per night, double occupancy. Rates include meals and nonalcoholic drinks. MC, V. **Amenities:** Restaurant; bar, lounge. *In room:* A/C, TV, fridge, hair dryer, no phone.

Expensive

In addition to the places listed below, **Posada Cayo Luna** (✆ **0237/221-1272;** www.posadacayoluna.com), **Posada La Cigala** (✆ **0414/236-5721;** www.lacigala.com), and **Posada La Gaviota** (✆ **0414/324-2092;** www.posadalagaviota.com) are other excellent options in this price range. Similarly, the well-run **Caracol Group** (✆ **237/221-1049;** www.caracolgroup.com) has two pretty *posadas,* and one live-aboard boat in Los Roques.

Posada Acquamarina ★ This is another small, Italian-run *posada,* but it sets itself apart by offering more amenities than most of the other options around. All the rooms here have air-conditioning, televisions, in-room sound systems, and minifridges. The best rooms are those around the central interior courtyard. Excellent Italian- and Venezuelan-inspired meals are served family style on the hotel's rooftop terrace. These folks also have their own airline, Blue Star (see above), as well as a small, rustic three-bedroom *posada* on the tiny Rasqui cay, for those looking for a romantic and isolated getaway.

Los Roques. ✆ **0412/310-1962** or ✆/fax 0212/267-5769. www.posada-acquamarina.com. 9 units. BsF700 per person per night, double occupancy. Rates include meals and nonalcoholic drinks. MC, V. **Amenities:** Restaurant; bar, lounge. *In room:* A/C, TV, fridge, hair dryer.

Moderate

In addition to the option reviewed below, **Posada Guaripete** (✆ **0212/286-4932;** www.posadaguaripete.com) offers clean rooms, all but one with air-conditioning.

Posada Acuarela ★ Artistic touches abound in this popular *posada.* The walls are inlaid with hand-painted tile, bits of colored glass and shell, and whole bottles. Each of the rooms features an original painting or two by the owner, Angelo Belvedere. The nicest room has a small private rooftop terrace up a steep flight of stairs. Meals are served family style in the common dining room, and Angelo is also an excellent chef. Five of the rooms feature air-conditioning.

Los Roques. ✆ **0237/221-1008** or ✆/fax 0212/952-3370. www.posadaacuarela.com. 12 units. BsF420–BsF570 per person per night, double occupancy. Rates include meals and nonalcoholic drinks. AE, MC, V. **Amenities:** Restaurant; bar, lounge; free Wi-Fi. *In room:* No phone.

Inexpensive

Los Roques has few true budget options. You'll find a couple of rather rustic *posadas* around the Plaza Bolívar. If your looking for a less expensive option, **Posada Doña Magalis** (✆ **0414/287-7554;** www.magalis.com) and **Posada El Botuto** (✆ **0416/621-0381;** www.posadaelbotuto.com) are your best bets.

You can also camp on Gran Roque and a few of the other cays. You'll need a permit, which is issued free by **Inparques** from its office at the western end of town. A few of the isolated cays are open to campers; ask at Inparques for the current list. ***Be forewarned:*** The few shops and general stores on Gran Roque have very limited supplies and often run out of even the most basic goods. If you plan on camping, come prepared. If you camp on any other island, you'll have to bring all your own food and water and make firm arrangements in advance to be picked up at a specific time on a specific day. Also, remember it gets very hot here, and many tents only increase the heat.

WHERE TO DINE

As mentioned above, most visitors to Los Roques come as part of a package tour or stay at an all-inclusive *posada.* There are, in fact, very few independent restaurants on Gran Roque. If you're not staying at an all-inclusive *posada,* or if you want to broaden your culinary horizons on the island, stop in at the **Bar & Restaurant Acuarena ★** (✆ **0414/131-1282;** www.aquarena.com.ve), which is on the water between the airstrip and Plaza Bolívar. You can grab a table on the sand and order up some fresh grilled fish, or just spend the night working through their extensive list of cocktails. They also have good breakfasts and lunches, as well as one of the better gift shops on the island. The restaurant is open daily from 6:30am to 11pm, and even has free Wi-Fi. Other options for independent dining include **Bora El Mar** and **Canto de la Ballena.**

Note: Lobster season runs November 1 through April 30. Technically, restaurants should not serve lobster outside of the season. If they do, it is either frozen or illegal.

LOS ROQUES AFTER DARK

A couple of small bars surround the Plaza Bolívar. Of these, the **Rasquatekey Bar** and **La Chuchera** are the most popular. If you're looking for a mellower vibe, try **Bar & Restaurant Acuarena** or **La Gotera.** For a sunset cocktail, **Bora El Mar, La Gotera,** and the rooftop bar at **Natura Viva** are your best options—but you'll want to arrive early as tables with views are limited. In general, hours of operation for bars are 4pm to midnight, although they are very seasonal—some close during low periods and some will stay open as long as there are customers buying drinks.

7 MERIDA, THE ANDES & LOS LLANOS ★★

Mérida: 680km (422 miles) SW of Caracas

Mérida is a picturesque and bustling college town set on a flat plateau, nestled in a narrow valley between two mountain rivers, the Albarregas and Chama. It is flanked by two high Andean ridges, the Sierra Nevada and Sierra La Culata. Mérida's narrow streets and colonial architecture make it a great city to wander at your leisure, while the roaring rivers, towering Andean peaks and rugged mountain terrain make it a prime base for some serious adventure. Thanks to the presence of the Universidad de los Andes (ULA), along with a bustling tourist industry, Mérida has a great assortment of cafes, restaurants, bars, and discos.

Despite the imposing snow-capped peaks that surround it, Mérida enjoys a mild, springlike climate year-round. Days are generally warm, although you'll probably need a light sweater or jacket at night. May through November is the rainy season, with August and September being the wettest months.

ESSENTIALS

Getting There

BY PLANE The closest commercial airport to Mérida is located about 1 hour away in El Vigia. More than a dozen commuter flights daily to El Vigia's **Juan Pablo Pérez Alfonso airport** (✆ **0275/881-6972;** airport code VIG) from Caracas's Simón Bolívar International Airport. The principal airlines serving this route are **Conviasa** (✆ **0500/266-84272;** www.conviasa.aero), **Santa Bárbara** (✆ **0800/865-2636**; www.sbairlines.com), and **Venezolana** (✆ **0501/VENEZOLANA** [836-3965]; http://ravsa.com.ve). Fares range from BsF320 to BsF450 each way, depending on season and demand. Flight time is roughly 1 hour.

Taxis are waiting for all arriving flights. One-way fare to Mérida should run around BsF150.

Downtown Mérida's **Alberto Carnevalli Airport** (✆ **0274/263-0722;** airport code MRD) has been closed to commercial commuter traffic since 2008, and there is little indication that things will change any time soon.

BY BUS Several bus lines have daily service between Caracas and Mérida. The most prominent are **Expresos Occidente** (✆ **0212/632-2670**), **Expresos Mérida** (✆ **0274/263-3430**), and **Expresos Los Llanos** (✆ **0274/263-5927**). Many buses depart

between 6:30 and 10pm and drive through the night. The trip takes 8 to 10 hours and costs around BsF65 to BsF90. Most buses leave from La Bandera Terminal, near La Bandera Metro stop, although Expresos Flamingo has its own terminal near the Parque del Este. The bus station in Mérida is located about 3km (2 miles) southwest of downtown on the Avenida Las Américas and is connected to downtown by regular *por puestos* and inexpensive taxis.

BY CAR The fastest route to Mérida from Caracas is via Barinas. It's mostly flat to Barinas, after which you rise quickly and dramatically into the Andes, passing through Santo Domingo, Apartaderos, and Mucuchies. This route takes between 9 and 11 hours. For a more scenic tour through the Andes, you can turn off at Guanare and head up to Trujillo. From Trujillo, the Trans-Andean highway passes through Valera, Timotes, and Paseo El Aguila (Eagle Pass), before heading into Mérida. If you come this way, you can drive to the summit of **Pico Aguila;** at 4,007m (13,143 feet), it's the highest point in Venezuela you can reach in a car.

Getting Around

Mérida is a town of many parks and plazas. The two most important are the **Plaza Bolívar,** which is the de facto center of town, and the **Plaza Las Heroínas,** which is located about 5 blocks south of Plaza Bolívar.

You can easily walk to most destinations and attractions in downtown Mérida. Taxis are relatively plentiful and inexpensive. Most rides in town will run you BsF8 to BsF15. There's also a good system of local buses and buses to nearby towns, which is a good way to get around for next to nothing. In 2007, Mérida inaugurated a **Trolebus,** fixed-route electric-bus units that runs from a point near the southwestern corner of the airport to Ejido further southwest of the city center.

Both **Budget** (✆ **0274/263-1768;** www.budget.com.ve) and **Dávila Tours** (✆ **0274/266-1711**) have offices in Mérida and rent cars for BsF150 to BsF300 per day.

Visitor Information

Cormetur, the Mérida Tourism Corporation (✆ **0800/637-4300**), has a half-dozen information booths around town, including locations at the airport in El Vigia, the Mérida bus terminal, and on the Plaza Las Heroínas. Office hours vary slightly according to location, but most are open Monday through Saturday from 8am to 6pm. Their main office is beside the now mostly dormant Mérida airport on Avenida Urdaneta and Calle 45, but you can get a copy of the map they distribute and their list of hotels and tour operators at any of their branches.

FAST FACTS Several currency-exchange houses and a host of banks are around town, although you are best off asking at your hotel or one of the tour operators to find someone who will exchange your dollars or euros at a more favorable rate.

If you need medical attention, ask at your hotel, or head to **Centro Clínico** on Avenida Urdaneta, opposite the airport (✆ **0274/262-9111**). It has an emergency room and a variety of doctors on staff with offices nearby. Or you can contact the bilingual doctor **Aldo Olivieri** (✆ **0274/244-0805**).

Scores of Internet cafes are all over town. Rates run between BsF1 and BsF3. The main **Ipostel** office is on Calle 21 between avenidas 4 and 5; there's also a branch office at the main bus terminal.

Mérida is a great place to brush up on your high school Spanish or take a crash course in the language. **The Iowa Institute,** Avenida 4 and Calle 18 (✆ **0274/252-6404;** www.iowainstitute.com), runs programs of between 1 week and 6 months. Class sizes are small, and homestays can be arranged. Costs run around BsF344 per week for classes, BsF440 per week for room and board with a local family. Alternately, you can try **CEVAM** (✆ **0274/263-1362;** www.cevam.org), which is tied to the U.S. Embassy in Venezuela and specializes in private lessons.

WHAT TO SEE & DO

Mérida's principal church, the **Basílica Menor de la Inmaculada Concepción** ★, took more than 150 years to complete, but the effort paid off in one of the most impressive and eclectic cathedrals in Venezuela. Originally based on the design of the 17th-century cathedral in Toledo, Spain, work was begun in 1803. A couple of earthquakes and several distinct periods of construction have left it a mixed breed, with artistic and architectural touches representing various epochs, including some beautiful stained-glass work and large frescos.

Within a 4-block radius of Plaza Bolívar, you'll find a handful of local museums. The small but interesting **Museo de Arte Moderno Juan Astorga Anta (Museum of Modern Art Juan Astorga Anta)** ★, Avenida 2 and Calle 22 (✆ **0274/252-9664**), is housed within the city's Cultural Arts Complex, where you can often find out what concerts, exhibits, and performances are happening around town, if none are happening in the complex's own performing arts center. The nearby **Casa de Cultura Juan Félix Sánchez (Juan Félix Sánchez Cultural House),** Avenida 3 and Calle 23 (✆ **0274/252-6101**), has rotating exhibits of local and popular artists. The **Museo Arqueológico (Museum of Archeology),** Edificio del Rectorado at the Universidad de los Andes, Avenida 3 and Calle 23 (✆ **0274/240-2344;** admission BsF2), has a small collection of archaeological relics, including tools, ceramics, and jewelry. The highlight here is a reconstructed pre-Columbian grave and a fairly well-preserved headless mummy. The **Museo de Arte Colonial (Museum of Colonial Art),** Avenida 4 and Calle 20 (✆ **0274/657-2340;** free admission), has a decent collection of mostly religious art and crafts from the colonial period. Both of the above museums are housed in perfectly preserved old colonial homes, with pretty central courtyards.

Finally, there's the **Jardín Botánico de Mérida (Mérida Botanical Gardens)** ★★, Avenida Alberto Carnevali (✆ **0274/240-1241;** admission BsF5; daily 9am–5pm), an extensive collection of neo-tropical flora. The gardens feature an extensive collection of bromeliads, as well as sections dedicated to medicinal plants, orchids, and aquatic species.

Outdoor Adventures & Tours

Scores of tour agencies and adventure tour companies are in and around Mérida, with the greatest congregation around the Plaza Las Heroínas. The competition is cutthroat and you can often find good deals by shopping around. However, be careful, as some of them are fly-by-night operations. I highly recommend the companies mentioned below, as their level of service, quality of guides and equipment, and safety standards are consistent and dependable. Whatever tour company you choose, be absolutely sure that you feel confident about the competence of the guides and the quality of the equipment.

Arassari Treks ★★, Calle 24 no. 8–301, behind the *teleférico* (✆/fax **0274/252-5879;** www.arassari.com); **Natoura Adventure Tours** ★★, Calle 31 between avenidas Don Tulio and 6 (✆ **303/800-4639** in the U.S., or 0274/252-4216 in Venezuela; www.natoura.com); and **Guamanchi Expeditions** ★, Calle 24 No. 8–86 (✆ **0274/252-2080;** www.guamanchi.com), are the most established and trustworthy tour companies in town. All offer the majority of the outdoor adventure options listed below, and then some. And all of them can help you with onward tours and trips to Los Llanos and most other destinations in Venezuela.

CANYONEERING This adventure sport, a mix of hiking, sliding, and rappelling down a river canyon, is full of thrills and chills. No experience is necessary, but you should be prepared to get very wet. A 6.3m (21-ft.) natural water slide is just one of the highlights. The cost for the full-day tour, with a snack and late lunch at the end (around 4pm), is BsF250 to BsF350 per person.

CLIMBING & TREKKING At 5,007m (16,423 feet), **Pico Bolívar** is Venezuela's highest peak. Crowned with a statue of its namesake hero, it's the most popular summit for visiting climbers. Although the simplest routes are not technically difficult, the sheer altitude and variable weather conditions make a summit climb here plenty challenging. Only experienced climbers in good shape should attempt it. The more challenging routes over steep rock and ice are for die-hard climbers.

Other high Andean summits here include **Pico Humbolt** (4,944m/16,216 ft.), **Pico La Concha** (4,922m/16,144 ft.), **Pico Bonpland** (4,883m/16,016 ft.), and **Pico El Toro** (4,755m/15,596 ft.). Several of these peaks can be combined into a multiday trek. Some require ropes, crampons, and ice-climbing gear. All should be attempted only with a guide, proper conditioning, and proper acclimation.

For those looking for less adrenaline and a touch of culture, multiday treks of the high paramo that visit several small towns and Andean villages can also be arranged. Bird-watchers can also hire specialized guides for day hikes and multiday treks. Although you can see hundreds of species in the area, one of the most sought-after sightings, albeit rare, is that of a giant Andean condor.

Prices for climbing and treks range from BsF200 to BsF400 per person per day, depending on group size, season, itinerary, and equipment rentals. Porters can be hired for around BsF80 per day.

HORSEBACK RIDING If walking or biking don't strike your fancy, you can saddle up and tour the area on horseback. Prices range from around BsF100 for a half-day tour to between BsF250 and BsF350 for a full-day tour. Overnight and multiday tours are also available.

MOUNTAIN BIKING The same Andean peaks and paramo that make this such a great area for mountain climbing and trekking also make it a prime area for mountain biking. A variety of options are available, from simple half-day jaunts to multiday adventures. Tours can be designed to suit your skill level, experience, and conditioning. Prices range from BsF200 to BsF400 per person per day. Rental of a decent bike should cost around BsF45 per day.

PARAGLIDING The high mountain walls of the Andes and near-constant thermal wind currents make the Mérida valley perfect for paragliding. You may not see a condor, but you will get a condor's-eye view of things. Experienced paragliders will want to fly solo, but beginners can also enjoy the thrill, strapped into the front of a double harness with an experienced pilot behind them. If conditions are right, air time can exceed 90 minutes. A typical 3-hour tour, with 20 to 40 minutes in the air, will cost BsF360 per person.

WHITE-WATER RAFTING Rafting here is possible year-round, but the high season is May through November. Rafting is conducted down in the lower elevations near Barinas, so a hefty car or van ride is involved, and the trips are generally a minimum of 2 days. The rivers run include the Acequias, the upper and lower Canagua, and the Sinigui, which range in difficulty from Class I to Class V. Both Arassari and Guamanchi operate river lodges that make the trips even more enjoyable. Prices run around BsF600 to BsF800 per person for a 2-day, 1-night adventure.

Because the rivers here run from the Andean foothills down to the plains of Los Llanos (see below). It's common to combine a rafting trip out of Mérida with an onward tour and stay in Los Llanos.

WHERE TO STAY

Moderate

In addition to the places listed below, the new **Casa Milla** (✆ **0274/657-5340;** casamillaposada@hotmail.com), offers up comfortable, well-kept rooms in a converted house fronting the pretty Plaza Milla. In the foothills above Mérida, **Hotel & Spa La Sevillana** (✆ **0274/266-3227;** www.andes.net/lasevillana) has the feel of a cozy B&B and offers great bird-watching all around.

Posada Casa Sol ★★ (Finds) This downtown option is the most stylish joint in Mérida. Artistic touches abound. Intricate wood and metal work ranges from random sculptures, spread around the rambling colonial-era building, to the entrance door, which is a work of art in itself. Rooms vary in size, but all are clean, inviting, and well kept, with firm beds, plush down comforters and tasteful decor. Most have high ceilings. My favorite rooms are the second-floor units with small balconies overlooking the central courtyard. Service is attentive and friendly. The hotel has no formal restaurant, although breakfast is served daily, as well as light snacks and drinks throughout the day.

Av. 4, between calles 15 and 16, Mérida. ✆ **0274/252-4164.** www.posadacasasol.com. 17 units. BsF290 double; BsF320 suite. Rates include taxes. MC, V. Parking nearby. **Amenities:** Free Wi-Fi. *In room:* TV, no phone.

Inexpensive

A backpacker and adventure-tourist hot spot, Mérida has scores of inexpensive *posadas* geared toward backpackers. Many are congregated in close proximity to the Plaza Las Heroínas. In addition to the places listed below, I also like the **Posada La Montaña** (✆ **0274/252-5977;** www.posadalamontana.com). It's quite easy to comparison shop and check out a handful before committing.

Posada Guamanchi Located just off the Plaza Las Heroínas, this is my favorite true budget hostel in Mérida. Rooms are impeccably clean, with simple furnishings, but lots of light. About half have private balconies, and some of these have good views of the mountains. Even if you don't get a room with a view, the common rooftop patio is a great place to hang out. If you want to cook for yourself, you're welcome to the shared kitchen here. These folks run one of the better tour operations in town, and also have a sister *posada* in the mountain village of Los Nevados.

Calle 24 no. 8–86, Mérida. ✆ **0274/252-2080.** www.guamanchi.com. 18 units. BsF90 double with shared bath; BsF120 double with private bath. MC, V. Limited free parking. *In room:* No phone.

Posada Luz Caraballo Located on the charming Plaza Milla (Sucre) at the northeast end of town, this is another solid option with plenty of colonial flavor. The rooms are spread over three floors connected by interior courtyards and verandas. Rooms are simple and clean; a few have mattresses a little too thin and soft for my taste, while others have comfortable, plush beds. All come with a small television. If possible, ask for one of the rooms in the "newer" wing, or request no. 30 or 35; the latter two have great views over tile roofs, over the plaza, and onto the Andes. The attached restaurant, El Andino, is popular and inexpensive.

Av. 2 no. 13–80, in front of Plaza Milla, Mérida. ✆ **0274/252-5441.** 36 units. BsF150 double. No credit cards. Limited free parking. **Amenities:** Restaurant. *In room:* TV, no phone.

WHERE TO DINE

Dozens of inexpensive Venezuelan restaurants are around town—and almost as many pizza places. Most are pretty good. Walk around and choose one whose menu and ambience strike your fancy. If there's trout on the menu, it's likely to be fresh and local.

Moments Heladería Coromoto

The **Heladería Coromoto ★★** (✆ **0274/252-3525**), Avenida 3 and Calle 29, in front of the Plaza El Llano, holds the Guinness world record for the most ice-cream flavors. Adventurous souls can sample smoked trout, garlic, beer, avocado, or squid. The eclectic and *long* list takes up two walls in the joint. The count currently exceeds 900 flavors, with roughly 100 choices available on any given day. It's open Tuesday through Sunday from 2 to 10pm.

Vegetarians should head to **La Fonda El Tinajero,** Calle 29, between avenidas 3 and 4 (✆ 0274/252-2465). For something a bit different, try **La Mama & Sushi** (✆ 0274/252-4851) on Calle 29, between avenidas 4 and 5, which is a combo sushi bar, Italian restaurant, and pizza joint. Another good spot for pizza is **L'Astilla** (✆ 0274/251-0832), which fronts the pretty Plaza Milla. For a light bite, I like the open-air dining at **T'Cafe** (✆ 0414/741-5288) on the corner of Avenida 3 and Calle 29, located conveniently across from Heladería Coromoto, if you're looking to cap things off with some dessert. Finally, there are a couple of excellent options a bit farther afield. Both **Cabañas Xinia & Peter ★★** (✆ **0274/283-0214**) and **Casa Solar ★** (✆ 0416/674-5653) serve up excellent international fare in elegant and intimate settings outside of town.

An interesting culinary note: In Mérida, and throughout much of the Andes region, *arepas* are made with wheat flour instead of the traditional cornmeal.

Entrepueblos ★★ Finds INTERNATIONAL This tiny restaurant serves up some of the most creative and eclectic fare in the region. Generous cuts of meat, chicken, and fresh fish come in a wide range of preparations with sauces based on everything from green peppercorns to prunes. Also look for the daily chalkboard specials and tempting desserts. Six small tables are crowded into the main dining room. However, I prefer the two tables on the front porch, even though they are roadside.

Av. 2 Bolívar no. 8–115, La Parroquia. ✆ **0274/271-0483** or 0416/674-1957. Reservations recommended. Main courses BsF40–BsF85. AE, DC, MC, V. Wed–Mon noon–11pm.

Infusion ★ Finds VEGETARIAN I like the relaxed and eclectic vibe of this new joint. The main dining area is an open-air, interior courtyard, with wrought-iron tables set under white-linen umbrellas. There are also a series of private rooms. You'll find a long list—two pages worth—of teas, as well as a range of salads, soups, sushi, and main courses, all vegetarian. The salads are excellent, as are the spring rolls. In the evenings, this is a real, local bohemian hangout, with occasional live music.

Av. 4 no. 13–14. ✆ **0274/251-3105** or 0416/577-4108. Reservations not necessary. Main courses BsF15–BsF25. MC, V. Mon–Sat noon–3pm and 6pm–midnight.

L'Abadia ★ INTERNATIONAL Tables and chairs are spread around a host of rooms and several interior and exterior courtyards covering two floors of this old building. The entire place exudes a sense of rustic elegance, and interesting decorative touches abound. My favorite seats are those on the second-floor covered patio. The menu is broad, and features salads, sandwiches, and pastas, as well as a few more hefty main dishes. You can get a steak or chicken breast with a variety of sauces that range from a creamy Roquefort sauce to an oriental preparation with ginger, soy sauce, and scallions. There are also a few vegetarian options and excellent desserts. The upstairs is home to a popular Internet cafe, tour operation, and good gift shop. These folks have opened a very similar sister restaurant, **La Abadía del Angel,** on Calle 21 between avenidas 5 and 6 (✆ **0274/252-8013**).

Av. 3, between calles 17 and 18. ✆ **0274/251-0933.** www.grupoabadia.com. Reservations not necessary. Main courses BsF45–BsF74. MC, V. Mon–Sat 9am–midnight.

La Trattoria Europa da Lino ★ (Finds) ITALIAN Delicious pastas and authentic Italian cuisine have defined this cozy place since Lino's family immigrated here in the 1950s. On the long list of pastas, many, including the gnocchi, tortelli, and agnolotti, are homemade. I like to start off with the Sicilian *caponatina,* a savory marinade of eggplant, peppers, olives, and carrots. Among the pastas, the tortelli stuffed with local squash is a standout. If you're hankering for a meat dish, I recommend the rabbit served with radicchio in a white wine–and-rosemary sauce. Couples looking to squeeze the most romance possible out of Mérida should grab a table in the dimly lit brick-walled side room. A good selection of Italian and Chilean wines are on offer at fair prices.

Pasaje Ayacucho no. 25–30, Vía Teleférico, in front of El Seminario. ✆ **0274/252-9555.** Main courses BsF25–BsF48. MC, V. Tues–Fri noon–3pm and 7–10pm; Sat–Sun noon–10pm.

Mogambo ★★★ (Finds) FUSION With old saxophones and photos of jazz artists on the wall, this homey bistro is at once elegant, comfortable, and lively. Moreover, a recent change in the kitchen has made this, hands down, the best restaurant in town. The creative menu ranges from a magret of duck served over couscous in a citrus sauce, to fresh fish with green mango served on a sweet potato cake. I like to start things off with the tomato-orange soup with serrano ham, or the fish cakes in wasabi foam. Presentations are artsy and the service is excellent. They also have the best wine list in the Venezuelan Andes. Live music on weekends makes this a great alternative to the dance clubs and rowdy bar scene.

Av. 4 and Calle 29. ✆ **0274/252-5643.** Main courses BsF38–BsF70. AE, MC, V. Tues–Sun 5:30–11pm.

MERIDA AFTER DARK

This is both a college town and a popular backpacker and adventure-tourism destination, so you'll find a relatively active nightlife here. In general, the bars get going around 9pm and shut down around midnight to 2am. Discos get cranking around 10pm and close their doors between 3 and 4am. None of the bars in town charge a cover; some of the dance clubs will occasionally charge BsF1 to BsF10 admittance, but it will usually get you a drink or two.

La Cucaracha Racing Bar, Alto Prado, and **El Bodegón de Pancho,** Centro Comercial Mamayeya, are both multienvironment establishments and two of the more popular nightspots in town. **El Hoyo Queque ★** and **Grada's Sports Bar,** Avenida 4 and Calle 19, are two happening bars almost always overflowing with the local college crowd; they're located straight across the street from each other. For a mellower scene, try **T'Café ★** (see above), which is popular with college kids and locals.

SIDE TRIPS FROM MERIDA

Mérida is surrounded by picturesque mountain towns and villages. These can be visited in a rental car or as part of guided tours. Most have quaint little *posadas* for overnight stays, and some even have pretty nice lodges and hotels.

Los Nevados ★, a tiny, isolated mountain village, is one of the more popular destinations. Trips here are often done in a circuit, with one leg conducted by jeep and the other by mule or foot. **Mucuchíes** is best known for its namesake breed of dog. On the road just outside of Mucuchíes, on the way to Barinas and Los Llanos, is the beautiful little stone church of **San Rafael de Mucuchies** ★, built by Juan Félix Sánchez. Another stone church, also built by Sánchez, can be seen in **El Tisure.** Other popular towns include **Tabay, Jají** ★, and **Mucutuy.** The trails, lakes, and waterfalls of the **Mucubají** ★★ section of the **Sierra Nevada National Park** make a great destination for a day trip.

Where to Stay in the Mountain Towns Around Mérida

The mountain towns outside Mérida have several pleasant options for spending a night or two. One of the nicest is the intimate **Cabañas Xinia & Peter** ★★, La Mucuy Baja, Tabay (✆ **0274/283-0214;** www.xiniaypeter.com), a delightful and artistically done retreat about 20 minutes outside Mérida. Close to Jají is the rustic **Hacienda El Carmen** (✆ **0414/639-2701;** www.haciendaelcarmen.com), a former coffee plantation that retains the ambience of its working past. Located about 60km (37 miles) outside Mérida, **Casa Solar** ★, Apartaderos (✆ **0416/674-5653;** www.casasolar.info), is a small lodge that bears the distinction of being the highest hotel in Venezuela at 3,500m (11,500 ft.).

A Side Trip to Los Llanos ★★

Located on plains that roll on for hundreds of miles south and east of the Andes, **Los Llanos** is an area of flat, mostly open cattle ground, punctuated with some isolated stands of gallery forest. During the latter part of the rainy season (July–Nov), the plains are almost entirely flooded, with only a few raised highways and service roads passable in anything that doesn't float. In the dry season, the land reemerges and wildlife congregates in dense herds and mixed flocks around the ponds and creeks left behind. Traditionally agricultural land, Los Llanos has also garnered fame as a destination for wildlife lovers and bird-watchers.

The quantity and variety of wildlife visible at the nature lodges located in Los Llanos is phenomenal—anaconda, caiman, capybara, deer, massive flocks of birds, and even wildcats are commonly sighted.

GETTING THERE Most folks visit Los Llanos as part of a package tour out of either Mérida or Caracas. In this case, your transportation will be taken care of. It is possible to reach the gates, or at the least, nearby towns of most of the *hatos* by bus as well, but since you have to coordinate your arrival time and pickup with the lodge, it is best that you work out any independent travel closely with the lodge beforehand.

Note: It's hot in Los Llanos year-round, and in the dry season, the sun can be downright brutal. Definitely bring sunscreen, but also make sure that you've got a wide-brimmed hat. Mosquitoes and other insects can also be plentiful here. Although repellent is recommended, I often prefer using lightweight long-sleeved shirts and pants. Also, be sure to bring glasses or sunglasses on the safari-style tours. When the trucks pick up a bit

Isolated Lodges, or Hatos

Hato is the local term for a very large expanse of land. It designates a ranch or farm much larger than a *finca* or a hacienda. With the international boom in ecotourism, *hato* has also become the local term for an isolated nature lodge. *Hatos* in Los Llanos range from almost luxurious lodges—with boats for river and lagoon excursions and large, open-air safari-style trucks for land tours—to basic camps with a zinc shelter over a concrete slab where hammocks are hung inside mosquito nets. Tours at the more basic *hatos* are usually conducted by foot or horseback and, occasionally, in boats.

Tips Choosing Your Hato

Both **Hato Piñero** and **Hato El Cedral** are long-standing nature lodges, with capable and bilingual guides offering a steady stream of wildlife-watching tours. At each, you will see enough birds, mammals, and reptiles to keep you pinned to your binoculars and reeling off shots on your camera. However, they are different: In a nutshell, Piñero will give you greater diversity (of species), while El Cedral will give you greater density. Piñero is considered a better spot for spotting jaguar and other wildcats, although their spotting is still extremely rare. You can sometimes spot as many as 100 different species of birds in 1 day at Piñero. On the other hand, the sheer number of capybara at El Cedral—more than 50,000—is mind-boggling. Moreover, El Cedral is perhaps the best spot for spotting anaconda, particularly in the dry season.

of velocity, particularly around dusk or on the night tours, you'll find your corneas attract insects like a semi's windshield.

WHAT TO SEE & DO Folks come to Los Llanos to **see and photograph wildlife ★★★**. And for that, they are richly rewarded. From pink river dolphins to giant anaconda, this is a wildlife lover's dream come true. Hundreds of bird species are also to be seen, many in massive flocks. Among the highlights are the jabiru and wood stork; scarlet macaw; numerous species of hawks, herons, and parrots; and large flocks of scarlet ibis. The hoatzin is one of the more bizarre and louder members of the avian world. Common mammals here include the white-tailed deer, red howler *(araguato)* and capuchin monkeys, giant anteater, gray fox, peccary, and giant river otter. Although difficult to spot (and far from guaranteed), jaguars, pumas, and ocelots are relatively common in Los Llanos. However, you *are* guaranteed to see large families of capybara *(chigüire)*, as well as dozens of spectacled caiman *(baba)*. Tours are conducted year-round, with a much higher percentage of boat tours in the rainy season, of course.

WHERE TO STAY & DINE In addition to the lodges listed below, most of the tour agencies in Mérida arrange trips to the Llanos. Price wars are waged on the streets of Mérida. However, by opting for the cheapest options you may find yourself in an overcrowded van and sleeping in primitive conditions. That said, 4-day, 3-night tours from Mérida run between BsF1,500 and BsF4,000 per person; the price includes transportation, meals, and a variety of tours. The price range generally reflects the level of luxury you'll find in transportation and accommodations.

Hato El Cedral ★ There are so many capybara, caiman, and anaconda here that it feels like a zoo. More than 350 species of birds have been recorded. The newer rooms here are quite large, with two double beds and high ceilings. The older rooms, which are spread around the pool, are somewhat smaller and have lower ceilings. All rooms are a bit spartan and could use some sprucing up. In 2009, Hato El Cedral was expropriated by the Venezuelan government, which has taken over operations. While they plan to continue running the hotel and ecotourism operation, they also plan to use some of the land here for agricultural and petroleum production. They even plan to harvest and process capybara for consumption. Moreover, to date, the Venezuelan government has a terrible track record in the hospitality business.

Near Mantecal. Mailing address: Av. La Salle, Edificio Pancho, Piso 5, PH, Los Caobos, Caracas. ✆ **0212/781-8995** or ✆/fax 0212/793-6082. www.elcedral.com. 25 units. BsF350–BsF400 per person double occupancy. Rates include 3 meals, 2 guided tours, and all nonalcoholic beverages. AE, MC, V. **Amenities:** Restaurant; lounge; postage stamp–size outdoor pool. *In room:* A/C, no phone.

Hato Piñero ★★ This pioneer nature lodge is the most charming of the *hatos.* A working farm and ranch, Piñero has the feel of a traditional hacienda. Rooms are comfortable but rustic, with polished concrete floors, and two built-in twin beds. The best features here are the high ceilings, whitewashed walls, and blue-trimmed wooden windows opening up to the outdoors and an interior hallway. Tours are conducted safari style or on horseback, and—during the rainy season—by boat. You'll want to check out the library and biological exhibitions at the lodge's own biological research center. Early on, Piñero declared much of its property a biological preserve, and they've maintained a steady stream of invited scientific researchers, student groups, and interns, who have their own residence and basic research facilities.

El Baúl. Mailing address: Edif. General, Piso 6, Ofic. 6-B, Av. La Estancia Chuao, Caracas. ✆ **0212/991-0079.** Fax 0212/991-6668. www.hatopinero.com. 11 units. BsF340–BsF495 per person double occupancy. Rates include 3 meals, 2 guided tours, all beverages, and taxes. Transportation by car from Caracas costs BsF409 round-trip for up to 4 persons. AE, MC, V. **Amenities:** Restaurant; lounge. *In room:* A/C, no phone.

8 CANAIMA, ANGEL FALLS & THE RIO CAURA ★★

Canaima: 725km (450 miles) SE of Caracas

Angel Falls is the world's tallest waterfall. It's an imposing sight, and the trip there is definitely an adventure. In addition to Angel Falls and hundreds of other tropical jungle waterfalls, Venezuela's southeastern region, or Gran Sabana, is known for its unique geological formations, or *tepuis*—massive steep-walled and flat-topped mesas that inspired Sir Arthur Conan Doyle's *The Lost World.* A large chunk of this region, more than 3 million hectares (7 million acres), is protected within **Canaima National Park,** the largest national park in Venezuela and the sixth largest in the world.

The small Pemón Indian village and tourist enclave of Canaima is the gateway to Angel Falls and much of this region. Set on the edge of a black-water lagoon ringed with soft, pink-sand beaches; fed by a series of powerful waterfalls; and surrounded by miles of untouched jungle, the word "idyllic" doesn't do this spot justice.

Located south of Ciudad Bolívar, and a fair bit north of Canaima, a trip along the **Río Caura** to **Para Falls** offers many of the same sights and experiences to be had on a trip to Canaima and Angel Falls, with a more undiscovered feel to it, and fewer fellow travelers.

ESSENTIALS

Because Canaima is such a popular destination, it can get quite busy during the high season, particularly from July to August and from November to January. During peak periods, prices can get inflated, and the river, lagoon, and waterfall tours can seem downright crowded.

Although flyovers are conducted year-round, trips to Angel Falls itself are only possible during the rainy season, when the water level is high enough in the rivers to reach its base. The unofficial season for tours to the foot of Angel Falls runs from June through November. October and November are regarded as the best months to visit, since the

Fun Facts The Tepuis

Formed over millions and millions of years, the sandstone *tepuis* of the Gran Sabana are geological and biological wonders. With vertical edges that plunge for thousands of feet, most are unclimbed and unexplored. The highest, Roraima, at 2,810m (9,217 ft.), towers over the savanna below. Auyántepui, or "Devil's Mountain," is some 700 sq. km (275 sq. miles) in area—roughly the size of Singapore. Given their age and isolation, the *tepuis* host an astounding number of endemic species, both flora and fauna. In some cases, as much as half of all species of flora and fauna on a given *tepui* will be endemic.

rains are winding down but the water level remains high. Depending on the river level, trips can sometimes be made as late as December and even January. August and September are definitely the rainiest months to visit, and although the falls are thick and impressive, visibility may be limited. Although there are no organized trips to Angel Falls in the dry season (Jan–May), this is also a good time to take advantage of low-season bargains and the relative desolation of Canaima. The dry season is a good time to visit the region as a beach destination, as the many pink- and white-sand beaches that line the rivers' edges throughout the dry season all but disappear during the rainy season.

Getting There

BY CAR There are no year-round serviceable roads into Canaima, and even in the dry season the road here is so long and arduous as to be an unviable option for travelers.

BY PLANE Most visitors to Canaima come on package tours that include air transport. If you decide to book your travel by yourself, be forewarned that flight schedules to and from Canaima change frequently and seasonally. Given the isolation and distance, flights here often sell out well in advance. It's recommended that you book your flights with a confirmed departure out of Canaima, so as to not find yourself waiting standby for several days.

There are no direct flights to Canaima from Caracas. To get there you must first fly to Ciudad Bolívar or Puerto Ordaz. **Aeropostal** (✆ **0800/284-6637;** www.aeropostal.com), **Aserca** (✆ **0800/648-8356;** www.asercaairlines.com), and **Rutaca** (✆ **0800/788-2221;** www.rutaca.com.ve) all have regular flights to both gateways from Caracas. Fares from Caracas to either city run BsF200 to BsF350 each way. **Serami** (✆ **0286/952-0424;** www.serami.com) flies to Canaima daily from Puerto Ordaz. Flights between Canaima and Puerto Ordaz or Ciudad Bolívar cost between BsF350 and BsF670 each way.

If you get to Ciudad Bolívar or Puerto Ordaz on your own, either by air or bus, you can usually find a tour or charter company with a trip heading to Canaima, although the scheduling and costs can vary immensely depending on demand. If you need to overnight in Ciudad Bolívar, be sure to check in to the **Posada Casa Grande** (✆ **0212/993-2939**), a gorgeous little hotel in the colonial center of the city.

Aerotuy (✆ **0212/212-3110;** www.tuy.com) runs daily day tours (BsF1,716 per person) to Canaima from Isla de Margarita, including a flyover of Angel Falls and a visit to Salto El Sapo. It also uses this flight to bring people to and from its own remote riverside hotel, **Arekuna Lodge.** The flight leaves Margarita at 8:30am and departs Canaima around 3pm. The hours are subject to change, as it often juggles its itinerary to Canaima and Arekuna. Space is limited and during the high season, these flights often sell out far, far in advance.

Fun Facts Jimmy Angel

Angel Falls are named after American bush pilot and gold-seeker Jimmy Angel, who first spotted the falls in 1935. Although earlier anecdotal reports exist about them, and certainly the local Pemón people knew of them, Jimmy Angel gets most of the credit. In 1937, Angel crash-landed his plane on the top of Auyántepui. No one was injured, but the pilot, his wife, and two companions had to hike for 11 days to descend the *tepui* and reach safety. For decades, the silver fuselage of *El Río Coroní* could be seen on the top of Auyántepui. In 1970, it was salvaged by the Venezuelan Air Force. The plane was restored and is currently on display at the airport in Ciudad Bolívar.

All visitors to Canaima must pay the BsF8 park entrance fee. The fee is collected at the airport upon arrival and is good for the duration of your stay.

Getting Around

Besides the few dirt tracks that ring the eastern edge of the lagoon and define the tiny village of Canaima, this region has virtually no roads. Transportation is conducted primarily by boat in traditional dugout canoes called *curiaras.* From Canaima, numerous tours are arranged to a half-dozen waterfalls, including Angel Falls, and neighboring indigenous communities. Aside from strolling around the small village of Canaima and walking along the edge of the lagoon or to the lookout over Ucaima Falls, you will be dependent upon your lodge or tour operator for getting around.

VISITOR INFORMATION & TOURS Almost all visitors to Canaima come as part of a prearranged package that includes meals, accommodations, and tours. These packages can be arranged with either the local lodges listed below or any number of agencies and operators in Caracas or abroad. Given the remote location, lack of roads, and limited accommodations, you should make reservations prior to your arrival. If you decide to visit on your own, there are usually several local tour agencies waiting for incoming flights at informal information desks at the small airport. Independent travelers can quickly shop around and try to arrange the best price and timing for a trip to Angel Falls, as well as local accommodations, which can range from a hammock under a simple roof to one of the nicer lodges mentioned below.

FALLS, FALLS & MORE FALLS: WHAT TO SEE & DO IN CANAIMA

Few organized adventure sports are regularly practiced in this region. Despite the scores of rivers, with ample rapids and white water, no one yet is offering any rafting or kayaking in the area. Aside from the relatively soft adventures mentioned below multiday treks around the region, including climbs of Auyántepui and Roraima, are possible. If you're interested in a multiday trek, you can ask one of the local tour operators in Canaima, or try **Akanan Travel & Adventure** ★★ (© **0212/715-5433** or 0414/116-0107; www.akanan.com), **Cacao Expeditions** ★★ (© **0212/977-1234;** www.cacaotravel.com), or **Lost World Adventures** ★★ (© **800/999-0558** in the U.S., or 0212/577-0303 in Caracas; www.lostworldadventures.com).

Angel Falls ★★★

With an uninterrupted drop of 807m (2,648 ft.) and a total drop of 979m (3,211 ft.), Angel Falls is an impressive sight—and as you are already aware, the tallest waterfall on earth. The vast majority of tourists who visit Angel Falls get to see it only from the window of their airplane. Almost all flights to Canaima, both commercial and charter, attempt a flyover of the falls. However, given the fact that Angel Falls is located up a steep canyon that is often socked in with clouds (especially in the rainy season), the flyovers are sometimes either aborted or offer limited views. Moreover, even on a good day, when the plane makes a couple of passes on each side, the view is somewhat distant and fleeting. If for some reason your flight doesn't make the pass in front of Angel Falls, you can arrange for a quick flyover for BsF150 to BsF260 per person, with a minimum of four persons. Ask at your hotel or check at the airport. ***Be aware:*** If you choose to purchase a flyover trip to Angel Falls, most operators will *not* refund your money, even if you don't catch the slightest glimpse of the falls.

If you want to really enjoy the splendor of Angel Falls, you'll have to take a trip there in a boat. Almost all the hotels and tour agencies in Canaima offer 1-, 2-, and 3-day tours to Angel Falls. As the route and distance traveled are the same, the only difference is the amount of time you actually spend at the falls—and whether or not you spend a night or two in a hammock at one of the rustic camps, near the base of the falls. Typically the tour begins at 5am with a pickup at your hotel and transfer to the tiny port atop Ucaima Falls. From here, you travel up the Carrao River, with a portage around some particularly rough rapids, to Isla Orquídea or another camp for a breakfast stop. After breakfast, it's back into the boats and on to the narrow Churún River, which snakes up Cañón del Diablo (Devil's Canyon) and over scores of rapids to Isla Ratoncito (Little Mouse Island) at the base of the falls. On average, the upriver journey takes 4 to 5 hours. Keep your eyes peeled and you might see a toucan, cock-of-the-rock, or some howler monkeys. Once at the base, you'll still need to hike for another hour or so uphill through tropical forest to reach the pools at the foot of the falls. The hike is somewhat strenuous and can be slick and muddy, but a swim in the refreshing pool at the foot of the massive falls makes it worth the effort. Back on Isla Ratoncito, you'll have lunch before boarding the boats once again for the trip back to Canaima. With the current, the trip is a bit faster and you should even get to visit Salto El Sapo (see below) before being dropped back off at your hotel around sunset.

Multiday tours sometimes leave later in the morning or afternoon, sacrificing a visit to the falls on the first day. However, once there, you get to spend a longer time at the foot of the falls, and/or visit the falls on consecutive days. Moreover, because of positioning, the sunrise and early morning sun directly hits the falls, while in the afternoon they are more backlit, with the sun setting behind Auyántepui.

Day tours from Canaima range from BsF215 to BsF538 per person. Two-day, one-night tours to Angel Falls can cost between BsF300 and BsF600. Be careful about trying to save a few dollars: Paying more for a respectable operator will often get you a boat with two working engines (required by law, but not always the case in practice), a more experienced captain (important, given the nature of the rivers), and a better and truly bilingual guide.

Other Area Falls ★★

Several distinct and impressive falls work together to form the Canaima lagoon. All of these are easily visited in organized boat trips out of town. The most popular of these falls is **Salto El Sapo,** which is located on the backside of small Anatoly's Island, on the north end of the lagoon. A visit to Salto El Sapo includes a 15-minute hike across the island, from the foot of Hacha Falls to the base of Salto El Sapo. After a swim in the pool here, you are led along a path that passes behind the falls (be prepared to get wet), then up around the other side, with a visit to the smaller El Sapito Falls, and then (when the water level permits) across the top. Walking behind El Sapo Falls in the rainy season is very impressive. Tours to Salto El Sapo often include lunch, or at the very least a refreshment.

Hacha, Golondrina, and **Ucaima falls** are located in a neat row fronting the lagoon. They can be observed and enjoyed from just about any point along the edge of the lagoon or by dugout canoe. At a 15-minute hike uphill from the small village, you'll find a little lookout built as part of the small hydroelectric plant on the top of Ucaima Falls. It's not Niagara, but it's a pretty good view. A 10-minute drive and then a 15-minute boat ride downstream are the wide and roaring **Yuri Falls.** A visit to Yuri Falls usually includes a short but interesting walk through the forest. All the hotels and tour operators in town offer trips to these waterfalls, in half- and full-day combinations, which often include a little bit of hiking, a little bit of swimming, and lunch and/or refreshments. Prices range from BsF75 to BsF150 for a half-day tour, and from BsF125 to BsF250 for a full-day tour.

Shopping

Several gift shops are located in and around the small village of Canaima. By far, the best of the bunch is **Makunaima Arte Indígena** ★ (✆ **0286/621-5415**), located just beyond Waku Lodge. This place has a broad and reasonably priced selection of local indigenous crafts, including Pemón blowguns, Yanomami baskets, and Piaroa masks, as well as quality jewelry, ceramics, and woodwork. Another good option—but with a much more limited selection—is the **Kayarinwa Gallery** (no phone), located right in the small village of Canaima. Unless you need toothpaste or some basic goods from their attached general store, avoid the **Canaima Souvenir Shop** (✆ **0414/884-0940**), which has a broad but overpriced selection of crafts. You'll also always find vendors selling jewelry, crafts, and souvenirs at the airport.

WHERE TO STAY & DINE

As previously mentioned, most visitors here come on prearranged packages that include transportation, meals, and tours. All the lodges listed below offer packages, but package prices vary greatly depending on whether or not you visit Angel Falls and how long you stay. Per-night rates are listed below, with the various tours as add-ons.

In addition to the places listed below, **Tapuy Lodge** (✆ **0212/993-2939**) is a pretty, cozy option built right on the lagoon's edge.

Finally, budget travelers can find several options for hanging a hammock, or sleeping in a rented hammock. Rates run around BsF22 to BsF33 per person per night. However, I think the best budget option is to head to the **Campamento Tomás Bernal** (✆ **0414/854-8234;** www.bernaltours.com) across the lagoon on Anatoly Island, with a convivial hostel-like vibe and mix of hammocks and simple rooms. Their hammock camp up near Angel Falls has an excellent early-morning view. There's usually a representative of Bernal Tours at the airport.

Jungle Rudy Campamento ★★ *Finds* Located a short boat ride up the Río Carrao above Ucaima Falls, this nature lodge is a wonderful and romantic retreat. The lodge was founded and built up over a period of decades by the late, legendary Rudy Truffino, and is still run by his family. The rooms are simple, with indigenous artifacts and wildlife photos on the walls. My favorite rooms feature small private terraces fronting the river. There are well-tended gardens and grounds, and two riverside swimming nooks formed by natural and sculpted rock formations. All the standard tours are offered, including to Salto El Sapo, Yuri Falls, and Angel Falls. Jungle Rudy's camp near the base of the falls is the plushest by far, and the only one where you sleep in a real bed instead of a hammock.

Canaima (Parque Nacional Canaima, Sector Laguna de Canaima, Gran Sabana, Edificio Bolívar). ✆/fax **0286/962-2359** in Canaima, or ✆/fax 0212/754-0244 in Caracas. www.junglerudy.com. 14 units. BsF1,000 per person per day. Rates include 3 meals, welcome cocktail, and airport transfers. AE, MC, V. **Amenities:** Restaurant; bar; free Wi-Fi. *In room:* No phone.

Waku Lodge ★★ Set right on the banks of the Canaima lagoon, with a fabulous direct view of the Hacha and Ucaima falls, this lodge has the plushest rooms in the area. All are spacious and modern, and feature a front patio with a couple of chairs and a hammock overlooking the grounds and the lagoon. Room nos. 11 to 15 actually have views of the waterworks. The restaurant is housed in a large, open-air structure with a thatched roof, and the lounge area features a television with DirecTV hookup. However, these folks handle a lot of the day-tour traffic, and there can be a bit of a cattle-car feel to the operation at times.

Canaima (Parque Nacional Canaima, Sector Laguna de Canaima, Gran Sabana). ✆ **0286/962-0559.** www.wakulodge.com. 15 units. BsF950 per person per day. Rates include 3 meals, a quick boat tour around the lagoon, and airport transfers. AE, MC, V. **Amenities:** Restaurant; bar. *In room:* A/C, no phone, free Wi-Fi.

A SIDE TRIP: RIO CAURA & PARA FALLS ★★★

The Río Caura is a major affluent of the Orinoco River. A trip up the Río Caura is a voyage to a remote and untouched land. All trips here begin in Ciudad Bolívar, a small colonial-era city on the banks of the Orinoco. From Ciudad Bolívar, it's a 4-hour drive to the tiny village of Las Trincheras, on the banks of the Río Caura. After an overnight in or near Las Trincheras, it's time for a 5-hour boat ride up the Caura. Along the way, if you're lucky, you'll see freshwater dolphins, and perhaps you'll fish for *cachamba,* a large and tasty river fish. This is an area of dense primary rainforest, and it is rich in tropical flora and fauna. You'll see (and hear) howler monkeys in the trees and catch sight of scarlet macaws flying overhead. The only civilization you'll pass along the way is the small Yekuana indigenous community of Nichere. At the end of the ride, you'll come to El Playón, another small indigenous community on a large, natural, freshwater beach set at the base of two converging and raging rapids. The beach here is incongruous, with soft white sand that seems as if it were imported from the Caribbean. At El Playón, you'll find accommodations in a series of large, circular, open-air ranchos, with hammocks strung around the circle. The accommodations and shared bathrooms are rustic but clean. Meals are simple and filling. From El Playón, it's a 3- to 4-hour hike to an overlook across from the impressive Para Falls. This is a full-day tour, and somewhat strenuous. The only inhabitants of this region are the Yekuana and, to a lesser extent, Pemón indigenous peoples. Both tribes excel in craftworks, and you'll have ample opportunities to buy ceramic wares, woodcarvings, and woven baskets, both in Nichere and El Playón.

Akanan Travel & Adventure (✆ **0212/715-5433** or 0414/116-0107; www.akanan.com) and **Cacao Expeditions** (✆ **0212/977-1234;** www.cacaotravel.com) are the two best operators working the Río Caura.

Most trips here are 6-day/5-night affairs, with an overnight in Ciudad Bolívar to start things off, followed by an early-morning departure for Las Trincheras. The second night is spent either in Las Trincheras or at Yokore Lodge. The next 2 nights are spent at El Playón, and the final night is spent back at Las Trincheras, allowing for an early departure for Ciudad Bolívar or Puerto Ordaz, in time for a connecting flight onward.

INDEX